Excel 4 Super Book

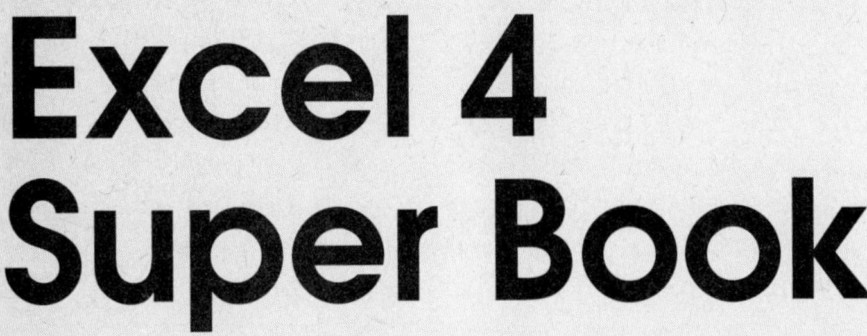

Excel 4 Super Book

Michael Griffin,
Paul McFedries,
Don Scellato, and
Debbie Walkowski

SAMS
A Division of Prentice Hall Computer Publishing
11711 North College, Carmel, Indiana 46032 USA

International Standard Book Number: 0-672-30256-X

Library of Congress Catalog Card Number: 92-081068

95 94 93 92   8 7 6 5 4 3 2 1

Interpretation of the printing code: the rightmost double-digit number is the year of the book's first printing; the rightmost single-digit number is the number of the book's printing. For example, a printing code of 92-1 shows that this copy of the book was printed during the first printing of the book in 1992.

Screen reproductions in this book were created by means of the program Collage Plus from Inner Media, Inc., Hollis, NH.

Printed in the United States of America.

Publisher
Richard K. Swadley

Associate Publisher
Marie Butler-Knight

Managing Editor
Elizabeth Keaffaber

Product Development Manager
Lisa A. Bucki

Acquisitions Manager
Stephen Poland

Development Editors
Faithe Wempen, Seta Frantz

Manuscript Editors
Barry Childs-Helton, Sara Black

Editorial Assistant
Hilary Adams

Cover Design
Tim Amrhein

Designer
Michele Laseau

Indexer
John Sleeva

Production Team
Claudia Bell, Terri Edwards, Mark Enochs, Tim Groeling, Dennis Clay Hager, Carla Hall-Batton, Phil Kitchel, Juli Pavey, Cindy Phipps, Linda Quigley, Caroline Roop, Angie Trzepacz, Julie Walker, Kelli Widdifield, Allan Wimmer, Phil Worthington

Special thanks to Avon Murphy and Catherine Kenny for assuring the technical accuracy of this book.

Table of Contents

Publishing and Printing Workshop

Graphics Workshop

Database Workshop

File Management Workshop

Advanced Topics Workshop

Macros Workshop

Projects Workshop

Command Reference

Introduction

With Excel for Windows, Microsoft has proven that their flagship spreadsheet product is still not only the easiest to use, but also one of the most powerful spreadsheets on the market. Incorporating over 70 percent of user requests, Microsoft Excel 4.0 offers the following new features:

- Improved toolbars, including a new Standard toolbar, additional toolbars, and customizable toolbars
- Shortcut menus that give you access to common commands with a click of the right mouse button
- The Scenario Manager, a tool that lets you save a variety of input values in a worksheet model and view the results of each
- The ChartWizard, which guides you through the typical steps for creating a chart
- Special support and help files for Lotus 1-2-3 users, and a macro interpreter that lets you run 1-2-3 macros in Excel
- The Analysis ToolPak, which includes a set of special statistical and engineering analysis tools that you can apply to different types of data to simplify the analysis process
- The Crosstab ReportWizard, which allows you to quickly summarize and compare information contained in a database
- An abundance of new standard functions (over 200 in total), grouped by category, as well as new macro sheet functions
- The ability to include multiple documents in a "workbook" so that you can open, work with, and save all files at once

- ▲ A zoom feature that allows you to view your worksheet at different levels of magnification or reduction
- ▲ A variety of new chart types, including 3-D surface area, 3-D bar, and radar charts

If you've just purchased or upgraded to version 4.0 of Excel, you know that the product includes two voluminous manuals that tell you more than any user would ever want to know about Excel. So, you may be wondering what this book—*Excel 4.0 Super Book*—offers that is of value to you? The answer is usability and simplicity.

Even though manuals provide every detail about a program (many you may never care to know), they are seldom organized in a fashion that makes the information easy to use and readily accessible. The Super Book from Sams is designed to be comprehensive, but most of all, to be useful to you, the user, who has real work to do and real problems to solve. This book is divided into three parts; one to help you review the basics, another to expand your skills using advanced features, and the last to help you put the skills you've learned to the test. Here's a brief review of the sections:

The Basics Workshop—This workshop describes the fundamental steps for opening, creating, saving, and printing worksheets, including basic tasks such as moving, copying, inserting, and deleting cells and creating basic formulas and functions. If you've used other spreadsheets, you'll find this section helpful for quickly learning the nuances of Excel.

The Advanced Workshops—This section includes six workshops of skill sessions that focus on the more advanced features of Excel. Rather than just describing the features, you'll learn practical ways of using them. These workshops guide you through the logical steps of

- ▲ Publishing and printing a document
- ▲ Creating and incorporating graphics in a document
- ▲ Creating and managing an Excel database

- ▲ Putting file management tips and techniques to use
- ▲ Using Excel's advanced calculation and analysis features
- ▲ Creating and running macros to simplify repetitive tasks

The Projects Workshop—This workshop provides a variety of practical and creative lessons for using Excel in "real-world" situations, from creating a checkbook register, to developing a customer database, to producing a bid comparison worksheet, to setting up a budget for a small business. The worksheets for completing the projects are included on the disk that came with the book. All you need to do is copy them to your hard drive, open them up, and enter your own data.

The *Command Reference* describes Excel commands and standard functions. Appendix A includes installation instructions, and Appendix B is a Windows primer to get you up and running with Windows, if you're not familiar with this graphical user interface.

Basic Skills Workshop

The Basic Skills Workshop introduces you to the fundamental skills you need to use Excel. This workshop includes lessons on basic operational skills, such as how to start and exit Excel, how to work with Excel's menus and dialog boxes, and how to control Excel's worksheet windows.

Skill Session

1

Starting and Exiting Excel

To run Excel 4 for Windows, you must install the program on your hard disk. If you have not yet installed the program, turn to Appendix A for complete instructions. During the installation process, Excel icons are installed under the Windows Program Manager in a group called Microsoft Excel 4.0. (You may have only one icon depending on the installation options you choose.)

Starting Excel

To start Excel 4 for Windows, you must first be running the Windows version 3.0 or later. Start Windows as you normally do, then follow these steps.

TIP: If you are not familiar with using the mouse, follow the keyboard steps to start Excel. Mouse techniques are discussed later in this skill session.

Using the mouse:

1. If it is not already open, open the Program Manager window by moving the mouse pointer (the arrow on the screen) to the Program Manager icon and double-clicking. After a few seconds, the Program Manager window is displayed.

2. If the Microsoft Excel 4.0 group window is not open inside of the Program Manager window, move the mouse pointer to the Microsoft Excel 4.0 group icon and double-click.

3. When the Microsoft Excel 4.0 window opens, move the mouse pointer to the program icon labeled Microsoft Excel 4.0 (shown in Figure 1.1) and then double-click. After a few seconds, Excel 4 for Windows appears on your screen in its own program window (see Figure 1.2).

Using the keyboard:

1. If it is not already open, select the Program Manager window by pressing Alt+Esc until the Program Manager icon is highlighted. Press Alt+spacebar to access the Control menu. Use the down arrow key to highlight Maximize, then press Enter. After a few seconds, the Program Manager window is displayed.

2. If the Microsoft Excel 4.0 group window is not open inside the Program Manager window, press Ctrl+F6 until the Microsoft Excel 4.0 group icon is highlighted and then press Enter.

3. When the Microsoft Excel 4.0 window opens, use the arrow keys to highlight the program icon labeled Microsoft Excel 4.0 (shown in Figure 1.1) and then press Enter. After a few seconds, Excel for Windows appears in its own window on your screen (see Figure 1.2).

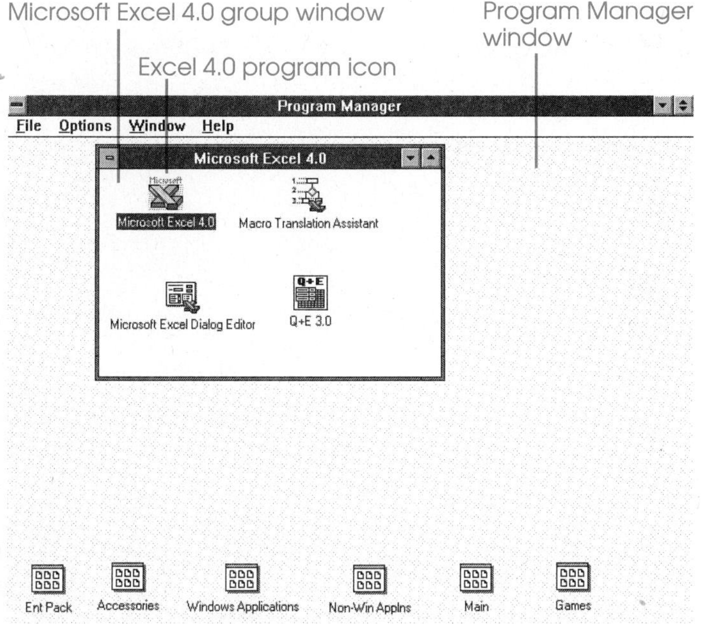

Figure 1.1 The Program Manager and the Microsoft Excel 4.0 group window.

The Excel Screen

The window shown in Figure 1.2 is the Excel program window, which contains a worksheet window called "Sheet1." The *worksheet window* is a grid, outlined on the bottom and right by scroll bars, on the left by row numbers and on the top by column labels. The worksheet window is separate from the program window because you can work on multiple worksheets at once in Excel, as you'll learn in Skill Session 6. The following paragraphs describe the screen shown in Figure 1.2.

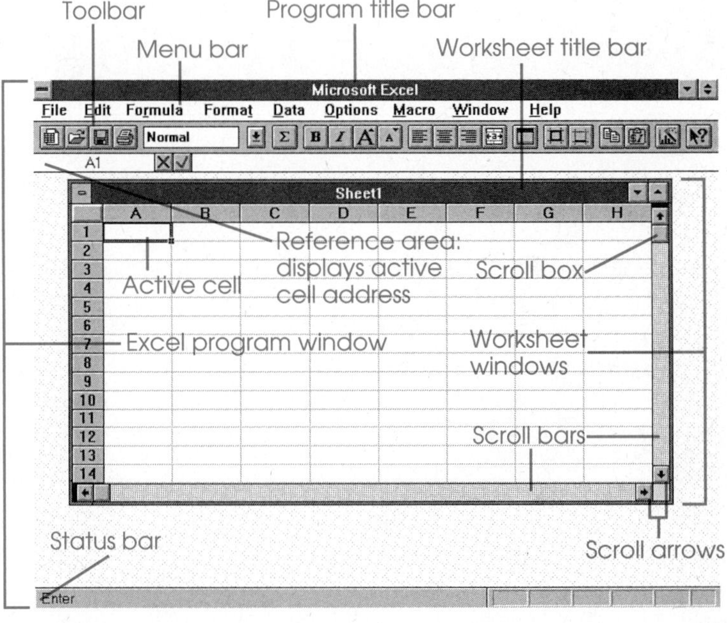

Figure 1.2 The Excel program window with the worksheet entitled Sheet1.

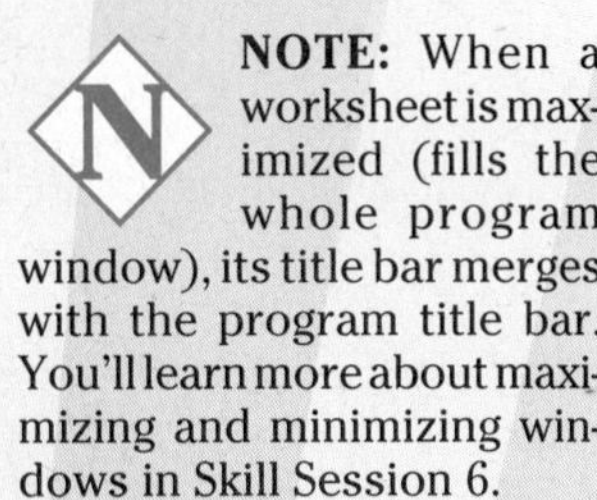

NOTE: When a worksheet is maximized (fills the whole program window), its title bar merges with the program title bar. You'll learn more about maximizing and minimizing windows in Skill Session 6.

At the top of the window is the *title bar* for the program, Microsoft Excel. When you save and rename a worksheet, the name appears in the worksheet's title bar. When you work with multiple windows, the title bar of the active window is highlighted and the title bars of inactive windows are grayed.

Just below the title bar is the *menu bar*. Each menu name opens to display a list of Excel's commands. You'll learn more about using menus and commands in Skill Session 2.

Below the menu bar is the *toolbar*. The toolbar displays graphic representations (tools) for some of Excel's most commonly used commands such as printing. (Notice that the fourth tool from the left is a picture of a printer.) The toolbar is designed for mouse users and makes selecting commands quick and easy. You'll learn about using the toolbar in Skill Session 4.

At the bottom of the program window is the *status bar*, where Excel displays messages or brief instructions.

Inside of the program window is the *worksheet window*. As displayed on your screen, the worksheet appears to have 8 columns and 14 rows. In fact, the worksheet actually contains 256 columns and 16,384 rows. Rows are numbered 1 through 16,384 and the columns are labeled A through Z, then AA, AB, AC, . . ., BA, BB, BC, and so on through column IV.

Each row and column intersection is called a *cell*. Cells are referred to by the *address* of their intersection (e.g., cell B5 or EA540). The outlined cell is called the *active* (or *current*) cell. The worksheet is bordered on the right and bottom by scroll bars, used for moving around the worksheet. Each scroll bar contains a *scroll box* and *scroll arrows*.

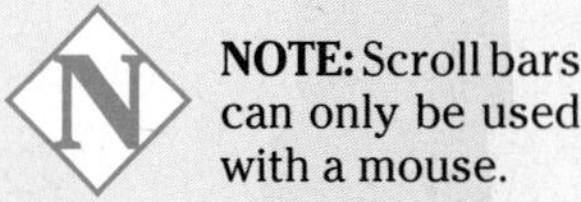

NOTE: Scroll bars can only be used with a mouse.

The *formula bar*, located just below the toolbar, is where you enter and edit data in the worksheet. The left end of the formula bar is called the *reference area* and always displays the current cell address. If you are using a mouse, the *cancel box* (an X) allows you to cancel an entry you've made; the *enter box* (a check mark) allows you to confirm an entry. The entry you type is displayed to the right of the enter box. (You'll begin entering information into the worksheet in Skill Session 5.) The formula bar contains a *cursor* (not visible in Figure 1.2) marking the spot where characters are inserted when you type.

Basic Mouse and Keyboard Techniques

Excel 4 for Windows is designed to be used with a mouse. If you are not using a mouse, basic keyboard techniques are included at the end of this section. Throughout this book, keyboard instructions are provided only when necessary or when the keyboard method is more efficient. In some cases, mouse users may want to use a combination of mouse and keyboard methods for selecting commands and maneuvering the worksheet.

Basic Mouse Techniques

The cross (or arrow) on your screen is called the *mouse pointer* and marks the location of the mouse in the worksheet area. When the mouse pointer is in a worksheet, it is shaped like a cross. When you move it into the Excel toolbar, menu bar, or scroll bar areas, the pointer becomes an arrow. When you move it onto the area to the right of the enter box on the formula bar, it becomes an I-beam.

You'll use the mouse to select commands, cells, or ranges of cells and to move around the worksheet. The following mouse terms apply throughout this book:

Point—Move the mouse pointer to a new location in the window.

Click—Quickly press and release the left mouse button once.

Double-click—Quickly press and release the left mouse button twice.

Drag—Press and hold the left mouse button as you move the mouse pointer to a new location, then release.

Unless otherwise indicated, these terms apply to the left mouse button.

With the mouse, you can use the scroll bars to move through the worksheet. Click on a scroll arrow to move up, down, right, or left one row or column at a time. Click and drag the scroll box to move to an approximate location in the worksheet.

Basic Keyboard Techniques

If you are not using a mouse, the primary keys you'll use for navigating the worksheet are the arrow keys. Press any arrow key to move one cell at a time. Press and hold any arrow key to move continuously through the rows or columns of a worksheet. These and other navigation keys are described in Table 1.1.

Table 1.1 Navigation keys used in Excel 4 for Windows

Key	*Function*
Up arrow, down arrow	Moves up one row or down one row at a time.
Right arrow, left arrow	Moves right one column or left one column at a time.
Tab, Shift+Tab	Moves left one column, moves right one column.

continues

Table 1.1 continued

Key	*Function*
Home	Moves to column A in the current row.
Ctrl+Home, Ctrl+End	Moves to cell A1 from anywhere in the worksheet.
Page Down, Page Up	Moves down or up one screen at a time.
End+right arrow	Moves from the current cell to the next cell in the current row that contains data. If remaining cells are blank, moves to the last cell in the current row.
End+left arrow	Moves from the current cell to the previous cell in the current row that contains data. If the remaining cells are blank, moves to the first cell in the current row.
End+up arrow	Moves from the current cell to the previous cell in the current column that contains data. If the remaining cells are blank, moves to the first row in the current column.
End+down arrow	Moves from the current cell to the next cell in the current column that contains data. If the remaining cells are blank, moves to the last row in the current column.

Exiting Excel

When you're ready to close Excel and return to the Windows Program Manager, follow these steps.

Using the mouse:

1. Point and click on File to open the menu.
2. Point and click on Exit (shown in Figure 1.3). The Excel window closes and returns you to the Windows Program Manager as it was when you left it.
3. If you have made any entries, you will be asked if you want to save changes before exiting. Answer accordingly.

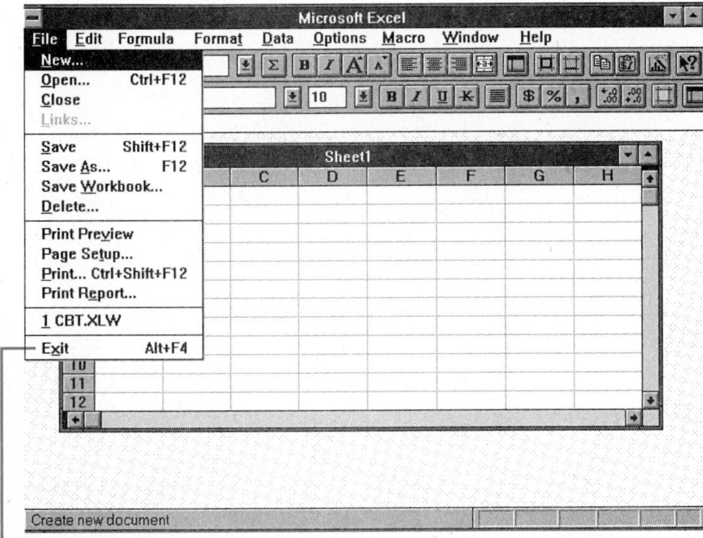

Use the Exit Command to exit Excel and return to the Windows Program Manager.

Figure 1.3 The Exit command on the File menu.

Using the keyboard:

1. Press Alt and then press F to open the **File** menu.
2. Press X to select **Exit**. The Excel window closes and returns you to the Windows Program Manager as it was when you left it.

3. If you have made any entries, you will be asked if you want to save changes before exiting. Answer accordingly.

Skill Session

2

Using Menus and Dialog Boxes

Aside from the data you enter into the worksheet, the majority of the work you do in Excel for Windows will be with *commands*. A command tells Excel what kind of task you want to perform (for example, underline an entry in a cell or print a worksheet). In this skill session, you'll learn how commands are organized on Excel menus, how to select commands and provide Excel with additional information about the tasks you want to perform, and how to get help when you need it.

The Excel Menu Structure

Excel commands are grouped by category under the menus listed on the menu bar. When you select a menu, it opens to reveal a list of commands. Figure 2.1 illustrates the list of commands under the **E**dit menu.

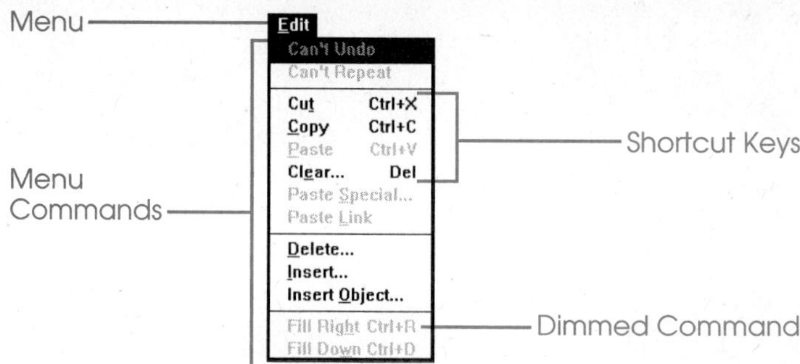

Figure 2.1 The commands on the Edit menu.

Excel has nine menus on the menu bar. Each menu name indicates the type of commands you'll find on the menu. For example, the Forma**t** menu contains commands that allow you to change the format of a worksheet (such as choosing a font, centering text, and adding dollar signs to numbers). The **E**dit menu contains commands that allow you to move, copy, cut, and paste cell entries as well as make other editing changes.

Notice in Figure 2.1 that some of the commands on the menu appear in light gray text. When a command is dimmed, it is unavailable because it doesn't apply to the work or task you are performing at the time. For example, you can't use the **P**aste command to insert an entry if you haven't used the Cu**t** or **C**opy command first. The commands appear in normal text on the menu when the task you're performing makes them available.

Making Menu Selections

In most cases, you'll open a menu before selecting a command. To open a menu using the mouse, point to the menu name and click. Once the menu is open, point to a command name and click to select a command.

Notice that one character in each menu name—and in each command on the menu—is underlined. This is called the *selection* letter. If you are using a keyboard instead of a mouse, you open a menu by first pressing Alt, then typing the selection letter for the menu name. For example, to open the **File** menu, press Alt+F. (Excel is not case sensitive; you can press F or f to select **File** menu.) Once the menu is open, select a command by pressing just the selection character—it's not necessary to press Alt again. Instead of using the selection character, you can use the arrow keys to select menus and commands. Press Alt, then the right or left arrow key to select menus. Once a menu is open, press the up or down arrow key to highlight a command.

Note: Throughout this book, the selection letter for every menu name and command name appears in boldface type. When you are instructed to select a command, the menu name appears first, immediately followed by the command name. For example, to select the **Print** command on the **File** menu, the instructions will say "select **File Print**."

In Skill Session 1, you learned that the status line displays messages and brief instructions. When you choose a menu or a menu command, the status line gives you a brief explanation of the menu or the command. This information can be especially helpful when you're first learning to use Excel.

Using Shortcut Keys

Some menu commands have *shortcut keys* associated with them. A shortcut key allows you to choose a command without opening the menu first. It is usually a two-key sequence that you can type to select a command. Shortcut keys appear to the right of the command name on the menu. In Figure 2.1, notice that the shortcut key for the Cut command is Ctrl+X. This means that, without opening the menu first, you can press Ctrl+X to use the Cut command. Obviously, when you first begin using Excel, you won't know these shortcut keys without looking at the menu first. But once you begin using them, you'll learn them quickly.

Using Shortcut Menus

After using Excel for a while, you'll find that you use some commands more frequently than others. Excel 4 for Windows features these commands on new *shortcut menus*, which you can access by pressing the right mouse button from anywhere in the worksheet. (If you're using a keyboard, press Shift+F10 to display a shortcut menu.) There are several shortcut menus in Excel 4; the one that is displayed depends on the type of task you're performing. For example, if you're working in the worksheet, the shortcut menu contains commands for editing and formatting cell entries. If you're working on a graphic object, the shortcut menu contains commands for moving and arranging objects. Several shortcut menus are shown in Figure 2.2.

You select a command from a shortcut menu the same way you do any other menu: point to the command and click, or press the selection letter.

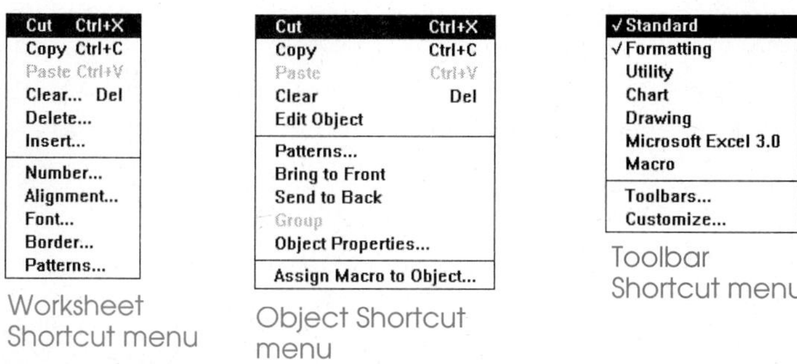

Figure 2.2 Shortcut menus used in Excel 4 for Windows.

Using Dialog Boxes

Menu commands that are followed by an ellipsis (such as the **D**elete command shown in Figure 2.1) display *dialog boxes*—small windows that appear on top of the Excel worksheet and disappear when you are finished using them. A dialog box asks you to provide more information about the command you have chosen, either by typing an entry or by selecting options. For example, the dialog box shown in Figure 2.3 is displayed when you select File Print. In this dialog box, you specify options such as the pages and the number of copies to print.

Dialog Box Elements

Dialog boxes vary in size, shape, and the number of settings and options. They may contain many different settings and, therefore, are often divided into named sections. (The Print Range box shown in Figure 2.3 represents a section of the Print dialog box.) Within each section, a dialog box can contain any of the following elements:

Text boxes—Text boxes either are blank or contain suggested text or data (such as the number of copies to print, as shown in Figure 2.3). When a text box is blank, you must either type an entry or leave it blank if you don't want to use the option.

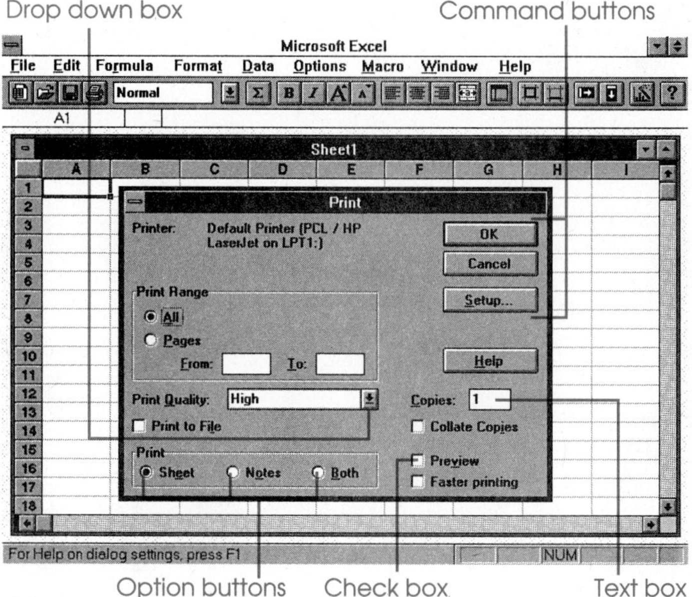

Figure 2.3 The File Print dialog box.

List boxes—List boxes display lists of options to choose from such as a list of file names. When the list is long, the box contains a vertical scroll bar that operates the same as other Windows scroll bars. You may select only one item from a list box.

Drop-down boxes—Similar to list boxes, drop-down boxes offer a list of options to choose from, but the full list is hidden until you reveal it by selecting the drop-down arrow. The Print Quality box in Figure 2.3 is an example of a drop-down box.

Option buttons—An option button is an open circle used to select one setting from a set (such as Sheet, Notes, or Both, as shown in Figure 2.3). You can select only one option button from the set. Option buttons turn on and off when you select them.

Check boxes—Settings that are preceded by an open square box are called check boxes (see the Preview check box in Figure 2.3). When the setting is selected, an x appears in the box. You may choose as many check boxes as you like in a dialog box. Check boxes turn on and off when you select them.

Command buttons—Almost all dialog boxes contain at least two command buttons: OK and Cancel. When you select OK, all the settings in the dialog box take effect. When you select Cancel, Excel ignores the settings and returns to the Excel worksheet without making any changes. Most dialog boxes also contain a Help command button, which you can select at any time to display help on the dialog box settings. Occasionally, dialog boxes contain command buttons that are followed by an ellipsis. These buttons open *subdialog boxes*, from which you can choose more specific settings.

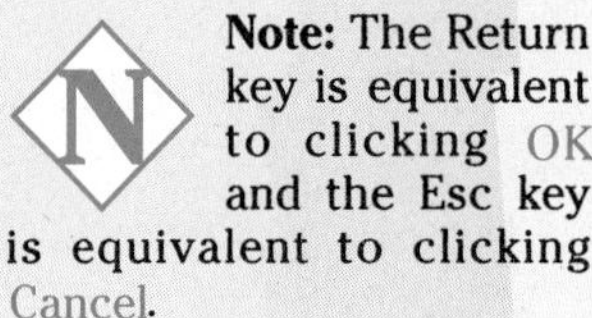

Note: The Return key is equivalent to clicking OK and the Esc key is equivalent to clicking Cancel.

Changing Dialog Box Settings with a Mouse

To change settings in a dialog box using the mouse, simply point to and click on the option, item, or button you want to select. To select an item from a list box, click on the item if it is displayed. If it is not displayed, use the scroll bar to display the item and then click on it. To make an entry in a text box, click on the box and then begin typing. To select an item from a drop-down box, click on the down arrow, then click on an item in the list.

Changing Dialog Box Settings with the Keyboard

To change settings in a dialog box using the keyboard, follow these guidelines:

- Press Tab to cycle from one section of the dialog box to the next. Press Shift+Tab to cycle backward one section at a time. As you move from one section to the next, a dotted line surrounds the selection at your current location.
- When you press Tab to move to a section of the dialog box, press the Spacebar to select a checkbox; press an arrow key to select an option button.
- Move immediately to a section or an option in the dialog box by pressing Alt and then the selection letter for the section or option. (Note that some dialog box sections do not have selection letters, but all dialog box options do.)

▲ To select an item from a list or drop-down box, press Alt and the selection letter for the box name. Use the up arrow or down arrow to select (highlight) an item in the list.

▲ To make an entry in a text box, press Alt and the selection letter for the box name and then type the entry.

Getting Help

Excel 4 for Windows provides extensive online help through the **H**elp menu, by pressing F1, or by selecting the Help tool on the standard toolbar. When you use the Help menu, you can choose a help topic. When you press F1, Excel provides *context-sensitive* help, that is, help that relates to the task you are currently working on. When you select the Help tool, the mouse pointer changes to a question mark. Point to any area on the worksheet, any menu, or any command to display the appropriate help topic. Excel also includes a help command button in every dialog box. Whenever you need help on dialog box settings, select this help button.

The **H**elp menu includes the commands shown in Table 2.1.

Table 2.1 Help menu commands

Help Menu Command:	*Meaning:*
Contents	Provides a list of task-oriented help topics.
Search	Displays a search window in which you can type any word or topic. Excel lists all locations in the Help file that cover the topic entered.
Product Support	Provides details on all product support services available for Excel.
Introducing Microsoft Excel and Learning Microsoft Excel	These options are only available if you install the Excel tutorials during Setup. Select either of these commands to start an Excel tutorial. If you have a worksheet open, you will be asked if you want to save changes before closing it.
Lotus 1-2-3	Provides help to Lotus 1-2-3 users by displaying a help topic on equivalent Excel commands.
Multiplan	Provides help to Multiplan users by displaying a help topic on equivalent Excel commands.
About Microsoft Excel	Lists the current version of Microsoft Excel and the name of the licensee.

When you select one of these commands, a separate Help window like the one shown in Figure 2.4 is displayed. Use the scroll bars, the arrow keys, or the

Page Up and Page Down keys to review the help topic displayed in the window.

Text that is displayed in green in a help screen is known as a "hot spot." Hot spots allow you to move quickly through help screens and zero in on the exact help you're looking for. Hot spots are displayed either with a solid underline or a dotted underline. When you move the mouse over a hot spot, the mouse pointer changes to a hand. Click on a hot spot with a solid underline to display a help screen for the hot spot topic. Click on a hot spot with a dotted underline to pop up a box that displays a definition for the hot spot text. Click anywhere on the screen to close a pop-up definition box.

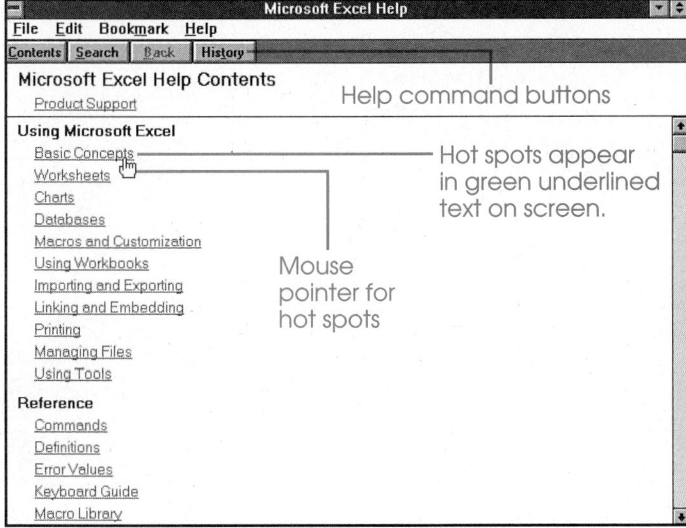

Figure 2.4 The Help window displays information about the selected topic

The command buttons displayed along the top of the Help window allow you to choose other help topics. The following describes these buttons and how they are used.

- **C**ontents: Displays the table of contents help screen. When you display a Contents help screen, (either by selecting **H**elp **C**ontents or the **C**ontents button from a Help screen) the topics listed are all hot spots. Click on the topic you want to view. In most cases, another list of topics is displayed which contains hot spots. Continue selecting topics from these hot spot lists until the topic information you want is displayed.

- **S**earch: Displays a search dialog box (shown in Figure 2.5) in which you can type any word or topic. Select **H**elp **S**earch, or select the **S**earch button from within a Help screen to display the Search dialog box. To search for a topic, enter a word or phrase in the text box. The upper list box displays matching (or the closest matching) entries from the Help files. Select an entry in this list, then select the Show Topics button to display a list of actual Help topics in the lower list box. Select a topic from the lower list, then select the **G**o To button. Excel displays the help screen for the topic chosen.

- **B**ack: Redisplays the help topic you viewed previously. Select this button at any point to return to the previous Help topic. When selected repeatedly, **B**ack retraces your steps through the Help files.

- His**t**ory: In a separate window, displays a history list of all help topics you have viewed during the current Excel session. Select the His**t**ory button to display the history list. Select any topic in the list to redisplay to the associated Help screen.

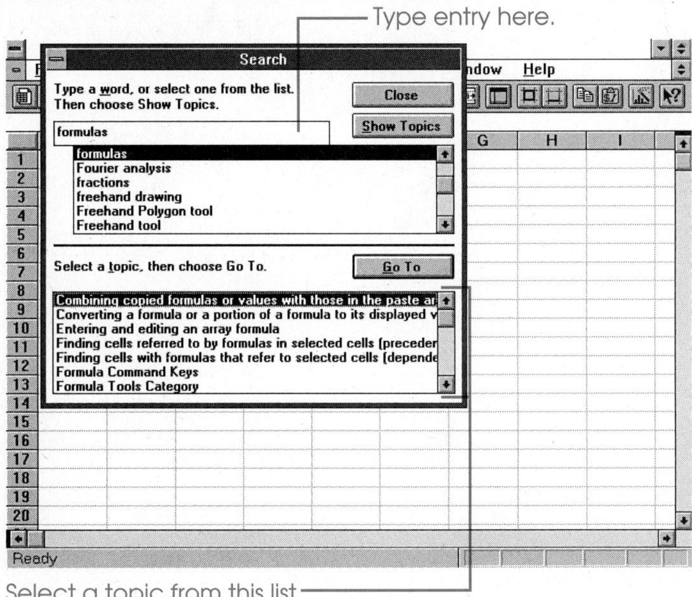

Figure 2.5 The Search dialog box.

Skill Session

3

Controlling Worksheet Windows

In Skill Session 1, you learned about the Excel program and worksheet windows and how to move around the worksheet using the mouse and the keyboard. In this skill session, you'll learn how to control the size, arrangement, and placement of the Excel windows on the screen and how to work with the control menu box.

Window Elements

Most Windows applications have some common characteristics, including the elements that make up a window. You learned about most of these elements in Skill Session 1. Those that were not covered in Skill Session 1 are listed below and shown in Figure 3.1.

▲ The control menu box

▲ The maximize button

▲ The minimize button

▲ The restore button

▲ The worksheet title bar (as a tool for moving a window)

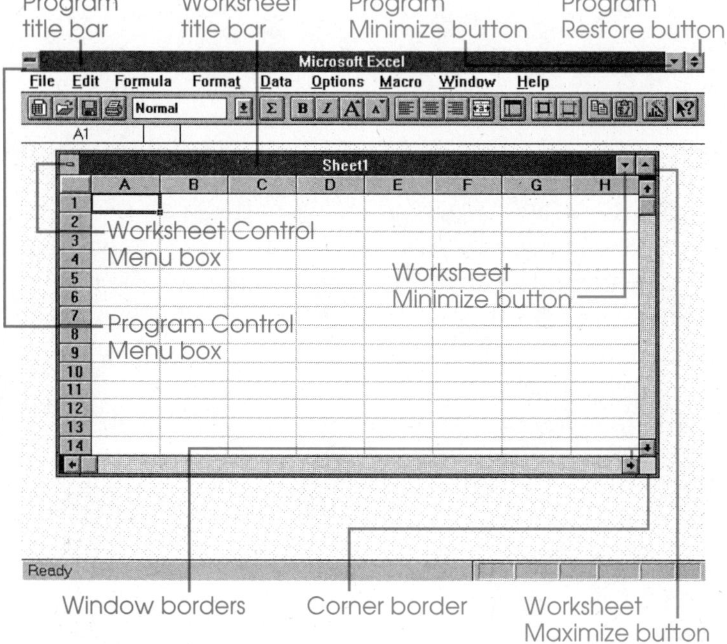

Figure 3.1 The Excel window and a worksheet window.

Notice that these elements appear in both the program window and in the worksheet window shown in Figure 3.1. This is because each window can be manipulated independently of the other. The exception to this is the program window, which contains a restore button in place of a maximize button. You'll learn why later in this skill session.

The Control Menu

The control menu box opens the Control menu, which contains a variety of commands for restoring, moving, resizing, and closing a window (see Figure 3.2). The Control menu for the *program* window (not the *worksheet* window) contains additional options that allow you to switch to or start other applications. (These options are not available in the worksheet window because the Excel program window controls the worksheet window.) Figure 3.2 illustrates the slight difference in commands between the program Control menu and the worksheet Control menu.

Figure 3.2 The commands on the program Control menu and the worksheet Control menu have slight differences.

The Control menus and their commands exist primarily for keyboard users, although mouse users can use the Control menus as well. For example, keyboard users must use the **R**estore, **M**ove, **S**ize, Mi**n**imize, Ma**x**imize, **C**lose, and Nex**t** Window commands on the Control menus to accomplish any of these tasks. Mouse users simply click the mouse on various screen elements to accomplish these tasks.

Using Control Menus with the Keyboard

The following general instructions describe how to select commands from the Control menus using the keyboard.

- To open the program window's Control menu, press Alt+spacebar. Excel opens the Control menu.
- If you want to open the worksheet's Control menu, press Alt+spacebar, then press the right arrow. Excel highlights the worksheet control menu box and opens the menu. Otherwise, skip to step 3.
- To cycle through each menu on the Excel menu bar, press Alt+spacebar, then continue to press the right arrow as each menu name is highlighted. After highlighting the last menu name (Help), Excel returns to the program control menu box, then cycles back to the worksheet control menu box. Press the left arrow to cycle backward.
- To select a command (from either the program or worksheet Control menu), press the underlined character for the command or use up- and down-Arrow keys. To close the Control menu without selecting a command, press Esc.

Using Control Menus with a Mouse

To access either of the Control menus using the mouse, click on the control menu box, then click on the command you want to use. To close the Control menu without selecting a command, click anywhere outside of the menu.

The remainder of this skill session uses these basic principles to describe the keyboard and mouse methods for maximizing, minimizing, moving, resizing, and so on.

Maximizing, Restoring, and Minimizing Windows

When you first start the Excel program, the program window may not fill the screen. Instead, the program window might be displayed at a reduced size. You can work with the Excel window at a reduced size if you choose, but most often you'll want to work with Excel at its maximum size. To *maximize* Excel—that is, to make the program window fill the screen—click the program window's maximize button. If you are using the keyboard, open the program Control menu, then select the Maximize command by pressing x. In Figure 3.3, the program window is maximized.

Maximizing the program window makes Excel easier to work with, but it doesn't automatically maximize the worksheet window. To display the worksheet window at its largest size, use the same method you just learned: Click on the worksheet's maximize button or select Control Maximize. Figure 3.4 shows both the program and the worksheet windows at their maximum size.

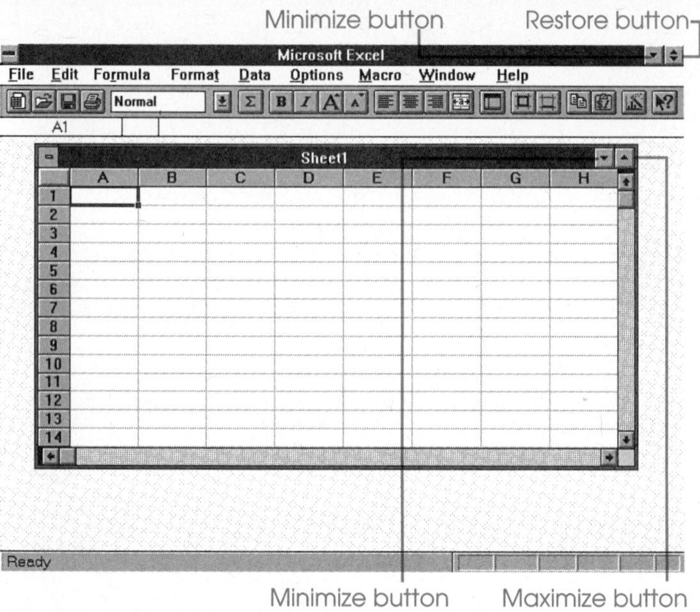

Figure 3.3 The program window and each worksheet window have separate maximize and minimize buttons.

You may have noticed that when you maximize a window, the maximize button in the upper right corner of the window no longer looks the same. In a maximized window, you do not need a maximize button, so it changes to a *restore* button, a double-headed arrow shown in Figure 3.4. The restore button returns a window to its previous size and position. To restore a window using the mouse, click on the restore button. Using the keyboard, select Control Restore.

When you minimize a worksheet, this icon is displayed ide the Excel program win- to remind you that a heet file is still open.

At this point, you have only two windows open on your screen—a reasonable number to manage. You can, however, have many windows open at once, as you'll learn in Skill Session 6. When you work with multiple windows, it's often helpful to minimize a window temporarily to clear some space on the screen. Minimizing a window doesn't close the file or the application, it simply reduces the window to an icon. To shrink a window to an icon using the mouse, click on the minimize button. Using the keyboard, select Control Minimize or press Ctrl+F9.

When you minimize the Excel program, this icon is displayed near the bottom of your screen to remind you that Excel is still running.

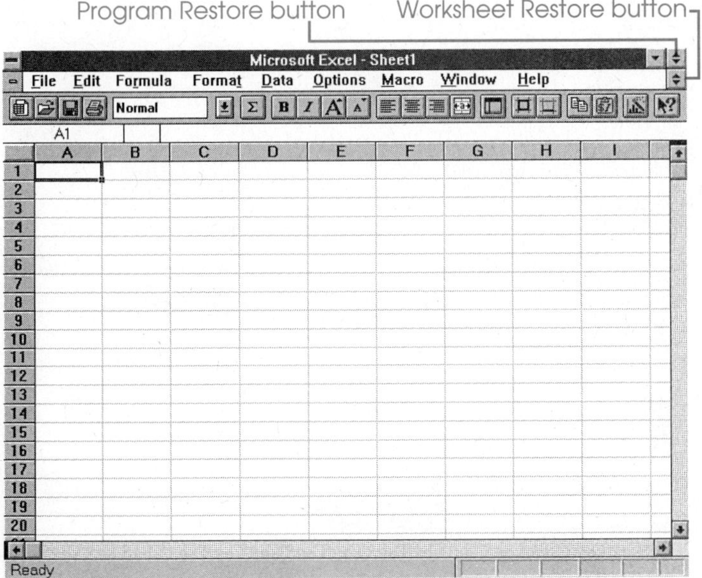

Figure 3.4 The Excel program window and the worksheet window are maximized.

You can shrink a worksheet window to an icon without shrinking the Excel window. You can't, however, shrink the Excel window to an icon and keep the worksheet window open on the screen. Because the worksheet window is dependent upon the Excel window, the worksheet window goes along with Excel when you shrink it to an icon.

Resizing a Window

When you use the minimize, maximize, and restore buttons or commands, you have no control over the size of a window; the size is automatically determined for you. But suppose you want to determine the size and shape of your windows. You can use the window borders or Control Size to resize a window to the dimensions you choose. Resizing a window gives you the flexibility to display whatever you like on your screen by allowing you to create more space.

To resize a window using a mouse, you use the window borders. The top, bottom, right, and left borders resize in one dimension only; the window corners resize the window in two dimensions at once. Drag a window border or a window corner to the dimensions you choose, releasing the mouse button when the window is the size you want.

When you point to a top or bottom border, the mouse pointer changes to this double-headed arrow.

When you point to a right or left border, the mouse pointer changes to this double-headed arrow.

When you point to a window/border corner, the mouse pointer changes to this double-headed arrow.

NOTE: When a window is maximized, you can't resize it using the borders. You must first restore the window to its previ- 's size (using the restore on or command), mak- borders visible, and the borders to resize v.

To resize a window using the keyboard, follow these steps:

1. Press Alt+spacebar to open the program Control menu. If you want to resize a worksheet window, press the right arrow until the worksheet Control menu opens.
2. Select **S**ize by pressing S. The mouse pointer changes to a four-headed arrow.
3. Use the arrow keys to resize the window and then press Enter. The window is automatically resized to the dimensions you choose.

TIP: You can skip steps 1 and 2 by pressing Ctrl+F8. Then follow step 3.

NOTE: When a window is maximized you cannot resize it using the **S**ize command. Use the **Re**store command to restore the window first, then use the **S**ize command or Ctrl+F8.

Moving a Window

One of the great advantages of the Microsoft Windows system is that you can work with more than one window on the screen at once—document windows or program windows. In order to do this, however, you need to be able to move windows wherever you want them on the screen. For example, if you are working on two Excel worksheets at the same time, you might want to move one of the Excel windows to the bottom of the screen, as shown in Figure 3.5. You can do this by resizing and moving each window to fit on the screen at once.

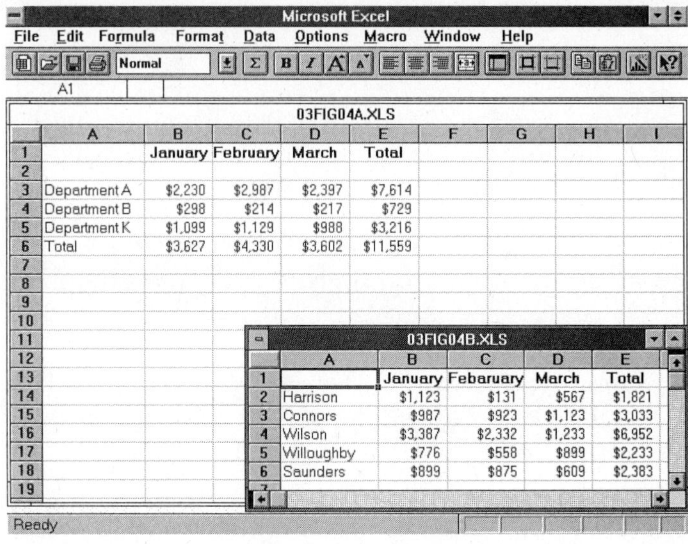

	A	B	C	D	E
1		January	February	March	Total
2					
3	Department A	$2,230	$2,987	$2,397	$7,614
4	Department B	$298	$214	$217	$729
5	Department K	$1,099	$1,129	$988	$3,216
6	Total	$3,627	$4,330	$3,602	$11,559

	A	B	C	D	E
1		January	Febaruary	March	Total
2	Harrison	$1,123	$131	$567	$1,821
3	Connors	$987	$923	$1,123	$3,033
4	Wilson	$3,387	$2,332	$1,233	$6,952
5	Willoughby	$776	$558	$899	$2,233
6	Saunders	$899	$875	$609	$2,383

Figure 3.5 The two open windows were resized and moved to convenient working positions.

To move a window using the mouse, simply click on the title bar and drag the window to a new location, releasing the mouse button when the window is positioned where you want it. To move a window using the keyboard, follow these steps:

1. Press Alt+spacebar to open the program Control menu. If you want to move a worksheet window, press the right arrow until the worksheet Control menu opens.

2. Select **M**ove from the menu by pressing M. The mouse pointer changes to a four-headed arrow.

3. Press the arrow keys to move the window to a new location on the screen. When the window is positioned where you want it, press Enter.

Try using the Move and Resize features together to arrange the open windows on the screen just how you want them.

TIP: You can skip steps 1 and 2 by pressing Ctrl+F7. Then follow step 3.

TIP: The dialog boxes you learned about in Skill Session 2 are a type of window. Occasionally they pop up and obscure the area of the worksheet you're working on. You can move a dialog box to any location on the screen using the steps you just learned.

NOTE: You cannot move a maximized window. Restore the window first, then move it.

Skill Session

4

Using Excel's Toolbars

In Skill Session 1, you learned that the toolbar displays pictures that represent Excel's most commonly used actions and commands (for example, printing). Each picture is called a *tool* and can be selected in place of a menu command if you are using a mouse. Using the toolbar saves you the trouble of opening a menu, selecting a command, and, in many cases, specifying settings and options in a dialog box.

Excel automatically displays the *Standard* toolbar and offers additional toolbars that you can display at your option. In this skill session, you'll learn how to use the Standard toolbar and get a brief introduction to Excel's additional toolbars.

Standard Toolbar Tools

When you start Excel, the Standard toolbar shown in Figure 4.1 is automatically displayed. Each tool on this toolbar, from left to right, is identified in Table 4.1.

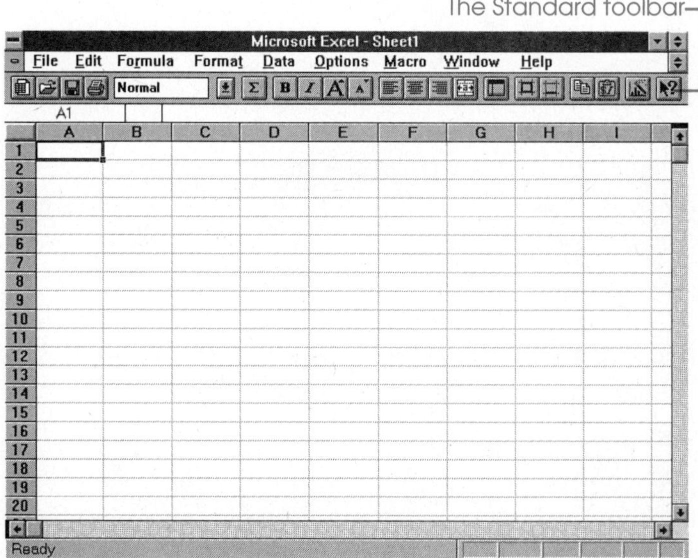

Figure 4.1 The Excel screen with the Standard toolbar.

Table 4.1 Standard toolbar tools

Icon	*Tool Name*	*Description*
	New Worksheet	Creates a new worksheet. Use instead of selecting **F**ile **N**ew.

Icon	Tool Name	Description
	Open File	Displays the File Open dialog box so you can open another worksheet. Use instead of File **O**pen.
	Save File	Saves the active worksheet. Use instead of File **S**ave.
	Print	Prints the active worksheet. Use instead of File **P**rint.
Normal	Style Box	Allows you to choose a cell style (for example, Currency or Comma). Use instead of Forma**t** **S**tyle.
Σ	Autosum	Automatically inserts the SUM function on the edit line and suggests the range of cells to sum.
B	Bold	Automatically bolds the entries in the selected cell range, text box, or chart. Use instead of Forma**t** Fon**t**.
I	Italic	Automatically italicizes the entries in the selected cell range, text box, or chart. Use instead of Forma**t** Fon**t**.
A	Increase Font	Increases the font size of the selected text to the next available size. Use instead of Forma**t** Fon**t**.

continues

Table 4.1 continued

Icon	*Tool Name*	*Description*
	Decrease Font	Decreases the font size of the selected text to the next available size. Use instead of Forma**t** Fon**t**.
	Left Align	Automatically left-aligns the entries in the selected cell range, text box, or chart. Use instead of Forma**t** **A**lignment.
	Center Align	Automatically centers the entries in the selected cell range, text box, or chart. Use instead of Forma**t** **A**lignment.
	Right Align	Automatically right-aligns the entries in the selected cell range, text box, or chart. Use instead of Forma**t** **A**lignment.
	Center Across	Automatically centers text across the columns range of selected columns. Use instead of Forma**t** **A**lignment.
	Autoformat	Automatically formats the selected range to the last table format applied using Forma**t** AutoFor**m**at.

Icon	*Tool Name*	*Description*
	Outline Border	Adds an outline border to the selected range of cells. Use instead of Forma**t** **B**order.
	Bottom Border	Adds a border to the bottom edge of the selected range of cells. Use instead of Forma**t** **B**order.
	Copy	Copies selected text onto the Clipboard. Use instead of **E**dit **C**opy. Use instead of **E**dit Paste **S**pecial.
	Paste Format	Pastes only the format of the selected cells to the new location.
	Chart Wizard	Allows you to create a new embedded chart or edit the selected chart using Chart Wizard.
	Help	Adds a question mark to the mouse pointer so you can point anywhere on the Excel screen to get help on that item.

Selecting Standard Tools

You must use a mouse to access the tools on the toolbar. Some tools (for example, the New Worksheet tool) require no action before selecting the tool. Other tools require you to select a cell or range of cells before selecting the tool. For instance, before selecting the Bold tool, you must tell Excel which cell or cells you want to bold; otherwise, Excel will bold the current cell. To select a cell, point to it and click. (Skill Session 7 discusses selecting ranges of cells.) To select a tool, point to it on the toolbar and then click.

In most cases, the tool takes immediate action. For example, if you choose the Increase Font tool, the font shown in the selected cell is immediately changed to the next largest size. In other cases, a dialog box may be displayed (for example, when you select the Open File tool). Use the dialog box as you normally would to complete the action.

Hiding and Displaying the Standard Toolbar

The Standard toolbar is automatically displayed when you start Excel, but you can hide it if you choose. Hiding the toolbar gives you more room in the worksheet window (a maximum of 22 rows) and simplifies the Excel window. You might choose to hide the toolbar when you are busy entering data and not using any formatting or enhancement features.

You can hide the toolbar using **O**ptions T**o**olbars or a shortcut menu. To hide the toolbar using the menu command:

1. Select Options Toolbars. Excel displays the Toolbars dialog box shown in Figure 4.2.
2. Select Standard from the Show T**o**olbars list box.
3. Select Hide.
4. Select Close to close the dialog box and return to Excel.

When you want to redisplay the toolbar, follow the same steps, selecting Show in step 3.

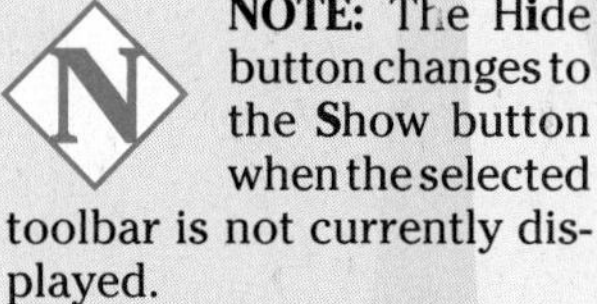

NOTE: The H**i**de button changes to the **S**how button when the selected toolbar is not currently displayed.

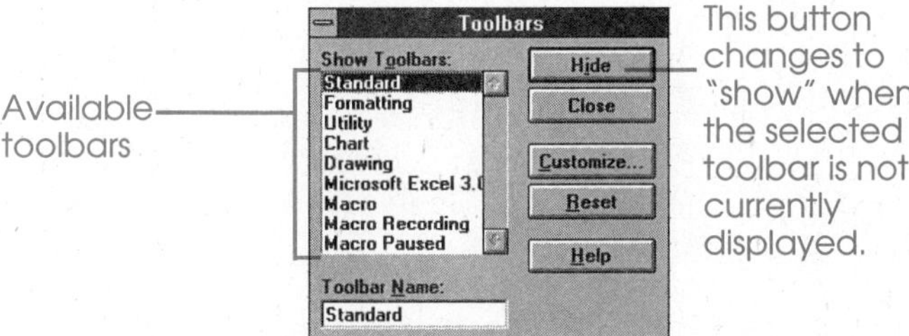

Figure 4.2 The Toolbars dialog box.

To hide the toolbar using the shortcut menu:

1. Move the mouse pointer to any blank area within the toolbar, then click the *right* mouse button. Excel displays the Toolbars shortcut menu shown in Figure 4.3. Notice that the Standard menu item has a check mark next to it, indicating that the toolbar is currently displayed.
2. Click on Standard to hide the toolbar.

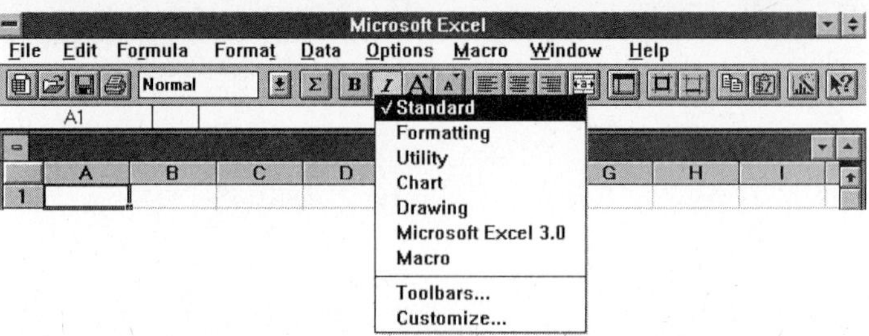

Figure 4.3 The Toolbars shortcut menu.

You can use the shortcut menu to redisplay the Standard toolbar by following the same steps. Note that when the Standard toolbar is hidden, it will not have a check mark next to it on the shortcut menu.

Using Other Toolbars

Excel offers additional toolbars shown in Figure 4.4. Each one contains tools that represents a particular activity (e.g., formatting). The complete list with descriptions of each toolbar is shown in Table 4.2.

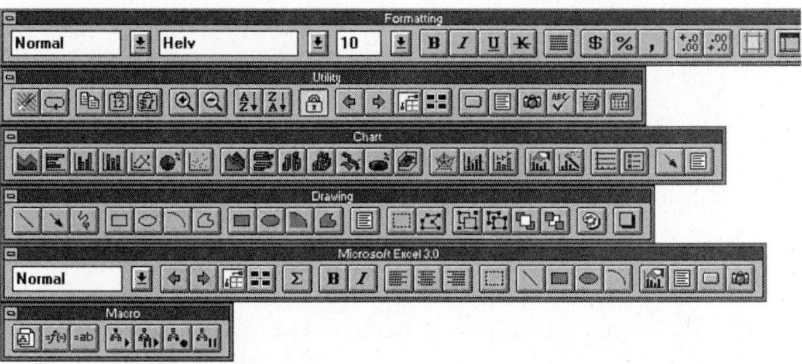

Figure 4.4 Excel's additional toolbars.

Table 4.2 Additional toolbars

Toolbar	*Description*
Formatting	Contains tools for changing all aspects of cell formatting, including font style and size; bold, italic, and underline accents; alignment options; currency, percent, decimal, and comma styles; and shading and shadowing options.
Utility	Contains tools for working more efficiently with the worksheet (for example, undo, repeat, copy, paste, zoom, sort, spell check, and outline).
Chart	Contains tools that allow you to edit an existing chart or create a new one. Most of the tools represent chart types (for example, pie, bar, area, and line), in addition to various 3-D chart types.
Drawing	Contains tools that allow you to add graphical elements to your worksheets (for example, lines, arrows, rectangles, ovals, and circles). Also contains several freehand drawing tools.
Microsoft Excel 3.0	Contains all the tools on the Standard toolbar from version 3.0 of Microsoft Excel. You may find this toolbar helpful while you are still learning to use Excel 4.0.
Macro	Contains the tools necessary for creating new macro sheets and recording, running, and resuming macros. Note that you can display individual toolbars (subsets of the Macro toolbar) for Macro Recording and Macro Paused.

To display or hide any of the additional toolbars, use the same steps you learned in the previous section.

Excel stacks each toolbar you choose below the menu bar. In Figure 4.5, the Standard, Formatting, and Drawing toolbars are displayed.

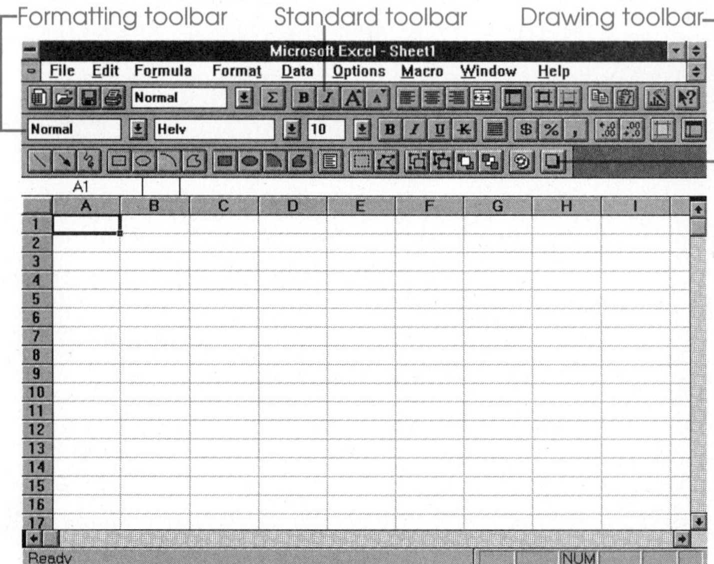

Figure 4.5 The Standard, Formatting, and Drawing toolbars are displayed.

Advanced Toolbar Options

Excel includes additional tools that are not displayed on any of the toolbars described in Table 4.2. These tools represent common Excel commands and activities for file operations, editing, formatting, creating formulas, and so on. You can use these tools by creating custom toolbars. In addition, Excel allows you to move toolbars to any location on the screen and change the shape of the window in which they are displayed. For information about creating custom toolbars and moving toolbars, see Skill Session 48 on managing toolbars.

Skill Session

5

Entering and Editing Data

Before you begin using the majority of Excel's commands, you need to know the basics of entering data into the worksheet. In this skill session, you'll learn about the different types of data you can enter in a cell, the conventions for entering each type, and how to reverse an entry when necessary.

Types of Data

You can enter two basic types of data in Excel cells: *constants* and *formulas*. A constant is a number, date, time, or text entry that you type directly into the cell. "245 ", "4/15/92", "11:59 am", and "Expenses" are all examples of constants. The term *constant* refers to the fact that the content of the cell doesn't change unless you change it.

A formula is a combination of numbers, mathematical operators, functions, names, and cell references that calculate a result. "=A5+A6-C3" is an example of a simple formula. Rather than displaying the formula itself in the cell, Excel displays the result of the formula. The result may change based on the values in the cells referenced by the formula. Formulas are briefly introduced in this skill session only for the purpose of distinguishing them from constants. Skill Session 10 discusses formulas in detail.

To enter data—both constants and formulas—you use Excel's formula bar shown in Figure 5.1. The *reference area* of the formula bar always displays the address of the active cell. In Figure 5.1, the reference area shown is A1. Notice the highlight around cell A1 indicates that it is the active cell. You click on the *cancel box* to cancel an entry and the *enter box* to confirm an entry. The entry you type appears to the right of the enter box as well as in the active cell. You must click on either the enter or the cancel box to complete an entry. (Or you can press Enter to confirm or Esc to cancel an entry.)

Entering Numbers

Numbers are numeric constants upon which Excel can perform a calculation. Entries made up of digits (0–9) are considered numbers.

In general, a number can contain no letters or symbols. However, there are a few special non-digit characters that Excel allows in number entries. For example, numbers can begin with any of these symbols:

```
+ - . $ %
```

Numbers can also include commas (if entered in the appropriate places to mark thousands), parentheses (if entered as a pair to denote a negative number), or the letters e or E (if used for scientific notation).

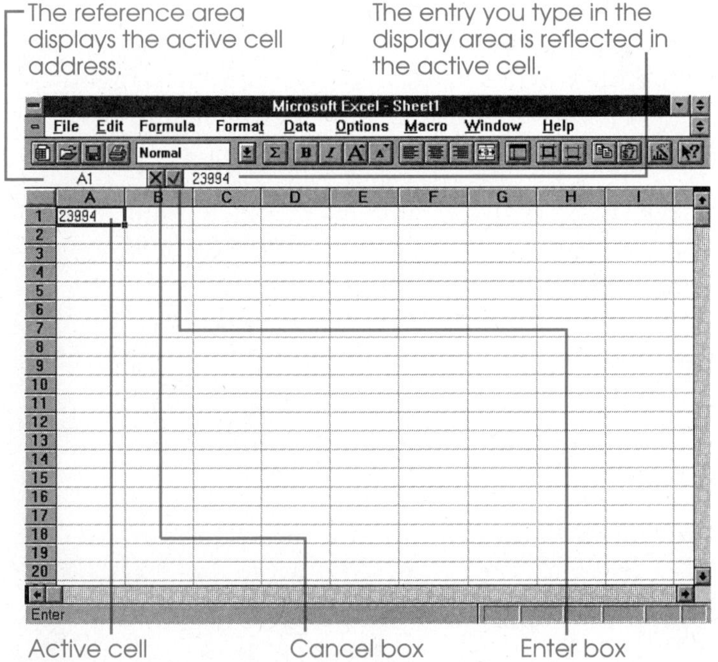

Figure 5.1 The reference area contains the active cell name and the cancel and enter boxes. The characters you type are shown in the active cell as well as on the formula bar.

To enter a number in a cell, follow these steps:

1. Select the cell in which you want to enter a number.
2. Type the entry. The entry you type appears in the formula bar as well as the cell.
3. Press Enter or click on the enter box in the formula bar to confirm the entry. Press Esc or click on the cancel box to cancel the entry.

NOTE: The cancel and enter boxes appear on the formula bar only when you are actually entering or editing a cell entry. In addition, some menu commands are grayed while you enter data in a cell. The commands become available again as soon as you complete the entry.

TIP: When you are entering data in a series of adjacent cells—for instance, across a single row—you can save some keystrokes by confirming each entry with an arrow key. When you press any of the arrow keys, you confirm the entry in the active cell and move to the next cell with just one keystroke.

TIP: If you make an error as you are typing an entry, press Backspace to delete characters to the left of the cursor and then continue typing.

TIP: If you're using Excel's default alignment options, you can tell quickly if an entry is a number by looking at the entry's alignment in the cell. By default, numbers are right-aligned, while text is left-aligned.

When you enter the addition character to signify a positive number, Excel ignores the character. To enter a negative number, type a minus sign (–) just before the number or enclose the number in parentheses. If you enter any characters that are not allowed in number entries, Excel will format the data as a *text* entry, a type of constant that you'll learn about shortly.

When the number you enter exceeds the cell width, Excel displays the number either in scientific notation or as a series of number signs (######) depending on the length of the number. You can correct this problem by widening the column (see Skill Session 16) or by changing the format of the cell (see Skill Session 13).

NOTE: Excel provides a variety of built-in cell formats, including dollar signs, percent signs, and commas. You can type these designators with the numbers you enter, or you can save yourself some keystrokes and have Excel add these designators automatically. See Skill Session 13 for information about formatting cells.

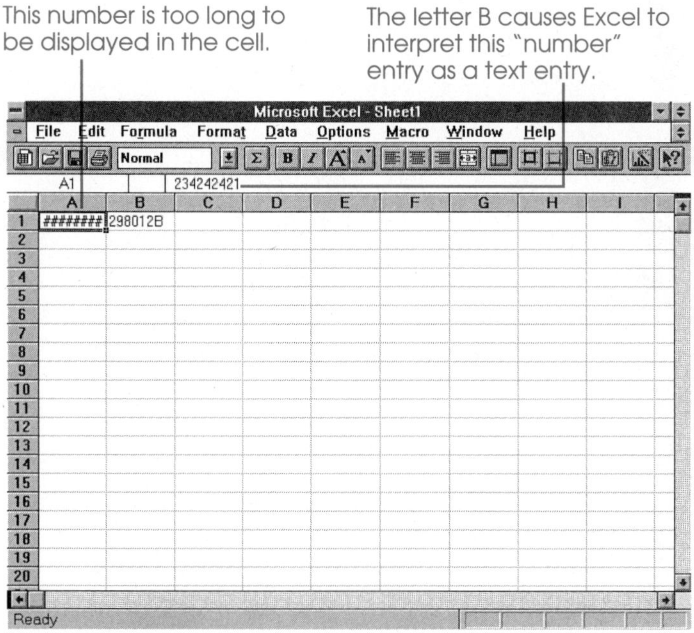

This number is too long to be displayed in the cell.

The letter B causes Excel to interpret this "number" entry as a text entry.

Figure 5.2 Number entries in a worksheet.

Dates and times are often entered as column or row headings in worksheets. Each is a type of constant that

Excel interprets as a number. You can enter dates and times in a variety of formats, or you can use one of Excel's standard *formats*. Format refers to the style in which the data are displayed in the cells. The entries shown in Table 5.1 represent Excel's built-in date and time formats. (In Skill Session 13, you'll learn more about formats and how to select them.) When you enter dates and times in any of these formats, the entry is displayed just as you typed it.

Table 5.1 Built-in date and time formats

Format	*Example*
m/d/yy	5/22/92
d-mmm-yy	3-May-92
d-mmm	3-May
mmm-yy	May-92
h:mm AM/PM	4:55 PM
h:mm:ss AM/PM	4:55:30 PM
h:mm (24 hour clock)	16:55
h:mm:ss (24 hour clock)	16:55:30
m/d/yy h:mm	5/3/92 4:55

If you enter a date or time that does not match one of the formats shown in Table 5.1, use the following general guidelines:

- Use slashes (/) or hyphens (-) as separators for dates.
- Enter the names of months in either uppercase or lowercase; Excel will adjust the capitalization.

- ▲ When entering a time, use the colon (:) to separate hours and minutes and seconds.
- ▲ If you add am or pm as designators to times, Excel automatically converts the lowercase designators to uppercase. (You can also type just **a** for AM or **p** for PM.)
- ▲ When you don't enter an AM or PM designator, Excel assumes AM.
- ▲ Unless you indicate AM or PM, Excel uses the 24-hour clock format.
- ▲ You may enter both the time and the date (in either order) in a single cell as long as they are separated by a space.

CAUTION: When you enter dates and times in a nonstandard format, Excel may convert the entry to a built-in format or to a text entry. Note that when a date or time is interpreted as a text entry, Excel cannot perform a calculation on the entry. To change a date or time format, see Skill Session 13.

Although Excel displays the date or time you enter in a recognizable format, it stores dates as serial numbers and times as decimal fractions. Excel uses these formats to perform calculations on date and time entries. To display a date as a serial number or a time as a decimal fraction, apply the General format using Forma**t** **N**umber. Refer to Skill Session 13 for information on applying number fonts.

Entering Text

Any entry that is not interpreted as a number, date, time, or formula is interpreted as a *text* entry. A text entry is a type of constant that contains alphabetic characters, punctuation marks and other symbols, or any combination of numbers, alphabetic characters, and symbols. Text is a catch-all category; if Excel cannot determine the entry type, it makes it a text entry. Table 5.2 includes examples of text entries and the reasons they are interpreted as text rather than some other type.

Table 5.2 Text entries

Entry	*Reason*
Utilities	All alphabetic characters.
Overdue	A combination of alphabetic characters and symbols.
1_5_92	A combination of numbers and symbols.
12511 15th Ave.	A combination of alphabetic characters and numbers.
123PFW01	A combination of alphabetic characters and numbers.
‘98053	Numeric entry preceded by a single quote.
’12/21/69	Combination of numbers and symbols preceded by a single quote. Without the single quote, this entry would be interpreted as a date.

In some cases, you may want to enter a number as a text entry (e.g., a part number or a postal ZIP Code). You can force Excel to interpret the number as a text entry by preceding the entry with a single quote (‘). Examples of these types of text entries are included in Table 5.2.

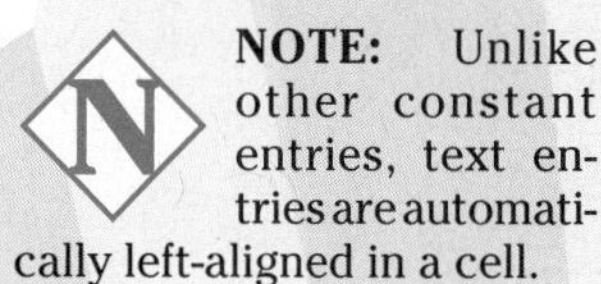

NOTE: Unlike other constant entries, text entries are automatically left-aligned in a cell.

To enter text in a cell:

1. Select the cell in which you want to enter text.

2. Type the text. The entry you type appears in the formula bar as well as the cell.

3. Press Enter or click on the enter box in the formula bar to confirm the entry. Press Esc or click on the cancel box to cancel the entry.

When the text you enter exceeds the column width, the entry will display in the next cell to the right, provided that cell is empty. If not, Excel stores the entry correctly but displays only those characters that will fit in the cell. You can display the entire contents by changing the column width (see Skill Session 16) or by wrapping the text to a new line in the same cell (see Skill Session 15).

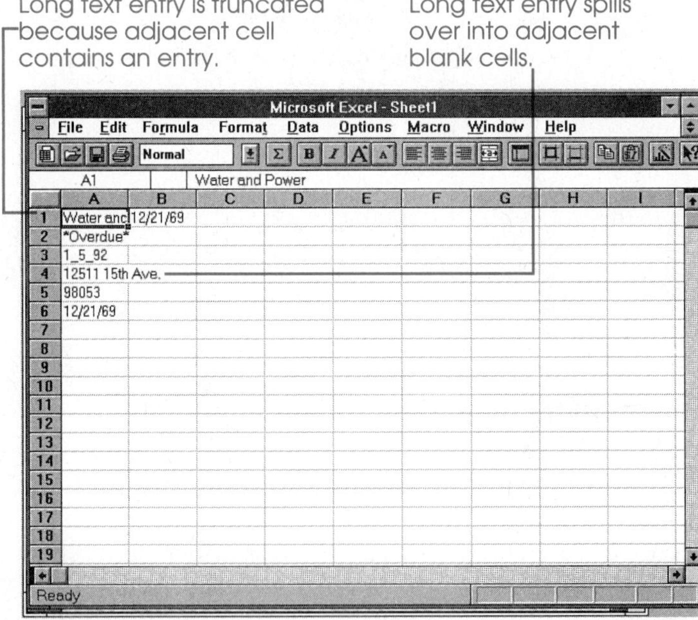

Figure 5.3 Text entries in a worksheet are automatically left-aligned.

Editing Data in Cells

You can edit cell entries in a worksheet at any time. *Editing* refers to the changes you make to the contents of a cell (e.g., replacing an existing entry, clearing a cell, correcting an error, or changing a cell entry).

When you need to change the entire contents of a cell, use these steps to replace the existing entry:

1. Select the cell to edit.
2. Type the new entry. Excel automatically replaces the previous entry with the text you type.
3. Confirm the entry by clicking on the enter box or pressing Enter. Cancel the new entry by pressing Esc or clicking on the cancel box.

Sometimes you want to erase the contents of a cell and leave it blank. Excel calls this *clearing* a cell. Follow these steps:

1. Select the cell you want to clear.
2. Select Edit Clear. Excel displays the Clear dialog box.
3. Select an option from the Clear box, then select OK or press Enter. Excel clears the cell.

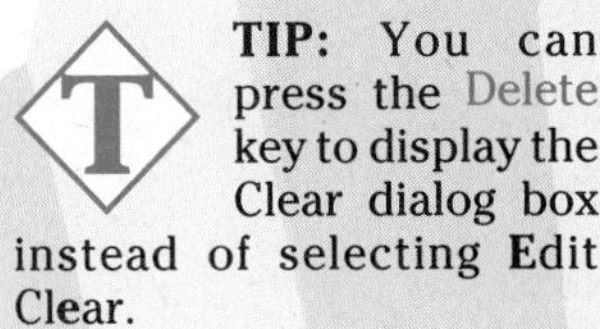

TIP: You can press the Delete key to display the Clear dialog box instead of selecting **Edit** Clear.

When a cell contains a long or complex entry, it's often easier to correct the entry than retype it. For these situations, you can use Excel's *edit key*, F2, which allows you to change selected characters in an entry. Follow these steps to correct an error or change an entry using the edit key:

1. Select the cell for which you want to correct or change the entry.

2. Press F2 to activate the formula bar. Excel places the cursor at the end of the entry in the formula bar. Use the right and left arrows to move the cursor.

3. Press Delete to delete characters to the right of the cursor or Backspace to delete characters to the left of the cursor.

4. To insert characters, move the cursor to the appropriate location and begin typing.

5. When the entry is correct, press Enter or click on the enter box.

Using Undo

One of Excel's most useful features is the *Undo* command, which allows you to reverse the most recent action taken. For example, if you type an entry in the wrong cell, you can restore the previous contents by using the **U**ndo command.

To reverse an entry, select Edit Undo Entry immediately after typing the entry. Note that the **U**ndo command reverses only the most recent action taken, so you must select the command immediately after typing an entry. If you take any other action after typing the entry, Excel reverses that action instead of reversing the entry you typed.

The **U**ndo command works not only with entries you type but also with Excel commands that you select. To remind you which action you are reversing, Excel adds

TIP: You can press Ctrl+Z instead of selecting the Undo to reverse the most recent action.

the name of the most recent command or action to the **E**dit **U**ndo command name. In the previous example, the command is called **U**ndo *Entry*. If you just formatted a cell, the command name would change to **U**ndo *Formatting*. As you work through later skill sessions and learn additional Excel commands, experiment with the **U**ndo command.

Click the Undo tool on the Utility toolbar to reverse the most recent action.

Attaching Cell Notes

Sometimes it's useful to attach comments to the data contained in a worksheet to explain the source of the data or to provide additional information. Using Excel's Fo**r**mula **N**ote command, you can attach comments to individual cells. Notes are not visible on the worksheet, but a note marker—a tiny box—is added to the upper right corner of the cell to indicate that a note is attached. If you want a note to be visible on the screen and on the printed copy, you can add a visible note enclosed in a text box. See Skill Session 21 for instructions on adding text box notes to a worksheet.

To create a note:

1. Select the cell in which you want to attach a note.
2. Select Fo**r**mula **N**ote. Excel displays the Cell Note dialog box. The address of the current cell is shown in the **C**ell text box.
3. In the **T**ext Note box, type the text for the note.

TIP: To add notes to cells without returning to the worksheet, click on Add instead of OK to enter a note, then enter a new cell address in the **C**ell text box and follow step 3. When all notes are entered, select OK and return to the worksheet.

4. Select OK or press Enter. Excel returns to the worksheet and places a note marker in the cell.

To read a note, follow these steps:

1. Double-click on the cell containing the note you want to read or select Formula Note. Excel displays the Cell Note dialog box.
2. From the Notes in the **S**heet list box, select the note you want to display. The note is displayed in the **T**ext Note box.
3. Repeat step 2 to read other notes.
4. Select Close to close the dialog box and return to the worksheet.

Use Delete in the Cell Note dialog box to delete notes that are no longer needed. You can also edit a note by selecting the text in the **T**ext Note box and retyping the entry. In Skill Session 43, you will learn about the Info window, where you can display cell notes.

Skill Session

6

Working with Worksheets and Workbooks

Before you start entering valuable information into an Excel worksheet, you need to know how to save your work, how to open new and existing worksheets, and how to work with multiple worksheets at the same time. You'll learn about each of these topics in this skill session, as well as how to create and add worksheets to a *workbook*, a special kind of document that contains several files.

Saving Worksheets

In Skill Session 1, you learned that the title bar displays the name of the current worksheet. When you start Excel, the title of the new worksheet in the worksheet window is Sheet1. As you open additional worksheets (you'll learn how to do this shortly), Excel automatically names them Sheet2, Sheet3, and so on. These are temporary names that Excel assigns to new worksheets.

NOTE: The terms *worksheet* and *file* are often used interchangeably. File is a generic term; a file can be a word processing document, a picture, an executable program, or a worksheet from a program like Excel. Worksheet is more specific; it refers to a type of file that contains spreadsheet data.

Until you save a file, none of the information you enter into Excel is stored on your computer's disk. Saving a worksheet permanently stores the file on your computer's disk and makes it available for you to recall later.

The file name you choose can be up to eight characters long and should not include asterisks (*), braces ([ ]), slashes (/), backslashes (\), greater than (>) or less than (<) symbols, vertical bars (|), or addition signs (+). Excel automatically adds the file extension .XLS. If you choose, you can save the worksheet under the temporary name that Excel assigns. When you do this, Excel also adds the .XLS file extension, as in Sheet3.XLS.

Excel has two commands for saving files: **S**ave and Save **A**s. Use the Save As command to save a new file or an existing file under a new name. Use Save to save all subsequent changes to a file under the same name.

To save a file using the Save **A**s command:

1. Select File Save As or press F12. Excel displays the Save As dialog box shown in Figure 6.1. The directory in which the file will be saved—the current directory—is displayed above the **D**irectories list box. The file name is highlighted in the File **N**ame text box.

2. In the File **N**ame text box, enter the new name for the file. (As you begin typing, the temporary file name is erased.) You don't need to type the .XLS file extension; Excel will add it automatically.

3. Select OK or press Enter.

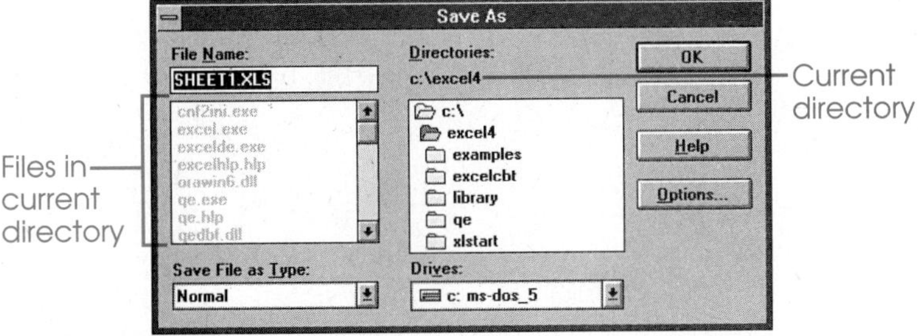

Figure 6.1 The Save As dialog box.

The Save **A**s command offers additional options for saving a file. These options and the guidelines for using them are described in Table 6.1.

Table 6.1 Save As dialog box options

Save File	*Guidelines*
Under a new name	Enter a new name for the file in the File **N**ame text box. The previous file under the old name remains intact.
In a different directory	Double-click on a directory in the **D**irectories list box. If necessary, use the scroll bar to display the complete list. The directory name displayed above the box will reflect the new name you choose.

continues

Table 6.1 continued

Save File	*Guidelines*
On a different disk drive	Select a different drive from the Drives drop-down box. The list of directories and files will reflect the new drive you choose.
In a different file format	From the Save File as **T**ype drop-down box, select a file format.
With a password	Select the **O**ptions button to display the Save Options dialog box. Enter a 15-character password in the **P**rotection Password box to require a password to open the file. Enter a 15-character password in the **W**rite Reservation Password box to require a password to save changes to the file. Check the **R**ead-Only Recommended box if you want to display a message recommending that the user open the file as read-only.
With a backup copy	Check the Create **B**ackup File box if you want Excel to automatically save a backup copy under the same file name with a .BAK file extension.

To use any of these additional save options, follow the steps you just learned for the Save **A**s command, choosing the appropriate settings in the dialog box before selecting OK or pressing Enter.

Once you have renamed and saved a file, select File Save or press Shift+F12 to save subsequent changes to the file. Because the file name is already known, Excel immediately saves the file without displaying a dialog box.

Click this tool on the Standard toolbar to save the active worksheet.

CAUTION: To avoid losing data, it's a good idea to save your file regularly as you're working—every 5 or 10 minutes if you're entering data continuously. In the event of a temporary power interruption or a hardware problem, your file will include only those changes that were made before you last saved the file.

Opening a New Worksheet

In Excel, you can open more than one worksheet at a time. One way to do this is to create a new worksheet while you're still working on the existing one. To open a new worksheet, follow these steps:

1. Select File New. Excel displays the New dialog box.
2. Select the Worksheet item from the list shown, then select OK or press Enter.

Whether the previous worksheet is visible or not depends on the size of your worksheet window. If the worksheet window is maximized, the new worksheet you create will be displayed on top of the old one in its own window. The previous worksheet file has not been closed or deleted; it is still intact and you can continue to make and save changes to it. When the worksheet menu is maximized and you have multiple

To create a new worksheet instantly, click on this tool on the Standard toolbar.

windows open, use the **W**indow menu to switch between active worksheets.

If the worksheet window is not maximized, the new worksheet you create will be displayed in its own window, leaving the left border and the title bar of the original worksheet window slightly visible. This arrangement style is called "cascaded." Each subsequent window you open will be arranged in this cascade style. Later in this skill session, you'll learn how to arrange worksheets and move from one worksheet window to another.

Opening a Saved Worksheet

Another way to work with multiple worksheets at once is to open a saved worksheet. Again, the existing worksheet remains open and intact. Follow these steps to open a saved worksheet:

1. Select File Open. Excel displays the File Open dialog box shown in Figure 6.2. The current directory is displayed above the **D**irectories list. The list box under File **N**ame lists all files stored in the current directory.

2. Select a file from the files list and then select OK or press Enter.

   If the file you want to open is located in a different directory or on a different drive or has a different file extension, follow these guidelines before selecting a file and closing the Open dialog box:

- ▲ If the file you want to open is located in a different directory, select the correct directory from the Directories list box. The files list will be updated to reflect the directory you choose.
- ▲ If the file you want to open is stored on a different drive, select the correct drive from the Drives drop-down list box. The directories and files lists are automatically updated to reflect the drive you choose.
- ▲ To select a file of a different file type, select the correct file extension in the List Files of Type drop-down list box. The directories and files lists are automatically updated to reflect the drive you choose.

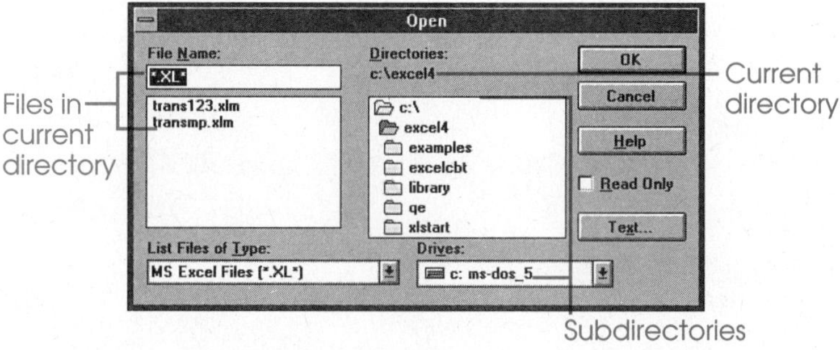

Figure 6.2 The File Open dialog box.

Arranging Multiple Worksheet Windows

As you've already learned, if the worksheet window isn't maximized when you open or create a new worksheet, the new worksheet windows are cascaded on top of the existing windows. (When a worksheet window is maximized, it fills the screen and is the only one displayed.)

Excel gives you several options for displaying multiple worksheets at once, making it easier to move from one to the other. You can resize and move each window manually, as you learned in Skill Session 3, or you can have Excel size and arrange windows for you.

Excel offers three arrangement styles: tiled, horizontal, and vertical. When you select the *tiled* option, Excel arranges all open windows in a tile pattern on the screen. The pattern changes depending on the number of windows that are open. When you choose the *horizontal* option, all open windows are "stacked" and run lengthwise across the screen. The *vertical* option places all open windows side by side across the screen. An example of each is shown in Figures 6.3, 6.4, and 6.5.

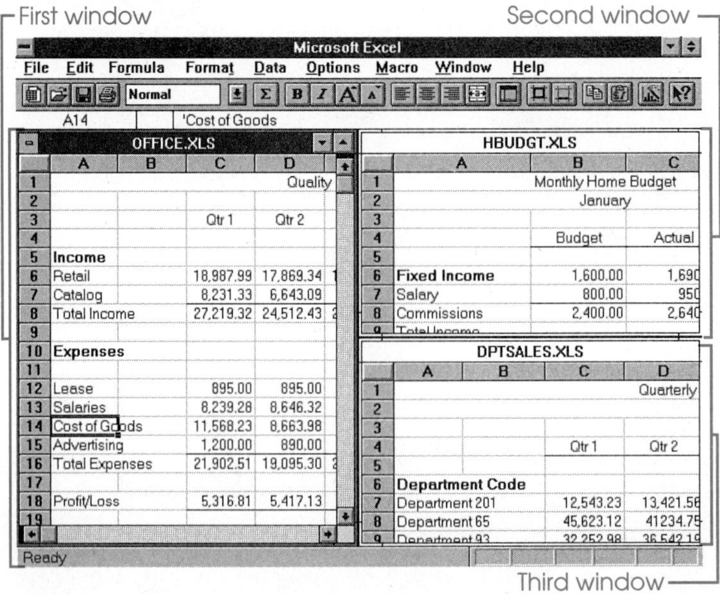

Figure 6.3 Three open windows are tiled.

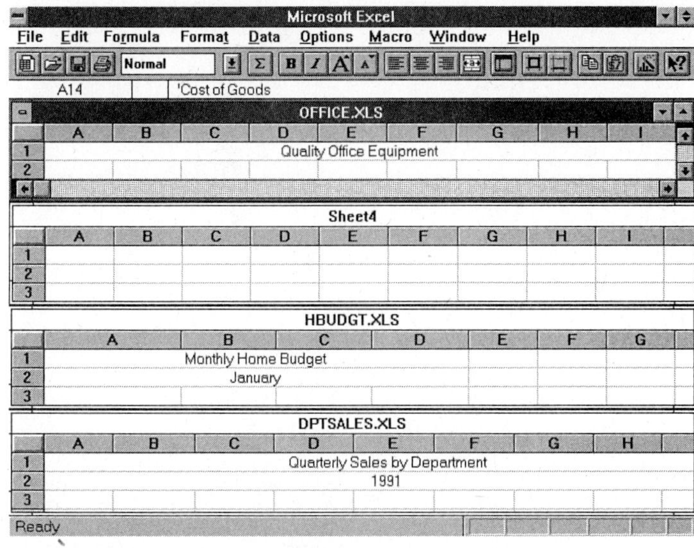

Figure 6.4 Four open windows are arranged horizontally.

Microsoft Excel
File Edit Formula Format Data Options Macro Window Help
Normal
B9

HBUDGT.XLS

	A	B	C
1		Monthly Home Budget	
2		January	
3			
4		Budget	Actu
5			
6	**Fixed Income**	1,600.00	1,
7	Salary	800.00	
8	Commissions	2,400.00	2,
9	Total Income		
10			
11	**Fixed Expenses**	650.00	
12	Rent	58.00	
13	Utilities	30.00	
14	Telephone	150.00	
15	Food	30.00	
16	Gasoline/Auto	120.00	
17	Insurance	210.00	
18	Tuition/Books	1,248.00	1,
19	Total Expenses		

OFFICE.XLS

	A	B	C	D	
1				Quality Offi	
2					
3			Qtr 1	Qtr 2	Q
4					
5	**Income**				
6	Retail		18,987.99	17,869.34	16,9
7	Catalog		8,231.33	6,643.09	7,5
8	Total Income		27,219.32	24,512.43	24,5
9					
10	**Expenses**				
11					
12	Lease		895.00	895.00	8
13	Salaries		8,239.28	8,646.32	8,1
14	Cost of Goods		11,568.23	8,663.98	9,9
15	Advertising		1,200.00	890.00	1,2
16	Total Expenses		21,902.51	19,095.30	20,2
17					
18	Profit/Loss		5,316.81	5,417.13	4,2
19					
20					

Ready

Figure 6.5 Two open windows are arranged vertically.

Select a window arrangement by following these steps:

1. Select Window Arrange. Excel displays the Arrange Windows dialog box.

2. From the Arrange box, select Tiled, Horizontal, Vertical, or None.

3. Select OK or press Enter.

NOTE: When you use the **Arrange** command, Excel automatically arranges all open windows; you can't arrange a subset of the open windows using this command.

Moving among Open Worksheets

Opening and displaying multiple worksheets is an advantage only if you can move among them efficiently. If you use one of Excel's arrangement styles so that all windows are visible on the screen, you can move easily from one worksheet to another just by clicking anywhere in the worksheet. Using the keyboard, press Ctrl+F6 until the title bar of the worksheet you want is highlighted.

When your worksheet window is maximized, only one open worksheet is visible at a time. To display a different worksheet, you use the **W**indow menu, which displays a numbered list of all open worksheets. A check mark appears to the left of the worksheet title that is currently displayed. To choose a worksheet to display, follow these steps:

1. Select Window. A numbered list of all open worksheets appears at the bottom of the menu.

2. Select the worksheet you want to display. (If you are using the keyboard, select the number that precedes the worksheet title.) Excel "hides" the previous worksheet and displays the worksheet you choose. The previous worksheet file is still open.

Closing Worksheets

When you finish working with a particular worksheet, you can close it without exiting Excel. This allows you to clear your screen of windows you're not using and continue working on others. To close a worksheet file:

1. Make the worksheet the active window by clicking anywhere in the window.
2. Select File Close. If you have not saved the most recent changes to the worksheet, Excel displays a dialog box asking if you want to save the worksheet.
3. Select Yes to save the worksheet and close the file. Select No to close the worksheet without saving changes. Select Cancel to return to the worksheet.

Saving Multiple Worksheets in a Workbook

With Excel 4, you can combine related files or worksheets into a workbook, allowing you to save, open, and close multiple files at once. A workbook can include any combination of worksheet files, charts, templates, and macro sheets. You must first create a workbook, adding the files you want to include and then save the workbook under a name you choose.

To create a new workbook:

1. Open all the worksheets, charts, templates, and macro sheets that you want to include in the workbook.

2. Select File New. Excel displays the New dialog box.

3. From the dialog box, select Workbook, then select OK or press Enter. Excel displays the Workbook Contents window.

4. Select Add in the Workbook window. Excel displays the Add to Workbook dialog box.

5. Select a file to add and then select Add.

6. When all files are added to the workbook, select OK or press Enter. Figure 6.6 illustrates the Workbook Contents window with files added to the current book.

Click on this tool to create a new workbook automatically and display the Workbook window. (Note that this is a custom tool that is only available if you have added it to a toolbar. See Skill Session 48 for instructions on customizing toolbars.)

When you click on the Next Worksheet icon, Excel moves to the next worksheet in the workbook, replacing the Workbook Contents window. Clicking on the Previous Worksheet icon takes you back to the previous worksheet. When you want to return to the Workbook Contents window, click on the Workbook Contents icon. Note that each time you move to a new worksheet file, the previous window is closed, unlike when you work with multiple worksheet windows. This is because the worksheet files are always accessible by selecting the Worksheet Contents window.

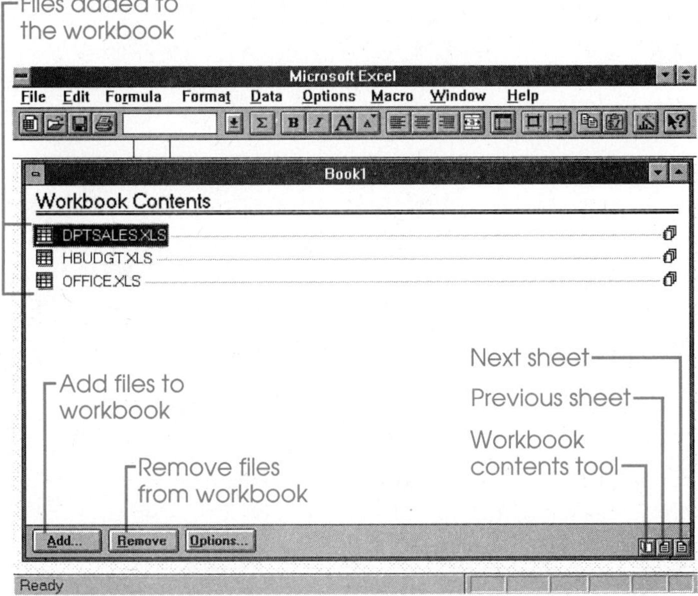

Figure 6.6 The Workbook Contents window.

You must save the workbook you create before closing the Workbook Contents window, or the workbook will not be created. As with any other type of file, you must name the workbook when you save it for the first time. Follow these steps to save a workbook for the first time:

1. From the Workbook Contents window, select File Save Workbook. Excel displays the Save As dialog box shown earlier in Figure 6.1. In the File Name text box, Excel inserts the temporary workbook name, Book*.XLW, where the asterisk is a number. Notice the file extension for workbook files is .XLW.

2. Enter a name for the workbook, then select OK.

To save the workbook under a different directory or on a different drive, refer to Table 6.1.

Closing and Opening Workbook Files

You close and open a workbook file just like you close or open any other Excel file—with the **F**ile **C**lose menu command and the **F**ile **O**pen menu command or tool on the Standard toolbar. If you try to close a workbook without saving changes to individual worksheets, Excel displays a message asking if you want to save the changes.

When you want to open a workbook, select File Open. Excel displays the Open dialog box shown earlier in Figure 6.2. If the workbook is stored in the current directory, the file name (with its .XLW extension) will be listed along with other worksheet files. Select the workbook file name, then select OK or press Enter.

Adding Additional Files to a Workbook

Once you create a workbook, you can add additional files at any time. You learned earlier how to add files that were currently open. Follow these steps to add files that are not currently open:

1. With the Workbook window open on your screen, select File Open. Excel displays the Open dialog box.

2. Select the file to open from the files list, then select OK or press Enter. Excel opens the file in its own window.

3. Click in the Workbook window. Use the Window menu to select the Workbook if the worksheet window is maximized. Click on Add. Excel displays the Add to Workbook dialog box.

4. Select the file to add, then select OK or press Enter. Excel adds the file to the existing list of workbook files.

5. After adding additional files, save the workbook. Or, when you close the workbook, click Yes to save the Save the Workbook prompt.

TIP: When you save files in a workbook, Excel remembers the size and arrangement of each window on the screen. The next time you open the workbook file, Excel restores each window exactly as you saved it.

Skill Session

7

Working with Ranges

By now, you have acquired some very basic knowledge of the Excel worksheet, menu commands, and tools—you should be feeling comfortable with the idea of entering data in a simple worksheet. In this skill session, you'll learn to use the worksheet much more efficiently by using ranges.

What Is a Range?

In simplest terms, a *range* is a group of cells. A range can be one row or column, multiple rows or columns, or even just one cell. A range can also be a group of adjacent cells that form a rectangular shape. Examples of separate rectangular ranges are shown in Figure 7.1. (It isn't possible to select multiple ranges at once. The rectangular areas outlined in Figure 7.1 are *examples* of ranges.)

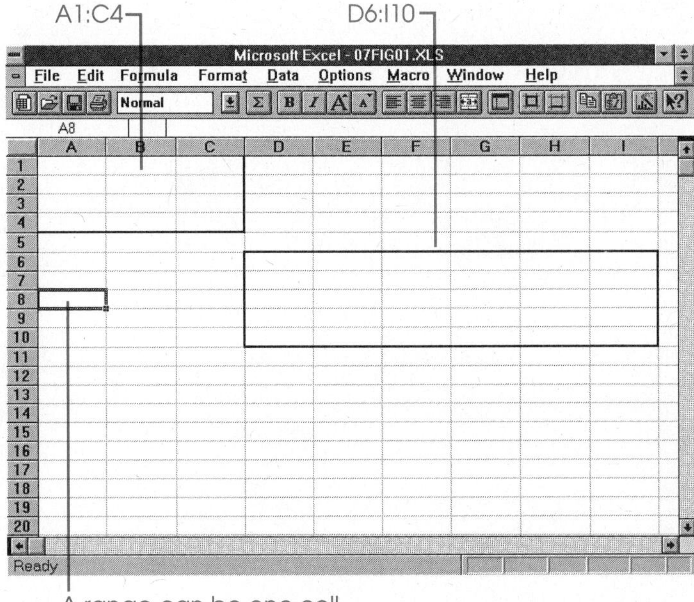

Figure 7.1 The rectangular areas represent separate ranges of cells.

A range can also be a nonadjacent groups of cells. Each portion of a nonadjacent range, however, must still be rectangular. Nonadjacent ranges are better seen than described. In Figure 7.2, each rectangular area is part of a single nonadjacent range.

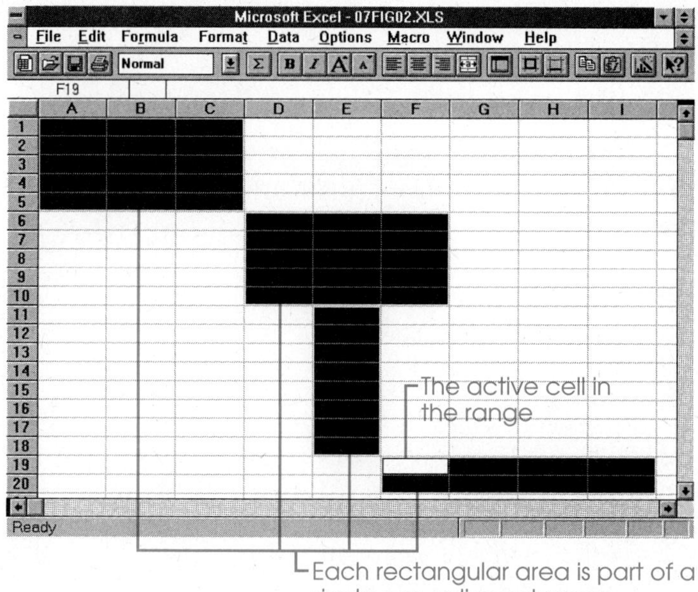

Figure 7.2 A nonadjacent range of cells.

A range of cells is designated by two cell addresses separated by a colon, as in A1:C4. The first cell address defines the upper-left corner of the range; the second cell address defines the lower-right corner. Therefore, the range A1:C4 includes cells A1, A2, A3, A4, B1, B2, B3, B4, C1, C2, C3, and C4. This range is illustrated in Figure 7.1.

Selecting a Range

Imagine how tedious it would be to assign a percent or dollar format to 20 separate cells or to move the contents of each of those cells—individually—to a new location. The advantage to selecting a range of cells is that you can use a command or apply a feature to every cell in the range simultaneously. This not only saves you time and keystrokes but also helps ensure consistency throughout the worksheet.

You can select cell ranges using either the mouse or the keyboard. Methods for selecting both a rectangular (or *adjacent*) range and a nonadjacent range are described below. (It should already be clear to you how to select a single cell!) Follow these steps to select a rectangular range of cells.

Using the mouse:

1. Point to the cell that will define the upper-left corner of the range.

2. Click and drag the mouse to the cell that will define the lower-right corner of the range. Excel shades the selected cells.

3. Release the mouse button. The highlighted cell is the active cell. (The active cell will always benefit the first cell in the range.)

Using the keyboard:

1. Using the arrow keys, move to the cell that will define the upper-left corner of the range.

2. Press and hold the Shift key.

3. Use the arrow keys to move to the cell that will define the lower-right corner of the range. Excel shades the selected cells.

4. Release the Shift key. The highlighted cell is the active cell.

The following steps show how to select a nonadjacent cell range.

Using the mouse:

1. Point to the cell that will define the upper-left corner of the first rectangular area.
2. Click and drag the mouse diagonally to the cell that will define the lower-right corner of the first rectangular area. Excel shades the selected cells.
3. Release the mouse button.
4. Press Ctrl, then repeat steps 1–3 to define the second rectangular area.
5. Repeat step 4 for all areas that will be included in the range. Excel shades all areas as a single range.

Using the keyboard:

1. Use the arrow keys to move to the cell where you want to begin selecting the first area.
2. Press and hold the Shift key while moving the arrow keys to select the first area. Excel shades the selected cells.
3. Press Shift+F8 to freeze that selection. The status line says ADD to let you know you can add a nonadjacent area to the range.
4. Move to the cell where you want to begin selecting the next area.
5. Press F8. The status line says EXT to let you know you can extend the current area.

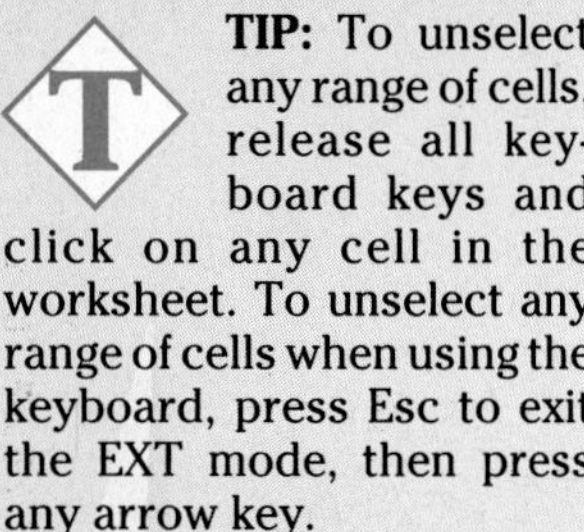

TIP: To unselect any range of cells, release all keyboard keys and click on any cell in the worksheet. To unselect any range of cells when using the keyboard, press Esc to exit the EXT mode, then press any arrow key.

6. Use the arrow keys to select the area.

7. Press Shift+F8 to freeze that selection.

8. Repeat steps 4–6 until all areas are selected.

Entering Data in a Range

NOTE: This method is similar to another entry shortcut you learned in Skill Session 5,in which you pressed an arrow key to confirm an entry. The range method is even more efficient, though, because the Enter key is easier to reach than the arrow keys. When entering data in a range, press any arrow key when you have finished.

When entering data in a range of cells, you can save some keystrokes by selecting the range before you enter the data. After selecting the range, type your entry into the active cell and then press Enter. Pressing Enter confirms the entry in the active cell and activates the next cell in the range—all with one keystroke.

When the range you select spans multiple rows and columns, pressing Enter moves the active cell down each row in the first column, then to the top of the next column and down each row, and so on until you reach the cell in the lower-right corner of the range. Pressing Enter again returns the active cell to the upper-left corner of the range. When the range you select is nonadjacent, the active cell follows this same pattern, moving from the first rectangular area to the next. When entering data in a contiguous range, press any arrow key when you have finished.

Naming a Cell Range

In Excel, you can assign a name to a range of cells in a worksheet. Naming a range allows you to refer to the range by name rather than by cell references. For example, if cells B15:B24 contain dollar amounts for January's expense items, you can name the range *JanuaryExpenses*.

Naming ranges becomes particularly valuable when you begin creating formulas because you can use range names rather than cell addresses. For example, the name *JanuaryProfit* is much easier to read and more descriptive than B12:B24. Follow these steps to create a range name.

1. Select the range of cells to name.
2. Select Formula Define Name. Excel displays the Define Name dialog box shown in Figure 7.3.
3. In the **N**ame text box, enter a name to assign to the range.
4. Check to see that the cell range shown in the **R**efers to text box is accurate, then select the Add button.
5. Select the Close button to close the dialog box and return to the worksheet.

Use the following guidelines when choosing a name:

- The name can be up to 255 uppercase or lowercase (or both) characters.
- The first character must be a letter or the underline character.
- Spaces are not allowed; use underlines or some

NOTE: The Name textbox displays the text in the first cell of the range. If the first cell contains a number, the textbox is blank.

NOTE: The cell reference shown in the Define Name dialog box includes dollar signs ($) before each row and column label. You can ignore these signs for now. In Skill Session 10, you'll learn what the dollar signs represent.

other character to represent spaces

▲ The name should not resemble a cell reference (e.g., Q1 or FY92).

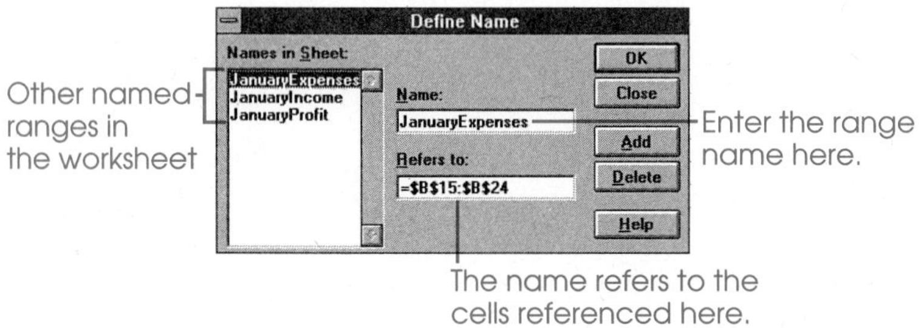

Figure 7.3 The Define Name dialog box.

Deleting Range Names

A worksheet that you use frequently is likely to undergo significant changes over time. You may move, copy, or delete entire blocks of data, as well as enter new data. After a while, you may discover that some of the ranges you named are no longer relevant, useful, or correct. You can delete a range name from the worksheet by following these steps:

1. Select Formula Define Name to display the Define Name dialog box shown in Figure 7.3.
2. From the Names in Sheet box, select the name you want to delete.

3. Select **D**elete.

4. To delete additional range names, repeat steps 2 and 3.

5. Select Close to close the dialog box and return to the worksheet.

Skill Session

8

Copying, Moving, and Clearing Cells

Spreadsheet programs like Excel wouldn't be very useful if you couldn't change your mind about the data you enter in a worksheet. Some of the most common activities are reorganizing, rearranging, and replacing data. You can't accomplish this without knowing the basic skills for copying, moving, and clearing cells.

Selecting Ranges for Copying and Moving

To copy or move cells, you must select the *source* range—the range from which you copy or move cells—and the *destination* range—the range to which you copy or move cells. Excel calls the destination range the *paste area* because you use the **P**aste command to place the selected cells into the range. When selecting the paste area, be sure the cells are blank; otherwise, they will be overwritten. It isn't necessary to select the entire range for the paste area—just select the cell where the moved or copied block's top left corner will be. Excel will copy or move the entire range accordingly.

Copying Cells

When you copy a cell or cells, Excel places a duplicate of *all* the cell contents—the entry, the cell format, and any notes attached to the cells—into the paste area, leaving the cells in the source range intact. If you don't want to copy all of these elements, Excel provides a special command that allows you to choose which of these (or other) elements to copy. See "Copying Special Elements" later in this skill session.

There are two ways to copy data using Excel: by using the **C**opy command, or by dragging the cells to a new location. The **C**opy command places a duplicate in the Clipboard, a temporary storage area. Follow these steps to copy data using Excel's menu commands.

1. Select the range of cells to copy. Excel shades and borders the selected cells.

2. Select Edit Copy or press Ctrl+C. Excel surrounds the selected cells with a moving border. Notice the status line tells you to select a destination.

3. Select the cell in the upper left corner of the destination range.

4. Press Enter. Excel pastes the Clipboard contents into the destination range.

Click this tool to copy the selected cells to the Clipboard.

To copy cell contents using the drag method, follow these steps.

1. Select the range of cells to copy. Excel shades and borders the selected cells.

2. Press and hold the Control key.

3. Move the mouse pointer to any point on the border surrounding the cells. The usual cross mouse pointer changes to an arrow with a plus (+) sign.

4. While continuing to hold the Control key, drag the mouse to the cell in the upper left corner of the paste area. As you drag the mouse, an outline of the cell range moves along with the mouse.

5. When the mouse is positioned correctly in the paste area, release the mouse button and the Control key. Excel pastes the selected cell contents into the paste area.

You may prefer to use the drag method to copy cells since it displays an outline of the entire range as you move the mouse.

The methods just described allow you to paste one copy of the selected range to the paste area. It is possible, however, to paste the copied cells to more than one area of the worksheet at once. For example, suppose you wanted to copy column headings from row 1 to rows 15, 25 and 35. It's quicker to copy the selection to all three rows at once. There are two ways to accomplish this: using the **P**aste command on the **E**dit menu, or by selecting a *non-adjacent* destination range.

To paste multiple copies of selected cells using the **P**aste command, follow these steps:

1. Select the range of cells to copy. Excel shades and borders the selected cells.
2. Select **E**dit **C**opy or press Ctrl+C. Excel surrounds the selected cells with a moving border. Notice the status line tells you to select a destination.
3. Select the cell in the upper left corner of the first destination range.
4. Select **E**dit **P**aste, or press Ctrl+V. Excel pastes the selected cells into the paste area and the selected cells remain active.
5. Select the cell in the upper left corner of the next destination range.
6. Repeat steps 4 and 5 as many times as necessary.
7. When you're ready to paste the last selection, press Enter. Excel pastes the selected cells into the paste area and makes the selected cells inactive.

Click this tool to copy the Clipboard contents to the worksheet. Note that this custom tool is only available if you have added it to a toolbar, see Skill Session 48.

To paste multiple copies of selected cells using the non-adjacent range method, follow these steps.

1. Select the range of cells to copy. Excel shades and borders the selected cells.

2. Select Edit Copy or press Ctrl+C. Excel surrounds the selected cells with a moving border. Notice the status line tells you to select a destination.

3. Select the nonadjacent range of destination cells.

4. Press Enter.

You can also paste copied cells into a destination range that is larger than the source range. For example, if you copy cells A1:A5 to cells B1:F5, the contents of A1:A5 are repeated in columns B through F. This is similar to copying to multiple areas of the worksheet except that the cells in the destination range are adjacent.

TIP: For instructions on selecting non-adjacent ranges, refer to Skill Session 7.

Copying Special Elements

The **E**dit Paste **S**pecial command is designed to allow you to copy selected elements of a cell's contents. For example, rather than copying the actual cell entry, you might want to copy only the cell's format or a note that is attached to the cell. When you use the **E**dit Paste **S**pecial command, Excel displays the Paste Special dialog box shown in Figure 8.1. Notice that the Paste box contains option buttons, which means you can select only one of the following options:

- Fo**r**mulas
- **V**alues
- Forma**t**s
- **N**otes

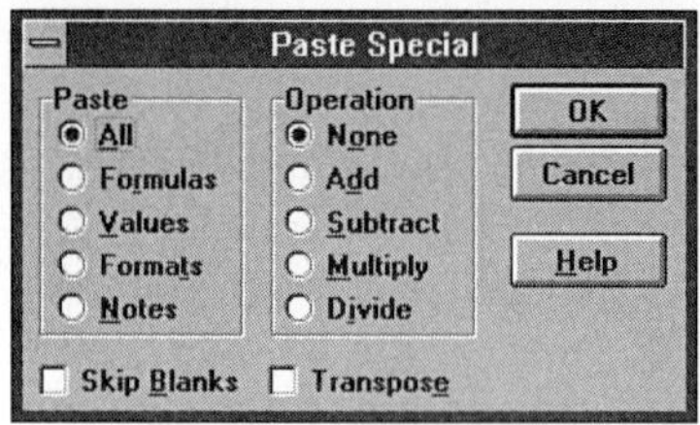

Figure 8.1 The Paste Special dialog box.

To copy all of these elements, select All. To copy more than one element, use the following steps to copy the first element, then repeat the steps for each additional element:

1. Select the range of cells to copy. Excel shades the selected cells.
2. Select Edit Copy. Excel surrounds the selected cells with a moving border. The status line tells you to select a destination.
3. Select the cell in the upper left corner of the destination range.
4. Select Edit Paste Special to display the Paste Special dialog box shown in Figure 8.1.
5. Select one of the options in the Paste box, then select OK and press Enter. Excel returns to the worksheet.

Inserting Copied Cells

In some cases, you may want to insert copied cells between existing cells. To make room for the copied cells, you could insert a new row or column first (refer to Skill Session 9 for this), but you might not want an entire row or column. To solve this problem, Excel provides a special command, **E**dit **I**nsert Paste, that allows you to insert copied cells without replacing entries in the existing cells and without adding new rows or columns to the worksheet.

You choose which direction to shift the surrounding cells—to the right or down (see Figures 8.2 and 8.3). Follow these steps to insert copied cells:

1. Select the range of cells to copy. Excel shades the selected cells.
2. Select Edit Copy. Excel surrounds the selected cells with a moving border.
3. Select the cell in the upper left corner of the destination range.
4. Select Edit Insert Paste to display the Insert Paste dialog box.
5. Select either the Shift Cells Right or the Shift Cells Down option, then select OK. Excel returns to the worksheet and inserts the copied cells.
6. Press Enter or Esc to make the selected cells inactive.

NOTE: If any of the surrounding cells are empty when you select Insert Paste, Excel may choose which direction to shift the cells without displaying the Insert Paste dialog box.

Filling Cells

An activity that is similar to copying cells is *filling* cells with data. Excel's fill commands allow you to enter repetitive data quickly. This command is especially useful for items that are the same amount each month (such as expense items). For example, if you want to enter a monthly mortgage or lease payment of $1,292.65, you can type the entry in the January column and automatically fill columns February through December with the same entry.

These cells will be copied and inserted into Cells D7:E8.

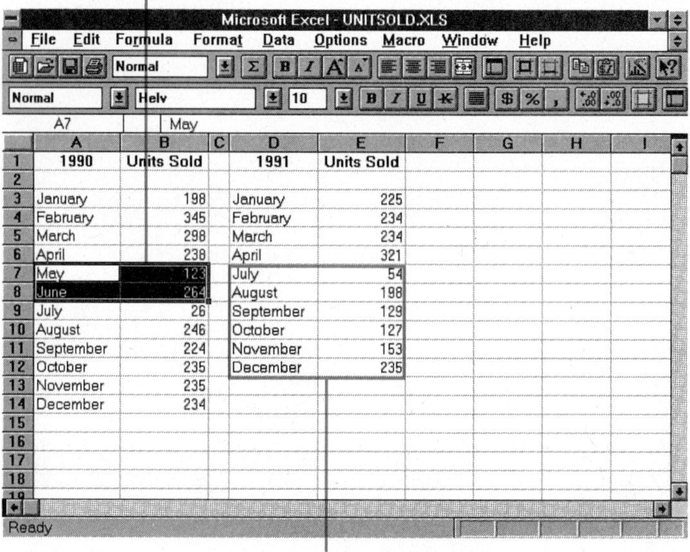

These cells will be shifted down to make room for the new cells.

Figure 8.2 The selected cells will be inserts into cells D7:E8. Current entries in cells D7:E12 will be shifted down.

NOTE: You must select the range to fill before using these commands.

Excel provides two fill commands: Fill Right and Fill Down. As shown in Figure 8.4, the Fill Right command fills selected cells across a row or rows. The Fill Down command fills selected cells down a column or columns. Each command copies the entry in the first selected cell to all other selected cells.

These cells were copied and inserted from A7:B8.

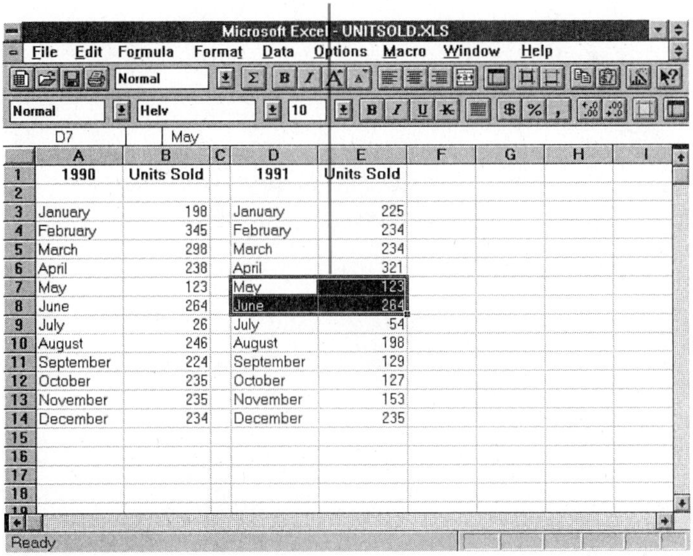

Figure 8.3 The worksheet after the selected cells are inserted.

Moving Cells

Excel moves cells by removing them from their source range and pasting them temporarily into the Clipboard, then pasting them into the destination range.

The steps for moving cells are very similar to those for copying cells. The result, however, is that the cells in the source range are cleared.

You can move cells in one of two ways:

▲ Using the Cut and Paste commands

▲ Dragging the cells to a new location

Like the Copy command, the Cut command places the selected cells into the Clipboard. The Paste command moves the cells from the Clipboard to the worksheet. Follow these steps to use the Cut and Paste commands for moving cells:

1. Select the range of cells to move. Excel shades the selected cells.

2. Select Edit Cut or press Ctrl+X. Excel surrounds the selected cells with a moving border. The status line tells you to select a destination.

3. Select the cell in the upper left corner of the destination range.

4. Press Enter or select Edit Paste. Excel moves the cells into the destination range.

Click on this tool in place of the Edit Cut command. (Note that this custom tool is only available if you have added it to a toolbar, see Skill Session 48.)

To move cell contents using the drag method, follow these steps:

1. Select the range of cells to move. Excel shades and borders the selected cells.

2. Move the mouse pointer to any point on the border surrounding the cells. The usual cross mouse pointer changes to a simple arrow.

3. Drag the range of cells to the destination range. As you drag the mouse, an outline of the cell range moves along with the mouse pointer.

4. When the range is positioned correctly in the paste area, release the mouse button. Excel moves the selected cells into the destination range.

Just as you can copy and insert cells at the same time, you can move and insert cells at the same time. This requires shifting the surrounding cells either down or to the right to make room for the new cells. Follow these steps:

1. Select the range of cells to move. Excel shades and borders the selected cells.

2. Select Edit Cut. Excel surrounds the selected cells with a moving border.

3. Select the cell in the upper left corner of the range where you want the cells inserted.

4. Select Edit Insert Paste to display the Insert Paste dialog box.

5. Select either the Shift Cells Right or the Shift Cells Down option, then select OK. Excel returns to the worksheet and inserts the moved cells.

For instructions on inserting cells, rows, or columns, see Skill Session 9.

Click on this tool to move the Clipboard contents to the worksheet. (Note that this custom tool is only available if you have added it to a toolbar, see Skill Session 48.

NOTE: When you move cells, *all* cell contents are moved to the new location. The Paste **S**pecial command, used for pasting selected cell elements to the new range, is *not* available when you move cells, only when you copy cells.

NOTE: If any of the surrounding cells are empty when you select Insert Paste, Excel may choose which direction to shift the cells without displaying the Insert Paste dialog box.

Clearing Cells

When you want to remove a cell's contents, you use Excel's Clear command. In effect, the Clear command erases a cell's contents. When you select the Clear command, Excel displays a dialog box allowing you to choose which elements of the selected cells to clear: the formats, formulas, notes, or all elements. Follow these steps to clear cells:

1. Select the range of cells to be cleared.
2. Select Edit Clear, or press Delete. Excel displays the Clear dialog box.
3. Select All, Formats, Formulas, or Notes, then select OK. Excel returns to the worksheet and clears the cells.

CAUTION: *Clearing* and *deleting* are two separate functions in Excel. Cleared cells are emptied of their contents but remain part of the worksheet. Deleted cells are actually removed from the worksheet, changing the structure of the surrounding rows and columns. This concept can be confusing to the new user, especially because the speed key for the Clear command is the Delete key. See Skill Session 9 for instructions on deleting cells.

Skill Session

9

Inserting and Deleting Cells, Rows, and Columns

In Skill Session 8, you learned some basic copying, moving, and erasing skills for rearranging and changing cells in a worksheet. Two other activities that have to do with rearranging and changing are *inserting* and *deleting* cells. Quite often, after you've created a worksheet, you'll want to insert cells between existing cells to make room for additional data, or you'll want to delete cells entirely from a worksheet. In this skill session, you learn how to insert and delete single cells, a range of cells, and entire rows and columns.

Inserting Cells and Cell Ranges

In Excel, you can insert a single cell or a range of cells anywhere in a worksheet. Whatever the case, the area you select should be the same size as the area you want to insert. For example, if you want to insert a range of cells three columns wide by four rows deep, the area you select in the worksheet should be exactly that size. Select the cell in the upper-left corner of the range where you want to insert cells (see Figure 9.1). If you want to insert a single cell, just select the cell where you want the new cell inserted.

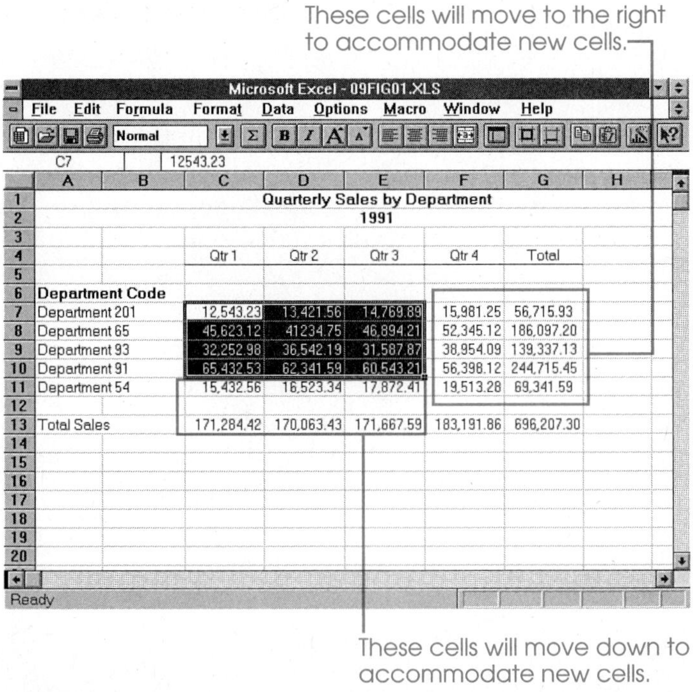

Figure 9.1 Selecting a range of cells to insert.

To accommodate the new cells, Excel gives you the choice of shifting the surrounding cells either to the right or down. Follow these steps to insert a cell or range of cells:

1. Move to the cell in the upper-left corner of the range where you want to insert a cell or cells.
2. Select the cell or range of cells.
3. Select Edit Insert. Excel displays the Insert dialog box.
4. Select Shift Cells Right or Shift Cells Down, then select OK. Excel returns to the worksheet and inserts the cell or range of cells you selected.

Inserting Rows and Columns

Rather than inserting a cell or range of cells, it's quite common to insert an entire row or column (for example, to add expense items or additional months to a worksheet). You can insert one row or column at a time, or you can insert multiple rows or columns. When you insert a row or rows, the rows just below the insertion point are automatically shifted down. Columns to the right of an inserted column are automatically shifted to the right.

To insert a single row, select any cell in the row where you want the new row inserted. For example, if you want a new row between rows 11 and 12, select any cell in row 12. To insert a single column between two existing columns, select any cell in the rightmost of the two columns. For instance, select any cell in column D to insert a column between columns C and D.

Follow these steps to insert a single row or column:

1. Select any cell in the row or column where you want a new row or column inserted.

2. Select Edit Insert. Excel displays the Insert dialog box.

3. Select Entire Row to insert a row or Entire Column to insert a column, then select OK. Excel returns to the worksheet and inserts the row or column you specified.

To insert multiple rows or columns, you must select the same number of cells for the number of rows or columns you want to insert. For example, if you want to insert three rows at row 5, make your selection include any cells in rows 5, 6, and 7. To insert four columns at column C, make your selection include any cells in columns C, D, E, and F. These examples are illustrated in Figure 9.2.

To insert multiple rows or columns, follow these steps:

1. Select the same number of cells for the number of rows or columns you want to insert (see Figure 9.2).

2. Select Edit Insert. Excel displays the Insert dialog box.

3. Select Entire Row to insert a row or Entire Column to insert a column, then select OK. Excel returns to the worksheet and inserts the rows or columns you specified.

TIP: You can insert rows or columns quickly by selecting the entire row or column before choosing Edit Insert. To select an entire row or column, click on the row number or the column letter. Select multiple rows or columns by dragging through the row numbers or the column letters.

If you have added this custom tool to a toolbar, click on it to insert the selected cell or range of cells.

If you have added this custom tool to a toolbar, click on it to insert the selected row or rows.

If you have added this custom tool to a toolbar, click on it to insert the selected column or columns.

To insert four columns at Column C, select any cells in these four columns.

Microsoft Excel - 09FIG01.XLS

	A	B	C	D	E	F	G	H
1			Quarterly Sales by Department					
2			1991					
3								
4			Qtr 1	Qtr 2	Qtr 3	Qtr 4	Total	
5								
6	Department Code							
7	Department 201		12,543.23	13,421.56	14,769.89	15,981.25	56,715.93	
8	Department 65		45,623.12	41234.75	46,894.21	52,345.12	186,097.20	
9	Department 93		32,252.98	36,542.19	31,587.87	38,954.09	139,337.13	
10	Department 91		65,432.53	62,341.59	60,543.21	56,398.12	244,715.45	
11	Department 54		15,432.56	16,523.34	17,872.41	19,513.28	69,341.59	
12								
13	Total Sales		171,284.42	170,063.43	171,667.59	183,191.86	696,207.30	

To insert three rows at row 5, select any cells in these three rows.

Figure 9.2 Cells to select to insert multiple rows or columns.

Deleting Cells and Cell Ranges

Just as you may want to insert cells in a worksheet, you'll also want to delete cells. When you delete cells, they are actually removed from the structure of the worksheet. The surrounding cells are shifted up or to the left to fill in the area where cells were deleted. Use the following steps to delete a cell or range of cells:

1. Select the cell or range of cells to delete.

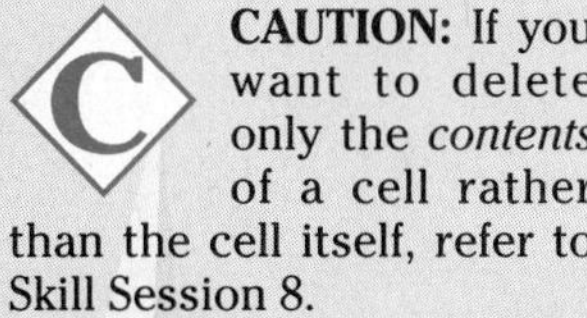

CAUTION: If you want to delete only the *contents* of a cell rather than the cell itself, refer to Skill Session 8.

2. Select Edit Delete. Excel displays the Delete dialog box.

3. Select Shift Cells Up or Shift Cells Left, then select OK. Excel deletes the selected cells and shifts the surrounding cells to fill in the worksheet.

Deleting Rows and Columns

In addition to deleting cells, you can also delete entire rows or columns in a worksheet. When you delete rows, all rows below the row you delete are shifted up to fill in the worksheet. All columns to the right of the column you delete are shifted to the left.

To delete a single row, select any cell in the row you want to delete. To delete a single column, select any cell in the column. Follow these steps:

1. Select any cell in the row or column you want to delete.

2. Select Edit Delete. Excel displays the Delete dialog box.

3. Select Entire Row or Entire Column, then select OK. Excel returns to the worksheet and deletes the row or column you selected.

To delete multiple rows or columns, select one cell in each row or column you want to delete. For example, if you want to delete rows 5 through 7, select any cell in rows 5, 6, or 7. To delete columns C through F, select any cell in columns C, D, E, or F. (For an illustration of these cells, refer to Figure 9.2.) To delete multiple rows or columns, follow these steps:

1. Select at least one cell in each row or column you want to delete. (See Figure 9.1 for an example of how to select cells.)

2. Select Edit Delete. Excel displays the Delete dialog box.

3. Select Entire Row or Entire Column, then select OK. Excel returns to the worksheet and deletes the rows or columns you specified.

TIP: You can delete rows or columns quickly by selecting the entire row or column before choosing Edit Delete. To select an entire row or column, click on the row number or the column letter. Select multiple rows or columns by dragging through the row numbers or the column letters.

If you have added this custom tool to a toolbar, click on it to delete the selected cell or range of cells.

If you have added this custom tool to a toolbar, click on it to delete the selected row or rows.

If you have added this custom tool to a toolbar, click on it to delete the selected column or columns.

Skill Session

10

Writing Formulas

If the only thing a spreadsheet program like Excel did was calculate numbers, it would still be a valuable tool, but a spreadsheet program's real power lies in its capability to *recalculate* results automatically whenever you change a number. This lets you not only record actual data but also forecast future data and create hypothetical numeric models. In this skill session, you learn how to create, display, and edit simple formulas—the key to calculation in spreadsheet programs.

What Is a Formula?

A *formula* is an equation that performs calculations on one or more numbers and returns a result. A formula can be as simple as one that adds two numbers or as complex as one that calculates the depreciation for a capital asset using the sum of the year's digits. A formula in a cell draws its input—that is, the numbers upon which it performs calculations—from references to other cells that contain numbers, from named cells, or from constants that you enter.

All formulas begin with an *equals sign* (=), which tells Excel that the entry is a formula rather than a number or text entry. In simple formulas, the equals sign is usually followed by a *cell reference* such as B25 or C13. The cell reference tells Excel where to get the first value on which the calculation will be made.

Cell references are usually separated by an *operator* such as + for addition or / for division. `=B4-B5` is an example of a simple formula that subtracts the value in B5 from the value in B4 and displays the result in cell B6, where the formula is located (see Figure 10.1).

`JanuaryIncome - JanuaryExpenses` is an example of a formula that references named cells. And finally, `=B13-(C25+3)/12` is an example of a formula that contains a combination of constants and cell references.

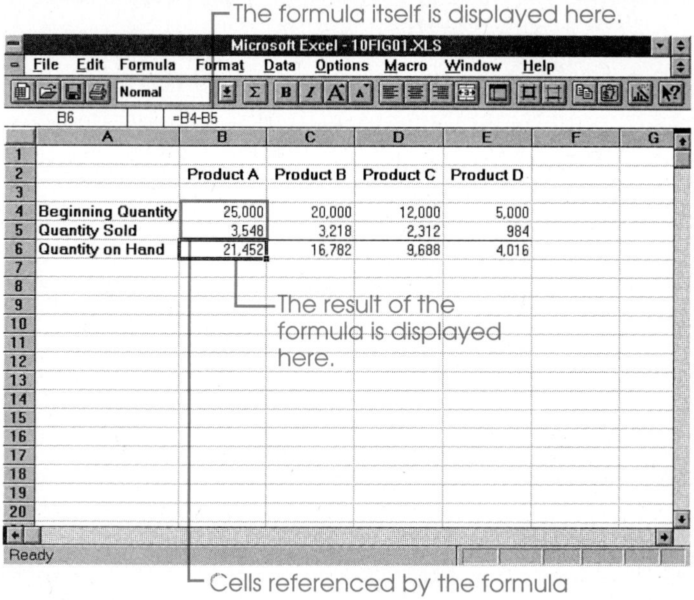

The formula itself is displayed here.

Microsoft Excel - 10FIG01.XLS

File Edit Formula Format Data Options Macro Window Help

B6 =B4-B5

	A	B	C	D	E
2		Product A	Product B	Product C	Product D
4	Beginning Quantity	25,000	20,000	12,000	5,000
5	Quantity Sold	3,548	3,218	2,312	984
6	Quantity on Hand	21,452	16,782	9,688	4,016

The result of the formula is displayed here.

Cells referenced by the formula

Figure 10.1 A simple formula that subtracts one value from another.

Entering Formulas

You can create a formula in any cell in a worksheet by typing cell references or by pointing to them. To select the reference cells to be used in the formula, click on the cell using the mouse, or use the arrow keys. The following steps illustrate the basic principles for creating simple formulas:

1. Select the cell where you want the formula result to appear.

2. Type = to begin the formula.
3. Select the cell to be used as the first number in the formula. Note the blinking outline as you move the pointer.
4. Enter an operator (for example, a plus sign). The cell selector returns to the cell you chose in step 1. Notice, also, that the formula is being "built" in the formula bar.
5. Select the cell to be used as the next number, or enter a constant.
6. Repeat steps 4–5 for all cell references and constants.
7. Press Enter or click on the Enter box in the formula bar to end the formula. Excel displays the results of the formula in the cell you chose in step 1.

When a formula requires parentheses, you can add them as you build the formula, or you can add them after the formula is complete by pressing F2 to activate the formula bar. See "Editing Formulas" later in this skill session.

The cell in which a formula is located displays the results of the equation; the formula itself is displayed in the formula bar when the cell is the active cell. If you change any of the values referenced by the formula, Excel recalculates the result automatically.

Operators and Operator Precedence

Excel allows you to enter four different types of operators in formulas: arithmetic, reference, text, and comparison. Descriptions and examples of each are shown in Table 10.1.

Table 10.1 Operators allowed in Excel formulas

Operator	*Description*	*Example Formula*
Arithmetic Operators		
+	Addition	`=B2+C25`
-	Subtraction	`=B3-F19`
*	Multiplication	`=C25*3`
/	Division	`=JanuarySales/10`
%	Percentage	`60%`
^	Exponential values	`=15^2*.5`
Reference Operators		
:	Ranges	`=A12:C12`
(space)	Intersection	`=A1:B5 B5:C10`
,	Union	`=JanSales,FebSales`
Text Operators		
&	To combine two or more text values into one (where F25 contains a text entry such as Dept. B21).	`="Totals Sales:" &F25`

continues

NOTE: In some of the examples in Table 10.1, text is used instead of cell references or numbers. Remember, this is not regular text; the words are references to named cells.

Table 10.1 continued

Operator	*Description*	*Example Formula*
Comparison Operators		
=	Equal to	`=2500`
>	Greater than	`=F17>3500`
<	Less than	`=Commission<1000`
>=	Greater than or equal to	`=C29>=12`
<=	Less than or equal to	`=Participants<=200`
<>	Not equal to	`=D16<>Sales`

When a formula contains values enclosed in parentheses, the contents of the innermost set of parentheses are evaluated first. Without parentheses, Excel evaulates in the order of precedence of individual operators. When two operators have the same priority, Excel evaluates from left to right. Table 10.2 lists the operators in order of precedence from highest to lowest.

Table 10.2 Operators and their order of evaluation

Operator	*Description*	*Order of Evaluation*
:	Range	1
(space)	Intersection	2
,	Union	3
–	Negative number	4
%	Percent	5
^	Exponent	6
* and /	Multiplication and division	7

Operator	*Description*	*Order of Evaluation*
+ and –	Addition and subtraction	8
&	Joining text	9
= < > <= >= <>	Comparison	10

Displaying Formulas in a Worksheet

Because most users want to see results in a worksheet, Excel automatically displays the result rather than the formula in a cell where a formula is located. When you don't remember the formula you entered to calculate a result, you can display the formula in the formula bar by selecting the cell where the result is displayed. Occasionally, you may want to display all formulas in a worksheet rather than the formulas' results. This feature can be useful when you are looking for a particular formula or when you are checking the accuracy of all formulas. Figure 10.2 illustrates a worksheet in which the formulas are displayed. To display formulas in a worksheet, follow these steps:

1. Select Options Display. Excel displays the Display Options dialog box.
2. In the Cells box, select the Formulas option.
3. Select OK. Excel returns to the worksheet and displays all formulas in their cells.

When you want to redisplay results rather than formulas, follow the same steps to turn off the Formulas option.

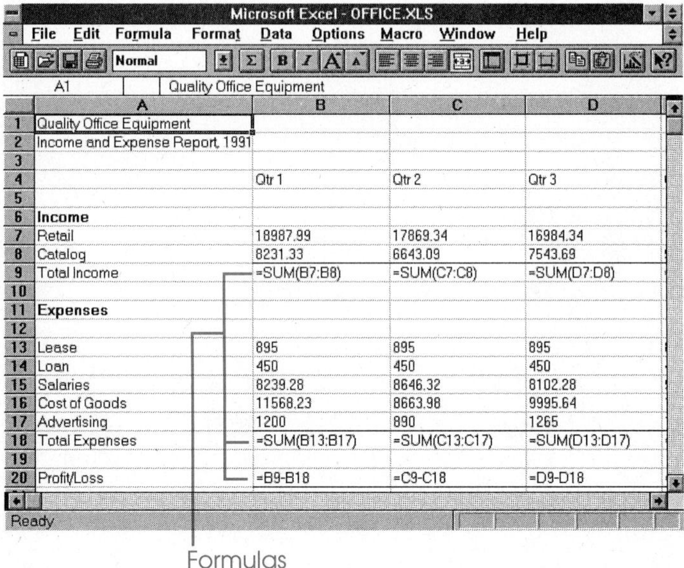

	A	B	C	D
1	Quality Office Equipment			
2	Income and Expense Report, 1991			
3				
4		Qtr 1	Qtr 2	Qtr 3
5				
6	**Income**			
7	Retail	18987.99	17869.34	16984.34
8	Catalog	8231.33	6643.09	7543.69
9	Total Income	=SUM(B7:B8)	=SUM(C7:C8)	=SUM(D7:D8)
10				
11	**Expenses**			
12				
13	Lease	895	895	895
14	Loan	450	450	450
15	Salaries	8239.28	8646.32	8102.28
16	Cost of Goods	11568.23	8663.98	9995.64
17	Advertising	1200	890	1265
18	Total Expenses	=SUM(B13:B17)	=SUM(C13:C17)	=SUM(D13:D17)
19				
20	Profit/Loss	=B9-B18	=C9-C18	=D9-D18

Figure 10.2 A worksheet displaying formulas rather than results.

Editing Formulas

Suppose your worksheet contains a complex formula that required much thought and planning to create. You have just discovered a minor error in the formula. You don't want to recreate the entire formula just to correct a simple error. Using the edit key, F2, you can change a formula without rebuilding it. In Skill Session 5, you used the edit key to correct number and text entries. You modify a formula using the same methods. Follow these guidelines:

- ▲ Select the cell containing the formula, then press F2 to access the formula bar.
- ▲ Use the right and left arrow keys to position the cursor.
- ▲ Press Backspace to delete characters to the left of the cursor or Delete to delete characters to the right of the cursor.
- ▲ Type new characters as needed. Characters you type are entered at the point of the cursor.
- ▲ Click on the Enter box or press Enter to confirm the changes and return to the worksheet, or click the Cancel box or press Esc to cancel the changes and return to the worksheet.

Using Relative and Absolute Cell Addressing

Earlier in this skill session you learned how to create a simple formula such as `=B14-B13`. This formula, entered in cell B15, subtracts the value in B13 from the value in B14 and puts the result in B15. The cell references in this formula are known as *relative* references because Excel does not interpret them literally. To Excel, this formula means *find the value in the cell one row up and subtract it from the value in the cell two rows up*. It could be said that a formula with relative cell addresses "follows directions" rather than going to specific cell addresses to find the values it calculates. If you copied this formula to cell D20, Excel would change the formula to =D19-D18. The directions Excel follows are still the same, but the cells the formula operates on are different.

NOTE: You must enter a separate dollar sign for each row number and each column letter; if you entered $B14-$B13, only the column, B, would stay constant; the row numbers would be subject to change.

When you want Excel to calculate values in specific cells, you create a formula that contains *absolute* cell references. Formulas always reference specific cells. It is only when you copy a cell that you should be concerned. Use absolute cell references when the cell reference should not change if the formula is copied. This means that no matter where the formula is located in the worksheet, it always operates on the values found in the referenced cells. With absolute references, the formula =B14-B13 would be typed as **=$B$14-$B$13**. The dollar signs ($) designate the absolute cell references. If you moved this formula to cell R39, it would still calculate on the values in cells B14 and B13 but place the result in cell R39.

How Excel Handles Moved, Copied, and Deleted Formulas

Before you move, copy, or delete formulas or the cells they reference, you should understand how Excel reacts to these changes. In some cases, you won't see any changes; in others, you will.

When Formulas and References Are Moved

When you move a cell that contains a formula, the cell references in the formula remain the same. Presumably, you still want the formula to calculate the same values—you're just changing the location of the result. For example, if the formula `=C3-C4` is located in cell C5 and you move the formula to cell D20, the formula is still `=C3-C4`.

When you move a cell that is referenced in a formula, Excel automatically adjusts the cell references in the formula so that the formula still calculates the same values. For example, if cell A3 contains the formula `=A1+A2` and you move cell A1 to cell C1, Excel adjusts the formula to `=C1+A2` so that the same values are used in the calculation. This is true whether the cell you move contains a value or a formula.

The general principle to remember when moving cells is that Excel assumes you want your formulas to calculate on the same numbers, so it will take whatever action is necessary to ensure that happens.

When Formulas and References Are Copied

When you copy a cell that contains a formula, you generally don't want the copied formula to calculate on the same values as the original formula. Therefore, when you copy a formula, Excel adjusts all relative cell references. For example, suppose your worksheet contains values in rows 12–16 of columns C–F and you want to total each column (see Figure 10.3). You can copy the formula in C17, which totals column C, into cells D17 through F17, knowing that the totals will reflect the values in each column rather than the values in column C.

The formula in cell C17

Microsoft Excel - OFFICE.XLS

File Edit Formula Format Data Options Macro Window Help

Normal

C17 =SUM(C12:C16)

	A	B	C	D	E	F	G	H	I
1			Quality Office Equipment						
2			Income and Expense Report, 1991						
3									
4									
5			Qtr 1	Qtr 2	Qtr 3	Qtr 4	Total		
6	**Income**								
7	Retail		18,987.99	17,869.34	16,984.34	19,898.78	73,740.45		
8	Catalog		8,231.33	6,643.09	7,543.69	9,321.42	31,739.53		
9	Total Income		27,219.32	24,512.43	24,528.03	29,220.20	105,479.98		
10									
11	**Expenses**								
12	Lease		895.00	895.00	895.00	895.00	3,580.00		
13	Loan		450.00	450.00	450.00	450.00	1,800.00		
14	Salaries		8,239.28	8,646.32	8,102.28	9,954.53	34,942.41		
15	Cost of Goods		11,568.23	8,663.98	9,995.64	11,653.65	41,881.50		
16	Advertising		1,200.00	890.00	1,265.00	1,490.00	4,845.00		
17	Total Expenses		22,352.51	19,545.30	20,707.92	24,443.18	87,048.91		
18									
19	Profit/Loss		4,866.81	4,967.13	3,820.11	4,777.02	18,431.07		
20									

Ready

In this cell, the formula is adjusted to =SUM (D12:D16).

Figure 10.3 When the formula in C17 is copied to D17:F17, cell references are automatically adjusted.

Copying a cell referenced by a formula has no effect on the formula. The original values the formula needs to perform its calculation are unchanged, so there is no reason for Excel to adjust cell references in the formula.

When You Clear or Delete Formulas and Cell References

When you clear a cell that contains a number or a formula, its value becomes zero. Any formulas that reference the deleted cell will simply operate on the cell with a value of zero. This may change some numbers in your worksheet, but it will not change cell references in formulas.

Unlike clearing a cell, when you delete a cell that is referenced in a formula, the cell no longer exists. Because the formula doesn't know where to find the cell, it can't perform an accurate calculation, so Excel returns the #REF! error value. This error is a signal to you that you need to adjust the formula so that it references the correct cell.

Deleting a formula has no effect on the worksheet, unless, of course, another formula refers to the deleted formula. In that case, the result is the same: The #REF! error value is returned because the formula doesn't know where to find the cell it references.

Skill Session

11

Using Built-In Functions

Using Excel's built-in functions can simplify the tasks involved in creating worksheets. By relying on functions to perform many of the calculations for which you would otherwise have to create a formula, you'll save time and reduce the possibility of calculation errors in your worksheets. In this skill session you'll learn what functions are and how to use them in your worksheets.

What Are Built-In Functions?

Built-in functions are formulas that are preprogrammed into Excel and designed to simplify the task of creating formulas. They often represent such common tasks as finding the sum or average of a range of numbers or calculating the monthly payment amount on a loan. Functions can also represent complex calculations, such as the DEVSQ function, which returns the sum of squares of deviations of data points from their sample mean. Excel contains over 200 built-in functions in a variety of categories including financial, statistical, logical, and mathematical. For a complete list and description of Excel worksheet functions.

Like formulas, functions perform calculations on values and return a number. (A value is a number, a reference to a cell containing a number, or a named cell.) The values upon which functions calculate are called *arguments*. Arguments are enclosed in parentheses and appear in the function just after the function name. The function below, PMT, uses the arguments shown to calculate a periodic payment on a loan or annuity. You supply the values for each argument in the form of constants or cell references.

```
=PMT(rate,nper,pv,fv,type)
```

Argument place holders

TIP: In the Function Reference, optional arguments are shown in italics. In Help, required arguments are shown in bold type and optional agruments are shown in normal type.

In certain functions, some arguments are optional. For example, to calculate a monthly loan payment, the PMT function only requires values for the *rate* (interest rate), *nper* (number of payment periods), and *pv* (present value of the loan) arguments—the *fv* (future value) and *type* (payment at end of period or beginning of period) arguments are optional.

```
=PMT(12%/12,60,-25000)
```

Function name

Values as arguments

In the preceding example, the PMT function calculates the monthly payment of $556.11 based on an interest rate of 12% (note that this figure is divided by 12 months), 60 payments, and a loan amount of $-25,000. (The loan amount is entered as a negative number since it is money borrowed. This ensures that the function returns a positive number for the monthly payment.) In this case, no values are supplied for the optional arguments, *fv* and *type*.

Rather than entering values as arguments to a function, you can enter cell references. For example, if the values 12%, 60, and -25,000 were entered in cells C3, C4, and C5, respectively, you could reference these cells in the following function to calculate exactly the same result:

```
=PMT(C3/12,C4,C5)
```

This function is illustrated in Figure 11.1.

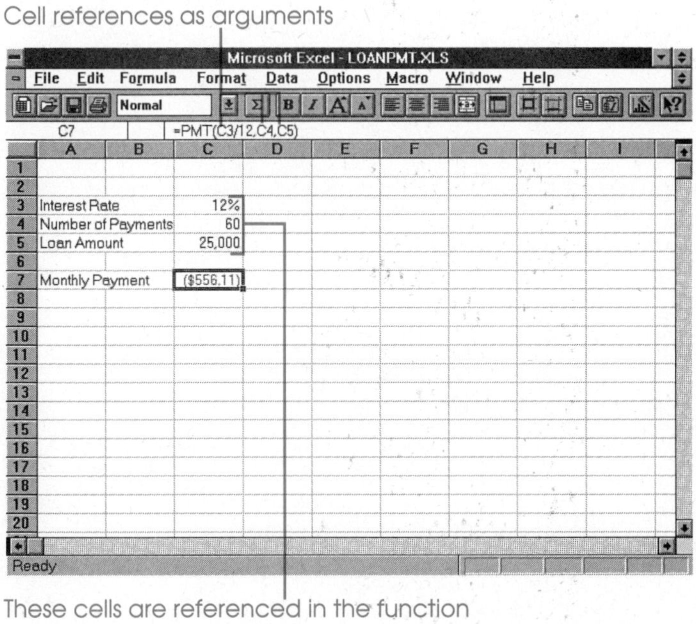

Cell references as arguments

These cells are referenced in the function

Figure 11.1 Cell references are used as arguments to the PMT function.

Using Built-in Functions

You can enter functions into a worksheet by typing the function name and its arguments, or by using Excel's Formula Paste Function command. When you use the Formula Paste Function command, Excel automatically enters into the formula bar the function name, and optionally, the argument names as place holders. You fill in the place holders with actual values or cell references.

Using the Paste Function command is the most efficient way to create functions in Excel because you don't have to remember the function names and arguments—you can choose them from the Paste Function dialog box shown in Figure 11.2. Follow these steps:

1. Select the cell in which you want the function result to appear.
2. Select Formula Paste Function. Excel displays the Paste Function dialog box shown in Figure 11.2.
3. Select a category in the Function Category box.
4. Select a function from the Paste Function box. Excel displays the selected function and its arguments below the Function Category box.
5. To have Excel automatically paste argument place holders into the function, make sure the Paste Arguments check box is selected.
6. Select OK. Excel pastes the function into the formula bar.

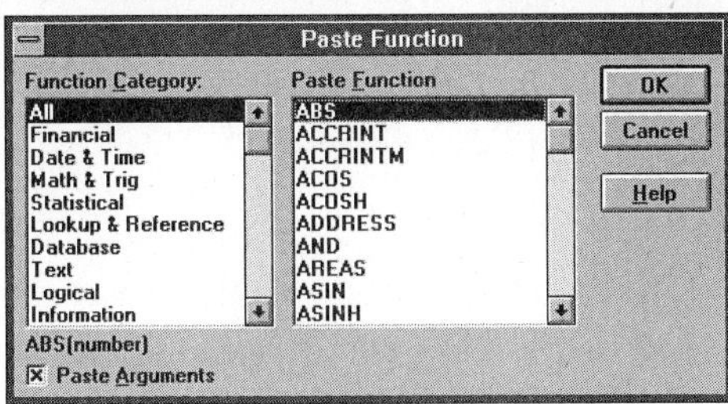

Figure 11.2 The Paste Function dialog box.

At this point, the formula bar is still active. To complete the function, replace the argument place holders in the formula bar with the actual values or with cell references. To eliminate optional arguments, delete the place holders. When the function is complete, press Enter or select the Enter box.

If you use some functions frequently, you may find it easier to simply type the function name and its arguments into the cell where you want the result displayed. If so, remember to precede the function name with an equals sign (=) and enclose all arguments in parentheses. Use commas to separate arguments and don't include spaces anywhere in the function.

You can use functions as part of other formulas by combining them with other operators and values. You can also use functions as arguments to other functions. These are called *nested* functions. In addition, Excel allows you to create custom functions. See Skill Session 47 for details on these advanced functions topics.

Using the Autosum Tool

One of the most common calculations in worksheets is addition—usually of the values in a row or a column. You can create a simple addition formula to add the values in a range of cells, but the more cells you reference, the more tedious the formula is to create. For example, to add the values in cells C3 through C10, a simple addition formula would look like this:

```
=(C3+C4+C5+C6+C7+C8+C9+C10)
```

Although this formula will calculate correctly, typing or pointing to each of these cell references is not the most efficient way to create it. Imagine how long it would take to create the same type of formula that referenced 75 or 100 cells. Excel's SUM function lets you replace this formula with the following formula:

```
=SUM(C3:C10)
```

The result is automatically calculated based on the value of the arguments you supply to the function.

The SUM function is used so frequently in worksheets that Excel added it as a tool in the Standard toolbar—it's called the *Autosum* tool. The Autosum tool goes one step farther than the SUM function by supplying a suggested cell range as the argument to the function. For example, if you click on the Autosum tool at the end of a column of numbers, Excel automatically assumes you want to sum the numbers in the column and supplies that cell range as the argument to the function. To use the Autosum tool, follow these steps:

1. Select the cell where you want the sum to be displayed.

2. Click on the Autosum tool. Excel inserts the SUM function and a suggested cell range enclosed in parentheses. The cell range is highlighted with a moving border.

3. If the suggested range is correct, press Enter or click the Enter box to complete the formula. If the suggested range is incorrect, enter the correct range, then press Enter or click the Enter box.

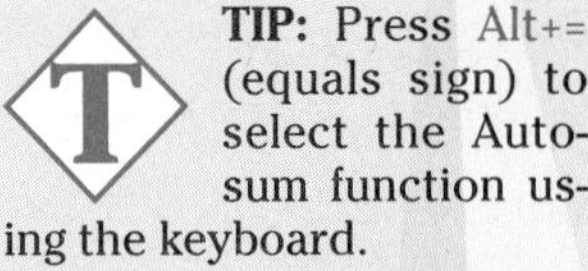

TIP: Press Alt+= (equals sign) to select the Autosum function using the keyboard.

Click on this tool in the Standard toolbar to automatically insert into the active cell the SUM function and a suggested range of cells to sum.

Skill Session

12

Basic Printing

This skill session focuses on the essentials of basic printing, including previewing a document before you print it. For a discussion of advanced printing topics, refer to Skill Session 22.

Preparing to Print

Before you print an Excel document, you need to consider three types of settings:

- ▲ Printer settings
- ▲ Page layout settings
- ▲ Print area

Printer settings determine how the printer itself operates during printing (for example, the print orientation such as portrait or landscape). The printer settings you choose in Excel affect *all* application programs on your computer whenever you print a document. Page layout settings, on the other hand, determine the appearance of the document on paper and affect only the current document. The print area refers to the portion of the document you want to print. In the following sections, you learn how to specify each of these settings. Note that the print settings are controlled by Windows and not Excel.

Setting Up Your Printer

TIP: To check whether your printer is installed, return to the Windows Program Manager and select the Control Panel icon, then select the Printers icon. The Printers box lists all the installed printers.

If you have been using your printer to print files from Windows applications other than Excel, chances are your printer is already installed and set up correctly. However, if Excel is the first Windows application you've used, or if you are printing for the first time, check to make sure the Windows print driver for your printer is installed and set up. If not, refer to your Microsoft Windows User's Guide for instructions on installing printers using the Windows Program Manager Control Panel.

TIP: Because printer settings are generally the same, you will rarely need to change them once they are set. Remember, however, that printer settings affect *all* applications on your computer, so if you change printer settings frequently in other applications, you might need to change them back again when you print from Excel.

Once your printer is installed correctly, you're ready to check the current printer settings. Printer settings apply to *all* documents in all application programs on your computer. If, for example, you change the paper size, this setting will remain in effect even when you print a document from another application.

You control printer settings from the Setup dialog box shown in Figure 12.1. (You'll learn how to access this dialog box in the next set of steps.) These settings will vary depending on the printer. A description of the settings in this dialog box follow:

Printer	Displays a list of all installed printers when you click on the drop-down box. If you have more than one printer installed on your computer, select a printer from the list.
Paper **S**ource	Displays the paper source when you click on the drop-down box. Refer to your printer manual to select the option recommended for your printer.
Paper Si**z**e	Displays paper size choices when you click on the drop-down box. The size you choose should match the actual paper size in your printer.
Memory	Displays the number of megabytes of memory when you click on the drop-down box. If you aren't sure how much memory is in your computer, use the default setting.
Orientation	Controls the print direction—Po**r**trait for vertical printing, **L**andscape for horizontal printing.
Graphics Resolution	Controls the print quality. To print quickly, choose the lowest setting. To print at high quality but at a slower speed, choose the highest setting.
Car**t**ridges	If your printer uses font cartridges, this box allows you to indicate the printer cartridges installed in your printer.

TIP: The setting you choose in the Setup dialog box affects all Windows programs because this is actually a Windows dialog box. The same dialog box is accessible through the Control Panel icon in the Windows Program Manager.

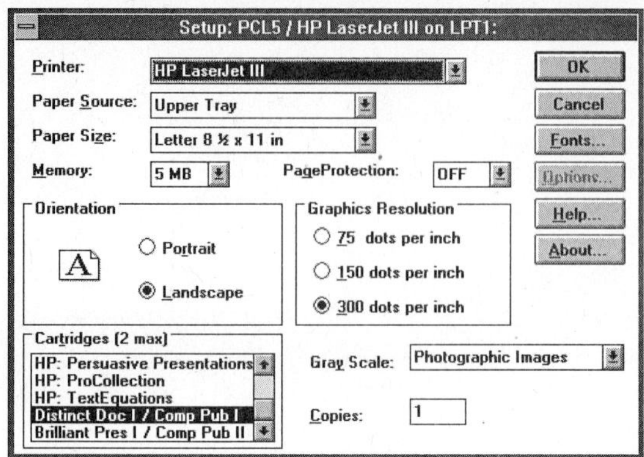

Figure 12.1 The Setup dialog box.

Follow these steps to change print settings in the Setup dialog box:

1. Select File Page Setup.
2. Select the Printer Setup command button. Excel displays the Printer Setup dialog box, which lists each installed printer.
3. Select a printer, then select the Setup button. Excel displays the Setup dialog box shown in Figure 12.1.
4. Select the settings you want to change, then select OK. Excel returns to the Printer Setup dialog box.
5. Select OK to close the Printer Setup dialog box. Excel returns to the Page Setup dialog box.
6. Select OK to close the Page Setup dialog box and return to the worksheet window.

Setting Page Layout

Now that your printer is set up, the next step is to check the settings that affect the appearance of the document you want to print. When you select File Page Setup, Excel displays the Page Setup dialog box shown in Figure 12.2. The settings in the Page Setup dialog box are described below:

Orientation	Choose Portrait to print vertically and Landscape to print horizontally.
Paper	Select the correct paper size from the Size drop-down box. The size you choose should match the actual paper size in your printer.
Margins	Specify the margin width in inches in the Left, Right, Top, and Bottom margin boxes. To center content on the page, select either the Horizontally or Vertically check box.
Page Order	Select Down, then Over to print down the page first, then move to the right. Select Over, then Down to print across the page first, then down.
Row & Column Headings	Check this box to include worksheet row and column headings on the printed copy.
Cell Gridlines	Check this box to include worksheet gridlines on the printed copy.

Black & White Cells	Select this box to print color-formatted cells in patterns. Leave the box blank to print cells in black and white only.
Start Page No.'s At	Enter the starting page number.

For instructions on setting Scaling options and using the command buttons in the Page Setup dialog box, refer to Skill Session 22.

NOTE: The Paper and Orientation settings appear in both the Setup dialog box for printers (Figure 12.1) and in the Page Setup dialog box (Figure 12.2), but these settings are *not* the same. The settings in the printer Setup dialog box apply to the printer itself and affect all documents and all applications on your computer. The settings in the Page Setup dialog box apply only to the active document and take precedence over printer settings.

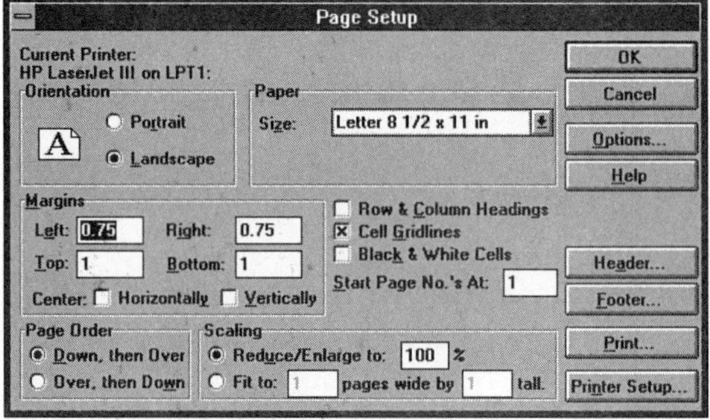

Figure 12.2 The Page Setup dialog box.

To set the page layout for an Excel document, follow these steps:

1. Make the document you want to print the active document.
2. Select File Page Setup. Excel displays the Page Setup dialog box shown in Figure 12.2.
3. Select the options you want to use and edit the options you want to change.

4. When all settings are correct, select OK.

NOTE: Excel saves the page setup settings with the document when you save it. These settings remain in effect until you change them.

Choosing the Print Area

Excel assumes you want to print the entire worksheet unless you specify otherwise. The *entire worksheet* is the range of all cells that contain entries. So, if the bulk of a worksheet's entries are in columns A through F and rows 1 through 16, but an entry also appears in cell K59, Excel automatically defines the print area as A1:K59.

Sometimes worksheets can become quite large, and you may want to print only a portion at a time. For instance, in the previous example, you might want to print only cells A1 through F16. To print a selected range of cells rather than the entire worksheet, you must set the print area. Once a print area is set, Excel prints only the cells in that range until you reset the print area. Follow these steps to set the print area:

1. Select the range of cells you want to print.
2. Select Options Set Print Area. Excel outlines the selected cells with a dotted line and names the selected range Print_Area. (Notice this name appears in the reference area of the formula bar.)

Click on this tool in the Utility toolbar to set the print area for the selected cells.

TIP: To change the current print area, select a new print area.

In Excel you can also select multiple cell ranges and print them on separate pages. In addition, you can select nonadjacent cell ranges for printing. Refer to Skill Session 22 for instructions on these advanced print topics.

Previewing a Print Job

The print preview feature in Excel allows you to see what your printed page will look like based on current printer and page settings. The preview feature is very helpful for checking such things as a document's page layout, page breaks, and margin and column widths.

The print preview feature displays your document at full-page size in a preview window like the one in Figure 12.3. The status bar displays the current page number and total number of pages. Descriptions of the buttons at the top of the preview window follow:

Next and **P**revious buttons	Use these buttons (or the Page Up and Page Down keys) to display the page you want to preview.
Zoom	Allows you to enlarge the document to its normal size. Select this button again to return to a full-page view of the document. You can also use this button to zoom in on a particular area of the document and use the scroll bars to see other areas.
Prin**t**	Prints the print area of the displayed document.

Setup	Displays the Page Setup dialog box so you can make changes to the page layout settings.
Margins	Displays margin and column markers in the document. You can use these markers to adjust margins.
Close	Closes the preview window and returns to the worksheet window.

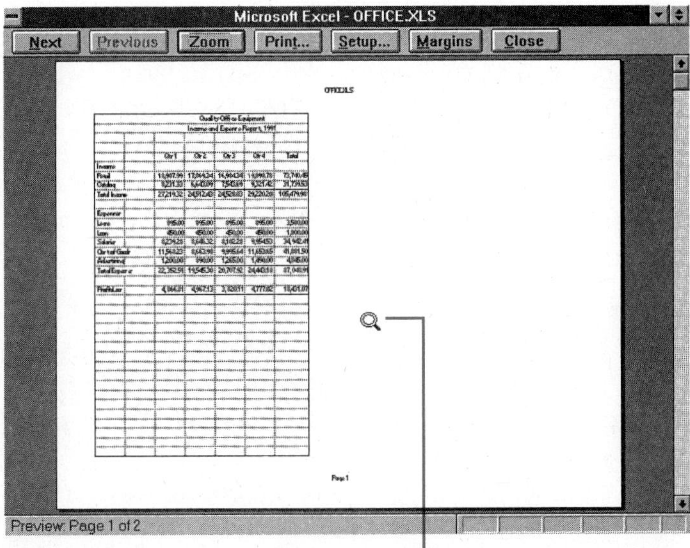

Figure 12.3 A worksheet displayed in the Preview screen.

Follow these steps to preview a document:

1. Make the document you want to preview the active document. Select the print area if necessary.

2. Select File Print Preview. Excel displays the active document at full-page size in a preview window.

3. Use the buttons at the top of the window to display the correct page, enlarge your view of the document, or change the page setup.

4. To close the preview window and return to the worksheet window, select the Close button.

Click on this tool to automatically display the active document in the Print Preview window. (Note that this is a custom tool that is only available if you have added it to a toolbar, see Skill Session 48.)

NOTE: You can't edit an Excel document in the preview window. Return to the worksheet window to edit the document.

TIP: To get the largest full-page view of a document, make sure the Excel window is maximized when you use the print preview feature. When the Excel window is reduced, Print Preview must display a full page view of the document in the reduced window, making the page more difficult to view.

In print preview, the mouse pointer changes to a magnifying glass when you move the mouse anywhere within the worksheet area. Click the magnifier anywhere in the worksheet to zoom in on a specific area. Click on any cell or select the Zoom button to return to a full-page view of the document.

Excel makes it easy for you to adjust margin and column widths in the print preview mode. When you select the Margins button, the Print Preview window displays dotted lines marking the top, bottom, left, and right margins. These margins reflect the settings in the Page Setup dialog box. At the top of the page, Excel displays column markers for each column within the print area. Each margin and column marker has a *handle*, a small solid box used for adjusting the width. When you move the mouse pointer over a handle, the pointer changes to a different shape to indicate that you can adjust the width. To adjust margin and column widths in the Print Preview window:

1. Select the Margins button if margin and column markers are not displayed.

2. Move the mouse pointer to the handle for the margin or column you want to adjust.

3. Drag the handle to a new location. Excel automatically adjusts the margin or column to the new width.

NOTE: When you want margins to be a precise width, select the Setup button in the Print Preview window to display the Page Setup dialog box. In this box, you can set precise widths for top, bottom, left, and right margins.

Printing

At this point, you have learned all the essentials for preparing to print a document. You have:

- ▲ Checked your printer set up
- ▲ Checked the document's page setup
- ▲ Set the print area, if desired
- ▲ Previewed the document

Now you're ready to print your document. When you select File Print, Excel displays the Print dialog box shown in Figure 12.4. The settings in this dialog box are described as follows:

Print Range	Select All to print all pages or Pages to print selected pages. When you select Pages, enter page numbers in the From and To boxes.
Print Quality	Displays choices for print quality when you click on the drop-down box. The choices are determined by the type of printer you have.
Copies	Enter the number of copies to print.

Print	Select Sheet to print just a worksheet, Notes to print only the notes in a worksheet, or Both to print both on separate pages.
Preview	Check this box to automatically display the preview window before printing.
Page Setup button	Displays the Page Setup dialog box.

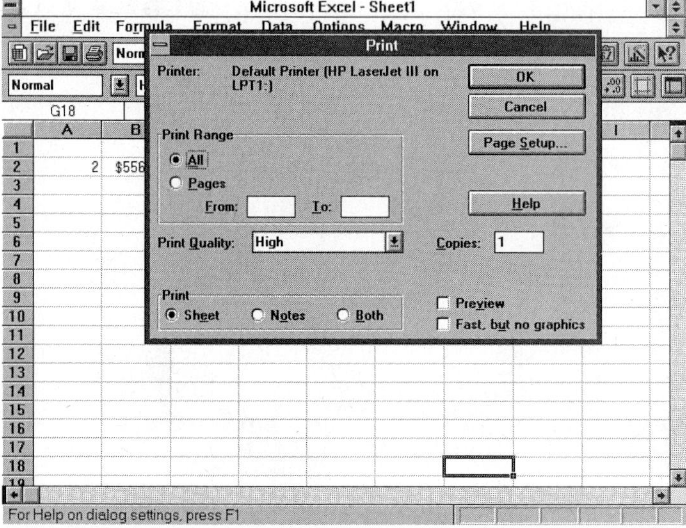

Figure 12.4 The Print dialog box.

Follow these steps to print an Excel document:

1. Make the document you want to print the active document.

2. Select File Print. Excel displays the Print dialog box shown in Figure 12.4.

Tip: Press Ctrl+Shift+F12 to display the Print dialog box.

Click on this tool in the Standard toolbar to print the active document, using default settings, without displaying the Print dialog box.

Tip: If you have more than one printer installed on your computer and want to use a different printer than the one shown in the Print dialog box, you must use the Printer Setup dialog box. Select File Page Setup and then select the Printer Setup command button. Excel displays the Printer Setup dialog box from which you can select the printer to use.

Publishing and Printing Workshop

This workshop leads you through all of Excel's extensive publishing and printing features. You'll learn how to format cells, create your own styles, spell check your worksheets, and print reports.

Skill Session

13

Formatting Numbers, Dates, and Times

One of the best ways to improve the readability of your worksheets is to display your data in a format that is logical, consistent, and straightforward. Formatting currency amounts with leading dollar signs, percentages with trailing percent signs, and large numbers with commas to separate thousands are a few of the ways you can improve your spreadsheet style.

This skill session shows you how to format numbers, dates, and times using the built-in Excel formatting options. You'll also learn how to create your own formats to gain maximum control over the appearance of your data.

Numeric Display Formats

When you enter numbers in a worksheet, Excel removes any leading or trailing zeros. For example, if you enter `0123.4500`, Excel displays `123.45`. The exception to this occurs when you enter a number that is wider than the cell. In this case, Excel tailors the number to fit into the cell by either rounding off some decimal places or by using scientific notation. A number such as 123.45678 is displayed as `123.4568`, and 123456789 is displayed as `1.23+08`. In both cases, the number is changed for display purposes only; Excel still retains the original number internally.

When you create a worksheet, each cell uses this format, known as the General number format, by default. If you would like your numbers to appear differently, you can choose from among the 13 other built-in numeric formats supplied by Excel. Table 13.1 lists these formats along with some examples.

Table 13.1 Excel's built-in numeric formats

Format	*1234.5*	*–1234.5*	*.4375*
General	1234.5	–1234.5	0.4375
0	1235	–1235	0
0.00	1234.50	–1234.50	0.44
#,##0	1,235	–1,235	0
#,##0.00	1,234.50	–1,234.50	0.44
$#,##0_);($#,##0)	$1,235	($1,235)	$0
$#,##0_);[RED] ($#,##0)	$1,235	($1,235)*	$0

Format	*1234.5*	*–1234.5*	*.4375*
$#,##0.00_);($#,##0.00)	$1,234.50	($1,234.50)	$0.44
$#,##0.00_);[RED]($#,##0.00)	$1,234.50	($1,234.50)*	$0.44
0%	123450%	–123450%	44%
0.00%	123450.00%	–123450.00%	43.75%
0.00E+00	1.23E+03	–1.23E+03	4.38E–01
# ?/?	1234 1/2	–1234 1/2	4/9
# ??/??	1234 1/2	–1234 1/2	7/16

* *This format displays negative numbers in red.*

The built-in formats use special symbols (e.g., #, 0, and ?) to create *format codes* that define how each format treats your numbers. You can use these symbols to create your own custom formats. See the section entitled "Customizing Numeric Formats," later in this skill session.

Changing the Numeric Format

The quickest way to format your numbers is to specify the format in the formula bar. For example, if you begin a dollar amount with a dollar sign ($), Excel automatically formats the number as currency. Similarly, if you type a percent sign (%) after a number, Excel automatically formats the number as a percentage. Here are some more examples of this technique (note that you can enter a negative value with either the negative sign (–) or parentheses ():

Number Entered	*Number Displayed*	*Format Used*
$1234.567	$1,234.57	Currency
($1234.5)	($1,234.50)	Currency
10%	10%	Percentage
123E+02	1.23E+04	Scientific
5 3/4	5 3/4	Fraction
0 3/4	3/4	Fraction
3/4	4-Mar	Date

NOTE: Excel interprets a simple fraction such as 3/4 as a date (March 4th, in this case). Always include a leading zero (followed by a space) if you want to enter a simple fraction from the formula bar.

Specifying the numeric format in the formula bar is fast and efficient because Excel guesses the format you want to use. Unfortunately, Excel sometimes guesses wrong (e.g., interpreting a simple fraction as a date). In any case, you don't have access to all the available formats (e.g., displaying negative dollar amounts in red). To overcome these limitations, you can select your numeric formats from the Number Format dialog box (see Figure 13.1). The Number Format dialog box is divided into four sections:

Category — This list box contains the various categories of numeric formats such as currency and percentage.

Format Codes — This list box displays the formats associated with each category.

Code — This text box displays the currently selected format and can be edited when you want to create your own custom formats.

Sample	This information line shows you an example of the effect of the currently selected format.

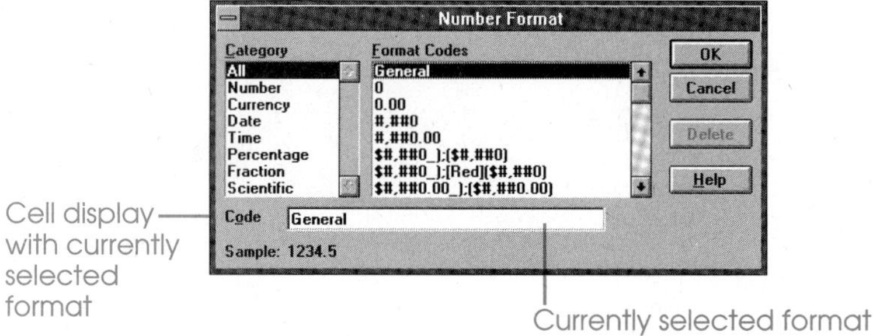

Figure 13.1 The Number Format dialog box.

To open the Number Format dialog box and select a format, follow these steps:

1. Select the cell or range of cells to which you want the new format to apply.
2. Select Format Number. The Number Format dialog box appears.
3. Select a format category from the **C**ategory list box. The listing of format codes changes to reflect the category you choose.
4. Select the numeric format from the **F**ormat Codes list box. The currently highlighted format appears in the C**o**de text line. The Sample information box shows a sample of the format applied to the current cell's contents.
5. Select OK or press Enter. Excel returns you to the spreadsheet with the new formatting applied.

Changing the Numeric Format:

1. Select the cell or range of cells to which you want the new format to apply.
2. Select Format Number.
3. Select a format category from the **C**ategory list box.
4. Select a numeric format from the **F**ormat Codes list box.
5. Select OK or press Enter.

TIP: To open the Number Format dialog box quickly, right-click on a cell or range (or press Shift+F10) and then select the Number option from the shortcut menu that appears (shown below).

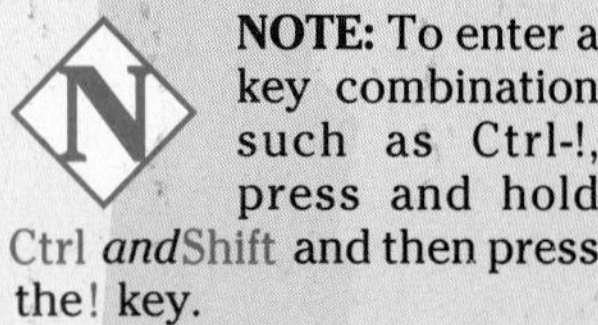

NOTE: To enter a key combination such as Ctrl-!, press and hold Ctrl *and* Shift and then press the ! key.

As an alternative to the Number Format dialog box, Excel offers several keyboard shortcuts for setting the numeric format. Select the cell or range you want to format and use one of the key combinations listed in Table 13.2.

Table 13.2 Shortcut keys for selecting numeric formats

Shortcut Keys	*Format*
Ctrl-~	General
Ctrl-!	#,##0.00
Ctrl-$	$#,##0.00_);($#,##0.00)
Ctrl-%	0%
Ctrl-^	0.00E+00

If you have a mouse, you can use the Formatting toolbar as another method for selecting numeric formats. Figure 13.2 shows the five available tools:

Currency Style Tool—Applies the $#,###0.00_);[RED]($#,##0.00) format.

Percent Style Tool—Applies the 0% format.

Comma Style Tool—Applies the #,##0.00 format.

Increase Decimal Tool—Increases the number of decimal places in the current format.

Decrease Decimal Tool—Decreases the number of decimal places in the current format until the integer is reached.

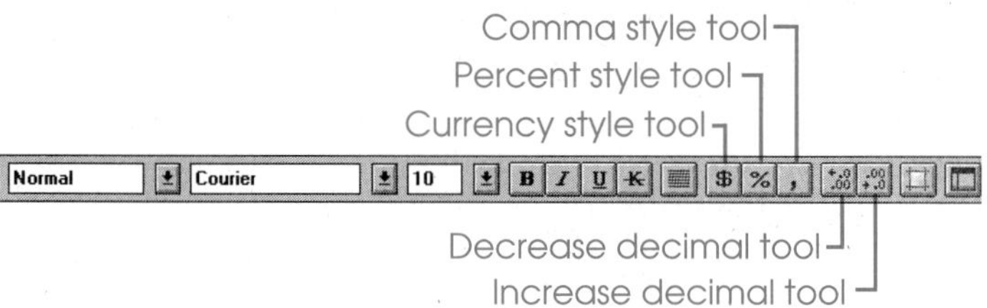

Figure 13.2 The numeric format tools from the Formatting toolbar.

Customizing Numeric Formats

You have a great deal of control over the display of your numbers with the built-in numeric formats, but they have their limitations. For example, no built-in format allows you to display a different currency symbol (e.g., the British Pound—£), or to display a ZIP Code with a leading zero (e.g., "01234"). To overcome these limitations, you need to create your own custom numeric formats. You can do this either by editing an existing format or by entering your own from scratch. The formatting syntax and symbols are explained in detail later in this section. To customize a numeric format, select the cell or range you want to format, and follow these steps:

1. Display the Number Format dialog box using one of the methods outlined in the previous section.
2. Select the format category that is appropriate for your custom format. The formats associated with the category appear in the Format Code list box.

Creating a Custom Numeric Format:

1. Display the Number Format dialog box.
2. Select the appropriate format category.
3. If editing an existing format, highlight it.
4. Select Code.
5. Edit the format code, or enter your own.
6. Select OK or press Enter.

3. If you are editing an existing format, highlight it in the **F**ormat Code list box. The format appears in the C**o**de text box. (If you are creating a format from scratch, skip to step 4.)

4. Click on the C**o**de text box or press Tab. A blinking cursor appears in the C**o**de text box.

5. Edit the displayed format code or enter your own format from scratch.

6. Select OK or press Enter. Excel returns you to the spreadsheet with the custom format applied.

Excel stores each new format definition at the end of the format list. If you edited an existing format, the original format is left intact, and the new format is added to the list. You can select your custom formats the same way as you select the built-in formats. To use your custom format in other worksheets, you need to copy a cell containing the format to that worksheet. See Skill Session 18 to learn about copying and moving cell formats.

Every Excel numeric format, whether it's built-in or customized, has the following syntax:

```
positive format;negative format;zero
format;text format
```

The four parts, separated by semicolons, determine how various numbers are presented. The first part defines how a positive number is displayed; the second part defines how a negative number is displayed; the third part defines how zero is displayed; the fourth part defines how text is displayed. If you leave out one or more of these parts (recall that the built-in formats only use one or two parts), numbers are controlled as follows:

Parts Used	*Format Syntax*
Three	positive format; negative format; zero format
Two	positive and zero format; negative format
One	positive, negative, and zero format

Table 13.3 lists the special symbols you use to define each of these parts.

Table 13.3 Numeric formatting symbols

Symbol	*Description*
General	Displays the number with the General format.
#	Holds a place for a digit and displays the digit exactly as typed. Displays nothing if no number is entered.
0	Holds a place for a digit and displays the digit exactly as typed. Displays zero if no number is entered.
?	Holds a place for a digit and displays the digit exactly as typed. Displays a space if no number is entered.
. (period)	Sets the location of the decimal point.
, (comma)	Sets the location of thousands (marks only the location of the first thousand).
%	Multiplies the number by 100 (for display only) and adds the percent (%) character.
E+ e+ E– e–	Displays the number in scientific format. E– and e– place a minus sign in the exponent; E+ and e+ place a plus sign in the exponent.

continues

Table 13.3 continued

Symbol	*Description*
/ (slash)	Sets the location of the fraction separator.
$ ( ) : – + space	Displays the character.
*	Repeats the character immediately following the symbol until the cell is full (doesn't replace other symbols or numbers).
_ (underscore)	Inserts a blank space the width of the character following the symbol.
\ (backslash)	Inserts the character following the symbol.
"*text*"	Inserts the text within the quotation marks.
@	Holds a place for text.
[*COLOR*]	Displays the cell contents in the specified color. See Skill Session 17.
[*condition value*]	Uses conditional statements to specify when the format is to be used.

Figure 13.3 shows some example custom formats. The format in Example 1 always displays four decimal places. Example 2 shows how you can reduce a large number to a smaller, more readable one by using the thousands separator; each comma represents three zeros (though Excel uses the original number in calculations). Use the format in Example 3 when you don't want to display any leading or trailing zeros. Example 4 shows a four-part format. In Example 5, the pound sign (£) is used in place of the dollar sign. To enter the pound sign, press Alt+0163 on your keyboard. Table 13.4 shows some common ANSI characters you can use.

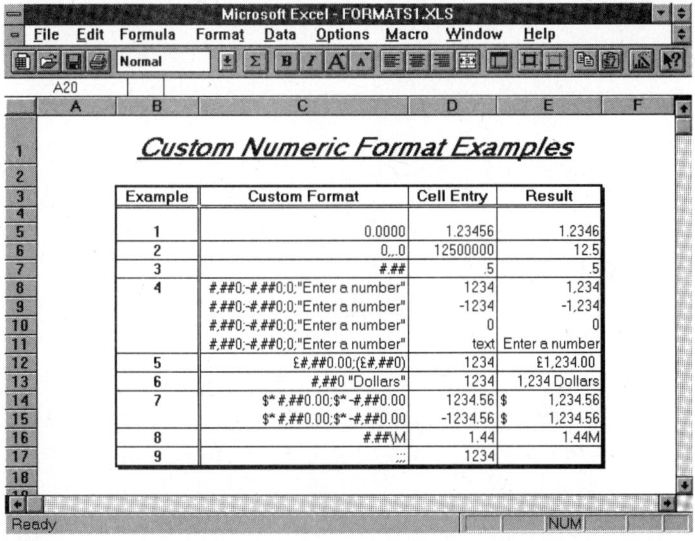

Custom Numeric Format Examples

Example	Custom Format	Cell Entry	Result
1	0.0000	1.23456	1.2346
2	0,,.0	12500000	12.5
3	#.##	.5	.5
4	#,##0;-#,##0;0;"Enter a number"	1234	1,234
	#,##0;-#,##0;0;"Enter a number"	-1234	-1,234
	#,##0;-#,##0;0;"Enter a number"	0	0
	#,##0;-#,##0;0;"Enter a number"	text	Enter a number
5	£#,##0.00;(£#,##0)	1234	£1,234.00
6	#,##0 "Dollars"	1234	1,234 Dollars
7	$* #,##0.00;$* -#,##0.00	1234.56	$ 1,234.56
	$* #,##0.00;$* -#,##0.00	-1234.56	$ 1,234.56
8	#.##\M	1.44	1.44M
9	;;;	1234	

Figure 13.3 Sample custom numeric formats

Table 13.4 ANSI character key combinations

Key Combination	*ANSI Character*
Alt+0163	£
Alt+0162	¢
Alt+0165	¥
Alt+0169	_
Alt+0174	_

Example 6 adds the text string "Dollars" to the format. Example 7 shows how you can line up your dollar signs flush left. In the format definition, each dollar sign is followed by an asterisk (*) and a space. This causes the cell to be filled with spaces over to the number. In Example 8, an "M" is appended to any number. This is useful if your spreadsheet units are in megabytes. Finally, the three semicolons used in Example 9 result in no number being displayed.

The formats used in Figure 13.3 were all designed to work with numbers or dollar values. You can create numeric formats for other types of entries such as telephone numbers, account numbers, and ZIP Codes. Figure 13.4 shows some examples of these types of formats.

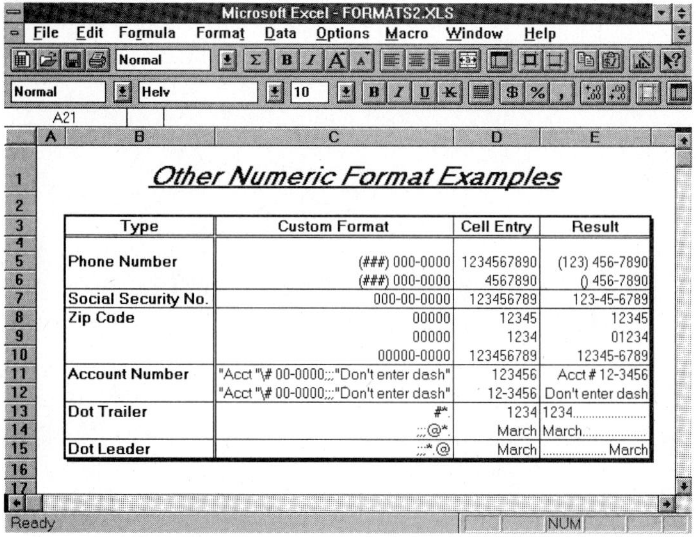

Other Numeric Format Examples

Type	Custom Format	Cell Entry	Result
Phone Number	(###) 000-0000	1234567890	(123) 456-7890
	(###) 000-0000	4567890	() 456-7890
Social Security No.	000-00-0000	123456789	123-45-6789
Zip Code	00000	12345	12345
	00000	1234	01234
	00000-0000	123456789	12345-6789
Account Number	"Acct "\# 00-0000;;;"Don't enter dash"	123456	Acct # 12-3456
	"Acct "\# 00-0000;;;"Don't enter dash"	12-3456	Don't enter dash
Dot Trailer	#*.	1234	1234......................
	;;;@*.	March	March..................
Dot Leader	;;;*.@	March	.... March

Figure 13.4 Other types of numeric formats.

Hiding Zeros

Worksheets look less cluttered and are easier to read if you hide unnecessary zeros. With Excel, you can either hide zeros throughout the entire worksheet or only in selected cells.

To hide all zeros, select Options Display and, in the Display Options dialog box that appears, uncheck the Zero Values box and then select OK or press Enter.

To hide zeros in selected cells, create a custom format that uses the following format syntax:

```
positive format;negative format;
```

The extra semicolon at the end acts as a placeholder for the zero format. Because there is no definition for a zero value, nothing is displayed. For example, the format $#,##0.00_);($#,##0.00); displays standard dollar values but will leave the cell blank if it contains zero.

TIP: If your worksheet contains only integers (no fractions or decimal places), you can use the format #,### to hide zeros.

Using Condition Values

The action of the formats you've seen so far have depended on whether the cell contents were positive, negative, zero, or text. Although this is fine for most applications, there are times when you'll need to format a cell based on different conditions. For example, you might want only specific numbers to take on a certain format or numbers within a certain range. You can achieve this by using the [*condition value*] format symbol. With this symbol, you set up conditional statements using the logical operators =, <, >, <=, >=, and <>, and the appropriate numbers. You then assign these conditions to each part of your format definition.

For example, suppose you have a worksheet where the data must be within the range –1,000 and 1,000. To flag numbers outside this range, you would set up the following format:

```
[>=1000]"Error: Value >= 1,000";
[<=-1000]"Error: Value
<= -1,000";0.00
```

The first part defines the format for numbers greater than or equal to 1,000 (an error message). The second part defines the format for numbers less than or equal to –1,000 (also an error message). The third part defines the format for all other numbers (0.00).

Date and Time Display Formats

If you include dates or times in your worksheets, you need to make sure that they are presented in a readable, unambiguous format. For example, most people would interpret the date 8/5/92 as August 5, 1992. However, there are countries where this date would mean May 8, 1992. Similarly, if you use the time 2:45, do you mean AM or PM? To avoid these kinds of problems, you can use the Excel built-in date and time formats listed in Table 13.5.

Table 13.5 Excel date and time formats

Format	*Display*
m/d/yy	8/23/92
d-mmm-yy	23-Aug-92
d-mmm	23-Aug
mmm-yy	Aug-92
h:mm AM/PM	3:10 PM

Format	Display
h:mm:ss AM/PM	3:10:45 PM
h:mm	15:10
h:mm:ss	15:10:45
m/d/yy h:mm	8/23/92 15:10

You use the same methods to select date and time formats as you used for numeric formats. In particular, you can specify the date and time format as you input your data. For example, entering **Oct-92** automatically formats the cell with the mmm-yy format. Also, you can use the following shortcut keys:

Shortcut Key	Format
Ctrl+#	d-mmm-yy
Ctrl+@	h:mm AM/PM
Ctrl+;	Current date (d-mmm-yy)
Ctrl+:	Current time (h:mm AM/PM)

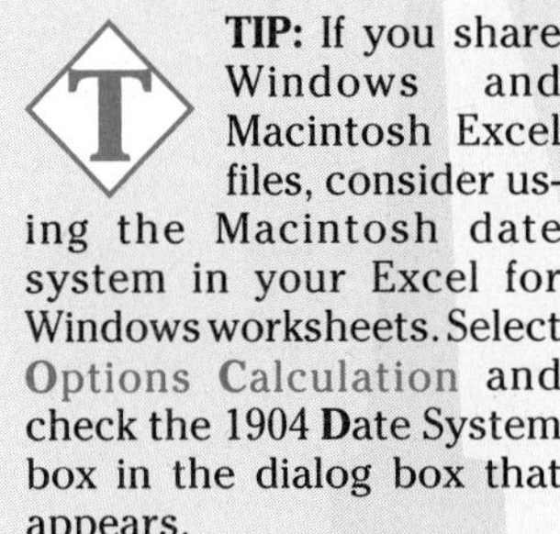
TIP: If you share Windows and Macintosh Excel files, consider using the Macintosh date system in your Excel for Windows worksheets. Select Options Calculation and check the 1904 **D**ate System box in the dialog box that appears.

Customizing Date and Time Formats

Although the built-in date and time formats are fine for most applications, you may need to create your own custom formats. For example, you might want to display the full month name (e.g., "August" instead of "Aug") or even the day of the week. Custom date and time formats are generally simpler than custom numeric formats. There are fewer formatting symbols, and you usually don't need to specify different formats for different conditions (although there are times when this is useful, as you'll see later). Table 13.6 lists the date and time formatting symbols.

Table 13.6 The date and time formatting symbols

Symbol	*Description*
	Date Formats
d	Day number without a leading zero (1 to 31)
dd	Day number with a leading zero (01 to 31)
ddd	Three-letter day abbreviation (e.g., Mon)
dddd	Full day name (e.g., Monday)
m	Month number without a leading zero (1 to 12)
mm	Month number with a leading zero (01 to 12)
mmm	Three-letter month abbreviation (e.g., Aug)
mmmm	Full month name (e.g., August)
yy	Two-digit year (00 to 99)
yyyy	Full year (1900 to 2078)
	Time Formats
h	Hour without a leading zero (0 to 24)
hh	Hour with a leading zero (00 to 24)

Symbol	*Description*
m	Minute without a leading zero (0 to 59)
mm	Minute with a leading zero (00 to 59)
s	Second without a leading zero (0 to 59)
ss	Second with a leading zero (00 to 59)
AM/PM, am/pm, A/P	Displays time using 12-hour clock
/ : . –	Symbols used to separate parts of dates or times
[*COLOR*]	Displays date or time in color specified
[*condition value*]	Uses conditional statements to specify when the format is to be used

Figure 13.5 shows some examples of custom date and time formats.

Deleting Custom Formats

The best way to get familiar with custom formats is try your own experiments. Just remember, however, that Excel stores each format you try. If you find that your format lists are getting too long or are cluttered with unused formats, you can delete formats by following these steps.

NOTE: You cannot delete built-in formats.

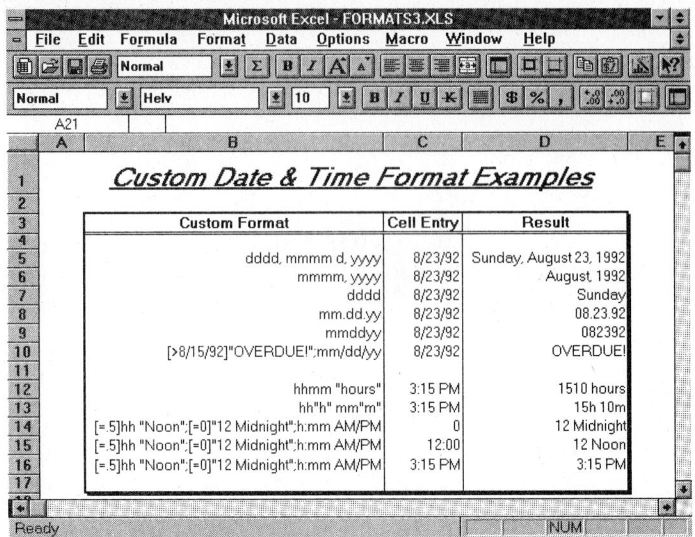

Custom Date & Time Format Examples

Custom Format	Cell Entry	Result
dddd, mmmm d, yyyy	8/23/92	Sunday, August 23, 1992
mmmm, yyyy	8/23/92	August, 1992
dddd	8/23/92	Sunday
mm.dd.yy	8/23/92	08.23.92
mmddyy	8/23/92	082392
[>8/15/92]"OVERDUE!";mm/dd/yy	8/23/92	OVERDUE!
hhmm "hours"	3:15 PM	1510 hours
hh"h" mm"m"	3:15 PM	15h 10m
[=.5]hh "Noon";[=0]"12 Midnight";h:mm AM/PM	0	12 Midnight
[=.5]hh "Noon";[=0]"12 Midnight";h:mm AM/PM	12:00	12 Noon
[=.5]hh "Noon";[=0]"12 Midnight";h:mm AM/PM	3:15 PM	3:15 PM

Figure 13.5 Example custom date and time formats.

Deleting a Custom Format:

1. Select Format Number.
2. Select the category of the format to delete.
3. Highlight the format in the **F**ormat Code list box.
4. Select Delete.
5. To delete other formats, repeat steps 2–4.
6. Select OK or press Enter.

1. Choose Format Number to display the Number Format dialog box.
2. Select the format category that contains the format you want to delete. The formats associated with the category appear in the **F**ormat Code list box.
3. Highlight the format in the **F**ormat Code list box.
4. Select Delete. Excel removes the format from the list.
5. To delete other formats, repeat steps 2–4.
6. Select OK or press Enter. Excel returns you to the spreadsheet.

Skill Session

14

Working with Fonts

Skill Session 13 showed you how to format your worksheet numbers, dates, and times. You learned that assigning appropriate formats to these numbers can greatly enhance the readability of your data. But no matter how skillfully you have applied your formatting, a worksheet full of numbers will still cause the eyes of your audience to glaze over very quickly. The next step in creating a presentation-quality report is to surround your numbers with attractive labels and headings.

This skill session teaches you about the extensive font capabilities of Excel 4 for Windows. You will learn about the various font attributes and how to apply them to your worksheets. Throughout this skill session, the emphasis will be on selecting fonts that improve the impact and effectiveness of your worksheets.

Learning About Fonts

The characters that you enter into your Excel worksheets have a number of attributes: the typeface, the type size, and the type style. Taken all together, these attributes define the character's *font*.

The first of these attributes, the *typeface*, refers to a distinctive graphic design of letters and numbers. Typefaces differ according to the shape and thickness of characters, as well as a number of other stylistic features. As Figure 14.1 shows, typefaces can be very different.

This is a typeface called Times Roman.

This is a typeface called Helvetica.

This is a typeface called Modern.

Figure 14.1 Some sample typefaces.

All typefaces are classified as either *serif* or *sans serif*. A serif typeface contains a fine cross stroke, or "foot," at the end of each main character stroke. For example, look at the capital T in the Times New Roman typeface in Figure 14.1. A sans serif typeface, such as the Helvetica example in Figure 14.1, does not contain these cross strokes. Here are some general rules for selecting worksheet typefaces:

- ▲ Use sans serif typefaces for numbers, headings, and titles. Sans serif characters tend to be wider and cleaner looking than their serif counterparts, which helps when displaying numbers or brief, but large, text entries.

- Use serif typefaces for lengthy sections of text. The elegant serif design makes smaller characters easy to read.
- When choosing a typeface for a report, take your audience into account. If you are presenting to a business group, you should use more conservative typefaces such as Bookman or Helvetica-Narrow. In more relaxed settings, you can try Avant Garde or even (in small doses) a calligraphic font such as Lucida Calligraphy).
- Try to limit yourself to two typefaces (at most) in a single worksheet. If you use more than that, your reports will look jumbled and confusing. It is much more effective to vary type size and style within a single typeface than to use many different typefaces.

NOTE: The number of typefaces you have available will depend on the printer you use and whether you have a printer font cartridge or font management program installed on your computer.

The next font attribute is the *size* of the typeface. Type size is a measure of the height of a font and is measured in *points*. There are 72 points in an inch so selecting a type size of 72 gives you letters approximately one inch high. (Technically, type size is measured from the highest point of a tall letter such as "h" to the lowest point of a descending letter such as "y.") Figure 14.2 shows some sample type sizes.

This is 12-point type.

This is 18-point type.

This is 36-point type.

Figure 14.2 The sample type sizes.

Use different type sizes in your worksheets to differentiate titles and headings from data:

- ▲ Use 24- or even 36-point type size for worksheet titles, but bear in mind that you want your title to fit on a single page. If your report has a subtitle, use a type size that is slightly smaller than the one used in the main title. For example, if your title is in 24-point type, make the subtitle 18-point type.
- ▲ Column and row headings look good in 12- or 14-point type, but, again, watch your size. If your headings are too large, you will have to widen your columns accordingly.
- ▲ For most reports, the standard 10-point type is fine for your data, although you will probably have to switch to a larger type (such as 12-point) if you plan to present your work on a slide or overhead.

The *type style* of a font refers to attributes such as regular, bold, and italic. Figure 14.3 shows examples of each of these attributes.

This is regular type

This is bold type

This is italic type

This is bold italic type

Figure 14.3 Some type style attributes.

Other type styles (often called type *effects*) include underlining and strikeout characters. Use any of these type styles to make sections of your worksheet stand out. Bold is often used for worksheet titles, and headings are often displayed as both bold and italic. In general, however, you should use these styles sparingly because overuse diminishes their impact.

Figure 14.4 shows an Excel spreadsheet that implements many of the features already described in this skill session. As you can see, fonts are a powerful way to improve your worksheet design. The next section shows you how to implement fonts in Excel.

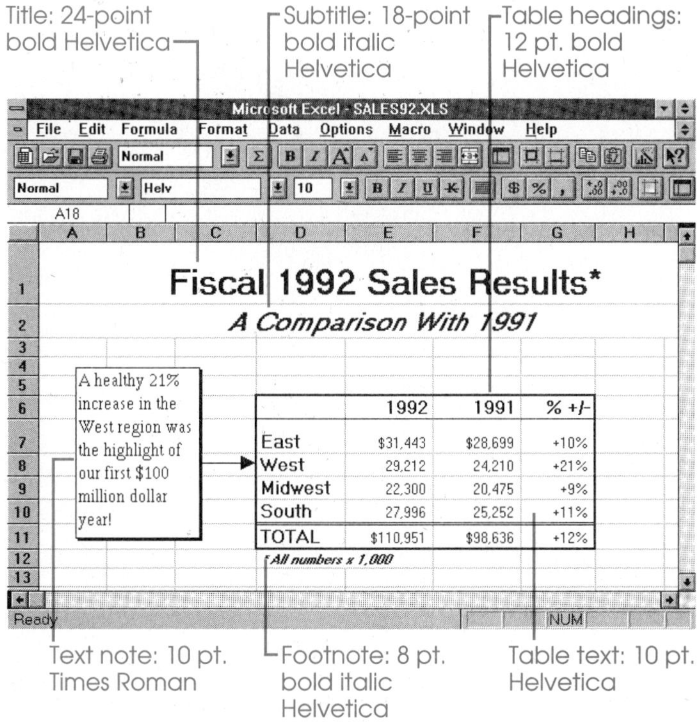

Figure 14.4 Using fonts effectively can greatly improve the look of your worksheets.

Using Fonts in Excel

With Excel, you can use up to 256 different fonts on a single worksheet, although, in practice, a presentation-quality report should only use a few fonts. (Remember that a font is a specific combination of typeface, size, and style. This means that 10-point Helvetica is a different font than 24-point Helvetica Bold.)

You can set all the font attributes from the Font dialog box (see Figure 14.5). This dialog box is divided into six areas:

Font	This is a list box of available typefaces (the terms font and typeface are often used interchangeably). Excel shows printer fonts with a printer graphic beside them, and TrueType fonts (the ones that come with Windows 3.1) with the TrueType logo.
Font Style	This is a list box of font styles available for the highlighted typeface.
Size	This is a list box that displays the available type sizes for the highlighted typeface.
Effects	Use this section to choose the Strikeout and Underline font effects.
Color	This is a drop-down list box that enables you to select a font color. See Skill Session 17 for a discussion of color.

Normal Font — Check this box to select Excel's default font. See Skill Session 18 to learn how to change the default font.

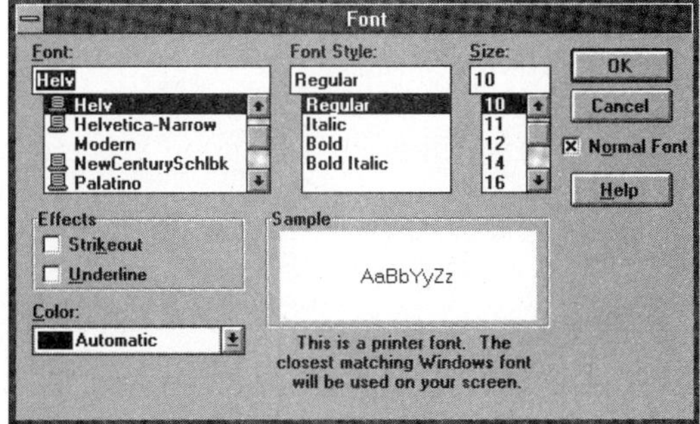

Figure 14.5 The Font dialog box.

Selecting a Font:

1. Select a cell or range to format.
2. Select Format Font.
3. Select a typeface.
4. Select a font style.
5. Select a type size.
6. Check any font effects you want.
7. Select OK or press Enter.

To select a font using the Font dialog box, follow these steps:

1. Select a cell or range of cells to format.
2. Select Format Font. The Font dialog box appears.
3. Select a typeface from the **F**ont list box. Excel displays the selected typeface in the Sample area.
4. Select a font style from the Font St**y**le list box. The style is displayed in the Sample area.
5. Select a type size from the **S**ize list box. Excel displays the size in the Sample area.
6. Check any font effects you want to use. Each time you select an effect, it is displayed in the Sample area.
7. Select OK or press Enter. Excel returns you to the worksheet and formats the cells with the font you chose.

TIP: To open the Font dialog box quickly, right-click on a cell or range of cells, or press Shift+F10, and then select the Font option from the shortcut menu that appears (shown below).

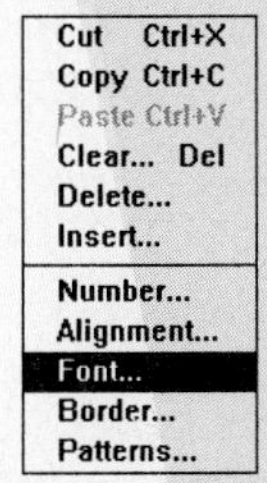

Selecting Fonts with the Toolbar

Besides using the Font dialog box, you can set all the font attributes using the Formatting toolbar (shown in Figure 14.6). The Formatting toolbar contains the following font tools:

Font Name Box—Displays the available typefaces.

Font Size Box—Displays the available type sizes for the selected typeface.

Bold Tool—Applies the bold style to the selected cells.

Italic Tool—Applies the italic style to the selected cells.

Underline Tool—Applies the underline effect to the selected cells.

Strikeout Tool—Applies the strikeout effect to the selected cells.

Figure 14.6 The Formatting toolbar font tools.

You can also use the Standard toolbar (see Figure 14.7) to apply certain font attributes:

Bold Tool—Applies the bold style to the selected cells.

Italic Tool—Applies the italic style to the selected cells.

Increase Font Size Tool—Increases the font to the next highest point size.

Decrease Font Size Tool—Decreases the font to the next lowest point size.

Figure 14.7 The Standard toolbar font tools.

Selecting Font Attributes with Shortcut Keys

If you don't have a mouse or you prefer to work with the keyboard, Excel provides a number of keyboard shortcuts that you can use to select font attributes. Table 14.1 lists these shortcut key combinations.

Table 14.1 Shortcut keys for selecting font attributes

Keys	*Action*
Ctrl+1	Applies Normal (default) font.
Ctrl+2 or Ctrl+B	Toggles bold style on or off.
Ctrl+3 or Ctrl+I	Toggles italic style on or off.
Ctrl+4 or Ctrl+U	Toggles underline effect on or off.
Ctrl+5	Toggles strikeout effect on or off.
Ctrl+F	Activates Font Name box. Use the arrow keys to select a font name.
Ctrl+P	Activates Font Size box. Use the arrow keys to select a font size.

NOTE: If the Formatting toolbar is not displayed when you press Ctrl+F or Ctrl+P, Excel opens the Font dialog box.

Skill Session

15

Formatting Other Cell Attributes

This skill session teaches you about other cell attributes, such as cell borders and patterns, and the alignment within cells and across ranges.

Aligning Cell Contents

When you place data into an unformatted cell, Excel aligns text entries with the left edge of the cell, numbers and dates with the right edge of the cell, and error and logical values in the center of the cell. This is the default General alignment scheme. Although this format is useful for distinguishing text entries from numerical ones, it tends to make a worksheet look messy and poorly organized. To remedy this, Excel allows you to apply a number of alignment options.

You set the Excel alignment attributes using the Alignment dialog box (see Figure 15.1). This dialog box is divided into four areas: Horizontal, Vertical, Orientation, and **W**rap Text. The Horizontal section contains the following options (see Figure 15.2 for an example of each option):

Click on this tool in the Standard toolbar to left-align cell contents.

Click on this tool in the Standard toolbar to center cell contents.

Click on this tool in the Standard toolbar to right-align cell contents.

Click on this tool in the Standard toolbar to center cell contents across selection.

Click on this tool in the Formatting toolbar to justify cell contents.

General	Uses the default alignment settings.
Left	Left-aligns the cell contents.
Center	Centers the cell contents.
Right	Right-aligns the cell contents.
Fill	Repeats the contents of the cell until the cell is filled.
Justify	Aligns the cell contents with the left and right edges of the cell. For text entries longer than the cell width, the cell height is increased to accommodate the text.
Center **a**cross selection	Centers the cell contents across the selected range of selection cells.

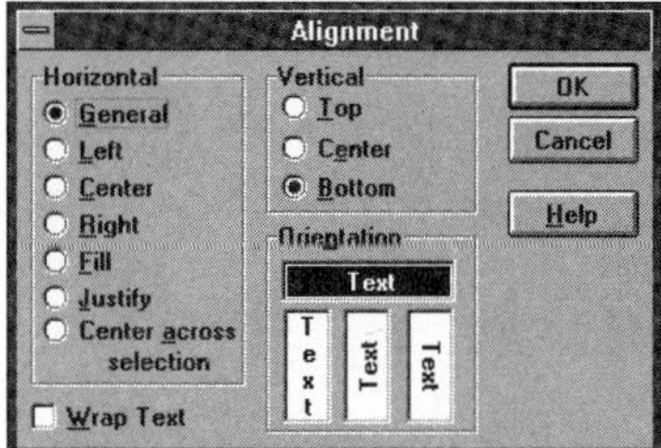

Figure 15.1 The Alignment dialog box.

	A	B	C
1	Left-aligned		
2	Centered		
3	Right-aligned		
4	FilledFilledFilledFilledFilled		
5	Here is an example of text that is justified. Notice that Excel aligns the text on the left and right.		
6	Centered across columns A->C		
7			

Figure 15.2 The horizontal alignment options.

If you increase the height of a row (explained in Skill Session 16), the Vertical section of the Alignment dialog box enables you to position cell entries vertically using the following options (see Figure 15.3 for an example of each option):

Top Aligns the cell contents with the top of the cell.

Center Aligns the cell contents with the center of the cell.

Bottom Aligns the cell contents with the bottom of the cell.

	A	B	C
1	Top	Center	Bottom
2			

Figure 15.3 The vertical alignment options.

The Orientation section of the Alignment dialog box enables you to orient your cell entries in four ways: left-to-right (normal), vertically, sideways with characters running from bottom to top, and sideways with characters running from top to bottom (though this does not necessarily mean the top and bottom of the cell boundaries). Figure 15.4 shows an example of each option.

Note: If you choose either the vertical or a sideways orientation with a long text entry, you will have to adjust the height of the cell to see all the text. See Skill Session 16 for instructions on adjusting row height.

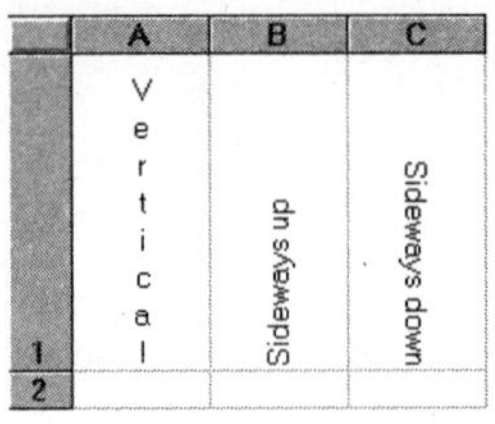

Figure 15.4 The orientation alignment options.

The final section of the Alignment dialog box, the **Wrap** Text option, enables you to wrap long cell entries so they are displayed on multiple lines in a single cell (see Figure 15.5). You can left-align, center, right-align, or justify wrapped entries.

Tip: You can enter carriage returns and tabs in your wrapped cells. To enter a carriage return, position the cursor in the formula bar and press Alt+Enter. For a tab, press Ctrl+Tab.

	A	B	C	D
1	Here is a long text entry that is not wrapped.			
2	Here is a long text entry that is wrapped.			

Figure 15.5 The Word Wrap alignment option.

Aligning Cell Contents:

1. Select the cell or range of cells that you want to align.
2. Choose Format Alignment.
3. Select your alignment options.
4. Select OK or press Enter.

Follow these steps to select alignment attributes with the Alignment dialog box:

1. Select the cell or range of cells that you want to align.

2. Choose Format Alignment to display the Alignment dialog box.

3. Select your alignment options as described previously.

4. Select OK or press Enter. Excel returns you to the worksheet with the new alignment activated.

Tip: To open the Alignment dialog box quickly, right-click on a cell or range, or press Shift+F10, and then select the Alignment option from the shortcut menu that appears (shown below).

Justifying Text in a Cell Range

If your worksheet has cells containing long text entries that extend over several columns, you can use Format Justify to rearrange the text so it fits neatly into a smaller cell range.

Figure 15.6 shows a worksheet where text has been imported from a word processing program. The highlighted range `A2:D17` defines the new four-column wide area for the text. Excel divides the text into smaller, four-column wide segments and copies each segment, in order, to the first cell in each row of the range. Figure 15.7 shows the results.

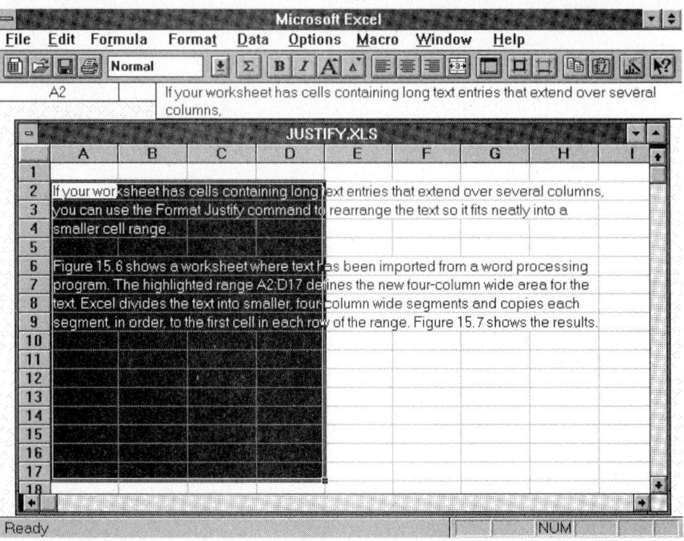

Figure 15.6 Highlight the new range into which you want the text to fit.

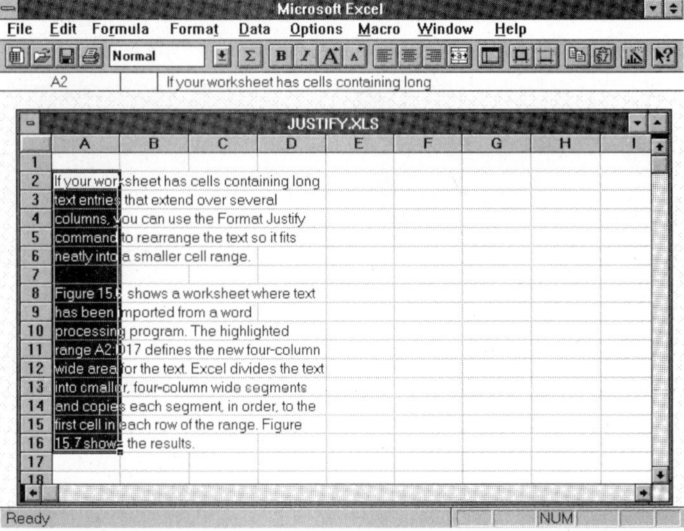

Figure 15.7 Excel fills only as much of the range as it needs to justify the text.

To justify your worksheet text, select the new range for the text and choose Format Justify. When selecting a range, keep the following points in mind:

- ▲ You must include the text to be justified as part of the range. Text not included in the range is not affected.
- ▲ Do not include numbers or formulas in the range. Excel will only justify text entries.
- ▲ If your selected range is too large, Excel only fills as much as it needs to justify the text. If your range is too small, Excel warns you with the dialog box shown in Figure 15.8.

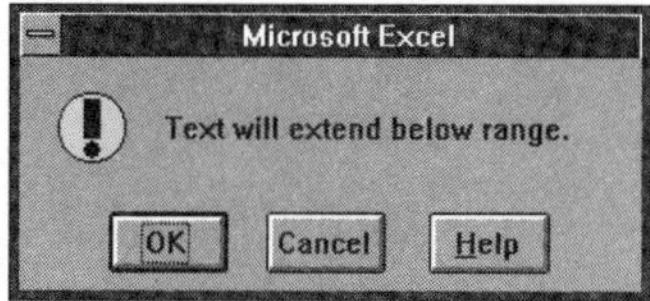

Figure 15.8 Excel warns you if the justified text will extend beyond the range you selected.

Caution: Before selecting OK (or pressing Enter) to extend the text below the range, make sure this will not write over any existing data.

Working With Cell Borders

With Excel 4 for Windows, you can place borders of various weights and patterns around your worksheet cells. This is useful for enclosing different parts of the worksheet, defining data entry areas, and marking totals. You apply cell borders using the Border dialog box (see Figure 15.9). This dialog box is divided into four sections: Border, Style, Color (see Skill Session 17), and Shade.

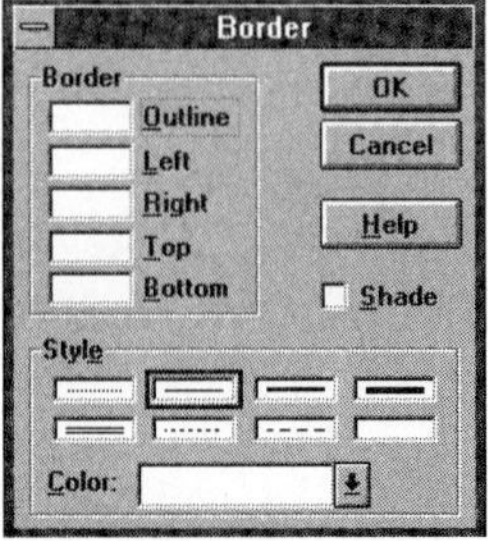

Figure 15.9 The Border dialog box.

The Border section contains five options:

Outline Applies the currently selected border style around the outer edges of the selected cells.

Left Applies the currently selected border style on the left edge of the selected cells.

Right Applies the currently selected border style on the right edge of the selected cells.

Top Applies the currently selected border style on the top edge of the selected cells.

Bottom Applies the currently selected border style on the bottom edge of the selected cells.

Tip: To see your borders better, turn off the worksheet gridlines by choosing Options Display and then deselecting the Gridlines option on the dialog box that appears.

Select this tool on the Standard Toolbar to apply an outline border to the selected cells.

Tip: Press Ctrl+Shift+& (ampersand) to toggle the outline border on or off around the selected cells.

Select this tool on the Standard toolbar to apply a bottom border to the selected cells.

Tip: Press Ctrl+Shift+_ (underscore) to remove all borders from the selected cells.

The Style section contains the eight border styles that you can use. Figure 15.10 demonstrates each of these styles (except the blank style).

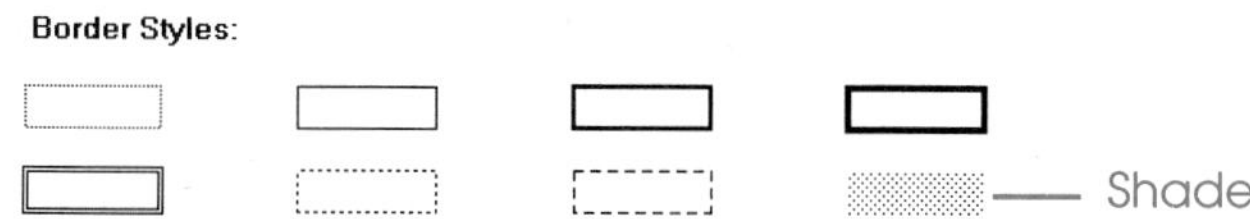

Figure 15.10 The Excel border styles.

The Shade option applies a shading pattern to each cell in the range. See the next section, "Working With Cell Patterns," for a complete discussion of shading effects.

Follow these steps to apply a border to a cell or range:

1. Select the cell or range of cells to be bordered.
2. Choose Format Border to display the Border dialog box.
3. Select the border location from the Border section of the dialog box. Excel displays a sample of the currently selected border style beside the Border option.
4. Select a different border style, if necessary. When you select a style, a sample appears in the box to the left of the Border option.
5. Select Shade, if necessary.
6. Select OK or press Enter. Excel returns you to the worksheet with the borders applied.

Formatting Cell Borders:

1. Select the cell or range to be bordered.
2. Choose Format Border.
3. Select the border location.
4. Select a border style.
5. Select Shade, if necessary.
6. Select OK or press Enter.

Tip: To open the Border dialog box quickly, right-click on a cell or range, or press Shift+F10, and then select the Border option from the shortcut menu that appears (shown below).

Cut Ctrl+X
Copy Ctrl+C
Paste Ctrl+V
Clear... Del
Delete...
Insert...
Number...
Alignment...
Font...
Border...
Patterns...

Figure 15.11 shows how you can use cell borders to create an invoice form. In a business document such as this, your borders should be strictly functional. You should avoid the merely decorative, and, as in Figure 15.12, you should make your borders serve a purpose whether it's marking a data area or separating parts of the form.

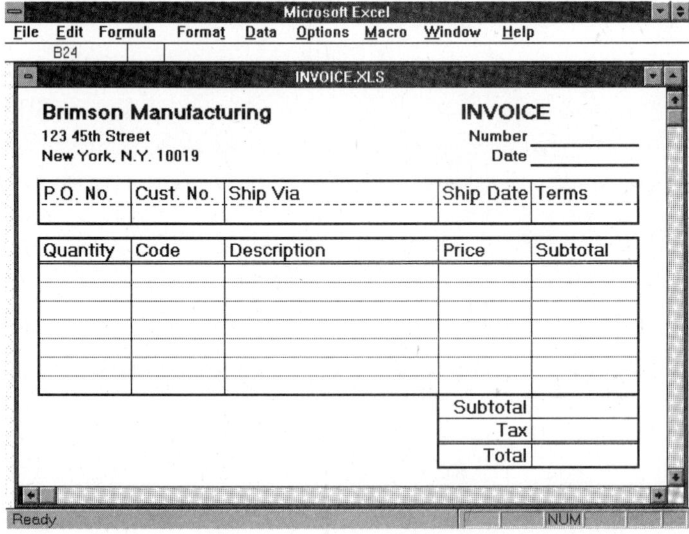

Figure 15.11 Use cell borders to create an invoice form.

Working With Cell Patterns

One of the most effective ways to make an area of your worksheet stand out is to apply a pattern or shading to the cells. By shading titles, headings, and important results, you give your reports a polished, professional-quality appearance.

Excel 4 for Windows offers 18 different patterns, as shown in Figure 15.12. You apply these patterns through the Patterns dialog box shown in Figure 15.13. This dialog box is divided into four areas: the **P**attern drop-down list box contains the 18 cell patterns; the **F**ore-ground and **B**ackground drop-down list boxes are used to set the pattern colors (see Skill Session 17 for instructions on using these color options); and the Sample area shows how the currently selected pattern options will appear on the worksheet.

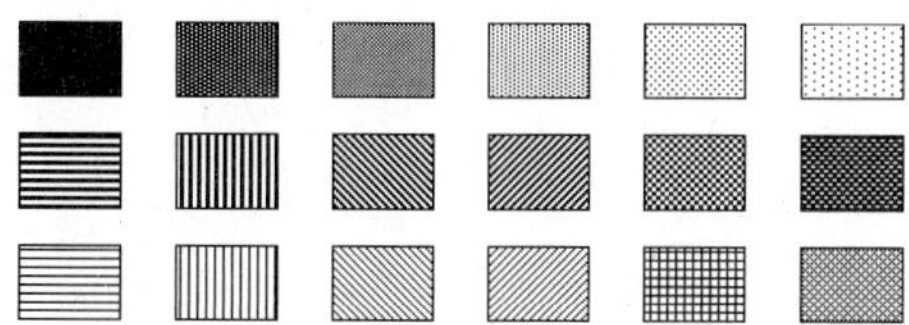

Figure 15.12 Excel offers 18 different cell patterns.

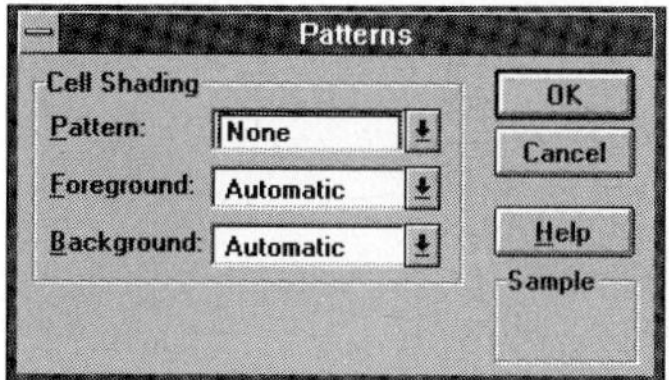

Figure 15.13 The Patterns dialog box.

To apply a pattern to a cell or range of cells, choose Format Patterns to display the Patterns dialog box and then select your pattern from the **P**attern list. When you select OK or press Enter, Excel returns you to the worksheet with the patterns applied.

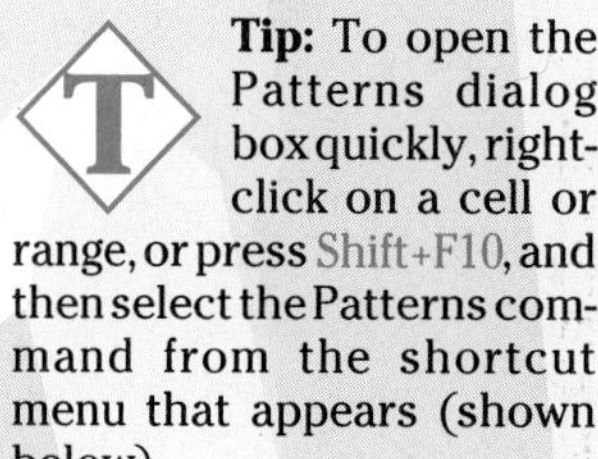

Tip: To open the Patterns dialog box quickly, right-click on a cell or range, or press Shift+F10, and then select the Patterns command from the shortcut menu that appears (shown below).

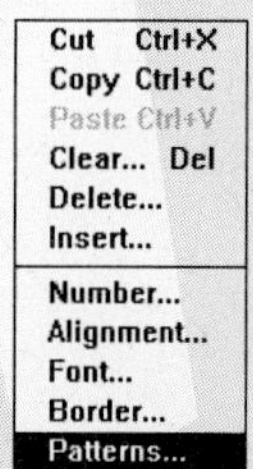

Figure 15.14 shows the Brimson Manufacturing invoice with some shading effects. Figure 15.15 shows another application of cell patterns. In this example, patterns are used to create a time line (also known as a Gantt chart) for a project management application. Each project task is listed on the left and the bars show where each task starts and ends. You can use different cell patterns to represent tasks not yet started, partially completed, fully completed, and delayed.

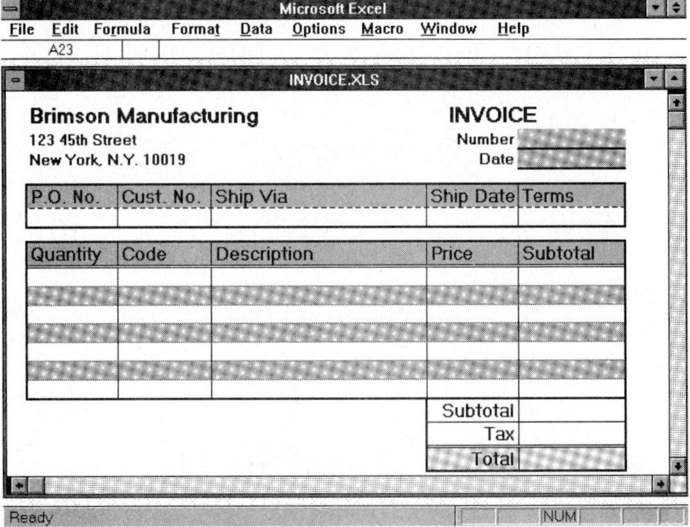

Figure 15.14 The Brimson Manufacturing invoice with shading effects.

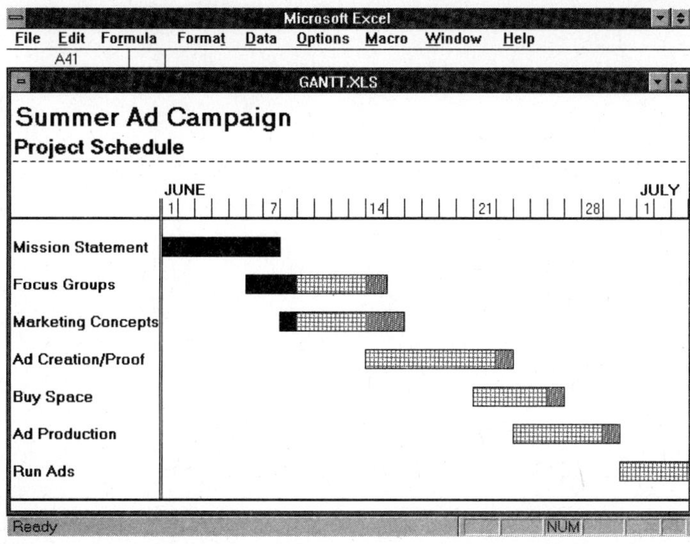

Figure 15.15 Using cell patterns to create a Gantt chart.

Skill Session

16

Working with Columns and Rows

One of the easiest ways to improve the appearance of your worksheet is to manipulate your rows and columns. This skill session teaches you how to adjust column widths and row heights and how to hide and unhide entire rows and columns in addition to gridlines and headings.

Adjusting Column Widths

You can use column width adjustments to improve the appearance of your worksheet in a number of different ways.

▲ If you're faced with a truncated text entry or a number that Excel shows as ######, you can enlarge the column so the entry will be displayed in full.

▲ If your worksheet contains many numbers, you can widen the columns to spread the numbers out and make the worksheet less cluttered.

▲ You can make your columns smaller to fit the entire worksheet onto your screen or onto a single printed page.

▲ You can adjust the column width for the entire worksheet to create a grid for a time line chart such as the one shown in Skill Session 15.

TIP: It often happens that you have a column of numbers where one number (such as a date) is wider than the column and appears as ######. Instead of widening the column to accommodate the number, change the number to `TEXT(number, format)`. Excel displays the number as text, and it will flow into the next column. For details, see the Function Reference that comes with Excel.

Excel measures column width in characters. When you create a new worksheet, each column uses a standard width of 8.43 characters. The actual column width you see on your screen depends on the width of the default font. For example, the standard column width with 10-point Helvetica (7 pixels) will be only half the size of the standard width with 20-point Helvetica (14 pixels). See Skill Session 18 for instructions on changing the default font. You can use any of three methods to adjust your column widths:

▲ Entering a specific column width

▲ Using the mouse to set the column width

- Having Excel set the width automatically with the Best Fit feature

Method One—Entering a Specific Column Width

With Excel, you can set column widths as small as 0 characters or as large as 255 characters. To enter a column width, follow these steps:

1. Select at least one cell in each column you want to adjust.
2. Select Format Column Width. Excel displays the Column Width dialog box, as shown in Figure 16.1. The **C**olumn **W**idth text box shows the width of the selected columns.(This box will be blank if you have chosen columns with varying widths.)
3. Enter the desired width in the **C**olumn **W**idth text box. To return a column to the Standard width, select the Use Standard Width check box.
4. Select OK or press Enter. Excel sets the column width and returns you to the worksheet.

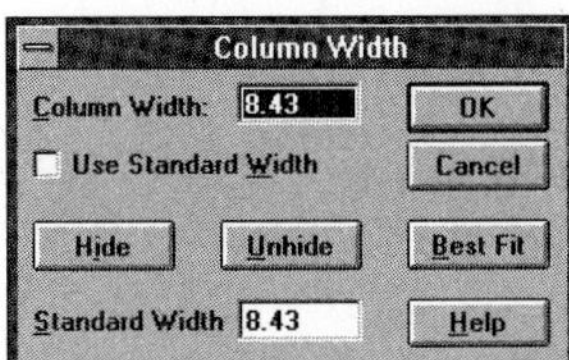

Figure 16.1 The Column Width dialog box.

Entering a Column Width:

1. Select cell(s) in each column you want to adjust.
2. Select Format Column Width.
3. Enter width or select Use Standard Width.
4. Select OK.

TIP: To open the Column Width dialog box quickly, right-click on the column heading, or press Ctrl+space bar to select the entire column and press Shift+F10. Then choose Column Width from the shortcut menu that appears (shown below).

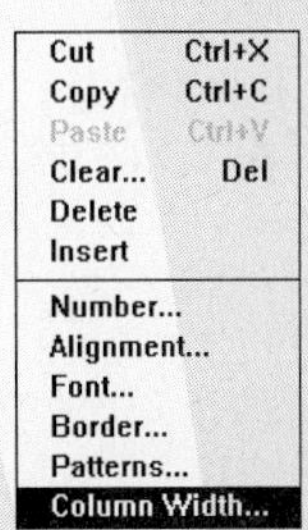

NOTE: If you are running Excel under Windows 3.1, your default font is 10-point MS Sans Serif.

When entering column widths, you can use an integer or a decimal number. However, if you enter a width such as 10.1 and call up the Column Width dialog box for the same column, you will notice that the **C**olumn Width text box actually says 10.14. What happened is that Excel adjusts the column width to the nearest pixel. For 10-point Helvetica (Excel's default font) a character unit has 7 pixels or roughly 0.143 characters per pixel. This means that Excel will round a column width of 10.1 to 10.14. Similarly, a width of 9.35 is rounded down to 9.29.

You can also use the Column Width dialog box to change the standard column width. To do so, display the Column Width dialog and enter the new number in the **S**tandard Width text box. When you select OK or press Enter, Excel sets each column to the new width.

Method Two—Using the Mouse to Set the Column Width

You can bypass the Column Width dialog box entirely by using your mouse to drag a column to the width you want. Here are the steps you need to follow to do this:

Adjusting Column Widths with the Mouse:

1. Point to right edge of column heading.
2. Press and hold left mouse button.
3. Drag pointer to desired width.
4. Release mouse button.

1. Move the mouse pointer to the column headings area and position the pointer at the right edge of the column you want to adjust. The mouse pointer changes to the shape shown in Figure 16.2.

2. Press and hold down the left mouse button. The formula bar displays the current column width and the column's right gridline turns into a dashed line (see Figure 16.2).

3. Drag the pointer left or right to the desired width. As you move the pointer, the formula bar displays the new width.

4. Release the mouse button. Excel adjusts the column width accordingly.

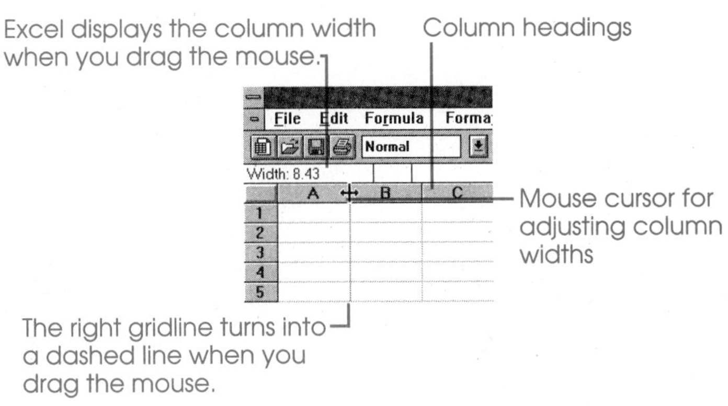
Excel displays the column width when you drag the mouse.
Column headings
File Edit Formula Forma
Normal
Width: 8.43
A B C
1
2
3
4
5
Mouse cursor for adjusting column widths
The right gridline turns into a dashed line when you drag the mouse.

Figure 16.2 You can use a mouse to adjust the column width.

You can use this technique to set the width of several columns at once. For every column you want to adjust, select the entire column (see Skill Session 7 for instructions on selecting multiple columns) and then perform the preceding steps on any one column. Excel will apply the new width to each selected column.

Method Three—Using Excel's Best Fit Feature

If you have a long column of entries of varying widths, it may take you a few tries to get the optimum column width. To avoid guesswork, you can have Excel set the width automatically using the Best Fit feature. When you use this feature, Excel examines the column's contents and sets the width slightly larger than the longest entry. Follow these steps to set the column width using Best Fit:

Adjusting Column Widths Using Best Fit:

1. Select cell(s) in each column you want to adjust.
2. Choose Format Column Width.
3. Select Best Fit.

1. Select each column you want to adjust.
2. Select Format Column Width to display the Column Width dialog box.
3. Select Best Fit. Excel adjusts the columns to their optimal width and returns you to the worksheet.

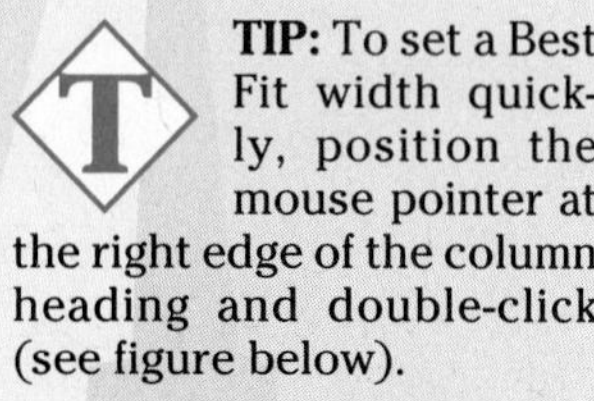

TIP: To set a Best Fit width quickly, position the mouse pointer at the right edge of the column heading and double-click (see figure below).

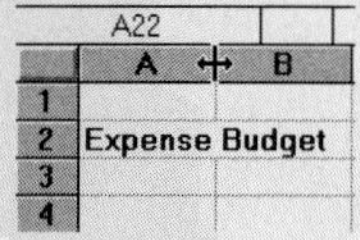

Adjusting Row Height

You can set the height of your worksheet rows using techniques similar to those used for adjusting column widths. Excel normally adjusts row heights automatically to accommodate the tallest font in a row. You can make your own height adjustments, however, to give your worksheet more breathing room or to reduce the amount of space taken up by unused rows.

CAUTION: When reducing a row height, always keep the height larger than the tallest font to avoid cutting off the tops of any characters.

Excel measures row height in *points*, the same units used for type size. When you create a new worksheet, Excel assigns a slightly taller standard row height of 12.75 points because the default font for each row is 10-point Helvetica. If you were to change the default font to 20-point Helvetica, each row height would increase accordingly. (See Skill Session 18 for instructions on changing the Normal font.)

NOTE: If you are running Excel under Windows 3.1, your default font is 10-point MS Sans Serif.

As with column widths, you can use three methods to adjust row heights:

- Entering a specific row height
- Using the mouse to set the row height
- Having Excel set the height automatically using the row's standard height

Method One—Entering a Specific Row Height

With Excel, you can set row heights as small as 0 points or as large as 409 points. To enter a row height, follow these steps:

1. Select at least one cell in each row you want to adjust.
2. Choose Format Row Height. Excel displays the Row Height dialog box, as shown in Figure 16.3. The **R**ow Height text box shows the height of the selected rows. (This box will be blank if you have chosen rows with varying heights.)
3. Enter the height you want in the **R**ow Height text box.
4. Select OK or press Enter. Excel sets the row height and returns you to the worksheet.

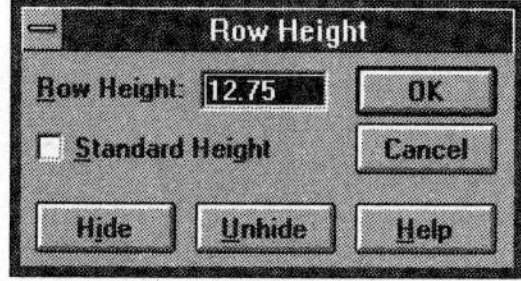

Figure 16.3 The Row Height dialog box.

Entering a Row Height:

1. Select cell(s) in each row you want to adjust.
2. Choose Format Row Height.
3. Enter height.
4. Select OK.

TIP: To open the Row Height dialog box quickly, right-click on the row heading, or press Shift+space bar to select the entire row and press Shift+F10. Then choose Row Height from the shortcut menu that appears (shown below).

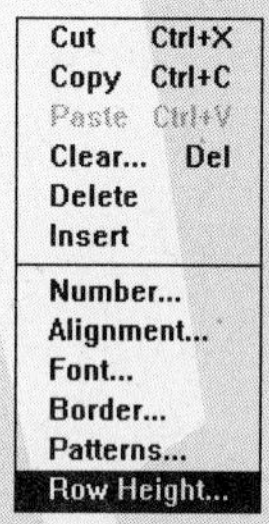

Method Two—Using the Mouse to Set the Row Height

Adjusting Row Heights with the Mouse:

1. Point to bottom edge of row heading.
2. Press and hold left mouse button.
3. Drag pointer to desired height.
4. Release mouse button.

You can bypass the Row Height dialog box entirely by using your mouse to drag a row to the height you want. Follow these steps to do this:

1. Move the mouse pointer to the row headings area and position the pointer at the bottom edge of the row you want to adjust. The mouse pointer changes to the shape shown in Figure 16.4.

2. Press and hold down the left mouse button. The formula bar displays the current row height and the row's bottom gridline turns into a dashed line (see Figure 16.4).

3. Drag the pointer up or down to the desired height. As you move the pointer, the formula bar displays the new height.

4. Release the mouse button. Excel adjusts the row height accordingly.

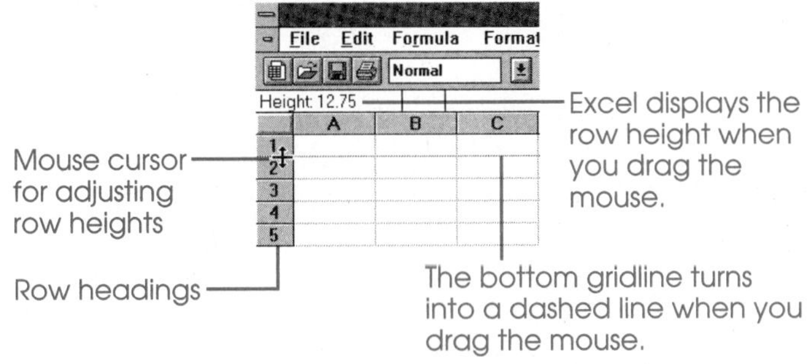
File Edit Formula Format
Normal
Height: 12.75
A
B
C
1
2
3
4
5
Excel displays the row height when you drag the mouse.
Mouse cursor for adjusting row heights
Row headings
The bottom gridline turns into a dashed line when you drag the mouse.

Figure 16.4 You can use a mouse to adjust the row height.

You can use this technique to set the height of several rows at once. For every row you want to adjust, select the entire row (see Skill Session 7 for instructions on selecting multiple rows), and then perform these steps on any one row. Excel will apply the new height to each row.

Method Three—Setting the Standard Height of a Row

If you have made several font changes and height adjustments to a long row of entries, you may need several tries to set an optimum row height. To avoid guesswork, you can have Excel set the height automatically to the best fit. This feature works slightly differently for rows than columns. With rows, Excel defines the *standard height* to be a height just large enough to accommodate the tallest font in the row. For a row where 10-point Helvetica is the tallest font, the standard height is 12.75 points. If a row contains one or more cells formatted to 18-point Helvetica, the row's standard height changes to 23.25 points. Follow these steps to set the optimum row height automatically:

1. Select at least one cell in each row you want to adjust.
2. Choose Format Row Height to display the Row Height dialog box.
3. Select Standard Height to turn on the Standard Height option.
4. Select OK or press Enter. Excel adjusts the rows to their optimal height and returns you to the worksheet.

Adjusting Row Heights Using Best Fit:

1. Select cell(s) in each row you want to adjust.
2. Choose Format Row Height.
3. Select Standard Height.
4. Select OK.

TIP: To set the standard height quickly, position the mouse pointer at the bottom edge of the row heading and double-click (see figure below).

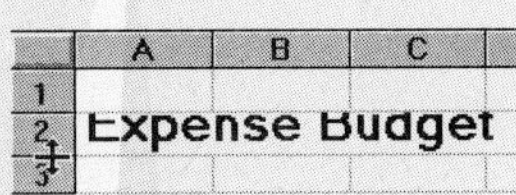

Hiding Columns and Rows

Your worksheets may contain sensitive information (e.g., payroll figures) or unimportant information (e.g., the period numbers used when calculating interest payments). In either case, you can hide the appropriate columns or rows when showing your worksheet to others. The data remain intact but are not displayed on the screen. The next two sections show you how to hide (and unhide) columns and rows.

Hiding and Unhiding Columns

When you hide a column, what you are really doing is setting the column width to 0. Hiding a column is just a special case of a column width adjustment, as the following steps demonstrate:

Hiding Columns:

1. Select cell(s) in each column you want to hide.
2. Choose Format Column Width.
3. Select Hide.
4. Select OK.

1. Select at least one cell in every column you want to hide.

2. Choose Format Column Width or use the shortcut menu to display the Column Width dialog box.

3. Enter `0` in the Column Width text box or select Hide. If you select the Hide button, Excel returns you to the worksheet with the columns hidden.

4. Select OK or press Enter. Excel returns you to the worksheet with the columns hidden.

TIP: A quick way to hide columns from the keyboard is to select a cell from each column and press Ctrl+0 (zero).

When you hide a column, the column letter no longer appears in the heading. For example, Figure 16.5 shows a worksheet with confidential payroll information in columns C, D, and E. Figure 16.6 shows the same worksheet with these columns hidden and their letters missing from the column heading. Despite this, you can still refer to cells in the hidden columns in formulas and searches.

TIP: To hide a column with a mouse, position the pointer on the right edge of the column heading, click the left button, and drag the pointer to the left, past the left edge of the column heading.

Microsoft Excel

File Edit Formula Format Data Options Macro Window Help

Normal

A19

PAYROLL.XLS

	A	B	C	D	E	F
1						
2			Salary	Commission	Total	Region Totals
3		*Eastern Reps:*				
4		Lynn Kuta	$56,000	$15,000	$71,000	
5		Michael Bubna	$58,000	$14,000	$72,000	
6		Jan Switzer	$62,000	$18,000	$80,000	
7			$176,000	$47,000	$223,000	$223,000
8		*Western Reps:*				
9		Rick Brown	$58,000	$14,000	$72,000	
10		Sharon Severn	$56,000	$15,000	$71,000	
11		Norman Sigurdson	$58,000	$16,000	$74,000	
12			$172,000	$45,000	$217,000	$217,000
13		*Region Totals*	$348,000	$92,000	$440,000	$440,000
14						

Ready NUM

Figure 16.5 Columns C, D, and E contain confidential information.

To unhide a range of columns, follow these steps:

1. Select at least one cell from each column on either side of the hidden columns. For example, to unhide columns C, D, and E, select a cell in columns B and F.
2. Choose Format Column Width or use the shortcut menu to display the Column Width dialog box.
3. Select Unhide. Excel unhides the columns and returns you to the worksheet.

Unhiding Columns:

1. Select cell(s) from each column on either side of hidden columns.
2. Choose Format Column Width.
3. Select Unhide.

TIP: A quick way to unhide columns from the keyboard is to select a cell on each side of the hidden columns and press Ctrl+Shift+0 (zero).

TIP: You can use a mouse to unhide a single column or the rightmost column of a group of hidden columns. Position the pointer as shown in the figure below and drag the pointer to the right to unhide the column.

Unhiding One of Several Columns:

1. Choose Formula Goto.
2. Enter cell address in column you want to unhide.
3. Select OK.
4. Choose Format Column Width.
5. Select Unhide.

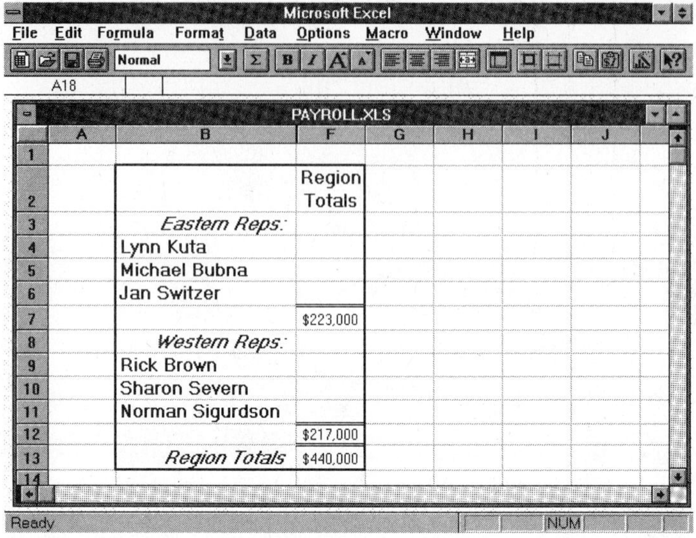

Figure 16.6 The same worksheet with columns C, D, and E hidden.

If you have just one column hidden, you can use these steps to unhide it. However, if you want to unhide a single column out of a *group* of hidden columns (e.g., column C out of columns C, D, and E), use the following steps:

1. Choose Formula Goto. Excel displays the Goto dialog box.
2. Enter a cell address in the column you want to unhide (e.g., if you are trying to unhide column C, enter **C1**).
3. Select OK or press Enter. Excel moves to the cell address.
4. Choose Format Column Width or use the shortcut menu to display the Column Width dialog box.
5. Select Unhide. Excel unhides the column and returns you to the worksheet.

Hiding and Unhiding Rows

Hiding rows is similar to hiding columns. Follow these steps:

1. Select at least one cell in every row you want to hide.
2. Choose Format Row Height or use the shortcut menu to display the Row Height dialog box. To display the Row Height command in the shortcut menu, the entire row must be selected.
3. Enter 0 in the Row Height text box or select Hide. If you select the Hide button, Excel returns you to the worksheet with the rows hidden.
4. Select OK or press Enter. Excel returns you to the worksheet with the rows hidden.

As with columns, when you hide a row, the row letter no longer appears in the heading, but you can still refer to cells in the hidden rows in formulas and searches.

To unhide a range of rows, follow these steps:

1. Select at least one cell from each row on either side of the hidden rows. For example, to unhide rows 3, 4, and 5, select a cell in rows 2 and 6.
2. Choose Format Row Height or use the shortcut menu to display the Row Height dialog box.
3. Select Unhide. Excel unhides the rows and returns you to the worksheet.

If you have just one row hidden, you can use these steps to unhide it. However, if you want to unhide a single row out of a *group* of hidden rows (e.g., row 3 out of rows 3, 4, and 5), use the following steps:

Hiding Rows:

1. Select cell(s) in every row you want to hide.
2. Choose Format Row Height.
3. Select Hide.
4. Select OK.

TIP: A quick way to hide rows from the keyboard is to select a cell from each row and press Ctrl+9.

TIP: To hide a row with a mouse, position the pointer on the bottom edge of the row heading and drag the pointer up *past* the top edge of the row heading.

Unhiding Rows:

1. Select cell(s) from each row on either side of hidden rows.
2. Choose Format Row Height.
3. Select Unhide.

TIP: A quick way to unhide rows from the keyboard is to select a cell from each row on either side of the hidden rows and press Ctrl+Shift+9.

Unhiding One of Several Rows:

1. Choose Formula Goto.
2. Enter cell address in row you want to unhide.
3. Select OK.
4. Choose Format Row Height.
5. Select Unhide.

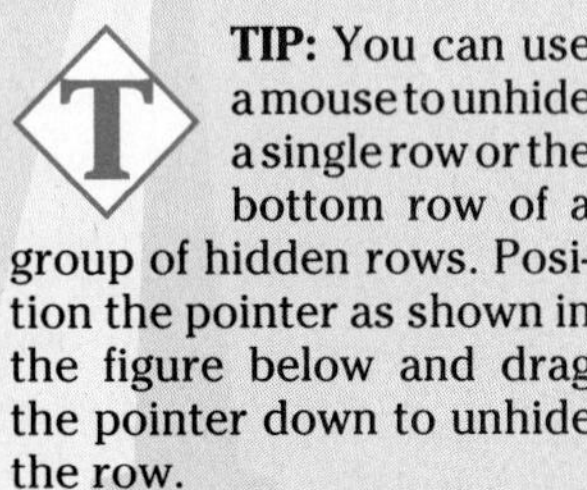

TIP: You can use a mouse to unhide a single row or the bottom row of a group of hidden rows. Position the pointer as shown in the figure below and drag the pointer down to unhide the row.

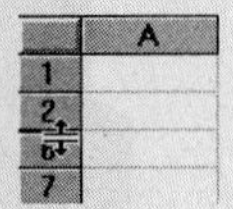

1. Choose Formula Goto. Excel displays the Goto dialog box.

2. Enter a cell address in the row you want to unhide (e.g., if you are trying to unhide row 3, enter **A3**).

3. Select OK or press Enter. Excel moves to the cell address.

4. Choose Format Row Height or use the shortcut menu to display the Row Height dialog box. To display the Row Height command in the shortcut menu, you must select the entire row.

5. Select Unhide. Excel unhides the row and returns you to the worksheet.

Hiding Gridlines and Headings

Excel allows you to hide both your worksheet gridlines and the row and column headings. This is useful if you are displaying your worksheet to others on-screen or on an overhead, or if you have set up a data entry application. Removing gridlines also helps your cell border and shading effects show up better.

Hiding Gridlines and Headings:

1. Choose Options Display.
2. Select Gridlines.
3. Select Row and Column Head.
4. Select OK.

To remove your worksheet gridlines and headings, follow these steps:

1. Choose Options Display. The Display Options dialog box appears.

2. To remove gridlines, select the Gridlines check box to remove the check mark.

3. To remove the headings, select the Row and Column Head check box to remove the check mark.

4. Select OK or press Enter. Excel returns you to the worksheet with your chosen display options in effect.

To restore gridlines or row and column headings, repeat these steps. When you reselect either the Gridlines or Row and Column Headings check box, the check mark reappears indicating that the option has been reactivated.

Skill Session

17

Using Color in Worksheets

The previous skill sessions in this Workshop have shown you how to turn a plain, unformatted worksheet into an attractive, professional-quality report. The final touch involves adding just the right amount of color to your presentation. With colors, you can emphasize important results, shape the layout of your page, and add subtle psychological effects.

If you do not have access to a color printer, you can still use color in your worksheets for on-screen presentation, or to convert worksheets and charts to overheads or slides using an offsite graphics service.

Excel 4 for Windows has extensive color capabilities. This skill session shows you how to add color to your cell contents, borders, and backgrounds using Excel's basic 16-color palette.

Excel's Color Palette

When applying colors to your worksheet elements, Excel allows you to choose from a palette of 16 colors. Figure 17.1 shows the default palette. Later in this skill session, you will learn how to customize this palette with your own colors.

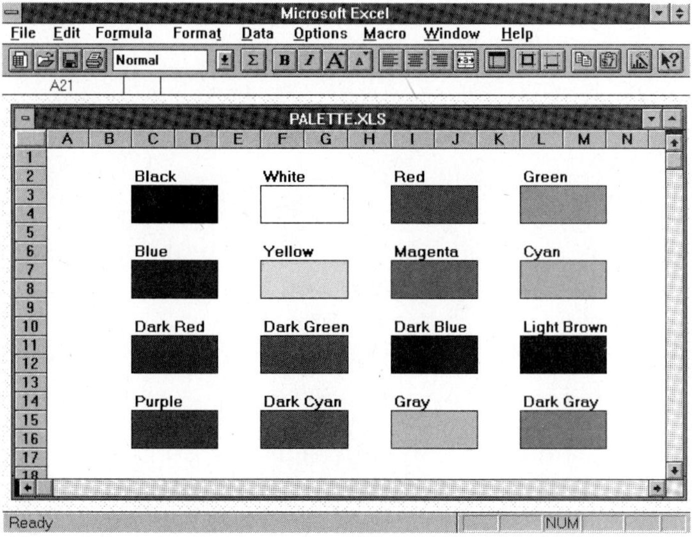

Figure 17.1 Excel's default 16-color palette.

Assigning Colors to Cell Contents

You can use any of the palette colors to format individual cell entries. Colors make worksheet titles and headings stand out or emphasize interesting results.

You can use two methods to change the color of cell contents:

- ▲ Using the Font dialog box. The Color drop-down list box contains the 16 palette colors.
- ▲ Using color symbols in custom numeric and date formats.

To apply a color to a cell using the Font dialog box, follow these steps:

1. Select the cell or range of cells you want to format.
2. Choose Format Font to display the Font dialog box.
3. Select Color to drop down the list box of colors.
4. Select a color from the list. The font in the Sample box changes color to match your selection.
5. Select OK or press Enter. Excel returns you to the worksheet with the color applied.

Assigning Colors to Cell Contents:

1. Select cell/range to format.
2. Choose Format Font.
3. Select Color.
4. Select a color from list.
5. Select OK.

You can gain even more control over the coloring of cell entries by using numeric formats. Recall the following currency formats from Skill Session 13:

```
$#,##0_);[RED]($#,##0)
$#,##0.00_);[RED]($#,##0.00)
```

In each example, the second part of the format applies the color red to any negative amount. By creating your own custom formats, you can apply a color to any number or range of numbers. Table 17.1 lists the 16 color symbols you can use in your custom numeric color formats.

Table 17.1 The color symbols to use in numeric formats

Symbol	*Color*	*Symbol*	*Color*
[BLACK]	Black	[COLOR 9]	Dark Red
[WHITE]	White	[COLOR 10]	Dark Green
[RED]	Red	[COLOR 11]	Dark Blue
[GREEN]	Green	[COLOR 12]	Light Brown
[BLUE]	Blue	[COLOR 13]	Purple
[YELLOW]	Yellow	[COLOR 14]	Dark Cyan
[MAGENTA]	Magenta	[COLOR 15]	Gray
[CYAN]	Cyan	[COLOR 16]	Dark Gray

The following format displays positive numbers in blue, negative numbers in red, zero values in green, and text in magenta:

```
[BLUE]0.00;[RED]-0.00;[GREEN]0;[MAGENTA]
```

You can add condition values to your formats to handle just about any situation.

IN ACTION: If you have an accounts receivable worksheet that contains a column showing the number of days that invoices are past due, use the format `[>90] [MAGENTA]###;###` to display numbers over 90 in magenta.

Assigning Colors to Borders and Patterns

In Skill Session 15, you learned that using cell borders and shading can make your worksheets appear more organized and dynamic. You can extend these advantages by applying colors to your borders and cell patterns.

To set the border color, follow these steps:

1. Select the cell or range of cells you want to format.
2. Choose Format Border to display the Border dialog box.
3. Select Color and click the down arrow or use the up and down arrows to drop down a list box of colors.
4. Select a color from the list. The font in the Sample box changes color to match your selection.
5. Select (or reselect) the border location and style.
6. Select OK or press Enter. Excel returns you to the worksheet with the color applied.

Assigning Border Colors:

1. Select cell/range to format.
2. Choose Format Border.
3. Select Color.
4. Select a color.
5. Select border location and style.
6. Select OK.

With patterns, you can fill your worksheet cells with any of the palette colors (this does not affect the color of your cell entries). To get a pattern color, you need to specify both a foreground and a background color. The foreground color is the color of the pattern itself. The background color is the color the pattern is displayed upon.

By mixing the pattern and its foreground and background colors, you can create different shades of any palette color. Figure 17.2 shows an example of this.

Here, in each of the Result columns, the foreground color used is Dark Cyan. In the first six columns, the background color is black and the pattern varies from Pattern 1 (solid) in the middle through to the widely spaced dots of Pattern 6 on the left. As you can see, the original color becomes progressively darker. In the last five columns, the background color is switched to white. In this case, as you move through the dot patterns, the original color becomes lighter. With this simple trick, you get an additional ten colors for every palette color.

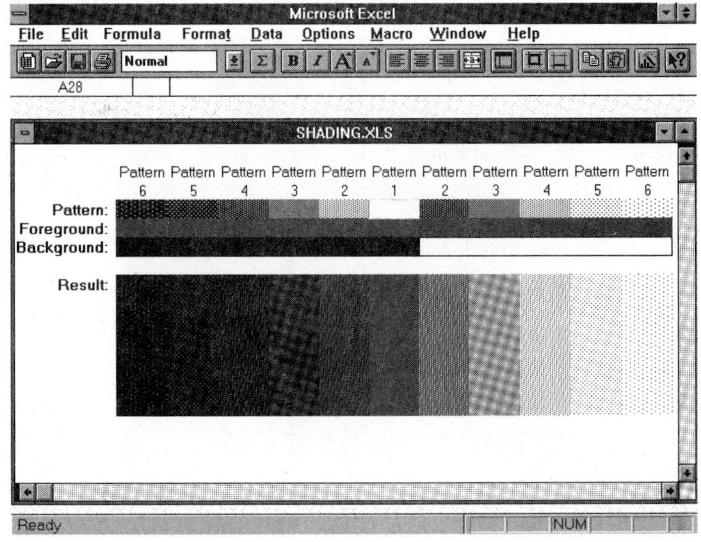

Figure 17.2 Use the dot patterns with dark or light background colors to produce shades of the foreground color.

Assigning Pattern Colors:

1. Select cell/range to color.
2. Choose Format Patterns.

Here are the steps to follow to set the pattern color:

1. Select the cell or range of cells you want to color.
2. Choose Format Patterns to display the Patterns dialog box.

3. Select a pattern from the Pattern list box. Your choice appears in the Sample box.

4. Select a color from the Foreground list box. The color is applied to the Sample pattern.

5. Select a color from the Background list box. The color is applied to the Sample pattern.

6. Select OK or press Enter. Excel returns you to the worksheet with the pattern applied.

3. Select pattern.
4. Select foreground color.
5. Select background color.
6. Select OK.

Use this tool on the Drawing toolbar to apply a foreground color to a cell or range. Repeatedly click on the tool to cycle through the palette colors. Hold down the Shift key while clicking to cycle through the palette backward.

Creating 3-D Effects

You can use contrasting border and pattern colors to achieve impressive 3-D effects in your worksheets. Begin by coloring each cell in the worksheet with a neutral (not too dark, not too light) color such as gray. (Depending on which color you use, you may have to bold most of your cell contents to make them show up properly). With 3-D effects, you can format an area to look as though it is raised up from the worksheet or depressed into the worksheet. To create a raised effect, follow these steps:

1. Select the top row of cells in the range and apply a white border.

2. Select the left column of cells in the range and apply a white border.

3. Select the bottom row of cells in the range and apply a black border.

4. Select the right column of cells in the range and apply a black border.

To create a depression effect, follow these steps:

1. Select the top row of cells in the range and apply a black border.

2. Select the left column of cells in the range and apply a black border.

3. Select the bottom row of cells in the range and apply a white border.

4. Select the right column of cells in the range and apply a white border.

Figure 17.3 shows a worksheet formatted with 3-D effects.

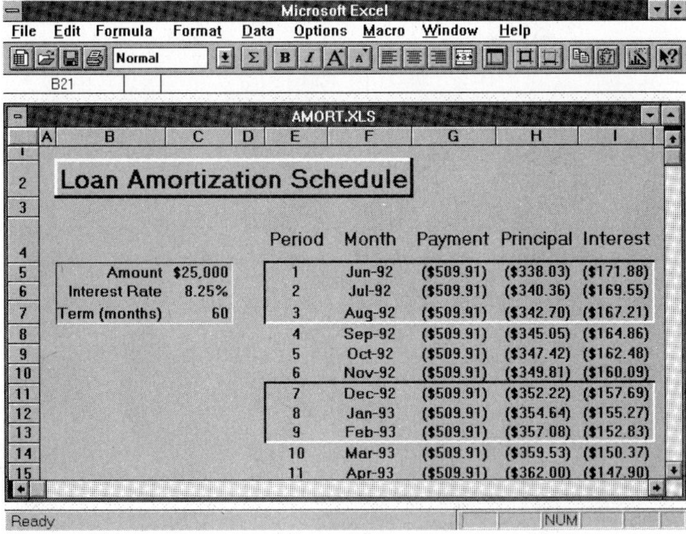

Figure 17.3 You can use borders and shading to create 3-D effects.

Assigning Colors to Gridlines and Headings

You can change the color of your worksheet gridlines and the numbers and text in the row and column headings. Here are the steps to follow to do this:

1. Choose Options Display. Excel displays the Display Options dialog box.
2. Select Gridline and Headings Color.
3. Select one of the 16 palette colors from the list box.
4. Select OK or press Enter. Excel returns you to the worksheet with the new color applied.

Assigning Gridline and Heading Colors:

1. Choose Options Display.
2. Select Gridline and Headings Color.
3. Select a color.
4. Select OK.

Customizing the Color Palette

As you have seen in this skill session, you use the Excel color palette throughout the program. The 16 default colors are usually fine for most applications, and you may never have any need for another color. However, if a particular shade would be just right for your presentation, Excel allows you to customize the color palette.

IN ACTION: If you use your corporate colors in presentations, create a custom palette containing several hues and shades of your company's colors.

You customize your own colors using the Color Picker dialog box (see Figure 17.4). You can use either of two methods to select a color. The first method comes from the fact that you can create any color in the spectrum by mixing the three primary colors, red, green, and blue. The Color Picker dialog allows you to enter specific numbers between 0 and 255 for each of these colors. A lower number means the color is less intense and a higher number means the color is more intense.

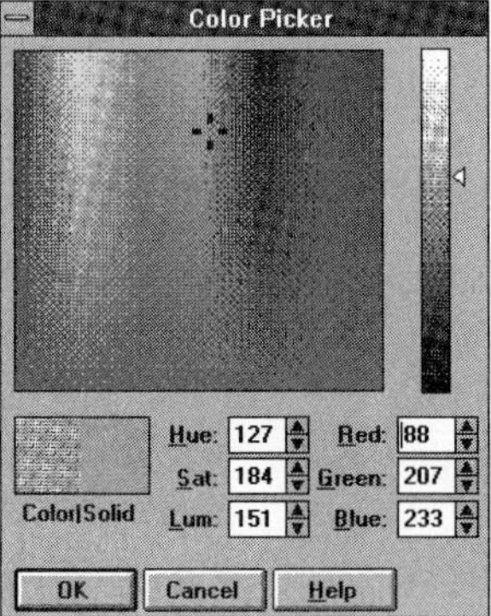

Figure 17.4 The Color Picker dialog box.

To give you some idea of how this works, Table 17.2 lists the first eight colors of the default palette and their respective red, green, and blue numbers.

NOTE: Whenever the three numbers are equal, you get a gray-scale number. Lower numbers are darker grays, higher numbers are lighter grays.

Table 17.2 The red, green, and blue numbers for eight default palette colors

Color	*Red*	*Green*	*Blue*
Black	0	0	0
White	255	255	255
Red	255	0	0
Green	0	255	0
Blue	0	0	255
Yellow	255	255	0
Magenta	255	0	255
Cyan	0	255	255

The second method for selecting colors involves setting three different attributes: hue, saturation, and luminance.

Hue. This number (which is more or less equivalent to the term *color*) measures the position on the color spectrum. Lower numbers indicate a position near the red end and higher numbers move through the yellow, green, blue, and violet parts of the spectrum. As you increase the hue, the color pointer moves from left to right.

Saturation. This number is a measure of the purity of a given hue. A saturation setting of 240 means that the hue is a pure color. Lower numbers indicate that more gray is mixed with the hue until, at 0, the color becomes part of the gray-scale. As you increase the saturation, the color pointer moves toward the top of the color palette.

Luminance. This number is a measure of the brightness of a color. Lower numbers are darker and higher numbers are brighter. The luminance bar to the right of the color palette shows the luminance scale for the selected color. As you increase the luminance, the slider moves toward the top of the bar.

Follow these steps to create a custom palette:

1. Choose Options Color Palette. Excel displays the Color Palette dialog box.
2. Select a color from the Color Palette. To reset the palette to the default colors, select Default.
3. Select Edit. The Color Picker dialog box appears with the selected color's numbers displayed.
4. To select a new color, use the arrows or manually enter new values in the text boxes. You can also use the mouse to move the color pointer in the color box and move the slider up or down the brightness bar.
5. (Optional) The Color¦Solid box shows the selected color on the left and the nearest solid color on the right. If you want to use the solid color, double-click on it.
6. Select OK or press Enter. Excel returns you to the Color Palette dialog.
7. Repeat steps 2–6 to customize other colors in the palette.
8. When you finish, press Enter or select OK in the Color Palette dialog box. Excel returns you to the worksheet with the new palette in effect.

Customizing the Color Palette:

1. Choose Options Color Palette.
2. Select a color.
3. Select Edit.
4. Select a new color.
5. Double-click on a solid color to select it. (Optional)
6. Select OK.
7. Repeat steps 2–6 to customize other colors.
8. Select OK.

TIP: In step 4, you can select a custom color quickly by clicking on a color in the Color Picker dialog's color palette. To set the luminance, click the appropriate area in the luminance bar or drag the slider.

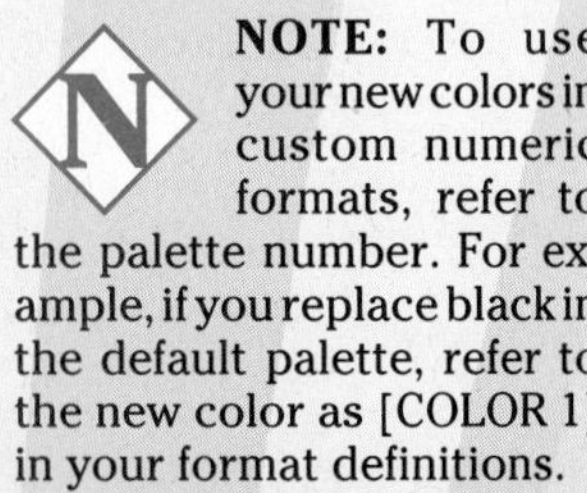

NOTE: To use your new colors in custom numeric formats, refer to the palette number. For example, if you replace black in the default palette, refer to the new color as [COLOR 1] in your format definitions.

Copying Custom Color Palettes

You can copy custom color palettes created in other worksheets by following these steps:

1. Use File Open to open the worksheet that contains the custom color palette.
2. Switch to the worksheet to which you want to copy the custom palette.
3. Choose Options Color Palette to display the Color Palette dialog box.
4. Select Copy Colors From. Excel displays a list of the open files.
5. Select the file that contains the custom colors you want to copy.
6. Select OK or press Enter. Excel copies the color palette into the current worksheet.

IN ACTION: Save color schemes that you use frequently (such as your company's colors or the colors of major clients) in their own files. You can then copy the colors into your current worksheet whenever you need them.

Copying Custom Color Palettes:

1. Open worksheet that contains custom color palette.
2. Switch to worksheet to which you want to copy the custom palette.
3. Choose Options Color Palette.
4. Select Copy Colors From.
5. Select file that contains custom colors to copy.
6. Select OK.

Using Excel's Custom Color Palettes

Loading a Custom Color Palette:

1. Choose File Open.
2. Open PALETTES.XLA in \LIBRARY\COLOR directory.
3. Choose Options Custom Palettes.
4. Select palette.
5. To preview palette, select Apply.
6. Select OK.

CAUTION: If you cannot find the file PALETTES.XLA, you will need to run the Excel setup program again to install it.

Excel 4 for Windows comes with a number of preset custom palettes that you can use in your worksheets. To load the palettes, follow these steps:

1. Choose File Open. Excel displays the Open dialog box.
2. Open the file PALETTES.XLA in the \LIBRARY \COLOR directory (this is a subdirectory of your main Excel directory).
3. Choose Options Custom Palettes. Excel displays the Custom Color Palettes dialog box, as shown in Figure 17.5.
4. Select a palette from the **P**alettes list box.
5. To preview the palette, select Apply.
6. Select OK or press Enter. Excel returns you to the worksheet with the new palette in effect.

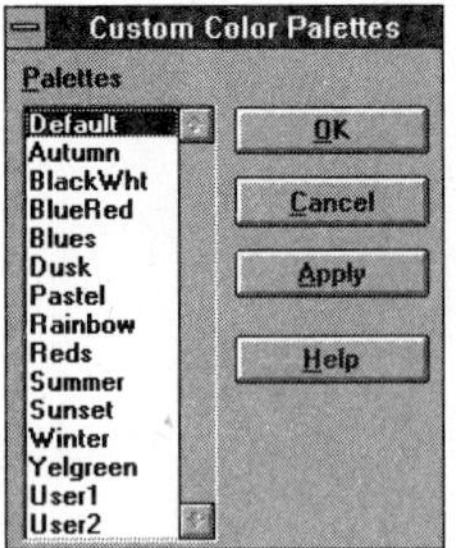

Figure 17.5 The Custom Color Palettes dialog box.

The files shown in the **P**alettes list box are worksheets that have customized color palettes. To return your worksheet to the default palette, select the DEFAULT.XLS file. If you want to modify one of these file palettes, select **File Open** to open the file, use **Window Unhide** to unhide the file, and then edit the palette. The two files USER1.XLS and USER2.XLS originally contain the default palette. You can edit these palettes to your own taste and recall them from the Custom Color Palettes dialog box at any time.

Using Color Effectively

You now know how to apply colors to your Excel worksheets, but that is only half the battle. Colors that are poorly matched or improperly applied can make a presentation look worse, not better. This section examines a few basics for using colors effectively in your worksheets.

With so many colors available, the temptation is to go overboard and use a dozen different hues on each page. However, using too many colors can confuse your audience and even cause eye fatigue. Try to stick to, at most, three or four colors. If you must use more, try to use different shades of three or four hues.

Before finalizing your color scheme, you need to make sure that the colors you have selected work well together. For example, blue and black are often difficult to distinguish and green/red combinations clash. Other color combinations to avoid are red/blue, green/blue, and brown/black. On the other hand, color combinations such as red/yellow, gray/red, and blue/yellow go well together, as do contrasting shades of the same color, such as black and gray.

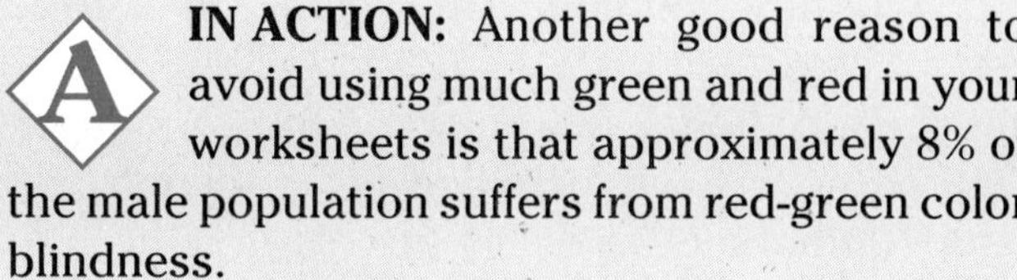

IN ACTION: Another good reason to avoid using much green and red in your worksheets is that approximately 8% of the male population suffers from red-green color blindness.

When selecting colors, think about the psychological impact that your scheme will have on your audience. Studies have shown that "cool" colors such as blue and gray, evoke a sense of dependability and trust. Use these colors for business meetings. For presentations that require a little more excitement, "warm" colors such as red, yellow, and orange can evoke a festive, fun atmosphere. For a safe, comfortable ambience, try using brown and yellow. For an environmental touch, use green and brown.

After you have settled on a color scheme, use it consistently throughout your presentation. Charts, clip art, and slides should all use the same colors.

Skill Session

18

Working with Cell Formats

Excel 4 for Windows contains powerful formatting features that can make your worksheets look their best. The problem is that you can end up spending more time working on the appearance of a spreadsheet than on the actual data. To remedy this, Excel offers a number of features that make your report formatting faster and more efficient.

This skill session shows you how to display cell format information, copy and move existing formats, define format styles, and use Excel's handy new AutoFormat feature.

> **TIP:** Worksheet templates and startup sheets give you easy access to your formats. See Skill Session 45 in the File Management Workshop for information about working with Excel templates.

Displaying Cell Format Information

With so many formatting options available, it is easy to lose track of which cells are formatted with which options. To help, Excel provides an Info window that can show you the attributes of any cell. To use the Info window to learn about a cell's formatting, follow these steps:

Displaying Cell Formatting in the Info Window:

1. Select the cell to learn about.
2. Choose Options Workspace.
3. Select Info Window.
4. Select OK.
5. Choose Info Format.
6. Choose Close from window Control menu.

TIP: To display the Info window quickly, select the cell you want and press Ctrl+F2.

NOTE: For more information on the Info window, see Skill Session 43 in the File Management Workshop.

1. Select the cell you want to learn about.

2. Choose Options Workspace. Excel displays the Workspace dialog box.

3. Select Info Window.

4. Select OK or press Enter. Excel displays the Info window.

5. Choose Info Format. Excel displays the cell format information in the Info window.

6. Choose Close from the window Control menu or press Ctrl+F4. Excel returns you to the worksheet.

Figure 18.1 shows an Info window displaying the formatting options of cell C12 from the PAYROLL worksheet.

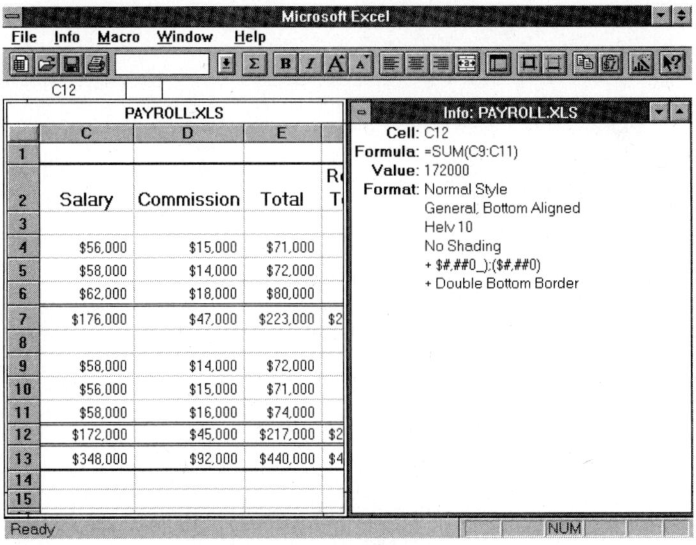

	C	D	E	
1				
2	Salary	Commission	Total	R T
3				
4	$56,000	$15,000	$71,000	
5	$58,000	$14,000	$72,000	
6	$62,000	$18,000	$80,000	
7	$176,000	$47,000	$223,000	$2
8				
9	$58,000	$14,000	$72,000	
10	$56,000	$15,000	$71,000	
11	$58,000	$16,000	$74,000	
12	$172,000	$45,000	$217,000	$2
13	$348,000	$92,000	$440,000	$4
14				
15				

Figure 18.1 The Info window displaying cell formatting.

Copying, Moving, and Deleting Cell Formats

Once you have formatted a cell the way you want it, you can use the same formatting in other parts of your worksheet by copying or moving the entire cell. When you move a cell, Excel pastes both the cell contents and the cell format to the new location.

Suppose you want to copy only the format and apply it to an existing cell. When you copy a cell, Excel gives you the option of copying the cell format only. To copy a cell format, follow these steps:

Copying Cell Formats:

1. Select cell/range to copy.
2. Choose Edit Copy.
3. Select paste location for range.
4. Choose Edit Paste Special.
5. Select Formats.
6. Select OK.

1. Select the cell or range you want to copy.
2. Choose Edit Copy. Excel surrounds the range with a moving border.
3. Select the paste location for the range.
4. Choose Edit Paste Special. Excel displays the Paste Special dialog box, as shown in Figure 18.2.
5. In the Paste section, select Formats.
6. Select OK or press Enter. Excel copies only the formats from the original cells.

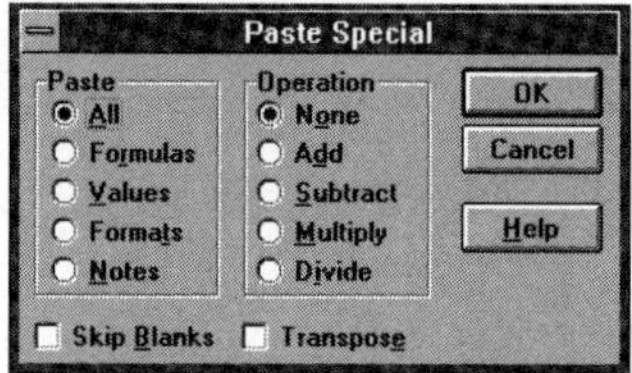

Figure 18.2 The Paste Special dialog box.

Use this tool in the Standard toolbar to paste cell formats.

IN ACTION: Create a worksheet called FORMATS.XLS, and enter samples of often-used formats. Save the file in Excel's XLSTART directory to open the worksheet each time you start Excel. You can use this file to copy your formats quickly to your current worksheet.

Deleting Cell Formats

When deleting a cell, Excel gives you the option of clearing only the cell format and leaving the cell contents intact. Here are the steps to follow to delete a cell format:

1. Select the cell or range with the formats you want to delete.
2. Choose Edit Clear or press Delete. Excel displays the Clear dialog box.
3. Select Formats.
4. Select OK or press Enter. Excel clears the cell formats.

Deleting Cell Formats:

1. Select cell/range with formats to delete.
2. Choose Edit Clear or press Delete.
3. Select Formats.
4. Select OK.

Working with Styles

Depending on the options you choose, formatting a single cell or range can take dozens of mouse clicks and keystrokes. If you plan to use a specific formatting combination repeatedly, don't reinvent the wheel each time. Using Excel's Style feature, you can summarize any combination of formatting options under a single style name.

Styles also save you time if you need to reformat your document. Normally, you would have to select every cell containing the format you want to change (including blank cells) and then make the adjustment. With styles, you just redefine the style, and all the associated cells will be updated automatically.

A style can contain many of the formatting features you have learned about in this Workshop, including fonts, alignment, borders, patterns, and number, date, and time formats. Excel comes with several built-in styles: Comma, Comma [0], Currency, Currency [0], Percent, and Normal. Normal is the default style for the entire worksheet.

Applying a Style

There are two methods you can use to apply a style to your worksheets:

▲ Select the style from the Style dialog box

▲ Select the style from the Style list box in the Standard toolbar

Here are the steps to follow to apply a style using the Style dialog box:

Applying a Style with the Style Dialog Box:

1. Select cell/range to format.
2. Choose Format Style.
3. Select desired style.
4. Select OK.

1. Select the cell or range that you want to format.

2. Choose Format Style. Excel displays the Style dialog box, as shown in Figure 18.3.

3. Select the style you want from the **S**tyle Name list box. A description of the formatting options included in the selected style appears in the Description information box.

4. Select OK or press Enter. Excel applies the style to the selected cells.

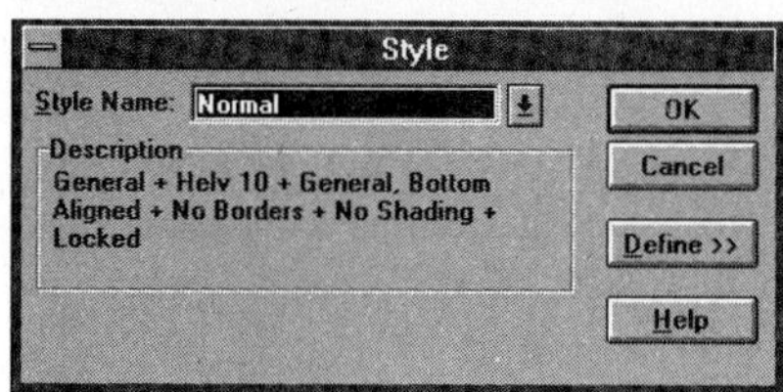

Figure 18.3 The Style dialog box.

To apply a style using the Standard toolbar, follow these steps:

1. Select the cell or range you want to format.
2. Click on the down arrow in the Standard toolbar (see Figure 18.4) to display the style list in the Style box.
3. Click on the style you want, or use the arrow keys to highlight the style and then press Enter. Excel applies the style to the selected cells.

Applying a Style with the Standard Toolbar:

1. Select cell/range to format.
2. Select Style box in Standard toolbar.
3. Click on desired style.

TIP: To access the Style box from the keyboard, press Ctrl+S.

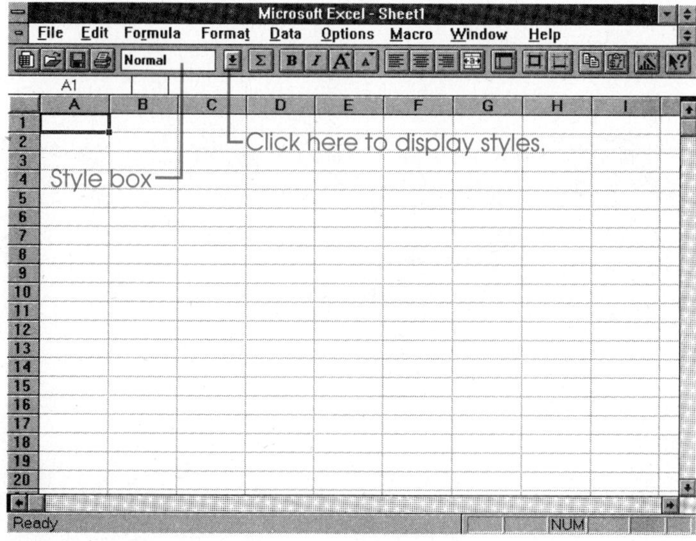

Figure 18.4 The Style box.

When you apply a style to a cell, Excel overwrites the cell's existing format. Similarly, if you apply a style first and then format the cell, the new formatting overwrites the style. In both cases, however, only defined attributes are changed. For example, if you apply the Percent style to a cell already formatted as left-aligned, the alignment does not change.

Creating a Style

Besides using the built-in styles supplied by Excel, you can define your own styles to suit your needs. Any style you create appears in the Style list for that worksheet. Excel provides three ways to define styles:

- By example
- By definition
- By merging styles from another document

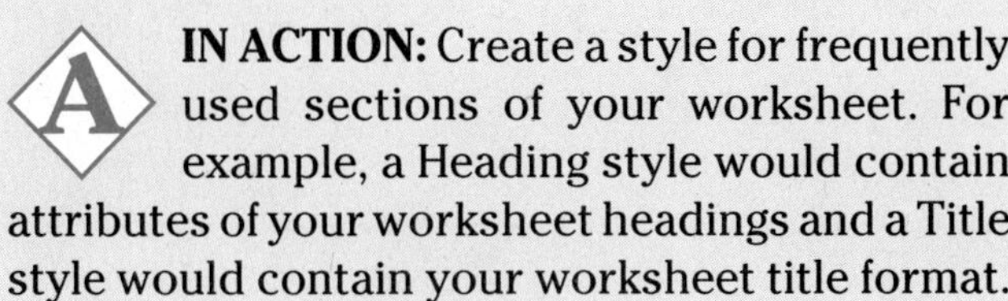

IN ACTION: Create a style for frequently used sections of your worksheet. For example, a Heading style would contain attributes of your worksheet headings and a Title style would contain your worksheet title format.

Creating a Style by Example

If you have a cell that contains a format combination that you want to use as a style, you can tell Excel to define a new style based on the cell format. This is called the *style by example* method. Here are the steps to follow for this method:

1. Select the cell that contains the format combination you want to turn into a style.
2. Choose Format Style. Excel displays the Style dialog box.
3. Type the new style name in the **S**tyle Name text box.
4. Select OK or press Enter. Excel adds the style name to the style list.

Creating a Style by Example:

1. Select cell that contains format example.
2. Choose Format Style.
3. Type new style name.
4. Select OK.

TIP: To create a style by example using the toolbar, select the example cell, type the new name in the Style box, and press Enter.

You can select multiple cells to use as an example. In this case, Excel assigns only those formats that the cells have in common. For example, suppose you have a cell that is left-aligned with a border and another that is left-aligned without a border. If you select both cells to use as your example, Excel will only define the new style as left-aligned.

Creating a Style by Definition

The second method for creating a style involves setting the specific format options using the Style dialog box. This is called the *style by definition* method. Follow these steps to create a style by definition:

Creating a Style by Definition:

1. Choose Format Style.
2. Enter new style name.
3. Select Define.
4. Check box for each attribute to include.
5. Select button for attribute to change.
6. Select desired formatting options and then select OK.
7. Repeat steps 5–6 to set other formatting options.
8. Select OK.

1. Choose Format Style to display the Style dialog box.
2. Enter the new style name in the **S**tyle Name text box.
3. Select Define. Excel expands the dialog box, as shown in Figure 18.5.
4. In the Style Includes section, activate the check box for each attribute you want to include in the style. If there are attributes you do not want included in the style, turn off the appropriate check boxes.
5. In the Change section, select a button for an attribute you want to change. Excel displays the appropriate dialog box for the attribute.
6. Select the formatting options you want to use in the new style and then select OK or press Enter to return to the Style dialog.
7. Repeat steps 5–6 to set the other formatting options you want to include in the style.
8. To accept the new style and define more, select Add and repeat steps 2–7. To apply the new style to the selected cells, select OK or press Enter. This also saves the new style. To accept the new style and not apply it to the selected cells, select Add to define the style, and then select Close.

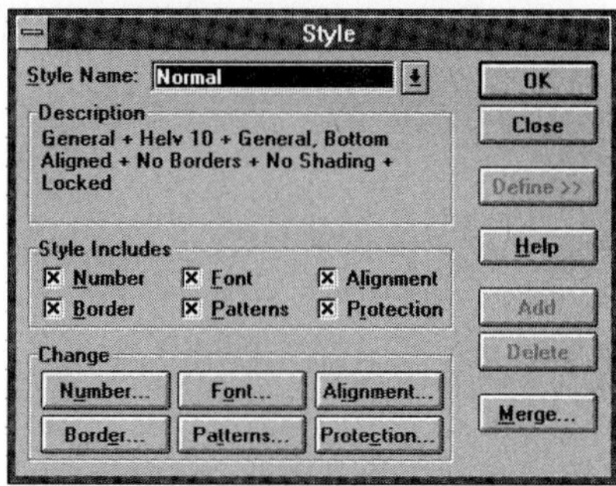

Figure 18.5 The expanded Style dialog box.

Merging Styles from Another Document

The third method for creating styles involves copying the existing styles from another document into your worksheet. This is called *merging* styles. This method is useful if you have other worksheets where you have already defined several styles. Instead of defining them again in the current worksheet, you simply copy them. Before proceeding, you need to have the document containing the styles open in the workspace, and the worksheet receiving the styles must be the active window. Follow these steps to merge styles:

1. Choose Format Style to display the Style dialog box.
2. Select Define to expand the dialog box.
3. Select Merge. The Merge Styles dialog box appears with a list of the files currently open in the workspace (see Figure 18.6).
4. Select the file with the styles you want to copy.

Merging Styles from Another Document:

1. Choose Format Style.
2. Select Define.
3. Select Merge.
4. Select file with styles to copy.
5. Select OK.
6. Choose style and select OK, or select Close.

CAUTION: If the receiving worksheet contains any styles with the same name as styles being merged, Excel displays a warning box. Select Yes to overwrite the existing styles or No to merge all styles except those with the same name.

5. Select OK or press Enter. Excel copies the styles from the file and returns you to the Style dialog box.

6. To apply one of the new styles, select it from the **S**tyle Name list box and then select OK or press Enter. Otherwise, select Close.

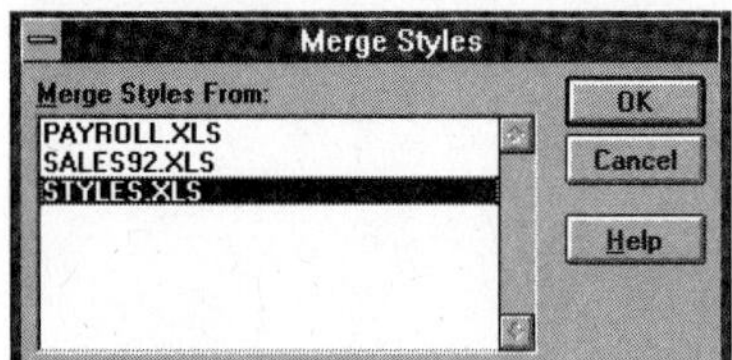

Figure 18.6 The Merge Styles dialog box.

IN ACTION: Create a new worksheet called STYLES.XLS and use it to store all your frequently used styles. To use the styles in the current worksheet, merge them from STYLES.XLS.

Redefining a Style

As you can see, styles can save you time when you have to apply many formats to a worksheet. Styles can also save you time by making it easier to reformat your documents. If you have used styles to format a worksheet, just redefine the style, and Excel will automatically update every cell containing the style to match the new style definition. You can also redefine any of Excel's built-in styles, including the Normal style, which is the default used for all cells in any new worksheet. You can redefine styles by

- Example
- Definition

Redefining a Style by Example

You can use the style by example method to redefine an existing style. Follow these steps:

1. Select a cell that contains the format you want to redefine.
2. Adjust the cell format so that it contains the new format you want.
3. Apply the style name again using the Toolbar or the Forma**t** **S**tyle command. Excel asks if you want to redefine the style (see Figure 18.7).
4. Select Yes to redefine the style. Excel redefines the style and updates any cells that contain the style.

Redefining a Style by Example:

1. Select cell that contains format to redefine.
2. Change cell format to new format.
3. Apply style name again.
4. Select Yes.

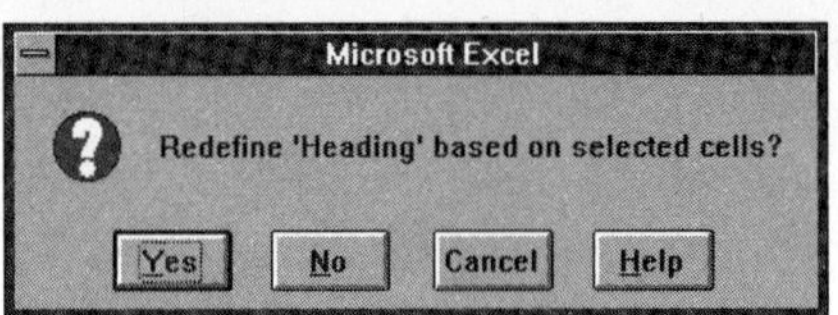

Figure 18.7 Excel asks if you want to redefine the style.

Redefining a Style by Definition

You can use the style by definition method to redefine an existing style. Here are the steps to follow:

Redefining a Style by Definition:

1. Choose Format Style.
2. Select Define.
3. Select style to redefine.
4. Adjust format attributes.
5. Select OK.

1. Choose Format Style to display the Style dialog box.
2. Select Define to expand the dialog box.
3. Select the style that you want to redefine from the Style Name list box. The style's current format attributes appear in the Description box.
4. Adjust the format attributes using the buttons located in the Change section of the dialog box.
5. To accept the new definition and keep the dialog box open, select Add. To accept the new definition without applying it, select Add and then Close. To apply the new definition, select OK or press Enter.

Deleting a Style

NOTE: You can't delete the Normal style.

To keep your style lists to a minimum, you should delete any styles you no longer use. When you delete a style, any associated cells revert to the Normal style.

(Any other formatting options you added on top of the style remain in effect.) Follow these steps to delete a style from a worksheet:

1. Choose Format Style to display the Style dialog box.
2. Select Define to expand the dialog box.
3. Select the style that you want to delete from the Style Name list box.
4. Select Delete. Excel deletes the style.
5. Repeat steps 3–4 to delete other styles.
6. Select OK or press Enter to return to the worksheet.

Deleting a Style:

1. Choose Format Style.
2. Select Define.
3. Select style to delete.
4. Select Delete.
5. Repeat steps 3–4 to delete other styles.
6. Select OK.

Using the AutoFormat Feature

Excel 4 for Windows offers a new feature that enables you to easily format any worksheet range. This feature, called *AutoFormat*, can automatically apply certain predefined format combinations to create attractive, professional-quality tables and lists.

There are 14 predefined AutoFormat tables. Each one uses selected format options to display numbers, fonts, borders, and patterns and to set cell alignment, column width, and row height. AutoFormat doesn't just apply a single format combination to each cell. Instead, it applies separate formatting for row and column headings, data, and summary lines (e.g., subtotals and totals). If you have your own formatting that

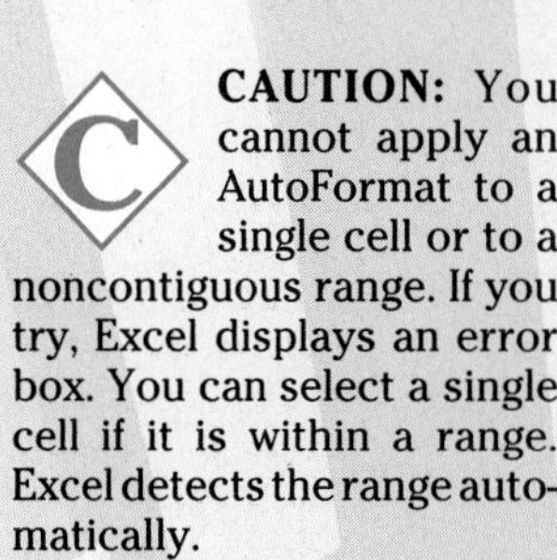

CAUTION: You cannot apply an AutoFormat to a single cell or to a noncontiguous range. If you try, Excel displays an error box. You can select a single cell if it is within a range. Excel detects the range automatically.

you want left intact, you can tell Excel to leave out the appropriate format options from the automatic format. For example, if you have already set up your font options, you can exclude the font formats from the AutoFormat table.

Here are the basic steps to follow to use the AutoFormat feature:

Using AutoFormat:

1. Select range to format.
2. Choose Format AutoFormat.
3. Select format combination from Table Format list box.
4. Select Options and uncheck format types to exclude.
5. Select OK.

1. Select the range you want to format.

2. Choose Format AutoFormat. Excel displays the AutoFormat dialog box, as shown in Figure 18.8.

3. Select a format combination from the Table Format list box. An example of each format appears in the Sample box.

4. To exclude formatting, select Options and, in the Formats to Apply section that appears, uncheck the format types you want to exclude. The displayed sample adjusts accordingly.

5. Select OK or press Enter. Excel applies the formatting to the range you selected.

Use this tool from either the Standard toolbar or the Formatting toolbar to apply the Classic 1 table format (or the most recently selected format) quickly.

When using the AutoFormat feature, keep the following points in mind:

▲ AutoFormat usually assumes that the top row and the left column in your range contain the range headings. To avoid improper formatting, be sure to include your headings when you select the range.

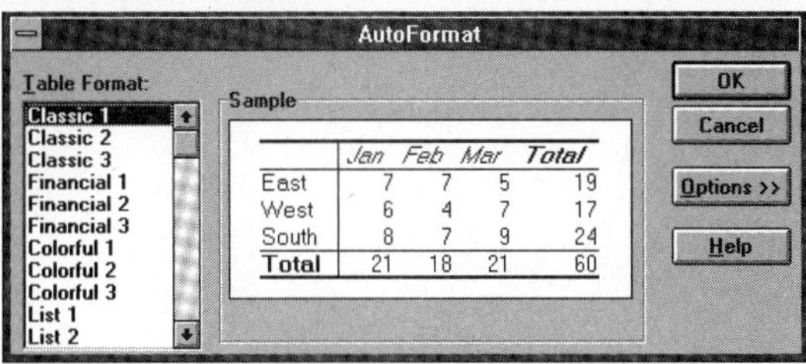

Figure 18.8 The AutoFormat dialog box.

- Each table format uses the typeface defined in the Normal font. To use a different typeface in all your AutoFormat tables, change the Normal font to the typeface you want.
- The Classic table formats are designed to be used in any worksheet to make your data more readable. Headings and totals are separated with borders or shading.
- The Financial table formats can be used in any worksheet that contains currency values. Initial data values and totals are formatted as currency.
- The Colorful table formats are suitable for on-screen or slide presentations or for reports produced on a color printer.
- The List table formats can be used with lists and databases. Shading and borders are used to make the data more readable.
- The 3D Effects table formats give your worksheets a professional-quality appearance suitable for any presentation.

Skill Session

19

Changing the Worksheet View

When you work with large and complex worksheets, only a small part of the total document fits into a single window. The result is that you spend much time scrolling through your worksheet and jumping back and forth between data areas. What you need is a way to view separate parts of a worksheet simultaneously.

This skill session shows you how to do just that. With Excel, you can view a single worksheet in multiple windows, split a single window into multiple panes, and even view the same worksheet with different formatting and display options.

Displaying Multiple Worksheet Windows

As a user of the Windows environment, you know what an advantage it is to have multiple applications running in their own windows. Most Windows applications take this concept a step farther by allowing you to open multiple documents in their own windows. But Excel goes one better by allowing you to open multiple windows for the *same* document.

When you open a second window on a worksheet, you are not opening a new file; instead, you are viewing the same file twice. You can navigate independently in each window, so you can display different parts of a worksheet at the same time. Excel even allows you to change the worksheet display for every window.

IN ACTION: You can change a value in one part of the worksheet and watch its effect in another part. This is invaluable for "what-if" analysis.

Opening a New Worksheet Window

To open another window for the current worksheet, choose Window New Window. When Excel opens the new window, it changes the names appearing in the worksheet title bar. Excel appends :1 to the title of the original window, it appends :2 to the title of the second window, and so on. Figure 19.1 shows an example using the SALES92.XLS worksheet. Notice that the original window now has the title SALES92.XLS:1 and the new window has the title SALES92.XLS:2.

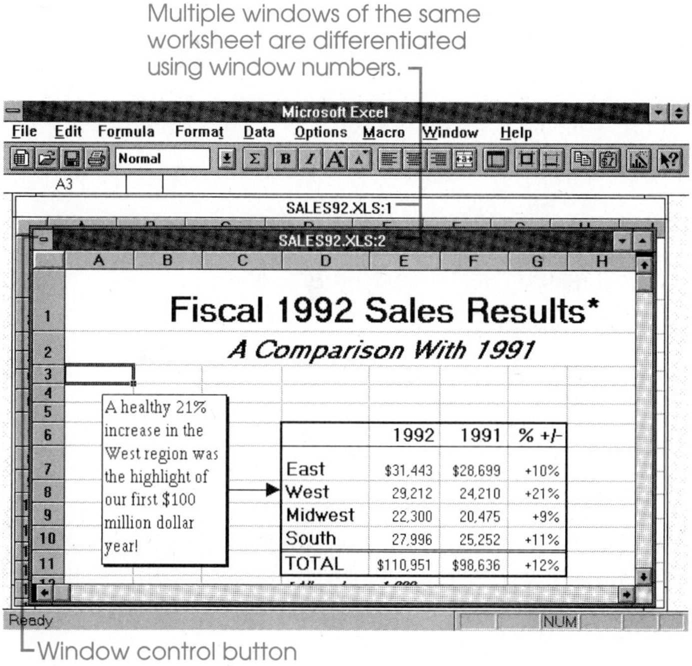

Multiple windows of the same worksheet are differentiated using window numbers.

Window control button

Figure 19.1 Two windows containing the same worksheet.

The number of windows you can open for a worksheet is limited only by your computer's memory. Any window you open can be moved and sized to suit your taste. Since each window is a view of the same worksheet, any editing or formatting changes you make in one window are automatically reflected in all the others.

IN ACTION: Use multiple windows to make data entry easier. Open one window for the data entry area and then use other windows to display a list of data codes (e.g., part numbers or general ledger accounts).

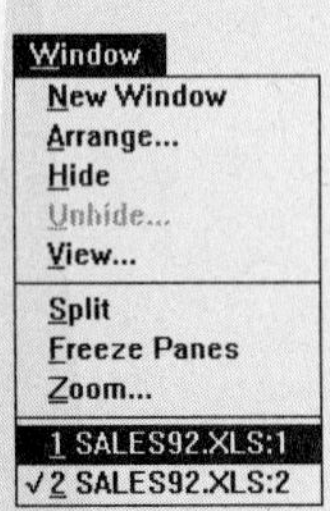

Use any of the following techniques to navigate among worksheet windows:

- Click on any visible part of a window to activate it.
- Pull down the **W**indow menu and select one of the windows listed at the bottom of the menu. Excel displays a check mark beside the currently active window.
- Press Ctrl+F6 to move to the next window. Press Ctrl+Shift+F6 to move to the previous window.
- Activate the window's Control menu by clicking on the window Control button (see Figure 19.1), or by pressing Alt+ - (hyphen). Select Next Window.

One of the most useful aspects of multiple worksheet windows is that you can set different display options (such as showing gridlines or row and column headings) in each window. For example, you could turn off gridlines in one window while trying out different formatting options in another. Here are the steps to follow to try this:

Setting Display Options for a Window:

1. Activate window to change.
2. Choose Options Display.
3. Select desired display options.
4. Select OK.

1. Activate the window in which you want to change the display.
2. Choose Options Display. The Display Options dialog box appears.

3. Select the display options you want for the window.

4. Select OK or press Enter. Excel returns you to the window with the new options in effect.

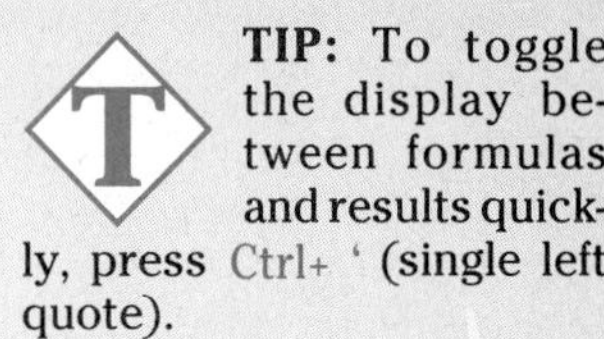

TIP: To toggle the display between formulas and results quickly, press Ctrl+ ‘ (single left quote).

> **IN ACTION:** To troubleshoot formula errors in complex worksheets, display formulas in one window and results in another. Figure 19.2 shows an example using the SALES92.XLS worksheet.

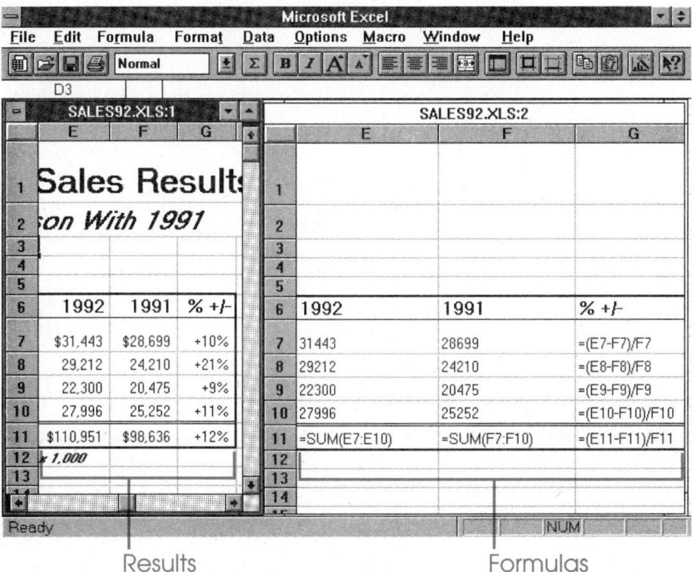

Figure 19.2 You can set different display options in each worksheet window.

Arranging Worksheet Windows

One of the problems with having several windows open at once is that they tend to get in each other's way. In most cases, it is preferable to give each window its own portion of the work area. Even though you can move and size windows yourself, you may prefer to have Excel handle this for you. You use the Arrange Windows dialog box, shown in Figure 19.3, to do this. The Arrange section contains the following options:

Tiled	Divides the work area into rectangles of approximately equal size (called *tiles*), and assigns each open window to a tile.
H**o**rizontal	Divides the work area into horizontal strips of equal size, and assigns each open window to a strip.
Vertical	Divides the work area into vertical strips of equal size, and assigns each open window to a strip.
None	Does not arrange windows. Use this option in conjunction with the synchronization options discussed later.

If you have other worksheets open at the same time and you only want to arrange the current worksheet windows, select Windows of **A**ctive Document from the Arrange Windows dialog box. This tells Excel to apply the selected Arrange option to the current worksheet windows only. When you select Windows of **A**ctive Document, Excel enables the following two options:

Sync Horizontal	Synchronizes the worksheet windows horizontally. If you scroll across a row in one window, the other windows also scroll.
Sync Vertical	Synchronizes the worksheet windows vertically. If you scroll up or down a column in one window, the other windows also scroll.

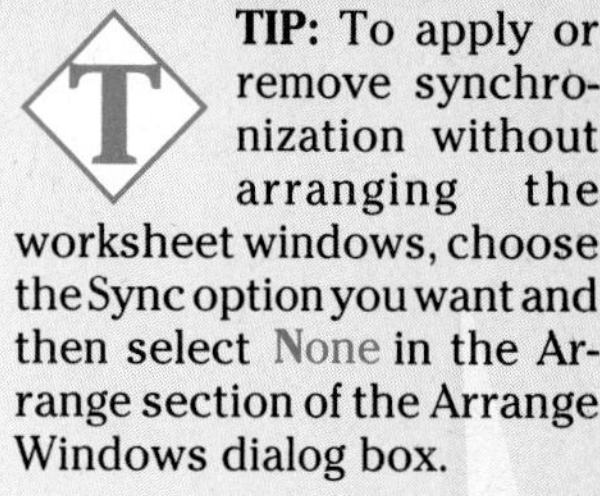

TIP: To apply or remove synchronization without arranging the worksheet windows, choose the Sync option you want and then select None in the Arrange section of the Arrange Windows dialog box.

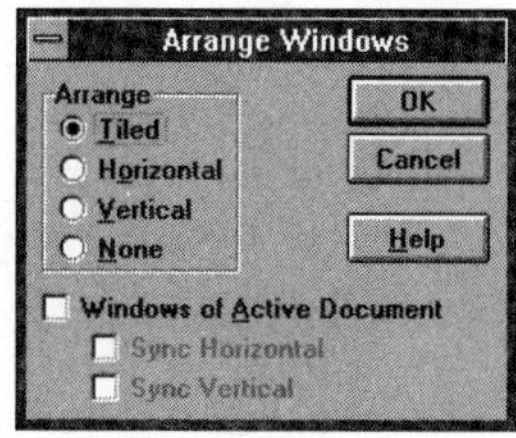

Figure 19.3 The Arrange Windows dialog box.

Figure 19.4 shows the SALES92.XLS windows arranged horizontally with both synchronization options selected. Excel indicates the synchronization by displaying `[HVSync]` in each window's title bar.

If you don't want to include a window in an arrangement, activate the window and choose Window Hide. Excel removes the window from the screen, but it remains open in memory. To view the window again, choose Window Unhide and select the window from the Unhide dialog box that appears.

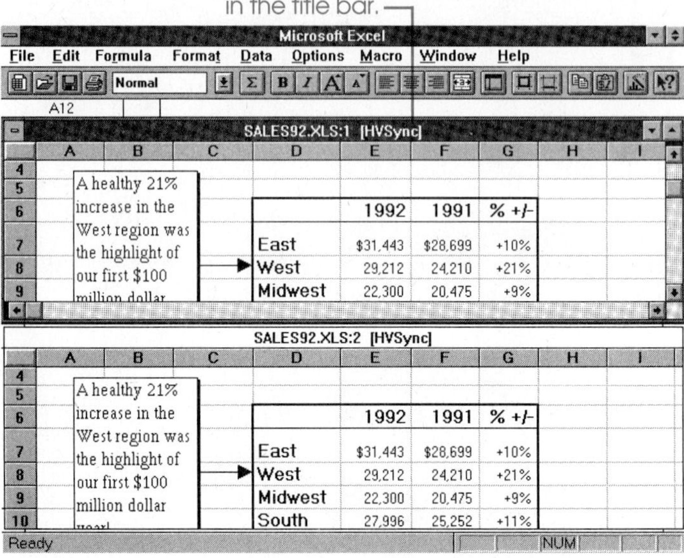

Figure 19.4 The SALES92.XLS windows arranged horizontally and synchronized.

Closing Worksheet Windows

If you find your work area getting cluttered with open windows, you can close a window by following these steps:

1. Select the window you want to close.
2. Activate the window Control menu by clicking on the Control box or by pressing Alt+ - (hyphen).
3. Select Close. Excel closes the window.

When you close a worksheet, Excel remembers the current window sizes and positions. The next time you open the worksheet, Excel arranges the windows in

Closing a Worksheet Window:

1. Select window to close.
2. Activate window Control menu.
3. Select Close.

NOTE: To close a window quickly, double-click on the Control button or press Ctrl+F4.

their previous positions. If you do not want Excel to save the window information, you need to close any unwanted windows.

Displaying Multiple Worksheet Panes

Another way to view different parts of a large worksheet simultaneously is to use Excel's Split feature. You can use Split to divide a worksheet into two or four *panes*, where each pane can display a different area of the document. The panes scroll together horizontally and vertically. You can also freeze the panes to the keep a worksheet area in view at all times.

Splitting a Window into Panes

Depending on the type of split you want, you can use any of three different methods to split your worksheets:

- ▲ Use Window Split to split the worksheet into four panes at the selected cell (Later, you can adjust the split to two panes, if you like).
- ▲ Use the horizontal or vertical split boxes to split the worksheet into two panes at a position you specify (horizontally or vertically, respectively).
- ▲ Use Control Menu Split to create either a two- or four-pane split at a position you specify.

Method One—Using the Window Split Command

When you use this method, Excel splits the worksheet into four *panes* at the currently selected cell. How do you know which cell to select? Let's look at an example. Figure 19.5 shows a worksheet called LOAN.XLS with cell D7 selected. When the worksheet is split using this method, the results are as shown in Figure 19.6. Notice that Excel places the *horizontal split bar* on the top edge of the selected cell's row, and the *vertical split bar* on the left edge of the selected cell's column. This is convenient because now the loan variables are in the upper left pane, the periods and months are in the lower left pane, the title and column headings are in the upper right pane, and the loan data is in the lower right pane. The panes are synchronized so that as you move down through the loan data, the period and month values also move down.

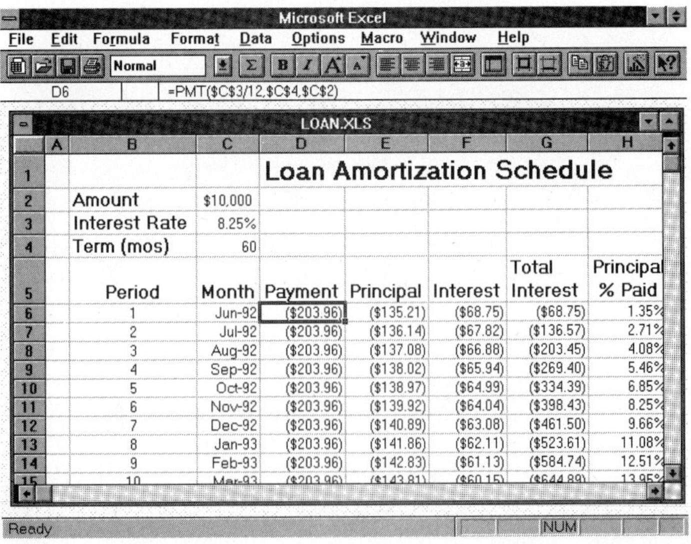

	A	B	C	D	E	F	G	H
1				Loan Amortization Schedule				
2		Amount	$10,000					
3		Interest Rate	8.25%					
4		Term (mos)	60					
5		Period	Month	Payment	Principal	Interest	Total Interest	Principal % Paid
6		1	Jun-92	($203.96)	($135.21)	($68.75)	($68.75)	1.35%
7		2	Jul-92	($203.96)	($136.14)	($67.82)	($136.57)	2.71%
8		3	Aug-92	($203.96)	($137.08)	($66.88)	($203.45)	4.08%
9		4	Sep-92	($203.96)	($138.02)	($65.94)	($269.40)	5.46%
10		5	Oct-92	($203.96)	($138.97)	($64.99)	($334.39)	6.85%
11		6	Nov-92	($203.96)	($139.92)	($64.04)	($398.43)	8.25%
12		7	Dec-92	($203.96)	($140.89)	($63.08)	($461.50)	9.66%
13		8	Jan-93	($203.96)	($141.86)	($62.11)	($523.61)	11.08%
14		9	Feb-93	($203.96)	($142.83)	($61.13)	($584.74)	12.51%
15		10	Mar-93	($203.96)	($143.81)	($60.15)	($644.89)	13.95%

Figure 19.5 The LOAN.XLS worksheet before splitting.

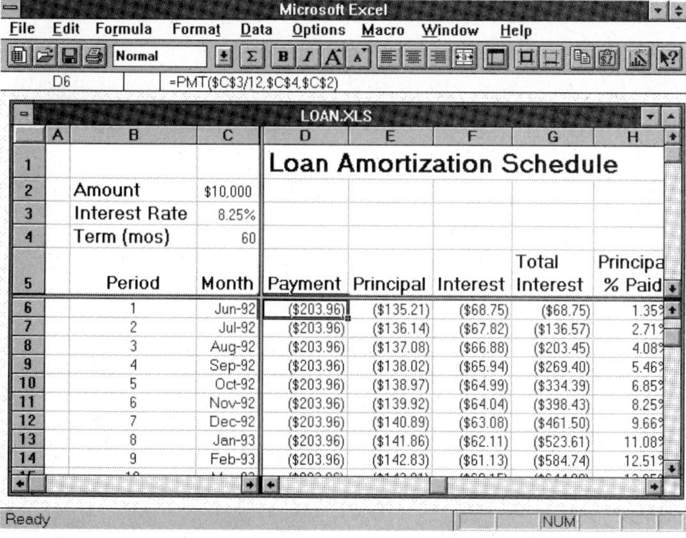

Figure 19.6 The LOAN.XLS worksheet after splitting.

Here are the steps involved in this method:

1. Select the cell where you want the worksheet to be split.
2. Choose Window Split. Excel displays split bars at the cell location.
3. If the split is not where you want it, you can adjust it by dragging the appropriate split bar. Alternatively, you can choose Window Remove Split and try again.

Using the Window Split Command:

1. Select cell where you want split.
2. Choose Window Split.
3. Drag appropriate split bar to adjust split.

TIP: To remove the splits, choose Window Remove Split.

Method Two—Using the Window Split Boxes

If you use a mouse, you can use the horizontal and vertical split boxes to create a two-pane split. The horizontal split box is the black area located between the vertical scroll bar up arrow and the window Maximize button (see Figure 19.7). The vertical split box is the black area between the horizontal scroll bar left arrow and the window border (see Figure 19.7).

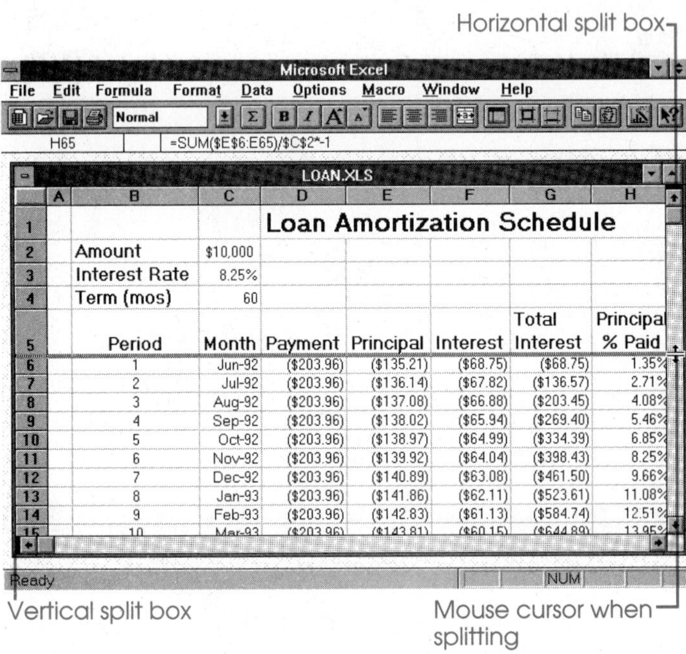

Figure 19.7 Using the split boxes to create a two-pane split.

Using Split Boxes to Split a Worksheet:

1. Point to desired split box.
2. Press and hold left mouse button.
3. Drag pointer to desired split location.
4. Release mouse button.

Follow these steps to split a worksheet using the split boxes:

1. Position the mouse pointer on the split box you want. The pointer changes to the shape shown in Figure 19.7.

2. Press and hold down the left mouse button. Excel displays a light gray bar to indicate the current split position.

3. Drag the pointer to the desired split location.

4. Release the mouse button. Excel splits the worksheet at the selected location. The split box moves to the split location.

TIP: To remove the split, drag the split box back to its original location or choose Window Remove Split.

Method Three—Using the Control Menu Split Command

With this method, you use either a mouse or your keyboard to split the worksheet into two or four panes. Follow these steps:

1. Open the window's Control menu by clicking on Control or by pressing Alt+ - (hyphen).

2. Choose Split. Excel displays horizontal and vertical gray bars at the currently selected cell.

3. Move the bars to the desired split location by moving the mouse pointer, or by using the keyboard arrow keys.

4. To split the worksheet, click on the mouse or press Enter.

Using the Control Menu Split Command:

1. Open window's Control menu.
2. Choose Split.
3. Move bars to desired split location.
4. Click on mouse or press Enter.

To remove the split, choose Control Split again, and move the gray bars to the upper left corner of the worksheet. (You can also remove the split by choosing Window Remove Split.)

TIP: To create a two-pane split, move the gray bar all the way to the top (for a vertical split), or all the way to the left (for a horizontal split).

Freezing Worksheet Titles

One of the problems with viewing multiple panes is that the work area can get confusing if some of the panes contain the same cells. For example, Figure 19.8 shows the LOAN.XLS worksheet split into four panes where each pane contains cell D8 in its upper left corner. Clearly, such a display is meaningless. To prevent this from happening, you can freeze your panes so that areas displaying worksheet titles or column headings remain in place.

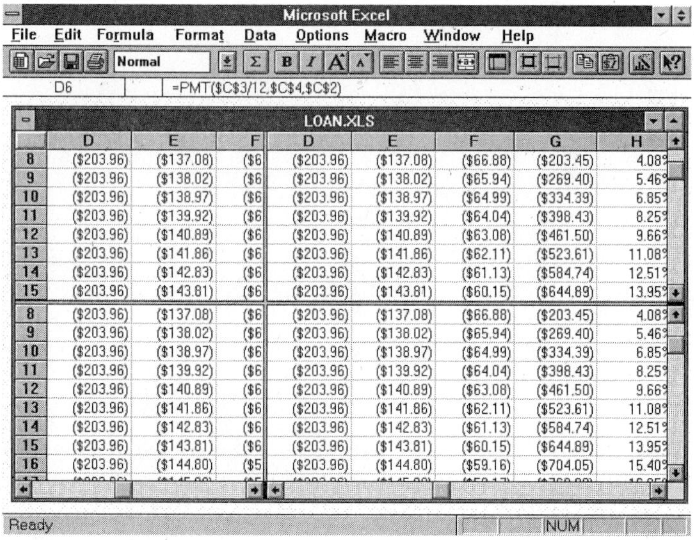

Figure 19.8 Split worksheets can become confusing.

Freezing Panes:

1. Split worksheet; arrange each pane as desired.
2. Choose Window Freeze Panes.

Here are the steps to follow:

1. Split the worksheet, and arrange each pane with the desired information (titles, headings, etc.).

2. Choose Window Freeze Panes. Excel replaces the thick, gray split bars with thin, black freeze bars.

Figure 19.9 shows the LOAN.XLS worksheet with frozen panes. In this case, the panes were frozen from the split position shown in Figure 19.6. In this example, the frozen panes provide the following advantages:

▲ No matter where you move up or down in the worksheet, the column headings and loan variables remain visible.

▲ As you move up or down in the worksheet, the values in the bottom panes remain synchronized.

▲ No matter where you move left or right in the worksheet, the period and month values remain visible.

▲ As you move left or right in the worksheet, the values in the two right panes remain synchronized.

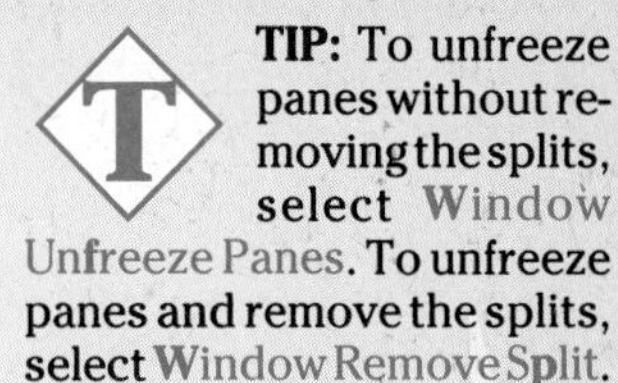

TIP: To unfreeze panes without removing the splits, select Window Unfreeze Panes. To unfreeze panes and remove the splits, select Window Remove Split.

Microsoft Excel

File Edit Formula Format Data Options Macro Window Help

H65 =SUM($E$6:E65)/$C$2*-1

LOAN.XLS

	A	B	C	E	F	G	H	I
1						:hedule		
2		Amount	$10,000					
3		Interest Rate	8.25%					
4		Term (mos)	60					
5		Period	Month	Principal	Interest	Total Interest	Principal % Paid	
57		52	Sep-96	($191.77)	($12.20)	($2,188.41)	84.18%	
58		53	Oct-96	($193.08)	($10.88)	($2,199.28)	86.11%	
59		54	Nov-96	($194.41)	($9.55)	($2,208.84)	88.05%	
60		55	Dec-96	($195.75)	($8.21)	($2,217.05)	90.01%	
61		56	Jan-97	($197.09)	($6.87)	($2,223.92)	91.98%	
62		57	Feb-97	($198.45)	($5.51)	($2,229.43)	93.96%	
63		58	Mar-97	($199.81)	($4.15)	($2,233.58)	95.96%	
64		59	Apr-97	($201.19)	($2.78)	($2,236.36)	97.97%	
65		60	May-97	($202.57)	($1.39)	($2,237.75)	100.00%	

Ready NUM

Figure 19.9 The LOAN.XLS worksheet with frozen panes.

Zooming In and Out

So far, you have seen a number of methods for viewing your worksheets in different ways. Most of these techniques help you to work more easily with large spreadsheets by enabling you to see different parts of the document simultaneously. Even though this is very valuable, what you often need is the ability to see the big picture, because even the largest window can display only a few dozen cells at most. Excel 4 for Windows offers a new Zoom feature that lets you see your worksheets with various degrees of *magnification*.

With Zoom, a magnification value of 100% represents the normal worksheet view. If you select a lower magnification, Zoom scales each cell smaller by the amount you specify and so displays more cells in the window. For example, if you choose the 50% magnification, the worksheet cells become smaller by half. If you choose a higher magnification, Zoom scales each cell larger. All your data and formatting options remain intact, and you can make changes to the worksheet at any magnification.

Zooming In On or Out from a Worksheet:

1. Choose Window Zoom.
2. Select Magnification value or enter your own value.
3. Select OK.

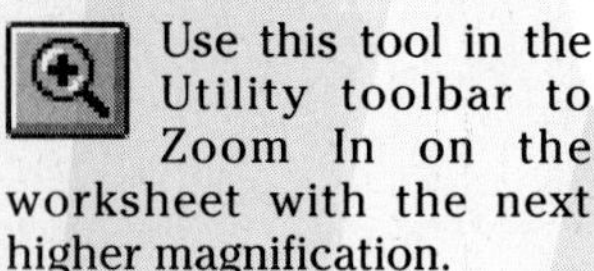

Use this tool in the Utility toolbar to Zoom In on the worksheet with the next higher magnification.

Use this tool in the Utility toolbar to Zoom Out from the worksheet with the next lower magnification.

Follow these steps to use the Zoom feature:

1. Choose Window Zoom. Excel displays the Zoom dialog box (see Figure 19.10).
2. Select a Magnification value from the choices presented or enter you own value in the **C**ustom text box (enter a number between 10 and 400).
3. Select OK or press Enter. Excel adjusts the Zoom magnification and redisplays the worksheet.

Figure 19.11 shows what a worksheet looks like at 25% magnification. There are nearly 2,000 cells visible in this view, and although you cannot see individual cells, you do get a good sense of the overall layout of your worksheet.

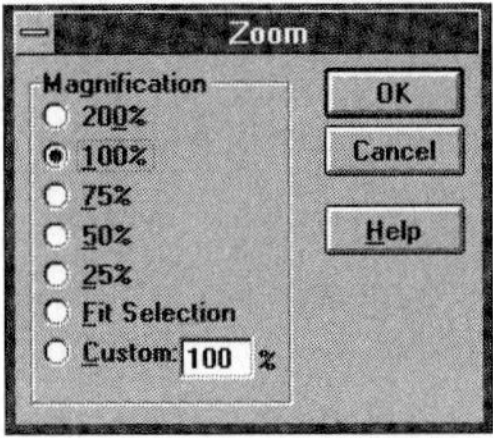

Figure 19.10 The Zoom dialog box.

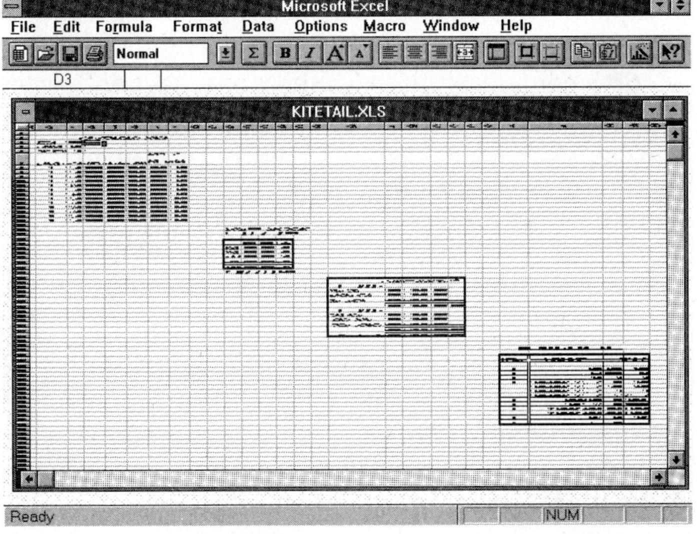

Figure 19.11 A Worksheet at 25% magnification.

IN ACTION: Figure 19.11 is a good example of the "kite tail" worksheet design (also called the "diamondback" design). Notice how the discrete work areas do not overlap in any column or row. This makes it easy to add, delete, or edit within each area of the worksheet.

Displaying Multiple Worksheet Views

Displaying the same file in multiple windows or panes is a great way to manage large worksheets. Unfortunately, sometimes managing the windows themselves can become time-consuming. You have to open each window, scroll to the worksheet area you want, set your display options, size the window, and position it where you can see it. Of course, you could save your window configurations with the worksheet and Excel will reinstate them every time you open the file. But you may not want all those windows active all the time. The solution, new with Version 4 of Excel, is to create different views of your worksheets.

TIP: The first view you create should be of your worksheet in its basic configuration (give it the name "Normal"). This way, you can always revert to this configuration from your other views.

A *view* is a specific worksheet configuration that can include the window size and position, panes and frozen titles, zoom magnification, selected cells, display options, row heights and column widths (including hidden rows and columns), and even print settings. Once you have saved a view, you can conveniently recall it any time from a list of views.

Creating a View

Creating a Worksheet View:

1. Set up worksheet with desired view.
2. Choose Window View.
3. Select Add.
4. Enter view name.
5. Select settings to include.
6. Select OK.

You use the **W**indow **V**iew command to create worksheet views. Here are the steps to follow:

1. Set up your worksheet (or one of your worksheet windows) with the view configuration you want.
2. Choose Window View. Excel displays the Views dialog box, as shown in Figure 19.12.

3. Select Add. Excel displays the Add View dialog box.

4. Enter the view name in the Name text box.

5. In the View Includes section, select the settings you want to include in the view.

6. Select OK or press Enter. Excel saves the view and returns you to the worksheet.

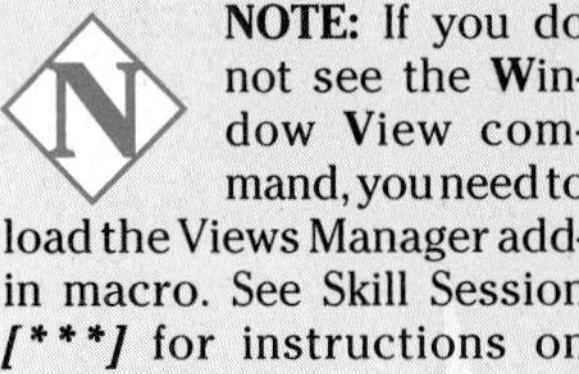

NOTE: If you do not see the **Win**dow **View** command, you need to load the Views Manager add-in macro. See Skill Session *[***]* for instructions on loading add-in macros.

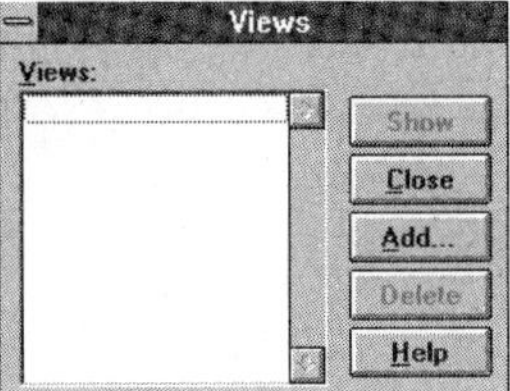

Figure 19.12 The Views dialog box.

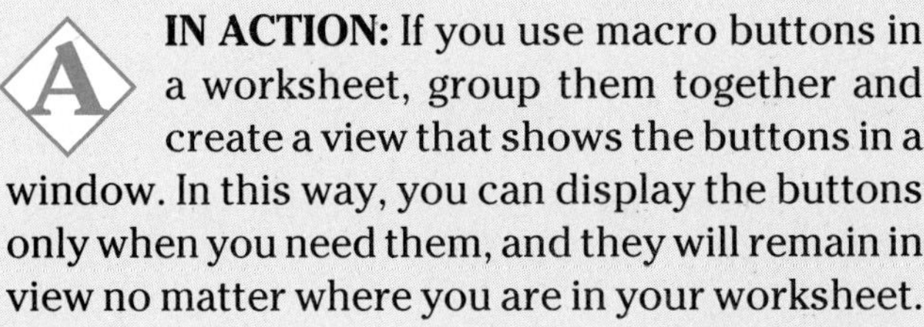

IN ACTION: If you use macro buttons in a worksheet, group them together and create a view that shows the buttons in a window. In this way, you can display the buttons only when you need them, and they will remain in view no matter where you are in your worksheet.

Displaying a View

One of the main advantages to views is that you can display them only when you need them. Excel makes displaying views easy. Here are the steps to follow:

Displaying a Worksheet View:

1. Choose Window View.
2. Highlight desired view.
3. Select Show.

1. Choose Window View to display the Views dialog box.

2. Highlight the view you want to use.

3. Select Show. Excel displays the view.

IN ACTION: If you use many complex calculations in your worksheets, set up a view that displays your formulas. When you need to troubleshoot a formula, just call up the view alongside your results.

To illustrate how you can use the View command, look at the example in Figure 19.13. It shows the overall structure of a worksheet called LEDGER.XLS. This worksheet contains a general ledger with three data areas: assets account codes, liabilities account codes, and customer account numbers. The idea is to have the three data areas visible so that a person entering data into the ledger can refer to them when needed.

To accomplish this, you need to set up four windows as follows:

- *LEDGER.XLS:1*—This window contains the general ledger itself. The window need only be large enough to display the ledger headings and a single line of data. The window is split and the headings are frozen.

- *LEDGER.XLS:2*—This window contains the assets account codes and is only wide enough to display the account description and the code. The window is split and the title is frozen.

▲ *LEDGER.XLS:3*—This window contains the liabilities account codes and is only wide enough to display the account description and the code. The window is split and the title is frozen.

▲ *LEDGER.XLS:4*—This window contains the customer account numbers and is only wide enough to display the customer name and the account number. The window is split and the title is frozen.

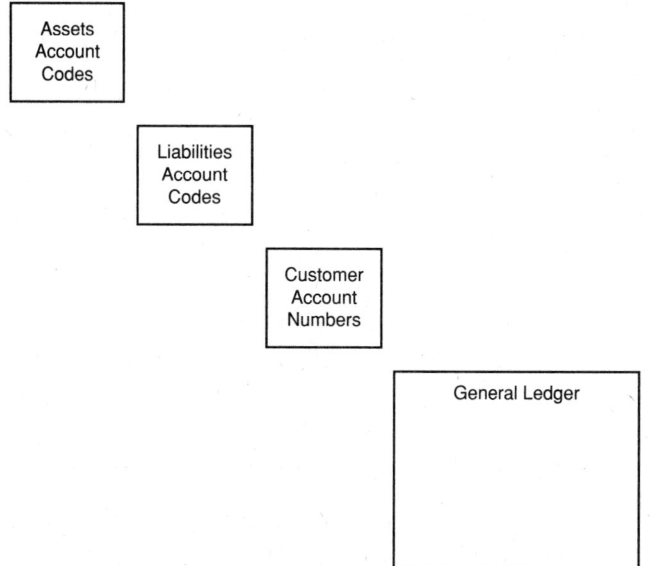

Figure 19.13 The structure of the LEDGER.XLS worksheet.

In each window, the gridlines and row and column headings are removed. The four windows are saved as views with the following names: Ledger, Asset Acct Codes, Liabilities Acct Codes, and Customer Accounts. Figure 19.14 shows the results.

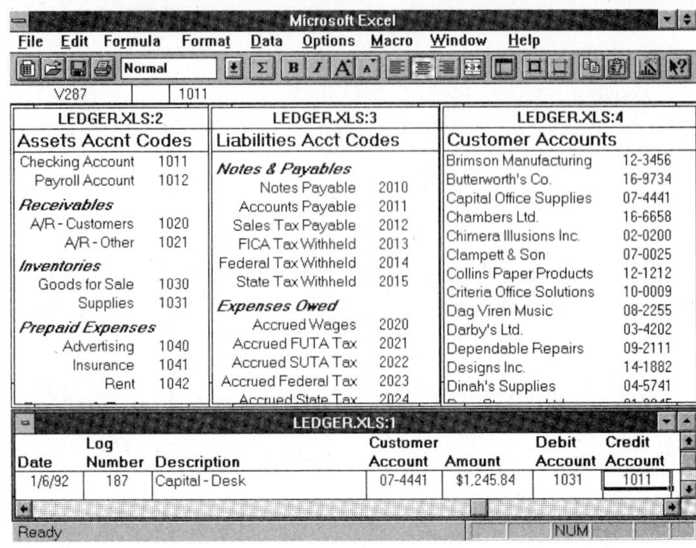

Figure 19.14 The LEDGER.XLS worksheet set up as four views.

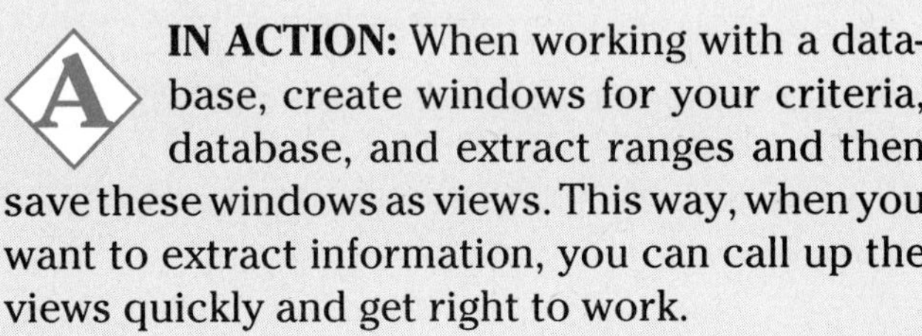

IN ACTION: When working with a database, create windows for your criteria, database, and extract ranges and then save these windows as views. This way, when you want to extract information, you can call up the views quickly and get right to work.

Deleting a View

To delete a worksheet view that you no longer need, follow these steps:

1. Choose Window View to display the Views dialog box.
2. Highlight the view you want to delete.
3. Select Delete. Excel removes the view name from the Views list.
4. Repeat steps 2–3 to delete other views.
5. Select Close to return to the worksheet.

Deleting a Worksheet View:

1. Choose Window View.
2. Highlight view to delete.
3. Select Delete.
4. Repeat steps 2–3 to delete other views.
5. Select Close.

Skill Session

20

Spell-Checking the Worksheet

One of the easiest ways to lose face in a presentation is to display a worksheet that contains spelling mistakes. No matter how professionally organized and formatted your report appears, a simple spelling error will stick out like a sore thumb. But mistakes do happen, especially if your presentation includes a large number of complicated documents. To help you catch those errors, Excel for Windows now includes a spell-checking utility.

This skill session shows you how to use the spell checker to check your entire worksheet, a range, or even a single word. You will also learn how to augment Excel's dictionary with your own custom dictionary.

Spell-Checking a Range

When you invoke the Spelling command, Excel compares each word in your selected range with those in its standard dictionary. If Excel doesn't find the word, it displays the Spelling dialog box (see Figure 20.1).

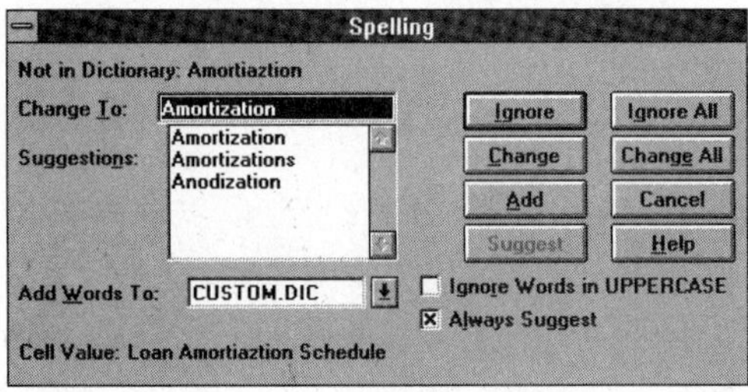

Figure 20.1 The Spelling dialog box.

The Spelling dialog box contains the following elements:

Not in Dictionary	This information box shows the word that Excel could not find.
Change **T**o	This text box contains the word that Excel has determined is closest to the unknown word. If you turn off the A**l**ways Suggest option, Excel displays the unknown word. In either case, you can enter your own correction in this box.
Suggestio**n**s	This list box contains all the words that Excel has determined are close to the unknown word. No suggestions appear if you turn off the A**l**ways Suggest option.

Ignore	Select this button to skip this instance of the word.
Ignore All	Select this button to skip all instances of the word.
Change	Select this button to change the unknown word to the word displayed in the Change To box.
Change All	Select this button to change all instances of the unknown word to the word displayed in the Change To box.
Add	Select this button to add the unknown word to the dictionary shown in the Add Words To box.
Suggest	Select this button to have Excel suggest corrections. This button is only active if you turn off the Always Suggest option.
Add Words To	This box displays the current custom dictionary. See the section entitled "Using Custom Dictionaries," later in this skill session.
Ignore Words in UPPERCASE	Select this option to have Excel skip uppercase versions of words that are found in the dictionary in lowercase. This option is off by default.

Always Suggest	Select this option to have Excel make suggestions for every unknown word. This option is on by default.
Cell Value	This information box displays the full contents of the cell containing the unknown word.

If you do not select a range for the spell check, Excel checks the entire worksheet including cell notes, embedded charts, macro buttons, headers, and footers. Follow these steps to spell-check a range or worksheet:

Spell-Checking a Range or Worksheet:

1. Select range to check.
2. Choose Options Spelling.
3. If Excel finds unknown word, select appropriate command button.
4. If prompted, select Yes to continue or No to end.
5. Select OK when the spell check is complete.

1. Select the range you want to check. (To check the entire worksheet, leave only the current cell selected.)
2. Choose Options Spelling. If Excel finds a word that is not in any open dictionary, the Spelling dialog box appears. If you have the Always Suggest option turned on, Excel usually suggests a new word.
3. Select the appropriate command button. For example, to continue the spell check, select the Ignore button.
4. If you are checking the entire worksheet and you began from a cell that was not at the beginning of the sheet, when Excel reaches the bottom, it asks if you want to continue the check from the beginning (see Figure 20.2). Select Yes to continue or No to end the spell check.
5. When Excel has finished checking the entire range or worksheet, it displays a message to that effect. Select OK or press Enter to return to the worksheet.

TIP: If you are spell-checking your entire worksheet, make cell A1 active before invoking the Spelling command. This prevents Excel from asking if you would like to continue checking at the beginning of the sheet.

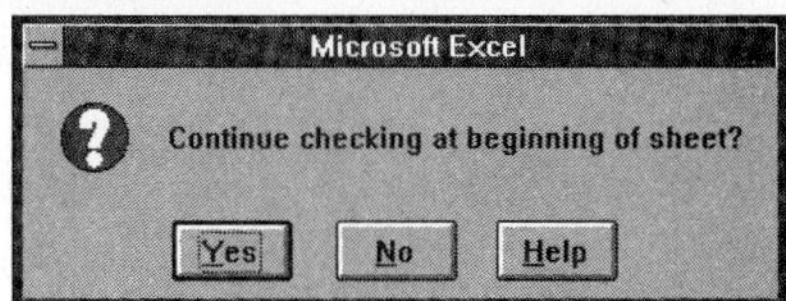

Figure 20.2 Excel asks if you want to continue checking at the beginning of the worksheet.

Spell-Checking a Single Word

Excel can check the spelling of a single word in the formula bar or in a text box or macro button. Here are the steps to follow:

1. Make the cell active; in the formula bar, highlight the word you want to check.
2. Choose Options Spelling. If Excel cannot find the word in any open dictionary, it displays the Spelling dialog box.
3. Select the appropriate options from the dialog box.
4. If Excel determines that the word is spelled correctly, it displays the message shown in Figure 20.3. If Excel did not find the word, then once you have made your choice in the Spelling dialog box, Excel tells you that the check is complete. In either case, select OK or press Enter to return to the worksheet.

Spell-Checking a Single Word:

1. Make cell active and highlight word to check.
2. Choose Options Spelling.
3. Select appropriate option when prompted.
4. Select OK.

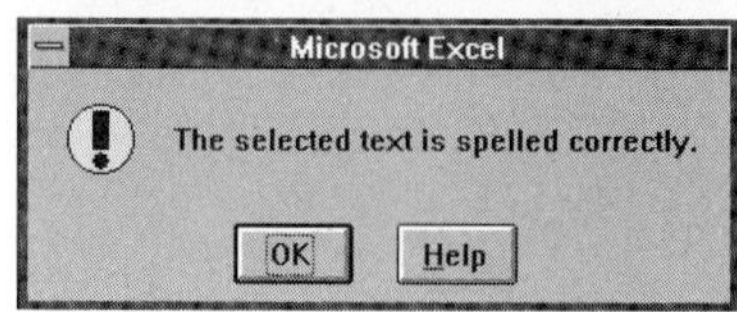

Figure 20.3 Excel tells you if the word is spelled correctly.

Using Custom Dictionaries

Although the dictionary Excel uses to check spelling is extensive, it obviously cannot include every word in the English language. You will find that Excel often flags names of people or companies, as well as unusual technical terms. To account for this, you can use custom dictionaries to hold words you use frequently but Excel does not recognize. The default custom dictionary is called CUSTOM.DIC. You can add your words to this dictionary or create your own. Follow these steps to create a custom dictionary:

Creating a Custom Dictionary:

1. Choose Options Spelling.
2. Enter name for new dictionary.
3. Press Enter.
4. Select Yes to create dictionary.
5. Continue with spell check or cancel to return to worksheet.

1. Choose **O**ptions **S**pelling to display the Spelling dialog box.
2. In the Add **W**ords To text box, enter the name for the new dictionary. (You do not need to add the extension .DIC to the dictionary name; Excel will do this for you.)
3. Press Enter. Excel asks if you want to create a new dictionary (see Figure 20.4).
4. Select Yes to create the dictionary.

5. You can continue with the spell check or cancel to return to the worksheet.

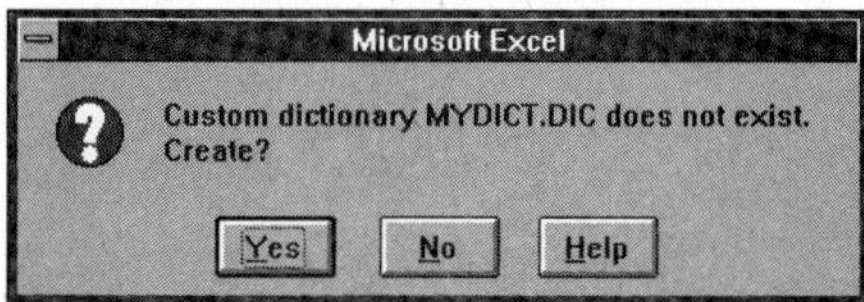

Figure 20.4 Excel asks you to confirm that you want to create the dictionary.

You can create as many different dictionaries as you need. For example, you could have a dictionary for technical terms used in your industry, another for employee or customer names, and another for common abbreviations. Keep in mind that you can only use one custom dictionary at a time.

Skill Session

21

Adding Comments with Text Boxes and Notes

This workshop has shown you many techniques for making your worksheets clearer and more readable. But a worksheet that is well organized can still be difficult to read if you use formulas and calculations that are obscure to others. Because you cannot always be there to explain your work, Excel allows you to add comments to your documents in the form of *text boxes* and *text notes*. You use text boxes to add explanatory remarks that sit "on top" of the worksheet. You use text notes to attach comments to individual cells. This skill session shows you how to work with both kinds of objects.

Working With Text Boxes

Many people like to add handwritten comments directly on their printed worksheets or on sticky notes. For a more professional look, or for those times when you are presenting your work on-screen or on a slide, add an Excel text box to your worksheet. A text box is simply a block of text that sits on the worksheet. The text box is a graphic "object," so you can position, size, edit, and format it independently of the worksheet cells. (For more information on Excel's graphic objects, especially information on object properties and formatting, see the appropriate skill sessions in this book's Graphics Workshop.)

Adding a Text Box

To create a text box, you need to display the Drawing toolbar. (See Skill Session 4 for information on displaying toolbars.) Here are the steps to follow to add a text note:

Adding a Text Box:

1. Click or double-click on Text Box tool.
2. Point where you want top left corner to be.
3. Press and hold left mouse button.
4. Drag pointer to where you want bottom right corner to be.
5. Release mouse button.

1. Click on the Text Box tool on the Drawing toolbar. (If you want to create more than one text box, double-click on the tool.) The regular mouse pointer changes to a cross-hair pointer.

2. Position the pointer where you want the top left corner of the text box to be.

3. Press and hold down the left mouse button.

4. Drag the mouse pointer to where you want the bottom right corner of the text box to be. As you drag the pointer, Excel draws an outline of the box.

5. Release the mouse button. If you are drawing only one box, Excel places a blinking insertion point cursor in the upper left corner of the box. If you double-clicked the Text Box tool, but you only want to draw a single box, skip to step 7.

6. If you are creating more boxes, repeat steps 2–5. When you have finished, click on the first box in which you want to enter text.

7. Type the text you want in the box. The text automatically wraps and scrolls within the box.

8. To add text to another box, click on the box (or press Tab to move to the next box), and enter the text you want.

9. When you are finished, click on an empty area of the worksheet, or press Esc.

6. If you are creating more boxes, repeat steps 2–5.
7. Type text you want in box.
8. To add text to another box, click on box or press Tab.
9. Press Esc.

This is the Text Box tool from the Drawing toolbar.

TIP: To make the text box a square, hold down Shift while dragging the pointer. To align the text box with the worksheet gridlines, hold down Alt while dragging the pointer.

IN ACTION: Use text boxes for short explanations or to point out key worksheet results. For longer, more technical comments, attach a text note to a cell (see the section entitled "Working With Text Notes" later in this skill session).

Making Text Box Adjustments

Once you have added a text box to a worksheet, you are free to edit the text contained in the box and to make adjustments to the size, shape, and position of the box. (For information on other formatting options such as alignment, fonts, and shading, see Skill Session 32 in the Graphics Workshop.)

Editing a Text Box:

1. Click on text box to edit.
2. Position cursor to insert text, or highlight text to change.
3. Edit text.
4. Click outside box, or press Esc.

CAUTION: If you click only once on the text box and then begin typing, Excel replaces the entire contents of the box with your typing. If this happens, immediately choose Edit Undo Typing.

TIP: When editing a text box, press Enter to start a new line. To enter a tab, press Ctrl+Tab.

Positioning a Text Box:

1. Click on text box and hold left mouse button.
2. Drag text box to desired location.
3. Release mouse button.

To edit the contents of a text box, follow these steps:

1. Click on the text box you want to edit.
2. Click inside the text box to position the cursor for inserting text, or highlight the text you want to change.
3. Edit the text using the same techniques you learned for editing cell contents.
4. When you are finished, click outside the box or press Esc.

IN ACTION: Use text boxes to show others your worksheet formulas. To enter a formula in a text box, first select the cell and highlight the formula in the formula bar. Then choose Copy, position the cursor in the text box, and Paste the formula into the box.

To adjust the position of a text box, follow these steps:

1. Click on the text box and hold down the left mouse button.
2. Drag the text box to the desired location. The box border changes to a dotted line as you drag the pointer.
3. Release the mouse button. Excel drops the box in the new location.

You can adjust the size of any text box to suit your needs. You size a text box by using *sizing handles*. These handles appear any time you select a text box. Excel displays eight handles for each box: one on each side of the box and one in each corner. You adjust the box size by dragging these handles with the mouse pointer. Here are the steps to follow:

Adjusting the Size of a Text Box:

1. Click on text box to adjust.
2. Position mouse pointer over a handle.
3. Press and hold down left mouse button.
4. Drag handle to desired location.
5. Release mouse button.
6. To adjust other parts of box, repeat steps 2–5.

1. Click on the text box you want to adjust. Excel changes the box border into a thicker, broken line and displays the sizing handles, as shown in Figure 21.1.
2. Position the mouse pointer over a handle. The changes to the shape are shown in Figure 21.1.
3. Press and hold down the left mouse button. The pointer changes to a cross-hair pointer.
4. Drag the handle to the desired location. As you drag the mouse, Excel displays the new border as a dashed line.
5. Release the mouse button. Excel adjusts the size of the text box.
6. To adjust other parts of the box, repeat steps 2–5.

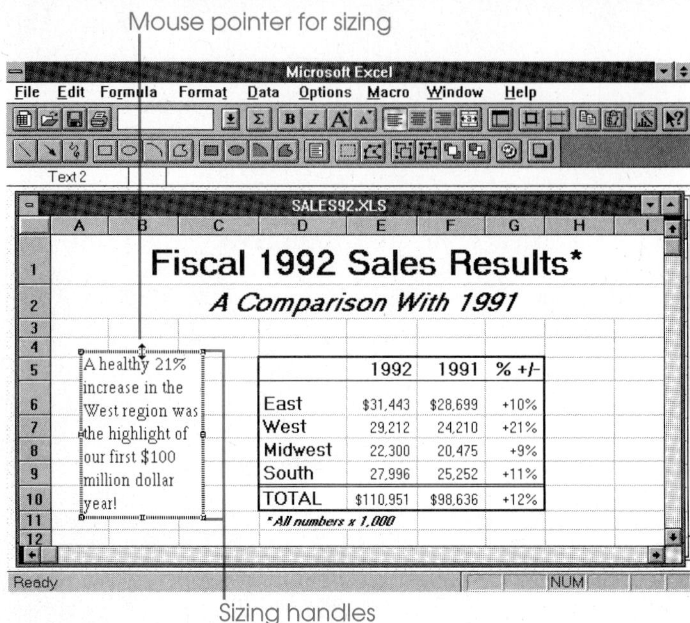

Figure 21.1 You can change the size of your text boxes.

Attaching an Arrow to a Text Box

Many of your text boxes will refer to specific worksheet cells or ranges. For added clarity, you can attach an arrow to the text box so that it points at the appropriate cell or range. Follow these steps to attach a text box arrow:

1. Click on the Arrow tool in the Drawing toolbar. To draw more than one arrow, double-click on the tool. The mouse pointer changes to a cross-hair pointer.

2. Position the cross-hair pointer where you want the arrow to start. For a text box, you usually start the arrow at the edge of the box nearest the cell that you want to single out.

3. Press and hold down the left mouse button.

4. Drag the pointer to where you want the arrow to point. Excel draws a line as you drag the mouse.

5. Release the mouse button. Excel adds an arrowhead to the line.

6. If you are drawing other arrows, repeat steps 2–5. When you are finished, click on an empty part of the worksheet or press Esc.

Figure 21.2 shows a worksheet with a text box and attached arrow. To move or adjust the size of an arrow, use the same techniques that you used for text boxes. Note that the resizing pointer is displayed as a cross-hair pointer, and not as an arrow.

Adding an Arrow to a Text Box:

1. Click or double-click on Arrow tool.
2. Position cross-hair pointer where you want arrow to start.
3. Press and hold down left mouse button.
4. Drag pointer to where you want arrow to point.
5. Release mouse button.
6. To draw other arrows, repeat steps 2–5. When done, press Esc.

This is the Arrow tool from the Drawing toolbar.

NOTE: You can adjust the style and weight of both the arrow line and the arrowhead. See Skill Session 32 in the Graphics Workshop.

Deleting a Text Box or Arrow

If your worksheet contains a text box or arrow that you no longer need, you can delete the object by following these steps:

1. Click on the text box or arrow. Excel displays the object's sizing handles.

2. Choose Edit Clear or press Delete. Excel removes the text box or arrow from the worksheet.

Deleting a Text Box or Arrow:

1. Click on text box or arrow.
2. Choose Edit Clear or press Delete.

TIP: In some cases, you may prefer to hide text boxes and arrows instead of deleting them. To do this, choose Options Display and select Hide All.

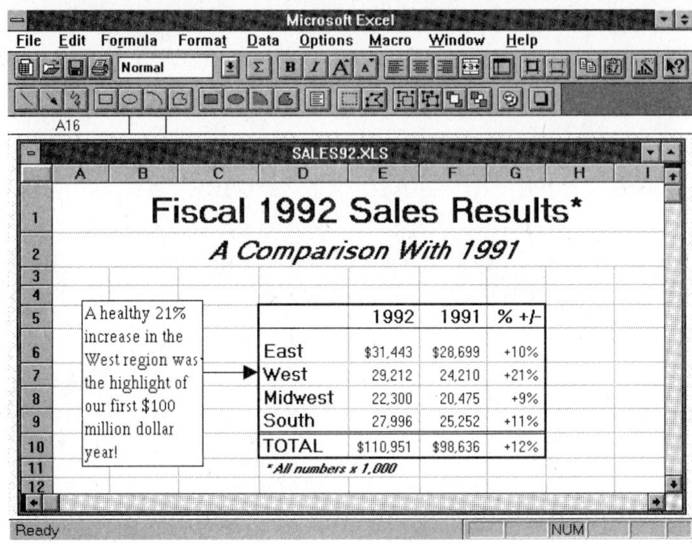

Figure 21.2 You can attach arrows to your text boxes.

Working with Text Notes

NOTE: You can print your worksheet notes separately. See Skill Session 22 to learn how to print notes.

If you don't want to display comments on your worksheet, you can attach text notes to specific cells. These notes remain hidden and can be viewed only within the Cell Note dialog box. A note indicator marks each cell that contains a note.

A text note is like a footnote in a book or report. They can be as long as you like, so you can use them for lengthy explanations of your worksheet assumptions without interfering with the appearance of the document. You can also use text notes for technical explanations, analysis of worksheet results, or even just your name.

IN ACTION: For audited worksheets, enter the name of the person who created the worksheet, the auditor, and the date of the last revision in a text note. Use a consistent cell for the note, such as A1. Be sure to protect each worksheet so no unauthorized revisions can be made. For more information on protecting worksheets, see Skill Session 41.

Adding a Text Note

You can add text notes to individual worksheet cells. Follow these steps:

1. Select the cell to which you want to add the note.
2. Choose Formula Note. Excel displays the Cell Note dialog box, as shown in Figure 21.3.
3. Enter the note in the Text Note box.
4. Select Add. Excel displays the cell address and the first few characters of the note in the Notes in Sheet list box.
5. To add a note to another cell, enter the cell address in the Cell box (or use the arrow keys to select a cell) and repeat steps 3–4.
6. Select OK or press Enter. Excel returns you to the worksheet.

Adding a Text Note:

1. Select cell to which you want to add note.
2. Choose Formula Note.
3. Enter note in the Text Note box.
4. Select Add.
5. To add a note to another cell, enter cell address in Cell box and repeat steps 3–4.
6. Select OK.

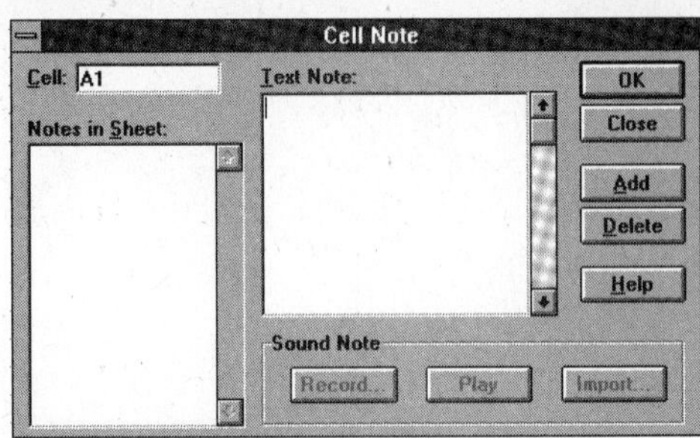

Figure 21.3 The Cell Note dialog box.

When you add a text note to a cell, a small red square (called a *note indicator*) appears in the upper right corner of the cell.

TIP: You can turn off the note indicators if you are presenting your worksheet on-screen. Select Options Workspace and turn off Note Indicator.

Viewing a Text Note

Viewing a Text Note:

1. Select cell containing note.
2. Choose Formula Note.
3. To display a note from a different cell, select note from Notes in Sheet list box.
4. Select Close.

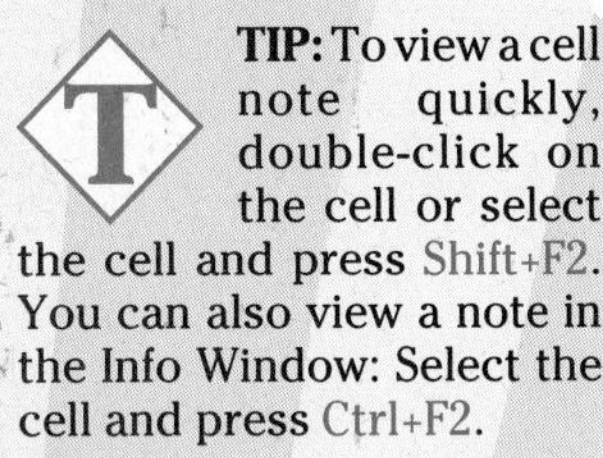

TIP: To view a cell note quickly, double-click on the cell or select the cell and press Shift+F2. You can also view a note in the Info Window: Select the cell and press Ctrl+F2.

To view a text note, follow these steps:

1. Select the cell containing the note.
2. Choose Formula Note to display the Cell Note dialog box. The note attached to the selected cell appears in the Text Note box.
3. All the worksheet text notes appear in the Notes in Sheet list box (see Figure 21.4). Select the note you want from this list to display another note. The note appears in the Text Note box.
4. Select Close to return to the worksheet.

Use this procedure to edit your text notes. After you have selected a note, use the same editing methods you use in the formula bar.

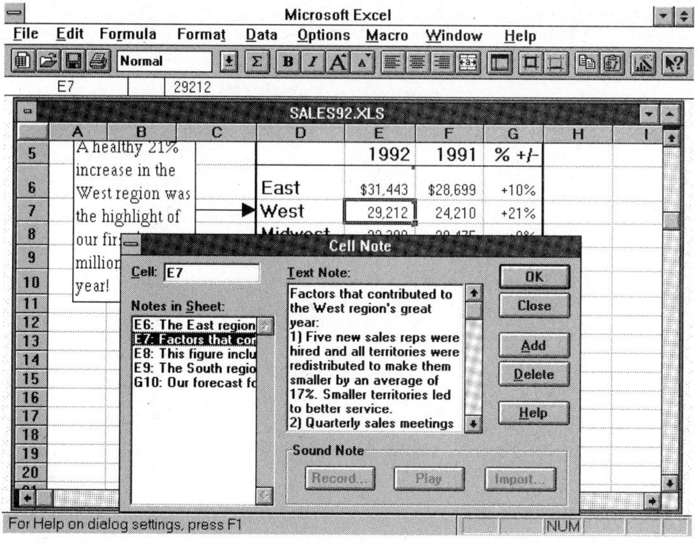

Figure 21.4 Select the text note you want to view from the Cell Note dialog box.

TIP: When entering or editing a text note, press Shift+Enter to start a new line and press Ctrl+Tab to enter a tab.

TIP: If you are not sure which cell contains the note you want, use Formula Find to search for a word or phrase from the note. In the Find dialog box, enter the word or phrase in the Find What box; in the Look in: section, select Notes.

Copying a Text Note

If you need to copy a text note to another cell, follow these steps:

1. Choose Formula Note to display the Cell Note dialog box.
2. Select the note you want to copy from the Notes in Sheet list box. The note appears in the Text Note box.
3. In the Cell box, enter the address of the cell to which you want to copy the note.
4. Select OK or press Enter. Excel copies the note to the new cell.

Copying a Text Note:

1. Choose Formula Note.
2. Select note to copy.
3. Enter address of cell to which you want to copy note.
4. Select OK.

TIP: You can also copy a text note using the cut-and-paste method: Select the cell and choose Edit Copy. Select the destination cell and choose Edit Paste Special. In the Paste Special dialog box, activate Notes and then select OK.

Deleting a Text Note

Deleting a Text Note:

1. Choose Formula Note.
2. Select note to delete.
3. Select Delete.
4. Select OK.
5. Select Close.

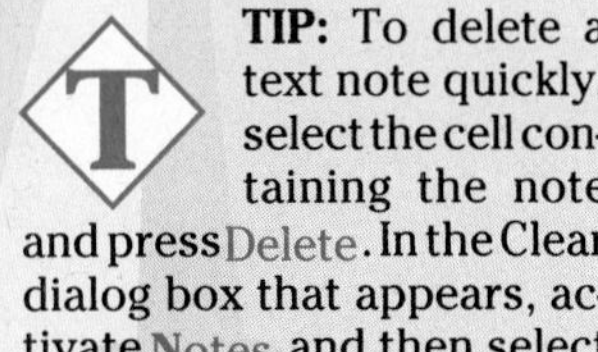

TIP: To delete a text note quickly, select the cell containing the note and press Delete. In the Clear dialog box that appears, activate Notes and then select OK or press Enter.

Deleting All Text Notes in a Worksheet:

1. Choose Formula Select Special.
2. Select Notes.
3. Select OK.
4. Choose Edit Clear or press Delete.
5. Select Notes.
6. Select OK.

If your worksheet contains notes that you no longer need, you can delete them by following these steps:

1. Choose Formula Note to display the Cell Note dialog box.
2. Select the note you want to delete from the Notes in Sheet list box. The note appears in the Text Note box.
3. Select Delete. Excel displays a message warning you that the note will be permanently deleted.
4. Select OK or press Enter. Excel returns you to the Cell Note dialog box with the note removed from the cell.
5. Select Close to return to the worksheet.

To delete all the notes in a worksheet, follow these steps:

1. Choose Formula Select Special. Excel displays the Select Special dialog box.
2. Select Notes.
3. Select OK or press Enter. Excel highlights all cells in the worksheet that contain notes.
4. Choose Edit Clear or press Delete. The Clear dialog box appears.
5. Select Notes.
6. Select OK or press Enter. Excel deletes the notes from the selected cells.

Skill Session

22

Advanced Print Operations

This skill session shows you how to get the most out of your printer with Excel. You will learn how to select different printers, adjust page breaks, add headers and footers to your document, and much more.

Selecting a Printer

If you have access to more than one printer, or if you have a printer with multiple modes (such as a LaserJet printer with a PostScript cartridge installed), you will need to use the Windows Control Panel to install a *driver* for each printer. After you have done this (see your Windows documentation for details), you can select the printer you want to use with Excel by following these steps:

Selecting a Printer:

1. Select File Page Setup.
2. Select the Printer Setup button.
3. Highlight desired printer.
4. (Optional) Select the Setup button.
5. Select OK.

1. Select File Page Setup. Excel displays the Page Setup dialog box.

2. Select the Printer Setup button. Excel displays the Printer Setup dialog box, as shown in Figure 22.1.

3. Highlight the printer you want to use.

4. (Optional) Select the Setup button to modify the printer's options.

5. Select OK or press Enter. Your selection becomes Excel's default printer, in all work sessions, until you specify another.

C **CAUTION:** If you choose the Setup button for the new printer, any adjustments you make to the printer options will affect *all* documents in *all* Windows applications. For individual worksheets, use Excel's Page Setup dialog box instead.

Adjusting Page Breaks

Excel breaks up large worksheets into pages, where the size of each page is a function of the paper size, the default font, and the margin settings in the Page Setup dialog box. Using these parameters, Excel sets automatic page breaks to delineate the print area for each page. Although you cannot adjust automatic page breaks, you can override them using manual page

T **TIP:** To see Excel's automatic page breaks before printing, run the Options Display command and select the Automatic Page Breaks option.

breaks. This allows you to control which data is printed on each page.

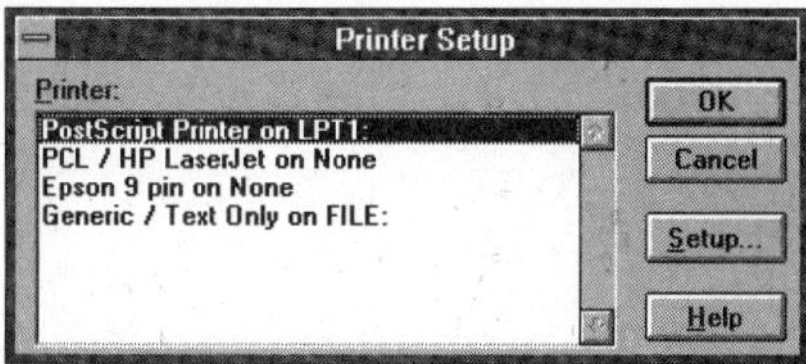

Figure 22.1 The Printer Setup dialog box.

Before setting a manual page break, you need to position the cell pointer correctly. Figure 22.2 illustrates the correct cell positions. In the BREAKS.XLS worksheet, the cell pointer is on cell C10. Inserting a manual page break here creates a horizontal break above the cell, and a vertical break to the right of the cell. In VBREAK.XLS, the break was inserted with the cell pointer in the first row. In this case, Excel inserts only a vertical break to the right of the cell. In HBREAK.XLS, the break was inserted with the cell pointer in the first column. Here, Excel inserts only a horizontal break above the cell.

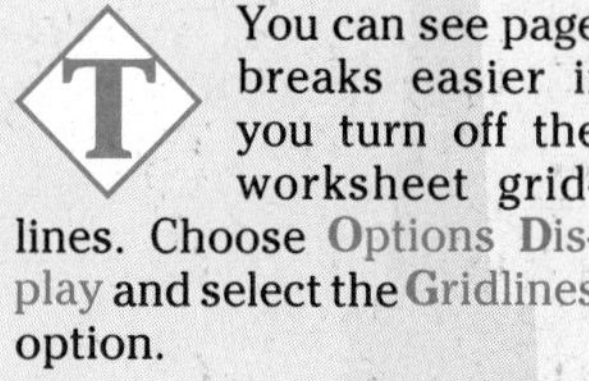

You can see page breaks easier if you turn off the worksheet gridlines. Choose Options Display and select the Gridlines option.

Follow these steps to insert a manual page break:

1. Position the cell pointer appropriately for the break you want.
2. Select Options Set Page Break. Excel inserts the page break at the cell you selected.

Inserting a Manual Page Break:

1. Position cell pointer.
2. Select Options Set Page Break.

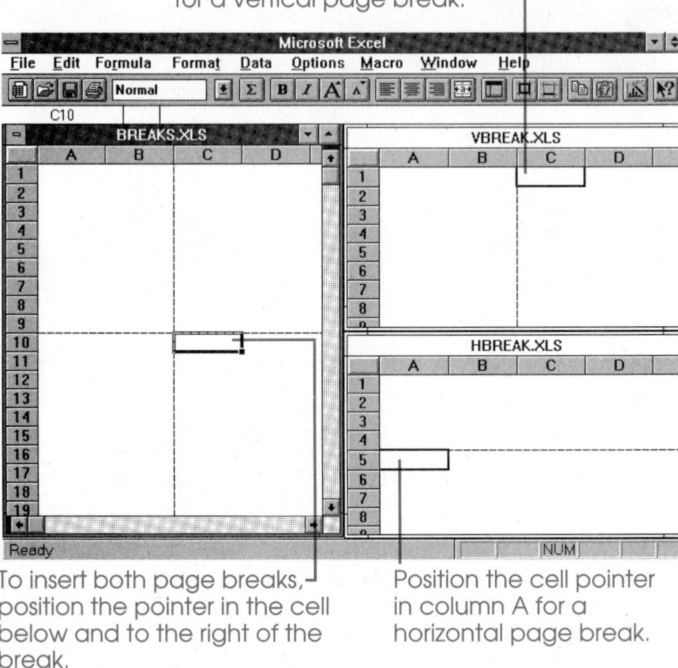
Position the cell pointer in row1 for a vertical page break.
Microsoft Excel
File Edit Formula Format Data Options Macro Window Help
Normal
C10
BREAKS.XLS
VBREAK.XLS
HBREAK.XLS
Ready
NUM
To insert both page breaks, position the pointer in the cell below and to the right of the break.
Position the cell pointer in column A for a horizontal page break.

Figure 22.2 Correct cell positions for inserting manual page breaks.

NOTE: Automatic and manual page breaks appear as dashed lines on your worksheet. You can tell them apart by noting that automatic page breaks use smaller dashes with more space between each dash.

To remove manual page breaks, select **O**ptions Re**move Page **B**reak. This command only appears if you position the pointer in any cell immediately below a horizontal page break, or in any cell immediately to the right of a vertical page break.

Fitting More Data on a Page

When you print a worksheet, you often end up with a couple of rows or columns that cannot fit on a page.

These are printed by themselves on a separate page, which is usually inconvenient and unattractive. This section examines several techniques you can use to fit more information on a page.

Adjusting the Normal Font

A worksheet's default column width and row height are functions of the *font* defined in the Normal style. In general, the smaller the type size of the Normal font, the more rows and columns will fit on a single printed page. For example, 10-point Helvetica prints 49 standard-height rows on a single page. However, if you reduce the Normal type size to 8 points, a single page will print 61 standard-height rows. Similarly, using a narrower font will increase the number of columns printed per page. For example, 10-point Helvetica prints 9 standard-width columns per page, but this increases to 12 standard-width columns if you use 10-point Helvetica Narrow.

NOTE: For instructions on adjusting the Normal style, see Skill Session 18.

Setting Smaller Margins

Since margins determine the amount of space surrounding your printed data, reducing margin size means more room on each page for printing. For example, reducing all four margins (right, left, top, and bottom) to 0.25" increases the number of columns printed from 9 to 11 and the number of rows from 49 to 58 (assuming that 10-point Helvetica is the Normal font). You adjust margins using the Page Setup dialog box (see Skill Session 12 for instructions on setting page margins).

NOTE: Some laser printers do not allow you to set your margins smaller than 0.25" because of physical limitations.

Changing the Paper Size and Orientation

If you are having trouble fitting all your rows on a page, try printing on longer paper. Changing the *paper size* from 8.5" by 11" to 8.5" by 14" will increase the number of rows per page from 49 to 66 (based on 10-point Helvetica, the "Normal" font). Use the Page Setup dialog box to select a paper size.

If you are having trouble getting all your columns to fit on a page, change the *paper orientation* from portrait to landscape in the Page Setup dialog box. Excel will print the worksheet sideways and increase the number of columns per page from 9 to 13. Just remember that this orientation reduces the number of rows printed per page.

Adjusting Rows and Columns

Make sure your rows are no taller (and your columns no wider) than they need to be. Select the entire print area, choose Format Row Height, and then select the Standard Height option. For columns, select Format Column Width and select Best Fit. Also, hiding any unnecessary rows and columns enables you to fit more important information on each page. (See Skill Session 16 for more information.)

IN ACTION: You can also use row adjustments to reduce the number of lines printed per page. For example, if you want to produce a double-spaced report, select every row in the print area, and use Format Row Height to double the height of each row.

Scaling Your Worksheet

If you have a PostScript printer or any other printer with scalable fonts, you can scale your worksheets to fit on a page. You specify a percentage reduction and Excel shrinks the printed worksheet proportionally, while maintaining all layout and formatting options. (You can also enlarge your worksheets.) Here are the steps to follow:

1. Select File Page Setup. Excel displays the Page Setup dialog box.
2. In the Scaling section, select Reduce/Enlarge to: and enter a number in the text box. To reduce the printout, enter a value between 10 and 100. To enlarge the printout, enter a value between 100 and 400.
3. Select OK or press Enter.

Scaling a Worksheet by a Percentage:

1. Select File Page Setup.
2. Enter a value in Reduce/ Enlarge to: text box.
3. Select OK.

Figure 22.3 shows a preview of a document that normally prints out on a little less than a page and a half. In this case, the worksheet was reduced to 70%; now the entire document prints on a single page.

If you find that you have to use a lot of trial and error to get the proper reduction setting, you can save some time by having Excel do it for you. All you do is specify the number of pages you want the document to fit on, and Excel handles the reduction automatically. If necessary, you can enter both a length and width for the printout. Here are the steps to follow:

1. Select File Page Setup. Excel displays the Page Setup dialog box.
2. In the Scaling section, select Fit to: and enter the number of pages wide and tall you want the printout to be.
3. Select OK or press Enter.

Scaling a Worksheet by a Percentage:

1. Select File Page Setup.
2. Enter values in Fit to: text boxes.
3. Select OK.

TIP: If you do not have a printer with scalable fonts, you can still scale your worksheets to fit a page. Select the entire print area, hold down the Shift key while you select Edit Copy Picture, and then scale the picture to the size you want. See Skill Session 34 for more information on working with pictures.

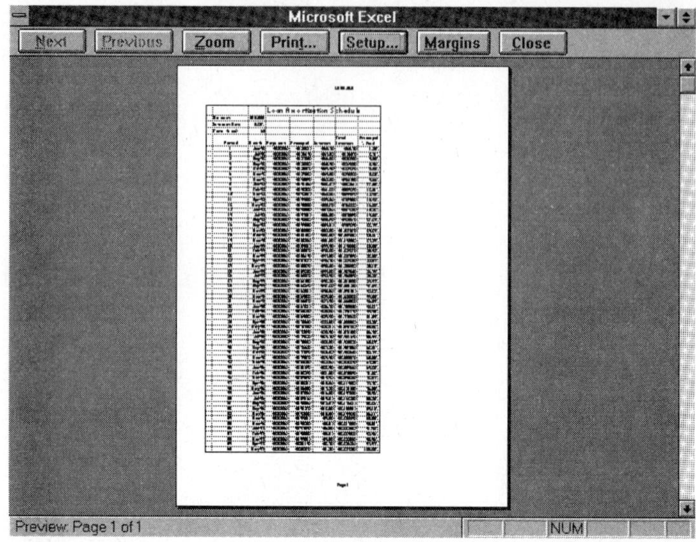

Figure 22.3 A worksheet reduced to 70%.

Adding Headers or Footers

You can add headers or footers that display information at the top or bottom of every printed page. You can enter six different items in a header or footer: a worksheet title or other text, the page number, the page count, the date, the time, and the file name. You can specify a font for any of these items, and you can place them on the left or right side of the page (or in the center).

IN ACTION: Use headers and footers to show things like the name of the worksheet author (or auditor), a copyright notice, or a list of linked worksheets.

Follow these steps to add a header or footer:

1. Select File Page Setup. Excel displays the Page Setup dialog box.
2. For a header, select the Header button. For a footer, select the Footer button. Excel displays either the Header or Footer dialog box (Figure 22.4 shows the Header dialog box).
3. Select either the Left, Center, or Right Section text box.
4. Enter text or select one of the buttons to insert a page number (&P), page count (&N), date (&D), time (&T), or file name (&F) code.
5. (Optional) Highlight any text you want to format and select the Font button.
6. Repeat steps 3–5 to enter any other text or codes.
7. Select OK or press Enter. Excel returns you to the Page Setup dialog box.
8. Select OK or press Enter. Excel adds the header or footer to the worksheet. Use File Print Preview to examine the header or footer before printing.

Adding a Header or Footer:

1. Select File Page Setup.
2. Select Header or Footer button.
3. Select Left, Center, or Right Section text box.
4. Enter text or select one of the buttons.
5. (Optional) Highlight any text and select Font button.
6. Repeat steps 3–5 to enter any other text or codes.
7. Select OK.

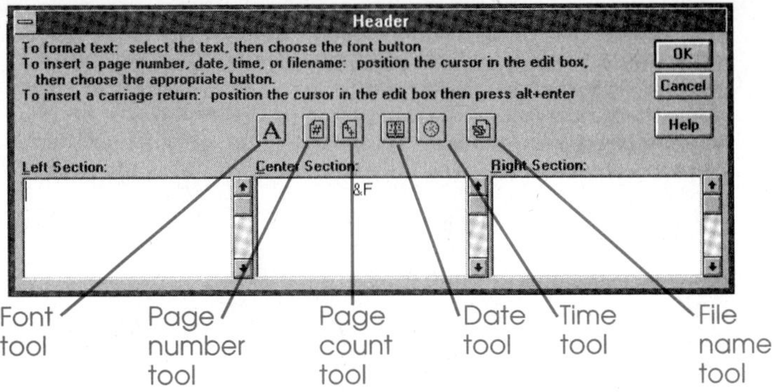

Figure 22.4 The Header dialog box.

Printing Text Notes

Printing Text Notes:

1. Select File Print.
2. Select Notes or Both.
3. Select any other print options.
4. Select OK.

In Skill Session 21, you learned how to attach text notes to individual worksheet cells. You can print these notes by following these steps:

1. Select File Print. Excel displays the Print dialog box.
2. In the Print section, select the Notes option to print notes only, or the Both option to print the worksheet and its notes.
3. Select any other print options as needed.
4. Select OK or press Enter. Excel executes the print operation.

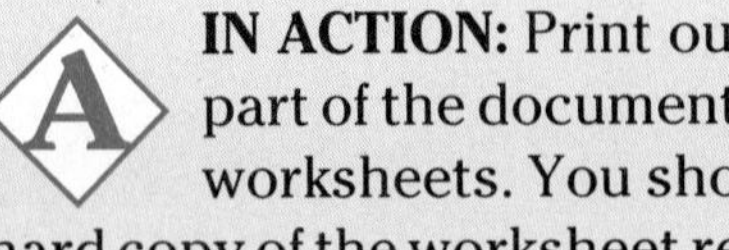

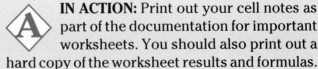

IN ACTION: Print out your cell notes as part of the documentation for important worksheets. You should also print out a hard copy of the worksheet results and formulas.

Printing Patterns and Colors

Printing patterns and colors on a black-and-white printer can be tricky because different printers can reproduce these elements in different ways. To illustrate, this section compares the printed output of patterns and colors for a LaserJet and a PostScript printer.

As you learned in Skill Session 17, you can produce shades of a foreground color by combining Excel's dot patterns with different background colors. While this is a handy way to produce attractive colors on your worksheet on-screen, your printer makes a big difference in how these colors are reproduced. Figure 22.5 shows a gray scale created by mixing dot patterns and colors. Figure 22.6 shows the same worksheet printed by a PostScript printer. As you can see, the dot pattern reproduction is inconsistent and several of the shades are almost indistinguishable. The LaserJet, on the other hand, reproduces the gray scale perfectly (see Figure 22.7). If you use dot patterns regularly in your worksheets, avoid using a PostScript printer, if possible.

Color output is a different story. As Figure 22.8 shows, the PostScript printer translates the default Excel palette into beautiful shades of gray, while the LaserJet output (shown in Figure 22.9) only produces satisfying results for a few colors. If you use solid colors regularly in your worksheets, a PostScript printer is a good choice.

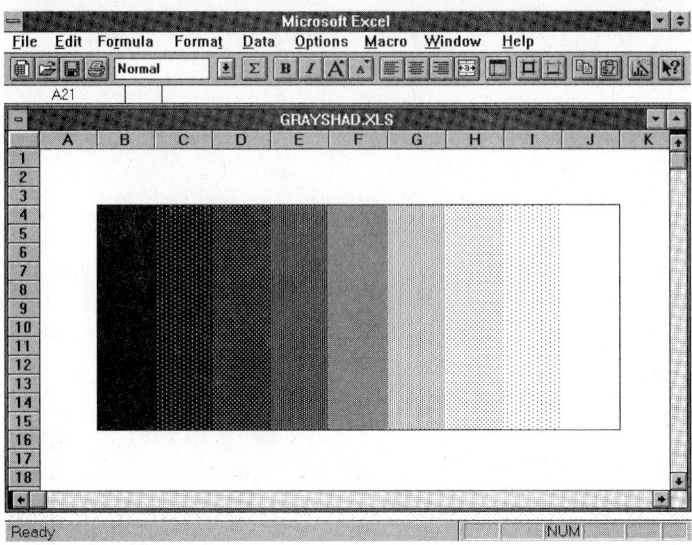

Figure 22.5 A gray scale produced by combining dot patterns and colors.

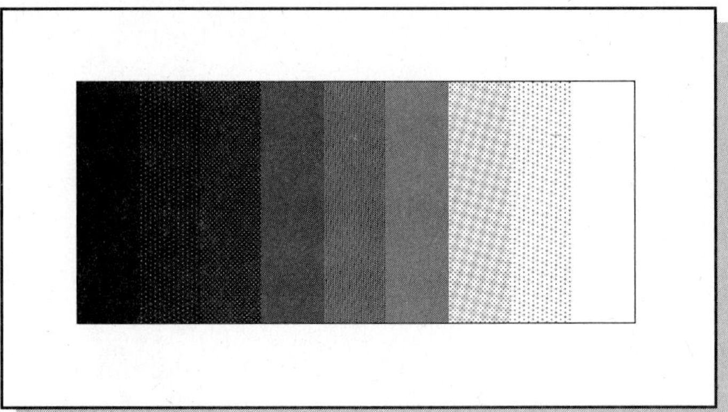

Figure 22.6 The gray scale printed on a PostScript printer.

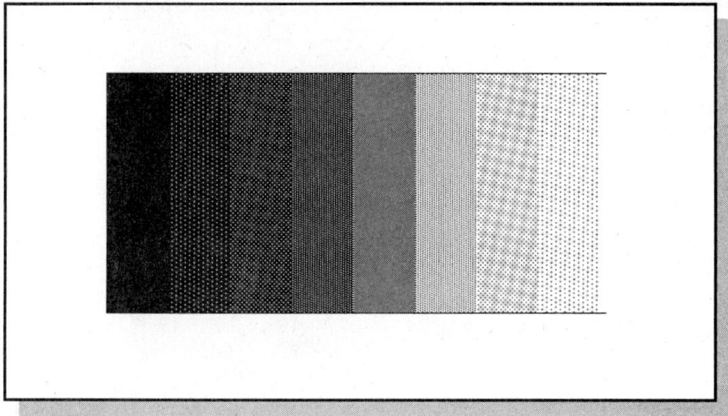

Figure 22.7 The gray scale printed on a LaserJet printer.

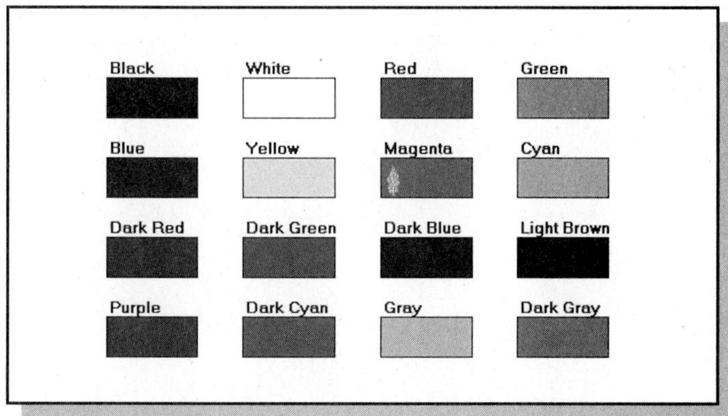

Figure 22.8 The default Excel color palette printed on a PostScript printer.

Black	White	Red	Green
Blue	Yellow	Magenta	Cyan
Dark Red	Dark Green	Dark Blue	Light Brown
Purple	Dark Cyan	Gray	Dark Gray

Figure 22.9 The default Excel color palette printed on a LaserJet printer.

Excel normally prints all text in black, no matter what color the text is on-screen. However, if you have a PostScript printer, you can get colored text to print in shades of gray by setting up your printer as a color printer. Here are the steps to follow:

Printing Gray-Scale Text:

1. Choose File Page Setup.
2. If needed, use Printer Setup to select a PostScript printer.
3. Select Options button.
4. Select a color PostScript printer from Printer list box.
5. Select OK.

1. Select File Page Setup to display the Page Setup dialog box.

2. Use Printer Setup to select your PostScript printer if it is not the Current Printer.

3. Select the Options button. Excel displays the PostScript Printer dialog box, as shown in Figure 22.10.

4. Select the Printer list box, and select a color PostScript printer (such as the NEC Colormate PS or the QMS ColorScript 100) from the list.

5. Select OK or press Enter. Excel returns you to the Page Setup dialog box.

6. Select OK or press Enter.

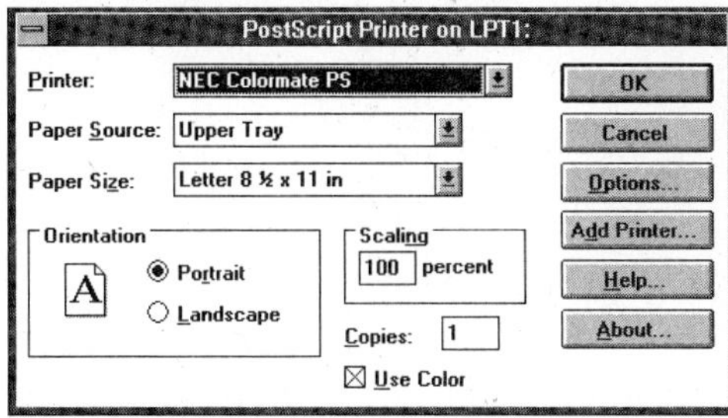

Figure 22.10 The PostScript Printer dialog box.

Figure 22.11 shows a sample printout using this technique.

This is blue text

This is red text

This is magenta text

This is green text

This is yellow text

Figure 22.11 Text colors printed as shades of gray.

Printing to a Text File

You can print your worksheets to a text file by using Windows 3.0's *FILE:* port. This is handy if you want to print a worksheet on an off-site printer, such as a color printer or a PostScript printer. You just select the appropriate printer driver, and print the worksheet to a file (as outlined below). When you get to the printer site, use DOS to copy the file to the printer. The output will be exactly the same as if it were printed directly from Excel.

IN ACTION: Use this procedure to copy worksheets to a file for printing later on a typesetting machine. Find out if your typesetter uses a Linotronic or Compugraphic model; select the appropriate printer driver; and then print the worksheet to a disk.

Printing to a Text File:

1. Switch to the Windows Program Manager, activate the Windows Control Panel, and select Settings Printers.
2. Highlight desired printer.
3. Select Configure (or Connect, in Windows 3.1).
4. Select FILE: port.

Follow these steps to print a worksheet to a text file:

1. Switch to the Windows Program Manager, activate the Windows Control Panel, and select Settings Printers. The Printers dialog box appears.
2. Highlight the appropriate printer in the Installed Printers list box.
3. Select the Configure button (if you are using Windows 3.1, select the Connect button). The Printers–Configure dialog box appears, as shown in Figure 22.12.
4. Select the FILE: port from the Ports list box.

5. Select OK or press Enter. The Control Panel returns you to the Printers dialog box.

6. Select OK or press Enter to return to the main Control Panel window.

7. Exit the Control Panel by selecting Settings Exit.

8. Use the Control menu to switch back to Excel; open the worksheet you want to print to a file.

9. In Excel, select File Page Setup Printer Setup, and select the printer you have just configured to the FILE: port.

10. Select File Print to display the Print dialog box.

11. Enter your print options and select OK or press Enter. Excel displays the Print to File dialog box, as shown in Figure 22.13.

12. Enter the name you want the file to have.

13. Select OK or press Enter. Excel copies the worksheet to the text file.

5. Select OK.
6. At the Printer's dialog box, select OK.
7. Select Settings Exit.
8. Switch back to Excel.
9. Select printer you just configured.
10. Select File Print.
11. Enter print options; select OK.
12. Enter name for file.
13. Select OK.

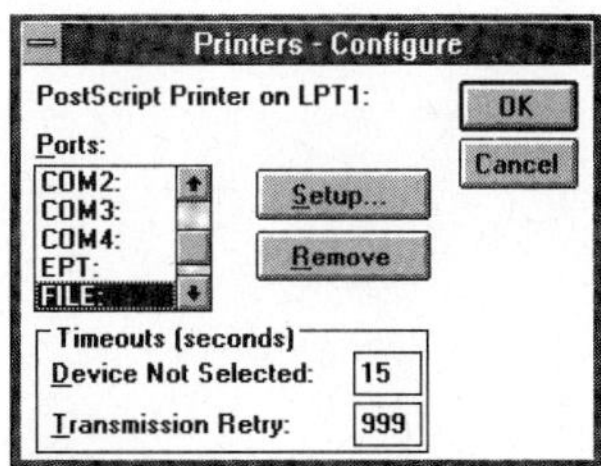

Figure 22.12 The Printers–Configure dialog box.

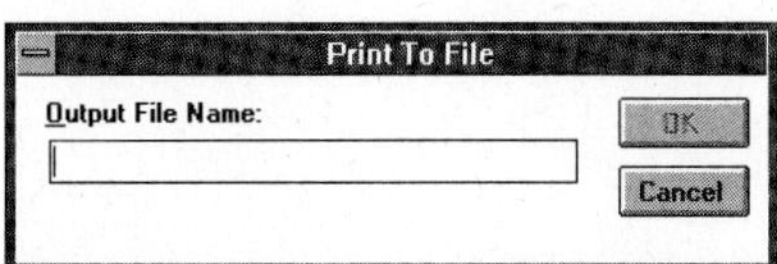

Figure 22.13 The Print to File dialog box.

Skill Session

23

Working with Reports

In Skill Session 19 of this Workshop, you learned how to create different *views* of your worksheets. A view, you will recall, contains specific settings for the display options, window position and size, row height and column width, and so on. These different views are real time-savers when you are manipulating a worksheet on-screen. Excel also includes a new feature, the *Report Manager*, that enables you to put together a sequence of views and print them out in a *report*. For maximum flexibility, you can specify different print settings with each view, and use these settings when printing your reports.

This skill session introduces you to Excel reports, and shows you how to create, edit, and print your own reports.

Creating Reports

If you are using views to create your report, first you need to define the print settings for each view. You can define page setup options, headers, footers, and even different printers (on different printer ports). Here are some guidelines to follow when defining your view print settings:

- ▲ Use the header or footer to display a title for each view.
- ▲ If a view is designed to show only a section of a worksheet (such as a list of account codes), be sure to use Options Set Print Area to restrict the printing to the view's data.
- ▲ Use Options Set Print Titles and Options Set Page Break as needed with each view.

When you create a report, you enter a report name, and then define the various *sections* of the report. (A section is a specific worksheet view, scenario, or a combination of the two.) Here are the steps to follow:

1. Choose File Print Report. Excel displays the Print Report dialog box.
2. Select the Add button. Excel displays the Add Report dialog box, as shown in Figure 23.1.
3. Enter a name for the report in the **R**eport Name text box.
4. Select the View drop-down list box. Excel displays a list of all the views associated with the worksheet.
5. Choose a view, if needed, from the list.

To Create a Report:

1. Choose File Print Report.
2. Select Add.
3. Enter name for report.
4. Select View drop-down list box.
5. Choose a view, if needed, from the list.
6. Select Scenario drop-down list box.
7. Choose a scenario, if needed, from the list.
8. Select Add.
9. Repeat steps 4–8 to include other sections.

6. Select the Scenario drop-down list box. Excel displays a list of all the scenarios associated with the worksheet.

7. Choose a scenario, if needed, from the list.

8. Select the Add button. Excel displays the view and scenario in the Current Sections list.

9. Repeat steps 4–8 to include other sections in the report.

10. Activate the Continuous Page Numbers option to print the report with consecutive page numbers.

11. Select OK or press Enter. Excel returns you to the Print Report dialog box.

12. Select Close. Excel returns you to the worksheet.

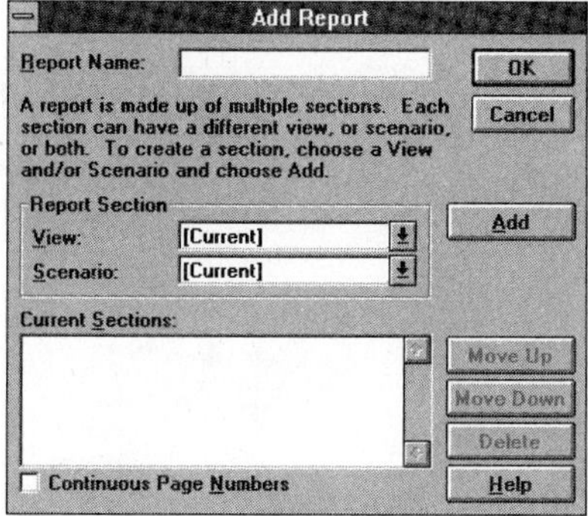

Figure 23.1 The Add Report dialog box.

You will recall from Skill Session 21 that window 1 shows the general ledger, window 2 shows the list of assets account codes, window 3 shows the list of liabilities account codes, and window 4 shows the customer account numbers. To get a listing of all account codes, for example, you would set up a report

10. Select Continuous Page Numbers, if needed.
11. Select OK.
12. Select Close.

NOTE: If the Print Report command does not appear on your **File** menu, select Options Add-ins and add REPORTS.XLA (the Report Manager add-in macro). If this file does not exist, run the Excel Setup program to install this macro.

that includes the two account code views. For each view, you would set the print area to include only the code list. When printing the complete general ledger, it would be useful to attach the account codes and customer account numbers. To do this, create a report that includes all four views (again, include the appropriate print areas in each view).

> **IN ACTION:** Document your complex worksheets by printing out hard copies of the results, formulas, variables used, and range names. Set up a view for each component, and then create a report called "Documentation." The LEDGER.XLS worksheet shown in Figure 23.2 provides a good example of the kinds of reports you can create.

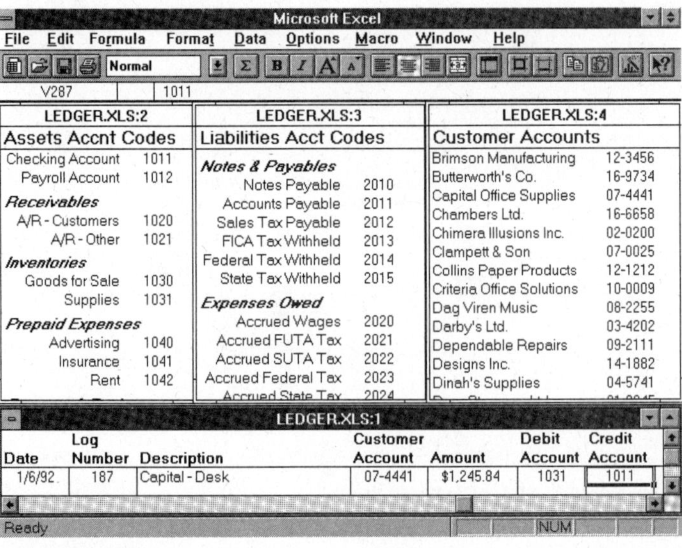

Figure 23.2 Four views of the LEDGER.XLS worksheet.

Editing Reports

Your reports will print in the order in which you selected the sections. If you want to change that order—or make any other modifications—you can edit your reports. Follow these steps:

1. Choose File Print Report. Excel displays the Print Report dialog box.

2. In the **R**eports box, highlight the report you want to edit.

3. Select the Edit button. Excel displays the Edit Report dialog box.

4. To add a section (or use a different combination of views and scenarios), choose the view and scenario from the Report Section, and select the Add button.

5. To change the section order, highlight the appropriate section in the Current **S**ections list and use the Move Up and Move Down buttons to place the section where you want it.

6. To delete a section, highlight the section in the Current **S**ections list, and select the Delete button.

7. Select OK or press Enter. Excel returns you to the Print Report dialog box.

8. Select the Close button to return to the worksheet.

To Edit a Report:

1. Choose File Print Report.
2. Highlight report to edit.
3. Select Edit.
4. To add a section, choose the view and scenario and select Add.
5. To change section order, highlight a section and use Move Up and Move Down to place it.
6. To delete a section, highlight the section and select Delete.
7. Select OK.
8. Select Close.

Printing a Report

To Print a Report:

1. Choose File Print Report.
2. Highlight report to print.
3. Select Print.
4. Select print options.
5. Select OK.

When you have defined the report to your satisfaction, you can print it out by following these steps:

1. Choose File Print Report. Excel displays the Print Report dialog box.
2. In the **R**eports box, highlight the report you want to print.
3. Select the Print button. Excel displays the Print dialog box, as shown in Figure 23.3.
4. Select the print options you want.
5. Select OK or press Enter. Excel prints the report.

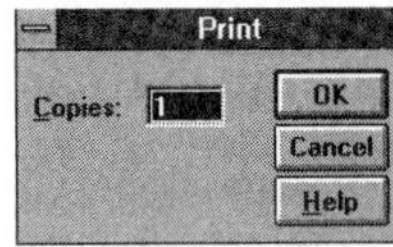

Figure 23.3 The Print dialog box.

Deleting a Report

To Delete a Report:

1. Choose File Print Report.
2. Highlight report to delete.
3. Select Delete.
4. Repeat steps 2 and 3 to delete other reports.
5. Select Close.

If you have a report you no longer use, you can delete it by following these steps:

1. Choose File Print Report. Excel displays the Print Report dialog box.
2. In the **R**eports box, highlight the report you want to delete.

3. Select the Delete button. Excel deletes the report from the Reports list.

4. Repeat steps 2 and 3 for other reports you want to delete.

5. Select Close. Excel returns you to the worksheet.

CAUTION: *Excel does not ask for confirmation* when you delete a report—so make sure each report you select is actually one you want to delete. To avoid mistakes, save your worksheet before making any deletions. This way, if you accidentally delete the wrong report, you can close the worksheet without saving your changes, and then re-open it to restore the report.

Graphics Workshop

The Graphics Workshop gives you an in-depth tour of Excel's charting and graphics features. The first part of the workshop includes sessions on creating and formatting charts, working with 3-D charts, and using chart overlays. The second part of the workshop covers topics such as drawing lines and shapes, formatting graphic objects, and creating slide shows.

Skill Session

24

Creating Charts

One of the best ways to analyze your worksheet data—or get your point across to other people—is to display your data visually in a chart. Excel gives you tremendous flexibility when creating charts; it enables you to place charts in separate documents, or directly on the worksheet itself. Not only that, but you have dozens of different chart formats to choose from—and you can further customize these charts to suit your own needs.

This skill session shows you the basics of creating and saving your Excel charts. You will learn how to create embedded charts and chart documents, and how to use Excel's new ChartWizard tool (which breaks down chart creation into a series of easy steps).

Chart Basics

Worksheet charts have their own terminology; you will need to become familiar with it. Figure 24.1 points out the various parts of a typical chart, and each part is explained in Table 24.1.

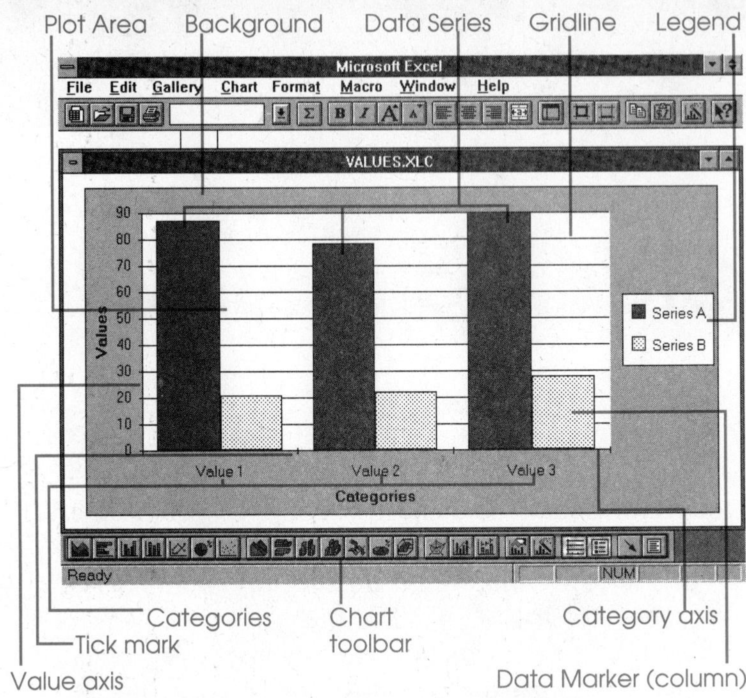

Figure 24.1 The elements of an Excel chart.

Table 24.1 The elements of an Excel chart

Element	*Description*
Background	The area on which the chart is drawn. You can change the color and border of this area.
Category	A grouping of data values on the category axis. Figure 24.1 has three categories: Value 1, Value 2, and Value 3.
Category axis	The axis (usually the X-axis) that contains the category groupings.

Element	*Description*
Data marker	A symbol that represents a specific data value. The symbol used depends on the chart type. In a column chart such as the one shown in Figure 24.1, each column is a marker.
Data series	A collection of related data values. Normally, the marker for each value in a series has the same pattern. Figure 24.1 has two series: Series A and Series B. These are identified in the legend.
Data value	A single piece of data. Also called a *data point.*
Gridlines	Optional horizontal and/or vertical extensions of the axis tick marks; these make data values easier to read.
Legend	A guide that shows the colors, patterns, and symbols used by the markers for each data series.
Plot area	The area bounded by the category and value axes containing the data points and gridlines.
Tick mark	A small line that intersects the category axis or the value axis, marking divisions in the chart's categories or scales.
Value axis	The axis (usually the Y-axis) that contains the data values.

Creating a Chart

Creating an Excel chart is usually straightforward and can often be done in only a few keystrokes or mouse clicks. However, a bit of background on how Excel converts your worksheet data into a chart will help you avoid some charting pitfalls.

When Excel creates a chart, it examines both the shape and the contents of the range you have selected. From this data, the program makes various assumptions to determine what should be on the category axis, what should be on the value axis, how to label the categories, and which labels should show within the legend.

The first assumption that Excel makes is that there are *more data categories than data series*. This makes sense because most graphs plot a small number of series over many different intervals. For example, a chart showing monthly sales and profit over a year has two data series (the sales and profit numbers) but 12 categories (the monthly intervals). Consequently, Excel assumes that the category axis (the X-axis) of your chart runs along the longest side of the selected worksheet range.

NOTE: If the range has the same number of rows and columns, Excel uses the columns as categories.

The chart shown in Figure 24.2 is a plot of the range B2:E4 in the VALUES1 worksheet. Since, in this case, the range has more columns than rows, Excel uses each column as a category. Conversely, Figure 24.3 shows the plot of a range with more rows than columns. In this case, Excel uses each row as a category.

The second assumption that Excel makes involves *the location of* labels for *categories and data series*.

- For a range with *more columns than rows* (such as in Figure 24.2), Excel uses the contents of the top row (row 2, in Figure 24.2) as the category labels, and the leftmost column (column B, in Figure 24.2) as the data series labels.

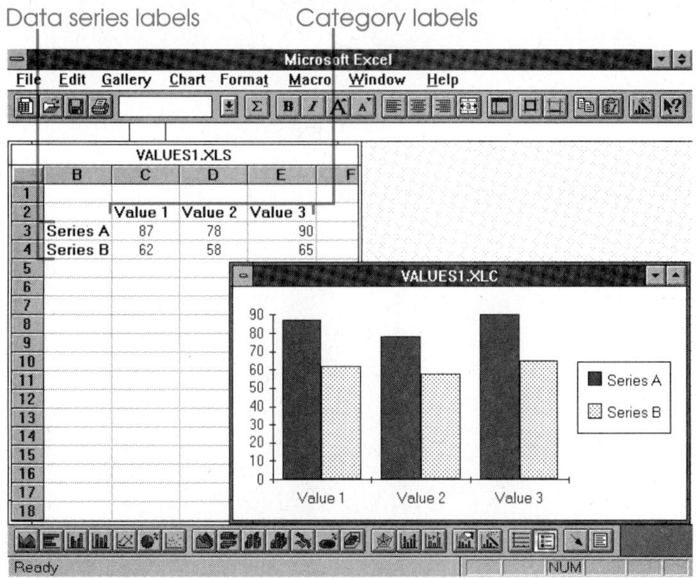

Figure 24.2 A range with more columns than rows.

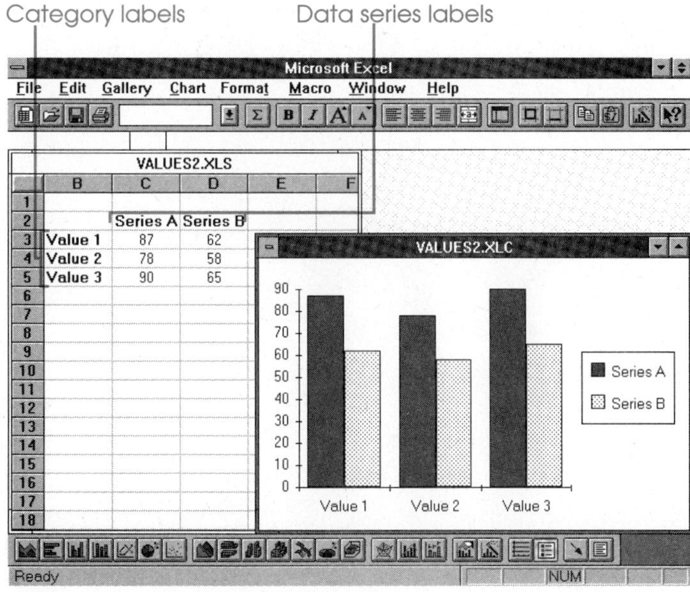

Figure 24.3 A range with more rows than columns.

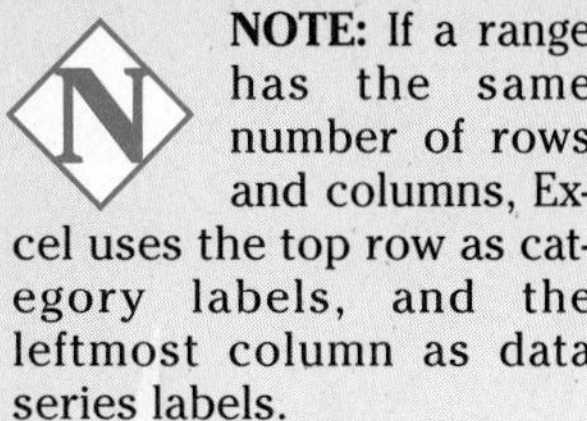

NOTE: If a range has the same number of rows and columns, Excel uses the top row as category labels, and the leftmost column as data series labels.

▲ For a range with *more rows than columns* (such as in Figure 24.3), Excel uses the contents of the leftmost column (column B, in Figure 24.3) as the category labels, and the top row (row 2, in Figure 24.3) as the data series labels.

If Excel examines your selected range and finds a label, number, or date in the upper-left cell, it cannot tell the correct plot for the chart. Instead, the program displays the New Chart dialog box (see Figure 24.4) so you can define how Excel should use the long side of the range. You have the following options:

Option	Description
First Data Series	Select this option if you are plotting a range without labels.
Category (X) Axis Labels	Select this option if you want Excel to use the first row or column as the category labels.
X-Values for XY-Chart	Select this option to use the long side of the range as X-values in an XY-chart (see Skill Session 25 for an explanation of XY-charts).

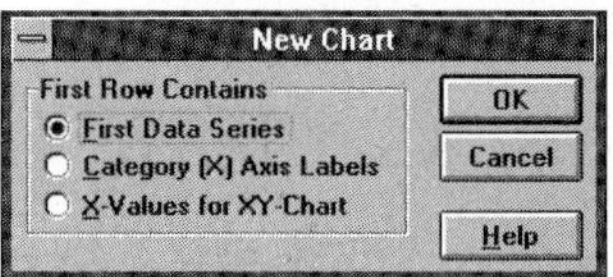

Figure 24.4 Excel displays the New Chart dialog box to define the long side of the selected range.

When plotting your worksheet data, you have two basic options: you can use the toolbar or the ChartWizard tool to create an *embedded chart* (which sits on top of your worksheet, and can be moved, sized, and formatted), or you can create a separate *chart document* by using the automatic or cut-and-paste methods. Whether you choose to embed your charts or store them in separate documents, the charts are linked with the worksheet data. Any changes you make to the data are automatically updated in the chart. The next few sections discuss each of these techniques.

> **IN ACTION:** Since you can print embedded charts along with your worksheet data, embedded charts are useful in presentations where you need to show plotted data and worksheet information simultaneously.

Creating an Embedded Chart Using ChartWizard

If you are unfamiliar with Excel charting methods, Excel 4's new *ChartWizard* feature can provide you with a shortcut to creating foolproof charts. The ChartWizard leads you through a 5-step process that begins with defining a worksheet range and ends with an embedded chart on your worksheet. Each step has its own dialog box that contains the step options and a number of buttons that enable you to skip steps, repeat steps, or start at the beginning. Table 24.2 summarizes these buttons.

Table 24.2 The ChartWizard navigation buttons

Button	*Action*
|<<	Returns you to Step 1 of ChartWizard.
< **B**ack	Returns you to the previous ChartWizard Step.
Next >	Moves to the next ChartWizard Step.
>>	Creates a chart using the current options you have selected and exits ChartWizard.
Cancel	Exits ChartWizard without creating a chart.

Creating a Chart with ChartWizard:

1. (Optional) Select cell range to plot.
2. Click on ChartWizard tool.
3. Create chart area.
4. If necessary, select desired cell range; select Next or press Enter.
5. Select a chart type; select Next or press Enter.
6. Select a chart format; select Next or press Enter.
7. Select desired layout options; select Next or press Enter.
8. Enter desired text options; select OK or press Enter.

Follow these steps to use ChartWizard:

1. *(Optional)* Select the cell range you want to plot. (You will get another chance to select a range later in the process.)

2. Click on the ChartWizard tool on the Chart toolbar. The mouse pointer changes to a cross hair.

3. Point the cross hair to the top-left corner of the area where you want to put the chart, and then drag the mouse to the bottom-right corner of that area. Excel displays a dashed box as you drag. When you release the mouse button, Excel displays the ChartWizard–Step 1 of 5 dialog box.

4. If you did not do so earlier, select the cell range you want to chart, and then select Next or press Enter. The ChartWizard–Step 2 of 5 dialog box appears.

5. Select a chart type and then select Next or press Enter. Excel displays the ChartWizard–Step 3 of 5 dialog box.

6. Select a chart format for the chart type you se-

lected and then select Next or press Enter. The ChartWizard–Step 4 of 5 dialog box appears (see Figure 24.5).

7. Select the options that define the layout of the data series and categories in your selected range. Select Next or press Enter. Excel displays the ChartWizard–Step 5 of 5 dialog box (see Figure 24.6).

8. Enter the text options you want (see Skill Session 27 for more information on adding text objects to a chart). Select OK or press Enter. Excel draws the chart on the worksheet.

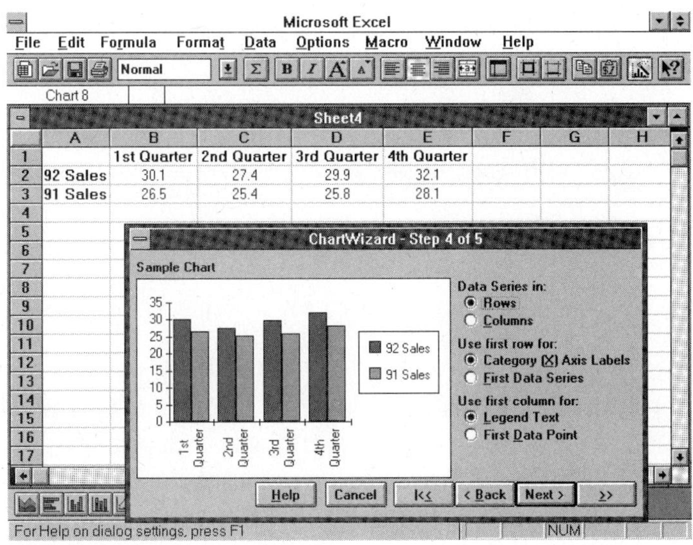

Figure 24.5 The ChartWizard–Step 4 of 5 dialog box.

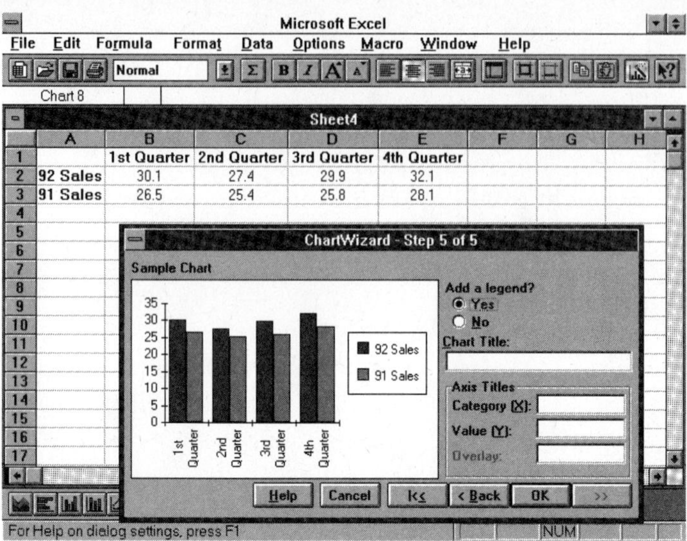

Figure 24.6 The Chart Wizard–Step 5 of 5 dialog box.

Creating an Embedded Chart with the Toolbar

If you are familiar with Excel charting, you may prefer to use the Chart toolbar to create your embedded charts. This method is much faster than the ChartWizard, since you are selecting from among the 17 preformatted chart types found on the Chart toolbar (see Figure 24.7). Make sure you have the Chart toolbar visible and then follow these steps:

Creating a Chart Using the Chart Toolbar:

1. Select cell range to plot.
2. Click on charting tool to use.

1. Select the cell range you want to plot.

2. On the Chart toolbar, click on the charting tool you want to use. To create more than one chart, double-click on the tool. The mouse pointer changes to a cross hair.

3. Point the cross hair to the upper-left corner of the area you want to use for the chart.

4. Click and drag the pointer to the bottom-right corner of the area you want to use for the chart. As you drag the mouse, Excel indicates your progress with a dashed box.

5. Release the mouse button. Excel draws the chart on the worksheet.

6. If you are creating multiple charts, repeat steps 3–5. Press Esc when you are done.

Figure 24.7 The Chart toolbar.

3. Point to upper-left corner of chart area.
4. Drag pointer to bottom-right corner of chart area.
5. Release mouse button.
6. Repeat steps 3 and 4, if needed, then press Esc.

TIP: To see the name of the chart type represented by each Chart toolbar tool, click and hold the mouse button on any tool. Excel displays the name in the status line.

TIP: To create a square chart area, hold down the Shift key while dragging the mouse. To align the chart with the worksheet gridlines, hold down the Alt key while dragging.

Creating a Chart in a Separate Document

If you don't want a chart taking up space in a worksheet, or if you want to print a chart on its own, you can create

Creating a Chart in a Separate Document:

1. Select cell range to plot.
2. Select File New.
3. Highlight Chart option in New list box.
4. Select OK.

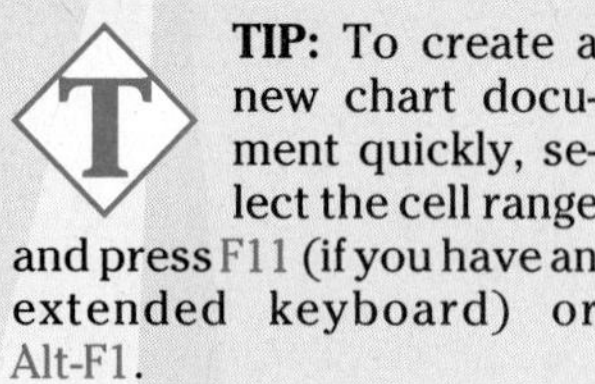

TIP: To create a new chart document quickly, select the cell range and press F11 (if you have an extended keyboard) or Alt-F1.

NOTE: When you save a chart document, Excel adds the extension `.XLC` to the file name you enter.

a separate chart document. Here are the steps to follow:

1. Select the cell range you want to plot.
2. Choose the File New command. Excel displays the New dialog box.
3. Highlight the Chart option in the New list box.
4. Select OK or press Enter. Excel opens a new document called `Chart1`, and draws the chart.

Excel displays the new chart using the default format. You can change this default to a new chart type and format (called the *preferred type*). See Skill Session 25 for instructions on setting your preferred chart type.

Creating Charts Using Cut-and-Paste

When you create a chart with the **F**ile **N**ew command, Excel automatically defines the category and value axes on the basis of the assumptions outlined earlier in this skill session. What happens, however, when your range does not fit the normal layout that Excel expects? To find out, take a look at Figure 24.8.

In this example, the plotted range has more data series (5) than data values (4). Excel therefore uses the series values on the category axis. There may be times when this is exactly what you want. If you need a more traditional arrangement, however, you will have to tell Excel to use the values on the long side of the cell as the data series. Here are the steps to follow:

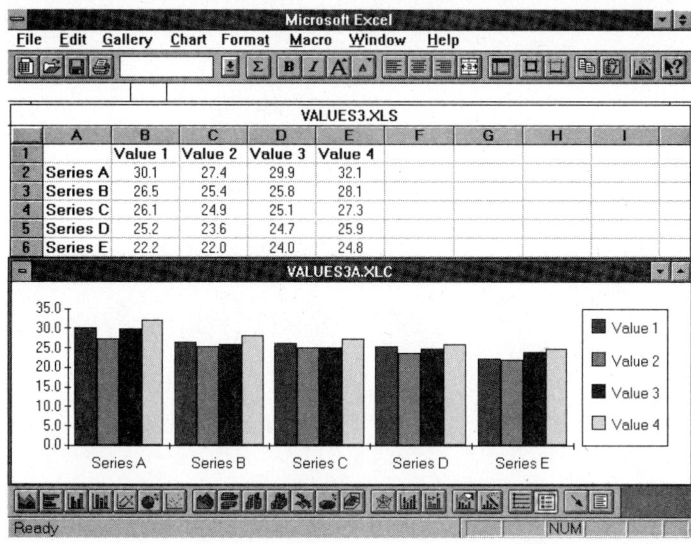

Figure 24.8 This range has more data series than data values, so Excel uses the series values as categories.

1. Select the range you want to plot.
2. Choose the Edit Copy command. Excel displays a moving border around the range.
3. Choose the File New command. Excel displays the New dialog box.
4. Highlight the Chart option in the New list box.
5. Select OK or press Enter. Excel opens a new, blank document.
6. Choose the Edit Paste Special command. The Paste Special dialog box appears, as shown in Figure 24.9.
7. In the Values (Y) in box, select Rows or Columns, depending on the layout of your range.
8. Select the other Paste Special options, as needed.

Creating a Chart Using Cut-and-Paste:

1. Select range to plot.
2. Select Edit Copy.
3. Select File New.
4. Highlight Chart option in New list box.
5. Select OK.
6. Select Edit Paste Special.
7. In Values (Y) in box, select Rows or Columns.
8. Select other Paste Special options.
9. Select OK.

9. Select OK or press Enter. Excel draws the chart.

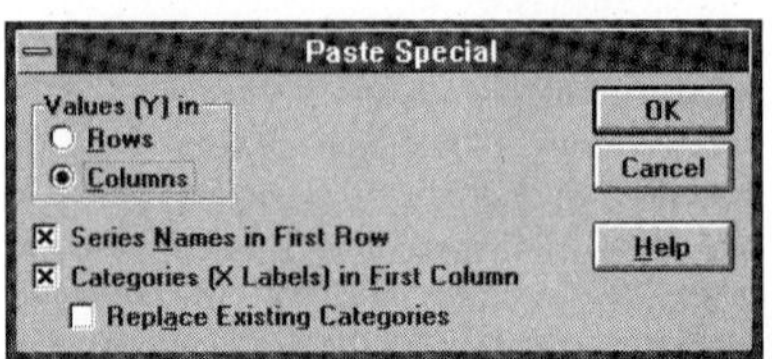

Figure 24.9 The Paste Special dialog box.

Figure 24.10 shows the VALUES3 worksheet plotted with the data series and values in the proper layout.

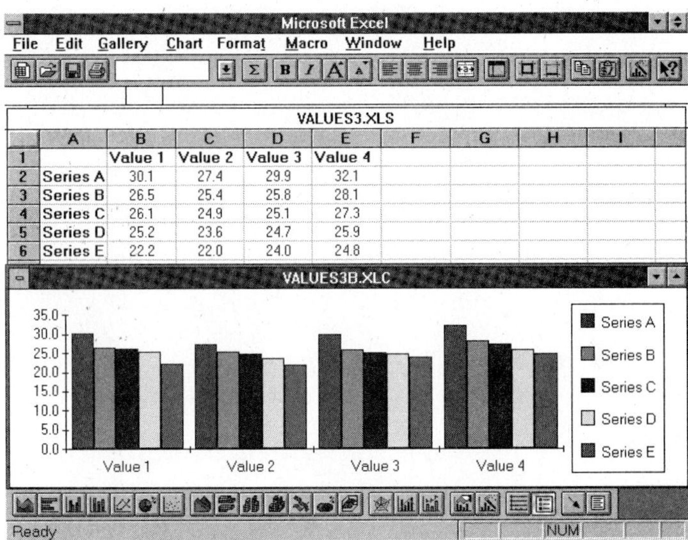

	A	B	C	D	E	F	G	H	I
1		Value 1	Value 2	Value 3	Value 4				
2	Series A	30.1	27.4	29.9	32.1				
3	Series B	26.5	25.4	25.8	28.1				
4	Series C	26.1	24.9	25.1	27.3				
5	Series D	25.2	23.6	24.7	25.9				
6	Series E	22.2	22.0	24.0	24.8				

Figure 24.10 The VALUES3 worksheet plotted with data series and values in the proper layout.

Embedding a Chart from a Separate Document

If you don't own a mouse, or if you would like to display a chart in a worksheet, you can still embed a chart by copying it from a chart document. Here are the steps to follow:

1. Activate the chart window and choose the Chart Select Chart command. Excel displays selection boxes around the chart.
2. Choose the Edit Copy command. Excel surrounds the chart with a moving border.
3. Activate the worksheet window and choose the Edit Paste command. Excel copies the chart onto the worksheet.

Embedding a Chart from a Chart Document:

1. Select Chart Select Chart.
2. Select Edit Copy.
3. Activate worksheet window and select Edit Paste.

Skill Session

25

Working with Chart Types

Whether you embed a chart in a worksheet or create a separate chart document, initially Excel plots your data using a simple column chart. If you prefer to use a different style, you can choose among Excel's 14 unique *chart types*. Each chart type contains a number of predefined formats; all told, there are nearly 100 different charts available.

This skill session explains and shows examples of seven of Excel's 2-D chart types: Area, Bar, Column, Line, Pie, Radar, and XY (for Combination charts see Skill Session 30; for 3-D charts, see Skill Session 29). You will learn how to select a different chart type by using either the Chart toolbar or the chart window's Gallery menu, and you will learn how to change the default chart.

Selecting a Chart Type

Depending on the chart, you can use one of three methods to select a different chart type:

- For an unformatted chart in a separate document or an unformatted embedded chart in a chart window, select the chart type from the **G**allery menu.
- For any unformatted chart, select a chart type from among the chart type tools on the Chart toolbar.
- For a chart already formatted with other options (such as gridlines or custom data markers), use Forma**t** **M**ain Chart to change only the chart type and leave the formatting intact.

TIP: To access the chart window commands for an embedded chart, double-click on the chart to open a chart window.

Selecting a Chart Type from the Gallery Menu

Follow these steps to use the chart window's Gallery menu to select a chart type:

1. Activate the chart window.
2. Pull down the **G**allery menu.
3. Select a chart type. Excel displays the formats available for charts in a Chart Gallery dialog box (Figure 25.1 shows one of these, which corresponds to the **A**rea chart type).

Selecting a Chart Type from the Gallery Menu:

1. Activate chart window.
2. Pull down **G**allery menu.
3. Select a chart type.
4. Select a chart format.
5. Select OK.

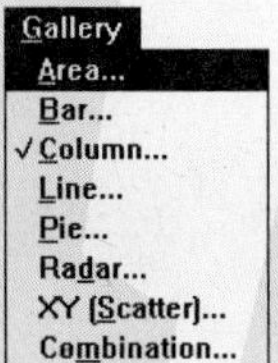

4. Select a chart format by clicking on the format, or by typing the format number. To see formats for other chart types, select the Next or Previous buttons.

5. Select OK or press Enter. Excel redraws the chart, using the new format.

CAUTION: When you select a new chart type, any formatting options you have added (such as gridlines and colors) are lost. See the section titled "Selecting a Chart Type for Formatted Charts," later in this skill session.

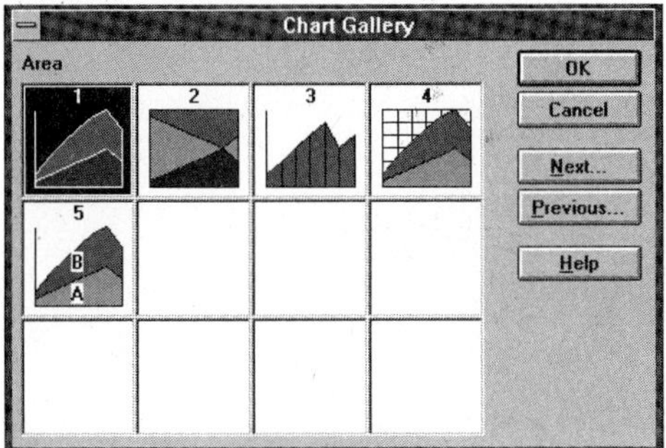

Figure 25.1 The Chart Gallery dialog box for the Area chart type.

Selecting a Chart Type from the Chart Toolbar

Follow these steps to select a chart type from the Chart toolbar:

1. Activate the chart window or select the embedded chart.

2. Click on the chart tool you want on the Chart toolbar. Excel redraws the chart, using the selected chart type.

Selecting a Chart Type from the Chart Toolbar:

1. Select chart.
2. Click on desired chart tool.

Selecting a Chart Type for Formatted Charts

To preserve any formatting options you have already applied to a chart, you can tell Excel to change *only* the chart type. Here are the steps to follow:

1. Activate the chart window (double-click on an embedded chart to place it in a window).
2. Choose Format Main Chart. Excel displays the Format Chart dialog box, as shown in Figure 25.2.
3. Select a chart type from the Main Chart Type list box. Excel displays several chart formats in the Data View area.
4. Select a chart format from the Data View area.
5. Select OK or press Enter. Excel redraws the chart while preserving your formatting options.

Selecting a Chart Type for Formatted Charts:

1. Activate chart window.
2. Select Format Main Chart.
3. Select a chart type.
4. Select a chart format.
5. Select OK.

TIP: For a brief description of each tool in the Chart toolbar, click and hold the left mouse button on any tool. Be sure to move the mouse pointer off the tool before releasing the button.

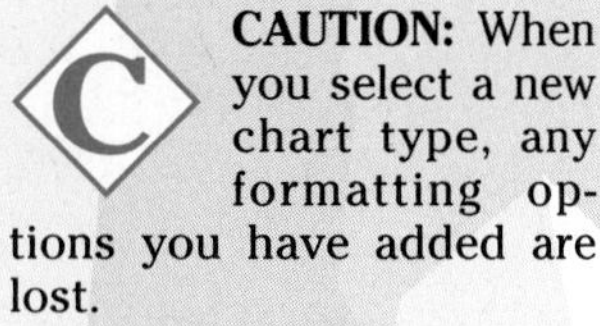

CAUTION: When you select a new chart type, any formatting options you have added are lost.

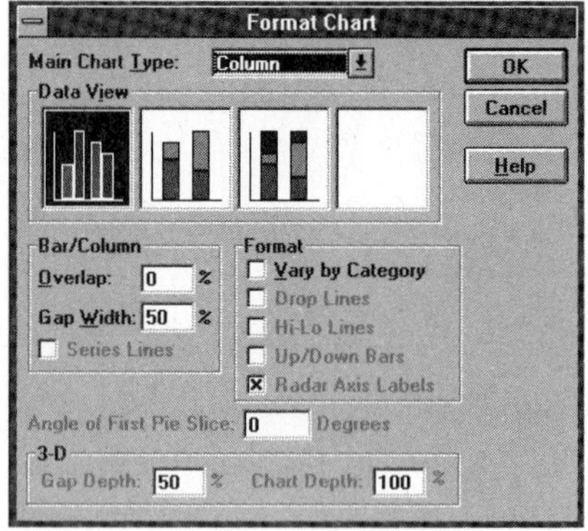

Figure 25.2 The Format Chart dialog box.

Working with 2-D Area Charts

Area charts show the relative contributions over time that each data series makes to the whole picture. The smaller the area a data series takes up, the smaller its contribution to the whole. For example, Figure 25.3 shows an area chart comparing yearly mortgage principal and interest over the 25-year term of a loan. The straight line across the top of the chart—at about $19,000—indicates the total yearly mortgage payment (the line is straight because the payments are constant over the term). The two areas below this line show the relative contributions of principal and interest paid each year. As you can see, the area representing yearly principal increases over time, which means that the amount of principal in each payment will increase as the term of the loan progresses.

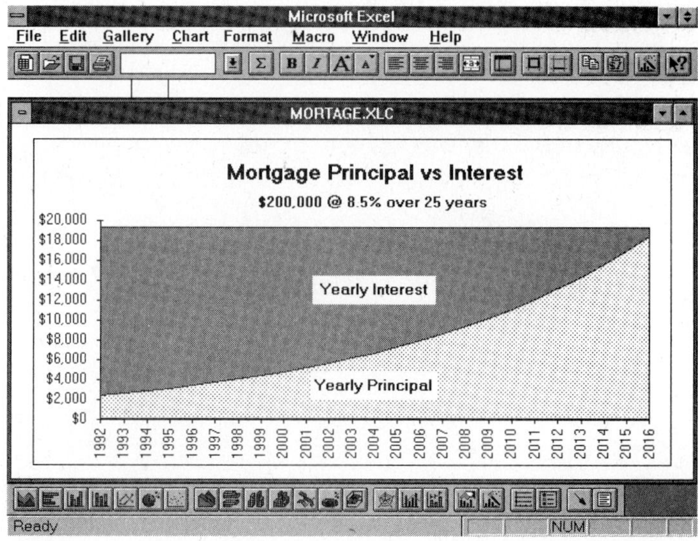

Figure 25.3 An area chart comparing mortgage principal and interest.

IN ACTION: Use area charts to show the relative contributions over time of individual expense categories, sales regions, and production costs.

Click on this tool on the Chart toolbar to select an area chart.

Excel offers five different area chart formats. To display the Area Chart Gallery, select Gallery Area.

Working with 2-D Bar Charts

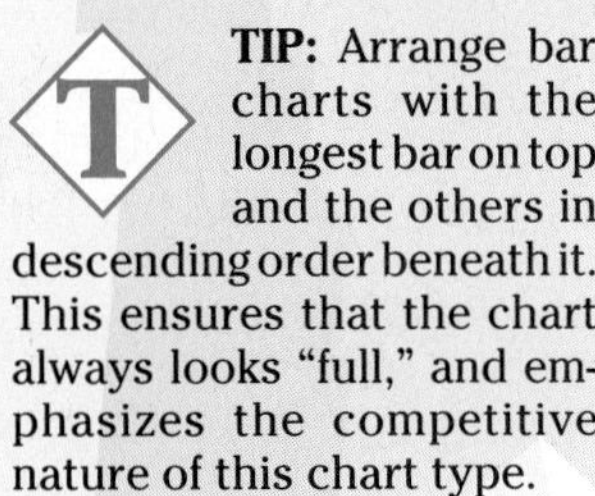

TIP: Arrange bar charts with the longest bar on top and the others in descending order beneath it. This ensures that the chart always looks "full," and emphasizes the competitive nature of this chart type.

Bar charts compare distinct items, or show single items at distinct intervals. A bar chart is laid out with categories along the vertical axis and values along the horizontal axis. This format lends itself to competitive comparisons, because categories appear to be "ahead" or "behind." For example, Figure 25.4 shows a comparison of parking tickets written in a single month by four officers. You can easily see that the officer on top is the "winner," because the top bar extends farther to the right than anyone else's.

IN ACTION: Use bar charts to show the results of sales contests, elections, sporting events, or any competitive activity.

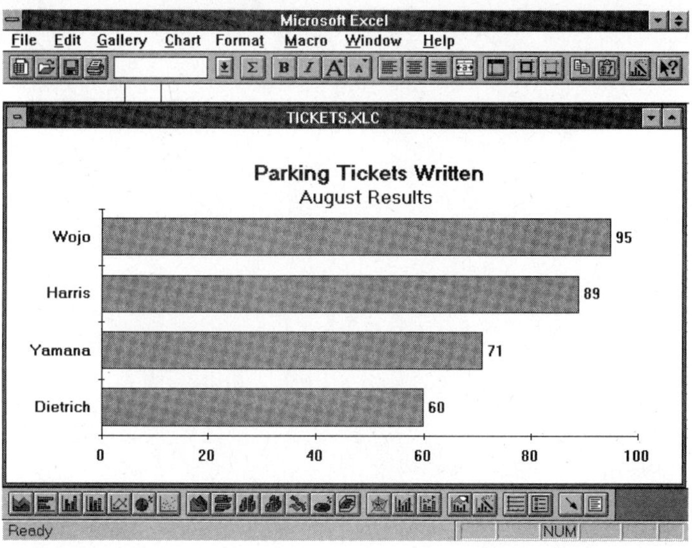

Figure 25.4 Bar charts are useful for competitive comparisons.

Excel offers ten different bar chart formats. To display the bar Chart Gallery, select **Gallery Bar**.

Click on this tool on the Chart toolbar to select a bar chart.

Working with 2-D Column Charts

Like bar charts, *column charts* compare distinct items or show single items at distinct intervals. However, a column chart is laid out with categories along the *horizontal* axis and values along the *vertical* axis (as are most Excel charts). This format is best suited for comparing items over time. For example, Figure 25.5 uses a column chart to show another view of the mortgage principal and interest comparison. In this case, it is easier to see the individual amounts for principal and interest, and how they change over time.

TIP: Try to keep the number of series in a column chart to a minimum. Having too many series causes the columns to become too narrow; the chart becomes confusing and difficult to read.

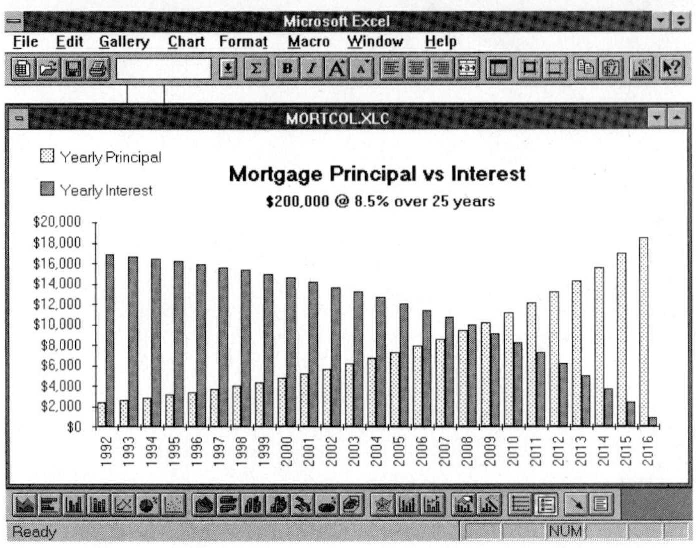

Figure 25.5 A column chart showing the mortgage principal and interest comparison.

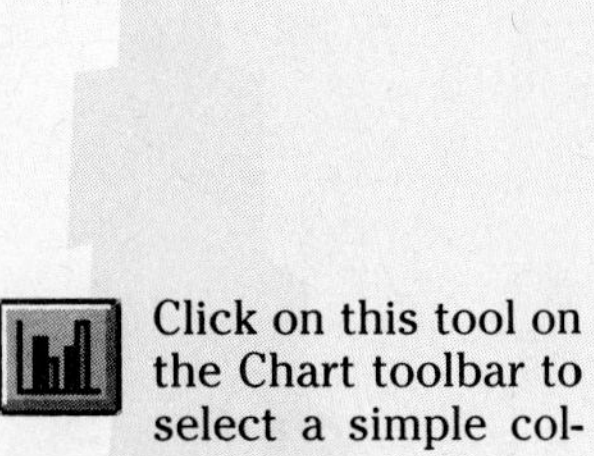

Click on this tool on the Chart toolbar to select a simple column chart.

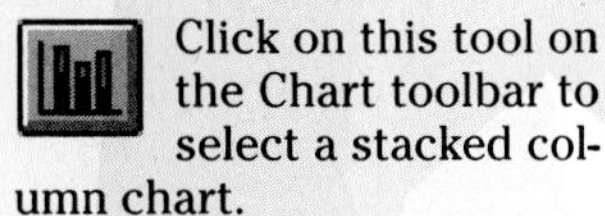

Click on this tool on the Chart toolbar to select a stacked column chart.

To display the column Chart Gallery, select Gallery Column. Excel offers ten different column chart formats, including *stacked* columns. A *stacked column chart* is similar to an area chart; series values are stacked on top of each other to show you the relative contributions of each series. While an area chart is useful for showing the flow of the relative contributions over time, a stacked column chart is better for seeing the contributions at discrete intervals. Figure 25.6 shows the mortgage principal and interest comparison as a stacked column chart.

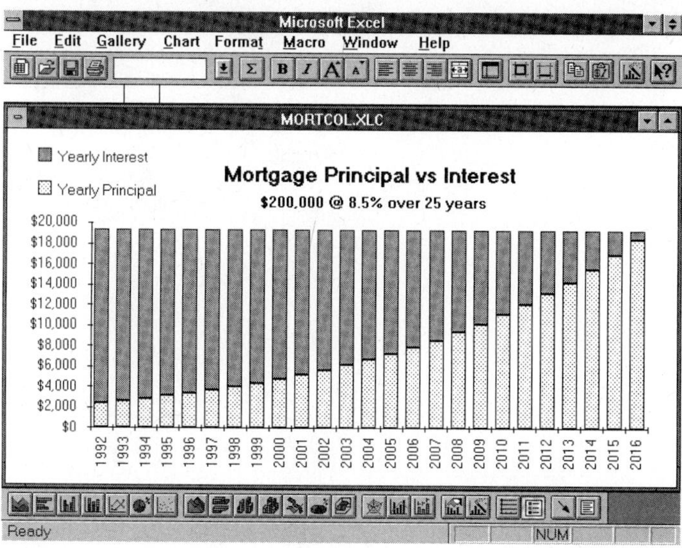

Figure 25.6 The mortgage principal and interest comparison as a stacked column chart.

Working with 2-D Line Charts

Line charts show how a data series changes over time. The category (X) axis represents a progression of even increments (such as days or months), and the series points are plotted on the value (Y) axis. Figure 25.7 shows a simple line chart that displays a month of daily closing figures for the Dow Jones Industrial Average.

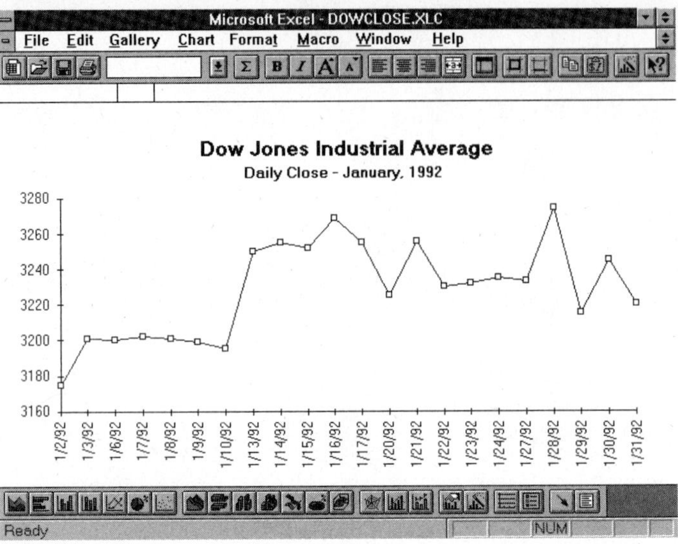

Figure 25.7 A line chart showing daily closes for the Dow Jones.

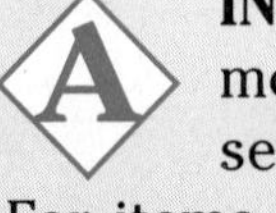

IN ACTION: Use line charts when you are more concerned with the *trend* of a data series than with the actual quantities. For items such as interest rates, inflation, and profits, it is often just as important to know the *direction* of the data as it is to know the specific numbers.

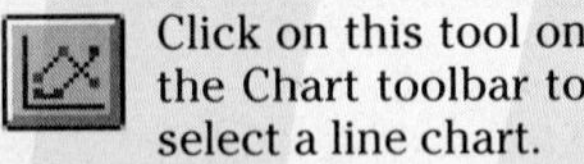

Click on this tool on the Chart toolbar to select a line chart.

To display the line Chart Gallery, select Gallery Line. Excel offers nine different line chart formats, including a *High- Low-Close chart*, which is useful for plotting stock market prices. Make sure your data is in High, Low, Close order, and then select format number 8 from the Chart Gallery. Figure 25.8 shows the Dow Jones Industrial Average plotted as a High, Low, Close chart.

Working with Radar Charts

Radar charts make comparisons within a data series and between data series relative to a center point. Each category is shown with a value axis extending from the center point. To understand this, think of a radar screen in an airport control tower. The tower itself is the central point, and the radar radiates a beam (a value axis). When the radar makes contact with a plane, a blip appears on the screen. In a radar chart, this is a data point and is shown with a data marker.

One common use for a radar chart is to make comparisons between products. For example, suppose you want to buy a new notebook computer. You decide to base your decision on six categories: price, weight, battery life, screen quality, keyboard quality, and service. To get a consistent scale, you rank each machine on a scale of, say, 1 to 10 for each category. When you graph this data on a radar chart, the computer that covers the most area is the better computer. Figure 25.10 shows an example of this kind of analysis. In this case, Notebook "A" is the better choice.

Excel offers five different radar chart formats. To display the radar Chart Gallery, select Gallery Radar.

Click on this tool on the Chart toolbar to select a radar chart.

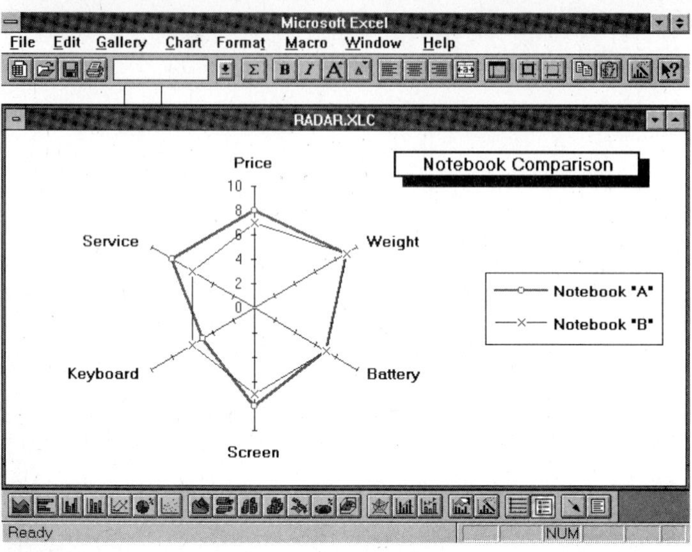

Figure 25.10 Using a radar chart to compare products.

Working with XY (Scatter) Charts

An *XY chart* (also called a *scatter chart*) shows the relationship between numeric values in two different data series, or it can plot a series of data pairs in XY coordinates. An XY chart is a variation of the line chart in which the category axis is replaced by a second value axis. Figure 25.11 shows a plot of Newton's Law of Gravitation where the X-axis represents the distance (r) between two objects, and the Y-axis represents the gravitational force between them.

NOTE: In Figure 25.11, the distance *r* is called the *independent variable* because you can control the series values. The force *F* is called the *dependent variable* because you cannot control these values. Excel always plots the independent variable on the X-axis and the dependent variable on the Y-axis.

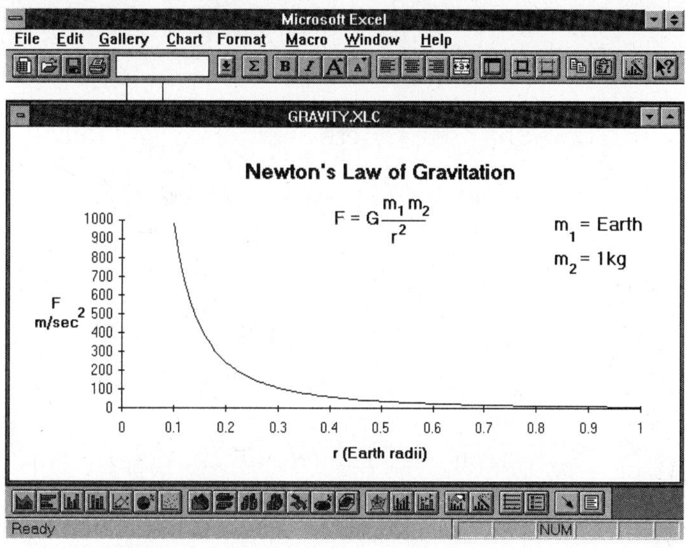

Figure 25.11 An XY chart of Newton's Law of Gravitation.

IN ACTION: Use XY charts for plotting items such as survey data, mathematical functions, and experimental results.

Excel offers five different XY chart formats. To display the XY Chart Gallery, select Gallery XY (Scatter).

Click on this tool on the Chart toolbar to select an XY chart.

Setting a Preferred Chart Type

Many people use the same type of chart regularly. For example, stockbrokers use High, Low, Close line charts, scientists use XY charts, and so on. If you have a specific chart type and format you prefer, you can tell Excel to use this type and format as the *default* for any new charts you create. Here are the steps to follow:

1. Create a chart (or activate an existing chart) with the type and format you prefer.

2. Run Gallery Set Preferred. Excel saves the chart type and format as the default.

To change any active chart to the preferred type, choose Gallery Preferred. You should note that the *preferred format* is only in effect for the current work session. You have to specify your preferred format each time you start Excel.

Setting the Preferred Chart Type:

1. Create chart with desired type and format.
2. Select Gallery Set Preferred.

Click on this tool in the Chart toolbar to change the active chart to the preferred type.

TIP: To save a preferred chart setting, select File Save Workbook or create a template that contains the preferred chart type. See the File Management Workshop for information on Excel workbooks and templates.

Skill Session

26

Enhancing Charts

After you have created a chart and selected the appropriate chart type, you can enhance the chart's appearance by formatting any of the various chart elements. This skill session shows you how to format chart axes, data markers, and gridlines as well as how to move and size an embedded chart.

Selecting Chart Elements

An Excel chart is composed of elements such as axes, data markers, gridlines, and text, each with its own formatting options. Before you can format an element, however, you need to select it. Table 26.1 lists the mouse techniques to use to select various chart items.

Table 26.1 Mouse techniques for selecting chart elements

To Select	*Click*
Entire chart	Just outside the plot area
Plot area	On an empty part of the plot area
Axis	On the axis or an axis label
Gridlines	On a gridline
Data series	On any marker in the series
Data marker	On the marker while holding down the Ctrl key
Chart object	On the object

TIP: To select the entire chart, select Chart Select Chart. To select the plot area, select Chart Select Plot Area.

If you do not have a mouse, or if you prefer to use the keyboard, you can navigate the chart elements using the arrow keys. To make navigating the chart easier, Excel divides the chart elements into the following *categories*:

Plot area	Text	Hi-lo lines
3-D floor	Arrows	Up-down bars
3-D walls	Gridlines	Series lines
Axes	Data series	Radar axis labels

A category can contain several elements. For example, the Axes category contains both the value axis and the category axis. You use the arrow keys to move between or within categories, as outlined in Table 26.2.

Table 26.2 Keyboard techniques for selecting chart elements

To Select	*Press*
First element in the next category	Up arrow
Last element in the previous category	Down arrow
Next element in the current category	Right arrow
Previous element in the current category	Left arrow

When you select a chart element, Excel displays the name of the element in the reference area of the formula bar, and it attaches *selection handles* to the element. For items that cannot be moved, such as the plot area or the chart title, the handles are white squares. For movable objects, such as arrows and legends, the handles are black squares. Figure 26.1 shows a chart with the plot area selected.

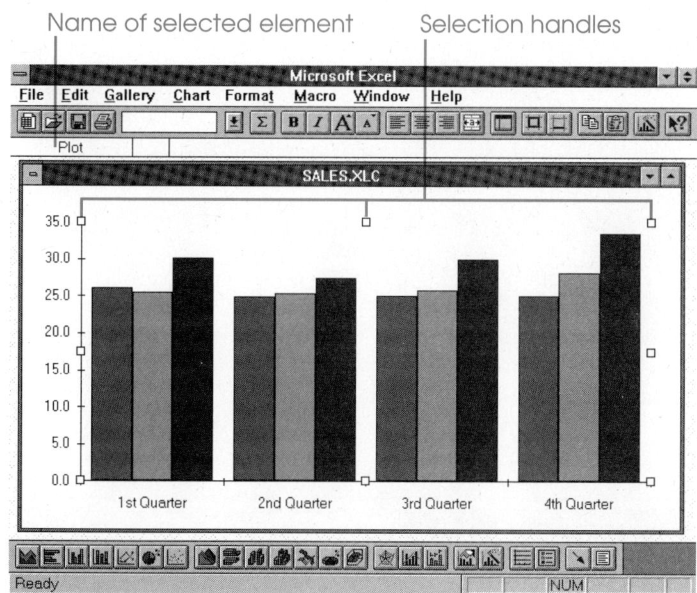

Figure 26.1 Excel surrounds selected chart elements with selection handles.

Formatting Chart Axes

Excel gives you a number of options for controlling the appearance of your chart axes. You can hide axes; set the typeface, size, and style of axis labels; format the axis lines and tick marks; and adjust the axis scale.

Hiding and Displaying Axes

If you like, you can hide a chart axis. This is useful if you add custom category or value labels to your chart (covered in Skill Session 27). For example, Figure 26.2 shows a line chart where custom category labels have been added to the plot area, making the category axis unnecessary.

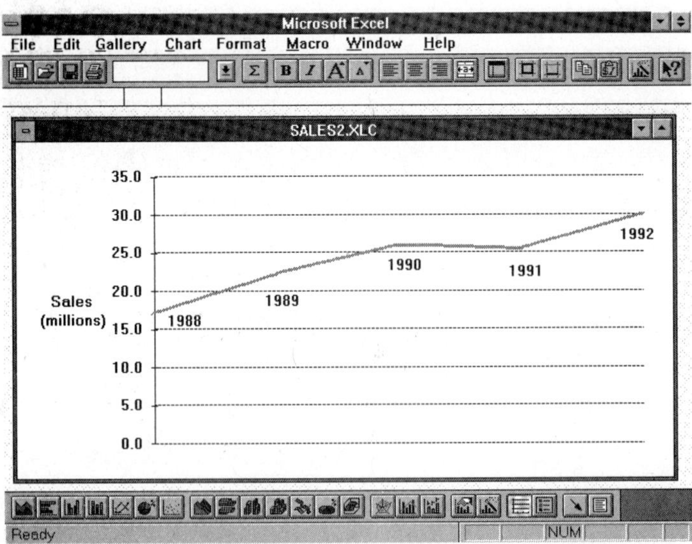

Figure 26.2 You may want to hide an axis when you use custom labels.

Follow these steps to hide an axis:

1. Select the axis you want to hide, using the techniques outlined earlier in this chapter.
2. Select Chart Axes. The Axes dialog box appears, as shown in Figure 26.3.
3. Deselect the check box for the axis you want to hide.
4. Select OK or press Enter. Excel hides both the axis and the axis labels from the chart.

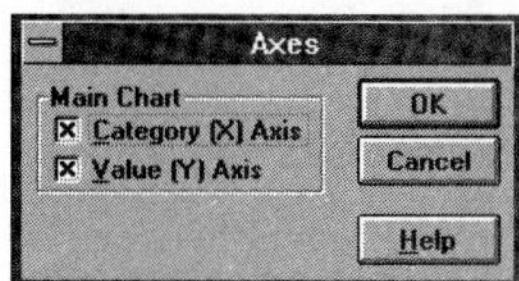

Figure 26.3 The Axes dialog box.

Hiding an Axis:

1. Select axis to hide.
2. Select Chart Axes.
3. Deselect check box for axis.
4. Select OK.

TIP: To open the Axes dialog box quickly, right-click on an axis, or select an axis and press Shift+F10, and then choose Axes from the shortcut menu that appears.

Formatting Axis Patterns

You can format the axis line with different styles, colors, or weights. You can also change the axis tick marks and reposition tick labels. Here are the steps to follow:

1. Select the axis you want to format.
2. Select Format Patterns. Excel displays the Patterns dialog box, as shown in Figure 26.4.
3. Enter the options you want in the Axis, Tick Mark Type, and Tick Labels sections.
4. Select OK or press Enter.

Formatting Axis Patterns:

1. Select axis to format.
2. Select Format Patterns.
3. Enter desired options.
4. Select OK.

TIP: To access the Patterns dialog box quickly, double-click on an axis. Alternatively, right-click on an axis, or select an axis and press Shift+F10. Then choose Patterns from the shortcut menu that appears.

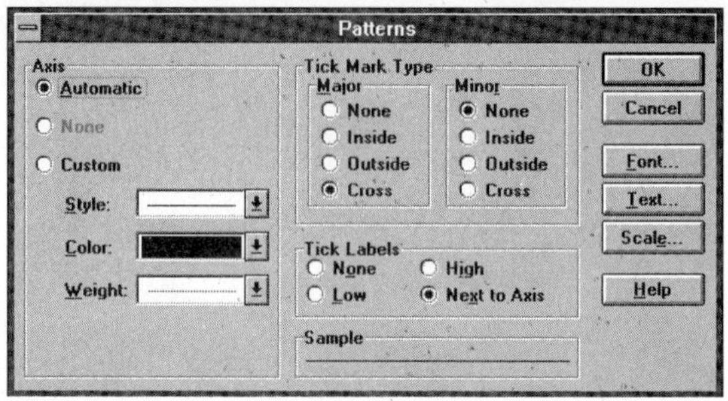

Figure 26.4 The Patterns dialog box.

Formatting Axis Labels

You can format both the font and, separately, the orientation of axis labels. To change the label font, follow these steps:

Formatting the Axis Label Font:

1. Select axis to format.
2. Select Format Font.
3. Enter desired options.
4. Select OK.

1. Select the axis you want to format.

2. Select Format Font. Excel displays the Font dialog box.

3. Enter the options you want for the typeface, style, size, effects, and color.

4. Select OK or press Enter.

TIP: To access the Font dialog box quickly, right-click on an axis, or select an axis and press Shift+F10, and then choose Font from the shortcut menu that appears.

When formatting the numbers used as value axis labels, Excel uses the format of the first number in the first data series. So, to change the format of your chart labels, simply reformat the appropriate worksheet cell.

Select an axis and click on any font tool (such as the Bold tool shown) from either the Standard or Formatting toolbar.

To change the label orientation, follow these steps:

1. Select the axis you want to format.
2. Select Format Text. Excel displays the Text dialog box, as shown in Figure 26.5.
3. Select the orientation you want.
4. Select OK or press Enter.

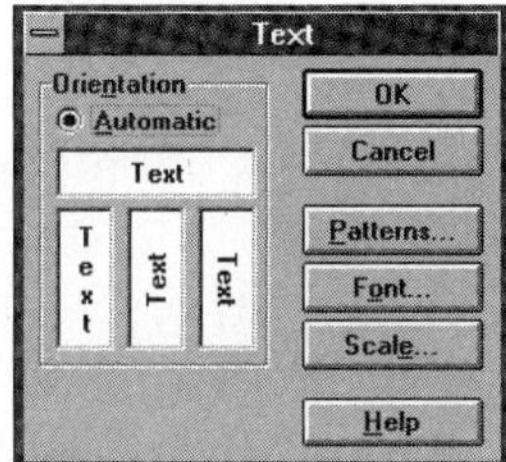

Figure 26.5 The Text dialog box.

Formatting Axis Label Orientation:

1. Select axis to format.
2. Select Format Text.
3. Enter desired options.
4. Select OK.

TIP: To access the Text dialog box quickly, right-click on an axis, or select an axis and press Shift+F10, and then choose Text from the shortcut menu that appears.

Formatting an Axis Scale

You can format the scale of your chart axes to set such things as the range of numbers on an axis and where the category and value axes intersect.

When you format the value axis scale, Excel displays the Axis Scale dialog box shown in Figure 26.6. The Minimum and Maximum numbers set the axis range, and the Major Unit and Minor Unit numbers control the frequency of tick marks. Use Category (X) Axis Crosses at or Category (X) Crosses at Maximum Value to set the position of the category axis.

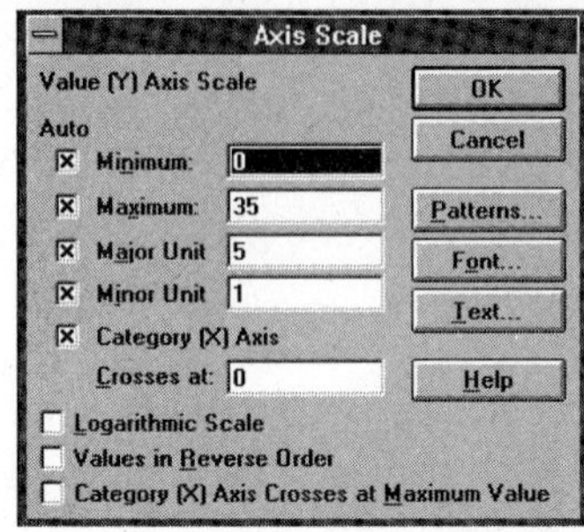

Figure 26.6 The Axis Scale dialog box for the value (Y) axis.

Formatting the value axis scale properly can make a big difference in the impact of your charts. For example, Figure 26.7 shows the sales chart presented earlier with the value axis range now reduced. As you can see, the trend of the data is now much clearer and more dramatic.

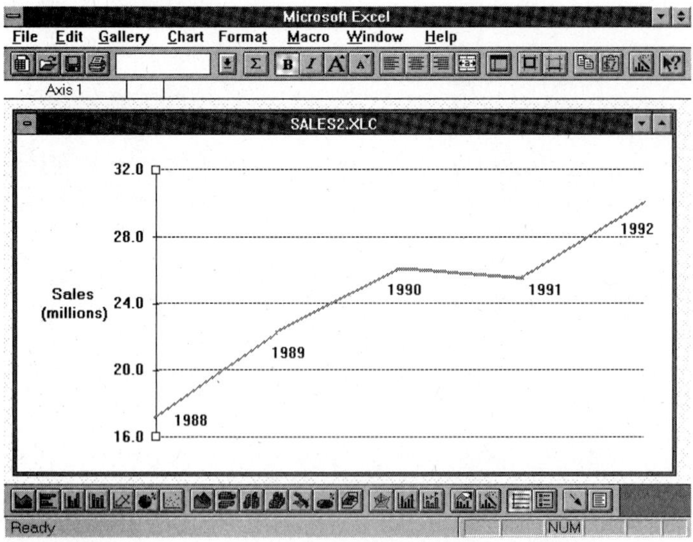

Figure 26.7 Reduce the value axis range to emphasize chart trends.

When you format the category axis scale, Excel displays the Axis Scale dialog box shown in Figure 26.8. Use the options in this dialog box to format the display of category labels and to position the intersection of the two axes.

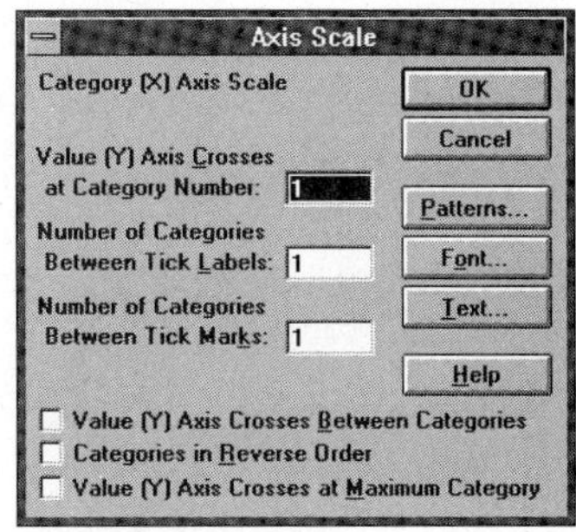

Figure 26.8 The Axis Scale dialog box for the category (X) axis.

Follow these steps to format an axis scale:

1. Select the axis you want to scale.
2. Select Format Scale to display the appropriate Axis Scale dialog box.
3. Select the scale options you want.
4. Select OK or press Enter.

Formatting an Axis Scale:

1. Select axis to scale.
2. Select Format Scale.
3. Select the scale options.
4. Select OK.

TIP: To access the Axis Scale dialog box quickly, right-click on an axis, or select an axis and press Shift+F10, and then choose Scale from the shortcut menu that appears.

Formatting Chart Data Markers

A *data marker* is the symbol that Excel uses to plot each number. Examples of data markers are small circles or squares for line charts, rectangles for column and bar charts, and pie slices for pie charts. Depending on the type of marker, you can format the color, pattern, marker style, or border.

Figure 26.9 shows the Patterns dialog box for an area, bar, column, or pie chart marker. Use the Border section to set the **S**tyle, **C**olor, and **W**eight of the marker border. Use the Area section to assign marker colors and patterns.

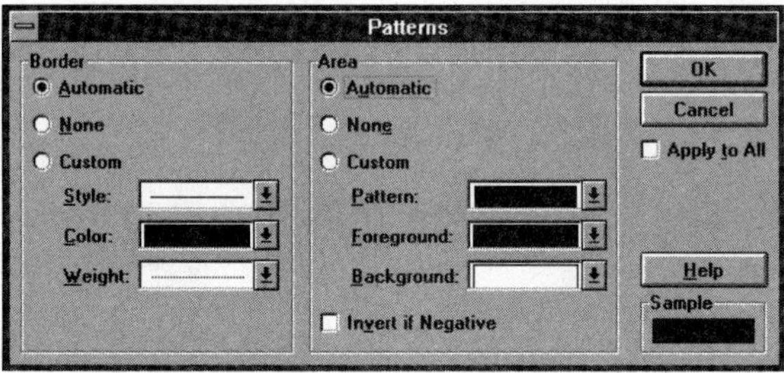

Figure 26.9 The Patterns dialog box for area, bar, column, and pie charts.

You get a different set of options when you format your line, XY, or radar chart markers, as shown in Figure 26.10. Use the Line section to format the **S**tyle, **C**olor, and **W**eight of the data series line and use the Marker section to format the marker Sty**l**e and **F**oreground and **B**ackground colors.

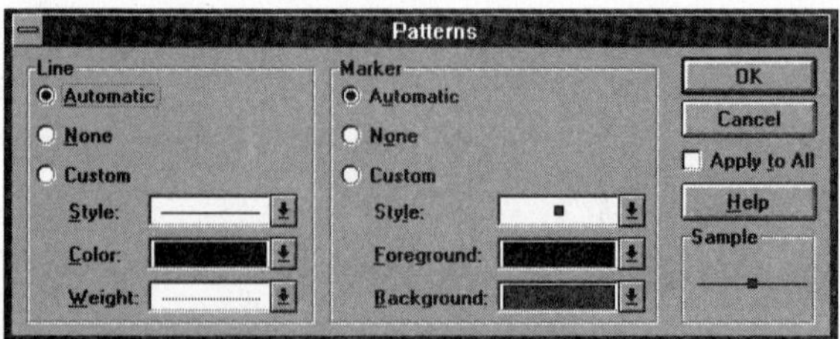

Figure 26.10 The Patterns dialog box for line, XY, and radar charts.

Follow these steps to format your chart data markers:

1. Select the series or marker you want to format.
2. Select Format Patterns to display the appropriate Patterns dialog box.
3. Select the marker options.
4. Select OK or press Enter.

Formatting Chart Data Markers:

1. Select series or marker to format.
2. Select Format Patterns.
3. Select desired marker options.
4. Select OK.

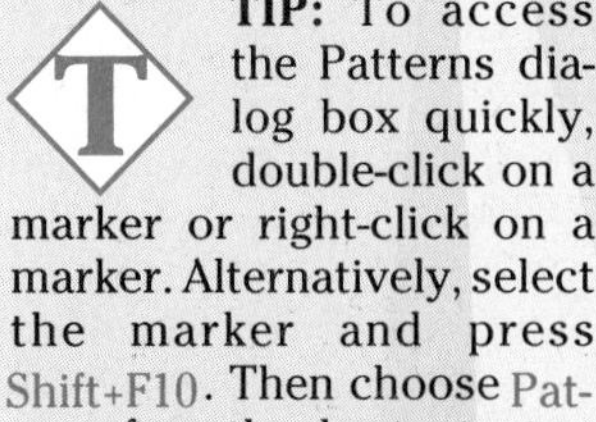

TIP: To access the Patterns dialog box quickly, double-click on a marker or right-click on a marker. Alternatively, select the marker and press Shift+F10. Then choose Patterns from the shortcut menu that appears.

Displaying and Formatting Chart Gridlines

Adding horizontal or vertical gridlines can make your charts easier to read. For each axis, you can display either a major or minor gridline (or both). The positioning of these gridlines is determined by the numbers you entered for the axis scales. For a value axis, major gridlines are governed by the Major Unit and minor gridlines are governed by the Minor Unit. For a category axis, major gridlines are governed by the number of categories between tick labels, and the minor gridlines are governed by the number of categories between tick marks. Follow these steps to display gridlines:

1. Select Chart Gridlines. Excel displays the Gridlines dialog box, as shown in Figure 26.11.
2. Select the gridlines you want to display.
3. Select OK or press Enter.

TIP: If you originally selected only a single data marker, you can apply your formatting to the entire data series by selecting Apply to All in the Patterns dialog box.

Displaying Gridlines:

1. Select Chart Gridlines.
2. Select gridlines.
3. Select OK.

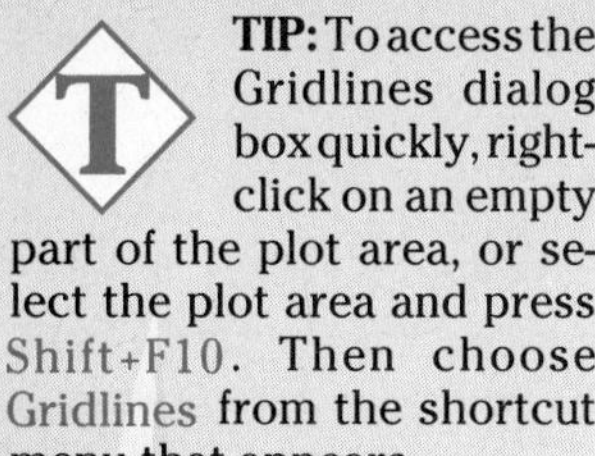

TIP: To access the Gridlines dialog box quickly, right-click on an empty part of the plot area, or select the plot area and press Shift+F10. Then choose Gridlines from the shortcut menu that appears.

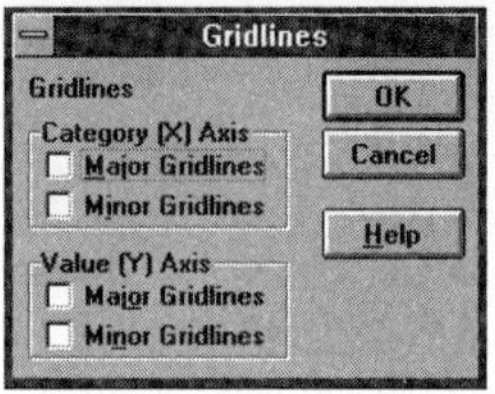

Figure 26.11 The Gridlines dialog box.

Click on this tool in the Chart toolbar to display value axis gridlines on your chart quickly.

Formatting Gridlines:

1. Select a gridline.
2. Select Format Patterns.
3. Select gridline options.
4. Select OK.

You can format the style, color, and weight of your gridlines by following these steps:

1. Select a gridline.
2. Select Format Patterns. Excel displays the Patterns dialog box.
3. Select the gridline options you want.
4. Select OK or press Enter.

TIP: To access the Patterns dialog box quickly, double-click on a gridline. Alternatively, right-click on a gridline, or select the gridline and press Shift+F10. Then choose Patterns from the shortcut menu that appears.

Formatting the Plot Area and Background

You can format borders, patterns, and colors for both the chart plot area and background. To format the plot area, follow these steps:

1. Select the plot area.
2. Select Format Patterns. Excel displays the Patterns dialog box.

Formatting the Plot Area:

1. Select plot area.
2. Select Format Patterns.
3. Select options for Border and Area.
4. Select OK.

3. Select the options you want for the Border and Area.

4. Select OK or press Enter.

Use the same steps to format the chart background. To add a shadow to the chart background, select Shadow in the Patterns dialog box.

TIP: To access the Patterns dialog box quickly, double-click on an empty part of the plot area. Alternatively, right-click on the plot area, or select the plot area and press Shift+F10. Then choose Patterns from the shortcut menu that appears.

Sizing an Embedded Chart

You can size charts embedded in a worksheet to suit your needs. Like other Excel objects, when you select an embedded chart, a number of *selection handles* appear around the chart. You size the chart by dragging these handles with your mouse pointer. Here are the steps to follow:

1. Select the chart you want to size. Excel displays selection handles around the chart, as shown in Figure 26.12.

2. Position the mouse pointer over the appropriate handle to adjust the chart. The pointer changes to a two-headed arrow (see Figure 26.12).

3. Drag the handle to the position you want.

4. Release the mouse button. Excel changes the chart size.

5. Repeat steps 2–4 to adjust other sides of the chart.

6. Press Esc or click outside the chart.

Sizing an Embedded Chart:

1. Select chart to size.
2. Position mouse pointer over a handle.
3. Drag handle.
4. Release mouse button.
5. Repeat steps 2–4, if needed.
6. Press Esc or click outside the chart.

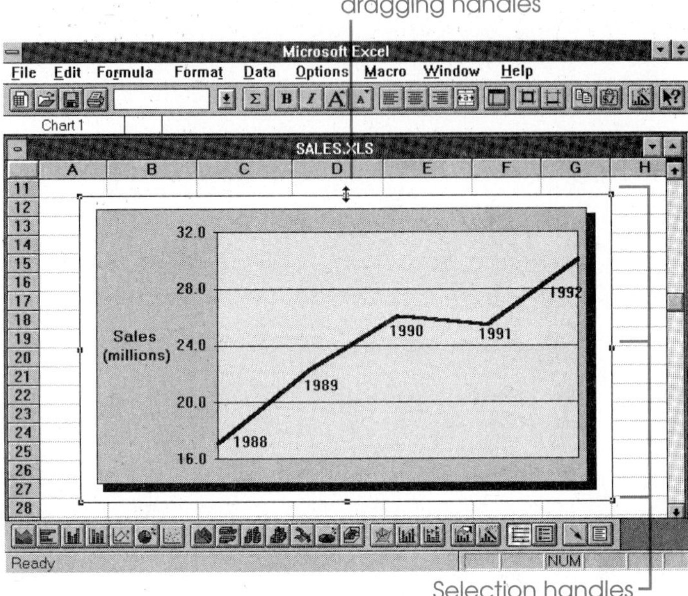

Figure 26.12 Size a chart by dragging the sizing handles.

Moving an Embedded Chart

Moving an Embedded Chart:

1. Select chart to move.
2. Point to edge of chart background.

As your worksheets grow, you may find that embedded charts are getting in the way. You can move these charts by following these steps:

1. Select the chart you want to move.
2. Position the mouse pointer on the edge of the chart background.

3. Drag the mouse pointer to position the chart where you want it. Excel displays the new chart position with a dashed outline.

4. Release the mouse button. Excel moves the chart.

5. Press Esc or click outside the chart.

3. Drag chart to desired position.
4. Release mouse button.
5. Press Esc or click outside chart.

Skill Session

27

Adding Objects to a Chart

Using charts in a presentation is a great way to make a point or display important information. But even an attractively formatted chart can be difficult to interpret without some guidelines. This skill session shows you how to add text, legends, arrows, and other graphic objects to your charts to make them easier to understand.

Adding and Formatting Chart Text

One of the best ways to make your charts more readable is to attach some descriptive text to various chart elements. Excel works with two types of text: *attached* and *unattached*. Attached text objects are connected to specific chart elements and cannot be moved or sized.

Examples of attached text are the chart title and the axis titles. Unattached text objects are text boxes that "float" on top of the graph and can be moved or sized as needed. Unattached text objects are useful for adding chart subtitles and comments. Figure 27.1 shows several text examples.

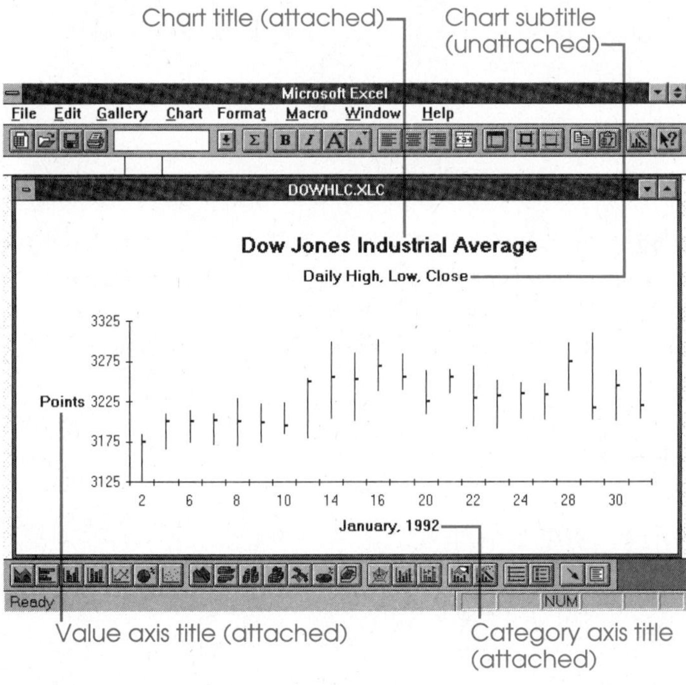

Figure 27.1 A chart with example text objects.

NOTE: If your chart is embedded in a worksheet, you need to display the chart in its own window before you can apply any formatting.

You add attached text using the Attach Text dialog box, shown in Figure 27.2. There are six Attach Text options:

Chart **T**itle	Adds a title centered above the chart.
Value (Y) Axis	Adds a title beside the value axis.

Value (Z) Axis	Adds a title beside the value axis of a 3-D chart.
Category (X) Axis	Adds a title below the category axis.
Series and **D**ata Point	Adds the series value to a specific data point.
Overlay options	Adds axis titles to overlay charts (see Skill Session 30).

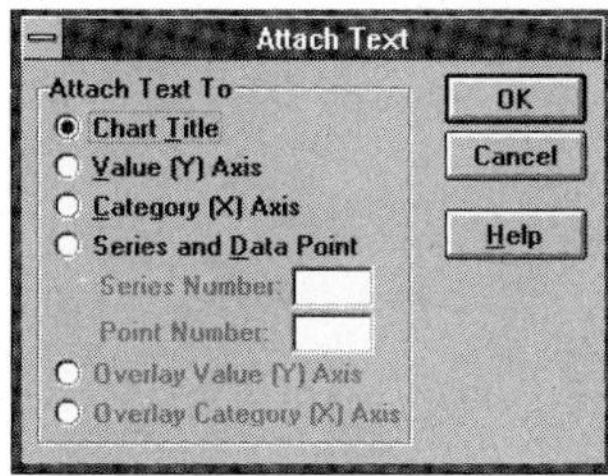

Figure 27.2 The Attach Text dialog box.

Follow these steps to add attached text to your chart (if you are adding a label to a data point, select the appropriate data marker before beginning these steps):

1. Select Chart Attach Text. Excel displays the Attach Text dialog box.
2. Select the text object you want to add. If you select Series and Data Point, enter a **S**eries Number and a **P**oint Number (for an area chart, enter a **S**eries Number only).
3. Select OK or press Enter. Excel adds temporary text to the location you specified. The white squares surrounding the text indicate that the text is

Adding Attached Text to a Chart:

1. Select Chart Attach Text.
2. Select text object to add.
3. Select OK.
4. Type in text.
5. Click on enter box or press Enter.

TIP: To start a new line when entering attached text, press Alt+Enter. To enter a tab, press Ctrl+Tab.

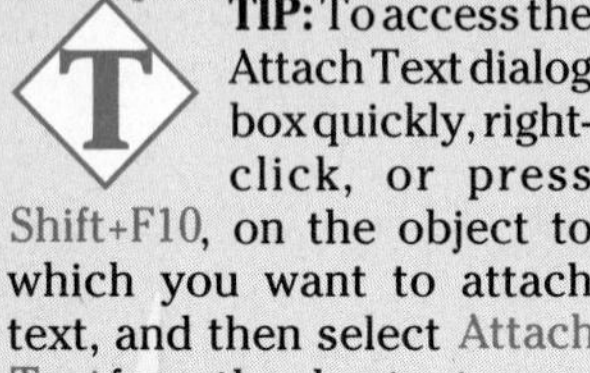

TIP: To access the Attach Text dialog box quickly, right-click, or press Shift+F10, on the object to which you want to attach text, and then select Attach Text from the shortcut menu that appears.

CAUTION: Before adding any unattached text to a chart, make sure that no existing text objects are selected; otherwise, they will be overwritten by the new text.

Adding Unattached Text to a Chart:

1. Type desired text.
2. Click on enter box or press Enter.

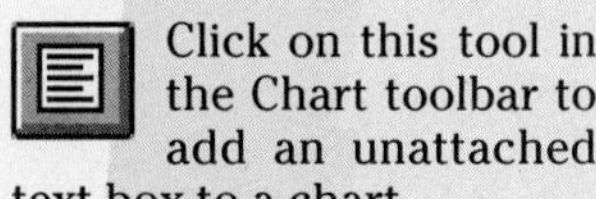

Click on this tool in the Chart toolbar to add an unattached text box to a chart.

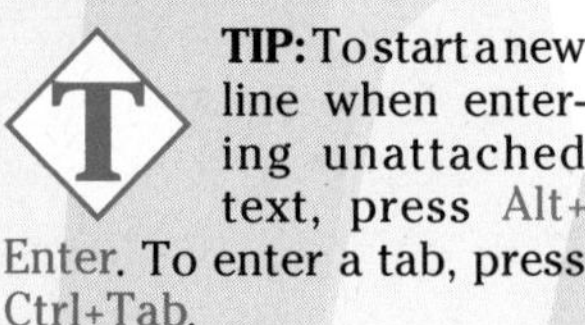

TIP: To start a new line when entering unattached text, press Alt+Enter. To enter a tab, press Ctrl+Tab.

currently selected. Note that these white squares are different from the black selection handles that you have seen around other graphic objects. White squares appear around objects that cannot be moved.

4. With the text selected, type in the text you want. Excel overrides any existing text and displays your typing in the formula bar.

5. Click on the enter box in the formula bar or press Enter.

To add unattached text, follow these steps:

1. Make sure no other text object is selected and type the text you want. Your typing appears in the formula bar.

2. Click on the enter box in the formula bar or press Enter. Excel adds the text box to the chart, surrounded by black selection handles.

Moving and Sizing Unattached Text

The main advantage of unattached text is that you can move and size it to suit your needs. If you have a mouse, the process is easy. To move text, simply drag the box to the new location. To size text, select the text box and then drag the selection handles (see Figure 27.3) to the dimensions you want.

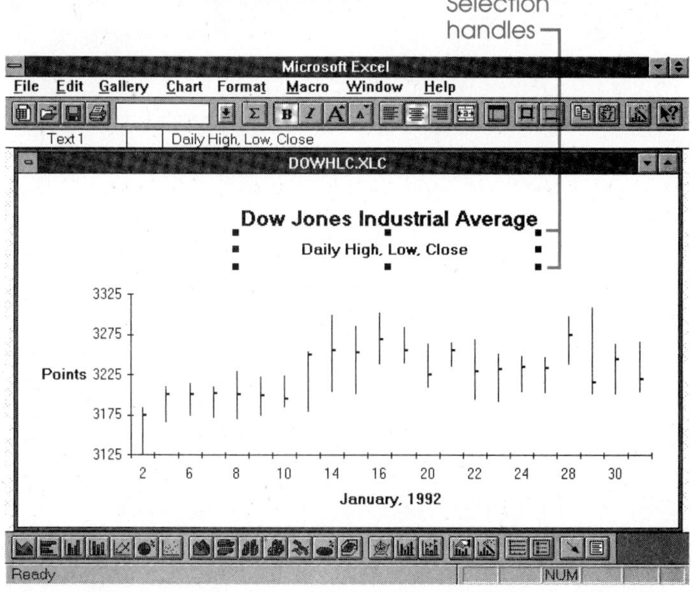

Figure 27.3 Drag text box selection handles to adjust the size of the box.

If do not have a mouse, or if you prefer to use the keyboard, follow these steps to move or size unattached text:

1. Use the arrow keys to select the text you want to adjust.
2. To move the text, select Format Move. To size the text, select Format Size.
3. Use the arrow keys to move or size the text box.
4. Press Enter to accept the new position or size.

Moving or Sizing Text with the Keyboard:

1. Select text.
2. Select Format Move or Format Size.
3. Use arrow keys to move or size text box.
4. Press Enter.

Formatting Chart Text

TIP: To open the Patterns dialog box quickly, double-click on the text box. You can also right-click on the text box, or select the text box and press Shift+F10. Then select Patterns from the shortcut menu that appears.

You can format your chart text (attached or unattached) to highlight the text or to make your chart conform to your presentation style. You can format the text box patterns (borders and colors), the text font, or the text alignment within the box.

To change the text box borders or colors, select the text object and select Format Patterns. The Patterns dialog box appears, as shown in Figure 27.4. The options in the Patterns dialog box enable you to set the **S**tyle, **C**olor, and **W**eight of your text border. Select the Sha**d**ow option to add a shadow to the text box. You can also select a **P**attern and its corresponding **F**oreground and **B**ackground colors for the text area.

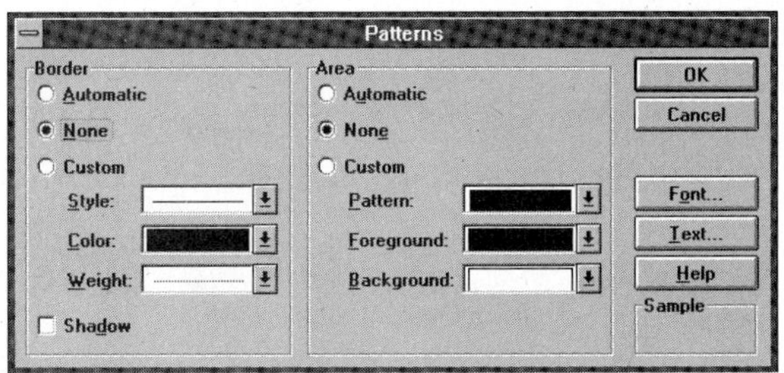

Figure 27.4 The Patterns dialog box allows you to change the text box border and color.

TIP: To open the Font dialog box quickly, right-click on the text box, or select the text box and press Shift+F10, and then select Font from the shortcut menu that appears.

To change the text font, select the Font button from the Patterns dialog box. Alternatively, if the Patterns dialog box is not displayed, select the text object and select Format Font. The Font dialog box appears, as shown in Figure 27.5. You have seen most of these options before except, perhaps, the three options in the Background area:

Auto**m**atic	Select this option to have the text box use the default background pattern.
Tra**n**sparent	Select this option to let the chart pattern beneath the text box show through.
Opa**q**ue	Select this option to have the text box background cover the chart pattern beneath it.

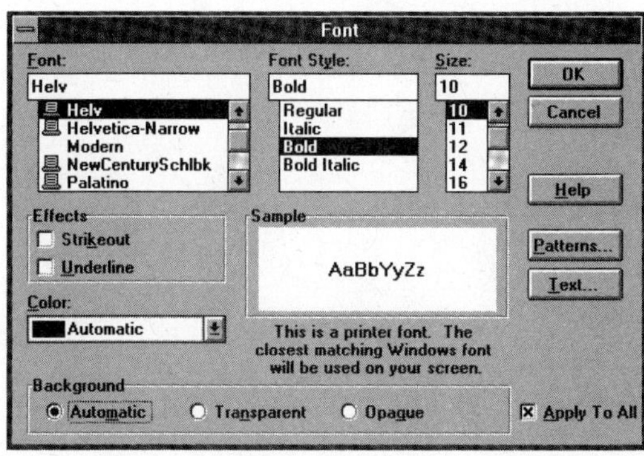

Figure 27.5 The Font dialog box.

Figure 27.6 shows a sample chart with transparent and opaque text objects.

To change the text alignment, select the Text button from the Patterns or Font dialog box. Alternatively, select the text object and select Format Text. The Text dialog box appears, as shown in Figure 27.7. You can set the horizontal or vertical alignment and the text orientation.

TIP: To open the Text dialog box quickly, right-click on the text box, or select the text box and press Shift+F10, and then select Text from the shortcut menu that appears.

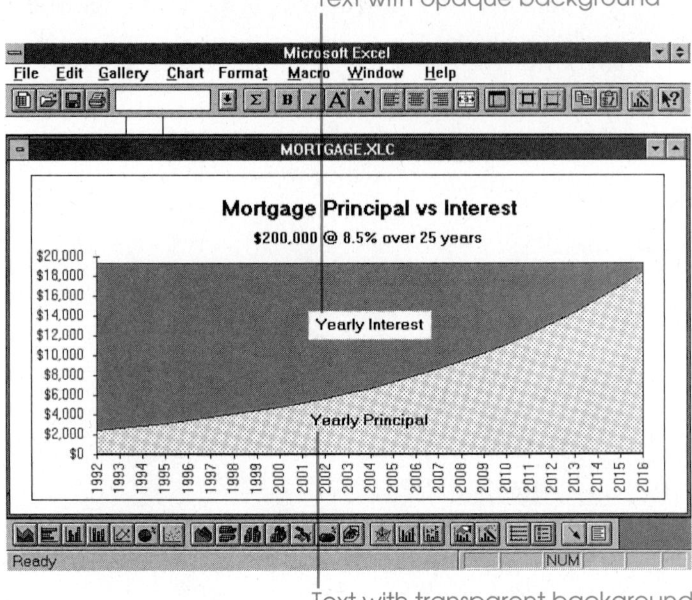

Figure 27.6 You can make your text object backgrounds transparent or opaque.

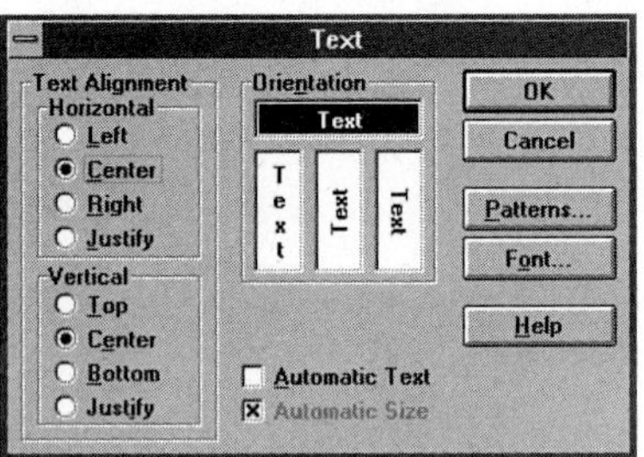

Figure 27.7 The Text dialog box.

Using Worksheet Text in a Chart

You can add text to a chart by linking a text object with a cell in a worksheet. For example, you can link the title you use in a chart to the title of the underlying worksheet. This way, if you change the worksheet title, Excel updates the chart automatically. Follow these steps to link chart text to a worksheet.

1. Select the chart text object that you want to link.
2. Type = (equals sign) to let Excel know you want to enter a formula.
3. Activate the worksheet and select the cell containing the text you want.
4. Select the enter box or press Enter. Excel adds the cell text to the chart text box. The newly selected text replaces the text that had been in the chart text box.

Linking Chart Text to a Worksheet Cell:

1. Select chart text object.
2. Type = (equals sign).
3. Select worksheet cell.
4. Select enter box or press Enter.

The reference that Excel uses for the chart text has the form *worksheet.XLS!address*, where *worksheet* is the worksheet name and *address* is the absolute cell address of the worksheet cell. For example, Figure 27.8 shows a chart title linked to a worksheet title. The formula reference is `=MORTGAGE.XLS!$J$2`.

Adding and Formatting a Chart Legend

If your chart includes multiple data series, you should add a legend to explain the series markers. This makes your chart more readable and makes it easier for others to distinguish each series.

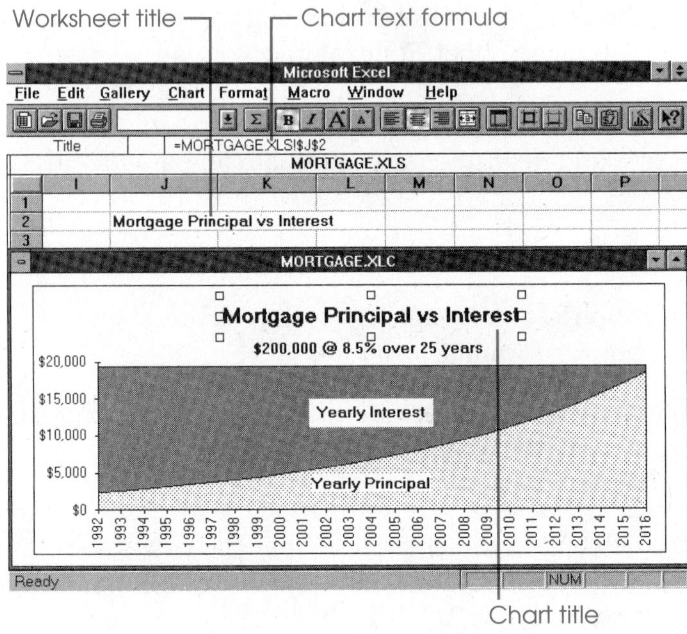

Figure 27.8 You can link chart text with worksheet cells.

Click on this tool in the Chart toolbar to add a legend to a chart. Click on the tool again to delete the legend.

To add a legend to a chart, simply select Chart Add Legend. Excel creates the legend automatically from the worksheet data. To delete a legend, select Chart Delete Legend (this command appears only when a legend exists on the chart).

You can format your legends with the same options that you used to format chart text. For example, to change the border and colors, select the legend and select Format Patterns. To change the legend font, select the legend and select Format Font. Figure 27.9 shows a chart with a formatted legend.

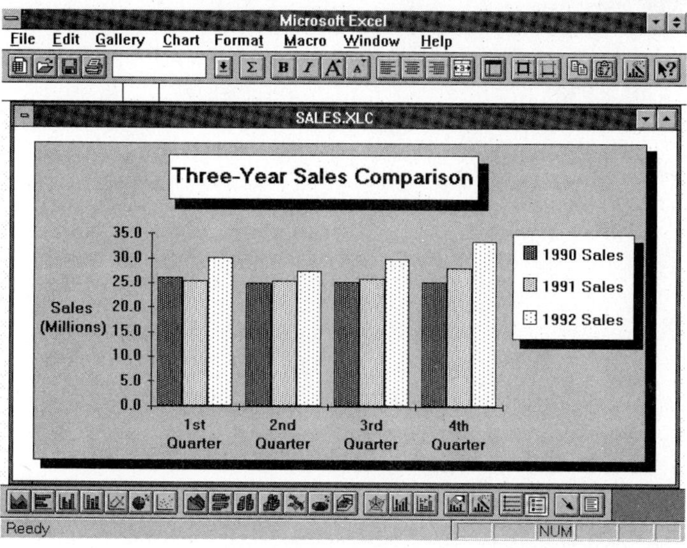

Figure 27.9 You can format your chart legends.

Although you cannot size a legend, you can move it to any position within the chart area. If you have a mouse, simply drag the legend to the location you want. From the keyboard, select the legend, select Format Legend, and, in the Legend dialog box that appears (see Figure 27.10), select the position you want.

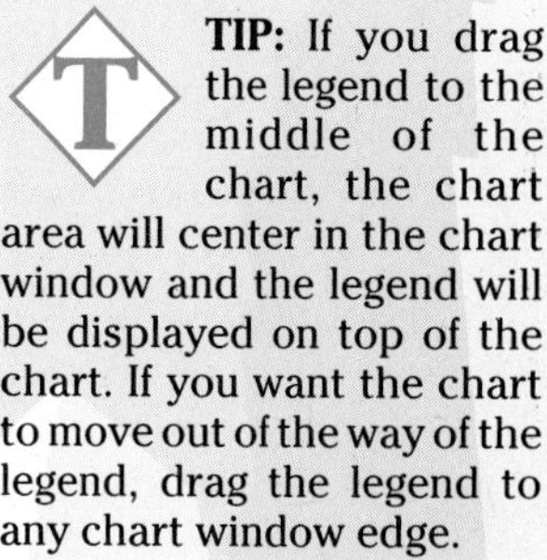

TIP: If you drag the legend to the middle of the chart, the chart area will center in the chart window and the legend will be displayed on top of the chart. If you want the chart to move out of the way of the legend, drag the legend to any chart window edge.

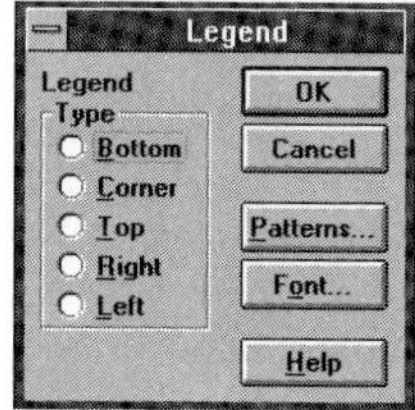

Figure 27.10 The Legend dialog box.

Adding and Formatting Chart Arrows

Even though you will often use chart text for general remarks, it is common to use text to point out a significant result or a specific data point that needs to be explained. When you do this, attach an arrow to the text that points at the appropriate data (see Figure 27.11).

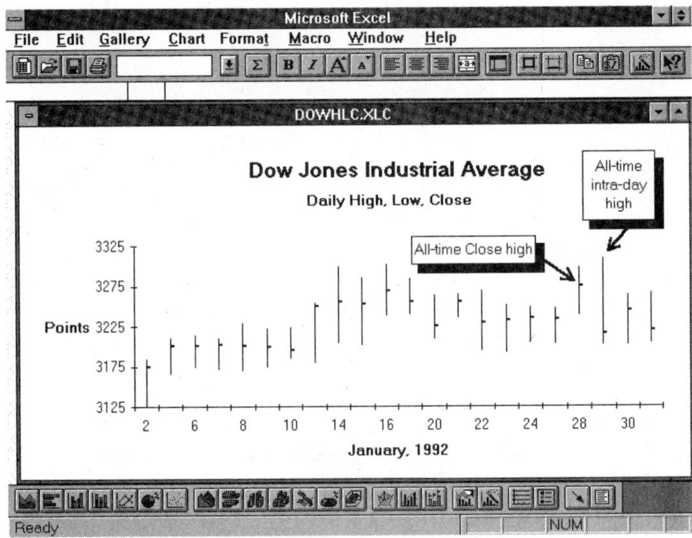

Figure 27.11 Use arrows to point out significant results.

Follow these steps to add an arrow to a chart:

Adding an Arrow to a Chart:

1. Select Chart Add Arrow.
2. Drag line to desired position.
3. Drag arrow head to desired position.

1. Select Chart Add Arrow. Excel displays an initial arrow that begins in the upper left corner of the chart area and points to the middle of the plot area.

2. Drag the selection handle at the start of the arrow so that it is next to the text box.

3. Drag the arrow head selection handle so that it points at the data you want to emphasize.

You can size an arrow by selecting it and following steps 2–3. You can also select Format Size and size the arrow using the keyboard arrow keys.

To move an arrow, position the mouse pointer on the shaft of the arrow and drag the arrow to the new position. From the keyboard, select the arrow, select Format Move, and move the arrow using the arrow keys.

You can format any arrow by selecting it and selecting Format Patterns. In the Patterns dialog box that appears (see Figure 27.12), you can format the **S**tyle, **C**olor, and **W**eight of the arrow shaft, as well as the Sty**l**e, Wi**d**th, and L**e**ngth of the arrow head.

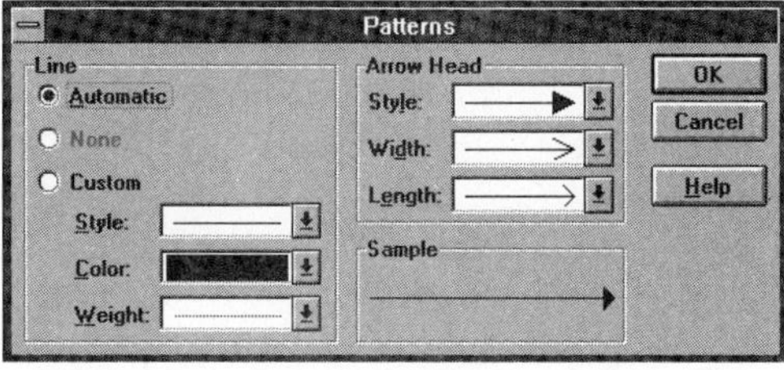

Figure 27.12 The Patterns dialog box for arrows.

IN ACTION: If you are interested in stock market technical analysis, you can draw stock chart trendlines by adding arrows and then removing the arrow heads. Figure 27.13 shows an example.

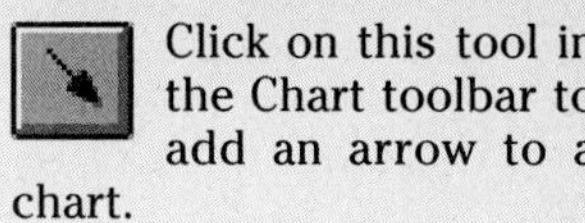

Click on this tool in the Chart toolbar to add an arrow to a chart.

TIP: To access the Patterns dialog box for arrows quickly, double-click on the arrow. Alternatively, you can right-click on the arrow, or select the arrow and press Shift+F10. Then select Patterns from the shortcut menu that appears.

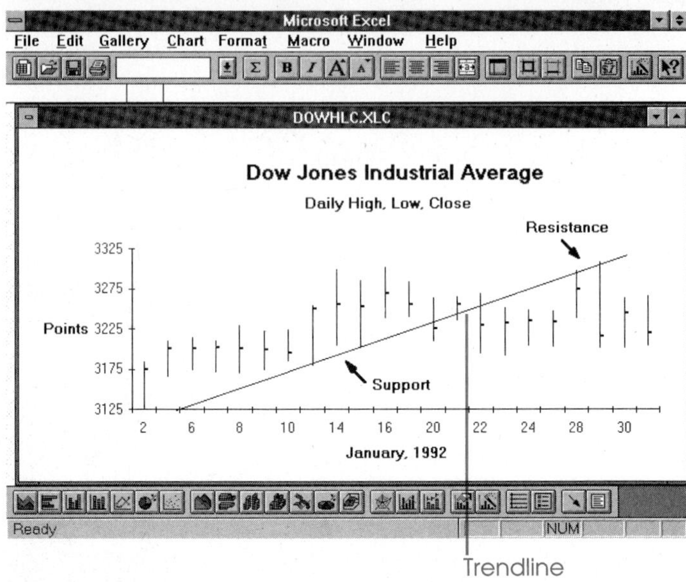

Figure 27.13 Use headless arrows to draw trendlines on stock charts.

To delete an arrow, select it, and then either select Chart Delete Arrow, Edit Clear, or press the Delete key.

Creating Picture Charts

For a different twist to your column, line, or radar charts, you can replace the regular data markers with graphic images imported from programs such as Windows Paintbrush or CorelDRAW!. Here are the steps to follow:

1. Copy the image you want from your graphics program to the Windows Clipboard.

2. In Excel, select the data series or data marker in which you want to use the picture.

3. Select Edit Paste. Excel pastes the picture onto the chart.

When you first paste the picture into the chart, Excel stretches the image according the number the marker represents. If you prefer, you can have Excel use stacks of the image to represent the number. Figure 27.14 shows an example of a stacked picture chart.

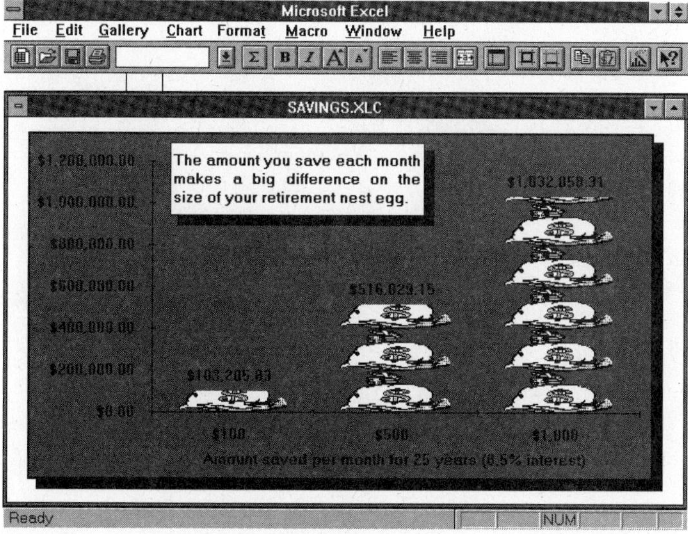

Figure 27.14 A stacked picture chart.

To change to a stacked picture, Select Format Patterns to display the Format Picture dialog box (see Figure

Creating a Picture Chart:

1. Copy image to the Windows Clipboard.
2. Select data series or data marker.
3. Select Edit Paste.

27.15). Select Stack to stack the images. To adjust the scale that Excel uses, select Stack and Scale and enter a number in the Units/Picture text box.

Figure 27.15 The Format Picture dialog box.

Skill Session

28

Data Series Editing

A chart is only as useful as the worksheet information on which it is based. If the chart data is out of date or erroneous, the chart itself will be of little use and it might even be misleading. Excel makes it easy to update your charts whenever you add or edit your worksheet data.

This skill session shows you the ins and outs of the series formulas used by Excel charts and how to use these formulas to edit your chart data series and even add new data series.

Changing Data Series Values

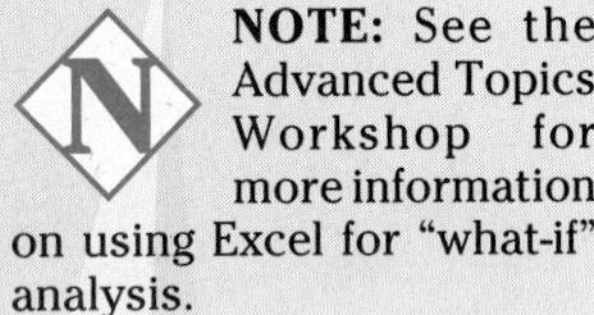

NOTE: See the Advanced Topics Workshop for more information on using Excel for "what-if" analysis.

The easiest way to update a chart is simply to edit the individual data series numbers in the associated worksheet. Because Excel maintains a link between the worksheet and the chart, the chart is automatically adjusted. This provides you with an extra "what-if" analysis tool. By arranging your worksheet and chart so that you can see both windows, you can plug numbers into the worksheet and watch the results on the chart.

For example, Figure 28.1 shows a worksheet that computes the future value of regular deposits to a retirement account. The accompanying chart shows the cumulative savings over time. (The numbers shown in the chart for 15, 20, and 25 years are linked to the appropriate cells; see Skill Session 27 for information on linking chart text and worksheet cells.) By plugging in different numbers for the interest rate, annual deposit, or deposit type, you can watch the effect on the total savings. Figure 28.2 shows the result when you change the annual deposit from $5,000 to $10,000.

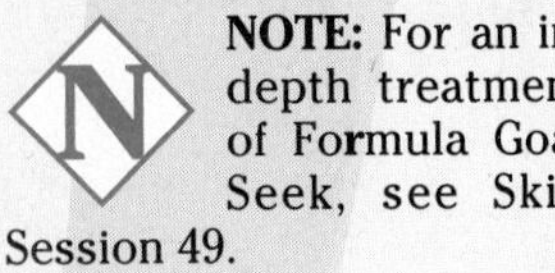

NOTE: For an in-depth treatment of Formula Goal Seek, see Skill Session 49.

Editing numbers in a worksheet and watching a linked chart update automatically is relatively straightforward. However, the link extends both ways, so it is possible to turn this process around. You can make changes to a chart data point, and Excel will update the worksheet automatically. You can do this with 2-D bar, column, line, and XY charts by using a mouse to drag a data marker to a new position. If the data marker represents a worksheet value, Excel adjusts the contents of the corresponding cell. If the data marker represents a formula, then Excel will use Formula Goal Seek to work backward and derive the appropriate formula input values.

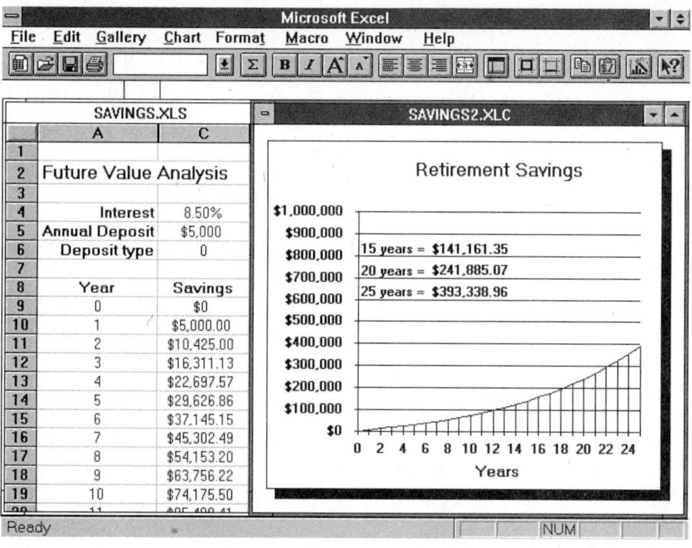

Figure 28.1 Using the chart as a "what-if" analysis tool.

Change the worksheet value and Excel updates the chart automatically.

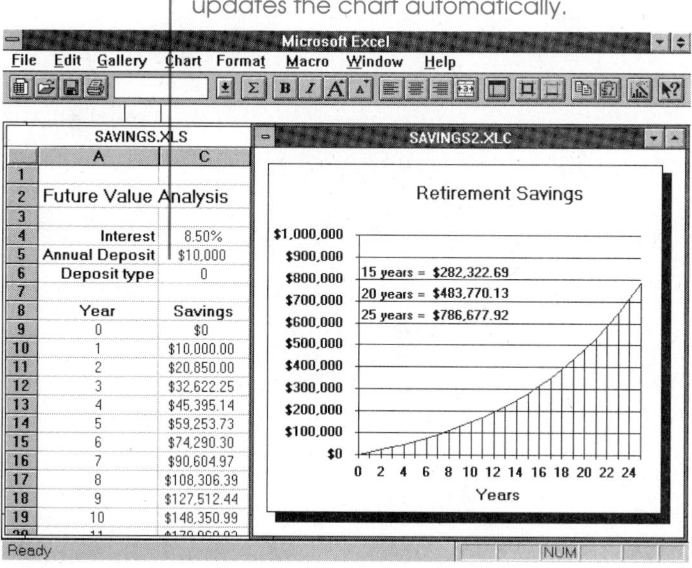

Figure 28.2 When you change a variable in the worksheet, Excel updates the chart automatically.

An example will help explain this process. Suppose your goal is to retire in 25 years with $1,000,000 in savings. Assuming a constant interest rate, how much do you need to set aside annually to reach your goal? The idea is to adjust the chart data marker at 25 years so that it is $1,000,000. Here are the steps to follow to do this:

Moving Data Markers to Change Worksheet Values:

1. Select data marker to adjust.
2. Drag black selection handle to desired number.
3. Release mouse button.
4. Enter appropriate numbers.
5. Select OK.
6. Select OK.

1. In the chart window, select the specific data marker you want to adjust. Excel adds selection handles to the marker. For the example, select the data marker corresponding to 25 years on the category axis.

2. Drag the black selection handle to the desired value. As you drag the handle, the current value appears in the formula bar reference area (see Figure 28.3).

3. Release the mouse button. If the marker references a number in a cell, Excel changes the number and redraws the chart. If the marker references a formula, as in the example, Excel displays the Goal Seek dialog box (see Figure 28.4). The **S**et cell: box shows the cell referenced by the data marker, the To **v**alue: box shows the new number you selected, and the By **c**hanging cell: box is the variable for the formula.

4. Enter the appropriate numbers. For the example, you would enter **C5** in the By **c**hanging cell: box to calculate the required annual deposit.

5. Select OK or press Enter. Excel displays the Goal Seek Status dialog box as it solves for the new number.

6. When the iteration is complete, select OK or press Enter.

Reference area displays the new value as you drag the handle.

Value axis marker moves as you drag the handle.

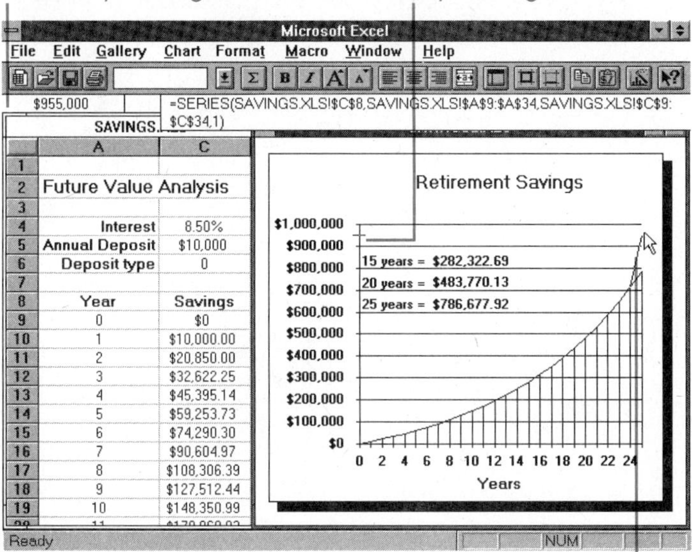

Drag the black selection handle to the desired value.

Figure 28.3 Drag the data point to the desired value.

Cell containing formula

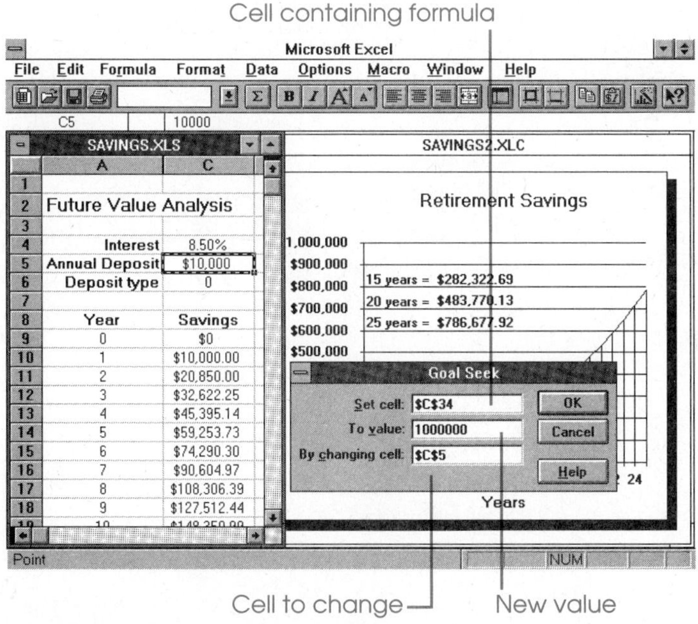

Cell to change

New value

Figure 28.4 If the data marker is derived from a formula, Excel runs Goal Seek.

> **IN ACTION:** Use this technique to make visual adjustments to profit targets. You can also use Goal Seek to recalculate profit variables such as sales and expense budgets.

Working With Series Formulas

To understand how Excel links a worksheet and a chart, and to use the more complex series editing techniques presented in the rest of this skill session, you need to understand the *series formula*.

Whenever you create a chart, Excel sets up a series formula to define each chart data series. This formula has four parts:

Series Name. This is the name of the series that appears in chart legends. It may be a reference to a worksheet label or a text string(in quotes). The general format is either *worksheet_name!cell_reference* (e.g., SALES.XLS!$A$3) or *"series name"* (e.g., "1992 Sales").

X-Axis Labels. These appear as text on the category (X) axis (or the X-axis numbers in an XY chart). An X-axis label may be a range or range name. The general format is *worksheet_name!range_reference* (e.g., SALES.XLS!$B$1:$E$1).

Y-Axis Values. These numbers are plotted on the value (Y) axis. A Y-axis value may be a range or range name. The general format is *worksheet_name!range_reference* (e.g., SALES.XLS! $B$2:$E$2).

Plot Order. This is an integer representing the order in which each series is plotted on the chart.

As shown in Figure 28.5, the series formula appears in the formula bar whenever you select a chart data series.

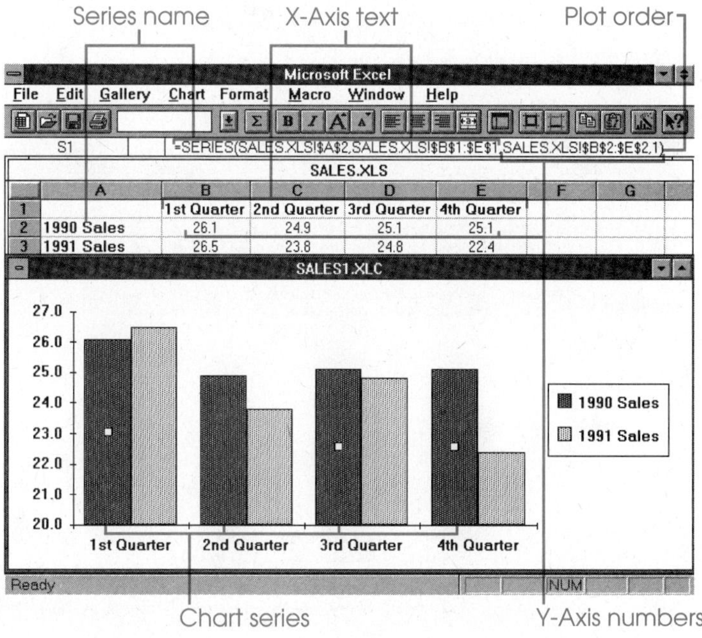

Figure 28.5 The series formula appears in the formula bar.

Editing a Data Series

TIP: Besides the steps outlined here, you can also edit the series formula in the formula bar. Just select the series you want to edit and make your changes to the formula.

When you make changes to an existing worksheet data series, Excel updates your charts automatically by referring to the series formula. However, if you make changes to an area of the worksheet *not* referenced by the series formula, Excel does not adjust the chart. If you extend or reduce a series on a worksheet, you have to tell Excel to extend or reduce the range in the series formula. For example, suppose a new column showing the yearly totals is added to the SALES.XLS worksheet (see Figure 28.6). The formula for each series needs to be updated to include the new column.

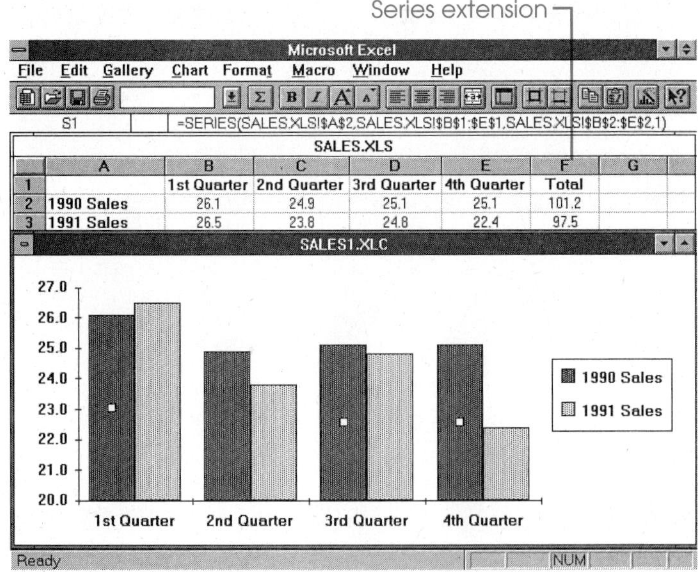

Figure 28.6 When you extend a worksheet series, Excel does not extend the series on the chart.

Follow these steps to edit a series formula:

1. Select Chart Edit Series. Excel displays the Edit Series dialog box, as shown in Figure 28.7.
2. Select the series you want to edit from the **S**eries list.
3. To change the series name, select the Name box; enter the appropriate cell reference or type in the name you want.
4. To change the category axis labels, select the X Labels box (X Values box if you are editing an XY chart) and edit the range. In the preceding example, the range would now be SALES.XLS! $B$1:$F$1.
5. To change the data series values, select the Y Values box and edit the range. In the example, the new range would be SALES.XLS!$B$2:$F$2.
6. To adjust the plot order of the series, enter the number you want in the **P**lot Order box. Excel automatically adjusts the plot order for the other series in the chart.
7. Repeat steps 2–6 to edit other series. When you select another series, Excel asks if you want to save your changes to the current series. Select Yes or press Enter.
8. When you have finished editing the series, select OK or press Enter.

Editing a Data Series:

1. Select Chart Edit Series.
2. Select series to edit.
3. Edit series name, if desired.
4. Edit category (X) axis text, if desired.
5. Edit value (Y) axis numbers, if desired.
6. Adjust plot order, if desired.
7. Repeat steps 2–6 to edit other series.
8. Select OK.

TIP: When changing cell references in the Edit Series dialog box, you can use a mouse or the keyboard to select the cell or range directly on the worksheet.

NOTE: Although Excel adjusts the scale range to accommodate the new data, you may have to adjust the Major Unit to get readable value axis labels.

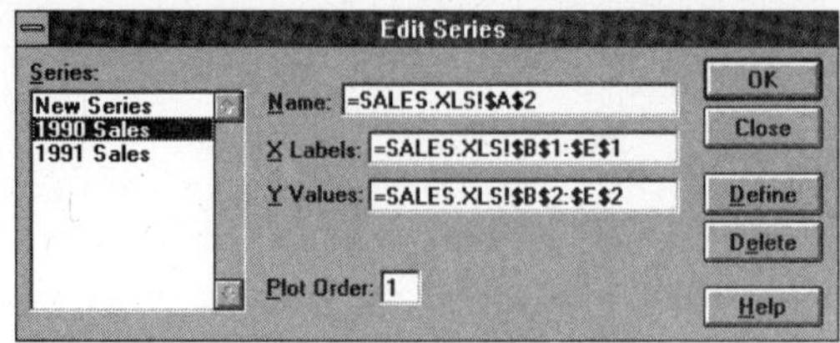

Figure 28.7 The Edit Series dialog box.

Figure 28.8 shows the SALES1.XLC chart with the series extended.

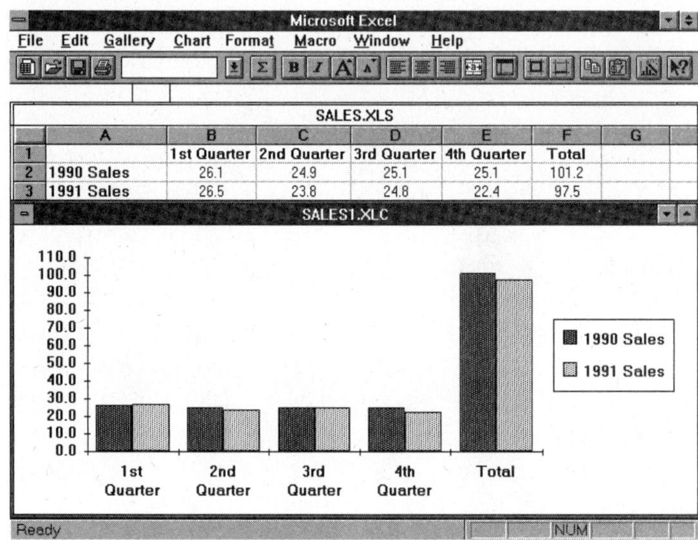

Figure 28.8 The SALES1.XLC chart with the extended series.

Editing a Data Series with ChartWizard

If you extend or reduce a worksheet series, you can use ChartWizard to update the chart series formulas (see Skill Session 24 for details on using ChartWizard). Here are the steps to follow:

1. With the chart you want to edit selected, choose the ChartWizard tool from the Chart or Standard toolbar. Excel displays the ChartWizard—Step 1 of 2 dialog box and a moving line appears in the worksheet around the current chart range.
2. Enter a new range or select the new range on the worksheet.
3. Select Next >. Excel displays the ChartWizard—Step 2 of 2 dialog box.
4. Select any other adjustment options, as needed.
5. Select OK or press Enter.

Editing a Data Series Using ChartWizard:

1. Select ChartWizard tool.
2. Enter new range.
3. Select Next >.
4. Select any other adjustment options.
5. Select OK.

Click on this tool in the Chart or Standard toolbar to run ChartWizard.

Adding a Data Series

Besides editing existing data series, you will often add new series to your worksheets. For example, Figure 28.9 shows the SALES.XLS worksheet with a new series added for 1992 sales. Again, Excel does not add this new data automatically to any associated chart, so you need to define a new series formula.

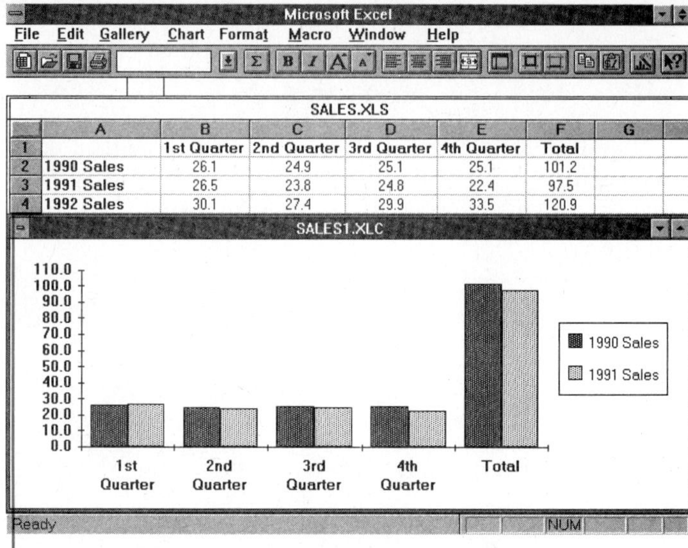

	A	B	C	D	E	F	G
1		1st Quarter	2nd Quarter	3rd Quarter	4th Quarter	Total	
2	1990 Sales	26.1	24.9	25.1	25.1	101.2	
3	1991 Sales	26.5	23.8	24.8	22.4	97.5	
4	1992 Sales	30.1	27.4	29.9	33.5	120.9	

Figure 28.9 When you add a new worksheet series, Excel does not add the series to the chart.

Editing a Data Series:

1. Select Chart Edit Series.
2. Select New Series from Series list.
3. Enter series name.
4. Edit category axis text, if needed.
5. Enter range for series values.
6. Enter plot order.
7. Select Define.
8. Repeat steps 2–7 to add other series.
9. Select OK.

Follow these steps to add a new series to a chart:

1. Select Chart Edit Series to display the Edit Series dialog box.
2. Select New Series from the **S**eries list.
3. Select the Name box and enter the cell reference for the series name or type in the name you want. For the preceding example, the reference would be SALES.XLS!$A$4.
4. Excel enters the current series category axis text in the **X** Labels box. You can edit this range, if needed.
5. Select the Y Values box and enter the range for the series values. In the example, the new range would be SALES.XLS!$B$4:$F$4.

6. Enter the plot order you want in the **P**lot Order box.

7. Select the Define button to add the series to the chart.

8. Repeat steps 2–7 to add other series.

9. When you have finished adding series, select OK or press Enter.

Figure 28.10 shows the SALES1.XLC chart with the new series added.

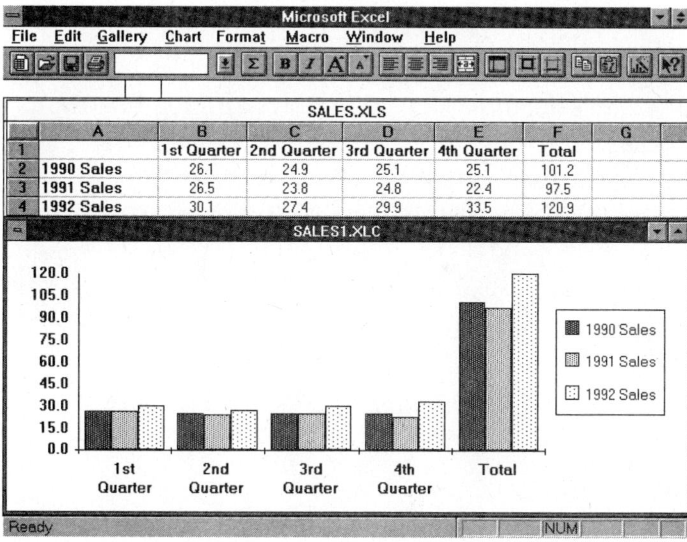

Figure 28.10 The SALES1.XLC chart with the added series.

Adding a Data Series with ChartWizard

To add a series with ChartWizard, follow the same steps that were outlined above for editing a data series with ChartWizard. When you redefine the range to be plotted, include the new data series.

Adding Data Series from Another Worksheet

When adding data series to your charts, you do not have to restrict yourself to data from a single worksheet. You can use the Edit Series dialog box to add series from any other worksheet. For example, suppose you wanted to add data from a worksheet called OLDSALES.XLS to the SALES1.XLS chart. You would just select Chart Edit Series and enter cell references from OLDSALES.XLS in the Edit Series dialog box. This is demonstrated in Figure 28.11.

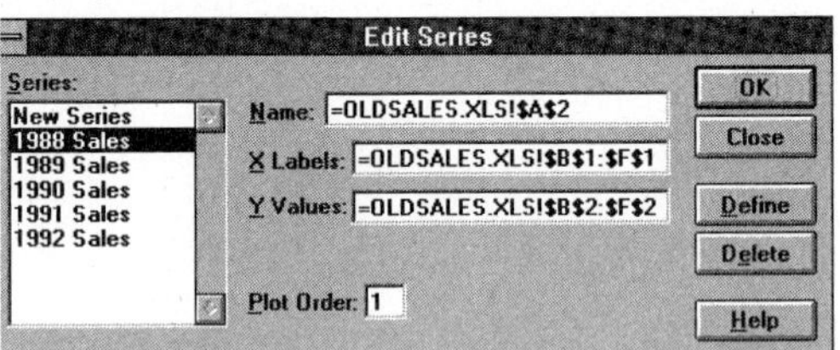

Figure 28.11 You can define series formulas for series in other worksheets.

Another technique for adding series from another worksheet is to copy the new series and then paste the numbers onto the chart. Here are the steps required:

1. Activate the worksheet from which you want to add a series.
2. Select the series that you want to copy (the new series should have the same number of data points as the existing series in the chart).
3. Select Edit Copy. Excel places a moving border around the highlighted range.
4. Activate the chart window.
5. Select Edit Paste Special. Excel displays the Paste Special dialog box.
6. Select the appropriate options.
7. Select OK or press Enter. Excel pastes the new series onto the chart.

Adding a Series from Another Worksheet:

1. Activate worksheet from which you want to add a series.
2. Select series to copy.
3. Select Edit Copy.
4. Activate chart window.
5. Select Edit Paste Special.
6. Select appropriate options.
7. Select OK.

Merging Charts

Another way of adding data series to a chart is to merge two similar charts. Follow these steps to merge charts:

1. Select the chart that contains the data series you want to add.
2. Select Chart Select Chart to select the entire chart.
3. Select Edit Copy. Excel displays a moving border around the chart.
4. Activate the chart to which you want to copy the series.
5. Select Edit Paste. Excel adds the new series to the chart.

Merging Two Charts:

1. Activate chart that contains data series to add.
2. Choose Chart Select Chart.
3. Select Edit Copy.
4. Activate chart to which you want to copy the series.
5. Choose Edit Paste.

CAUTION: Selecting Edit Paste copies both the data series and their formats to the chart. To keep the formatting of the active chart, select Edit Paste Special instead. Then choose Formulas from the Paste Special dialog box that appears.

TIP: Select the series and press Delete to display the Clear dialog box quickly.

CAUTION: Once you delete a series you cannot retrieve it. As a precaution, save the chart before performing any deletions. This way, if you accidentally delete a series, you can close the chart without saving changes and reopen it with the deleted series restored.

Deleting a Data Series:

1. Select Chart Edit Series.
2. Select series to delete.
3. Select Delete.
4. Repeat steps 2–3 to delete other series.
5. Select OK.

IN ACTION: Use this technique to combine charts from other departments for budget or sales presentations. For best results, the data in each chart should have the same layout.

Deleting Data Series

To delete a data series from a chart, select the series, select Edit Clear, and choose Series from the Clear dialog box that appears (see Figure 28.12).

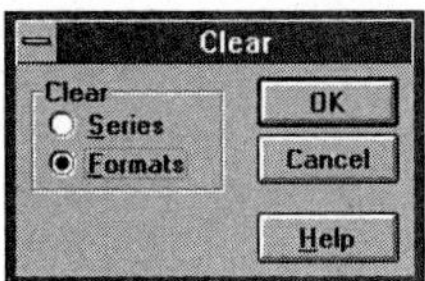

Figure 28.12 The Clear dialog box.

Alternatively, you can delete series from the Edit Series dialog box. Here are the steps to follow:

1. Select Chart Edit Series to display the Edit Series dialog box.
2. In the **S**eries list, select the series you want to delete.
3. Select the Delete button. Excel removes the series from the chart.
4. Repeat steps 2–3 to delete other series.
5. Select OK or press Enter.

Skill Session

29

Working with 3-D Charts

Besides the various 2-D chart types you learned about in Skill Session 25, Excel also offers a number of 3-D charts. 3-D charts are very striking and so are suitable for presentations, flyers, and newsletters. (If you are using charts to help with data analysis, or if you just need a quick chart to visualize your data, you are probably better off sticking with the simpler 2-D charts.) Excel has six different 3-D chart types—area, bar, column, line, pie, and surface. You can select, format, and edit your 3-D charts using the same techniques that you learned for 2-D charts. This skill session introduces you to each 3-D chart type and shows you how to manipulate the depth and perspective for each chart.

Working with 3-D Area Charts

Like their 2-D counterparts, 3-D area charts show the relative contributions over time of each data series. Figure 29.1 shows the 3-D version of the Mortgage Principal vs Interest chart.

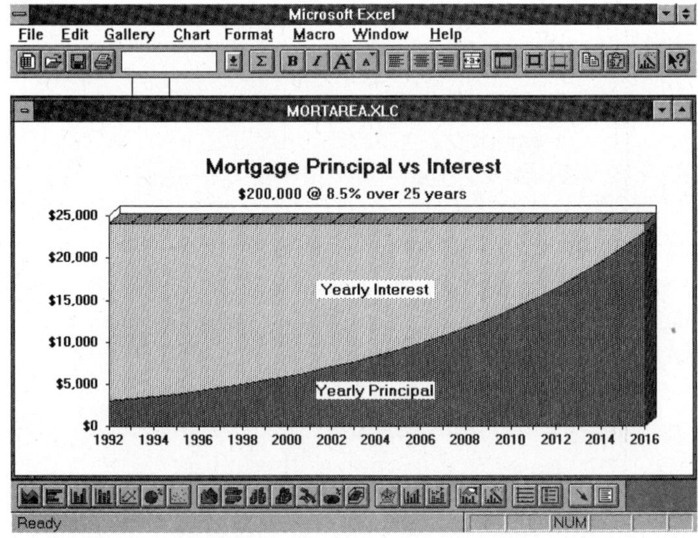

Figure 29.1 3-D area chart comparing mortgage principal and interest.

IN ACTION: Use 3-D charts in presentations to show the relative contributions of individual expense categories, sales regions, and production costs.

To display the 3-D area Chart Gallery, select Gallery 3-D Area. Excel offers seven different predefined area chart formats, three of which enable you to show separate area plots for each data series (something the 2-D area chart cannot do). In this variation, the emphasis is not on the relative contribution of each series to the whole, but, rather, on the relative differences among the series. Figure 29.2 shows an example.

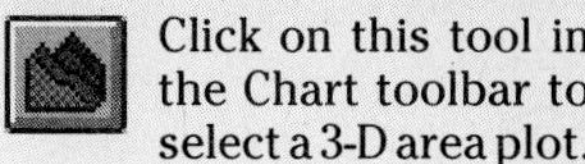

Click on this tool in the Chart toolbar to select a 3-D area plot.

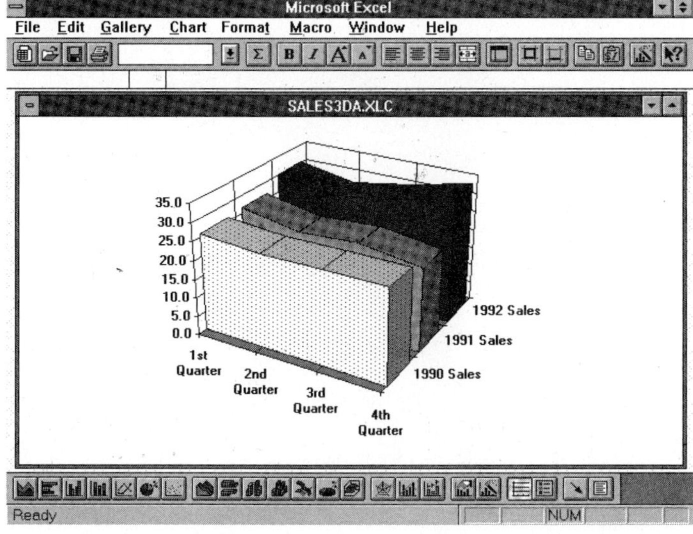

Figure 29.2 A 3-D area chart showing separate series areas.

Working with 3-D Bar Charts

Like 2-D bar charts, 3-D bar charts are useful for portraying competitive comparisons. For example,

Figure 29.3 shows a comparison of a company's sales increases by region. In this format, it is clear that the West region is the "winner" because its bar extends farthest to the right.

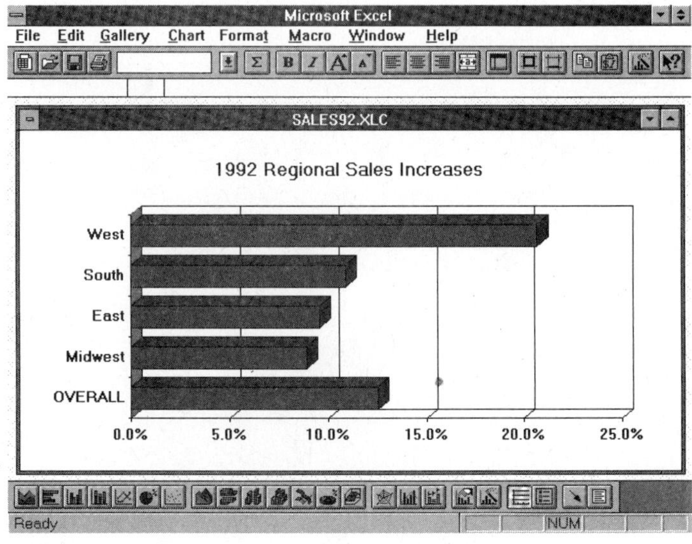

Figure 29.3 Use 3-D bar charts for competitive comparisons.

IN ACTION: Use 3-D bar charts when presenting the results of sales contests, elections, or sporting events.

Click on this tool in the Chart toolbar to select a 3-D bar chart.

Excel offers four different 3-D bar chart formats. To display the 3-D bar Chart Gallery, select Gallery 3-D Bar.

Working with 3-D Column Charts

You use 3-D column charts to compare multiple, distinct data items or to show individual data items over distinct intervals. Figure 29.4 shows a basic 3-D column chart that compares the quarterly sales data over 3 years.

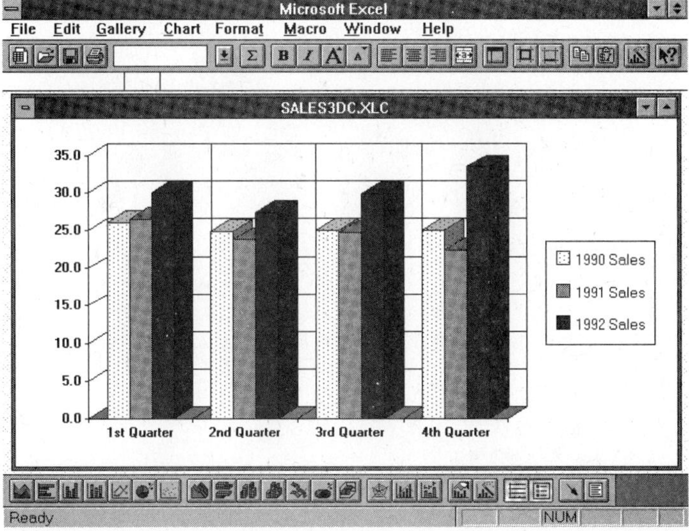

Figure 29.4 3-D column charts compare multiple data series.

To display the 3-D column Chart Gallery, select Gallery 3-D Column. Excel has seven different 3-D column formats, including three that use a three-dimensional plot area. In these charts, there are three axes: the category axis remains the X-axis, a new *series axis* becomes the Y-axis, and the value axis becomes the Z-axis. The advantage of this design is that it enables you to compare data both within a data series and

Click on this tool in the Chart toolbar to select a standard 3-D column chart.

Click on this tool in the Chart toolbar to select a 3-D column chart with a three-dimensional plot area.

among data series in the same chart. For example, Figure 29.5 updates the sales chart to the three-axis format. To see the quarterly progression for each year (i.e., each data series), read the data markers left to right *across* the graph. To compare series, read the data markers from front to back *into* the graph.

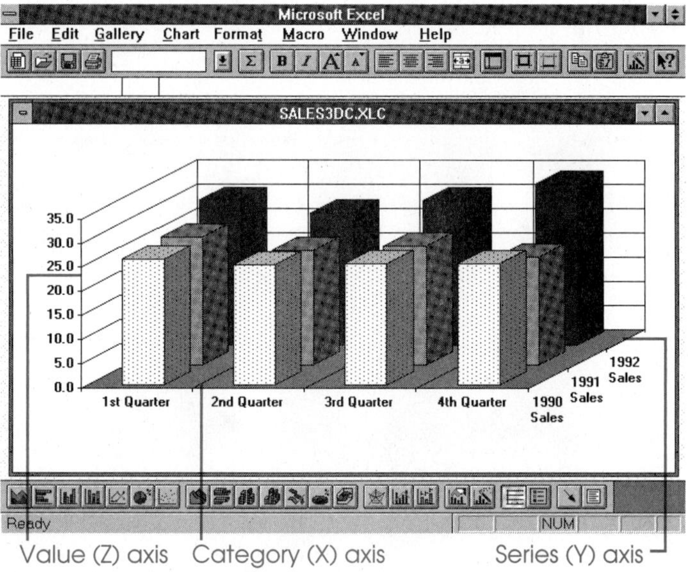

Figure 29.5 An Excel column chart with a three-dimensional plot area.

Working with 3-D Line Charts

3-D line charts (also called *ribbon* charts) show how data series change over time using a three-dimensional plot area: the category (X) axis, the series

(Y) axis, and the value (Z) axis. The individual lines are plotted as ribbons, which makes it easier to see each line and to distinguish each series when they intersect. Figure 29.6 shows a 3-D plot of the Dow Jones Industrial Average (the daily close and a 10-day moving average).

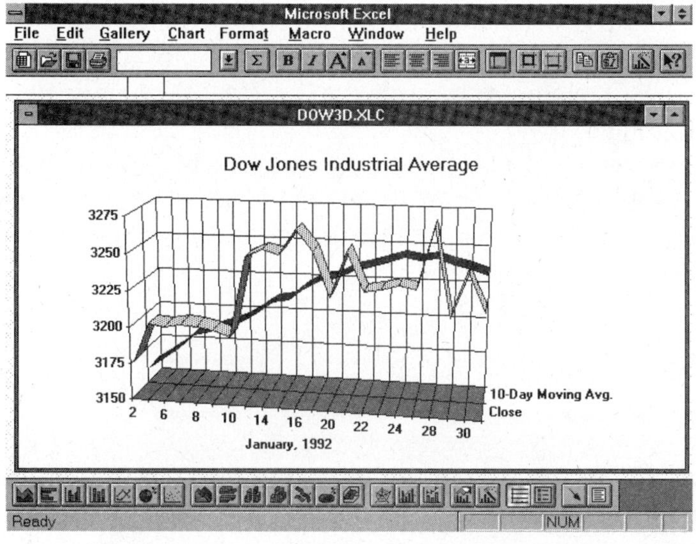

Figure 29.6 3-D line charts plot series as ribbons.

> **IN ACTION:** Use 3-D line charts to see the trends underlying stock, bond, and futures prices. Also, economic indicators such as interest rates, the money supply, and inflation are best seen with this type of chart.

To display the 3-D line Chart Gallery, select Gallery 3-D Line. There are four different 3-D line formats available.

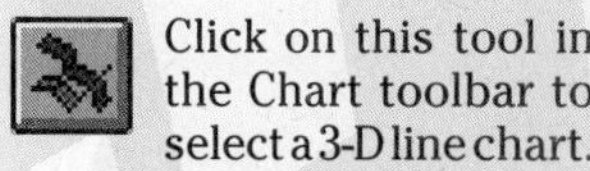

Click on this tool in the Chart toolbar to select a 3-D line chart.

Working with 3-D Pie Charts

Like 2-D pie charts, 3-D pie charts show the proportion of the whole that is contributed by each number in a single data series. A shallow cylinder (the "pie") represents the whole and each "slice" represents an individual series value. Figure 29.7 shows a pie chart of the Earth's elements. As shown in the figure, you can highlight any of the pie slices by pulling them out from the pie. To move a slice, either drag it with your mouse pointer or select the slice, select Format Move, and then use the keyboard arrow keys to move the slice to the desired position.

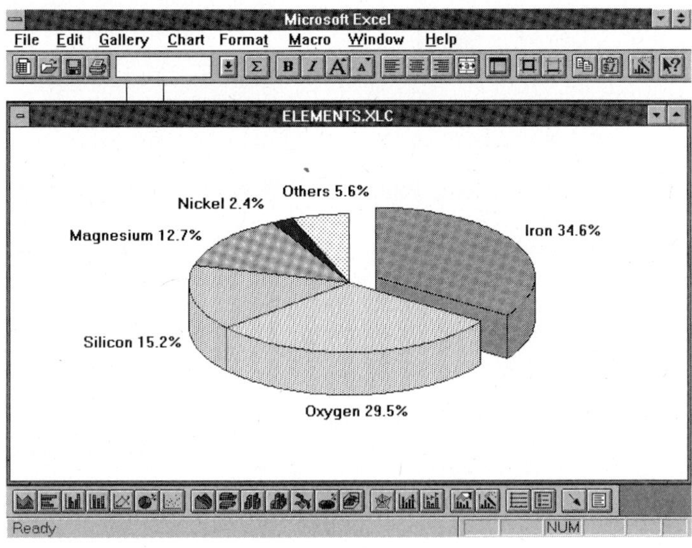

Figure 29.7 A 3-D pie chart of the Earth's elements.

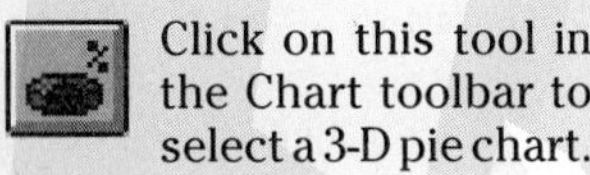

Click on this tool in the Chart toolbar to select a 3-D pie chart.

To view the 3-D pie Chart Gallery, select Gallery 3-D Pie. Excel offers seven different 3-D pie formats.

Working with 3-D Surface Charts

Excel 4 for Windows offers a new type of 3-D chart—the surface chart. You use this type of chart to analyze two sets of data and determine the optimum combination of the two. For example, consider a simplified company where profit is a function of sales expenses and shipping costs. Sales expenses affect profits because with too few salespeople or sales materials, revenues would drop and so would profits. Conversely, you can spend *too much* on sales support and this, too, reduces profit. Using a similar analysis, you can determine that spending too little or too much on shipping costs will also lead to lower profits. These relationships are summarized in the surface chart shown in Figure 29.8.

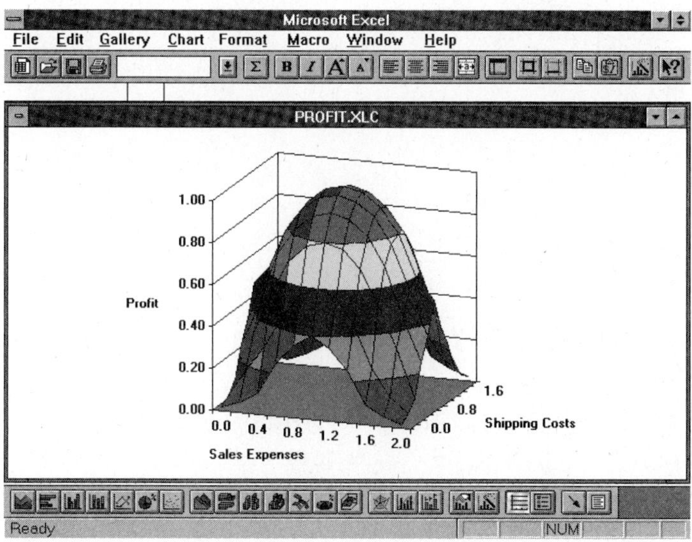

Figure 29.8 A surface chart showing the relationship among sales and shipping costs and profit.

A surface chart is like a topological map. The chart colors do not represent individual data series; instead, they represent points from both series that are at the same value (i.e., the same height on the Z-axis). In Figure 29.8, each color represents a correlation between sales expenses and shipping costs that produce a certain level of profit. The area defined by the highest color, and therefore the highest profit, is the optimum combination of sales and shipping costs.

Click on this tool in the Chart toolbar to select a 3-D surface chart.

To view the 3-D surface Chart Gallery, select Gallery 3-D Surface. Excel has four different 3-D surface formats: 3-D surface chart, 3-D wireframe chart, 2-D contour chart, and 2-D wireframe contour chart.

IN ACTION: A contour chart shows you what the 3-D surface looks like from directly overhead. Use contour charts to help analyze the specific series combinations that produce an optimum result.

Changing the 3-D View

When you use 3-D charts, you will sometimes find that some data points in the back of a chart are obscured behind taller data markers in the chart foreground. This can mar the look of an otherwise attractive chart. Fortunately, Excel allows you to change a number of aspects of the 3-D view to try to get a better perspective on your data.

Excel's 3-D View dialog box (see Figure 29.9) handles these adjustments.

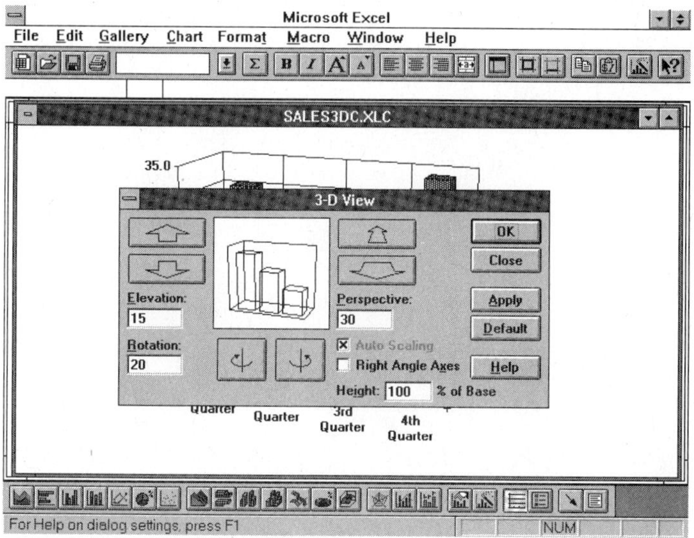

Figure 29.9 The 3-D View dialog box.

Within this dialog box you can set the six options: **E**levation, **R**otation, **P**erspective, Auto **S**caling, Right Angle A**x**es, and Hei**g**ht.

Elevation controls the height from which you look at the chart and is measured in degrees. For most 3-D charts, you may enter an elevation value between –90 and 90. A 0-degree elevation puts you on the floor of the plot area; 90 degrees means that you are looking at the chart from directly overhead; –90 degrees means that you are looking at the chart from directly underneath. Figure 29.10 shows a 3-D column chart from an elevation of 80 degrees. For a 3-D bar chart, the acceptable range of elevation is between 0 and 44 degrees. For pie charts, the range is from 10 to 80 degrees.

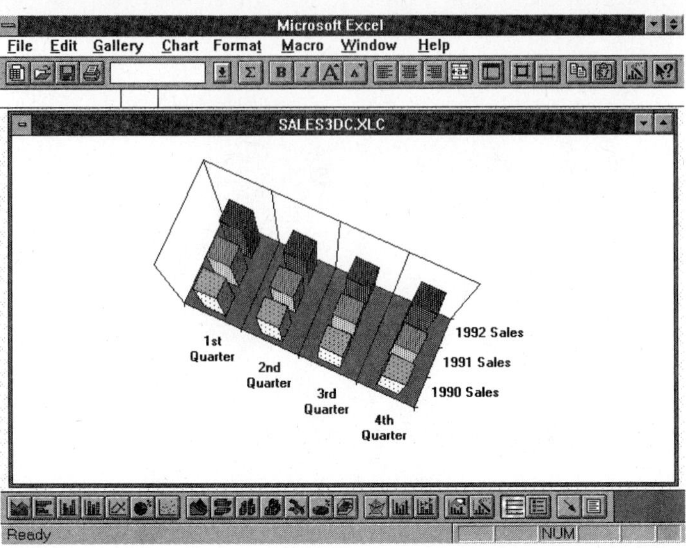

Figure 29.10 A 3-D column chart from an elevation of 80 degrees.

Rotation, also measured in degrees, controls the rotation of the chart around the vertical (Z) axis. For most 3-D charts you can enter a value between 0 and 360 degrees. A 0-degree rotation puts you directly in front of the chart; 90 degrees brings you to the side of the chart; 180 degrees shows you the back of the chart with the series now in reverse order. For a 3-D bar chart, the acceptable range of rotation is between 0 and 44 degrees. For pie charts, the rotation represents the angle of the first slice where 0 degrees puts the left edge of the slice at 12 o'clock, 90 degrees puts it at 3 o'clock, and so on. Figure 29.11 shows the pie chart of the Earth's elements (first shown in Figure 29.7) rotated to 300 degrees.

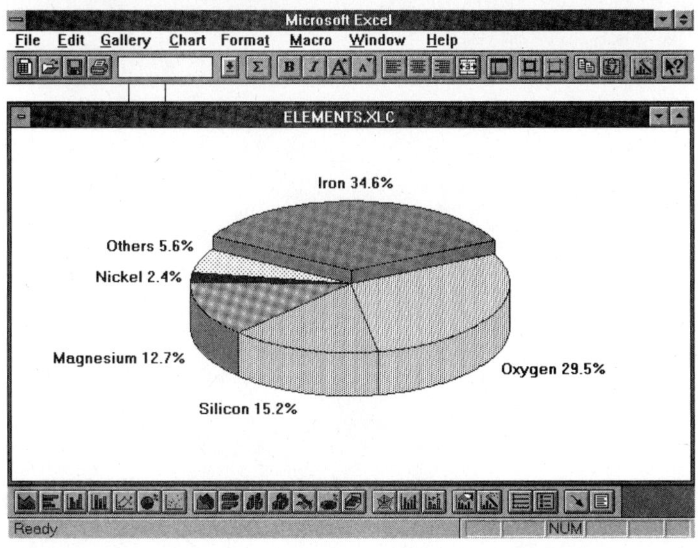

Figure 29.11 Changing the rotation in a pie chart changes the angle of the first slice.

Perspective controls the sense of distance (or *perspective*) that a chart conveys. More perspective (you can enter a value as high as 100 degrees) means that data markers at the back of the chart are shown relatively smaller than those at the front. Pie charts and 3-D bar charts do not have a perspective setting. Figure 29.12 shows a column chart with a high perspective value.

The Auto **S**caling option tells Excel to scale the chart automatically so that it always fills the entire chart window. This option is available only if you select the Right Angle A**x**es option.

The Right Angle A**x**es option controls the orientation of the chart axes. When you select this option, Excel draws the axes at right angles to each other and disables the **P**erspective option.

TIP: If your chart lines appear overly jagged, activate the Right Angle A**x**es option. The chart lines that define the walls and markers will run horizontally and vertically and should appear straight.

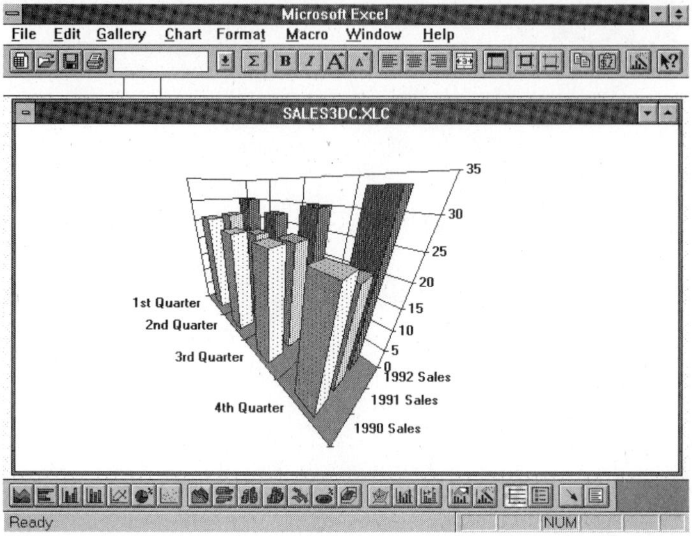

Figure 29.12 Use a high perspective value to add a sense of distance to a chart.

The Height option controls the height of the vertical (Z) axis. The height is measured as a percentage of the category (X) axis. This option is unavailable when you select Auto Scaling.

Adjusting the 3-D View:

1. Select Format 3D-View.
2. Select 3-D view options.
3. Select Apply.
4. Select OK.

Follow these steps to adjust the 3-D view of a chart:

1. Select Format 3D-View. Excel displays the 3-D View dialog box.

2. Select the 3-D view options that you want. The sample chart in the dialog box shows the effect of each change.

3. To see how your changes will look on the actual chart, select Apply. Excel changes the chart view but leaves the dialog box open.

4. To change the view permanently, select OK or press Enter.

TIP: To return a chart to its default view, select the Default button.

Plotting a Multicategory 3-D Chart

The three-dimensional equivalent of the 2-D XY chart is called the *multicategory* chart. You will recall that an XY chart (a variation of the line chart) plots the relationship between two sets of numbers—an independent variable and a dependent variable. Similarly, the multicategory 3-D chart (a variation of the 3-D column chart) plots the relationship among *two* independent variables (i.e., two categories) and a dependent variable. Excel plots the categories on the X- and Y-axes and plots the values on the Z-axis.

As an illustration, consider the earlier example of the company profit that is a function of both sales expenses and shipping costs. In that example, both types of costs are independent variables and the profit is the dependent variable. Figure 29.13 shows how you would set up a multicategory 3-D chart to analyze the relationship among these variables.

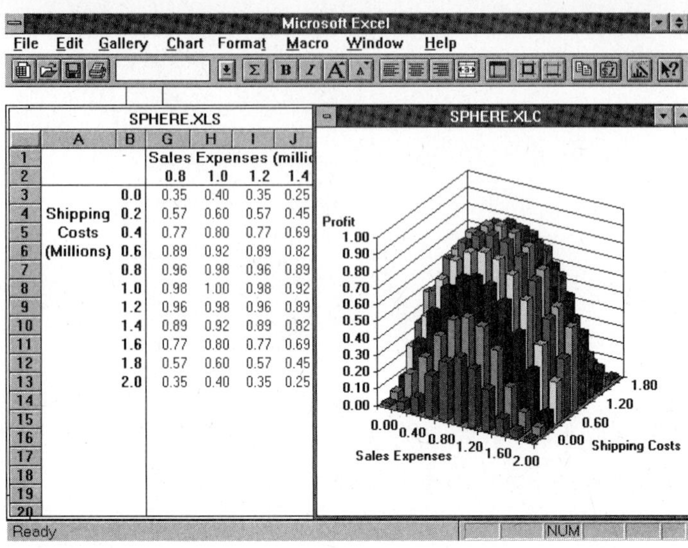

Figure 29.13 A multicategory 3-D chart.

Skill Session

30

Working with Chart Overlays

All the charts you have seen so far have used a single value axis (except XY charts) and a single chart type. With Excel, you can *overlay* one chart on another to produce combination charts that display two different chart types simultaneously. The two types can even use different units and different value axes.

This skill session shows you how to use Excel's preformatted combination charts and how to add and format your own overlay charts.

Working With Excel's Combination Charts

CAUTION: Converting an existing chart to a combination type will overwrite any formatting you have applied. To maintain your formatting, add your own overlay. See the section entitled "Adding an Overlay Chart" for instructions.

The easiest way to create a combination chart is to select one of Excel's six preformatted combination types. Simply select Gallery Combination to display the combination Chart Gallery dialog box (see Figure 30.1).

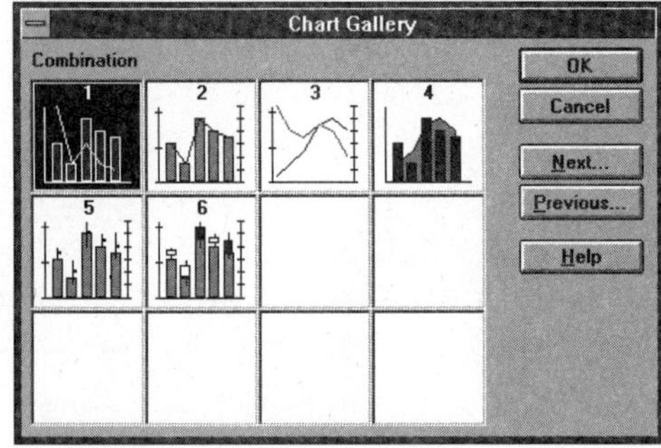

Figure 30.1 The combination Chart Gallery dialog box.

Click on this tool on the Chart toolbar to select a combination chart that overlays a line chart on a column chart.

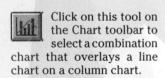

Click on this tool on the Chart toolbar to select a combination chart that overlays a high, low, close chart on a column chart.

Excel creates combination charts by overlaying one chart on another. Table 30.1 outlines the chart types used in each of the combination chart formats.

Combination charts are useful for showing how distinct series are related. For example, Figure 30.2 shows a chart that overlays a Dow Jones daily high, low, close line chart on a column chart showing daily volume. The line chart value axis (showing units in points) is on the right and the column chart value axis (showing units in millions of shares) is on the left.

Table 30.1 Excel's combination charts

Combination	*Description*
1	A column chart overlaid by a line chart.
2	A column chart overlaid by a line chart that uses a separate value (Y) axis. The overlay axis appears on the right side of the plot area.
3	A line chart overlaid by a second line chart that uses a separate value (Y) axis. The overlay axis appears on the right side of the plot area.
4	An area chart overlaid by a column chart.
5	A column chart overlaid by a high, low, close line chart that uses a separate value (Y) axis. The overlay axis appears on the right side of the plot area.
6	A column chart overlaid by an open, high, low, close chart that uses a separate value (Y) axis. The overlay axis appears on the right side of the plot area.

IN ACTION: Use combination charts to look for relationships between distinct data series such as house purchases and interest rates, product prices and inflation, or widget production and the price of tea in China.

TIP: Scale the axes on your combination charts to prevent the series from interfering with each other. See Skill Session 26 for information on formatting your chart axes.

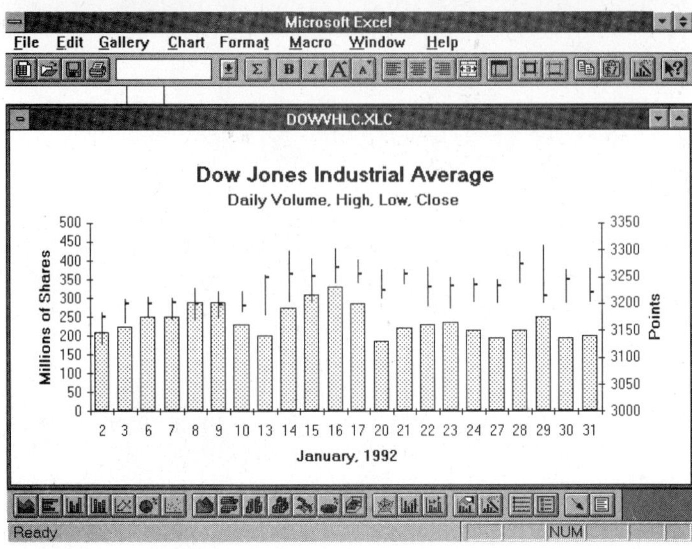

Figure 30.2 A chart combining a line chart type with a column chart type.

Adding an Overlay Chart

If you want to create a combination chart not found among Excel's Chart Gallery charts, or if you have chart formatting that you want to preserve, you can add your own overlay chart by selecting Chart Add Overlay. When you select this command, Excel splits the chart into a main chart and an overlay and attempts to divide the data series equally between the two charts. The first half of the series (in plot order) appears in the main chart, and the second half appears in the overlay chart (if there is an odd number, the extra series goes to the main chart).

As an example, Figure 30.3 shows a chart with three series: sales figures for 1991 and 1992, and a series that plots the growth from 1991 to 1992. The growth series would make more sense as a line chart, so an overlay is added (see Figure 30.4).

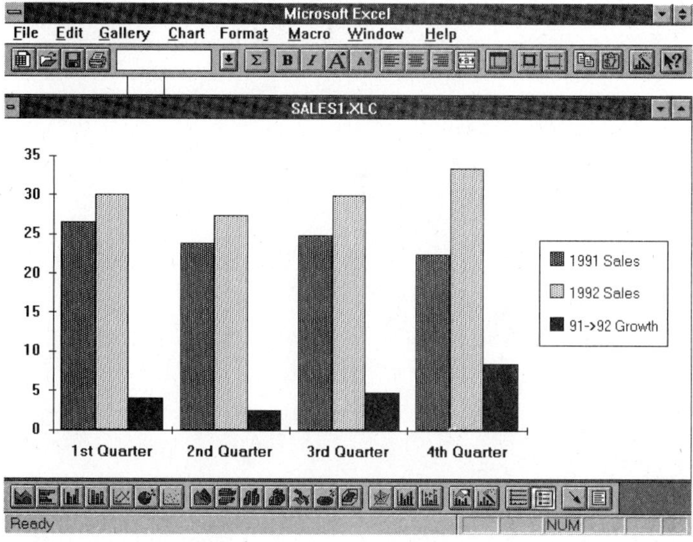

Figure 30.3 The growth series would be better as a line chart.

Adjusting the Overlay Data Series

When it distributes the data series between the main chart and an overlay, Excel arbitrarily splits the series according to plot order. But this split may not always be what you want. To illustrate, suppose in the preceding example that there were *three* years of data (1990, 1991, and 1992) and you select Chart Add Overlay. At first, Excel plots the first two series (1990 Sales and

1991 Sales) in the main chart and the other two series (1992 Sales and 90->92 Growth) in the overlay as line charts (see Figure 30.5).

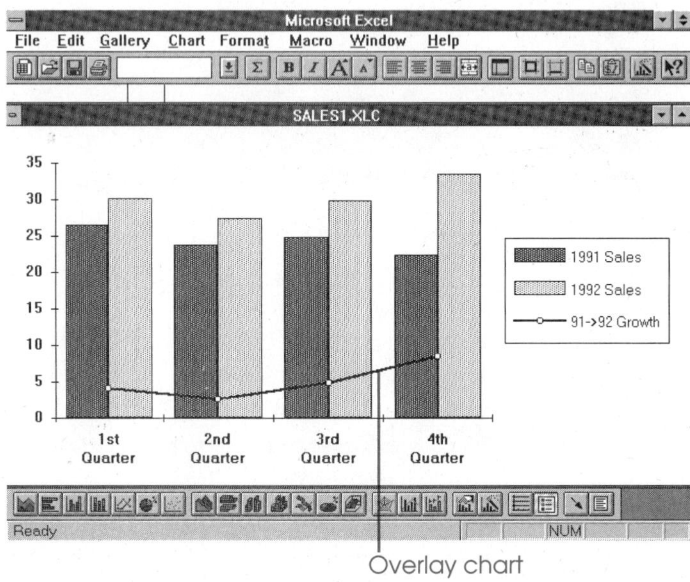

Figure 30.4 The growth series as a line chart overlay.

You can fix this by telling Excel which of the data series should be the first overlay series. Here are the steps to follow:

Changing the Overlay Data Series:

1. Select Format Overlay.
2. Select First Overlay Series.
3. Enter series number.
4. Select OK.

TIP: To display the overlay Format Chart dialog box quickly, right-click on the plot area or chart background, or select either area and press Shift+F10. Then select Overlay from the shortcut menu that appears.

1. Select Format Overlay. Excel displays the Format Chart dialog box, as shown in Figure 30.6.

2. In the Series Distribution section, select First Overlay Series. Excel highlights the text box.

3. Enter the number of the first series you want to appear in the overlay. To correct the preceding example, you would change this number from 3 to 4.

4. Select OK or press Enter.

Third and fourth data series appear in the line chart overlay.

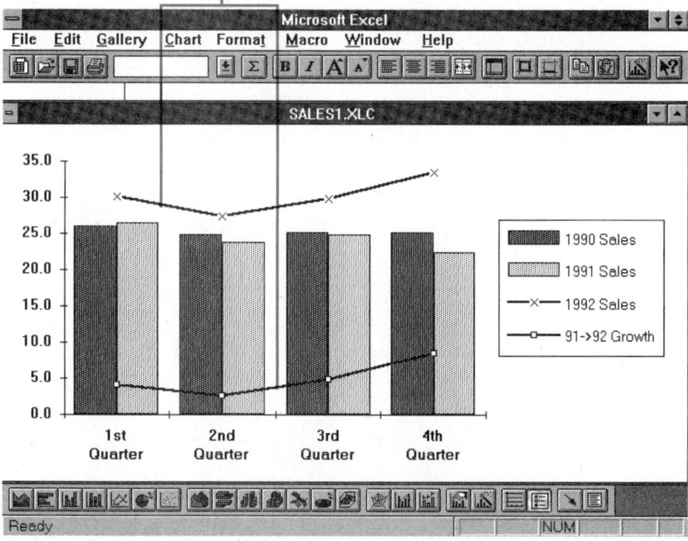

Figure 30.5 Excel arbitrarily splits the series between the main chart and the overlay.

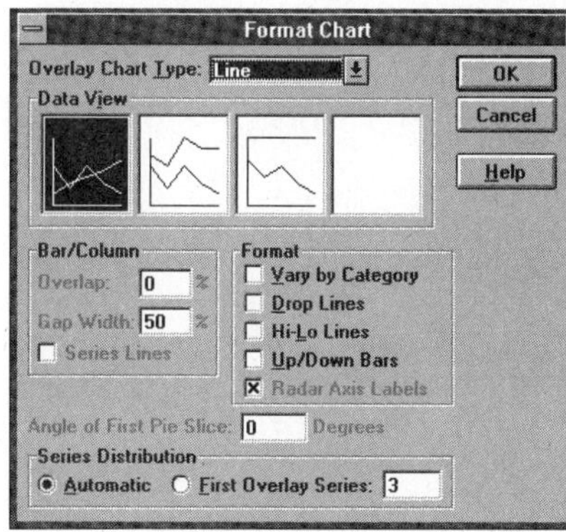

Figure 30.6 The Format Chart dialog box for overlay charts.

NOTE: See Skill Session 28 for instructions on changing data series plot order.

The other way to adjust which data series appears in the overlay is to change the plot order. For example, suppose you have four data series and want the first two to appear in the overlay instead of the last two. All you need to do is change the plot order of the first two series, and Excel will use them for the overlay automatically.

Changing the Overlay Chart Format

When Excel adds an overlay to a chart, it uses a line chart as the default format. If you would prefer a different chart type, follow these steps to make the change:

Changing the Overlay Chart Format:

1. Select Format Overlay.
2. Select a chart type.
3. Select a chart format.
4. Enter other format options.
5. Select OK.

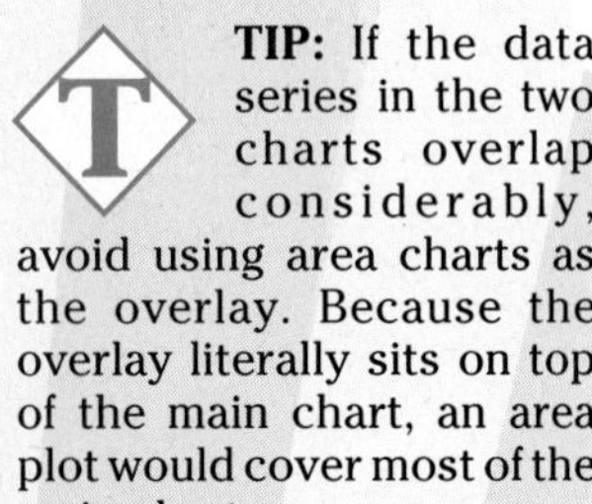

TIP: If the data series in the two charts overlap considerably, avoid using area charts as the overlay. Because the overlay literally sits on top of the main chart, an area plot would cover most of the main chart.

1. Select Format Overlay to display the Format Chart dialog box.
2. Select a chart type from the Overlay Chart Type list. Excel displays several chart formats.
3. In the Data View section, select a chart format.
4. Enter other format options, as needed.
5. Select OK or press Enter.

If the main chart and the overlay use different units or have data series with different value ranges, you can add a second value axis for the overlay. For example, consider the line chart shown on Figure 30.7. This chart attempts to compare the effect of altitude on the force of gravity and on a person's weight. Unfortunately, because the numbers in each series use different ranges, the comparison is not an effective one. The solution is to overlay one series on the other, display two different axes, and then adjust each axis scale for best effect. Figure 30.8 shows the result.

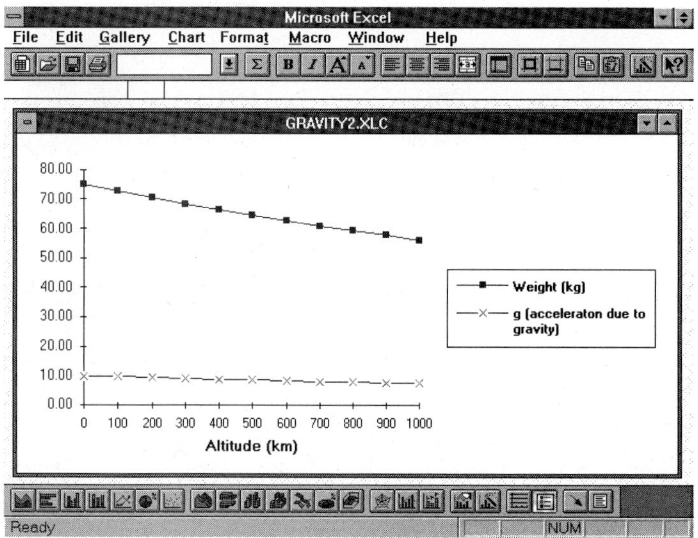

Figure 30.7 Series with different ranges can produce ineffective charts.

Follow these steps to add an overlay value or category axis:

1. With the overlay added, select Chart Axes. Excel displays the Axes dialog box, as shown in Figure 30.9.
2. In the Overlay section, select the overlay axes you want to appear.
3. Select OK or press Enter. Excel adds the axes to the chart.
4. Scale each axis as needed.

Adding Overlay Axes:

1. Select Chart Axes.
2. Select overlay axes.
3. Select OK.
4. Scale each axis as needed.

TIP: To display the Axes dialog box quickly, right-click on an axis (or on the chart background), or select an axis and press Shift+F10. Then select Axes from the shortcut menu that appears.

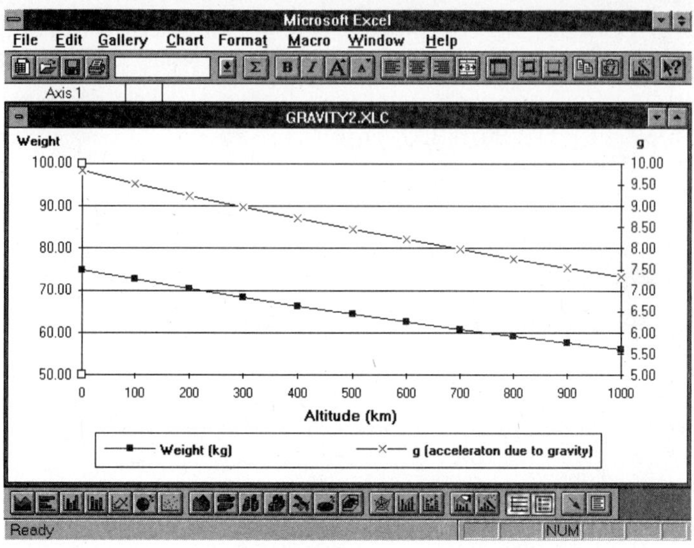

Figure 30.8 Overlaying one series and adjusting the axes ranges lead to a better comparison.

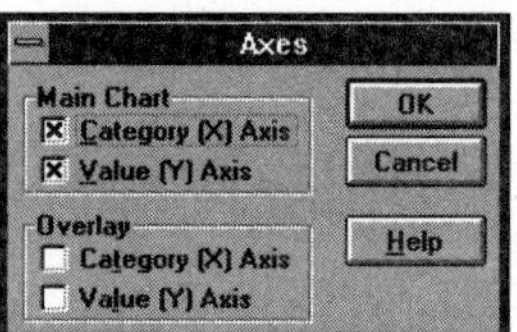

Figure 30.9 The Axes dialog box showing overlay options.

Deleting an Overlay

To delete an overlay, select Chart Delete Overlay (this command appears only when an overlay chart is present). You can also delete an overlay by selecting another chart type from the Chart Gallery or by clicking on a chart tool in the Chart toolbar. However, you will also delete any formatting in the active chart. To preserve your formatting, use Chart Delete Overlay. If you delete an overlay by accident, you can restore it by immediately selecting Edit Undo Delete Overlay.

Creating 3-D Combination Charts

Excel does not allow you to combine 3-D charts, as a rule, but you can use some tricks to manufacture your own 3-D combination charts.

The basic idea is to embed a 3-D chart (the main chart) in a worksheet and then superimpose a second 3-D chart (the overlay) on top of the first. By making the top chart's background and plot area invisible, the bottom chart will show through and you will have your combination. Here are some tips to follow when trying this on your own:

- If you want to compare numbers, make sure both charts use the same range on the value axis.
- Use the same numbers for elevation, rotation, and perspective for both charts.
- You will use the walls, floor, and axes of the main chart, so you will need to hide these elements in the overlay.
- Copy the main chart to the worksheet first, then copy the overlay.

▲ Once you have copied the overlay to the worksheet, hide the background so you can see through to the main chart. Leave the borders, however, because you will need them to move and size the overlay.

▲ Move and size the overlay, as needed, to make it fit into the plot area of the main chart (see Skill Session 32 for instructions on moving and sizing worksheet objects).

Figure 30.10 shows an example of a 3-D combination chart constructed in this manner.

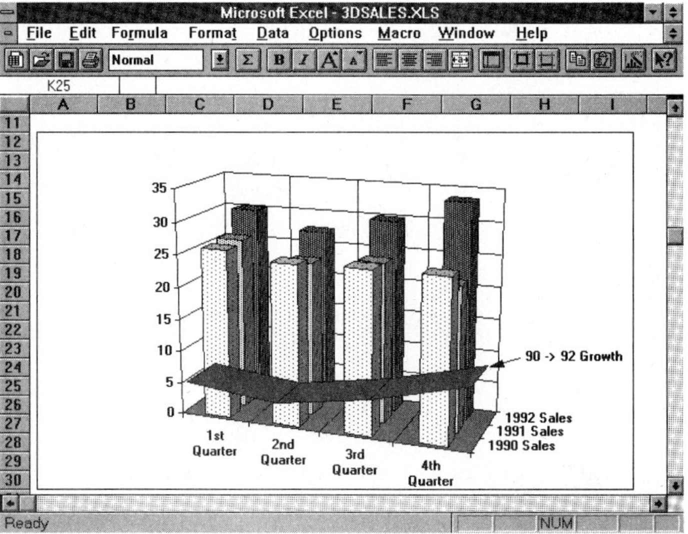

Figure 30.10 A 3-D combination chart.

Skill Session

31

Adding Graphic Objects to a Worksheet

Excel 4 for Windows gives you a powerful set of drawing tools to create and enhance graphic objects on your worksheets. You can add lines, circles, or polygons; you can import graphics from external sources; and you can even export pictures of your worksheets to use in other programs.

This skill session shows you the basics of adding graphic objects to a worksheet either by drawing them yourself using the Drawing toolbar or by importing graphics from outside Excel.

Using the Drawing Toolbar

The Excel 4 for Windows Drawing toolbar contains a number of tools you can use to create your own graphic objects. With these tools, you can add lines, rectangles, ovals, arcs, and polygons to your worksheets. Table 31.1 summarizes the 11 drawing tools.

Table 31.1 Excel's drawing tools

Tool	*Name*	*Description*
	Line	Draws a straight line.
	Arrow	Draws an arrow.
	Freehand	Draws a freehand line.
	Rectangle	Draws a rectangle or square.
	Oval	Draws an oval or circle.
	Arc	Draws an arc or circle segment.
	Freehand Polygon	Draws a polygon from a combination of freehand and straight lines.
	Filled Rectangle	Draws a rectangle or square filled with a background pattern and color.

Tool	*Name*	*Description*
	Filled Oval	Draws an oval or circle filled with a background pattern and color.
	Filled Arc	Draws an arc or circle segment filled with a background pattern and color.
	Filled Freehand Polygon	Draws a freehand polygon filled with a background pattern and color.

The Drawing toolbar makes creating your own graphic objects easy. In most cases, you just click on the tool and then drag on the worksheet to create the object. Figure 31.1 shows several examples of objects you can create with the drawing tools.

Drawing Lines

You can create three kinds of lines with Excel's drawing tools: straight lines, arrows, and freehand lines. Use lines to point out important worksheet information or as part of a more complex graphic such as a company logo. Follow these steps to create a line:

Drawing a Line:

1. Click on a line-drawing tool.
2. Position the crosshair.
3. Press and hold down left mouse button.
4. Drag mouse to where you want line to end.
5. Release mouse button.
6. Repeat steps 2–5 to draw other lines.
7. Press Esc.

TIP: To restrict straight lines and arrows to horizontal, vertical, and 45-degree angles, hold down Shift while drawing. To create lines along the worksheet gridlines or diagonally between cell corners, hold down Alt while drawing.

1. Click on a line-drawing tool. To draw multiple lines, double-click on the tool. The mouse pointer changes to a crosshair.

2. Position the crosshair where you want to begin the line.

3. Press and hold down the left mouse button.

4. Drag the mouse to where you want the line to end. If you are drawing a freehand line, drag the mouse in the shape of the line you want.

5. Release the mouse button. Excel places black selection handles on each end of the line. If you are drawing an arrow, Excel adds an arrowhead automatically.

6. If you are drawing multiple lines, repeat steps 2–5.

7. To finish drawing multiple lines, click on an empty part of the worksheet or press Esc.

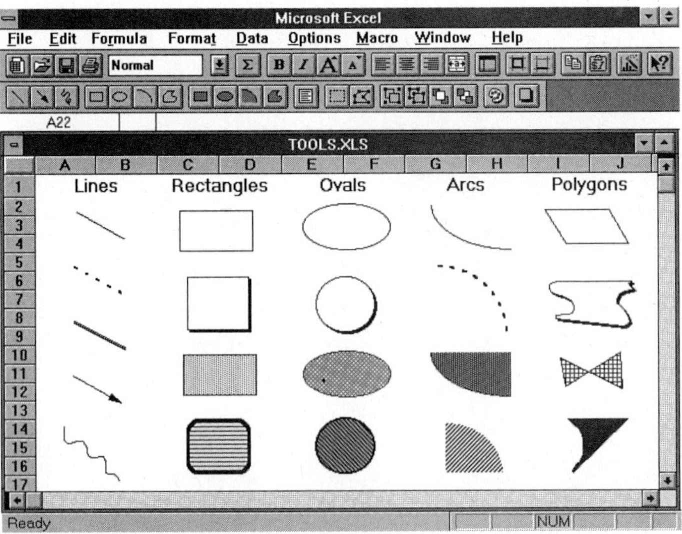

Figure 31.1 Excel's drawing tools let you create many different graphic objects.

IN ACTION: Excel does not give you an option for double underlining words in text or cell notes, but you can create your own by using two straight lines.

Figure 31.2 demonstrates some ways to use lines in a worksheet.

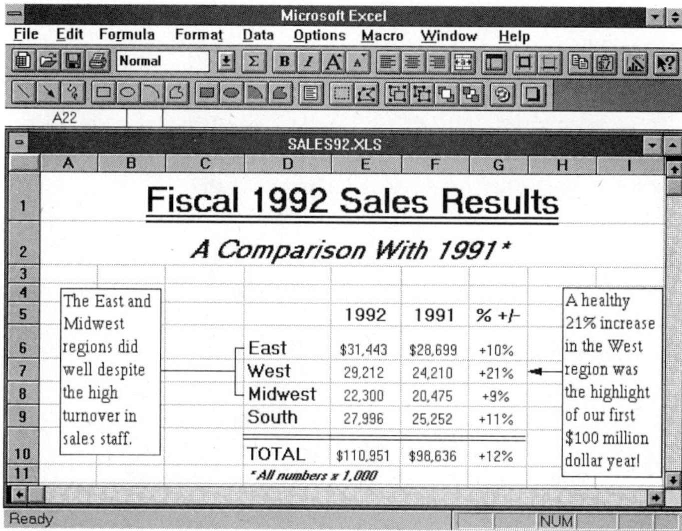

Figure 31.2 Some examples of Excel line objects in a worksheet.

Drawing Shapes

You can create three kinds of predefined shapes with Excel's drawing tools: rectangles, ovals, and arcs (a fourth shape—the polygon—is discussed in the next section). You will use shapes most often as part of more complex graphics such as a company logo. Follow these steps to create a shape:

1. Click on a shape-drawing tool. To draw multiple shapes, double-click on the tool. The mouse pointer changes to a crosshair.
2. Position the crosshair where you want to begin the shape.
3. Press and hold down the left mouse button.
4. Drag the mouse until the shape has the size and form you want.
5. Release the mouse button. Excel places black selection handles around the shape.
6. If you are drawing multiple shapes, repeat steps 2–5.
7. To finish drawing multiple shapes, click on an empty part of the worksheet or press Esc.

Drawing a Shape:
1. Click on a shape-drawing tool.
2. Position the crosshair.
3. Press and hold down left mouse button.
4. Drag mouse to draw the shape.
5. Release mouse button.
6. Repeat steps 2–5 to draw other shapes.
7. Press Esc.

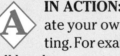

TIP: To make your rectangles square or your ovals circular, hold down Shift while drawing. To align your shapes with the worksheet gridlines, hold down Alt while drawing.

IN ACTION: You can use shapes to create your own custom worksheet formatting. For example, instead of using Excel's cell borders, create your own with the Rectangle tool (see Figure 31.3).

Figure 31.3 shows some examples of shapes used in a worksheet. The arrowhead on the end of the arc was accomplished by attaching an arrow with a very short shaft.

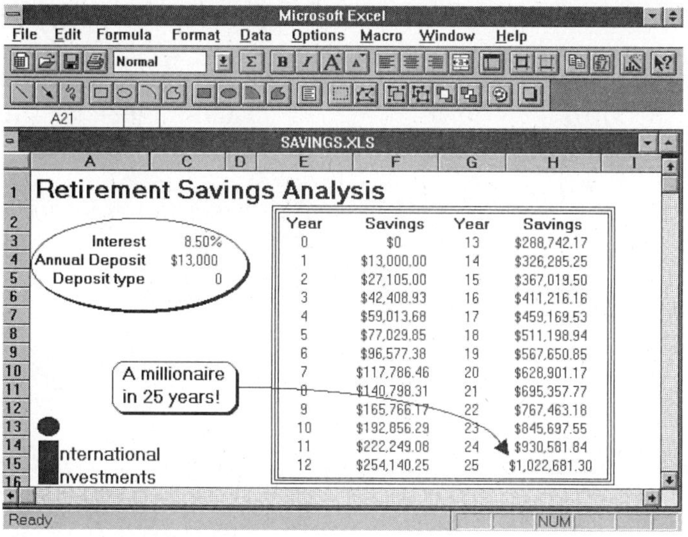

Figure 31.3 Some example shapes on a worksheet.

Drawing a Polygon

The Freehand Polygon tool is new with Excel 4 for Windows. This tool enables you to combine freehand lines with straight lines to create a polygon of any shape or size. Here are the steps to follow to use this tool:

1. Click on the Freehand Polygon tool. To draw multiple polygons, double-click on the tool. The mouse pointer changes to a crosshair.

2. Position the crosshair where you want to begin the polygon.

3. To draw freehand, press and hold down the left mouse button. To draw a straight line, click the left mouse button.

Drawing a Polygon:

1. Click on Freehand Polygon tool.
2. Position crosshair.
3. To draw freehand, press and hold down left mouse button. To draw a straight line, click left mouse button.

4. Move mouse to draw.
5. Release mouse button (freehand) or click left mouse button (line).
6. Repeat steps 3–5 to add other freehand or straight lines.
7. Double-click to finish drawing the polygon.

4. Move the mouse to draw the object you want.

5. To finish freehand drawing, release the mouse button. To finish drawing a straight line, click the left mouse button.

6. Repeat steps 3–5 to add other freehand or straight lines.

7. Double-click to finish drawing the polygon.

8. If you are drawing multiple polygons, repeat steps 2–7.

9. To finish drawing multiple polygons, click on the tool or press Esc.

Polygons are useful for creating complex shapes. In Figure 31.4, a polygon has been added around the sales figures and shaded to create a 3-D effect.

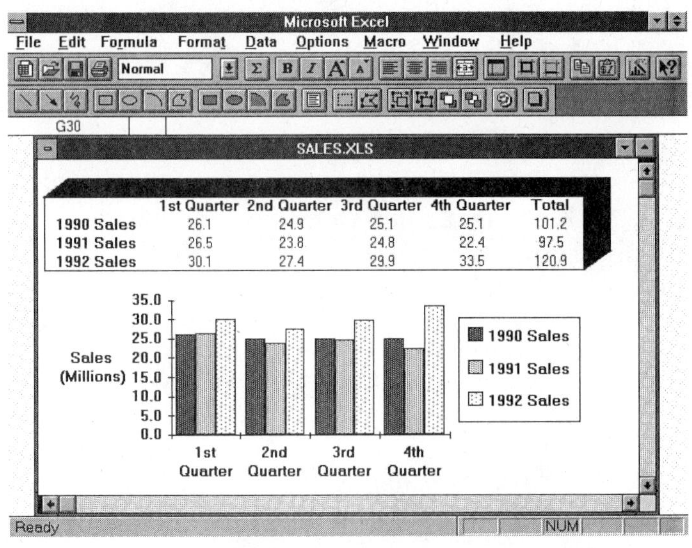

Figure 31.4 Use polygons for complex shapes.

Importing Graphics from Other Applications

Although the drawing tools that come with Excel are handy for creating simple graphics effects, a more ambitious image will require a dedicated graphics program such as Windows Paintbrush or CorelDRAW!. With these programs you can create professional-quality graphics and then import them into your Excel worksheet. If the application supports DDE (Dynamic Data Exchange) or OLE (Object Linking and Embedding), you can maintain a link between the object and the original program. Follow these steps to import a graphic image from another file:

1. Activate the graphics application.
2. Select the graphic image you want to import.
3. Copy the image to the Windows Clipboard. (Note: in most Windows applications, select Edit Copy.)
4. Activate Excel and select the worksheet you want to receive the graphic.
5. Select Edit Paste to copy the image to the worksheet.

Use the images you import from dedicated graphics applications to enhance the appearance of your worksheets. Figure 31.5 shows the SAVINGS.XLS worksheet with an imported money-related graphic.

Importing a Graphic Object:

1. Activate graphics application.
2. Select graphic image.
3. Copy image to Windows Clipboard.
4. Activate Excel worksheet.
5. Select Edit Paste.

TIP: If the graphics application supports OLE, use Edit Paste Link to establish a link between the two applications or Edit Insert Object to embed an object from the application. If the application allows you to import the graphic as different data types, use Edit Paste Special. See Skill Session 41 for more information.

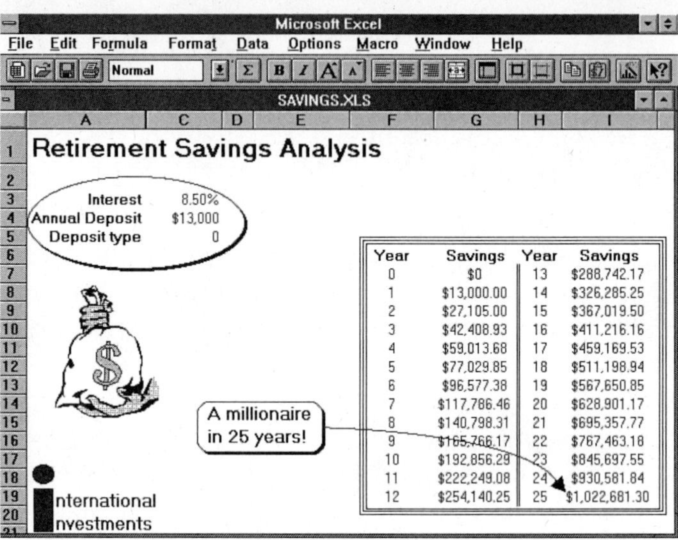

Year	Savings	Year	Savings
0	$0	13	$288,742.17
1	$13,000.00	14	$326,285.25
2	$27,105.00	15	$367,019.50
3	$42,408.93	16	$411,216.16
4	$59,013.68	17	$459,169.53
5	$77,029.85	18	$511,198.94
6	$96,577.38	19	$567,650.85
7	$117,786.46	20	$628,901.17
8	$140,798.31	21	$695,357.77
9	$165,766.17	22	$767,463.18
10	$192,856.29	23	$845,697.55
11	$222,249.08	24	$930,581.84
12	$254,140.25	25	$1,022,681.30

Figure 31.5 Importing graphics from other programs can improve the appearance of your worksheets.

IN ACTION: If you have access to a digital scanner, scan in your company logo and import the file to use for presentations and reports.

If you do not have the time or the skill to create your own images, consider using a *clip art* library. Clip art is professional-quality artwork that is commercially available in libraries of several hundred or more images. Some graphics programs, such as CorelDRAW! and Microsoft PowerPoint, include clip art collections. If you find that you use certain images repeatedly, create a worksheet to hold copies of these images. This will save you from having to search through massive clip art libraries every time you need an image. Figure 31.6 shows a worksheet containing several images imported from the CorelDRAW! clip art library.

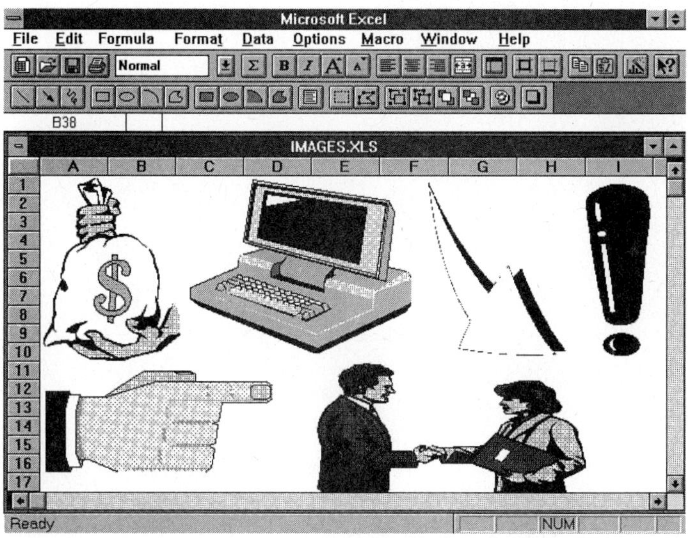

Figure 31.6 Copy often-used images to a separate file for easy access.

Skill Session

32

Editing Graphic Objects

Once you have added a graphic object to your worksheet, you can edit the object by changing the line or border style, the fill pattern, or the size. You can also easily move, copy, and delete graphic objects. This skill session shows you how to perform these basic graphic-editing tasks.

Selecting Graphic Objects

Before you can edit a graphic object, you need to select it. Here are the steps to follow to select any graphic object:

Selecting a Graphic Object:
1. Point to border of graphic.
2. Click mouse button.
3. To select other objects, hold down Ctrl and repeat steps 1 and 2.

1. Position the mouse pointer over the border of the graphic. The pointer changes to an arrow.
2. Click the mouse button. Excel displays selection handles around the object and shows the object identifier in the formula bar reference area (e.g., Line 1 or Oval 5).
3. To select other objects, hold down the Ctrl key and repeat steps 1 and 2.

Every graphic object has an invisible, rectangular *frame*. For a line or rectangle, the frame is the same as the object itself. For all other objects, the frame is a rectangle that completely encloses the shape or image. When you select an object, Excel displays black *selection handles* around the frame. Figure 32.1 shows several selected objects.

Formatting Lines

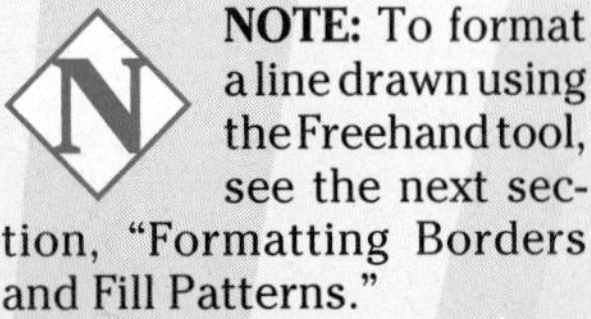

NOTE: To format a line drawn using the Freehand tool, see the next section, "Formatting Borders and Fill Patterns."

Figure 32.2 shows the Patterns dialog box for drawing lines. Using the options in this dialog, you can control the **S**tyle, **C**olor, and **W**eight of the line, and in the Arrow Head section, you can format the Sty**l**e, Wi**d**th, and

Length of an arrow's head. You can also add an arrowhead to a plain line or remove an arrowhead from an arrow. Figure 32.3 shows some formatted lines and arrows.

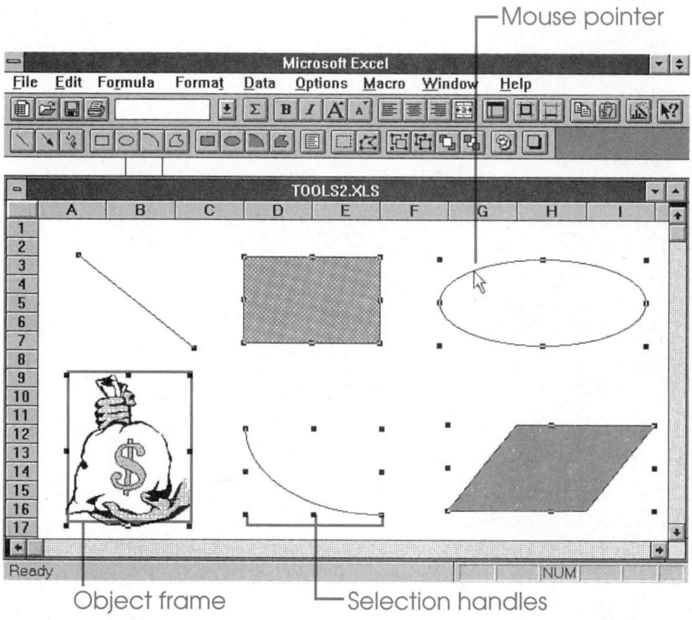

Figure 32.1 Selected objects display handles around the object's frame.

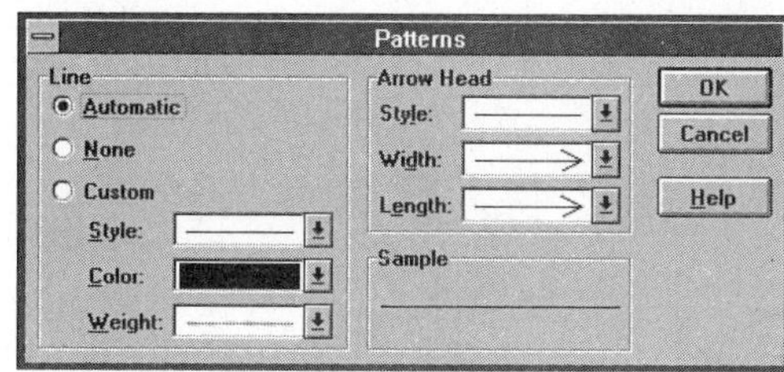

Figure 32.2 The Patterns dialog box for a drawn line.

TIP: To display the line Patterns dialog box quickly, double-click on the line. Alternatively, you can right-click on the line, or select the line and press Shift+F10. Then select Patterns from the shortcut menu that appears.

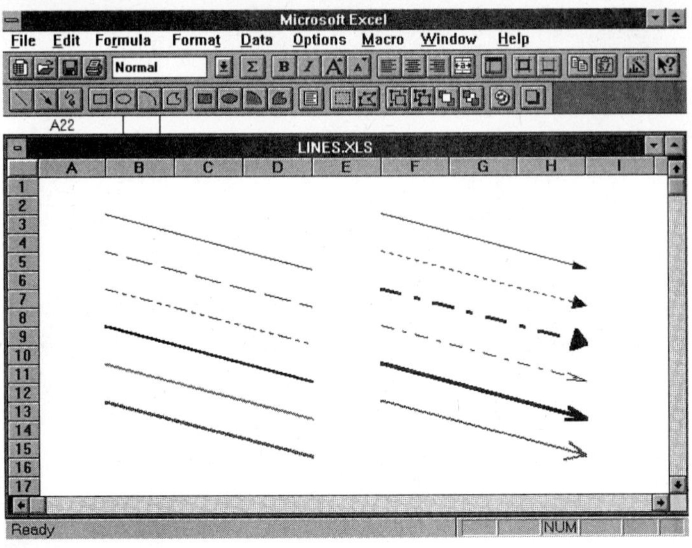

Figure 32.3 Some formatted lines and arrows.

Formatting a Line:

1. Select line.
2. Select Format Patterns.
3. Choose line options.
4. Select OK.

Click on this tool in the Drawing toolbar to cycle the line through the color palette. To cycle backward through the palette, hold down the Shift key while clicking.

Follow these steps to format a line:

1. Select the line you want to format.
2. Select Format Patterns to display the Patterns dialog box.
3. Choose the line options you want.
4. Select OK or press Enter.

Formatting Borders and Fill Patterns

For all other types of Excel graphic objects—including freehand lines—you can format the border and fill pattern using the Patterns dialog box shown in Figure 32.4. In this dialog box, you can set the **Style**, **Color**, and

Weight of the border, the fill **P**attern, and the **F**oreground and **B**ackground colors. You also have the option of adding a Sha**d**ow to a rectangle, oval, polygon, or freehand line. The **R**ound Corners option is available only for rectangles. Figure 32.5 shows a few examples of objects with formatted borders and fill patterns.

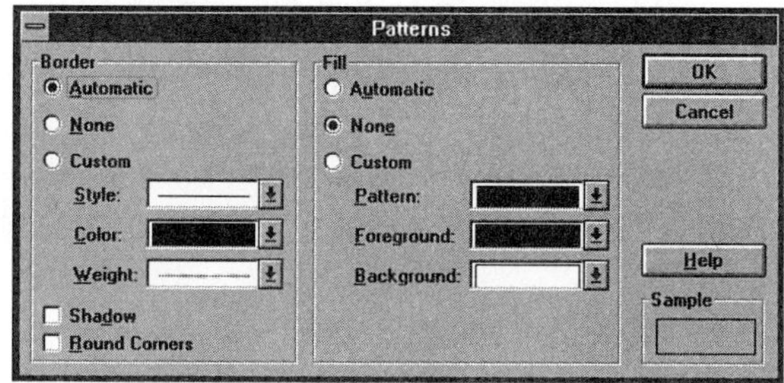

Figure 32.4 The Patterns dialog box for formatting object borders and fills.

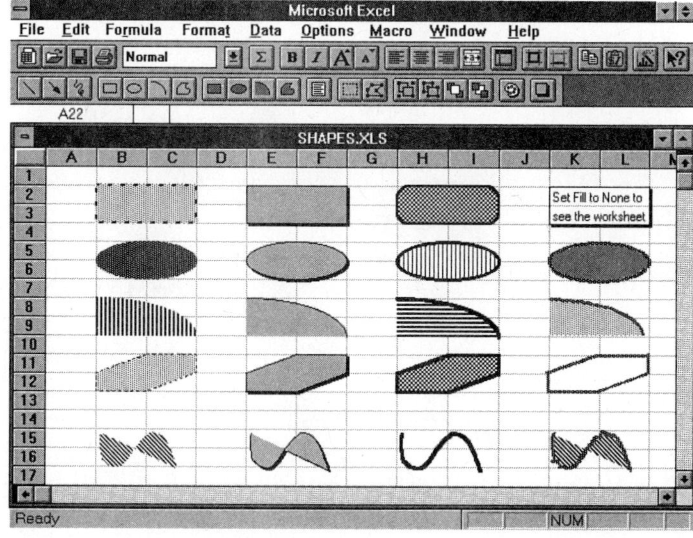

Figure 32.5 Some example objects with formatted borders and fill patterns.

Click on this tool in the Drawing toolbar to cycle the foreground color through the color palette. To cycle backward through the palette, hold down Shift while clicking.

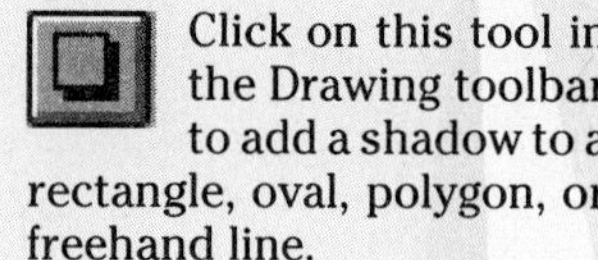

Click on this tool in the Drawing toolbar to add a shadow to a rectangle, oval, polygon, or freehand line.

Formatting Borders and Fill Patterns:

1. Select object.
2. Select Format Patterns.
3. Choose format options.
4. Select OK.

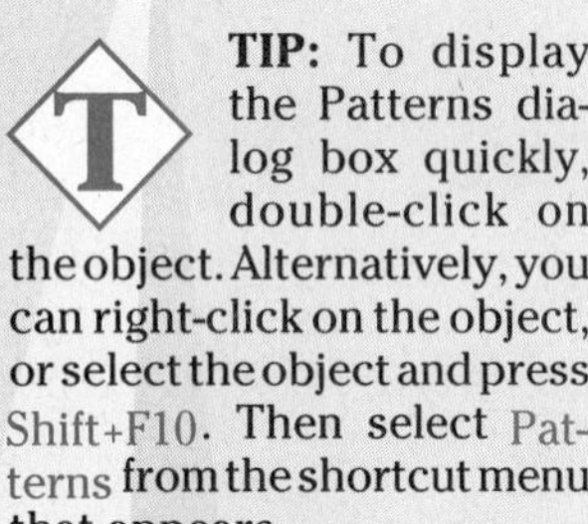

TIP: To display the Patterns dialog box quickly, double-click on the object. Alternatively, you can right-click on the object, or select the object and press Shift+F10. Then select Patterns from the shortcut menu that appears.

Follow these steps to format borders and fill patterns:

1. Select the object you want to format.
2. Select Format Patterns to display the Patterns dialog box.
3. Choose the formatting options you want.
4. Select OK or press Enter.

Sizing Graphic Objects

Sizing a Graphic Object:

1. Select object.
2. Position mouse pointer over a handle.
3. Drag handle to desired position.
4. Release mouse button.

TIP: To keep the same proportions when sizing an object, hold down Shift and drag a corner handle. To size the object with the worksheet gridlines, hold down Alt while dragging.

You can resize any graphic object to change its shape or dimensions. Here are the steps to follow:

1. Select the object you want to size. Excel displays the black selection handles around the object's frame.
2. Position the mouse pointer over the handle you want to move. The pointer changes to a two-headed arrow (see Figure 32.6). To change the size horizontally or vertically, use the appropriate handle on the middle of a side. To change the size in both directions at once, use the appropriate corner handle.
3. Drag the handle to the position you want. The pointer changes to a cross hair.
4. Release the mouse button. Excel redraws the object and adjusts the frame size.

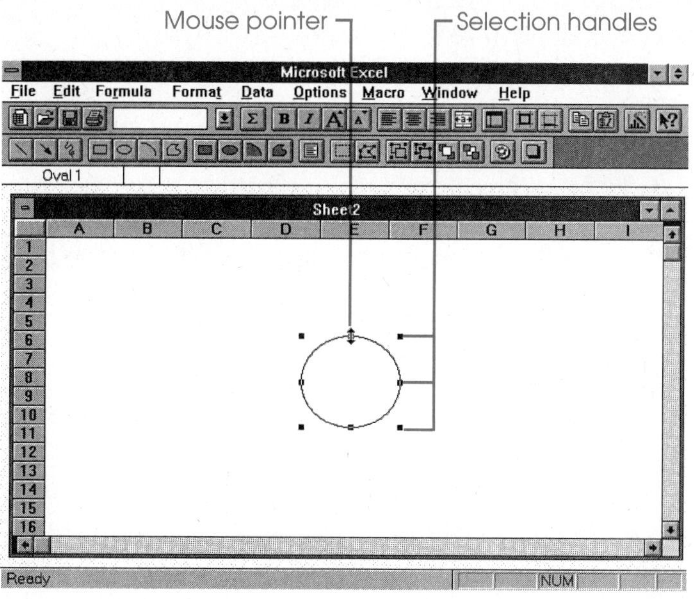

Figure 32.6 Drag a selection handle to size a graphic object.

NOTE: When you scale an image such as a clip art graphic, the scaling percentages for height and width appear in the formula bar reference area. The original graphic was 100% × 100%.

Editing Polygons

To change the size of a polygon, you can either use the procedure outlined in the previous section or edit the polygon using the Reshape tool. When you click on the Reshape tool, Excel displays *selection squares* at each vertex of the selected polygon. (Several vertices appear along each freehand line and one vertex appears at the beginning and end of every straight line.) You can then move, add, or delete vertices to get the shape you want. Here are the steps to follow:

To Edit a Polygon:

1. Select polygon.
2. Click on Reshape tool.
3. Drag a vertex to move it.
4. Press Shift and drag a line to add a vertex.
5. Press Shift and click on a vertex to delete it.
6. Click on Reshape tool.

The Reshape tool from the Drawing toolbar.

1. Select the polygon you want to edit.

2. Click on the Reshape tool. Excel displays the selection squares at each vertex of the polygon.

3. To move a vertex, position the mouse pointer over the vertex (the pointer changes to a cross hair; see Figure 31.7), and then drag the vertex to the position you want. Excel redraws the polygon with the new vertex position.

4. To add a vertex, press Shift and position the mouse pointer over the appropriate polygon line (the pointer changes to a cross hair with a square; see Figure 31.7). Drag the line to the new vertex point. Excel adds the vertex and redraws the polygon.

5. To delete a vertex, press Shift, position the mouse pointer over the vertex (the pointer changes to an "X"; see Figure 31.7), and then click once. Excel deletes the vertex and redraws the polygon.

6. When you have finished editing the polygon, click on the Reshape tool.

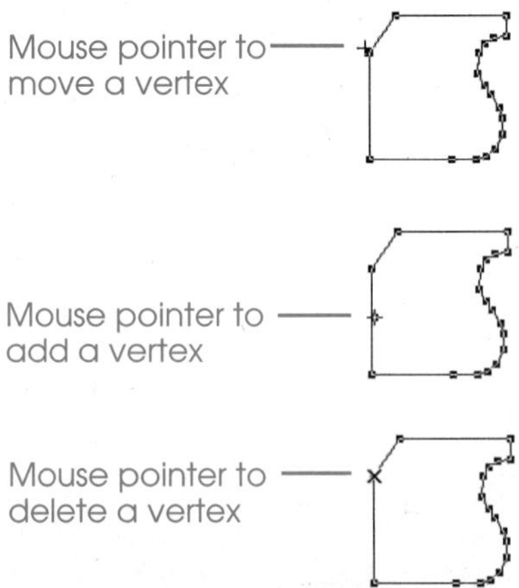

Figure 32.7 Excel displays a different mouse pointer for moving, deleting, or adding a vertex.

Moving Graphic Objects

You can move any graphic object to a different part of the worksheet by following these steps:

1. Select the object you want to move. Excel displays the black selection handles around the object's frame.
2. Position the mouse pointer on any edge of the object. The pointer changes to an arrow.
3. Drag the object to the position you want.
4. Release the mouse button. Excel redraws the object in the new position.

You can also move graphic objects using the cut-and-paste method. Follow these steps:

1. Select the object you want to move. Excel displays the black selection handles around the object's frame.
2. Select Edit Cut. Excel cuts the objects from the worksheet.
3. Move the cell selector to the new position.
4. Select Edit Paste. Excel redraws the object in the new position.

Moving a Graphic Object by Dragging:

1. Select object.
2. Position mouse pointer over an edge.
3. Drag object to new position.
4. Release mouse button.

TIP: To move the object with the worksheet gridlines, hold down Alt while dragging. To move the object only horizontally or vertically, hold down Shift while dragging.

Moving a Graphic Object by Cutting and Pasting:

1. Select object.
2. Select Edit Cut.
3. Move cell selector to new position.
4. Select Edit Paste.

TIP: To cut and paste an object quickly, right-click on the object, or select the object and press Shift+F10, and then select either Cut or Paste from the shortcut menu that appears.

Copying Graphic Objects

Copying a Graphic Object by Dragging:

1. Select object.
2. Press Ctrl and position mouse pointer over an edge.
3. Drag pointer to new position.
4. Release mouse button.

If you want multiple copies of the same object, you do not have to draw each one. Instead, follow these steps to make as many copies of the object as you need:

1. Select the object you want to copy. Excel displays the black selection handles around the object's frame.
2. Press Ctrl and position the mouse pointer on any edge of the object. The pointer changes to an arrow with a plus sign (see Figure 32.8).
3. Drag the pointer to the position you want.
4. Release the mouse button. Excel copies the object in the new position.

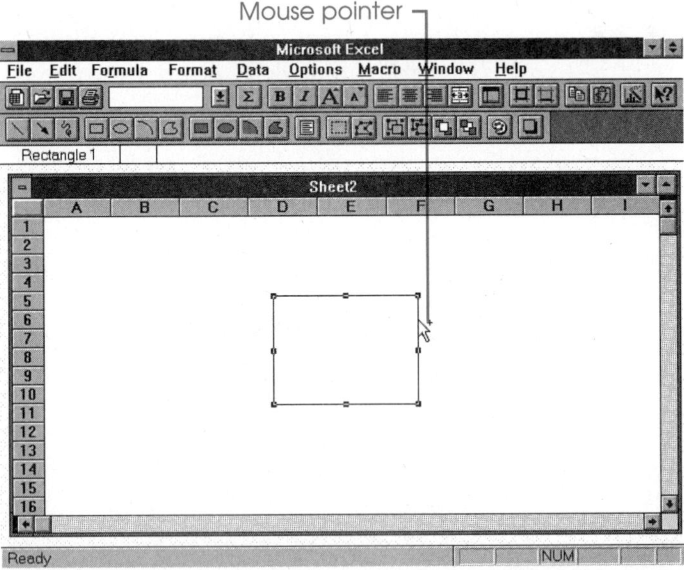

Figure 32.8 Mouse pointer for copying an object by dragging.

You can also use Edit Copy to copy graphic objects. Here are the steps to follow:

1. Select the object you want to copy. Excel displays the selection handles around the object's frame.
2. Select Edit Copy.
3. Position the cell selector in the approximate position you want for the copy.
4. Select Edit Paste. Excel pastes a copy of the object at the selected cell.

Copying Graphic Objects by Cutting and Pasting:

1. Select object.
2. Select Edit Copy.
3. Position cell selector.
4. Select Edit Paste.

TIP: To copy and paste an object quickly, right-click on the object, or select the object and press Shift+F10, and then select either Copy or Paste from the shortcut menu that appears.

Deleting Graphic Objects

To delete a graphic object that you no longer need, follow these steps:

1. Select the object you want to delete. Excel displays the selection handles around the object's frame.
2. Select Edit Clear. Excel deletes the object.

Deleting Graphic Objects:

1. Select object.
2. Select Edit Clear.

TIP: To delete an object quickly, select it and press Delete. Alternatively, you can right-click on the object, or select the object and press Shift+F10. Then select Clear from the shortcut menu that appears.

Skill Session

33

Working with Graphic Objects

Now that you know how to create and edit graphic objects, this skill session illustrates several techniques to make working with graphics faster and more efficient. You'll learn about working with multiple objects, hiding objects, and taking pictures with Excel's Camera tool.

Selecting Multiple Graphic Objects

If you use graphics often, you could easily end up with a dozen or more objects in a worksheet. If you then want to rearrange or reformat the worksheet, it becomes time-consuming to move or format each object individually. To get around this, Excel allows you to select all the objects you want and work with them simultaneously.

Excel offers a couple of methods for selecting multiple objects. If you just need a few objects, or if the objects you need are scattered widely throughout the worksheet, hold down Ctrl and select each object individually. If the objects you want are grouped together, you can use Excel's Selection tool to select them all quickly. Here are the steps to follow:

The Selection tool from the Drawing toolbar.

Selecting Multiple Objects with the Selection Tool:

1. Click on Selection tool.
2. Position pointer in top left corner of selection area.
3. Press and hold left mouse button.
4. Drag pointer to bottom right corner of selection area.
5. Release mouse button.
6. Click on Selection tool or press Esc.

1. Click on the Selection tool. The mouse pointer changes to a cross hair.
2. Position the pointer at the top left corner of the area you want to select.
3. Press and hold down the left mouse button.
4. Drag the pointer to the bottom right corner of the area you want to select. As you drag the pointer, Excel indicates the selected area with a dashed border (see Figure 33.1).
5. Release the mouse button. Excel places selection handles around each object in the selection area.
6. To end the selection, click on the Selection tool or press Esc.

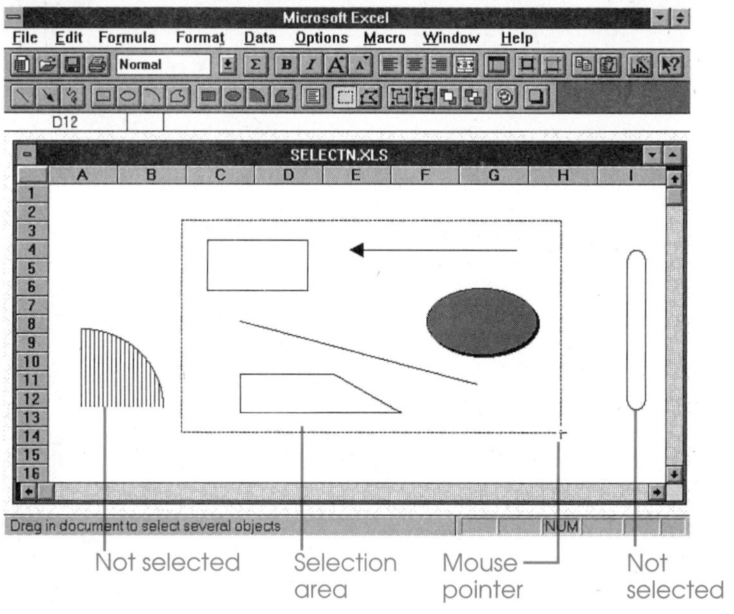

Figure 33.1 Make sure the selection area completely encloses each object you want to select.

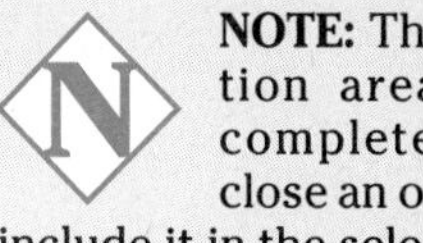

NOTE: The selection area must completely enclose an object to include it in the selection.

TIP: If you miss any objects, make sure the Selection key is still active and then, while holding down the Ctrl key, repeat steps 2–5 for the other objects you want to include.

TIP: To select all graphic objects in a worksheet, select Formula Select Special and then choose Objects from the Select Special dialog box that appears. To deselect all objects, simply click on any empty part of the worksheet or press Esc.

After you have your multiple selection, you can format, size, move, copy, or delete all of the objects at once. Note, however, that you will need to format lines and shapes separately because they use different formatting options. To exclude an object from the selection, hold down Ctrl and click on the object's border. To exclude a number of objects from the selection, hold down Ctrl and use the Selection tool to reselect the objects.

Grouping Graphic Objects

Excel 4 for Windows allows you to create object *groups*. A group is a collection of objects that you can format, size, or move as though it were a single object. To select the entire group, you need only select a single object from the group. Here are the steps to follow:

Grouping Graphic Objects:

1. Select objects.
2. Select Format Group.

1. Select the objects you want to group together.
2. Select Format Group. Excel creates an invisible, rectangular frame around the objects.

Use the Group tool on the Drawing toolbar to group selected objects.

IN ACTION: If you have combined a number of graphic objects into a design or logo, group the elements so you can move or size them together.

Excel treats a group as a single graphic object with its own frame. In Figure 33.2, for example, an oval, a rectangle, and a text box have been grouped together. Any sizing, move, or copy operations act on each member of the group. If your group mixes line and shape objects, you will only be able to format the shapes. To format the lines, you need to ungroup the objects and work on the lines separately.

To ungroup objects, follow these steps:

Ungrouping Graphic Objects:

1. Select group.
2. Select Format Ungroup.

1. Select the group.
2. Select Format Ungroup. Excel removes the group but leaves the individual objects selected.

Use the Ungroup tool on the Drawing toolbar to ungroup graphic objects.

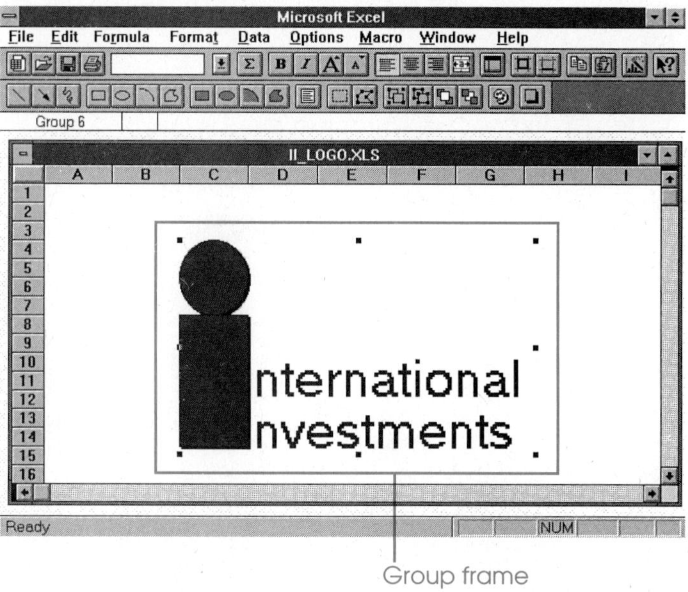

Figure 33.2 Excel treats grouped graphics as a single object.

Hiding Graphic Objects

One of the problems with graphic objects is that they take longer to display than regular worksheet elements. The more detailed the graphic or the more graphics on-screen, the longer Excel takes to redraw the screen. Even with today's powerful 386 and 486 machines, this can make scrolling through a worksheet cumbersome and time-consuming.

To get around this problem, you can temporarily "hide" all worksheet objects so that Excel does not redraw them every time you scroll past. You have two options you can use when hiding graphic objects:

Hi**d**e All	Suppresses the display of all graphic objects.
Show Placeholders	Displays a gray rectangle in place of all embedded charts and pictures (see Figure 33.3). Lines, shapes, and polygons are still shown.

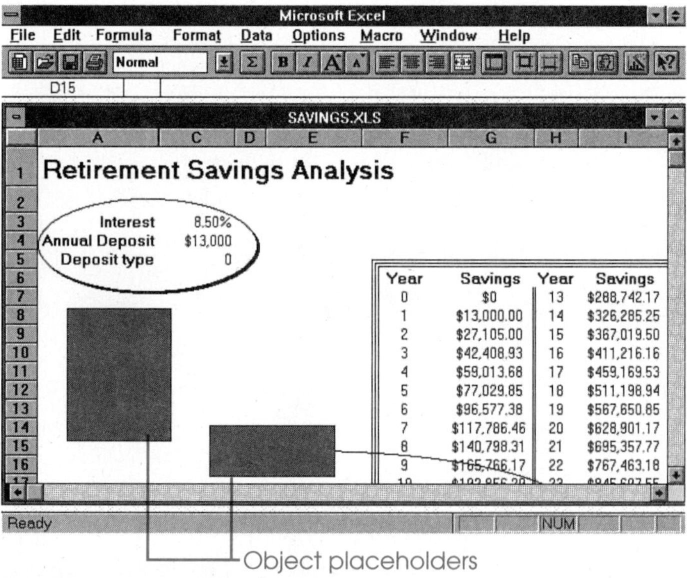

Figure 33.3 For faster screen redraws, you can hide objects with placeholders.

Follow these steps to hide graphic objects:

1. Select Options Display. The Display Options dialog box appears.
2. Select the option you want from the Objects section.
3. Select OK or press Enter.

Hiding Graphic Objects:

1. Select Options Display.
2. Select desired option.
3. Select OK.

TIP: To show the hidden objects, select Options Display and then select Show All.

TIP: Press Ctrl+6 to cycle through showing placeholders, hiding all objects, and showing all objects.

Controlling Object Placement

Most of your graphic objects are probably positioned relative to specific worksheet cells. For example, you might have a text box with an arrow to explain the contents of a cell or a rectangle around a worksheet table. In each of these cases, if you move or size the worksheet cells, you will want the graphic to move or size along with them. You can control this with the options found in the Object Properties dialog box (shown in Figure 33.4):

Move and Size with Cells	Attaches the object to the cells underneath the object. When you move or size the cells, the object is moved or sized accordingly. This is the default option for drawn objects.

Move but Don't Size with Cells	Attaches the object only to the cell underneath its top left corner. When you move this cell, the object moves with it, but does not change size. This is the default option for embedded charts and pictures.
Don't Move or Size with Cells	Object is not attached to the cell underneath it.

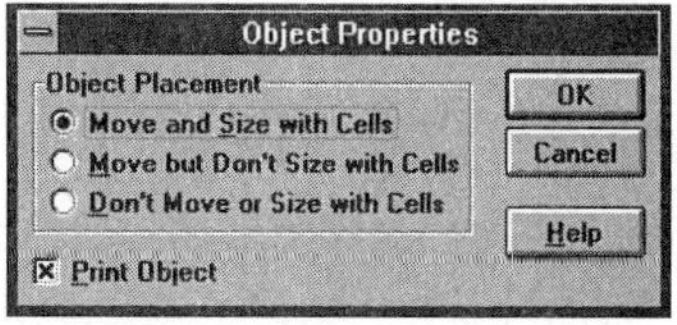

Figure 33.4 The Object Properties dialog box.

IN ACTION: Use the **M**ove but Don't Size with Cells option for logos and designs that you want to remain the same size.

Setting an Object's Placement:

1. Select object.
2. Choose Format Object Properties.
3. Select placement option.
4. Select OK.

Follow these steps to attach an object to its underlying cells:

1. Select the object.
2. Select Format Object Properties. Excel displays the Object Properties dialog box.
3. Select the placement option you want.
4. Select OK or press Enter.

To illustrate this property, Figure 33.5 shows three copies of a graphic image where each copy has been given a different placement option. Figure 33.6 shows the same graphics after one row has been inserted and another has had its height increased.

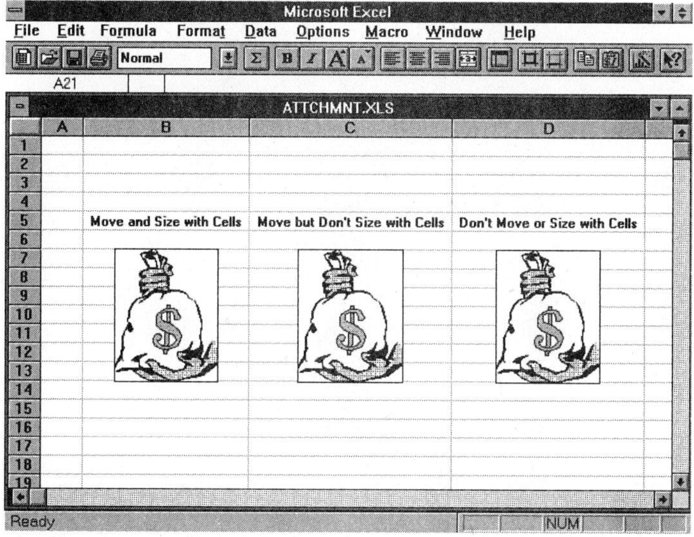

Figure 33.5 Three objects with different placement options.

TIP: To display the Object Properties dialog box quickly, right-click on the object, or select the object and press Shift+F10, and then select Object Properties from the shortcut menu that appears.

NOTE: The Object Properties dialog box has a fourth option: **Print** Object. Deactivate this option when you do not want the selected object to print with the worksheet.

Ordering Overlapped Graphic Objects

Whenever you have two graphic objects overlapping each other, the most recently created object will cover part of the earlier object. In this sense, the newer object is "in front" of the older one. You can change the order of overlapped objects by selecting an object and then selecting either Format Send to Back or Format Bring to Front.

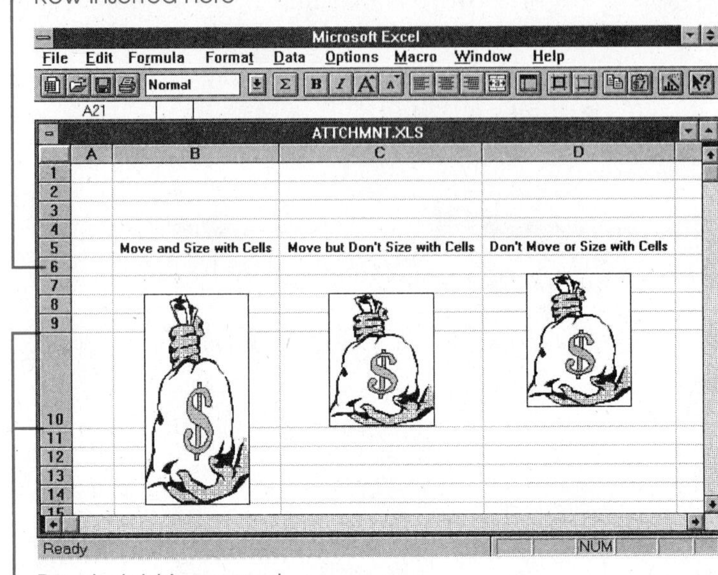

Figure 33.6 The placement options determine how an object is affected by cell movement or sizing.

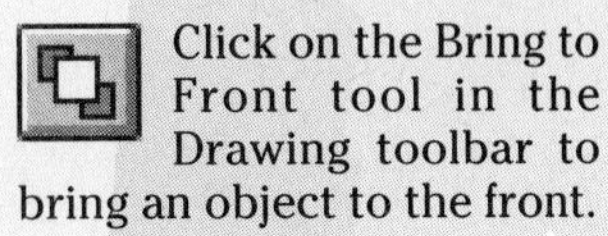

Click on the Bring to Front tool in the Drawing toolbar to bring an object to the front.

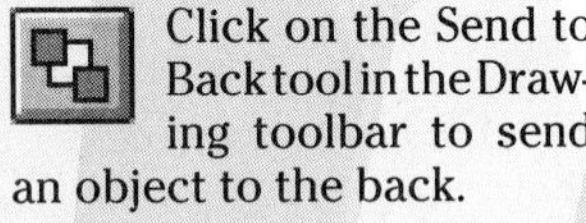

Click on the Send to Back tool in the Drawing toolbar to send an object to the back.

Figure 33.7 shows a filled rectangle in front of a text box. By selecting the rectangle and selecting Format Send to Back, the rectangle becomes an attractive shadow effect (see Figure 33.8).

Working with Pictures

Excel allows you to take *pictures* of your worksheet cells, graphic objects, and charts. In the same way that a photograph captures an image of a particular scene, an Excel picture captures an image of the selected range or object. You can then treat the picture as you would any other graphic object: you can place it anywhere in the current or another worksheet, you can size it, copy it, and even format it to suit your needs. If you take a picture of a range of cells, you also have the option of linking the picture to the original cells. This way, if the numbers in any range change, Excel updates the picture automatically.

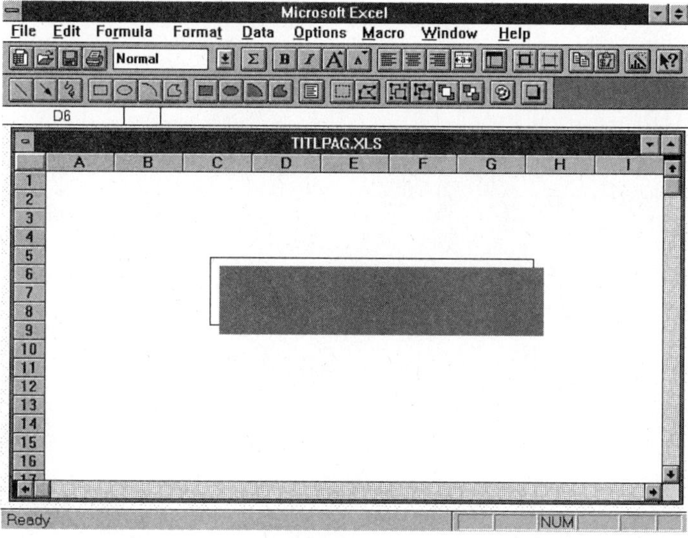

Figure 33.7 The filled rectangle covers the text box underneath.

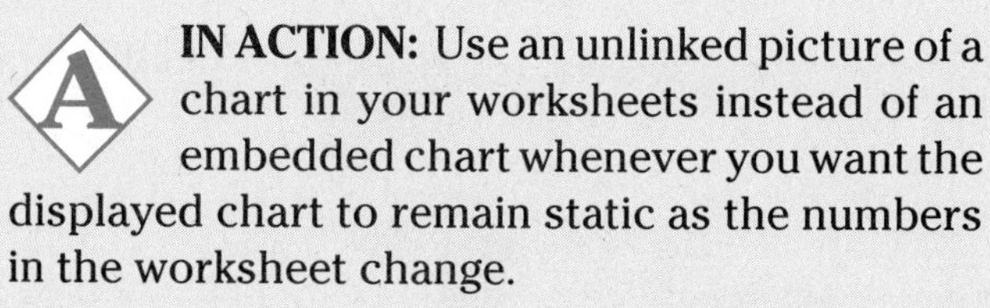

IN ACTION: Use an unlinked picture of a chart in your worksheets instead of an embedded chart whenever you want the displayed chart to remain static as the numbers in the worksheet change.

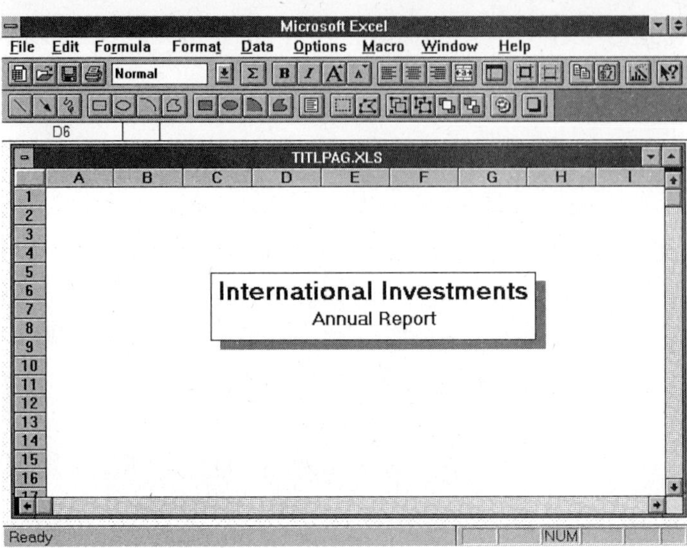

Figure 33.8 Selecting Send to Back enables you to use the rectangle to create a shadow effect.

When you copy a picture, you set the copy options using the Copy Picture dialog box, shown in Figure 33.9. To set the appearance of the picture, you have two options:

As Shown on **S**creen	Copies the picture as it appears on-screen, including the row and column headings for cell ranges.
As Shown when **P**rinted	Copies the picture as it appears when printed but does not copy row and column headings for cell ranges.

Figure 33.9 The Copy Picture dialog box.

Which of these options you choose depends on what you are copying and what kind of printer you have. The As Shown when **P**rinted option has the advantage of not copying row and column headings. However, if you select this option and are using a black and white printer, Excel will convert all colors in the selection to black and white. In general, the best choice is usually As Shown on **S**creen. If you do not want the row and column headings copied, select **O**ptions **D**isplay and turn off the row and column headings before copying the range.

In some cases, the Copy Picture dialog box also gives you the choice of either a Picture or a **B**itmap format. The Pic**t**ure format is the default and copies a drawing of the image that scales proportionately when you size the picture. The **B**itmap format gives you a picture made up of different colored pixels.

If you want to copy a picture of a cell range, graphic object, or chart, but you do not want Excel to update the picture every time the data changes, you need to copy an unlinked picture. Here are the steps to follow:

Copying an Unlinked Picture:

1. Select object to copy.
2. Hold down Shift and select Edit Copy Picture.
3. Choose desired copy options.
4. Select OK.
5. Activate receiving worksheet.
6. Select upper left corner of destination.
7. Select Edit Paste.

1. Select the range, object, or chart you want to copy.
2. Hold down Shift and select Edit Copy Picture. Excel displays the Copy Picture dialog box.
3. Select the copy options you want.
4. Select OK or press Enter.
5. Activate the worksheet to which you want to copy the picture.
6. Select the cell at the upper left corner of the area where you want to copy the picture.
7. Select Edit Paste. Excel pastes the picture onto the worksheet.

IN ACTION: Use Excel pictures anytime you need to view or print a range or chart on the same worksheet. Pictures are useful for doing worksheet analysis or data entry without setting up separate windows or panes.

Copying a Linked Picture of a Cell Range:

1. Select range to copy.
2. Hold Shift and select Edit Copy Picture.
3. Select copy options.
4. Select OK.

If you want to copy a picture of a cell range, graphic object, or chart, and you want Excel to update the picture every time the data changes, you need to copy a linked picture. Here are the steps to follow:

1. Select the range you want to copy.
2. Hold down Shift and select Edit Copy Picture. Excel displays the Copy Picture dialog box.
3. Select the copy options you want.
4. Select OK or press Enter.

5. Activate the worksheet to which you want to copy the picture.

6. Select the cell at the upper left corner of the area where you want to copy the picture.

7. Hold down Shift and select **E**dit Paste **L**ink. Excel pastes the picture onto the worksheet and displays the linked range in the formula bar.

5. Activate receiving worksheet.
6. Select cell where you want to copy the picture.
7. Hold Shift and select **E**dit Paste **L**ink.

Excel updates linked pictures of ranges automatically whether you change the numbers or the formatting of the original cells. For example, if you change the font or alignment in the original range, the picture, font, and alignment also change.

To copy a linked picture of a cell range quickly, select the Camera tool from the Utility toolbar. To paste the picture, click the left mouse button.

You can make changes to a linked cell picture quickly by double-clicking on the picture. Excel activates the worksheet and selects the range for you automatically. When you change the cells, Excel updates the picture.

IN ACTION: Use Excel pictures to copy worksheet cells, objects, or charts to another Windows application. Copy the picture, activate the application, and then choose **E**dit **P**aste.

Skill Session

34

Creating Slide Shows

Excel 4 for Windows offers some powerful tools for creating slide show presentations. A new template makes creating slide shows fast and easy, and you can even include video and audio transition effects between slides. This skill session shows you how to create, edit, and run Excel slide shows.

Working with the Slide Template

Opening the Slide Template:

1. Select File New.
2. Highlight Slides.
3. Select OK.

You use a special template included with Excel 4 for Windows to create your slide shows. To open the template, follow these steps:

1. Select File New. Excel displays the New dialog box.
2. From the New list, highlight Slides.
3. Select OK or press Enter. Excel opens the slide show template, as shown in Figure 34.1.

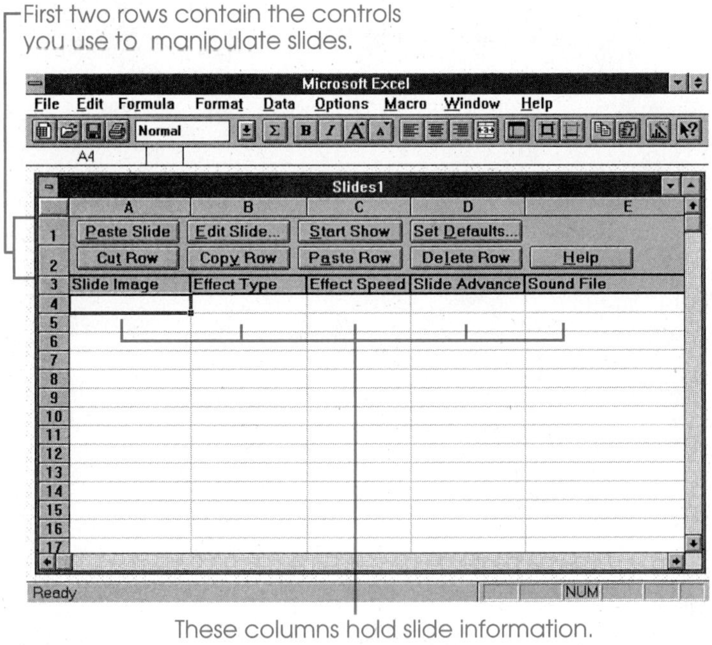

First two rows contain the controls you use to manipulate slides.

	A	B	C	D	E
1	Paste Slide	Edit Slide...	Start Show	Set Defaults...	
2	Cut Row	Copy Row	Paste Row	Delete Row	Help
3	Slide Image	Effect Type	Effect Speed	Slide Advance	Sound File

These columns hold slide information.

Figure 34.1 The slide template.

The first two rows of the template contain a number of command buttons that you use to manipulate your slides. With these buttons, you can add or delete slides, edit the slide settings, and change the slide order. Excel stores the information for each slide in columns A through E, beginning in row 4. This information includes a reduced image of the slide and the settings for the transition effects.

Creating a Slide

To create a slide, you copy the desired cell range or chart onto the Windows Clipboard. Excel uses the Clipboard contents to create a new slide in the slide template. Excel then displays the Edit Slide dialog box, as shown in Figure 34.2. This dialog box contains three sections:

Transition Gallery. This section sets the video transition effects. The **E**ffect list contains over 40 different video transitions, and the **S**peed slider bar controls the transition speed. Use the **T**est button to see an example of the transition effect.

Advance. Slide advance can be either **M**anual or Time**d**. If you choose Time**d**, you enter the number of seconds between slides.

Sound. This section sets the audio transition effects. Select Choose to open a sound file. The Test Sou**n**d button plays a sample of the sound. The Cl**e**ar button closes the sound file.

NOTE: To use audio transition effects, you must have Windows Multimedia Extensions Version 1.00 or later or Windows 3.1 (and an appropriate sound board) or later.

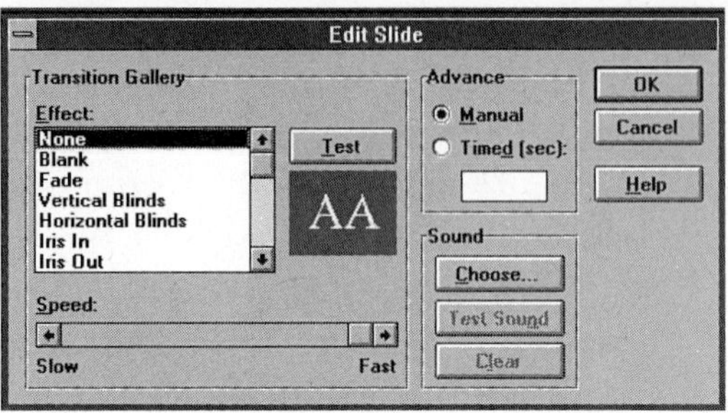

Figure 34.2 The Edit Slide dialog box.

Follow these steps to create a slide from a worksheet range:

Creating a Slide from a Worksheet Range:

1. Activate worksheet.
2. Highlight cell range.
3. Select Edit Copy.
4. Activate slide template.
5. Select Paste Slide.
6. Select desired options.
7. Select OK.

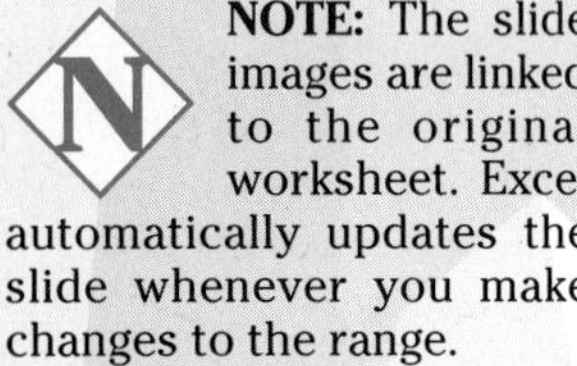

NOTE: The slide images are linked to the original worksheet. Excel automatically updates the slide whenever you make changes to the range.

1. Activate the worksheet containing the cell range you want to include in the slide.

2. Highlight the cell range.

3. Select Edit Copy. Excel displays a moving border around the selection.

4. Activate the slide template.

5. Select Paste Slide on the slide template. (When you move the mouse cursor over the slide template buttons, the pointer changes to a hand with a pointing finger.) Excel pastes a reduced image of the range in the Slide Image column and displays the Edit Slide dialog box.

6. Select the options you want.

7. Select OK or press Enter. Excel enters the slide settings on the template.

IN ACTION: Make sure your slides are simple and readable with plenty of open space. Your audience should not have to guess what the point of the slide is. Try to use a consistent design scheme in all your slides. A company logo or other graphic in a corner and consistent colors will give your presentation continuity.

Figure 34.3 shows a slide template with several worksheet slides.

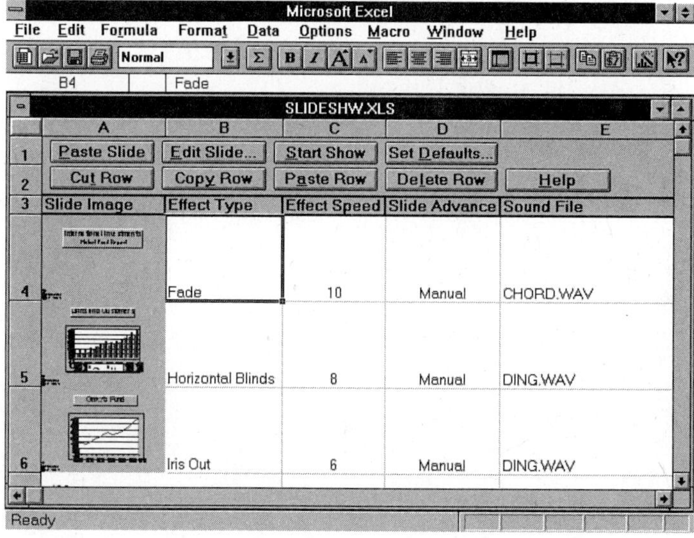

Figure 34.3 An Excel slide show.

Creating a Slide from a Chart:

1. Activate chart.
2. Select Chart Select Chart.
3. Select Edit Copy.
4. Activate slide template.
5. Select Paste Slide.
6. Select desired options.
7. Select OK.

TIP: You can use graphics from other applications in your Excel slide shows. Simply copy the image to the Clipboard and select Paste Slide on the slide template.

Follow these steps to create a slide from a chart:

1. Activate the chart you want to include in the slide.
2. Select Chart Select Chart. Excel displays selection handles around the chart.
3. Select Edit Copy. Excel displays a moving border around the chart.
4. Activate the slide template.
5. Select Paste Slide. Excel pastes a reduced image of the chart in the Slide Image column and displays the Edit Slide dialog box.
6. Select the options you want.
7. Select OK or press Enter. Excel enters the slide settings on the template.

Editing Slide Transition Effects

Editing Slide Transition Effects:

1. Select a cell in the slide row.
2. Select Edit Slide.
3. Enter desired options.
4. Select OK.

You can edit the transition effects of any slide or group of slides that appears on the slide show template. Here are the steps to follow:

1. Select at least one cell from the row containing the slide information you want to edit (do not select the slide itself). To edit more than one slide, select a cell from each row.
2. Select Edit Slide. Excel displays the Edit Slide dialog box.

3. Enter the options you want.

4. Select OK or press Enter. Excel updates the slide information.

If you find that you use the same transition settings for most of your slides, you can set up a default setting by following these steps:

1. Select Set Defaults. Excel displays the Set Defaults dialog box.

2. Select the transition effects you want to use as defaults.

3. Select OK or press Enter.

Setting Default Transition Effects:

1. Select Set Defaults.
2. Select transition effects.
3. Select OK.

NOTE: The new default transition effects do not change the settings for any existing slides. To change the transition options for existing slides, use Edit Slide instead.

Moving a Slide

Changing the order of a slide is as easy as cutting and pasting a row in the slide template. Here are the steps to follow:

1. Select at least one cell in the row containing the slide you want to move (do not select the slide itself).

2. Select Cut Row. Excel cuts the slide from the template.

3. Select a cell in the row above which you want to insert the slide. To move the slide to the end, select a cell in any empty row.

4. Select Paste Row. Excel inserts the slide above the selected row.

Moving a Slide:

1. Select a cell in the slide row.
2. Select Cut Row.
3. Select a cell in the row above which you want to insert the slide.
4. Select Paste Row.

Copying a Slide

Copying a Slide:

1. Select a cell in the slide row.
2. Select Copy Row.
3. Select a cell in the row above which you want to insert the copy.
4. Select Paste Row.

If you want to use the same slide at another point in your presentation, you do not have to create the slide again. Instead, follow these steps to copy the existing slide:

1. Select at least one cell in the row containing the slide you want to copy (do not select the slide itself).
2. Select Copy Row.
3. Select a cell in the row above which you want to insert the copy. To copy the slide to the end, select a cell in any empty row.
4. Select Paste Row. Excel inserts the copy above the selected row.

Deleting a Slide

Deleting a Slide:

1. Select a cell in the slide row.
2. Select Delete Row.

If you no longer need a slide, you can delete it from the template by following these steps:

1. Select at least one cell in the row containing the slide you want to delete (do not select the slide itself).
2. Select Delete Row. Excel deletes the row.

Running a Slide Show

When you want to run a slide show, press Start Show. Excel displays the Start Show dialog box, as shown in

Figure 34.4. This dialog box allows you to set two options:

Repeat show until Esc is pressed	Select this option to run the slide show in a continuous loop.
Initial Slide	Use the slider bar to specify the first slide in the show.

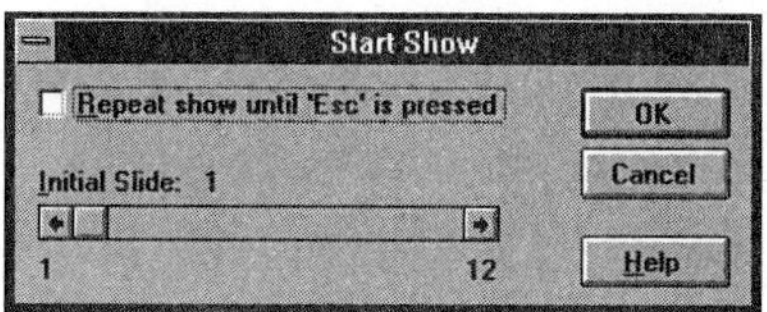

Figure 34.4 The Start Show dialog box.

When you have chosen your options, select OK or press Enter. Excel displays the first slide, sized to fit the screen.

If you set your slides to advance at timed intervals, Excel automatically performs the transition from one slide to the next. If you are using the manual advance, Excel pauses on each slide until you are ready. To advance to the next slide, click the left mouse button.

Interrupting a Slide Show

You can interrupt a slide show at any time by pressing Esc. When you do, Excel displays the Slide Show Options dialog box, as shown in Figure 34.5. In this dialog box, you have the following options:

Slide **N**umber	If you want to switch to a different slide, select the slide number from the slider bar.

Goto	Select this button to resume the slide show at the Slide **N**umber.
Stop	Select this button to end the slide show.
Continue	Select this button to resume the slide show from the same slide where it was interrupted.

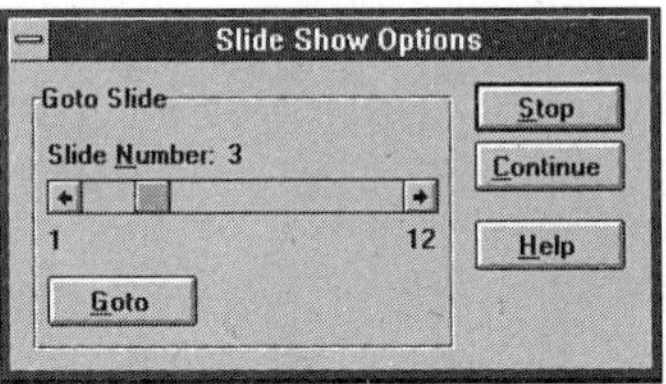

Figure 34.5 The Slide Show Options dialog box.

Running a Slide Show on a Different Computer

Running a Slide Show on a Different Computer:

1. Activate Excel on the other computer.
2. Open slide show template file.
3. Select Options Unprotect Document.
4. Select File Links.

If you want to run your slide show on another computer equipped with Excel, you need to make sure the slide template is linked to the Slide Show Add-in file (called SLIDES.XLA) on the other computer. Here are the steps to follow:

1. Activate Excel on the other computer.
2. Open the slide show template file as outlined earlier in this skill session.
3. Select **O**ptions Un**p**rotect Document. This enables you to change the file's links.
4. Select **F**ile **L**inks. Excel displays the Links dialog box.

5. Highlight SLIDES.XLA in the **L**inks list box.
6. Select **C**hange. Excel displays the Change Links dialog box.
7. Highlight SLIDES.XLA (this file should be in the \LIBRARY\SLIDES subdirectory).
8. Select OK or press Enter. Excel updates the links and returns you to the Links dialog box.
9. Select Close.
10. Run the slide show.

5. Highlight SLIDES.XLA.
6. Select **C**hange.
7. Highlight SLIDES.XLA.
8. Select OK.
9. Select Close.
10. Run slide show.

Database Workshop

This workshop introduces you to Excel databases. You'll learn basic skills such as creating and sorting a database and setting database criteria, as well as more advanced skills including database functions and crosstab tables.

Skill Session

35

Creating and Sorting a Database

This skill session introduces you to Excel databases. You'll learn what databases are, what you can use them for, and how to create them in your Excel worksheets.

What Is a Database?

A *database* is a collection of related information with an organizational structure that makes it easy for you to find or extract data from its contents. For example, a phone book is a database organized by name, and a library card catalogue is a database organized by book title.

In Excel 4 for Windows, the term *database* means a range of worksheet cells that has the following properties:

> **NOTE:** In spreadsheet databases, the term *field* can mean either a column or an individual cell, depending on whether you are talking about the entire database or a single record.

Field. A single type of information such as a name, address, or phone number. In Excel databases, each column (or any cell in a column) is a field.

Field name. You assign a unique name to every database field (worksheet column). These names are always found in the first row of the database.

Record. A collection of associated fields. In Excel databases, each row is a record.

Database range. The worksheet range that includes all the records, fields, and field names of the database.

As an example, suppose you want to set up an accounts receivable database. A simple system would include information such as the account name, account number, invoice number, invoice amount, due date, date paid, and a calculation of the number of days overdue. Figure 35.1 shows how this would be implemented as an Excel database.

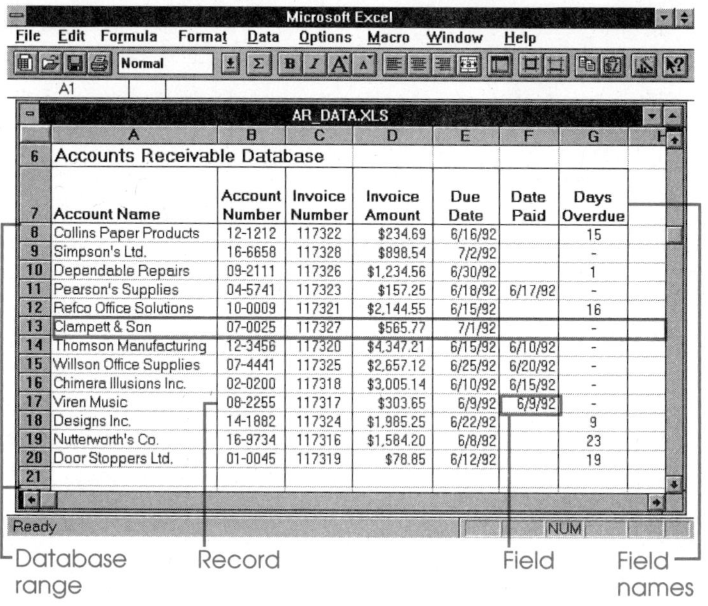

	A	B	C	D	E	F	G
6	Accounts Receivable Database						
7	Account Name	Account Number	Invoice Number	Invoice Amount	Due Date	Date Paid	Days Overdue
8	Collins Paper Products	12-1212	117322	$234.69	6/16/92		15
9	Simpson's Ltd.	16-6658	117328	$898.54	7/2/92		-
10	Dependable Repairs	09-2111	117326	$1,234.56	6/30/92		1
11	Pearson's Supplies	04-5741	117323	$157.25	6/18/92	6/17/92	-
12	Refco Office Solutions	10-0009	117321	$2,144.55	6/15/92		16
13	Clampett & Son	07-0025	117327	$565.77	7/1/92		-
14	Thomson Manufacturing	12-3456	117320	$4,347.21	6/15/92	6/10/92	-
15	Willson Office Supplies	07-4441	117325	$2,657.12	6/25/92	6/20/92	-
16	Chimera Illusions Inc.	02-0200	117318	$3,005.14	6/10/92	6/15/92	-
17	Viren Music	08-2255	117317	$303.65	6/9/92	6/9/92	-
18	Designs Inc.	14-1882	117324	$1,985.25	6/22/92		9
19	Nutterworth's Co.	16-9734	117316	$1,584.20	6/8/92		23
20	Door Stoppers Ltd.	01-0045	117319	$78.85	6/12/92		19
21							

Figure 35.1 An accounts receivable database.

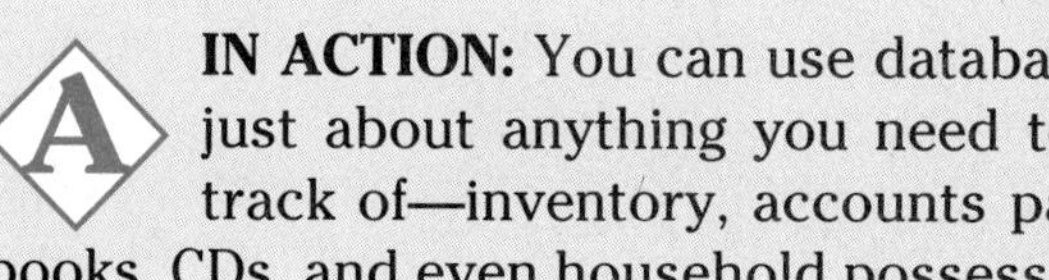

IN ACTION: You can use databases for just about anything you need to keep track of—inventory, accounts payable, books, CDs, and even household possessions.

Planning a Database

You need to plan your database before you create it. What kind of information do you want to include? How much detail do you need for each record? What field names do you want to use? By asking yourself these questions in advance, you save yourself the trouble of redesigning your database later on.

The most important step in creating a database is determining the information you want it to contain. Although a database can be as large as the entire worksheet, in practice you want to minimize the size of the range. This saves memory and makes managing the data easier. To that end, you should strive to set up all your databases with only essential information.

For example, if you are building an accounts receivable database, you should include only information that relates to the receivables. In this case, you need two kinds of information: invoice data and customer data. The invoice data would include the invoice number, the amount, the due date, and the date paid. You would also include a calculated field that determines the number of days overdue. For the customer, you would need, at least, a name and an account number. You do not need to include their address or phone number because this information is not essential to the receivables data.

TIP: Different but related databases need to have a *key field* that is common to each. For example, the accounts receivable and customer information databases could both contain an account number field. This enables you to cross-reference entries in both databases.

This last point brings up the idea of *data redundancy*. In many cases, you will be setting up a database as part of a larger application. You may have databases, for example, not only for accounts receivable, but also for accounts payable, customer information, part numbers, and so on. You don't need to include information such as addresses and phone numbers in the receivables database, because you should have that data in a more general customer information database. To include this data in both places is redundant.

Once you know what kind of information to include in your database, you need to determine the level of detail for each field. For example, if you are including address information, do you want separate fields for the street address, city, state, and ZIP Code? For a phone number, do you need a separate field for the area code? In most cases, the best approach is to split up the data into the smallest elements that make sense. This will give you maximum flexibility when it comes to sorting and extracting information.

The next stage in planning your database is to assign names to each field. Although you can assign names as long as 255 characters, you should try to use shorter names to prevent your fields from becoming too wide. Field names must appear in the first row of the database, they must be unique, and they must be text or text formulas. If you need to use numbers, format them as text.

TIP: If you need to use a longer field name, turn on the Word Wrap alignment option to keep the field width small. See Skill Session 15.

The final step in planning your database is to determine its position in the worksheet. If the worksheet contains only the database, then you just need to leave 5 or 6 rows blank at the top of the worksheet for the criteria range (see Skill Session 37 for information on setting database criteria). If the worksheet contains other data, then you need to position the database so that it will not interfere with this data. Here are two guidelines to follow:

- Since you will be adding records (rows) and fields (columns) to the database, you need to position the range so that it does not overlap horizontally or vertically with any other data. This "kite tail" design is illustrated in Figure 35.2.

- In most databases, the extract range is situated directly below the database. (See Skill Session 37 for information on extracting database information.) In theory, the extract range can extend to the bottom of the worksheet. Therefore, you need to position the database so that there is no other data below it that could be overwritten by the extract range.

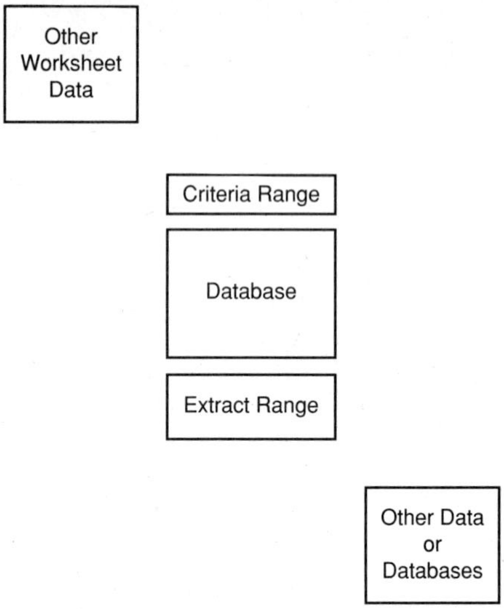

Other Worksheet Data

Criteria Range

Database

Extract Range

Other Data or Databases

Figure 35.2 Use a "kite tail" design to position your databases.

Defining a Database

Once you have settled on a plan for your database, you are ready to build the basic database structure. Here are the steps to follow:

Defining a Database:

1. Enter field names.
2. Add a single row of data.
3. Select database range.
4. Select Data Set Database.

1. Enter the field names in the first row of the area you are using for the database.

2. Add a single row of data (a record) in the row directly beneath the field names.

3. Select the range that includes the field names, the first row of data, and the blank row beneath the data (see Figure 34.3).

4. Select Data Set Database. Excel creates a named range called Database and displays this name in the formula bar reference area.

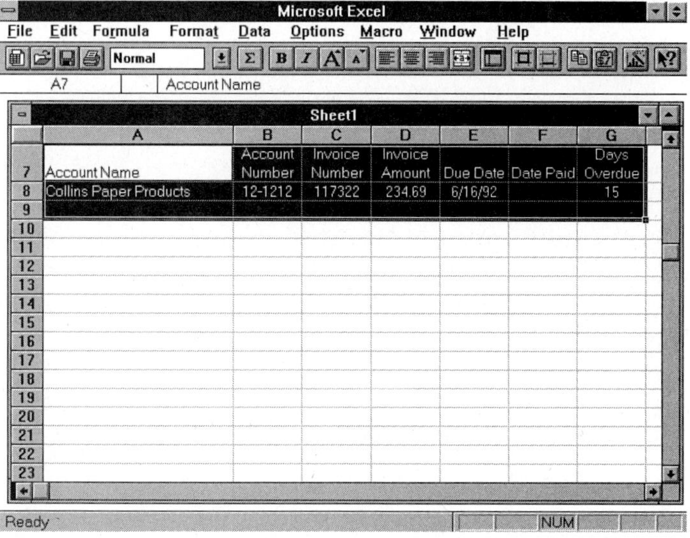

Figure 35.3 Select the field names, records, and a blank row when defining a database.

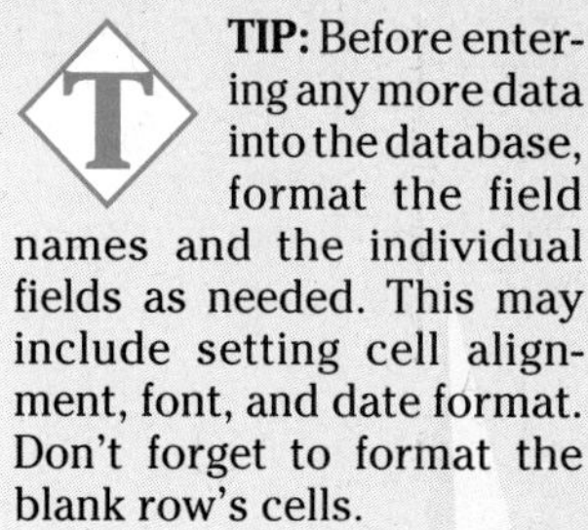

TIP: Before entering any more data into the database, format the field names and the individual fields as needed. This may include setting cell alignment, font, and date format. Don't forget to format the blank row's cells.

Entering Data

The most straightforward way of entering information into a database is simply to type directly into the worksheet rows. You must be careful, however, that you enter the new records within the database range. Excel does not include records entered outside of this area as part of the database. (To include these records, you would have to redefine the range.)

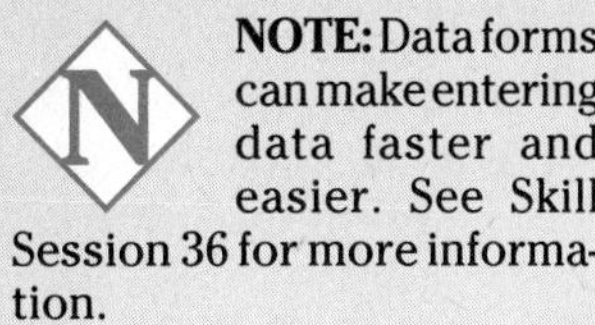

NOTE: Data forms can make entering data faster and easier. See Skill Session 36 for more information.

To avoid accidentally entering records outside the database range, enter records only after you have inserted a new row in the range. When you insert a row within a range, Excel automatically redefines the range and copies the field formats into the new row. This is why you originally defined the range with an extra blank row. To add a record at the bottom of the database, select the blank row and select Edit Insert.

Entering and deleting database records and fields is analogous to inserting and deleting rows and columns in a regular worksheet application. Table 35.1 summarizes these database commands.

Table 35.1 Basic database commands

Database Action	*Excel Commands*
Add a record	Select a row and select **E**dit **I**nsert.
Add a field	Select a column and select **E**dit **I**nsert.
Delete a record	Select the row and select **E**dit **D**elete.
Delete a field	Select the column and select **E**dit **D**elete.

Adding or Deleting Within a Range:

1. Highlight a record or field.
2. Select Edit Insert or Edit Delete.
3. Select appropriate Shift Cells option.
4. Select OK.

If you do not want to add or delete an entire row or column (e.g., if you have other worksheet data in the way), you can perform an insert or delete within the database range. To do this, follow these steps:

1. If you are inserting or deleting a row, select a database record (make sure you include each field in the record). If you are inserting or deleting a column, select a database field (make sure you include each record in the field).

2. Select either Edit Insert or Edit Delete. Excel displays either the Insert or Delete dialog box (Figure 35.4 shows the Insert dialog box).

3. Select the appropriate Shift Cells option. For example, if you are inserting a row, select Shift Cells Down.

4. Select OK or press Enter.

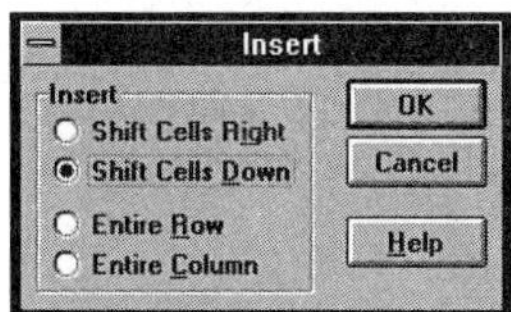

Figure 35.4 The Insert dialog box.

Entering database information can be a tedious chore. To speed up the process, Excel offers a number of shortcut keys. These are summarized in Table 35.2.

Table 35.2 Excel data entry shortcut keys

Press	*To*
Tab	Confirm the entry and move to the field on the right.
Shift+Tab	Confirm the entry and move to the field on the left.
Enter	Confirm the entry and move to the record below.
Shift+Enter	Confirm the entry and move to the record above.
Ctrl+"	Copy the number from the same field in the record above.

continues

TIP: If pressing Enter or Shift+Enter does not move you to another record, select Options Workspace and, in the dialog box that appears, activate the Move Selection after Enter option.

Table 35.2 continued

Press	*To*
Ctrl+'	Copy the formula from the same field in the record above.
Ctrl+;	Enter the current date.
Ctrl+:	Enter the current time.

Working with Database Ranges

Defining a Database Range Name:

1. Select database range.
2. Select Formula Define Name.
3. Enter name in Name text box.
4. Select OK.

When you define a database, Excel gives the range the name Database. Only one range per worksheet can have this name, so if you plan on defining other databases on the same worksheet, you need to create your own range names. To do this, follow these steps:

1. Select the database range you want to name.
2. Select Formula Define Name. Excel displays the Define Name dialog box, as shown in Figure 35.5.
3. Enter a name in the Name text box.
4. Select OK or press Enter. Excel displays the new range name in the formula bar reference area.

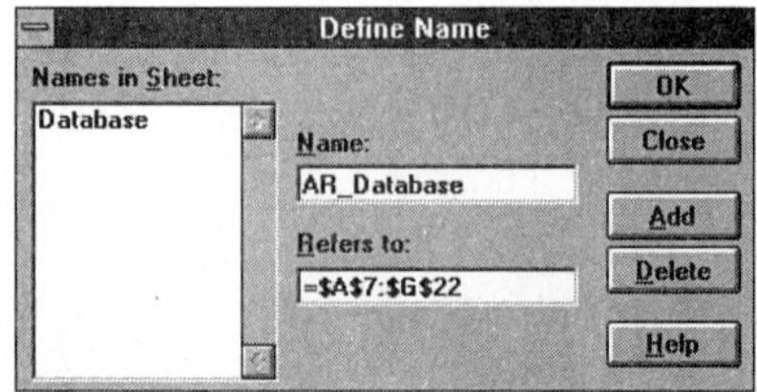

Figure 35.5 The Define Name dialog box.

IN ACTION: Names such as AR_Database, AP_Database, and Parts_Database make databases easier to find and remember. Legal range names must begin with a letter or underscore character, they cannot include spaces, and they can be a maximum of 255 characters.

Naming each of your worksheet databases also makes it easier to navigate among them using the **G**oto command. Here are the steps to follow:

1. Select Formula Goto or press F5. Excel displays the Goto dialog box, as shown in Figure 35.6.
2. Highlight a database range name in the **G**oto list.
3. Select OK or press Enter. Excel moves to and highlights the range.

Navigating Databases Using Goto:

1. Select Formula Goto or press F5.
2. Highlight database range name.
3. Select OK.

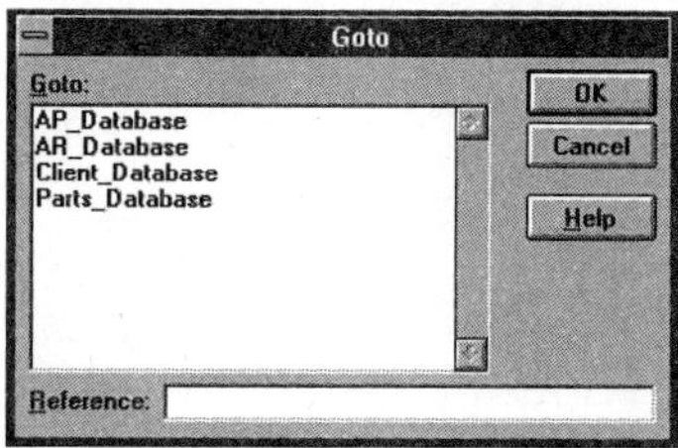

Figure 35.6 The Goto Dialog box.

Sorting a Database

One of the advantages of a database is that you can rearrange the records so that they are sorted alphabetically or numerically. This allows you to view the data in order by customer name, account number, part number, or any other field. You can even sort on multiple fields. This would enable you, for example, to sort a client list by state and then by name within each state.

The sorting procedure is determined by the options in the Sort dialog box shown in Figure 35.7. The three sort *keys* specify the fields that Excel sorts on. The **1**st Key text box contains an absolute reference to a cell in the field that determines the overall sort order. In Figure 35.7, this key is the Due Date field (column E). All records that have the same Due Date are then sorted by the **2**nd Key, the Account Name field (column A). Finally, if there are records that have the same Due Date *and* the same Account Name, these are sorted by the **3**rd Key, the Invoice Amount field (column D). Depending on your needs, you can enter just a single key, two keys, or all three.

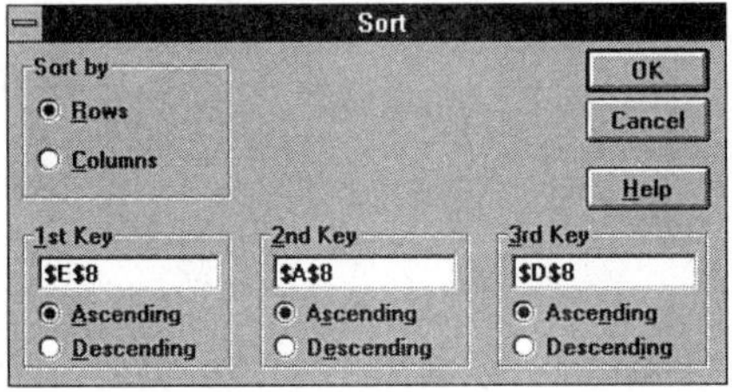

Figure 35.7 The Sort dialog box.

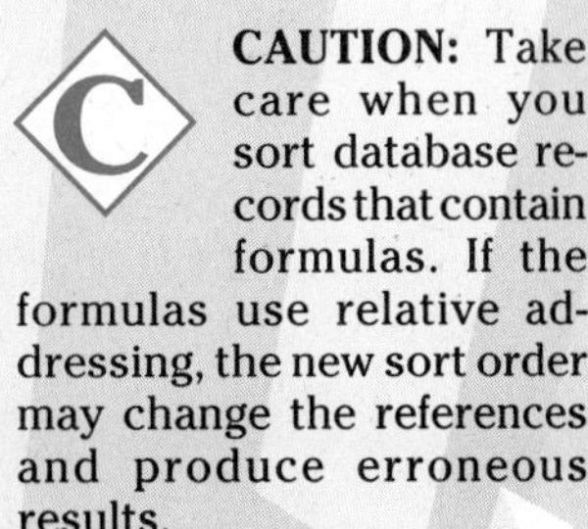

CAUTION: Take care when you sort database records that contain formulas. If the formulas use relative addressing, the new sort order may change the references and produce erroneous results.

For each key, you can specify whether the field is sorted in **A**scending order or **D**escending order. If you are sorting **R**ows, ascending order is from top to bottom. If you are sorting **C**olumns, ascending order is from left to right. Descending order reverses the order for each. Table 35.3 summarizes Excel's ascending sort priorities.

Table 35.3 Excel's ascending sort order

<table>
<tr><th>Type (in priority order)</th><th>Order</th></tr>
<tr><td>Numbers</td><td>Largest negative to largest positive</td></tr>
<tr><td>Text</td><td>Space ! " # $ % & ' ( ) * + , - . /
0 through 9 (when formatted as text)
: ; < = > ? @
A through Z (Excel ignores case)
[\ ] ^ _ ' { | } ~</td></tr>
<tr><td>Logical</td><td>False before True</td></tr>
<tr><td>Error</td><td>All error values equal</td></tr>
<tr><td>Blank</td><td>Always sorted last (ascending or descending)</td></tr>
</table>

Here are the steps to follow to sort a database:

1. Highlight the range you want to sort. For each record in the range, be sure to select every field to avoid scrambling the database.
2. Select Data Sort. Excel displays the Sort dialog box.
3. Enter the sort options you want.
4. Select OK or press Enter. Excel sorts the range.

Sorting a Database:

1. Highlight range to sort.
2. Select Data Sort.
3. Enter sort options.
4. Select OK.

Select the Sort Ascending tool in the Utility toolbar to perform an ascending one-key sort on the active field in the selection.

Select the Sort Descending tool in the Utility toolbar to perform a descending one-key sort on the active field in the selection.

Sorting on More Than Three Keys

You are not restricted to just three key fields when you sort an Excel database. By performing consecutive sorts, you can use as many keys as there are fields.

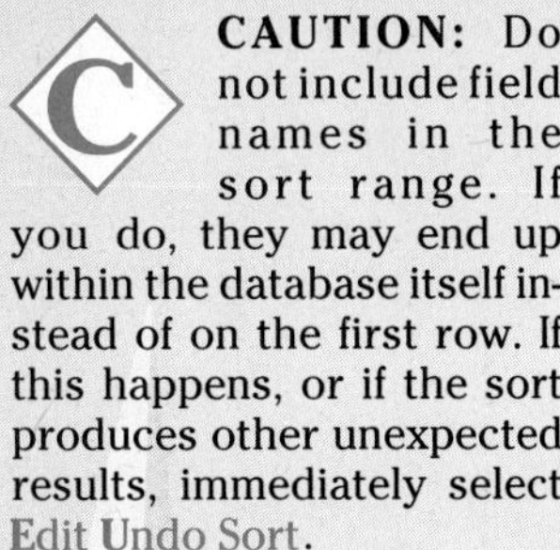

CAUTION: Do not include field names in the sort range. If you do, they may end up within the database itself instead of on the first row. If this happens, or if the sort produces other unexpected results, immediately select Edit Undo Sort.

As an example, suppose you have a customer database that you want to sort by the following keys (in order of importance): Region, State, City, ZIP Code, and Name. To use five keys, you need to perform two consecutive sorts. The first sort uses the three *least* important keys: City, ZIP Code, and Name. Of these three, City is the most important, so it is the **1**st Key, ZIP Code is the **2**nd Key, and Name is the **3**rd Key. When this sort is complete, you need to run another using the remaining keys, Region and State, where Region is the **1**st Key and State is the **2**nd Key.

By running multiple sorts where you always use the least important keys first, you can sort on as many keys as you like.

Using a Database in Natural Order

It is sometimes handy to see the order that records were entered into a database. This is called the *natural* order of the data. Normally, you can restore a database to its natural order by selecting Edit Undo Sort immediately after a sort.

TIP: Use the **D**ata Se**r**ies command to quickly enter a sequence of numbers (such as the record numbers for you database). See Skill Session 45 for instructions.

Unfortunately, after several sort operations, it is no longer possible to restore the natural order. The solution to this is to create a new field, called Record, in which you assign consecutive numbers as you enter the data. The first record is 1, the second is 2, and so on. To restore the database to its natural order, you just sort on the record field. Figure 35.8 shows the Accounts Receivable database with a record field.

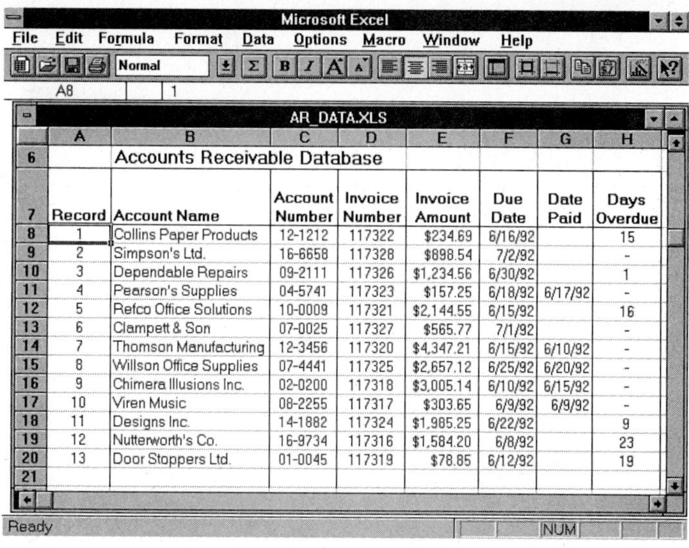

Accounts Receivable Database

Record	Account Name	Account Number	Invoice Number	Invoice Amount	Due Date	Date Paid	Days Overdue
1	Collins Paper Products	12-1212	117322	$234.69	6/16/92		15
2	Simpson's Ltd.	16-6658	117328	$898.54	7/2/92		-
3	Dependable Repairs	09-2111	117326	$1,234.56	6/30/92		1
4	Pearson's Supplies	04-5741	117323	$157.25	6/18/92	6/17/92	-
5	Refco Office Solutions	10-0009	117321	$2,144.55	6/15/92		16
6	Clampett & Son	07-0025	117327	$565.77	7/1/92		-
7	Thomson Manufacturing	12-3456	117320	$4,347.21	6/15/92	6/10/92	-
8	Willson Office Supplies	07-4441	117325	$2,657.12	6/25/92	6/20/92	-
9	Chimera Illusions Inc.	02-0200	117318	$3,005.14	6/10/92	6/15/92	-
10	Viren Music	08-2255	117317	$303.65	6/9/92	6/9/92	-
11	Designs Inc.	14-1882	117324	$1,985.25	6/22/92		9
12	Nutterworth's Co.	16-9734	117316	$1,584.20	6/8/92		23
13	Door Stoppers Ltd.	01-0045	117319	$78.85	6/12/92		19

Figure 35.8 The Record field tracks the order in which records are added to a database.

Skill Session

36

Working with Data Forms

Excel databases are powerful information management tools, but creating and maintaining them can be tedious and time-consuming. To save you time and make data entry easier, Excel creates a *data form* with each database. You can use this form to add, edit, delete, and find database records quickly. You can even create your own custom forms to suit the way you work.

This skill session shows you how to use data forms. You will learn how to use the form to edit, delete, and find existing records and to add new records to the database. You will also learn how to create your own customized data form.

What Is a Data Form?

A *data form* is a dialog box that simplifies database management in the following ways:

- ▲ The dialog box shows only one record at a time, which makes data entry and editing easier.
- ▲ You can view many more fields in a form than you can see on your screen. In fact, depending on the size of your screen, you can view as many as 18 fields in a single form.
- ▲ When you add or delete records with the data form, Excel adjusts the database range automatically.
- ▲ You get an extra level of safety when adding or deleting records. Excel does not allow you to overwrite other worksheet data, and it seeks confirmation for record deletions.
- ▲ Novice users or data entry clerks are insulated from the normal database commands. Simple command buttons allow them to add, delete, and find data.

Once you have defined a database, you can view the form by selecting **D**ata F**o**rm. Figure 36.1 shows the data form for the Accounts Receivable database.

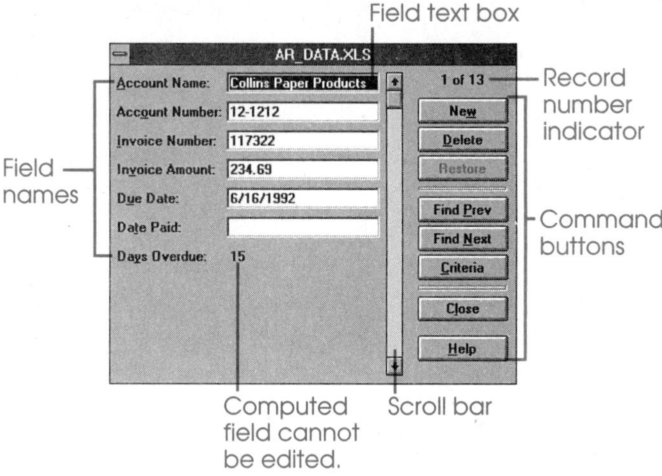

Figure 36.1 An Excel data form.

When constructing the data form, Excel begins with the field names and adds a text box for each editable field. Excel includes fields that are the result of a formula or function (e.g., the Days Overdue field in Figure 36.1) for display purposes only; you cannot edit these fields. The scroll bar enables you to move quickly through the database. The record number indicator in the top right corner of the dialog box keeps track of the current database row. The dialog box also includes several command buttons for adding, deleting, and finding records.

NOTE: The record number indicator is unaffected by the database sort order. The first record below the field names is always record 1.

Editing Records

You can use the data form to edit any fields in your database records, with the exception of computed or protected fields. Here are the steps to follow:

Editing a Database with the Data Form:

1. Select Data Set Database and define range.
2. Select Data Form.
3. Select a record.
4. Edit the fields.
5. Repeat steps 3–4 for other records.
6. Select Close.

CAUTION: When you make changes to a record, Excel saves the changes permanently when you scroll to another record. Before leaving a record, check each field to make sure it contains the data you want. To restore a record to its original data, select the Restore button in the data form dialog box.

1. Select Data Set Database to define the database range.
2. Select Data Form to display the Data Form dialog box.
3. Select the record you want to edit.
4. Edit the fields you want to change.
5. Repeat steps 3–4 for other records you want to edit.
6. Select Close to finish editing the database.

If you prefer to use your keyboard to navigate the data form, Excel offers a number of shortcuts and techniques to speed up the process. These are summarized in Table 36.1.

Table 36.1 Data form keyboard techniques

Key	*Result*
Alt+underlined letter in field name	Selects the field if it is editable.
Alt+underlined letter in command button	Selects the command button.
Tab	Moves to the next editable field.
Shift+Tab	Moves to the previous editable field.
Enter	Moves to the next record.
Shift+Enter	Moves to the previous record.
Down arrow	Moves to the same field in the next record.

Key	*Result*
Up arrow	Moves to the same field in the previous record.
Page Down	Moves to the same field ten records down.
Page Up	Moves to the same field ten records back.
Ctrl+Page Down	Moves to the last record.
Ctrl+Page Up	Moves to the first record.

Adding Records

Adding records with the data form is fast and easy. Here are the steps to follow:

1. Select Data Set Database to define the database range.
2. Select Data Form to display the Data Form dialog box.
3. Select New. Excel scrolls to the first blank record and displays `New Record` as the record number indicator.
4. Fill in the fields for the new record.
5. Select New or press Enter. Excel displays another blank record.
6. Repeat steps 4 and 5 for other records you want to add.
7. Select Close to finish adding new records.

Adding Records with the Data Form:

1. Select Data Set Database and define range.
2. Select Data Form.
3. Select New.
4. Fill in the fields.
5. Select New or press Enter.
6. Repeat steps 4 and 5 to add other records.
7. Select Close.

When you add records with the data form, Excel adds them to the bottom of the database without inserting a new row (the database range is automatically adjusted to include the new record). If there is no room to extend the database range, Excel displays the warning message shown in Figure 36.2. To add new records, you must either move the other data or extend the database range.

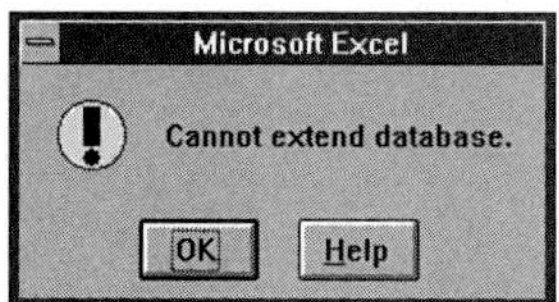

Figure 36.2 Excel warns you when the database range runs out of room.

Deleting Records

Follow these steps to delete records using the data form:

1. Select Data Set Database to define the database range.
2. Select Data Form to display the Data Form dialog box.
3. Select Delete. Excel warns you that the record will be deleted permanently (see Figure 36.3).
4. Select OK or press Enter to confirm the deletion. Select Cancel to end the deletion. Excel returns you to the data form.

Deleting Records with the Data Form:

1. Select Data Set Database and define range.
2. Select Data Form.
3. Select Delete.
4. Select OK.

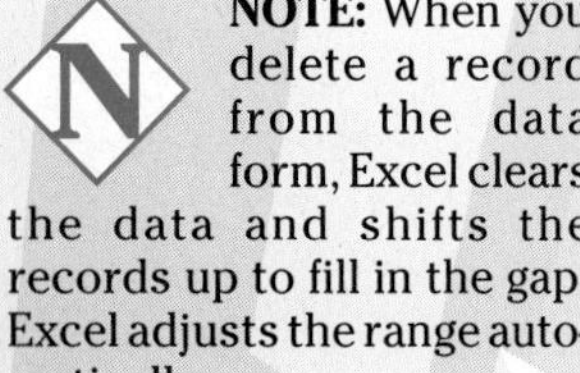

NOTE: When you delete a record from the data form, Excel clears the data and shifts the records up to fill in the gap. Excel adjusts the range automatically.

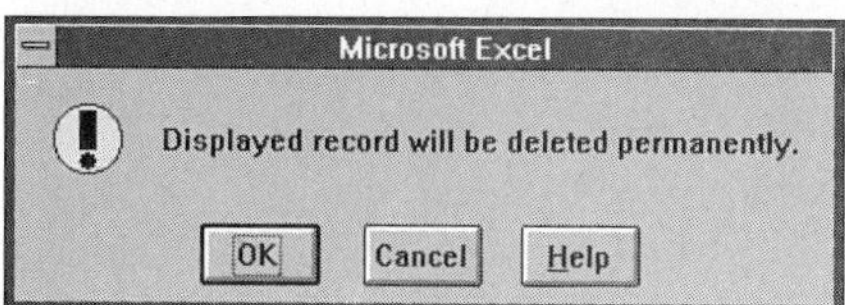

Figure 36.3 Excel warns you that the record will be deleted permanently.

Finding Records

Although the data form enables you to scroll through a database, you may find that, for larger databases, you need to use the form's search capabilities to find what you want quickly. You can find specific records in the database by first specifying the *criteria* that the search must match. Excel then compares each record with the criteria and displays the first record that matches. For example, you might want to find all invoices that are over $1,000.00 or those that are at least one day past due.

NOTE: You can perform simple searches with the data form. For more complex search criteria, select Data Find. See Skill Session 37 for instructions.

You construct the search criteria using text, numbers, and comparison operators such as equal to (=) and greater than (>). For example, to find all the invoices that are over $1,000.00, you would enter **>1000** in the Invoice Amount field. To find an account named Read (and not Reader or Reading), you would enter **=read** in the Account Name field. Here are the steps to follow:

1. Select Data Set Database to define the database range.

2. Select Data Form to display the Data Form dialog box.

Finding Records with the Data Form:

1. Select Data Set Database.
2. Select Data Form.
3. Select Criteria.
4. Select field to search.
5. Enter criterion.
6. Repeat steps 4 and 5 if you want to use multiple criteria.
7. Select Find Next and Find Prev to search.

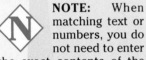

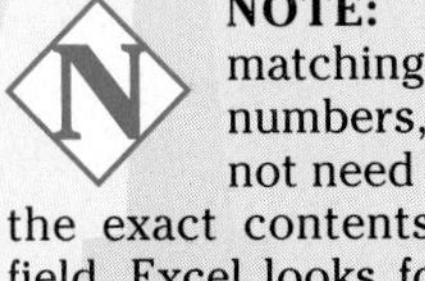

NOTE: When matching text or numbers, you do not need to enter the exact contents of the field. Excel looks for those fields that *begin* with the criteria. For example, entering **de** will find both Dependable Repairs and Designs Inc. (Notice, too, that Excel does not match upper- and lowercase.)

3. Select Criteria. Excel displays the Criteria data form (see Figure 36.4).

4. Select the field you want to use for the search.

5. Enter the criterion.

6. Repeat steps 4–5 if you want to use multiple criteria.

7. Use Find Next and Find Prev to move up or down to the next record that matches the criteria. If there are no matching records, select Form to return to the data form.

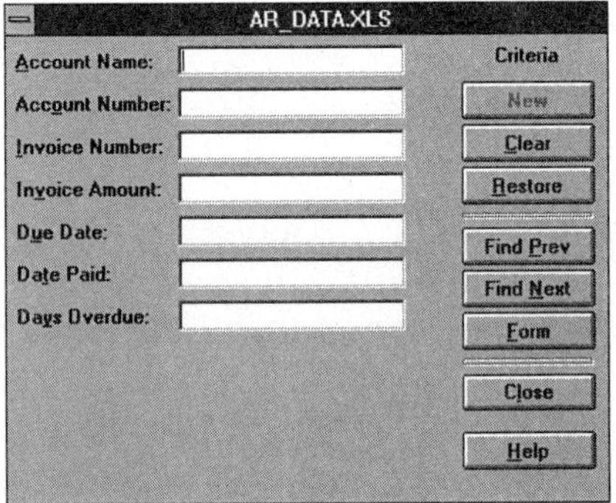

Figure 36.4 The Criteria data form.

To hone your searches, you can use multiple criteria. For example, Figure 36.5 shows a form with three criteria entered. In this case, Excel will search for all invoices that are past due, are over $1,000.00, and have the word "Office" in the account name. Note that all three criteria must be satisfied before Excel will find a match.

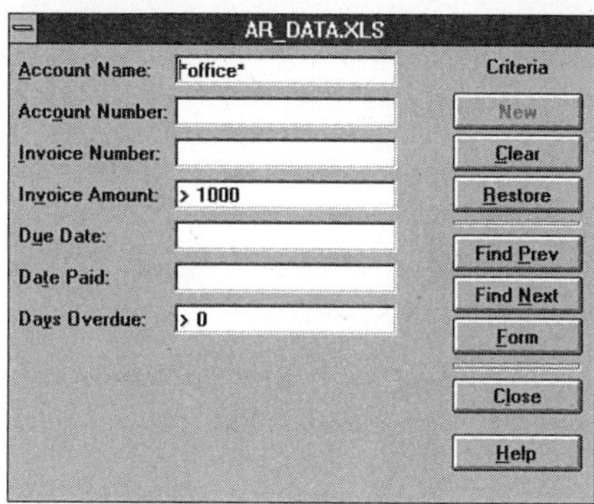

Figure 36.5 You can enter multiple criteria to hone your searches.

Another feature demonstrated in Figure 36.5 is the use of *wildcard* characters. Use the asterisk (*) to substitute for any number of characters. In Figure 36.5, `*office*` finds Refco Office Solutions or Wilson Office Supplies. Use the question mark (?) to substitute for a single character. For example, enter **Re?d** to find Read, Reid, or Reed.

TIP: To search for an actual question mark or asterisk, precede it with a tilde (~). For example, to find PAID?, enter **PAID~?**.

Using a Custom Data Form

The data form makes entering database information faster and easier, and most users find that the default form that Excel creates is adequate for their needs. However, if you would prefer a different layout, or a title, or instructions to the user, you can create your own custom form. Figure 36.6 shows an example of a custom data form.

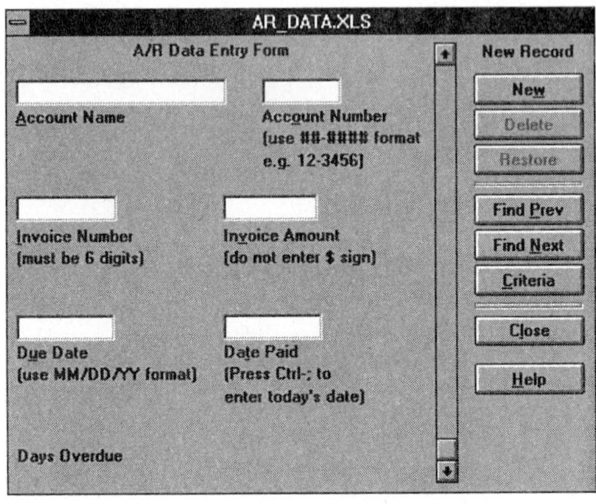

Figure 36.6 A custom data form.

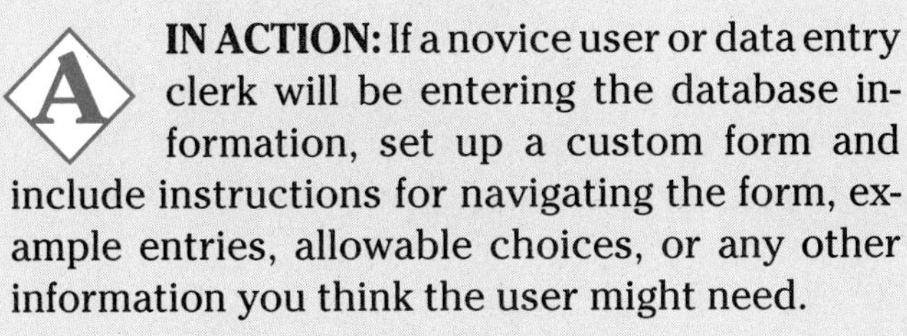

IN ACTION: If a novice user or data entry clerk will be entering the database information, set up a custom form and include instructions for navigating the form, example entries, allowable choices, or any other information you think the user might need.

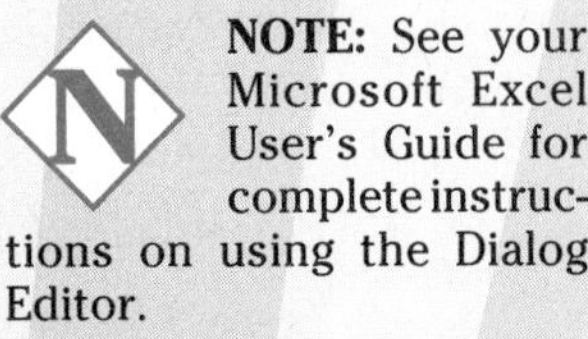

NOTE: See your Microsoft Excel User's Guide for complete instructions on using the Dialog Editor.

The easiest way to create a custom data form is to use the Dialog Editor utility that comes with Excel. The Dialog Editor is a dialog box creation program that enables you to define and position text, edit boxes, command buttons, and other dialog box elements. For a custom data form, you will only need to create edit boxes and explanatory text for each field. Excel adds the data form command buttons automatically. Follow these steps to start the Dialog Editor:

1. Select Control Run. The Run dialog box appears.
2. Choose Dialog Editor.
3. Select OK or press Enter. Windows loads the Dialog Editor program.

To define your data form, you need to do the following for each field:

- Add an edit box.
- Associate the edit box with a database field.
- Size the box.
- Add explanatory text such as the field name or instructions to the user.

Here are the steps to follow (these steps assume you have the Dialog Editor running):

1. Select Item Edit Box. A dialog box appears asking for the type of data that will be entered into the box.
2. Choose the field type and select OK or press Enter. An edit box is added to the dialog.
3. Select Edit Info, enter the field name in the **Init/** Result field, and then select OK or press Enter.
4. Move or size the field as needed.
5. Select Item Text to display a text element in the dialog box.
6. Select Edit Info, enter the text you want in the **Text** field, and then select OK or press Enter.
7. Move or size the text as needed.
8. Repeat steps 1–7 for each field in the database.

Starting the Dialog Editor:

1. Select Control Run.
2. Choose Dialog Editor.
3. Select OK.

Creating a Custom Data Form:

1. Select Item Edit Box.
2. Choose field type and select OK.
3. Select Edit Info, enter field name in **Init/Result**, and select OK.
4. Move or size field as needed.
5. Select Item Text.
6. Select Edit Info, enter text in **Text**, and select OK.
7. Move or size text as needed.
8. Repeat steps 1–7 for each field.

Copying the Custom Data Form to the Worksheet:

1. Select Edit Select Dialog.
2. Select Edit Copy.
3. Activate database worksheet.
4. Choose a cell in an empty area.
5. Select Edit Paste.
6. Select Formula Define Name.
7. In Name text box, enter `Data_Form`.
8. Select OK.

TIP: To include a hot key for a field, enter an ampersand (&) before one of the letters of the field name text (e.g., `&Account Name`). Excel underlines the letter in the dialog box.

Once you have set up the dialog box, you need to copy the definition to the worksheet and set it up as a data form. Here are the steps to follow:

1. In the Dialog Editor, select Edit Select Dialog.
2. Select Edit Copy to copy the dialog box definition to the Clipboard.
3. Activate the Excel worksheet that contains the database.
4. Select a cell in an empty area of the worksheet.
5. Select Edit Paste. Excel pastes the dialog box definition to the worksheet.
6. Select Formula Define Name. Excel displays the Define Name dialog box.
7. In the Name text box, enter `Data_Form`. This tells Excel to use your dialog box as the default data form.
8. Select OK or press Enter.

Figure 36.7 shows the dialog box definition for the custom data form shown in Figure 36.6 (the definition has been formatted for clarity). Each row describes a single element of the dialog box and contains the following data:

Type. Identifies the dialog element. For example, 5 is text, 6 is a text edit box, and so on.

X Pos, Y Pos. The screen coordinates of the element.

Width, Height. The dimensions of the element. (No number means that Excel uses the default dimensions for the element.)

Text. The dialog box text elements. Note the ampersands (&) used to define hot keys for each field.

Init/Result. The database field names.

Type of element
Dialog box text
Field names

Microsoft Excel

File Edit Formula Format Data Options Macro Window Help

AR_DATA.XLS

	I	J	K	L	M	N	O
22	Accounts Receivable Custom Data Form						
23	Type	X Pos	Y Pos	Width	Height	Text	Init/Result
24		75	50	434	312		
25	5	130	5			A/R Data Entry Form	
26	6	10	30	213			Account Name
27	5	10	50			&Account Name	
28	6	260	30	80			Account Number
29	5	260	50			Acc&ount Number	
30	5	260	65			(use ##-#### format	
31	5	260	80			e.g. 12-3456)	
32	7	10	110	101			Invoice Number
33	5	10	130			&Invoice Number	
34	5	10	145			(must be 6 digits)	
35	8	220	110	95			Invoice Amount
36	5	220	130			In&voice Amount	
37	5	220	145			(do not enter $ sign)	
38	6	10	190	100			Due Date
39	5	10	210			D&ue Date	
40	5	10	225			(use MM/DD/YY format)	
41	6	220	190	100			Date Paid
42	5	220	210			Da&te Paid	
43	5	220	225			(Press Ctrl-; to	
44	5	220	240			enter today's date)	
45	9	10	260	45			Days Overdue
46	5	10	280			Days Overdue	

Position of the element within the dialog box
Dimensions of the elements
Dialog box dimensions

Figure 36.7 The custom data form definition.

To make changes to your custom data form once you have exited the Dialog Editor, you can edit the cells in the definition. If you add or delete a line, however, you must redefine the Data_Form range.

Skill Session

37

Managing Database Records

So far in this workshop, you have learned simple techniques for managing data either directly on the worksheet or by using a data form. These techniques are fine for small databases, but they can be cumbersome and time-consuming on databases that contain dozens or even hundreds of records. This skill session shows you more sophisticated techniques for finding, editing, and deleting records in large databases.

Setting Database Criteria

Whether you want to find, extract, or delete records in a large database, your first step is to define the *criteria* for the records you want to work with. Criteria are conditions that you want the records to satisfy. For example, if you want to see all receivables invoices that are more than 90 days past due, then your criterion is that the record must have a value greater than 90 in the Days Overdue field.

Before you can enter any criteria, you must set up and define a *criteria range*. A criteria range has some or all of the database field names in the top row, with a blank row directly underneath. You enter your criteria in the blank row under the appropriate field name, and Excel searches the database for records with field values that satisfy the criteria. You can place the criteria range anywhere on the worksheet outside the database range. One common position for the criteria range is a couple of rows above the database range. Follow these steps to set up a criteria range:

Defining a Criteria Range:

1. Copy database field names to criteria range.
2. Select field names and one blank row.
3. Select Data Set Criteria.

1. Copy the database field names to the first row of the criteria range.

2. Select the field names in the criteria range and one blank row beneath them.

3. Select Data Set Criteria.

CAUTION: Make sure you use exactly the same field names in the criteria range as in the database. If the names are different, Excel's search and extract commands may not work properly.

Figure 37.1 shows the Accounts Receivable database with a criteria range defined.

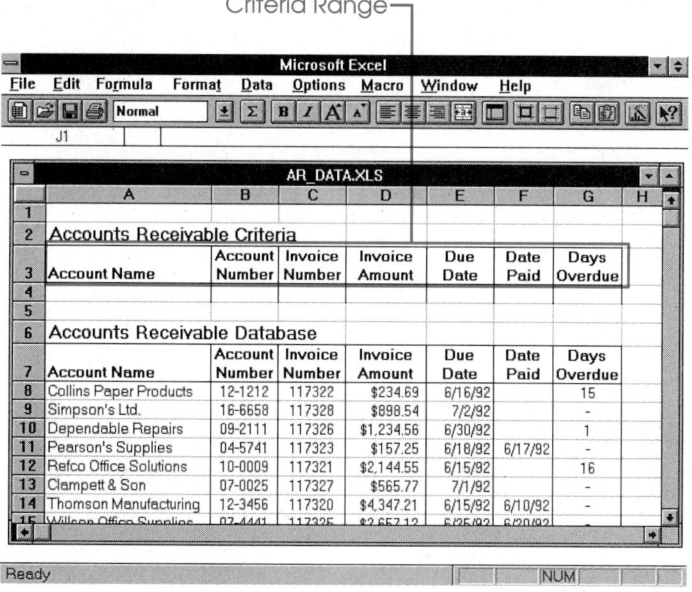

Figure 37.1 The Accounts Receivable database with a criteria range.

Using Comparison Criteria

The simplest types of criteria are the *comparison criteria*. With these, Excel performs a comparison test on each record in the database to see if any match your criteria. To search for text, numbers, or dates, you simply enter the characters, numbers, or date in the appropriate field in the criteria range. In the Accounts Receivable database, for example, to work with all records that have a Due Date of June 16, 1992, you would enter `6/16/92`in the Due Date field of the criteria range. Similarly, to find invoice number 117330, you would enter `117330` in the Invoice Number field.

You can extend the comparison criteria to include a range of values. This enables you to look for, say, all invoices that are 90 days or more past due, or all invoice amounts less than $1,000.00. You use the basic comparison operators listed in Table 37.1 to specify the range you want to use. To define your criteria, you combine one of the comparison operators with text or numbers. For the above examples, you would enter `>=90` in the criteria range Days Overdue field, and you would enter `<1000` in the Invoice Amount field.

Table 37.1 The comparison operator

Operator	*Description*
=	Equal to
>	Greater than
<	Less than
>=	Greater than or equal to
<=	Less than or equal to
<>	Not equal to

There are times when you don't need to find an exact match for your text criteria. For example, you may not be sure how to spell a person's name, or you may want to search only for a substring of a field. To do this, you can use special characters, called *wild cards*, to substitute for one or more characters. Use the question mark (?) wild card to substitute for a single character. For example, entering `re?d` will match Read, Reid, and Reed. The other wild card is the asterisk (*). Use this symbol to substitute for any group of characters. For example, entering `*carolina` will find North Carolina and South Carolina.

NOTE: Whenever you use a simple text search, Excel automatically adds an asterisk at the end of the text criteria. So entering `simpson` will find Simpson, Simpson's, and Simpson & Son. To find an exact match, you would type `="=Simpson"`.

TIP: To include a wild card as part of the criteria, precede the character with a tilde (~). For example, to find PAID?, enter `PAID~?`.

Using Multiple Criteria

For more complex comparison criteria, you can use multiple fields in the criteria range. For example, to work with all invoices that are 90 days or more past due and are over $4,000.00, you would enter `>=90` in the Days Overdue field and `>4000` in the Invoice Amount field. Note that both conditions must be true before Excel will find a match. You can enter criteria for any number of fields in the criteria range.

A different kind of multiple criteria is needed when you want one condition or another to be satisfied. For example, you might want to work with invoices that are 90 or more days past due *or* that are over $4,000.00. To set up these criteria, you would enter `>=90` in the Days Overdue field and then, on a new line, you would enter `>4000` in the Invoice Amount field. Figure 37.2 shows how this is done. In this case, Excel matches any record that satisfies either one of these conditions. Note that you must redefine the criteria range to include the new line.

CAUTION: When you no longer need the second line, always reset the criteria range back to its original form. If you leave a blank line in the criteria range, Excel will match every record in the database.

You can combine these two types of multiple criteria to create complex conditions. Figure 37.3 shows multiple criteria that must meet one of the following conditions before a match is found:

- Days Overdue is greater than or equal to 90 *and* the Account Name begins with "Collins" or
- Days Overdue is less than 60 *and* the Invoice Amount is greater than $4,000.00 or
- The Invoice Amount is less than $100.00

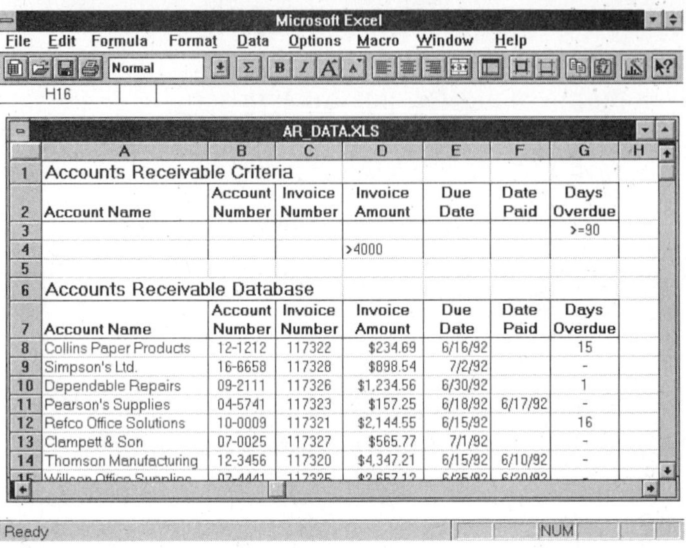

Microsoft Excel — AR_DATA.XLS

	A	B	C	D	E	F	G	H
1	Accounts Receivable Criteria							
2	Account Name	Account Number	Invoice Number	Invoice Amount	Due Date	Date Paid	Days Overdue	
3							>=90	
4				>4000				
5								
6	Accounts Receivable Database							
7	Account Name	Account Number	Invoice Number	Invoice Amount	Due Date	Date Paid	Days Overdue	
8	Collins Paper Products	12-1212	117322	$234.69	6/16/92		15	
9	Simpson's Ltd.	16-6658	117328	$898.54	7/2/92		-	
10	Dependable Repairs	09-2111	117326	$1,234.56	6/30/92		1	
11	Pearson's Supplies	04-5741	117323	$157.25	6/18/92	6/17/92	-	
12	Refco Office Solutions	10-0009	117321	$2,144.55	6/15/92		16	
13	Clampett & Son	07-0025	117327	$565.77	7/1/92		-	
14	Thomson Manufacturing	12-3456	117320	$4,347.21	6/15/92	6/10/92	-	

Figure 37.2 Use a separate line to have Excel match one condition or another.

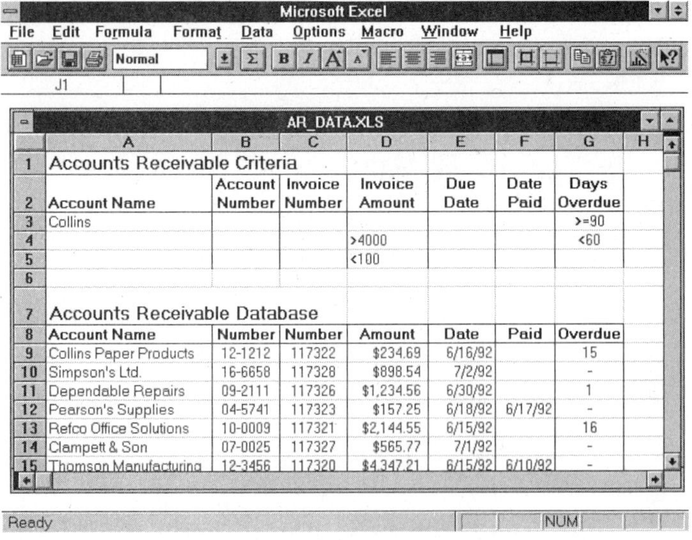

Microsoft Excel — AR_DATA.XLS

	A	B	C	D	E	F	G	H
1	Accounts Receivable Criteria							
2	Account Name	Account Number	Invoice Number	Invoice Amount	Due Date	Date Paid	Days Overdue	
3	Collins						>=90	
4				>4000			<60	
5				<100				
6								
7	Accounts Receivable Database							
8	Account Name	Number	Number	Amount	Date	Paid	Overdue	
9	Collins Paper Products	12-1212	117322	$234.69	6/16/92		15	
10	Simpson's Ltd.	16-6658	117328	$898.54	7/2/92		-	
11	Dependable Repairs	09-2111	117326	$1,234.56	6/30/92		1	
12	Pearson's Supplies	04-5741	117323	$157.25	6/18/92	6/17/92	-	
13	Refco Office Solutions	10-0009	117321	$2,144.55	6/15/92		16	
14	Clampett & Son	07-0025	117327	$565.77	7/1/92		-	
15	Thomson Manufacturing	12-3456	117320	$4,347.21	6/15/92	6/10/92	-	

Figure 37.3 You can create complex conditions by combining multiple criteria.

Using Computed Criteria

The fields in your criteria range are not restricted to the database fields. You can create *computed criteria* that use a calculation to match records in the database. The calculation can refer to one or more database fields, or even to cells outside the database, and must return either TRUE or FALSE. Excel selects those records that return TRUE.

To use computed criteria, add a column to the criteria range and enter the formula in the new field. Make sure that the name you give the criteria field is different from any field name in the database. For the formula cell references, use the first row of the database. For example, to select all records where the Date Paid is equal to the Due Date in the accounts receivable database, you would enter the following formula:

```
=F7=E7
```

Equals sign tells Excel the criterion is a formula.

Criterion uses a logical expression to select elements.

Note the use of relative addressing. If you want to reference cells outside the database, use absolute addressing.

Figure 37.4 shows a more complex example. The goal is to select all records where the invoice was paid at least 10 days before the due date. The new criteria, range column, Early, contains the following formula:

```
=IF(ISBLANK(F7),FALSE(),E7-F7>=10)
```

If the Date Paid field (column F) is blank, then the invoice has not been paid and the formula returns FALSE. Otherwise, the logical expression E7-F7>=10 is evaluated. If the Date Paid (column E) is at least 10 days before the Due Date, the expression returns

TIP: Your computed criteria formulas will be easier to read if you use the database field names instead of cell references. If the field name contains blanks, substitute an underscore character. For example, for the Due Date field, enter `due_date`.

TIP: Use Excel's AND, OR, and NOT functions to create *compound criteria*. For example, to select all records where the Days Overdue value is less than 90 *and* greater than 30, enter `=AND(G7<90, G7>30)`.

TRUE, and Excel selects the record. In Figure 37.4, the Early field displays FALSE because the formula evaluates to FALSE for the first row in the database.

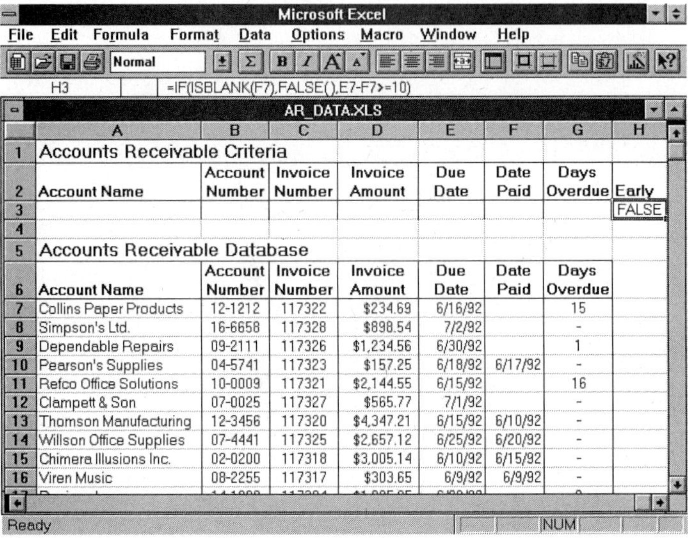

	A	B	C	D	E	F	G	H
1	Accounts Receivable Criteria							
2	Account Name	Account Number	Invoice Number	Invoice Amount	Due Date	Date Paid	Days Overdue	Early
3								FALSE
4								
5	Accounts Receivable Database							
6	Account Name	Account Number	Invoice Number	Invoice Amount	Due Date	Date Paid	Days Overdue	
7	Collins Paper Products	12-1212	117322	$234.69	6/16/92		15	
8	Simpson's Ltd.	16-6658	117328	$898.54	7/2/92		-	
9	Dependable Repairs	09-2111	117326	$1,234.56	6/30/92		1	
10	Pearson's Supplies	04-5741	117323	$157.25	6/18/92	6/17/92	-	
11	Refco Office Solutions	10-0009	117321	$2,144.55	6/15/92		16	
12	Clampett & Son	07-0025	117327	$565.77	7/1/92		-	
13	Thomson Manufacturing	12-3456	117320	$4,347.21	6/15/92	6/10/92	-	
14	Willson Office Supplies	07-4441	117325	$2,657.12	6/25/92	6/20/92	-	
15	Chimera Illusions Inc.	02-0200	117318	$3,005.14	6/10/92	6/15/92	-	
16	Viren Music	08-2255	117317	$303.65	6/9/92	6/9/92	-	

Figure 37.4 Use a separate criteria range column for calculated criteria.

Finding Records

In Skill Session 36 you learned how to perform basic database searches using the data form fields. Now, with your criteria range set up, you can try more sophisticated searches using **Data Find**. Here are the steps to follow:

1. Set up a criteria range if you have not already done so.
2. Enter your criteria in the range.
3. Select Data Find. Excel highlights the first record that matches the criteria. If no records match the criteria, Excel displays a message to that effect.
4. Use the techniques outlined in Table 37.2 to navigate the selected records.
5. To exit Find, select Data Find again or press Esc.

Table 37.2 Mouse and keyboard techniques for navigating the found records

Action	*Results*
Mouse Techniques	
Click on up or down scroll bar arrow	Finds next or previous matching record.
Click above or below the scroll box	Finds next or previous matching record at least one window away.
Drag the scroll box	Finds next or previous matching record in the database area selected.
Keyboard Techniques	
Press the Down arrow	Finds next matching record.
Press the Up arrow	Finds previous matching record.
Press Page Down	Finds next matching record at least one window away.
Press Page Up	Finds previous matching record at least one window away.
Tab	Moves the selected field in the matching record to the right.
Shift+Tab	Moves the selected field in the matching record to the left.

Finding Records:

1. Set up a criteria range.
2. Enter criteria.
3. Select Data Find.
4. Navigate selected records.
5. Select Data Find or press Esc.

TIP: To search from the first database record, either select a cell in the first record or select a cell outside the database range. To start the search from a specific record, select a cell in that record. To search backward through the database, press Shift when you select Data Find.

Figure 37.5 shows an example criteria that find all records where the invoice is at least 60 days overdue and is over $4,000.00. Note the use of the split screen to keep the criteria range and database field names in view.

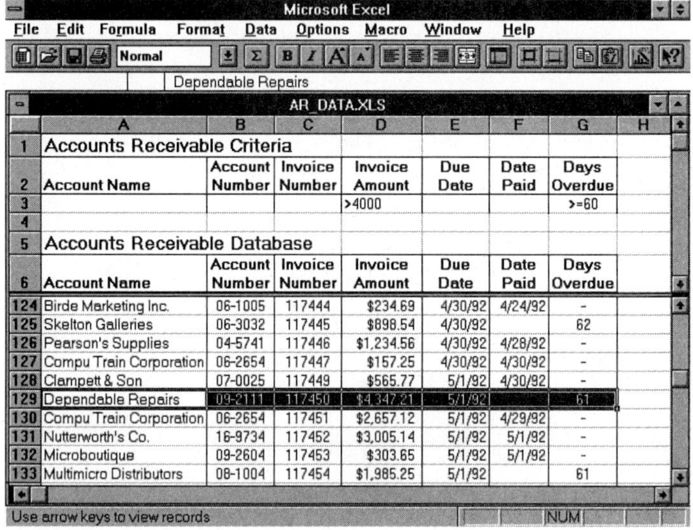

Figure 37.5 Use criteria to find database records.

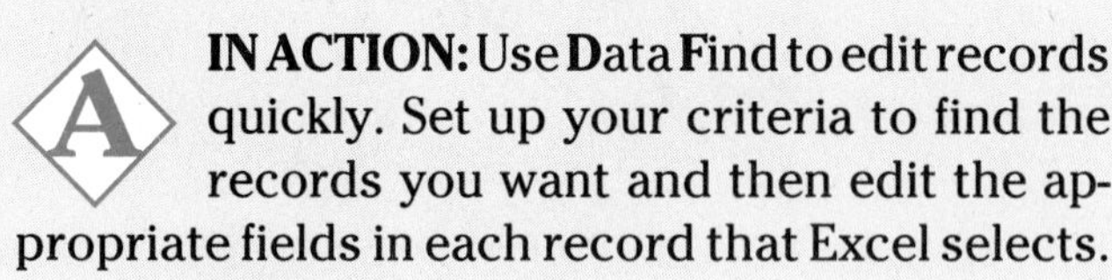

IN ACTION: Use **Data Find** to edit records quickly. Set up your criteria to find the records you want and then edit the appropriate fields in each record that Excel selects.

Deleting Records

You can delete unneeded records quickly by setting up the appropriate criteria and selecting **Data Delete**.

Here are the steps to follow:

1. Set up a criteria range if you have not already done so.
2. Enter your criteria in the range.
3. Select Data Delete. Excel displays a warning that the matching records will be permanently deleted (see Figure 37.6).
4. Select OK or press Enter. Excel deletes the matching records and shifts the database rows up to fill in the gaps.

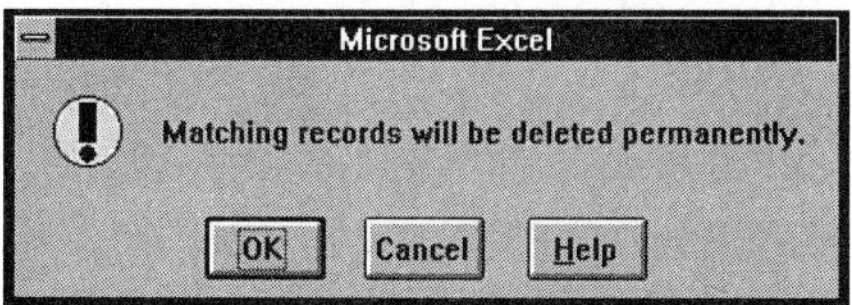

Figure 37.6 Excel warns you that the records will be permanently deleted.

IN ACTION: Select **D**ata **D**elete to remove defunct accounts from a customer database or invoices written off as bad debts.

Extracting Records

One of the most powerful of Excel's database features is **D**ata **E**xtract. With this command, you can extract a subset of a database to another part of the worksheet.

Deleting Records:

1. Set up a criteria range.
2. Enter your criteria.
3. Select Data Delete.
4. Select OK.

CAUTION: To guard against accidentally deleting the wrong records, always save your database before selecting Data Delete. If you make a mistake, close the file without saving any changes.

The subset that is extracted depends on the conditions you set up in the criteria range. For example, in the Accounts Receivable database, you could extract all invoices that are more than 90 days past due.

To extract records from a database, you must first set up and define an extract range. This procedure is similar to setting up a criteria range, except that you can define two types of extract range—limited and unlimited. A *limited* extract range includes only the database field names and a specified number of rows. If your criteria match more records than will fit in the extract range, the extra records are left out. To make sure you get every matching record, you can also define an *unlimited* extract range. This range includes only the database field names. If needed, Excel will fill in the extract range to the bottom of the worksheet. Follow these steps to define an extract range:

Defining an Extract Range:

1. Copy database field names.
2. Highlight range.
3. Select Data Set Extract.

CAUTION: If you set up an unlimited extract range, make sure that there are no worksheet data beneath the range. If the extract is large enough, Excel will overwrite any data in the range.

1. Copy the database field names to the area you want to use for the extract range.

2. Highlight the range you want to use for the extracted records (including the field names). For an unlimited range, highlight only the field names. For a limited range, highlight the field names and the number of rows you want to use.

3. Select Data Set Extract.

Figure 36.7 shows an extract range set up for the Accounts Receivable database.

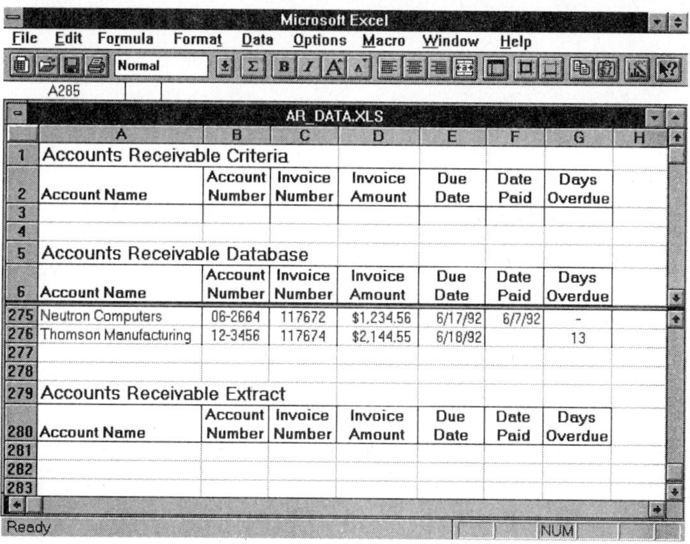

Figure 36.7 An extract range for the accounts receivable database.

To extract records from the database, follow these steps:

1. Set up the extract range if you have not already done so.
2. Enter the criteria for the records you want to extract.
3. Select **Data Extract**. Excel records the matching records in the extract range. If you run out of room in the range, Excel displays a message.

Extracting Records:

1. Set up extract range.
2. Enter criteria.
3. Select **Data Extract**.

NOTE: When the extract range includes a database field with a formula, only the value of the field is extracted. If the result in the calculated field changes, the extract is not updated.

IN ACTION: Use **D**ata **E**xtract to produce database reports. Once you have extracted the information you want, format it, run **O**ptions Set Print **A**rea on the extract range, and then print out the information.

Figure 37.8 shows the results of an extract in the Accounts Receivable database. Notice how the two records extracted meet the criteria entered in the criteria range.

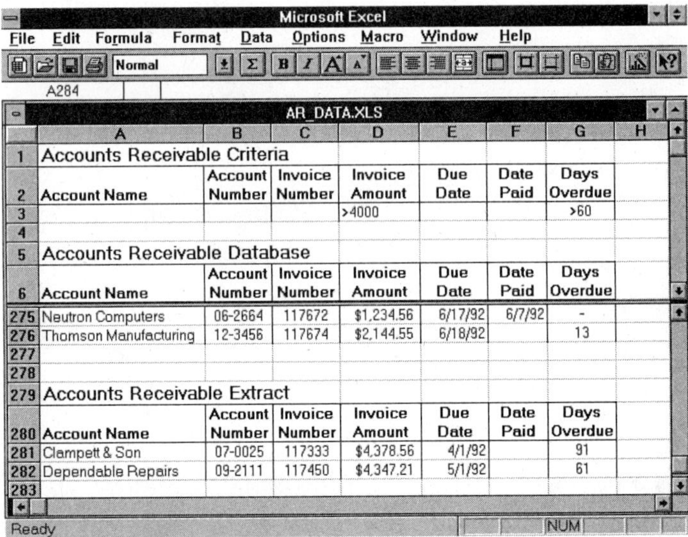

	A	B	C	D	E	F	G	H
1	Accounts Receivable Criteria							
2	Account Name	Account Number	Invoice Number	Invoice Amount	Due Date	Date Paid	Days Overdue	
3				>4000			>60	
4								
5	Accounts Receivable Database							
6	Account Name	Account Number	Invoice Number	Invoice Amount	Due Date	Date Paid	Days Overdue	
275	Neutron Computers	06-2664	117672	$1,234.56	6/17/92	6/7/92	-	
276	Thomson Manufacturing	12-3456	117674	$2,144.55	6/18/92		13	
277								
278								
279	Accounts Receivable Extract							
280	Account Name	Account Number	Invoice Number	Invoice Amount	Due Date	Date Paid	Days Overdue	
281	Clampett & Son	07-0025	117333	$4,378.56	4/1/92		91	
282	Dependable Repairs	09-2111	117450	$4,347.21	5/1/92		61	
283								

Figure 37.8 The results of an extract in the Accounts Receivable database.

Skill Session

38

Using Database Functions

A database is really just a worksheet range, so you can analyze your data using many of the same methods that you would use for regular worksheet cells. Typically, this involves using formulas and functions to answer questions and produce results. Excel goes one step further by offering a number of database-specific functions. These functions can work with entire databases or subsets defined by a criteria range. This skill session introduces you to the database functions, shows you how to use them, and gives examples of each.

About Database Functions

If you want to calculate the sum of a database field, you could enter **SUM(*range*)**, and Excel would produce the result. If you only want to sum a subset of the field, however, you would have to specify the particular cells to use as arguments. For example, Figure 38.1 shows a parts database where each part is assigned to a particular division within the company. To sum the Total Cost field for all Division 3 parts, you would have to enter cells F8, F9, and F12 as arguments for the SUM( ) function. If the database contains hundreds of records, however, this process quickly becomes impractical.

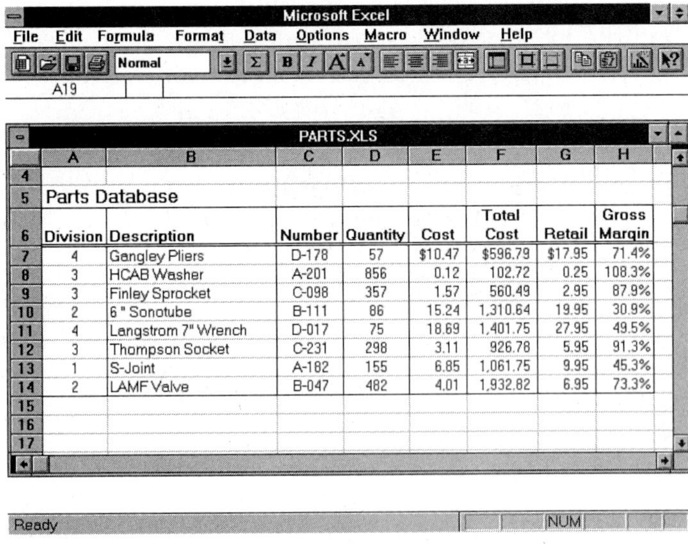

Parts Database

Division	Description	Number	Quantity	Cost	Total Cost	Retail	Gross Margin
4	Gangley Pliers	D-178	57	$10.47	$596.79	$17.95	71.4%
3	HCAB Washer	A-201	856	0.12	102.72	0.25	108.3%
3	Finley Sprocket	C-098	357	1.57	560.49	2.95	87.9%
2	6 " Sonotube	B-111	86	15.24	1,310.64	19.95	30.9%
4	Langstrom 7" Wrench	D-017	75	18.69	1,401.75	27.95	49.5%
3	Thompson Socket	C-231	298	3.11	926.78	5.95	91.3%
1	S-Joint	A-182	155	6.85	1,061.75	9.95	45.3%
2	LAMF Valve	B-047	482	4.01	1,932.82	6.95	73.3%

Figure 38.1 A parts database.

The solution is to use the database equivalent of the SUM( ) function: DSUM. The DSUM( ) function, like all the database functions, takes three arguments—a database range, a field name, and a criteria range. DSUM() looks at the specified field in the database and sums only those records that match the criteria set forth in the criteria range. For the preceding example, you could enter **3** in the Division field of the criteria range and then execute the DSUM() function to get the result you want.

Excel offers 13 different database functions. These are summarized in Table 38.1.

Table 38.1 The database functions

Function	*Returns*
CROSSTAB( )	Structure and content of a cross-tabulation table. (See Skill Session 39 for a complete discussion of cross-tabulation tables.)
DAVERAGE( )	Average of the values in a specified field for matching records.
DCOUNT( )	Count of the matching records.
DCOUNTA( )	Count of the nonblank matching records.
DGET( )	Value of a specified field for a single matching record.
DMAX( )	Maximum value in a specified field for the matching records.
DMIN( )	Minimum value in a specified field for the matching records.
DPRODUCT( )	Product of the values in a specified field for the matching records.

continues

Table 38.1 continued

Function	*Returns*
DSTDEV( )	Estimated standard deviation of the values in a specified field if the matching records are a sample of the population.
DSTDEVP( )	Standard deviation of the values in a specified field if the matching records are the entire population.
DSUM( )	Sum of the values in a specified field for the matching records.
DVAR( )	Estimated variance of the values in a specified field if the matching records are a sample of the population.
DVARP( )	Variance of the values in a specified field if the matching records are the entire population.

Entering Database Functions

Every database function has the following structure:

```
Dfunction(database, field, criteria)
```

where D*function* is a function name, such as DSUM( )or DAVERAGE( ).

The *database* argument specifies the range of cells that make up the database you want to work with. You can either use the range address or the range name if one is defined. (If you set up the database with **D**ata Set Data**b**ase, Excel gives the name Database to the range.)

The *field* argument is the name of the field on which you want to perform the operation. You can use either the field name itself as the argument or the *field number* (where the leftmost field is field number 1, the next field is field number 2, and so on). If you use the field name, you must enclose the name with double quotation marks (e.g., "total cost").

The *criteria* argument specifies the range of cells that hold the criteria you want to work with. You can either use the range address or the range name if one is defined. (If you set up the criteria range with **D**ata Set **C**riteria, Excel gives the name Criteria to the range.)

You enter database functions in the same way as any other Excel function. You type an equal sign (=) and then enter the function—by itself, or combined with other Excel operators in a formula. The following are all valid database functions:

```
=DSUM(A6:H14, "total cost", A1:H3)
=DSUM(Database, "total cost", Criteria)
=DSUM(AR_Database, 3, Criteria)
=DSUM(1992_Sales, "Sales", A1:H13)
```

TIP: You can use any worksheet range that has column headings as the *database* argument. This enables you to use the database functions on any type of data in a worksheet.

TIP: To perform an operation on every record in the database, leave all the criteria fields blank. This causes Excel to select every record in the database.

NOTE: In some of the examples shown here, the default range names, Database and Criteria, are used for the *database* and *criteria* function arguments. In the other examples, these defaults are replaced by different values. In the following function descriptions, these default range names are used to illustrate the functions. Keep in mind, however, that you can use your own range names or range addresses as function arguments.

Using DAVERAGE()

NOTE: Excel does not differentiate between upper- and lowercase in database function arguments.

The DAVERAGE function calculates the average *field* value in the *database* records that match the *criteria*. Figure 38.2 shows an example. The goal is to calculate the average Gross Margin for all parts assigned to Division 2. The database range is named Database, and the criteria range is named Criteria. To restrict the operation of the DAVERAGE() function, a "2" is entered in the criteria range Division field. The following function is entered in cell H16:

```
=DAVERAGE(database, "gross margin", criteria)
```

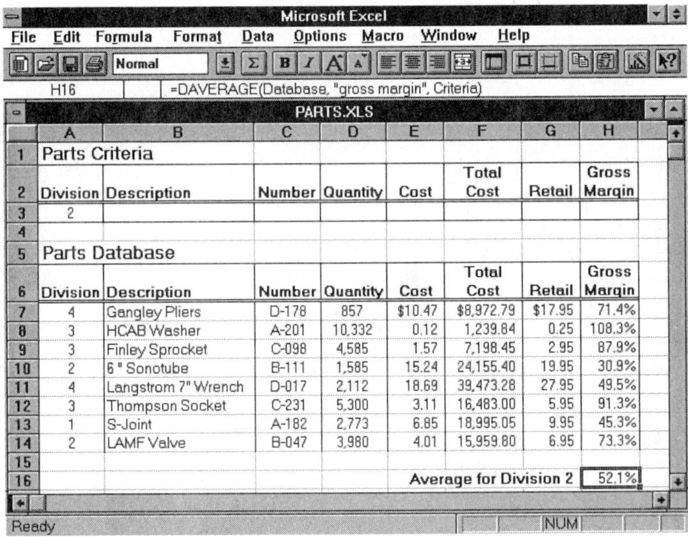

	A	B	C	D	E	F	G	H
1	Parts Criteria							
2	Division	Description	Number	Quantity	Cost	Total Cost	Retail	Gross Margin
3	2							
4								
5	Parts Database							
6	Division	Description	Number	Quantity	Cost	Total Cost	Retail	Gross Margin
7	4	Gangley Pliers	D-178	857	$10.47	$8,972.79	$17.95	71.4%
8	3	HCAB Washer	A-201	10,332	0.12	1,239.84	0.25	108.3%
9	3	Finley Sprocket	C-098	4,585	1.57	7,198.45	2.95	87.9%
10	2	6" Sonotube	B-111	1,585	15.24	24,155.40	19.95	30.9%
11	4	Langstrom 7" Wrench	D-017	2,112	18.69	39,473.28	27.95	49.5%
12	3	Thompson Socket	C-231	5,300	3.11	16,483.00	5.95	91.3%
13	1	S-Joint	A-182	2,773	6.85	18,995.05	9.95	45.3%
14	2	LAMF Valve	B-047	3,980	4.01	15,959.80	6.95	73.3%
15								
16					Average for Division 2			52.1%

Figure 38.2 Use DAVERAGE() to calculate the field average in the matching records.

Using DCOUNT() and DCOUNTA()

The DCOUNT function counts the number of *database* records that match the *criteria* and that contain numeric entries in the *field*. For this function, the *field* argument is optional. If you do not specify a *field*, Excel counts all the nonblank records in the *database* that satisfy the *criteria*. Figure 38.3 demonstrates this use of the DCOUNT( ) function. In this example, the criteria range is blank so DCOUNT( ) counts all the records in the database.

Microsoft Excel

File Edit Formula Format Data Options Macro Window Help

H16 =DCOUNT(Database, , Criteria)

PARTS.XLS

	A	B	C	D	E	F	G	H
1	Parts Criteria							
2	Division	Description	Number	Quantity	Cost	Total Cost	Retail	Gross Margin
3								
4								
5	Parts Database							
6	Division	Description	Number	Quantity	Cost	Total Cost	Retail	Gross Margin
7	4	Gangley Pliers	D-178	857	$10.47	$8,972.79	$17.95	71.4%
8	3	HCAB Washer	A-201	10,332	0.12	1,239.84	0.25	108.3%
9	3	Finley Sprocket	C-098	4,585	1.57	7,198.45	2.95	87.9%
10	2	6" Sonotube	B-111	1,585	15.24	24,155.40	19.95	30.9%
11	4	Langstrom 7" Wrench	D-017	2,112	18.69	39,473.28	27.95	49.5%
12	3	Thompson Socket	C-231	5,300	3.11	16,483.00	5.95	91.3%
13	1	S-Joint	A-182	2,773	6.85	18,995.05	9.95	45.3%
14	2	LAMF Valve	B-047	3,980	4.01	15,959.80	6.95	73.3%
15								
16							Total Records	8

Ready NUM

Figure 38.3 Omit the field name to count all nonblank records that match the criteria.

If you do enter a *field* argument, make sure you use a numeric field, because the DCOUNT() function ignores text entries. For example, entering the formula

`=DCOUNT(Database, "Description", Criteria)` for the parts database would return `0` because the Description field contains only text. If you want to get a count on a text field, use the DCOUNTA function, instead. This function counts the nonblank *database* records that match the *criteria* for any type of field. Figure 38.4 shows an example of this function that counts all records by examining the Description fields. For this example, one of the Descriptions was cleared to show that DCOUNTA() counts only nonblank cells.

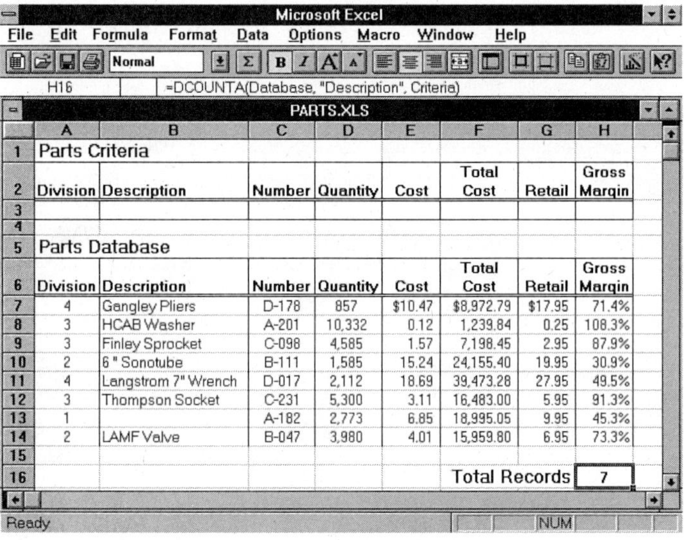

	A	B	C	D	E	F	G	H
1	Parts Criteria							
2	Division	Description	Number	Quantity	Cost	Total Cost	Retail	Gross Margin
3								
4								
5	Parts Database							
6	Division	Description	Number	Quantity	Cost	Total Cost	Retail	Gross Margin
7	4	Gangley Pliers	D-178	857	$10.47	$8,972.79	$17.95	71.4%
8	3	HCAB Washer	A-201	10,332	0.12	1,239.84	0.25	108.3%
9	3	Finley Sprocket	C-098	4,585	1.57	7,198.45	2.95	87.9%
10	2	6 " Sonotube	B-111	1,585	15.24	24,155.40	19.95	30.9%
11	4	Langstrom 7" Wrench	D-017	2,112	18.69	39,473.28	27.95	49.5%
12	3	Thompson Socket	C-231	5,300	3.11	16,483.00	5.95	91.3%
13	1		A-182	2,773	6.85	18,995.05	9.95	45.3%
14	2	LAMF Valve	B-047	3,980	4.01	15,959.80	6.95	73.3%
15								
16							Total Records	7

Figure 38.4 Use DCOUNTA() to count records using any type of field.

Using DGET()

The DGET function extracts the value of a single *field* from the record that matches the *criteria*. If there are no matching records, DGET() returns #VALUE!. If there is more than one matching record, DGET() returns #NUM!. DGET() is typically used to query the database for a specific piece of information. For example, in the parts database, you might want to know the cost of the Finley Sprocket. To extract this information, you would enter **Finley Sprocket** in the criteria Description field, and your formula would be

```
=DGET(Database, "Cost", Criteria)
```

A more interesting application of this function would be to extract the name of a part that satisfies a certain condition. For example, you might want to know the name of the part that has the highest gross margin. Creating this application requires two steps:

1. Set up the criteria to match the highest value in the Gross Margin field.
2. Add a DGET() function to extract the Description of the matching record.

Figure 38.5 shows how this is done. For the criteria, a new field is created called Highest Margin. As the text box shows, this field uses the following computed criteria:

```
=H7=MAX($H$7:$H$14)
```

The range $H$7:$H$14 is the Gross Margin field (note the use of absolute references). Excel will match only the record that has the highest Gross Margin. The DGET() function is straightforward:

```
=DGET(Database, "Description", Criteria)
```

This formula returns the Description of the part with the highest Gross Margin.

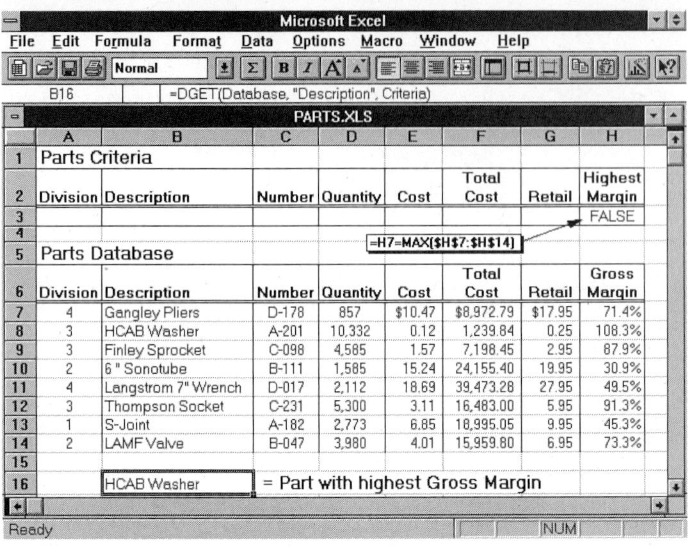

	A	B	C	D	E	F	G	H
1	Parts Criteria							
2	Division	Description	Number	Quantity	Cost	Total Cost	Retail	Highest Margin
3								FALSE
4								
5	Parts Database							
6	Division	Description	Number	Quantity	Cost	Total Cost	Retail	Gross Margin
7	4	Gangley Pliers	D-178	857	$10.47	$8,972.79	$17.95	71.4%
8	3	HCAB Washer	A-201	10,332	0.12	1,239.84	0.25	108.3%
9	3	Finley Sprocket	C-098	4,585	1.57	7,198.45	2.95	87.9%
10	2	6 " Sonotube	B-111	1,585	15.24	24,155.40	19.95	30.9%
11	4	Langstrom 7" Wrench	D-017	2,112	18.69	39,473.28	27.95	49.5%
12	3	Thompson Socket	C-231	5,300	3.11	16,483.00	5.95	91.3%
13	1	S-Joint	A-182	2,773	6.85	18,995.05	9.95	45.3%
14	2	LAMF Valve	B-047	3,980	4.01	15,959.80	6.95	73.3%
15								
16		HCAB Washer	= Part with highest Gross Margin					

Figure 38.5 A DGET( ) function to extract the name of the part with the highest margin.

Using DMAX() and DMIN()

The DMAX and DMIN functions return the maximum and minimum *field* value, respectively, out of the *database* records that match the *criteria*. These functions are most often used in analyzing statistical populations. For example, you could use these functions to calculate the *range* of the values in a field. The range is defined as the difference between the largest and smallest number in the sample and is a crude measure of the sample's variance.

Figure 38.6 shows a database of defects found among 12 work groups in a manufacturing process. In this example, the database is named Defects, and two criteria ranges are used: one for each of the group leaders, Johnson and Perkins. The table shows a number of calculations. First, DMAX() and DMIN() are calculated for each criteria. The range is then calculated using the following formula (Johnson's groups):

```
=DMAX(Defects, "defects", Criteria1) -
DMIN(Defects, "defects", Criteria1)
```

You could, of course, simply refer to the cells containing the DMAX() and DMIN() results.

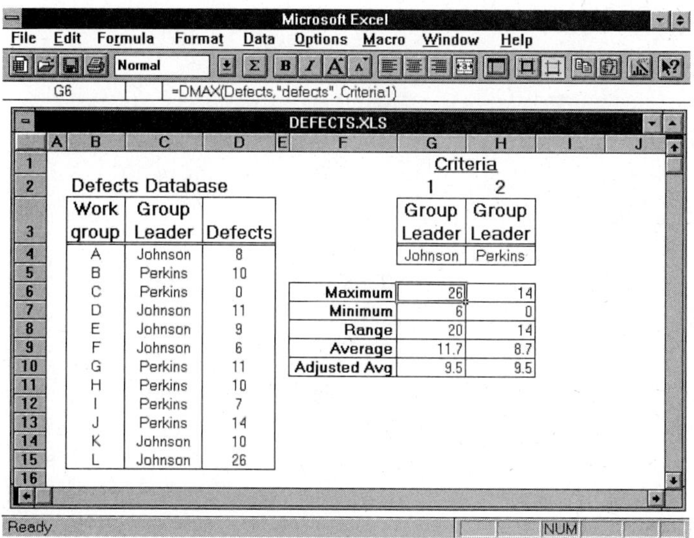

Figure 38.6 Using functions to analyze a database of defects in a manufacturing process.

The next line uses DAVERAGE() to find the average number of defects for each group leader. Notice that the average for Johnson's groups (11.7) is significantly higher than that for Perkins' groups (8.7). However, Johnson's average is skewed higher by one anomalously large number (26), and Perkins' average is skewed lower by one anomalously small number (0). The last line, Adjusted Avg, uses the DMAX() and DMIN() functions to remove the largest and smallest number for each sample and then recalculates the average. As you can see, without the anomalies, the two leaders have the same average.

Using DSTDEV() and DSTDEVP()

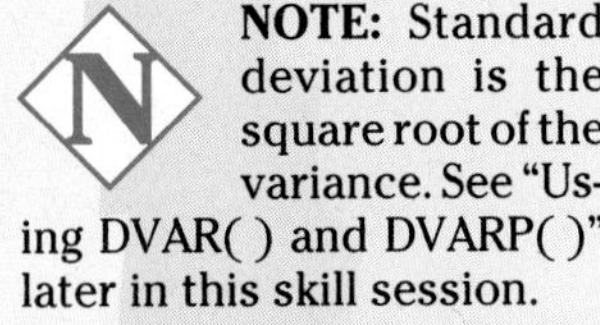

NOTE: Standard deviation is the square root of the variance. See "Using DVAR( ) and DVARP( )" later in this skill session.

The DSTDEV function returns the estimated standard deviation of the *fields* for the *database* records that match the *criteria*. Standard deviation is a measure of the dispersion in the selected fields. The higher the variation from the average, the higher the standard deviation. The DSTDEV() function assumes that the matching records are a sample of the population. If the matching records encompass the entire population, use the DSTDEVP() function, instead. Figure 38.7 shows the two standard deviation functions applied to the defects database.

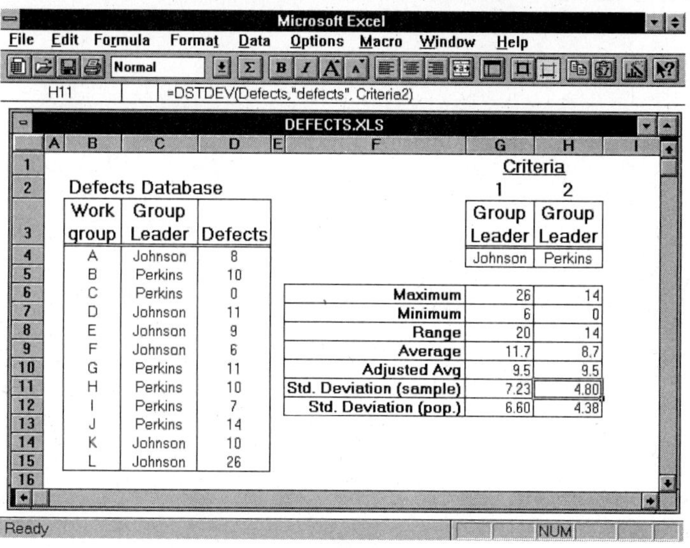

Figure 38.7 Standard deviation in the defects database.

Using DSUM() and DPRODUCT()

The DSUM function returns the sum of the *fields* for the *database* records that match the *criteria*. Figure 38.8 shows a DSUM() function that adds up the Total Cost for parts assigned to Division 3 that have a Gross Margin of more than 90%.

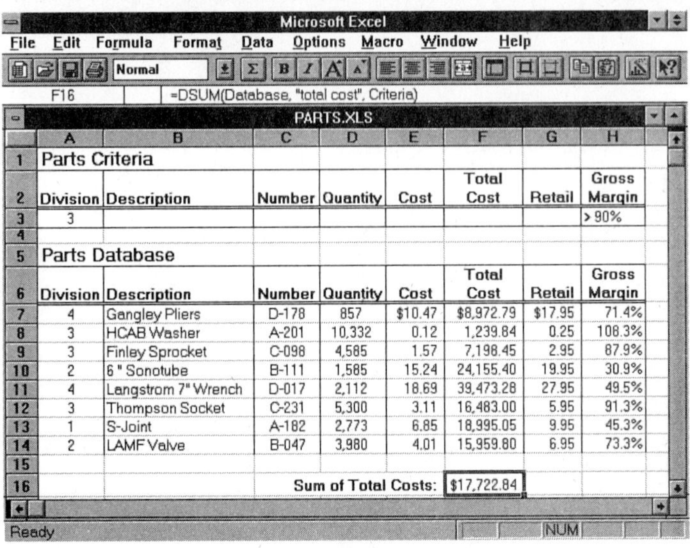

	A	B	C	D	E	F	G	H
1	Parts Criteria							
2	Division	Description	Number	Quantity	Cost	Total Cost	Retail	Gross Margin
3	3							> 90%
4								
5	Parts Database							
6	Division	Description	Number	Quantity	Cost	Total Cost	Retail	Gross Margin
7	4	Gangley Pliers	D-178	857	$10.47	$8,972.79	$17.95	71.4%
8	3	HCAB Washer	A-201	10,332	0.12	1,239.84	0.25	108.3%
9	3	Finley Sprocket	C-098	4,585	1.57	7,198.45	2.95	87.9%
10	2	6" Sonotube	B-111	1,585	15.24	24,155.40	19.95	30.9%
11	4	Langstrom 7" Wrench	D-017	2,112	18.69	39,473.28	27.95	49.5%
12	3	Thompson Socket	C-231	5,300	3.11	16,483.00	5.95	91.3%
13	1	S-Joint	A-182	2,773	6.85	18,995.05	9.95	45.3%
14	2	LAMF Valve	B-047	3,980	4.01	15,959.80	6.95	73.3%
15								
16					Sum of Total Costs:	$17,722.84		

Figure 38.8 Use the DSUM() function to add fields from selected records.

The DPRODUCT function is similar to DSUM(), except that it multiplies the *fields* from the *database* records that match the *criteria*.

Using DVAR() and DVARP()

The DVAR function returns the estimated variance of the *fields* for the *database* records that match the *criteria*. Like standard deviation, variance is a measure of the dispersion in the selected fields. (Standard deviation is the square root of the variance.) The DVAR() function assumes that the matching records are a sample of the population. If the matching records encompass the entire population, use the DVARP() function instead. Figure 38.9 shows the two variance functions applied to the defects database.

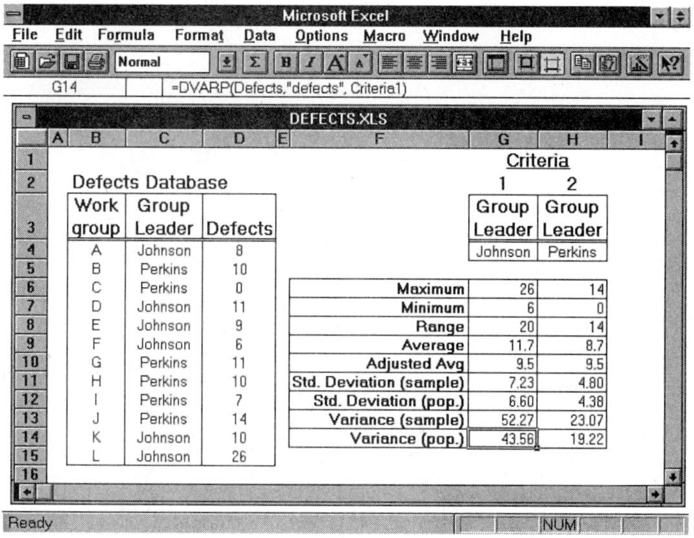

Figure 38.9 Variance in the defects database.

Skill Session

39

Using Crosstab Tables

Databases can contain hundreds or even thousands of records. Analyzing that much data can be a nightmare without the right kinds of tools. Excel 4 offers a new data analysis tool called *cross tabulation tables* (crosstab tables, for short) that enable you to summarize hundreds of records into a concise tabular format. This skill session introduces you to crosstab tables and shows you a variety of ways to use them with your own databases.

What Are Crosstab Tables?

To understand crosstab tables, you need to see where they fit in with Excel's other database analysis features. Database analysis has several levels of complexity. The simplest level involves the basic lookup and retrieval of information. For example, if you have a database that lists the company sales reps and their territory sales, you could use a data form to search for a specific rep to look up the sales in his or her territory.

The next level of complexity uses more sophisticated lookup and retrieval systems where the criteria and extract techniques discussed in Skill 37 are used. You can then apply the database functions as described in Skill 38 to find answers to your questions. For example, suppose each sales territory is part of a larger region and you want to know the total sales in, say, the East region. You would set up your criteria to match all territories in the East region and use the DSUM() function to get the total. To get more specific information, such as total East region sales in the second quarter, you just add the appropriate conditions to your criteria.

NOTE: You must have a mouse to use the Crosstab ReportWizard because most of the ReportWizard's commands and buttons are nor accessible from the keyboard.

The next level of database analysis applies a single question to multiple variables. For example, if the company in the previous example has four regions, you might want to see separate totals for each region broken down by quarter. One solution would be to set up four different criteria and four different DSUM() functions. But what if there were a dozen regions? Or a hundred? Ideally, you need some way of summarizing the database information into a "sales table" that has a row for each region and a column for each quarter. This is exactly what crosstab tables do. With Excel's Crosstab ReportWizard, you can create your own tables with just a few mouse clicks.

In the simplest case, crosstab tables work by summarizing the data in one field (called a *value field*), and breaking it down according to the data in another field. The unique values in the second field (called the *row categories*) become the row headings. For example, Figure 39.1 shows a database of sales by sales representatives. With a crosstab table, you can summarize the numbers in the Sales field and break them down by region. Figure 39.2 shows the resulting crosstab table. Notice how Excel uses the four unique categories in the Region field (East, West, Midwest, and South) as row headings.

Microsoft Excel — SALES.XLS

Region	Quarter	Sales Rep	Sales
East	1st	A	192,345
West	1st	B	210,880
East	1st	C	185,223
South	1st	D	165,778
Midwest	1st	E	155,557
South	1st	F	180,567
West	1st	G	200,767
Midwest	1st	H	165,663
East	2nd	A	173,493
West	2nd	B	200,003
East	2nd	C	170,213
South	2nd	D	155,339
Midwest	2nd	E	148,990
South	2nd	F	175,656
West	2nd	G	190,290
Midwest	2nd	H	159,002
East	3rd	A	175,776

Figure 39.1 A database of sales by sales representatives.

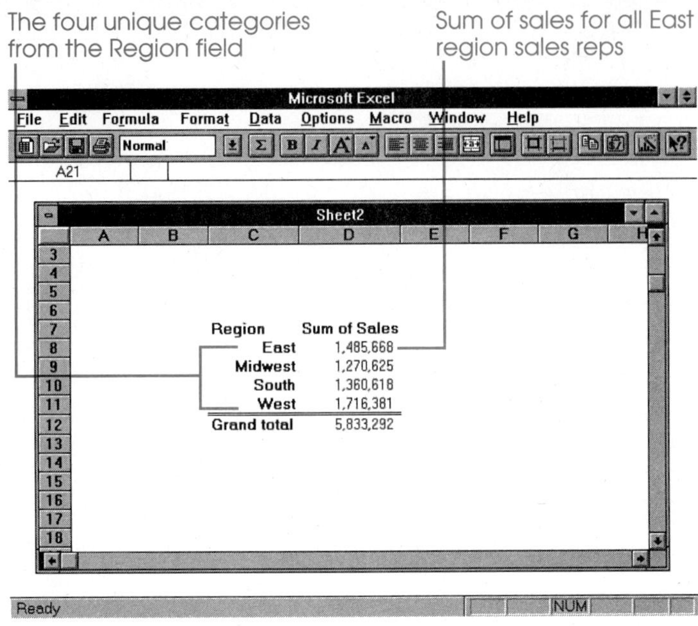

Figure 39.2 A crosstab table showing total sales by region.

IN ACTION: Use crosstab tables to break down expenses by department or, if you do freelance work, by client.

You can add a further breakdown to your data by specifying a third field (the unique entries of which are called the *column categories*) to use for column headings. Figure 39.3 shows the resulting crosstab with the four categories in the Quarter field (1st, 2nd, 3rd, and 4th) used to create the columns.

The four unique categories from the Quarter field

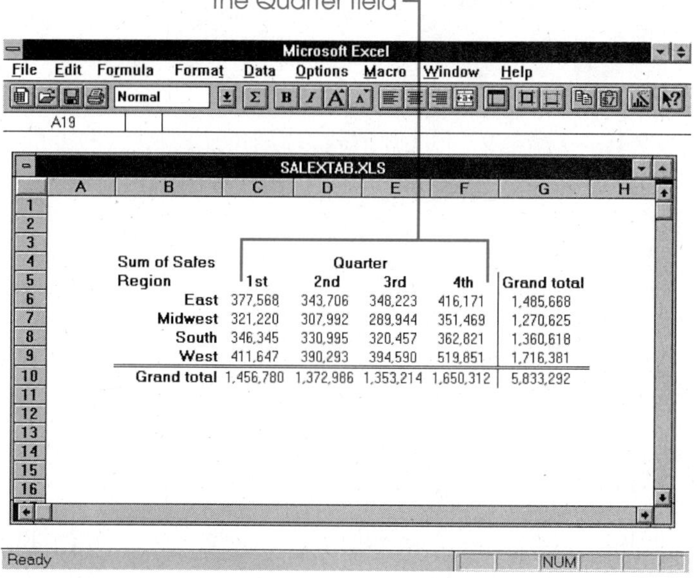

Figure 39.3 A crosstab table showing sales by region for each quarter.

Crosstab tables have tremendous flexibility. For the table layout, you can have multiple value fields and subheadings for your rows and columns, and you can change the table headings to suit your needs. For the table values, you can use criteria to include only matching records in the table, and you can add custom subtotals for average, maximum and minimum, etc. The next section shows you how to create a crosstab table.

IN ACTION: Use multiple value fields to compare actual sales or expenses with budgeted amounts.

Creating a Crosstab Table

Excel provides you with the Crosstab ReportWizard to help you create and modify your crosstab tables. The Crosstab ReportWizard uses a four-step approach that enables you to build a crosstab table from scratch. Here is a summary of the four steps:

1. Define the table row headings by specifying the field containing the row categories.

2. Define the table column headings by specifying the field containing the column categories.

3. Identify the field values to be used for summarizing the row and column categories.

4. Create the table.

The Crosstab ReportWizard dialog boxes contain a number of buttons that enable you to navigate the ReportWizard quickly. These buttons are summarized in Table 39.1 and shown in Figure 39.4.

Crosstab ReportWizard provides annotated explanations of the available options as you proceed. At each step, you can specify a number of options such as subtotal types and groupings. This section just outlines the steps to create a basic crosstab table. For more information on the options available, see the section entitled "Setting Crosstab Table Options" later in this chapter.

Table 39.1 Crosstab ReportWizard navigation buttons

Click on	*To*
Explain	Display more information about the current step.
Cancel	Close the Crosstab ReportWizard without creating the table.
|<<	Go back to the first step.
<Back	Go back to the previous step.
Next>	Go to the next step.
>>|	Go to the last step.

Figure 39.4 The CrossTab ReportWizard navigation buttons.

Throughout the rest of this chapter, the Orders database shown in Figure 39.5 will be used as an example. This is a database of orders placed in response to a 3-month marketing campaign. Each record shows the date of the order, the product ordered (there are four types: printer stand, glare filter, mouse pad, and copy holder), the quantity and net dollars ordered, the promotional offer selected by the customer (1 Free with $10 purchase or Extra Discount), and the advertisement to which the customer is responding (direct mail, magazine, or newspaper).

ORDERS DATABASE

Date	Product	Quantity	Net $	Promotion	Advertisement
6/1/92	Printer stand	11	$119.68	1 Free with 10	Direct mail
6/1/92	Glare filter	6	77.82	Extra Discount	Magazine
6/1/92	Mouse pad	15	100.95	Extra Discount	Newspaper
6/1/92	Glare filter	11	149.71	1 Free with 10	Magazine
6/2/92	Mouse pad	22	155.32	1 Free with 10	Magazine
6/2/92	Mouse pad	3	20.19	Extra Discount	Newspaper
6/2/92	Copy holder	5	33.65	Extra Discount	Direct mail
6/2/92	Printer stand	22	239.36	1 Free with 10	Newspaper
6/2/92	Glare filter	10	129.70	Extra Discount	Magazine
6/3/92	Mouse pad	22	155.32	1 Free with 10	Magazine
6/3/92	Printer stand	8	82.96	Extra Discount	Direct mail
6/3/92	Printer stand	22	239.36	1 Free with 10	Direct mail
6/3/92	Copy holder	55	388.30	1 Free with 10	Magazine
6/3/92	Mouse pad	25	168.25	Extra Discount	Newspaper
6/3/92	Glare filter	22	299.42	1 Free with 10	Magazine
6/4/92	Printer stand	11	119.68	1 Free with 10	Magazine

Figure 39.5 The Orders database that will be used as an example throughout this chapter.

Figure 39.6 shows a simple crosstab table for the Orders database. In this example, the quantity shipped is summarized by product and advertisement. The row headings were taken from the Product field, and the column headings were taken from the Advertisement field. The following steps show you how to create a basic crosstab table such as this one:

Creating a Crosstab Table:

1. Set up and define database.
2. Choose Data Crosstab.
3. Select Create a New Crosstab.

1. Set up and define a database, if you have not already done so. Wait until you are familiar with crosstab tables before setting any criteria.

2. Select Data Crosstab. Excel displays the Crosstab ReportWizard—Introduction dialog box.

3. Select Create a New Crosstab. Excel displays the Crosstab ReportWizard—Row Categories dialog box, as shown in Figure 39.7.

4. From the Fields in Database list, select the field you want to use for the row headings and then click on Add. Excel displays the field name in the Include as Row Categories list. For the Orders database, you would select the Product field.

5. Select Next>. Excel displays the Crosstab ReportWizard—Column Categories dialog box, as shown in Figure 39.8.

6. From the Fields in Database list, select the field you want to use for the column headings and then click on Add. For the Orders database, you would select the Advertisement field.

7. Select Next>. Excel displays the Crosstab ReportWizard—Value Fields dialog box, as shown in Figure 39.9.

8. From the Fields in Database list, select the field you want to use for the field values and then click on Add. For the Orders database, select the Quantity field.

9. Select Next>. Excel displays the Crosstab ReportWizard—Final dialog box.

10. Select Create It. Excel displays the table in a new worksheet.

4. Highlight field and then click on Add.
5. Select Next>.
6. Highlight field and then click on Add.
7. Select Next>.
8. Highlight field and then click on Add.
9. Select Next>.
10. Select Create It.

NOTE: If the Crosstab option does not appear on the **Data** menu, you need to install the Crosstab ReportWizard add-in macro. See your Microsoft Excel User's Guide for instructions.

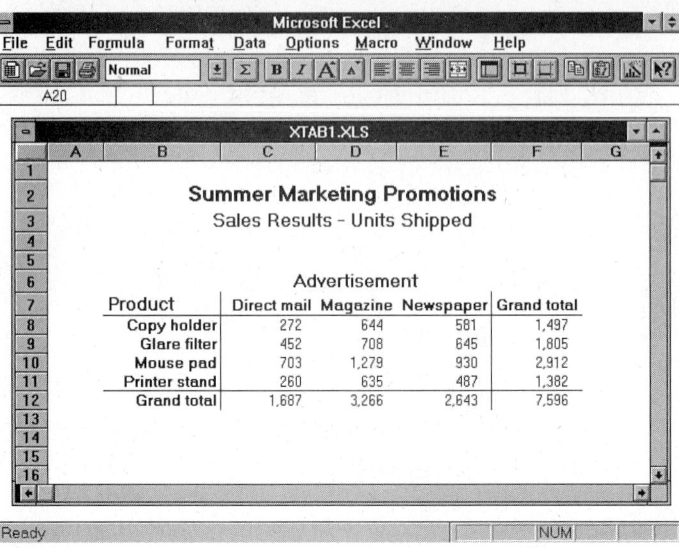

Summer Marketing Promotions

Sales Results - Units Shipped

	Advertisement			
Product	Direct mail	Magazine	Newspaper	Grand total
Copy holder	272	644	581	1,497
Glare filter	452	708	645	1,805
Mouse pad	703	1,279	930	2,912
Printer stand	260	635	487	1,382
Grand total	1,687	3,266	2,643	7,596

Figure 39.6 A simple crosstab table from the Orders database.

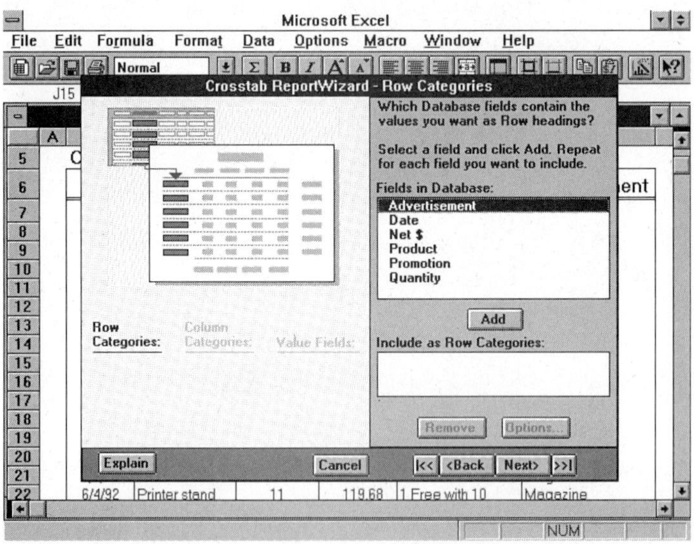

Figure 39.7 The Crosstab ReportWizard—Row Categories dialog box.

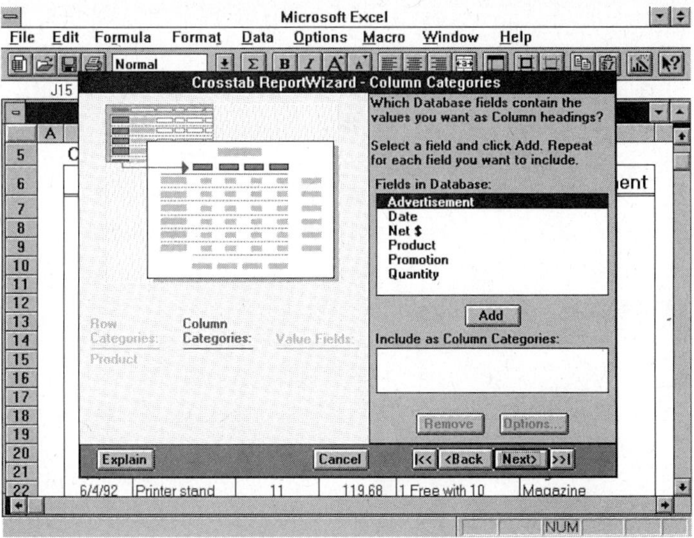

Figure 39.8 The Crosstab ReportWizard—Column Categories dialog box.

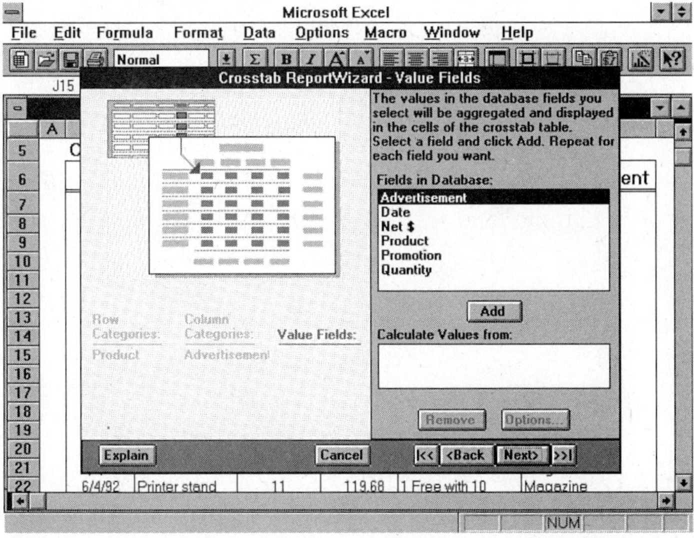

Figure 39.9 The Crosstab ReportWizard—Value Fields dialog box.

TIP: To remove the outline symbols, select Options Display and turn off Outline Symbols.

When Excel creates a crosstab table, it begins by extracting the database information you requested and uses this information to build the basic table structure. Then it calculates the table values and displays the final result in a new worksheet. Depending on the type of computer you have and the size of the database, this process can take a few seconds or a few minutes. Figure 39.10 shows what the example crosstab table looks like when it is first created. Notice that Excel automatically outlines the table. This enables you to collapse the rows or columns of large tables into a single Grand Total. (See your Microsoft Excel User's Guide for more information on outlining.) You can format the crosstab into your preferred tabular style.

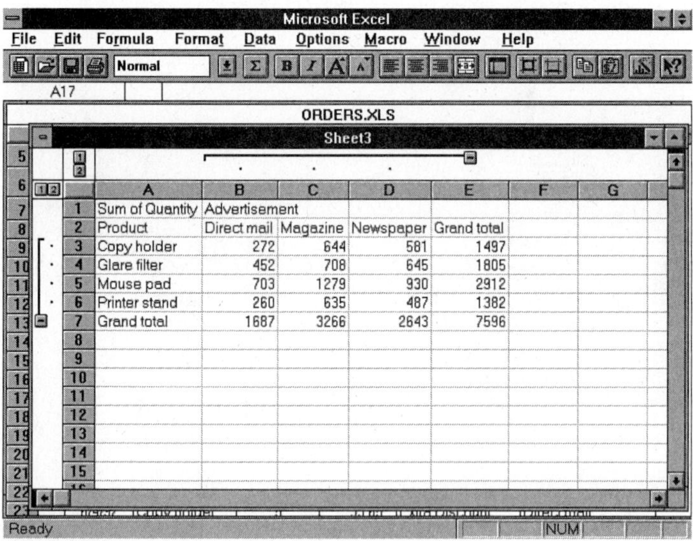

Figure 39.10 The Orders database crosstab table.

Setting Crosstab Table Options

Each Crosstab ReportWizard dialog box offers a number of options that you use to set up the table to suit your needs. You can set options for the row and column categories, value fields, or the table as a whole. The next few sections discuss these options in detail. To follow along, select Data Crosstab and then select the Modify Current Crosstab button.

Row and Column Category Options

When you add a field in either the Row Categories or Column Categories dialog boxes, the Options button becomes active. Select this button to display a list of options available for the selected field. Figure 39.11 shows the Crosstab ReportWizard—Row Categories Options dialog box.

For date and numeric fields, the In Groups of: box allows you to group the categories into manageable ranges. In date fields, for example, you have a number of options, including weeks, months, and quarters. For numeric fields, you can enter any number as a grouping range.

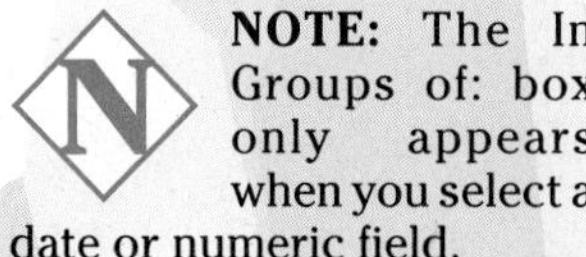

NOTE: The In Groups of: box only appears when you select a date or numeric field.

To restrict the field values used as row headings, enter a beginning and ending value in the Starting at and Ending at boxes.

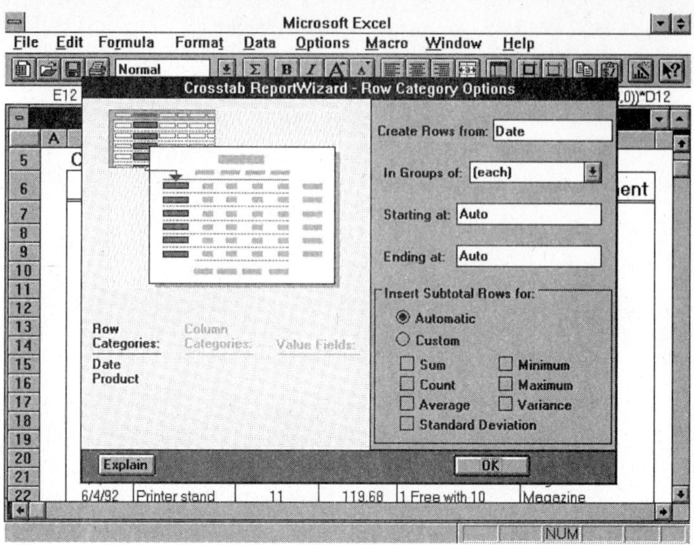

Figure 39.11 The Crosstab ReportWizard—Row Category Options dialog box.

You can also display individual subtotal lines for each row or column category. You can subtotal on sum, count, average, standard deviation, minimum, maximum, or variance. Select your subtotal options from the check boxes in the Insert Subtotal Rows for section.

When you have finished entering your row and column category options, select OK.

Value Field Options

The value field has a different set of options, as shown in the Value Field Options dialog box in Figure 39.12.

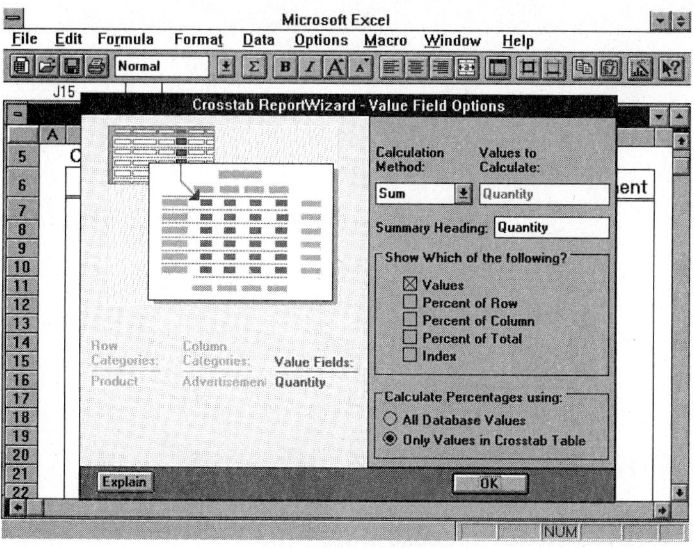

Figure 39.12 The Crosstab ReportWizard—Value Field Options.

The Calculation Method list box contains the various methods you can use to summarize the value field data. Your choices are Sum, Count, Average, Minimum, Maximum, Standard Deviation, and Variance. If you are using a number field, the default operation is Sum. If you use a text field, the default operation is Count.

Excel uses the operation and the value field name to create a table heading. For example, if the operation is Sum and the value field is Quantity, the heading is "Sum of Quantity." If you want to use a word or phrase other than the field name in the heading, enter the text you want in the Summary Heading box.

Use the Show Which of the following? section to select the types of entries to display. You can display the entries just as values; as percentages of the row, column, or total; or as an index.

Use the Calculate Percentages using section to determine how Excel calculates the table values. If your crosstab table entries are only a subset of the database, but you want to see calculations such as percentages based on the entire database, select All Database Values. Otherwise, leave the default Only Values in Crosstab Table selected, as this is much faster.

When you have finished entering your row and column category options, select OK.

Table Creation Options

After you have selected the fields to use in your table, you can also select several options that affect the overall table. Select Set Table Creation Options from the Crosstab ReportWizard—Final dialog box. The Crosstab ReportWizard—Create Options dialog box appears, as shown in Figure 39.13.

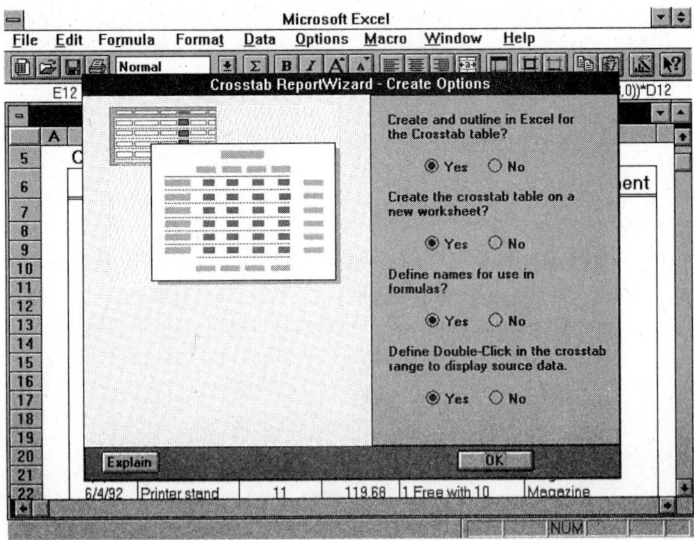

Figure 39.13 The Crosstab ReportWizard—Create Options dialog box.

Select Yes in the first option, Create an outline in Excel for the Crosstab table?, to enable Excel's outlining feature for your table. Outlines are useful for collapsing large tables into summary rows and columns.

Select Yes in the next option, Create the crosstab table in a new worksheet, to have Excel automatically open a new worksheet for your table. If you prefer to display the table in the database worksheet, note that you can only have one crosstab table per worksheet. To include other crosstabs in the same worksheet, create a picture of the table and embed it in the worksheet with Edit Paste Link. See Skill Session 33 for details.

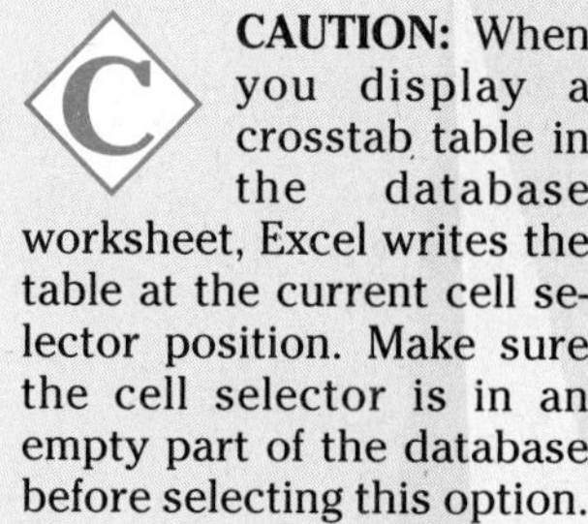

CAUTION: When you display a crosstab table in the database worksheet, Excel writes the table at the current cell selector position. Make sure the cell selector is in an empty part of the database before selecting this option.

If you select Yes in the Define names for use in formulas? option, Excel will create names for the table values (e.g., "Grand_Total" or "Advertisement") that you can use as formula references.

The final option, Define Double-Click in the crosstab range to display source data, enables you to double-click on any table cell to "drill down" and see the source data that created the cell total.

Modifying Crosstab Tables

After you have created a crosstab table, you can recalculate the table at any time, or you can make changes to the table definition either by using the Crosstab ReportWizard or by modifying the CROSSTAB() functions associated with the table.

Recalculating a Crosstab Table

Recalculating a Crosstab Table:

1. Activate crosstab table worksheet.
2. Select Data Crosstab.
3. Select Recalculate Current Crosstab.

If you edit the database, Excel does not automatically update the crosstab table. To recalculate the table, follow these steps:

1. Activate the worksheet containing the crosstab table.
2. Select Data Crosstab.
3. Select Recalculate Current Crosstab. Excel rebuilds the table using the existing options.

Modifying a Crosstab Table

Modifying a Crosstab Table:

1. Activate crosstab table worksheet.
2. Select Data Crosstab.
3. Select Modify Current Crosstab.
4. Redefine crosstab.

You can use the Crosstab ReportWizard to modify the table definition. Here are the steps to follow:

1. Activate the worksheet containing the crosstab table.
2. Select Data Crosstab.
3. Select Modify Current Crosstab.
4. Make your changes to the crosstab definition.

Changing Row and Column Headings

You can change the row and column headings in your crosstab table by modifying the CROSSTAB() functions directly on the worksheet. Excel defines each row and column heading with a CROSSTAB() function that has the format

```
=CROSSTAB(heading, expression)
```

where *heading* is the row or column heading you see in the table and *expression* is information Excel uses to calculate the table. To get a new heading, you simply edit the first argument in the appropriate CROSSTAB() function. For example, to change a column heading called "Grand Total" that is defined by the function CROSSTAB("Grand Total", "Grand Total:") to the heading "Product Total," you would change the function to CROSSTAB("Product Total", "Grand Total:").

Using Multiple Fields for Row and Column Categories

You are not restricted to just one field for your row or column categories. You can select multiple fields, and Excel organizes them as a hierarchy. The first field you include as a row or column category is considered the main category, the next field is treated as a subcategory of the first, and so on. For example, Figure 39.14 shows a crosstab table from the Orders database where the rows are organized by date and then by product.

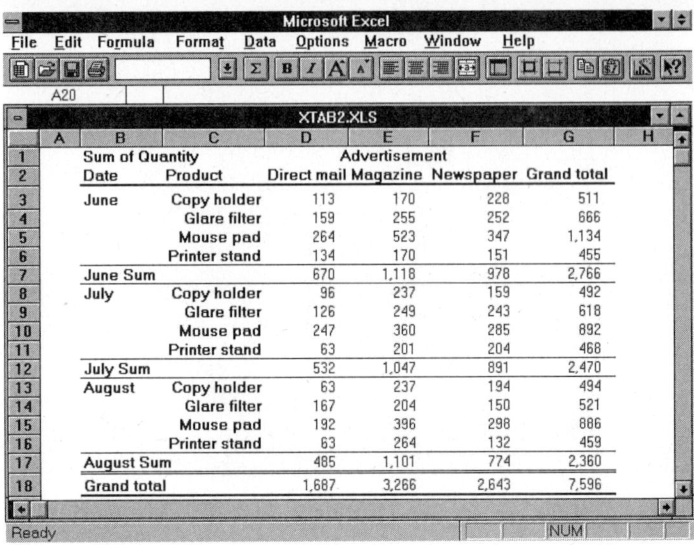

Sum of Quantity		Advertisement			
Date	Product	Direct mail	Magazine	Newspaper	Grand total
June	Copy holder	113	170	228	511
	Glare filter	159	255	252	666
	Mouse pad	264	523	347	1,134
	Printer stand	134	170	151	455
June Sum		670	1,118	978	2,766
July	Copy holder	96	237	159	492
	Glare filter	126	249	243	618
	Mouse pad	247	360	285	892
	Printer stand	63	201	204	468
July Sum		532	1,047	891	2,470
August	Copy holder	63	237	194	494
	Glare filter	167	204	150	521
	Mouse pad	192	396	298	886
	Printer stand	63	264	132	459
August Sum		485	1,101	774	2,360
Grand total		1,687	3,266	2,643	7,596

Figure 39.14 You can use multiple fields to define your row and column categories.

Using Multiple Fields for Row and Column Categories:

1. Select Data Crosstab.
2. Select Create a New Crosstab or Modify Current Crosstab.
3. Highlight main row category field and select Add.
4. Repeat step 3 to include other fields.
5. Select Next>.
6. Highlight main column category field and select Add.
7. Repeat step 6 to include other fields.
8. Select other table options and create table.

Follow these steps to include multiple rows or column categories in your crosstab tables:

1. Select Data Crosstab.

2. If you are defining a new crosstab table, select Create a New Crosstab. If you are making changes to an existing crosstab, select Modify Current Crosstab.

3. If you are modifying an existing crosstab, first use the Remove button to remove any existing row categories (if necessary). Then highlight the field that you want to use for the main row category and click on Add. For the Orders database example, you would select the Date field.

4. Repeat step 3 for other row categories you want to include in the table. Select the fields in order of priority. For the Orders database example, you would select the Product field.

5. Select Next> to enter the column categories.

6. If you are modifying an existing crosstab, first use the Remove button to remove any existing column categories (if necessary). Then highlight the field that you want to use for the main column category and click on Add.

7. Repeat step 6 for other column categories you want to include in the table. Select the fields in order of priority.

8. Select your other table options, as needed, and create the table.

Using Multiple Value Fields

Just as you can include multiple fields for your crosstab row and column categories, so can you include multiple value fields. This is useful for comparing related numbers within the same category. For example, Figure 39.15 shows an Orders database crosstab table that uses both the Quantity and Net $ fields.

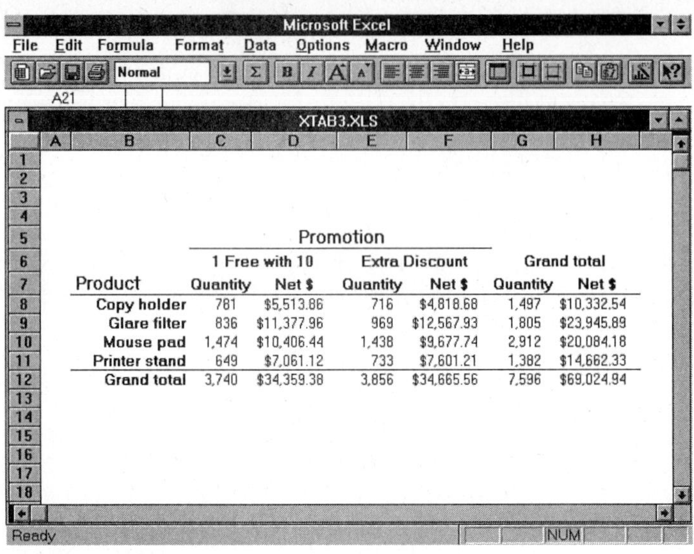

Product	Promotion					
	1 Free with 10		Extra Discount		Grand total	
	Quantity	Net $	Quantity	Net $	Quantity	Net $
Copy holder	781	$5,513.86	716	$4,818.68	1,497	$10,332.54
Glare filter	836	$11,377.96	969	$12,567.93	1,805	$23,945.89
Mouse pad	1,474	$10,406.44	1,438	$9,677.74	2,912	$20,084.18
Printer stand	649	$7,061.12	733	$7,601.21	1,382	$14,662.33
Grand total	3,740	$34,359.38	3,856	$34,665.56	7,596	$69,024.94

Figure 39.15 You can use multiple value fields in your crosstab tables.

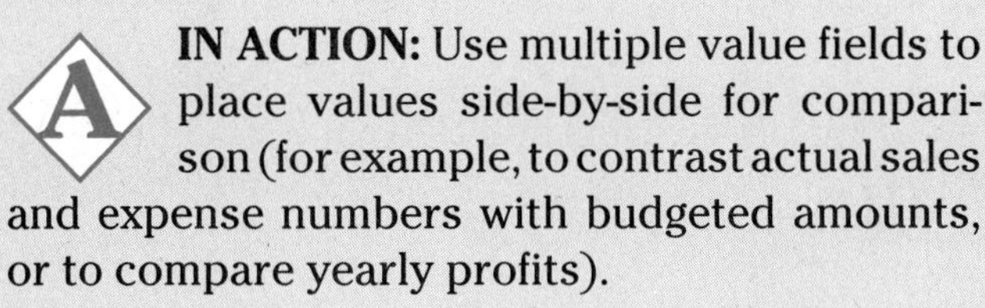

IN ACTION: Use multiple value fields to place values side-by-side for comparison (for example, to contrast actual sales and expense numbers with budgeted amounts, or to compare yearly profits).

When you use multiple value fields, you have a choice of formats that you can use. The format used in Figure 39.15 is called the *inner column* format because both value fields are displayed side-by-side within each column category. Figure 39.16 displays the same information in *outer column* format. In this case, the value fields are displayed outside of the column categories. You can also select *inner row* and *outer row* formats.

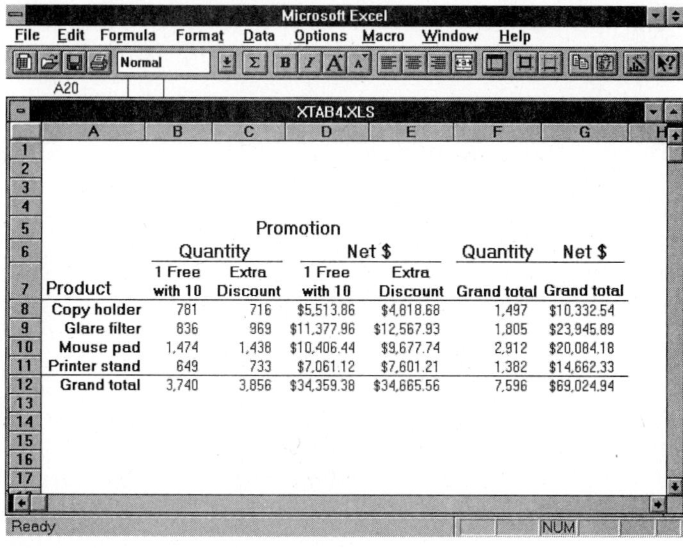

Microsoft Excel

XTAB4.XLS

	Promotion					
	Quantity		Net $		Quantity	Net $
Product	1 Free with 10	Extra Discount	1 Free with 10	Extra Discount	Grand total	Grand total
Copy holder	781	716	$5,513.86	$4,818.68	1,497	$10,332.54
Glare filter	836	969	$11,377.96	$12,567.93	1,805	$23,945.89
Mouse pad	1,474	1,438	$10,406.44	$9,677.74	2,912	$20,084.18
Printer stand	649	733	$7,061.12	$7,601.21	1,382	$14,662.33
Grand total	3,740	3,856	$34,359.38	$34,665.56	7,596	$69,024.94

Figure 39.16 The outer column format.

Follow these steps to include multiple value fields in a crosstab table definition:

1. Select Data Crosstab.
2. If you are defining a new crosstab table, select Create a New Crosstab. If you are making changes to an existing crosstab, select Modify Current Crosstab.
3. Add the fields for your row and column categories.
4. In the Crosstab ReportWizard—Value Fields dialog box, select the first field you want to use to calculate the table values, and then select Add.
5. Repeat step 4 for other value fields you want to include in the table. For the Orders database example, select the Quantity and Net $ fields.

Using Multiple Value Fields:

1. Select Data Crosstab.
2. Select Create a New Crosstab or Modify Current Crosstab.
3. Add fields for your row and column categories.
4. Select first value field and then click on Add.
5. Repeat step 4 for other value fields.
6. Select Next>.
7. Select layout option.
8. Select Next>.
9. Create table.

6. Select Next>. Excel displays the Crosstab ReportWizard—Multiple Value Field Layout dialog box.

7. Select the layout option you want.

8. Select Next>.

9. Select other table options, as needed, and create the table.

Skill Session

40

Using Q+E

So far in this workshop, you have been using databases defined as ranges in Excel worksheets. You can also use Excel to access external database files from programs such as dBASE III Plus, dBASE IV, ORACLE, or Microsoft SQL Server. Excel 4 for Windows comes with an add-in program called Q+E that enables you to work with these external files. This skill session shows you the basics of the Q+E program and explains how to use external databases within Excel.

About Q+E

Q+E is a small but powerful database application designed to provide you with easy access to various database formats. You can use Q+E as a stand-alone program or as an add-in to Excel. When used as a stand-alone program, you can display and manipulate database files in the Q+E window (see Figure 40.1). When used as an add-in, Q+E provides links to an external database via DDE (Dynamic Data Exchange). Excel modifies most of its database commands to take advantage of this link and work with external databases directly within a worksheet.

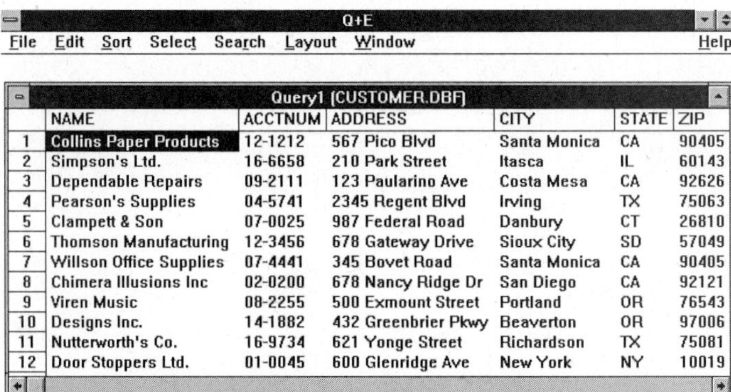

	NAME	ACCTNUM	ADDRESS	CITY	STATE	ZIP
1	Collins Paper Products	12-1212	567 Pico Blvd	Santa Monica	CA	90405
2	Simpson's Ltd.	16-6658	210 Park Street	Itasca	IL	60143
3	Dependable Repairs	09-2111	123 Paularino Ave	Costa Mesa	CA	92626
4	Pearson's Supplies	04-5741	2345 Regent Blvd	Irving	TX	75063
5	Clampett & Son	07-0025	987 Federal Road	Danbury	CT	26810
6	Thomson Manufacturing	12-3456	678 Gateway Drive	Sioux City	SD	57049
7	Willson Office Supplies	07-4441	345 Bovet Road	Santa Monica	CA	90405
8	Chimera Illusions Inc	02-0200	678 Nancy Ridge Dr	San Diego	CA	92121
9	Viren Music	08-2255	500 Exmount Street	Portland	OR	76543
10	Designs Inc.	14-1882	432 Greenbrier Pkwy	Beaverton	OR	97006
11	Nutterworth's Co.	16-9734	621 Yonge Street	Richardson	TX	75081
12	Door Stoppers Ltd.	01-0045	600 Glenridge Ave	New York	NY	10019

Figure 40.1 Q+E displays external database files in query windows.

The name Q+E comes from the program's two main functions: querying and editing database files. A *query* is a request to the database for specific information. It combines criteria and extract conditions with functions to display the data you want to see. With Q+E, you can construct queries by executing individual pull-down menu commands or by writing query statements using SQL (Structured Query Language).

You can also use Q+E to edit and maintain your database files. You can add and delete records, modify field contents, join databases, and even create new database files. The beauty of Q+E is that you can do all this with many different database formats while maintaining a consistent interface that takes full advantage of the Windows environment.

If you want to use Q+E as a stand-alone program, double-click the Q+E 3.0 icon in the Microsoft Excel 4.0 program group. See your Q+E for Microsoft Excel User's Guide for complete instructions on using Q+E. The rest of this skill session deals with using Q+E as an Excel add-in.

Opening Q+E within Excel

You use Q+E within Excel by opening the QE.XLA add-in macro sheet. Here are the steps to follow:

1. Select File Open. Excel displays the Open dialog box.
2. Change to the directory containing the QE.XLA file. This should be in QE, a subdirectory of your main Excel directory.
3. Highlight QE.XLA.
4. Select OK or press Enter.

Opening Q+E within Excel:

1. Select File Open.
2. Change to QE directory.
3. Highlight QE.XLA.
4. Select OK.

NOTE: If you cannot find the QE.XLA file on your hard drive, you probably chose not to install Q+E during the Excel setup. To install Q+E, rerun the setup program and select only the Q+E option at the Installation Options screen.

When you open QE.XLA, Excel loads Q+E into memory and modifies the **D**ata menu commands so that they work with external databases. In addition, three new commands are added to the Data menu:

Paste F**i**eldnames	Copies selected field names from a database to use as headings in a criteria or extract range.
SQL **Q**uery	Enables you to write an SQL query to extract information from an external database.
Acti**v**ate Q+E	Switches to the Q+E program.

Working with External Databases

When working with worksheet (internal) databases, you must define the database range using Data Set Data**b**ase. Once you have opened the QE.XLA file, you can use Data Set Data**b**ase to define either an internal or external database. You can use the same command to open multiple external databases and switch between them.

IN ACTION: When you open multiple databases, Q+E allows you to join those that have common fields. This is useful for extracting records from one database based on criteria in another. See the section entitled "Joining External Databases" later in this skill session.

Defining an External Database

Q+E can create links between a number of popular database file formats, including dBASE II, dBASE III Plus, and dBASE IV, SQL Server, ORACLE and even text files containing data from other programs. The number of these database systems, or *sources*, that you can access depends on the drivers you installed during the Excel setup. You must specify which source you want to use for the external databases you are defining. Note that you can only define multiple external databases if they are from a single source.

Follow these steps to define an external database for use within Excel:

1. Open QE.XLA, if you have not already done so.
2. Select Data Set Database. Excel displays the Set Database dialog box, as shown in Figure 40.2.
3. Choose External Database.
4. Select OK or press Enter. Excel displays the Set External Database dialog box, as shown in Figure 40.3.

Defining an External Database:

1. Open QE.XLA.
2. Select Data Set Database.
3. Choose External Database.
4. Select OK.
5. Select a source from Source list box.
6. Highlight file.
7. Select OK.
8. Select Change or Add, if needed, and repeat steps 6 and 7.
9. Select OK.

5. Select a source from the **S**ource list box. If the source you want does not appear on this list, select Sources for other options.

6. Use the **Di**rectories and **F**iles lists to highlight the file you want.

7. Select OK or press Enter. Excel returns you to the Set Database dialog box and displays the file you chose.

8. To change the file or add another, select Change or Add and repeat steps 6 and 7.

9. Select OK or press Enter.

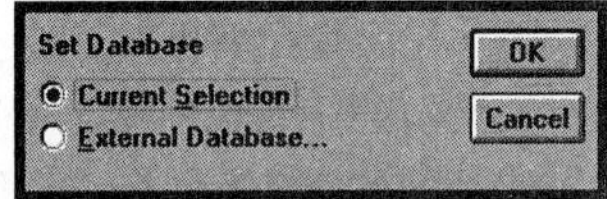

Figure 40.2 The Set Database dialog box.

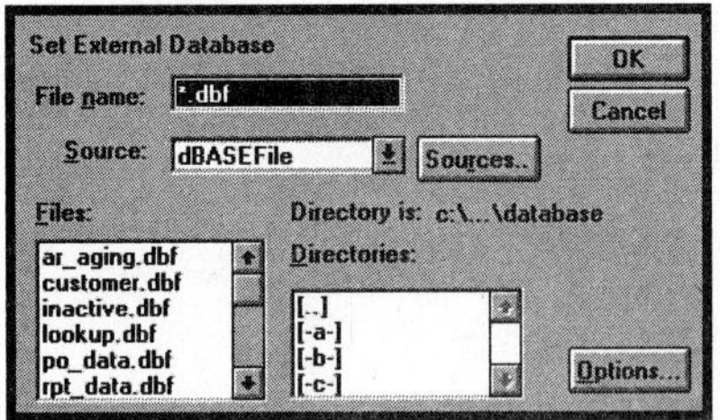

Figure 40.3 The Set External Database dialog box.

When you define an external database, Excel does not display it on-screen. Instead, the file is linked to Excel through Q+E. This allows you to set up criteria and extract ranges in your worksheet or write SQL queries to get the information you want from the database. If you want to view the contents of the file, select Data Activate Q+E to activate Q+E and open the file.

Changing the External Databases

Once you have defined an external database, you can change to another file at any time and define as many additional databases as your computer's memory will permit. Here are the steps to follow:

1. Select Data Set Database. Excel displays the Set Database dialog box showing the current source and the defined external databases (see Figure 40.4).
2. To change the files, select Change. Excel displays the Set External Database dialog box.
3. Choose a new file and then select OK or press Enter. Excel replaces the original databases with the selected file.
4. To add files, select Add. Excel displays the Set External Database dialog box.
5. Choose an additional file and then select OK or press Enter. Excel adds the file to the list of defined databases.
6. Select OK or press Enter.

Changing or Adding External Databases:

1. Select Data Set Database.
2. To change files, select Change.
3. Choose a new file; select OK.
4. To add files, select Add.
5. Choose an additional file; select OK.
6. Select OK.

NOTE: You can only add external databases that are from the same source. For example, if the currently defined files are dBASE files, the additional databases must also be dBASE files.

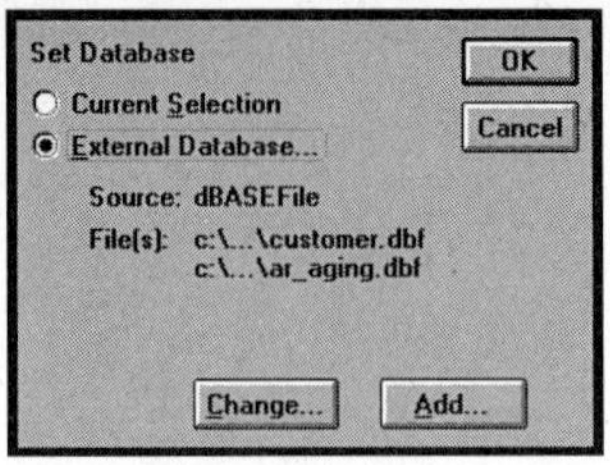

Figure 40.4 The Set Database dialog box showing the currently defined external databases.

Switching Between Internal and External Databases

Excel's **D**ata menu commands operate differently depending on whether you are using an internal worksheet database or one or more external databases. You need to specify which type of database you want the commands to operate on. Here are the steps to follow to do this:

Switching between Internal and External Databases:

1. Select **D**ata Set Data**b**ase.
2. Choose Current **S**election or **E**xternal Database.
3. Select OK.

1. Select **D**ata Set Data**b**ase to display the Set Database dialog box.

2. To use the commands on an internal database, choose Current **S**election. Otherwise, choose **E**xternal Database.

3. Select OK or press Enter.

Pasting Field Names from an External Database

To work with information from an external database, you will generally set up a criteria range and then select the appropriate **D**ata menu command. If you want to extract information from the database, you will also need to set up an extract range.

Although you cannot see the database from your worksheet, you can still set up criteria or extract ranges by using Paste Fieldnames to copy some or all the database field names to the worksheet. You then define your ranges as you would with an Excel database.

The syntax of the field names depends on the number of external databases you have defined. If you have defined only one, the field names appear as they do in the database. If you have defined more than one external database, each field name is prefaced by the database name. For example, in a database named CUSTOMER that has an ADDRESS field, the name appears as `customer.ADDRESS`.

Follow these steps to paste field names:

Pasting Field Names from an External Database:

1. Position the cell selector.
2. Select Data Paste Fieldnames.

1. Position the cell selector where you want the field names to begin.
2. Select Data Paste Fieldnames. Excel displays the Paste Fieldnames dialog box, as shown in Figure 40.5.

3. Select Paste All or select names with Ctrl+spacebar.
4. To paste fields in a different order, select Order Fields.
5. Select field names in order; select Add.
6. Select Paste.

3. To paste all the field names to the worksheet, select Paste All. Excel pastes the field names and returns you to the worksheet.

4. To paste only selected names, hold down Ctrl and either click on each field name you want, or select each name with the arrow keys and press spacebar. Skip to step 7.

5. If you want to paste the fields in a different order, select Order Fields. The dialog box expands, as shown in Figure 40.6.

6. In the order you want, select the field names from the Available Fields list and, for each name, select Add. To clear a single field name from the Selected Fields list, select Remove. To clear all the field names, select Clear All.

7. Select Paste. Excel pastes the field names to the worksheet.

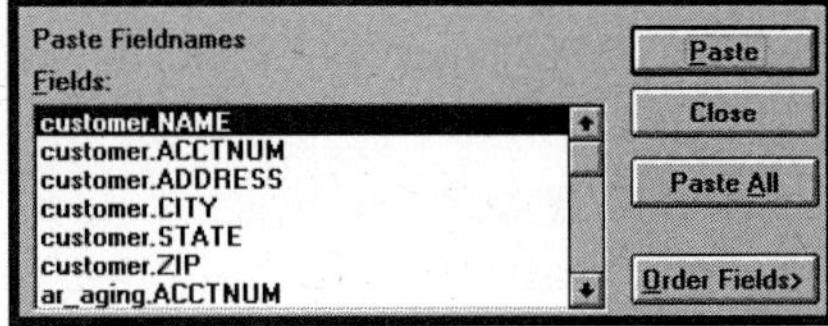

Figure 40.5 The Paste Fieldnames dialog box.

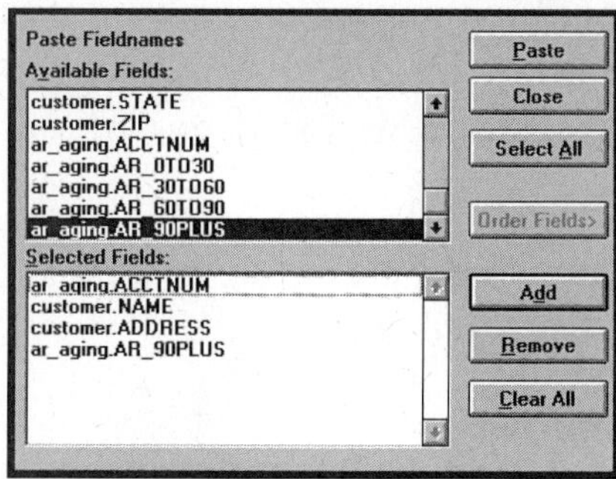

Figure 40.6 Use the expanded dialog box to paste field names in a different order.

Entering Criteria

You set up a criteria range for an external database in the same way as you would for a worksheet database. After you have pasted the field names you want, highlight the range and then select Data Set Criteria.

When you enter your criteria, you follow most of the techniques outlined in Skill Session 37 with two exceptions.

The first exception is that Q+E is case-sensitive when it evaluates criteria. You must use the same upper- and lowercase formats that are found in the database. For example, suppose you are setting criteria for a database with a STATE field that contains only two-letter state abbreviations in uppercase. If you enter, say, "ca" (for California) as part of your criteria, Q+E will not match any records because all the California records will have "CA" in the STATE field.

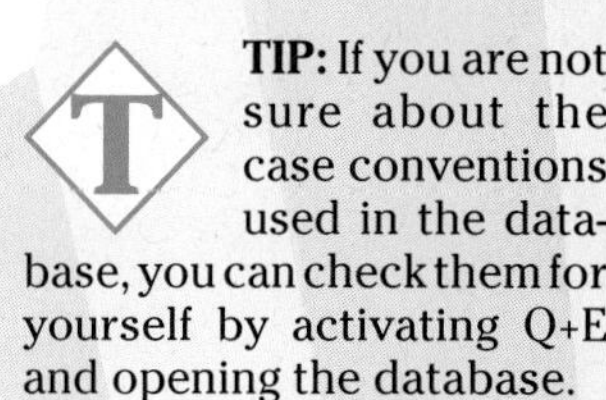

TIP: If you are not sure about the case conventions used in the database, you can check them for yourself by activating Q+E and opening the database.

The second exception is that Q+E evaluates computed criteria differently. As you learned in Skill Session 37, when you set up computed criteria for a worksheet database, you have to follow two conventions:

- ▲ You must create a new field name that does not exist in the database.
- ▲ You must use logical expressions where other fields are referenced by their cell addresses in the first row of the database.

For example, in Skill Session 37, you saw a sample computed criterion that tested for invoices that were paid at least 10 days before they were due. The criterion was set up as follows (this is rearranged slightly from the original):

```
Early
=F7<=E7-10
```

where *Early* was the name of the new field and *E7* and *F7* were the Due Date field and Date Paid field, respectively (row 7 was the top row of the database).

To create the same computed criterion for an external database, you must use a syntax that is closer to an SQL query and that has the following conventions:

- ▲ You must use the existing database field names. (You cannot create new names.)
- ▲ You refer to other fields using the field name so that the criteria conditions become simple comparative statements.
- ▲ You cannot use Excel functions or cell references.

The example criterion given above would become

```
DATE_PAID
<=DUE_DATE-10
```

Extracting Records from an External Database

Once you have set up your criteria range, you can extract the information you need from an external database. You set up your extract range the same way you would for a worksheet database. Select **Data Paste Fieldnames** to get the fields you need for the extract. Then highlight the cells and select **Data Set Extract** to define the range. Figure 40.7 shows the criteria and extract ranges set up for a dBASE file called CUSTOMER.

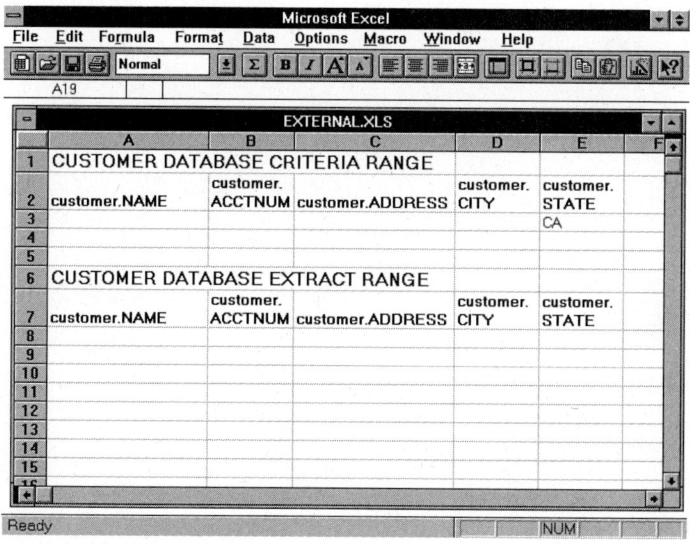

Figure 40.7 The criteria and extract ranges for the CUSTOMER database.

Extracting Records from an External Database:

1. Enter criteria.
2. Select Data Extract.
3. Select OK.
4. Select Linked or Unlinked.
5. Select Save As or Paste.

Follow these steps to extract records from an external database:

1. Enter your criteria in the criteria range.
2. Select Data Extract. Excel asks if you want to extract unique records only.
3. Select OK or press Enter. Excel performs the query and notifies you of the number of records received from the file (see Figure 40.8).
4. To maintain a link with the file through Q+E, select the Linked option. Otherwise, leave the Unlinked option selected.
5. To save the information as a text file, select Save As and enter a file name in the dialog box that appears. Otherwise, select Paste. Excel pastes the records into the extract range.

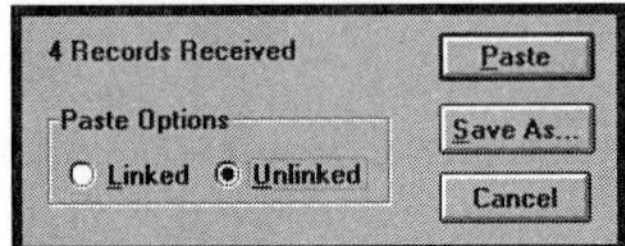

Figure 40.8 Excel notifies you of the number of records received.

Figure 40.9 shows the results of the query for all customers from California.

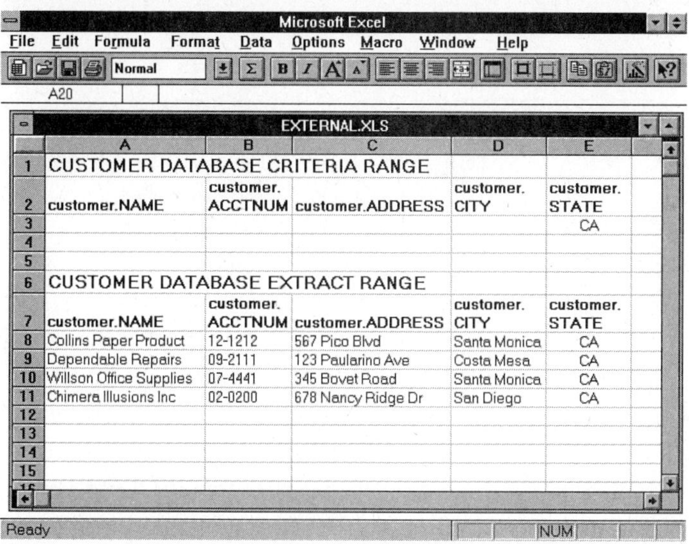

	A	B	C	D	E
1	CUSTOMER DATABASE CRITERIA RANGE				
2	customer.NAME	customer. ACCTNUM	customer.ADDRESS	customer. CITY	customer. STATE
3					CA
4					
5					
6	CUSTOMER DATABASE EXTRACT RANGE				
7	customer.NAME	customer. ACCTNUM	customer.ADDRESS	customer. CITY	customer. STATE
8	Collins Paper Product	12-1212	567 Pico Blvd	Santa Monica	CA
9	Dependable Repairs	09-2111	123 Paularino Ave	Costa Mesa	CA
10	Willson Office Supplies	07-4441	345 Bovet Road	Santa Monica	CA
11	Chimera Illusions Inc	02-0200	678 Nancy Ridge Dr	San Diego	CA

Figure 40.9 The result of the CUSTOMER database query.

Joining External Databases

Q+E has a powerful feature that enables you to join two or more databases. To take advantage of this feature, your databases must have at least one field in common. The fields do not need to have the same names, but the data within each field must be of a common type. For example, if one database has an ACCTNUM field and another has a CUST_ID field, you can join the two databases as long as these fields have similar contents (account numbers, in this case).

Q+E joins databases by using the common field to cross-reference information from one database to the other. As an example, both the CUSTOMER database used previously and another dBASE file, AR_AGING.DBF, have a common field called ACCTNUM. AR_AGING is a database of accounts receivable aging where each record contains an account number and the amount the account still owes that is between 0 and 30 days old, 30 to 60 days old, and so on. The idea is to look up the accounts receivable information in the AR_AGING database and cross-reference with the CUSTOMER database to get the account name, address, etc.

To join these two files, you use the full name of one of the common fields (say, customer.ACCTNUM) as a field in the criteria range, and you use the full name of the other field as the actual criterion. Figure 40.10 shows how this is done. In this case, the query is designed to extract all records with invoices that are more than 90 days past due and show the account name and address. Figure 40.11 shows the result of the extraction.

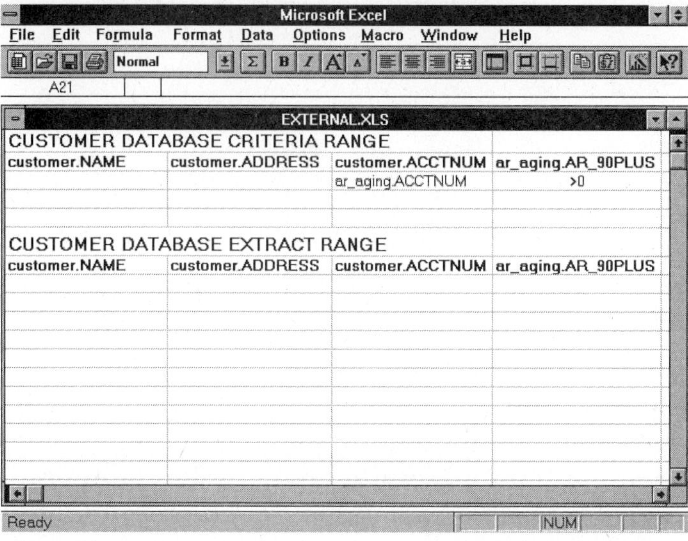

Figure 40.10 Use a common field name as a criterion to join two databases.

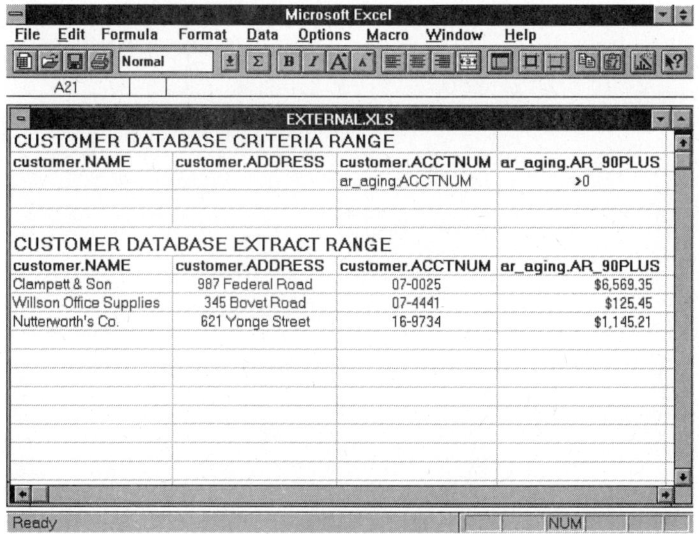

Figure 40.11 The result of the extraction.

File Management Workshop

To work efficiently and effectively with your file documents, it is crucial to develop file management skills. If you seek better ways to plan your applications, organize your files, and protect your documents then this workshop has been written for you. This workshop details various skills that allow you to protect your document files and selected data within those files, share document information via linking and importing, combine data through consolidation, revise multiple documents concurrently with the group edit feature, and better understand the structure and nature of your file documents through the operation of the Info Window.

Skill Session

41

Protecting Data in Documents

As a single user, you may not have the need to protect your documents (worksheet, chart, macro sheet, or workbook). However, if you are one of a number of users who have access to the same documents, there may be certain documents you want to protect from being changed or viewed. Documents containing confidential or sensitive information often need some type of protection; documents containing complex formulas, macros, or charts may also need protection (to prevent others from copying or destroying your work).

Excel allows for different degrees of security and layers of protection. Lower-level protection includes locking and hiding cells. Locking means Excel prevents the user from making changes, and informs the user with a message that locked cells cannot be changed. Documents you want to safeguard from changes—but don't need to protect from being opened—can be protected by locking all cells or specific cells, or by hiding cells so their contents cannot be seen by other users.

Without other types of protection, locking or hiding cells offers (at best) limited security; many users will know how to unlock or unhide cells. However, locked or hidden cells can be *password-protected*. When a user tries to change locked cells that are protected by a password—or tries to display password-protected hidden cells—Excel requires a password before unlocking or unhiding the cells. This level of protection is more secure than either locking or hiding cells alone; assigning a password to documents prevents their being opened without the password.

You can also save a file in such a way that when a user opens it, a message will recommend opening the file in a *Read-Only state*. When a file is opened as Read-Only, the user can read the file, but cannot save it under the same name.

Locking All Cells in a Document

Locking All Cells in a Document:

1. Choose Options Protect Document.
2. Click the Cells check box.
3. Choose OK or press Enter.

You can protect the contents of all cells in a document (such as a worksheet or macro sheet) from changes by *locking* the cells. When a user tries to enter data into (or edit) locked cells, Excel displays a message informing the user that the cells are locked and cannot be changed. To lock cells, follow these steps:

1. Choose Options Protect Document. The Protect Document dialog box, shown in Figure 41.1 appears.

2. Turn on the Cells check box by clicking on the check box. (Initially, by default the Cells check is selected; therefore, if there is an X showing in the Cells check box, this step is not needed.)

3. Choose OK or press Enter.

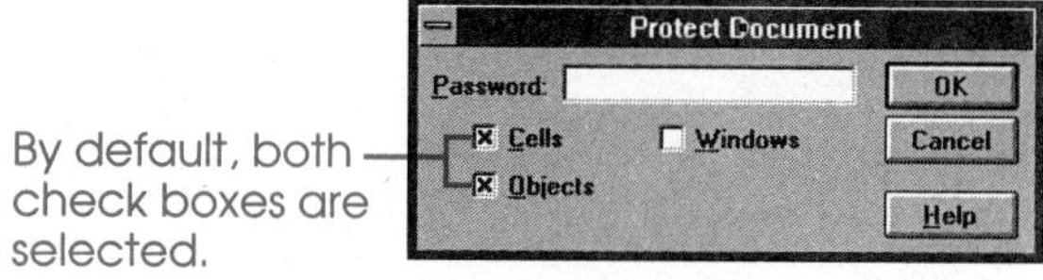

Figure 41.1 The Protect Document dialog box.

Unlocking Ranges of Cells in a Protected Worksheet

You do not have to lock all the cells of a worksheet. You can be selective—unprotecting some cells, leaving others protected. For example, if you want to lock all the cells of a worksheet with the exception of the range C6..C10 (where you may be frequently entering or editing data), follow these steps:

1. Make sure the worksheet is unprotected. If the worksheet is protected, choose Options Unprotect Document.

2. Select the cells you want to unprotect (unlock).

3. Choose Format Cell Protection. The Cell Protection dialog box shown in Figure 41.2 appears.

Unlocking a Range of Cells:

1. Choose Options Unprotect Document.
2. Select the cells you want to unlock.
3. Choose Format Cell Protection.

4. Click the Locked check box to turn off the cell locking, and then choose OK or press Enter.
5. Choose Options Protect Document.

4. Turn off the Locked check box. The Locked check box should now be empty (if it contains an X, the cell locking is still enabled).

5. Choose OK or press Enter.

6. Choose Options Protect Document.

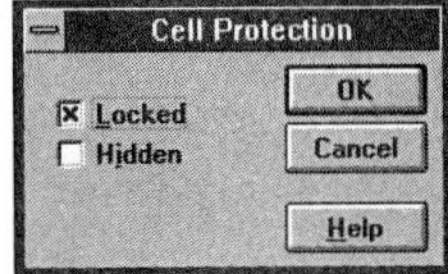

Figure 41.2 The Cell Protection dialog box.

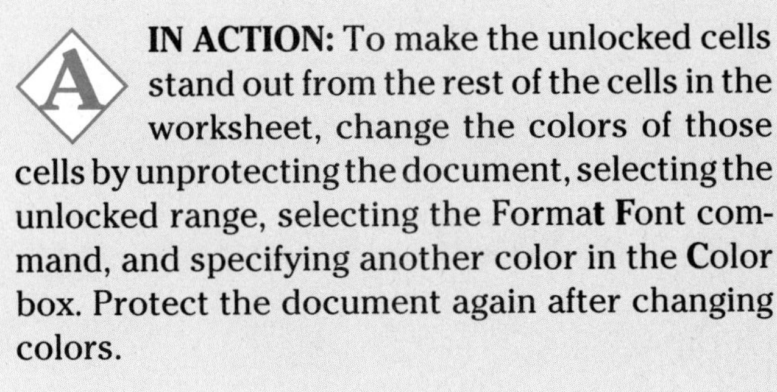

IN ACTION: To make the unlocked cells stand out from the rest of the cells in the worksheet, change the colors of those cells by unprotecting the document, selecting the unlocked range, selecting the Forma**t** **F**ont command, and specifying another color in the **C**olor box. Protect the document again after changing colors.

After unlocking ranges of a worksheet, you may decide that you want some of those ranges to be once again protected. This is sometimes the case when developing a worksheet or making revisions to a worksheet. To re-lock ranges, follow these steps:

Re-locking a Range of Cells:

1. Choose Options Unprotect Document.
2. Select the unlocked range, and then choose Format Cell Protection.

1. Choose Options Unprotect Document.

2. Select the unlocked range.

3. Choose Format Cell Protection. The Cell Protection dialog box appears.

4. To enable cell locking, turn on the Locked check box by clicking on it, or tabbing to it and pressing the spacebar. (The Locked check box should now contain an X.)

5. Choose OK or press Enter.

6. Choose Options Protect Document. The Protect Document dialog box appears.

7. Choose OK or press Enter.

3. Choose OK or press Enter.
4. Choose Options Protect Document.
5. Choose OK or press Enter.

Click the Lock Cell tool on the Utility toolbar to prevent selected cells and objects from being changed when the document is protected. If a cell or object is locked, this tool appears selected. To unlock a cell or object, select the Lock Cell tool.

Protecting Worksheet Cells with a Password

To add further security to the locking of cells in a worksheet, you can protect locked cells with a password. This type of password protection should not be confused with *file password protection* (covered later in this Skill Session). By assigning a password to locked cells, you can prevent other users from unlocking the cells. If a locked cell has no password protection, a knowledgeable Excel user can strip away the locking protection, and make changes to the cells. To protect worksheet cells with a password, follow these steps:

1. Unprotect the document if necessary, and then select the cells you want to protect.

Locking a Range with a Password:

1. Select the cells you want to protect, and then choose Format Cell Protection.
2. Click on the Locked check box; choose OK or press Enter.
3. Choose Options Protect Document.
4. Turn on the Cells check box by clicking on it.
5. In the Password box, type a password; choose OK or press Enter.
6. In the Re-enter Protection Password box, type your password again to confirm it.
7. Choose OK or press Enter.

2. Choose Format Cell Protection. The Cell Protection dialog box appears.

3. Select the Locked check box. (Caution: With a new worksheet, the **L**ocked check box is turned on (contains an X), therefore, be careful not to turn it off. You may find that this step is not needed if you are working with a new worksheet.)

4. Choose OK or press Enter.

5. Choose Options Protect Document. The **P**rotect Document dialog box appears.

6. Turn on the Cells check box by clicking on the check box. (Initially, by default the **C**ell check is selected; therefore, if there is an X showing in the **C**ells check box, this step is not needed.)

7. In the **P**assword box, type a password. Choose a password that you will remember but will also prevent others from turning off document protection. A password can be any combination of letters, numbers, or symbols, up to 255 characters long. Also, passwords are case-sensitive. (Case-sensitive means that Excel distinguishes between lowercase letters and uppercase letters.)

8. Choose OK or press Enter. The Confirm Password dialog box appears.

9. In the Re-enter Protection Password box, type your password again to confirm it. (NOTE: If in this step you do not type a password that exactly matches the one entered in Step 7, Excel will redisplay the Protect Document dialog box; you will have to enter the password once again, and then confirm it.

10. Choose OK or press Enter.

Hiding Cell Formulas

You may be willing to develop worksheets for others (or share your own worksheet), and still prefer not to share the formulas you have used. For some worksheet developers, such formulas are a type of programming code that should be *copy-protected*. To prevent a cell's formula from being displayed in the formula bar when a document is protected (in other words, to *copy protect* it), follow these steps:

1. Select the cells you want to protect.
2. Choose Format Cell Protection. The Cell Protection dialog box appears.
3. Make sure that Hidden is turned on; if the Hidden check box is not checked, you can click on it (or tab to it and press the space bar) to turn it on.
4. Choose OK or press Enter.
5. Choose Options Protect Document. The Protect Document dialog box appears.
6. Make sure that Cells is turned on (checked); if it is not, clicking on the Cells check box (or tabbing to it and pressing the space bar) will turn it on.

Hiding Cell Formulas:

1. Select the cells you want to protect, and then choose Format Cell Protection.
2. Turn on the Hidden check box, and then choose OK or press Enter.
3. Choose Options Protect Document.
4. Turn on the Cells check.
5. In the Password box, type a password; choose OK or press Enter.
6. In the Re-enter Protection Password box, type your password again to confirm it.
7. Choose OK or press Enter.

TIP: You can turn off locked or hidden cell protection quickly by choosing Options Unprotect Document, typing the password (if any) in the **Pass**word box, and choosing OK or pressing Enter. Remember, however, that this procedure will turn off protection for all the cells in the document.

8. In the **P**assword box, type a password.
9. Choose OK or press Enter. The Confirm Password dialog box appears.
10. In the Re-enter Protection Password box, type your password again to confirm it.
11. Choose OK or press Enter.

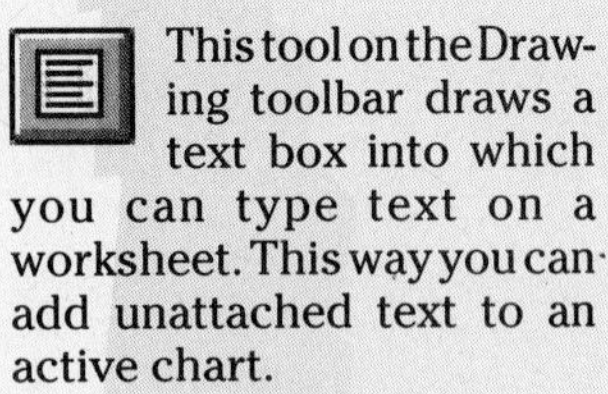

This tool on the Drawing toolbar draws a text box into which you can type text on a worksheet. This way you can add unattached text to an active chart.

Protecting an Object

In addition to protecting worksheet cells, you can lock and or hide *graphic objects* or *text* in a text box. (Skill Sessions 31 and 32 cover the creation and editing of graphic objects.) You can use the tools on Excel's Drawing toolbar to draw graphic objects, then add them to worksheets and macro sheets. In addition, you can import graphics (as pictures) from other applications to enhance the appearance of your worksheets and macro sheets. The Text Box tool on the Utility toolbar enables you to create a text box on worksheets and macro sheets; then you can add text with an automatic word wrap. (Skill Session 21 covers creating text boxes and notes.)

Figure 41.3 shows a worksheet with simple graphic object and a text box. The graphic object is the line that extends from cell B9 to the rounded text box that contains text. To protect the graphic object (so it can't be deleted, formatted, moved, or sized), follow these steps:

1. Select the graphic object by pointing to it and clicking. Excel displays selection handles around the graphic object.

2. Choose Format Object Protection. As shown in Figure 41.4, the Object Protection dialog box appears.

3. Turn on the Locked check box. (*Caution:* With a new worksheet, the Locked check box contains an X, showing it is turned on; be careful not to turn it off. For this reason, you may find this step is not needed if you are working with a new worksheet.)

4. Choose OK or press Enter.

5. Choose Options Protect Document. The Protect Document dialog box appears.

6. Turn on the Objects check box by clicking on it (or tabbing to it and pressing the space bar); deselect the Cells option if you want to lock objects only. (Initially, by default, the **O**bjects check box is selected; therefore, if there is an X showing in the box, this step is not needed.)

7. (Optional) If you want to lock the object with a password, enter a password in the **P**assword box.

8. Choose OK or press Enter. (If you protected the object with a password, the Confirm Password dialog box appears. In the Reenter Protection Password box, type your password again to confirm it.)

9. Choose OK or press Enter.

Protecting an Object:

1. Select the graphic object, and then choose Format Object Protection.
2. Select the Locked check box, and then choose OK or press Enter.
3. Choose Options Protect Document.
4. If necessary, turn on the Objects check box.
5. Choose OK or press Enter.

You can use the Selection tool on the Drawing toolbar to select and protect a group of objects. After clicking the Selection tool, you complete the selection procedure by dragging the mouse—which allows you to draw a rectangle around the group of objects you want to select. Once your rectangle has enclosed all these objects, release the mouse button. The objects will be displayed with selection handles.

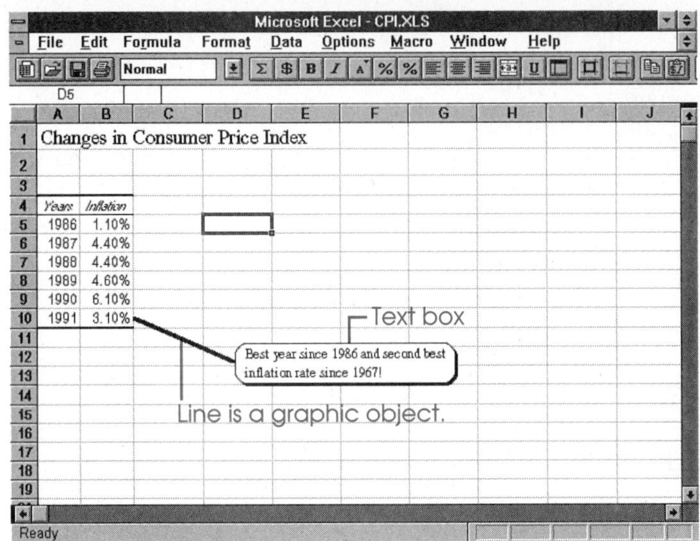

Figure 41.3 A worksheet with a graphic object and a text box.

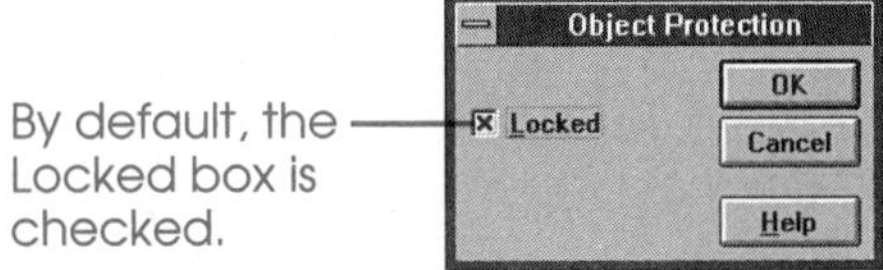

Figure 41.4 The Object Protection dialog box.

A text box is a type of object; you can protect it with a series of steps similar to those used for other objects. Text box protection can take one of three forms.

- *A text box can be locked*, which means the text in the box can be edited or formatted, but the box itself cannot be deleted, formatted, moved, or sized.

- *The text in a text box can be locked* so it can't be edited or formatted, while still allowing the box itself to be formatted, moved, sized, or deleted.
- *Both the text box and the text inside it can be locked,* so that the text box itself cannot be deleted, formatted, moved, or sized and the text in the text box can be locked so that it can't be edited or formatted.

To protect a text box and its contents, follow these steps:

1. Select the text box by pointing to the box and clicking. Excel displays selection handles around the text box, as shown in Figure 41.5.
2. Choose Format Object Protection. As shown in Figure 41.6, the Object Protection dialog box appears, showing two check boxes: **L**ocked and Locked **T**ext.
3. Select:
   - only the Locked check box to prevent the text box from being deleted, formatted, moved, or sized. (*Caution:* With a new worksheet, the **L**ocked check box contains an X, showing it is turned on; be careful not to turn it off.)
   - only the Locked Text check box to prevent editing and formatting of the text within the text box but allow the text box to be formatted, moved, sized, or deleted. (*Caution:* With a new worksheet, the Locked **T**ext check box contains an X, showing it is turned on; be careful not to turn it off.)

Protecting a Text Box:

1. Select the text box, and then choose Format Object Protection.
2. Select the Locked check box, and/or the Locked Text check box, and choose OK or press Enter.
3. Choose Options Protect Document.
4. Turn on the Objects check box.
5. Choose OK or press Enter.

- both the Locked and the Locked Text check boxes to prevent the text box itself from being deleted, formatted, moved, or sized and the text in the text box from being edited or formatted. (*Caution:* With a new worksheet, both the **L**ocked and Locked **T**ext boxes are turned on; be careful not to turn them off).

4. Choose OK or press Enter.

5. Choose Options Protect Document. The Protect Document dialog box appears.

6. Turn on the Objects check box (deselect Cells if you want to protect objects only). Initially, by default, the **O**bjects check box is selected—therefore, if there is an X showing in the box, this step is not needed.

7. (Optional) If you want to lock the object with a password, enter a password in the **P**assword box.

8. Choose OK or press Enter. (If you choose to protect the object with a password, the Confirm Password dialog box appears in the Re-enter Protection Password box, type your password again to confirm it.

9. Choose OK or press Enter.

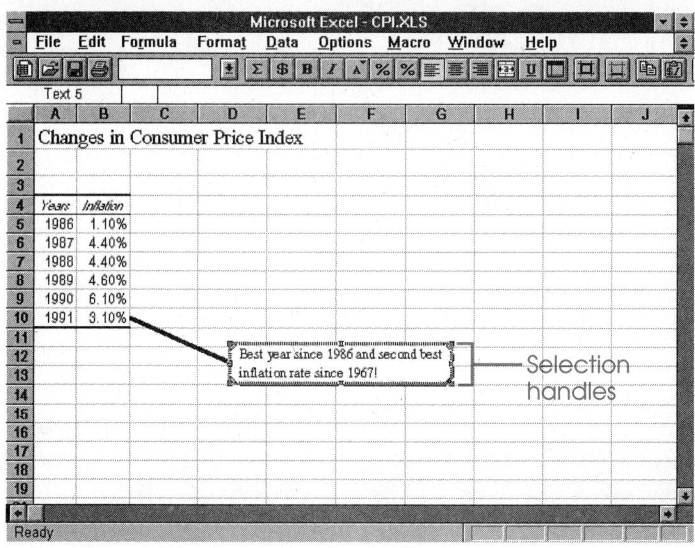

Figure 41.5 A selected text box.

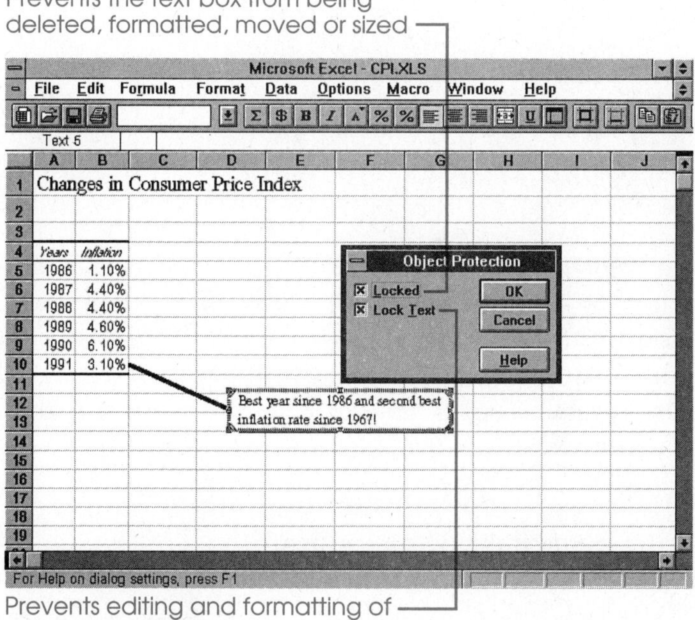

Figure 41.6 The Object Protection dialog box.

Protecting a Chart

Charts can be saved as separate documents, or can be embedded in a worksheet. In either case, charts can be protected. To protect a chart saved as a separate document, follow these steps:

Protecting a Separate Document Chart:

1. Switch to the chart window; choose Chart Protect Document.
2. Select the Chart check box; choose OK or press Enter.
3. If you typed a password, type the password again, and then choose OK or press Enter.

1. Switch to the chart window. If the chart document is not open, choose File Open to open the chart document. If the chart document is open, choose Window and select the chart name.
2. Choose Chart Protect Document. The Protect Document dialog box appears, as shown in Figure 41.7.
3. Select the Chart check box.
4. (Optional) To prevent others from turning off document protection, type a password in the **P**assword box.
5. Choose OK or press Enter.
6. If you typed a password, the Confirm Password dialog box appears. Type the password again, and then choose OK or press Enter.

An *embedded chart* is a dynamic chart that has been added to—and is lodged in—a worksheet (as shown in Figure 41.8). For more information on how to create an embedded chart, see Skill Session 24, "Creating Charts." To protect a chart embedded in a worksheet, follow these steps:

Protecting an Embedded Chart:

1. Choose Options Protect Document.

1. Choose Options Protect Document. The Protect Document dialog box appears.

2. To protect the chart formats, select the Objects check box; to protect the data from which the chart is plotted, also select the Cells check box.

3. (Optional) To prevent others from turning off document protection, type a password in the **P**assword box.

4. Choose OK or press Enter.

5. If you typed a password, the Confirm Password dialog box appears. Type the password again, and then choose OK or press Enter.

2. Select the Objects check box and/or Cells check boxes.

3. (Optional) Protect the chart with a password if desired.

4. Choose OK or press Enter.

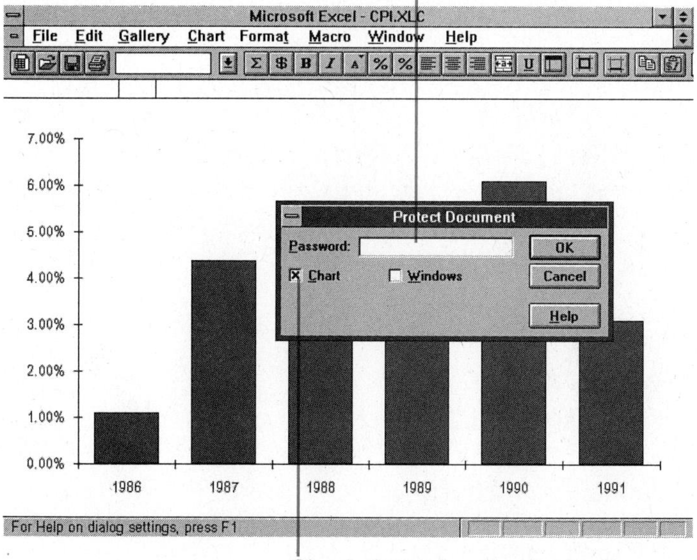

Figure 41.7 The Protect Document dialog box (chart window).

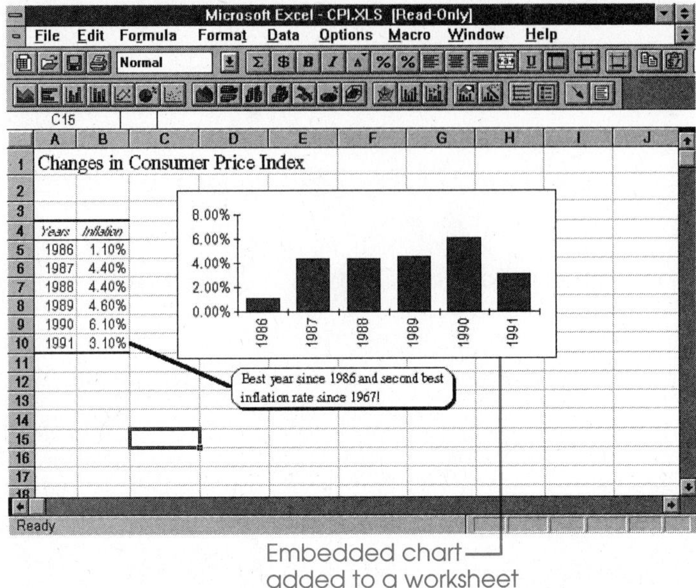

Figure 41.8 A bar chart embedded in a worksheet.

Unprotecting a Chart:

1. Switch to the chart document or to the worksheet in which the chart is embedded.
2. Choose Chart Unprotect or Options Unprotect menu.
3. Type the password in the Password box.
4. Choose OK or press Enter.

Regardless of whether a chart is a separate document or embedded in a worksheet, the steps for unprotecting it are the same. To unprotect a chart, follow these steps:

1. Switch to the chart document (or to the worksheet in which the chart is embedded).
2. Choose Chart Unprotect (for charts that are separate documents) or Options Unprotect menu (for embedded charts).
3. If the chart is protected with a password, type the password in the **P**assword box.
4. Choose OK or press Enter.

Protecting and Hiding Windows

Skill Session 3 covers the techniques you can use to control, resize, and move document windows. A document window contains the individual documents—worksheets, charts, workbooks, and macro sheets—that you are working with. You can apply a type of protection to document windows that will prevent others from moving, sizing, or closing your document window. You can also hide an open document window from the view of other users. The steps for hiding a document window are explained in a separate section that follows.

NOTE: If your worksheet has only one window and you hide it, you will need to use File Unhide to redisplay it.

To protect document windows against being moved, sized, or closed by other users, follow these steps:

1. Move and size the window or windows within your workspace so they are the way you want them.
2. If the active document is a worksheet, a macro sheet, or a workbook, choose Options Protect Document; if the active document is a chart, choose Chart Protect Document. The Protect Document dialog box appears.
3. Select the Windows check box. (Optional: If you want to protect the window with a password, type a password in the **P**assword box.)
4. Choose OK or press Enter. (Optional: If you have assigned a password, the Confirm Password dialog box appears; type the password again, and choose OK or press Enter.)

Protecting Document Windows:

1. Move and size the windows.
2. Choose Options Protect Document (for worksheet, macro sheet, or workbook) or Chart Protect Document (for charts).
3. Select the Windows check box, and type a password in the **P**assword box.
4. Choose OK or press Enter.
5. Type the password again; choose OK or press Enter.

TIP: You can close a protected window—and the file as well—by choosing File Close.

Turning off a document window's protection is easy: choose Options Unprotect Document (for worksheets, macro sheets, and workbooks) or Chart Unprotect Document (for charts) from the menu. If the document is protected with a password, type the password in the **P**assword box, and then choose OK or press Enter.

Hiding a Document Window

In addition to preventing a document window from being moved, sized, or closed, you can *hide* an active document window (it is still open, but cannot be seen by other users). Hiding a worksheet document is another way of preventing sensitive or confidential information from being discovered by unauthorized users. To hide a document window, choose Window Hide. If the document is password-protected, the document password dialog box appears; then you must enter the password to hide the window.

Hiding a Document Window:

1. Make the document window active.
2. Choose Window Hide.

Unhiding a Document Window:

1. Choose Window Unhide.
2. Select the document from the Unhide list box.
3. Select OK or press Enter.

Once a document window is hidden, you can unhide it by following these steps:

1. Choose Window Unhide. The Unhide dialog box appears, as shown in Figure 41.9.
2. Select the document window you want to unhide from the **U**nhide list box.
3. Select OK or press Enter.

Select the name of the document window that you want to unhide.

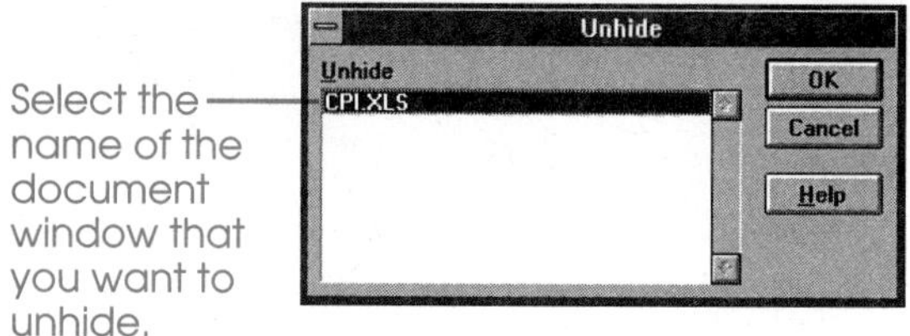

Figure 41.9 The Unhide dialog box.

> **IN ACTION:** When you arrange your documents, you may not want to arrange all the document windows. For example, you may want to exclude a document from a tiled arrangement. To exclude certain windows from being arranged, hide those windows before choosing Window Arrange.

Protecting a Document File with a Password

As you may know from reviewing previous sections of this Skill Session, you can protect your documents by locking and hiding cells, objects, charts, and windows. You can add a higher degree of security to your documents by assigning passwords when you apply protection. For example, you may lock a portion of a worksheet—and assign a password to that lock, so that no one without that password can unlock those cells. Unless you take additional steps, however, other users can open the document that contains those password-locked cells. If you don't want other users to have that ability, you can assign a password to your document at the time you save it. To assign a password to a document, follow these steps:

Assigning a Document Password:

1. Choose File Save As.
2. In the File Name box, type a name for the document, and then choose the Options button.
3. In the Protection Password box, type a password, and then choose OK or press Enter.
4. In the Re-enter Protection Password box, type the password again.
5. Choose OK or press Enter twice.

1. Choose File Save As. The File Save As dialog box appears.

2. In the File Name box, type a name for the document or accept the default name.

3. Choose the Options button. The Save Options dialog box appears, as shown in Figure 41.10.

4. In the Protection Password box, type a password. As you type, asterisks(*) appear in place of the typed characters.

5. Choose OK or press Enter. The Confirm Password dialog box appears.

6. In the Re-enter Protection Password box, type the password again to confirm it.

7. Choose OK or press Enter. The File Save As dialog box appears again.

8. Choose OK or press Enter to save the protected document.

A password can contain up to 16 characters; these can include spaces, symbols, and numbers, as well as letters. To open a password-protected document, you must enter the password while matching uppercase and lowercase letters exactly.

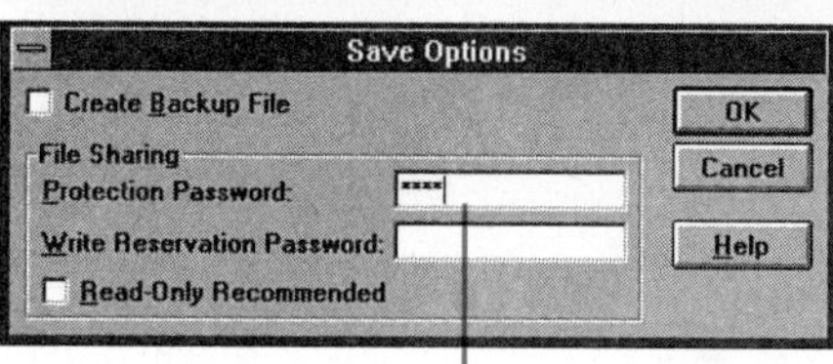

Figure 41.10 The Save Options dialog box.

Removing password protection from a protected document involves using the File Open and File Save As commands to replace the protected version of the document with an unprotected version. To remove password protection, follow these steps:

1. Choose File Open. The File Open dialog box appears.
2. In the File Name text box, enter the name of the document or select a file from the list.
3. Choose OK or press Enter. The Password dialog box appears.
4. Enter the password in the password text box.
5. Choose OK or press Enter. The document opens.
6. Choose File Save As. The File Save As dialog box appears.
7. Choose the Options button. The Save Options dialog box appears.
8. If the password text box is not selected (it is selected by default), double-click on the password text box, and then double-click on the password itself; the password is displayed as asterisks (*) in the Protection Password box.

Removing a Document Password:

1. Choose File Open.
2. In the File Name text box, enter the name of the document, and then choose OK or press Enter.
3. Enter the password in the Password text box, and then choose OK or press Enter.
4. Choose File Save As, and then choose the Options button.
5. Select the password in the Protection Password box, press the Del key.
6. Choose OK or press Enter three times.

TIP: Since you cannot open a password-protected document—or remove its protection—unless you know the password, keep a list of document names and their passwords in a safe and secure place.

8. Press the Del key to remove the password.

9. Choose OK or press Enter. The Save As dialog box appears.

10. Choose OK or press Enter to save the unprotected document.

11. Choose OK or press Enter to confirm replacement of the protected document with an unprotected version.

Creating a Read-Only File

A *Read-Only file* is another type of document protection you can apply to a document at the time you save it. A Read-Only file has particular advantages. The user cannot make changes to the file and then save it under the same file name. If changes are made to a document that has been opened as Read-Only, the changed document can only be saved under a name that is different from that of the Read-Only file. The Read-Only file itself remains intact. To save a document as a Read-Only file, follow these steps:

1. Choose File Save As. The File Save As dialog box appears.

2. In the File Name box, type a name for the document.

3. Choose Options. The Save Options dialog box appears.

Saving a Document as Read-Only:

1. Choose File Save As.
2. In the File Name box, type a name for the document.
3. Choose Options.
4. Select the Read-Only Recommended check box.
5. Choose OK or press Enter twice—first to turn on Read-Only status, and again to save the document.

4. Select the Read-Only Recommended check box to turn on Read-Only status, as shown in Figure 41.11.

5. Choose OK or press Enter. The File Save As dialog box appears.

6. Choose OK or press Enter.

When a user opens a Read-Only document, a message appears requesting that the user open the file as Read-Only. If the Read-Only Recommended check box is not checked (as shown in Figure 41.12), the message to the user is displayed before the document is opened. If the Read-Only check box is checked, then the file opens automatically as Read-Only. The file's status will appear in brackets next to the document name in the Title bar, as follows: `[Read-Only]`. If the user chooses not to open the document as a Read-Only file, the document can be changed and saved.

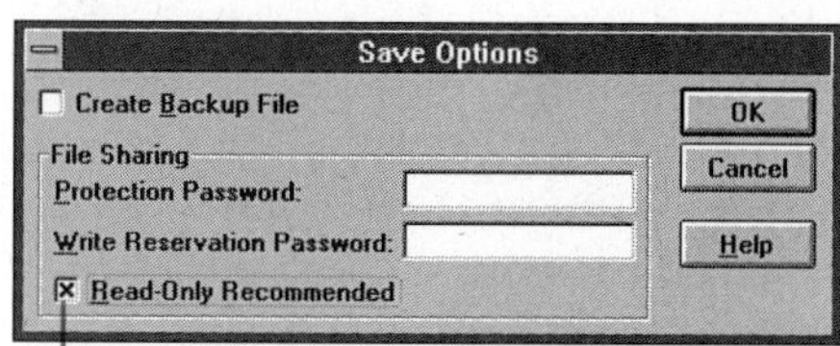

Figure 41.11 The Save Options dialog box with Read-Only Recommended selected.

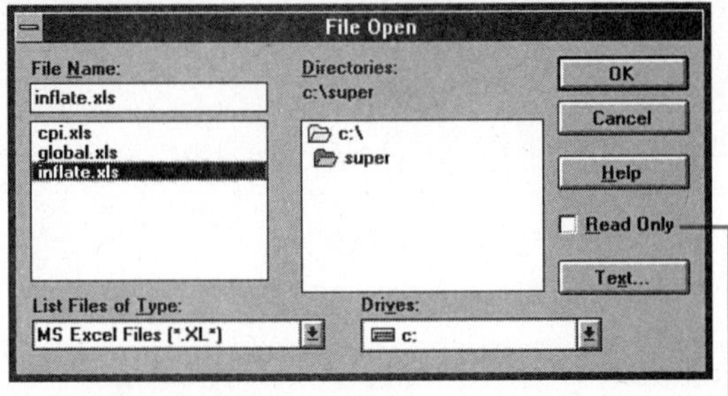

Select to have Excel display a message suggesting the user open the file as a read-only document.

Figure 41.12 The File Open dialog box.

The Read-Only feature is, accordingly, a type of honor system. The user of a Read-Only file can open it without the Read-Only status enabled. For example, if the Read-Only check box in the File Open dialog box is clear (unchecked), then the file will not open automatically as Read-Only; rather, Excel displays a message (prior to opening the file) which recommends that the file be opened as Read-Only. The Read-Only recommendation message reads as follows:

```
File should be opened as Read-Only unless
changes to it need to be saved. Open as
Read-Only?
```

Then the user is given the choice of selecting the Yes or No option buttons.

If the user selects Yes, then the file opens as Read-Only; the user cannot replace it with a new version. If the user selects No, then the file opens without the Read-Only limitation, therefore it can be revised and saved. When you create a Read-Only file, your hope is that a user who opens it will choose to open it under Read-Only status. (The Read-Only file feature does not guarantee that the user will open a Read-Only file as a restricted file.)

Skill Session

42

Advanced File Operations

Using a Startup Directory

You can save documents in a *startup directory* so that they will automatically open each time you start Excel. The startup directory is named XLSTART, and is located in the same directory that contains EXCEL.EXE. You can save worksheets, charts, macro sheets, workbooks, and add-ins in the XLSTART subdirectory if you want them to open automatically when you start EXCEL. For example, suppose you are preparing the annual budget for your department; over the next few weeks, most of your Excel sessions will involve working with a file named BUDGET.XLS. As a time-management technique, you may want to open BUDGET.XLS each time you start Excel; that way you can go right into

Placing files in the Startup Directory:

1. Open the document you want to have open automatically.
2. Choose File Save As.
3. In the File Name text box, enter the XLSTART path name and the document name.
4. Choose OK or press Enter.

your budgetary tasks. If you have made XLSTART a subdirectory of a directory named EXCEL, that subdirectory now serves as your startup directory. You can place BUDGET.XLS in the startup directory by following these steps:

1. Choose File Open to open BUDGET.XLS.
2. Choose File Save As. The File Save As dialog box appears.
3. In the File Name text box, enter the path name of the XLSTART (the startup directory) and the document name (which is **C:\EXCEL\XLSTART\BUDGET.XLS** in this example). An alternative is to use the list boxes to select appropriate subdirectories.
4. Choose OK or press Enter.

In Action: If you start each work day by starting Excel, give serious thought to the work you are used to doing next; determine if there are some documents you want automatically opened each day. For example, you may start each day with a To Do list. Why not put that To Do list in an Excel worksheet named TODO.XLS, and save it in the XLSTART directory?

Specifying an Alternate Startup Directory

You can also specify an *alternate startup directory*; then, each time you start Excel, all documents in this additional startup directory will be opened automatically—along with the documents of the standard startup directory. Some network users may find it valuable to set up an alternate startup directory, since the standard startup directory is shared, and resides on the network server; this way they have their own startup directories. As an Excel network user, you can create your own startup directory by following these steps:

1. Choose File Open. The File Open dialog box appears.
2. Select ALTSTART.XLA from the LIBRARY directory (located in the same directory that contains EXCEL.EXE).
3. Choose OK. The alternate startup directory dialog box appears.
4. In the Change **to**: text box, enter the complete path and filename of the alternate startup directory.
5. Choose OK or press Enter.

Tip: To cancel a startup document so that it will not open when you start up Excel, move the document out of the startup directory into another directory.

Specifying an Alternate Startup Directory:

1. Choose File Open.
2. Select ALTSTART.XLA from the LIBRARY directory.
3. Choose OK.
4. In the Change **to**: text box, enter the complete path of the alternate startup directory.
5. Choose OK or press Enter.

Linking Worksheets

With Excel you can create *dynamic links* between worksheets. A link between worksheets is dynamic if changes in the source data in one worksheet trigger immediate changes in other linked worksheets. When linking worksheets, you work with a *source worksheet* and *dependent worksheets*. The source worksheet contains the information that is to be linked to another worksheet. (This *source data* can be a worksheet cell,

cell range, or defined name.) The dependent worksheet contains the links to the source worksheet.

The dependent worksheet's role in the dynamic link is easy to remember: it *depends* on information contained in another worksheet (the source worksheet). You can make the linking of worksheets easier if you arrange the source and dependent worksheets in tiled windows. Tiling the worksheet windows will enable you to use the mouse pointer to switch back and forth between the dependent and source worksheets, select source data, and link it dynamically into the dependent worksheet.

Linking Two or More Worksheets:

1. Choose File Open to open the worksheets you want to link.
2. Choose Window Arrange Tiled.
3. Switch to the source worksheet window.
4. Select the cell containing the information to link, and then choose Edit Copy.
5. Switch to the dependent worksheet window.
6. Select the cell that will contain the link.
7. Choose Edit Paste Link.

To create a link between two or more Excel worksheets, follow these steps:

1. Choose File Open to open the two or more worksheets you want to link.
2. Choose Window Arrange. The Arrange Windows dialog box appears.
3. To display all windows in the workspace at the same time (so as to make it easier to create the links), select Tiled.
4. Switch to the source worksheet window by moving the mouse pointer to that window and clicking it once.
5. Select the cell (or cell range) containing the information to be linked.
6. Choose Edit Copy. A moving, broken-line border called a *marquee* appears around the selected cell or range.

7. Switch to the dependent worksheet window by moving the mouse pointer and clicking on that window.

8. Use the mouse to select the cell (or the upper-left corner of the range) that will contain the link.

9. Choose Edit Paste Link. Excel then creates the external reference formula that links the worksheets.

Figure 42.1 shows two worksheets (EARNINGS.XLS and INCOME.XLS) in a Tiled workspace. To link the total earnings in cell B6 from EARNINGS.XLS (source worksheet) to cell B3 of INCOME.XLS (the dependent worksheet), you would follow these steps:

1. Switch to the source worksheet window EARNINGS.XLS by moving the mouse pointer to that window and clicking on it once.

2. Use the mouse to select the cell B6.

3. Choose Edit Copy. A moving marquee appears around B6.

4. Switch to the dependent worksheet window INCOME.XLS by moving the mouse pointer and clicking on that window.

5. Use the mouse to select the cell B3.

6. Choose Edit Paste Link.

In this example, Excel creates an *external reference formula* (the same one shown in Figure 42.2): `='EARNINGS.XLS'!$B$6`. The first component of the external reference (='EARNINGS.XLS) is the name of the source worksheet. The second part of the reference (after the exclamation point) contains the cell, range, or named range. By using this syntax, an external cell reference formula can be typed into a dependent worksheet.

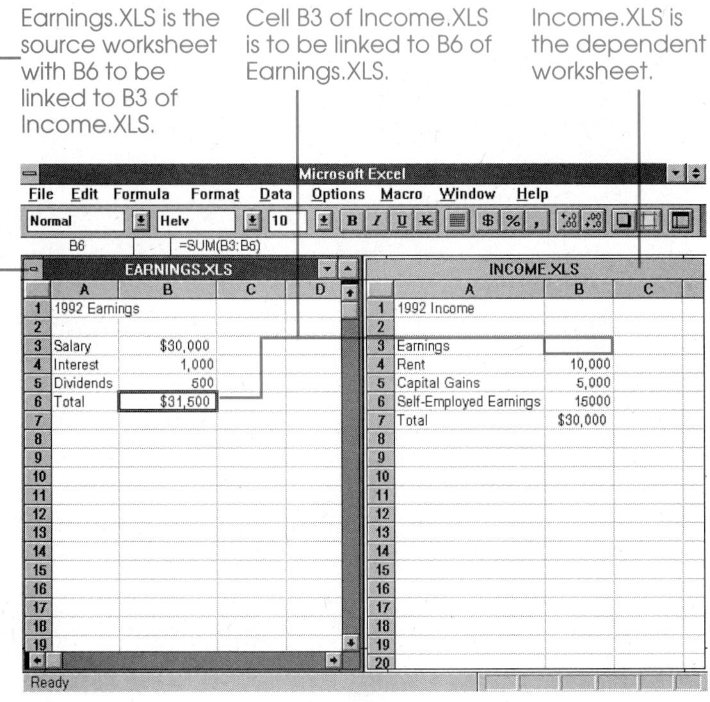

Figure 42.1 EARNINGS.XLS and INCOME.XLS in a Tiled workspace.

Note: You can also use a defined name to refer to the cell or cells to be used in an external reference formula. For example, if the source cell is named TOTAL, the external reference formula would be written as follows:

```
='C:\FINANCE\EARNINGS.XLS'
!TOTAL
```

You can also link the current worksheet to an unopened worksheet by entering an external reference formula that includes the *path* to the source worksheet. For example, if EARNINGS.XLS is an unopened worksheet in the FINANCE directory, and you want to link to B6 of EARNINGS.XLS, you could enter the following in your cell reference in the current worksheet.

```
='C:\FINANCE\EARNINGS.XLS'!$B$6
```

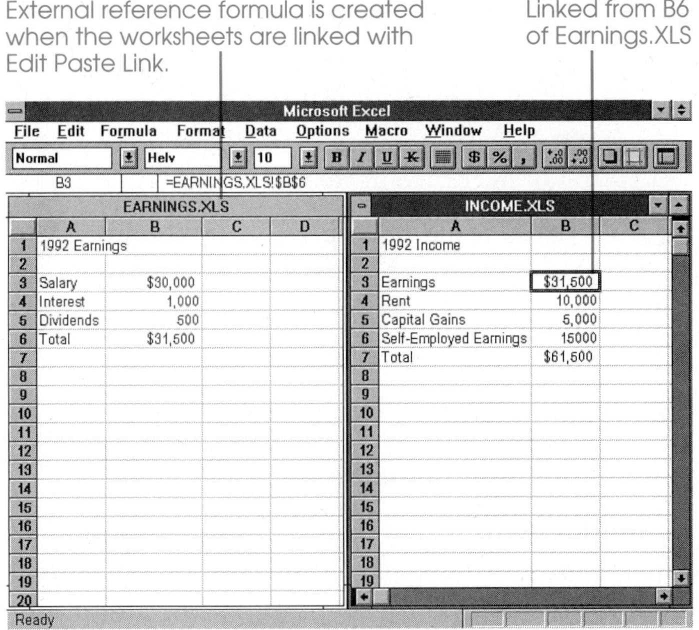

Figure 42.2 External reference formula.

Information on how to create defined names is presented in Skill Session 7, "Working with Ranges."

Using an External Reference in a Formula

External references can be used in formulas. An external reference is a reference to a cell or range of cells in another worksheet. As with the procedure for creating a cell link with another worksheet, you can make it easier to create the formula that does the linking by opening both the source and dependent worksheets, and then arranging them in Tiled windows in your workspace (use Windows Arrange). Then you can complete the process by following these steps:

Note: External references can be used in functions. For example (assuming the worksheet EARNINGS.XLS is the current directory), if you wanted to add the external reference value =EARNINGS.XLS!$B$6 to the values found in the range A10:A15 of the current worksheet, your function would be as follows:

```
=SUM(A10:A15,
EARNINGS.XLS!$B$6)
```

Using an External Reference in a Formula:

1. Select the cell where you want to enter the formula.
2. Start entering the formula.
3. Enter the external reference, or use the mouse to switch to the source worksheet window.
4. Continue entering the formula, and then click on the Enter box or press Enter.

Tip: To view the source worksheet of an external reference, you can double-click on the cell containing the external reference; Excel will open (if it is not already open), switch to the source worksheet, and display the source data.

Saving Linked Documents

1. Switch to the source worksheet.
2. Choose File Save As.
3. Specify the source worksheet name.
4. Choose OK.
5. Repeat steps 1–4 in other source document.
6. Save dependent worksheets.

1. Select the cell where you want to enter the formula.
2. Start entering the formula. If you are not starting the formula with the external reference, enter the formula up to the operator that will precede the external reference.
3. Enter the external reference, or switch to the source worksheet window by moving the mouse pointer to that window and clicking on it once. Excel enters the external reference into the formula.
4. Continue entering the formula. When you have finished the formula, click on the Enter box or press Enter.

You should save source worksheets before saving the dependent worksheet. As a part of this procedure, you can ensure that the formulas in the source document have been recalculated—and that the external references in the dependent worksheet are current—by following these steps:

1. Switch to the source worksheet by clicking on it with the mouse pointer, or by using the Window menu to select it from the list of open documents.
2. Choose File Save As from the menu. The File Save as dialog box appears.
3. Enter the source worksheet name in the File Name text box.
4. Choose OK.
5. Repeat steps 1 through 4 for any other source worksheets.
6. Switch to the dependent worksheet by clicking on it with the mouse pointer, or by using the Window menu to select it from the list of open documents.

7. Save the dependent worksheet(s) by repeating steps 2 through 4.

Opening Linked Worksheets and Updating Links

When you open a dependent worksheet, Excel gives you the option of *updating links* by displaying the question: `Update references to unopened documents?` If you want the references updated, you select Yes; if you choose not to update the references, you select No.

If you open all source worksheets and then open the dependent worksheet, the dependent worksheet's external reference formulas will update automatically. You can also update external references in the dependent worksheet by choosing File Links. For example, if your dependent worksheet is INCOME.XLS and you want to update its external links to EARNINGS.XLS, you would follow these steps:

1. Switch to the dependent worksheet (INCOME.XLS) by clicking on it with the mouse pointer, or by using the Window menu to select it from the list of open documents.
2. Choose File Links. The Links dialog box appears, as is shown in Figure 42.3.
3. In the **Links** list box, select the source worksheet (EARNINGS.XLS) by clicking on its name.

Updating External References or Opening a Source Worksheet:

1. Switch to the dependent worksheet.
2. Choose File Links.
3. Select the source worksheet(s) in the **Links** list box.
4. Choose Update or Open.

Tip: You can select more than one source worksheet in the **Links** list box by holding down Ctrl and clicking on the name of each worksheet.

Caution: If you rename a source worksheet, the dependent worksheet must also be opened at the time of the renaming. That way, Excel does an automatic update of the worksheet name in the dependent worksheet's external reference.

4. To update external references in the dependent worksheet, choose Update.

5. To open the selected worksheets, choose Open.

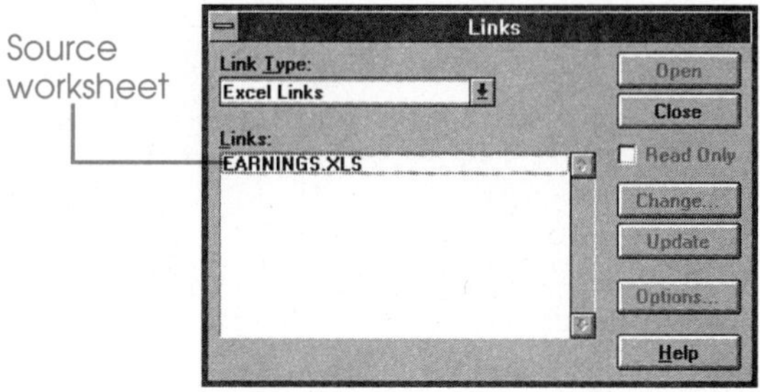

Figure 42.3 The Links dialog box.

Importing Data with the Clipboard

The *Clipboard* is a temporary holding area for the information you cut or copy. The Clipboard is always available when you want to transfer information during a Windows session. Information that you cut or copy to the Clipboard remains on the Clipboard until you clear it—by cutting or copying new data to it, or by exiting Windows.

You can cut or copy information from an application onto the Clipboard, and then transfer that information from the Clipboard to other applications. For example, you can use **E**dit Cu**t** or **E**dit **C**opy to transfer information from an Excel document to the Clipboard—and then paste it into another Windows application—or you can *import* data into Excel by using the Clipboard.

Since Clipboard contents remain on the Clipboard until you cut or copy new information to the Clipboard (or exit Windows), you can import (paste) the same information repeatedly. To import data from the Clipboard into Excel, follow these steps:

Importing Data into Excel Using the Clipboard:

1. Start Excel.
2. Go to the source application and select the information.
3. Choose the other application's Edit Cut or Copy command.
4. Use File Open to open the Excel document to which you want to import the data.
5. Select the cell in the upper-left-hand corner of the area where you want to paste the Clipboard data.
6. Choose Edit Paste.

Use this tool to paste the contents of the Clipboard into a worksheet, macro sheet, chart, project window, or into the formula bar.

1. Start Excel.
2. Go to the source application and select the information you want to transfer to the Clipboard. (You can cut or copy text, graphics, or a combination of text and graphics to the Clipboard).
3. Choose the application's Edit Cut or Copy command. The selected information is transferred to the Clipboard. Cut removes the information from the application and transfers it to the Clipboard; Copy transfers a copy of the information, and leaves the original information unchanged in the application.
4. Open the Excel document to which you want to import the data. The Excel document must be made active to import the data from the Clipboard. To make a document active, either click on the document with the mouse, or choose the document name from the list that appears when you choose Window.
5. Select the cell in the upper-left-hand corner of the area where you want to paste the Clipboard data. To select the cell, use the *cell pointer movement keys* (arrow keys), or click on the cell of your choice with the mouse.
6. Choose Edit Paste.

Linking Excel with Other Windows Applications

Importing data from another Windows application by using the Clipboard and the Excel **E**dit **P**aste command does not create a dynamic link. A dynamic link is more than just a copy of data—it is "alive"; it reveals new information as information in the source document is changed. You can create dynamic links between Excel and other Microsoft Windows applications. These links can work two ways:

- ▲ *Link a source Excel worksheet to a dependent document of another Microsoft Windows application,* so that changes in the Excel worksheet are immediately reflected in the dependent document.
- ▲ *Link a source document of another Microsoft Windows application to a dependent Excel worksheet,* so that changes in the source document are immediately reflected in the Excel worksheet.

Your Excel worksheet data and charts can often be utilized in other Windows applications. The assumptions and results of an Excel worksheet calculation could be linked to a word processing document, for example, to enhance the effectiveness of your communication. With a link in place *inside* a word processing document, related changes in the source worksheet would change linked parts of the word processing document automatically.

For example, Figure 42.4 shows a worksheet that computes a monthly loan payment. If you wanted to include that calculation and its assumptions (loan amount, interest rate, and term) in a word processing document, dynamic linking might be the answer.

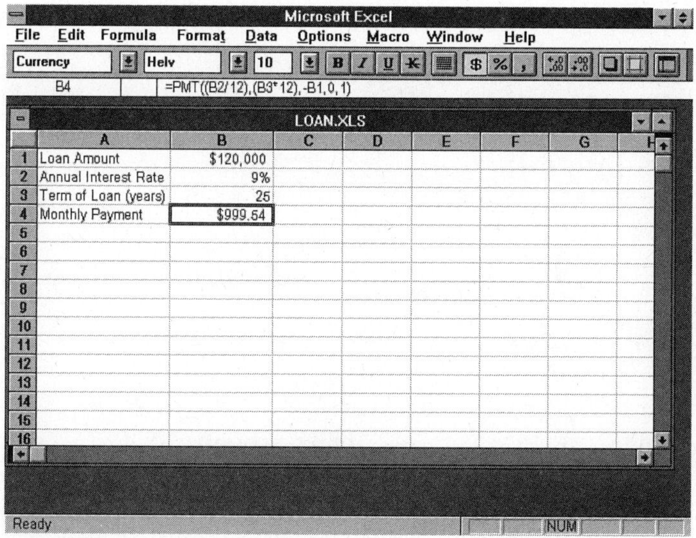

Figure 42.4 Excel worksheet that calculates a loan payment.

By linking the worksheet loan payment calculation to a word processing document, you could have any change in the variables of worksheet calculation—such as a different loan amount, rate, or term—updated automatically in the word processing document. File-linking Excel worksheets to other applications brings this capability of *"what-if" analysis* into the other applications. Figure 42.5 shows the results.

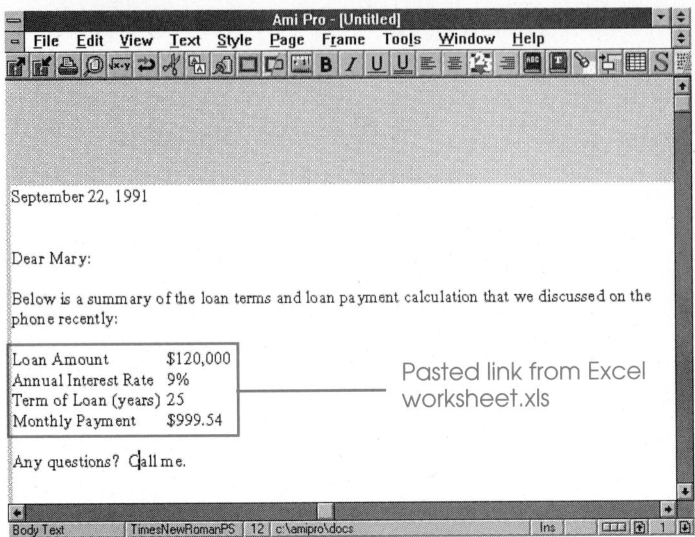

Figure 42.5 The Excel worksheet from Figure 42.4, linked to an Ami Pro document.

Linking the Excel worksheet from Figure 42.4 to a word processing document, so that it produces results similar to those in Figure 42.5, can be accomplished by following these steps:

Linking Excel with Other Windows Applications:

1. Open the Excel worksheet and the other application document.
2. Switch to the Excel source worksheet.
3. Select the worksheet data you want to link, and then choose Edit Copy.
4. Switch to the document window in the other application.
5. Place the insertion point where you want the link to be, and then choose Paste Link.

1. Open the source worksheet in Microsoft Excel and the dependent document in the other Windows application.
2. Switch to the Excel source worksheet.
3. Select the worksheet data (or embedded chart) you want to copy into the dependent document in the other application.
4. Choose Edit Copy.
5. Switch to the dependent document window in the other application.

6. Place the insertion point where you want to paste the source worksheet data.

7. Choose Paste Link. The source worksheet data will now be linked to the dependent document.

Note: The procedure in step 7 (choosing Paste Link) may be different in other applications. Consult the dependent Windows application's documentation about how to link to that application. Also, make sure the application whose document you want to link to an Excel worksheet can support *dynamic data exchange (DDE)* or *object linking and embedding (OLE)*.

Use this tool from the Utility toolbox to copy data that you want to link to another application.

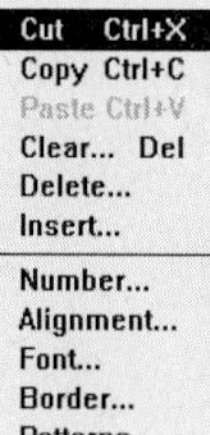

After selecting the worksheet data to be linked, there are two other methods you can use to copy the data besides using the **E**dit menu. You can display the shortcut menu by clicking the right mouse button and then selecting Copy, or you can press Ctrl+C to copy that data.

Linking Another Application to Excel

You can link an Excel worksheet to a dependent document in another Microsoft Windows application, and you can link a source document from that Windows application to a dependent Excel worksheet. The processes are similar. In the latter case, both the dependent Excel worksheet and the source document in the other application must be opened; you follow the other application's procedure for selecting and copying data. Once the source data is copied, you switch to the dependent Excel worksheet and follow two familiar procedures:

- ▲ Select the cell which is in the upper-left corner of the range that will contain the linked data.
- ▲ Choose **E**dit Paste **L**ink.

Note: After you have copied data from the other application, and then have chosen the Excel **E**dit command, you could find that the Paste **L**ink command is unavailable. This usually means that the other application does not support linking, or cannot supply the data in a format recognized by Microsoft Excel.

In Action: For better organization, keep linked worksheets together in a single workbook. For more information on how to create and manage workbooks, see Skill Session 5 ("Working with Worksheets and Workbooks") and Skill Session 44 ("More About Workbooks").

Importing Files

Excel makes it easy to import data and files from other applications. This capability enables you to use Excel to calculate, analyze, and chart the data those applications produce. In fact, importing files from many types of other applications is no different from opening an Excel document. There are 15 file formats that Excel recognizes. Files saved in these formats can be imported automatically through the Excel File **O**pen command. Table 42.1 shows the file formats Excel can open.

Table 42.1 File Formats Excel Can Open

Format	*Type of document*
CSV	Comma-separated values.
DBF 2	dBase II.
DBF 3	dBase III.
DBF 4	dBase IV.
DIF	Data interchange format.
FMT	Formatting information for Lotus 1-2-3 Release 2.*x* WYSIWYG.
FM3	Formatting information for Lotus 1-2-3 for Windows and 3.1.
Normal	Standard Excel format.
SYLK	Microsoft Multiplan.
Text	ANSI text for Windows.
WKS	Lotus 1-2-3 Release 1A.
WK1	Lotus 1-2-3 Release 2.*x*.
WK3	Lotus 1-2-3 Release 3.*x* and Lotus 1-2-3 for Windows.
Excel 2.*x*	Excel for Windows version 2.1.
Excel 3.0	Excel version 3.0.

To open a file that is in one of the formats shown in Table 42.1, follow these steps:

Importing a File from Another Application:

1. Choose File Open.
2. Specify a file type in the List Files of Type box.
3. Select or type the name of the file you want to open.
4. Choose OK or press Enter.

1. Choose File Open. The File Open dialog box appears.

2. Change which file types are listed in the File Name box by selecting a different file type in the List Files of Type box. If the file type you want to display is not shown in the List Files of Type box, select All Files (*.*) in the List Files of Type box.

3. In the File Name box, type the name of the file you want to open, or select it from the list.

4. Choose OK or press Enter.

Importing ASCII Data

Many applications save data in their own unique file formats—which are often incompatible with those of other applications. An *ASCII (American Standard Code for Information Interchange)* file is a format that can be read by many applications; it serves as a common denominator between programs that produce incompatible file formats. Some applications allow you to save a file in the application's own resident format, or in other popular formats; many other applications (such as word processing programs) only allow you to save files in the native format or in the ASCII format. Figure 42.6 shows an example of an ASCII file created with a word processing program.

Notice that each piece of information in the ASCII output (such as name, department, salary, title, and performance rating) is separated by semicolons (;) which are called delimiters. A *delimiter* is a character, space, or tab used to separate one item of data from another. Excel recognizes delimiters as column separations. To create an ASCII file from a word processing program and successfully import it into Excel, you need to separate text with delimiters for Excel to break it into multiple columns. Otherwise, the entire entry for each line will be placed in column A. For example, the first row of data in the ASCII example file is:

```
Abelard P.;Accounting;$25,000;Clerk;1
```

```
Abelard P.;Accounting;$25,000;Clerk;1
Boone  D.;Receiving;$30,000;Manager; 2
Browne T.;Receiving;$15,000;Staff 1;2
Browning E.;Accounting;$35,000;Manager;2
Carroll L.;Plant;$40,000;Manager;1
Chaucer G.;Accounting;$20,000;Clerk 1;3
Darwin C.;Plant;$21,000;Mechanic;4
Keats J.;Receiving;$22,000;Staff;3
Lear E.;Shipping;$40,000;Manager;1
Milton J.;Plant;$25,000;Mechanic;2
Shelley P.;Shipping;$27,000;Shipper 1;1
Walsh W.;Shipping;$27,500;Shipper 1;5
Yeats W.;Plant;$28,000;Mechanic;2
```

Figure 42.6 An example of an ASCII file created with a word processing program, using semicolons as delimiters.

The person's name *Abelard P.* will be placed in Excel column A when imported, the department name *Accounting* will be placed in Excel column B when imported, and so on. The second row of ACSII data will be imported in the same way: *Boone D.* will be placed in Excel column A when imported, the department name *Receiving* will be placed in Excel column B when imported, and so on.

Assuming that the ASCII file shown in Figure 42.6 is named SALARY.TXT, you would follow these steps to import it into Excel.

Importing an ASCII File into Excel:

1. Choose File Open.
2. Select the directory in which the ASCII file is saved.
3. Select the Text File (*.TXT;*.CSV) format.
4. Select the ASCII file name, and then choose Text.
5. Select the column delimiter.
6. Select DOS or OS/2(PC-8).
7. Choose OK (or press Enter) twice in succession.

1. Choose File Open. The File Open dialog box appears.

2. Under **D**irectories, select the directory in which the ASCII file is saved by double-clicking on the directory name in the Directories list box.

3. Select the Text File (*.TXT;*.CSV) format from the List File of **T**ype list box (as shown in Figure 42.7), or enter *. (followed by the text file extension) in the File **N**ame text box. For example, if you know that the ASCII file has been saved with a .TXT extension, you can enter `*.TXT` in the File **N**ame text box. As shown in Figure 42.8, the files with the extension you specified are displayed in the File Name list box.

4. From the File **N**ame list box, select the ASCII file name; the file name will appear in the File **N**ame text box, or you can enter the file name directly in the File **N**ame text box. In this example, the file name that would be selected or entered is SALARY.TXT.

5. Choose Text. The Text File Options dialog box appears.

6. Under Column Delimiter, select the method used in the ASCII file of separating one data item from another. As shown in Figure 42.9, the Semicolon has been selected as the delimiter because the data in SALARY.TXT was separated with semicolons (;). However, other choices of delimiters include: Tab, Comma, Space, None, Custom.

7. Under File Origin, select DOS or OS/2(PC-8).

8. Choose OK, and then return to the File Open dialog box.

9. Choose OK or press Enter and the ASCII file is imported into an Excel worksheet, as shown in Figure 42.10.

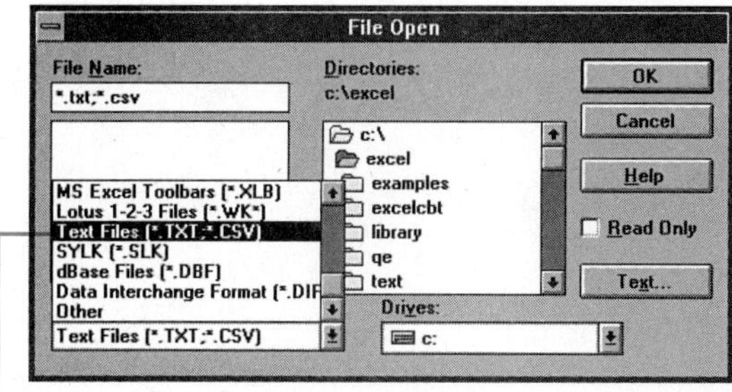

Figure 42.7 The List Files of Type list box.

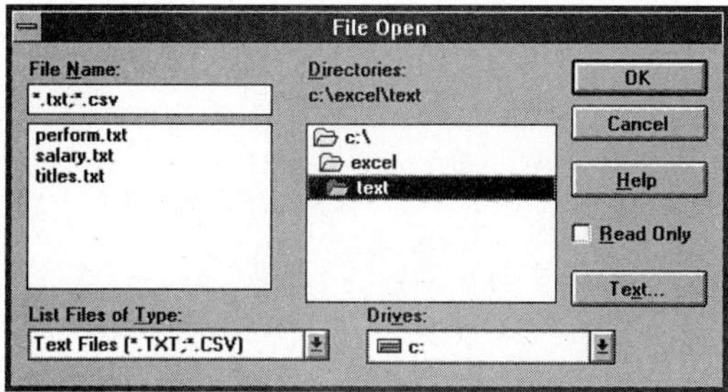

Figure 42.8 The files with the specified extension displayed in the File Name List Box.

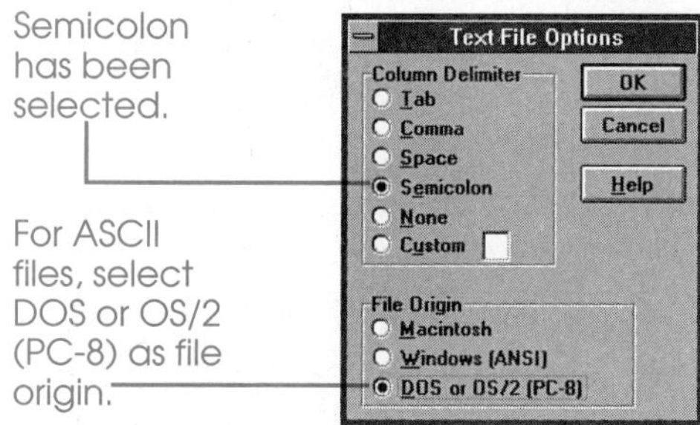

Figure 42.9 The Text File Options dialog box.

Tip: If you have a choice of delimiters when creating an ASCII with another application, it is recommended that you *avoid using the comma as a delimiter* in situations where some of the data are numbers that use the comma to separate thousands. When you use the comma as the delimiter, Excel will recognize the comma as the end of one piece of data, and therefore split numbers into two or more columns. For example, if the comma is the delimiter and the number 25,000 is imported into the Excel worksheet from an ASCII file, Excel will place `25` in one column, and then `000` in the next column.

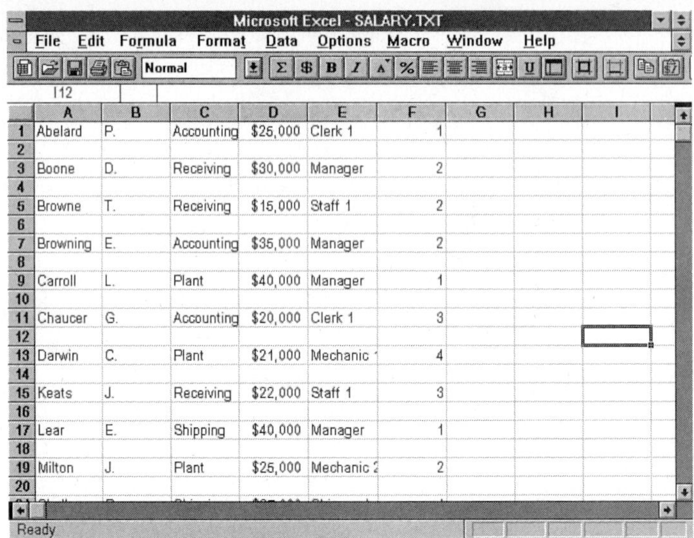

Figure 42.10 SALARY.TXT: an ASCII file imported into an Excel worksheet.

Consolidating Worksheets

Importing data and linking worksheets are two methods of getting information from one document to another. Another method of sharing data is through the consolidation of worksheet data. Consolidation is a procedure that can summarize data from other worksheets. For example, if each of three salespersons in a department keep track of their travel expenses on separate Excel worksheets, those worksheets could be consolidated into one travel expense report for the department.

When consolidating data, you must specify the *source areas* (the ranges in the other worksheets from which the data originates), and the *destination area* (the range of a worksheet that will hold the consolidated data and the source areas). For example, Figure 42.11 shows the source areas (B2:B12) of a data consolidation. The three travel expense worksheets (EXP1.XLS, EXP2.XLS, and EXP3.XLS) can be consolidated into a destination area that begins at B1 of the EXPTOTAL.XLS worksheet. This type of consolidation involves adding numbers that have identical positions in each of the worksheets to be consolidated. This process of *consolidation by position* is useful when you are consolidating a series of identical worksheets whose arrangement is identical to that of destination areas. The results of consolidating the source areas of Figure 42.11 are shown in Figure 42.12.

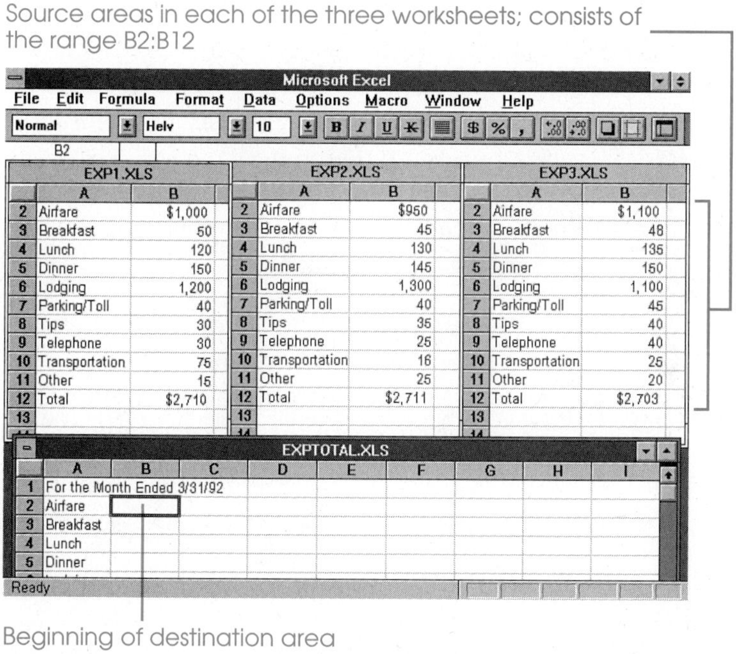

Source areas in each of the three worksheets; consists of the range B2:B12

Microsoft Excel

File Edit Formula Format Data Options Macro Window Help

Normal Helv 10

B2

EXP1.XLS

	A	B
2	Airfare	$1,000
3	Breakfast	50
4	Lunch	120
5	Dinner	150
6	Lodging	1,200
7	Parking/Toll	40
8	Tips	30
9	Telephone	30
10	Transportation	75
11	Other	15
12	Total	$2,710
13		

EXP2.XLS

	A	B
2	Airfare	$950
3	Breakfast	45
4	Lunch	130
5	Dinner	145
6	Lodging	1,300
7	Parking/Toll	40
8	Tips	35
9	Telephone	25
10	Transportation	16
11	Other	25
12	Total	$2,711
13		

EXP3.XLS

	A	B
2	Airfare	$1,100
3	Breakfast	48
4	Lunch	135
5	Dinner	150
6	Lodging	1,100
7	Parking/Toll	45
8	Tips	40
9	Telephone	40
10	Transportation	25
11	Other	20
12	Total	$2,703
13		

EXPTOTAL.XLS

	A	B	C	D	E	F	G	H	I
1	For the Month Ended 3/31/92								
2	Airfare								
3	Breakfast								
4	Lunch								
5	Dinner								

Ready

Beginning of destination area

Figure 42.11 Expense Reports: EXP1.XLS,EXP2.XLS, and EXP3.XLS.

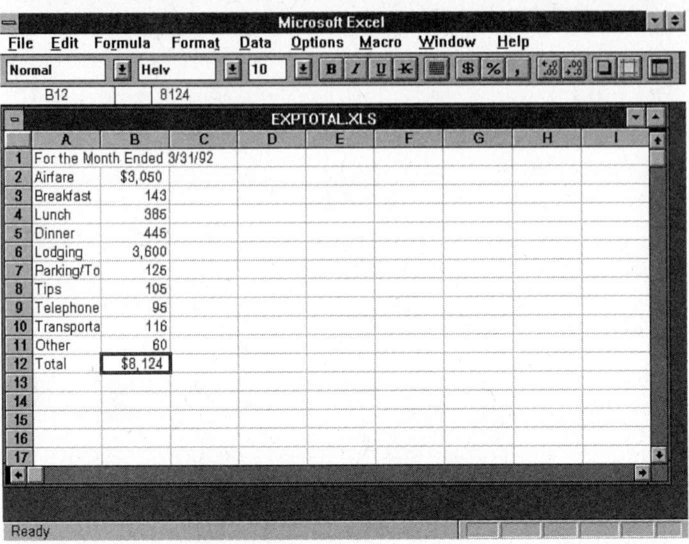

Figure 42.12 Consolidated expense reports.

You can also *consolidate by category*; similar data in different locations within source worksheets can be consolidated. Excel uses labels, rows, or column titles to determine categories. For example, you can have Excel sum all column ranges (in several source worksheets) labeled "Postage"; Excel will add together all source ranges that begin with "Postage" as the text in the first row of the column.

When source areas contain similar data—but source areas are arranged differently from destination areas—use labels to consolidate data by category. To consolidate the data from multiple worksheets in this manner, follow these steps:

Consolidating Worksheets:

1. Select the destination area.
2. Choose Data Consolidate.

1. Select the destination area you want to contain the consolidated data.

2. Choose Data Consolidate. The Consolidate dialog box appears, similar to the one in Figure 42.13.

3. In the **R**eference box, enter a reference to the source area you want to consolidate. To enter the references of open worksheets, you can select the source area with the mouse . Also, you can choose Browse to display a dialog box from which you can locate and select unopened files. If you do select an unopened file, its full path and file name will be entered into the **R**eference text box. Then you must add a name (or a reference to a cell or range) to complete the source reference.

4. Choose Add. The reference appears in the All References text box.

5. Repeat steps 3 and 4 for all the source areas you want to consolidate. Each time you complete step 4 a new source reference should appear in the All References text box.

6. Under **F**unction select the function you want to use to consolidate the source areas. The choices of functions available for a consolidation are shown in the Figure 42.14. (The SUM function is the default.) For more information about these functions, see the Functions section of the Command Reference.

7. Under Use Labels In, select Top Row if you want to consolidate by category and the label you want Excel to use as the category will be found in the first row of the source range. Select Left Column if you want to consolidate by category and the label is to be found in the left column. To consolidate by position, don't select either of the check boxes under Use Labels In.

8. Choose OK or press Enter.

3. Enter a reference to a source area in the **R**eference box, and then choose Add.
4. Repeat step 3 to specify more source areas.
5. Under Use Labels In, select Top Row or Left Column to consolidate by category.
6. Choose OK or press Enter.

If you consolidate by category using labels, you must include in your source area selection (in step 3 above) the labels you want to appear in the destination area. If you consolidate by position using references, however, you should not include category labels in the source area selection.

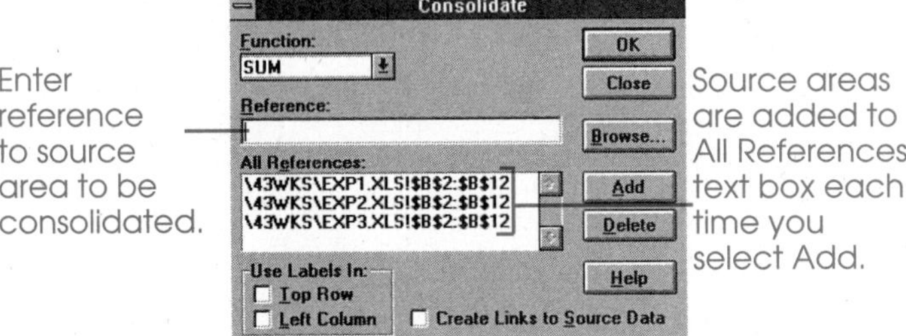

Figure 42.13 The Consolidate dialog box.

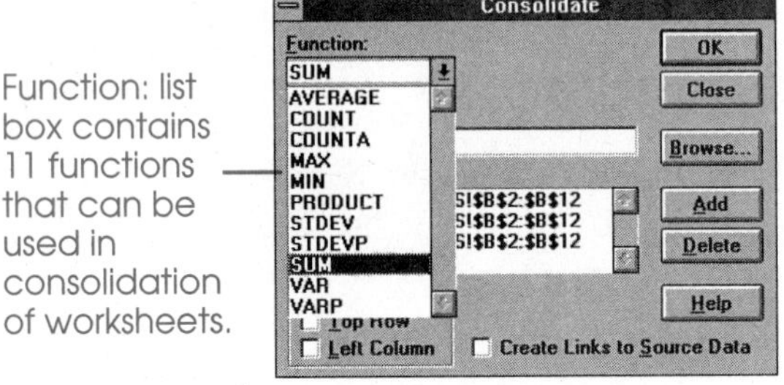

Figure 42.14 Functions that can be used with Data Consolidate.

Tip: As you enter references in the **R**eference text box of the Consolidate dialog box, the dialog box may block you from using the mouse to select source references. If you need to move the Consolidate dialog box out of the way, click and drag the title bar.

Creating Links to Source Data When Consolidating

When consolidating data, you can create links to the source data so that the destination area will be updated automatically whenever the source data changes.

When you create *consolidation links*, Excel inserts rows or columns in the destination area to hold the linking formulas for the consolidated cells. The inserted rows or columns are collapsed in *summary rows or columns*, and can be expanded at any time to reveal the consolidation links.

The destination area is outlined with linking formulas; these are placed in hidden rows or columns, subordinate to positions (or categories) in the destination area. For example, Figure 42.15 shows a destination worksheet that holds the linked source data of three expense reports.

Microsoft Excel - EXPTOTAL.XLS

File Edit Formula Format Data Options Macro Window Help

Normal Helv 10

B4 =EXP3.XLS!$B$2

	A	B	C	D	E	F	G	H	I
1	For the Month Ended 3/31/92								
5	Airfare	$3,050							
9	Breakfast	143							
13	Lunch	385							
17	Dinner	445							
21	Lodging	3,600							
25	Parking/Toll	125							
29	Tips	105							
33	Telephone	95							
37	Transportatic	116							
41	Other	60							
45	Total	$8,124							
46									
47									
48									
49									
50									
51									
52									
53									

Ready

Rows 2, 3, 4 are hidden—they are rows that contain the linked source data.

Figure 42.15 Destination worksheet that holds linked source data.

Notice the row numbering scheme in Figure 42.15. Rows 1,5,9,13,17,21,25,29,33,37,41, and 45 are visible. The rows in between (2,3, and 4) are hidden, because they contain the linked cells—and are therefore subordinated in the outline. The airfare total of $3,050 (found in B5) is the sum of cells B2:B4 (the collapsed rows that contain the links). Figure 42.16 shows the collapsed rows (2 through 4) expanded.

Contain the linking formulas

Microsoft Excel - EXPTOTAL.XLS

File Edit Formula Format Data Options Macro Window Help

Normal | Helv | 10

B2 =EXP1.XLS!$B$2

	A	B	C	D	E	F	G	H	I
1	For the Month Ended 3/31/92								
2		$1,000							
3		$950							
4		$1,100							
5	Airfare	$3,050							
9	Breakfast	143							
13	Lunch	385							
17	Dinner	445							
21	Lodging	3,600							
25	Parking/Toll	125							
29	Tips	105							
33	Telephone	95							
37	Transportatic	116							
41	Other	60							
45	Total	$8,124							
46									
47									
48									
49									
50									

Ready

Figure 42.16 Destination worksheet that holds linked source data, with summary rows expanded to display linked references.

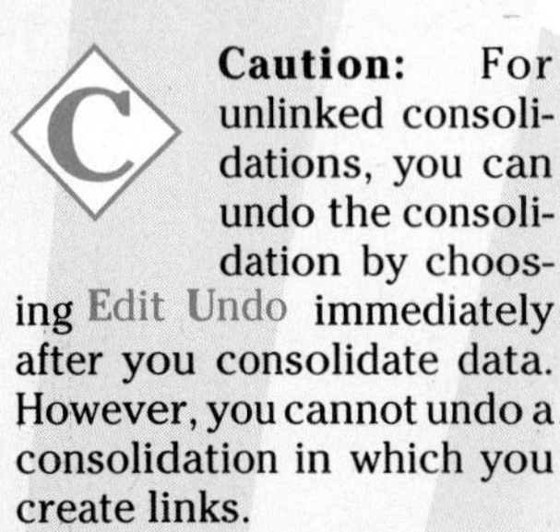

Caution: For unlinked consolidations, you can undo the consolidation by choosing Edit Undo immediately after you consolidate data. However, you cannot undo a consolidation in which you create links.

Figure 42.16 reveals that cells B2, B3, and B4 contain the following linking references, respectively:

```
=EXP1.XLS!$B$2,
=EXP2.XLS!$B$2,
```
and
```
=EXP3.XLS!$B$2.
```

To link source data in a consolidation, follow the steps for consolidating data (as detailed in the previous section); these include selecting the destination area you want to contain the consolidated data, choosing Data Consolidate, entering source area references, selecting a Function, and specifying consolidation—either by category (Top Row or Left Column) or by position. All you need do after that is select the Create Links To Source Data check box, and then choose OK or press Enter.

If you make a mistake when selecting source references, you can remove a reference from a consolidation. To correct the mistake, access the All References box of the Consolidate dialog box, and select the source area reference you want to remove. Then simply select the Delete button, and complete the process by selecting OK or pressing Enter.

Note: If a worksheet has a range named Consolidate Area, Excel uses that range as the permanent destination area for any consolidation on that worksheet.

Editing a Group of Worksheets

If you need to make changes to a worksheet that you would like duplicated in a group of worksheets start a group editing session. Once a group editing session is started, changes in the active sheet are made to the remainder of the worksheets in the group. To start a group editing session follow these steps:

1. Use File Open to open the worksheets that you want to work with as a group.
2. Switch to the worksheet in which you want to make changes, and select a cell where you will make the first change. This cell is called the *active cell*; any change in this cell will be replicated in that same cell location in other worksheets in the group.

Starting a Group Edit Session:

1. Open the worksheets you want to edit as a group.
2. Select the cell you want to edit first.

3. Choose Option Group Edit.
4. Select the worksheets for the group by holding down Ctrl and clicking on the worksheet name in the Select **G**roup box.
5. Choose OK or press Enter.

3. Choose **O**ptions **G**roup Edit. The Group Edit dialog box appears, as shown in Figure 42.17 (which displays a list of all open worksheets in the Select **G**roup box). By default, all sheets in the list are selected; if you have previously started a group editing session, however, those sheets involved in that editing session will be selected.

4. Select the worksheets you want to group together for editing by holding down Ctrl and clicking on the worksheet name in the Select **G**roup box.

5. Choose OK or press Enter. Excel adds `[Group]` to the titles in the title bars of the worksheets in the group.

After executing these five steps, you can begin editing the group of worksheets. To enter data into the same cells of all the worksheets in the group, simply begin entering data into the cell of your choice in the active worksheet. As you enter the data, you will see it appear in the formula bar of the active cells, and once you click on the Enter box or press Enter, the data will be duplicated in the same location in all the worksheets of the group.

After starting the group editing session (by following the previous steps), you can copy cell contents, formulas, and formatting from the active worksheet to the other worksheets in the group by following these steps:

Copying Contents, Formulas, and Formatting to All Worksheets in a Group:

1. Select the cells you want to copy.
2. Choose Edit Fill Group.
3. Select All, Formats, or Formulas.
4. Choose OK or press Enter.

1. In the active worksheet, select the cells you want to copy.

2. Choose Edit Fill **G**roup. The Fill Workgroup dialog box appears, as in Figure 42.18.

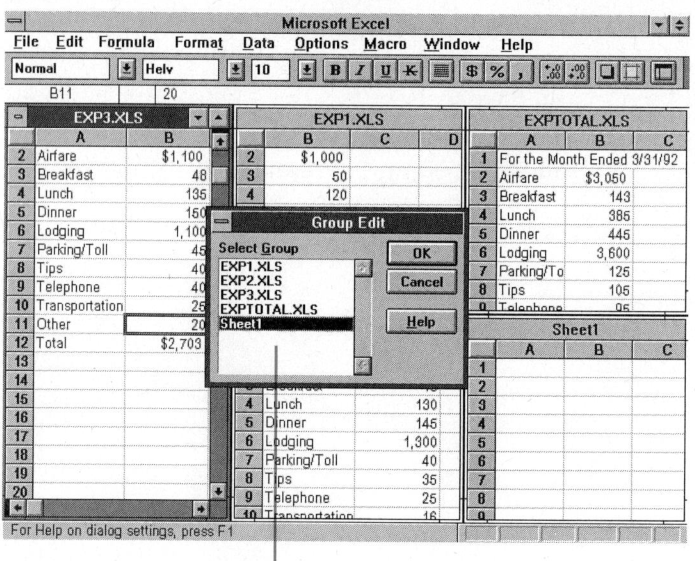
Displays all open worksheets

Figure 42.17 The Group Edit dialog box.

3. To copy cell contents, formulas, and formatting, select All. To copy only the formulas, select Formulas; to copy only formatting, select Formats.

4. Choose OK or press Enter.

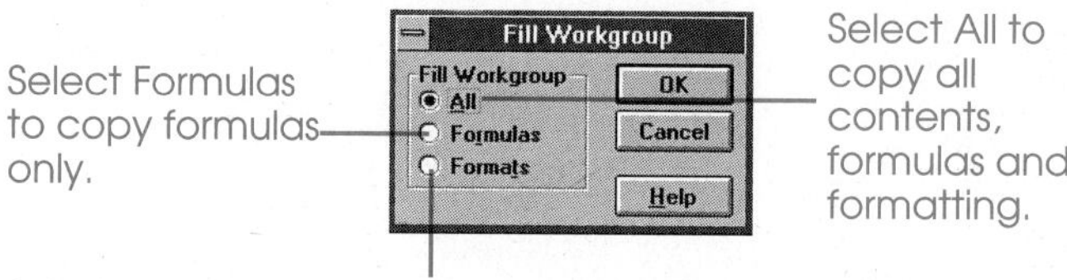
Select Formulas to copy formulas only.
Select All to copy all contents, formulas and formatting.
Select Formats to copy formats only.

Figure 42.18 The Fill Workgroup dialog box.

Tip: If you want to view all worksheets in a group to see how your edits affect them choose Window Arrange; select Tiled, Horizontal, or Vertical; and choose OK or press Enter.

To end a group editing session, switch out of the active worksheet into another worksheet (by clicking to it, or by choosing a worksheet from the list in the **W**indow menu). When you end a group editing session, the `[Group]` mode identifier disappears from the title bars of the worksheets in the group.

Skill Session

43

Using the Info Window

The *Info Window* displays detailed information about the active cell of a worksheet. By opening the Info Window, you can view the formula, value, format, protection, and name of the active cell. The Info Window can also display the note, if any, that is attached to an active cell. (Skill Session 5 discusses adding a cell note.) You can also use the Info Window to print a report that shows information about a selected range of cells in a worksheet.

When working with the Info Window, you specify the type of information you want to see. For example, if you want to see only the notes, formatting and protection status of the active cell, you can customize the Info Window so that it displays just that information.

You can get a "feel" for how a worksheet is constructed by scanning it with the Info Window. When used in conjunction with the **S**elect Special command (from the Excel Fo**r**mula menu), the Info Window can track relationships between formulas and the cells they reference.

For more information on how to use the Info Window with the Formula Select Special command, see the section "Scanning Cells with the Info Window" later in this skill session.

Opening the Info Window

Before you can view or print the data from an Info Window, you must first open it. Opening the Info Window is accomplished through the **O**ptions **W**orkspace command. Once opened, the Info Window appears on the right side of the worksheet as the active window, displaying its own menus.

Opening the Info Window:

1. Choose Options Workspace.
2. Turn on Info **W**indow check box.
3. Choose OK.

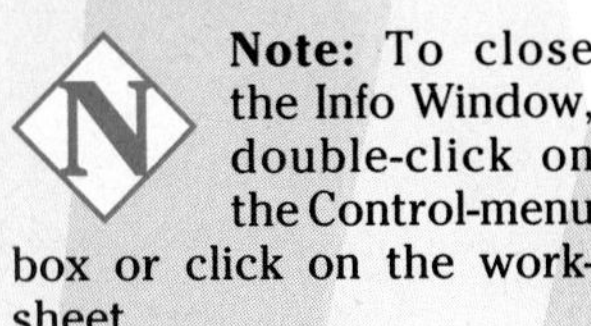

Note: To close the Info Window, double-click on the Control-menu box or click on the worksheet.

To open the Info Window, follow these steps:

1. Choose Options Workspace. The Workspace Options dialog box appears as shown in Figure 43.1.
2. Under Display, turn on the Info **W**indow check box.
3. Choose OK or press Enter. The Info Window appears, displaying the information for the selected cell (see Figure 43.2). Viewing the contents of the Info Window moves you from cell to cell in the worksheet, so you must choose Window Arrange to see more than one window in the workspace at one time.

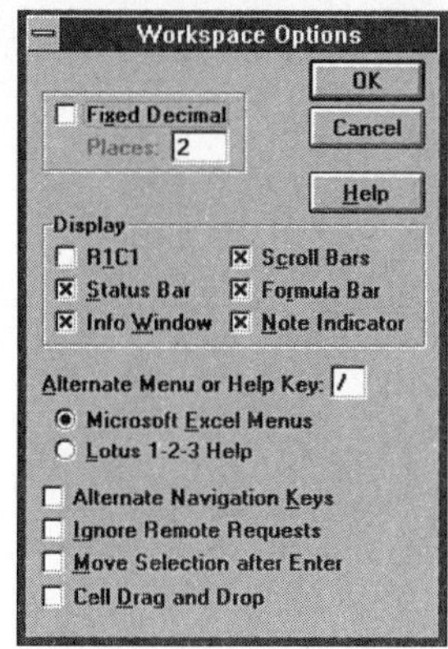

Figure 43.1 The Workspace Options dialog box.

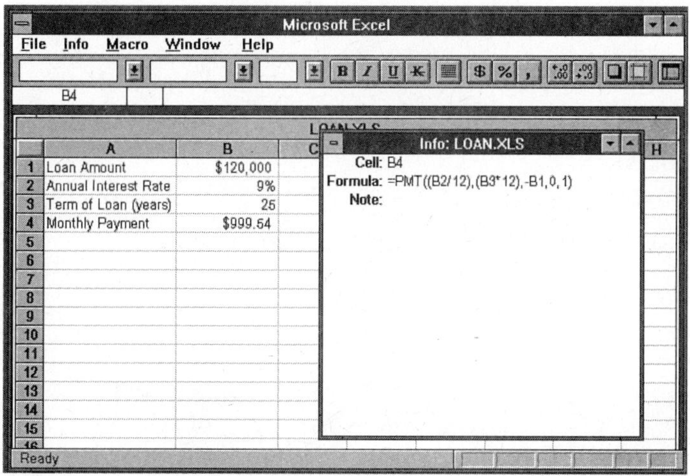

Figure 43.2 By default, the Info Window displays the active cell's reference, formula, and note.

Changing the Info Window Display

The first time you open the Info Window, it displays (by default) the active cell's reference, formula, and note, as shown in Figure 43.2. If that information is not what you want to view, however, you can change and customize the Info Window (to some extent) to meet your needs. When the Info Window is active, you can select any one of nine types of information about a cell by choosing the **I**nfo menu and selecting any number of the choices shown in Table 43.1.

Table 43.1 Information the Info Window can display

Info Menu Selection	*What It Displays*
Cell	The cell's reference
Fo**r**mula	The contents of the cell
Value	The value in the cell in General Format
Forma**t**	The number format, alignment, font, borders, and shading of cell
Pr**o**tection	The protection status of cell
Na**m**es	The cell and range names that include references to cell
Precedents	A dialog box is displayed, from which you select one of two options: **D**irect Only (which displays only the direct precedents that the cell refers to), and **A**ll Levels (which displays both direct and indirect precedents that the cell refers to).

Info Menu Selection	*What It Displays*
Dependents	A dialog box containing two options: **D**irect Only (which displays only the direct dependents that refer to the cell), and **A**ll Levels (which displays both direct and indirect dependents that refer to the cell)
Note	The note, if any, attached to the active cell

The type of information that the Info Window is set to display is indicated by a check mark next to its corresponding command name on the **I**nfo menu, as shown in Figure 43.3. To display additional information in the Info Window, follow these steps:

Selecting Information to Display in an Info Window:

1. Make Info Window active.
2. Choose Info.
3. Select a command.

1. Make the Info Window active. It will appear at the right side of the workspace, along with the Info menu.
2. Choose Info.
3. Select one of the commands without a check mark. (Or, to turn off information that is being displayed, select one of the commands with a check mark.)

Tip: To work on the worksheet while keeping the Info Window in view, use the Window Arrange command and choose the Tiled option. The worksheet and the Info Window will be displayed in one workspace at the same time.

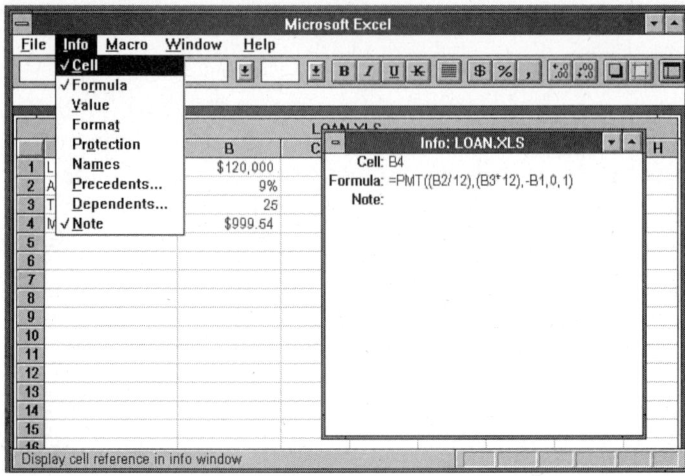

Figure 43.3 The Info menu of the Info Window.

Moving Between the Info Window and the Worksheet

Moving between the Info Window and the worksheet is easy. As with any other document window, you can make the Info Window active by selecting it from the **W**indow menu. For example, if the Info Window is open but not visible, follow these steps to switch to the Info Window:

1. Choose Window.

2. Select 1 Info: from the list of document names. As shown in Figure 43.4, a check mark will appear next to the Info Window name in the **W**indow list, and then the Info Window will be displayed.

Moving Between the Info Window and Worksheet:

1. Choose Window.
2. Select 1 Info: or the worksheet name from the list.

If both the Info Window and the worksheet are visible, use the mouse pointer to click on the window you want to switch to (make active).

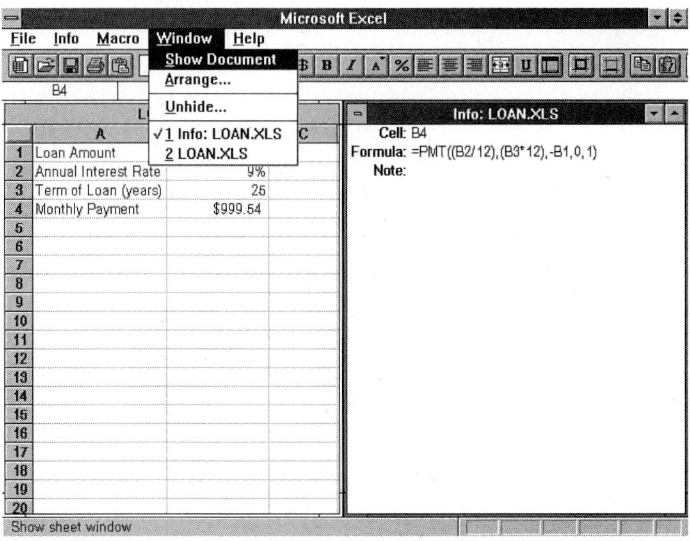

Figure 43.4 The Window menu lists the open documents of Document Names.

Scanning Cells Using the Info Window

If you need a quick understanding of a particular worksheet's structure (and the relationships of its formulas), the Info Window can help. With the Info Window, you can use the **S**elect Special command from the Formula menu to scan a worksheet; you can also track the relationships between formulas and the cells they reference. The Fo**r**mula **S**elect Special

Scanning Cells with the Info Window:

1. Choose Options Workspace.
2. Turn on Info Window check box.
3. Select OK.
4. Choose Window Arrange.
5. Select Tiled.
6. Select OK.
7. Make worksheet window active.
8. Choose Formula Select Special.
9. Select an option to scan.
10. Select OK.
11. Press Tab to move from cell to cell.

command allows you to select cells that have the characteristics you specify. Excel displays the information for the selected cell in the Info Window if you follow these steps:

1. Choose Options Workspace. The Workspace Options dialog box appears.
2. Under Display, turn on the Info Window check box.
3. Select OK or press Enter.
4. Choose Window Arrange. The Arrange Windows dialog box appears.
5. Select Tiled.
6. Select OK or press Enter. The worksheet and the Info Window will be displayed in one workspace at the same time.
7. Make the worksheet window active by clicking on it, or by selecting it from the Window menu.
8. Choose Formula Select Special. As shown in Figure 43.5, the Select Special dialog box appears.
9. Select one of the options for the type of information for which you want Excel to scan, as summarized in Table 43.2.
10. Select OK. Excel selects all cells containing the type of information (or formula) you selected, and displays information about the cell in the Info Window.
11. Press Tab to move from cell to cell.

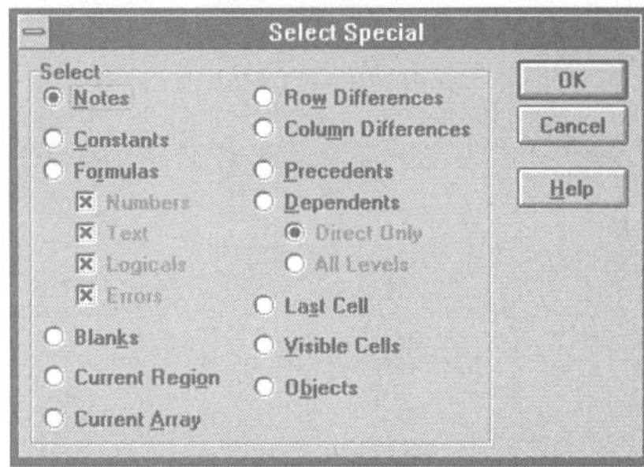

Figure 43.5 The Select Special dialog box.

Table 43.2 Summary of select special options

Option	*What it Selects*
Notes	All cells containing a note
Constants	All cells containing constants, depending upon which of the following check boxes you select: Numbers (selects constant numbers), Text (selects constant text), Logicals (selects cells containing the logical values TRUE and FALSE that were entered as constants), and Errors (selects cells containing error values that were entered as constants)
Fo**r**mulas	All cells containing formulas, depending upon which of the following check boxes you select: Numbers (selects cells with formulas that produce numbers), Text (selects cells with formulas that produce text), Logicals (selects cells with formulas that produce the logical values TRUE and FALSE), and Errors (selects cells with formulas that produce error values)
Blan**k**s	All blank cells

continues

Table 43.2 continued

Option	*What it Selects*
Current Region	A rectangular range of cells around the active cell. The range selected is an area bounded by any combination of blank rows and blank columns.
Current Array	The entire array to which the active cell belongs, if any
Row Differences	Cells whose contents are different from the comparison cell in each row. For each row, the comparison cell is in the same column as the active cell.
Column Differences	Cells whose contents are different from the comparison cell in each column. For each column, the comparison cell is in the same row as the active cell.
Precedents	Cells to which the formulas in the selected cells refer. Direct Only selects only cells directly referred to by formulas in the selection. All Levels selects all cells referred to (directly or indirectly) by cells in the selection.
Dependents	Cells with formulas that refer to the cells in the current selection. Direct Only selects only cells with formulas that refer directly to the cells in the selection. All Levels selects all cells that refer (directly or indirectly) to cells in the selection.
Last Cell	The last cell that contains data or formatting in the worksheet or macro sheet
Visible Cells	The visible cells on a worksheet, so that any changes you make affect only the visible cells and not the hidden rows or columns
Objects	All graphic objects, including buttons and text boxes

To search the entire worksheet, select a single cell before choosing Formula Select Special and to search only a specific range, select just that range, then choose Formula Select Special.

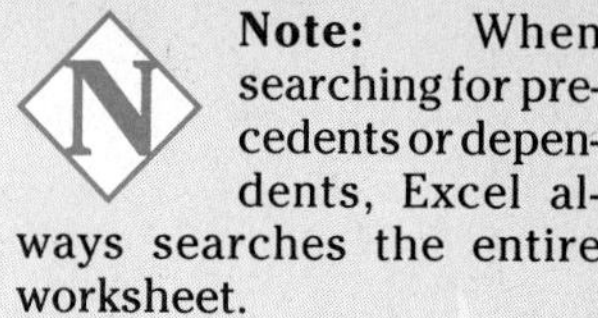

Note: When searching for precedents or dependents, Excel always searches the entire worksheet.

Tip: It is more efficient to use Formula Paste Name to find range names than to use Info Window. To make a list of the range names used in your worksheet, determine where you want to paste the list of names and select the upper-left cell of where you want the names listed. Make sure you choose an area where there will be sufficient room for all the names and references so that you don't paste over critical data or formulas. The list will occupy two columns—one for names and one for references. Choose Formula Paste Name. Select Paste List from the Paste Names dialog box.

Generating Info Window Reports

With the Info Window active, you can print reports showing any number of the nine types of information about a cell or range of cells. The length of the report depends upon the number of cells you select before you print the report. If you select one cell, the Info Window report will show information on only the one selected cell and if you select a range of cells, the report will disclose information about all the cells in the selected range.

Printing Information from the Info Window:

1. Select cells whose information you want to print.
2. Switch to Info Window.
3. Choose File Print.
4. Select OK.

To print Info Window information for a selected range of cells, follow these steps:

1. Select the cells for which you want to print the Info Window information.
2. Switch to the Info Window. If the Info Window is open but not visible, you can choose Window and select Info Window from the list. If the Info Window is open and visible, you can use the mouse to click on the window. (If the Info Window is not open, follow the steps in the previous section, "Opening the Info Window.")
3. Choose File Print. The Print dialog box appears.
4. Select OK. Excel prints the Info Window information for the cells selected in Step 1.

Comparing Worksheets

Sometimes it's difficult to determine the differences in similar worksheets. For example, you may improve a worksheet with a few revisions, and then have difficulty (at a later date) determining whether the old or new version is the improved version. Excel allows you to compare two similar worksheets, and prepare a report that shows the differences between them. This *comparison report* provides a list of the cells that differ between two versions. To prepare a comparison report of two worksheets, follow these steps:

1. Choose File Open. The Open File dialog box appears.

2. Select the file COMPARE.XLA located in the LIBRARY subdirectory of the directory in which you installed Excel.

3. Select OK.

4. Choose File Open, select the two worksheets you want to compare, and select OK.

5. Switch to one of the worksheets.

6. Choose Formula Compare. The Worksheet Comparison dialog box appears.

7. In the Compare To Sheet box, select the other worksheet.

8. Select OK. As shown in Figure 43.6, Excel creates a new worksheet, and enters a list of differing cells (and their contents) into it.

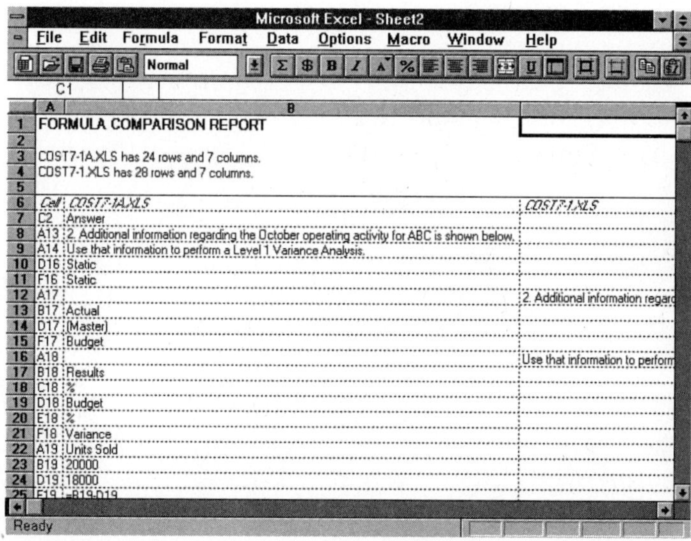

Figure 43.6 A list of cells that differ between two worksheets.

Comparing Two Worksheets:

1. Choose File Open.
2. Select COMPARE.XLA from LIBRARY subdirectory.
3. Select OK.
4. Open the two worksheets to compare.
5. Switch to one of them.
6. Choose Formula Compare.
7. In the Compare To Sheet box, select the other worksheet.
8. Select OK.

Working With Summary Information

Viewing and Updating Worksheet Summary Information:

1. Choose File Open.
2. Select SUMMARY.XLA from LIBRARY subdirectory.
3. Select OK.
4. Choose Edit Summary Info.
5. Edit summary information.
6. Select OK.

To document your worksheets properly, you may find it wise to enter *summary information* (such as the title, author, and creation date), and store it with the worksheet. Summary information can be stored with the worksheet—and updated each time the worksheet is revised—by using the *document summary macro*. You can run the document summary macro by following these steps:

1. Choose File Open.
2. Select the file SUMMARY.XLA located in the LIBRARY subdirectory of the Excel directory.
3. Select OK.
4. Choose Edit Summary Info. As shown in Figure 43.7, the Summary Info dialog box is displayed, containing current summary information about the active worksheet.
5. Make the changes you want to the summary information.
6. Select OK or press Enter.

When you save the worksheet, the summary information is saved automatically with the worksheet and anytime you want to view the summary information you can repeat the steps detailed above.

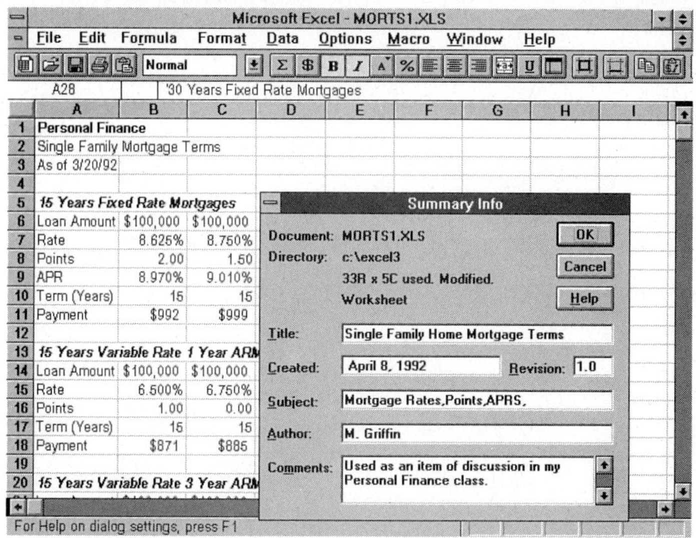

Figure 43.7 Summary Info dialog box is displayed.

Skill Session

44

More about Workbooks

Skill Session 6 covers how to save worksheets as a workbook and how to open and close workbooks. This skill session gives more details on how to manage workbooks. It shows how to add and delete documents from a workbook and how to move and copy documents between multiple workbooks.

A *workbook* is a type of Excel file in which you can store documents and any combination of worksheets, macro sheets, and charts. The advantages of organizing related documents in a workbook include easier file management and quicker movement among related documents. Also, a workbook can be shared with other users who might need access to a collection of documents. For example, if you are working on next year's master budget, it may make sense to bind all the subsidiary budgets (e.g., the sales forecast, the manufacturing costs budget, and the marketing and advertising budget) into one workbook.

Organizing documents in a workbook is also a good time management technique. When a workbook is opened, all the documents in the workbook are automatically opened; when you close the workbook, all its files are closed.

Adding Documents to a Workbook

After you have created a workbook by choosing File New Workbook (see Skill Session 6), one way that you can add a document by dragging it to the workbook. If the document is a worksheet or macro sheet, you can add it to a workbook by dragging the Select All button to the workbook window or to a workbook icon. Figure 44.1 shows the Select All button of a worksheet. If the document that you want to add to the workbook is a chart, you must select the entire chart and drag one of the selection squares to the workbook window or workbook icon. The selection squares appear around the chart when you click on the chart. After you drag the document to the workbook and release the mouse button, the document name appears listed in the contents of the workbook, as shown in Figure 44.2.

Adding a Document to a Workbook:

1. Switch to window of document that you want to add to a workbook.
2. Drag Select All button to workbook window or icon.

To add a document to a workbook, follow these steps:

1. Switch to the window of the document that you want to add to a workbook by either using the mouse to click on that window or by selecting the document from the **W**indow menu list.

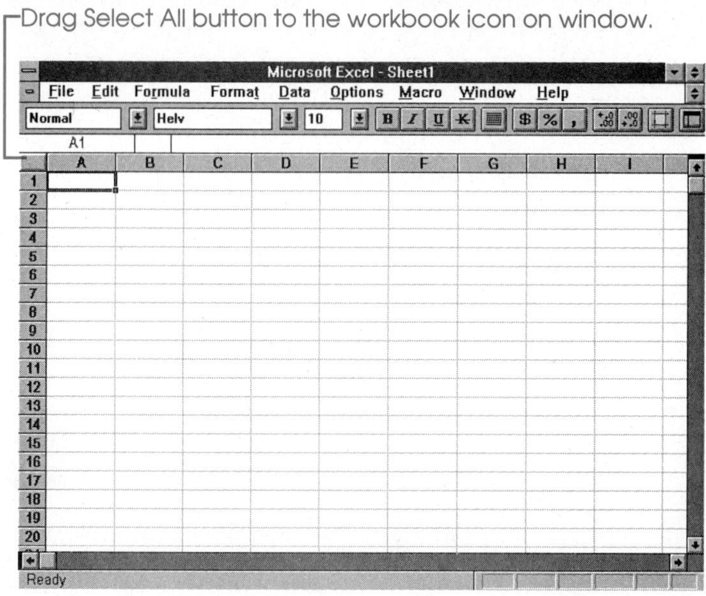

Figure 44.1 The Select All button of a worksheet.

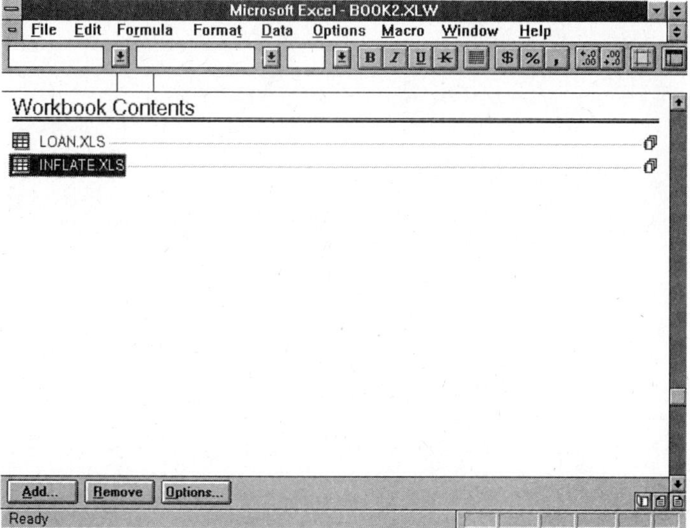

Figure 44.2 The Workbook Contents.

2. In the case of a worksheet or macro sheet, drag the Select All button to the workbook window or icon. If the document is a chart, select the entire chart and drag one of the selection squares. Excel adds the document to the workbook after you release the mouse button. The document name appears in the contents of the workbook.

You can also add an open document to a workbook while the workbook window is active. The advantage to this approach is that you can easily add any documents that are open but have not been previously added to the workbook by selecting them from a list of document names.

Adding a Document to a Workbook while in the Workbook Window:

1. Choose Add.
2. Select open document from **S**elect Document to Add list and select Add.
3. Select Close.

To add open documents to a workbook while in the workbook window, follow these steps:

1. Choose the Add button. As shown in Figure 44.3, the Add To Workbook dialog box appears listing any open documents that have not been added to the workbook.

2. If the document that you want to add is an open document, select it from the **S**elect Documents to Add list, and select the Add button. The document appears in the contents of the workbook. If the document is not open, select Open. The Open dialog box appears. Select the file to open and choose OK or press Enter. The document will then appear in the Contents of the workbook. The Add to Workbook dialog box reappears.

3. If you want to add another document to the workbook, repeat step 2.

4. When finished selecting documents to add to the workbook, select Close.

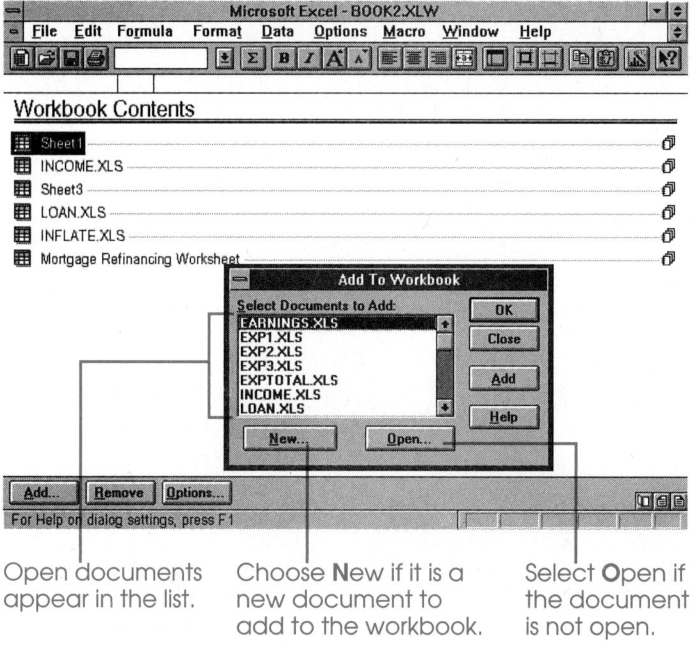

Figure 44.3 The Add To Workbook dialog box.

In step 2, the Add To Workbook dialog box displays all open, unbound documents. An *unbound* document is one that is saved as a separate file, not as part of a workbook file.

Tip: When selecting a document to add to a workbook, you can select several documents in sequence and add them all at once by holding down the Shift key while selecting the documents. If you want to select a group of documents that are out of sequence, hold down the Ctrl key while making your selections. You must then either click on Add or OK to add the files to the workbook.

Tip: You can open a worksheet from within a workbook window by double-clicking on the document icon.

Moving among Workbook Documents

You can move among workbook documents in sequence or in any order you desire. When moving in sequence, you cycle through the documents according to the order in which they are listed in the contents of the workbook. To display the document listed above the active document in the contents of the workbook, click the left paging button found in the lower right corner of the document window, as shown in Figure 44.4. To move to the document listed below the active document, click the right paging button, which is also located in the lower right corner of the document window.

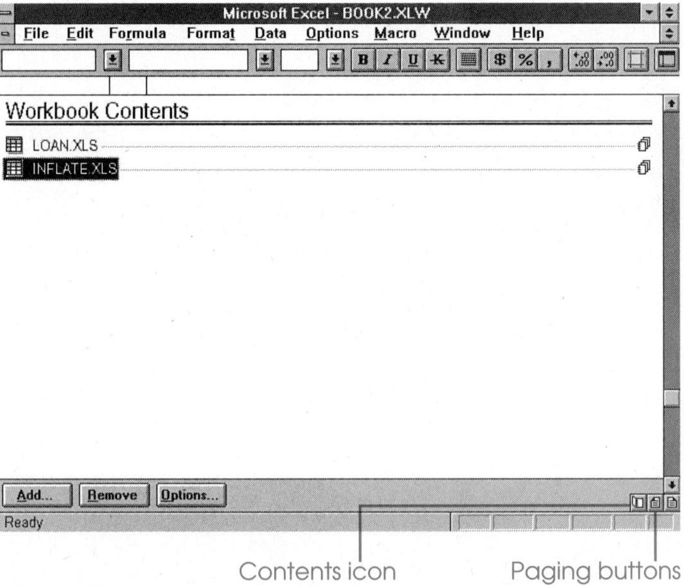

Figure 44.4 The workbook paging buttons and contents icon.

You can also move to any document in a workbook by double-clicking on the document name from the Workbook Contents list that appears when you click on the Contents icon. As shown in Figure 44.4, the Contents icon is located near the left and right paging buttons in the lower right corner of the document window. To move to a workbook document, follow these steps:

Moving to a Workbook Document:

1. Click on Contents icon.
2. Select document name from shortcut menu list.

1. Click on the Contents icon. The Workbook Contents appear.
2. Select the document you want to move by double-clicking the document name.

The order of the documents in the workbook is initially determined by the order in which the documents were added to the workbook. However, you can reorder the document list by dragging documents into new positions in the workbook contents list. For example, if FILE1.XLS in currently listed first in a contents that has four documents (FILE1.XLS, FILE2.XLS, FILE3.XLS, and FILE4.XLS) and you want to move it to the fourth (last) position, you could drag the FILE1.XLS document icon to the fourth position in the workbook. After dragging the document to the new position in the contents and releasing the mouse button, the documents appear in their new order.

Removing Documents from a Workbook

When you no longer want to include a document in a workbook, you have three options of removing it. All three methods begin by selecting the document in the

Contents window of the workbook. Then you can proceed to remove the document by either dragging the document out of the workbook, choosing Remove, or choosing Edit Clear. Each of the three methods is summarized in Table 44.1.

Table 44.1 Removing a document from a workbook

Method	*Steps*
Dragging	Select the document from Workbook Contents and drag it to any other place in the Excel workspace.
Choosing Remove	Select the document from Contents and choose the Remove button.
Choosing Edit Clear	Select the document from Contents and choose Edit Clear.

If you want to remove a document from one workbook and add it to another workbook, you can do it by dragging the document from the source workbook to the destination workbook. For example, if the worksheet REFI.XLS is in BOOK1.XLW and you want to move it to BOOK2.XLW, select REFI.XLS from the contents of BOOK1.XLW and drag it to BOOK2.XLW. Place it where you want it positioned in the contents list and release the mouse button. You can drag the document to an opened workbook window or to a workbook icon. If the destination workbook is an opened window, choose Window Arrange Tiled so that you can see both the source and destination workbooks simultaneously as you move the document.

Copying a Document from One Workbook to Another

You can also use the dragging method to copy a document from one workbook to another. Before you drag the copy of the document to the destination file, however, you must hold down the Ctrl key. A copy of a document can be deposited in a workbook opened to a window or to a workbook icon. When Excel copies the document to the destination workbook, the document remains either saved or listed in the destination workbook, depending upon its status in the source workbook. For example, if the worksheet REFI.XLS is a saved document in BOOK1.XLW and is copied to BOOK2.XLW, it will also be a saved file in BOOK2.XLW. When a document is saved in a workbook, it becomes part of the workbook file. Listed documents can be shared by several workbooks.

To copy a document from one workbook to another using the dragging method, follow these steps:

Copying a Document to Another Workbook by Dragging:

1. Hold down Ctrl.
2. Select document to copy.
3. Drag it to destination workbook.

1. Hold down the Ctrl key.
2. Select the document that you want to copy.
3. Drag the document that you want to copy to the destination workbook. Before you release the mouse button, place the document copy at the point in the contents list where you want it positioned and then release the mouse button. The document and icon name appear in the contents list of the destination workbook.

Copying a Document to Another Workbook by Using Copy and Paste:

1. Select the document you want to copy.
2. Choose Edit Copy.
3. Select the destination workbook window.
4. Choose Edit Paste.

You can also use the **C**opy and **P**aste commands to copy a document to another workbook (which must be open if you use this method). This procedure is similar to copying and pasting any type of data in Excel. The steps are as follows:

1. While in the workbook window, select the document that you want to copy.

2. Choose Edit Copy. A moving border appears around the selected document.

3. Select the destination workbook window and select the document above which you want to place the copy document.

4. Choose Edit Paste. The copied document appears in the destination workbook window.

Binding and Unbinding Workbook Documents

The documents in a workbook can be either bound or unbound. A *bound document* is a file that is saved within the workbook and does not exist separately from the workbook. An *unbound document* is listed in the contents of a workbook but is not part of the workbook file; it exists as a separate file and can be listed in other workbooks. Binding documents in the workbook is handy when you want to keep related documents in one file for security reasons, organization, or immediate user access to a group of related documents. Documents should be unbound if you want to include a document in two or more workbooks.

When a document is added to a workbook, Excel assumes that it is a bound document. When you save a workbook, unless you specify otherwise, all newly added documents are bound. To unbind a document in a workbook, follow these steps:

1. While in the Workbook Contents window, select the document you want to unbind in the workbook.
2. Choose the Options button. The Documents Options dialog box appears, as shown in Figure 44.5.
3. Select the Separate File check box.
4. Choose OK or press Enter. The Document icon on the far right side of the document in the Workbook Contents window resembles unbound pages.

Unbinding Documents:

1. Select document to unbind.
2. Choose Options.
3. Select Separate File.
4. Choose OK.

In Action: Click the Document icon to the right of the document name in the Workbook Contents window to change the document status from bound to unbound. The Document icon changes to resemble unbound pages. Click on it again to change the document status from unbound to bound. The icon changes back to the bound appearance.

To bind a document in a workbook, you follow these steps:

1. While in the Workbook Contents window, select the document you want to bind in the workbook.

Binding Documents:
1. Select document to bind.
2. Choose Options.
3. Select Workbook File.
4. Choose OK.

2. Choose the Options button. The Documents Options dialog box appears, as shown in Figure 44.5.

3. Select the Workbook File option button in the Documents Options dialog box.

4. Choose OK or press Enter. The Document icon on the far right side of the document in the Workbook Contents window resembles unbound pages.

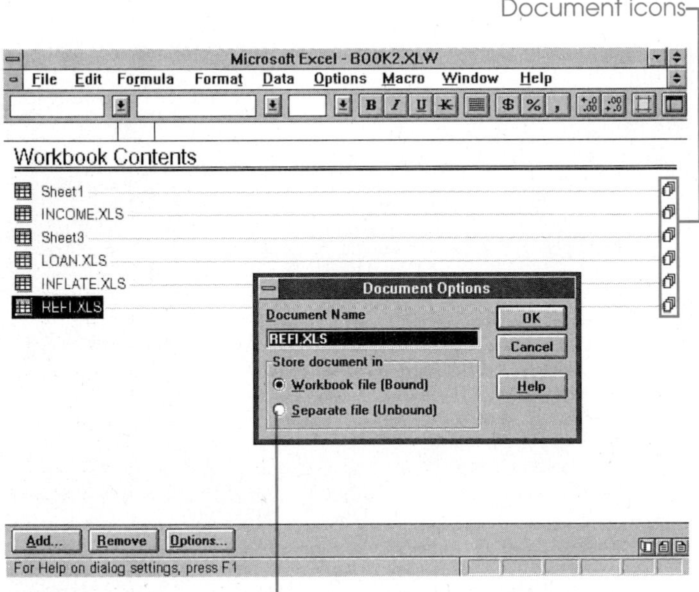

Figure 44.5 The Documents Options dialog box.

Giving a Bound Workbook Document an Extended Name

You can give bound documents names with up to 31 characters. The document name can include any combination of characters and spaces. This feature allows you to be much more descriptive when naming your bound documents than you can be when naming unbound documents that are restricted to the DOS 8-character file name limit. For example, if you have a worksheet that allows you to determine whether it is prudent to refinance your home mortgage and that file is bound in a workbook, you could name the worksheet Mortgage Refinancing Worksheet (28 characters including spaces).

To give a bound workbook an extended name, follow these steps:

1. In the Workbook Contents window, select the bound document to which you want to give an extended name.
2. Choose Options. The Document Options dialog box appears.
3. Under **D**ocument Name, type a name up to 31 characters long.
4. Choose OK or press Enter. The new extended document name appears in the Workbook Contents window, as shown in Figure 44.6.

Extending Name:

1. Select document to which you want to give an extended name.
2. Choose Options.
3. Under **D**ocument Name, type a name.
4. Choose OK.

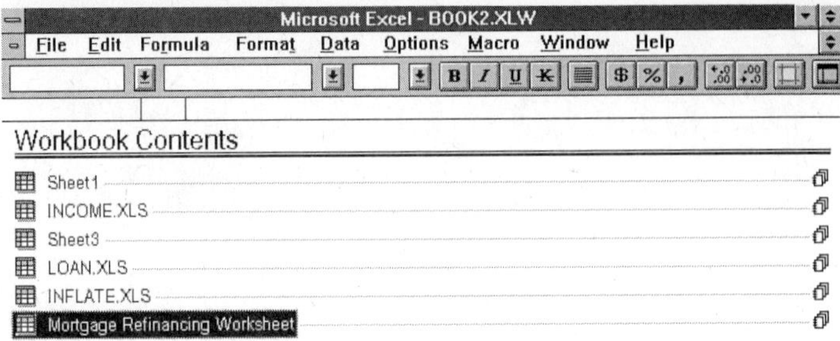

Figure 44.6 Workbook Contents window.

Skill Session

45

Creating and Using Templates

A *template* is a document you create and then save so that it can be used as a model for similar documents that you will work with in the future. Templates contain text, formatting, macros, and formulas that you anticipate using with new data. For example, you may create a tax planning worksheet that allows you to enter the IRS 1040 form data and then calculates the tax liability. The template would contain all the text for income, adjustments to income, and deductions; formulas and data tables for calculating the tax liability; and all formatting such as font types and lines. If you save the IRS 1040 worksheet as a template, you can use that model every few months to recalculate tax liability, without disturbing the original model. When you create a new document from a template, Excel opens an exact copy of the template file, not the template file itself.

Creating a New Template

The procedure for creating a new template begins just like the creation of a new document. You create a worksheet, chart, or macro sheet with all the styles, formats, text, formulas, and macros you want; or you can open an existing document that you want to use as a template. Then follow these steps:

Creating a New Template

1. Choose File Save As.
2. Type template name.
3. Select Template.
4. Choose OK.

Note: You can save frequently used templates in your startup directory (the default startup directory is XLSTART). The advantage of saving a frequently used template in the startup directory is that its name is displayed in the New dialog box when you choose File New. For more information on how to save a file in your startup directory see Skill Session 43.

1. Choose File Save As.
2. In the File Name text box type the name you want for the template.
3. In the Save File As Type box, select Template, as shown in Figure 45.1. Microsoft Excel adds the extension .XLT to the template name in the File Name text box.
4. Choose OK or press Enter.

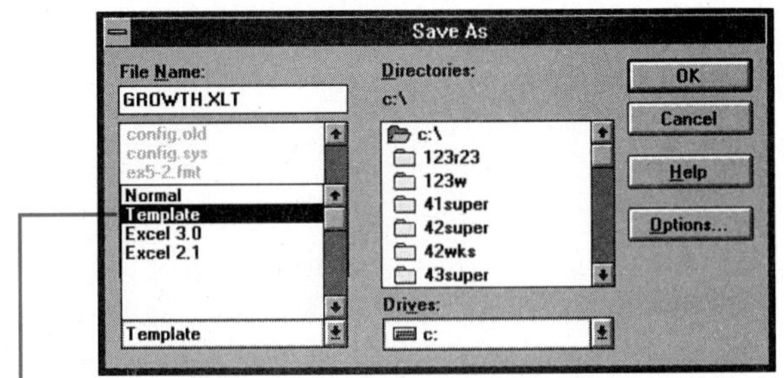

Figure 45.1 The Save As dialog box.

In Action: Worksheet style has become an important characteristic of business reporting. Everyone is now a publisher: applying formats, styles, fonts, italic, and boldface to reports, charts, and schedules. After you have discovered a style that properly communicates your message, save the worksheet as a template. That way, you capture a style you can use again and again.

Opening a Template

For the most part, you open a template document the same way you open any Excel document by choosing File Open. The exception to this rule is when a template has been saved in the startup directory. You can open a template when it is in the startup directory and when it is in any other directory.

Follow these steps to open a template when it is in the startup directory:

1. Choose File New. The New dialog box appears.
2. Select the template name from the New dialog box.
3. Choose OK or press Enter.

Opening a Template when It Is in the Startup Directory:

1. Choose File New.
2. Select the template name.
3. Choose OK or press Enter.

Opening a template from any other directory is straightforward. Use the following steps:

1. Choose File Open. The Open dialog box appears.

Opening a Template When It Is in Any Other Directory:

1. Choose File Open.
2. Select the template name.
3. Choose OK or press Enter.

Tip: When opening a template by choosing File Open, you can list templates only by selecting Microsoft Excel Templates (*.XLT) in the List Files Of Type box.

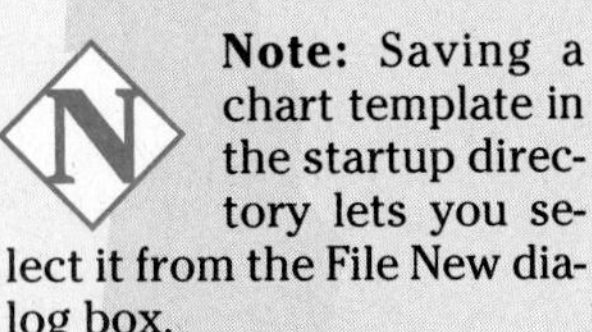

Note: Saving a chart template in the startup directory lets you select it from the File New dialog box.

2. Select the template on which you want to base a new document by entering the template name in the File Name text box.

3. Choose OK or press Enter.

When you open a template, you are actually opening a copy of the template while the original template remains intact. When you open a copy of a template, Excel gives it a temporary name. For example, if the template is named LOAN.XLT, Excel names the temporary name of the opened copy LOAN1.XLT.

Chart Templates

Using a data series, you can create charts and then save those charts as templates to be used with new data series. Whatever formatting characteristics you give to the chart template when you create it will be used on any new data series that you want to chart using the template. For example, assume that you create a 3-D chart with a customized 3-D view (elevation, rotation, perspective), gridlines, and text and save it as a template named CHART1.XLT. If you then enter a new data series in a worksheet, you can have it plotted using the same formatting characteristics that you used to create CHART1.XLT.

When you create a new chart from a chart template, the data series that were used to create the chart on the original template are not used for the new chart. Instead, the data that you select in the active worksheet is used to supply the data series for the new chart. Excel plots worksheet data based on the shape and contents of the worksheet selection. Before opening a chart template, select the data series in the worksheet that you want the template to plot. For more information on how to create charts and how to control how Excel plots a data series, see Skill Session 24.

> **In Action:** One of the advantages of templates is style consistency. For example, if you want all your 3-D bar charts to have the same look, you can create a 3-D bar chart using any data series and then experiment with such characteristics as text, arrows, colors, and patterns. When you have captured the style you desire, save the chart as a template. Any time you need to create a 3-D bar chart, the template is available to keep you consistent.

Below is a summary of the steps to follow when creating chart templates:

1. Using a data series, create a chart with all the formatting characteristics that you desire.
2. Choose File Save As. The Save As dialog box appears.
3. In the File Name text box, type the name you want for the template.
4. In the Save File As Type box, select Template. Excel adds the extension .XLT to the template name in the File Name text box.
5. Choose OK or press Enter.

Creating Chart Templates:

1. Create chart with desired formats.
2. Choose File Save As.
3. Enter template name.
4. Select Template.
5. Choose OK.

Using a chart template involves entering a data series in a worksheet and then opening the chart template so

Opening a Chart Template:

1. Enter a data series in a worksheet.
2. Select range of worksheet cells.
3. Choose File Open.
4. Enter template name.
5. Choose OK.

that you can apply the formats. The following steps detail how to use a chart template:

1. When you are ready to work with the chart template, enter a data series in a worksheet.

2. Select the range of worksheet cells containing the data series that you want to plot with the template.

3. Choose File Open (or File New, if the chart has been saved in the startup directory). The Open dialog box appears.

4. Select the chart template by entering the template name in the File **N**ame text box or by selecting it from the File **N**ame list.

5. Choose OK or press Enter. The data series that you selected is plotted in a new chart window using all the formatting characteristics of the template.

Editing a Template

When you open a template, Excel protects the original template file by opening a copy of the template. The original template file stays intact. However, you can override the protection and open the original template, make changes to it, and save the revision for future use. You may, for example, have created TAX.XLT to help you compute the 1992 income tax liability of your clients. After 1993 arrives, you can edit TAX.XLT so that it reflects the new 1993 tax rates.

To edit a template, follow these steps:

1. Choose File Open. The Open dialog box appears.
2. Enter the name of the template that you want to edit in the File Name text box or select it from the File Name list.
3. Hold down Shift and choose OK, or press Enter. Excel opens the original template for editing.
4. Make your revisions to the template.
5. Choose File Save. Excel saves the revised template using its original name.

Editing a Template:

1. Choose File Open.
2. Enter name of template to edit.
3. Hold Shift and choose OK, or press Enter.
4. Revise template.
5. Choose File Save.

Note: You must hold down Shift when you choose OK in step 3; otherwise, Excel will open a copy of the template and will not allow you to change the original template.

Advanced Topics Workshop

This workshop includes skills sessions that will show you preferred ways to work with ranges of data, how to build formulas that utilize powerful functions, and how to create your own custom functions. Excel is a program that can be almost tailor made to meet your needs. Custom functions are one of the features that give Excel flexibility. Another example of Excel's flexibility can also be seen in the skill session that shows you how to create a custom toolbar and then save it for future use.

Skill Session

46

Advanced Range Operations

Working with large worksheets can be difficult. Making revisions to ranges of text, formulas, and data in large worksheets can be cumbersome. Searching for specific data, replacing old data with new data, and formatting and entering data series can be time-consuming. However, some advanced range operations can help you be more efficient when working with large worksheets.

This skill session details some advanced range operations that make it easier to work with large ranges of data. It shows you how to use the Fo**r**mula **F**ind or the Fo**r**mula R**e**place commands as well as the **E**dit Paste **S**pecial command. You'll also learn how you can convert existing data in a worksheet to a new format by copying data from one range and pasting it in a transposed format in a new range.

This skill session can show you how to experiment with Automatic Range Formatting, if formatting numbers, switching fonts, adding borders, and changing alignment never really seems to give your reports the style and professional image that you seek. Finally, you'll learn how to manipulate your worksheets that involve data series of incremental numbers or dates.

Finding Data

When creating or revising large worksheets you may need to search the worksheet to find certain data. Searching for data in a large worksheet can be a cumbersome task if you have to search cell by cell. Fortunately, Excel gives you the capability to find data in an efficient manner through the Formula Find command. By choosing Formula Find, you can search for any letter, number, or punctuation mark and tell Excel to look for your search data in cell formulas, cell values, or cell notes.

Before beginning a search, you can select a range to search. If you don't select a range, Excel will search the entire worksheet. To search a worksheet or macro sheet for some specified data, follow these steps:

Searching a Worksheet:

1. Select area to search.
2. Choose Formula Find.
3. Type characters to search for.
4. Select Formulas, Values, or Notes.
5. Select Whole or Part.
6. Select Rows or Columns.
7. Select Match Case.
8. Choose OK.
9. Press F7 to find next occurrence.

1. Select the area of the worksheet or macro sheet you want to search. If no range is selected, the entire worksheet or macros sheet will be searched.

2. Choose Formula Find. As shown in Figure 46.1, the Find dialog box appears.

3. In the Find What box, type the characters you want to search for.

4. Under Look in, select the type of search: Formulas, Values, or Notes.

5. Under Look at, select Whole if you want the search to find only cells that exactly match the Find What box . Select Part if you want the search to find all cells that include the characters in the Find What box.

6. Under Look by, select the direction in which you want Excel to search. If you select Rows, Excel searches across rows. If you select Columns, Excel searches down columns.

7. Select Match Case if you want Excel to use the exact combination of upper- and lowercase characters you entered in the Find What box.

8. Choose OK or press Enter. Excel finds the first occurrence.

9. Press F7. Excel finds the next occurrence.

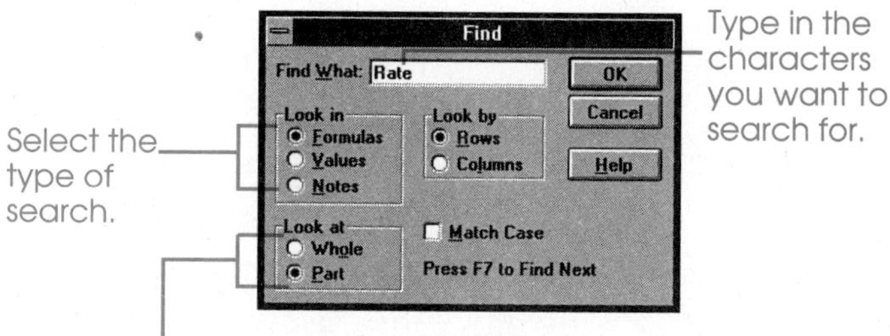
Find
Find What: Rate
OK
Cancel
Help
Look in
Formulas
Values
Notes
Look by
Rows
Columns
Look at
Whole
Part
Match Case
Press F7 to Find Next
Type in the characters you want to search for.
Select the type of search.
Select Whole to search for exact matches or Part to search for all cells that include the characters in the Find What box.

Figure 46.1 The Find dialog box.

You may use the two wildcards ? and * when you enter the characters in the Find What box. The ? replaces any one character, whereas * replaces any number of characters. Because Excel recognizes ? and * as wildcards, if you want to search for either the actual characters ? or *, you must precede the character with

Tip: While using Formula Find to search a worksheet, you can go back to a previous search occurrence by holding down the Shift key and pressing F7.

Tip: To display the Find dialog box so you can specify search options, hold down the Shift key and press F5.

a tilde (~). For example, if you want to search for ?, enter ~? in the Find What box.

Finding and Replacing Data

If you want to find data and replace it with new data, use Formula Replace. The Formula Replace command does not search notes or the numbers produced by formulas. It searches and replaces only the contents of cells. Like the Formula Find command, before beginning a search, you can select a range to search. If you don't select a range, Excel will search the entire worksheet. To find and replace data, follow these steps:

Finding and Replacing Data:

1. Select area to replace characters.
2. Choose Formula Replace.
3. Type characters to search for.
4. Type characters to use instead.
5. Select Whole or Part.
6. Select Rows or Columns.
7. Select Match Case.
8. Choose Replace All or Find Next then Replace.
9. Choose Close.

1. Select the area of the worksheet or macro sheet in which you want to replace characters. If no range is selected, the entire worksheet or macro sheet will be searched.

2. Choose Formula Replace. As shown in Figure 46.2, the Replace dialog box appears.

3. In the Find What box, type the characters you want to search for. You can include any letter, number, punctuation mark, or wildcard in your search. To search for an actual wildcard (* or ?), precede it with a tilde (~).

4. In the Replace With box, type the characters you want to use in place of the characters you entered in the Find What box.

5. Under Look at, select Whole if you want the search to find only cells that exactly match the Find What box. Select Part if you want the search to find all cells that include the characters in the Find What box.

6. Under Look by, select the direction in which you want Excel to search. If you select Rows, Excel will search across rows. If you select Columns, Excel will search down columns.

7. Select Match Case if you want Excel to use the exact combination of upper- and lowercase characters you entered in the Find What box.

8. Choose Replace All if you want Excel to find and replace all occurrences automatically. Or choose Find Next if you want to find the first and then next occurrence of the characters; then choose Replace to replace the specified characters. After you choose Replace, Excel automatically finds the next occurrence.

9. When finished, choose Close.

Enter the characters you want to use in place of the characters in the Find What box.

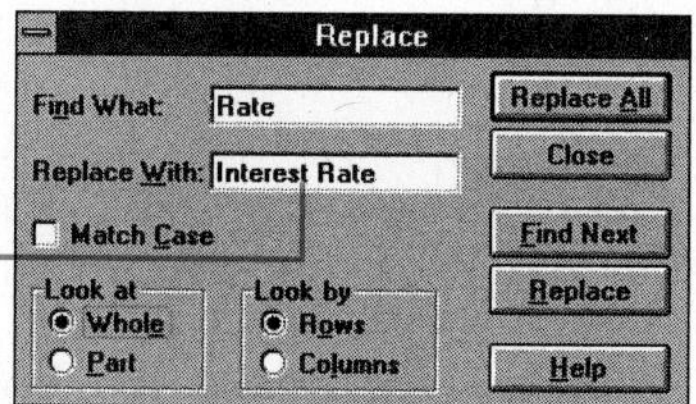

Figure 46.2 The Replace dialog box.

Caution: Replace All replaces all occurrences in the worksheet area you selected (or the entire worksheet if you don't select a range). To reverse the Replace All command, after selecting Close, choose Edit Undo Replace or hold down Ctrl and press Z.

Tip: If the worksheet location that you want to search is named, press F5, and the Goto dialog box appears. You can specify the cell location or name in the Reference box and then choose OK or press Enter. Excel will select the specified cell or range.

Transposing Data in a Range

When building worksheets, you may need to reposition data in a worksheet so that a column range of data is displayed in a row range or vice versa. Repositioning data in a column range to a row range format or from a row to a column format is called *transposition*. Excel allows you to transpose data with the **E**dit **C**opy and **E**dit Paste **S**pecial commands. For example, Figure 46.3 shows a Sales Budget with data in column ranges. The data may need to be spread horizontally across a budget to make it easier to prepare a purchases and cash budget, which is traditionally prepared horizontally. The ranges A4:A15, B4:B15, and C4:C15 contain the months, unit sales, and dollar sales in column ranges. Displaying these items horizontally means that they must be transposed into row ranges. Figure 46.4 shows the results of transposing the data from Figure 46.3 so that it is displayed horizontally (in rows).

To transpose ranges from columns to rows or from rows to columns, follow these steps:

Transposing Data:

1. Select cells to transpose.
2. Choose Edit Copy.
3. Select upper left cell of paste area.
4. Choose Edit Paste Special.
5. Select Transpose.
6. Choose OK.

To copy a range, select the range and select the Copy tool from the Utility toolbar.

1. Select the cells you want to transpose.

2. Choose Edit Copy. A moving border appears around your selection.

3. Select the upper left cell of the paste area.

4. Choose Edit Paste Special. As shown in Figure 46.5, the Paste Special dialog box appears.

5. Select Transpose.

6. Choose OK and press Enter.

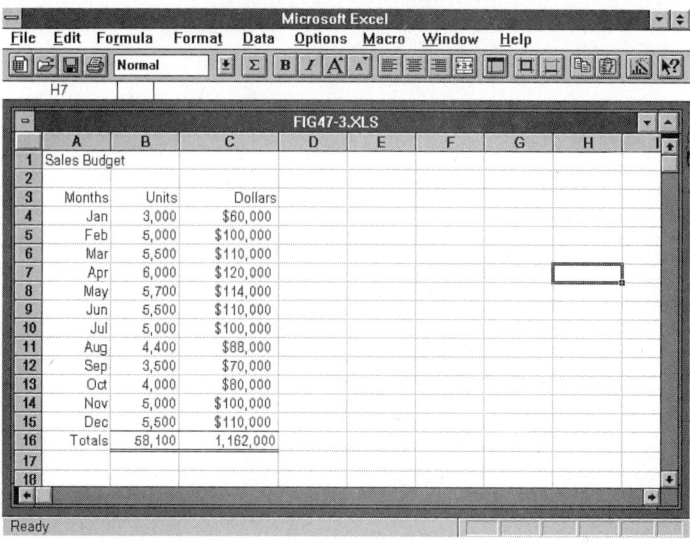

Microsoft Excel — FIG47-3.XLS

	A	B	C
1	Sales Budget		
2			
3	Months	Units	Dollars
4	Jan	3,000	$60,000
5	Feb	5,000	$100,000
6	Mar	5,500	$110,000
7	Apr	6,000	$120,000
8	May	5,700	$114,000
9	Jun	5,500	$110,000
10	Jul	5,000	$100,000
11	Aug	4,400	$88,000
12	Sep	3,500	$70,000
13	Oct	4,000	$80,000
14	Nov	5,000	$100,000
15	Dec	5,500	$110,000
16	Totals	58,100	1,162,000

Figure 46.3 Sales budget with its elements displayed in column ranges.

Microsoft Excel - FIG47-3.XLS

	E	F	G	H	I	J	K	L	M	N	O
1											
2											
3	Months	Jan	Feb	Mar	Apr	May	Jun	Jul	Aug	Sep	Oct
4	Units	3,000	5,000	5,500	6,000	5,700	5,500	5,000	4,400	3,500	4,000
5	Dollars	$60,000	$100,000	$110,000	$120,000	$114,000	$110,000	$100,000	$88,000	$70,000	$80,000

Figure 46.4 Transposed data from Figure 46.3 sales budget.

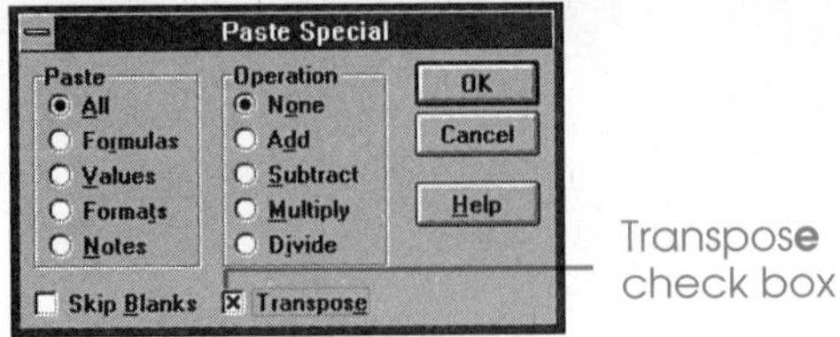

Figure 46.5 The Paste Special dialog box.

Sorting Worksheet Data

You can sort a selected range of cells in a worksheet by using the Data Sort command. Before you sort worksheet cells, you should select the range you want to sort. Only selected cells will be sorted; any unselected cells are not rearranged. To sort a worksheet range follow these steps:

Sorting Worksheet Data:

1. Select range to sort.
2. Choose Data Sort.
3. Select Rows or Columns.
4. Specify sort references.
5. Select Ascending or Descending.
6. Choose OK.

Select the range of cells you want to sort then select the Sort Ascending tool from the Utility toolbar to rearrange the rows of a selection in an ascending order.

1. Select the range you want to sort. (If you are sorting a database, exclude the field names.)
2. Choose Data Sort. The Sort dialog box is displayed.
3. Under Sort By, select the Rows button to sort by rows or the Columns button to sort by columns.
4. In the 1st Key box, enter the reference of your first sort key by typing the reference or by using the mouse to select the first key cell. The 1st Key specifies the column to sort by when sorting rows or the row to sort by when sorting columns. To sort by more than one key, enter references in the 2nd Key and 3rd Key boxes.

5. Select the Ascending or Descending button for each key you specify, to indicate whether you want the sort to be performed in ascending or descending order.

6. Choose OK or press Enter.

Select the range of cells you want to sort then select the Sort Descending tool from the Utility toolbar to rearrange the rows of a selection in descending order.

Using Automatic Range Formatting

In Skill Sessions 13–14, you can learn to apply a variety of formats to ranges of cells. These formats, available through the Excel Format menu, include formatting for numbers, borders, fonts, patterns, alignment, column width, and row height. Formatting ranges involves selecting a range of cells and applying a desired format by choosing Format and then selecting the format. Proper formatting allows you to customize your reports and enhance their message. However, formatting numbers, borders, and fonts is time-consuming. Unless you have developed a good style from prior experience with spreadsheet publishing, the results of formatting are often disappointing. Improper use of number formats and inappropriate mixes of fonts and borders can create "noisy" or busy-looking reports that diminish the intended message.

Excel includes a handy feature called AutoFormat, which automatically formats a range of cells using one of several built-in table formats. These built-in formats are well-designed and can give your reports a professional look. To format a range of cells using AutoFormat, follow these steps:

Formatting a Range Using AutoFormat:

1. Select range to format.
2. Choose Format AutoFormat.
3. Select an automatic format.
4. (Optional) Select Options and clear check boxes of options not to change.
5. Select OK.

1. Select the range you want to format.
2. Choose Format AutoFormat. As shown in Figure 46.6, the AutoFormat dialog box appears.
3. Under Table Format, select one of the automatic formats. As you select a format, a sample of the format is displayed in the Sample box.
4. (Optional) Select Options. The options shown in Figure 46.7 are displayed. These options are explained in Table 46.1. Clear the check boxes for the types of formatting you don't want to change. As you turn on or off an option, the effect is shown in the Sample box.
5. Select OK or press Enter.

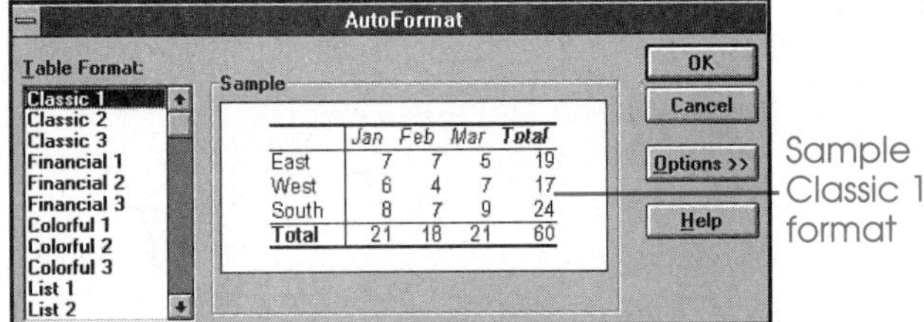

Figure 46.6 The AutoFormat dialog box.

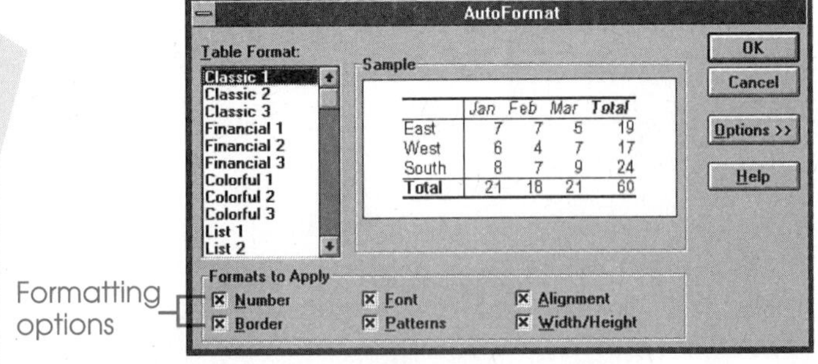

Figure 46.7 The AutoFormat dialog box with options displayed.

Table 46.1 Summary of AutoFormat options

Option	*Description*
Number	Determines how numbers, currency, dates, and times are displayed in selected cells.
Border	Adds solid border lines, shading, or both in certain cells.
Font	Determines fonts for text in certain cells.
Alignment	Determines alignment for the contents of certain cells.
Width/Height	Determines the width of certain columns and the height of certain rows.
Patterns	Determines the fill pattern of cells.

When performing an AutoFormat command, Excel may display a message telling you that it could not detect a table around the active cell. This happens when you have selected only one cell that has no adjacent nonblank cells. To correct this situation, select the desired range and choose Forma**t** AutoFor**m**at again. If you select one cell in a range of adjacent nonblank cells, AutoFormat selects the entire range, called the *current region*, and applies the selected table format.

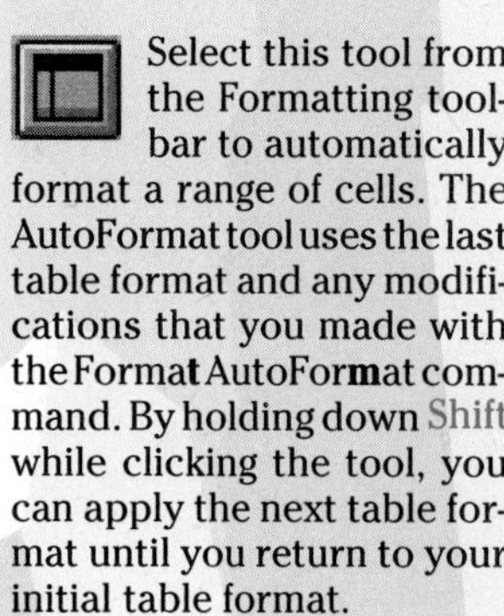

Select this tool from the Formatting toolbar to automatically format a range of cells. The AutoFormat tool uses the last table format and any modifications that you made with the Forma**t** AutoFor**m**at command. By holding down Shift while clicking the tool, you can apply the next table format until you return to your initial table format.

> **In Action:** When working with financial reports, such as the one shown in Figure 46.8, consider formatting the report using the Financial 1 table format. The Financial 1 table format is a traditional style that formats the first and last dollar amounts in a column as currency with no decimal places and double underlines totals.

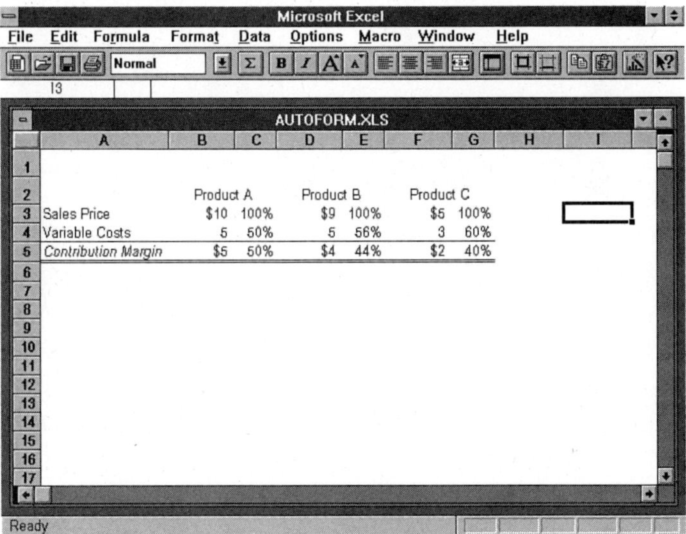

Figure 46.8 A financial report formatted using the Financial 1 table format of AutoFormat.

Creating a Series

When working with large amounts of data, it is sometimes necessary to extend a series of numbers. For example, when creating a list of 350 customers, you may want to assign a number to each customer's record. You could enter the first customer number and then, upon deciding what type of increment you want to use for each of the remaining 349 record numbers, enter the remaining numbers. Fortunately, once you decide what type of incremental increase or decrease you want in a series of numbers, you can extend a data series by using the Data Series command. By choosing Data Series, Excel will enter either numbers or dates that have constant incremental increases or decrease.

The **D**ata Se**r**ies command is particularly useful when entering a series of dates. For example, if you are tracking the value of the stocks in your investment portfolio by valuing them once a week, you could use **D**ata Se**r**ies to enter a series of dates automatically in 7-day increments. To extend a data series, follow these steps:

1. Select the first cell you want in your series.
2. Enter the starting number of the series.
3. Starting with the cell containing the starting number, select the cells in the row or column that you want to fill.
4. Choose Data Series. As shown in Figure 46.9, the Series dialog box is displayed.
5. Under Series in, select either Rows or Columns. Select Rows if you want to fill the series across

Extending a Data Series:

1. Select first cell in series.
2. Enter starting number of series.
3. Select cells in row or column to fill.
4. Choose Data Series.
5. Select Rows or Columns.
6. Select type of series.
7. If you selected **D**ate option, select a unit.
8. Enter **S**tep Value.
9. (Optional) Enter St**o**p Value.
10. Choose OK.

rows or Columns if you want to fill the series down columns.

6. Under Type, select the type of series. The choices of **L**inear, **G**rowth, **D**ate, and Auto**F**ill are summarized in Table 46.2.

7. If you selected the **D**ate option, select a unit of either D**a**y, **W**eekday, **M**onth, or **Y**ear, under Date Unit. The date unit determines whether a series of dates will increase by days, weekdays, months, or years.

8. In the **S**tep Value box, enter a number by which you want to increment the series. A positive number causes the series to increase; a negative number causes it to decrease. If you choose the AutoFill option, the Step Value is ignored.

9. (Optional) To stop the series at a specific number or date, enter the number or date in the St**o**p Value box.

10. Choose OK or press Enter.

Table 46.2 Summary of the type of series options

Type of Series	*Description*
Linear	Adds a step value to each cell value in turn.
Growth	Multiplies the number of each cell in turn by your entry in the **S**tep Value box.
Date	Calculates a series of dates according to your selected option under Date Unit.

Type of Series	Description
AutoFill	Fills blank cells in a selection with a series based on data included in the selection.

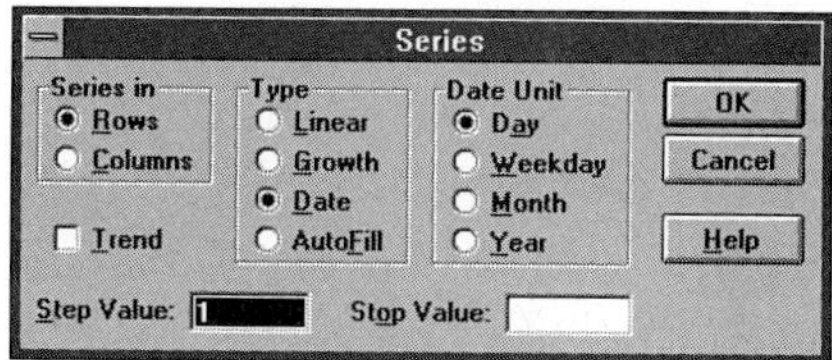

Figure 46.9 The Series dialog box.

You can use the AutoFill feature to extend a series by dragging the fill handle. The fill handle is the small black square at the bottom right of the selection. However, you should experiment with this method because Excel guesses at the type of series you want to create by the data type and incremental changes between cells in your initial selection. Table 46.3 shows some examples of data series guesses made by the AutoFill feature. Figure 46.10 shows the fill handle of a data series of part numbers that have been selected. If that data series is extended using the AutoFill feature, Excel guesses that you want to use a step value of 5.

Table 46.3 Samples of AutoFill operations on a selected cell or range of cells

Data Series in Selection	*Series Created by AutoFill*
1, 2	3, 4, 5, . . .
1, 3	5, 7, 9, 11, . . .
Mon	Tues, Wed, Thurs, . . .
1-Jan, 1-Mar	1-May, 1-Jul, 1-Sept, . . .

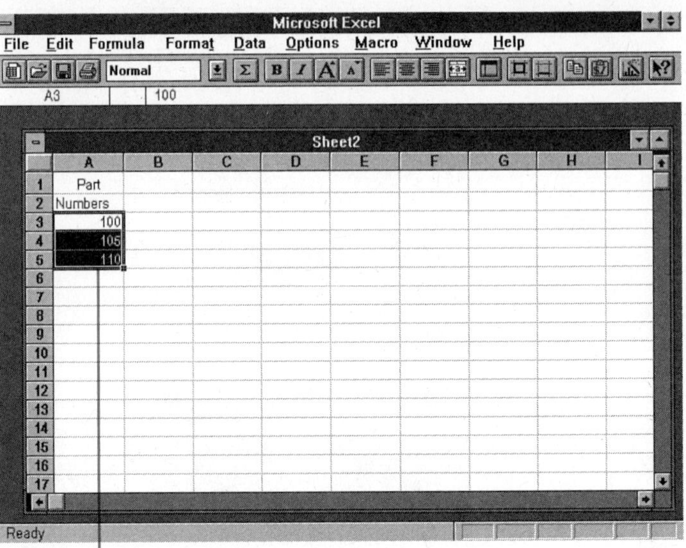

Fill handle of a selected range

Figure 46.10 A selected range.

Extending a Data Series by Dragging the Fill Handle:

1. Enter and select starting numbers.
2. Drag the fill handle to fill.

To use the AutoFill feature to extend a series by dragging follow these steps:

1. Select the first cell you want in your series and enter the starting number, or select two or more cells and enter the first several starting numbers.

2. With the cell or cells selected, drag the fill handle in the direction you want to fill and release the mouse button when you have reached the end of the range you want to fill. The AutoFormat feature will take a guess and fill the range with a series.

Skill Session

47

Advanced Formulas and Functions

This skill session reviews how you can build a formula by pasting a function into a formula and how you can create your own custom functions to make complex calculations easier to perform. In addition, this skill session also details how you can control calculations and audit your worksheets.

Pasting a Function into a Cell

When creating Excel documents, you can use built-in functions to perform calculations. A function, which is also explained in Skill Session 11, performs an operation on a series of numbers and then returns the result of the operation. You can enter functions alone or as part of a formula and can access them through the Formula Paste Function command. Using Formula Paste Function is efficient because it can paste the function into a cell or into a formula, and, therefore, you don't have to type the function.

Pasting a Function:

1. Select cell to enter a function or formula.
2. Choose Formula Paste Function.
3. Select type of function to use.
4. Select function to paste.
5. Select Paste Arguments.
6. Choose OK.

Note: If you selected a function with more than one form, you may have to choose OK twice in step 6—once to close the Paste Function dialog box and again to insert the selected function.

Select the Paste Function tool on the Macro toolbar to open the Paste Function dialog box so that you can paste a function.

Tip: To open the Paste Function dialog box so that you can paste a function, hold down Shift and press F3.

To paste functions, follow these steps:

1. Select the cell where you want to enter a function or where you want to insert it into a formula. If the cell contains a formula, the formula will appear in the formula bar. You must then place the insertion point where you want to insert the function.

2. Choose Formula Paste Function. As shown in Figure 47.1, the Paste Function dialog box appears.

3. In the Function Category box, select the category that describes the type of function you want to use. A list of the functions in the selected category are displayed in the Paste Function box. For example, Figure 47.1 shows that the Financial functions category has been selected in the Function Category box, and the financial functions are listed in the Paste Function box. If you want to view a list of all available functions, select the All in the Function Category box.

4. In the Paste Function box, select the function you want to paste.

5. If you want to include the function's arguments along with the pasted function, select the Paste Arguments check box.

6. Choose OK or press Enter. The function will be pasted into the cell or inserted into a formula. If you are simply pasting the function into a cell (the

formula bar is not currently active), Excel places the function, preceded by an equal sign, in the selected cell and replaces any existing cell contents. The function is displayed in the formula bar, and the first argument is highlighted; you can replace the formulas with the correct text.

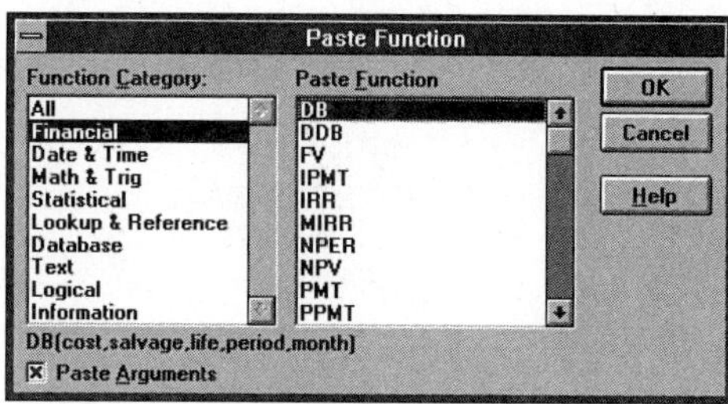

Figure 47.1 The Paste Function dialog box.

In step 5 of the routine of pasting a function, when the Paste **A**rguments check box is checked, a function's argument names will be inserted into the formula bar along with the function's name. For example, Excel pastes SYD(cost,salvage,life,per) for the SYD financial function (which calculates the sum-of-years' digits depreciation for an asset for a specified period) when you select the Paste Arguments check box. Choosing to paste the arguments is an efficient way of entering the arguments. Excel pastes placeholders to remind you that argument values are needed for the function to perform its operation. With the argument placeholders pasted, you can then replace them with actual arguments (e.g., cell references). Otherwise, as shown in Figure 47.2, you can leave the argument names intact and create range names that exactly match the arguments.

When you create range names (by using Formula Define Name or Formula Create Names) that exactly match the argument names, Excel uses the values in the named cells as the argument values. If the Paste **A**rguments check box is unchecked, Excel pastes the function without the arguments. For example, if the Paste **A**rguments check box is unchecked, Excel pastes SYD(), and you must then enter the argument placeholders by entering the actual arguments you want to use.

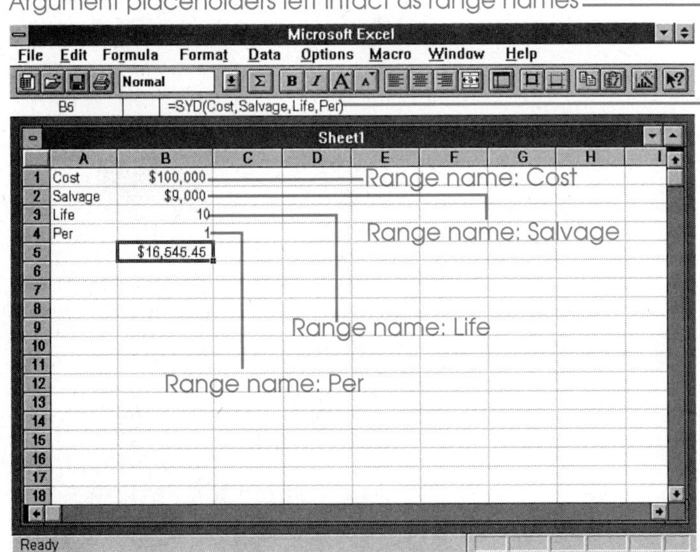

Figure 47.2 Function arguments.

Creating Custom Add-In Functions

You are not limited to the built-in Excel functions. If there is a calculation that you would like to have access to as a function, Excel allows you to build your own customized function. Any formulas or set of formulas that you can enter on a worksheet can be written as a custom function. You create a custom function by entering and saving it on a macro sheet. The three crucial parts of a custom function are the arguments, formulas, and numbers.

Like a built-in function, custom functions need arguments to perform the tasks or operations of the function. As you build the custom function, you must define the arguments by using the Argument function. The **Argument** function syntax is as follows:

ARGUMENT(*name_text,data_type_num,reference*)

Each of the arguments of the Argument function are described in Table 47.1.

Table 47.1 Description of the arguments of the Argument function

Argument	*Description*
name_text	Specifies the argument name (optional argument if you specify a *reference* argument).
data_type_num	Specifies the type data that the user must enter in the custom function argument. Table 47.2 shows a summary of data types.
reference	Specifies a reference to a cell or cell range on the macro sheet (optional argument if you specify a *name_text*).

Table 47.2 Summary of data types that can be used as data_type_num arguments

Number	*Data Type*
1	Number
2	Text
4	Logical
8	Reference
16	Error
64	Array

In addition to defining the arguments of a custom function, you can use the RESULT function to specify a data type for the result of the function. The RESULT function is required if you want the custom function to return an array or a reference. An *array* is a rectangular area of cells that share one common formula. It is used to build formulas that produce multiple results or that operate on a group of arguments arranged in rows or columns. In a later section of this skill session, "Creating and Using an Array Formula," you'll learn how to create and use array formulas.

If you use the result function, it must be the first function in the custom function. The RESULTS function syntax is as follows:

```
RESULT(type_num)
```

The *type_num* argument specifies the data type of the number returned by the custom function.

If you omit the RESULT function, Excel assumes the result type is 7, which is the sum of the data types 1,2, and 3 (numbers, text, and logical) and means that numbers, text, and logical values are allowed.

You build a custom function one row at a time. Excel performs the tasks and calculates the formulas in a custom function—beginning in the first cell of the custom function, and proceeding down the column until it comes upon a RETURN function. A RETURN function returns the result of the custom function to the worksheet or macro sheet in which you use the custom function. The syntax of a RETURN function is as follows:

```
RETURN(reference)
```

The *reference* argument of the RETURN function specifies the cell reference where the function is calculated.

To create a custom function, follow these steps:

1. Use File New or File Open to open a new or exiting macro sheet.
2. To specify the data type to be returned by the custom function, enter the RESULT function as the first function in the macro sheet.
3. Enter the ARGUMENT function for each argument in the custom function.
4. Enter the formulas of the custom function.
5. Enter the RETURN function.
6. Select the first cell of the custom function.
7. Choose Formula Define Name. As shown in Figure 47.3, the Define Name dialog box appears.
8. In the **N**ame box, enter a name for the custom function.
9. To display the custom function name in the Paste Function dialog box, select Function.

Creating a Custom Function:

1. Open macro sheet.
2. Enter RESULT function as first function.
3. Enter ARGUMENT function for each argument.
4. Enter formulas of custom function.
5. Enter RETURN function.
6. Select first cell of custom function.
7. Choose Formula Define Name.
8. Enter name for custom function.
9. Select Function.
10. Select category.
11. Choose OK.
12. Save macro sheet.

10. In the Category box, select a category or enter a new category.

11. Choose OK or press Enter.

12. Use File Save to save the macro sheet, or File Save As to save it under a new name.

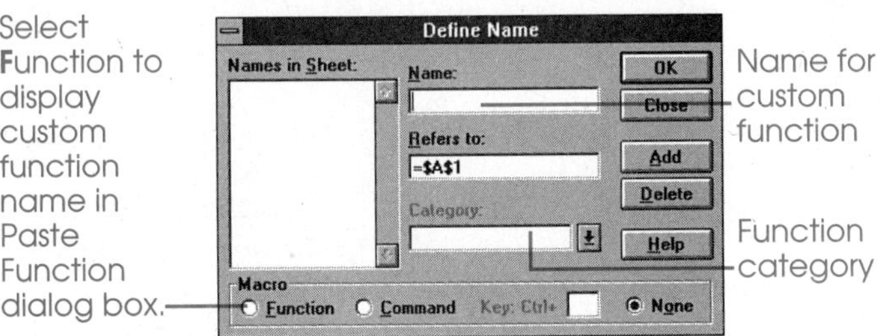

Figure 47.3 The Define Name dialog box.

Creating a Custom Function: An Example

The process of creating a custom function can be confusing; therefore, the following simple example illustrates the process. Assume you want to create a function that calculates the amount you must save each year to accumulate some future amount. This type of calculation is called a *sinking fund*. The sinking fund formula is complex and difficult to remember and, therefore, is a good candidate for a custom function. The sinking fund formula follows:

$$\text{Payment} = \text{Future Value}/((((1+\text{Interest Rate})^{\text{Periods}})-1)/\text{Interest Rate})$$

You can design a custom function that calculates this formula using the following arguments:

Future_Value

Interest_Rate

Periods

To design the sinking fund function, follow these steps:

1. Choose File New. The New dialog box appears.
2. Under New, select Macro Sheet.
3. Choose OK or press Enter.
4. Enter the RESULT function as the first function in the macro sheet. As shown in Figure 47.4, the RESULT function for the sinking fund is `RESULT(1)`. The *type_num* argument is 1 to specify that the data type of the sinking fund function is a number.
5. Enter the ARGUMENT function for each argument (Future_Value, Interest_Rate, and Periods) in the custom sinking fund function. In Figure 47.4 the arguments are shown in cells A3:A5.
6. Enter the formula. In Figure 47.4 the formula is shown in cell A6.
7. Enter the RETURN function. For the sinking fund function, the RETURN function is **`RETURN(A6)`**, which tells Excel that the value to return for the function is in cell A6.
8. Select the first cell of the custom function, which in this case is A2.
9. Choose Formula Define Name.
10. In the **N**ame box, enter a name for the custom function, which in this case is **`Sink`**.

Creating a Custom Function:

1. Choose File New.
2. Select Macro Sheet.
3. Choose OK.
4. Enter RESULT function.
5. Enter ARGUMENT function for each argument.
6. Enter formula.
7. Enter RETURN function.
8. Select first cell of custom function.
9. Choose Formula Define Name.
10. In the **N**ame box, enter name for custom function.
11. Select the Function option.
12. In the Category box, select a category.
13. Choose OK.
14. Use File Save As to save the macro sheet.

11. To display the custom function name in the Paste Function dialog box, select Function.

12. In the Category box, select a category. Because the Sink function calculates an annuity payment, the Financial category is an appropriate selection.

13. Choose OK or press Enter.

14. Use File Save to save the macro sheet or File Save As to save it under a new name.

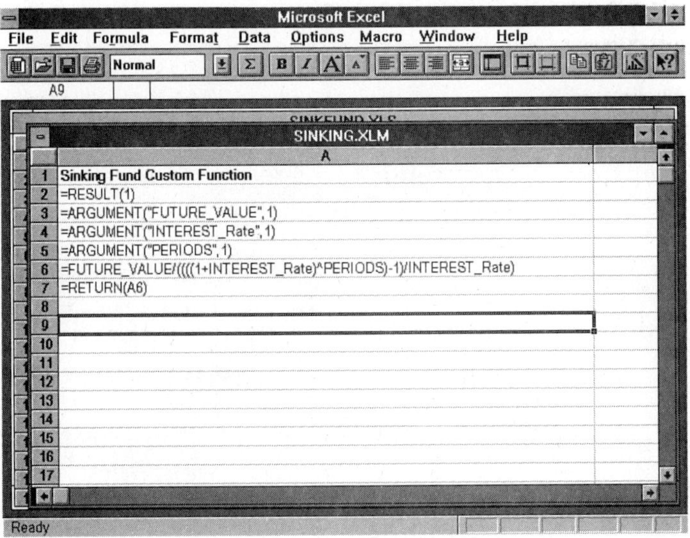

Figure 47.4 The Sink custom function.

Figure 47.5 shows the Sink custom function in action. It was used to calculate the amount that would have to be saved each year, for 5 years, at 9% interest, to have $10,000 accumulated. Notice the syntax of the Sink function in B4:

```
=SINKING.XLM!Sink(Future_Value,Interest_Rate,
Periods)
```

The *SINKING.XLM!* refers to the macro sheet that contains the custom function and is pasted as part of the function when you use Paste Function.

Note: In order to use a custom function, the macro sheet must be open.

In Action: Consider the types of calculations that you frequently perform. Ask yourself if some of these calculations could be designed as custom functions. If your commonly used calculations and formulas can be created as custom functions, the advantage is that you can paste them into your worksheet as needed.

Results of Sink custom function　　Custom function syntax

Microsoft Excel

File Edit Formula Format Data Options Macro Window Help

B4 =SINKING.XLM!sink(Future_Value,Interest_Rate,Periods)

SINKFUND.XLS

	A	B
1	Future Value	$10,000
2	Interest Rate	9%
3	Periods	5
4	Sinking Fund Amount	$1,671

Ready

Figure 47.5 The Sink custom function in action.

Creating and Using an Array Formula

Worksheets often contain rectangular ranges of data called arrays. For example, the range B3:D4 in Figure 47.6 is an array. If you need to perform calculations on a rectangular range of cells, you may create an *array formula*. Array formulas are time and memory savers. Rather than entering a series of similar formulas, a time- and memory-consuming process, you can use the array formula to enter one formula that will perform and repeat the same calculation on all cell ranges.

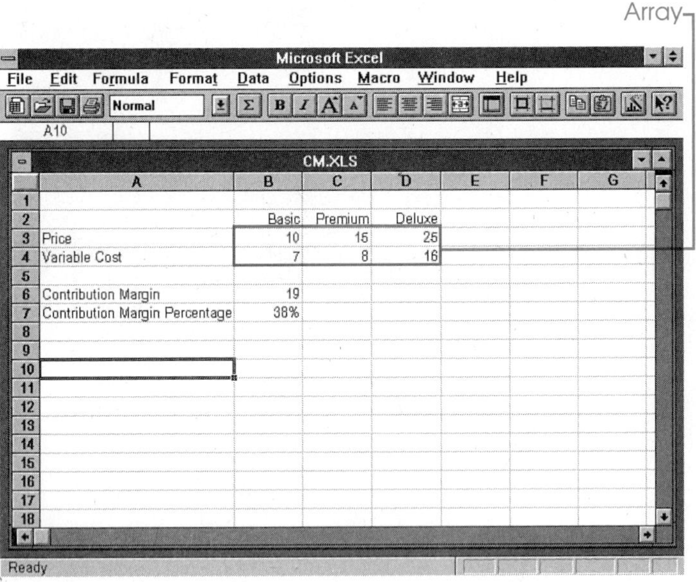

Figure 47.6 An array.

With a rectangular range of values entered on a worksheet, you can enter an array formula by following these steps:

1. Select the cell or range of cells in which you want to enter the array formula.

2. Enter the formula using normal formula-building methods.

3. Hold down the Ctrl and Shift keys and press Enter to enter the array formula into the cell or cells. Excel will place braces ({ }) around the array formula.

Figure 47.7 shows an array formula in cell B6 that calculates the contribution margin of a product line. The contribution margin is the sale price less the variable costs. The B6 contribution margin array formula reads as follows:

```
{=SUM(B3:D3-B4:D4)}
```

The array formula subtracts the total variable costs (B4:D4) from the sum of the selling prices (B3:D3). The result of a contribution margin of the $19 could have also been calculated in a series of formulas. The array formula accomplished the same result in one formula, however.

Another example of an array formula is shown in cell B7 of Figure 47.8, where the formula {=SUM(B3:D3-B4:D4)/SUM(B3:D3)} calculates the contribution margin percentage (Contribution margin/Total Sales Price). Notice that it finds the difference between the sums of two ranges (=SUM(B3:D3-B4:D4)) and divides that result by the sum of another range (SUM(B3:D3)) by using one formula that uses references all within the B3:D4 array.

Entering an Array Formula:

1. Select cells to enter the array formula.
2. Enter formula.
3. Hold down Ctrl and Shift and press Enter.

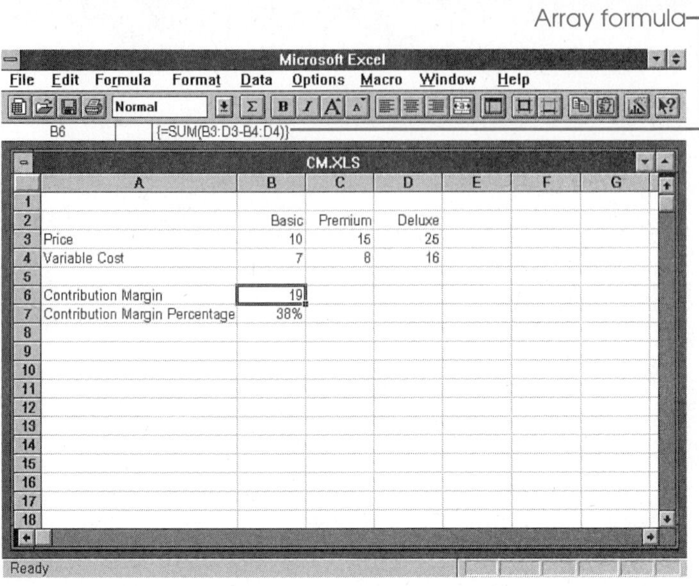

Figure 47.7 Using the array formula to calculate a contribution margin.

Tip: To edit an array formula, select any cell in the array range (the range that contains the array formula), click to the formula bar, edit the formula as you would any type of formula, and then hold down the Ctrl and Shift keys and press Enter to enter the formula back into the cell(s).

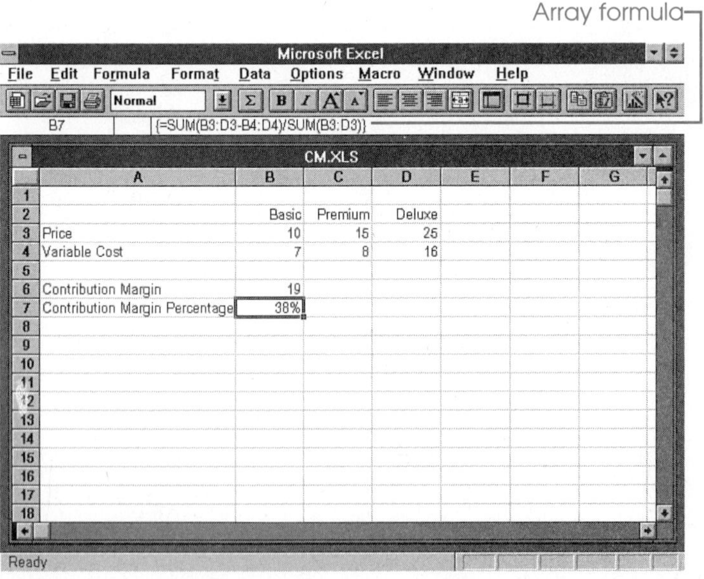

Figure 47.8 Another example of an array formula.

Controlling Calculations

By default, worksheets calculate automatically, each time you change the value in a cell. However, you can control the way that Excel calculates. For example, you can set Excel to calculate only upon your request, which is called *manual calculation* or to calculate all formulas in a worksheet automatically except for those in data tables. To control calculation, review the options available in Table 47.3 and follow these steps:

1. Choose Options Calculation. As shown in Figure 47.9, the Calculations Options dialog box appears.
2. Select the calculation options, as described in Table 47.3.
3. Choose OK or press Enter.

Setting Calculation Options for Open Worksheets:

1. Choose Options Calculation.
2. Select calculation options.
3. Choose OK.

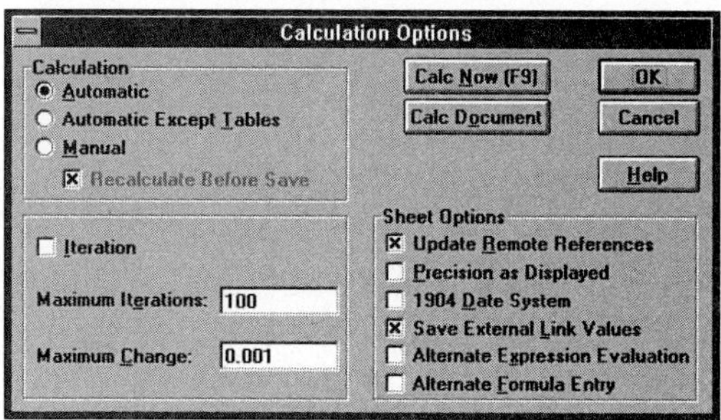

Figure 47.9 The Calculation Options dialog box.

You can also begin manual recalculation by holding down the Ctrl key and pressing the equal sign (=) or by just pressing F9. To calculate only the active worksheet and update only the charts on the worksheet and open charts linked to the worksheet, hold down the Shift key and press F9.

Table 47.3 Summary of Excel calculation options

Option	*Description*
Automatic	Calculates all dependent formulas every time you make a change to a number, formula, or name.
Automatic Except **T**ables	Calculates all dependent formulas except data tables. You can calculate tables by choosing Calc **N**ow in the Calculations Options dialog box or by pressing F9.
Manual	Calculates open documents only when you choose Calc **N**ow in the Calculations Options dialog box or press F9. (Note: When you choose **M**anual calculation, the Recalculate Before **S**ave check box of the Calculations Options dialog box is automatically selected.)
Iteration	Limits iteration for goal seeking or for resolving circular references. An iteration is one round of calculation. Some calculations require more than one iteration. Unless you specify otherwise, Excel stops after 100 iterations or when all values change by less than 0.001. You can limit iteration by changing Maximum It**e**rations, Maximum **C**hange, or both.
Calc **N**ow	Calculates all open worksheets, including data tables, and updates all open chart documents.
Calc D**o**cument	Calculates only the active worksheet and updates only the charts on the worksheet and open charts linked to the worksheet.

Option	*Description*
Update **R**emote References	Calculates formulas that include references to other applications. When cleared, formulas use the last number received from the other application.
Precision as Displayed	Changes stored numbers in cells from full precision (15 digits) to whatever format is displayed. The displayed numbers are then used for calculations.
1904 **D**ate System	Changes the starting date from which all dates are calculated from January 1, 1900 to January 2, 1904.
Save External **L**ink Values	Saves copies of numbers contained in an external document linked to your worksheet.
Alternate **Ex**pression Evaluation	Evaluates text strings to 0, Boolean expressions to 0 or 1, and database criteria according to the rules used in Lotus 1-2-3.
Alternate **F**ormula Entry	Converts formulas entered with Lotus 1-2-3 syntax into Microsoft Excel syntax.

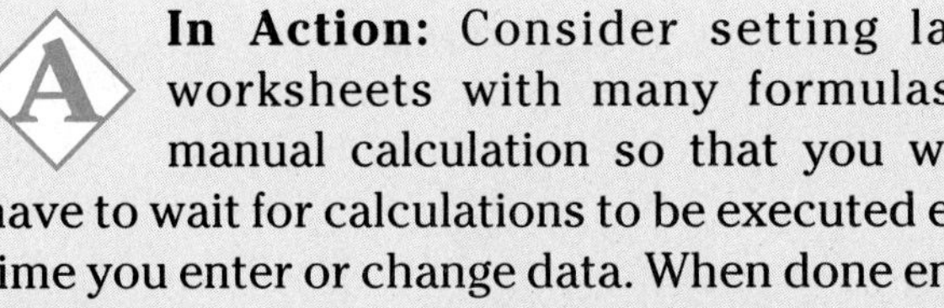

In Action: Consider setting large worksheets with many formulas to manual calculation so that you won't have to wait for calculations to be executed each time you enter or change data. When done entering data, set back to automatic to calculate your formulas.

To begin a manual recalculation select the Calculate Now tool, which is found in the Utility toolbar.

Auditing Worksheets

Excel contains an add-in macro named AUDIT.XLA, which is called the Worksheet Auditor. The Worksheet Auditor can help you find errors and understand the structure and data flow of the worksheet. The output of the Worksheet Auditor is a series of reports that the Auditor generates by creating a new worksheet of audit results. Descriptions of the four reports generated by the Worksheet Auditor Macro are shown in Table 47.4.

Table 47.4 Reports generated by the Worksheet Auditor

Report	*Description of Report*
Audit Report	A report of potential errors on your worksheet (e.g., cells with error values, references to blank cells, references to cells containing text, all cells that are part of circular references, and questionable or potentially unused worksheet names).
Map	A report that is a map of your worksheet's contents.
Interactive Trace	A report of cell dependencies in your worksheet.
Worksheet Info	A report of detailed information about your worksheet (e.g., the document name, path, protection status, version of Excel, name of operating system, size of active area, and number of hidden cells).

To generate a Worksheet Audit report, decide on the type of report you want (see Table 47.4) and then follow these steps:

1. Choose File Open and open the Worksheet Auditor add-in macro named AUDIT.XLA, which is found in the LIBRARY directory in the directory in which you installed Excel. LIBRARY is a subdirectory of your Excel program directory.

2. Choose Formula Worksheet Auditor. (Note: Worksheet Auditor will appear as a choice under the Formula menu only if you opened AUDIT.XLA.) As shown in Figure 47.10, the Worksheet Auditor dialog box appears.

3. Under Worksheet Auditor, select one of the four reports choices: Generate Audit Report, Map Worksheet, Interactive Trace, or Worksheet Information, as described in Table 47.4.

4. Choose OK or press Enter. If your report choice is either Map Worksheet or Worksheet Information, the Worksheet Auditor opens a new sheet and generates the report. If your choice of report is either the Audit Report or the Interactive Trace, go on to step 5.

5. If you selected Generate Audit Report in the Audit Report dialog box, clear the check boxes for the types of auditing you don't want included in the report. Table 47.5 describes the types of audits available. If you selected Interactive Trace in the Interactive Trace control panel, choose the command buttons for the cell dependencies you want to trace.

Generating a Worksheet Audit Report:

1. Open Worksheet Auditor add-in macro named AUDIT.XLA.
2. Choose Formula Worksheet Auditor.
3. Select a report choice.
4. Choose OK.
5. Select type of auditing or choose command buttons for the cell dependencies to trace.
6. Choose OK.

6. If you selected either Generate Audit Report or Interactive Trace, choose OK to generate the report.

Figure 47.10 The Worksheet Auditor dialog box.

Tip: To get a quick overview of the structure of your worksheet, follow these steps to generate a map of the worksheet:

1. Choose Formula Worksheet Auditor.
2. Select **M**ap Worksheet.
3. Choose OK.

Table 47.5 Description of types of audits generated by Worksheet Auditor (Generate Audit Report)

Types of Audits	*Description of Audit*
Errors	Cells with error values
Reference to **B**lank	Formulas that refer to blank cells
References To **T**ext	Formulas that refer to cells containing text
Circular Reference	All cells that are part of circular references
Names	Questionable or potentially unused worksheet names

An example of a map of a worksheet is shown in Figure 47.11.

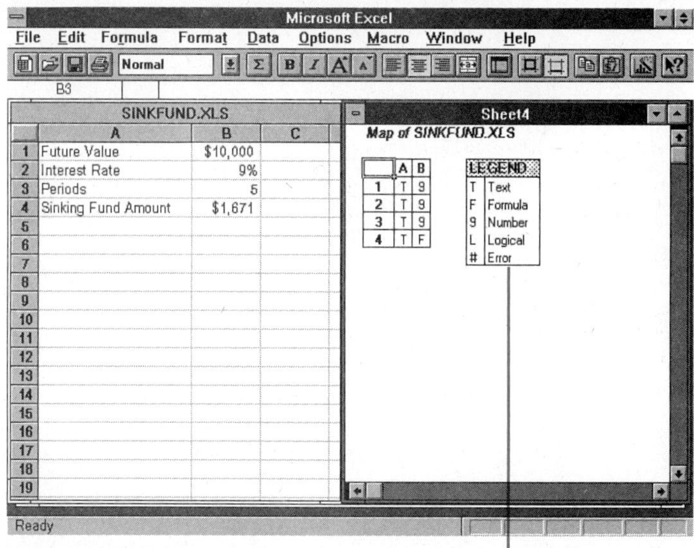

Figure 47.11 A map of a worksheet.

> **In Action:** If developing worksheet applications is a relatively new practice for you, consider using the Worksheet Auditor each time you complete a worksheet. Not only will the Auditor help identify errors or potential problems, but it may also help you develop a proper worksheet style. For example, the Map report, which looks at worksheet layout, can disclose faulty positioning of the input, calculation, and output sections of your worksheet.

Managing the Toolbars

Excel initially displays only the Standard toolbar. You can display any of the other toolbars as you need them. You can also customize toolbars to meet your needs more precisely. In this skill session, you'll learn how to add a tool to or delete it from a toolbar and how to create new customized toolbars.

Adding a Tool to a Toolbar

You can customize a toolbar so that it includes any group of tools. If the current grouping of tools is not serving most of your needs, you can add tools to the toolbar by following these steps:

Adding a Tool to the Toolbar:

1. Choose Customize.
2. Select category of tools.
3. Position tool on a displayed toolbar.

Tip: To move a tool to a new location on the toolbar, choose Customize from the toolbar shortcut menu and then drag the tool to the new location on the same toolbar. You can also use this same procedure to move a tool from one toolbar to another displayed toolbar.

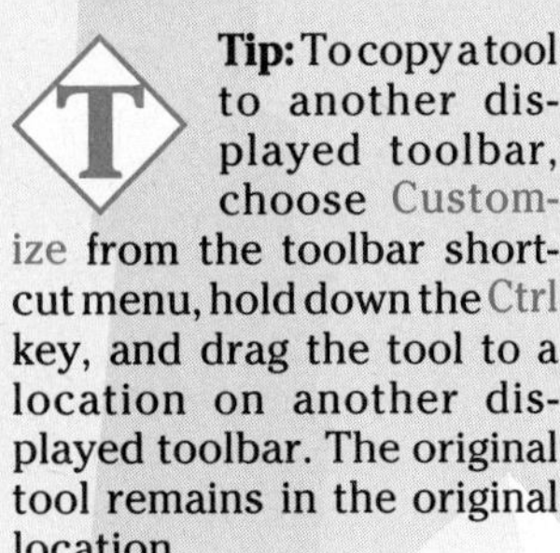

Tip: To copy a tool to another displayed toolbar, choose Customize from the toolbar shortcut menu, hold down the Ctrl key, and drag the tool to a location on another displayed toolbar. The original tool remains in the original location.

Note: When you delete a built-in tool from the toolbar, it is not permanently deleted, only removed from the toolbar itself.

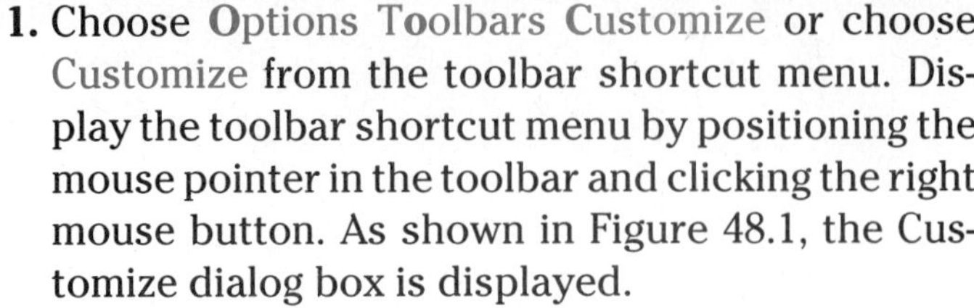

1. Choose **O**ptions T**o**olbars **C**ustomize or choose Customize from the toolbar shortcut menu. Display the toolbar shortcut menu by positioning the mouse pointer in the toolbar and clicking the right mouse button. As shown in Figure 48.1, the Customize dialog box is displayed.

2. In the **C**ategories box, select the category of tools from which you want to add tools. Excel displays the tools icons for that category in the Tools box. (Note: To display a description of a tool, click on the tool icon in the Tools box.)

3. Drag the tool from the Tools box to the position on a displayed toolbar where you want to add the tool. Excel resizes the toolbar to make room for the added tool. Make sure the toolbar you want to customize is displayed on the screen.

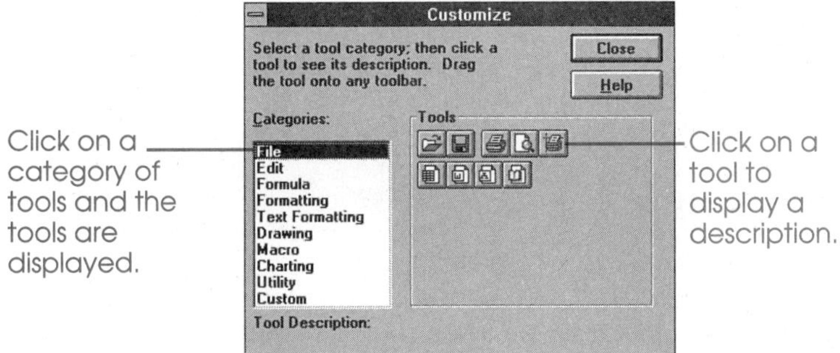

Figure 48.1 The Customize dialog box.

Deleting a Tool from a Toolbar

You can edit a toolbar by deleting tools that you rarely use. To delete a tool from a toolbar, you can either drag it or use the Toolbar menu. Both methods are detailed here.

To delete a tool from a toolbar by dragging it, follow these steps:

1. From the **O**ptions menu or the toolbar shortcut menu, choose Toolbars.
2. Drag the tool off the toolbar and place it anywhere there is no toolbar. The tool disappears from the toolbar.

To delete a tool from the toolbar using a menu command, follow these steps:

1. From the **O**ptions menu or the toolbar shortcut menu, choose Toolbars.
2. Select the tool that you want to delete.
3. Position the mouse pointer on the tool that you want to delete, and click with the right mouse button. The shortcut menu appears.
4. Choose Delete Tool. The tool disappears from the toolbar.

Deleting a Tool from a Toolbar by Dragging It:

1. Choose Toolbars.
2. Drag tool off toolbar.

Deleting a Tool from the Toolbar Using a Menu Command:

1. Choose Toolbars.
2. Select tool to delete.
3. Click with right mouse button.
4. Choose Delete Tool.

Note: The mouse pointer must be on a tool in order for the Delete Tool command to be displayed.

Caution: When you delete a customized tool, it is permanently deleted. If you want to delete a custom tool from a toolbar but want it available for future use, create a toolbar for storing unused tools and then move the tool that you want to delete to this storage toolbar. Custom tools are created to run macros. For more information on this topic, see the section of Skill Session 54 entitled "Creating a Custom Tool." Remember: you cannot delete built-in tools permanently; they are only removed from the toolbar.

Creating a New Customized Toolbar

Excel provides over 130 tools that are initially displayed in one of nine built-in toolbars. As you work with Excel, you may find that the groupings of tools within each of the nine toolbars do not always provide you with the proper mix of tools. As you may have seen in the earlier sections of this skill session, you can add and delete tools from toolbars to design toolbars that meet your needs. You can also create a new toolbar from scratch and include in it any grouping of tools. After you create a new toolbar, you can display it when you need its unique mix of tools. After you have created a toolbar, you cannot rename it without deleting it and recreating it.

Creating a New Toolbar:

1. Choose Toolbars.
2. Type name of new toolbar.
3. Choose Customize.
4. Select category of tools.
5. Position tool on new toolbar.
6. Repeat steps 4–5 to add more tools.
7. Choose Close.

To create a new toolbar, follow these steps:

1. From the **O**ptions menu or the toolbar shortcut menu, choose T**o**olbars. As shown in Figure 48.2, the Toolbars dialog box is displayed.
2. In the Toolbar **N**ame box, type the name you want to assign to the new toolbar.
3. Choose **A**dd or **C**ustomize. As shown in Figure 48.3, the Customize dialog box appears, and Excel displays a new blank toolbar so that you can add tools to the new toolbar.
4. In the **C**ategories box, select the category of tools from which you want to add tools to the new toolbar. The tools for the selected category are shown in the Tools box.
5. Drag the tool from the Tools box to the position on the new toolbar where you want to add the tool.

You can also drag tools from a displayed toolbar to the new toolbar. This moves the tool from the original toolbar to the new toolbar. If you want to copy a tool from a displayed toolbar, without affecting the original toolbar, hold down the Ctrl key while you drag the tool to the new toolbar. As shown in Figure 48.4, the new toolbar expands as you add tools to it.

6. Repeat steps 4–5 until you have added all the tools you want. (If you change your mind, you can remove the tool from the toolbar by dragging it off the toolbar and placing it anywhere there is no toolbar.)

7. When finished building your new toolbar, Choose Close and the new toolbar will be saved.

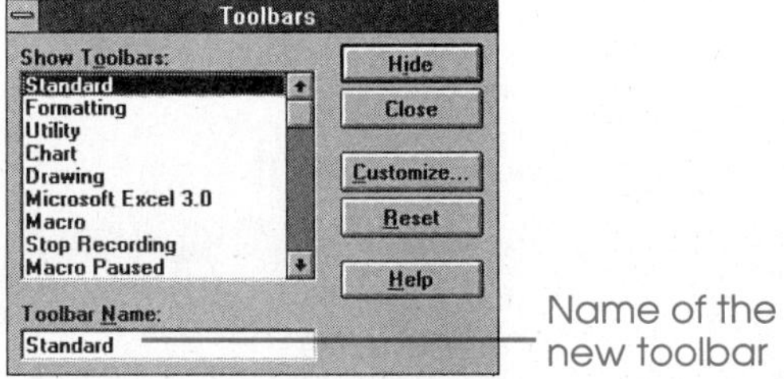

Figure 48.2 The Toolbars dialog box.

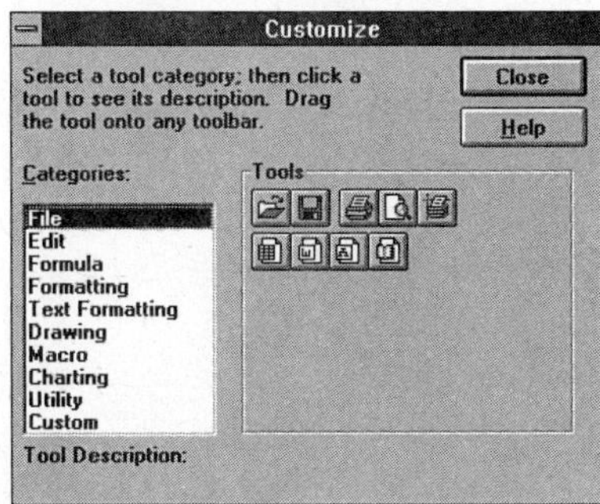

Figure 48.3 The Customize dialog box.

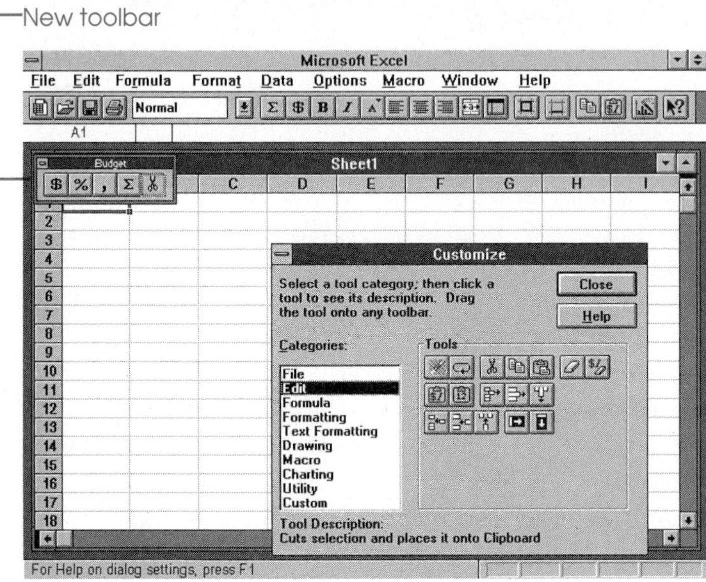

Figure 48.4 New toolbar expands to make room for new tools.

Tip: When you use the shortcut menu, you need only select the toolbar itself to display that toolbar.

When you want to display a custom toolbar, from the **O**ptions menu or the toolbar shortcut menu, choose T**o**olbars to display the Toolbar dialog box. Under Show T**o**olbars, select the toolbar and then select **S**how.

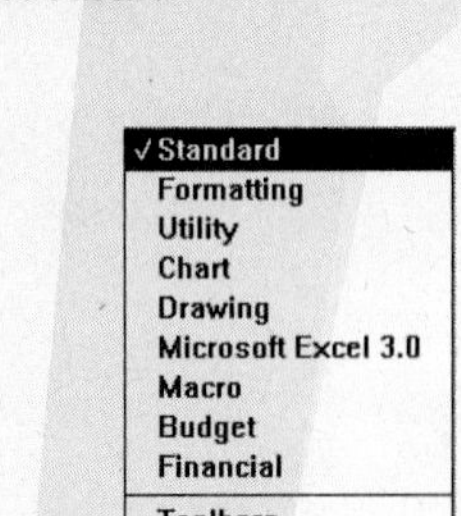

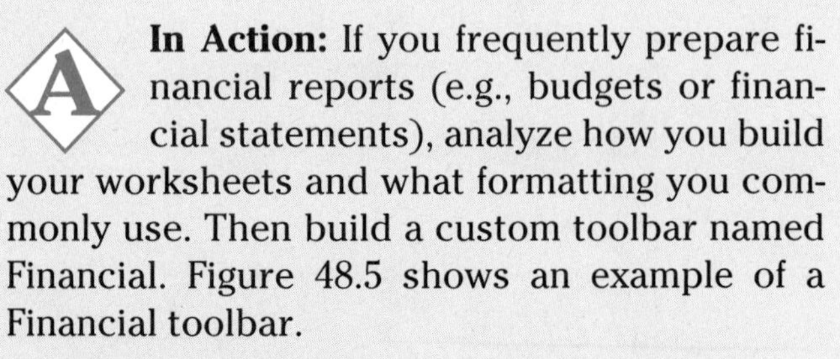

In Action: If you frequently prepare financial reports (e.g., budgets or financial statements), analyze how you build your worksheets and what formatting you commonly use. Then build a custom toolbar named Financial. Figure 48.5 shows an example of a Financial toolbar.

Figure 48.5 Custom toolbar named Financial.

To create a new toolbar by dragging, follow these steps:

Creating a New Toolbar by Dragging:

1. Choose Toolbars.
2. Choose Customize.
3. Select category of tools.
4. Position tool from Tools box where there is no toolbar.

1. From the **O**ptions menu or the toolbar shortcut menu, choose T**o**olbars.

2. Choose **C**ustomize.

3. In the **C**ategories box, select the category of tools from which you want to add tools to the new toolbar. The tools for the selected category are shown in the Tools box.

4. Drag a tool from the Tools box out of the dialog box and place it where there is no toolbar, or hold down the Ctrl key and drag a tool from a displayed toolbar. Excel creates a toolbar for the tool and names it Toolbar 1 or, if Toolbar 1 already exists, Toolbar 2, and so on.

Deleting a Custom Toolbar

If you want to delete a custom toolbar, keep in mind that a deletion cannot be undone. To delete a custom toolbar, use the following steps:

Deleting a Custom Toolbar:

1. Choose Toolbars.
2. Select custom toolbar to delete.
3. Select Delete.
4. Choose Close.

1. From the **O**ptions menu or the toolbar shortcut menu, choose T**o**olbars. The Toolbars dialog box appears.

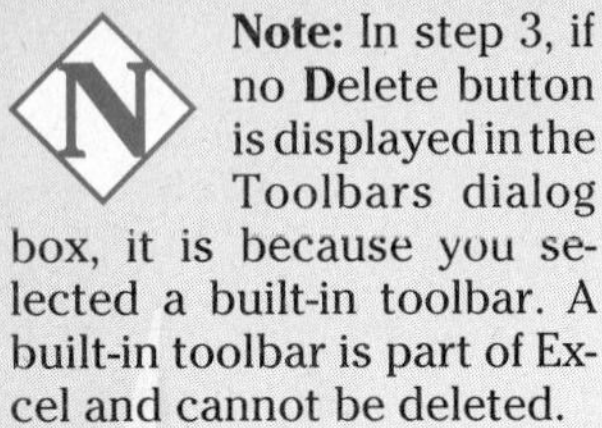

Note: In step 3, if no **D**elete button is displayed in the Toolbars dialog box, it is because you selected a built-in toolbar. A built-in toolbar is part of Excel and cannot be deleted.

2. In the Show T**o**olbars box, select the custom toolbar that you want to delete.

3. Select **D**elete; Excel displays a prompt asking you to verify the deletion. Answer accordingly to the prompt. The custom toolbar is removed from the Show T**o**olbars box.

4. Choose Close.

Grouping Tools in a Toolbar

Grouping Tools in a Toolbar:

1. Choose Toolbars.
2. Position tool in the toolbar.
3. Release mouse button.

The grouping of tools in a toolbar is a way of organizing tools so that they are easier to find. For example, you could position formatting tools in one grouping and file tools in another.

To group tools follow these steps:

1. From the **O**ptions menu or the toolbar shortcut menu, choose Toolbars.

2. On the toolbar, drag the tool that you want to group with another tool toward that tool.

3. Release the mouse button when you have positioned the tool where you want it in the toolbar.

If there is a space between two tools that you would like to delete, use the steps previously detailed to move the tools so that their borders are touching.

Skill Session

49

Using Goal Seeker

Sometimes problem solving involves setting a goal and then working backward to see what it takes to reach the goal. Excel has a feature called Goal Seeker that can help you find an unknown value that will make goal achievement possible. In other words, the Goal Seeker solves for one unknown variable. In this skill session, you will learn how to use the Goal Seeker to reach your goals by finding solutions to unknown variables.

The Goal Seeker

The Goal Seeker is useful when the goal you are trying to achieve is well defined and you have only one variable that you want to vary to achieve the goal. Assume, for example, that you have a product that sells for $15 and has a variable cost per unit of $3 and that your business has $30,000 of fixed costs. You could use the Goal Seeker to compute the number of units that you need to sell to break even.

The *breakeven point* is where the number of units sold produces revenue that is exactly equal to total costs (fixed costs plus total variable costs). At the breakeven point, there is neither a profit nor a loss. The number of units to be sold to break even is the unknown variable that Excel will find when you choose Formula Goal Seek.

Solving for an Unknown Variable

Finding a Solution Using Goal Seeker:

1. Select cell containing desired formula.
2. Choose Formula Goal Seek.
3. Enter target value.
4. Enter cell reference of unknown variable.
5. Choose OK.
6. Choose OK.

To solve for an unknown variable using goal seeking, follow these steps:

1. Select the cell containing the formula for which you want to find a specific solution. For example, Figure 49.1 shows that cell B4 has been selected so that the breakeven point can be calculated by having the goal seeker calculate the number of units that need to be sold to make the value in B4 (Operating Income) equal to zero.

2. Choose Formula Goal Seek. As shown in Figure 49.2, the Set Cell box in the Goal Seek dialog box displays the cell selected in step 1.

3. In the To value box, enter the target value. In Figure 49.3, `0` was entered in the To value box to set the operating income equal to zero in order to calculate the breakeven point.

4. In the By changing cell box, enter the reference of the cell whose value you want Excel to change to achieve the desired result. In Figure 49.3, the B6 cell reference for units sold was entered. Note: The cell you enter in the By changing cell box must be one that the formula referred to in the Set cell box depends on, and it must contain a number, not a formula.

5. Choose OK or press Enter. As shown in Figure 49.4, Excel displays the Goal Seek Status dialog box, which tells you if a solution has been reached.

6. If Excel reaches the solution you want for your formula, choose OK or press Enter. Excel enters the solution value in the cell that you referenced in the By changing cell box in step 4. If you don't want to accept the Goal Seeker solution, select Cancel to restore the original value.

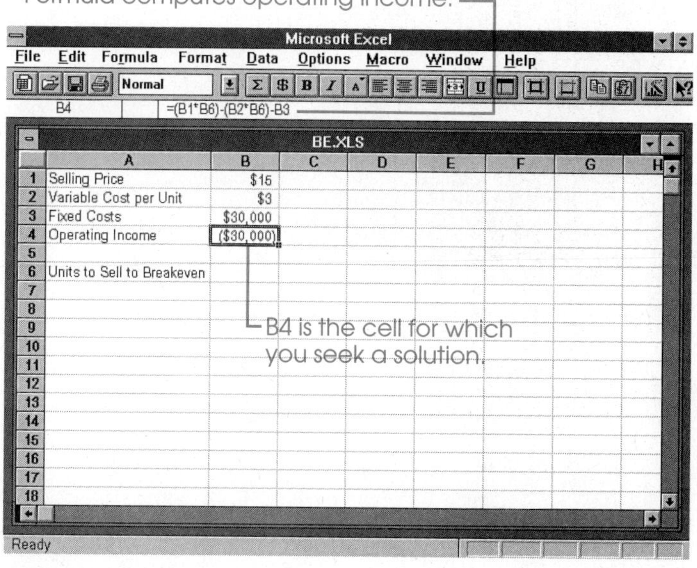

Figure 49.1 Breakeven point example.

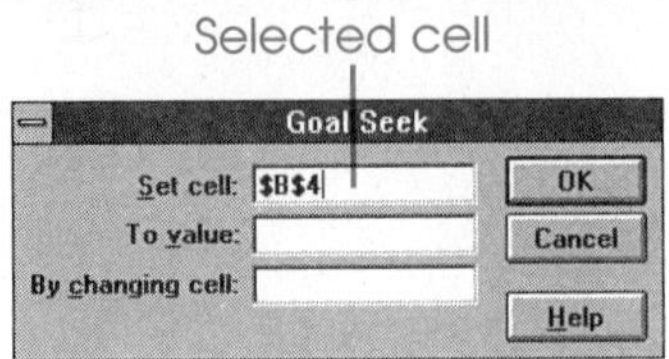

Figure 49.2 Goal Seek dialog box.

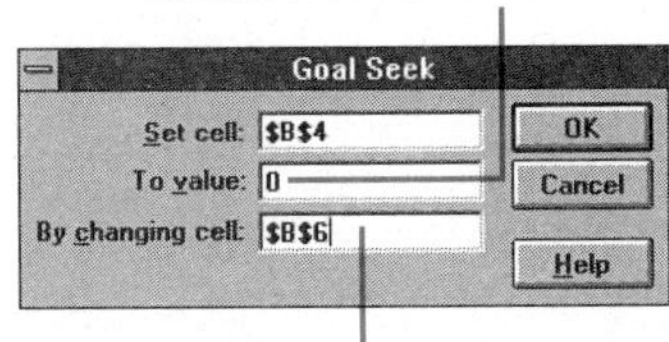

Figure 49.3 To value box of the Goal Seek dialog box.

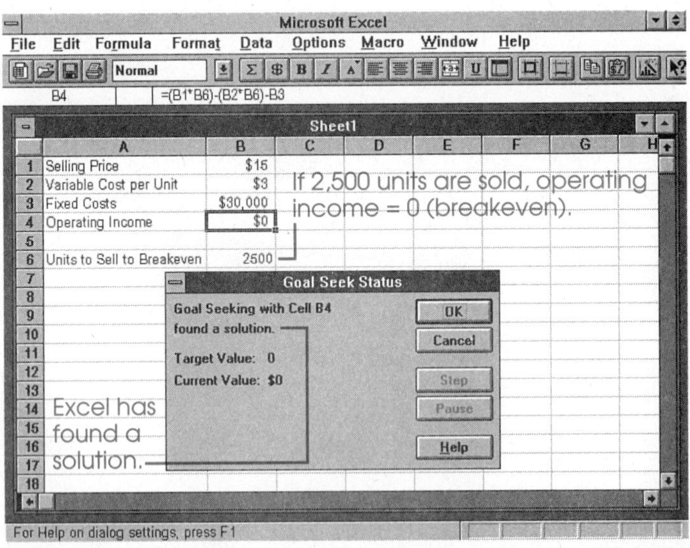

Figure 49.4 Goal Seek Status dialog box.

When you choose OK in step 6, Excel replaces the old value with the new solution value. If you immediately decide that you don't want the original value replaced, you can choose Edit Undo Goal Seek or hold down the Ctrl key and press Z to restore the original value.

> **IN ACTION:** You can use the breakeven model from Figures 49.1–49.4 and the Goal Seeker to compute the number of units you need to sell to achieve a target operating income. Figure 49.5 shows that the text in cell A6 has been revised to `Units to Sell to Achieve Target Profit` and the To value has been changed to $35,000—a target operating income. Figure 49.6 shows that if 5,417 units are sold (B6), $35,000 (B4) operating income will be realized.

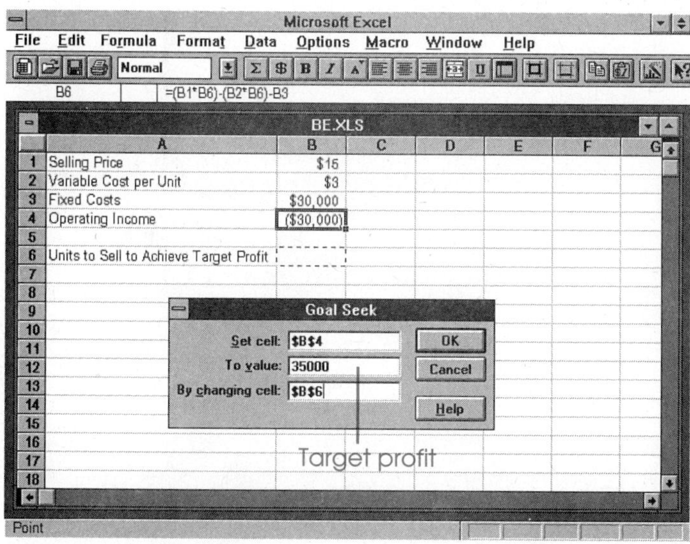

Figure 49.5 Using Goal Seeker to achieve a target profit.

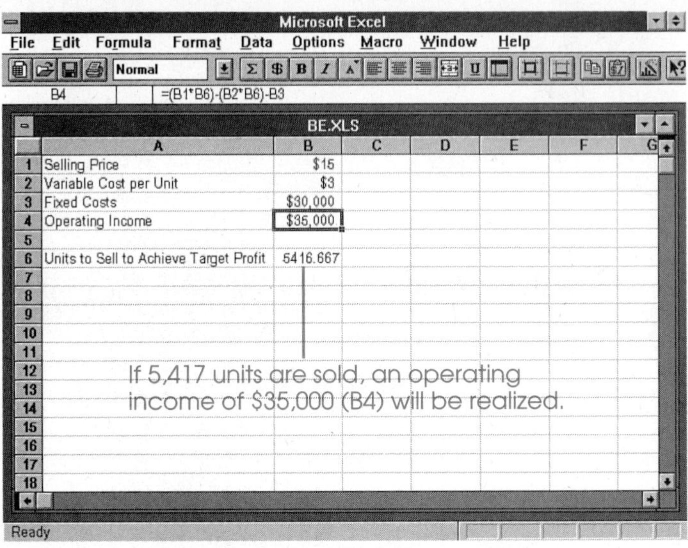

Figure 49.6 Goal Seeker target profit solution.

Skill Session

50

Using Scenario Manager

The Scenario Manager creates and saves different sets of data as separate *scenarios* (which are a type of "what-if" analysis, created by using different sets of input values). Scenarios allow you to view multiple outcomes based on different assumptions.

With the Scenario Manager, you can also create a separate summary report that shows the changing cell values, and the resulting cell values for each scenario.

Creating the Model in Scenario: Setting Up the Situation

To use the Scenario Manager you need a *worksheet model*—a worksheet (or set of worksheets) designed to help you examine scenarios. To create scenarios, you specify the *changing cells* and the values you want to appear in them. Changing cells hold the modified assumptions of each scenario. With each change you make to the changing cells, a different scenario will be created.

When you create scenarios, you add them to the Scenario list. Then, when you want to use a scenario, you can select it from the Scenario list and show it on a worksheet. To create a scenario, follow these steps:

Creating a Scenario:

1. Design worksheet model.
2. Choose Formula Scenario Manager.
3. Specify cells to change.
4. Choose Add.
5. Type name of scenario.
6. Enter input values.
7. Choose Add and repeat steps 4 and 5.
8. Choose OK.

1. Design a worksheet model.
2. Choose Formula Scenario Manager. As shown in Figure 50.1, the Scenario Manager dialog box is displayed. If the Scenario Manager command does not appear on the Formula menu, run the Setup program to install it.
3. In the **C**hanging Cells box, specify the cells you want to change by entering cell references or selecting the cells from the worksheet that you want to change. If you want to specify more than one cell, separate the references with commas. If you use the mouse pointer to select multiple changing cells, hold down Ctrl while you select the cells.
4. Choose Add. As shown in Figure 50.2, the Add Scenario dialog box appears.
5. In the **N**ame box, type the name of your scenario.
6. There is an *input cell box* for each changing cell you specify. Enter input values in each input cell box.

   The current values on the sheet are suggested for input values.

If you have more than nine changing cells, only the values of the first nine can be edited in the Add Scenario dialog box. The current sheet values are used for the others.

7. If you want to add the scenario to the list, and then create additional scenarios, choose Add and repeat steps 5 and 6. (If you want to return to the Scenario Manager dialog box without adding the current scenario, choose Cancel.)

8. When you are finished adding scenarios, choose OK or press Enter.

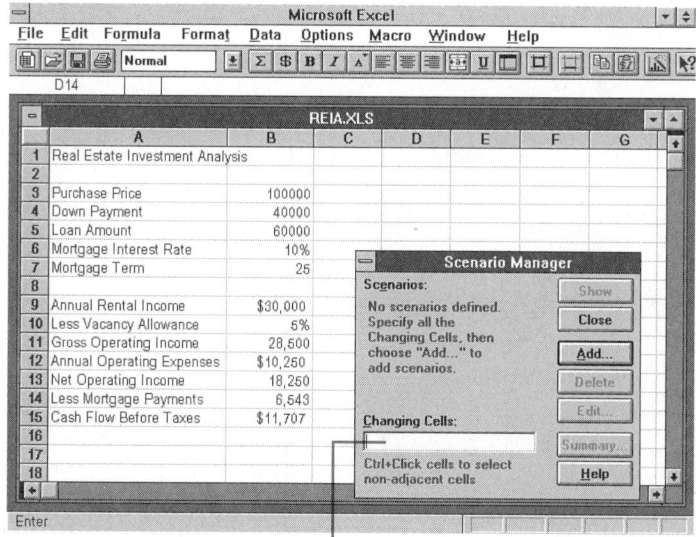

Specify the cells you want to change by entering cell references or by selecting the cells from the worksheet.

Figure 50.1 The Scenario Manager dialog box.

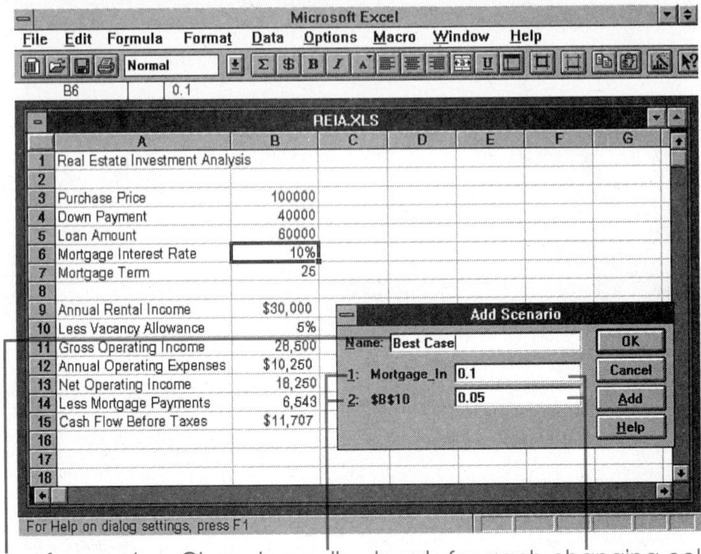

Figure 50.2 The Add Scenario dialog box.

Displaying a Scenario on the Worksheet

After using Formula Scenario Manager to create a scenario, you are ready to use the "what-if" feature of the Scenario Manager by displaying a scenario on the worksheet. To display data from a scenario on the active worksheet, follow these steps:

Displaying a Scenario:

1. Choose Formula Scenario Manager.
2. Select scenario.
3. Choose Show.
4. Choose Close.

1. Make the worksheet on which you want to use the scenario active, and choose Formula Scenario Manager. The Scenario Manager dialog box is displayed.

2. As shown in Figure 50.3, the Scenarios box displays scenarios that have been created previously. From the Scenarios box, select the scenario you want to show.

3. Choose Show. The changing cell values for the scenario you selected will appear in the changing cells on the worksheet, which is then recalculated to reflect the new values.

4. Repeat steps 2 and 3 to display other scenarios.

5. When finished, choose Close.

Tip: To delete a scenario, choose Formula Scenario Manager, select the scenario that you want to delete from the **Scenarios** box, choose Delete, and select Close. *Use caution when deleting scenarios; a deletion cannot be canceled or undone.*

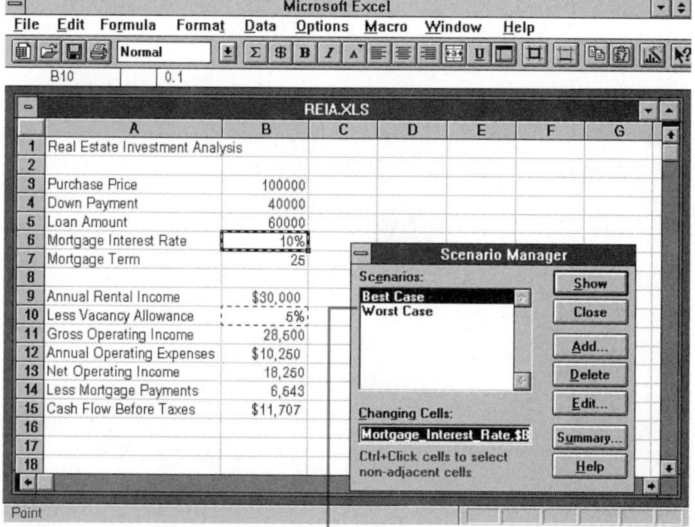

Scenario previously created. Select the one that you want to show in the worksheet.

Figure 50.3 The Scenarios box displays scenarios created previously.

Editing a Scenario

You can change both the name of an existing scenario and the values for each changing cell. To edit a scenario, follow these steps:

Editing a Scenario:

1. Choose Formula Scenario Manager.
2. Select scenario to edit.
3. Choose Edit.
4. Edit scenario name in Name box.
5. Edit values.
6. Choose OK.

1. Choose Formula Scenario Manager. The Scenario Manager dialog box is displayed.
2. In the **S**cenarios box, select the scenario you want to edit.
3. Choose Edit. As shown in Figure 50.4, the Edit Scenario dialog box is displayed.
4. If you want to rename the scenario, type a name in the Name box. To change the input values, edit the values for each changing cell and then choose OK. If you want to create a new scenario, click on Add from the Edit Scenario dialog box, enter names and values, and then choose OK.
5. Edit the values for each changing cell.
6. Choose OK.

To change just the input values for a scenario, choose Formula Scenario Manager, select the scenario you want to edit from the **S**cenarios box, choose Edit, edit the values for each changing cell, and then choose OK.

Creating a Report

You can generate a report that shows the scenarios that you created with their input values (changing cell values) and any result cells you want to display. A result cell is a cell that is recalculated when you show a new scenario. To create a summary report follow these steps:

Creating a Report:

1. Choose Formula Scenario Manager.

1. Choose Formula Scenario Manager. The Scenario Manager dialog box is displayed.

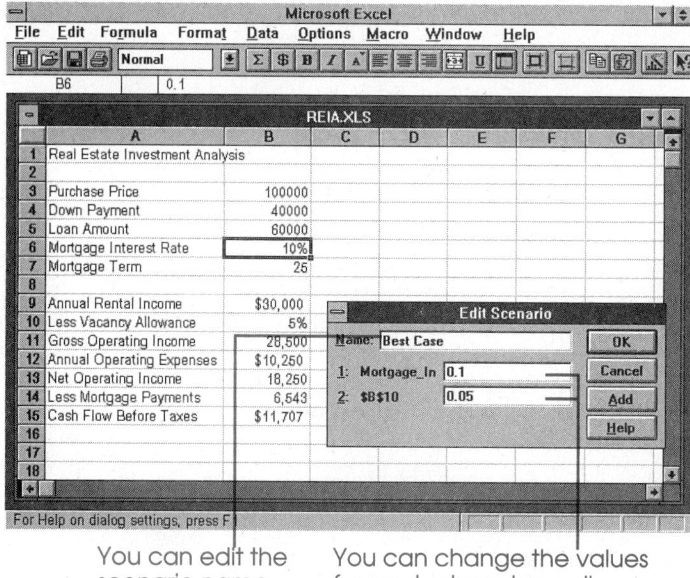

Figure 50.4 The Edit Scenario dialog box.

2. Select Summary. As shown in Figure 50.5, the Scenario Summary dialog box is displayed.

3. In the **R**esults Cells box, specify the cells that contain the significant results of each scenario by selecting the cells or typing the cell references. These cells should have formulas that refer to changing cells. If you include nonadjacent cells, select them by holding down Ctrl and then clicking each cell, or separate the cell references with a comma.

4. Choose OK. As shown in Figure 50.6, Excel creates a summary table of your scenarios on a separate worksheet.

2. Select Summary.
3. Specify cells that contain results.
4. Choose OK.

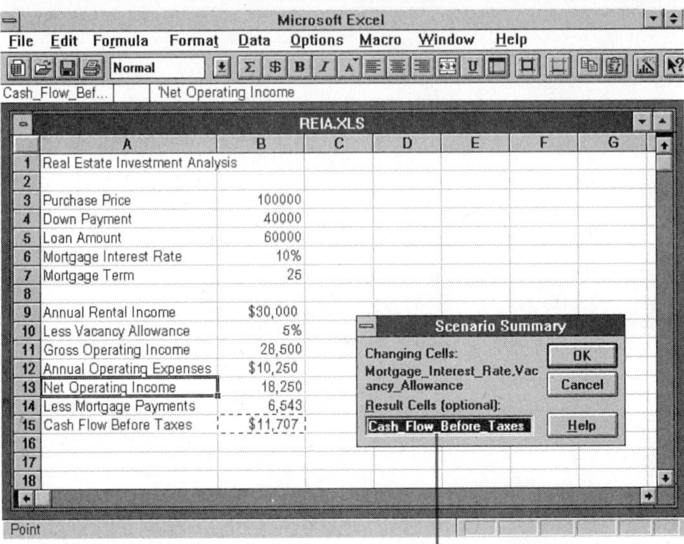

Specify the cell or cells containing the significant results of each scenario.

Figure 50.5 The Scenario Summary dialog box.

The summary report is easier to read if you define names for both the changing and result cells. Figure 50.6 shows that the Changing Cells have the following defined names: `Mortgage_Interest_Rate` and `Vacancy_Allowance`. The Result Cell was named `Cash_Flow_Before_Taxes`. By defining names for the changing and result cells, the report better describes the scenarios. You can look at the Figure 50.6 and know that the two scenarios involve the effects of changing both the mortgage interest rate and vacancy allowance on the cash flow before taxes from the real estate investment.

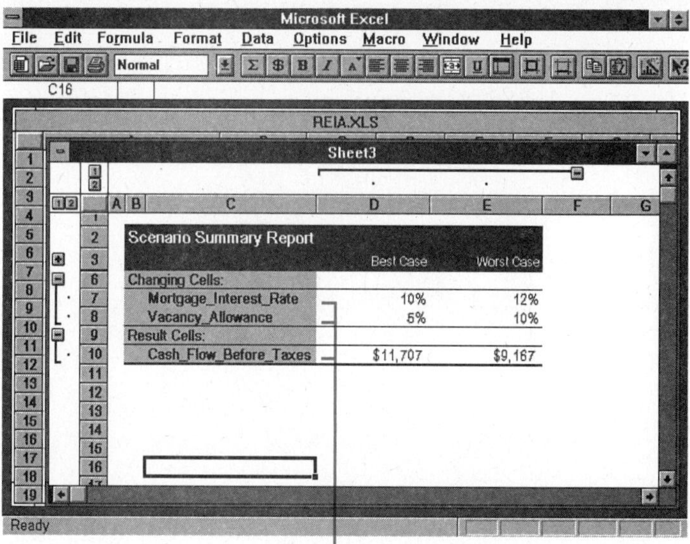

Changing and Result cells have defined names that make the summary report easier to interpret.

Figure 50.6 Summary table of scenarios.

Skill Session

51

Using Solver

Skill Session 49 details how to use Goal Seeker, an Excel feature that can help you find an unknown value that will make goal achievement possible. The Goal Seeker performs the algebraic task of solving for one unknown variable. The Solver is a more sophisticated backsolving function. Whereas Goal Seeker allows you to set a goal and solve for one unknown variable, the Solver can determine optimal solutions to business problems by changing *several* variables—while working within constraints you define. These features of Solver can give you the capability of doing business problem-solving simulations you may never have attempted before.

The Solver allows you to use Excel worksheets to perform goal-seeking, backsolving, and optimization analysis in minimal time—and without a knowledge of complex quantitative methods. An example of such methods, *linear programming*, is a technique for determining optimal business solutions—the best use of resources such as money, materials, labor, facilities, and time. The drawback to linear programming is that it is a stepwise, complicated, and time-consuming method.

In essence, the Solver makes linear and nonlinear problem solving simple and fast—by allowing you to define a problem, set constraints, analyze data, and show a variety of possible answers to the problem you have defined.

Setting Up a Solver Problem

The starting point for using Solver is to design a *worksheet model* to help you examine a particular business problem. For example, if you want to know the number of subs you need to make to achieve a certain net income, you could design an income statement model. With the worksheet that contains the model active, choose Formula Solver—and follow these four steps to a solution:

1. Specify a *target cell* (a cell whose value is to be maximized, minimized, or made to reach a certain value).

2. Specify the *changing cells* (the cells whose values are to be adjusted until a solution is found). Changing cells are the unknowns or variables of the problem.

3. Specify *constraint cells* (the cells whose values must fall within certain limits or satisfy target values). A constraint can be either a cell or cell range.

4. Solve the problem.

When you solve a problem with Solver, its solution values appear in the adjustable cells on the worksheet model. When Solver has found an optimal solution, you can then create three types of reports that summarize the results of a successful solution process. Creating Solver reports is covered in a subsequent section of this skill session.

To define a problem with Solver, follow these steps:

1. With the worksheet model active, choose Formula Solver. As shown in Figure 51.1, the Solver Parameters dialog box appears.

2. In the Set Cell box, enter a cell reference or name for the target cell (which you want to maximize, minimize, or assign a certain value). In Figure 51.1, the target cell is E7 which will contain a grand total of the contributions calculated with the formula: units sold × contribution margin. The result is the Total Contribution Margin for three products. You can type the target cell reference in the Set Cell box, or select the cell on the worksheet; the target cell must contain a formula.

3. If you want the target cell's value (just referenced in the Set Cell box) to be as large as possible, select the Max option. If you want the target cell's value to be as small as possible, select the Min option. If you want the target cell to have a certain value, select Value and then type the number you have chosen in the Value Of box.

4. In the By Changing Cells box, enter a name or reference for each cell you want Solver to change. In Figure 51.1, the changing cells—the unknown variables of the problem—are the units sold (which are in the range B4:B6). If you want to enter more

Defining a Problem with Solver:

1. Choose Formula Solver.
2. Name the target cell.
3. Select Max, Min, or Value Of.
4. Name each cell to be changed.
5. Select Add.

Caution: If you are solving a minimization problem and select the Min option, keep in mind that the Solver may find a negative number for the Set Cell (target cell). If you don't want a negative value as the Set Cell solution, add a constraint that specifies the Set Cell must contain a number greater than or equal to 0 (zero).

than one reference, and the references are not in a range, separate the references with commas. To select a series of nonadjacent ranges, hold down Ctrl while you select the cells or ranges.

5. Select Add to define the constraints of the problem. As shown in Figure 51.2, the Add Constraint dialog box is displayed. In the next section, "Specifying Constraints," you can follow the steps for adding constraints to a Solver problem.

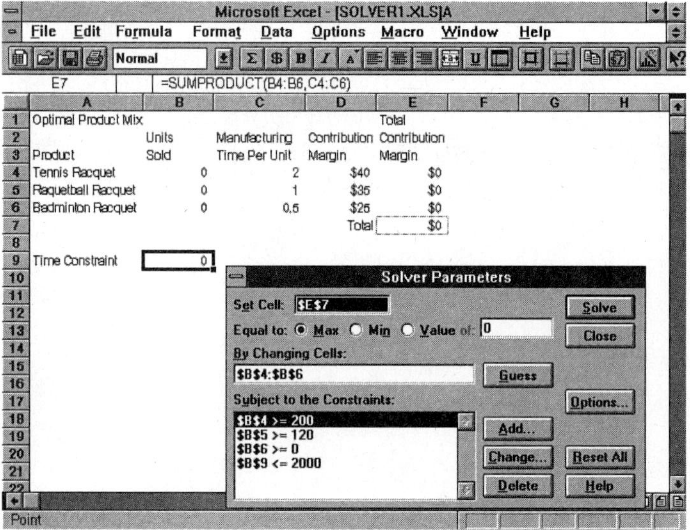

Figure 51.1 The Solver Parameters box.

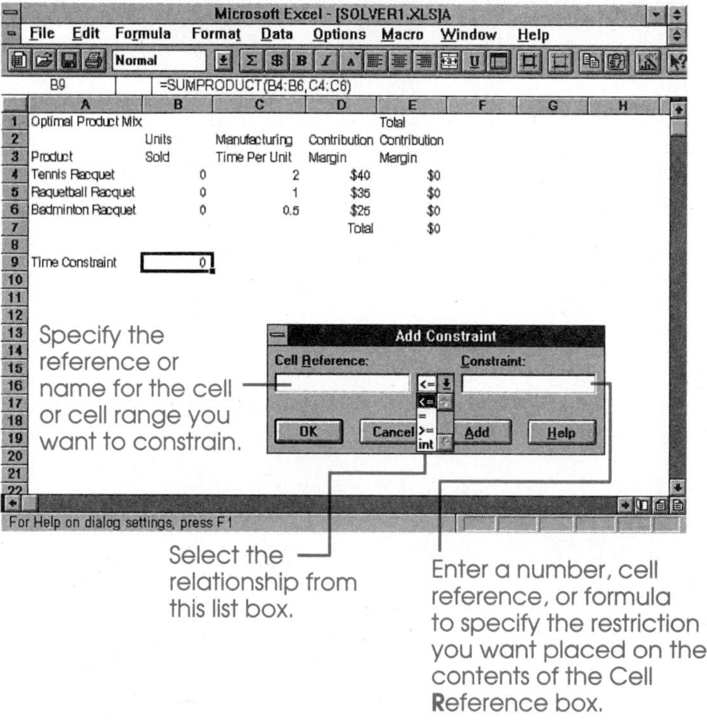

Figure 51.2 The Add Constraint dialog box.

Specifying Constraints

With a target cell (set cell) and the changing cells defined, the next task in using Solver is to specify the *constraints*. These are the many variables and limitations involved in business problem-solving (such as money, time, and personnel). For example, the worksheet model in Figure 51.1 shows a product mix of tennis, racquetball, and badminton racquets with the following limitations (constraints):

1. The total number of manufacturing hours are no greater than 2,000.

2. At least 200 tennis racquets must be manufactured.

3. At least 120 racquetball racquets must be manufactured.

4. No less than zero badminton racquets can be manufactured. (This constraint seems obvious, but it must be made. Otherwise, Solver could possibly produce a result of "negative manufacturing" to arrive at an optimal solution.)

The four constraints shown above are really *logical statements*; they can be expressed as logical formulas that must be entered, one by one, in the Add Constraint dialog box (see Figure 51.2).

Table 51.1 is a summary of how these four constraints would be entered into the Add Constraint Dialog Box. Solver will search for answers that satisfy each of the constraints.

Table 51.1 Constraints for the Figure 51.1 Solver problem

1. The total number of manufacturing hours (Cell $B$9) are no greater than 2,000.

Cell Reference	Relationship	Constraint
$B$9	<=	2000

2. At least 200 tennis racquets ($B$4) must be manufactured.

Cell Reference	Relationship	Constraint
$B$4	>=	200

3. At least 120 racquetball racquets ($B$5) must be manufactured.

Cell Reference	Relationship	Constraint
$B$5	>=	120

4. No less than zero badminton racquets ($B$6) can be manufactured.

Cell Reference	Relationship	Constraint
$B$6	>=	0

With a target cell (set cell) and the changing cells defined, follow these steps to add constraints to a Solver problem:

Adding Constraints to a Solver Problem:

1. Choose Add.
2. Specify reference for the cell/range to constrain.
3. Specify the relationship.
4. Enter number, cell reference or name, or formula.
5. Select Add.
6. Select OK.

1. Choose Formula Solver to display the Solver Parameters dialog box, and then select Add from this box. As shown in Figure 51.2, the Add Constraint dialog box is then displayed.

2. In the Cell Reference box, specify the reference or name for the cell or cell range whose value you want to constrain. You can specify the cells by entering the reference or name, or by selecting the cells from the worksheet.

3. In the unnamed list box between the Cell Reference box and the Constraint box (see Figure 51.2), select the relationship you want between the referenced cell (or cell range) and the constraint. You can select <=, =, >=, or int, which represent less than or

equal to, equal to, greater than or equal to, and integer respectively. If you choose int, the Constraint box is unavailable. If you don't select a relationship, Excel uses <= by default.

4. In the Constraint box, enter a number, cell reference, cell name, or a formula. The entry in the Constraint box specifies a restriction you want placed on the contents of the Cell Reference box. You can specify the cells by entering the reference or name or by selecting the cells from the worksheet.

5. Select Add to accept the constraint and to add another constraint without returning to the Solver Parameters dialog box.

6. When you are finished adding constraints, select OK or press Enter. The Solver Parameters dialog box appears with the constraints displayed in the Subject To The Constraints box.

Changing Constraints

You can change cell references, relationships, and constraints by following these steps to change constraints:

Changing Constraints:

1. Choose Formula Solver.
2. Select constraints to change.
3. Select Change.
4. Make changes to constraints.
5. Choose OK.

1. With the worksheet model active, Choose Formula Solver. The Solver Parameters dialog box is displayed.

2. In the Subject To The Constraints box, select the constraint that you want to change.

3. Select Change.

4. Make your changes to the constraint.
5. Select OK or press Enter to save the changes you made to the constraints.

Deleting Constraints

You can delete constraints by following these steps:

1. With the worksheet model active, choose Formula Solver. The Solver Parameters dialog box is displayed.
2. In the Subject To The Constraints box, select the constraint that you want to delete.
3. Choose Delete to delete the constraint.

Deleting Constraints:

1. Choose Formula Solver.
2. Select constraint to delete.
3. Choose Delete.

Solving

The Solver finds the solution to problems through a trial-and-error process called iterations. With each iteration, a set of changing cell values are used by Excel to recalculate your worksheet model and tested to see if they meet the constraints and set cell goal. The iteration process ends when a solution is found that falls within Excel's acceptable precision level (or when no further progress can be made toward meeting the constraints and set cell goal). To solve a previously defined problem, follow these steps:

Solving a Previously Defined Problem:

1. Choose Formula Solver.
2. Choose Solve.
3. Select Keep Solver Solution or Restore Original Values.
4. Choose OK.

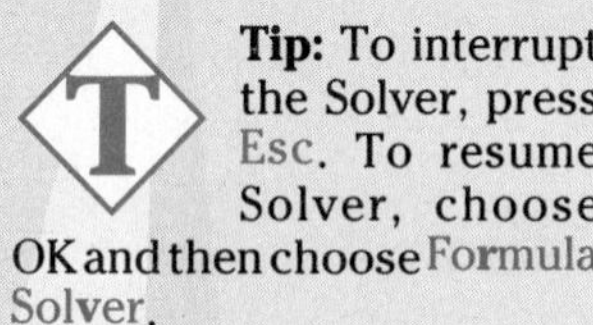

Tip: To interrupt the Solver, press Esc. To resume Solver, choose OK and then choose Formula Solver.

1. With the worksheet model active and the problem defined by a set cell and changing cells (see previous section), choose Formula Solver. The Solver Parameters dialog box appears.

2. Choose Solve. A message is displayed in the Excel status bar informing you that Excel is solving the problem. Then, as shown in Figure 51.3, the Solver dialog box appears containing a completion message.

3. If you want to keep the solution, in other words, you want the solution values to be reflected in the changing cells of the worksheet model, select Keep Solver Solution. If you want to restore the worksheet's original data, select Restore Original Values.

4. Choose OK or press Enter.

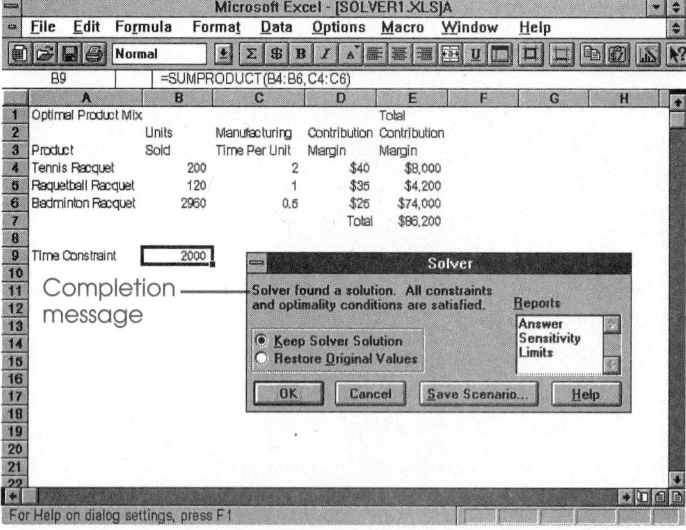

Figure 51.3 The Solver dialog box.

The Solver dialog box is displayed when the Solver has found a solution that satisfies the constraints and it shows the results of the last calculation, using the adjustable cell values that are closest to the solution you want. It also displays one of the following completion messages:

> `Solver found a solution. All constraints and optimality conditions are satisfied.`
>
> `All constraints are satisfied within the Precision setting and, if appropriate, a maximum or minimum value has been found for the cell in the Set Cell box.`
>
> `Solver has converged to the current solution. All constraints are satisfied.`
>
> `The value in the cell specified in the Set Cell box is virtually unchanged for the last five trial solutions. A solution may have been found, but it is also possible that the iterative solution process is making very slow progress.`

Solver may also display one of several unsuccessful completion messages or error messages. For help with interpreting these messages, see the Troubleshooting section of the *Microsoft Excel User's Guide, Book 2,* Chapter 2, "Performing What-If Analysis on a Worksheet."

Saving Results as Scenarios

Skill Session 50 describes how you can set up a worksheet model, define changing cells, and specify inputs to those cells, to create alternate solutions. These solutions (called scenarios) are a way of analyzing data—specifically, they apply "what-if" analysis to your worksheet models. You can save the changing cell values Solver generates—and keep them as a scenario—by following these steps:

Saving Cell Values as a Scenario:

1. Select Save Scenario.
2. Enter name for scenario.
3. Choose OK.

1. After Solver has finished its iterations and has found a solution, the Solver dialog box is displayed (see Figure 51.3), select Save Scenario. As is shown in Figure 51.4, the Save Scenario dialog box is displayed.

2. In the Scenario Name box, enter a name for the scenario.

3. Choose OK or press Enter. Excel saves the values for the changing cells that were generated by Solver as a named scenario. When you choose Formula Scenario, the name that you specified in step 2 will appear in the Scenarios list box of the Scenario Manager dialog box and if you select Show, the scenario values would be used in the worksheet model.

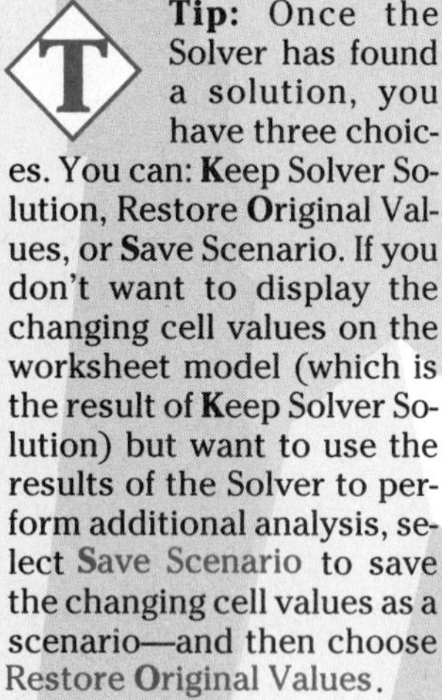

Tip: Once the Solver has found a solution, you have three choices. You can: **K**eep Solver Solution, Restore **O**riginal Values, or **S**ave Scenario. If you don't want to display the changing cell values on the worksheet model (which is the result of **K**eep Solver Solution) but want to use the results of the Solver to perform additional analysis, select Save Scenario to save the changing cell values as a scenario—and then choose Restore Original Values.

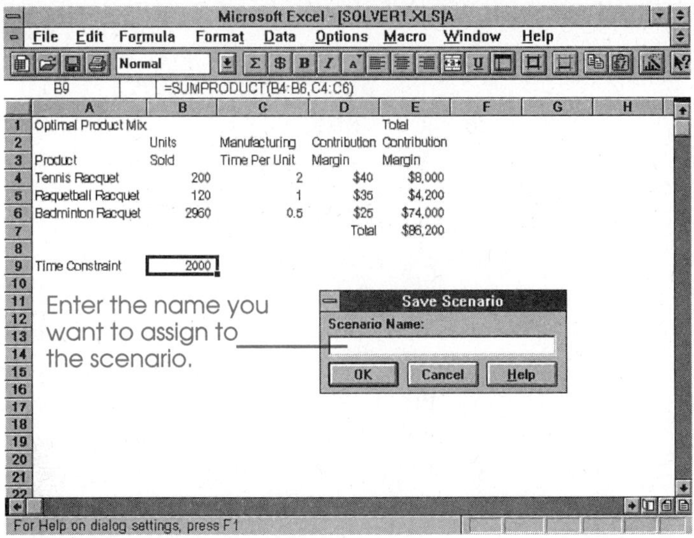

Figure 51.4 The Save Scenario dialog box.

Creating a Solver Report

When the Solver has found a solution to your defined problem, the Solver dialog box is displayed (see Figure 51.3), giving you the option of generating three types of reports that summarize the results of the Solver process. If you choose to generate a Solver report, each report will appear in its own worksheet window. The three reports are described below:

Answer Report lists the cell named in the Set Cell box and the adjustable cells, along with their original and final values. It also shows the constraints and information about the constraints. An example of the Answer Report is shown in Figure 51.5.

Limits Report lists the cell named in the Set Cell box, and the adjustable cells—along with their respective values, upper and lower limits, and target results. The *lower limit* is the smallest value that the adjustable cell can take while still satisfying the constraints and holding all other adjustable cells fixed. The *upper limit* is the greatest such value. The *target result* is the value of the cell in the Set Cell box, when the adjustable cell is at its lower or upper limit. An example of the Limits Report is shown in Figure 51.6.

Sensitivity Report provides information about how sensitive the solution is to small changes in the Set Cell formula or in the constraints. For nonlinear models, the report provides dual values (reduced gradients and Lagrange multipliers). For linear models, the report includes dual values (reduced costs and shadow prices) and objective coefficient and constraint right-hand side ranges. An example of the Sensitivity Report is shown in Figure 51.7.

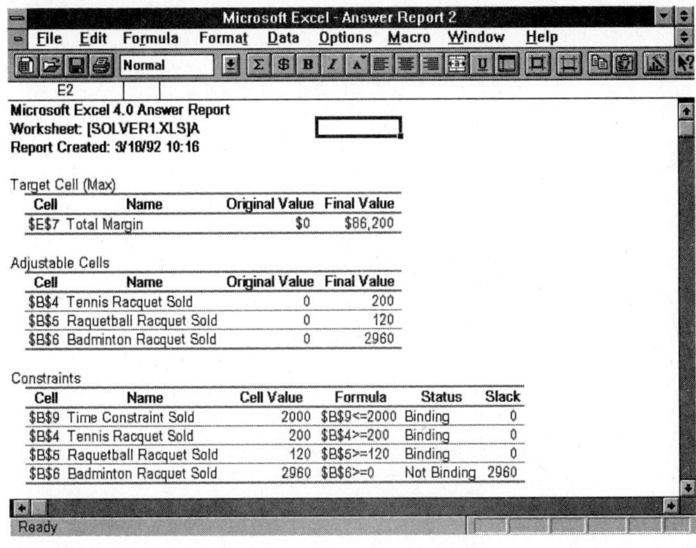

Microsoft Excel - Answer Report 2

File Edit Formula Format Data Options Macro Window Help

Microsoft Excel 4.0 Answer Report
Worksheet: [SOLVER1.XLS]A
Report Created: 3/18/92 10:16

Target Cell (Max)

Cell	Name	Original Value	Final Value
$E$7	Total Margin	$0	$86,200

Adjustable Cells

Cell	Name	Original Value	Final Value
$B$4	Tennis Racquet Sold	0	200
$B$5	Raquetball Racquet Sold	0	120
$B$6	Badminton Racquet Sold	0	2960

Constraints

Cell	Name	Cell Value	Formula	Status	Slack
$B$9	Time Constraint Sold	2000	$B$9<=2000	Binding	0
$B$4	Tennis Racquet Sold	200	$B$4>=200	Binding	0
$B$5	Raquetball Racquet Sold	120	$B$5>=120	Binding	0
$B$6	Badminton Racquet Sold	2960	$B$6>=0	Not Binding	2960

Ready

Figure 51.5 The Answer Report.

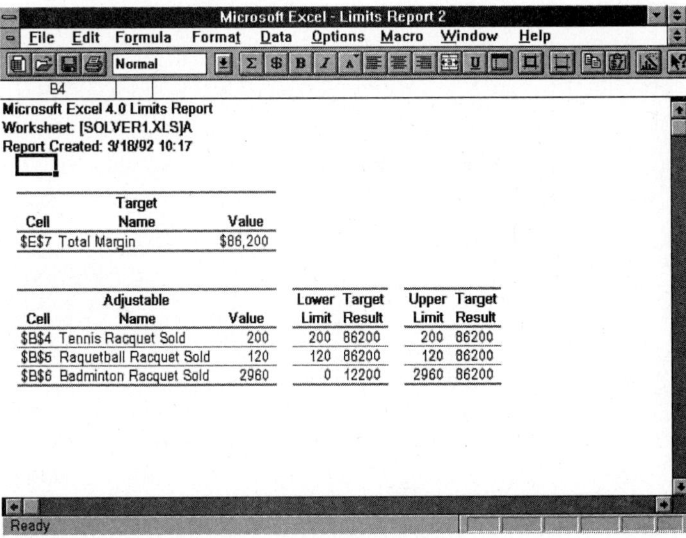

Microsoft Excel - Limits Report 2

File Edit Formula Format Data Options Macro Window Help

Microsoft Excel 4.0 Limits Report
Worksheet: [SOLVER1.XLS]A
Report Created: 3/18/92 10:17

Cell	Target Name	Value
$E$7	Total Margin	$86,200

Cell	Adjustable Name	Value	Lower Limit	Target Result	Upper Limit	Target Result
$B$4	Tennis Racquet Sold	200	200	86200	200	86200
$B$5	Raquetball Racquet Sold	120	120	86200	120	86200
$B$6	Badminton Racquet Sold	2960	0	12200	2960	86200

Ready

Figure 51.6 The Limits Report.

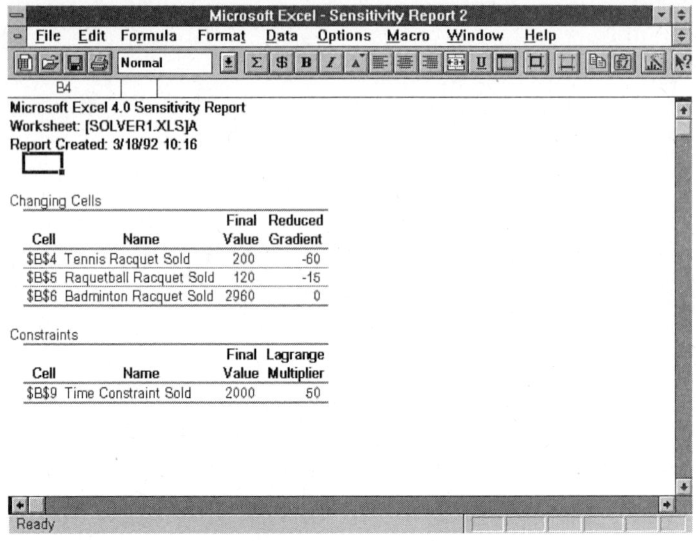

Microsoft Excel 4.0 Sensitivity Report
Worksheet: [SOLVER1.XLS]A
Report Created: 3/18/92 10:16

Changing Cells

Cell	Name	Final Value	Reduced Gradient
$B$4	Tennis Racquet Sold	200	-60
$B$5	Raquetball Racquet Sold	120	-15
$B$6	Badminton Racquet Sold	2960	0

Constraints

Cell	Name	Final Value	Lagrange Multiplier
$B$9	Time Constraint Sold	2000	50

Figure 51.7 The Sensitivity Report.

Generating a Solver Report:

1. Choose **K**eep Solver Solution or Restore **O**riginal Values.
2. Select desired reports.
3. Choose OK.

To create a Solver report, follow these steps:

1. After defining a Solver problem and running a solution, choose **K**eep Solver Solution or Restore **O**riginal Values from the Solver dialog box. If you choose **K**eep Solver Solution, Excel will replace the original worksheet values with the new solution values and will generate the report(s) that you select in step 2. If you choose Restore **O**riginal Values, Excel will generate the report(s) you select in step 2, using the Solver results—and will then restore the original worksheet values.

2. In the **R**eports list box, select any number of the three reports. If you want to select all three reports, hold down Shift or Ctrl as you select the reports.

3. Choose OK or press Enter. Excel creates a separate worksheet for each of the reports.

Macros Workshop

Macros are small programs that you create within Excel to accomplish specific tasks. By your learning to create and run macros, you can automate every day tasks and complex interactive applications. The first skill session of this workshop demonstrates the macro recorder which is a tool that allows you to record the commands you make and the other actions you take with Excel so that they can be executed again in the future. The macro recorder is useful for creating rather simple macros. Complicated macro applications require you to write the macro by using the Excel macro programming language which includes over 400 macro functions.

Skill Session

52

Recording a Macro

Excel lets you record a set of instructions, called *command macros*, for automating an Excel task. Command macros speed up your work and make you a more efficient Excel user. Macros are ideal for repetitive or complex tasks, and the possibilities of macro applications are limited only by your knowledge of Excel and your imagination. Recorded on a macro sheet, macros can be designed to automate tasks that you normally perform with the keyboard or mouse, such as using commands or entering data.

This skill session shows you how you can use the **M**acro Re**c**ord command to record macros. After choosing Macro Record, you use the keyboard and the mouse to choose commands and enter data, while Excel creates the macro instruction (called a *macro function*) for each action you take, and enters that instruction on an open macro sheet. Once recorded, the command macro can be run by selecting the macro name from a list using the **M**acro **R**un command or by pressing a shortcut key combination. Very sophisticated command macros can also be created by entering formulas and functions directly in cells on a macro sheet. These formulas and functions tell Excel how to perform each step of the macro. For more information on how to write a command macro, see Skill Session 53, and for more information on macro functions, see the macro command reference section of this book.

Recording a Macro

You can record a macro on a new, a global, or an existing macro sheet. A global macro sheet takes much of the work out of managing macros. Each time you start up Excel, the global macro sheet is automatically opened. Therefore, any macros saved in the global macro sheet are available when working in any Excel worksheet.

Recording a Macro on a New or Global Macro Sheet:

1. Choose Macro Record.
2. Type a name.
3. Type a shortcut key.
4. Select Global Macro Sheet.
5. Choose OK.
6. Carry out the actions.
7. Choose Macro Stop Recorder.

Select the Record Macro tool from the Macro toolbar to display the Record Macro dialog box so that you can begin recording your actions.

To record a macro on a new or global macro sheet, follow these steps:

1. Choose Macro Record. As shown in Figure 52.1, the Record Macro dialog box appears. Excel enters a suggested macro name in the Name box and a proposed shortcut key in the Key box. You can execute the macro command by selecting the macro name or by pressing the shortcut key combination. In Figure 52.1, the suggested macro name is Record2 and the shortcut key is Ctrl+A.
2. In the Name box, type a name or accept the proposed name.
3. In the Key box, type a shortcut key or accept the proposed key.

4. Select the Global Macro Sheet radio button if you want your macros saved in a global macro sheet (which Excel opens automatically when you start Excel), or select Macro Sheet to create a new macro sheet.

5. Choose OK or press Enter.

6. Use the keyboard and/or mouse to carry out the actions you want to record.

7. When you have finished performing the task that you want to automate, stop recording by choosing Macro Stop Recorder. As shown in Figure 52.2, Excel records the macro commands in a macro sheet.

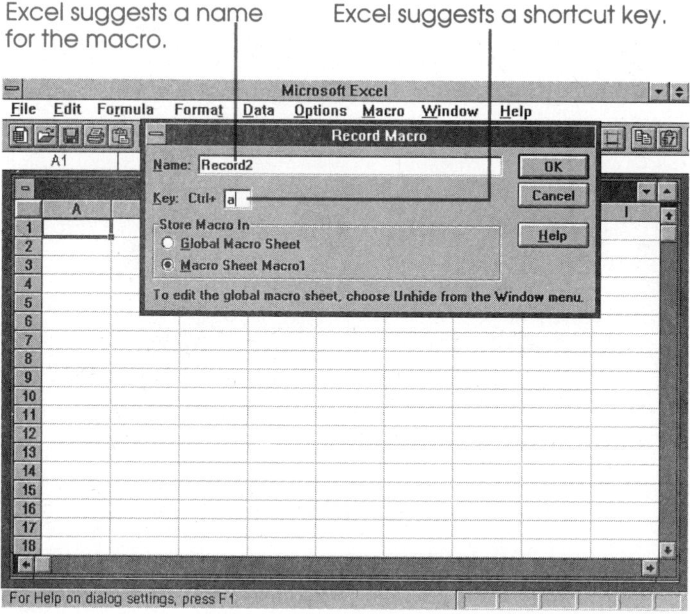

Figure 52.1 The Record Macro dialog box.

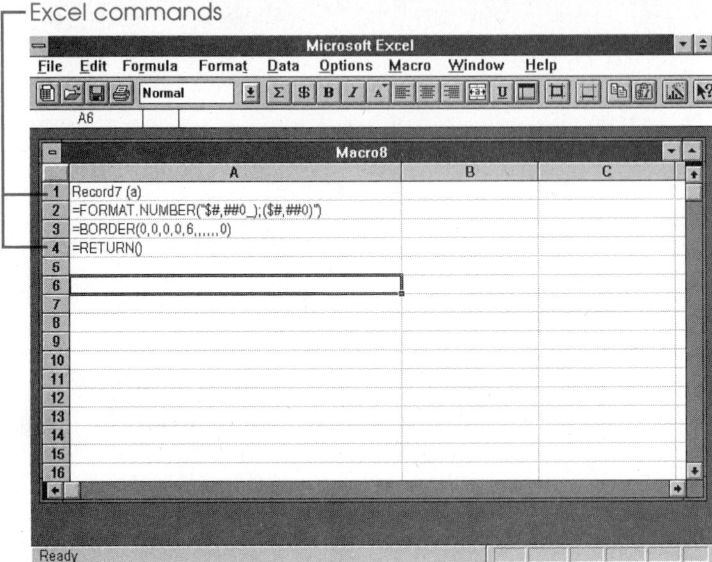

Figure 52.2 Macro commands recorded in a macro sheet.

Recording a Macro on an Existing Macro Sheet:

1. Open an existing macro sheet.
2. Select cell to begin recording.
3. Choose Macro Set Recorder.
4. Switch to document to carry out actions.
5. Choose Macro Record.
6. Type a name.
7. Type a shortcut key.
8. Choose OK.
9. Carry out actions to record.
10. Choose Macro Stop Recorder.

To record a macro on an existing macro sheet, follow these steps:

1. Open an existing macro sheet by choosing File Open, select the name of the macro sheet, and choose OK.
2. Select the cell on the macro sheet where you want to begin recording.
3. Choose Macro Set Recorder.
4. Switch to the document on which you will carry out the actions.
5. Choose Macro Record.
6. In the Name box, type a name or accept the proposed name.

7. In the **K**ey box, type a shortcut key or accept the proposed key. The name of your macro sheet appears as the chosen option under Store Macro In.

8. Choose OK or press Enter.

9. Carry out the actions you want to record.

10. To stop recording, choose Macro Stop Recorder.

Displaying the Macro Toolbar

The tools on the Macro toolbar can perform tasks such as macro recording, running, stepping through the currently selected command macro one cell at a time, resuming a macro operation after the macro has been paused, inserting a selected function into the formula bar, and inserting a selected name into the formula bar.

To display the Macro toolbar, follow these steps:

1. Choose Options Toolbars. The Toolbars dialog box is displayed.

2. Select the Macro toolbar.

3. Choose Show. The Macro toolbar is displayed.

Displaying the Macro Toolbar:

1. Choose Options Toolbars.
2. Select Macro toolbar.
3. Choose Show.

You can also display or hide a toolbar from the Toolbar shortcut menu. You can display the Toolbar shortcut menu by positioning the mouse pointer in the currently displayed toolbar and clicking the right mouse button. From the toolbar shortcut menu, choose Macro to display or hide the Macro toolbar. Excel places a check mark next to the name of each displayed toolbar.

Macro Toolbar Tools

Table 52.1 describes each of the tools in the Macro toolbar and their shortcut keys.

Table 52.1 Macro toolbar tools

Tool	*Name*	*Description*
	New Macro Sheet	Creates a new macro sheet. Clicking this tool is the same as choosing **F**ile **N**ew and selecting Macro Sheet. *Shortcut keys: Ctrl+F11*
=f(x)	Paste Function	Displays the Paste Function dialog box so that you can insert a selected function into the formula bar. *Shortcut keys: Shift+F3*
=ab	Paste Names	Displays the Paste Name dialog box so that you can insert a selected name into the formula bar. *Shortcut key: F3*
	Run Macro	Runs the currently selected macro, starting at the active cell.
	Step Macro	Displays the Single Step dialog box that you can step through the currently selected command macro one cell at a time, starting at the active cell.

Tool	*Name*	*Description*
	Record Macro	Displays the Record Macro dialog box so you can record your actions and commands to create a macro.
	Resume Macro	Resumes a macro operation after the macro has been paused.

Skill Session

53

Writing a Command Macro

This skill session describes how to use the **M**acro Re**c**ord command to open a macro sheet and record the macro. You can also create a macro by entering Excel commands yourself into a macro sheet. If you design and enter your own macro, the process should begin with a plan of what you want the macro to accomplish.

Planning the Macro

The first step in creating a macro is planning what you want the macro to do. Before you enter the keystrokes and commands, you have to think about the tasks that you want to automate. For complex tasks, planning a macro may involve taking notes, writing down specifications, or drawing a flow chart. For simple tasks, the planning may be much more informal so that you map out the macro in your mind.

After you know what you want a macro to do, you must decide where to locate the macro. There are three choices: a new macro sheet, an existing macro sheet, or a global macro sheet. If you locate a macro on a global macro sheet, you have an advantage in that you can use it with all your applications without opening a macro sheet each time you want to run the macro. For more information on creating and using a global macro sheet, see Skill Session 55.

To open a new macro sheet, follow these steps:

1. Choose File New. As shown in Figure 53.1, the New dialog box appears.
2. In the New box, select Macro Sheet.
3. Choose OK or press Enter. As shown in Figure 53.2, a macro sheet is displayed.

Opening a New Macro Sheet:

1. Choose File New.
2. Under New, select Macro Sheet.
3. Choose OK.

Select the New Macro Sheet tool from the Macro toolbox to open a new macro sheet.

Tip: You can also open a new macro sheet by holding down Ctrl and pressing F11 or by holding down both Alt and Ctrl and pressing F1.

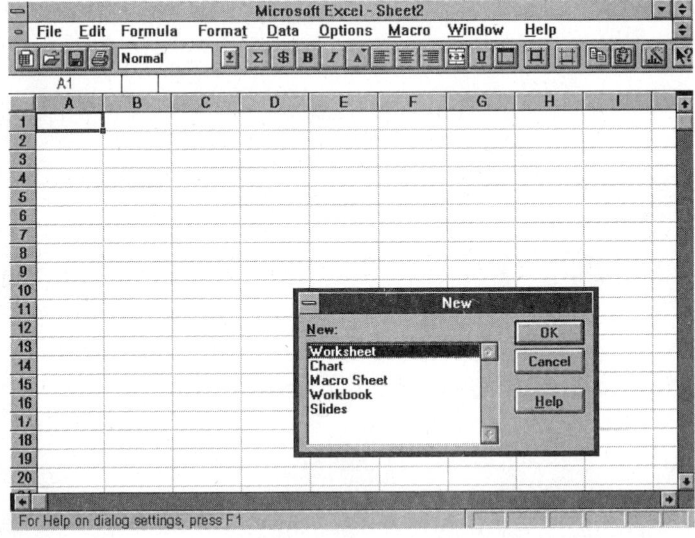

Figure 53.1 The New dialog box.

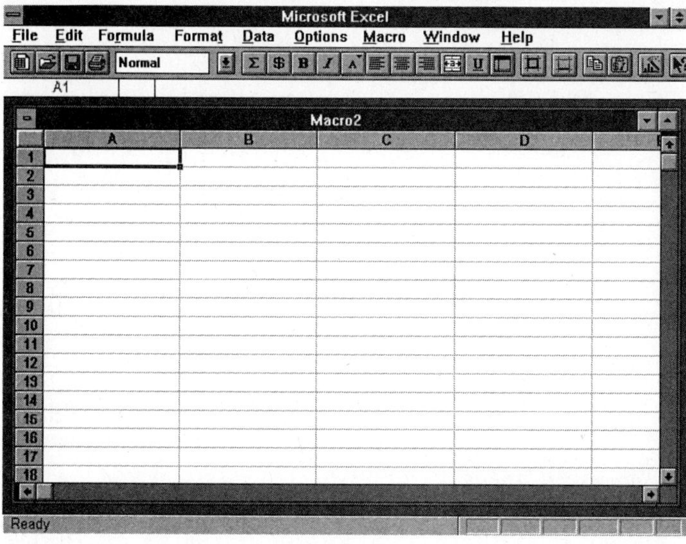

Figure 53.2 A new macro sheet.

To write a macro to an existing macro sheet, you must first open the macro sheet. The steps for opening an existing macro sheet follow:

1. Choose File Open. The Open dialog box is displayed.
2. In the File Name text box, enter the name of the macro sheet or select the name of the macro sheet from the File Name list box. (If the macro sheet is not in the current directory, select its directory from the Directories list box and then enter the macro sheet name in the File Name text box or select the macro sheet from the File Name list box.)
3. Choose OK or press Enter. Excel displays the macro sheet.

Opening an Existing Macro Sheet:

1. Choose File Open.
2. Select name of macro sheet.
3. Choose OK.

Select this tool from the Standard toolbox to display the Open dialog box so that you can open an existing macro sheet Open File tool.

Tip: To display the Open dialog box so that you can open a macro sheet, hold down Ctrl and press F12. You can also hold down Alt+Ctrl and press F2.

With the plan for your macro in place, you are ready to write the macro commands. You should be aware of the following basic macro rules before writing a macro:

- Many macro commands are command equivalent functions. Command equivalent macro functions perform the same task as choosing a particular command from an Excel menu. For example, the macro command =FILE.CLOSE is the equivalent to choosing File Close. When Excel comes upon =FILE.CLOSE in a macro, it closes the active document. For more information on the syntax of macro functions, see the Macro Commands reference section in this book.

- If a command equivalent macro displays a dialog box with option buttons, the option buttons are represented by numbers. For example, the macro command for arranging the windows of a workspace horizontally is =ARRANGE.ALL(2), which is the equivalent of **W**indow **A**rrange H**o**rizontal. The Horizontal option button in the Arrange Windows dialog box is the second option button shown in the dialog box.

- If a command equivalent macro displays a dialog box with check boxes, the logical values TRUE or FALSE determine whether a check box is selected or turned off. A TRUE argument selects the check box, and the FALSE argument clears the check box. For example, the command macro =PROTECT.DOCUMENT(FALSE,TRUE,FALSE) clears the Cells check box, selects the Windows check box, and clears the Objects check box of the Protect Document dialog box.

- Data to be entered into text boxes that are shown in dialog boxes are represented by text values. For example, the command macro =FORMULA.FIND

("Dollars",1,2,1,1,FALSE) executes the Formula Find command to seek out cells that contain the text `Dollars`. In the Find What text box of the Find dialog box, you must enter your search data, which in this case is **`Dollars`**.

- Numbers or text values represent list boxes. For example, the macro command =SHOW.TOOLBAR (7,TRUE) selects and displays the Macro toolbox, which is the third toolbox in the Toolbars dialog box. The following command macro selects the TimesNewRomanPS font from the Font list box of the Font dialog box:

```
=FORMAT.FONT("TimesNewRomanPS",10,FALSE,
FALSE,FALSE,FALSE,0)
```

- For every macro function, there is a specific syntax. The syntax includes the name of the function and all required and optional arguments. For example, the macro function that closes the active document is FILE.CLOSE, which has the following syntax: FILE.CLOSE(*save_logical*). The argument *save_logical* is a logical value specifying whether to save the file before closing it. If the *save_logical* value is TRUE, then Excel saves the file. If the *save_logical* value is false, Excel does not save the file. If the *save_logical* value is omitted from the function and if you have made changes to the file, Excel displays a dialog box asking you if you want to save the file; otherwise, the file will be closed.

- Excel ignores blank cells and text entries in macro sheets and continues on with any macro commands that come after blank cells.

- Recording part of a command macro by using Macro Record (Skill Session 52 describes how to use the Macro Record command) and then editing the macro is often faster than writing the macro from scratch. The **M**acro Re**c**ord saves typing time and helps to ensure proper syntax.

Naming a Macro

As discussed in Skill Session 52, you can name a macro at the time that you record it by choosing Macro Record and entering the name of the macro in the **N**ame box of the Record Macro dialog box or by accepting the Excel proposed name. After you have finished recording the macro, Excel enters the macro name in the first row of the macro, as shown in Figure 53.3. The macro name must be a valid Excel name.

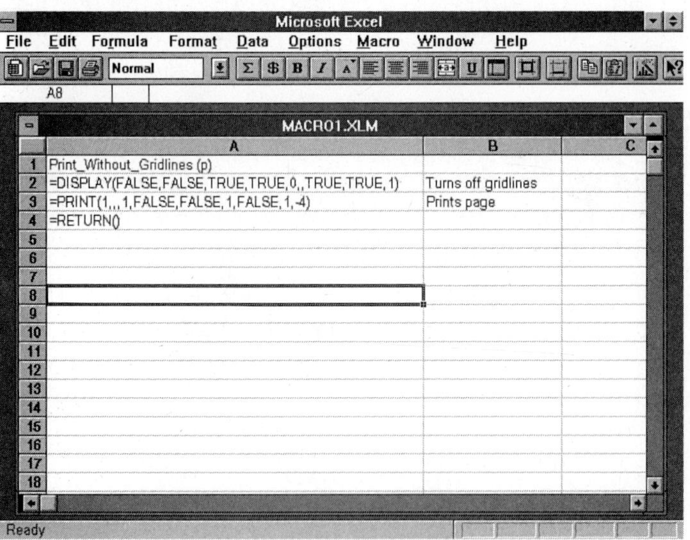

Figure 53.3 A macro that turns off gridlines and prints the worksheet.

To name a macro, follow these guidelines:

- ▲ The name should be descriptive. For example, the macro name Print_Without_Gridlines tells you more about the macro than MACRO1.
- ▲ The first character of the macro name must be a letter or the underscore character, whereas other characters can be letters, numbers, periods, and underlines.
- ▲ Spaces are not allowed in macro names; however, you can use underscores to represent spaces. For example, the macro name Print_Without_Gridlines uses two underscores instead of spaces.
- ▲ A macro name can be up to 255 characters long.
- ▲ You can use upper- or lowercase letters; however, Excel does not distinguish between upper- and lowercase letters in names.

You can also define a macro name without using the **M**acro Re**c**ord command. For example, if you were editing a macro by entering new or revised macro commands directly into the macro sheet and wanted to assign a new name to the macro, you would follow these steps:

Naming a Macro:

1. Select cells containing the macro.
2. Choose Formula Define Name.
3. Specify the name.
4. Specify the cell reference.
5. Select Command.
6. Specify a shortcut key.
7. Choose OK.

1. Select the cells in the macro sheet containing the macro you want to name.
2. Choose Fo**r**mula **D**efine Name. As shown in Figure 53.4, the Define Name dialog box appears.
3. In the **N**ame box, type the name you want to assign to the macro or accept the proposed name.

   If the active cell—or a cell immediately above or to the left of the active cell—contains text, Excel

Tip: To display the Define Name dialog box, hold down the Ctrl key and press F3.

Note: As Figure 53.5 shows, when macro sheets are minimized, their icons are different from other Excel documents to distinguish them from worksheet, graph, and workbook icons.

suggests that text as the macro's name by entering it in the Name text box.

4. In the **R**efers to box, type the cell reference or accept the proposed reference. Excel proposes the selected cell or range as the cell reference. If you type a reference, it must begin with an equal sign (=).

5. Under Macro, select Command.

6. (Optional) If you want to specify a shortcut key for running the macro, type a letter or a number in the **K**ey: Ctrl+ box.

7. Choose OK or press Enter to add the macro name and to close the dialog box.

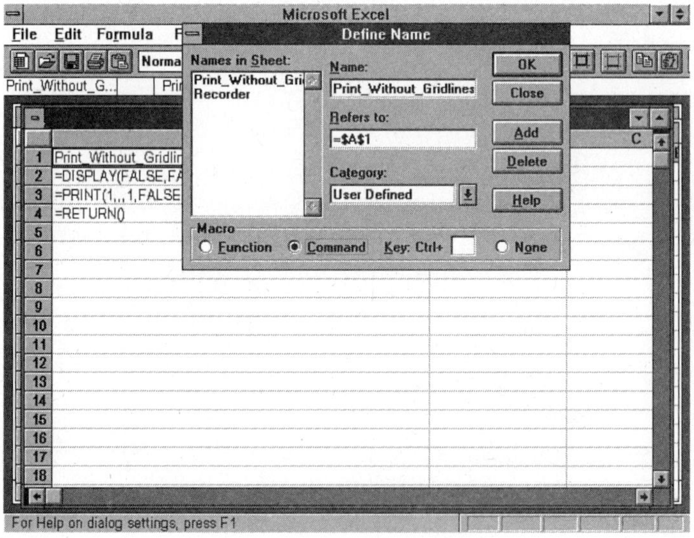

Figure 53.4 The Define Name dialog box.

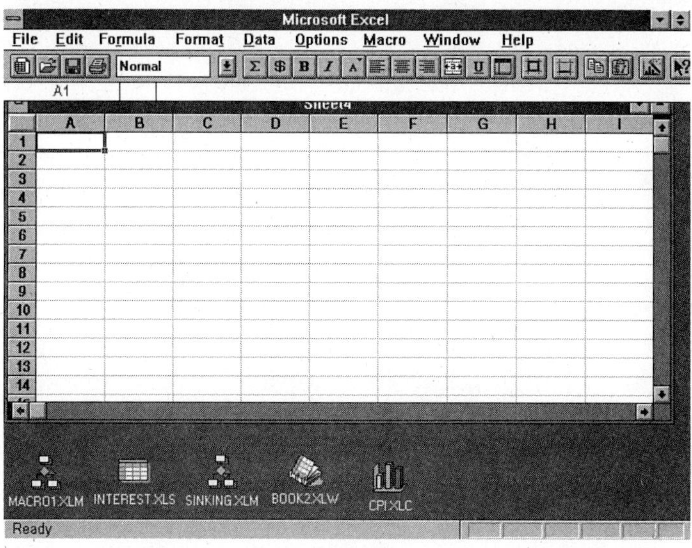

Figure 53.5 Document icons.

Documenting a Macro

Macro instructions are not always easy codes to read and interpret. Therefore, it is wise to document macros. Macro documentation is text that you enter in cells adjacent to the macro commands. You have already seen macro documentation in Figure 53.3 where the macro's name and shortcut key `[Print_Without_Gridlines (p)]` are entered in A1 and comments about the tasks performed by each command are entered in column B. Excel ignores text entries in a macro sheet when running a macro. To document a macro, follow these steps:

Documenting a Macro:

1. Record a macro.
2. Enter the macro's name and shortcut key.
3. Enter comments in the cells.

1. Record or write the macro.
2. Enter the macro's name and shortcut key in the cell above the first macro command.
3. Enter explanatory comments in the cells adjacent to the right of the cells containing the macro formulas.

Macro documentation is crucial if you are creating and working with numerous macros; it brings meaning to the macro and outlines its steps. Macro documentation is also helpful when revising macros.

You can attach notes to macro commands to annotate their purpose. Figure 53.6 shows a note that was attached to cell A4 of a macro. The documentation appears in the Text Note box of the Cell Note dialog box. The creating, viewing, and printing of text notes is covered in greater detail in Skill Session 22.

Attaching a Documentation Note to Macro:

1. Select cell.
2. Choose Formula Note.
3. Type explanatory text.
4. Choose OK.

To create or edit a note to a macro command, follow these steps:

1. Select the cell that contains the macro command that you want to document.
2. Choose Formula Note (or if the cell already has a note, double-click the cell). As shown in Figure 53.6, the Cell Note dialog box is displayed.
3. In the Text Note box, type explanatory text for the new note or edit the text of the existing note. The text you type wraps to the next line. To insert a line or paragraph break, press Ctrl+Enter.
4. Choose OK or press Enter. Excel attaches the note to the cell.

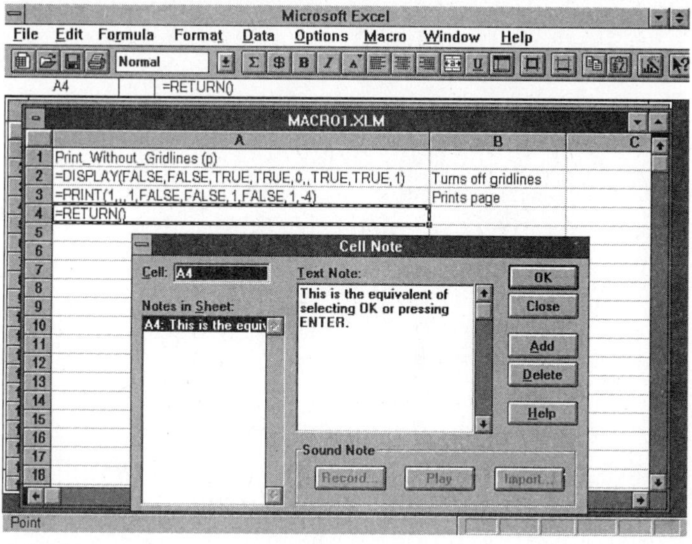

Figure 53.6 The Cell Note dialog box.

When you want to view macro documentation that has been added as text notes, follow these steps:

Viewing Notes in a Macro Sheet:

1. Select a cell.
2. Choose Formula Note.
3. Select note.
4. Choose Close.

1. In the macro sheet, select a cell that contains a macro command.
2. Choose Formula Note (double-click the cell). The Cell Note dialog box is displayed, and a list of all notes in the worksheet is shown in the Notes in Sheet box. To scroll through the list, use the scroll bar.
3. Select the note you want to view by clicking on your choice in the Notes in Sheet box. The text of the note is displayed in the Text Note box.
4. When you are finished viewing the notes, choose Close.

Debugging a Macro

Despite careful planning, recording, entering, revising, documenting, and naming a macro, you may find that the macro contains an error. Don't be discouraged by macro errors. Macro writing is often a trial and error process. Most macro errors are obvious and can be cleared up quickly.

When a macro contains an error, it will not perform the tasks that you had planned or Excel will interrupt the macro—not allowing it to finish executing the commands. Macro errors can result from a variety of mistakes such as incorrectly written commands, improper macro function syntax, and typing errors.

There are two effective ways of finding the source of macro errors so that they can be corrected. One way is to use an Excel feature that allows you to "step" through the macro commands, one at a time. By using the macro Step feature, you can verify which commands are working correctly and which are not. Another effective means of discovering errors in a macro is by using the Macro Debugger—an add-in macro that helps you to resolve errors in your macros. The Macro Debugger is covered in the next section.

Stepping through a Macro

Stepping through a Macro:

1. Choose Macro Run.
2. Specify macro to run.
3. Choose Step.
4. Choose Step Into or Step Over.

To step through a macro, follow these steps:

1. With the macro sheet open, choose Macro Run. The Run Macro dialog box appears.
2. In the **R**un box, select the macro you want to run or type the name or reference of the macro in the Reference box.

3. Choose **Step**. As shown in Figure 53.7, the Single Step dialog box appears. The first formula in the macro appears in the Single Step dialog box. The Single Step dialog box shows which cell in the macro is about to be calculated and what formula is in that cell.

4. The Single Step dialog box contains seven options that are described in Table 53.1. To step through, or carry out, the next macro instruction, choose **Step Into** or **Step Over**. **S**tep Into steps through user-defined functions. Step **O**ver carries out, but does not step through, user-defined functions. Continue to choose **Step Into** or **Step Over** until the macro completely executes.

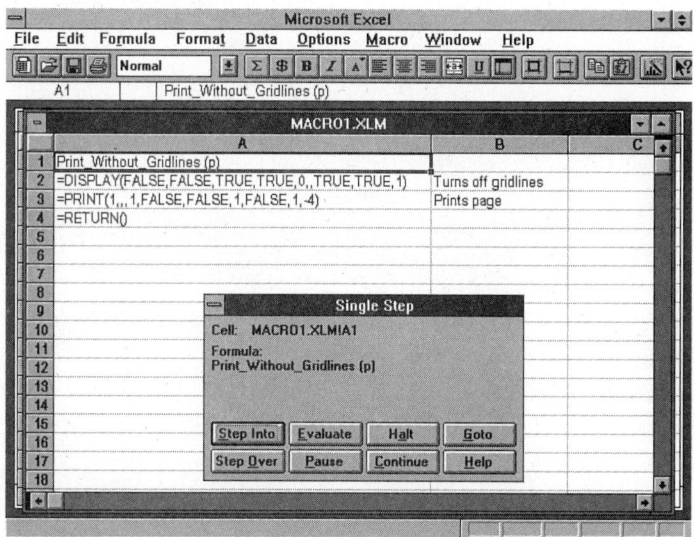

Figure 53.7 The Single Step dialog box.

Table 53.1 The options of the Single Step dialog box

Option	*Task*
Step Into	Executes the next instruction in the macro, including user-defined function calls.
Step **O**ver	Executes the next instruction in the macro. Carries out, but does not step through, user-defined function calls.
Evaluate	Calculates each part of the formula in the active cell. If chosen repeatedly, this button will Step Into the macro, not Step Over.
Pause	Closes the dialog box and suspends the macro, allowing you to perform other tasks.
H**a**lt	Stops the macro.
Continue	Runs the rest of the macro without single-stepping.
Goto	Stops the macro and selects the cell currently being evaluated on the macro sheet.

You can also make a macro step automatically each time it is run by entering the STEP function into the macro. If you use the STEP function, you can test a macro by stepping through it either by using the **M**acro **R**un command or by executing the macro with its shortcut keys. When developing and testing macros, a wise technique is to enter the STEP function in the first cell of a macro so that each time you test run it, you can step through it. After you have completely debugged the macro and are satisfied with its performance, you can remove the STEP function from the macro.

To use the STEP function in a macro:

1. Enter `=STEP()` in a cell where you want the macro to start stepping. If there is no empty cell above the cell where you want to start the automatic stepping, insert a cell.

2. Run the macro. Excel runs the macro until it encounters the STEP function and then displays the Step dialog box.

With a macro sheet active, you can select the Step Macro tool from the Macro toolbox to step through a macro.

Tip: After encountering an error when stepping through a formula, you can jump to the error function to examine and correct the error. When you discover an error, the Macro Error dialog box is displayed. Select Goto, and Excel jumps to the cell that contains the error.

Running the Macro Debugger

The Macro Debugger is a macro that can help you debug the macros that you create. To use the Macro Debugger, you must open the DEBUG.XLA file. When you run the Macro Debugger you can set *tracepoints* and *breakpoints* at key cells of the macro that you're debugging. A tracepoint is a location where the macro stops and enters the single-step mode. At a tracepoint, you can trace the macro's execution, continue the execution, or halt the macro. A breakpoint is a location where the macro pauses, displaying the values of a group of cells that you have specified. After reaching a breakpoint, you can also choose to continue to run the macro, enter the single-step mode, or halt the macro.

Note: Document protection must be off before you run the Macro Debugger.

To run the Macro Debugger, follow these steps:

Running the Macro Debugger:

1. Choose File Open.
2. Activate macro sheet to debug active.
3. Choose Macro Debug.
4. Select the cell.
5. Choose Debug Set Breakpoint.
6. Choose Debug Breakpoint Output and specify a variable.
7. Choose Add and select OK.

1. Choose File Open to open DEBUG.XLA, which is located in the LIBRARY subdirectory of the directory where Excel was installed.

2. Make the macro sheet you want to debug active.

3. Choose Macro Debug. As shown in Figure 53.8, the Macro Debugger menu bar is displayed.

4. Select the cell in the macro before which you want to set the tracepoint or breakpoint.

5. Choose Debug Set Trace Point or Debug Set Breakpoint. If you choose to set tracepoints, repeats steps 4–5 for each tracepoint that you want to set. If you set a breakpoint, the Set Breakpoint dialog box is displayed. If you want Excel to display a message when it encounters a breakpoint, type a message in the Alert String box and then choose OK or press Enter.

6. If you chose Debug Set Breakpoint in step 5, choose Debug Breakpoint Output to tell Excel which variable values to display at the breakpoint. As shown in Figure 53.9, the Breakpoint Output dialog box is displayed. In the Variables to Output text box, specify a variable by typing the reference or name, or switch to the sheet and click on the cell.

7. If you chose Debug Set Breakpoint in step 5, choose Add to add the variable to the Variables to Output scroll box, and then select OK. (Use Add if you are using multiple variables; if you are using only one variable, you need only select OK.)

After you set the tracepoints or breakpoints and specified the variables to be displayed at the breakpoints, you are ready to run the macro.

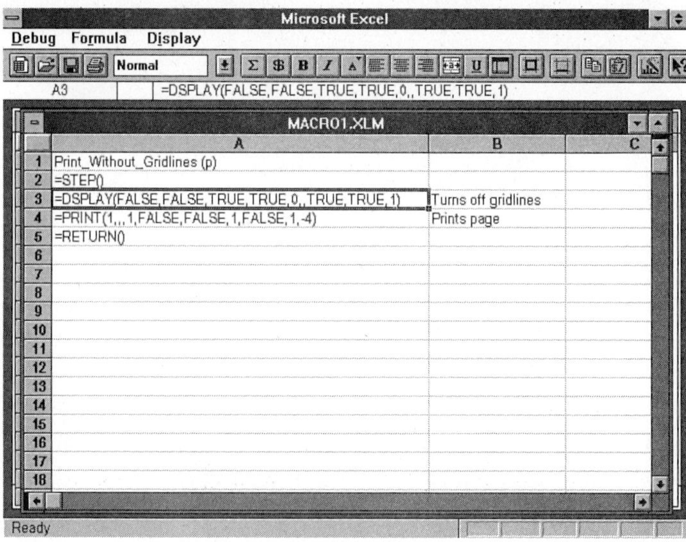

Figure 53.8 The Macro Debugger menu bar.

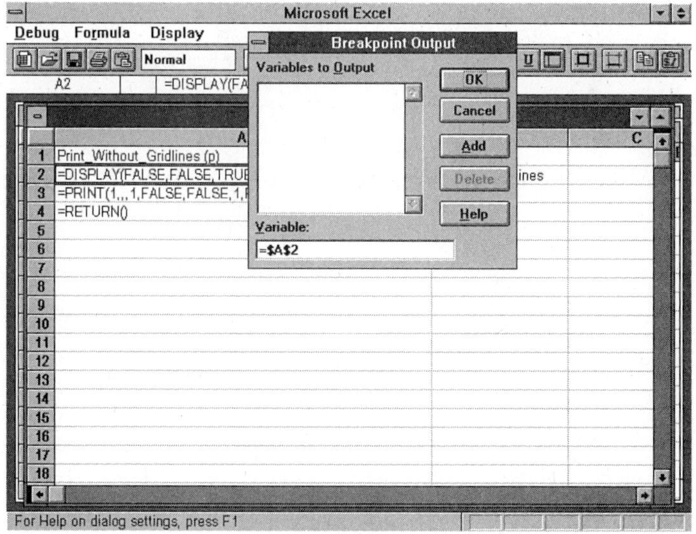

Figure 53.9 The Breakpoint Output dialog box.

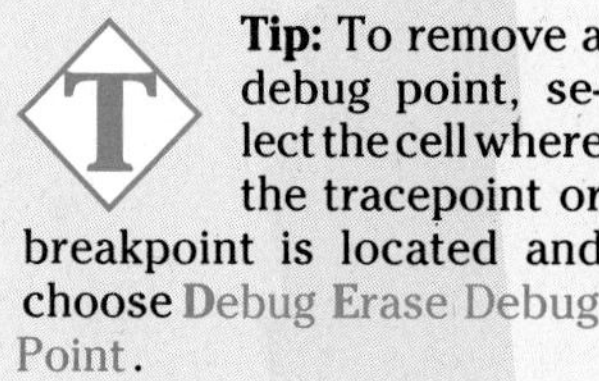

Tip: To remove a debug point, select the cell where the tracepoint or breakpoint is located and choose Debug Erase Debug Point.

Running a Macro with Macro Debugger:

1. Choose Debug Run Macro.
2. Specify name of macro.
3. Choose OK.

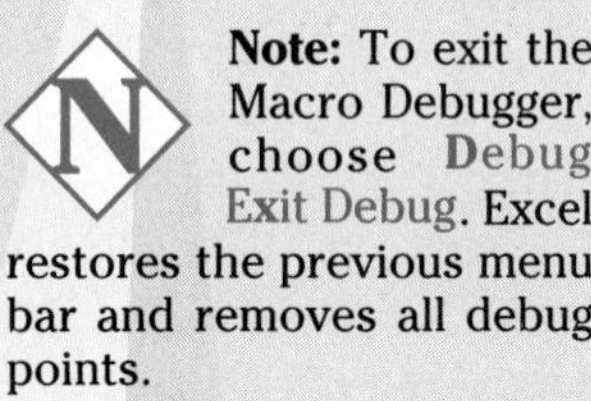

Note: To exit the Macro Debugger, choose Debug Exit Debug. Excel restores the previous menu bar and removes all debug points.

To run a macro with the Macro Debugger, follow these steps:

1. Choose **D**ebug **R**un Macro. The Run Macro dialog box is displayed.
2. In the **R**un box, specify the name of the macro.
3. Choose OK or press Enter.

The macro runs, and the breakpoint dialog box appears when a breakpoint is found. Choose Continue to continue running the macro, Step to enter single-step mode, or Halt to stop the macro. When a tracepoint is found, the macro switches to single-step mode.

Summary of Macro Debugger Commands

The Macro Debugger displays its own menu bar, as shown in Figure 53.8. Table 53.2 summarizes the commands on the Macro Debugger menu bar.

Table 53.2 Summary of other Macro Debugger menu commands

Menu	*Command*	*Task*
Formula	**Hi**dden Names	Displays the definitions of any hidden names on the active document
Formula	**N**ote	Same as the Formula Note command

Menu	*Command*	*Task*
Formula	**G**oto	Same as the Formula Goto command
Formula	**F**ind	Same as the Formula Find command
Formula	Select **D**ebug Points	Selects all the cells on your macro sheet with breakpoints or tracepoints
Formula	Select **E**rrors	Selects all the cells with formulas that result in errors
Display	**F**ormulas/ Values	Switches between displaying formulas and displaying values on the macro sheet
Display	**A**rrange All	Displays all open, displayed windows on your screen at once
Display	**S**how Info	Same as the Show Info check box in the Workspace dialog box that you open from the Options menu

Saving a Macro

After planning, writing, naming, documenting, and debugging a macro, the final step is saving the macro. You save a macro by saving the macro sheet that contains the macro. Saving a macro sheet uses the same procedure you use to save any Excel document.

To save a macro sheet for the first time, follow these steps:

Saving a Macro Sheet:

1. Choose File Save As or File Save.
2. Type desired name for macro sheet.
3. Select OK.

1. Choose File Save As (or File Save). The File Save As dialog box appears.
2. In the File Name text box, type the name you want for the macro sheet. If you don't type an extension, Excel adds the extension .XLM after you save the macro sheet.
3. Select OK or press Enter.

If you are saving a revised version of a previously saved macro sheet and you want to use the same name, choose File Save.

Select the Save File tool from the Standard toolbox to save changes made to the active macro sheet. If the macro sheet has not been previously saved, click on this tool to display the Save As dialog box instead of saving the file.

In Action: If a macro is to be used with a group of worksheets, bind the worksheets and macro sheet in a workbook. Another option is to save the workbook file, including that macro sheet, as an unbound document so that the workbook will access the latest macro sheet version when you update the macro sheet.

Skill Session

54

Running a Macro

This session details the various ways to run a macro. Macros can be activated by using the **M**acro **R**un command, pressing the macro's shortcut key combination, selecting the Macro Run tool, or clicking a button that you have assigned to the macro. No matter which method of macro execution you use, you must begin by opening the macro sheet.

Opening the Macro Sheet

A macro sheet must be open to execute its macro commands. You use the same procedure to open an existing macro sheet as you use to open any Excel document. To open a macro sheet, follow these steps:

1. Choose File Open. The Open dialog box is displayed.

2. Enter the macro sheet name in the File Name text box or select the macro sheet name from the File Name list. The File Name box displays a list of the Excel files in the current directory.

   To list only the macro sheets, enter `*.XLM`. (*.XLM is the extension Excel adds to a macro sheet when you save it, unless you specify a different extension.) Alternatively, you can select macros in the List Files of Type list box.

   To see a list of Excel files in another directory, select the directory from the **D**irectories box.

3. Choose OK or press Enter.

Opening a Macro Sheet:

1. Choose File Open.
2. Specify macro sheet name.
3. Choose OK.

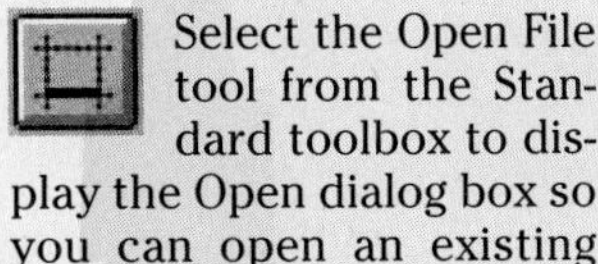

Select the Open File tool from the Standard toolbox to display the Open dialog box so you can open an existing macro sheet.

TIP: To display the Open dialog box so you can open an existing macro sheet, press Ctrl+F12.

NOTE: You don't have to open the global macro sheet to run its macros. So that macros in the global macro sheet are always available for execution, Excel automatically opens the global macro sheet when you start up Excel. For more information on how to create and use the global macro sheet, see Skill Session 55.

Running a Macro

There are four ways to run a macro:

- ▲ Choosing the **M**acro **R**un command
- ▲ Pressing the shortcut key combination
- ▲ Selecting the Macro Run tool from the Macro toolbox
- ▲ Clicking a button that you have assigned to the macro

This section covers the first three methods listed above, while the next two sections of this skill session cover how to create and use macro buttons.

To run a macro using the **M**acro **R**un command, follow these steps:

1. With the macro sheet open, choose Macro Run. As shown in Figure 54.1, the Run Macro dialog box appears.
2. In the **R**un box, select the name of the macro you want to run.
3. Choose OK or press Enter.

You can also run a macro by holding down Ctrl and pressing the shortcut key that you assigned to the macro when it was created. For example, Figure 54.2 shows a macro named Dollars that you can execute in one of two ways. You can choose Macro Run, select it from the **R**un box, and then choose OK. You can also run this macro by pressing Ctrl+A.

Running a Macro Using Macro Run:

1. Choose Macro Run.
2. Select name of macro.
3. Choose OK.

Select the Run Macro tool on the Macro toolbox to run a macro. Before you click on the Run Macro tool, a macro sheet must be active and the pointer must be in the macro you want to run. The macro runs from the active cell without displaying the Run dialog box.

TIP: To stop a macro while it is running, press Esc. When the Single Step dialog box appears, choose Halt to stop the macro.

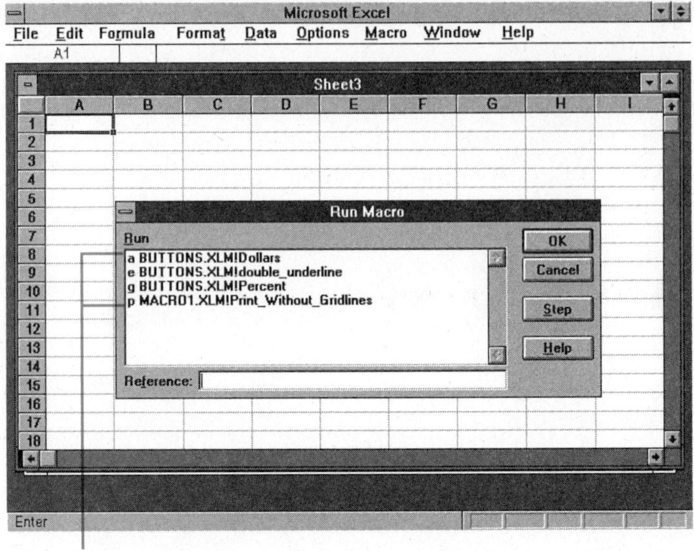

Figure 54.1 The Run Macro dialog box.

Creating a Macro Button

You can also run macros by selecting a *button*. A button is a graphic object that you place on a worksheet and to which you assign a macro. You use the Button tool on the Utility toolbox to add a button to a worksheet. A button looks like the buttons you find in dialog boxes. However, you can format the text in a button and move or size a button. When you are ready to run a macro that has been assigned to a button, you move the mouse pointer to the button. As it passes over the button, the mouse pointer changes to a hand, and then you can click on the button.

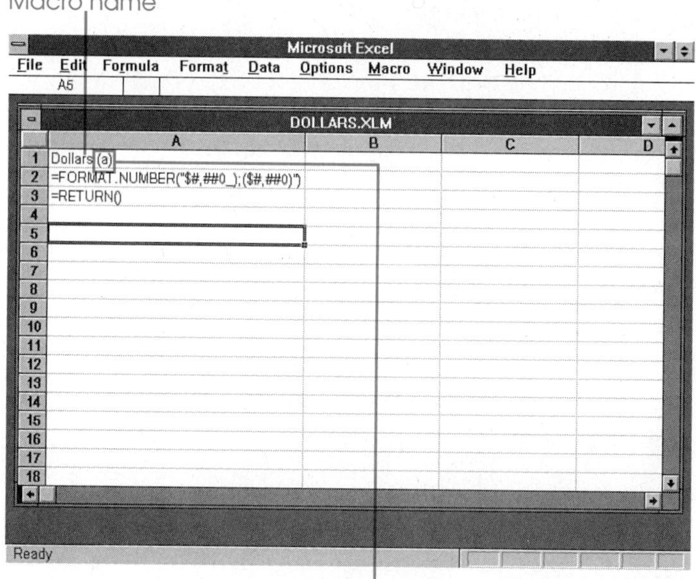

Figure 54.2 A macro named Dollars.

To create a macro button, follow these steps:

1. Click on the Button tool on the Utility toolbox. Figure 54.3 shows the Button tool. The mouse pointer changes to a cross hair.
2. Point to where you want to locate the left top corner of the button and drag the mouse to create a button. Excel displays the Assign To Object dialog box, as shown in Figure 54.4.
3. If you want to assign a macro to the new button, select a macro from the Assign **M**acro box and then choose OK or press Enter. Excel automatically enters the text "Button", followed by a number (e.g., "Button 1"). If you are not ready to assign a macro to the button, choose the Cancel button to close the dialog box.

Creating a Macro Button:

1. Click on Button tool.
2. Drag mouse to create button.
3. Select a macro and choose OK.
4. Edit button.
5. Click anywhere.

4. To edit or format the button, select the button if the button is not selected. Square handles appear around the button. To select a button with a macro assigned to it, hold down the Ctrl key while clicking the button. This selects the button without running the macro. Position the insertion point where you want to make changes and proceed to edit or format the text.

5. Click anywhere other than on the button.

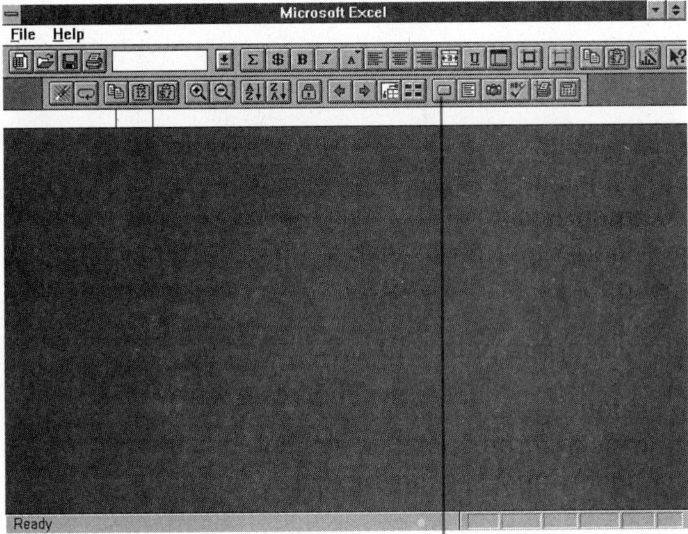

Figure 54.3 The Button tool.

Assigning a Command Macro to a Button

You may create a button and then later decide what macro to assign (or reassign) to that button. To assign a command macro to an existing button, follow these steps:

1. Open the macro sheet containing the macro you want to assign. If you are using a macro from the global macro sheet, you don't need to open a macro sheet because Excel opens the global macro sheet automatically when you begin an Excel session.
2. Select the button by clicking on it.
3. Choose Macro Assign To Object or press the right mouse button to display the shortcut menu and then select Assign Macro to Object. The Assign to Object dialog box is displayed.
4. In the Assign Macro box, select the macro you want to assign or type the macro name (name of the macro sheet, exclamation point, macro name) in the Reference box.
5. Choose OK or press Enter.

Assigning a Command Macro to an Existing Button:

1. Open macro sheet.
2. Click on button.
3. Choose Macro Assign To Object.
4. Select macro to assign.
5. Choose OK.

TIP: To delete a button on a worksheet or macro sheet, select the button you want to delete and then press the Del key or choose Edit Clear.

TIP: To perform a variety of tasks on a button (cut, clear, change alignment or fonts, and assign a macro), hold down the Ctrl key and press the right mouse button to display the shortcut menu.

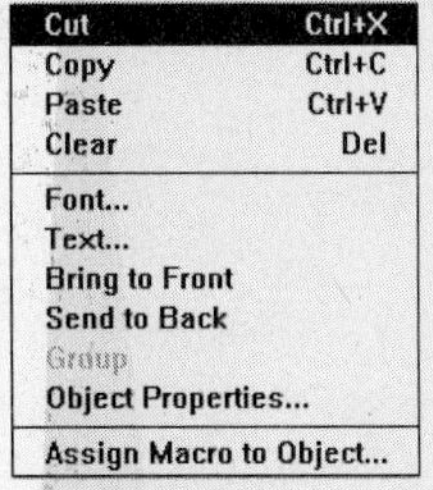

TIP: To select a button with a macro assigned to it, hold down the Ctrl key while clicking the object. This selects the button without running the macro.

> **IN ACTION:** Create buttons for frequently used macros and position them close to the worksheet data that you are working with. Figure 54.5 shows three buttons, each of which have been attached to the formatting macros shown in Figure 54.6.

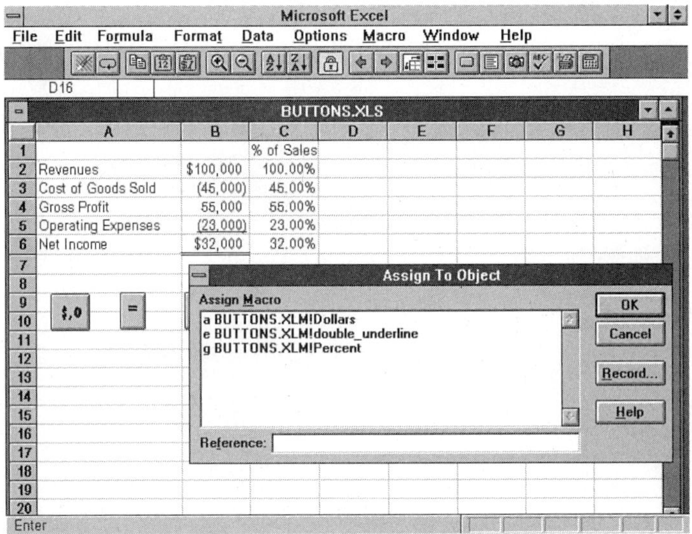

Figure 54.4 The Assign To Object dialog box.

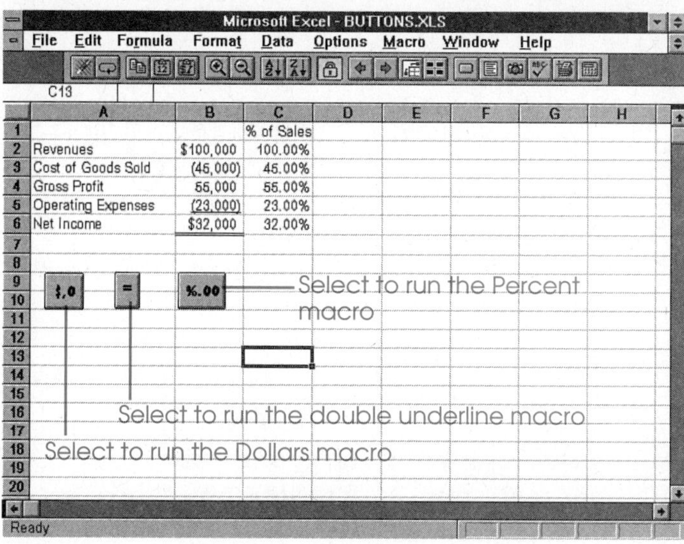

Figure 54.5 Three buttons attached to three formatting macros.

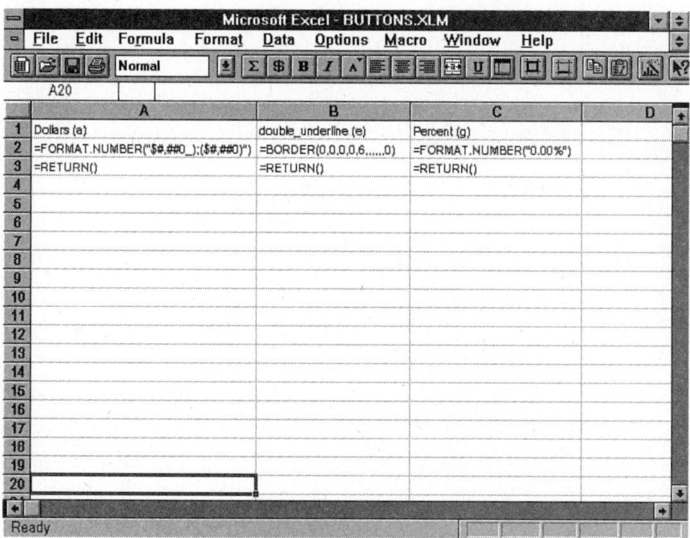

Figure 54.6 The three formatting macros for the buttons in Figure 54.5.

Aligning or Formatting Button Text

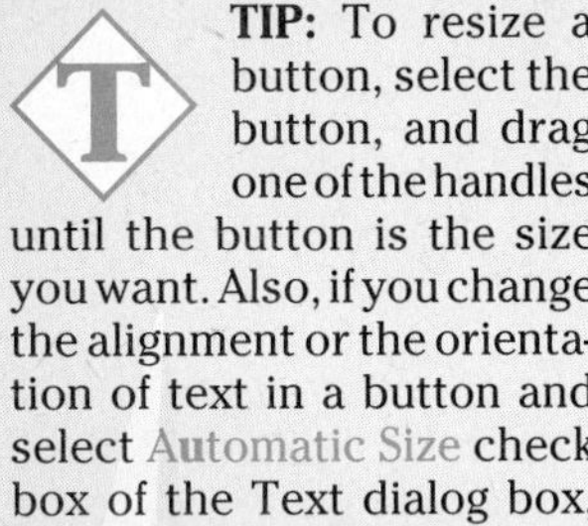

TIP: To resize a button, select the button, and drag one of the handles until the button is the size you want. Also, if you change the alignment or the orientation of text in a button and select Automatic Size check box of the Text dialog box, Excel resizes the button to fit exactly around the text.

Changing Alignment or Fonts of Button Text:

1. Select the button.
2. Choose Format Text or Format Font.
3. Select the text or font options.
4. Choose OK.

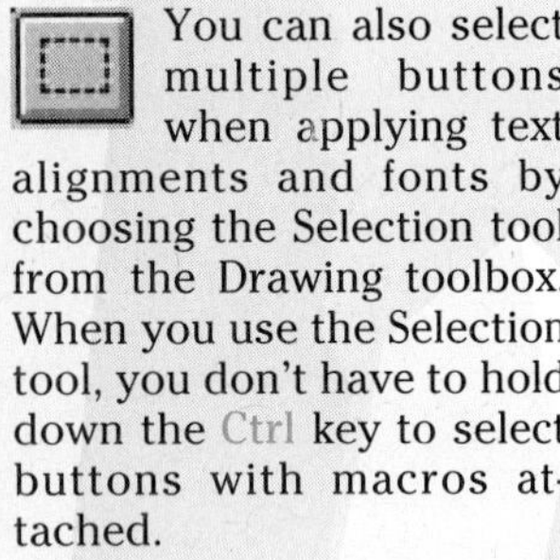

You can also select multiple buttons when applying text alignments and fonts by choosing the Selection tool from the Drawing toolbox. When you use the Selection tool, you don't have to hold down the Ctrl key to select buttons with macros attached.

You can change the alignment or formatting of the text font within a button in a manner similar to worksheet text alignment and formatting. Figure 54.7 shows some of the possibilities.

To change alignment or fonts of button text, follow these steps:

1. Select the button. If the button has a macro attached to it, select it by holding down the Ctrl key while clicking.
2. Choose Format Text or Format Font, or use the shortcut menu.
3. Just as you would for worksheet text, select the text alignment options or font, font style, and font size that you want.
4. Choose OK or press Enter to apply your changes.

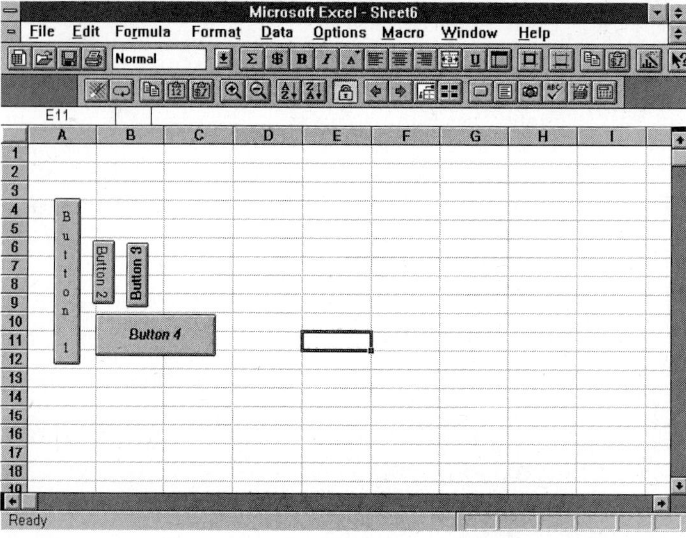

Figure 54.7 A sample of button text alignment and fonts.

Creating a Custom Tool

You create a custom tool by writing or recording a macro then assigning that macro to a custom tool. To execute a macro that has been assigned to a custom tool, you select the custom tool from the toolbar to which you have added the custom tool. Excel provides custom tools with a variety of tool faces, which you can examine by choosing **O**ptions T**o**olbar **C**ustomize and selecting Custom. To assign a macro to a custom tool, follow these steps:

Assigning a Macro to a Custom Tool:

1. Choose Options Toolbars.
2. Choose Customize.
3. Select Custom.
4. Drag the tool to the desired position.
5. Select name of command macro.
6. Choose OK.
7. Choose Close.

You can also choose Customize from the toolbar shortcut menu.

1. Choose Options Toolbars. The Toolbars dialog box appears.

2. Choose Customize. The Customize dialog box appears.

3. In the **C**ategories box, select Custom. The custom tools, as shown in Figure 54.8, are displayed.

4. Drag the tool you want from the Tools box to the position on the toolbar where you want to add the tool. The Assign To Tool dialog box appears.

5. In the Assign **M**acro box, select the name of the command macro you want to assign to the tool, or type a macro name or cell reference in the Reference box. Only command macros on the global macro sheet or other open macro sheets are listed in the Assign **M**acro box.

6. Choose OK or press Enter. The Customize dialog box appears.

7. Choose Close.

You can also create a custom tool face in a graphics application, copy that picture to the Windows Clipboard, and paste the tool face onto a blank custom tool. For example, you could create a custom tool face in Windows Paintbrush and paste that picture to a blank custom tool. However, keep in mind that the picture you create in a graphics program should be the same size as the built-in tool faces so that it fits properly on the blank custom tool. Excel will scale large pictures so that they will fit on the blank tool; however, the scaling can cause distortion of the picture. You can make sure that your picture is the same size as the built-in tool faces by copying the blank custom tool to your graphics application and then designing your custom tool face on the blank tool. To create a custom tool face, follow these steps:

1. Copy the blank tool by choosing Options Toolbars. The Toolbars dialog box appears.
2. Choose Customize. The Customize dialog box appears.
3. In the Categories box, select Custom. The custom tools are displayed.
4. Select the blank tool. A selection box appears around the selected blank tool.
5. Choose Edit Copy Tool Face. The blank tool face is copied to the Windows Clipboard.
6. Switch to the graphics application that you will use to design the custom tool face. For example, you could switch to the Windows Paintbrush application.
7. Using the graphic application's commands, paste the blank tool face.
8. Design the custom tool face and then copy it to the Windows Clipboard.
9. Switch to Microsoft Excel.
10. Choose Options Toolbars. The Toolbars dialog box appears.
11. Choose Customize. The Customize dialog box appears.
12. In the Categories box, select Custom. The custom tools are displayed.

Creating a Custom Tool Face:

1. Choose Options Toolbars Customize.
2. Select Custom.
3. Select the blank tool.
4. Choose Edit Copy Tool Face.
5. Switch to graphics application.
6. Paste the blank tool face.
7. Design custom tool face and copy to Windows Clipboard.
8. Switch to Microsoft Excel.
9. Choose Options Toolbars Customize.
10. Select Custom.
11. Select blank custom tool and drag it into toolbar.
12. Select Cancel.
13. Choose Edit Paste Tool Face.

13. Select the blank custom tool and drag it into a toolbar. The Assign to Tool dialog box appears.

14. Select Cancel. The blank custom tool remains selected in the toolbar to which it was added.

15. Choose Edit Paste Tool Face. The picture overlays the standard grey button background.

Skill Session

55

Creating and Using a Global Macro Library

You can choose to record your macros to a global macro sheet. Excel opens the global macro sheet each time you begin a session. The global macro sheet is a file of macros that are available for execution regardless of the Excel document that you are working with. You can run global macros at any time because the global macro sheet is always open even though it is, by default, hidden from view. By recording a macro to the global macro sheet, you free yourself from having to save, name, or open macro sheets because Excel manages those tasks for you. In this skill session, you can learn how to record a macro to the global macro sheet and how to hide and unhide the global macro sheet.

Recording a Macro to the Global Macro Sheet

Recording a Macro on a Global Macro Sheet:

1. Choose Macro Record.
2. Type a name.
3. Type a shortcut key.
4. Select Global Macro Sheet.
5. Choose OK.
6. Carry out actions to record.
7. Choose Macro Stop Recorder.

Select the Record Macro tool from the Macro toolbox to display the Record Macro dialog box so that you can begin recording your actions to a global macro sheet.

You can add a macro to the global macro sheet as you would add a macro to a new macro sheet by choosing **M**acro **R**ecord. You can also revise a global macro sheet by unhiding the global macro sheet and making your revisions.

To record a macro on a global macro sheet, follow these steps:

1. Choose **M**acro **R**ecord. As shown in Figure 55.1, the Record Macro dialog box appears. Excel enters a suggested macro name in the **N**ame box and a proposed shortcut key in the **K**ey box.
2. In the **N**ame box, type a name or accept the proposed name.
3. In the **K**ey box, type a shortcut key or accept the proposed key.
4. Select **G**lobal Macro Sheet.
5. Choose OK.
6. Use the keyboard and mouse to carry out the actions you want to record.
7. When you have finished performing the task that you want to automate, stop recording by choosing **M**acro Stop Re**c**order.

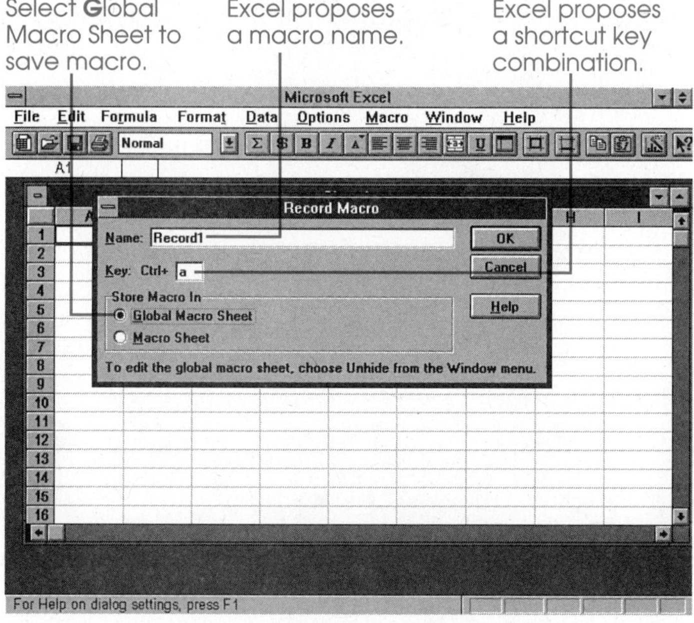

Figure 55.1 The Record Macro dialog box.

Displaying the Global Macro Sheet

By default, the global macro sheet is hidden from view. To edit the global macro sheet, you must unhide it by following these steps:

1. Choose Window Unhide. As shown in Figure 55.2, the Unhide dialog box is displayed.
2. Select GLOBAL.XLM from the **U**nhide list box.
3. Choose OK. As shown in Figure 55.3, the GLOBAL.XLM macro sheet is displayed.

Unhiding and Revising the Global Macro Sheet:

1. Choose Window Unhide.
2. Select GLOBAL.XLM.
3. Choose OK.
4. Make revisions.
5. Select Yes to save changes.

4. Make revisions to GLOBAL.XLM just as you would with any macro sheet. (See Skill Session 53 for more details on how to edit a macro sheet.)

5. When you finish your session (by selecting either File Close or File Exit), Excel will automatically ask you if you want to save the changes made to GLOBAL.XLM. Select Yes.

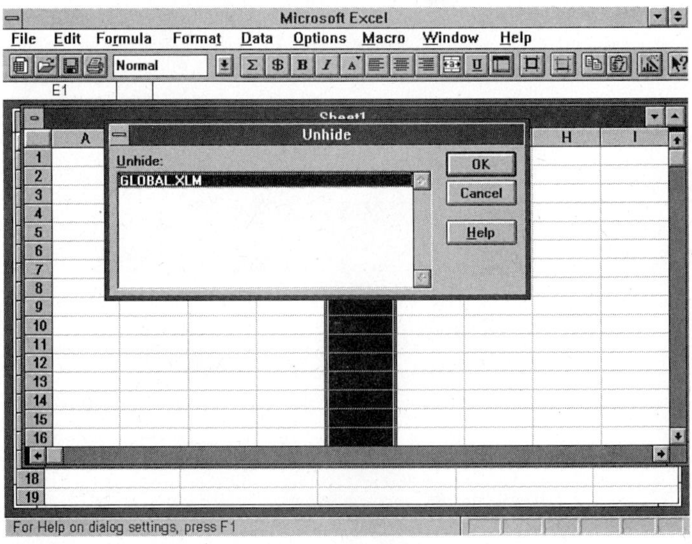

Figure 55.2 The Unhide dialog box.

Tip: To hide a displayed global macro sheet, choose Window Hide.

If you make changes to GLOBAL.XLM, but forget to hide it before you save it, it will be visible each time you start Excel. To hide GLOBAL.XLM, close all other windows first, and then choose Window Hide.

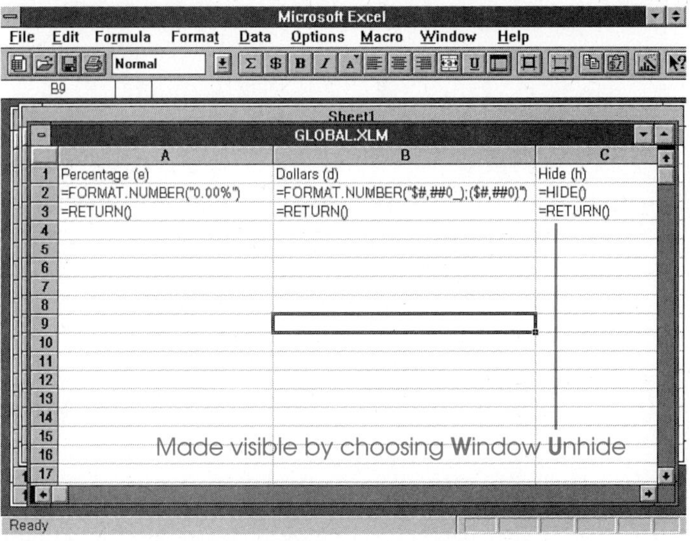

Figure 55.3 The GLOBAL.XLM macro sheet.

In Action: To become a more efficient Excel user, list those frequently used commands that are common to many of your documents and for which a toolbox tool is not available. Record a macro for each one of these frequently used commands and save them to the global macro sheet. As you work with your documents, create macro buttons (see Skill Session 54) and assign macros from the global macro sheet to the buttons.

Note: Excel saves the global macro sheet (GLOBAL.XLM) to the startup directory named XLSTART. Do not delete the startup directory, because you would lose your global macro sheet and Excel would have no place to save a new global macro sheet.

Projects Workshop

The disk that accompanied this book holds 12 worksheets. Each requires only that you enter the information that pertains to your situation. Step-by-step instructions are provided for using each worksheet. Note, however, that you may have to make slight adjustments to the template fonts, depending on the fonts and printer your system supports.

	A	B	C	D	E	F	G
1							
2			**Personal Net Worth Statement**				
3							
4		**Name(s): Wilson Taylor**		**Date: January 5, 1993**			
5		**Address: 1565 18th Avenue, Coral Gables, FL**					
6							
7				**Assets**			
8	**Cash and Equivalents**						
9		Cash on hand	$75				
10		Savings Account Balance	4,300				
11		Checking Account Balance	2,350				
12		Money Market Fund Balance	1,800				
13		Savings Bonds	400				
14		Certificates of Deposit	5,000				
15		Treasury Bills	1,000				
16		Loans to Others	100				
17		Total Cash on Hand	15,025				
18							
19	Value of Easily Convertible Assets						
20		Mutual Funds	3,500				
21		Stocks	2,800				
22		Bonds	1,200				
23		Treasury Notes	1,000				
24		Life Insurance Policies	12,000				
25		Other	500				
26		Total Convertible Assets	21,000				
27							
28	Value of Long Term Assets						
29		Home	253,000				
30		Other Real Estate	350,000				
31		IRAs, Keoughs, etc.	12,000				
32		Profit Sharing Plan	28,000				
33		Pension Lump Sum	225,000				
34		Other	2,000				
35		Total Long Term Assets	870,000				
36							
37	Value of Personal Possessions						
38		Automobile (s)	12,000				
39		Household Furnishings	35,000				
40		Clothing	4,000				
41		Jewelry	7,500				
42		Art, Antiques, etc.	1,500				
43		Other	500				
44		Total Personal Possessions	60,500				
45							
46		**Total Assets**	$966,525				
47							
48				**Liabilities**			
49	Unpaid Bills (Monthly Amounts)						
50		Taxes	$220				
51		Mortgage or Rent	1,800				
52		Insurance	150				
53		Utilities	55				
54		Alimony, Child Support					
55		Charge Card Balances	150				
56		Other	300				
57		Total Unpaid Bills	2,675				
58							
59	Loans (Total Due)						
60		Home Mortgage	$135,000				
61		Home Improvement Loan	$6,500				
62		Automobile(s)	$5,500				
63		Education	$4,500				
64		Charge Card Accounts	$1,200				
65		Insurance Loans	$350				
66		Home Equity Loans	$4,500				
67		Second Mortgage	$12,000				
68		Other Loans	$500				
69		Total Loans	170,050				
70							
71		**Total Liabilities**	$172,725				
72							
73	**Summary**						
74		**Total Assets**	$966,525				
75		**Total Liabilities**	$172,725				
76		**Net Worth**	$793,800				
77							

Project

1

Preparing a Net Worth Statement

The first project in the Projects Workshop is a *Net Worth Statement.* A Net Worth Statement is the personal equivalent of the financial statement for a business. It lets you understand your financial standing in the light of easily attainable cash, less convertible assets, and how your assets (cash and possessions) compare with your debt. Net worth is a convenient tool that lets you plan for your financial future, and measure your progress against any plans you make. If you wish to buy real estate (or any other major item), you can also use a Net Worth Statement as a valuable tool to assist you in completing loan applications.

The *Net Worth template* that accompanies this project is called NWORTH.XLS. It is a straightforward template that contains no complex mathematical formulas. Its operation will be described as you perform each step. To use the template, all you need do is open it, follow the instructions, and fill in the blanks. Sources for the relevant data are suggested as you follow the instructions. Once you've learned how to use the template in its current state, you will be provided with a number of suggestions (and illustrations) for adapting the template to your needs. These adaptations can involve expanding the template to include additional information and additional years, or linking the template to other templates. Follow along to put the NWORTH.XLS template to work.

As you work with this project, you will be using the following features of Excel:

- ▲ Opening a file
- ▲ Entering your own data
- ▲ Saving the file under a new name
- ▲ Adding a new row
- ▲ Expanding column width
- ▲ Adding labels
- ▲ Centering text
- ▲ Using drag and drop to fill right
- ▲ Selecting nonadjacent cells

Opening the Net Worth Worksheet

1. Choose File Open.
2. Select NWORTH.XLS from the list box. (Switch to the directory where you have copied NWORTH.XLS first, if necessary.)
3. Click on OK or press Enter. NWORTH.XLS opens.

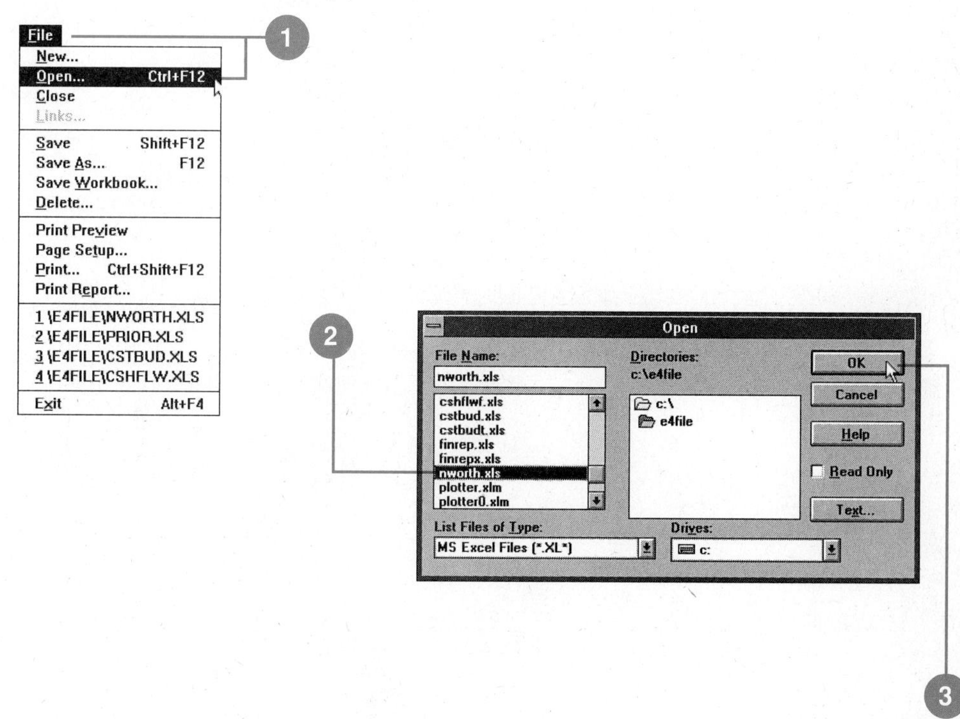

Entering Your Data

Entering Your Data on the First Screen

1. Select cell B4. Type your name and your spouse's name if you are married.
2. Select cell F4. Type the current date.
3. Select cell B5. Type your address.
4. Select cell C9. Enter any cash on hand as of the statement date.
5. Select cell C10. Enter the most current balance from your savings account books.
6. Select cell C11. Enter the current checking account balance for all your checking accounts. Adjust the amount to reflect current deposits and debits.
7. Select cell C12. Enter the current account balance for your money market accounts.
8. Select cell C13. Enter the current value of your Savings Bonds.
9. Select cell C14. Enter the cash value of your certificates of deposit.
10. Select cell C15. Enter the cash value of your treasury notes.
11. Select cell C16. Enter the cash value of any loans you have made to others.
12. Look at cell C17. This cell uses Excel's SUM( ) function to total entries in cells C9:C16.
13. Press Page Down to display the second screen for NWORTH.XLS.

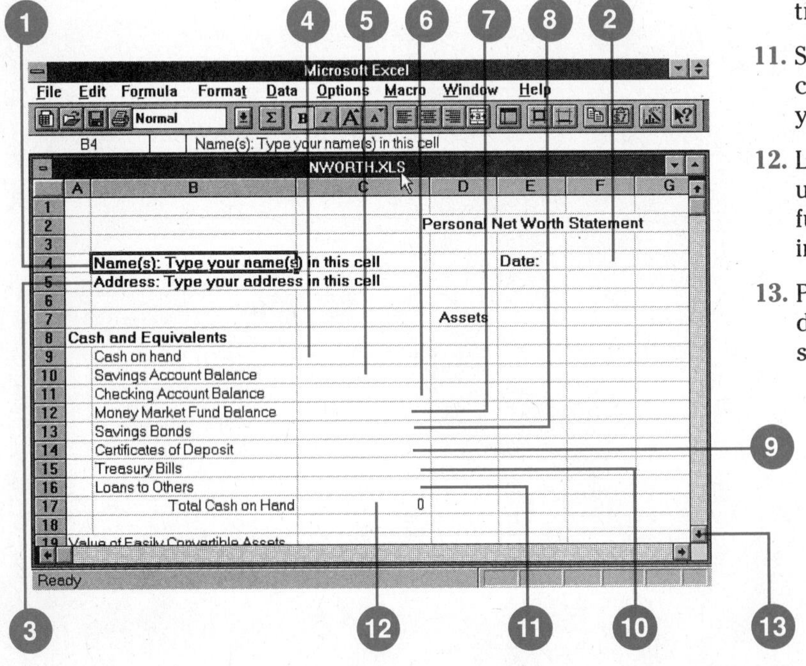

Entering Your Data on the Second Screen

1. Select cell C20. Enter the current cash value of your mutual funds.
2. Select cell C21. Enter the current cash value of your stocks.
3. Select cell C22. Enter the cash value of your bonds.
4. Select cell C23. Enter the value of your treasury notes.
5. Select cell C24. Enter the current cash value of your life insurance policies.
6. Select cell C25. Enter the cash value of any other easily convertible assets.
7. Review cell C26. The worksheet totals your easily convertible assets from cells `C20:C25`.
8. Select cell C29. Enter the current value of your home.
9. Select cell C30. Enter the value of other real estate you own.
10. Select cell C31. Enter the value of your IRAs and Keough Savings.
11. Select cell C32. Enter the cash value of your Profit Sharing or Employee Investment Plan.
12. Select cell C33. Enter the value of the current lump sum amount for your pension.
13. Select cell C34. Enter the value of your other long-term assets.
14. Review the contents of cell C35 for your long-term assets total. Press Page Down.

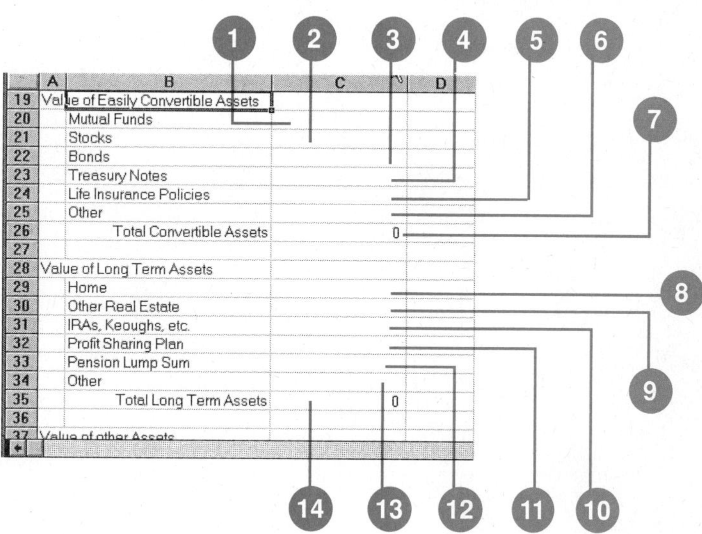

Entering Your Data on the Third Screen

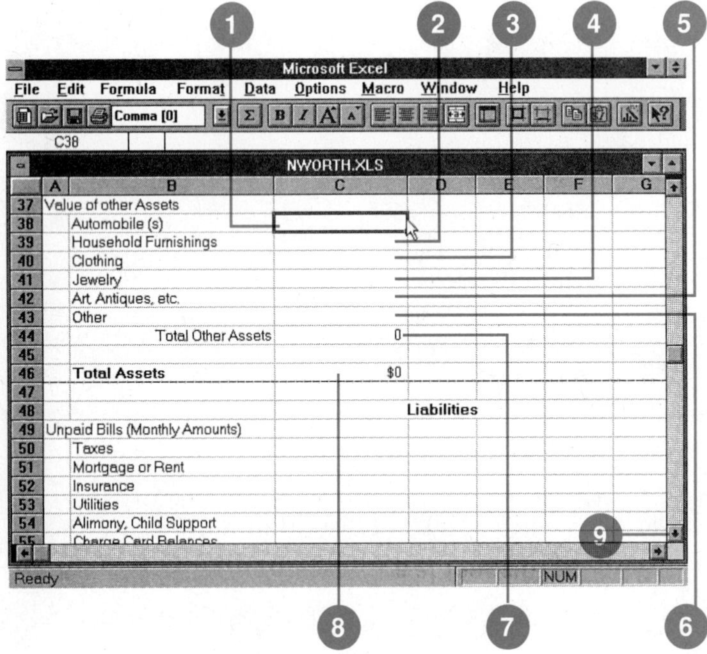

1. Select cell C38. Enter the value of your automobiles.
2. Select cell C39. Enter the value of your household furnishings.
3. Select cell C40. Enter the value of your clothing.
4. Select cell C41. Enter the value of your jewelry.
5. Select cell C42. Enter the value of any art or other collectibles you possess.
6. Select cell C43. Enter the value of any other personal property.
7. Review cell C44. This cell contains the total value of your personal possessions.
8. Review the content of cell C46. This cell contains the total value of all of your assets.
9. Scroll down until row 48 is at the top of the screen display.

Entering Your Short Term Expenses

1. Select cell C50. Enter any taxes due within the next 30 days.
2. Select cell C51. Enter the monthly amount of your mortgage or rent.
3. Select cell C52. Enter your average monthly insurance amount for all of your insurance policies.
4. Select cell C53. Enter the average monthly amount you pay for utilities.
5. Select cell C54. Enter any alimony and child support that you must pay.
6. Select cell C55. Enter the average amount you pay each month on any charge cards.
7. Select cell C56. Enter any other monthly amounts you pay for automobile and other loans.
8. Check the contents of cell C57. This cell contains the total of all of your monthly payments.
9. Scroll down the worksheet until row 59 is at the top of the screen display.

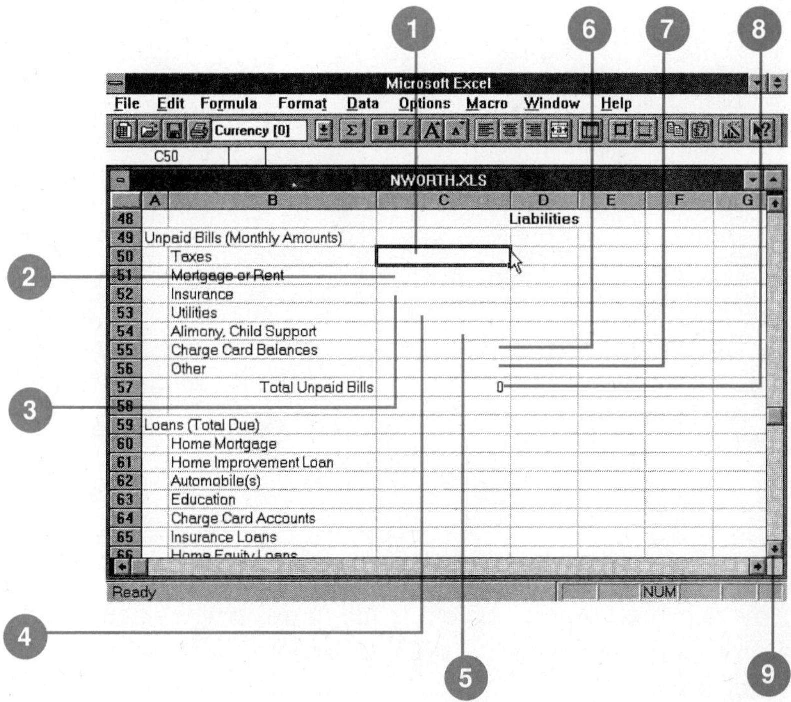

Entering Total Loan Amounts, Calculating Total Liabilities, and Calculating Net Worth

1. Select cell C60. Enter the total amount outstanding on your home mortgage.
2. Select cell C61. Enter the total amount outstanding on your home improvement loan.
3. Select cell C62. Enter the outstanding amount on your automobile loans.
4. Select cell C63. Enter any outstanding education loan amounts.
5. Select cell C64. Enter the total owed on your charge card accounts.
6. Select cell C65. Enter any outstanding insurance loan amounts.
7. Select cell C66. Enter the outstanding amounts of any home equity loans.
8. Select cell C67. Enter the outstanding amount of any second mortgage.
9. Select cell C68. Enter the outstanding amount of any other loans you may have taken out.
10. Look at cell C69. This cell contains the outstanding amounts of all your loans.
11. Review cell C71. It contains a number that equals the sum of all your liabilities.
12. Look at cell C74. It contains the value of all your assets.
13. Look at cell C75. It contains the value of all of your liabilities.
14. Examine cell C76. This cell contains your net worth. Net Worth is equal to total assets minus total liabilities.

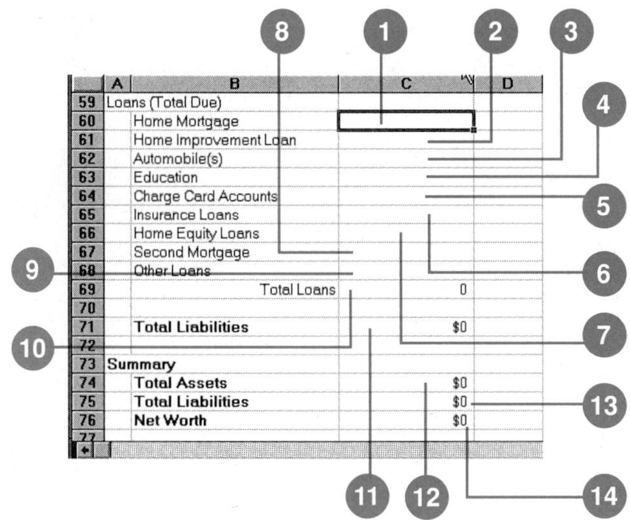

Now is a good time to save this file under a new name. Follow the steps listed next to save the file under any name you wish.

Saving NWORTH.XLS Under a New Name

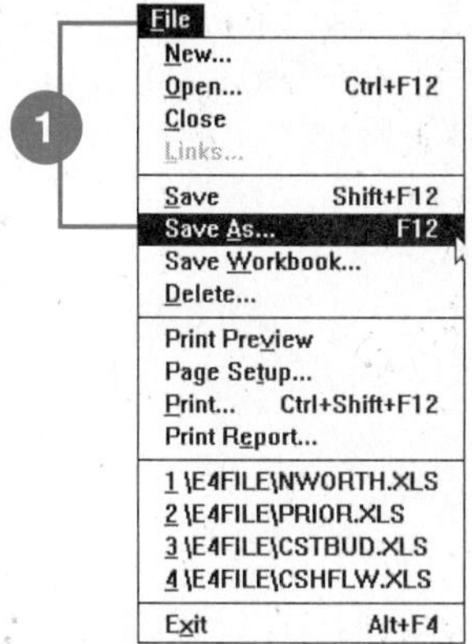

Use the **File** Save **As** command to save a file under a new name (this prevents an existing file from being overwritten with your current changes), in a new location such as in a new directory or on another disk, and in a new format. The procedure for saving a file under a new name is described in the following steps:

1. Choose File Save As.
2. Select the text NWORTH in the File Name text box.
3. Type a name of eight characters or less.
4. Press Enter or click on OK.

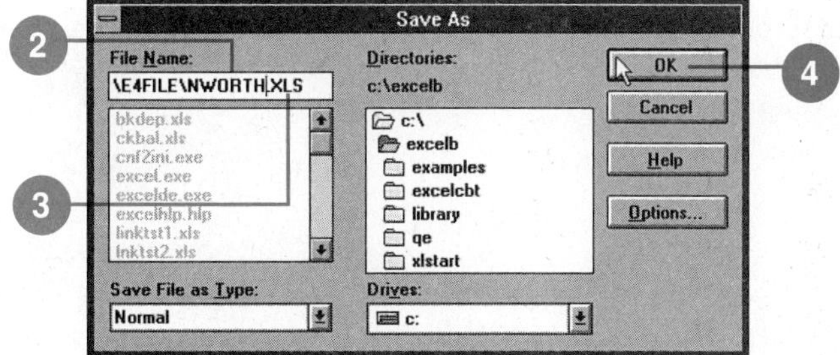

Customizing NWORTH.XLS

The *Net Worth worksheet* entitled NWORTH.XLS may not suit your situation. You may wish to make some changes to the worksheet that better suit your needs. The steps presented next are suggestions for customizing NWORTH.XLS. You may wish to make these changes, or they may suggest other changes. The suggested changes involve expanding the Net Worth worksheet to compare your financial situation over two years. They also involve renaming a few of the cells. A number of the entries on this worksheet (such as the checkbook balance, the value of your stocks, or the value of your inventory) may be entered by linking these entries to other worksheets. Linking is also used in the projects dealing with inventory, checkbook balancing, and the management of a stock portfolio. You may wish to add new rows to contain more items, or delete any rows containing items that don't apply to your situation. Feel free to do so.

Adding a New Row

The first step in customizing NWORTH.XLS is adding a new row to identify the years covered by the worksheet.

1. Select row 8.
2. Choose Edit Insert.

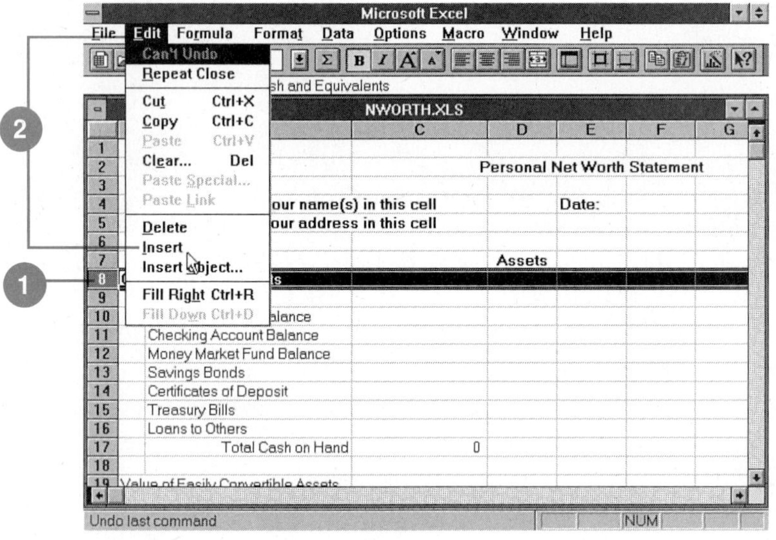

Expanding a Column Width

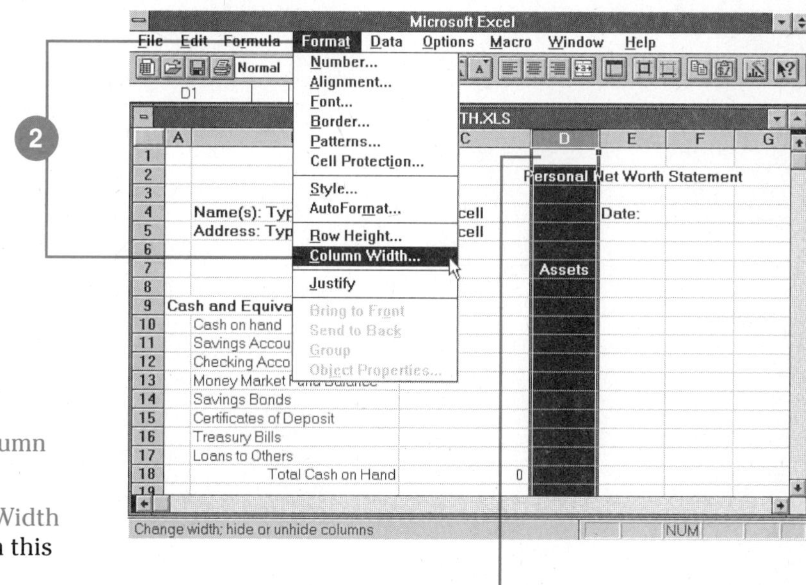

1. Select column D.
2. Choose Format Column Width.
3. Select the Column Width text box. Type 17 in this box.
4. Press Enter or click on OK.

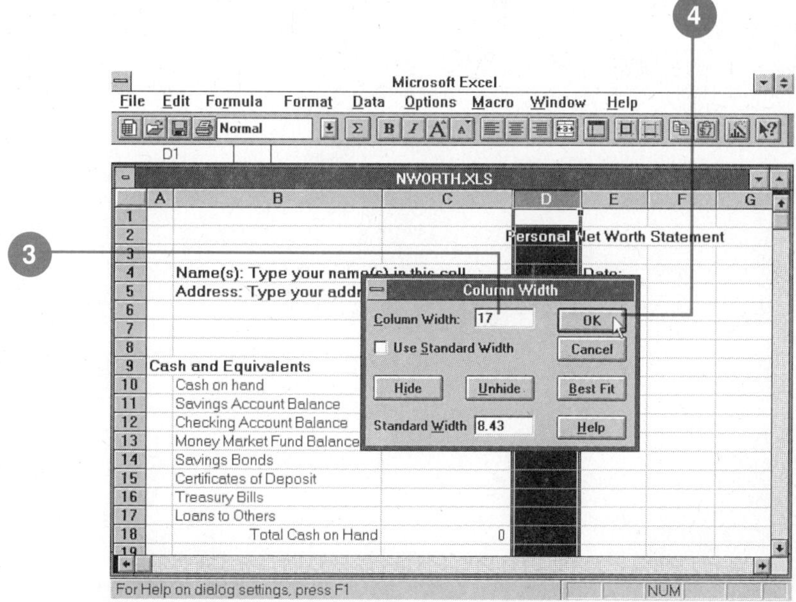

Adding Labels and Centering Text

The labels described below are being added to the worksheet to enable you to track your networth over several years. By tracking your progress you will know if it is shrinking, staying the same, or (better yet) growing.

1. Select cell C8. Type **1992**.
2. Select cell D8. Type **1993**.
3. Select cells C8 and D8.

4a. Click on the Center Text tool on the Standard toolbar or use Steps 4b through 4d.

4b. Choose Format Align.

4c. Select Center from the Horizontal options.

4d. Press Enter or click on OK.

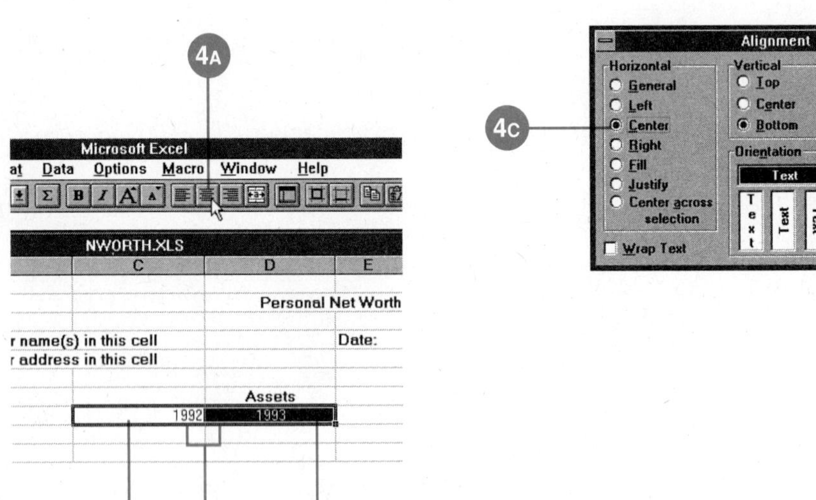

Using Autofill to Fill Right

This example takes you through the use of "autofill." Autofill is a convenient tool used to copy formulas into adjacent cells. It saves you time in constructing worksheets.

Follow the steps in this section on your NWORTH.XLS template.

1. Select cell C18.
2. Move the mouse pointer to the lower right corner of the cell. The pointer changes to a plus sign (+).
3. Drag the plus-sign cursor to the right until cell D18 is highlighted.
4. Release the mouse button.

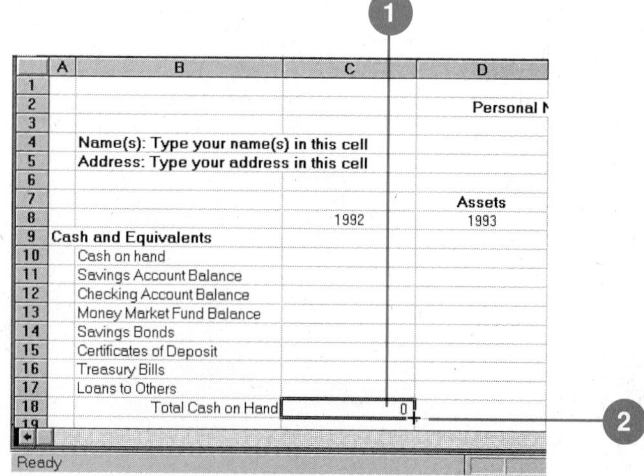

If you don't have a mouse, once you've selected the original cell and destination cell(s), press Ctrl+R to fill right.

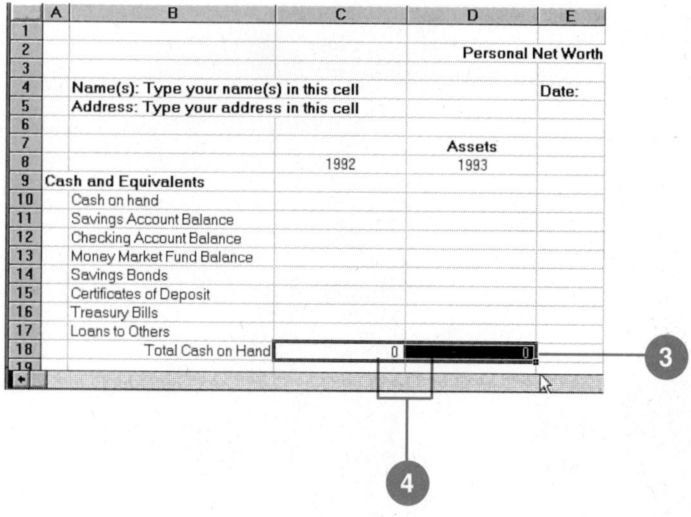

Selecting Nonadjacent Cell Ranges and Filling Formulas Right

The track illustrated below is another time saver. It takes less time to select nonadjacent cells and execute a command to copy, format, or otherwise manipulate the contents of such cells than it takes to make indiviudal selections and execute the same command many times.

1. Select cells C27:D27.
2. Press Ctrl.
3. Select cells C36:D36. Note that all four cells are highlighted.
4. Press Ctrl+R.

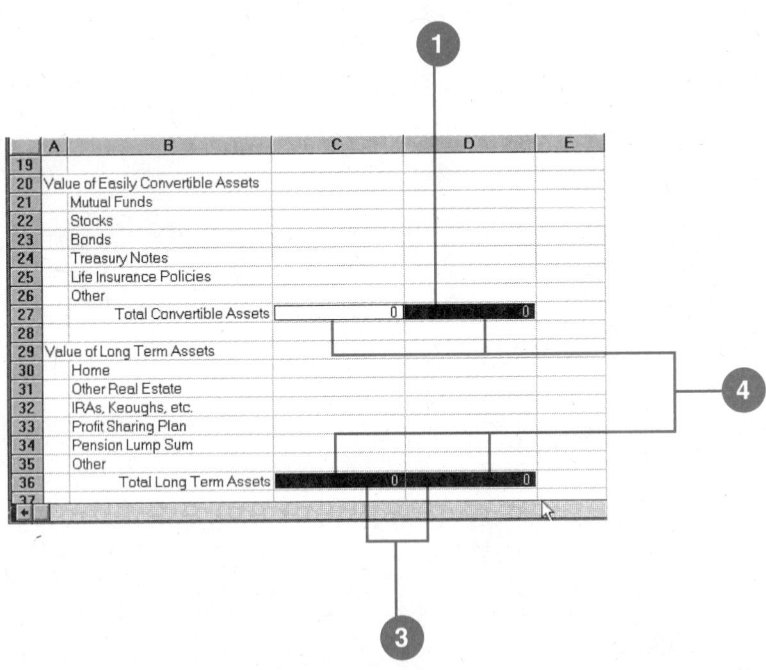

Filling Right More Formulas

1. Select cells C45:D45. Press Ctrl.
2. Select cells C47:D47. Press Ctrl.
3. Select cells C58:D58.
4. Press Ctrl+R.
5. Select cells C70:D70. Press Ctrl.
6. Select cells C72:D72. Press Ctrl.
7. Select cells C75:D77.
8. Press Ctrl+R.

After you've finished this step, you're ready to add data. Go back and add the appropriate data in cells D8 through 68.

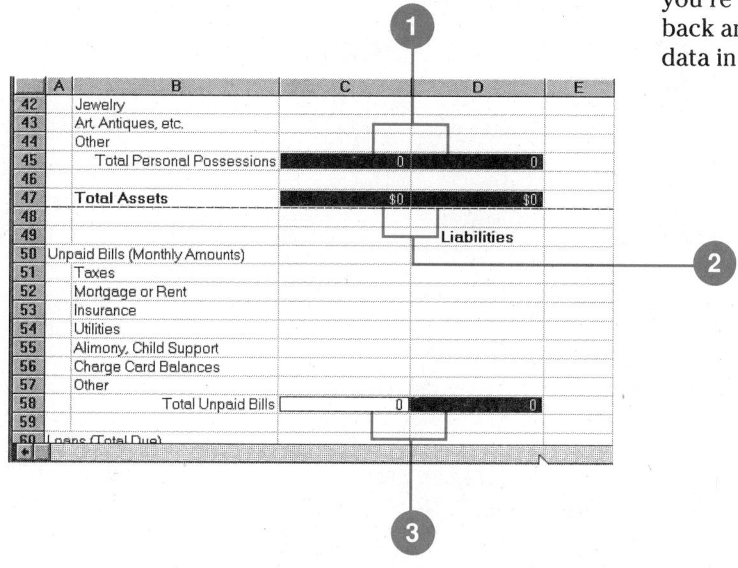

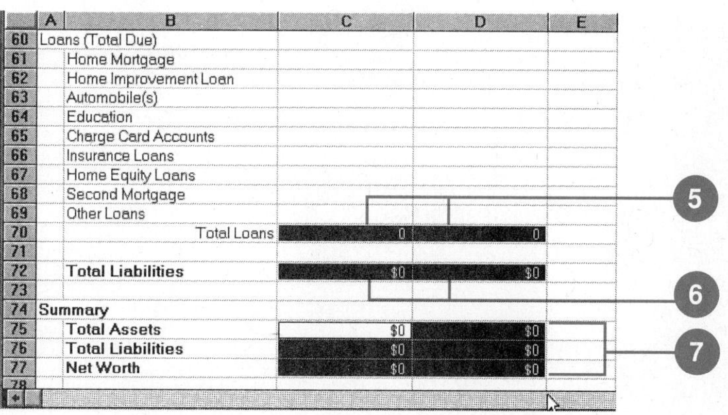

Using NWORTH.XLS

Now that you've built (and customized) NWORTH.XLS, you can:

- Print it for your files, or share with your financial advisor.
- Update it quarterly or annually, and compare the net growth (or decline) of the numbers representing your net worth, individual assets, and liabilities.
- Use it to support a loan application.
- Convert it to a net worth statement for your business.
- Use it as a planning tool to examine investment options by projecting change in value of new investments and projecting the costs to support the investments.

To convert this template to a net worth statment for a small business, take the following steps:

- Insert the appropriate name and address information in cells B4 and B5.
- Change the labels in cells B10:B16 to reflect the nature of your business' accounts, loans, and other cash advances.
- Change the labels in cells B20:B25 to better describe the convertible assets of your business.
- Change the labels in cells C38:C43 to describe the value of the smaller assets of your business. You may wish to consult an accountant or your financial staff regarding the treatment of depreciation in completing this portion of the worksheet.

- ▲ Change the labels in cells B50:B56 to reflect the nature of the short term expenses associated with your business.
- ▲ Change the labels in cells B60:B68 to reflect the amounts associated with long term debt for your business.
- ▲ Add new rows or take out rows as required to make the statement more attractive.

Summary

The Net Worth worksheet is a tool you may use to understand your current financial situation. You may create a version that contains your plans for future investments, debt payment, changes in insurance, or other important personal financial issues. You may use it to track your progress from year to year (or quarter to quarter if your situation is especially dynamic). The worksheet can be used to provide the information requested on loan applications for a home, an automobile, or other major investments. A Net Worth statement is fundamental of sound personal financial management.

The next project is a home inventory worksheet. The home inventory worksheet is a simple tool to keep track of your personal possessions and their value. You may link the home inventory worksheet to the Net Worth worksheet; the link will supply the data dealing with personal possessions automatically.

	A	B	C	D	E	F	G
1				Household Inventory			
2							
3	***Property of:***	Joe Smith					
4	***Address:***	123 Any Street, USA					
5				Inventory Recapitulation			
6			**Purch Price**	**Repl Value**	**No of Items**		
7	All items:		4705	4960	15		
8	Based on Criteria	Criteria	4705	4960	15		
9							
10							
11							
12							
13	Criteria Area						
14	***Description***	***Location***	***Type***	***Purch Date***	***Purch Price***	***Repl Value***	
15							
16							
17							
18	Database Area						
19	Description	Location	Type	Purch Date	Purch Price	Repl Value	
20	"Sacred Ground"	Family Room	Art	5/18/91	550	800	
21	Record Changer	Family Room	Electronics	3/15/89	120	90	
22	Color TV	Family Room	Electronics	5/18/89	375	280	
23	Stereo Receiver	Family Room	Electronics	2/18/90	450	420	
24	Amplifier	Family Room	Electronics	7/19/90	180	150	
25	CD Player	Family Room	Electronics	9/12/90	450	400	
26	VCR	Family Room	Electronics	9/19/90	325	280	
27	Large Speakers	Family Room	Electronics	9/22/90	480	450	
28	Small Speakers	Family Room	Electronics	4/18/91	280	250	
29	Tan Armchair	Family Room	Furniture	4/14/85	190	250	
30	TV Table	Family Room	Furniture	6/18/87	65	75	
31	Brown Sofa	Family Room	Furniture	2/15/88	840	1100	
32	Oak End Tables	Family Room	Furniture	8/15/88	180	220	
33	Coffee Table	Family Room	Furniture	5/17/89	175	150	
34	Bookcase	Family Room	Furniture	2/11/91	45	45	

Project

2

Household Inventory Database

The worksheet presented as Project 2 is a simple database for managing and valuing your personal possessions. The database is maintained by using Excel's Data Form dialog box. The data fields in the database describe each possession, a household location, a "type" classifier for each item, a purchase date, a purchase price, and a replacement price. These fields are adequate for managing most personal possessions. Fifteen items are supplied to allow you to practice using criteria to analyze the data in the database. You will enter one practice record to learn how to use the Data Form. After you have finished using the data provided for practice, you may delete this data and enter your own.

As you use this simple Excel database, you need to understand a few basic principles concerning databases in Excel. First, you must name each database field. Field names must be located at the head of the columns that make up the database. The range of cells that make up the database must be named Database. This naming is usually accomplished by using the **D**ata Set Data**b**ase command. Excel has a number of database functions such as DSUM (totals the values in a database field), DCOUNT (returns the number of items in a specified database field), and DAVERAGE (returns the average of the values in a database field). DSUM and DCOUNT are used in the worksheet described here. These functions and the others not named require that you define database criteria. You use criteria to constrain the database records according to specific requirements associated with the values in database fields. Criteria are defined by specifying values to be associated with data in certain data fields in a database.

The worksheet supplied on disk for this chapter is called HHINV.XLS. This worksheet may be used to print a list for insurance purposes. Print the database and put it in your safe deposit box along with other important papers such as deeds. Update it quarterly. It may also be used to supply data to the Net Worth statement described in Project 1. Another use is to provide information that may be used on a loan application. Finally, the worksheet is a tool to organize your life.

HHINV.XLS is organized in a manner that should be explained. Cells C7:E8 contain a recapitulation of the data in the database. This recapitulation lets you look at your entire household inventory and at slices of the inventory based on item type, purchase price, date purchased, and replacement value. Row 8 contains the information about items constrained by the criteria that are entered in the Criteria Area of the worksheet.

> The formula in cell C7 is =DSUM(Database,"Purch Price",Criteria).
>
> The formula in cell C8 is =DSUM(Database,"Purch Price",A14:F15).

The formula in D7 is =DSUM(Database,“Repl Value”,Criteria).

The formula in cell D8 is =DSUM(Database,“Repl Value”,A14:F15).

The formula in cell E7 is =DCOUNT(Database,“Purch Price”,Criteria).

The formula in cell E8 is =DCOUNT(Database,“Purch Price”,A14:F15).

The formulas in row 8 depend upon the criteria you define in the Criteria Area. Cells A14:F15 are called the Criteria Area. This range of cells has been named Criteria by using the Data Set Criteria command; hence, “Criteria” appears in cell B8. You use it to set the criteria used that constrain the data by any of the criteria contained in row 14. Thus, if you type `Furniture` in cell C15 under the word “Type,” the numbers in cells C8, D8,and E8 will reflect only the sums and count for the records in the database that contain a type of furniture. You may use this tool to obtain the purchase price, replacement value, and count of items in your household inventory based on any of the criteria you may want to use. For example, you can find the number and value of each piece of furniture that cost you more than $50. You can also find the count and value of all items purchased later than 1/12/88.

Open HHINV.XLS using the technique described in Project 1 (Skill Session 6 also covers opening worksheets). After you've opened the worksheet, follow the instructions described next.

Getting Acquainted with HHINV.XLS

HHINV.XLS is a basic database that lets you manage your personal possessions. By following the steps described below, you can become familiar with its layout.

- ▲ Cell B3 is used to identify the owners of the items described in the inventory. In this cell, enter your name and your spouse's name if you are married.
- ▲ Cell B4 is used to specify the address of the items being inventoried. Enter your address in this cell.
- ▲ Cells A7:E8 contain a recapitulation of the purchase price, replacement value, and number of items in the inventory. Row 7 contains the information about all of the items in the database.
- ▲ Row 8 contains the purchase price, replacement value, and number of items in your inventory based on the criteria you specify in cells A15:F16.
- ▲ Cells A14:F16 are defined as the Criteria Area on the worksheet. Like a database, a Criteria Area must include the field names and the cells that will be used to enter the criteria. You will use these cells to look at data in a constrained fashion. This procedure is described later in this project.
- ▲ Cells A19:F34 currently make up the database itself.

Getting Acquainted with the Household Inventory Database

Click the vertical scroll arrow in the lower right corner of the worksheet to view the database.

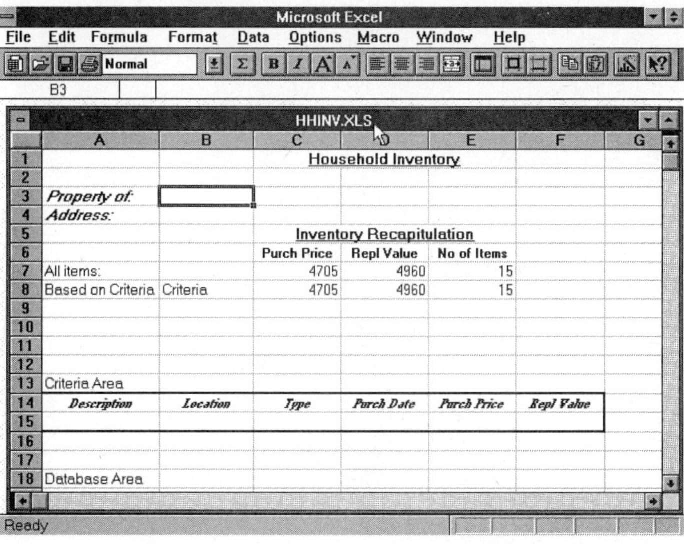

The worksheet section described below is the database itself. Each of its features is discussed for you.

- ▲ Each of the fields in the household inventory database are defined in row 19. Each cell in this row contains a field name that is associated by Excel with the data that is entered in the column containing the field name below the row containing the field name.
- ▲ The field names in this database are Description (A19), Location (B19), Type (C19), Purch Date (D19), Purch Price (E19), and Repl Value (F19).
- ▲ Rows 20–34 contain database records. A record is a complete set of information about each item in a database. You will be adding a record to this database for practice using Excel's Data Form. Later you will delete all of the practice records and start your own database.

Click on the vertical scroll bar at some point above the vertical scroll arrow. This will take you back one page on the HHINV.XLS worksheet. If you don't want to use the mouse, press Page Up.

Entering a New Database Record with Excel's Data Form

One of Excel's convenient database tools is the Data Form. This tool may be used to add, delete, and find data in a database. The following steps introduce you to the use of the Data Form.

1. Choose Data Form.

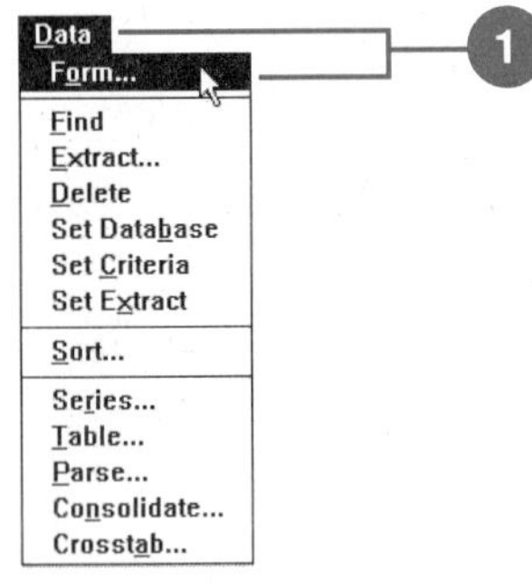

2. Select the New button.
3. Choose the Description text box and type **`Microwave`**.
4. Choose the Location text box and type **`Kitchen`**.
5. Choose the Type text box and type **`Appliance`**.
6. Select the Purch Date text box and type **`3/12/90`**.
7. Select the Purch Price text box and type **`325`**.
8. Choose the Repl Value text box and type **`280`**.
9. Select Data and the Close button. The Data Form closes, and the new record is added to the bottom of the database range. (You may tab between text boxes or select each box with the mouse in the previous steps.)

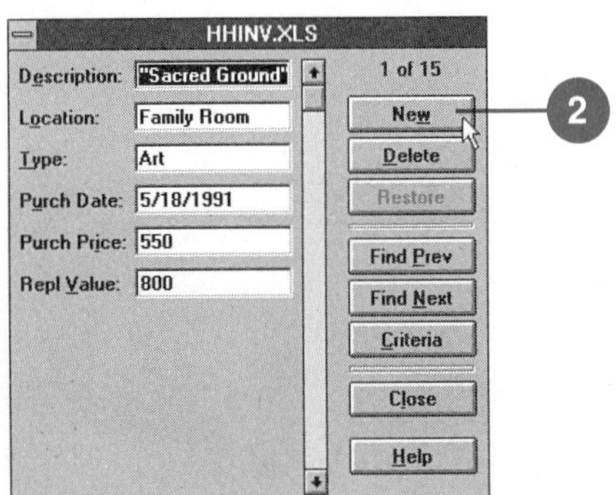

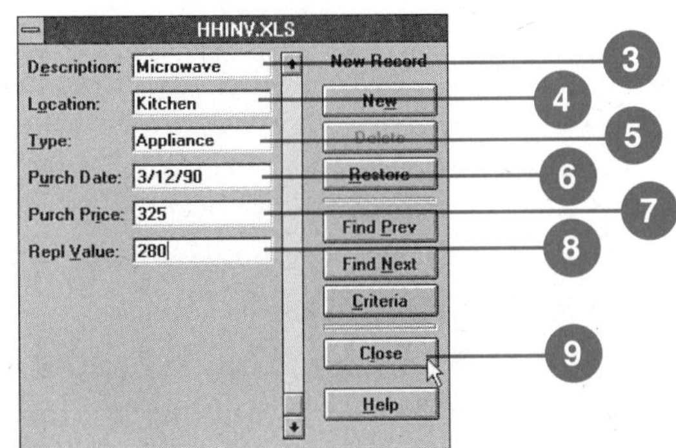

Checking the Summary Results and Viewing the New Record

The steps described below are typical of steps taken to make use of summary data from a database. This data should help you understand your current situation in high level terms.

1. Return to the first page of HHINV.XLS and look for the new values in cells C7:E8.
2. Scroll down the worksheet until row 19 is at the top of the worksheet window.
3. Look at row 35 to see the new database record and new row.
4. Return to the first page of the worksheet.

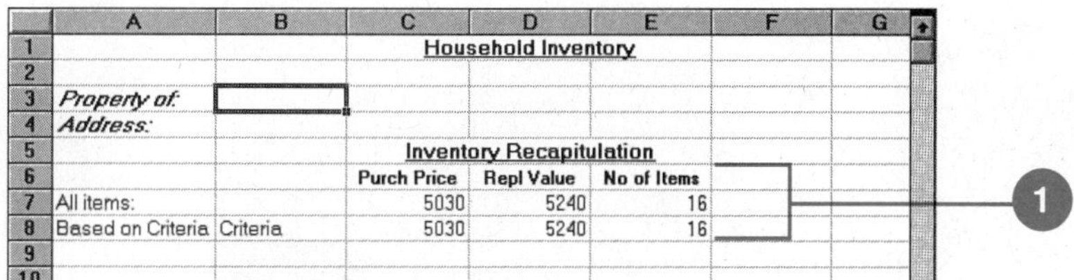

	A	B	C	D	E	F	G
1			Household Inventory				
2							
3	*Property of:*						
4	*Address:*						
5			Inventory Recapitulation				
6			Purch Price	Repl Value	No of Items		
7	All items:		5030	5240	16		
8	Based on Criteria	Criteria	5030	5240	16		
9							
10							

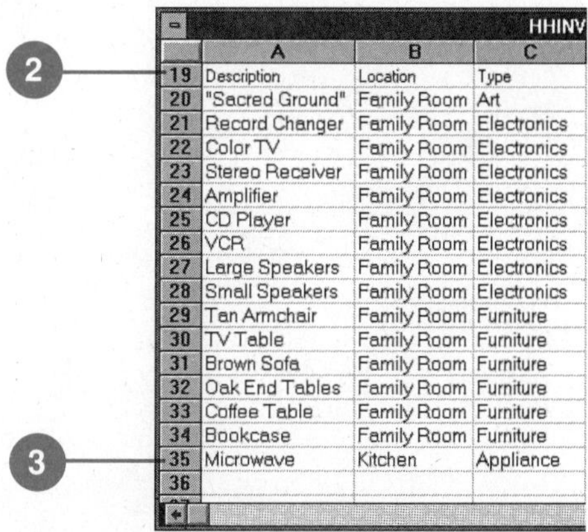

	A	B	C
19	Description	Location	Type
20	"Sacred Ground"	Family Room	Art
21	Record Changer	Family Room	Electronics
22	Color TV	Family Room	Electronics
23	Stereo Receiver	Family Room	Electronics
24	Amplifier	Family Room	Electronics
25	CD Player	Family Room	Electronics
26	VCR	Family Room	Electronics
27	Large Speakers	Family Room	Electronics
28	Small Speakers	Family Room	Electronics
29	Tan Armchair	Family Room	Furniture
30	TV Table	Family Room	Furniture
31	Brown Sofa	Family Room	Furniture
32	Oak End Tables	Family Room	Furniture
33	Coffee Table	Family Room	Furniture
34	Bookcase	Family Room	Furniture
35	Microwave	Kitchen	Appliance
36			

Using Criteria to Constrain Data to Find Specific Results

Many databases contain large amounts of information that may be examined in a number of ways. Criteria are used to focus your view of the data in your database by setting conditions such as "costing more than," "costing less than," and so on! This example illustrates this practice.

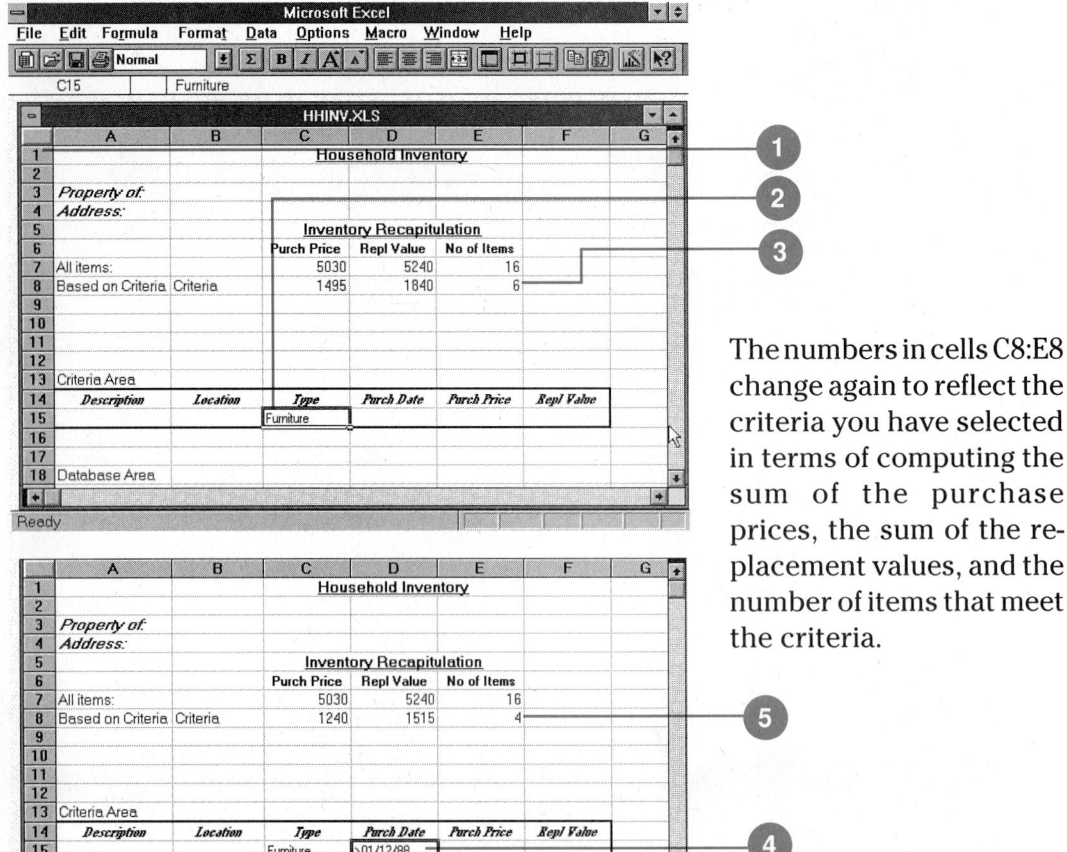

1. Use Page Up to return to the first page of the worksheet window.
2. Enter the furniture in cell C15.
3. Check cells C8:E8. If you count the database records that are identified with a "Type" of "Furniture," you will find that the count matches the number in cell E8.
4. Enter **>01/12/88** in cell.
5. Check cells C8:E8.

The numbers in cells C8:E8 change again to reflect the criteria you have selected in terms of computing the sum of the purchase prices, the sum of the replacement values, and the number of items that meet the criteria.

Sorting Data in Ascending Order

Data on a worksheet is often more convenient to use if it is selected in alphabetic or numeric order. This example illustrates the way to sort data in an Excel database.

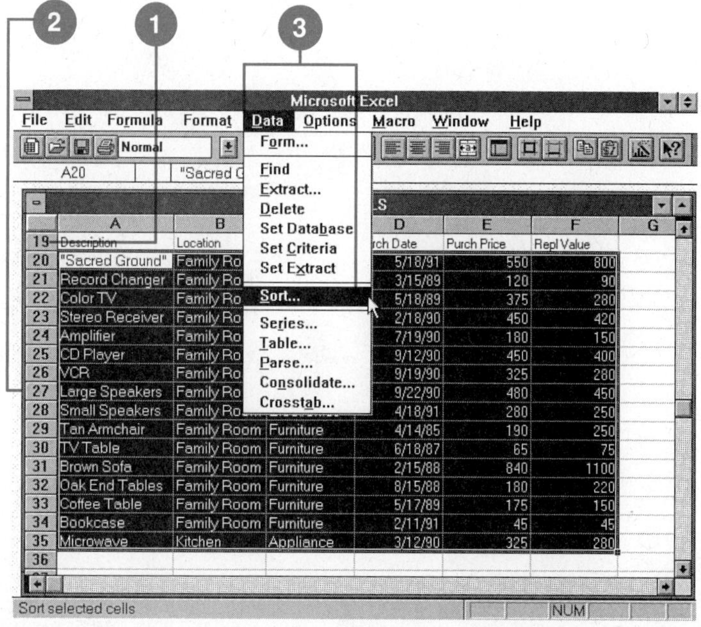

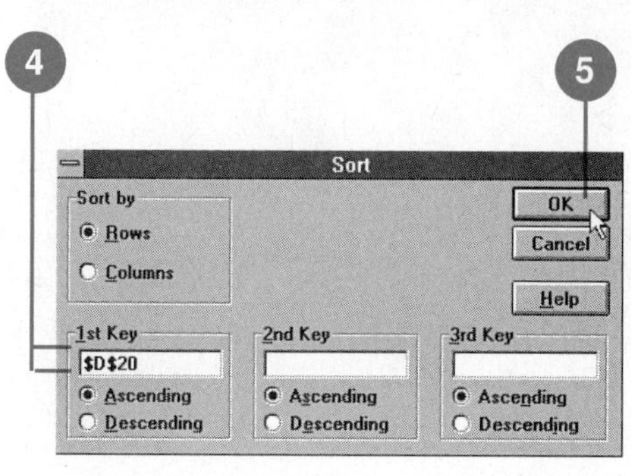

6

	A	B	C	D	E	F
19	Description	Location	Type	Purch Date	Purch Price	Repl Value
20	Tan Armchair	Family Room	Furniture	4/14/85	190	250
21	TV Table	Family Room	Furniture	6/18/87	65	75
22	Brown Sofa	Family Room	Furniture	2/15/88	840	1100
23	Oak End Tables	Family Room	Furniture	8/15/88	180	220
24	Record Changer	Family Room	Electronics	3/15/89	120	90
25	Coffee Table	Family Room	Furniture	5/17/89	175	150
26	Color TV	Family Room	Electronics	5/18/89	375	280
27	Stereo Receiver	Family Room	Electronics	2/18/90	450	420
28	Microwave	Kitchen	Appliance	3/12/90	325	280
29	Amplifier	Family Room	Electronics	7/19/90	180	150
30	CD Player	Family Room	Electronics	9/12/90	450	400
31	VCR	Family Room	Electronics	9/19/90	325	280
32	Large Speakers	Family Room	Electronics	9/22/90	480	450
33	Bookcase	Family Room	Furniture	2/11/91	45	45
34	Small Speakers	Family Room	Electronics	4/18/91	280	250
35	"Sacred Ground"	Family Room	Art	5/18/91	550	800

1. Scroll the worksheet window until row 19 is at the top of the window.
2. Select cells A20:F35.
3. Choose Data Sort.
4. Change the entry in the 1st Key text box to read `$D$20`.

Excel sorts all the items in the database from cell 20 until it encounters a blank cell (D36). The Ascending button has been selected for you already by Excel. Don't change this selection unless you wish your data to be sorted in Descending order.

5. Press Enter or click OK.
6. Check column D. All the entries have been sorted according to the dates in column D.

Clearing the Database for Your Use

The next step is to clear the database for your own use (you can also close without saving, and reopen HHINV.XLS). You may not want to clear this data if you plan to follow the practice customization described later.

1. Select all the records in the database (A20:F35).
2. Choose Edit.
3. Choose Clear or press Del.
4. Select Formulas. Press Enter or click OK.

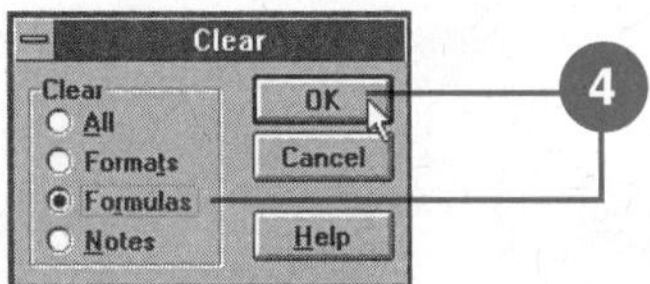

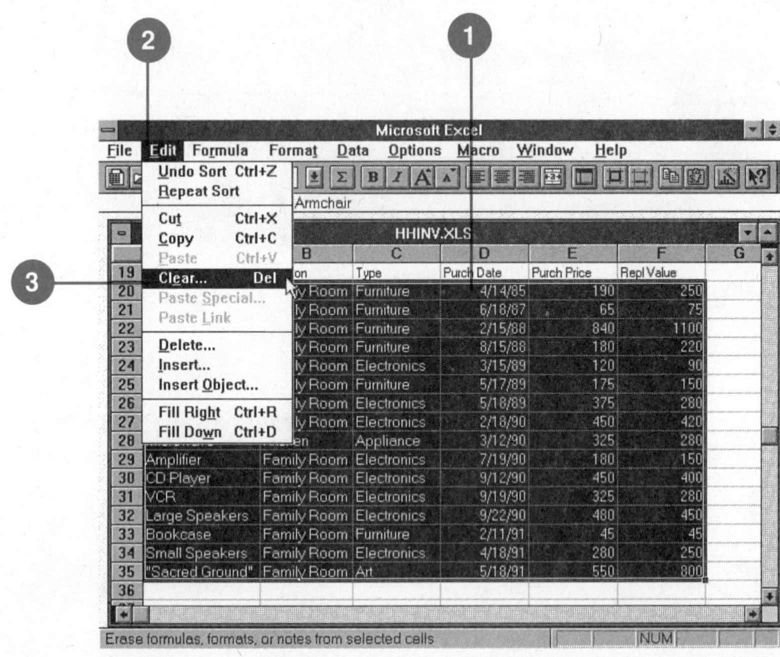

Clearing the Criteria

The practice data in the database are cleared from the worksheet allowing you to enter any data you wish. The final step in getting the household inventory database ready to use after the practice session is to clear the criteria used in practice.

1. Scroll the worksheet until row 1 is at the top of the worksheet window.
2. Select cells C15:D15.
3. Choose Edit Clear or press Del.
4. Press Enter or click OK to clear the practice data.

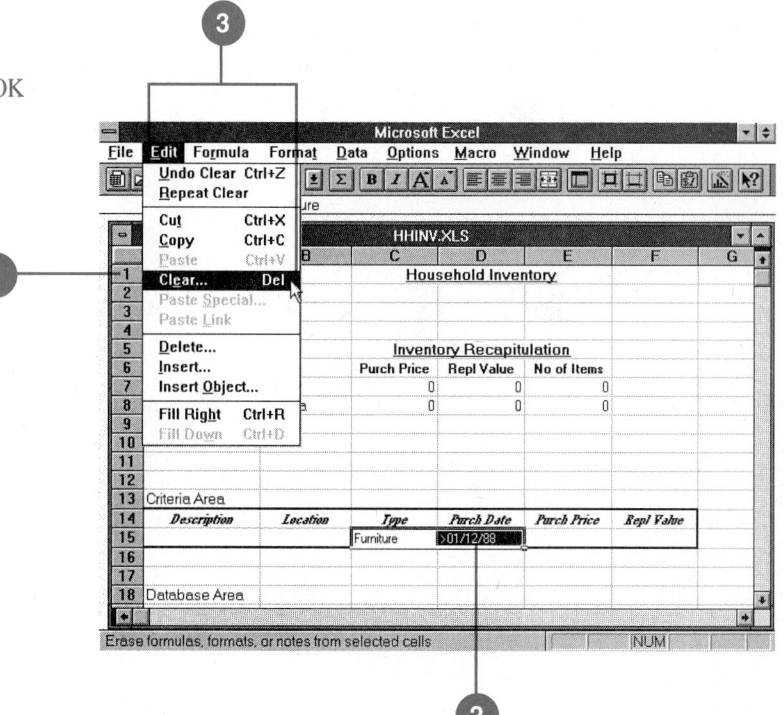

Accessing the Data Form to Enter Your Data

Now you're ready to enter your own household inventory data in the database and use the criteria to analyze the data.

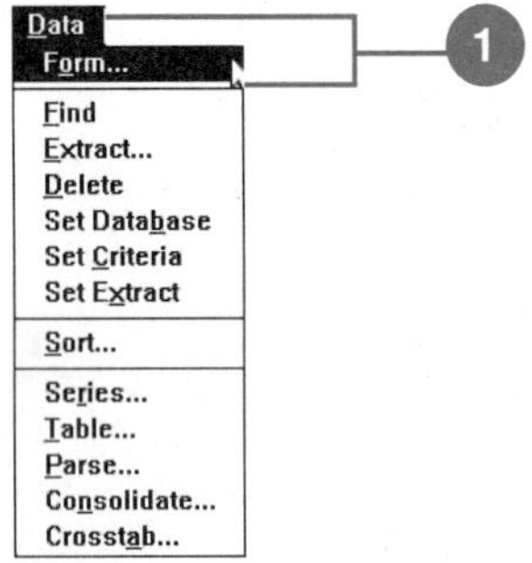

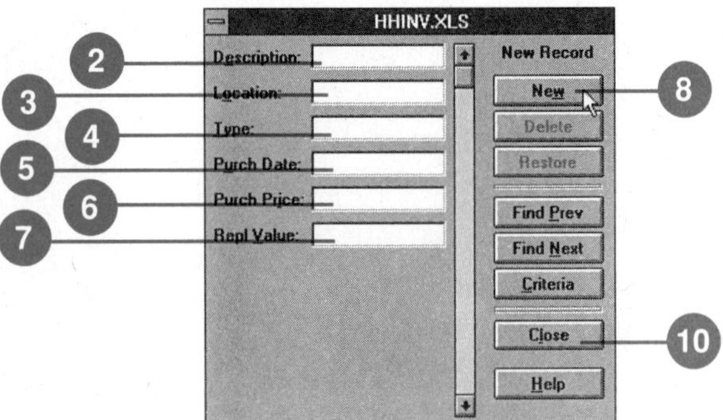

1. Select Data Form.
2. Select the Description text box and type the description of the first item.
3. Select the Location text box and type the location of the first item.
4. Select the Type text box and enter any standard type description.
5. Select the Purch Date text box and type the purchase date of the first item.
6. Select the Purch Price text box and type the purchase price of the item to the nearest dollar.
7. Select the Repl Value text box and type the estimated replacement value of the item.
8. Select New.
9. Repeat steps 3–9 to enter all items in your household.
10. Select the Close button.

Customizing HHINV.XLS

The HHINV.XLS household inventory worksheet is a basic format. The practice just offered is also very basic. In addition to changing the structure of the database by adding and deleting fields, expanding the Criteria Area, and using computed fields as is described next, you may also want to retain the practice data and use it to experiment further with the use of the Data Form and with other advanced uses of Excel databases. If you want to use the practice data in such a manner, save HHINV.XLS under a new name after you've cleared the practice data. Use the newly named file for your own database and reopen HHINV.XLS for additional practice.

You may want to explore the use of the Data Form further. To do this, retain the practice data or use your own data and refer to the skill sessions in this book that deal with databases and the use of data forms. Try the activities described in the Excel documentation and refer to Excel's help features as needed. The Excel documentation offers detailed descriptions and examples of using the Data Form to find constrained data within a database. It also explains how to use the Data Form to update (change) records, how to find specific records, and how to delete specific records. None of these uses of the Data Form is difficult.

The next customization steps describe adding a computed field (column) to HHINV.XLS, deleting a field and expanding the Criteria Area to provide a different look at the data in your database. Each of these customization steps is typical of steps taken to expand or contract databases in Excel. You can do the next examples with the practice data in the database to better illustrate the impact of the changes on an existing database. Therefore, you may want to wait until you've redesigned the database to suit your needs before you clear the practice data as described earlier.

Adding a New Field to HHINV.XLS

Adding a new field is simple. You add new fields by adding new columns and giving the new columns a field name in the row that contains field names. There is a trick to adding the new columns (database fields). You might want to consider these situations:

▲ If you add a new column before the first column included in the database range, or after the last column in the database range, you will need to select once again the *entire* database range—including the row that contains the field names—and use Data Set Database to reset the database for Excel.

▲ If you add the new columns anywhere between the first column and the last column included in the database range, Excel automatically includes the new column without requiring you to reset the range.

▲ If you don't want to insert columns above the database area, you can select as much of the desired column as lies within the database before you select **E**dit **I**nsert.

1. Scroll down the worksheet until row 19 is the top row.
2. Select column F by clicking on the column header.
3. Choose Edit Insert.
4. Select cell F19 and type **`Sale Price`**.
5. Press Enter or click the Enter button.

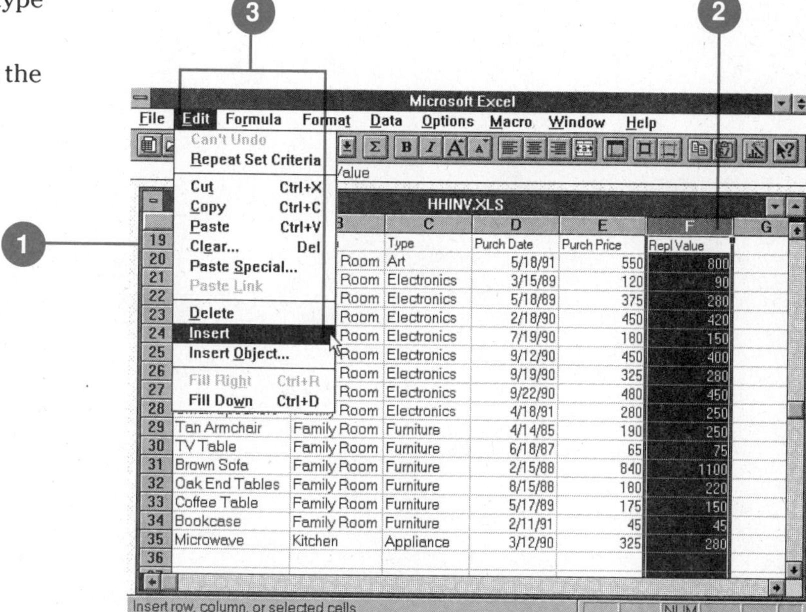

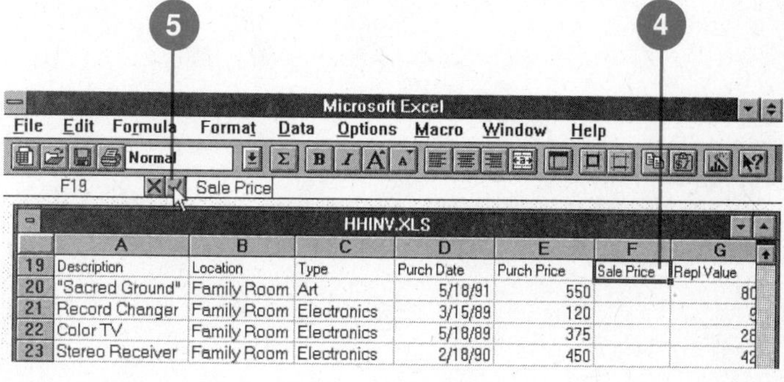

Adding a New Field to the Criteria Area

As you use databases of your own within Excel, you may add fields to existing databases or decide to add criteria. When this situation occurs, use the steps described below to expand or change the criteria area of your database.

1. Scroll back to the top row of the worksheet.
2. Select cell F14. Enter **Sale Price**.

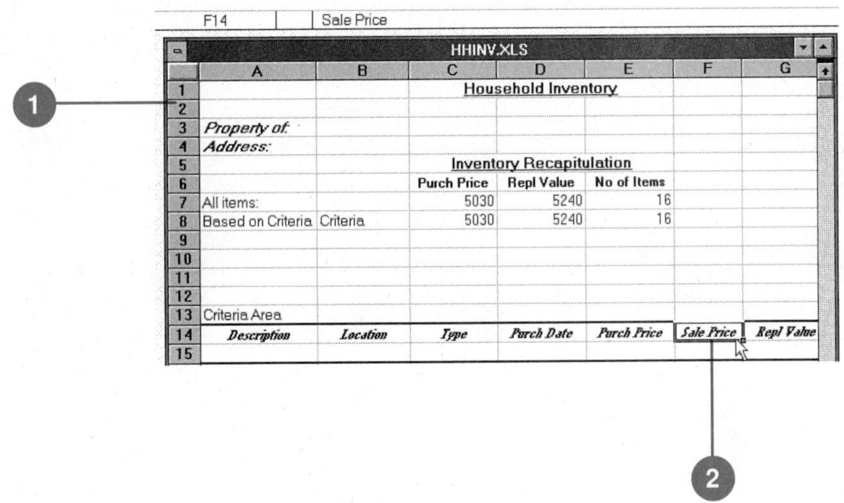

Using the Data Form to Update an Existing Database Record

Sometimes data within a database record must be changed to keep the record up to date. The data form may be used to make such changes in selected records.

1. Choose Data Form.
2. Select the Criteria button.
3. Select the Description text box and type the description of any record you want to find, such as `Microwave`.
4. Select the Find Next button. A Data Form containing the first record that contains the specified criteria is displayed.
5. Select the Sale Price text box and type a price, such as `250`.
6. Select the Close button.

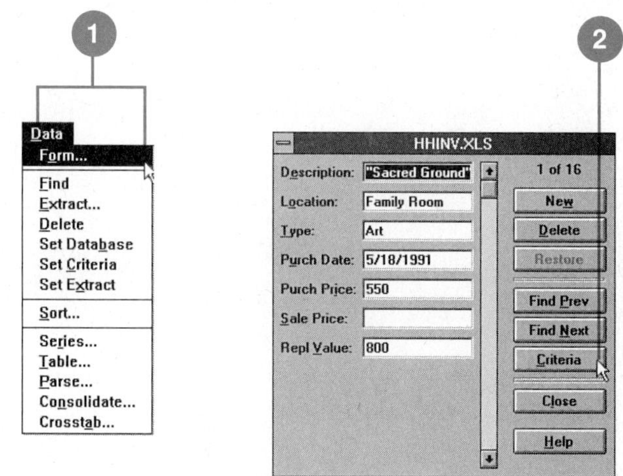

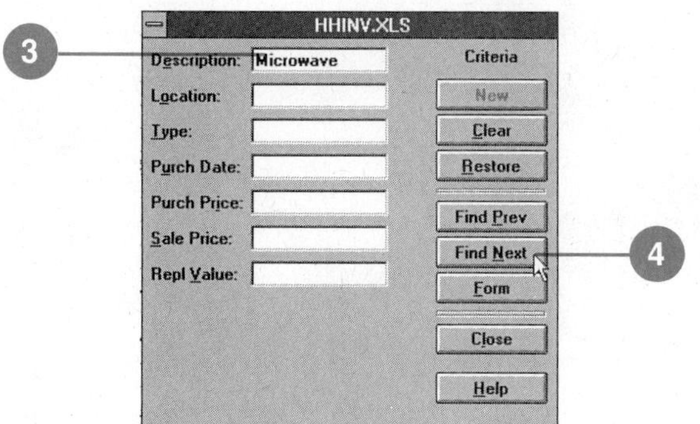

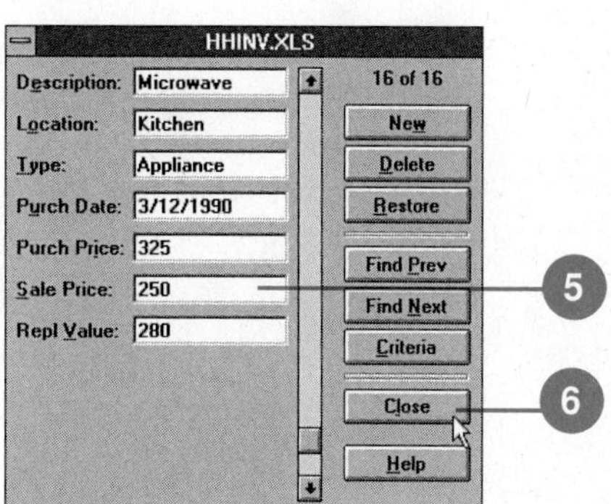

Creating a Computed Database Field

The next step is to add another field to the database. This field is a computed field that calculates the profit or loss from the sale of an item in the inventory.

Making a field a computed field is also quite simple. All you need to do is enter the formula required to make the calculation in the first cell in the column that contains the field that is to be computed. After you enter the formula, you just need to use Edit Fill Down or the Drag and Drop Fill Down shortcut to copy the formula into all the cells in the column that are included in the database. (Use **O**ptions **W**orkspace to be sure the Cell Drag and Drop check box is enabled.)

1. Select column G.
2. Choose Edit Insert.

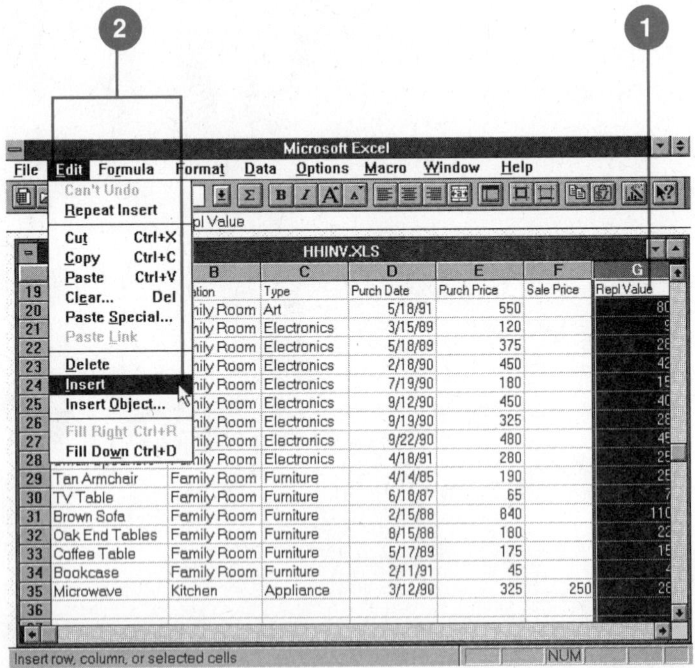

3. Select cell G19. Type **`Profit/(Loss)`** and press Enter.

4. Select cell G20. Type **`=IF(F20>0,E20-F20,0)`** and press Enter.

5. Choose Format.

6. Select Number from the **C**ategory list box.

7. Select (#,##0);(#,##0) from the **F**ormat Codes list box.

8. Press Enter or click OK.

9. Print to the lower right corner of cell G20. The pointer will change to a smaller plus sign.

10. Drag the pointer to the lower left corner of cell G35. Release the mouse button.

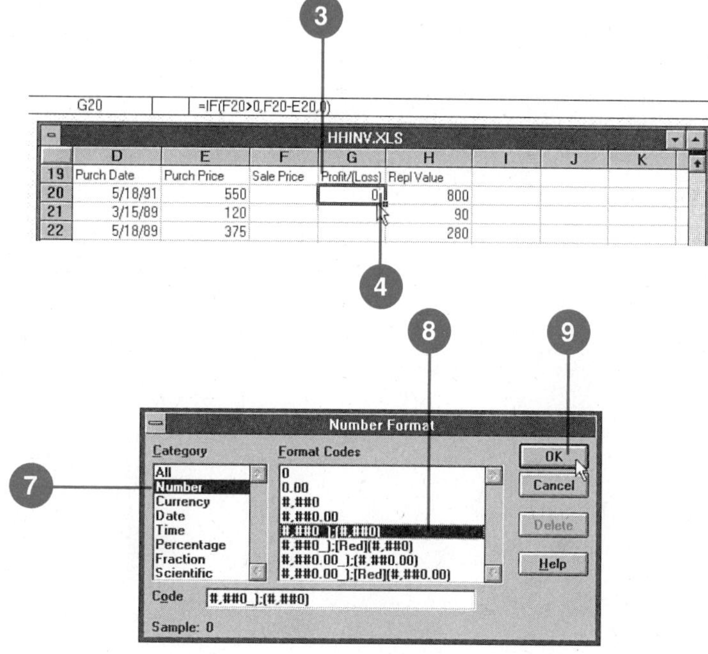

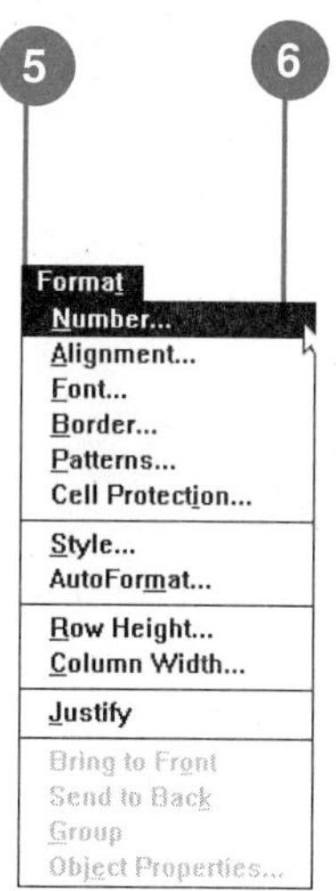

HHINV.XLS

	D	E	F	G	H
19	Purch Date	Purch Price	Sale Price	Profit/(Loss)	Repl Value
20	5/18/91	550		0	800
21	3/15/89	120			90
22	5/18/89	375			280
23	2/18/90	450			420
24	7/19/90	180			150
25	9/12/90	450			400
26	9/19/90	325			280
27	9/22/90	480			450
28	4/18/91	280			250
29	4/14/85	190			250
30	6/18/87	65			75
31	2/15/88	840			1100
32	8/15/88	180			220
33	5/17/89	175			150
34	2/11/91	45			45
35	3/12/90	325	250		280
36					

10

Computed Fields in the Data Form

The following steps illustrate Excel's treatment of computed fields on the Data Form.

1. Choose Data Form. The Data Form appears.
2. Look at the Profit/(Loss) field. Excel doesn't display text boxes for computed fields.
3. Select the Close button.

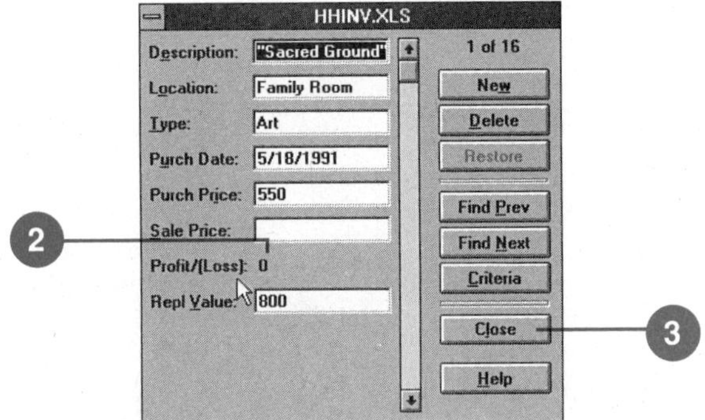

Removing a Data Field in the Middle of a Database

If you want to remove a data field from the middle of a database, it would be impractical to delete the entire column that contains the field. It's easier to use the Drag and Drop feature of Excel as described next.

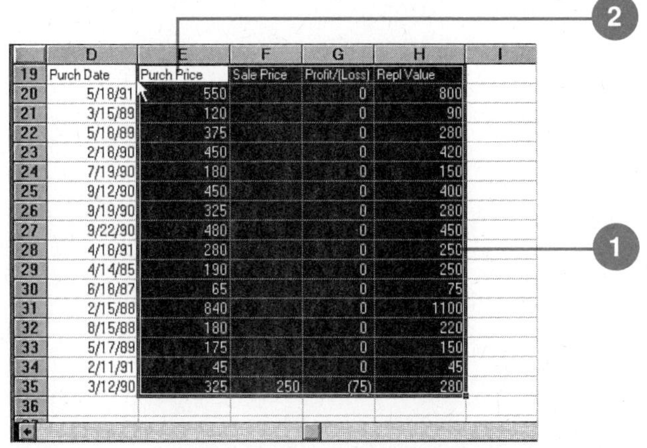

	D	E	F	G	H	I
19	Purch Date	Purch Price	Sale Price	Profit/(Loss)	Repl Value	
20	5/18/91	550		0	800	
21	3/15/89	120		0	90	
22	5/18/89	375		0	280	
23	2/18/90	450		0	420	
24	7/19/90	180		0	150	
25	9/12/90	450		0	400	
26	9/19/90	325		0	280	
27	9/22/90	480		0	450	
28	4/18/91	280		0	250	
29	4/14/85	190		0	250	
30	6/18/87	65		0	75	
31	2/15/88	840		0	1100	
32	8/15/88	180		0	220	
33	5/17/89	175		0	150	
34	2/11/91	45		0	45	
35	3/12/90	325	250	(75)	280	
36						

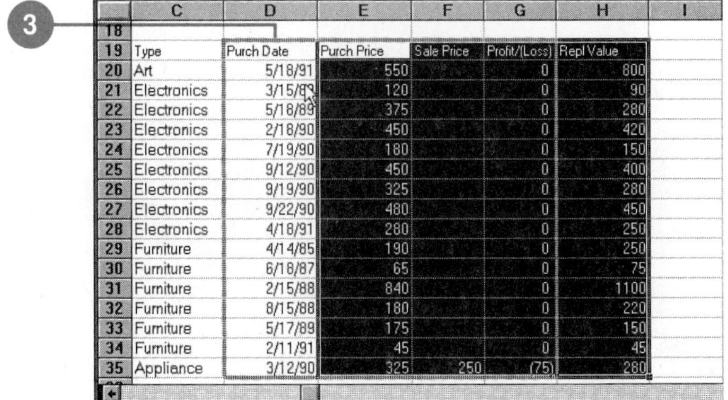

	C	D	E	F	G	H	I
18							
19	Type	Purch Date	Purch Price	Sale Price	Profit/(Loss)	Repl Value	
20	Art	5/18/91	550		0	800	
21	Electronics	3/15/89	120		0	90	
22	Electronics	5/18/89	375		0	280	
23	Electronics	2/18/90	450		0	420	
24	Electronics	7/19/90	180		0	150	
25	Electronics	9/12/90	450		0	400	
26	Electronics	9/19/90	325		0	280	
27	Electronics	9/22/90	480		0	450	
28	Electronics	4/18/91	280		0	250	
29	Furniture	4/14/85	190		0	250	
30	Furniture	6/18/87	65		0	75	
31	Furniture	2/15/88	840		0	1100	
32	Furniture	8/15/88	180		0	220	
33	Furniture	5/17/89	175		0	150	
34	Furniture	2/11/91	45		0	45	
35	Appliance	3/12/90	325	250	(75)	280	

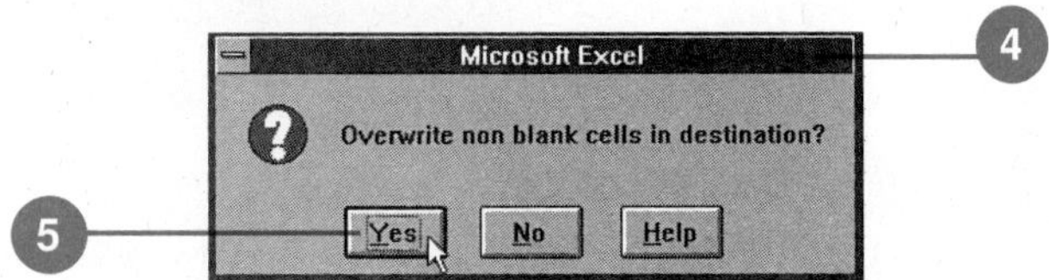

1. Select cells E19:H35.
2. Point to the left side of the selected cell so the pointer changes from a plus sign to an arrow.
3. Drag the selection to the left until the border of the selection overlaps the left side of column D.
4. Release the mouse button. An alert box appears.
5. Press Enter or click the Yes button.

If you don't use a mouse, you need to make the selection (E19:H35), use Edit Cut, select cell C19, and use Edit Paste to perform the same actions that were just described. You can use either approach to eliminate a field and its data in a database by using Cut and Paste techniques. With either approach, the Purch Date field is removed.

Deleting a Database Field from a Nonsensitive Location

Deleting a field from a nonsensitive location is simple. (A *nonsensitive* location is one where there's no critical data above or below the database area in the column you want to delete.) Just delete the column that contains a field you want to delete. As you delete the column, be sure that you don't also remove other important material from the worksheet. You may need to use **E**dit Cu**t** and **E**dit **P**aste or Drag and Drop, as just described, instead of **E**dit **D**elete to remove the unwanted fields.

If you wanted to remove the Repl Value field from the practice database, you need to use **E**dit **D**elete because removing this column does disrupt formulas or entries elsewhere on the worksheet.

1. Select column G.
2. Choose **E**dit **D**elete.

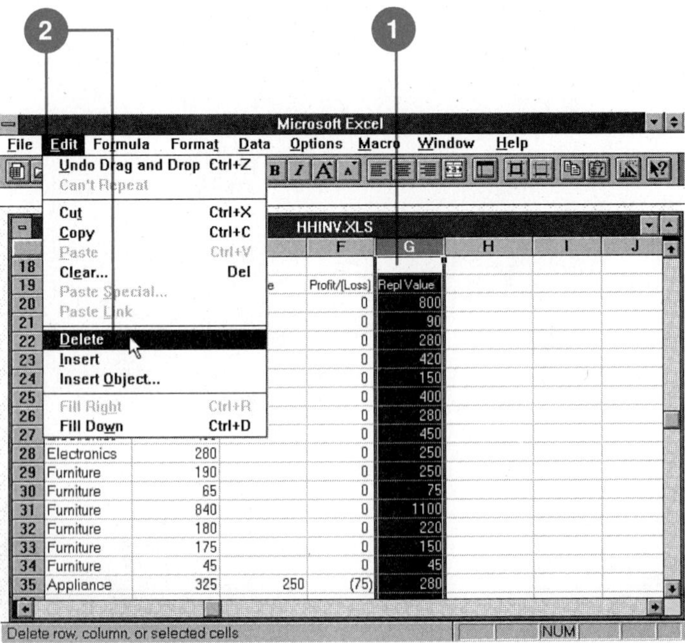

Making Adjustments for Deleted Database Fields

Sometimes when you remove a database field, you need to make adjustments elsewhere on the worksheet that include the database. In the case of the practice data, you need to remove the recapitulation cells for the Repl Value field because you removed the field from the database. As you change your own databases, make sure you make similar adjustments.

1. Scroll back to the first page of the worksheet.
2. Select cells E6:E8.
3. Point to the left side of the selection so the pointer changes to an arrow.
4. Drag the left border of the selection to the left until it overlaps the left side of column D. Release the mouse button.

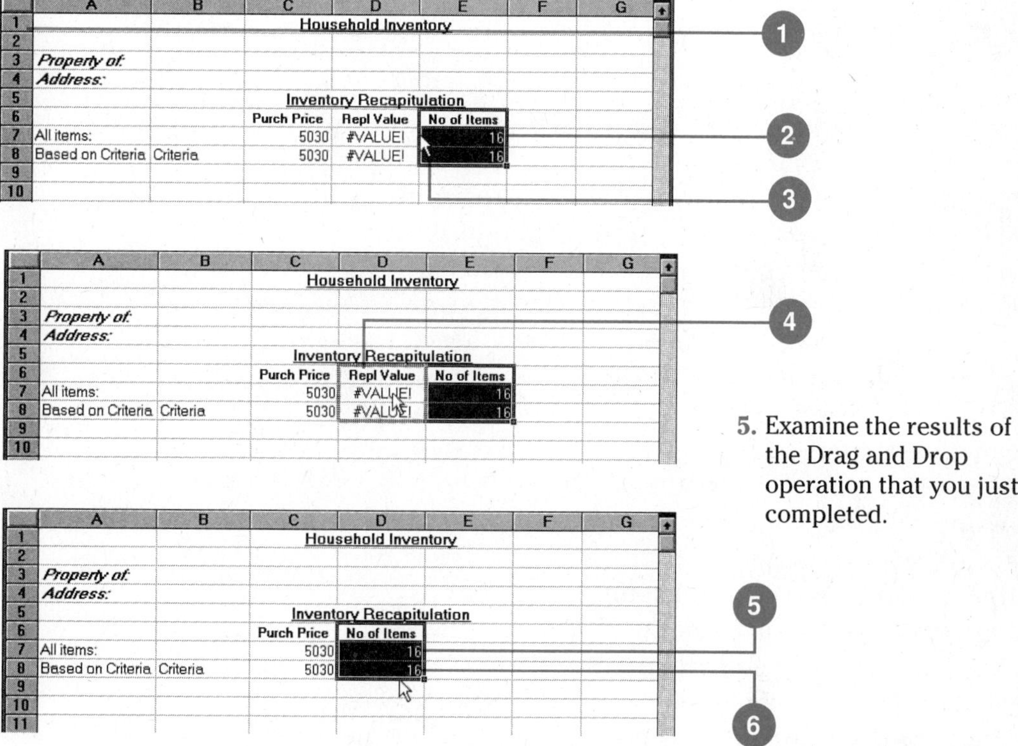

5. Examine the results of the Drag and Drop operation that you just completed.
6. Examine the Criteria Area. It adjusts to compensate for the removal of the last field.

The final customization step discussed here is the expansion of the Criteria Area. Take care when making this expansion if you still want to maintain the integrity of the formulas used in the recapitulation section of the worksheet. The care that you exercise involves including a blank row at the bottom of the Criteria Area to protect the formula that calculates the values for the entire database. The example stresses exercising this protective caution.

Summary

Project 2 deals with a typical household inventory in the form of an Excel database. It presents a simple database for recording and managing your personal possessions. The fields in the database describe each item, its location, its date of purchase, its purchase price, and its replacement value. All these fields are fundamental to managing personal possessions. The worksheet that contains this database is called HHINV.XLS. It also contains an area for recapitulating the number of items in the database, their total purchase price, and their total replacement value. By using a Criteria Area, the worksheet allows you to select only specific data from the database in accordance with criteria associated with each database field. You maintain the database by using Excel's Data Form to add records, change records, and find specific records in the database. The customization section of the project deals with adding fields to the database, deleting fields, and adjusting the Criteria Area and recapitulation area for the changes made in the database.

	A	B	C	D	E	F	G
1							
2			**Personal Net Worth Statement**				
3							
4		**Name(s): Wilson Taylor**		**Date: January 5, 1993**			
5		**Address: 1565 18th Avenue, Coral Gables, FL**					
6							
7				**Assets**			
8	**Cash and Equivalents**						
9		Cash on hand	$75				
10		Savings Account Balance	4,300				
11		Checking Account Balance	2,350				
12		Money Market Fund Balance	1,800				
13		Savings Bonds	400				
14		Certificates of Deposit	5,000				
15		Treasury Bills	1,000				
16		Loans to Others	100				
17		Total Cash on Hand	15,025				
18							
19	Value of Easily Convertible Assets						
20		Mutual Funds	3,500				
21		Stocks	2,800				
22		Bonds	1,200				
23		Treasury Notes	1,000				
24		Life Insurance Policies	12,000				
25		Other	500				
26		Total Convertible Assets	21,000				
27							
28	Value of Long Term Assets						
29		Home	253,000				
30		Other Real Estate	350,000				
31		IRAs, Keoughs, etc.	12,000				
32		Profit Sharing Plan	28,000				
33		Pension Lump Sum	225,000				
34		Other	2,000				
35		Total Long Term Assets	870,000				
36							
37	Value of Personal Possessions						
38		Automobile (s)	12,000				
39		Household Furnishings	35,000				
40		Clothing	4,000				
41		Jewelry	7,500				
42		Art, Antiques, etc.	1,500				
43		Other	500				
44		Total Personal Possessions	60,500				
45							
46		**Total Assets**	$966,525				
47							
48				**Liabilities**			
49	Unpaid Bills (Monthly Amounts)						
50		Taxes	$220				
51		Mortgage or Rent	1,800				
52		Insurance	150				
53		Utilities	55				
54		Alimony, Child Support					
55		Charge Card Balances	150				
56		Other	300				
57		Total Unpaid Bills	2,675				
58							
59	Loans (Total Due)						
60		Home Mortgage	$135,000				
61		Home Improvement Loan	$6,500				
62		Automobile(s)	$5,500				
63		Education	$4,500				
64		Charge Card Accounts	$1,200				
65		Insurance Loans	$350				
66		Home Equity Loans	$4,500				
67		Second Mortgage	$12,000				
68		Other Loans	$500				
69		Total Loans	170,050				
70							
71		**Total Liabilities**	$172,725				
72							
73	**Summary**						
74		**Total Assets**	$966,525				
75		**Total Liabilities**	$172,725				
76		**Net Worth**	$793,800				
77							

Project

3

Check Register

When you manage your money carefully, you need to have some sense of your current and future financial position. Your checking account represents an important aspect of your financial life. It is both a source of cash and a substitute for cash. Today there are many ways to deposit and withdraw money from your account. You may deposit funds directly with deposit slips. You may also transfer funds electronically. Withdrawals may be made by writing a check, using an automatic payment, transferring funds electronically, and using special banking cards to withdraw funds from a machine at a bank or in a store or other retail business.

All this freedom and reliance on automation makes it difficult to manage a checking account and to avoid problems with the account. The tool most frequently used to manage a checking account is the *check register*. A check register is a list of deposits, written checks, automatic banking card transactions, and electronic transactions. It usually includes a record of the date of the transaction, the check number for a check, the payee, and the amount of the check or transaction. Some check registers also include notations and comments about the nature of the expenditure. You can use this information to determine the influence of a transaction on your tax situation or to record the nature of each transaction to provide information for budget use. If you want to borrow money for any major purchase or to apply for a credit card, one of the questions on the application for the loan or credit card is your current checking account balance. If you want to keep track of how you spend your money, maintaining an accurate and complete check register is important.

The Check Register Worksheet

Project 3 is a check register worksheet called CKREG.XLS. The worksheet is designed to handle about one month's transactions. To keep it small and simple, you should start a new worksheet each month and store the old worksheet under a name that lets you find it easily if you need to refer to it. It allows you to enter each deposit you make, each check you write, each electronic fund transfer, and each automatic banking card transaction you make. One section of the worksheet presents the total for each of these transaction types along with the current account balance. Another section allows you to record data from your monthly bank statement and use this data to balance your checkbook. The customization section of the project deals with expanding the worksheet to assist you with budget management. It also presents a method to link this worksheet to your net worth statement. You can also use this same method to link your home inventory worksheet and other worksheets to the net worth statement.

Open CKREG.XLS and browse through the worksheet. Cells A2:E6 are used to gather general information about the bank account, the owner of the account, and the month being recorded. Cells A7:E11 are used to balance your checkbook. Cells A13:F22 recap your banking activity. Cells C16:C22 deal with current checkbook activity rather than statement activity. Cells A16:F21 deal with statement activity. Cells A25:Q65 are the check register. Your day-to-day entries are made in cells B31:E63. Cells A31:A63 are used to balance your register against your bank statement by indicating whether a transaction has been posted to the statement or not. Cells F31:O63 use IF statements to separate transactions into categories. In CKREG.XLS, these categories are bank transaction types. To use this worksheet, follow the steps described here to register your checks and balance your checkbook.

Starting Out with CKREG.XLS

The steps described in this section are used to start the check register. They provide the background for record keeping and start the calculations.

1. Open CKREG.XLS. Type your name and your spouse's name in cell C3.
2. Type the account number in cell C4.
3. Type a description of the account type in cell C5.
4. Enter the statement month in cell C6.
5. Enter the beginning balance for the statement month in cell C9.
6. After you receive your bank statement for the Statement month, enter the ending statment balance in cell E10.

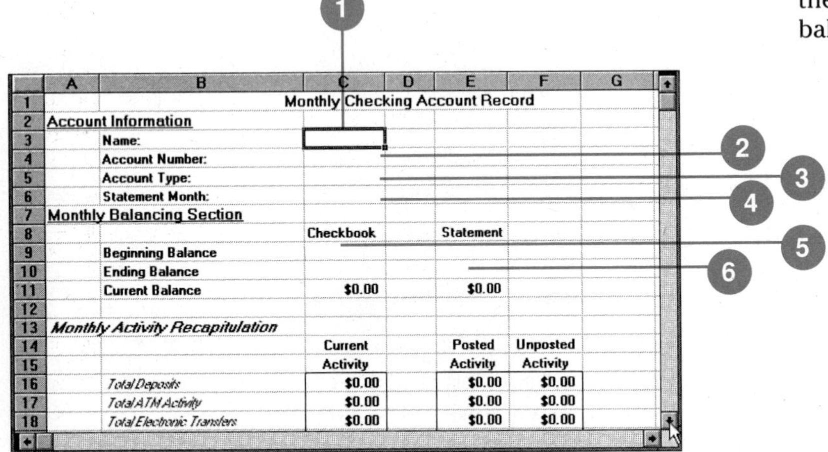

Understanding the Check Register

CKREG.XLS is straightforward in structure. Following is an overview of how it is setup.

- ▲ Cell C11 automatically displays your current checkbook balance for you as you make entries in the check register during the month. The formula in cell C11 is =C22. Cell C22 contains a calculation for the current balance.
- ▲ Cell E11 contains a calculation that uses the ending balance from your monthly statement and the data from cells F16 and F21 to calculate the

current balance according to your bank statement. The formula in cell E11 is =E10+F16-F21. In plain English, the formula means that the Current Balance per the statement adjusted for unposted activity equals the Ending Balance on the statement plus all unposted deposits and minus all unposted debits. Debits are Automatic Teller Machine (ATM) activity, Electronic Transfers, Checks, and Bank Charges. If the amounts in cells C11 and E11 don't match, you've made an error on your check register or your bank has made an error on the statement. Check both of these documents carefully for misrecorded amounts, missing deposits, missing checks, or other erroneous transactions.

- Cell C16 contains the total of all the deposits recorded in the check register. The formula in this cell is an array formula that uses a code in cells D31:D64 associated with an amount in cells E31:D64 to calculate the sum of deposits. If the formula finds a code of D for a deposit in a cell in column D, it accepts the amount in column E adjacent to this cell as a deposit and adds to any other cells in column E having a D in the adjacent cell in column D. The formula in cell C16 is `{=SUM(IF(D31:D64="D",E31:E64,0))}`.
- The formula in cell C17 calculates the sum of all ATM transactions in column E based on codes in adjacent codes in column D. The code in column D that denotes an ATM transaction is an A. It uses the same approach as in cell C16. The formula in this cell is `{=SUM(IF(D31:D64="A",E31:E64,0))}`.
- The formula in cell C18 calculates the sum of all of the Electronic Transfers in column E based on a code in adjacent cells in column D. The code in

column D that denotes an electronic transfer is an E. The formula in this cell is {=SUM(IF(D31:D64="E",E31:E64,0))}.

- The formula in cell C19 calculates the sum of all checks recorded in column E based on a code in adjacent cells in column D. The code in column D that denotes a check is C. The formula in this cell is {=SUM(IF(D31:D64="C",E31:E64,0))}.
- The formula in cell C20 calculates the sum of all the bank charges in column E based on a code in adjacent cells in column D. The code in column D that denotes a bank charge is MC. The formula in this cell is {=SUM(IF(D31:D64="MC",E31:E64,0))}.
- The formula in cell C21 sums all of the debits contained in cells C17:C20. The formula in this cell is =SUM(C17:C120).
- The formula in cell C22 calculates the current checkbook balance based on the entries made in the register. The formula in this cell is =(C9+C16)-(C21). It adds the starting balance to all deposits and subtracts all debits to arrive at this balance.
- Cells E16:E21 contain the totals for all posted account activity, based on reviewing your monthly statement and entering (in column A) a **Y** for debits and deposits that appear on your statement, and an **N** for activities that don't appear. This code is entered in cells A31:A64 when you receive your monthly account statement.
- Cells F16:F21 contain the totals for all unposted activity based on reviewing your monthly statement and entering the **N** in column A for each transaction that doesn't appear on your bank statement.

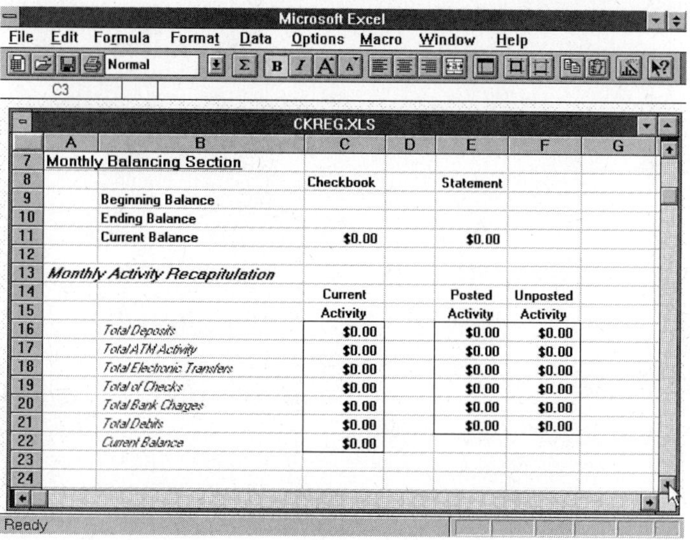

Using the Check Register

As you use your bank account after you've balanced your checkbook for the previous month, enter your banking activity in cells B31:E63. If you must add new rows to the worksheet to accommodate more activity than the worksheet allows, insert the new rows above row 64 to protect the formulas in row 65. Inserting new rows is described in the section of this project that deals with customization.

The activity codes for use with the check register are noted in rows 25 and 26. These codes should be used in column D for each entry made in the register to identify the nature of the entry.

1. Scroll down until row 23 is at the top of the window.
2. Enter the check number or activity description of the first transaction of the month in cell B31.
3. Enter the date of the first transaction in cell C31.
4. Enter the code for the first transaction in cell D31.
5. Enter the amount of the first transaction in cell E31.
6. Use cells B32:E63 to enter the same information row by row for subsequent activity. (See the example printout at the start of the project.)
7. You need to keep the labels in rows 28–39 scrolled out of view. Scroll back up until row 25 is at the top of the display.
8. Point to the split bar with the mouse pointer, press the left mouse button, and drag the line to a point just below row 30.
9. Complete column A after you receive your bank statement. If an item listed in column B appears on your statement, put a Y in column A next to this transaction. Otherwise, type N.

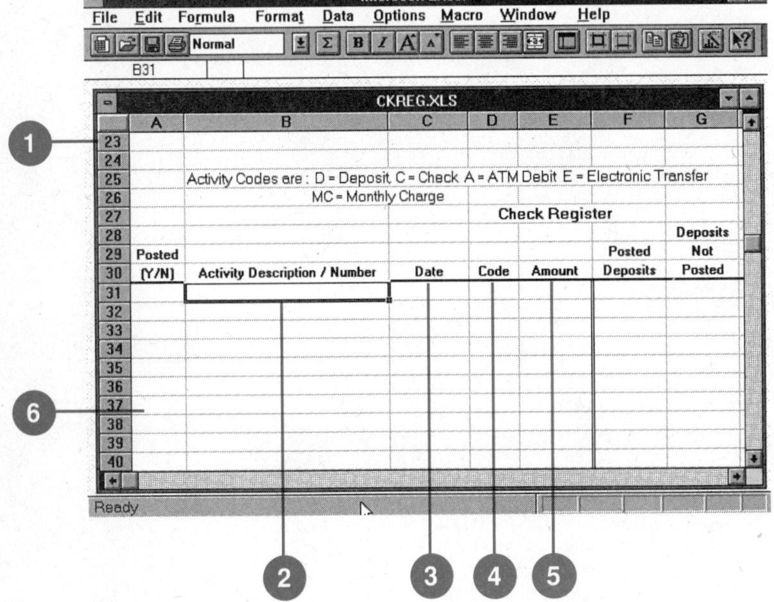

Tracking Monthly Activity

After you've marked cleared or posted transactions in column A (starting at row 31), columns F–O perform certain calculations for you automatically. The formulas in these columns have been copied down through row 64 of CKREG.XLS. Table P3.1 explains the entries in each of these columns.

Table P3.1 Calculations performed by CKREG.XLS

Column	*Description*
F	Reflects all deposits that have been posted in your bank statement.
G	Reflects all deposits in your check register that don't appear in your bank statement.
H	Contains the amounts for all the checks you indicate have been cleared on your bank statement.
I	Contains the amounts for any checks you have indicated have not been posted to your bank statement.
J	Contains the amounts for any ATM activity you indicate has been posted to your bank statement.
K	Contains the amounts for all ATM transactions you indicate haven't been posted to your bank statement.
L	Contains the amounts for all electronic funds transfers you indicated have been posted to your bank statement.
M	Contains the amounts for all electronic funds transfers that haven't been posted to your bank statement.

continues

Table P3.1 continued

Column	*Description*
N	Contains the amounts for all bank charges that have been posted to your account statement.
O	Contains the amounts for any bank charges you know about that haven't been posted to your bank statement.

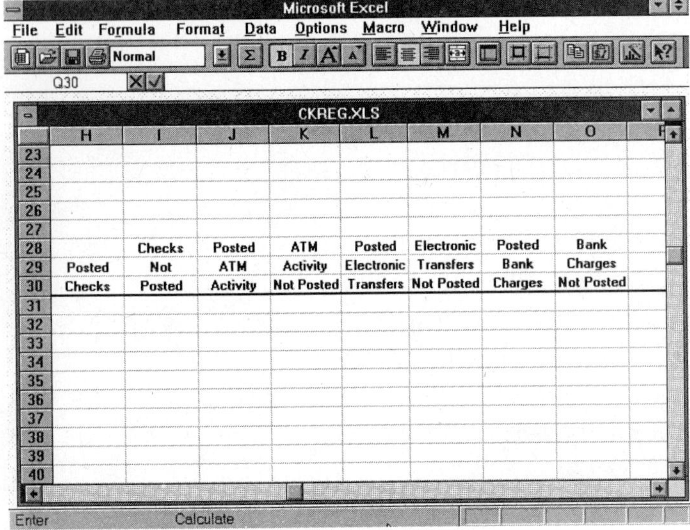

Viewing Monthly Totals

CKREG.XLS automatically totals all the columns of data it has calculated. The totals are contained in row 65 of the worksheet. To view them, you must scroll until that row appears on-screen. All the values in row 65 tie to the formulas in cells E16:F21.

Note that cell B64 contains a note that reads `Last Row–Insert New Rows Above This Row`. Even though there are formulas in row 64 and the formulas in row 65 include row 64, it is a buffer row that allows you to insert additional rows without changing the formulas in row 65. If you insert new rows above row 64, Excel automatically adjusts the formulas in row 65.

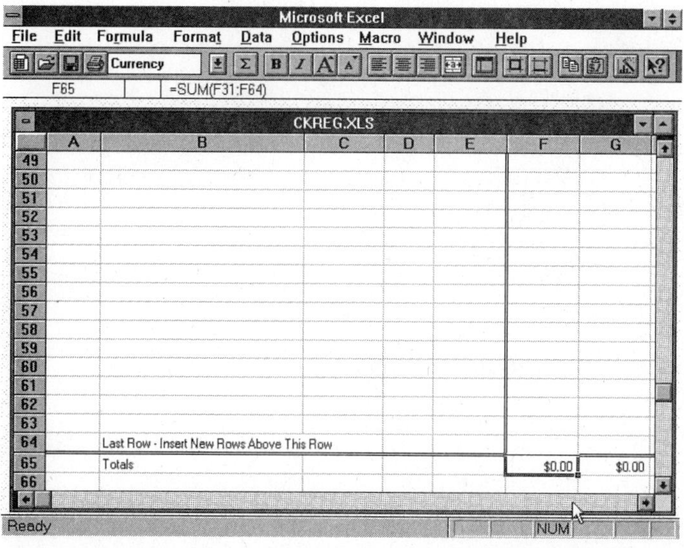

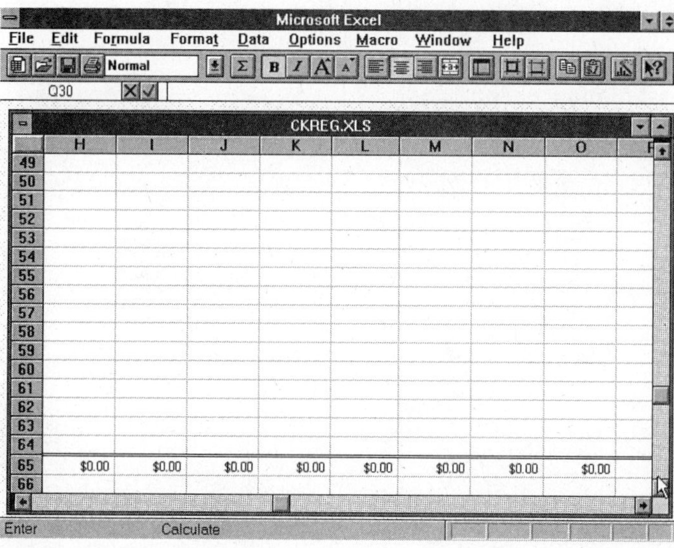

Table P3.2 explains the totals that appear in row 65 of the worksheet.

Table P3.2 Totals in row 65 of CKREG.XLS

Cell	*Totals*
F65	The amounts of all posted deposits you have recorded.
G65	The amounts of all unposted deposits you have recorded.
H65	The amounts of all posted checks you have recorded.
I65	The amounts of all unposted checks you have recorded.
J65	The amounts of all posted ATM activity you have recorded.
K65	The amounts of all unposted ATM activity you have recorded.
L65	The amounts of all posted Electronic Transfers you have recorded.
M65	The amounts of all unposted Electronic Transfers you have recorded.
N65	The amounts of all posted monthly bank charges you have recorded.
O65	The amounts of all unposted monthly bank charges you have recorded.

Linking CKREG.XLS to NWORTH.XLS

One of Excel's extremely powerful features is its capability to link data from one worksheet directly to another worksheet in a manner that can update the linked worksheet to reflect changes made to the origin worksheet any time the linked worksheet is opened. If you want to maintain a dynamic net worth statement, you can link the cell containing the current balance from CKREG.XLS to the cell in the net worth statement project worksheet (NWORTH.XLS) that contains the same information. After you've completed the check register for the current month, you can open the net worth worksheet and update it. When you use the Personal Budget Worksheet presented as Project 4, you may want to link each month's check register to the budget worksheet instead of rekeying the information from the check register to the budget worksheet to capture the current expense data for comparison with the budget.

Before you take the steps described next, make sure both NWORTH.XLS (or your own net worth file) and CKREG.XLS (or your own file for the most current month) are open. Also make sure CKREG.XLS is the active window.

Establishing the Link Between CKREG.XLS and NWORTH.XLS

As mentioned above, you can save time by linking one worksheet that contains information needed by another worksheet directly to the worksheet that needs the information. The steps in this section describe how to make sure a link.

1. Select the cell that contains the current balance (C11) for the month you choose to link to your net worth statement.
2. Choose **Edit Copy**.
3. Switch to NWORTH.XLS by choosing it from the bottom of the **W**indow menu.
4. Select the cell on your net worth worksheet that contains the value for your checking account balance (C11 or its counterpart).
5. Choose **Edit Paste Link**.
6. Examine cell C11 or its counterpart on your net worth worksheet. It will contain a formula displayed in the formula bar in the example.

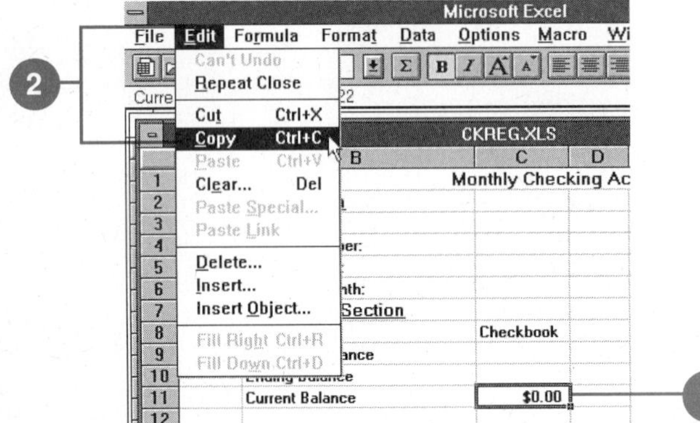

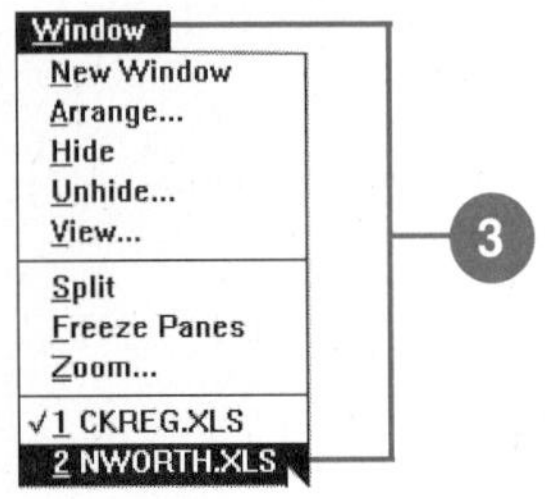

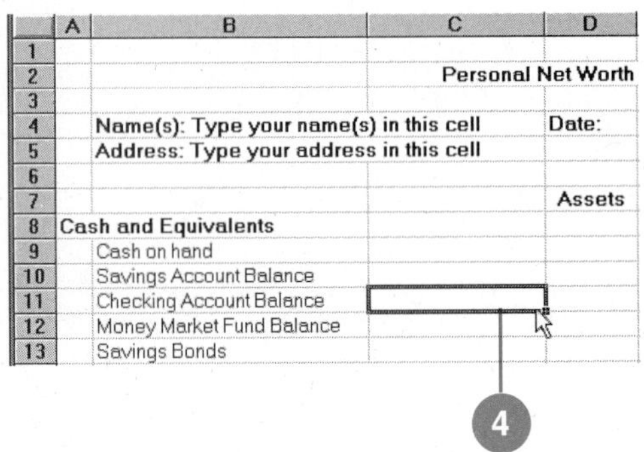

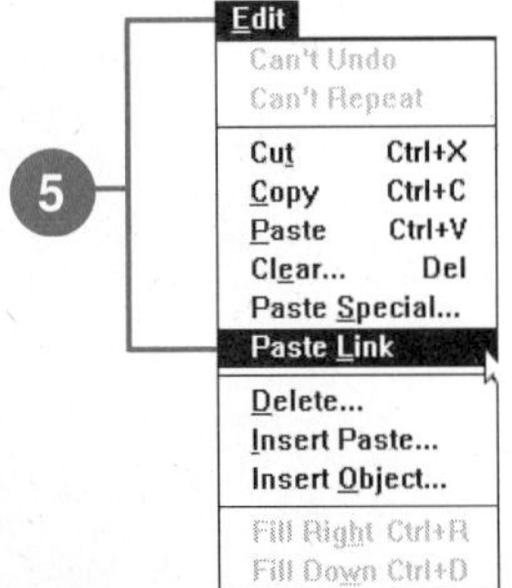

	A	B	C	D	E
1					
2			Personal Net Worth Statemen		
3					
4		Name(s): Type your name(s) in this cell		Date:	
5		Address: Type your address in this cell			
6					
7				Assets	
8	Cash and Equivalents				
9		Cash on hand			
10		Savings Account Balance			
11		Checking Account Balance	0		
12		Money Market Fund Balance			
13		Savings Bonds			
14		Certificates of Deposit			

6

Customizing CKREG.XLS

You may find that some of the features of CKREG.XLS don't suit you. If that is the case, customize the worksheet in whatever manner best suits your needs. One idea for customization is presented next.

As originally designed, CKREG.XLS measures monthly activity by bank transaction to assist you in balancing your checkbook. You can easily extend it to assist you in tracking your actual monthly expenses to compare these expenses to a budget. If you aren't interested in the nature of your banking transactions, you may want to replace the section of the worksheet that deals with recording the transactions with a section that is structured in a manner similar to the extension described next. When you customize the worksheet for your own use, change the labels and codes to better suit your needs. Codes should be somewhat mnemonic to make them easy to remember when you record your checking account transactions. When you use codes on a worksheet, you should also include a legend that describes each code. The legend is a useful reminder if you use the worksheet infrequently. It also helps anyone else who might use the worksheet to understand it. Remember to change the formulas in the section to use your codes.

Adding New Category Names

Your check register may not contain all of the categories included in CKREG.XLS. If not, don't use the categories that don't apply to you. You may use different categories. If you do, follow the steps described in this section.

1. Scroll your check register worksheet to place row 19 at the top of the worksheet window and to place Column P at the extreme left.
2. Select cell P30. Enter the label that best describes the first expense category you want to track (e.g., Medical).
3. Select cell Q30. Enter the label for the second expense category.
4. Select cell R30. Enter the label for the third expense category.
5. Continue adding labels until you have a column for each category you want to track.
6. If necessary, adjust the font size and style if you run out of cells that have already been formatted for you. Also extend the border along the bottom of row 30.

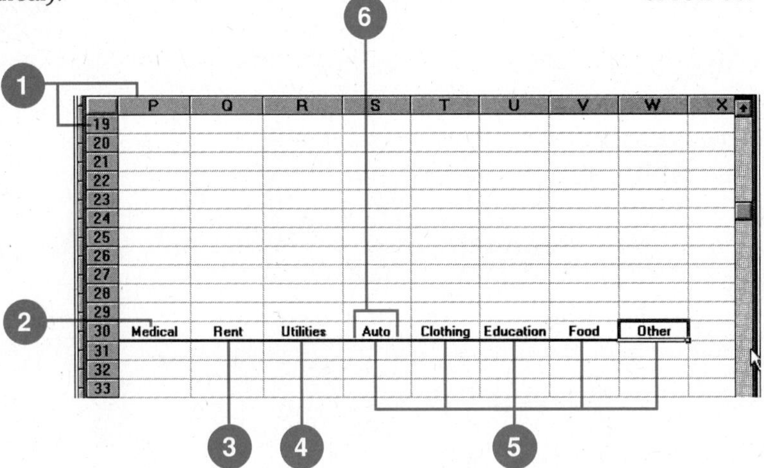

Adding Two New Rows for Additional Legend

If you add new expense categories, you should expand your legend to explain the codes that describe the new categories. Follow the steps described below to change the legend and to insert new rows to accommodate the expanded legend.

1. Scroll CKREG.XLS until row 19 is at the top and column A is at the left.
2. Select rows 27 and 28.
3. Choose Edit Insert. Two blank rows are added above row 27.

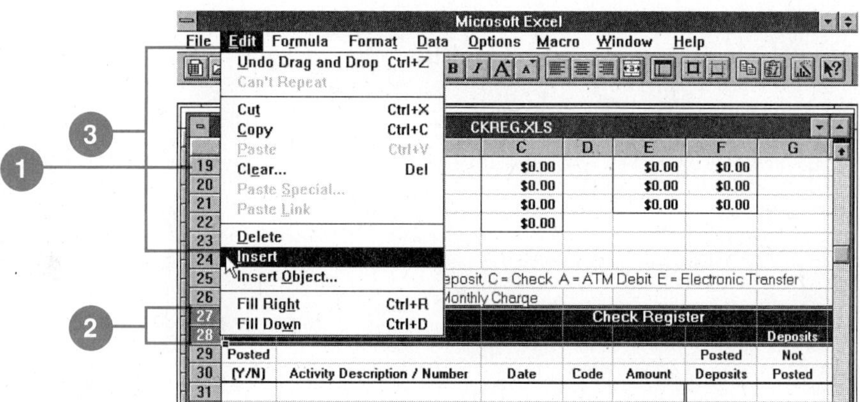

Adding a New Legend to Explain Expense Codes

1. Select cell B27. Enter the codes that pertain to the expense labels you added to row 30. For example, you might enter **MED=Medical** as one of the codes.
2. If necessary, select cell B28 and enter additional codes.
3. Select cell D31. Enter the abbreviation **Act** to differentiate the activity code from the expense code you will be adding to a new column in the worksheet.

	A	B	C	D	E	F	G
19		Total of Checks	$0.00		$0.00	$0.00	
20		Total Bank Charges	$0.00		$0.00	$0.00	
21		Total Debits	$0.00		$0.00	$0.00	
22		Current Balance	$0.00				
23							
24							
25		Activity Codes are : D = Deposit, C = Check A = ATM Debit E = Electronic Transfer					
26		MC = Monthly Charge					
27		Expense Codes are: MED = Medical, R = Rent, U = Utilities, AU = Auto, CL = Clothing,					
28		ED = Education, F = Food, OTH = Other					
29				Check Register			
30							Deposits
31	Posted			Act		Posted	Not
32	(Y/N)	Activity Description / Number	Date	Code	Amount	Deposits	Posted
33							
34							

Creating a New Expense Codes Column

If you wish to use all of the existing expense codes and add new expenses codes, you will need to insert new columns for each new expense code. Follow the steps described in this section for each such situation.

1. Select column B.
2. Choose Edit Insert.
3. Make sure column B is still selected.
4. Choose Format Column Width.
5. Change the Column Width text box value to 5.
6. Click OK or press Enter.
7. Select cell B31. Enter `Exp` as an abbreviation for "Expense" to this cell. Press Enter.
8. Select cell B32. Enter `Code`. Press Enter.

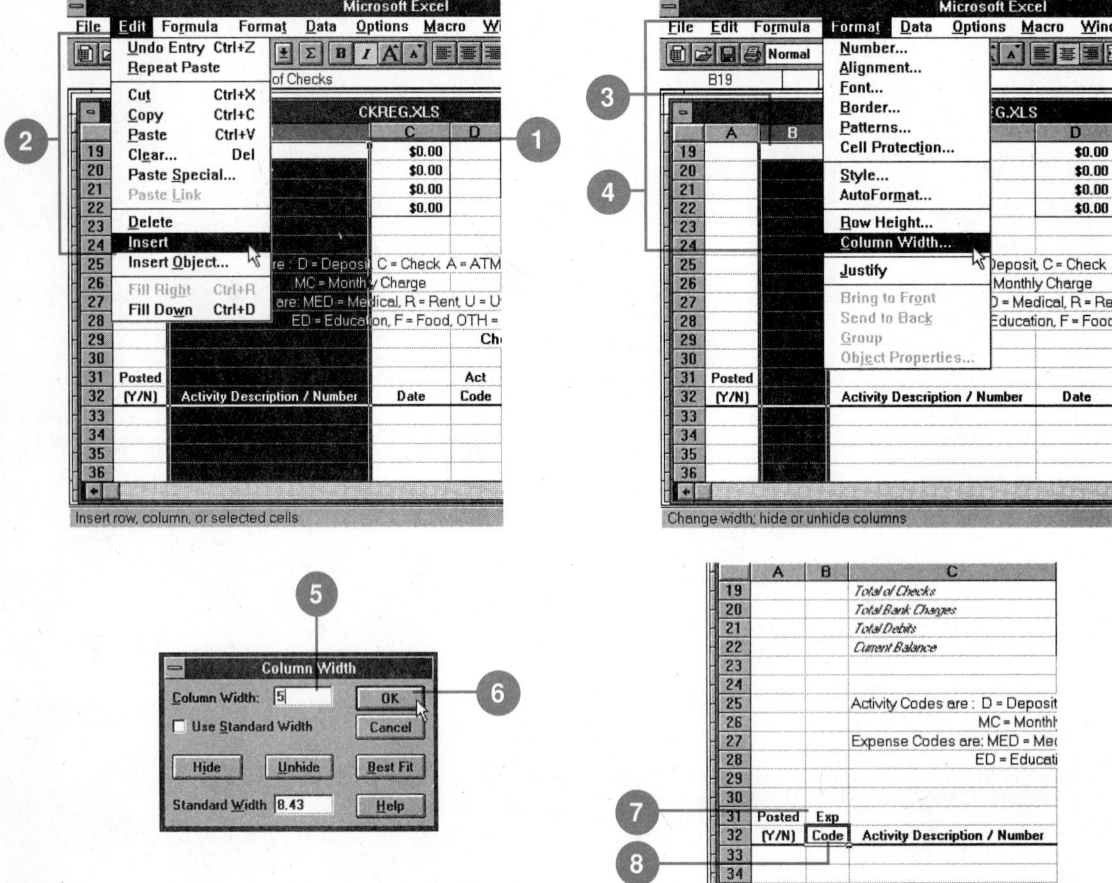

Adding Formulas to the Expense Record Section of CKREG.XLS

When you add new expenses codes, you will need formulas in the cells in the columns used for these codes to calculate the amounts to be entered. The steps in this section describe how to add such formulas to the worksheet.

1. Scroll the worksheet to the right until column Q is the leftmost column.
2. Select cell Q33. Enter the formula `=IF(B33="MED",F33," ")` and press Enter. Excel will enter the value in cell F33 into cell Q33 if the value in cell A33 is MED (or any other code you have created and included in the formula).
3. Select cell R33. Enter the formula `=IF(B33="R",F33," ")` and press Enter. Replace the R in the formula with the next code you intend to use.
4. Continue entering formulas in the remaining cells in row 33 that are associated with labels in row 32.

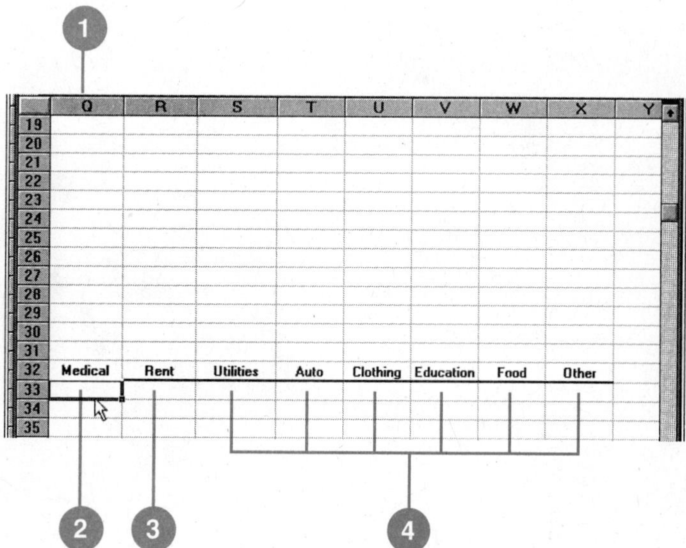

Copying Formulas Into the Expense Record Section of CKREG.XLS

When you add a new formula to one of the cells in a column, this forumla should be copied into all of the cells in the column.

1. Select all the cells that contain formulas to be used in the Expense Record section of your worksheet (Q33:X33 in the example.)
2. Point to the lower right corner of the selection.
3. Drag the square handle until all the cells between Q33 and X66 have been highlighted. (Or select all the columns containing formulas for updating the Expense Record section.)
4. Release the mouse button.

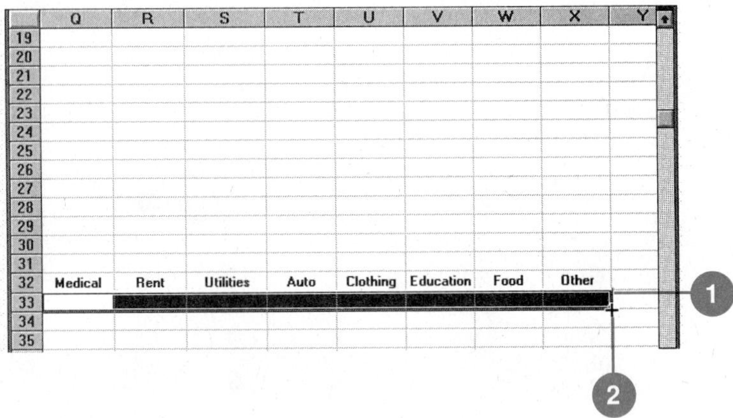

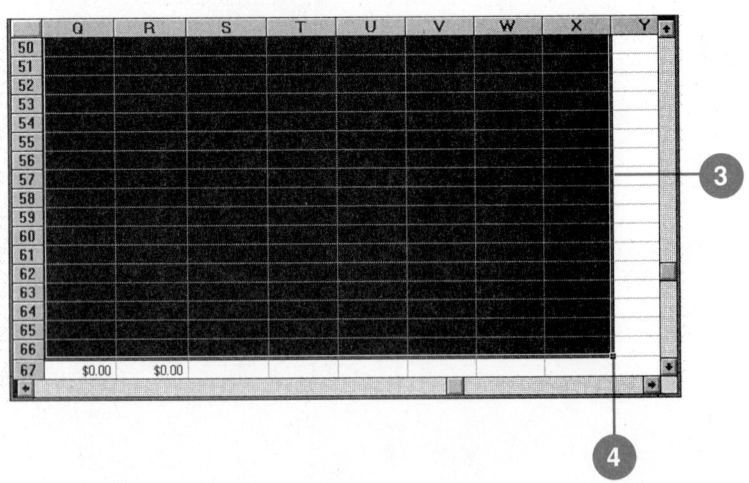

Formatting the Border at the Bottom of the Expense Record Section

When you add new forumlas and copy them down a column Excel usually removes any borders from the bottom cell of a column. Follow the steps in this section to restore the border.

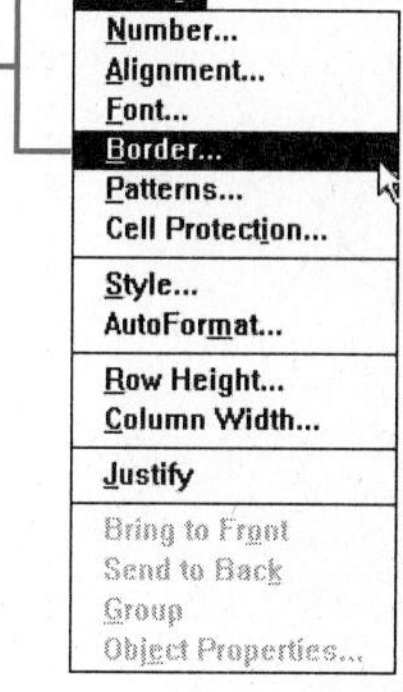

1. Select those cells in row 66 that contain formulas (cells Q66:X66).
2. Choose Format Border.
3. Choose the double line from the Style options.
4. Choose Bottom from the Border options.
5. Click OK or press Enter.

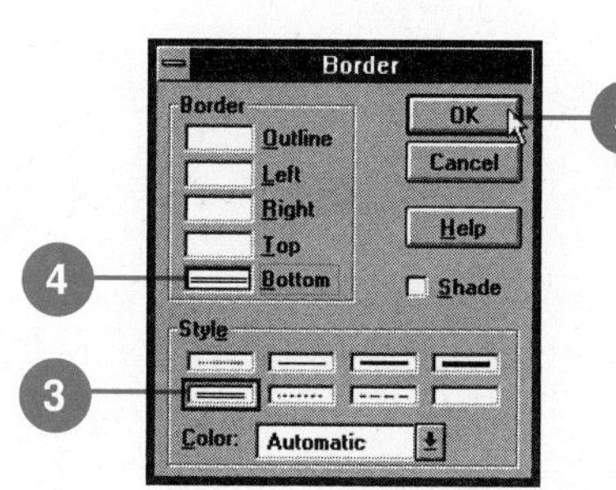

Copying Formulas to Calculate Each Expense Category Total

Now that you have added a new expense column and have added formulas to track the expenses, you will want to compute a total for the month for these expenses.

1. A formula is provided for you in cells Q67 and R67. Select cell R67.

2. Drag the copy handle through the range of cells in row 67 that extends from cell R67 until the end of your version of this section is reached (R67:X67).

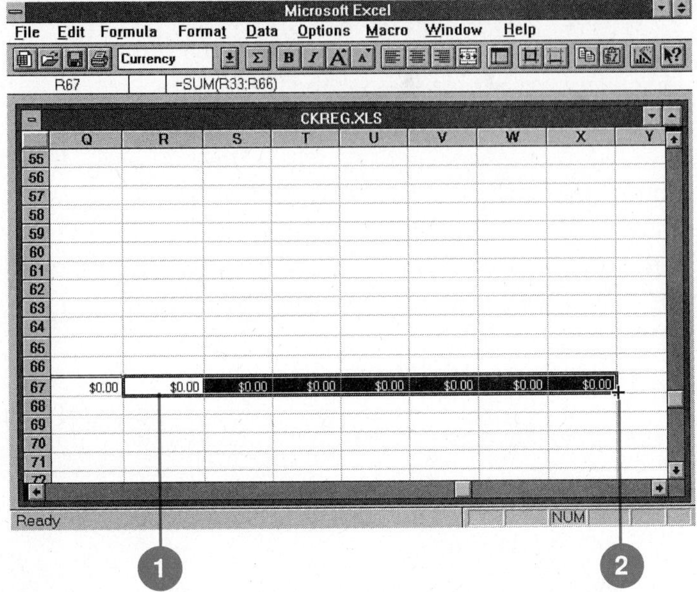

Adding a Monthly Recap of Expenses to CKREG.XLS

As a convenience, it is a good idea to recap all of the monthly expenses in one place on the worksheet. Follow the steps listed below in this section to add such a recap to CKREG.XLS.

1. Select cell I14. Enter Expense.

2. Select cell I15. Enter Category.

3. Select cell J14. Enter Amount.

4. Select cell J15. Enter Spent.

5. Enter labels into cells I16:I23 that describe the expenses you are tracking. If you need to, insert more rows above row 23.

6. Select cell J16. Enter the formula =Q67.

7. Enter the appropriate formulas in the remaining cells of the expense recap portion of the worksheet (=R67 for the next expense category and so on).

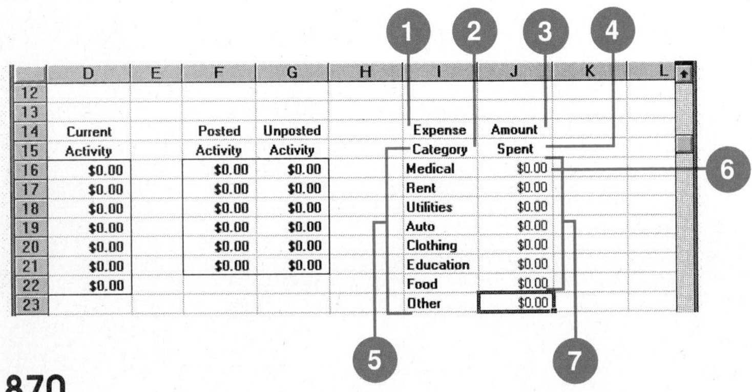

Adding New Rows for Checking Account Transactions

You may have more transactions in your account in any month than CKREG.XLS currently allows. If this is the case, follow the steps in this section to accommodate more transactions.

1. Select a number of rows equal to the number of new rows you want to insert (rows 61:63 in the example).
2. Choose Edit Insert.
3. Select any cell containing a formula that is immediately above the first cell in the new rows (e.g., G60).
4. Drag the border on the right side of this cell to the end of the row that contains the formulas (X60).
5. Point to the handle in the lower right corner of the rightmost cell of the selection.
6. Drag the handle down to select all the new rows and release the mouse button.

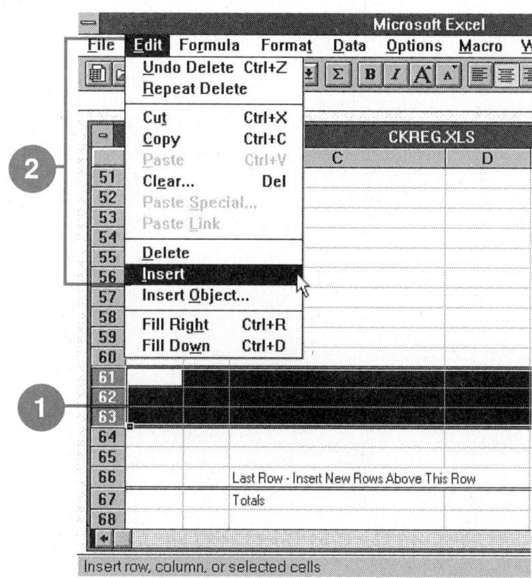

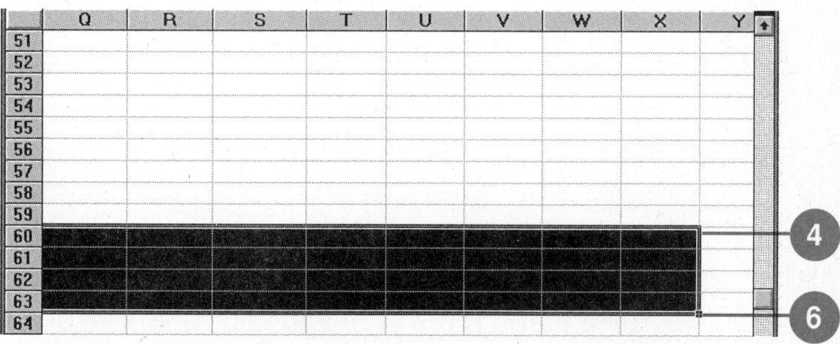

Checking the Array Formulas After New Rows Have Been Added to CKREG.XLS

To be sure that Excel has done what you expect, check it by following the steps described in this section.

1. Scroll to cell A1.
2. Select cell D16.
3. Look at the formula in the cell as it is displayed in the formula bar. Excel automatically expands the formula to accommodate the new rows you added to the worksheet.

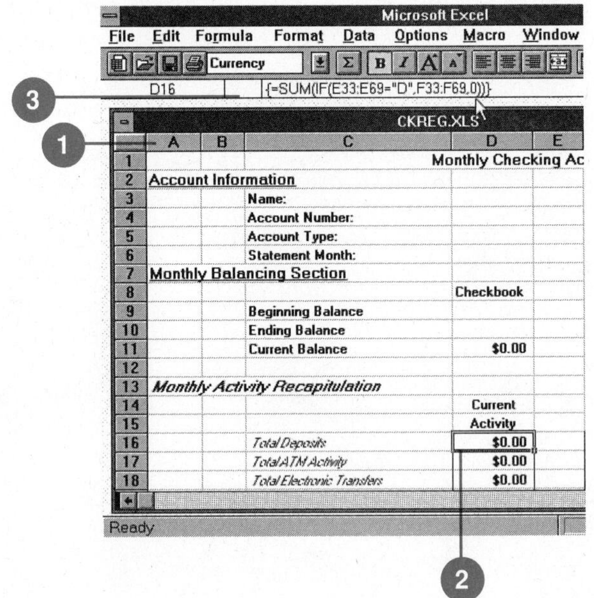

Summary

Managing your bank accounts is extremely important if you intend to borrow money, if you are living on a limited income, or if you want to live within some predetermined means based on the income available to you. Banks provide a manual check register to enable you to keep track of your banking transactions. For a checking account, this register is called a *checkbook*. It may take another form for other types of accounts. Banks also issue regular statements to confirm their records about your banking transactions. It is important to balance your checkbook regularly to ensure that neither you nor your bank has made an error in record keeping.

This project provides you with a worksheet called CKREG.XLS to balance your checkbook and to keep track of the nature of your bank transactions. It is intended for tracking a single month. If you choose to customize the worksheet, suggestions are made to allow you to track categories of expenses for comparison with a budget. If you choose to link data from this worksheet to another worksheet such as the net worth statement described in Project 1, the process of linking worksheets is described for you. Finally, the process of adding new rows to the check register portion of the worksheet is also described.

The next project describes the use of Excel to prepare and monitor a personal budget.

	A	B	C	D	E	F	G	H	I	J	K	L	M	N
1														
2			Personal Budget Worksheet											
3	**Name:**													
4	**Year:**													
5	Same for All Months (Y/N)	Y												
6	*Budget Entry Area*													
7	*Expense Description*	*Jan*	*Feb*	*Mar*	*Apr*	*May*	*Jun*	*Jul*	*Aug*	*Sep*	*Oct*	*Nov*	*Dec*	*Total*
8	***Monthly Income***	1,800	1,800	1,800	1,800	1,800	1,800	1,800	1,800	1,800	1,800	1,800	1,800	21,600
9	Rent/Mortgage	650	650	650	650	650	650	650	650	650	650	650	650	7,800
10	Property Taxes	75	75	75	75	75	75	75	75	75	75	75	75	900
11	Insurance	25	25	25	25	25	25	25	25	25	25	25	25	300
12	Food	250	250	250	250	250	250	250	250	250	250	250	250	3,000
13	Clothing	35	35	35	35	35	35	35	35	35	35	35	35	420
14	Utilities	65	65	65	65	65	65	65	65	65	65	65	65	780
15	Entertainment	25	25	25	25	25	25	25	25	25	25	25	25	300
16	Education	15	15	15	15	15	15	15	15	15	15	15	15	180
17	Transportation	35	35	65	65	65	75	75	75	75	75	75	75	790
18	Automobile	45	45	45	45	45	45	45	45	45	45	45	45	540
19	Phone	30	30	30	55	55	55	55	55	55	55	55	55	585
20	Medical/Dental	25	25	25	25	200	25	25	25	25	25	25	25	475
21	Other	65	65	65	65	65	65	65	65	65	65	65	65	780
22	Total	1,340	1,340	1,370	1,395	1,570	1,405	1,405	1,405	1,405	1,405	1,405	1,405	16,850
23	Available for Savings	460	460	430	405	230	395	395	395	395	395	395	395	4,750
24	Shortfall													
25														
26	*Actual Expense Entry Area*													
27	*Expense Description*	*Jan*	*Feb*	*Mar*	*Apr*	*May*	*Jun*	*Jul*	*Aug*	*Sep*	*Oct*	*Nov*	*Dec*	*Total*
28	***Monthly Income***	1,850	1,905											3,755
29	Rent/Mortgage	650	650											1,300
30	Property Taxes													0
31	Insurance	65	35											100
32	Food	220	280											500
33	Clothing	65	120											185
34	Utilities	95	90											185
35	Entertainment	15	65											80
36	Education		150											150
37	Transportation	40	45											85
38	Automobile	25	45											70
39	Phone	65	85											150
40	Medical/Dental	65	320											385
41	Other	95	75											170
42	Total	1,400	1,960	0	0	0	0	0	0	0	0	0	0	3,360
43	Available for Savings	450												395
44	Shortfall		(55)											
45														

	A	B	C	D	E	F	G	H	I	J	K	L	M	N
46	*Budget to Actual Comparison Area*													
47	*Expense Description*	*Jan*	*Feb*	*Mar*	*Apr*	*May*	*Jun*	*Jul*	*Aug*	*Sep*	*Oct*	*Nov*	*Dec*	*Total*
48	***Monthly Income***	50	0	0	0	0	0	0	0	0	0	0	0	50
49	Rent/Mortgage	0	0	0	0	0	0	0	0	0	0	0	0	0
50	Property Taxes	0	0	0	0	0	0	0	0	0	0	0	0	0
51	Insurance	(40)	(10)	0	0	0	0	0	0	0	0	0	0	(50)
52	Food	30	(30)	0	0	0	0	0	0	0	0	0	0	0
53	Clothing	(30)	(85)	0	0	0	0	0	0	0	0	0	0	(115)
54	Utilities	(30)	(25)	0	0	0	0	0	0	0	0	0	0	(55)
55	Entertainment	10	(40)	0	0	0	0	0	0	0	0	0	0	(30)
56	Education	0	(135)	0	0	0	0	0	0	0	0	0	0	(135)
57	Transportation	(5)	(10)	0	0	0	0	0	0	0	0	0	0	(15)
58	Automobile	20	0	0	0	0	0	0	0	0	0	0	0	20
59	Phone	(35)	(55)	0	0	0	0	0	0	0	0	0	0	(90)
60	Medical/Dental	(40)	(295)	0	0	0	0	0	0	0	0	0	0	(335)
61	Other	(30)	(10)	0	0	0	0	0	0	0	0	0	0	(40)
62		(100)	(695)	0	0	0	0	0	0	0	0	0	0	
63														

Project

4

Personal Budget

Do you ever wonder where all your money goes? If you're like most of us, it probably happens once in a while. If you have a limited income, are planning a large purchase, or just wonder what happens to your money during a typical month, a budget is a necessary evil. A simple budget helps you reach your financial goals and helps you understand how you spend your money.

The worksheet that is included in this project is called HBUD.XLS. It is divided into three parts. The first section of the worksheet is for you to enter your budget. This section is located in cells A6:N24. It is used to capture budgeted income and expenses for each month of the year. Cell B5 contains a Yes/No indicator that lets you extend the entries for the first month through the whole year automatically by placing a **Y** in this cell. If you put an **N** in the cell, you will be able to enter budget figures month by month and budget item line by budget item line. Using a **Y** and adjusting individual cells is much easier. Both methods are explained.

Finally, the three rows at the bottom of this section of the worksheet provide a total of the budgeted costs (row 22), the amount available for savings (row 23), and the amount of any monthly shortfall between income and expenses (row 24). Rows 22 and 23 provide you with a tool for planning for cash flow differences through the year as part of your budgeting process. For example, a planned shortfall in April to pay taxes needs to be prepared for in previous months by planned savings.

The second section of the worksheet is intended for the entry of your actual expenses for each budget category as the year progresses. At the end of each month, you use your check register, credit card slips, receipts, and other sources to record your expenses in each category. If you are using CKREG.XLS, the worksheet provided in Project 3, to record your checking account transactions for each month of the year, you may use the technique explained in Project 3 to link the check register's expense recap to the HBUD.XLS worksheet. You might also work up a simple worksheet to track your monthly expenses. The section of HBUD.XLS devoted to recording actual costs is included in cells A26:N44. Row 28 lets you enter your actual monthly income. This should be your take home pay. Rows 29–41 allow you to record monthly expenses in each budget category. Row 42 contains the total expenses for each month. Row 43 contains formulas that compute any funds that should be available for savings at the end of the month. Row 44 computes any shortfall. If you have a shortfall, you probably had to use savings or a credit card for purchases.

The final section of the worksheet computes the amount you are over or under budget in each category for each month. This section of the worksheet is in cells A46:N62. Row 48 computes any monthly amounts over or under your budgeted income amounts. Rows 49–61 compute the positive or negative differences for each budget item.

Finally, suggestions are offered at the end of the project for changing labels as a means of customizing this worksheet. If you need to add rows to the worksheet, follow the description included in Project 3. If you want to link this worksheet to the check register worksheet, refer to the description in Project 3.

The following pages describe how to use HBUD.XLS. Open the worksheet. (I recommend saving it under another name before you get started, as well, so you keep the original template intact.)

Entering General Information

To personalize your budget, enter the information requested in this section.

1. Make sure row 1 is at the top of the worksheet and column A is on the far left.
2. Select cell B3. Enter your name.
3. Select cell B4. Enter the year being budgeted.
4. Select cell B5. To have the amounts you enter for the first month automatically entered into the cells for the rest of the year, enter a Y. If you want to enter monthly amounts, cell by cell, enter an N.

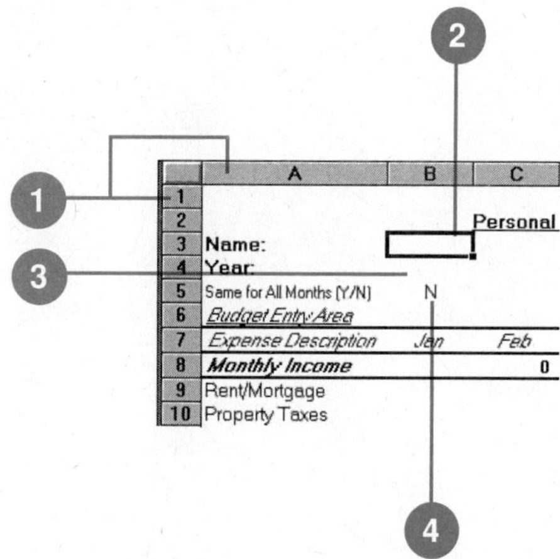

Entering Monthly Budget Data

Now you can begin entering the monthly budget amounts into rows 8–21 of HBUD.XLS. Each row contains a category, and the months run from Jan. through Dec. across the row. Use your records from the previous year or make an educated guess at the amounts for each category. If you have particular plans for spending in the coming year, enter the information relative to such planned expenditures in the appropriate row in the column for the month in which you plan to spend the money.

1. Scroll down until row 7 is at the top.
2. Enter your expected monthly take home income in row 8.
3. Enter expected expenses for each of the categories listed in rows 9–21.
4. Check the total expenses for each month in row 22.
5. Check row 23 to see the difference between your planned income and expenses for each month. If monthly expenses exceed income, the cell in row 23 will be blank.
6. View row 24 to see any shortfall between planned monthly income and expenses.
7. Column N computes the annual amounts budgeted for each budget category contained in column A.

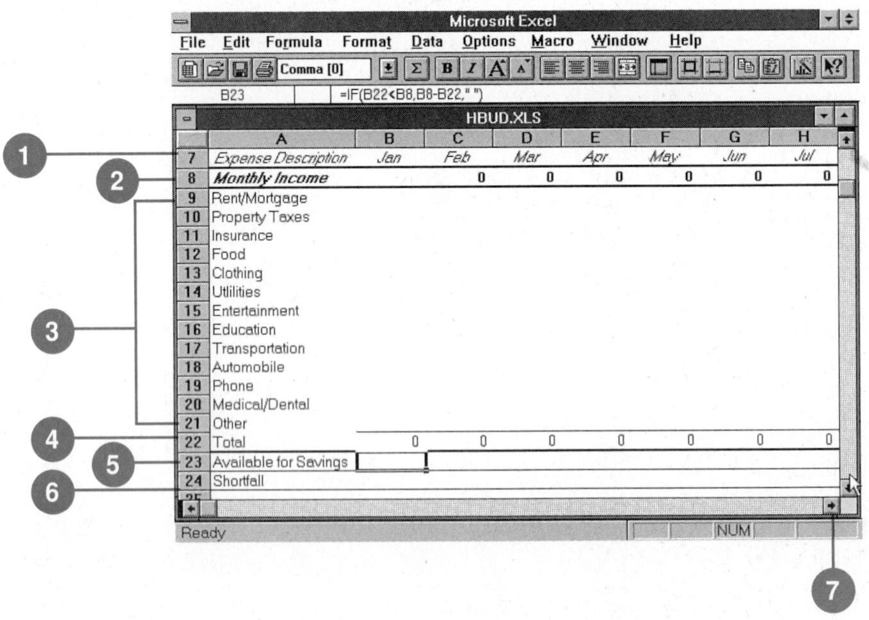

Entering Actual Cost Data

A budget gains real meaning when it is compared to your actual spending. The section of the worksheet described below allows you to enter your actual expenses for each month of the year.

1. Scroll until cell A27 is at the top left corner of the window.
2. Enter your actual take home income for each month in row 28.
3. Record your actual expenses for each budget category in rows 29–41.
4. Check row 42 to see your actual monthly expenses.
5. Check row 43 to see the monthly funds available for savings.
6. Check row 44 for any shortfall between income and expenses.
7. Scroll to column N to see totals for each budget cost category.

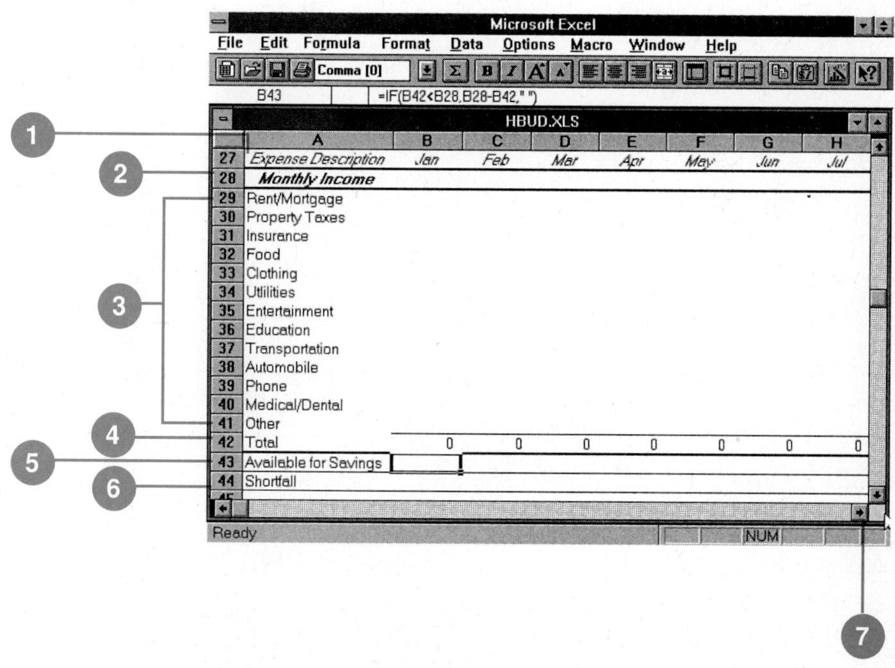

Using the Budget-to-Actual Comparison Section of HBUD.XLS

Once you have set your budget and begin to enter your actual income and spending, it helps to compare budget-to-actual to understand any differences.

1. Scroll until cell A46 is at the top left corner of the window.
2. Check row 48 to see the difference between actual and budgeted monthly take home income.
3. Check rows 49:61 to see the positive, negative (shown in parentheses), or zero differences between actual and budgeted expenses.

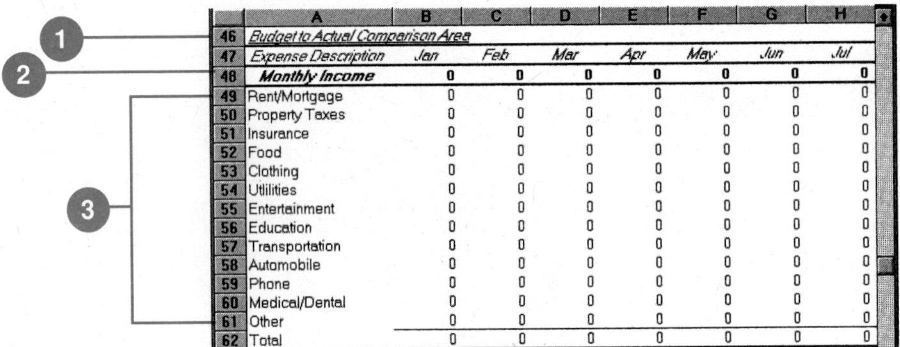

	A	B	C	D	E	F	G	H
46	*Budget to Actual Comparison Area*							
47	*Expense Description*	*Jan*	*Feb*	*Mar*	*Apr*	*May*	*Jun*	*Jul*
48	***Monthly Income***	**0**	**0**	**0**	**0**	**0**	**0**	**0**
49	Rent/Mortgage	0	0	0	0	0	0	0
50	Property Taxes	0	0	0	0	0	0	0
51	Insurance	0	0	0	0	0	0	0
52	Food	0	0	0	0	0	0	0
53	Clothing	0	0	0	0	0	0	0
54	Utilities	0	0	0	0	0	0	0
55	Entertainment	0	0	0	0	0	0	0
56	Education	0	0	0	0	0	0	0
57	Transportation	0	0	0	0	0	0	0
58	Automobile	0	0	0	0	0	0	0
59	Phone	0	0	0	0	0	0	0
60	Medical/Dental	0	0	0	0	0	0	0
61	Other	0	0	0	0	0	0	0
62	Total	0	0	0	0	0	0	0

Using AutoFill Right with Budget Entry

Now that you understand what to expect from each section of the worksheet, it's time to try one or two methods of entering budget data. You've already manually entered data. The second methods—using AutoFill, or the copy handle—is easier and automatic.

1. Scroll back up to row 6.
2. Select cell B8. Enter your monthly take home income.
3. Select the cells in column B for other categories and enter the estimated monthly expenditure for January.
4. Grab the copy handle in the lower right corner of cell B8.
5. Drag to the right until you reach the cell prior to the cell where another change will be made (G8 in the example).
6. Select the cell in which the new value should begin (H8 in the example). Enter the new value.
7. Grab the copy handle in the lower right corner of the cell.
8. Drag to the last cell that will use this value (cell M8 in the example) and release the mouse button.

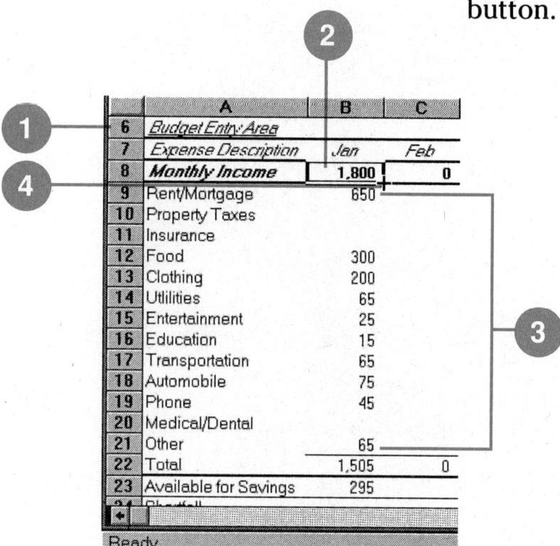

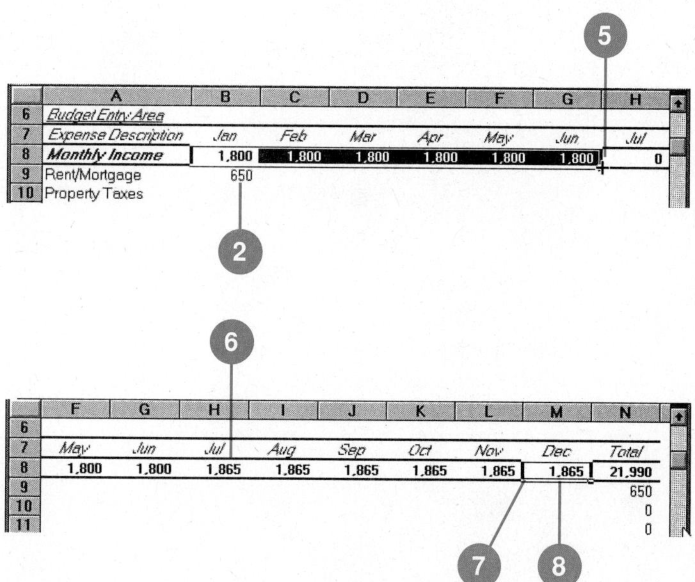

Selecting Nonadjacent Rows for Filling Right

In situations where you wish to fill formulas or formats across cells in a worksheet, you can save time by selecting nonadjacent rows and using autofill.

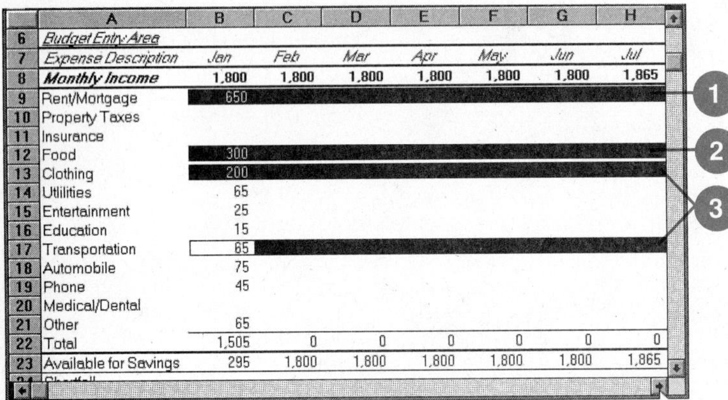

	A	B	C	D	E	F	G	H
6	Budget Entry Area							
7	Expense Description	Jan	Feb	Mar	Apr	May	Jun	Jul
8	Monthly Income	1,800	1,800	1,800	1,800	1,800	1,800	1,865
9	Rent/Mortgage	650						
10	Property Taxes							
11	Insurance							
12	Food	300						
13	Clothing	200						
14	Utilities	65						
15	Entertainment	25						
16	Education	15						
17	Transportation	65						
18	Automobile	75						
19	Phone	45						
20	Medical/Dental							
21	Other	65						
22	Total	1,505	0	0	0	0	0	0
23	Available for Savings	295	1,800	1,800	1,800	1,800	1,800	1,865

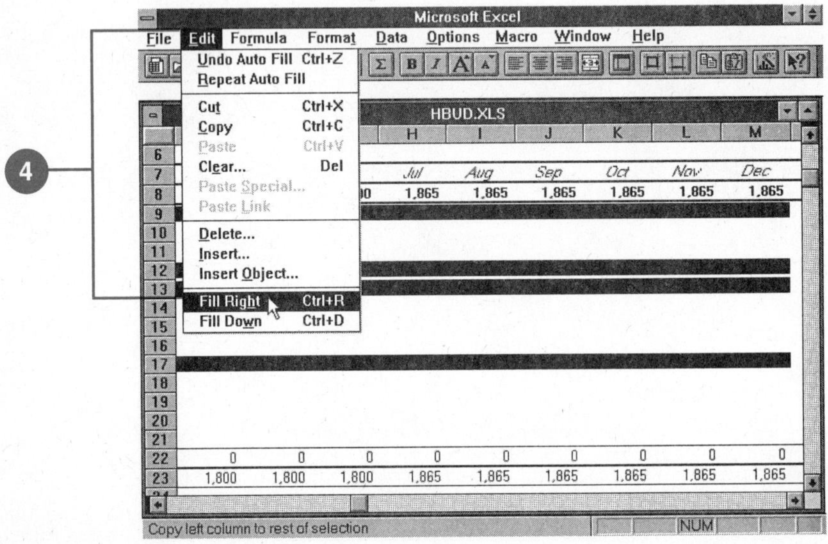

1. Select cell B9 and then drag to select all the cells in the row that you want to copy the entry (from B9) into.
2. Press and hold down Ctrl and then select a second row (row 12 in the example).
3. Continue to hold down Ctrl while you select additional rows (rows 13 and 17 in the example) until all rows that contain data you want to copy are selected.
4. Choose Edit Fill Right.

5. Scroll to the right to make sure all the data you wanted to copy has been copied in each row.

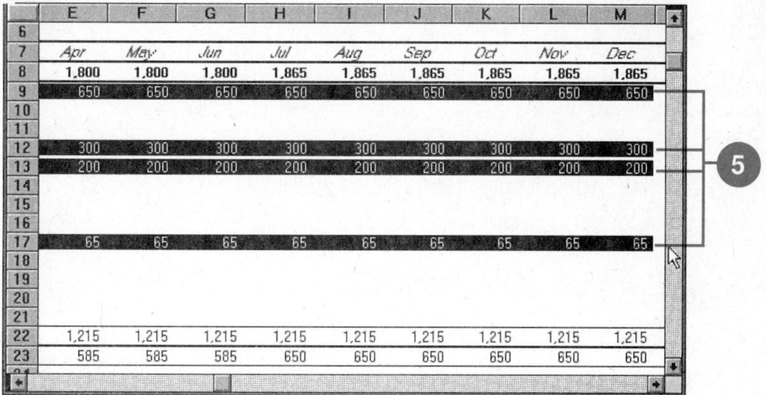

	E	F	G	H	I	J	K	L	M
6									
7	*Apr*	*May*	*Jun*	*Jul*	*Aug*	*Sep*	*Oct*	*Nov*	*Dec*
8	**1,800**	**1,800**	**1,800**	**1,865**	**1,865**	**1,865**	**1,865**	**1,865**	**1,865**
9	650	650	650	650	650	650	650	650	650
10									
11									
12	300	300	300	300	300	300	300	300	300
13	200	200	200	200	200	200	200	200	200
14									
15									
16									
17	65	65	65	65	65	65	65	65	65
18									
19									
20									
21									
22	1,215	1,215	1,215	1,215	1,215	1,215	1,215	1,215	1,215
23	585	585	585	650	650	650	650	650	650

Editing Monthly Budget Data

After you've completed the entries involving copying data across columns, there will be budget preparation situations that require entries in single months or adjustments to entries made by copying data across columns.

1. Enter the data in selected cells one at a time until you have completed all of your data entry.

2. Review the totals in rows 23 and 24.

1

	A	B	C	D	E	F	G	H
7	*Expense Description*	*Jan*	*Feb*	*Mar*	*Apr*	*May*	*Jun*	*Jul*
8	***Monthly Income***	**1,800**	**1,800**	**1,800**	**1,800**	**1,800**	**1,800**	**1,865**
9	Rent/Mortgage	650	650	650	650	650	650	650
10	Property Taxes				750			
11	Insurance		65				65	
12	Food	300	300	300	300	300	300	300
13	Clothing	200	200	200	200	200	200	200
14	Utilities	65	55	55	45	35	25	25
15	Entertainment	25						
16	Education	15						
17	Transportation	65	65	65	65	65	120	65
18	Automobile	75						
19	Phone	45	45	45	45	45	45	45
20	Medical/Dental			85				120
21	Other	65	65	65	65	65	65	65
22	Total	1,505	1,445	1,465	2,120	1,360	1,470	1,470
23	Available for Savings	295	355	335		440	330	395
24	Shortfall				(320.00)			

2

Using the AutoFill Feature of HBUD.XLS

If you intend to use the figures for January as your budget for each month of the year or if you need to make a few adjustments to these figures, HBUD.XLS has a feature that allows you to automatically copy these figures into every month.

1. Enter the budget amounts for each category for January.
2. Select cell B5.
3. Enter a Y. Excel copies the data entered in columns A–M. (If you made a mistake typing Y, you can cancel it by selecting Edit Undo Entry immediately.)
4. Scroll through the worksheet and check the results.

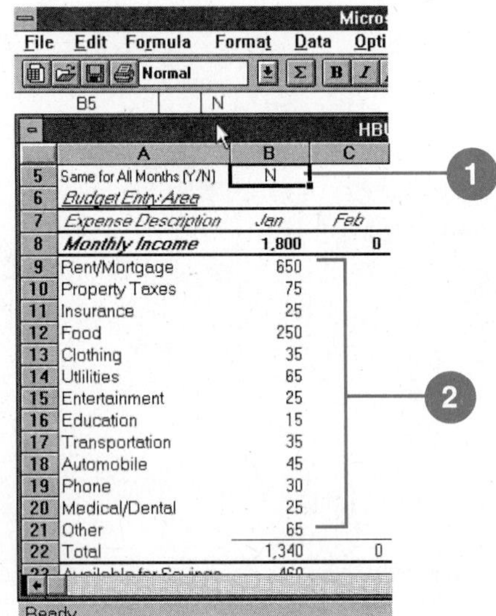

	A	B	C
5	Same for All Months (Y/N)	N	
6	*Budget Entry Area*		
7	*Expense Description*	*Jan*	*Feb*
8	***Monthly Income***	**1,800**	**0**
9	Rent/Mortgage	650	
10	Property Taxes	75	
11	Insurance	25	
12	Food	250	
13	Clothing	35	
14	Utilities	65	
15	Entertainment	25	
16	Education	15	
17	Transportation	35	
18	Automobile	45	
19	Phone	30	
20	Medical/Dental	25	
21	Other	65	
22	Total	1,340	0

	A	B	C	D	E	F	G	H
5	Same for All Months (Y/N)	Y						
6	*Budget Entry Area*							
7	*Expense Description*	*Jan*	*Feb*	*Mar*	*Apr*	*May*	*Jun*	*Jul*
8	***Monthly Income***	**1,800**	**1,800**	**1,800**	**1,800**	**1,800**	**1,800**	**1,800**
9	Rent/Mortgage	650	650	650	650	650	650	650
10	Property Taxes	75	75	75	75	75	75	75
11	Insurance	25	25	25	25	25	25	25
12	Food	250	250	250	250	250	250	250
13	Clothing	35	35	35	35	35	35	35
14	Utilities	65	65	65	65	65	65	65
15	Entertainment	25	25	25	25	25	25	25
16	Education	15	15	15	15	15	15	15
17	Transportation	35	35	35	35	35	35	35
18	Automobile	45	45	45	45	45	45	45
19	Phone	30	30	30	30	30	30	30
20	Medical/Dental	25	25	25	25	25	25	25
21	Other	65	65	65	65	65	65	65
22	Total	1,340	1,340	1,340	1,340	1,340	1,340	1,340

Editing Individual Entries

Sometimes you will need to adjust entries made in actual costs when newer or more complete information becomes available. The example in this section, illustrates how such changes are made.

1. Select cells (such as F20) and enter the new data.
2. To change several cells in a row (e.g., D17:F17, G17:H17, or F19:H19), use the AutoFill technique.

	A	B	C	D	E	F	G	H
5	Same for All Months (Y/N)	Y						
6	*Budget Entry Area*							
7	*Expense Description*	*Jan*	*Feb*	*Mar*	*Apr*	*May*	*Jun*	*Jul*
8	***Monthly Income***	**1,800**	**1,800**	**1,800**	**1,800**	**1,800**	**1,800**	**1,800**
9	Rent/Mortgage	650	650	650	650	650	650	650
10	Property Taxes	75	75	75	75	75	75	75
11	Insurance	25	25	25	25	25	25	25
12	Food	250	250	250	250	250	250	250
13	Clothing	35	35	35	35	35	35	35
14	Utlilities	65	65	65	65	65	65	65
15	Entertainment	25	25	25	25	25	25	25
16	Education	15	15	15	15	15	15	15
17	Transportation	35	35	65	65	65	75	75
18	Automobile	45	45	45	45	45	45	45
19	Phone	30	30	30	55	55	55	55
20	Medical/Dental	25	25	25	25	200	25	25
21	Other	65	65	65	65	65	65	65
22	Total	1,340	1,340	1,370	1,395	1,570	1,405	1,405

2 1

Customizing HBUD.XLS

The customization described next involves adding new labels to the worksheet and adding a totals row to the actual-to-budget comparison section of the worksheet. HBUD.XLS is also useful for a small business or even a department or office in a large business. Essentially all you need to do to adapt the worksheet for such situations is change the labels, add new rows for additional budget and cost items, and add new columns as required for account codes or similar data. If you need to add new rows or columns, follow the examples in Project 3. If you need to change labels, follow the examples described next. Remember to copy formulas into new rows and columns as described in Project 3. Also remember to copy titles into each section of the worksheet to ensure that it is consistent as you customize it.

Changing a Label

When you customize this worksheet, you may find that the cost categories or income categories that have been included don't meet your needs. Change the labels as described in this section. Be sure to reflect the changes through all three sections of the worksheet.

1. Select the cells containing labels you want to change (e.g., A9).
2. Type the new label in the formula bar. Press Enter.

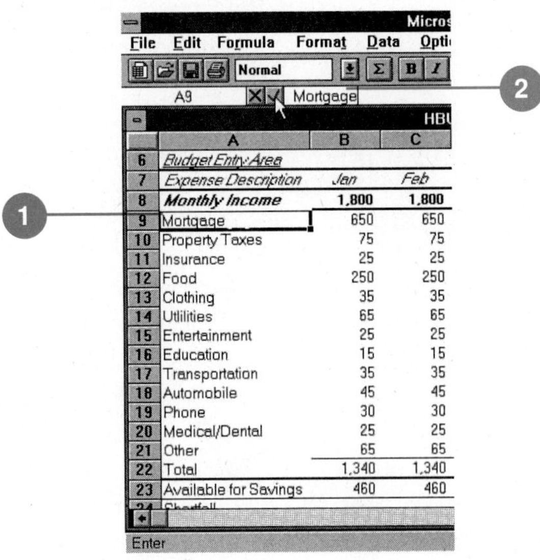

Copying the New Label to Other Sections of the Worksheet

After you change a label in the budget area of the worksheet, you'll need to copy it to the Actual Expense and Budget-to-Actual sections using the steps described next.

1. Select the cell containing the new label (e.g., A9).
2. Choose Edit Copy.
3. Scroll the worksheet to the next section where the label will be used.
4. Select the destination cell that will contain the new label (e.g., A29).
5. Press Enter.

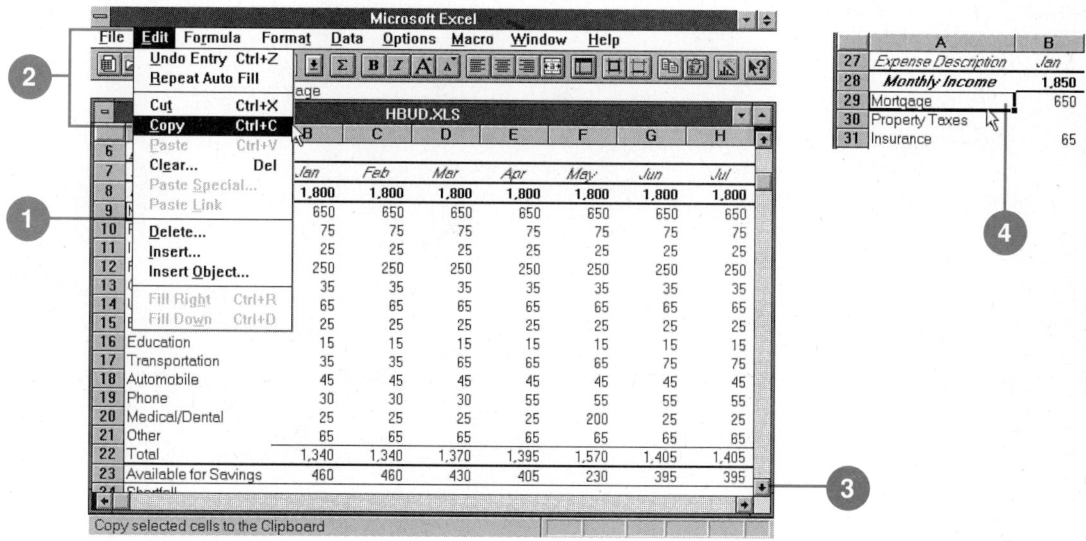

Using AutoSum to Total the Monthly Budget Actual Differences

The AutoSum tool on the toolbar is a time saver. The example in this section illustrates its use.

1. Select the cell in row 62 in the column you want to total (e.g., B62).
2. Click on the AutoSum button on the Standard toolbox.
3. Check the formula bar to view the sum formula that Excel entered. It includes cells B49:B61, the range between the selected cell and a blank cell or border.
4. In this example, because you should include your income in the formula, replace the 9 in 49 with an 8 in the formula. Press Enter.

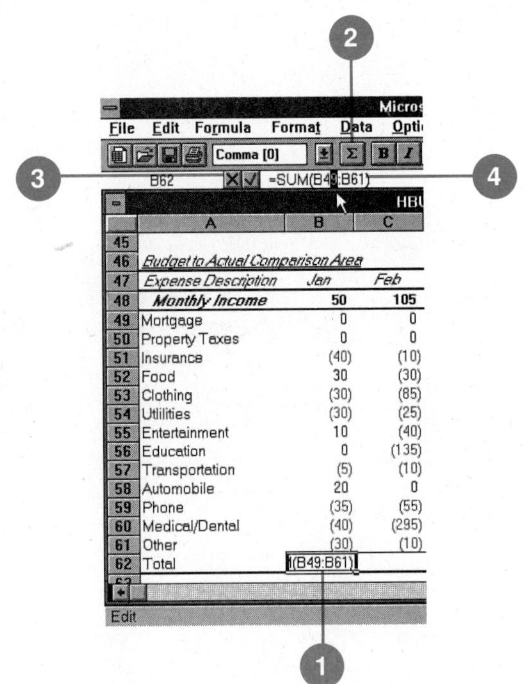

Using AutoFill to Copy the Formula Across a Row

1. Select the cell containing the formula you want to copy (B62 in this case).
2. Drag the handle in the lower right corner of the cell to copy the formula across the row (into B62:N62). This change will allow you to see how much total difference there was between your budget and your actual expenses.

	A	B	C	D	E	F	G	H
46	*Budget to Actual Comparison Area*							
47	*Expense Description*	*Jan*	*Feb*	*Mar*	*Apr*	*May*	*Jun*	*Jul*
48	***Monthly Income***	**50**	**105**	**0**	**0**	**0**	**0**	**0**
49	Mortgage	0	0	0	0	0	0	0
50	Property Taxes	0	0	0	0	0	0	0
51	Insurance	(40)	(10)	0	0	0	0	0
52	Food	30	(30)	0	0	0	0	0
53	Clothing	(30)	(85)	0	0	0	0	0
54	Utilities	(30)	(25)	0	0	0	0	0
55	Entertainment	10	(40)	0	0	0	0	0
56	Education	0	(135)	0	0	0	0	0
57	Transportation	(5)	(10)	0	0	0	0	0
58	Automobile	20	0	0	0	0	0	0
59	Phone	(35)	(55)	0	0	0	0	0
60	Medical/Dental	(40)	(295)	0	0	0	0	0
61	Other	(30)	(10)	0	0	0	0	0
62	Total	(100)	(590)	0	0	0	0	0
63								

Summary

Project 4 deals with preparing budgets and tracking actual costs against budgeted amounts. Making budgets and tracking your expenses and income against your budget in the manner described in this project allows you to manage your cash flow through the year. It lets you anticipate months when you will be required to spend more than you bring in. It also lets you plan savings to use in such months. The approach taken here is also useful in planning for savings and expenses associated with major purchases. You can also use it to perform "what-if" experiments by changing the values in the budget section of the worksheet or by entering projected expenses in the actual cost section of the worksheet. If you use the worksheet in this manner, format the projected values in italics or use some other means to differentiate them from actual expenses entered in the worksheet.

The next project provides you with a tool to track stock performance.

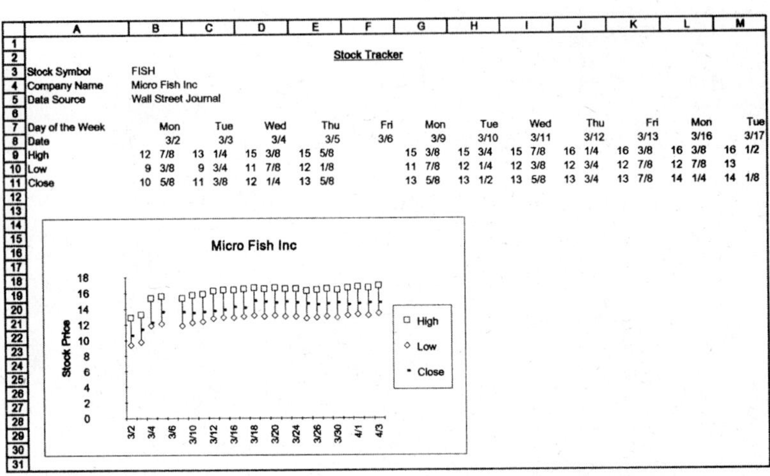

	A	B	C	D	E	F	G	H	I	J	K	L	M
1													
2						**Stock Tracker**							
3	Stock Symbol	FISH											
4	Company Name	Micro Fish Inc											
5	Data Source	Wall Street Journal											
6													
7	Day of the Week	Mon	Tue	Wed	Thu	Fri	Mon	Tue	Wed	Thu	Fri	Mon	Tue
8	Date	3/2	3/3	3/4	3/5	3/6	3/9	3/10	3/11	3/12	3/13	3/16	3/17
9	High	12 7/8	13 1/4	15 3/8	15 5/8		15 3/8	15 3/4	15 7/8	16 1/4	16 3/8	16 3/8	16 1/2
10	Low	9 3/8	9 3/4	11 7/8	12 1/8		11 7/8	12 1/4	12 3/8	12 3/4	12 7/8	12 7/8	13
11	Close	10 5/8	11 3/8	12 1/4	13 5/8		13 5/8	13 1/2	13 5/8	13 3/4	13 7/8	14 1/4	14 1/8

	N	O	P	Q	R	S	T	U	V	W	X	Y	Z
1													
2													
3													
4													
5													
6													
7	Wed	Thu	Fri	Mon	Tue	Wed	Thu	Fri	Mon	Tue	Wed	Thu	Fri
8	3/18	3/19	3/20	3/23	3/24	3/25	3/26	3/27	3/30	3/31	4/1	4/2	4/3
9	16 5/8	16 1/2	16 5/8	16 1/2	16 1/2	16 1/4	16 3/8	16 1/2	16 3/8	16 5/8	16 3/4	16 5/8	16 7/8
10	13 1/8	13	13 1/8	13	13	12 3/4	12 7/8	13	12 7/8	13 1/8	13 1/4	13 1/8	13 3/8
11	15	14 7/8	14 3/4	14 7/8	14 3/4	14 5/8	14 1/2	14 5/8	14 3/4	14 1/2	14 5/8	14 3/4	14 3/4
12													

Project

5

Tracking Stock Prices

If you invest your discretionary savings in the stock market, you may occasionally want to analyze the activity of a particular stock over a period of time. This analysis may cause you to hold on to the stock in a volatile market because the trend of activity of the stock appears to be flat or somewhat rising. It may also cause you to buy a stock because it appears to have stabilized during a downward cycle and has started to rise. You may also decide to sell a stock because its price is dropping at a rate that is faster than you desire. The worksheet included as Project 5 is a simple worksheet that lets you track the progress of a single stock.

Project 5 consists of a worksheet entitled STKTRK.XLS. This worksheet lets you enter a start date, which should be a Monday. Then, it automatically fills in all of the subsequent working days for a five-week period. It also fills in the day of the week immediately above the date being tracked. Space is provided for you to enter stock price data for the daily high, low, and close prices for the stock being tracked. The format for entry in the cells used to capture this data is called Fraction. This format allows you to enter a whole number followed by a space followed by the fraction itself. This format is available in Excel from the dialog box displayed by the Format Number command from the menu bar. You may use this worksheet to enter stock price activity each day until the five-week period is over. You should open a blank version of the worksheet for any five-week period. You should also open a blank version of the worksheet if you want to track more than one stock. As you enter the stock price data for the stock you are tracking, STKTRK.XLS displays an embedded chart that shows the stock activity in the "High, low, close" format presented in many publications that record and present stock price activity.

You can change the format of certain portions of this chart in the customization section of the project. This worksheet allows you to change the font size for the Category (X) Axis of the chart to fit more dates on the chart. You can also add text that describes the Value (Y) Axis of the chart. Finally, a method for compensating for the days that the stock market is closed is also described.

If you are ready to use STKTRK.XLS, open it now. (Don't forget to save it under a new name to keep the original template intact.) Table P5.1 details the structure of the opening screen of the worksheet.

Table P5.1 STKTRK.XLS opening screen

Location	*Description*
Cell B3	The stock symbol.
Cell B4	The company name. This name is automatically displayed as the title for the embedded chart.
Cell B5	Your data source. This data source could be a newspaper such as the *Wall Street Journal*. It could also be some electronic bulletin board if you are a sophisticated computer user.
Row 7	Cells that automatically display the day of the week associated with the dates entered in row 8. The entries in this row extend from cell B7 to cell Z7. There is no need for you to enter any data in row 7.
Cell B8	Date. After you enter a date in this cell, the formulas in row 8 between cell C8 and cell Z8 are filled in automatically. The entries in this row will follow a typical five-day week pattern. You should start your track with a Monday, so be sure to enter a date for a Monday in cell B8 when you begin your data entry.
Cells B9:Z9	The high daily stock price for the stock you are tracking. In this row, make entries by entering a whole number followed by a space followed by a fraction.
Cells B10:Z10	The low stock price for the stock being tracked. Make entries in this row in the same way as entries made in row 9.

continues

Table P5.1 continued

Location	*Description*
Cells B11:Z11	The daily closing price of the stock you are tracking. Use the same fraction type for entries in this row as are used for entries in rows 9 and 10.
Cell A14	The upper part of the embedded chart used to graphically present the price activity for the stock you are tracking.

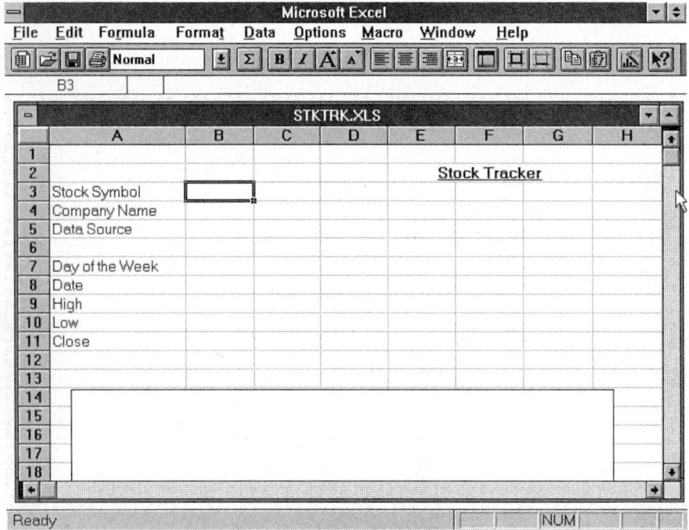

If you scroll down until row 13 is at the top of the screen, you'll see the embedded chart that displays the results of the data that you enter at the top of the worksheet. Table P5.2 explains the elements of this chart.

Table P5.2 Elements of the worksheet chart

Element	*Description*
Value (Y) Axis	Displays a range starting with 0 and ending with 1. The values on this axis change accordingly when you enter stock price data in cells B9:Z11.
Category (X) Axis	Shows no values. Values will automatically be displayed when you begin to enter data in cells B8:Z8.
Legend	This will not change unless you customize the chart in some fashion to alter the legend's location or content.

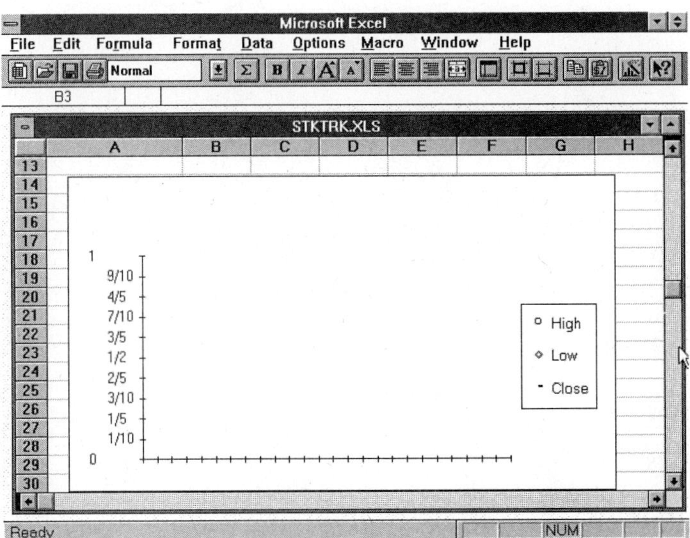

Entering Stock Information and Starting Date to STKTRK.XLS

To keep your files straight, you should enter the stock symbol, company name, data source for stock prices, and the starting date for tracking.

1. Select cell B3. Enter the stock symbol for the stock you are going to track.
2. Select cell B4. Enter the company name for the stock you are going to track.
3. Check the embedded chart. It automatically displays the name of the company you entered in cell B4.
4. Select cell B5. Enter the source of the data you are using to track the stock prices.
5. Select cell B8. Enter the start date for tracking the stock. Make sure this date is the date for a Monday. Press Enter.

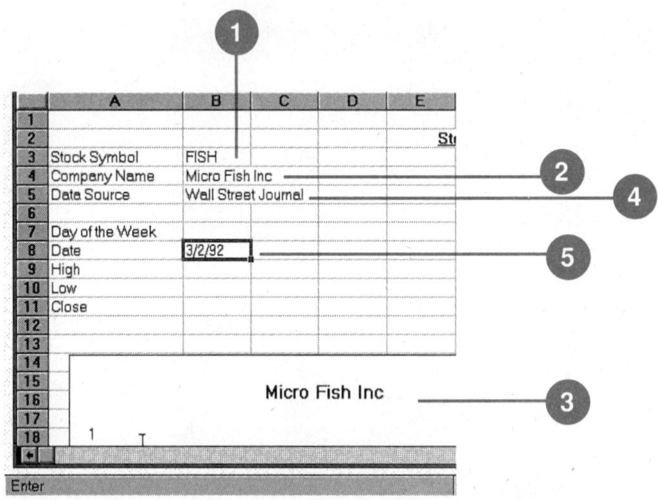

6. Check row 8. The worksheet formulas have filled the week's dates following the start date you entered in cell B8.

7. Check row 7. The worksheet formulas have entered days above each date in row 8.

8. Scroll the worksheet down until row 14 is at the top of the worksheet window.

9. Check the chart. The company name you entered appears as the chart title. The start date you entered and the subsequent dates generated by the worksheet are reflected on the X-axis of the chart. Note that Excel spaces these dates to show every other day, rather than every day.

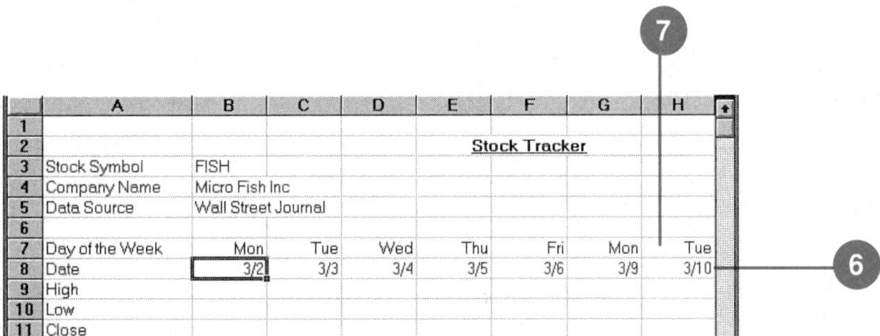

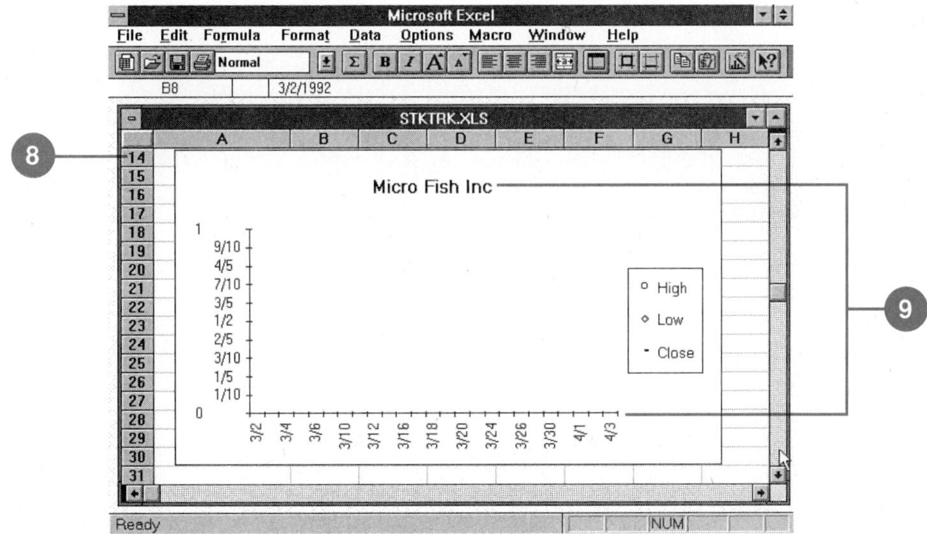

Entering Stock Price Information in STKTRK.XLS

As you consult your source for daily stock prices, enter the prices as described below.

1. Scroll the worksheet until row 1 is at the top again.
2. Select cell B9. Enter the daily high price for the stock being tracked for the first day that you track it. Enter this price as a fraction by entering the whole number of the price followed by a space followed by the fraction.
3. Select cell B10. Enter the daily low price (as a fraction) for the stock.
4. Select cell B11. Enter the daily closing price (as a fraction) for the stock.
5. Enter the second day's price activity in column C.
6. Enter subsequent activity in columns D–Z.

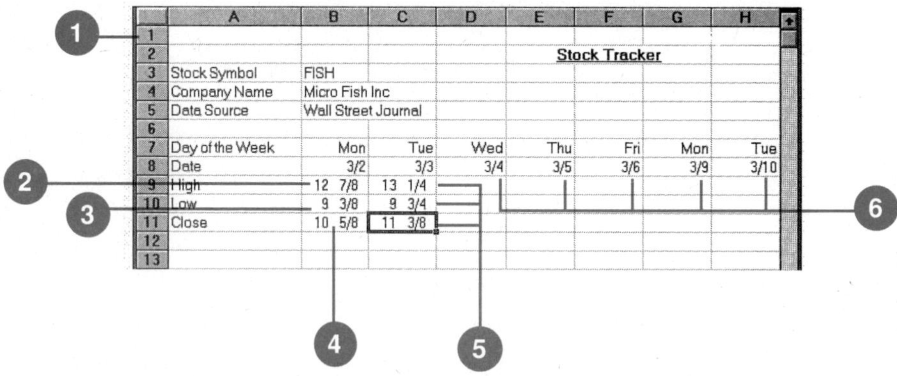

When you have filled in every column through column Z, open a blank version of the worksheet and start again.

Viewing the Adjusted Embedded Chart

The embedded chart described below reflects your daily entries of the high, low, and close prices for the stock you are tracking. Consult the chart daily for a graphic representation of the activity of the stock. Print it frequently if you wish.

1. Scroll the worksheet down until row 14 is at the top.
2. Check the Y-axis, which now reflects the range of value entries.
3. Check the high, low, and close values for the first two entries, which are displayed with distinctive markers for each value entered for a particular date.

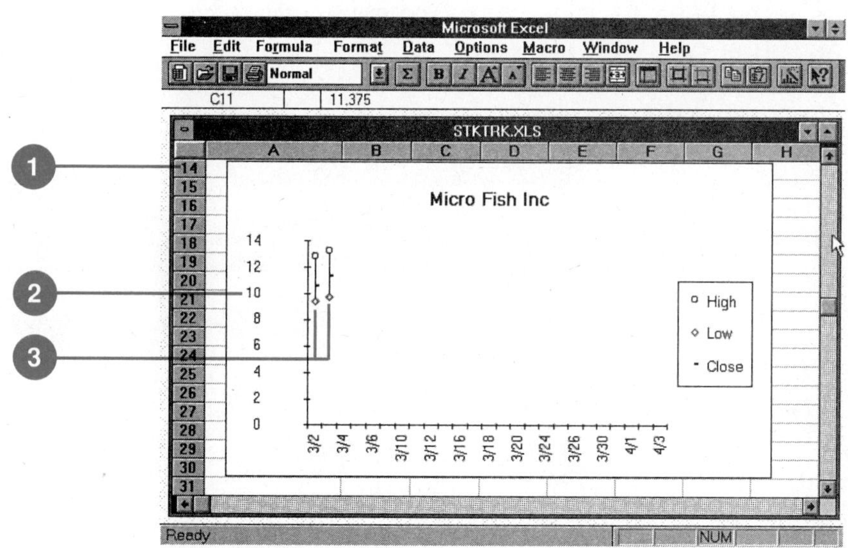

Customizing STKTRK.XLS

You can take a few simple steps if you want to customize the chart that is embedded in STKTRK.XLS. It is easy to change the markers used to identify the three stock prices. It's also easy to change the font size used for the X-axis and to add text that describes the Y-axis. Each of these changes is described in the customization section that follows.

Moving an Embedded Chart to a Chart Window for Editing

If you wish to edit any of the features of an embedded chart, you must first convert it to a chart window. The steps in this section describe how to change an embedded chart to a chart window for editing.

1. Double-click on the embedded chart to display it in a chart window.
2. If the Chart toolbar appears at any point other than the top of the display, drag it to a point just below the Standard toolbar.

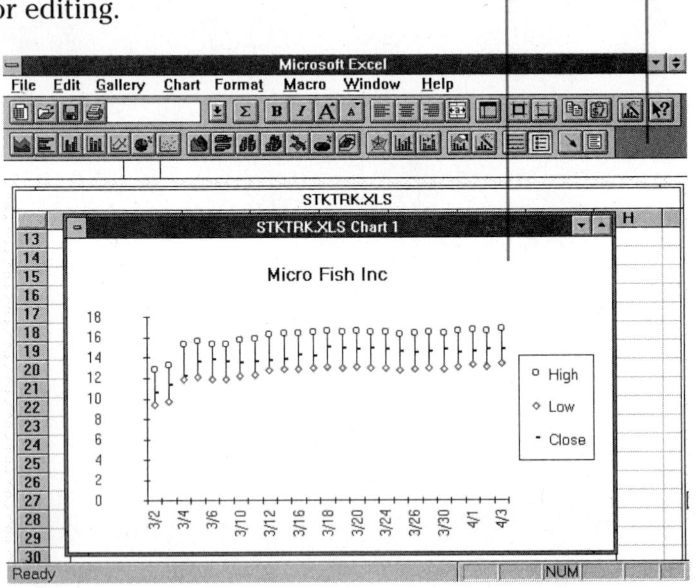

Editing a Chart Series to Alter the Marker

The possible change that you might wish to make to a chart is to change the markers that are used to signify each point plotted in a data series on the chart. Follow the steps described in this section to make this change. You would make such changes for clarity or for aesthetic reasons.

1. Select the data series that will have a marker change by pointing to the leftmost point on the chart for the series and clicking (High in this example).
2. The formula for the series appears in the formula bar.
3. The leftmost point, center point, and rightmost point of the series will show a box.
4. Select Format Patterns.

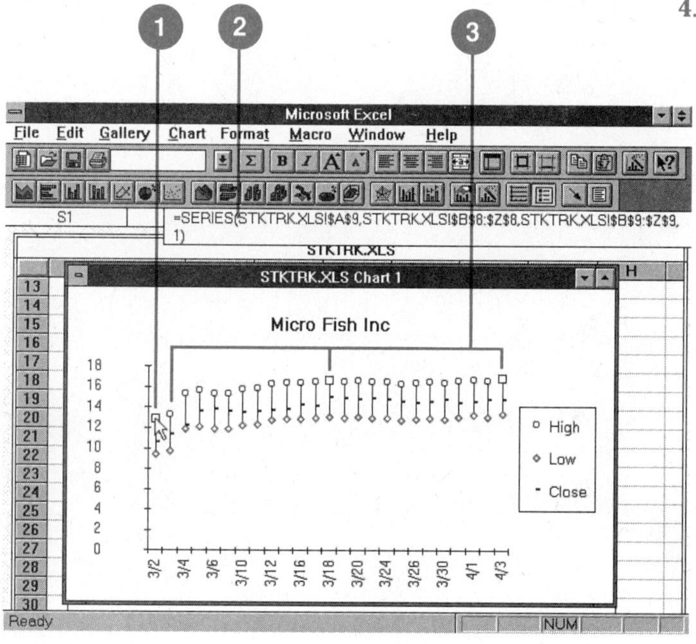

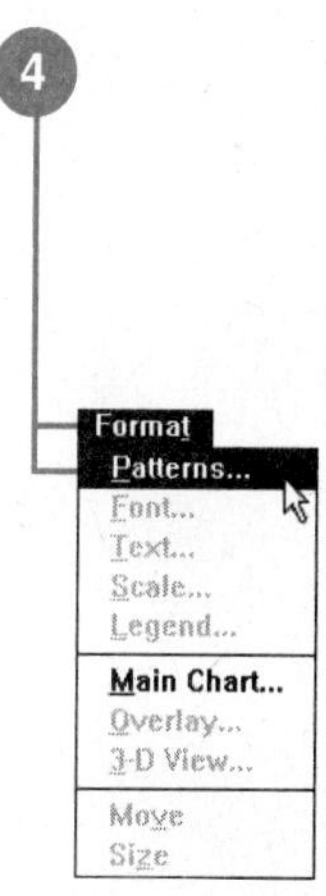

5. Select the Style drop list.
6. Select the symbol you want to use as a marker for the high daily price of the stock.
7. Click OK or press Enter.
8. Check the new markers for the high daily price data series.

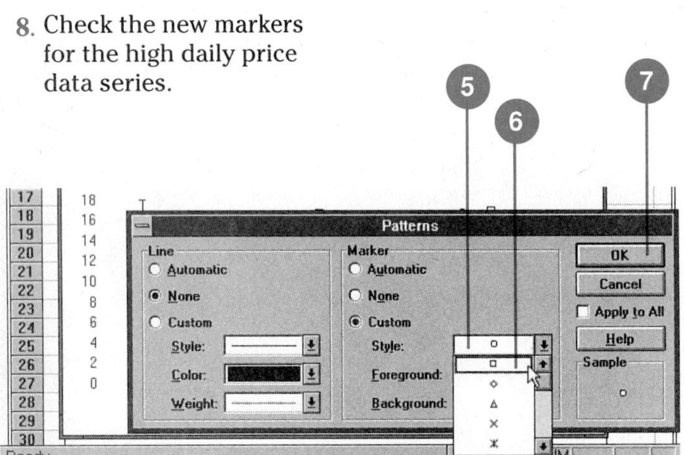

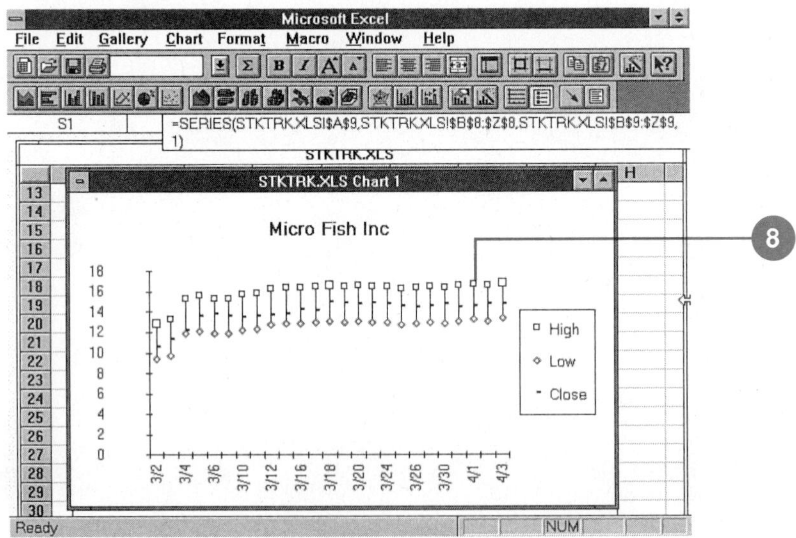

Changing the Font Size on a Chart Axis

Another change you may wish to make to an existing chart would be to change the font or font size used in titles or other labels. These steps describe how to change the font size of the chart's X-axis.

1. Select the X-axis by clicking on any of its dates.
2. Check to be sure a small square is displayed at each end of the axis.
3. Choose Format Font.
4. Select a size (such as 9) from the **S**ize list.
5. Click OK or press Enter. The Font dialog box closes.
6. Check the X-axis. In this case, all the dates from the worksheet appear due to the smaller font size.

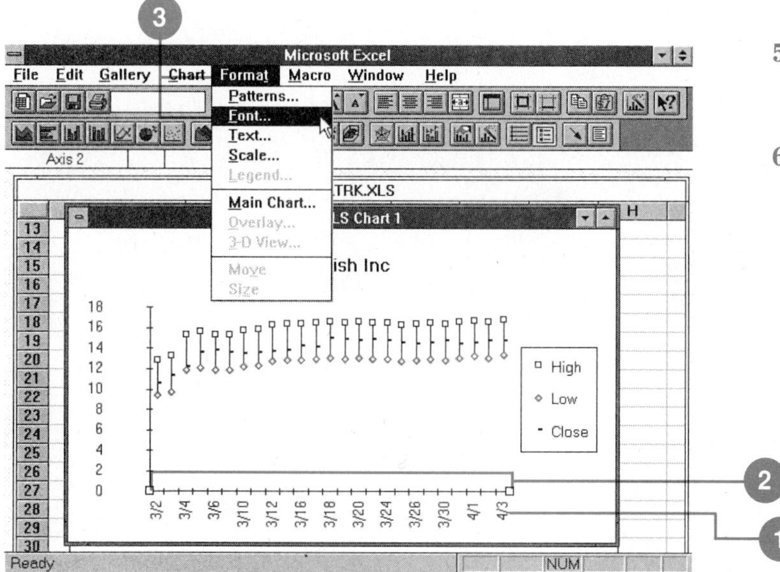

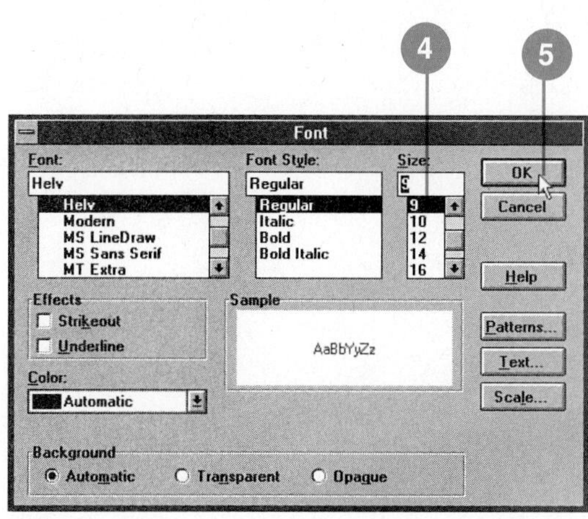

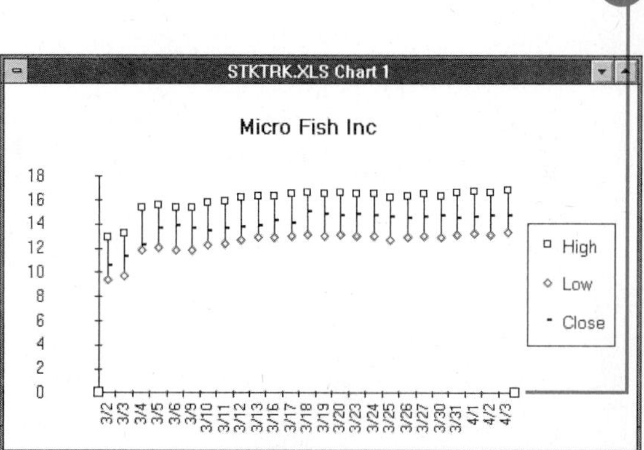

Adding Text to the Value (Y) Axis of a Chart

It usually helps the user of a chart if the axes of the chart are labelled to reflect their meaning or use. The steps below describe how to add text that describes the Y-axis of the stock tracking chart.

1. Click on the chart to select it.
2. Check to see that eight small squares appear around the chart border.
3. Choose Chart Attach Text.
4. Select the Value (Y) Axis radio button.
5. Click OK or press Enter to close the dialog box.

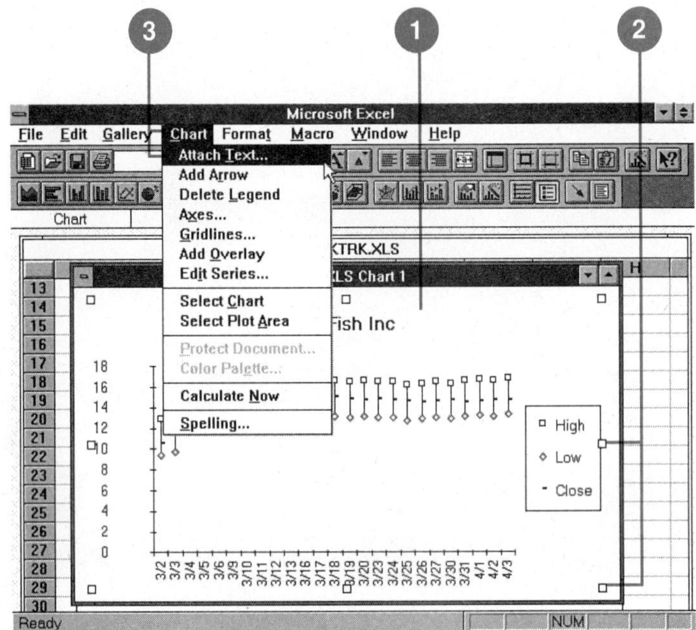

6. Be sure the letter "Y" appears with selection squares beside the Y-axis of the chart.

7. Type Stock Price or any other description you want to use for the Y-axis.

8. Press Enter. The text you just entered is displayed beside the Y-axis. If you want to add text to the X-axis, you can follow the same steps. Remember to select Category (X) Axis from the Radio Buttons in the attached text dialog box and to look for the letter "X" below the X-axis before typing "date" in the formula bar.

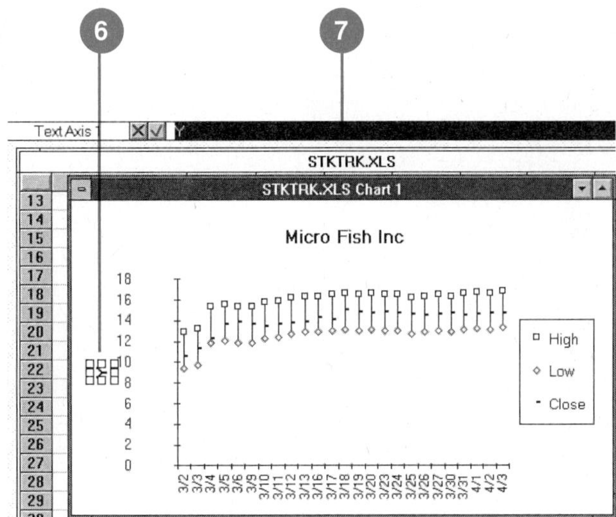

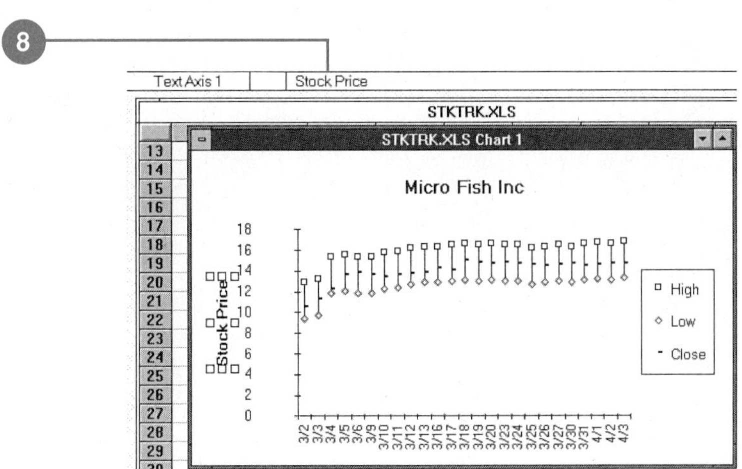

Closing the Chart Window

After you finish customizing the chart, you must close the chart window.

1. Open the chart window's Control menu.
2. Choose Close.
3. The window closes and the embedded chart reappears.

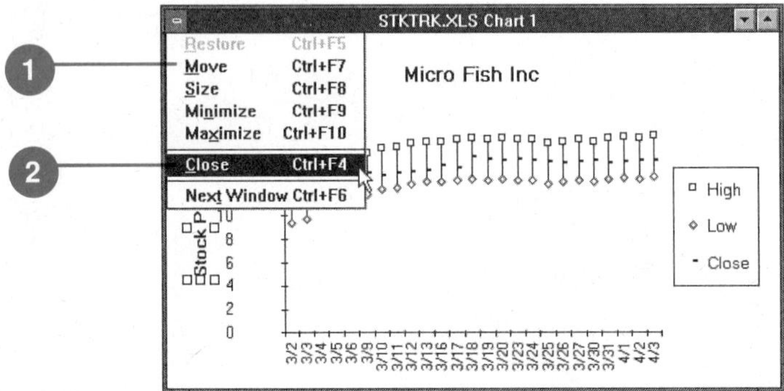

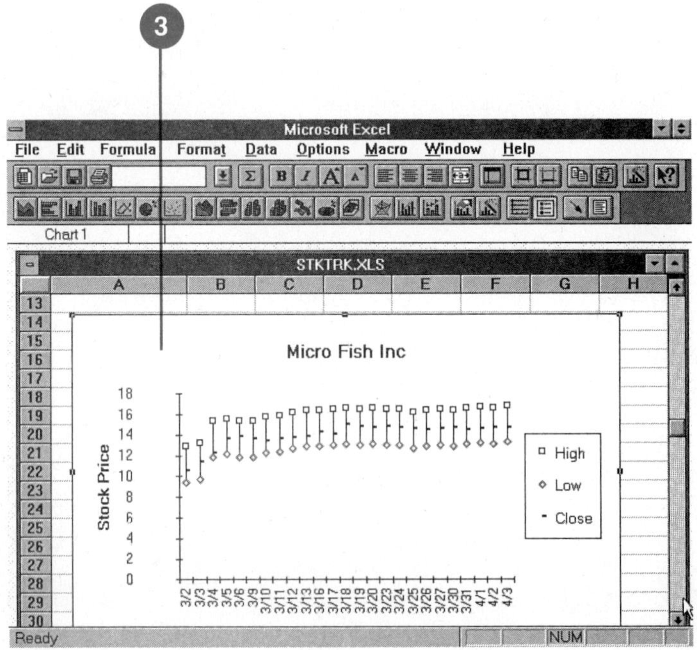

Reselecting the Worksheet

After you close the chart window, the embedded chart is still selected in the worksheet. Use the following steps to return to work with the worksheet.

1. Click in any cell outside of the embedded chart.
2. A plain border appears around the chart. The handles will be absent.

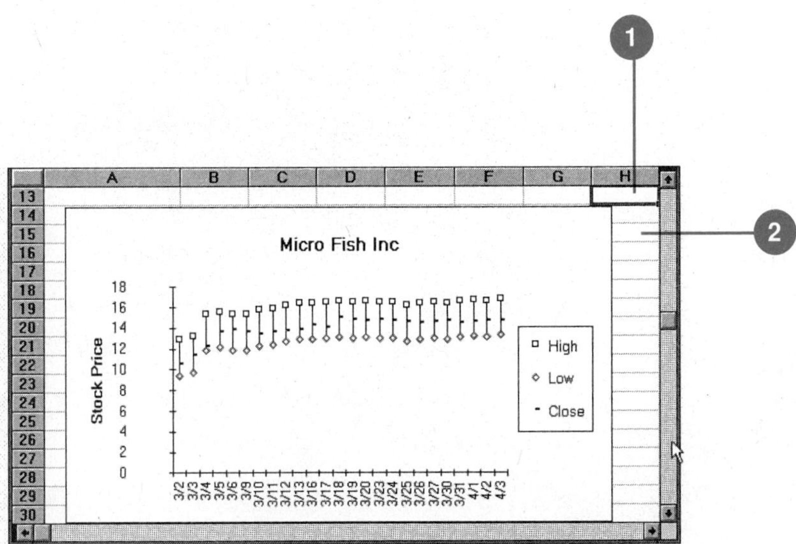

Saving STKTRK.XLS under a New Name

If you want to keep an original blank version of STKTRK.XLS available to use with additional stocks or to track a stock for an additional five-week period, you should save the document under a new name. This procedure is described next.

1. Choose File Save As or press F12. The Save As dialog box appears.
2. Select the File Name text box. Type a new file name in this box. Use some sort of mnemonic abbreviation that will help you find the file when you want to reopen it. MFSH392 is used in the example to signify "Micro Fish Inc 3/92."
3. Click OK or press Enter. The file is saved under a new name. Close it if you are finished with it.

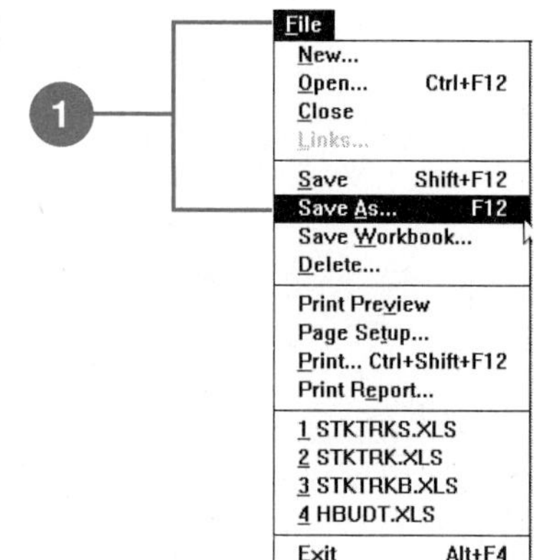

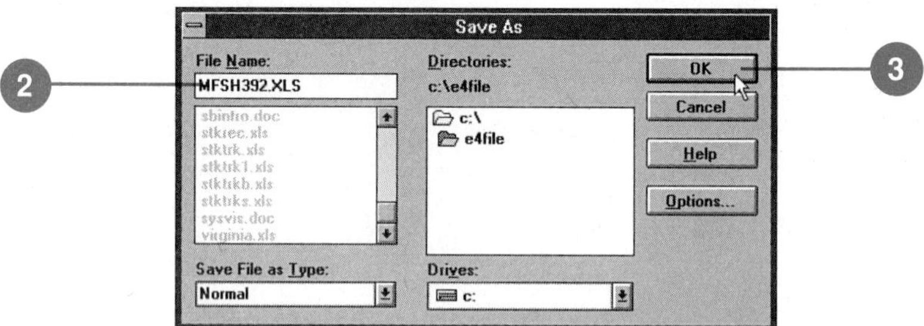

Compensating For Stock Market Closure

There will be times when you are tracking the progress of a stock and the stock market will be closed. The best way to compensate for the lack of data on such days is to enter no data. Otherwise, you will need to alter several formulas on the worksheet. This lack of data will leave a blank space on the chart for the day with no data. The impact of not entering the data for a particular day is illustrated in the following steps.

1. When you encounter a day when the stock market is closed, leave the cells in the column for that date blank (cells F9:F11 in the example).
2. Scroll the worksheet window down to examine the chart.
3. Check the chart for missing data. Anytime you fail to enter data for a particular date, the line for that date won't be displayed. Don't enter zeros in the cells for such dates, or there will be a marker at the zero point for such a day.

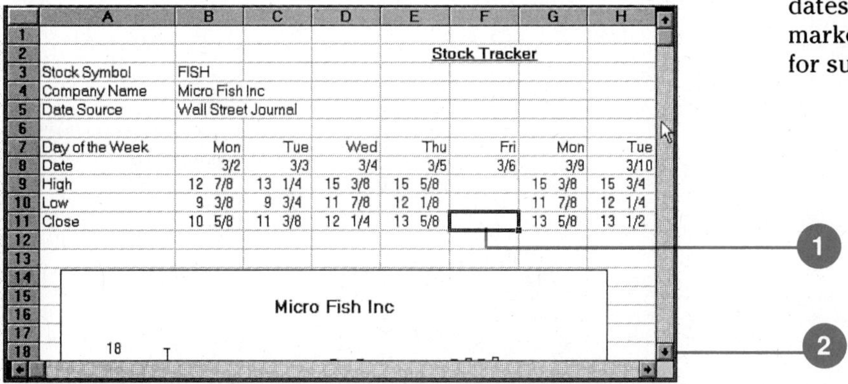

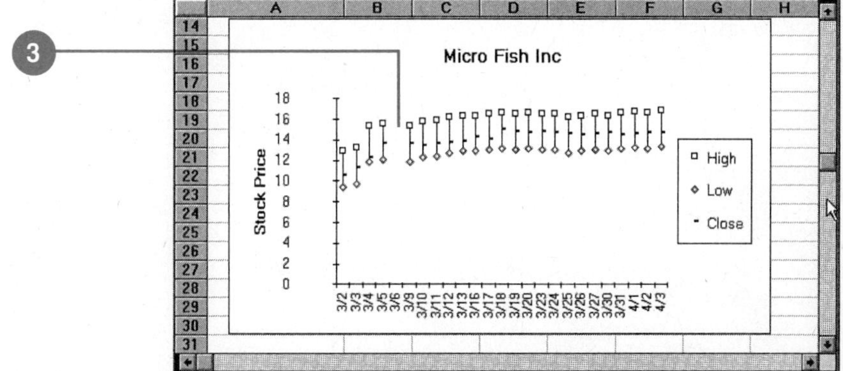

Summary

This project provides you with a tool to track the daily price changes for a single stock. This type of tracking a stock's high, low, and close price is useful for determining whether you should buy or sell a stock. If the trend is rising slightly or flat in a volatile situation, you may want to keep the stock. If the price is rising at a rate that interests you, you may want to buy shares before it goes too high. If the price is dropping at a rate that is too fast for you, you may want to sell.

	A	B	C	D	E	F
4	**Date of Bid**	3/12/92				
5						
6	**Customer Information**					
7	**Name**	Marvin Jones, Inc				
8	**Address**	1212 N West Road				
9	**City, State, Zip**	Minneapolis, Mn				
10	**Attention**	Marvin Jones				
11						
12	**Project Particulars**					
13	**Project Description**	Provide, Deliver, and Install 3 Rope Winders at Customer Address				
14						
15	**Bidding Firm Information**					
16	**Name**	Winder Rope Machines				
17	**Address**	1855 Center Street				
18	**City, State, Zip**	Hempville, Al				
19	**Contact**	George Winder				
20	**Phone**					
21						
22	**Bid Particulars**					
23	**Labor Hours Needed**	**Hours**	**Rate**	**Labor Cost**		
24	Straight Time - Prepare Shipment	14.00	$14.65	$205.10		
25	Unpack and Install	25.00	$18.65	$466.25		
26	Train Staff	35.00	$15.35	$537.25		
27	Overtime			$0.00		
28				$0.00		
29	**Total Labor Cost**	74.00			$1,208.60	
30						
31				**Materials**		
32	**Materials Needed for Project**	**Units**	**Unit Rate**	**Cost**		
33	Rope Winders	3	$15,465.00	$46,395.00		
34	Anchor Sets	3	$280.00	$840.00		
35	Feeder Assemblies	3	$1,200.00	$3,600.00		
36	Storage Reels	12	$180.00	$2,160.00		
37	Reel Handlers	3	$450.00	$1,350.00		
38	Reel Stackers	1	$1,800.00	$1,800.00		
39						
48						
49	**Total Materials**				$56,145.00	
50						
51	**Other Costs**					
52	Transportation			$2,800.00		
53	Packing Materials			$170.00		
54						
55						
56	**Total Other Costs**				$2,970.00	
57						
58				**Grand Total**	$60,323.60	
59						
64						
65		**Materials Lookup Table**				
66						
67	**Material Description**	**Unit Rate**				
68	Anchor Sets	$280.00				
69	Expansion Kits	$2,200.00				
70	Feeder Assemblies	$1,200.00				
71	Reel Handlers	$450.00				
72	Reel Stackers	$1,800.00				
73	Rope Winders	$15,465.00				
74	Shipping Kits	$1,300.00				
75	Storage Reels	$180.00				
76						

Project

6

Bid Worksheet

Large and small businesses often must bid on providing their goods and services. The bid process is fundamental to the competitive nature of most business activity. Excel can help you formalize this process in your organization. It can also provide a record of how each bid was derived and allow adjustments to bids as required without much additional work.

The bid worksheet included with this book is called PRJBID.XLS. It is a simple worksheet in its uncustomized version. The suggested customization of the worksheet introduces you to lookup tables. This worksheet assumes that you know your costs and markups. It also assumes that your labor rates and materials rates include your margins for profit. The customization section of this project discusses a method of expanding the worksheet to start with your costs and arrive at your billable rates. The worksheet itself doesn't take this approach for the sake of simplicity.

PRJBID.XLS starts with a section (A4:B20) that allows you to enter the date of bid, customer information, project description information, and information about your own firm. All the labels in this section are in column A. You enter your data in column B. The next section of the worksheet is the bid itself. Rows 23–29 describe labor use, labor hours, and labor rates. Labor costs are computed automatically after you enter labor hours and your billable labor rate. Rows 31–49 compute materials costs. They allow you to enter a list of materials associated with the bid, the units at which these materials are billed, and your billable rate for these materials. The worksheet automatically calculates the total materials costs after you have entered the unit and unit rate associated with each item of materials associated with the bid. Rows 51–56 are devoted to other costs associated with the bid. These costs might include shipping expenses or materials preparation or packaging costs. This section of the worksheet is set up like the materials section. It expects flat rate cost to be inserted in the total cost cell of the activity described.

If you are ready to try this worksheet, open it and continue with the steps for this project. (Save the worksheet under a new name to keep the original template intact.)

Entering General Bid Information

Use the first section of the worksheet to enter information about the bid itself, as described in this section.

1. Enter the date of the bid in cell B4.
2. Enter the name of the customer of the bid in cell B7.
3. Enter the street address of the customer in cell B8.
4. Enter the city, state, and ZIP Code of the customer in cell B9.
5. Enter the attention name for your customer in cell B10.
6. Enter a brief description of the project in cell B13. If you need more space for this description, enter the additional information in cell B14.

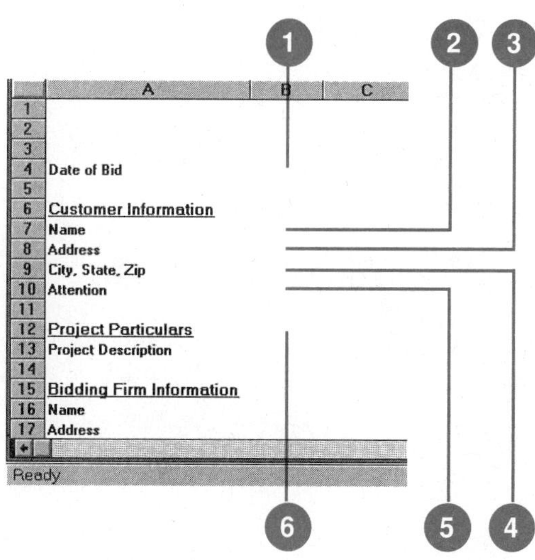

Entering Labor Information

This section of the worksheet is devoted to gathering general information about the company making the bid, and the company to which the bid is being tendered; it is also for the entry of labor use and labor price information for the bid.

1. Scroll down the worksheet until row 14 is at the top.
2. Enter the name of your business in cell B16.
3. Enter your firm's address in cell B17.
4. Enter the city, state, and ZIP Code for your firm in cell B18.
5. Enter the name of the person in your firm who has the authority to negotiate this bid in cell B19.
6. Enter the phone number of the individual named in cell B19 into cell B20.
7. Enter descriptions for the labor hours included in the bid (like `Packing Materials for Shipment` or `Training Customer's Staff`) in cells A24:A28.
8. Enter the hours associated with each labor description in cells B24:B28.
9. Enter your billable rate (including your margin) for each row that includes a description of labor use in cells C24:C28.
10. Check cells D24:D28. The worksheet calculates the total labor costs for each labor category.
11. Check cell B29 to see total labor hours.
12. Check cell E29 to find the total labor cost included in the bid. This cell is offset one column to focus attention on the total cost of providing labor rather than on the details.

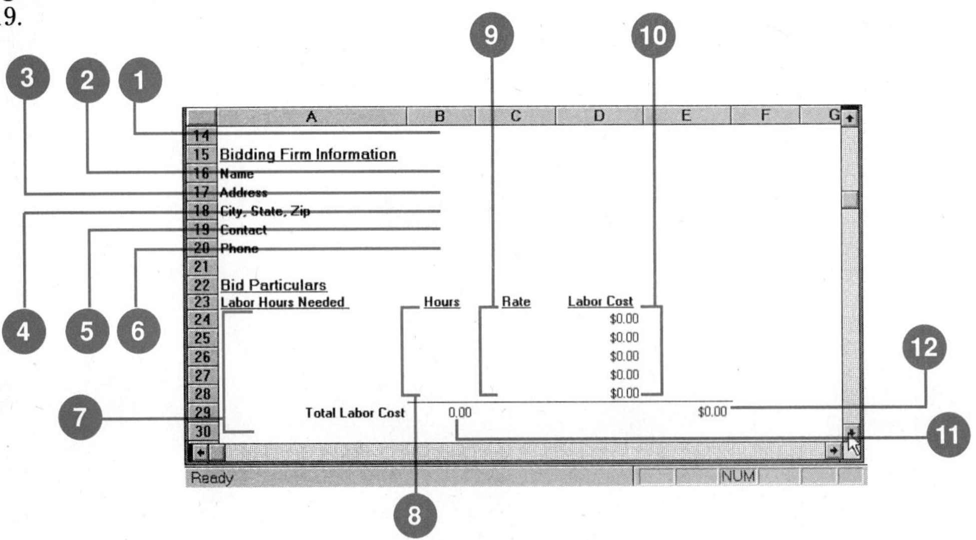

Presenting and Calculating Materials Costs

Many bids require the provision of materials to complete the work being bid. This section of the worksheet allows the bidder to list the materials to be used, and the price of these materials.

1. Scroll down until row 31 is at the top of the worksheet.
2. Enter the descriptions for project materials (e.g., `Number 2 Pencils` or `Reams, Number 20 Bond Paper`) included in the bid in cells A33:A48.
3. Enter the units for each material listed in column A into cells B33:B48.
4. Enter your unit charge for each material in cells C33:C48.
5. Check cells D33:D48 to see the total cost of each material.
6. The worksheet calculates total materials cost for the bid in cell E49.

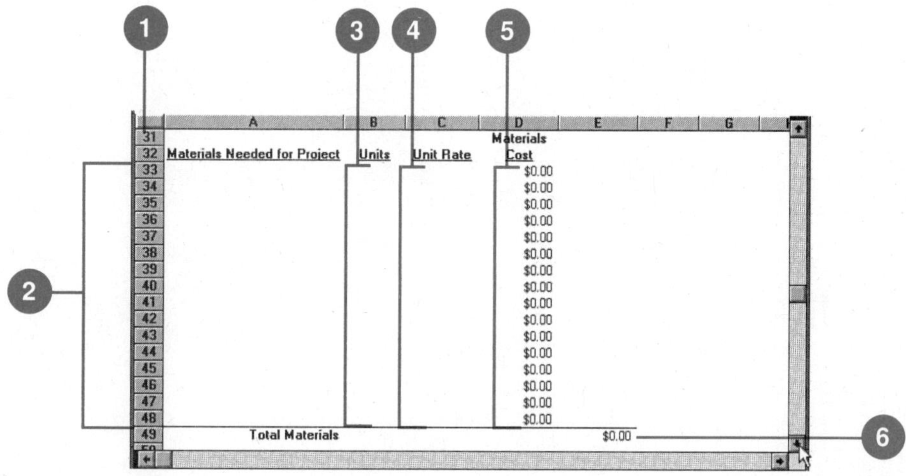

Estimating Other Costs and Total Costs

A bid may require that services or expenses other than labor and materials be expended. The worksheet section described in this section allows the bidder to list and describe such costs as shipping, parking, and other costs not included in labor and materials.

1. Scroll down the worksheet until row 50 is at the top.
2. Enter descriptions of any other costs associated with the bid in cells A52:A55.
3. The worksheet assumes that the costs in this category are flat-rate costs. Enter the billable rates for these costs directly into cells D52:D55.
4. Check cell E56 to see the total for other costs.
5. The worksheet calculates a grand total for the bid in cell E58.

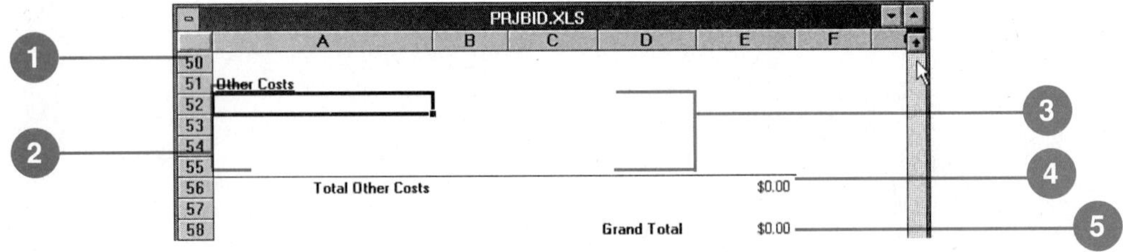

Clearing the Worksheet Title Before Using the Bid

Before you print and mail the bid or present it to your customer, you'll need to clear the worksheet title. Use the steps in this section to do so.

1. Scroll back to the top of the worksheet.
2. Select cell D2.
3. Choose Edit Clear or press Delete. Press Enter or click on OK.

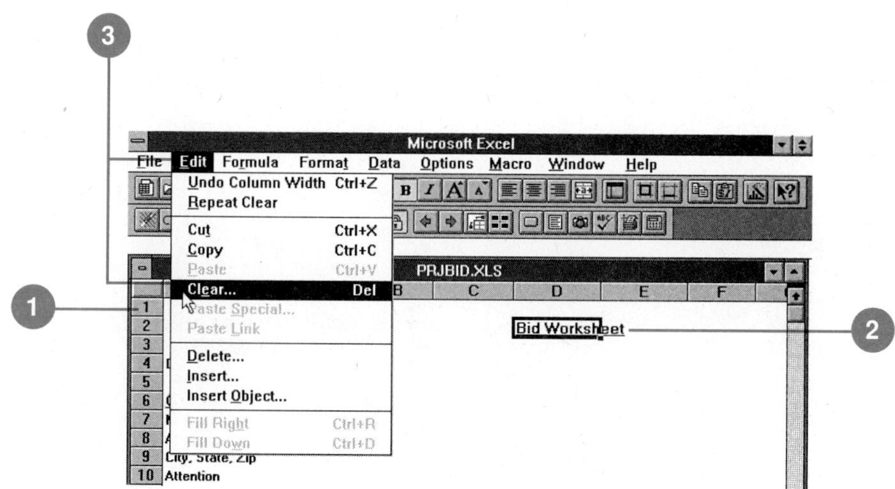

Using File Page Setup Before Printing

When you have completed your entries in PRJBID.XLS and are ready to print the worksheet, you need to first set up the page.

1. Select File Page Setup.
2. Adjust the left and right margins to 0.5.
3. Adjust the top and bottom margins to 0.5.
4. Center the worksheet horizontally.
5. Try to reduce the printed worksheet to 90%. This will work with many printers.
6. When you have completed any other changes you wish to make, press Enter or click OK.

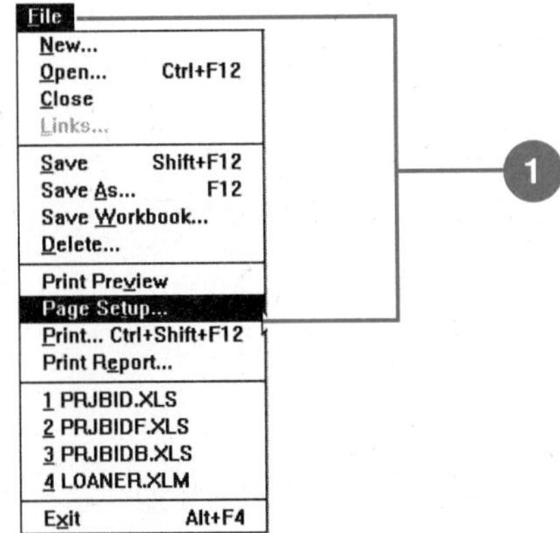

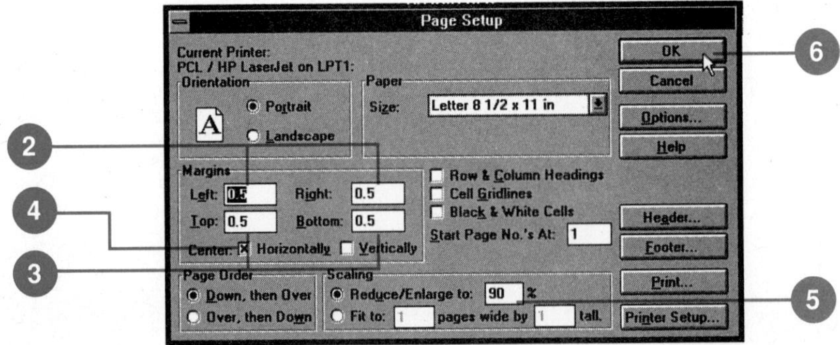

Previewing the Print Job

To get an idea of what your finished worksheet will look like when it is printed, use the Print Preview command.

1. Choose File Print Preview.
2. The symbols at the top of the image indicate the column widths. Adjust the column widths by dragging these symbols. (Click on the **Margins** button to display these symbols, if needed.)
3. The symbols with dotted lines indicate the document margins. Adjust the margins by dragging these symbols.
4. Point the magnifying glass pointer and click the left mouse button to zoom in and out. Zoom in now.

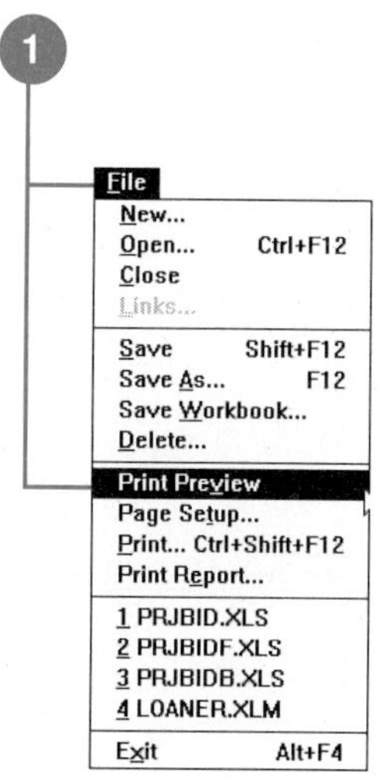

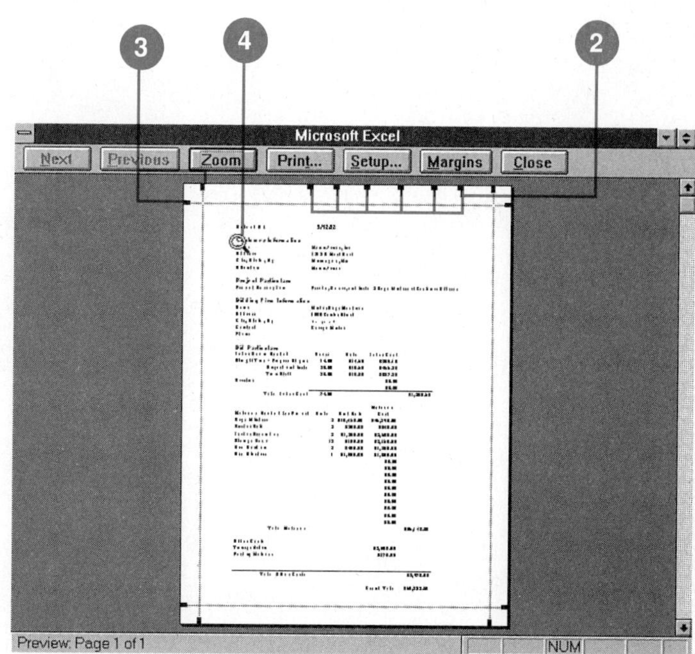

5. Move around the magnified image using the scroll bars.

6. The buttons at the top let you move through the pages, zoom, print, switch to page setup, turn the margin and column width symbols on and off, or close the preview.

7. If you discover something that doesn't look right in printed form, you'll need to switch back to the worksheet to make the adjustment. Use the **Close** button.

8. If everything looks fine on the Print Preview screen, select Print.

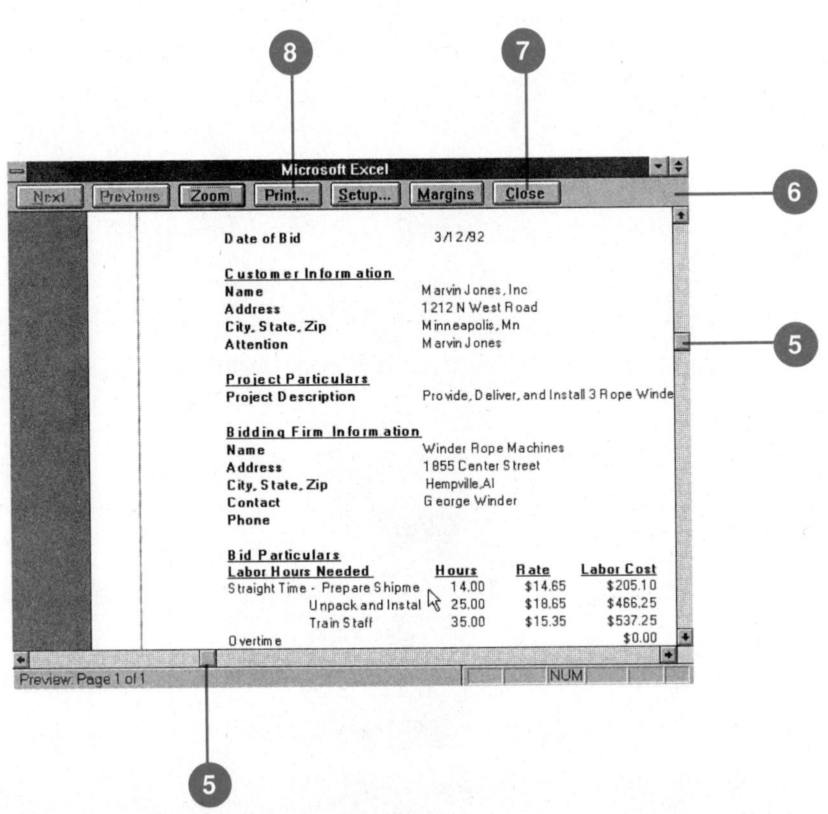

Customizing PRJBID.XLS

You can customize PRJBID.XLS in a number of different ways. You may change any of the labels on the worksheet by selecting any cells containing labels you don't like or need and redoing these labels. You may also add columns and rows as required to accommodate your approach to making bids. This type of customization has already been described in other projects. Another type of customization is building additional worksheets that calculate your actual costs for each aspect of a bid, add in your margins, and calculate your billable costs. These worksheets could be linked to PRJBID.XLS. Another customization that can be quite useful would be to partially automate your calculations by adding lookup tables to PRJBID.XLS that look up unit rates and plug them into the appropriate cells in the Materials section. This customization is described in detail next.

Adjusting Column Width for a Lookup Table

As you add new tables to a worksheet, you may find that the calculations in the cells within the table produce results that won't fit within some cells in the table without an error message. You may compensate for such an occurrence by using a smaller font size, or by expanding the column width for the column containing such cells. The steps in this section describe the expansion of the column width.

1. Scroll down the worksheet to a section that is below or beside the limits of the printed worksheet. (In the example, scroll down until column 58 is at the top of the display.)
2. Select cell B65. Type `Materials Lookup Table`.
3. Select cell A67. Type `Material Description`.
4. Select cell B67. Type `Unit Rate`.
5. As you build lookup tables, you may need to adjust column width to accommodate any text or numbers. Select the column to be expanded.
6. Choose Format Column Width. The Column Width dialog box appears.
7. Enter the new width (11) in the **C**olumn Width text box.
8. Press Enter or click OK.

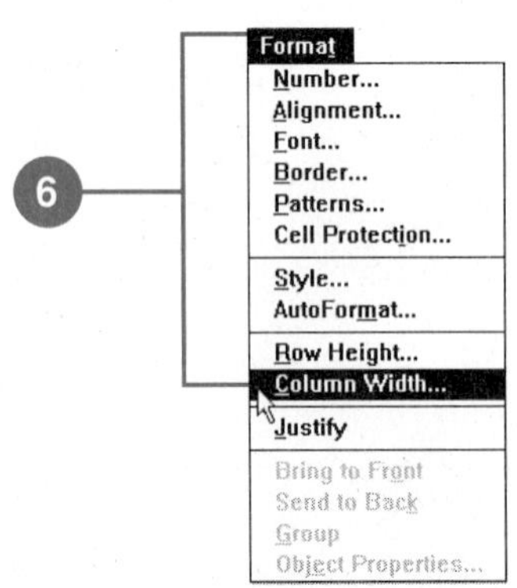

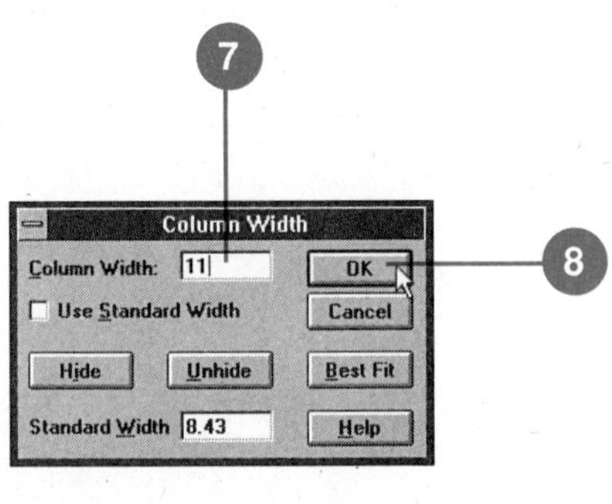

Using Format Font in the Lookup Table

If the expansion of a column width won't work, isn't aesthetic, or isn't otherwise desirable, try changing the font size of any cells that must be adjusted to produce a readable result.

1. Select the cell range that will contain the lookup table, including the labels (cells A65:C78).
2. Choose Format Font. The Format Font dialog box appears.
3. Select a font size (such as 9) from the **Size** list.
4. Click OK or press Enter.

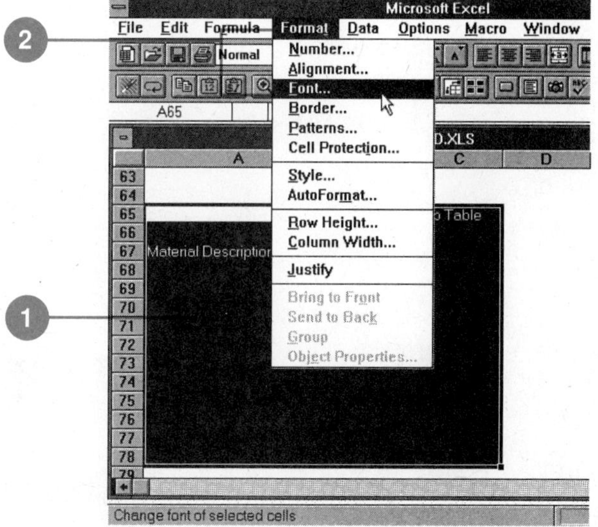

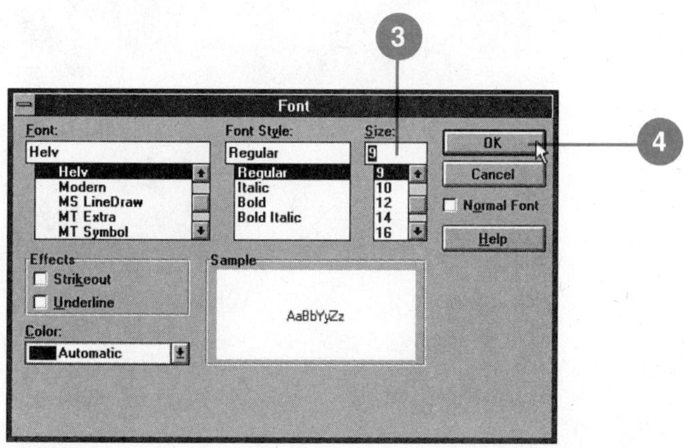

Using the Decrease Font Size Tool

An alternative to using Format Font is to use the Decrease Font Size tool from the Standard toolbox.

1. Select the cell range to contain the smaller or larger font (cells A65:B78).

2. Click on the Decrease Font Size tool on the Standard toolbox.

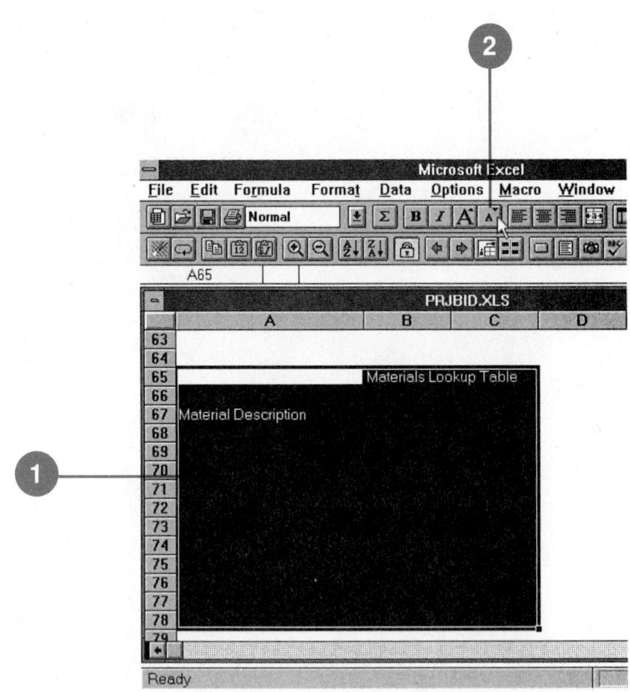

Boldfacing the Lookup Table Labels

Labels are more easily used and identified in tables if they are presented in a bold format.

1. Select cell B65. Press and hold down the Ctrl key.
2. Select cell A67.
3. Select cell B67. Release the Ctrl key. All three cells will be highlighted.
4. Click on the Bold tool on the Standard toolbox.

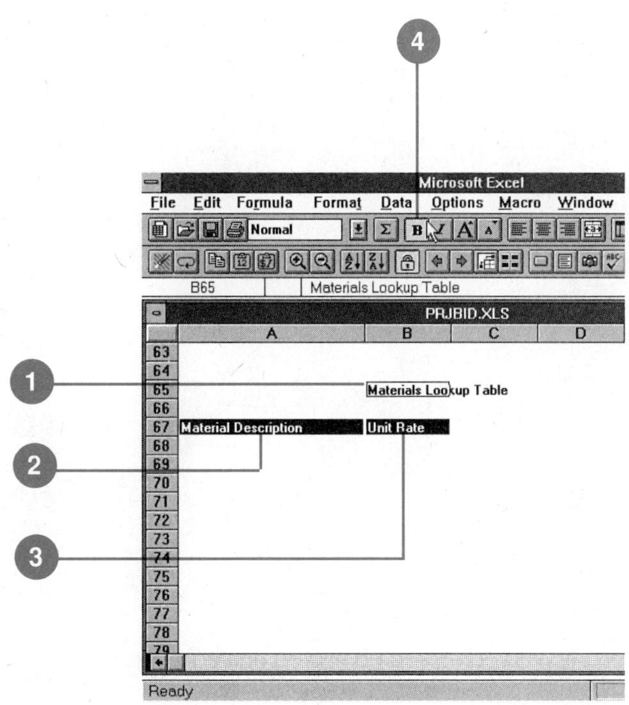

Setting Up a Lookup Table

You'll start your lookup table by entering values in the far left column of the area you want to contain the table. The values in this column could be numbers, letters, or text as illustrated in the example. In the case of this worksheet, they should be the materials you'll be including on bid worksheets. The values in this column are sorted later because Excel searches a column with its VLOOKUP() function or a row with its HLOOKUP() function until it encounters a value equal to or greater than the lookup value in the formula. If the values in the lookup column or lookup row aren't in sorted order, it will stop at the first value it encounters with a greater value than the lookup value supplied.

In the next column or columns, you enter the values Excel should return when it encounters the lookup value in the first column. You may have more than one column or row of values associated with each lookup value in a lookup table. The row or column index number in a lookup formula instructs Excel which row or column to reference.

1. Enter the list of items that will be included in the first column of the lookup range (A68:A75).
2. Enter in the next column (B68:B75) the values that should be returned from the lookup table when the lookup value is encountered.

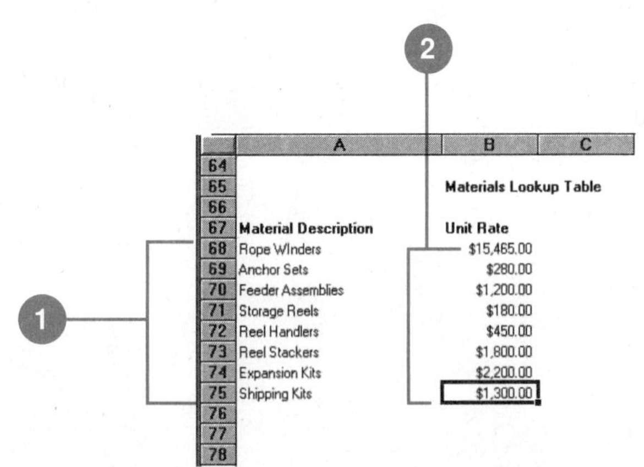

2
A
B
C
Materials Lookup Table
Material Description
Unit Rate
Rope Winders
$15,465.00
Anchor Sets
$280.00
Feeder Assemblies
$1,200.00
Storage Reels
$180.00
Reel Handlers
$450.00
Reel Stackers
$1,800.00
Expansion Kits
$2,200.00
Shipping Kits
$1,300.00
1

3. Select the entire lookup table cell range (A68:B75).
4. Choose Data Sort.
5. The **1**st Key text box should contain the address of the top left cell of the table ($A$68). Correct the entry if necessary.
6. Press Enter or click OK.
7. Check to be sure the table is sorted with the values in the first column (A) in alphabetical order.

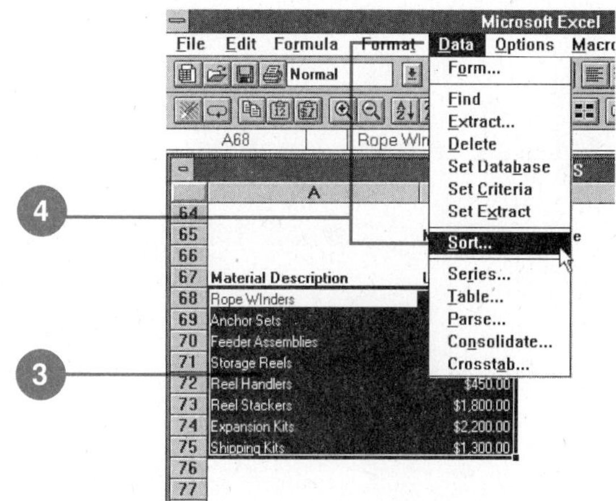

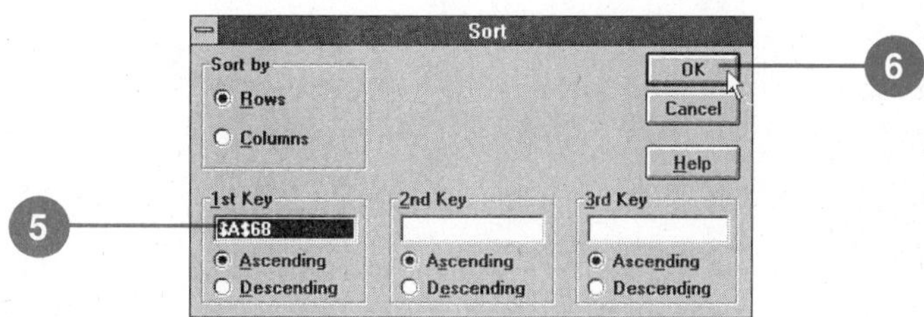

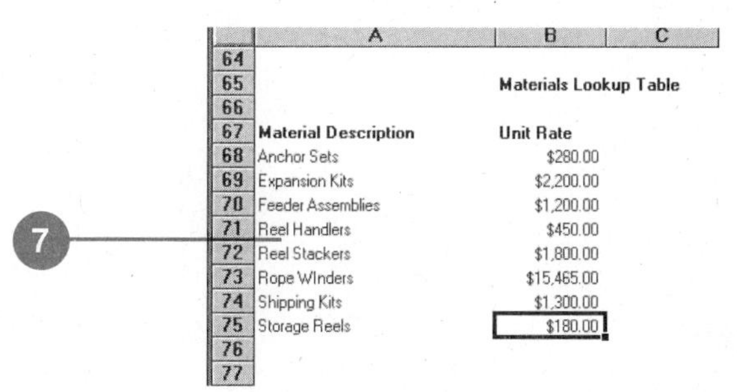

	A	B	C
64			
65		Materials Lookup Table	
66			
67	Material Description	Unit Rate	
68	Anchor Sets	$280.00	
69	Expansion Kits	$2,200.00	
70	Feeder Assemblies	$1,200.00	
71	Reel Handlers	$450.00	
72	Reel Stackers	$1,800.00	
73	Rope WInders	$15,465.00	
74	Shipping Kits	$1,300.00	
75	Storage Reels	$180.00	
76			
77			

Pasting Lookup Functions into the Materials Section

Once a lookup table has been built, you will need to change the formulas in the cells that refer to the lookup table in order to take advantage of the table.

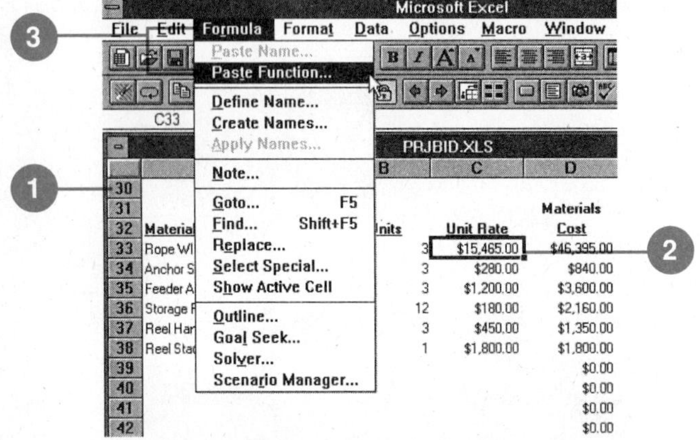

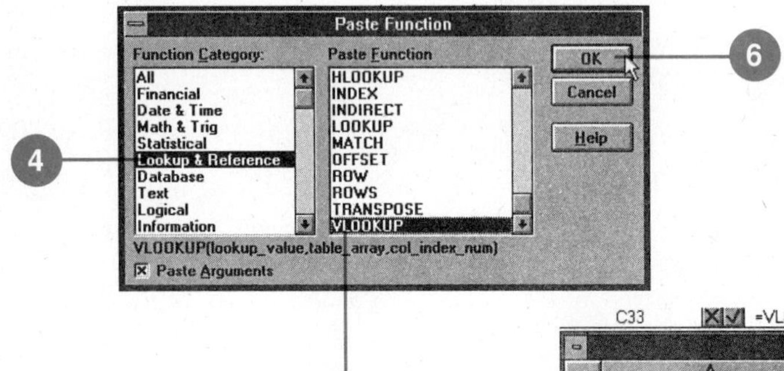

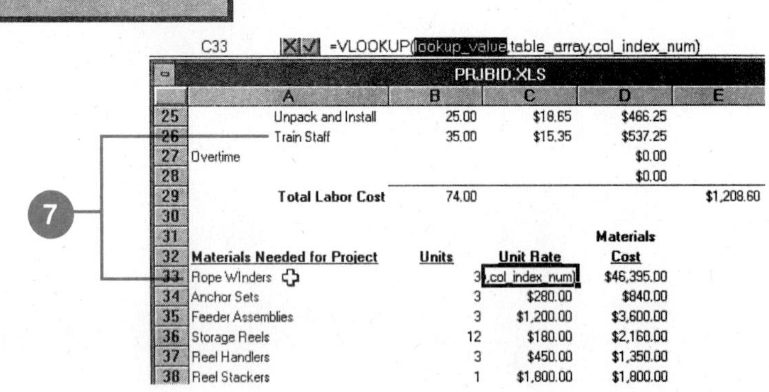

1. Scroll up the worksheet until row 30 is at the top.
2. Select cell C33. This cell contains the first unit rate.
3. Choose Formula Paste Function.
4. Choose Lookup & Reference from the Function Category list box.
5. Scroll down the list in the Paste Function list box until VLOOKUP is visible and select it.
6. Press Enter or click OK. The arguments for the VLOOKUP function are pasted into the selected cell on the worksheet. On the formula bar, `lookup_value` is highlighted.
7. Select cell A33 or type **A33** to replace `lookup_value` in the formula.

8. Double-click on table_array in the formula bar.

9. Scroll down the worksheet until row 63 is at the top.

10. Select all the cells that should be included in the lookup table (A68:B75). When you release the mouse button, the formula will reflect this cell range.

11. Select col_index_num in the formula bar.

12. Type 2 and press Enter. Excel will extract the value in the second table column when it encounters the lookup value in the first table column. (HLOOKUP would extract a value from the second *row* in the table.)

13. Check the worksheet. Cell C33 contains the unit price from the lookup table for the item listed in cell A33. The formula in the formula bar reflects the editing you've done.

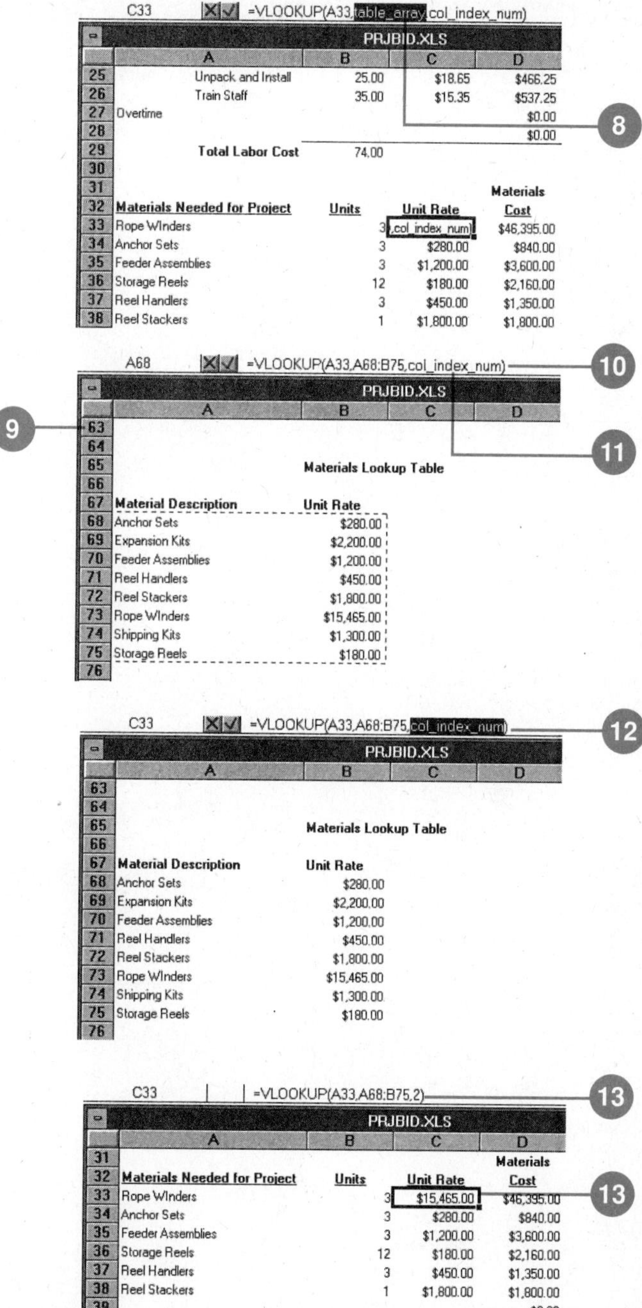

Changing the Table Array in the Lookup Formula to an Absolute Reference

Normally when you copy a formula from one cell to another in Excel, it assumes you want any cell references to be relative cell references in the new location for the formula. With your lookup table, you don't want Excel to make this assumption because the location of the lookup tables remains static on the worksheet and all the formulas that refer to the lookup table must recognize this static location.

1. Select cell C33.
2. Select the cell range A68:B75 in the formula bar.
3. Choose Formula Reference from the menu bar or press F4. The cell reference will change to $A$68:$B$75.

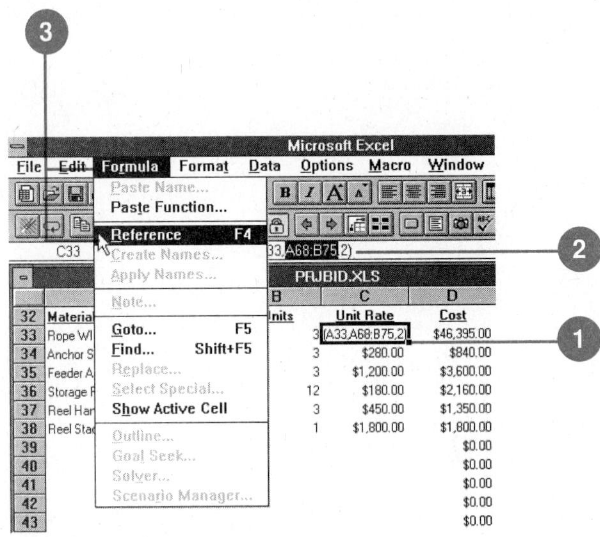

Adding an IF Statement and Using AutoFill to Copy the Lookup Formula

Unless you add an IF statement to the formula to write a space in the cell in which the formula resides if there is no value in column A in the reference cell, you will see an error message that will be printed when you print your worksheet. The IF statement that you add returns a value from the lookup table for the reference value in column A if there is a value in column A. Otherwise, it writes a space into the cell containing the formula.

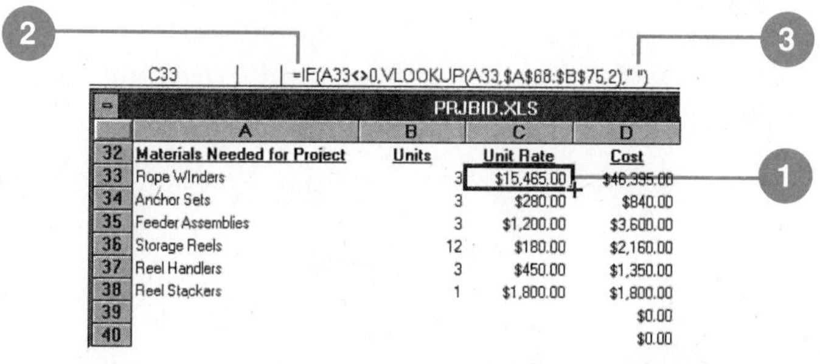
C33 =IF(A33<>0,VLOOKUP(A33,$A$68:$B$75,2)," ")

PRJBID.XLS

	A	B	C	D
32	Materials Needed for Project	Units	Unit Rate	Cost
33	Rope Winders	3	$15,465.00	$46,395.00
34	Anchor Sets	3	$280.00	$840.00
35	Feeder Assemblies	3	$1,200.00	$3,600.00
36	Storage Reels	12	$180.00	$2,160.00
37	Reel Handlers	3	$450.00	$1,350.00
38	Reel Stackers	1	$1,800.00	$1,800.00
39				$0.00
40				$0.00

C33 =IF(A33<>0,VLOOKUP(A33,$A$68:$B$75,2)," ")

PRJBID.XLS

	A	B	C	D
35	Feeder Assemblies	3	$1,200.00	$3,600.00
36	Storage Reels	12	$180.00	$2,160.00
37	Reel Handlers	3	$450.00	$1,350.00
38	Reel Stackers	1	$1,800.00	$1,800.00
39				#VALUE!
40				#VALUE!
41				#VALUE!
42				#VALUE!
43				#VALUE!
44				#VALUE!
45				#VALUE!
46				#VALUE!
47				#VALUE!
48				#VALUE!
49	Total Materials			
50				

5
4

1. Select cell C33.
2. Place the insertion point cursor immediately to the right of the equal sign in the formula bar. Type `IF(A33<>0,`.
3. Place the insertion point cursor immediately to the right of the close parentheses in the formula. Type `," ")`. Make sure there is a space between the quotation marks. Press Enter. This procedure will edit the formula in the formula bar to contain the IF statement.
4. Drag the AutoFill handle in the lower right corner of cell C33 down to the point where cell C48 is highlighted. The formula is copied down the rate column in the Materials section.
5. Check the display. An error message, #VALUE!, appears in column D where no values are displayed. The same error message appears in cell E49. Excel can't deal with a space or text in a cell where it is expecting a number to execute a formula. You can correct this situation by adding another IF statement to the formulas in column D.

Adding an IF Statement to the Materials Cost Formula

The next steps will help you add the IF statement to the formula and eliminate the error messages appearing in the bid worksheet.

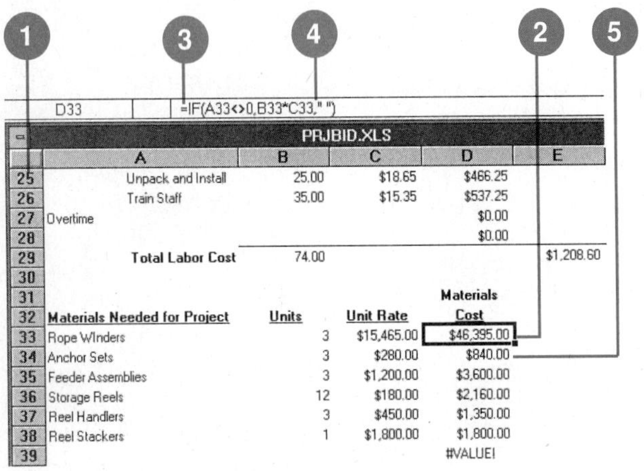

	A	B	C	D	E
25	Unpack and Install	25.00	$18.65	$466.25	
26	Train Staff	35.00	$15.35	$537.25	
27	Overtime			$0.00	
28				$0.00	
29	Total Labor Cost	74.00			$1,208.60
30					
31				Materials	
32	Materials Needed for Project	Units	Unit Rate	Cost	
33	Rope Winders	3	$15,465.00	$46,395.00	
34	Anchor Sets	3	$280.00	$840.00	
35	Feeder Assemblies	3	$1,200.00	$3,600.00	
36	Storage Reels	12	$180.00	$2,160.00	
37	Reel Handlers	3	$450.00	$1,350.00	
38	Reel Stackers	1	$1,800.00	$1,800.00	
39				#VALUE!	

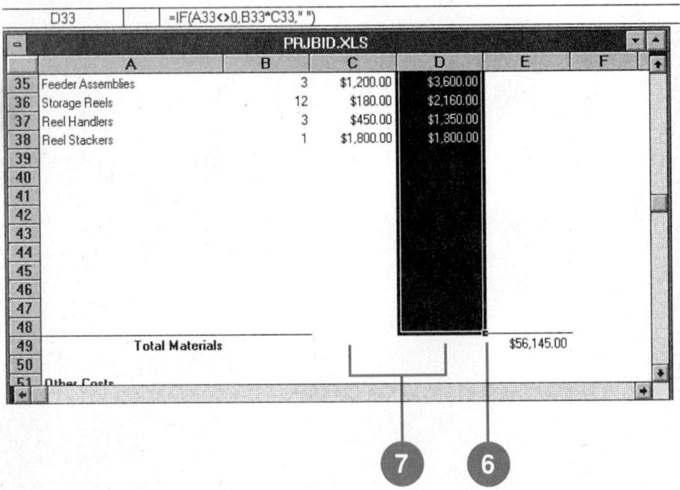

	A	B	C	D	E	F
35	Feeder Assemblies	3	$1,200.00	$3,600.00		
36	Storage Reels	12	$180.00	$2,160.00		
37	Reel Handlers	3	$450.00	$1,350.00		
38	Reel Stackers	1	$1,800.00	$1,800.00		
39						
40						
41						
42						
43						
44						
45						
46						
47						
48						
49	Total Materials				$56,145.00	
50						
51	Other Costs					

1. Scroll up the worksheet until row 25 is at the top.
2. Select cell D33.
3. Place the insertion point cursor in the formula bar immediately to the right of the equal sign. Type `IF(A33<>0,`.
4. Place the insertion point cursor immediately to the right of the last 3 in the formula. Type `," ")`. Make sure that there is a space between the quotation marks. Press Enter.
5. Grab the AutoFill handle in the lower right corner of cell D33.
6. Drag the AutoFill handle down column D until cell D48 is highlighted. Release the mouse button to copy the formula.
7. Examine cells C48 and D48. The preceding copy operations removed the border along the bottom of each of these cells.

Replacing the Cell Border

When formulas are copied from one cell to another with AutoFill, the formatting of the origin cell or cells is also copied. This usually means that borders are removed. The steps in this section describe how to compensate for this occurrence.

1. Select cells C48 and D48.
2. Click on the Bottom Border tool in the Standard toolbox.

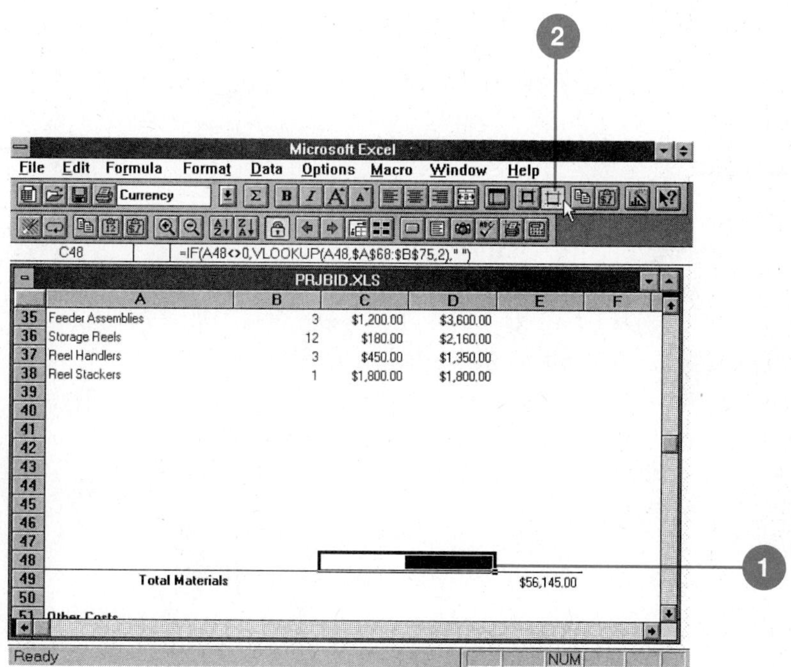

Summary

Project 6 introduced a worksheet, PRJBID.XLS, that allows a small business manager or owner to prepare a bid for providing goods or services to a customer. The preparation of bids by any business large or small is a characteristic of today's highly competitive business world. It usually requires that the bidder formally indicate how much labor and materials will be required to provide the goods or services requested. It also requires that the prices for the goods or services provided be supplied on the bid itself. Some bids contain waivers and other legal protection for the bidder. If you require such protection, add a page to the worksheet to accommodate this need.

PRJBID.XLS allows you to capture critical information about your customer, to capture information about your firm, to describe briefly what is being bid, and to calculate and present your billable costs associated with the bid. The worksheet as presented requires manual entry of all of the labor and materials units associated with the bid. It also requires the manual entry of the billable unit rates associated with the bid. The customization portion of the project introduces a simple lookup table to automatically insert unit rates for materials.

	A	B	C	D	E
1					
2			**Bid Comparison Worksheet**		
3					
4	**Project Under Bid:**	Acquisition of five 486 Computers			
5	**Project Description:**	Acquire and install five 486 computers.			
6					
7	**Work To Be Done For:**		Engineering Department		
8					
9	**Company Bidding**	AlphaComp	BetaComp	DeltaComp	**Minimum**
10	**Address**	1412 10th St	1818 Henry Rd	14 W 18th Avenue	**Of All Bids**
11	**Phone**	422-8877	422-1567	423-1814	**Received**
12	**Contact**	Chris Wilson	Matt Winters	Judy Winston	
13					
14	**Bid Specifications**				
15	**Labor Hours**				
16	Install Computers	5.00	6.00	5.00	5.00
17	Train Staff	8.00	12.00	12.00	8.00
18	**Totals**	13.00	18.00	17.00	13.00
19					
20	**Labor Costs**				
21	Install Computers	$120.00	$100.00	$100.00	$100.00
22	Train Staff	$180.00	$160.00	$155.00	$155.00
23	**Totals**	$300.00	$260.00	$255.00	$255.00
24					
25	**Materials**				
26	5 ea 486 computers	$17,250.00	$15,750.00	$14,250.00	$14,250.00
27	5 ea 12" Color Monitors	$2,125.00	$1,550.00	$1,775.00	$1,550.00
28	5 ea Surge Suppressors	$125.00	$99.75	$107.50	$99.75
29	5 ea Windows 3.0	$495.00	$525.00	$649.75	$495.00
30	5 ea MS Excel 4.0	$1,625.00	$1,550.00	$1,612.50	$1,550.00
31	5 ea MS Word 2.0	$1,625.00	$1,550.00	$1,612.50	$1,550.00
32					$0.00
33					$0.00
34					$0.00
35	**Total Materials Costs**	$23,245.00	$21,024.75	$20,007.25	$19,494.75
36					
37	**Total Cost of Bid**	$23,545.00	$21,284.75	$20,262.25	$19,749.75
38					

7

Bid Comparison Worksheet

In many businesses, major acquisitions and construction work undergo a bid process before a vendor or contractor can be selected. These businesses compare the bids to better evaluate what each bidder is offering. The bid process provides the business manager or owner with a tool to carry out further negotiations if such negotiations are required.

Project 7 consists of a bid comparison worksheet called BIDCMP.XLS. This worksheet lets you gather information about three bids for the same goods or services. It then looks at each item of the bid and reports the minimum amount for each item. The worksheet also provides subtotals for labor and materials associated with the bid. Finally, it provides totals for each bidder. The customization section of this project deals with adding new rows to accommodate more labor activity and a new column to accommodate another bidder. Open BIDCMP.XLS before proceeding.

Using Excel's Window Zoom Command

Excel 4.0 provides you with a valuable tool for working with worksheets that are larger than a normal worksheet window. This tool is the **W**indow **Z**oom command. It allows you to fit more of a worksheet into a window, or less, depending on how you use it.

1. Make sure BIDCMP.XLS is open and row 1 is at the top of the worksheet window.
2. Choose **W**indow **Z**oom.
3. Choose **C**ustom from the Magnification radio buttons.
4. Type **90** in the text box next to the Custom button.
5. Press Enter or click OK.

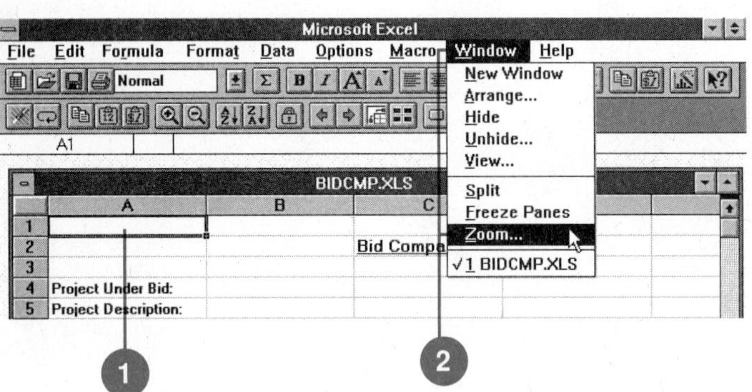

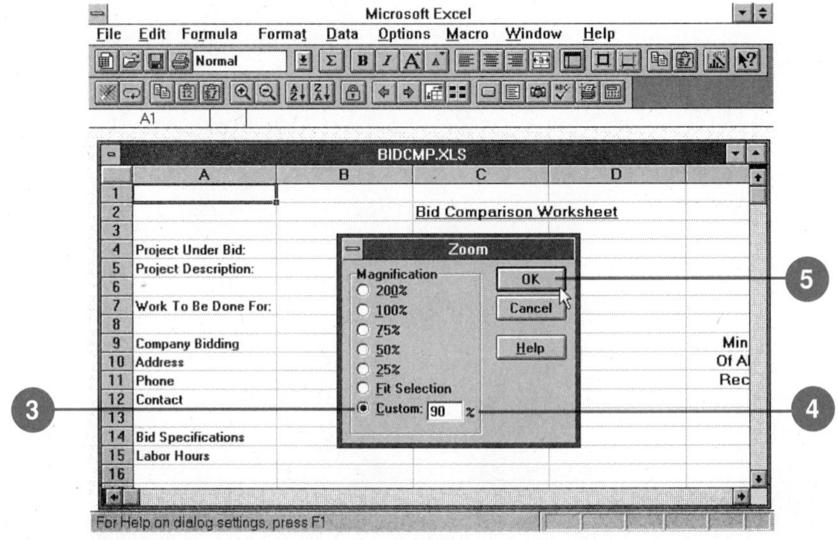

Moving the Worksheet Window

At times, the worksheet window as displayed on your computer may be too small or in an inconvenient location. Follow these steps to move it and resize it.

1. Point to the worksheet window title bar with the mouse pointer. Press the left mouse button.
2. Drag the worksheet window until the upper left corner fits snugly under the formula bar and against the left side of the screen display.
3. Point to the lower right corner of the worksheet window and press the left mouse button. The pointer should become a diagonal double-headed arrow.
4. Drag the pointer down and to the right until the worksheet fills the lower portion of the screen.

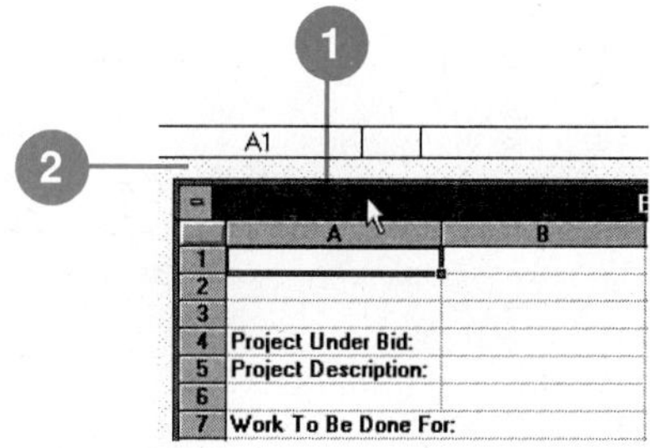

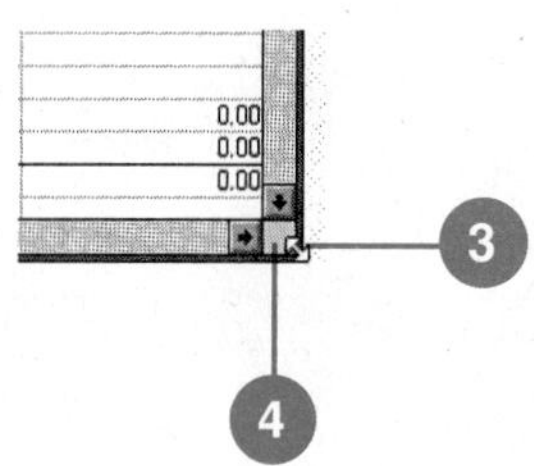

Entering Data in the First Section of BIDCMP.XLS

The first section of BIDCMP.XLS is used to enter information about the company receiving the bid and the companies competing for the bid. This information places the bid in context, and allows it to be explained and understood. The bottom portion of the screen allows labor-related information to be entered.

1. In cell B4, enter a project name for the bid.
2. In cell B5, enter a brief description of the bid.
3. In cell C7, enter the name or department that represents the customer of the bid.
4. In cells B9:B12, enter the bidding company's name, address, phone number, and contact name for the first bid.
5. In cells C9:C12, enter the bidding company name, address, phone number, and contact name for the second bid.
6. In cells D9:D12, enter the bidding company name, address, phone number, and contact name for the third bid being evaluated.
7. In cells A16:A17, briefly describe the manner in which labor will be used to accomplish the project under bid.
8. In cells B16:B17, enter the hours associated with the labor activity described in column A for the first bidder.
9. In cells C16:C17, enter the hours associated with labor for the second bidder.
10. In cells D16:D17, enter the same information for the third bidder.
11. Cells B18:D18 reflect the total labor hours for each bidder.
12. Cells E16:E17 reflect the minimum labor hours bid by the three bidders.
13. Cell E18 reflects the total of all minimum labor hours bid.

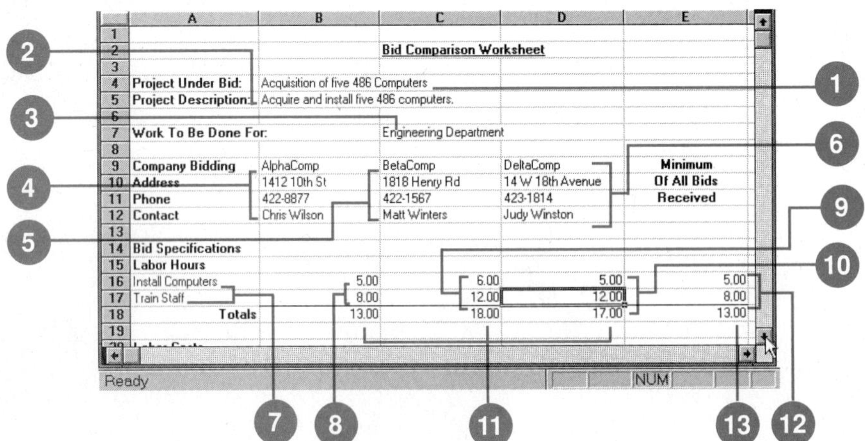

Bid Comparison Worksheet
Project Under Bid:
Acquisition of five 486 Computers
Project Description:
Acquire and install five 486 computers.
Work To Be Done For:
Engineering Department
Company Bidding
Address
Phone
Contact
AlphaComp
1412 10th St
422-8877
Chris Wilson
BetaComp
1818 Henry Rd
422-1567
Matt Winters
DeltaComp
14 W 18th Avenue
423-1814
Judy Winston
Minimum
Of All Bids
Received
Bid Specifications
Labor Hours
Install Computers
Train Staff
Totals
5.00
8.00
13.00
6.00
12.00
18.00
5.00
12.00
17.00
5.00
8.00
13.00
Ready
NUM

Splitting the Worksheet into Panes

When you are working at the extremities of a worksheet, and it is too high or too wide to allow you to see important labels, you need a tool to let you view these labels. Splitting the worksheet into *panes*—and freezing the panes—is Excel's solution to this problem.

1. Scroll down the worksheet until row 9 is at the top.
2. Point to the split bar in the upper right corner of the worksheet window and press the left mouse button.
3. Drag the split bar to a point just below row 12. Release the mouse button.

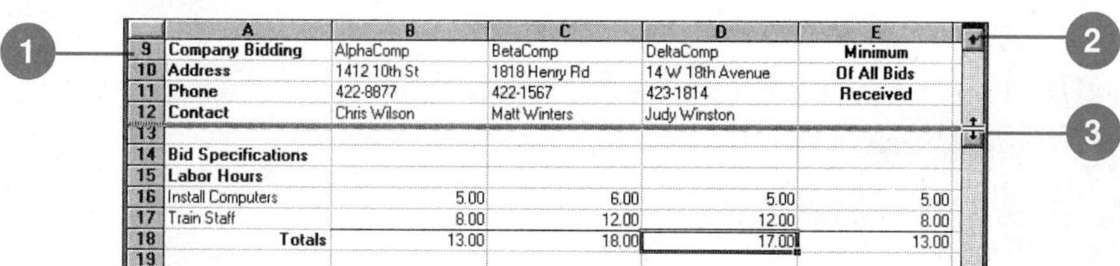

	A	B	C	D	E
9	Company Bidding	AlphaComp	BetaComp	DeltaComp	Minimum
10	Address	1412 10th St	1818 Henry Rd	14 W 18th Avenue	Of All Bids
11	Phone	422-8877	422-1567	423-1814	Received
12	Contact	Chris Wilson	Matt Winters	Judy Winston	
13					
14	Bid Specifications				
15	Labor Hours				
16	Install Computers	5.00	6.00	5.00	5.00
17	Train Staff	8.00	12.00	12.00	8.00
18	Totals	13.00	18.00	17.00	13.00
19					

Using the Window Freeze Panes Command

1. Ensure that the pane is positioned properly.
2. Choose Window Freeze Panes.

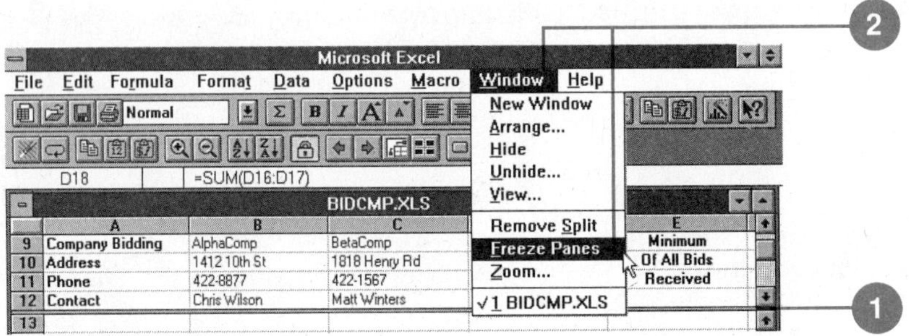

Completing the Data Entry for Labor Costs

If the bids you receive involve labor costs, the worksheet section described here lets you describe and enter these costs for each bidder.

1. In cells A21:A22, enter a description of the labor costs.
2. In cells B21:B22, enter the labor costs from the first bidder.
3. In cells C21:C22, enter the labor costs from the second bidder.
4. In cells D21:D22, enter the labor costs from the third bidder.
5. Cells B23:D23 show the total labor costs for each bidder.
6. Cells E21:E22 show the minimum bid made by the three bidders for each item of labor cost.
7. Cell E23 reflects the total of all the minimum amounts bid.
8. Scroll down the worksheet until row 24 is at the top.
9. In cells A26:A34, enter descriptions of the materials.

10. In cells B26:B34, enter the cost of each material for the first bidder.

11. In cells C26:C34, enter the cost of each material for the second bidder.

12. In cells D26:D34, enter the cost of each material for the third bidder.

13. Cells B35:D35 reflect the total cost of materials for each bidder.

14. Cells E26:E34 reflect the minimum cost of materials bid by the three bidders.

15. Cell E35 reflects the total of all the minimum amounts for materials contained in the three bids.

16. Cells B37:D37 reflect the total cost of labor and materials submitted by each bidder.

17. Cell E37 reflects the total of all the minimum amounts bid for labor and materials in the three bids.

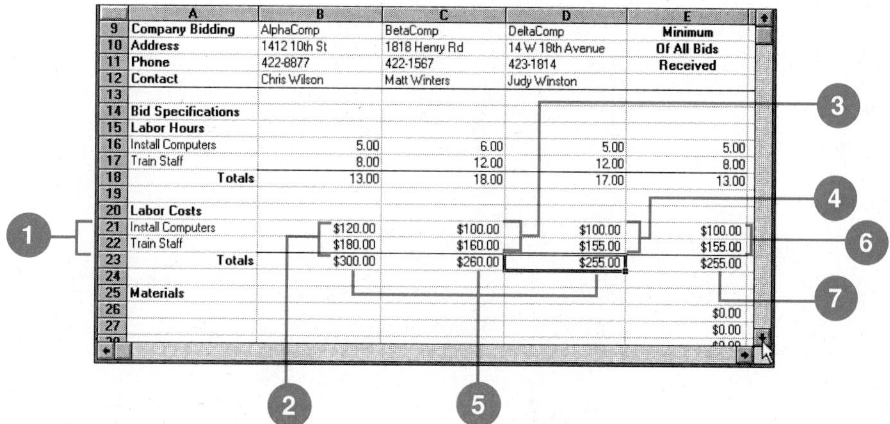

	A	B	C	D	E
9	Company Bidding	AlphaComp	BetaComp	DeltaComp	Minimum
10	Address	1412 10th St	1818 Henry Rd	14 W 18th Avenue	Of All Bids
11	Phone	422-8877	422-1567	423-1814	Received
12	Contact	Chris Wilson	Matt Winters	Judy Winston	
13					
14	Bid Specifications				
15	Labor Hours				
16	Install Computers	5.00	6.00	5.00	5.00
17	Train Staff	8.00	12.00	12.00	8.00
18	Totals	13.00	18.00	17.00	13.00
19					
20	Labor Costs				
21	Install Computers	$120.00	$100.00	$100.00	$100.00
22	Train Staff	$180.00	$160.00	$155.00	$155.00
23	Totals	$300.00	$260.00	$255.00	$255.00
24					
25	Materials				
26					$0.00
27					$0.00

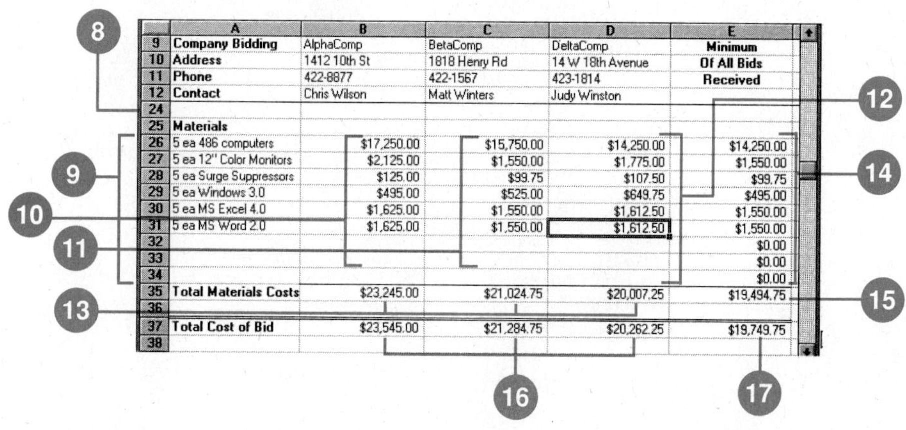

	A	B	C	D	E
9	Company Bidding	AlphaComp	BetaComp	DeltaComp	Minimum
10	Address	1412 10th St	1818 Henry Rd	14 W 18th Avenue	Of All Bids
11	Phone	422-8877	422-1567	423-1814	Received
12	Contact	Chris Wilson	Matt Winters	Judy Winston	
24					
25	Materials				
26	5 ea 486 computers	$17,250.00	$15,750.00	$14,250.00	$14,250.00
27	5 ea 12" Color Monitors	$2,125.00	$1,550.00	$1,775.00	$1,550.00
28	5 ea Surge Suppressors	$125.00	$99.75	$107.50	$99.75
29	5 ea Windows 3.0	$495.00	$525.00	$649.75	$495.00
30	5 ea MS Excel 4.0	$1,625.00	$1,550.00	$1,612.50	$1,550.00
31	5 ea MS Word 2.0	$1,625.00	$1,550.00	$1,612.50	$1,550.00
32					$0.00
33					$0.00
34					$0.00
35	Total Materials Costs	$23,245.00	$21,024.75	$20,007.25	$19,494.75
36					
37	Total Cost of Bid	$23,545.00	$21,284.75	$20,262.25	$19,749.75
38					

In the example, note that there is a difference of about $500 between the combined minimums and the lowest bid. The third bidder is higher than the lowest bidder in the price of surge suppressors, color monitors, Windows software, Excel software, and Word software. You may be able to negotiate this bidder down to the lowest bid level. You could also purchase these items from the lowest bidder.

Using the Window Remove Split Command

When you have completed your data entry, you may want to remove the pane that is splitting your worksheet window.

1. Choose Window Remove Split.
2. Examine rows 12 and 13. The solid line that represents the pane is gone.
3. Check to see that the split bar is back in its corner of the worksheet window.

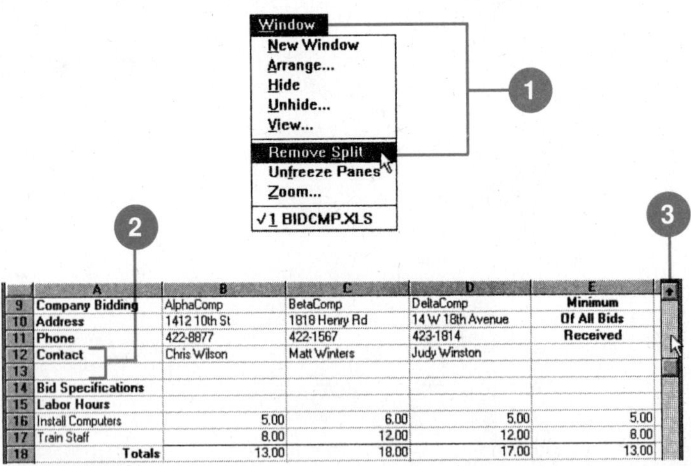

	A	B	C	D	E
9	Company Bidding	AlphaComp	BetaComp	DeltaComp	Minimum
10	Address	1412 10th St	1818 Henry Rd	14 W 18th Avenue	Of All Bids
11	Phone	422-8877	422-1567	423-1814	Received
12	Contact	Chris Wilson	Matt Winters	Judy Winston	
13					
14	Bid Specifications				
15	Labor Hours				
16	Install Computers	5.00	6.00	5.00	5.00
17	Train Staff	8.00	12.00	12.00	8.00
18	Totals	13.00	18.00	17.00	13.00

Now is a good time to save your copy of the bid comparison worksheet under a new name. The next section of this project deals with customizing BIDCMP.XLS.

Customizing BIDCMP.XLS

Customizing the bid comparison worksheet can be a simple matter of inserting new rows to allow for more labor hours, labor costs, or materials costs, or to include city, state, and ZIP Code if your bidders are not in your local area. It can also entail adding another column to accommodate another bidder. This type of customization is described later. There is really no reason to overcomplicate the worksheet with lookup tables because they cannot be used when comparing bids. If your bidders submit their bids on Excel worksheets or worksheets files that may be converted to Excel files, you may want to link this worksheet to the worksheets containing the bids. This procedure was described earlier in the Projects Workshop (Projects 1, 3, and 4). As you work through the customization examples, you should start with a blank copy of BIDCMP.XLS.

Inserting a New Row for Additional Labor Hours

The bids you receive may contain additional items associated with labor use. If these items exceed the items provided, you will need to add new worksheet rows for each such item.

1. Select one of the rows used to capture labor hours (row 17).
2. Choose Edit Insert.
3. Repeat the insertion at row 23 because you will have a labor cost associated with the labor hours captured in the new labor hours row.

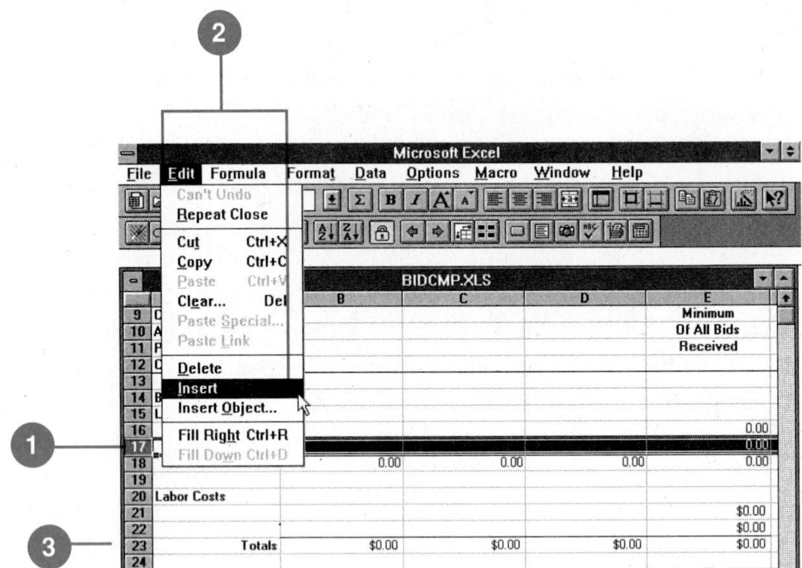

Copying a Formula into a New Row

When you add new rows to a worksheet, you will need to ensure that any cells in the new rows that should contain a formula do contain one. The steps that follow describe how to copy formulas into appropriate cells in inserted rows.

1. Select a cell in the row (E16).
2. Point to the AutoFill handle. Drag it down until cell E17 is highlighted. Release the mouse button.
3. If you have inserted a new row for labor costs, select cell E22.
4. Drag the AutoFill handle down until cell E23 is highlighted. Release the mouse button. This copies the formula from cell E22 into the blank cell E23.

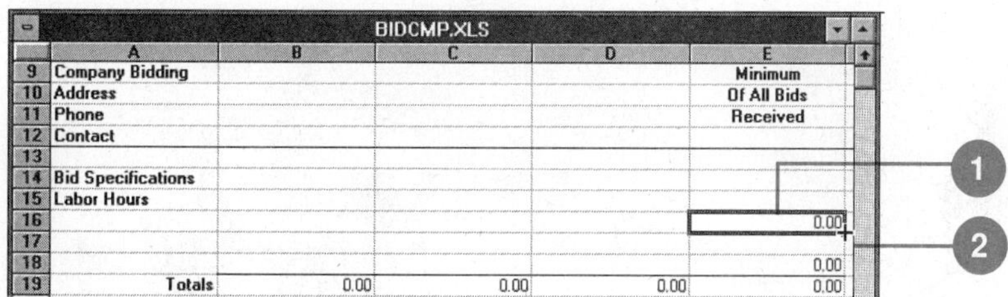
BIDCMP.XLS

	A	B	C	D	E
9	Company Bidding				Minimum
10	Address				Of All Bids
11	Phone				Received
12	Contact				
13					
14	Bid Specifications				
15	Labor Hours				
16					0.00
17					
18					0.00
19	Totals	0.00	0.00	0.00	0.00

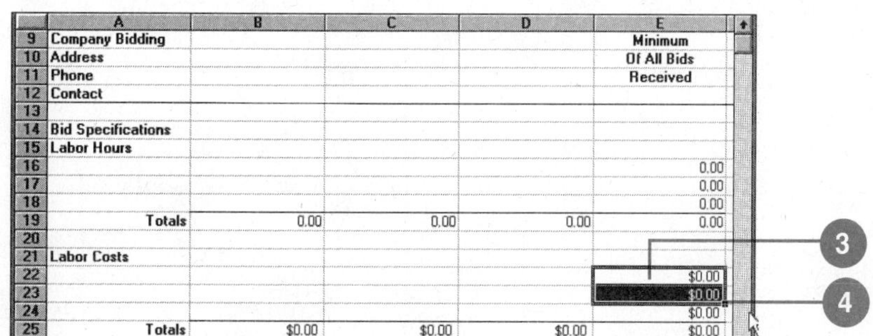

	A	B	C	D	E
9	Company Bidding				Minimum
10	Address				Of All Bids
11	Phone				Received
12	Contact				
13					
14	Bid Specifications				
15	Labor Hours				
16					0.00
17					0.00
18					0.00
19	Totals	0.00	0.00	0.00	0.00
20					
21	Labor Costs				
22					$0.00
23					$0.00
24					$0.00
25	Totals	$0.00	$0.00	$0.00	$0.00

Inserting a New Column for an Additional Bidder

If you collect more than three bids for a project, you will need to insert a new column for each additional bid.

1. Select the original column D.
2. Choose Edit Insert. A new column is inserted to the left of column D.

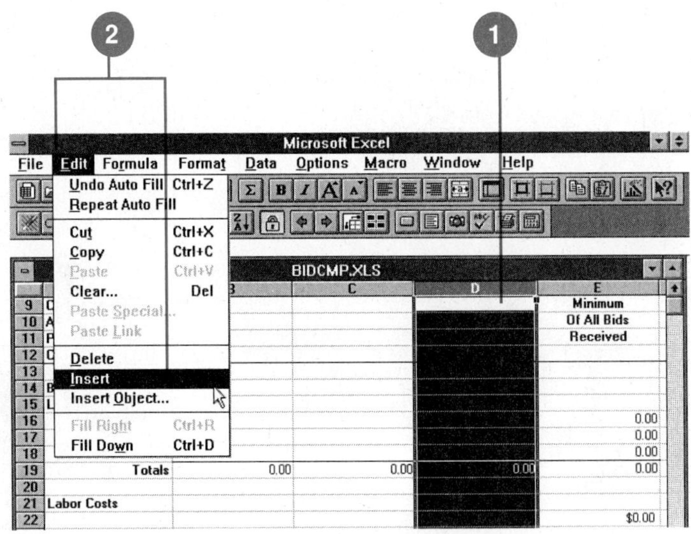

Using the Format Column Width Command

When you add new columns to a worksheet, you may need to adjust the width of a new column to conform to that of the other columns adjacent to the inserted column.

1. Examine the new column D. It's much narrower than the other bidder data columns.
2. Choose Format Column Width.
3. Change the value in the Column Width text box to 17.43 or whatever column width you're using on your copy of the worksheet.
4. Click OK or press Enter.

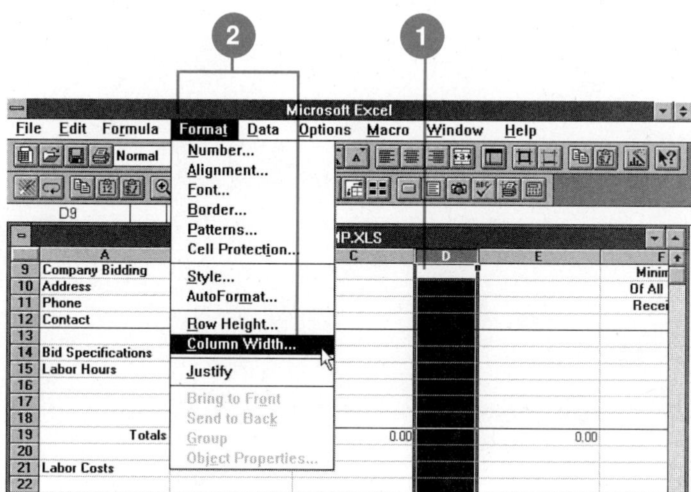

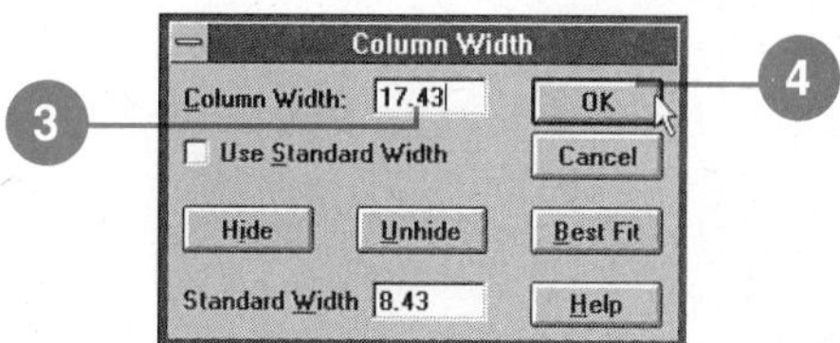

Filling Nonadjacent Cells

To copy formulas across a worksheet, it is much faster to use the method described in the steps that follow than to copy formulas row by row.

1. Press and hold the Ctrl key; select cells C19:D19.
2. Select cells C25:D25. Release the Ctrl key.
3. Scroll the worksheet down until row 25 is visible near the top.
4. Press and hold Ctrl; select cells C37:D37.
5. While holding down Ctrl, select cells C39:D39. Release the Ctrl key.
6. Choose Edit Fill Right or press Ctrl+R.

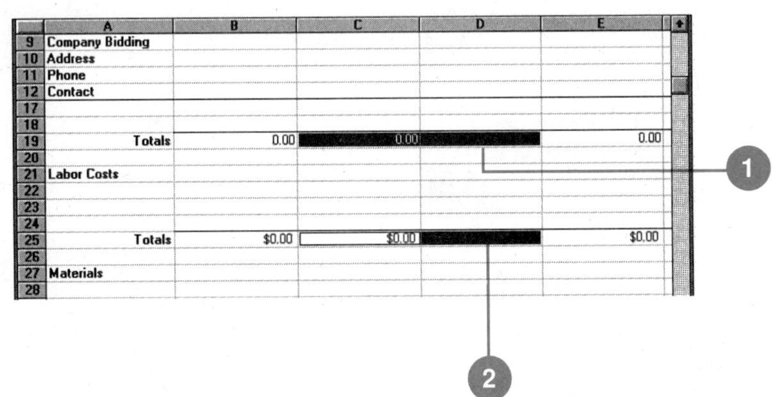

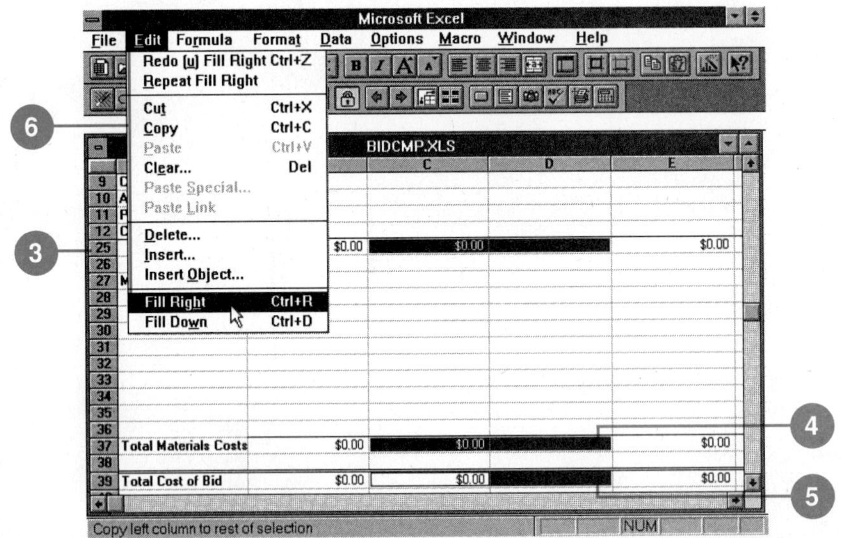

Summary

The worksheet BIDCMP.XLS allows you to compare three bids. The formal comparison of bids is a powerful tool for anyone in any business involved in buying goods or services. By comparing bids, you can place yourself in a stronger negotiating situation with the bidders. You can also justify the selection of one bidder over another based on a clearly presented set of facts. If the bid comparison analysis includes a recognition of the minimum amounts bid for each item contained in the bid, you may use this information to negotiate with the lowest bidder to bring this bidder to the lowest level for all items. You may also choose to split the purchase of goods and services to the lowest bidder for each item if this isn't too hard or too expensive to coordinate.

In addition to allowing you to compare three bids, this worksheet calculates the minimum amount bid for each item listed on the bid and also totals the bid amounts for each bidder. You can easily customize this worksheet to add items to the list by inserting rows or to accommodate additional bidders by inserting new columns.

	A	B	C	D	E	F	G	H	I
1									
2	Business Name	Pop's Pizza Parlor							
3	Bank Account Number	01023-14435							
4	Bank Name	Bank of the North							
5	Date	3/19/92							
6									
7	Section 1 Coins and Currency								
8		Coins &		Count	Value	Count	Value		
9		Currency		For Cash	For Cash	For	For		
10		Value	Count	Drawer	Drawer	Deposit	Deposit		
11	Pennies	$0.01	520	220	$2.20	300	$3.00		
12	Nickels	$0.05	50	50	$2.50	0	$0.00		
13	Dimes	$0.10	120	70	$7.00	50	$5.00		
14	Quarters	$0.25	135	35	$8.75	100	$25.00		
15	Half Dollars	$0.50	30	20	$10.00	10	$5.00		
16	One Dollar	$1.00	93	43	$43.00	50	$50.00		
17	Two Dollars	$2.00	1	0	$0.00	1	$2.00		
18	Five Dollars	$5.00	15	5	$25.00	10	$50.00		
19	Ten Dollars	$10.00	20	5	$50.00	15	$150.00		
20	Twenty Dollars	$20.00	15	5	$100.00	10	$200.00		
21	Fifty Dollars	$50.00	3	0	$0.00	3	$150.00		
22	One Hundred Dollars	$100.00	6	0	$0.00	6	$600.00		
23	Five Hundred Dollars	$500.00	2	0	$0.00	2	$1,000.00		
24	One Thousand Dollars	$1,000.00	1	0	$0.00	1	$1,000.00		
25					$248.45		$3,240.00		
26									
27	Section II - Checks	Check	Check						
28	Bank Identification Number	Number	Amount						
29	64-31/1221		$127.29						
30	64-31/1221		$119.65						
31	72-33/1033		$109.66						
32	72-33/1033		$17.67						
33	72-33/1033		$27.29						
49									
50			$401.56						
51									
52	Section III - Credit Card Slips	Card	Card						
53	Credit Card Number	Name	Amount						
54	1022-3794-2237	Diner's	$119.65						
55	67-4545-6789	Visa	$167.88						
56	88-8989-9065	AMEX	$110.44						
74									
75			$397.97						
76									

	J	K	L	M	N	O	P
1							
2				Bank Deposit Slip			
3							
4			Date of Deposit:	3/19/92			
5			Firm Making Deposit:	Pop's Pizza Parlor			
6			Bank Name:	Bank of the North			
7			Bank Account Number:	01023-14435			
8							
9			Cash Deposited				
10			Units	Count	Amount		
11			$0.01	300	$3.00		
12			$0.05	0	$0.00		
13			$0.10	50	$5.00		
14			$0.25	100	$25.00		
15			$0.50	10	$5.00		
16			$1.00	50	$50.00		
17			$2.00	1	$2.00		
18			$5.00	10	$50.00		
19			$10.00	15	$150.00		
20			$20.00	10	$200.00		
21			$50.00	3	$150.00		
22			$100.00	6	$600.00		
23			$500.00	2	$1,000.00		
24			$1,000.00	1	$1,000.00		
25			Subtotal Cash		$3,240.00		
26			Checks Deposited (See Attached List)				
27			Total Checks		$401.56		
28			Credit Card Slips (See Attached List)				
29			Total Credit Card Slips		$397.97		
30			Total Deposit		$4,039.53		
31							
32							
33							

Project

8

Cash Drawer Record and Bank Deposit Slip

One important aspect of running a small retail or service business is the daily closing of the cash drawer and the preparation of a bank deposit slip. This task is usually done manually with the aid of a calculator. The worksheet included for this project, BKDEP.XLS, automates the process of recording daily receipts, allows an amount to be withheld for making change on the next business day, and prepares a bank deposit slip for the day's receipts. Although using the Excel worksheet takes about as long as the manual process, it eliminates many mathematical errors other than errors caused by transposed numbers. It also provides a day-to-day record of cash receipts that may be stored on disk and referred to as needed. Data from daily worksheets may be linked to a summary worksheet.

BKDEP.XLS is broken into five sections. The first section is in range A1:B5. This worksheet section is used to gather general information about the business making the deposit, the bank for which the deposit is being prepared, and the bank account to which the deposit is being made. It also captures the date of the deposit. The second section of the worksheet is in cells B7:G25. This section is used to gather information about the cash collected during the business day. It also allows you to set aside cash to start the next business day and computes the difference between cash collected and cash withheld to arrive at the cash deposit amount. Data from this section of the worksheet automatically feed the deposit slip portion of the worksheet. The third section of the worksheet is in cells A27:B50. This worksheet section is used to list checks to be deposited. This worksheet section is printed to support the deposit slip as an attachment. It also feeds the deposit slip section of the worksheet. The fourth section of the worksheet is in cells A52:C75. This worksheet section is used to list credit card transactions for each day. This section of the worksheet also feeds the deposit slip portion of the worksheet. The final section of the worksheet is a deposit slip. It derives all of its information from the other sections of the worksheet.

The suggestions for customizing this worksheet include adding a new column for more information about checks and adding new labels to the checks list section of the worksheet. The steps undertaken in this project include using named portions of the worksheet to define a print area and to expedite printing.

Open BKDEP.XLS when you are ready to start.

Entering Data in BKDEP.XLS

Begin entering data into the worksheet. Part of the worksheet requires that you count all of the cash from your cash drawer and from your reserves each business day.

1. Enter the name of the business making the deposit in cell B2.
2. Enter the account number of the bank account in which the deposit is being made in cell B3.
3. Enter the name of the bank in cell B4.
4. Enter the date of the deposit in cell B5.
5. In cells C11:C24, enter the count for each denomination of cash from your cash drawer. The cells represent each denomination of cash normally encountered in an American business today.
6. In cells D11:D24, enter the count for each denomination that you want to use as change for the next day.
7. Column E automatically computes the amount of cash that will be available the next day.
8. Column F computes the count for each denomination of cash deposited in your checking account.
9. Column G computes the amount of money to be deposited in your bank account.
10. Cell E25 contains the total amount of money to be held for the cash drawer for the next business day.
11. Check cell G25 to see the total amount of cash to be deposited. The values in column G are transferred automatically into the deposit slip portion of the worksheet.

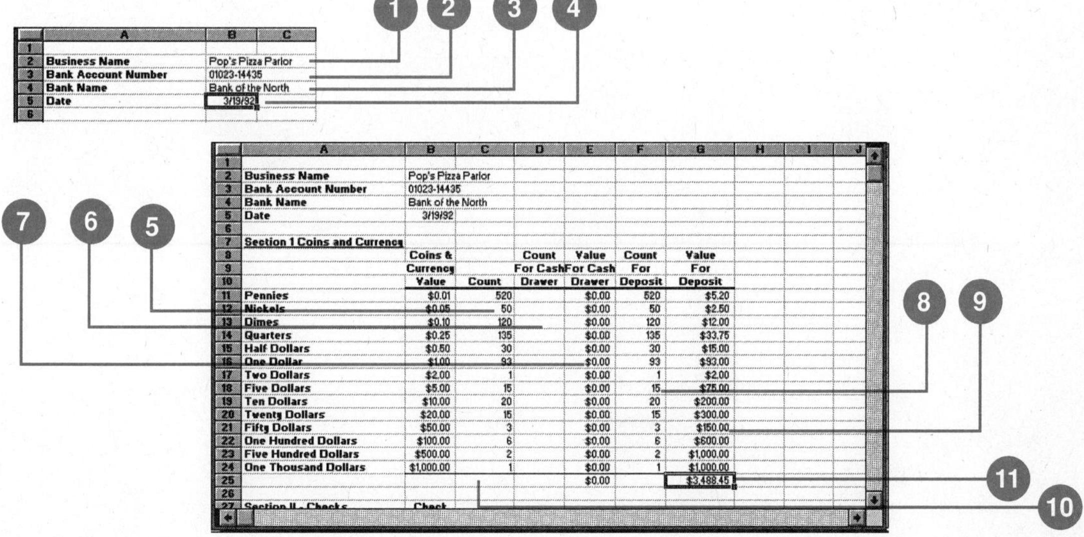

	A	B	C
1			
2	Business Name	Pop's Pizza Parlor	
3	Bank Account Number	01023-14435	
4	Bank Name	Bank of the North	
5	Date	3/19/92	
6			

	A	B	C	D	E	F	G	H	I	J
1										
2	Business Name	Pop's Pizza Parlor								
3	Bank Account Number	01023-14435								
4	Bank Name	Bank of the North								
5	Date	3/19/92								
6										
7	Section 1 Coins and Currency									
8		Coins &		Count	Value	Count	Value			
9		Currency		For Cash	For Cash	For	For			
10		Value	Count	Drawer	Drawer	Deposit	Deposit			
11	Pennies	$0.01	520		$0.00	520	$5.20			
12	Nickels	$0.05	50		$0.00	50	$2.50			
13	Dimes	$0.10	120		$0.00	120	$12.00			
14	Quarters	$0.25	135		$0.00	135	$33.75			
15	Half Dollars	$0.50	30		$0.00	30	$15.00			
16	One Dollar	$1.00	93		$0.00	93	$93.00			
17	Two Dollars	$2.00	1		$0.00	1	$2.00			
18	Five Dollars	$5.00	15		$0.00	15	$75.00			
19	Ten Dollars	$10.00	20		$0.00	20	$200.00			
20	Twenty Dollars	$20.00	15		$0.00	15	$300.00			
21	Fifty Dollars	$50.00	3		$0.00	3	$150.00			
22	One Hundred Dollars	$100.00	6		$0.00	6	$600.00			
23	Five Hundred Dollars	$500.00	2		$0.00	2	$1,000.00			
24	One Thousand Dollars	$1,000.00	1		$0.00	1	$1,000.00			
25					$0.00		$3,488.45			
26										
27	Section II - Checks	Check								

Entering Data about Checks to be Deposited

This section of the worksheet contains enough space for 20 checks. If your business receives more than 20 checks, add enough new rows to accommodate the number of checks you normally receive.

1. Scroll down the worksheet until row 26 is at the top.
2. In cells A29:A49, enter the Bank Identification Number for each check collected. This number generally appears in the upper right corner of every check. If your bank requires another number on a bank deposit slip, record that number instead.
3. List the amount of each check received in cells B29:B49.
4. Check cell B50 to see the total dollar amount of all checks listed.

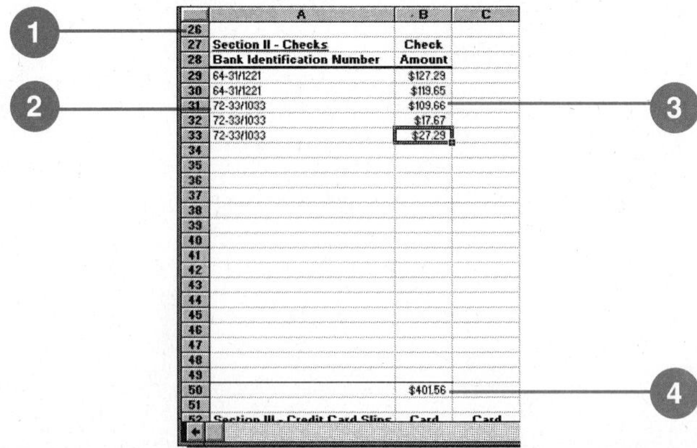

Entering Credit Card Slip Information

This worksheet allows for 21 credit card transactions to be recorded and assumes your bank treats these as normal deposits. If you have more than 21 of these transactions to record, add new rows by using the **E**dit **I**nsert command.

1. Scroll down the worksheet until row 51 is at the top.
2. List the credit card account numbers for all credit card transactions in cells A54:A74.
3. List the credit card name in cells B54:B74 for each credit card account number.
4. List the dollar amounts of each credit card transaction in cells C54:C74.
5. Check cell C75 to see the total dollar value for all credit card transactions.

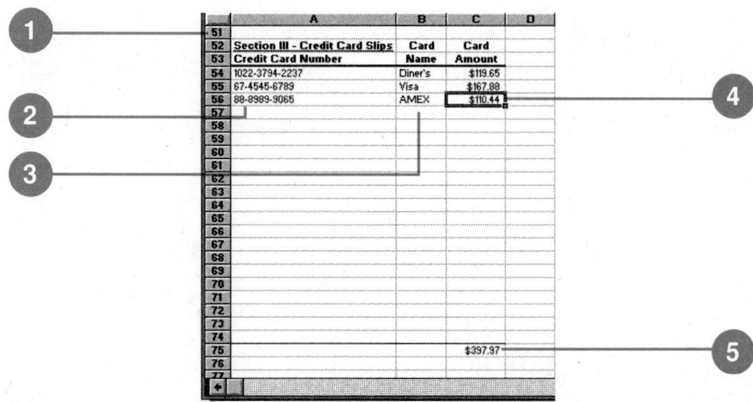

Understanding the Deposit Slip Section of BKDEP.XLS

The deposit slip portion of BKDEP.XLS extends from K1 to O31. It reflects data you entered in the left portion of the worksheet. Table P8.1 explains the entries in this section of the worksheet.

Table P8.1 The deposit slip portion of BKDEP.XLS

Cell	*Contents*
M4	The date of the deposit (the value you entered in cell B5).
M5	The value you entered in cell B2. It is the name of the firm making the deposit.
M6	The bank name you entered in cell B4.
M7	The bank account number you entered in cell B3.
M11:M24	The counts of coins and currency contained in cells F11:F24. This is the difference between the cash drawer count and the count of coins and currency to be retained for cash drawer change.
N11:N24	The dollar value for each denomination of coins and currency to be deposited. These values are calculated automatically for you.
N25	The total dollar amount of all coins and currency to be deposited.

Cell	*Contents*
N27	The total dollar value of all checks to be deposited. This is the total computed by the worksheet in cell B50.
N29	The total dollar value of all credit card transactions to be credited to your account. This value is equal to the value in cell C75.
N30	The total amount of the deposit. It's equal to the sum of the values in cells N25, N27, and N29.

Using the Formula Goto Command

You will use the Formula **G**oto command to move to the deposit slip portion of BKDEP.XLS.

1. Choose Formula Goto or press F5. The Formula Goto dialog box appears.
2. Choose Deposit Slip from the **G**oto list box.
3. Press Enter or click OK. The active cell in the worksheet moves to the upper left cell of the named cell range. The active cell is now cell K1 and the entire deposit slip portion of the worksheet is highlighted.

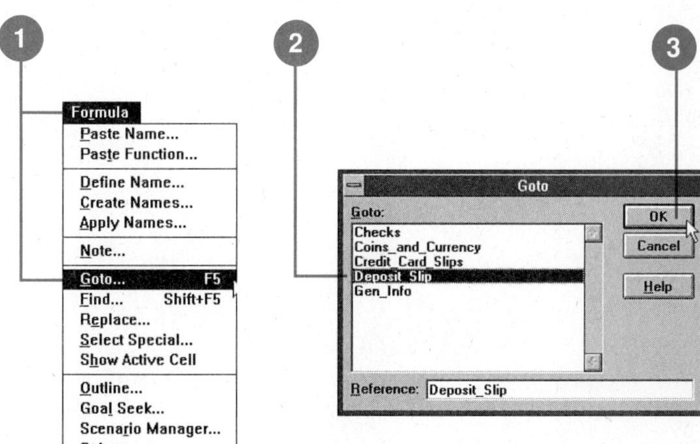

Selecting the Print Area

1. Make sure cells K1:O31 are selected.
2. Choose **O**ptions Set Print **A**rea, which instructs Excel to print only the selected section of the worksheet.

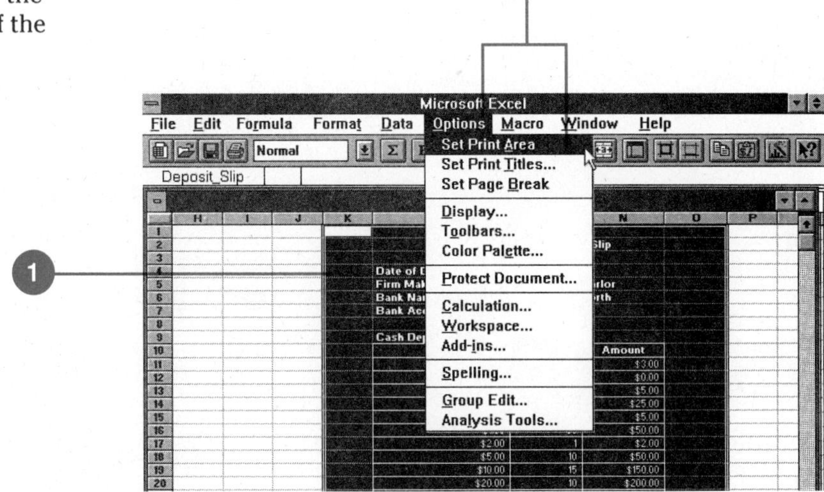

Setting Up the Printout

1. Choose File Page Setup. The Page Setup dialog box appears.
2. Select Center: Horizontally.
3. Make sure Cell **G**ridlines is not selected.
4. Choose the Header button. The Header dialog box appears.
5. Select the &F symbol in the **C**enter Section portion of the dialog box.

   Press to remove this symbol and prevent CKDEP.XLS from being printed at the top of each page.
6. Press Enter or click OK to return to the Page Setup dialog box.
7. Select the Footer button to display the Footer dialog box.

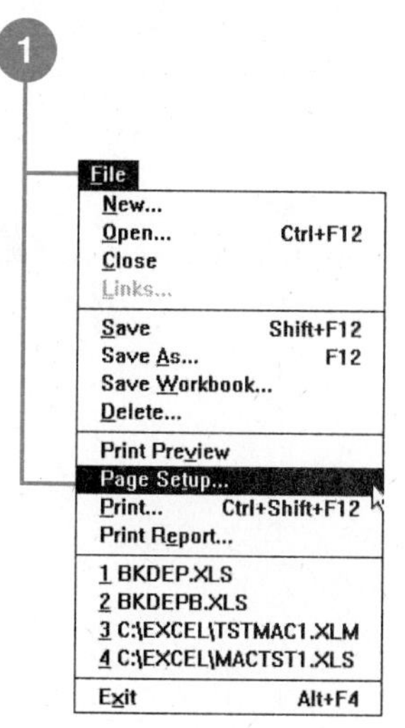

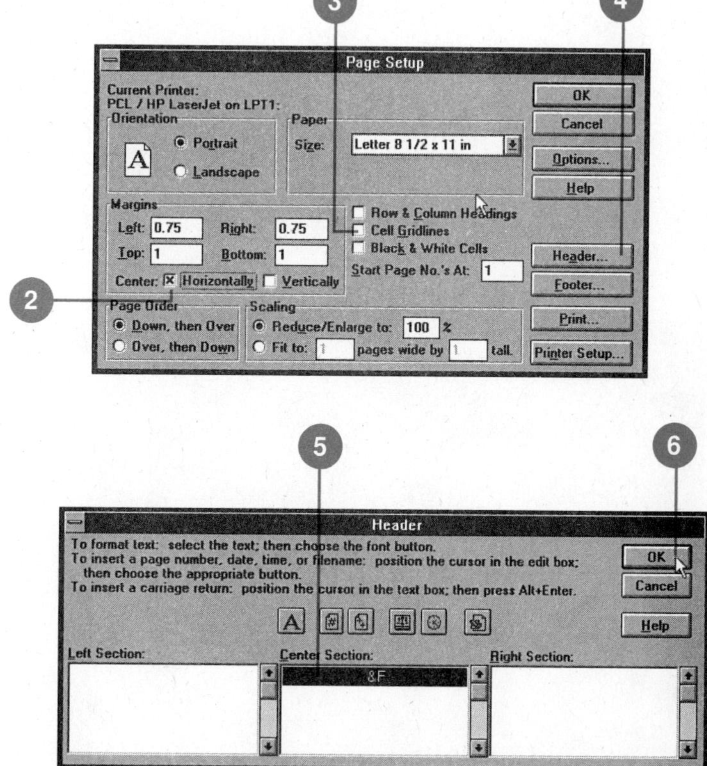

8. Select the Page & P value in the Center Section of the dialog box.
9. Press Backspace to remove the number. This prevents the page number from printing.
10. Press Enter or click OK to return to the Page Setup dialog box.
11. Select the **Print** button. The Print dialog box appears.
12. Press Enter or click OK. The deposit slip section of the worksheet is printed.

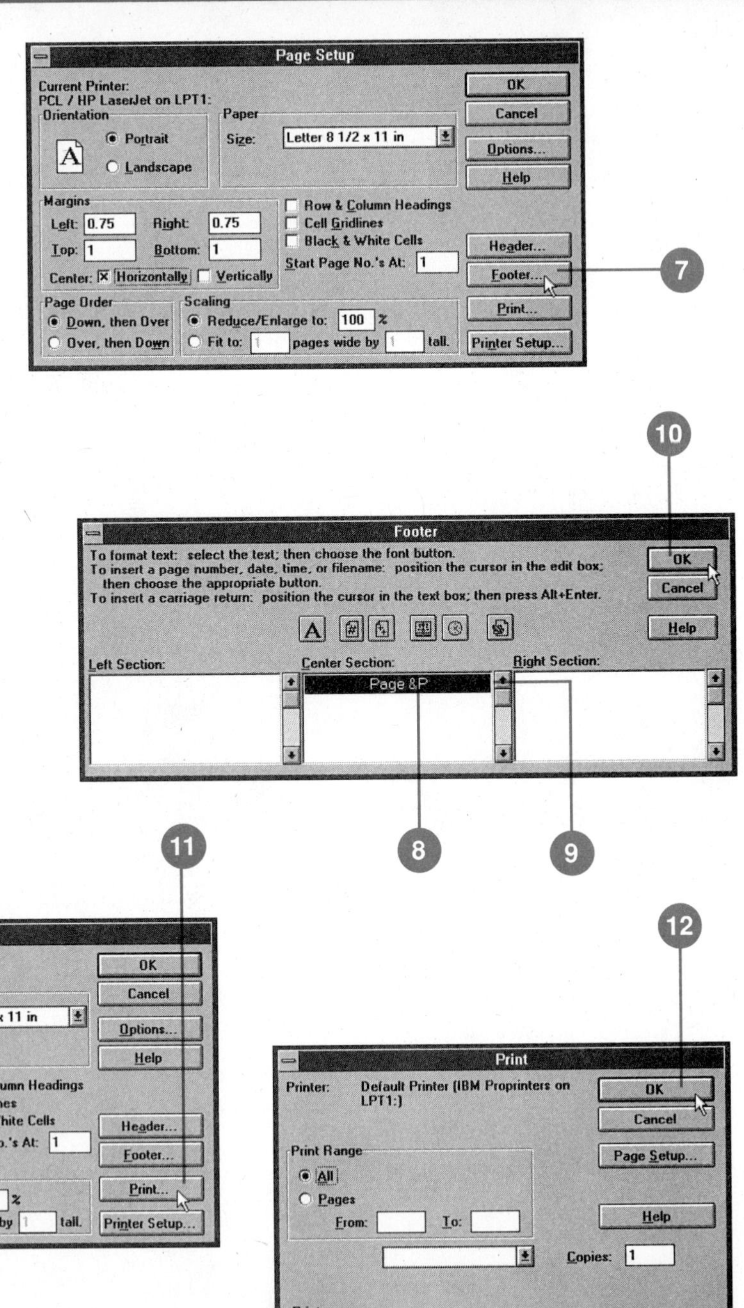

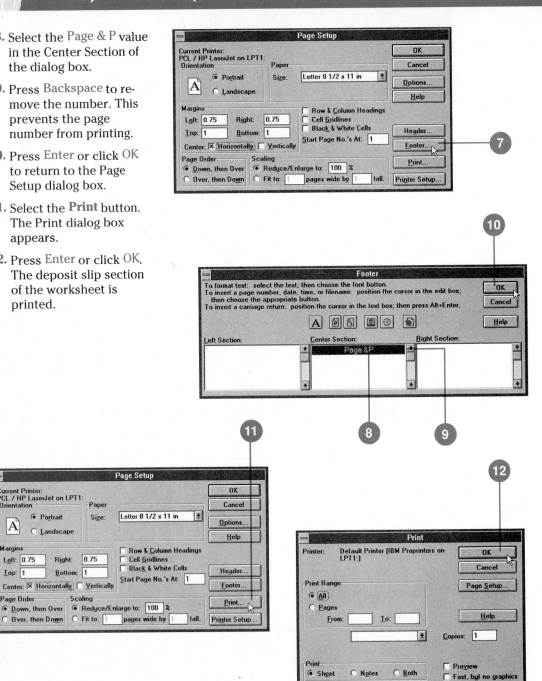

Printing the Checks Received

Now you should print the information that supports the deposit slip, starting with the checks you entered.

1. Choose Formula Goto or press F5. The formula Goto dialog box appears.
2. Select Checks from the list.
3. Press Enter or click OK.
4. Choose Options Set Print Area.
5. Select File Print or press Ctrl+Shift+F12. The Print dialog box appears.
6. Press Enter or click OK.

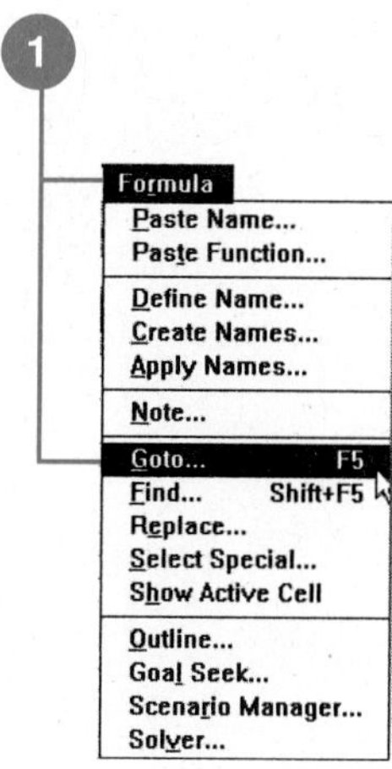

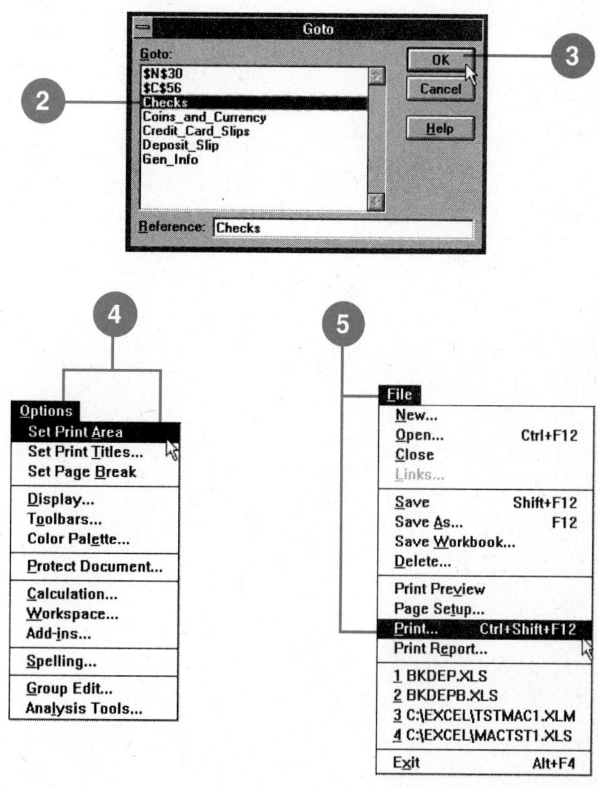

Printing the Credit Card Slip List

1. Choose Formula Goto or press F5. The formula, Goto dialog box appears.
2. Select Credit_Card_Slips from the dialog box.
3. Press Enter or click OK.
4. Choose Options Set Print Area.
5. Choose File Print or press Ctrl+Shift+F12. The Print dialog box appears.
6. Press Enter or click OK.

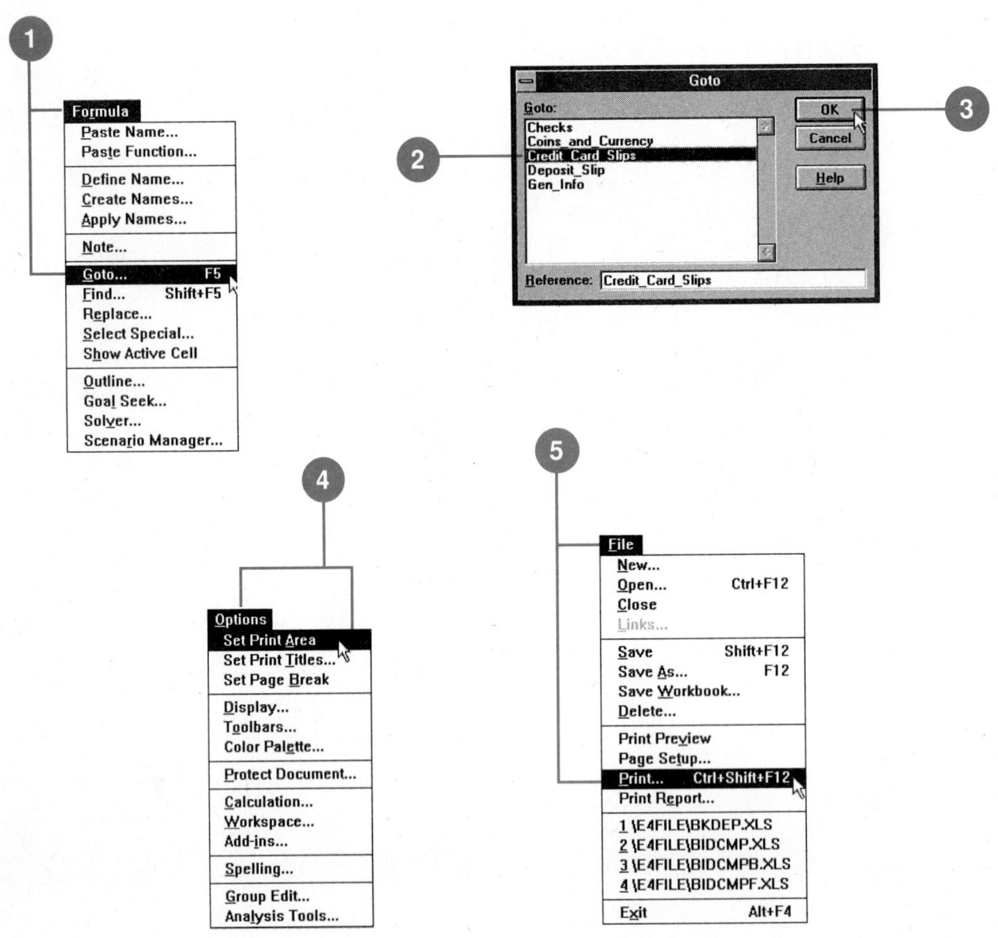

Clearing the Print Area on a Worksheet

Anytime you use the **O**ptions Set Print **A**rea command, this command names the selected range of cells "Print Area". To clear the current print area on any worksheet, you just need to delete the name from the formula Define Name dialog box.

1. Choose Formula **D**efine Name. The Formula Define Name dialog box is displayed.
2. Select Print Area from the Names in **S**heet list.
3. Select the Delete button.

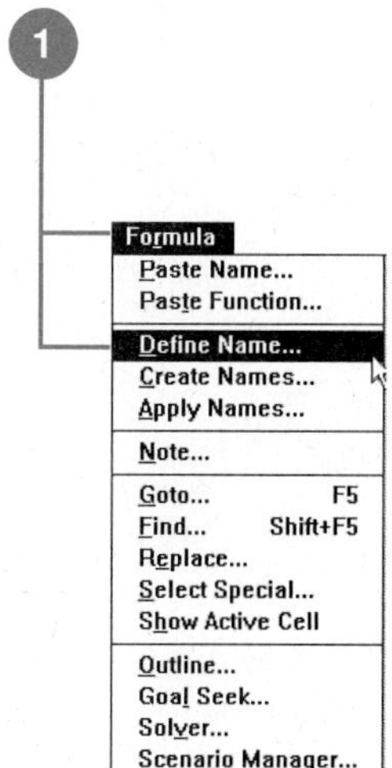

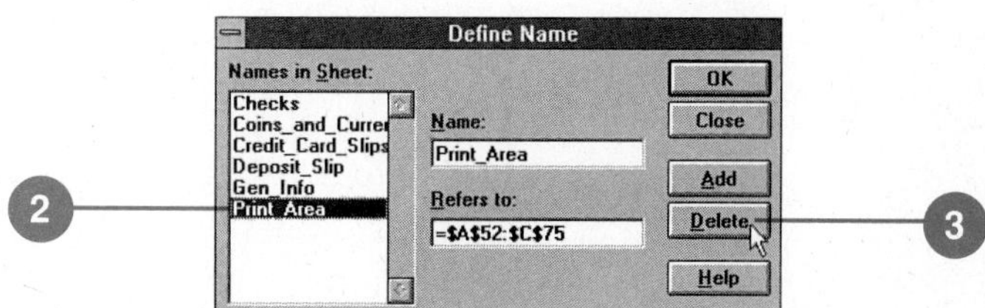

Customizing BKDEP.XLS

BKDEP.XLS is a rudimentary worksheet used to capture cash drawer data, plan for the next day's change for the cash drawer, and produce a deposit slip. Your bank dictates the nature of the information on the deposit slip. If the bank requires another format, you will need to negotiate the use of the format in this worksheet with the bank or change the worksheet to meet the needs of your bank. Obtain a copy of your bank's deposit slip and make any adjustments you need to make to the deposit slip section of the worksheet and to the sections of the worksheet that are sources of data for the deposit slip. Many banks accept deposit slips that use the format of the deposit slip included in this worksheet. Discuss this with your banker.

If your bank requires that you capture additional information not found on BKDEP.XLS, change the labels on the worksheet accordingly and capture this information instead of the information called for in this project. If you need more room for a longer list of checks or a longer list of credit card transactions, add rows to the worksheet by using the **E**dit **I**nsert command. If you need to add a new column of information such as the check number for each check listed or the name of the person who wrote each check, follow the steps described next.

Adding a New Column to the Checks List

The following procedure is the equivalent of the **E**dit Cu**t** and **E**dit **P**aste commands.

1. Select the entire range of cells that you want to move to a new location (cells B27:B50).
2. Point to the border on the right side of the selected cell range. Press the left mouse button. A shaded outline is displayed around the selection.
3. Drag the selection to its new location (one column over to cells C27:C50). Release the mouse button.

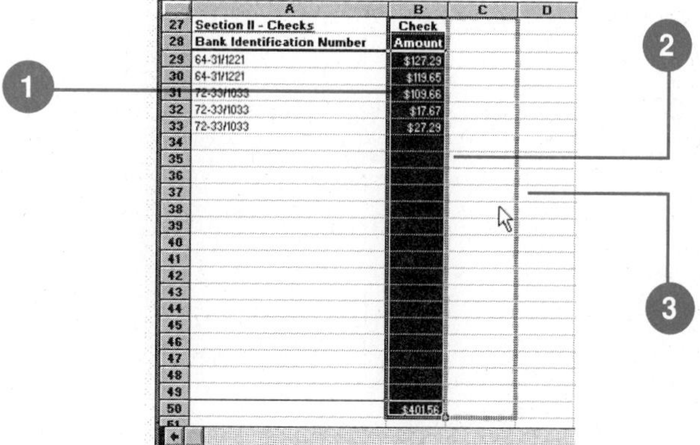

Adding a Label and Border to the New Column

1. Select cell B27 if you require a two part label. Enter the label for the column (`Check`). Press Enter.
2. Select cell B28 for the second part of a two part label or the only part of a single part label. Enter the label you require (`Number`). Press Enter.
3. Choose Format Border. The Border dialog box appears.
4. Choose the third line style from the left.
5. Choose Bottom from the list of borders.
6. Click OK or press Enter to add the heavier border to the bottom of the selected cell.

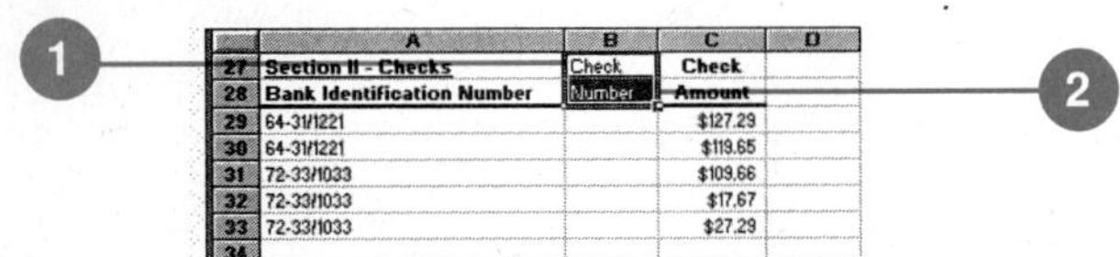

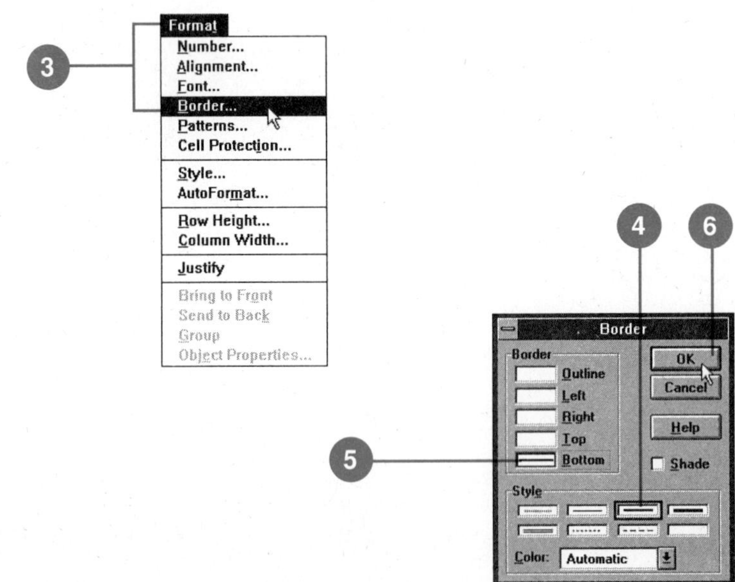

Using the Bottom Border Tool on the Standard Toolbar

1. Select cell B49, the bottom cell of the cell range in the new column.
2. Click the Bottom Border tool on the Standard toolbar.

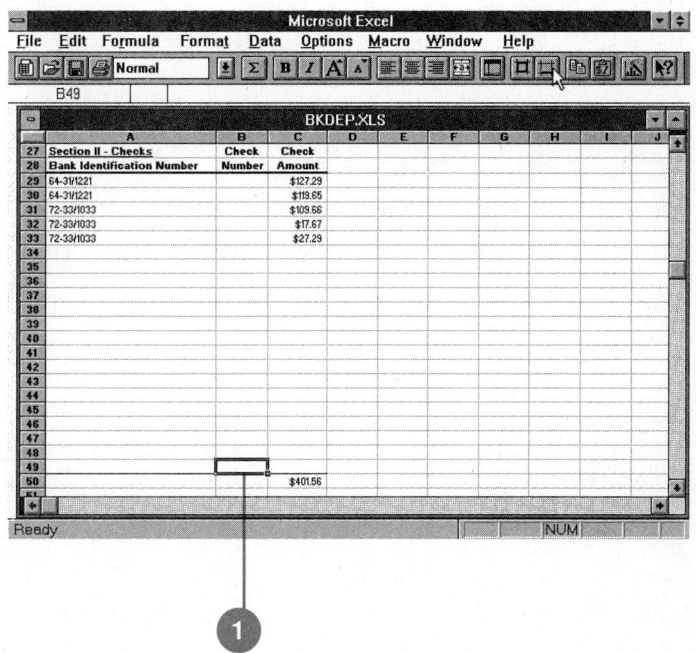

Summary

BKDEP.XLS is a worksheet that enables you to record your cash at the end of a business day. It also allows you to set aside cash to start the next business day. The worksheet automatically computes the amount and nature of your bank deposit by subtracting the dollar value of the cash retained for change from the total dollar values you enter in the worksheet. It also allows you to list checks and credit card transactions. After you enter this data, the worksheet automatically enters the totals from these lists into the deposit slip section of the worksheet and calculates a total deposit amount.

Recording your daily receipts and preparing a deposit slip is normally done manually unless your business has been automated and you capture such data with your automated tools. BKDEP.XLS allows you to use Excel to automate this process to a small degree.

Minor customization is described in this project. It involves adding a new column to the check list section of the worksheet. Although the addition of new rows to accommodate more checks and more credit card transactions is discussed at some length, this customization is not described in detail. Earlier projects describe this type of customization in greater detail.

	A	B	C	D	E	F	G
1			**Loan Qualification Worksheet**				
2	***Asking / Bid Price***	270,000					
3	***Down Payment***	54,000					
4	***Loan Amount***	**216,000**		**Loan Qualification Decision Ratios**			
5	***Loan Period in Years***	30		Loan to Value Ratio		80.00%	
6	Loan Period in Months	**360**	**Qualifying Ratio 1: If Loan to Value Ratio is 80% and Qualifying**				
7	***Annual Interest Rate***	10.25%	**Ratio ((Principal + Interest)/Gross Income) is less than 28% or if**				
8	Monthly Interest Rate	**0.8542%**	**Loan to Value Ratio is 90% and Qualifying Ratio is less than**				
9	***Period to Calculate***	360	**25%, you qualify.**			**@ 80%**	**@ 90%**
10	***Tax Rate to Apply***	1.0300%		Qualifying Ratio 1		25.81%	25.81%
11	***Insurance Rate to Apply***	0.5000%		Do you qualify ?		**YES**	**NO**
12	***Total Other Payments***	-235		Maximum Mortgage Paymen		2100	1875
13	***Gross Monthly Income***	7,500	**Qualifying Ratio 2: If Loan to Value Ratio is 80% and Qualifying**				
14	Payment Amounts For This Period		**Ratio ((Principal+Interest+Taxes+Insurance+Other Payments)/**				
15	Interest Payment	**-16.39**	**Gross Income is less than 36% or if Loan to Value Ratio is 90%**				
16	Principal Paid	**-1,919.19**	**and Qualifying Ratio is less than 33%, you qualify.**				
17	Average Monthly Tax	**-231.75**				**@ 80%**	**@ 90%**
18	Average Monthly Insurance	**-90.00**		Qualifying Ratio 2		33.23%	33.23%
19	Total Payment	**-2,257.33**		Do you qualify ?		**YES**	**NO**
20				Maximum Debt Payment		2700	2475

Project

9

Home Loan Qualification Worksheet

Purchasing a home or other real estate is the biggest single purchase most individuals or families make. In some cases, this purchase is a business or investment decision. Almost anyone who prepares loan application documents for this type of purchase wonders, "Will I qualify for this loan?" Sometimes a realtor or a representative of a lending institution can answer this question.

Most lenders use some pretty basic rules of thumb in determining whether you are qualified. These rules of thumb are only one of the tools they use to make their decision. They also examine your loan application sheet, your credit history, your work history, and your overall financial situation. They use the rules of thumb and other criteria in an attempt to minimize the risk of lending money. Although your home or property is collateral for a loan, the lending institutions really want to see you retain ownership.

The worksheet that is part of Project 9 is called LOANQ.XLS. It gives you an idea of how much you can afford to borrow to purchase a home or other real estate. It also estimates your monthly payments and generates an amortization schedule. A macro sheet called LOANERQ.XLM supports LOANSQ.XLS. This macro sheet contains macros to create an amortization schedule, print the table, and clear the table from the worksheet. You can execute these macros by using buttons on LOANSQ.XLS, by pressing a Ctrl key sequence, or by using the **M**acro **R**un command from the macro bar.

The customization example for this project involves building a reference table on LOANSQ.XLS to feed one of the cells that is important to the loan qualification. You may want to use similar tables to feed other cells in the loan qualification area of the worksheet. You can use the same approach as that used in the example for the cell containing the gross monthly income, the tax rate, and the insurance rate.

Using LOANSQ.XLS

Although LOANSQ.XLS appears busy, it is divided into logical sections. The worksheet section in cells A2:B13 is used to gather information about the loan. Enter data in cells B2 (Asking/Bid Price), B3 (Down Payment), B5 (Loan Period in Years), B7 (Annual Interest Rate), B9 (Period to Calculate), B10 (Tax Rate to Apply), B11 (Insurance Rate to Apply), B12 (Total Other Payments), and B13 (Gross Monthly Income). The remaining cells in this cell range contain calculations. Do not enter data in these cells. They are B4 (Loan Amount), B6 (Loan Period in Months), and B8 (Monthly Interest Rate). These cells contain calculations.

Cells A15:B19 contain calculations dealing with monthly payments for interest, principal, taxes, and insurance. The section on the right side of the worksheet contains three buttons that are assigned to macros, a cell containing the Loan to Value Ratio, two qualifying ratios used by lenders, and estimates of maximum mortgage payments for each qualifying ratio. The Loan-to-Value Ratio is a fundamental ratio that lenders use to measure the size of the loan compared to the value of the property being purchased. The more you pay as a down payment on the property, the easier it is to qualify for the loan. You may want to experiment with the size of the down payment if you don't qualify for a loan.

Qualifying Ratio 1 is the Mortgage Payment to Income Ratio. This ratio compares your gross income to the mortgage payment. The lender usually defines the mortgage payment as being the principal plus the interest for this ratio. The conservative lender requires that your Mortgage Payment to Income Ratio must be no greater than 25% for loans with a Loan-to-Value Ratio of 90% or more. This ratio is computed in cell G10. Such lenders require that your Mortgage Payment to Income Ratio must be no greater than 28% for loans with a Loan to Value Ratio of less than 90%. This ratio is computed in cell F10. Remember, this is a rule of thumb. Talk it over with your lender if you are reasonably close to these percentages.

Qualifying Ratio 2 is the Long-Term Debt Ratio. This ratio compares your gross income with the mortgage payment plus an amount for insurance and tax payments for the property plus any amounts for regular payments you are making on long-term debts. This ratio, which must be less than 33% for a loan with a Loan-to-Value Ratio of 90% or more, is displayed in cell G18. It must be less than 38% for a Loan to Value Ratio less than 90% and is displayed in cell F18.

After the Long-Term Debt Ratio and the Mortgage Payment to Income Ratio are known, you may also calculate the maximum mortgage payment you can afford. To do this, apply the ratio used by the lender to your gross income. The maximum mortgage payment for both qualifying ratios is calculated in cells F12:G12 for the Mortgage Payment to Income Ratio and in cells F20:G20 for the Long-Term Debt Ratio.

When you open the blank version of LOANSQ.XLS, you will see two types of error messages displayed. These error messages recognize that dependent cells for making calculations are blank. All the error messages disappear when you begin to enter numbers. The customization section discusses the use of IF() statements to prevent these error messages from being displayed. The first error message appears in cells B15, B16, and B19. It is `#NUM!`. Cell B15 calculates the interest payment for the loan. It contains the formula

> `=IPMT(`*rate*(B8)`,`*per*(B9)`,`*nper*(B5)`,`*pv*(B4)`,`*fv*(optional)`,`*type* (optional—if used, enter 0 for interest payments due at end of period and 1 if due at beginning of period)`)`

The error value is returned because cells B4, B5, B8, and B9 contain zeros. It appears in the other cells mentioned for the same reason.

Cells F5, F10:G10, F11:G11, F18:G18, and F19:G19 contain the error message `#DIV/0!`. This error message means that one of the cells that the formula in the cell displaying the message depends upon contains a value of zero. In this case, it is the dependent cell B13. As soon as you enter a value for your gross monthly income, this error message disappears.

Let's start using LOANSQ.XLS. Open LOANERQ.XLS and LOANSQ.XLS and follow the examples described next.

Entering Basic Home Purchase Information

The steps described in this section are used to enter basic information about the loan you are contemplating. When you enter the values in cells B3 and B13, it is unnecessary to enter commands.

1. Enter the Asking/Bid Price for the home you want to purchase in cell B2 (or enter the maximum price you think you can afford). (The cells are pre-formatted for the proper number format.)
2. Enter the down payment you intend to make in cell B3. (Start with 10% of the loan amount.)
3. Enter the loan period in years in cell B5.
4. Enter the annual interest rate you expect to pay in cell B7.
5. Enter the period to calculate in cell B9. The total payment is the same throughout the loan unless there is a "balloon" payment at the end.
6. Do not enter any data in cells B10, B11, or B12.
7. Enter your gross monthly income (pre-tax) in cell B13. Most lenders allow you to apply only a percentage of income from rental property (about 75%).
8. Check the results in cells B15, B16, and B19. These results represent your mortgage payment (principal and interest only).
9. Check the results in cells F5, F10:G10, F11:G11, and F12:G12.

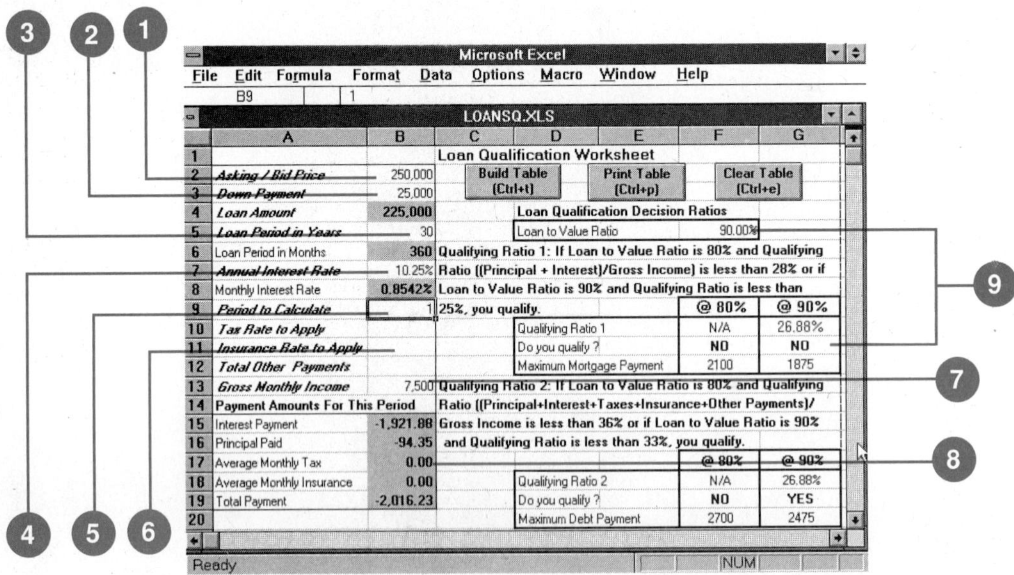

At this point, the results in F10:G12 represent the loan qualifications based on the mortgage payment, not on your long-term debt. Later, you'll enter long-term debt information to see how it affects your ability to qualify for a loan. This information will be entered in cells B10, B11, and B12.

Changing the Period to Calculate

To see the difference between the distribution of your interest payment to principal and interest at the beginning of the loan compared to the end of the loan, use the following steps. The results in cells B15 and B16 will be radically different!

1. Change the value in cell B9 to the value that's in cell B6.
2. Check the results in cells B15 and B16.

Microsoft Excel

File Edit Formula Format Data Options Macro Window Help

B9 360

LOANSQ.XLS

	A	B	C	D	E	F	G
1			Loan Qualification Worksheet				
2	*Asking / Bid Price*	250,000	Build Table (Ctrl+t)		Print Table (Ctrl+p)		Clear Table (Ctrl+e)
3	*Down Payment*	25,000					
4	*Loan Amount*	225,000		Loan Qualification Decision Ratios			
5	*Loan Period in Years*	30		Loan to Value Ratio		90.00%	
6	Loan Period in Months	360	Qualifying Ratio 1: If Loan to Value Ratio is 80% and Qualifying				
7	*Annual Interest Rate*	10.25%	Ratio ((Principal + Interest)/Gross Income) is less than 28% or if				
8	Monthly Interest Rate	0.8542%	Loan to Value Ratio is 90% and Qualifying Ratio is less than				
9	*Period to Calculate*	360	25%, you qualify.			@ 80%	@ 90%
10	*Tax Rate to Apply*			Qualifying Ratio 1		N/A	26.88%
11	*Insurance Rate to Apply*			Do you qualify ?		NO	NO
12	*Total Other Payments*			Maximum Mortgage Payment		2100	1875
13	*Gross Monthly Income*	7,500	Qualifying Ratio 2: If Loan to Value Ratio is 80% and Qualifying				
14	Payment Amounts For This Period		Ratio ((Principal+Interest+Taxes+Insurance+Other Payments)/				
15	Interest Payment	-17.08	Gross Income is less than 36% or if Loan to Value Ratio is 90%				
16	Principal Paid	-1,999.15	and Qualifying Ratio is less than 33%, you qualify.				
17	Average Monthly Tax	0.00				@ 80%	@ 90%
18	Average Monthly Insurance	0.00		Qualifying Ratio 2		N/A	26.88%
19	Total Payment	-2,016.23		Do you qualify ?		NO	YES
20				Maximum Debt Payment		2700	2475

Ready NUM

Entering Tax, Insurance, and Other Loan Information

To enter this information, you'll need to consult your realtor and insurance agent to find out the tax and insurance rates you can expect to pay. Long-term debt includes such payments as automobile loans, credit card payments, and payments for other loans. Your prospective lender can guide you by telling you what is expected.

Some lenders may be satisfied with using Mortgage Payment to Income Ratio by itself. Others use both ratios. When they do, if you fail to qualify on either of the two ratios, you would fail to qualify for the loan. If you are close to qualifying on any of these ratios, consult your lender. They might still allow the loan.

1. Enter the annual property tax rate in cell B10.
2. Enter the annual insurance rate in cell B11.
3. Enter the total monthly payment amount for any long-term debts you may have accrued in cell B12.
4. Check the results in cells B15:B19.
5. Check the results in cells F18:F20.
6. The results in cells F5 and F10:G12 are still valid. They represent another perspective of qualification.

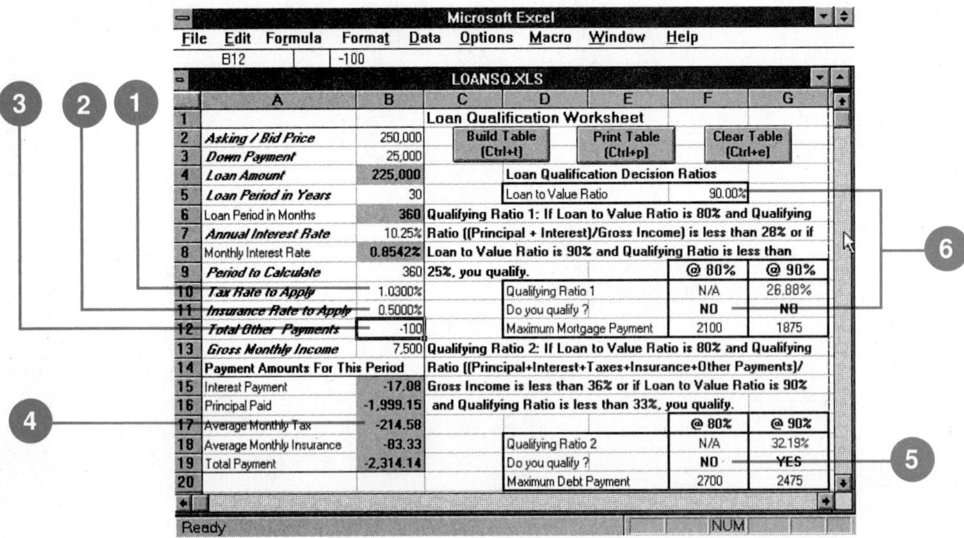

Changing the Loan Amount

If you fail to qualify for the first amount you try—or if you wish to see how much you can borrow—experiment with the values entered in cell B2. In the first case, reduce the amount until you qualify. In the second case, increase the amount until you no longer qualify.

1. Increase the loan amount in cell B2 (to **270,000** in the example).
2. Enter a 10% down payment (**27,000** in the example).
3. Check B15:B19 to see the new payment information.
4. Check the results in cells F10:G12.
5. Check the results in cells F18:G20.

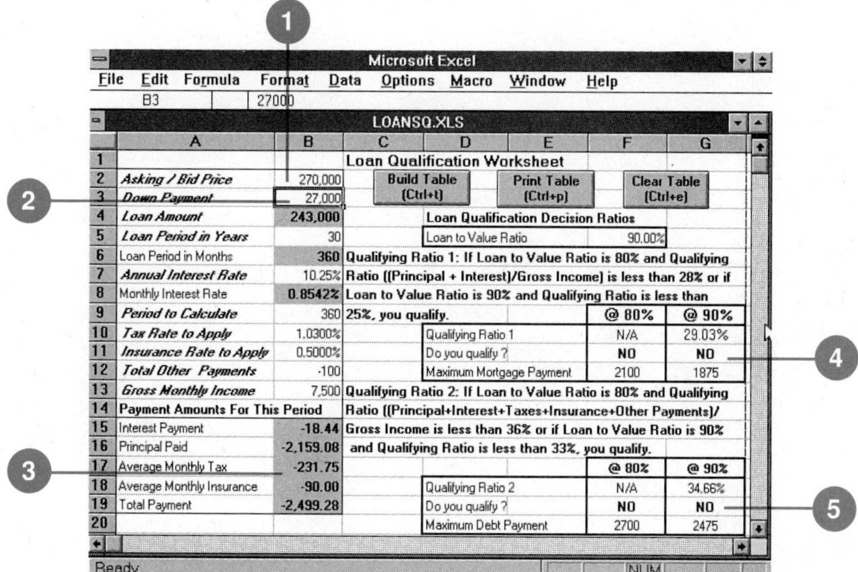

In the example, you wouldn't qualify based on the mortgage payment qualifier or the long-term debt qualifier.

Changing the Down Payment Amount

The down payment amount influences the ratio used by the lender. If you don't qualify at 10% down, try inserting **20%** down in cell B3.

1. Change the amount in cell B3 to 20% of the loan amount (**54,000** in the example).
2. Check the results in cell F5 to be sure the correct Loan to Value Ratio is expressed.
3. Check the results in cells F10:G12.
4. Check the results in cells F18:G20.

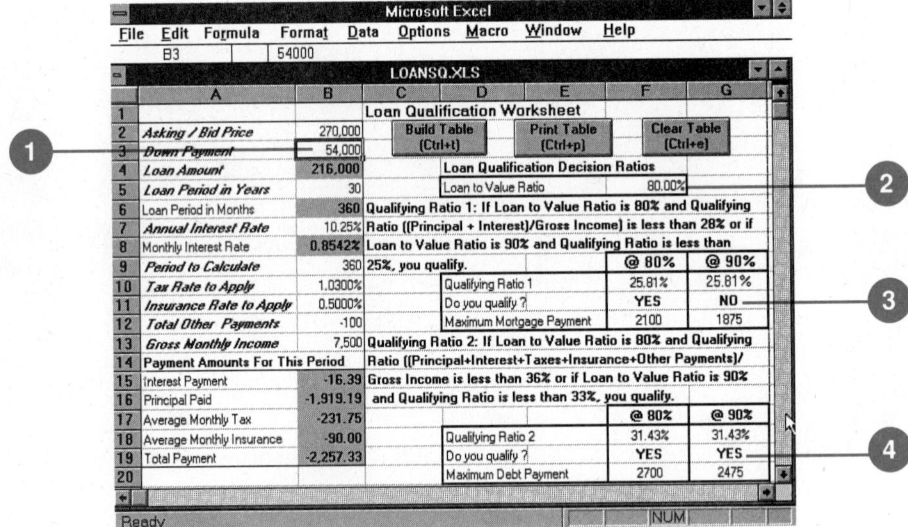

In the example, you would qualify in three of the four tests.

Building an Amortization Table

Make sure LOANERQ.XLM is open before you try this step. Also make sure LOANSQ.XLS is the active worksheet.

1. Click on the Build Table button at the top of the worksheet or press Ctrl+T.
2. The worksheet builds an amortization table for you for the number of years entered in cell B5.

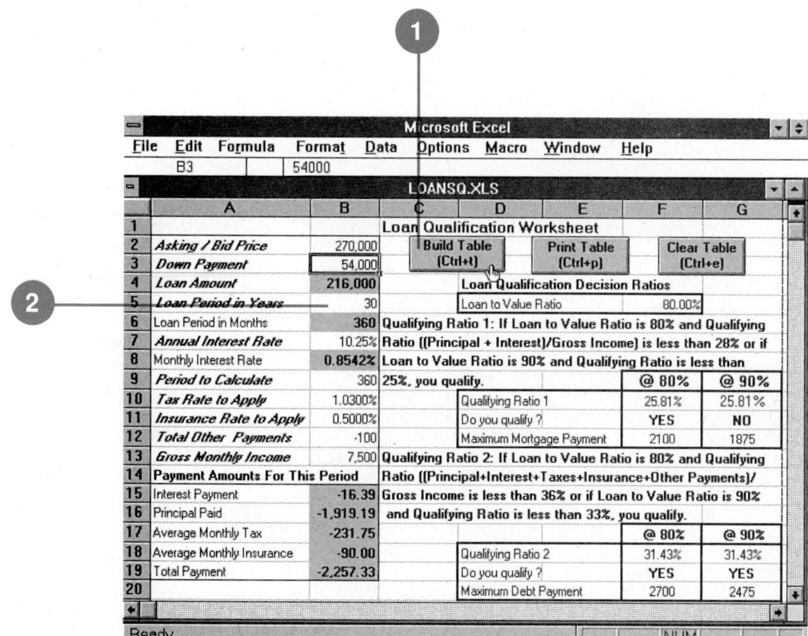

When the amortization table is complete, row 14 will be at the top of the worksheet. Table P9.1 explains the entries in the amortization table.

Table P9.1 The amortization table built on your worksheet

Column	*Contains*
A	An entry for each of the periods of the loan
B	The interest paid in each period
C	The principal paid for each period
D	The total mortgage payment (principal and interest) for each period
E	The accumulated interest to date for the loan for each period
F	The accumulated principal to date for the loan for each period
G	The total mortgage payment for the loan for each period

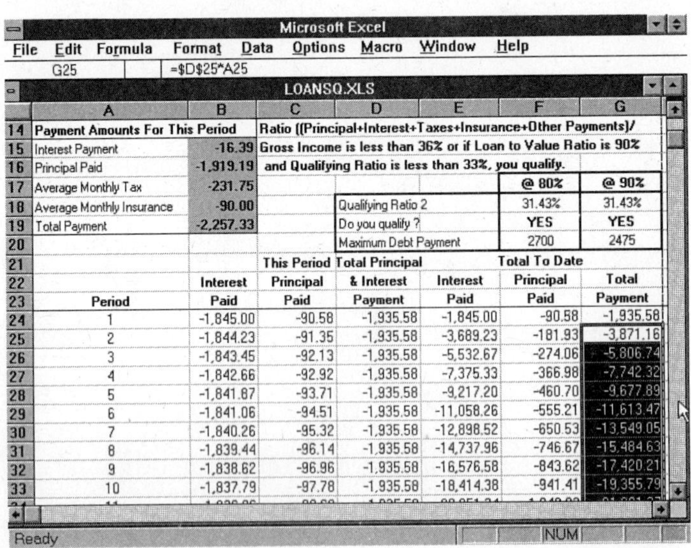

	A	B	C	D	E	F	G
14	Payment Amounts For This Period		Ratio ((Principal+Interest+Taxes+Insurance+Other Payments)/				
15	Interest Payment	-16.39	Gross Income is less than 36% or if Loan to Value Ratio is 90%				
16	Principal Paid	-1,919.19	and Qualifying Ratio is less than 33%, you qualify.				
17	Average Monthly Tax	-231.75				@ 80%	@ 90%
18	Average Monthly Insurance	-90.00		Qualifying Ratio 2		31.43%	31.43%
19	Total Payment	-2,257.33		Do you qualify ?		YES	YES
20				Maximum Debt Payment		2700	2475
21			This Period	Total Principal		Total To Date	
22		Interest	Principal	& Interest	Interest	Principal	Total
23	Period	Paid	Paid	Payment	Paid	Paid	Payment
24	1	-1,845.00	-90.58	-1,935.58	-1,845.00	-90.58	-1,935.58
25	2	-1,844.23	-91.35	-1,935.58	-3,689.23	-181.93	-3,871.16
26	3	-1,843.45	-92.13	-1,935.58	-5,532.67	-274.06	-5,806.74
27	4	-1,842.66	-92.92	-1,935.58	-7,375.33	-366.98	-7,742.32
28	5	-1,841.87	-93.71	-1,935.58	-9,217.20	-460.70	-9,677.89
29	6	-1,841.06	-94.51	-1,935.58	-11,058.26	-555.21	-11,613.47
30	7	-1,840.26	-95.32	-1,935.58	-12,898.52	-650.53	-13,549.05
31	8	-1,839.44	-96.14	-1,935.58	-14,737.96	-746.67	-15,484.63
32	9	-1,838.62	-96.96	-1,935.58	-16,576.58	-843.62	-17,420.21
33	10	-1,837.79	-97.78	-1,935.58	-18,414.38	-941.41	-19,355.79

Using the Formula Select Special Command

You'll need to scroll through the amortization table to check the information month by month. You can also jump to the end of the table quickly if you're just interested in checking the amortization figures for the last several months of the loan. One method you may use to find the end of the amortization table is to scroll down the worksheet until you reach the end by using the scroll arrow or scroll bar. This method is really slow if you are dealing with a large table. A simpler method is to use the Formula Select Special command.

1. Choose Formula Select Special. The Select Special dialog box appears.
2. Select the Last Cell radio button.
3. Click OK or press Enter.

There is a third method to get to the last active cell in the worksheet that is the easiest of all. Press Ctrl+End.

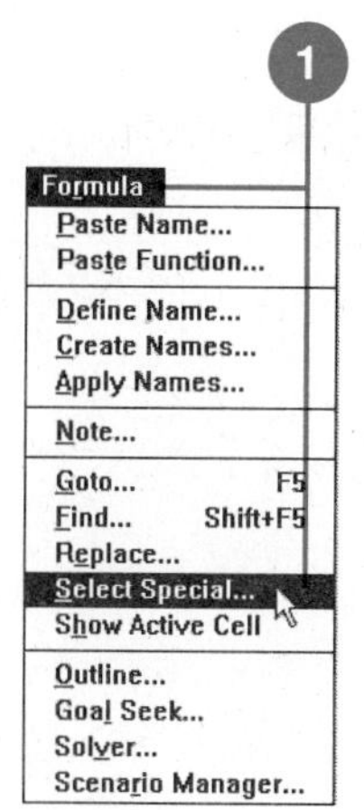

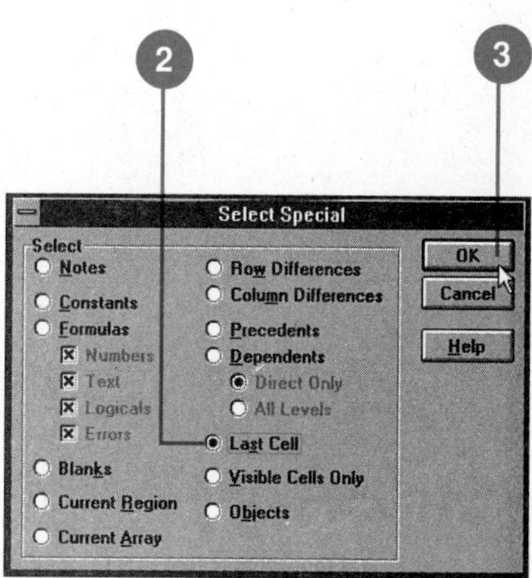

If you use any of the procedures already described, you will end up at the last cell in the worksheet. To return to the first page of the worksheet, press Ctrl+Home.

Printing the Amortization Table

You may wish to see a printed copy of the amortization table. If you do, follow the steps described in this section.

1. Move to the top of the worksheet.
2. Click on the Print Table button or press Ctrl+P. Excel prints the entire amortization table.

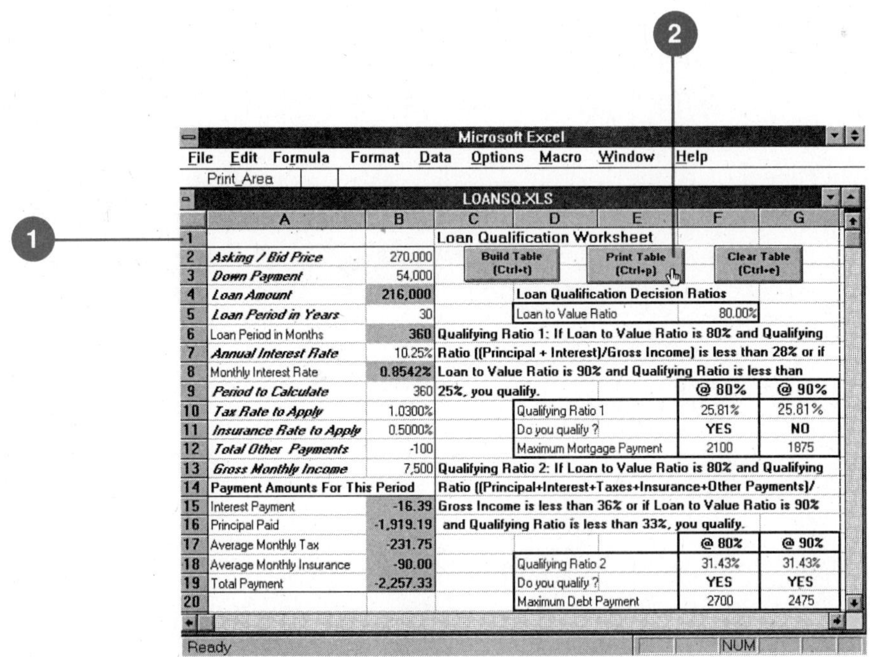

Clearing the Amortization Table

To make sure that any new amortization tables you build or print don't contain any old data, you may use the Clear Table button to save time in clearing the old amortization table from the worksheet.

1. Move to the top of the worksheet.
2. Click on the Clear Table button or press Ctrl+E.
3. The cell selector will move to area where the amortization table was located. Scroll back to the top of the worksheet.

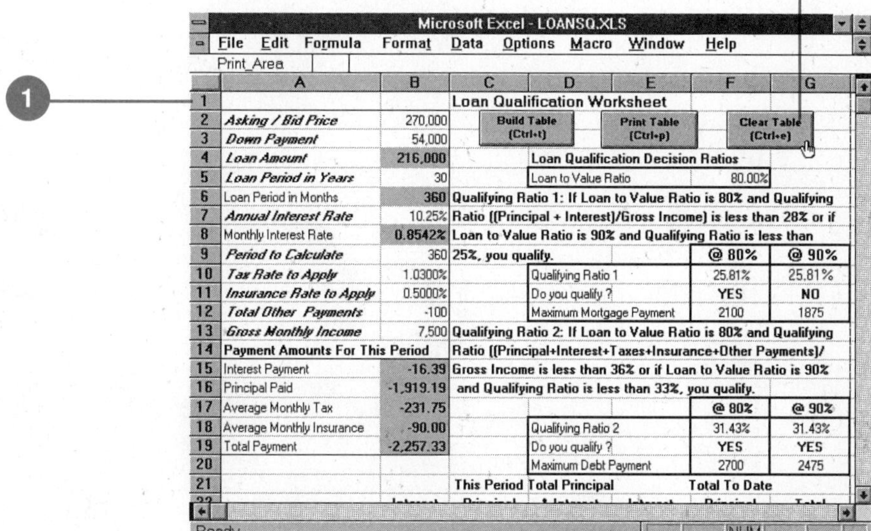

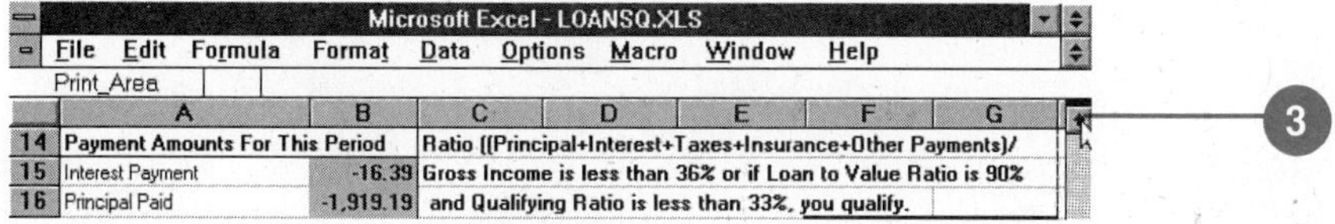

Printing the Loan Qualification Portion of the Worksheet

You need to take a couple of steps to print the loan qualification area. You have to specify a print area. And, because the Print Table button and macro sets rows 21:23 as a row of titles for the amortization table, you have to instruct Excel to stop using them to avoid having these rows applied to any other printed section of the worksheet.

1. Select cells A1:G20.
2. Choose **O**ptions Set Print Area.
3. Choose Fo**r**mula **D**efine Name. The Define Name dialog box appears.
4. Choose Print Titles from the Names in **S**heet list.
5. Select the **D**elete button.

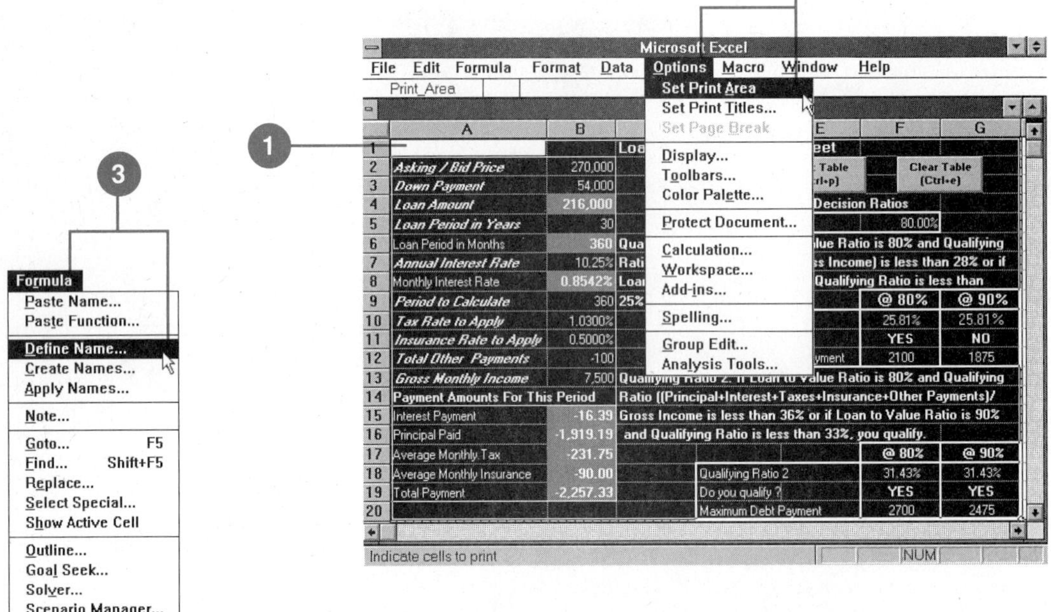

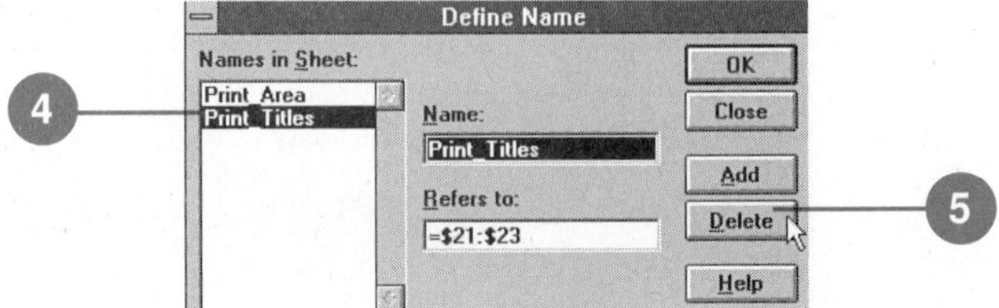

6. Check the Names in Sheet list to make sure Print Titles no longer appears.
7. Press Enter or click OK.
8. Choose File Print or press Ctrl+Shift+F12. The Print dialog box appears.
9. Select the parameters you want to use.
10. Press Enter or click OK.

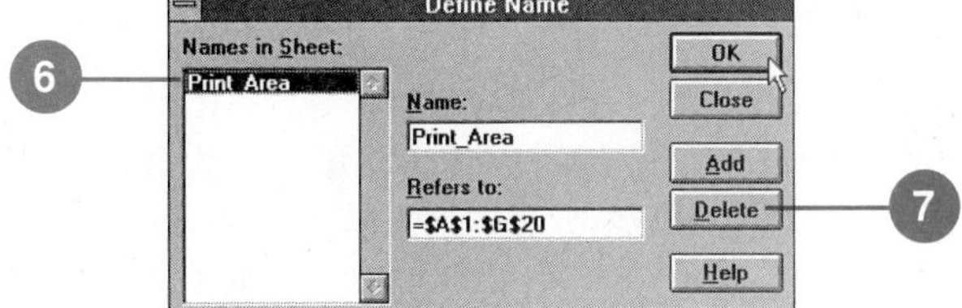

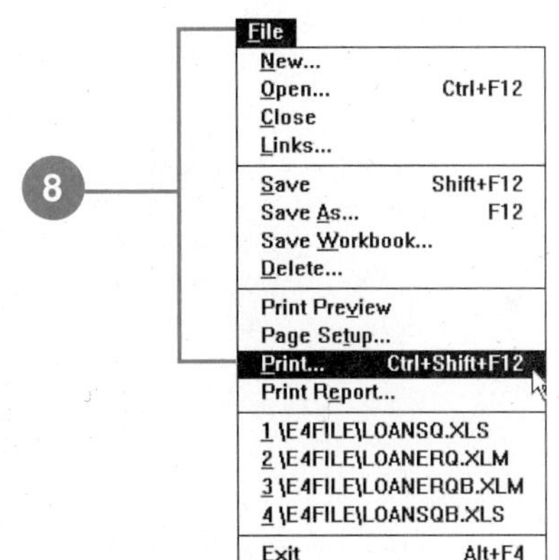

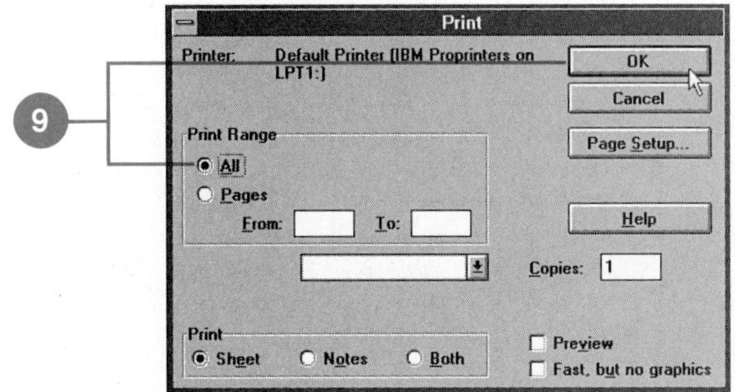

Customizing LOANSQ.XLS

To customize LOANSQ.XLS, you can easily add reference tables to the worksheet to provide more detailed information about loan payments or income. Another customization is altering the formulas used to compute the qualification ratios to avoid showing the error messages. You might also want to change these formulas to reflect different percentages of income if the lender's policies differ from the rules of thumb used on the worksheet. The following procedures help you create an example reference table and change the qualifying ratio formulas.

Decreasing Font Size Using the Standard Toolbar

If you add a table to the worksheet, you may want to make it a smaller font size to differentiate the table contents from other worksheet areas. To do so, use a tool on the Standard toolbar. If that toolbar does not currently appear, add it to the worksheet display before continuing.

1. Add appropriate labels to the range of cells you want to use for a table. (Some examples are shown in Figure 9.19.)
2. Select the worksheet cells that will contain the table.
3. Click on the Decrease Font Size tool on the Standard toolbar.

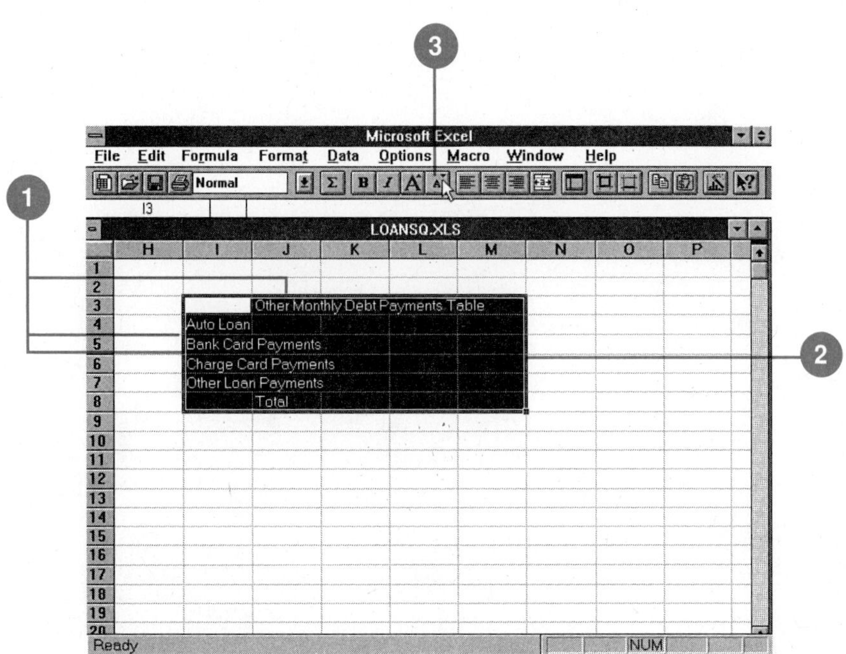

Using the Format Number Command

When you build a new table or add numeric data to a worksheet, you will often find that the cells used for the table or the data are already formatted by Excel, in the "General" format. If you wish to use another format, the Format Number command must be used.

1. Ensure that the cell range for the table has been selected.
2. Choose Format Number. The Number Format dialog box appears.
3. Choose Currency from the Category list.
4. Choose $#,##0.00_):($#,##0.00) from the Format Codes list.
5. Press Enter or click OK.

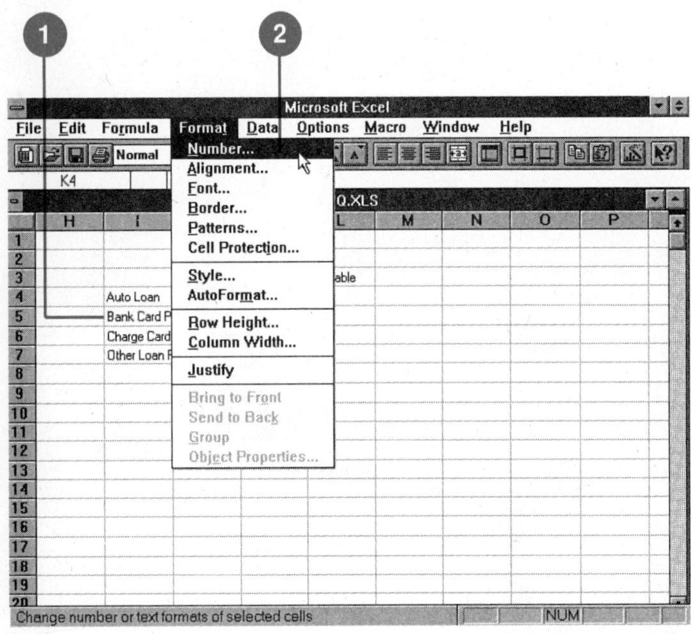

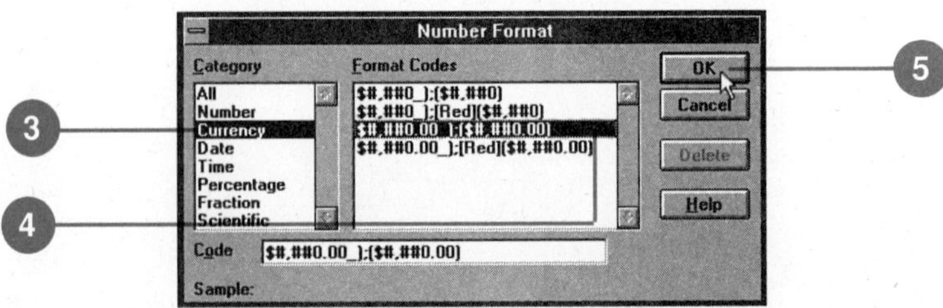

Adding a Sum Formula

Since you are going to pass the sum of all the monetary debt to LOANSQ.KLS, it is necessary to produce this sum. The following example describes the use of the AutoSum button. This button saves keystrokes when you are creating a worksheet.

1. Select the cell (K8) immediately below the last cell of the range of cells containing the values for each column in the table.
2. Click on the AutoSum button on the toolbar. A SUM() formula is inserted in the selected cell.
3. A marquee surrounds the range of cells included in the formula. Press Enter.

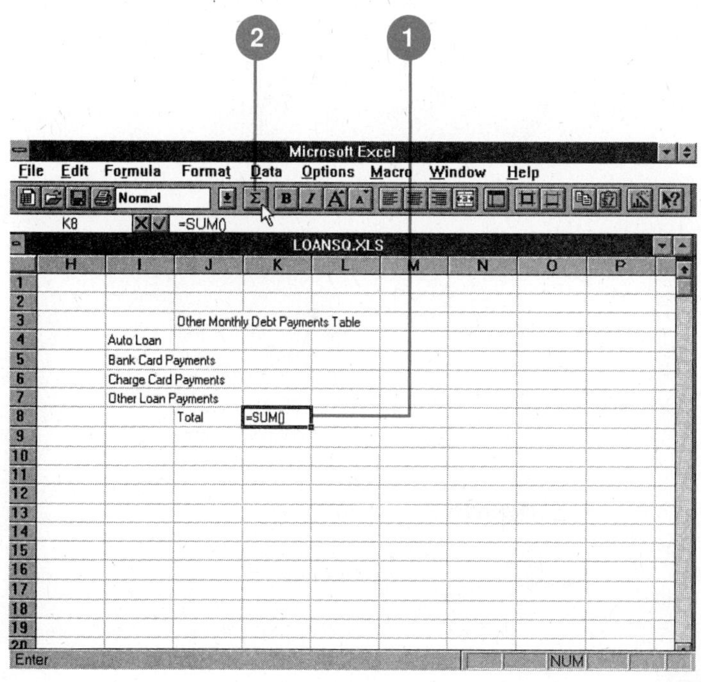

Using the Shortcut Menu to Turn Off a Toolbar

Removing toolbars from the screen display enables more of the active worksheet to appear. You can use a shortcut menu to quickly hide a displayed toolbar.

1. Point to the Standard toolbar and press the right mouse button. A shortcut menu appears.
2. Select the toolbar you want to hide (Standard). The toolbar disappears.

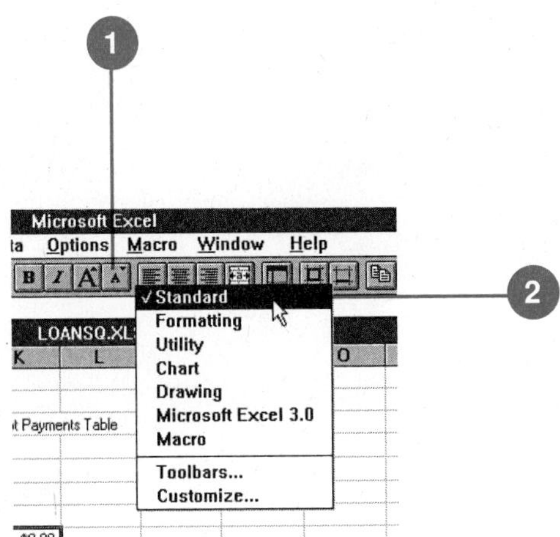

Completing the Reference Table

Once the reference table has been completed, enter the values in the table. The formula in cell B12 must be changed to allow the table to be used to feed data to the main portion of the worksheet.

1. Enter values in the cells of the table (K4:K7 in the example) that will be used to calculate a sum used by LOANSQ.XLS.
2. Scroll the worksheet until cell A1 is in the upper left corner.
3. Select the cell that will contain the total from your table (B12 in the example).
4. Change the formula in the cell to obtain its value from the reference table cell (=-K8 in the example). Be sure to enter the negative sign.
5. Press Enter.

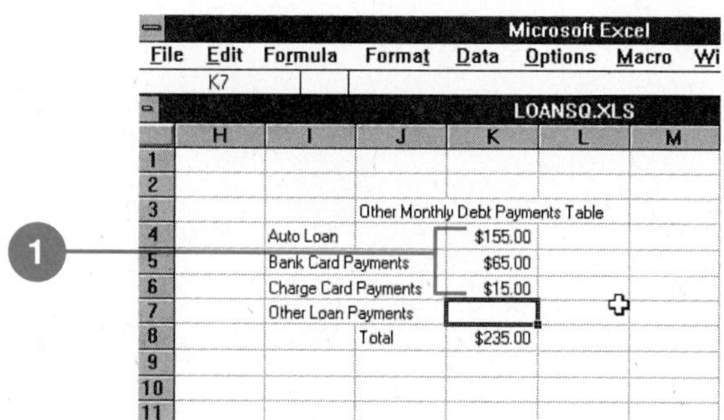

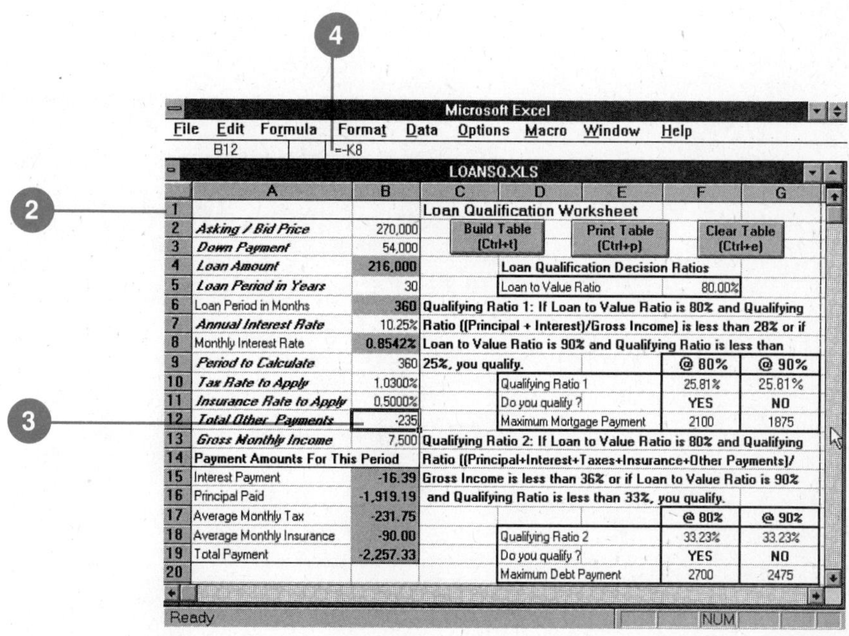

Preventing an Error Message from Being Displayed

Normally, the formula in cell F10 causes `N/A` to be displayed in the cell instead of the error message. You can change the formula so that the error message does not appear, and you can try the same approach in the other cells that display error messages. Choose a precedent cell that contains a blank or a zero to be included in the condition portion of the IF() statement.

(`=IF(`*condition,*`)`)

1. Select cell F10.
2. Change the formula to read as follows: **`=IF(B13<>0,IF(F5<=0.8,(B15+B16)/B13,"N/A"),"N/A")`**
3. Press Enter.

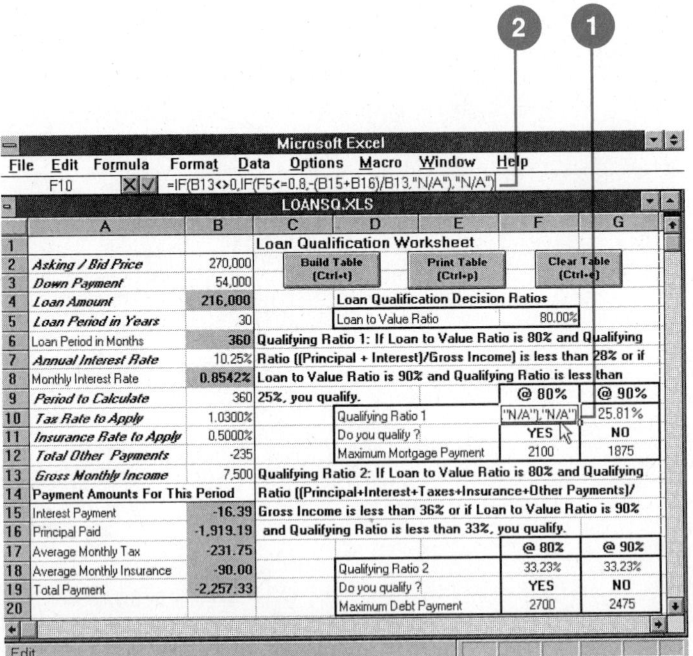

Changing the Qualification Parameter

If your lender uses a rule of thumb that is different from the rule of thumb used on LOANSQ.XLS, you may change the formula.

1. Select cell F11.
2. Change the value `.28` in the formula to `.30` or another value. Press Enter.

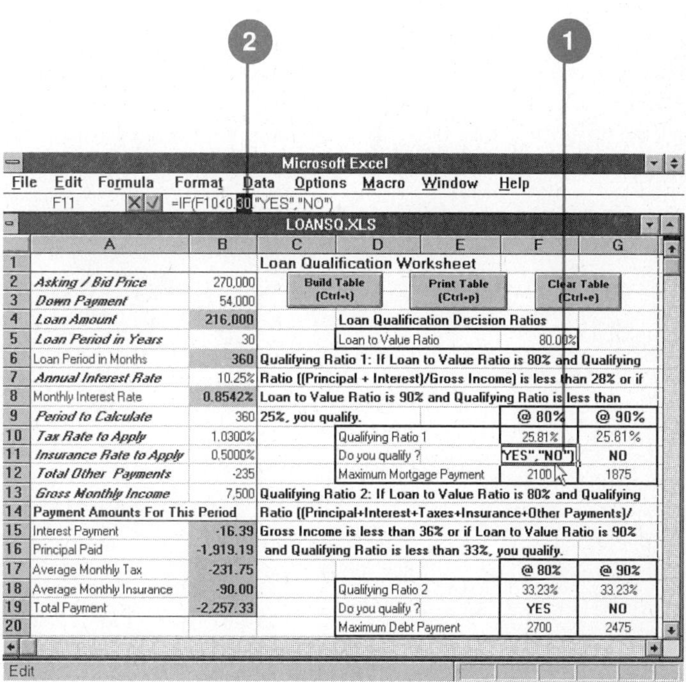

Summary

It helps to know whether you qualify for a loan before you apply. If you have this information, you can make adjustments by increasing the down payment, making a lower bid, decreasing your other debt obligations, or whatever is required to make your situation more attractive to a lender. If you haven't found a property to purchase, it helps to have an idea of how much you can afford.

LOANSQ.XLS, the worksheet for this project, lets you estimate your mortgage payments by using some of Excel's built-in financial functions. It also lets you estimate whether you qualify for a loan under conditions normally used by lenders. Finally, it lets you build, print, and clear an amortization table on the worksheet by using three macros that are included in LOANERSQ.XLS.

	P	Q	R	S	T	U
49						
50	Customer Database					
51	First Name	Last Name	Company	Title	Acct Num	Address
52	Louis	DePalma	Sunshine Cab Company	Dispatcher	123456	123 45th Street
53	Rob	Petrie	The Alan Brady Show	Screenwriter	987654	987 Somwhere Drive
54	Herb	Tarlek	WKRP	Sales Mgr	121212	456 Pitty-Pat Lane
55	Bert	Campbell	Campbell Construction	Owner	654321	1234 Harris Avenue
56	Ricky	Riccardo	DesiLu	Bandleader	456789	456 Lucy Street
57	Mary	Richards	WJN News	Producer	876543	6543 Tinker Way
58	Woody	Boyd	Cheers	Bartender	456654	432 Hayseed Road
59						
60						

	V	W	X	Y	Z	AA
49						
50						
51	City	State	Zip Code	Phone Num	Fax Num	Memo
52	New York	NY	10019	(212) 123-4567	(212) 987-6543	Birthday: Feb 29
53	New Rochelle	NY	98765-4321	(203) 987-6543	(203) 876-5432	Wife's name is Laura
54	Cincinnati	OH	45678	(513) 555-2345	(513) 555-3456	Likes plaid suits
55	Danbury	CT	12345-0001	(203) 444-5566	(203) 444-5567	Wife: Mary; Sons: Danny, Jody, Bob
56	New York	NY	65432-0002	(987) 654-3210	(987) 654-3211	Friend of Fred Mertz
57	Minneapolis	MI	00009-9999	(345) 678-9999	(345) 678-8888	Has spunk
58	Hanover	IN	46032	(111) 222-3333	(111) 222-4444	
59						
60						

Project

10

Creating a Customer Database

In business, managing information is often as important as crunching numbers. With this is mind, Excel provides extensive database capabilities that enable you to enter, edit, sort, find, and extract the information you want. Each of these database features and some advanced topics such as crosstab tables and accessing non-Excel databases are explained thoroughly in the Database Workshop (in Skill Sessions 35–39).

This project provides you with a ready-to-use Excel database, CUSTOMER.XLS, designed to hold customer information. With this database, you can enter your customer's name, company, title, account number, address, phone number, and fax number. There is also a memo field that can hold general comments. Of course, you do not have to restrict yourself to entering only customer data. You can use this database for contacts, colleagues, friends, family, or even a mailing list. Be sure to save each type of database under a different name. See the section entitled "Saving CUSTOMER.XLS Under a New Name."

The Customer Database file that you use in this project is called CUSTOMER.XLS. This file contains only the database range, a criteria range, and an extract range. Besides entering the database information, you will also work with the databases in the following ways:

- ▲ Use the data form to enter, edit, and find data.
- ▲ Sort the database.
- ▲ Enter criteria and use the criteria to find and delete database records.
- ▲ Extract information from the database.
- ▲ Customize the database to suit your own needs.

This project assumes that you are familiar with Excel databases and with terminology such as "criteria" and "extract." If you need to refresh your memory, read the relevant sections in the Database Workshop.

Opening the Customer Database

To follow along with the steps in this project, you need to open the CUSTOMER.XLS file. Before you do so, note the file called CUSTOMER.XLM that was included on the disk that came with this book. This is a macro sheet that is opened automatically when you open CUSTOMER.XLS. This sheet contains several macros and custom menu options that you will be using in this project. If you want to look at this file, open CUSTOMER.XLS, select Window Unhide, and then select CUSTOMER.XLM from the list that appears.

1. Choose File Open.
2. Select the drive and directory where you copied the disk files.
3. Highlight the CUSTOMER.XLS file.
4. Select OK or press Enter.

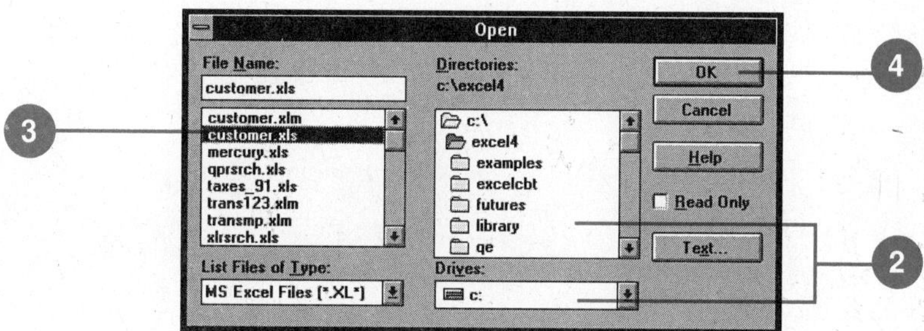

About CUSTOMER.XLS

The Customer Database consists of 12 fields, as outlined here.

Field	*Description*
First Name	The customer's first name.
Last name	The customer's surname.
Company	The name of the company the customer works for.
Title	The customer's job title.
Acct Num	The account number of either the customer or the company the customer works for.
Address	The customer's street address. This field is formatted as word wrap, so you can enter multiple lines, if necessary.
City	The customer's city.
State	The customer's state.
Zip Code	The customer's ZIP Code. This field has been formatted to accept both the normal five-digit ZIP Codes and the newer nine-digit codes. Note that a dash is added automatically whenever you enter a nine-digit code. For example, if you enter **123456789**, the data appears as 12345-6789.
Phone Num	The customer's phone number. This field has been formatted to accept a number with or without the area code and to enter the dash automatically. For example, if you enter **1234567**, the number appears as 123-4567. If you enter **1234567890**, the number appears as (123) 456-7890.

Field	*Description*
Fax Num	The customer's fax number. This field uses the same formatting as the Phone Num field.
Memo	Miscellaneous comments about the customer (e.g., birthdays, children's names, favorite color). The field is formatted as word wrap, so you can enter as much information as you need.

When you first open CUSTOMER.XLS, the Customer Database consists of the range P51:AA53 (the range name is Database). The field titles are frozen so that if your database grows past the bottom of the screen, the headings still remain in view. If you get lost while navigating the screen, either of the following methods should return you to the first record in the database:

- Press Ctrl+Home.
- Choose Formula Goto (or press F5) and select First_Rec from the list.

Entering Data

This section shows you how to enter your customer data directly into the database fields. For an alternative data entry method that uses the data form, see the section entitled "Using the Data Form."

Entering a Customer Record

If you are entering your first record in the database, you can type the data directly on the worksheet (be sure to use Row 52 in CUSTOMER.XLS) without further preparation. If you are entering subsequent records, you must first insert a new row in the database, and then use that row for the new record. (See the next section for information on inserting database rows.)

When entering the data, press the left arrow key when you have completed a field. This will take you to the next field automatically.

1. Select the First Name field and enter the customer's first name.
2. Select the Last Name field and enter the customer's last name.
3. Select the Company field and enter the customer's company.
4. Select the Title field and enter the customer's job title.
5. Select the Acct Num field and enter the customer's account number.

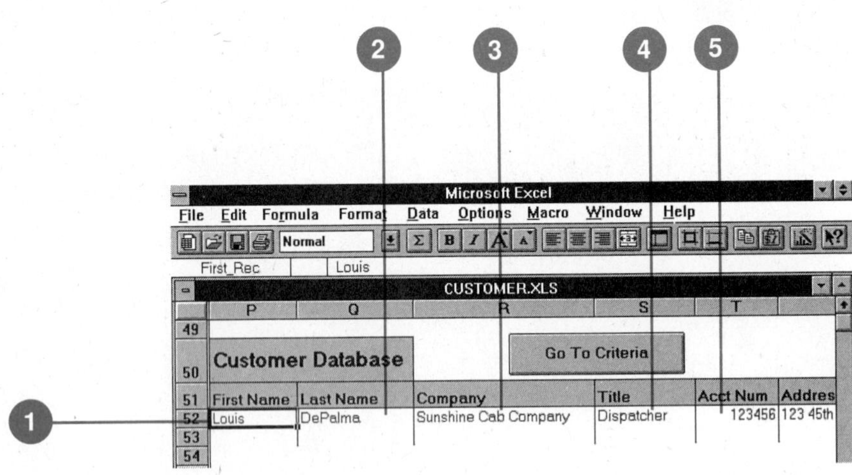

6. Select the Address field and enter the customer's street address. Remember that you can use multiple lines, if necessary.

7. Select the City field and enter the customer's city.

8. Select the State field and enter the customer's state.

9. Select the Zip Code field and enter the customer's ZIP Code. Remember that a dash is added automatically to nine-digit codes.

10. Select the Phone Num field and enter the customer's phone number. The area code is optional. Remember that the dash and area code brackets are added automatically.

11. Select the Fax Num field and enter the customer's fax number. The area code is optional. Remember that the dash and area code brackets are added automatically.

12. Select the Memo field and enter any miscellaneous information you may have about the customer. Use multiple lines, if necessary.

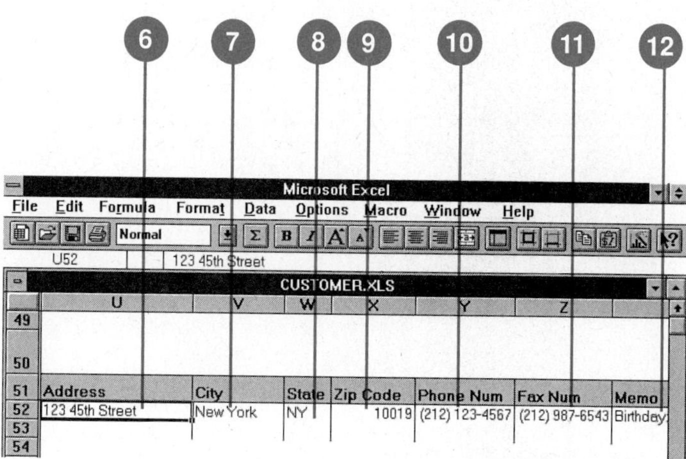

Inserting Database Rows

After you have entered your first record in the database, you need to insert a new database row for each record you want to add. Inserting a new row ensures that the Database range is extended to cover all your data.

1. Select a cell in the row immediately below the last record in the database.
2. Choose Edit Insert.
3. Select Entire Row.
4. Select OK or press Enter.

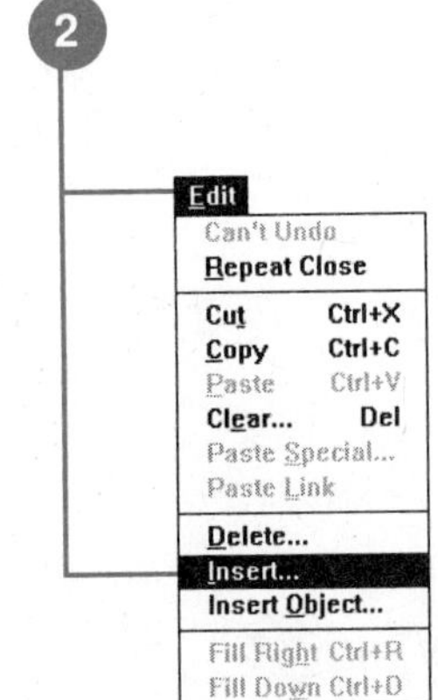

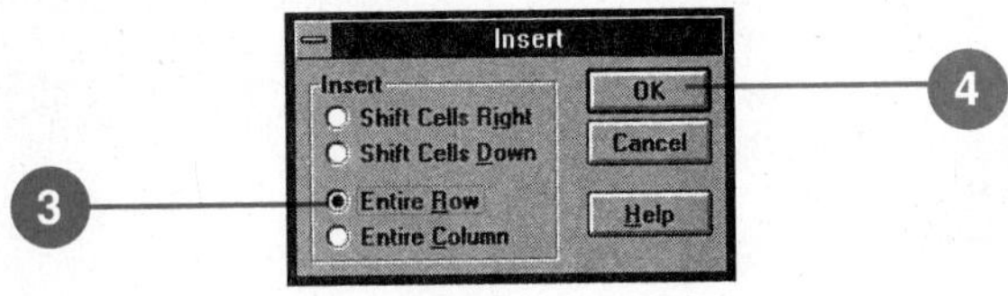

Deleting Customer Records

To save memory, you should delete those customer records that you no longer need or that you have duplicated.

1. Select a cell in the record you want to delete.
2. Choose Edit Delete.
3. Select Entire Row.
4. Select OK or press Enter.

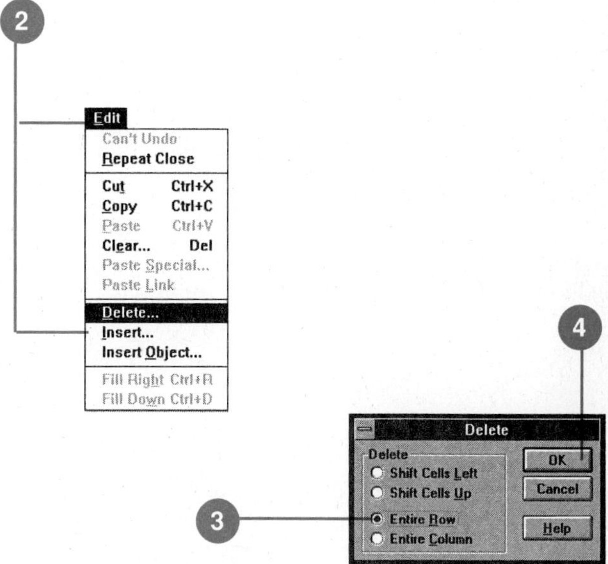

Using the Data Form

Anytime you set up an Excel database, the program automatically creates a *data form*. You can use the data form to add, edit, find, and delete database records quickly. The data form has two major advantages over working with the database range directly:

- ▲ It shows all the fields in a single dialog box.
- ▲ It automatically adjusts the database range whenever you add or delete records.

Entering Records with the Data Form

You can use the data form to add new records to the Customer Database. You do not need to insert a new row because Excel adjusts the database for you.

1. Choose Data Form. Excel displays the CUSTOMER.XLS dialog box.
2. Select New. Excel displays a new blank record.
3. Enter the customer data.
4. Repeat steps 2 and 3 to enter information for other customers.
5. Select Close.

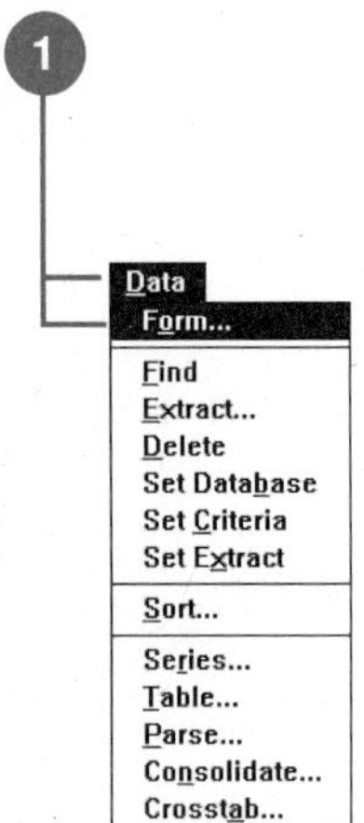

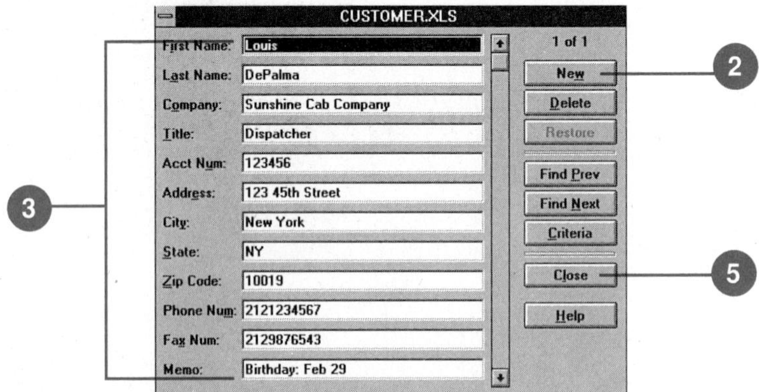

Deleting Records with the Data Form

You can erase unneeded customer records quickly by using the Delete button in the data form.

1. Choose Data Form. Excel displays the CUSTOMER.XLS dialog box.
2. Select the record you want to delete.
3. Select the Delete button. Excel warns you that the record will be permanently deleted.
4. Select OK or press Enter. Excel deletes the record.
5. Repeat steps 2 through 4 to delete other records.
6. Select Close.

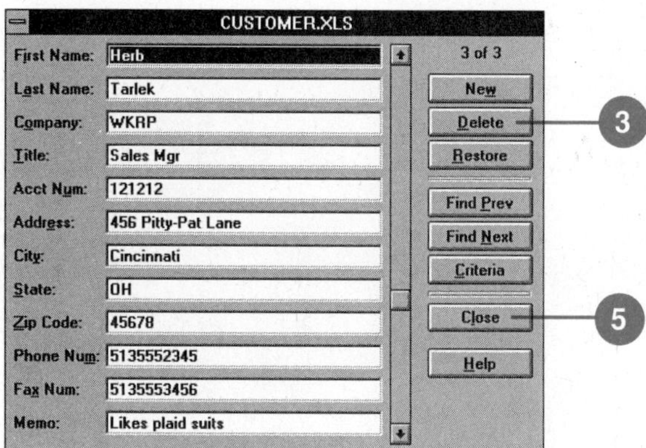

Finding Records with the Data Form

As your database grows, it becomes increasingly time-consuming to select the records you want to examine, edit, or delete. The data form helps by providing a Find feature that searches through your records to find customers that meet the criteria you have set.

1. Choose Data Form. Excel displays the CUSTOMER.XLS dialog box.
2. Select the Criteria button.
3. Select the Clear button to remove previously entered criteria.
4. Enter your criteria in the appropriate fields.
5. To search forward through the database, select the Find Next button. To search backwards, select the Find Prev button.
6. Select Close.

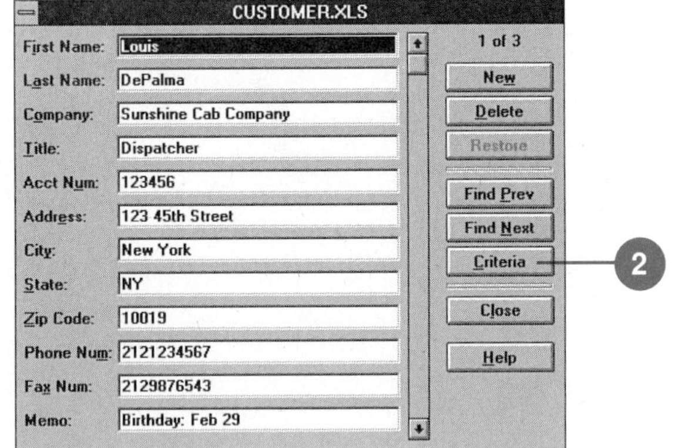

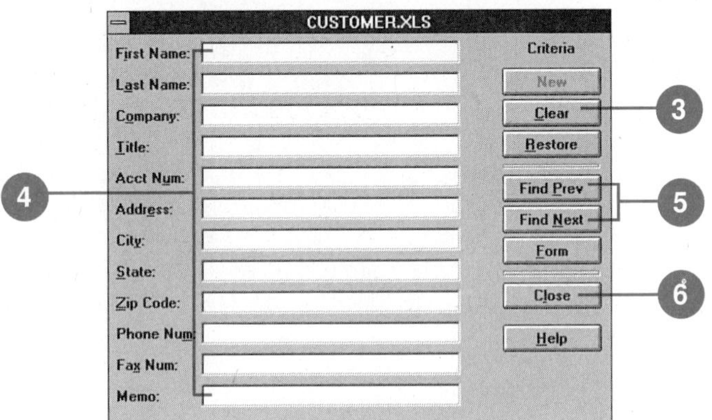

Sorting the Database

When you add records to the database, you generally enter them in random order. This is not a problem because you can easily sort the database on a single field or a combination of fields. Sorting makes it easier to find records or to check for duplicated records.

1. Highlight the range you want to sort. For each record, be sure to include every field.
2. Choose Data Sort.
3. Select Rows in the Sort by box.
4. In the 1st Key field, enter a cell address from the field you want to use for the overall sort order.
5. Select whether you want the **1**st Key to be **A**scending or **D**escending.
6. If necessary, use the **2**nd Key field to enter a cell address from the field you want to use for the second-level sort order.
7. Select whether you want the **2**nd Key to be A**s**cending or Descending.
8. If necessary, use the **3**rd Key field to enter a cell address from the field you want to use for the third-level sort order.
9. Select whether you want the **3**rd Key to be Ascending or Descending.
10. Select OK or press Enter.

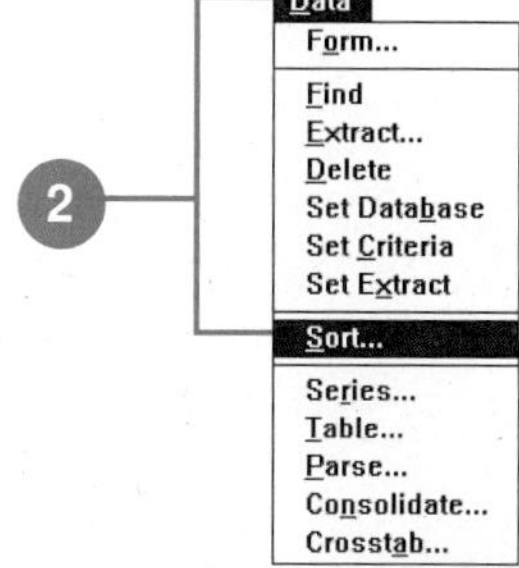

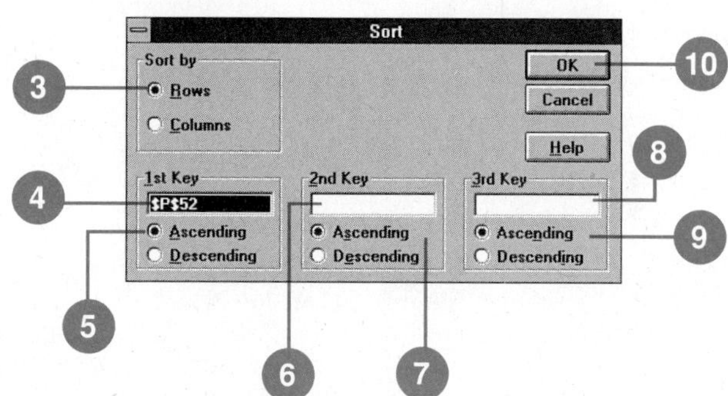

Entering Criteria

If you want to use more sophisticated criteria to find, delete, or extract customer records, you need to use the criteria range supplied with the CUSTOMER.XLS worksheet. The default criteria range is given by the coordinates A3:L4 (the range is named Criteria).

1. Select the Go To Criteria macro button or choose Data Go to Criteria (this is an extra Data menu command that is added automatically when you load the CUSTOMER.XLS worksheet).

2. Enter your criteria in the appropriate fields.

3. Select the Go To Database macro button or choose Data Go to Database (this is an extra Data menu command that is added automatically when you load the CUSTOMER.XLS worksheet).

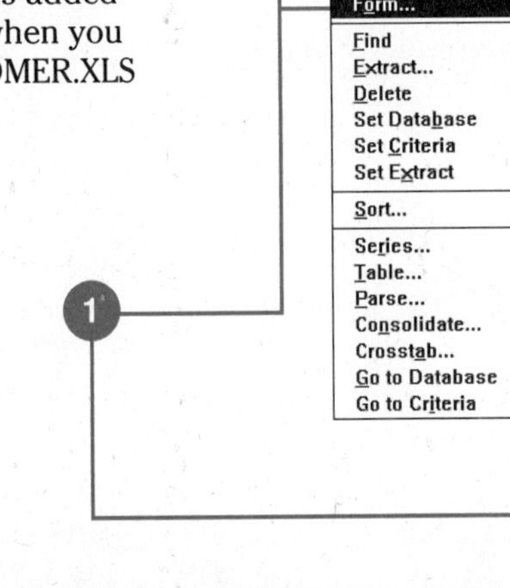

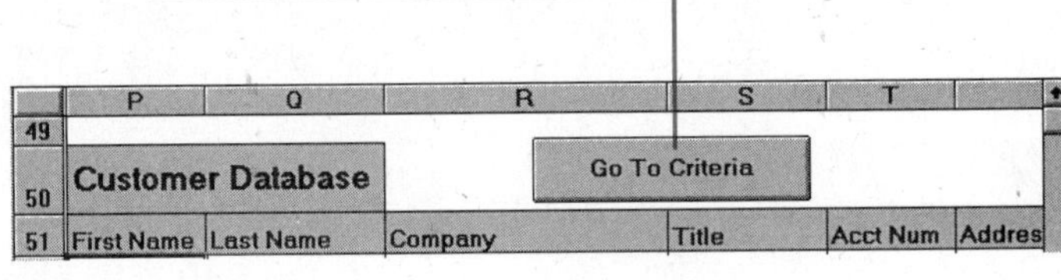

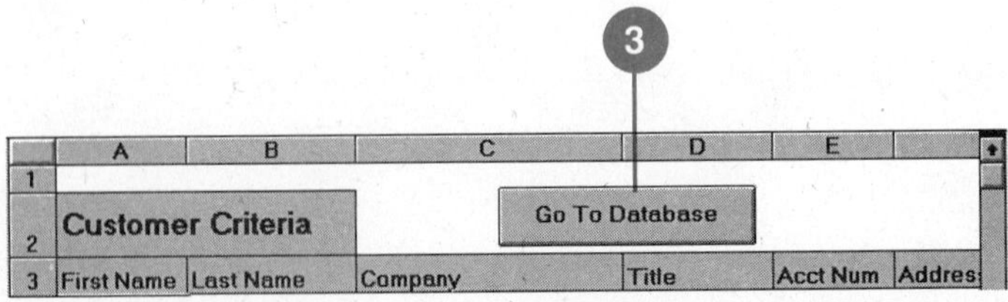

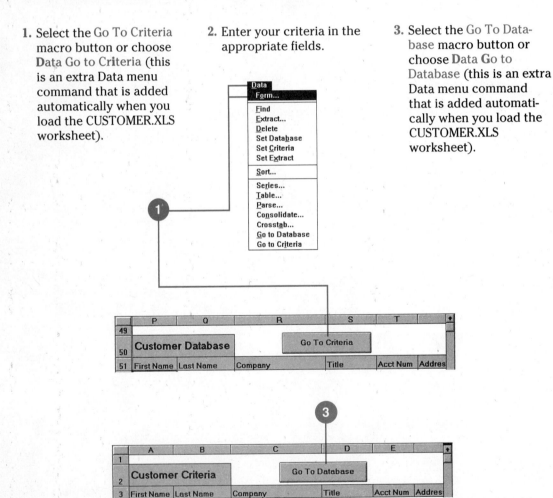

Finding Customer Records

You can use the criteria you enter in the Criteria range to find customer records. No matter how many records match your criteria, Excel highlights only one record at a time. You use the arrow keys to navigate the matching records.

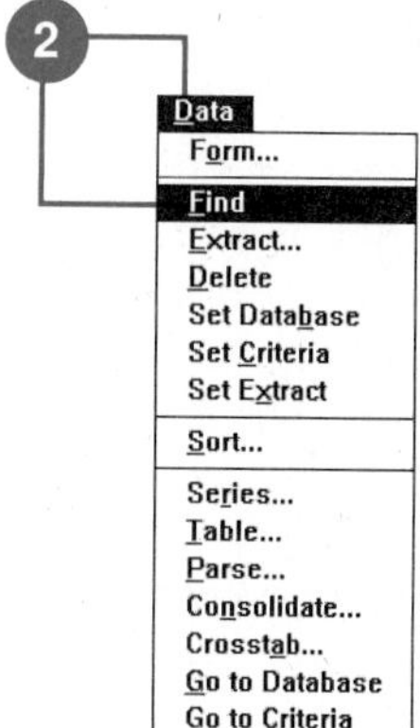

1. Enter your criteria and return to the Database range.
2. Choose Data Find. Excel highlights the first record that meets your criteria.
3. Use the arrow keys to find other records that meet the criteria.
4. Press Esc to exit the Find procedure.

Deleting Customer Records

The Criteria range is also useful for deleting customer records with the Data Delete command. Note that Excel deletes all matching records permanently, so use this command carefully.

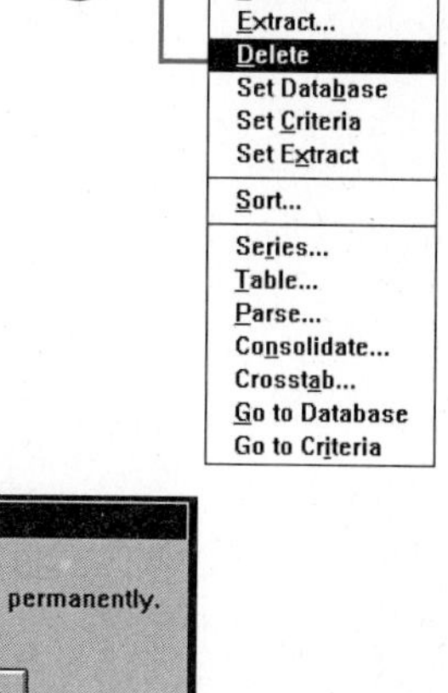

1. Enter your criteria and return to the Database range.
2. Choose Data Delete. Excel warns you that the records matching your criteria will be permanently deleted.
3. Select OK or press Enter.

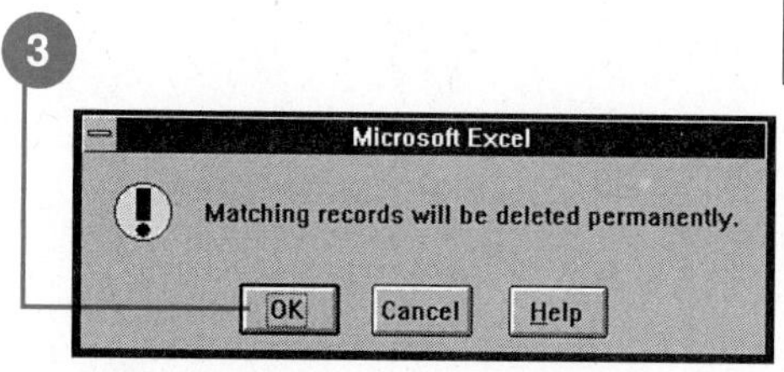

Extracting Customer Records

One of Excel's most powerful database features is the **D**ata E**x**tract command. With this command, you can extract a subset of the Customer Database and display it in the extract range. The subset you extract depends on the conditions you set up in the criteria range. The CUSTOMER.XLS file includes an extract range at coordinates A8:L8 (this range is called Extract).

1. Move to the Criteria range.
2. Enter your criteria for the extracted records.
3. Choose Data Extract. Excel finds all customer records that match your criteria and displays them in the extract range.

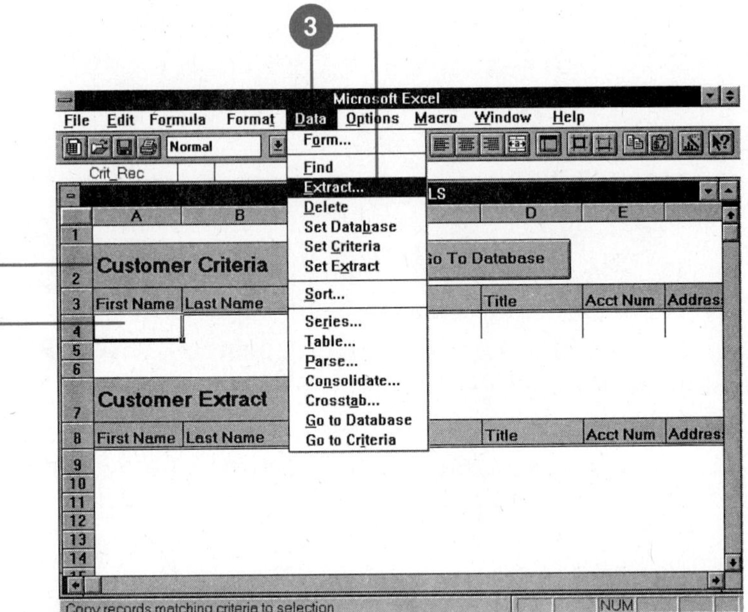

Customizing CUSTOMER.XLS

The Customer Database may not suit your needs exactly. You may want to delete some of the fields, rename one or more fields, or even add fields of your own. These are all straightforward operations and, if you follow the instructions given in the next few sections, you should have no problems. The only thing you need to watch for is that you maintain the proper range definitions for the database, criteria, and extract areas. If you have any doubts about these ranges, you can check them with the Fo**r**mula **D**efine Names command or you can simply redefine the appropriate range.

Renaming Database Field Names

If you prefer a different name for one or more of the database fields, you can easily rename the fields.

1. If you are not already there, move to the Database range.
2. Select the field name you want to rename.
3. Enter the new name.
4. Repeat steps 2 and 3 for other fields you want to rename.
5. Move to the Criteria range.
6. Repeat steps 2 through 4 for the Criteria range. Move to the Extract range.
7. Repeat steps 2 through 4 for the Extract range.
8. Return to the Database range.

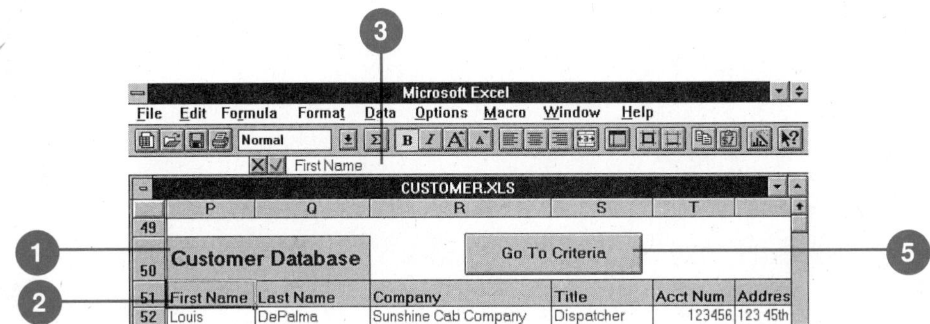

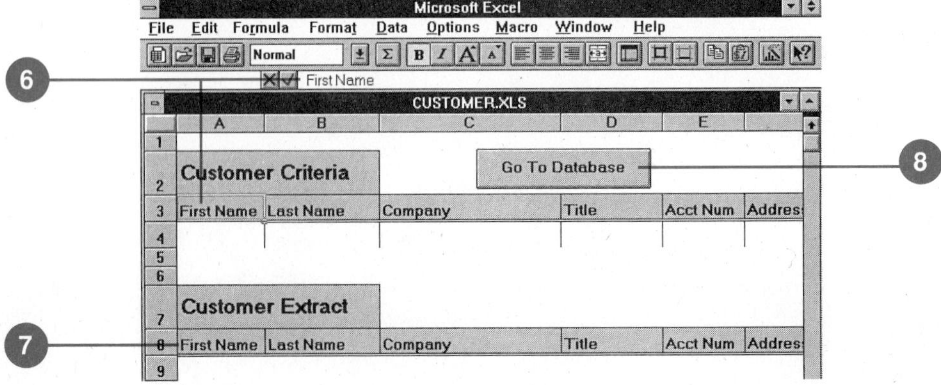

Deleting Database Fields

If you do not need one or more of the fields in the Customer Database, you can delete the appropriate columns.

1. If you are not already there, move to the Database range.
2. Select any cell in each field you want to delete.
3. Choose Edit Delete.
4. Select Entire Column.
5. Select OK or press Enter. Excel deletes the fields.
6. Move to the Criteria range.
7. Repeat steps 2 through 5 for the Criteria range. Move to the Extract range.
8. Repeat steps 2 through 5 for the Extract range.
9. Return to the Database range.

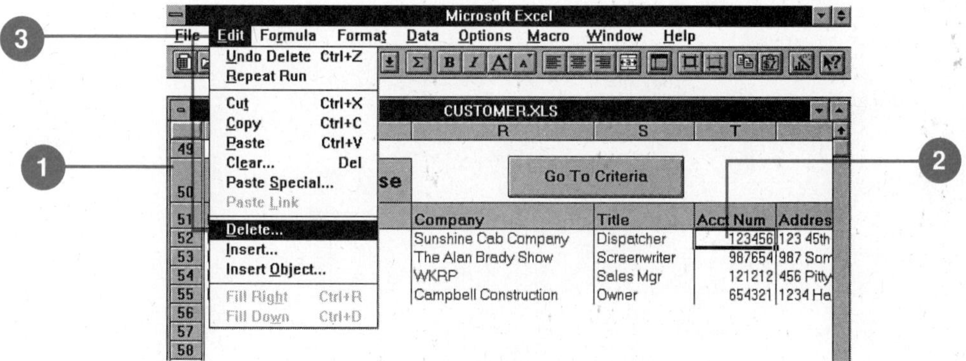

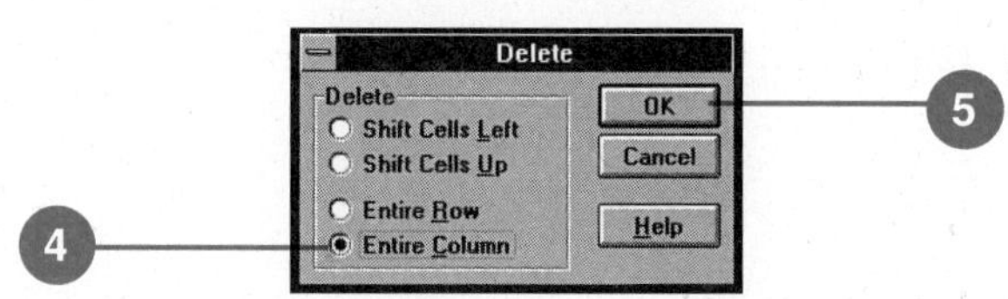

Adding a Database Field

You can add your own fields to the Customer Database.

1. If you are not already there, move to the Database range.
2. Select any cell in the field to the right of where you want to insert your own field. To make sure your field is included in the Database range, do not select a field outside the range.
3. Choose Edit Insert. Excel displays the Insert dialog box.
4. Select Entire Column.
5. Select OK or press Enter. Excel inserts the field.
6. Move to the Criteria range.
7. Repeat steps 2 through 5 for the Criteria range. Move to the Extract range.
8. Repeat steps 2 through 5 for the Extract range.
9. Return to the Database range.

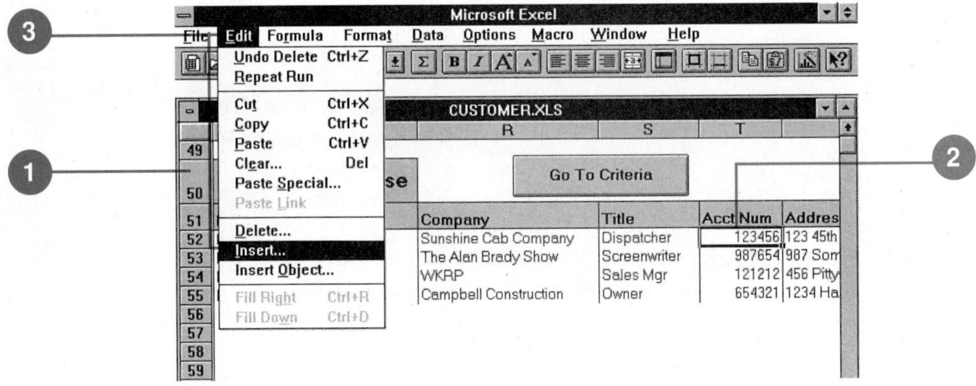

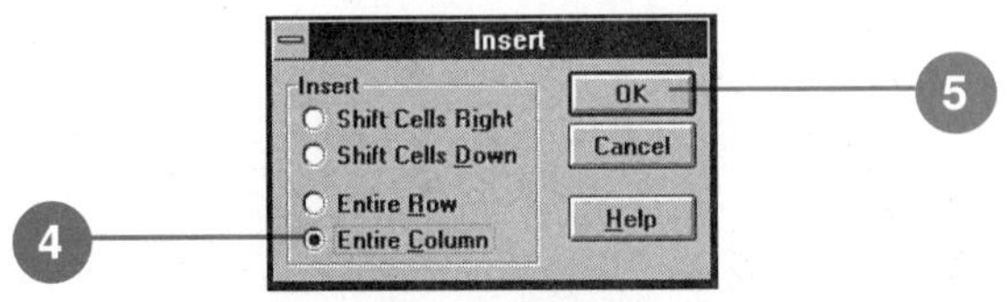

Saving CUSTOMER.XLS Under a New Name

Besides information about customers, you can use CUSTOMER.XLS to store information about friends, family, colleagues, and contacts. To preserve the default CUSTOMER.XLS worksheet, you need to save your work under a different name.

1. Choose File Save As.
2. Replace the file name in the File Name text box with the new name you want to use.
3. Select OK or press Enter.

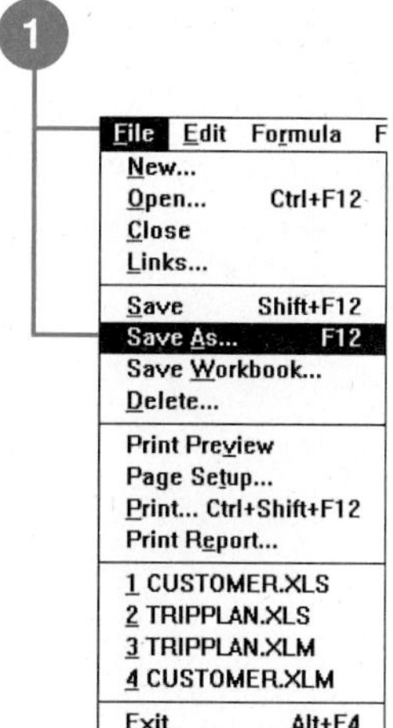

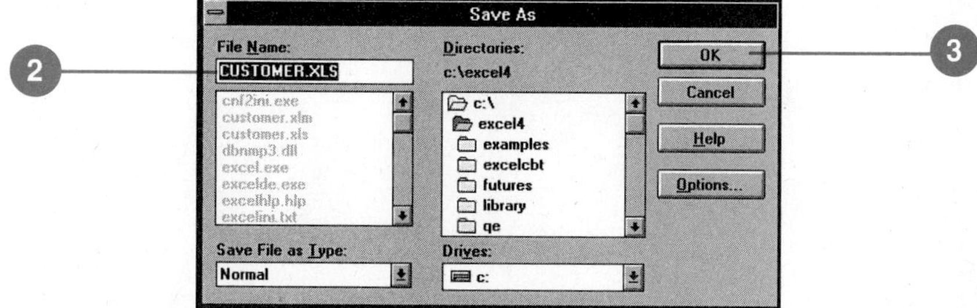

Summary

In any business, managing information is often as important as managing money. A well-designed database can save you time and effort by organizing the flow of information that crosses your desk. This project presented you with a database designed to manage customer information. You can use the template to enter data such as the customer's name, address, company, account number, and phone number. Once you have entered your data, you can use various methods to find, delete, and extract the information you need. Besides information on customers, you can also use this template to store data on other business contacts, colleagues, friends, and family.

	A	C	D	E	F	G	H	I	J	K	L	M	N	O
1		**Sales Forecast Worksheet**												
2		**Regression Analysis by Month**												
3														
4	Actual:	Jan	Feb	Mar	Apr	May	Jun	Jul	Aug	Sep	Oct	Nov	Dec	Total
5	1985	265.3	285.0	280.1	288.9	286.9	292.5	295.0	292.0	295.2	303.3	323.5	320.1	3,527.8
6	1986	330.8	361.1	356.3	348.4	353.6	347.2	344.6	340.0	350.6	389.6	401.5	410.2	4,333.9
7	1987	391.4	402.8	397.4	412.8	432.5	440.2	433.7	441.1	445.0	451.2	452.2	465.0	5,165.3
8	1988	451.2	455.1	465.0	463.3	458.7	475.5	480.2	480.6	479.2	488.3	490.2	495.3	5,682.6
9	1989	355.2	498.3	510.1	505.0	515.3	510.2	505.8	499.3	522.6	515.4	523.9	530.3	5,991.4
10	1990	550.5	560.6	600.4	590.2	605.3	606.0	614.8	603.5	620.4	609.7	616.6	612.3	7,190.3
11	1991	588.4	606.3	612.4	622.4	627.7	625.0	630.4	633.3	638.0	642.0	651.5	646.9	7,524.3
12	Frcst:													
13	1992	615.0	661.1	688.5	686.8	698.4	697.4	703.3	699.8	713.8	702.9	706.5	704.3	8,277.7
14	1993	664.1	713.2	745.6	743.1	755.8	754.0	761.1	757.3	772.6	757.2	759.5	756.1	8,939.4
15	1994	713.1	765.3	802.6	799.4	813.3	810.6	818.9	814.8	831.3	811.5	812.6	807.9	9,601.2
16	1995	762.1	817.3	859.7	855.6	870.7	867.2	876.7	872.2	890.1	865.8	865.7	859.6	10,262.9
17														
18														
19		**Regression Analysis for Consecutive Months**												
20														

	From January, 1985			From January, 1987			From January, 1989		
22		Actual	Frcst		Actual	Frcst		Actual	Frcst
23	Jan-90	550.5	554.5	Jan-90	550.5	554.3	Jan-90	550.5	545.6
24	Feb-90	560.6	559.1	Feb-90	560.6	558.7	Feb-90	560.6	551.0
25	Mar-90	600.4	563.7	Mar-90	600.4	563.1	Mar-90	600.4	556.3
26	Apr-90	590.2	568.3	Apr-90	590.2	567.4	Apr-90	590.2	561.7
27	May-90	605.3	572.9	May-90	605.3	571.8	May-90	605.3	567.1
28	Jun-90	606.0	577.5	Jun-90	606.0	576.2	Jun-90	606.0	572.5
29	Jul-90	614.8	582.1	Jul-90	614.8	580.5	Jul-90	614.8	577.9
30	Aug-90	603.5	586.8	Aug-90	603.5	584.9	Aug-90	603.5	583.2
31	Sep-90	620.4	591.4	Sep-90	620.4	589.3	Sep-90	620.4	588.6
32	Oct-90	609.7	596.0	Oct-90	609.7	593.7	Oct-90	609.7	594.0
33	Nov-90	616.6	600.6	Nov-90	616.6	598.0	Nov-90	616.6	599.4
34	Dec-90	612.3	605.2	Dec-90	612.3	602.4	Dec-90	612.3	604.7
35	Jan-91	588.4	609.8	Jan-91	588.4	606.8	Jan-91	588.4	610.1
36	Feb-91	606.3	614.4	Feb-91	606.3	611.1	Feb-91	606.3	615.5
37	Mar-91	612.4	619.0	Mar-91	612.4	615.5	Mar-91	612.4	620.9
38	Apr-91	622.4	623.6	Apr-91	622.4	619.9	Apr-91	622.4	626.2
39	May-91	627.7	628.2	May-91	627.7	624.3	May-91	627.7	631.6
40	Jun-91	625.0	632.8	Jun-91	625.0	628.6	Jun-91	625.0	637.0
41	Jul-91	630.4	637.4	Jul-91	630.4	633.0	Jul-91	630.4	642.4
42	Aug-91	633.3	642.1	Aug-91	633.3	637.4	Aug-91	633.3	647.8
43	Sep-91	638.0	646.7	Sep-91	638.0	641.7	Sep-91	638.0	653.1
44	Oct-91	642.0	651.3	Oct-91	642.0	646.1	Oct-91	642.0	658.5
45	Nov-91	651.5	655.9	Nov-91	651.5	650.5	Nov-91	651.5	663.9
46	Dec-91	646.9	660.5	Dec-91	646.9	654.9	Dec-91	646.9	669.3
47	Jan-92		665.1	Jan-92		659.2	Jan-92		674.6
48	Feb-92		669.7	Feb-92		663.6	Feb-92		680.0
49	Mar-92		674.3	Mar-92		668.0	Mar-92		685.4
50	Apr-92		678.9	Apr-92		672.3	Apr-92		690.8
51	May-92		683.5	May-92		676.7	May-92		696.2
52	Jun-92		688.1	Jun-92		681.1	Jun-92		701.5

Project 11

Sales Forecasting Worksheet

In these complex and uncertain times, forecasting business performance has become increasingly important. Today, more than ever, managers at all levels need to make intelligent predictions of future sales and profit trends as part of their overall business strategy. By forecasting sales 6 months, a year, or even 3 years down the road, you can anticipate related needs such as employee acquisitions, warehouse space, and raw material requirements. Similarly, a profit forecast enables you to plan the future expansion of your company.

Business forecasting has been around for many years and a number of methods have been developed, some more successful than others. The most common forecasting method is the qualitative "seat-of-the-pants" approach where a manager (or a group of managers) estimates future trends based on experience and knowledge of the market. This method, however, suffers from an inherent subjectivity and a short-term focus, because most managers tend to extrapolate from recent experience and ignore the long-term trend. Other methods, such as averaging past results, are more objective but are generally useful only for forecasting a few months in advance.

This project uses a technique called *linear regression analysis*. Regression is a powerful statistical procedure that has become a popular business tool. In its general form, you use regression analysis to determine the relationship between a dependent variable (e.g., car sales) and one or more independent variables (e.g., interest rates and disposable income). The model created for this project uses the simplest case where sales is considered to be a function of time. Essentially, this model determines the trend over time of past sales and extrapolates the trend in a straight line to determine future sales.

This project uses sales as an example; however, you can use the worksheet to forecast expenses, profits, or any other quantity for which you have historical data. Be sure to save each type of forecast under a different name. See the section entitled "Saving FORECAST.XLS Under a New Name."

Opening the Worksheet

The sales forecast worksheet is called FORECAST.XLS. To follow along with the steps in this project, you need to open this file.

1. Choose File Open.
2. Select the drive and directory where you copied the disk files.
3. Highlight the FORECAST.XLS file.
4. Select OK or press Enter.

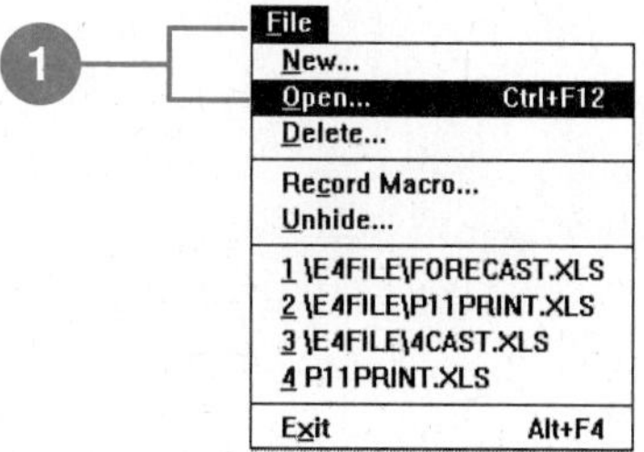

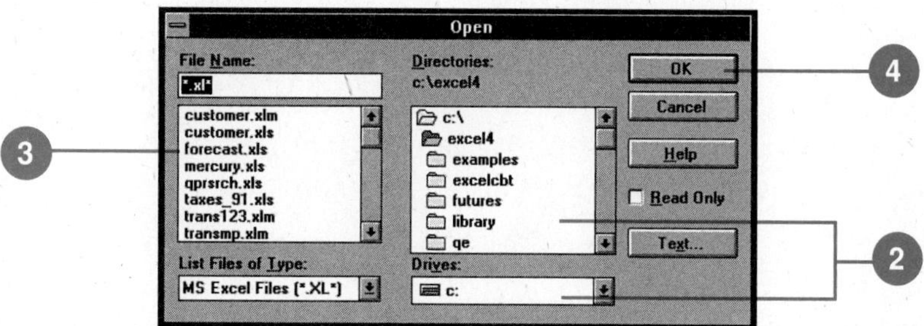

About FORECAST.XLS

The FORECAST.XLS worksheet is divided into two areas. The first area, Regression Analysis by Month, displays two tables where each column is a specific month and each row is a specific year. The INPUT table (the range C6:N12) enables you to enter up to 7 years of historical data by month. The OUTPUT table (range C14:N17) displays forecasts for each month for up to 4 years. This area of the worksheet also includes a Total column (Column O) that automatically sums the data for each year. You can use this column to establish a 4-year forecast based on the yearly totals.

The second area of the worksheet, Regression Analysis for Consecutive Months, displays four tables with three columns each to show the month, the actual sales (up to the current month), and a forecast (up to December 1995). Each table is designed to establish the overall monthly sales trend from a given point in time. TABLE 1 begins with January 1985, TABLE 2 with January 1987, TABLE 3 with January 1989, and TABLE 4 with January 1991. The actual sales in each table are linked to the INPUT table in the Regression Analysis by Month section. This saves you from having to reenter your sales numbers.

As you can see, the sales forecast worksheet can provide you with a great deal of information, most of which should be useful no matter what type of business you are in. However, certain types of analysis are more useful in different situations:

- If your business exhibits a pronounced seasonal sales trend, then you should get the most use out of the Regression Analysis by Month section. For example, if your company normally experiences high sales in November and December, and low sales in January and February, you need to see individual trends for each of these months.
- If your company's sales stepped up (i.e., jumped to a higher level as a result of, say, acquiring another company) at some point in the past, include only data since the step-up occurred. The earlier data will tend to make your forecasts too low. For example, if the step-up occurred in 1986, do not use TABLE 1 (because it includes data from 1985).

The worksheet forecasts all use a variation of Excel's TREND function. This function has the general form

TREND(*known_y's*, *known_x's*, *new_x's*, *const*)

In this function, *known_y's* is a range representing the known dependent variables, *known_x's* is a range representing the known independent variables, *new_x's* is a range representing the forecast independent variables, and *const* is an optional constant used by the function. This function uses linear regression to establish a straight-line trend through the *known_y's* and *known_x's*. After the trend is found, the function extends the straight line to determine the forecast values associated with the *new_x's*.

In FORECAST.XLS, the following variation of TREND is used:

TREND(*sales_data*, , *time_period*)

Here, *sales_data* is a named range representing the actual sales you enter, and *time_period* specifies the time period you want to forecast. By leaving out the *known_x's* argument, Excel substitutes the default array {1, 2, 3 . . .}. This is equivalent to calculating the trend over time.

As an example, suppose the named range Jan contains the actual January sales from 1985 through 1991, for a total of 7 months of data. The function TREND(Jan,8) tells Excel to calculate the forecast for the eighth time period or, in this case, January 1992.

Entering Historical Data

The sales forecast worksheet is driven entirely by the historical data you enter into the INPUT table. The steps in this section assume you are entering data for all 7 years. If you do not have that much data, see the section entitled "Using Less Historical Data" later in this chapter. If you would like to use more data, see the section entitled "Using Less Historical Data in the INPUT Table."

1. Select cell C6 (January 1985).
2. Enter the amount.
3. Repeat steps 1–2 for the other months of the year. Do not enter anything in the Total column.
4. Repeat steps 1–3 for the other years.
5. Press F9 to calculate the forecasts.

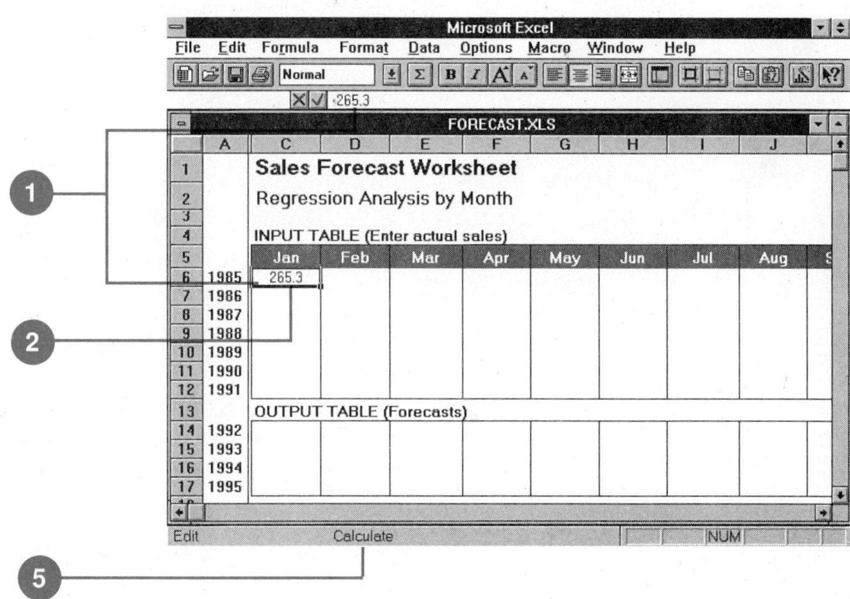

Using Less Historical Data in the INPUT Table

The INPUT table assumes that you have 7 years worth of historical data to enter. The OUTPUT table also makes this assumption, and its TREND functions are set up accordingly. You may want to use less data in your forecasts for a number of reasons:

- ▲ You do not have 7 years of data.
- ▲ You do not feel you need to enter that much data.
- ▲ You have entered the data for all 7 years but want to set up a monthly forecast for a smaller number of years.

For each of these situations, you can easily customize the INPUT table to handle fewer years by redefining the data ranges associated with each month. For example, January has a range named Jan given by the coordinates C6:C12 (the years 1985 to 1991). The January 1992 forecast is given by the function TREND(Jan,,ROWS(Jan)+1). Because this function references only the Jan range, updating Jan automatically updates the forecast. Other months are similar. For example, February has a range named Feb from D6:D12, and so on.

You can use one of two methods to customize the INPUT table:

- ▲ You can delete each row that contains a year you do not need.
- ▲ You can redefine the individual data ranges.

Deleting an INPUT Table Year

When you delete a row from the INPUT table, Excel automatically redefines the data ranges. Use this method if you are sure you will never use the years you delete.

1. Select a cell in the row containing the year you want to delete.
2. Choose Edit Delete. Excel displays the Delete dialog box.
3. Select Entire Row.
4. Select OK.
5. Repeat steps 1–4 for other years you want to delete.
6. Press F9 to recalculate the forecasts.

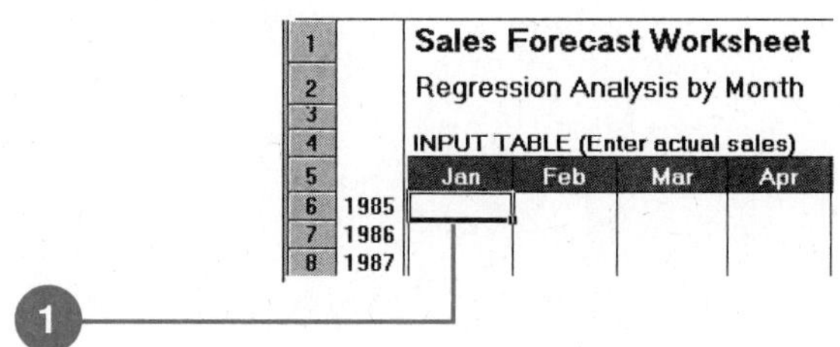

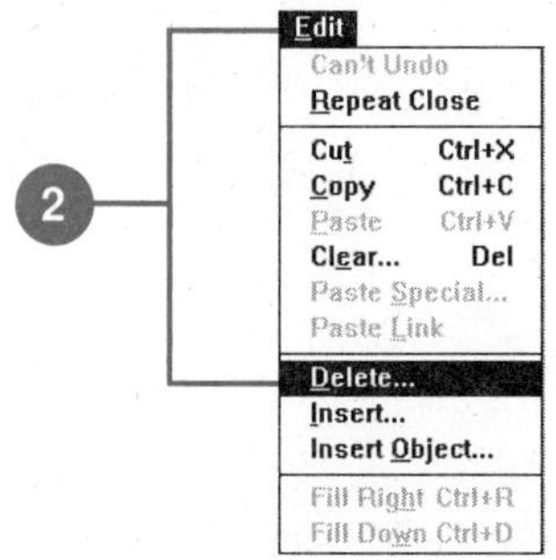

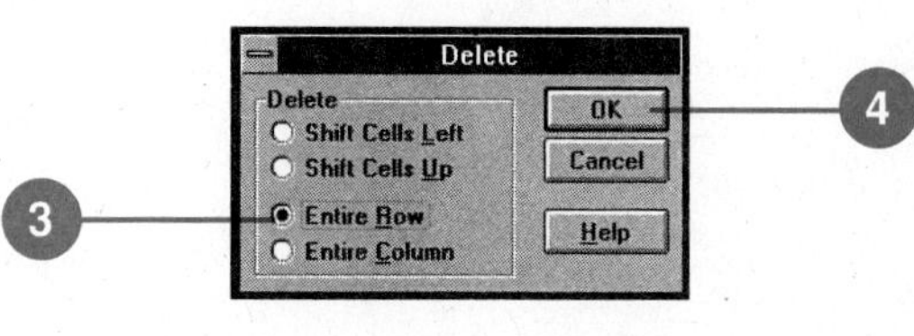

Redefining the INPUT Table Data Ranges

If you prefer to leave the INPUT table intact, you can modify the monthly forecasts to use fewer years by redefining the data range associated with each month. The name of each data range is the same as the label for each INPUT table column (i.e., Jan, Feb, Mar, etc.). For example, to change the January data range so that it references only the years 1988 to 1991, you would redefine the coordinates of the Jan range to C9:C12.

1. Choose Formula Define Name.
2. In the Names in **S**heet list box, select the range name for the month you want.
3. In the **R**efers to text box, enter the new range.
4. Select the Add button. Excel redefines the range.
5. Repeat steps 2–4 for the other months. Be sure to include the Total range to update the yearly forecasts.
6. Select OK or press Enter.
7. Press F9 to recalculate the forecasts.

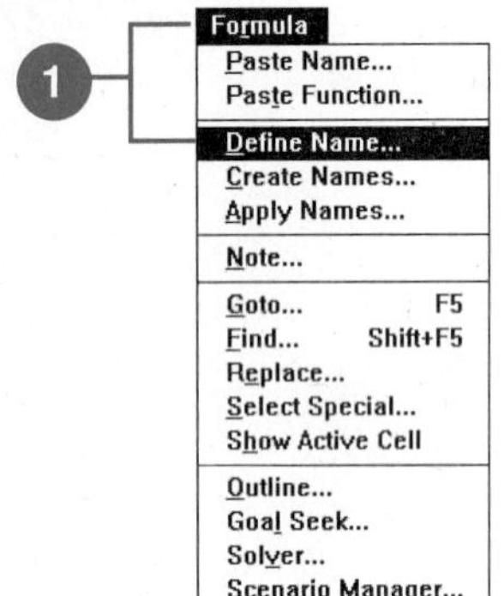

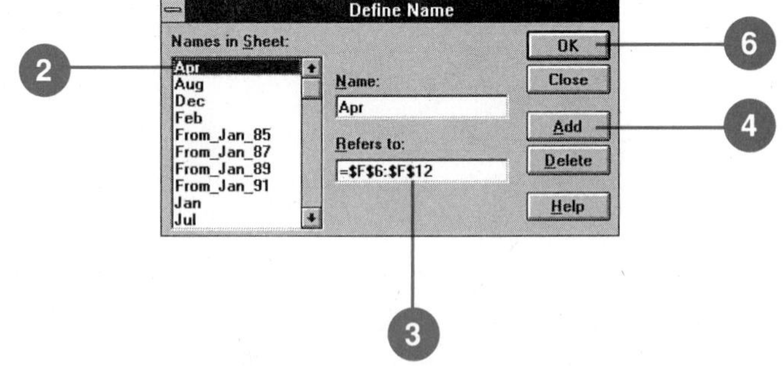

Using More Historical Data in the INPUT Table

Although 7 years of data should be adequate for most of your needs, you may want to analyze your data over the very long term. To do this, you will need to add years prior to 1985 to both the INPUT table and TABLE 1. This section shows you how to make the necessary customizations to the INPUT table. For TABLE 1, see the section entitled "Using More Historical Data in TABLE 1."

To add a year to the INPUT table, you must first insert a row at the top of the table and then redefine the data ranges as you learned in the section entitled "Using Less Historical Data in the INPUT Table."

Adding a Row to the INPUT Table

To make room for the new data, you need to add a row at the top of the table. To get a Total for the added year, you also need to copy the SUM formula in Column O.

1. Select a cell in the row below the column labels.
2. Choose Edit Insert.
3. Select Entire Row.
4. Select OK or press Enter.
5. Select cell A6.
6. Enter the year.

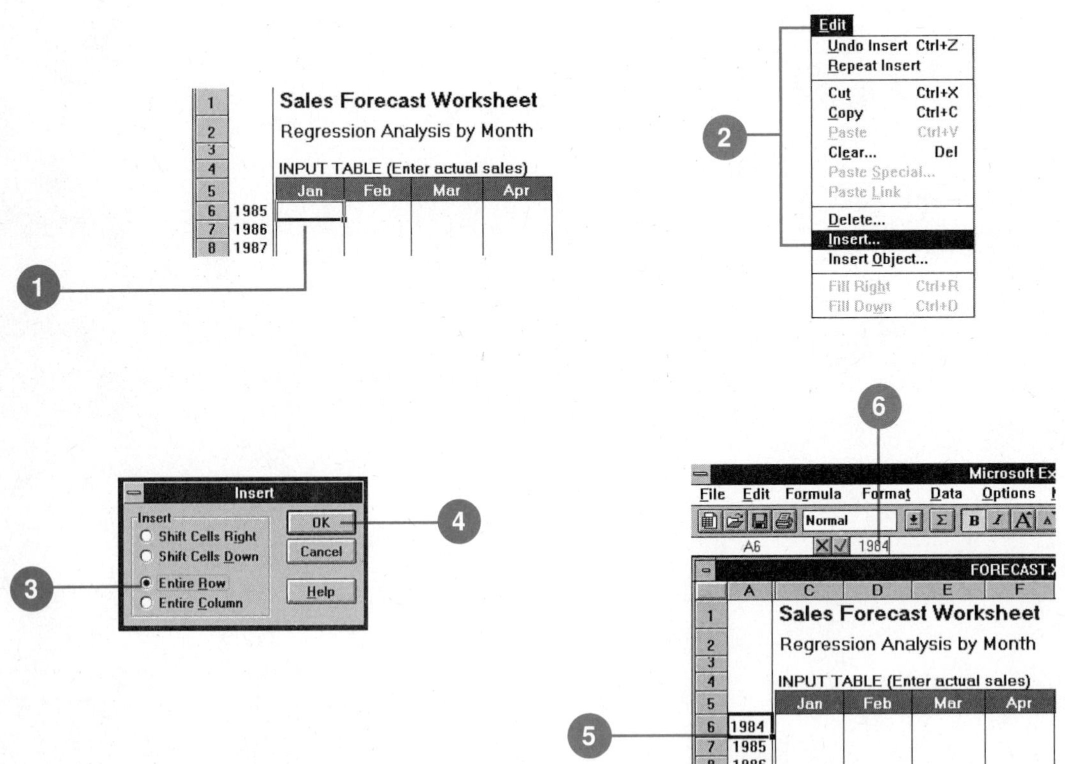

7. Select cell O7.
8. Choose Edit Copy.
9. Select cell O6.
10. Choose Edit Paste Special. Excel copies the formula to the new year.
11. Select the range A7:O7 and choose Edit Copy.
12. Select cell A6 and choose Edit Paste Special.
13. In the Paste Special dialog box, select Formats, and then select OK or press Enter.
14. Repeat steps 2–3 to add other years.
15. Enter the data for the new years.

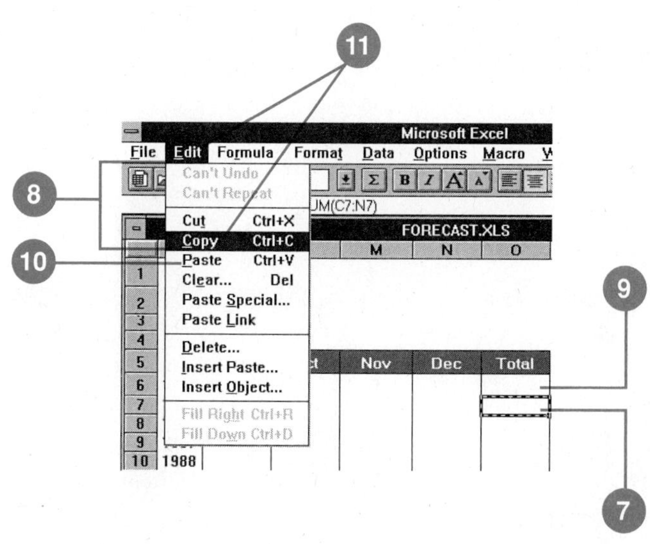

Redefining the INPUT Table Data Ranges

After you have added the data for the new years, you need to redefine the INPUT table data ranges before you can recalculate your forecasts.

1. Choose Formula Define Name.
2. In the Names in **S**heet list box, select the range name for the month you want.
3. In the **R**efers to text box, enter the new range.
4. Select the Add button. Excel redefines the range.
5. Repeat steps 2–4 for the other months. Be sure to include the Total range to update the yearly forecasts.
6. Select OK or press Enter.
7. Press F9 to recalculate the forecasts.

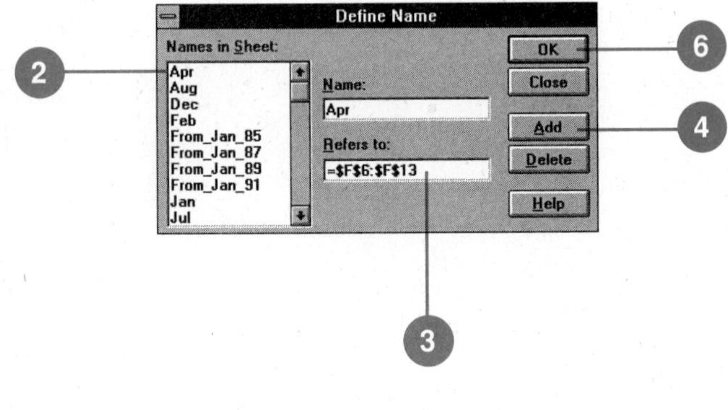

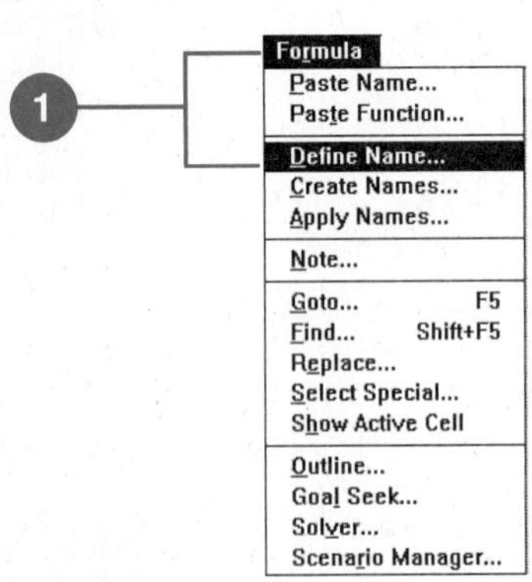

Using More Historical Data in TABLE 1

Before you add years to TABLE 1, you need to understand how the Regression Analysis for Consecutive Months tables work. As an example, consider TABLE 1. The forecasts generated in this table, although similar to those in the OUTPUT table, operate in a slightly different way. Here, the trend is calculated starting with the first month. These "forecasts" show you the trend line generated by the regression analysis. (As an exercise, you should graph the Actual data with the Forecast values. Use a line chart for best results.) The data range used in TABLE 1 is called From_Jan_85 and is defined by the coordinates D24:D107 (these coordinates will be different if you have added rows to the INPUT table). The time periods are taken from the numbers you see in Column A. The other TABLES operate similarly.

To use more historical data in TABLE 1, you need to perform three steps:

1. Add the new historical data to the INPUT table. (See the section entitled "Using More Historical Data in the INPUT Table.")
2. Insert the appropriate number of rows in TABLE 1.
3. Adjust the data range and time periods and fill in the new forecast formulas.

Adding Rows to TABLE 1

To make room for the new data, you need to add an appropriate number of rows at the top of TABLE 1. This section assumes you want to add a single year of data (1984) and that you have already modified the INPUT table.

1. Highlight the range C25:D36.
2. Choose Edit Insert.
3. Select Shift Cells Down.
4. Select OK or press Enter. Excel inserts 12 new rows.

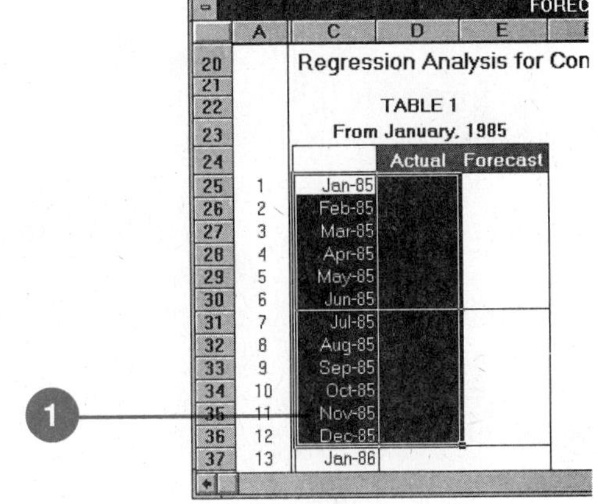

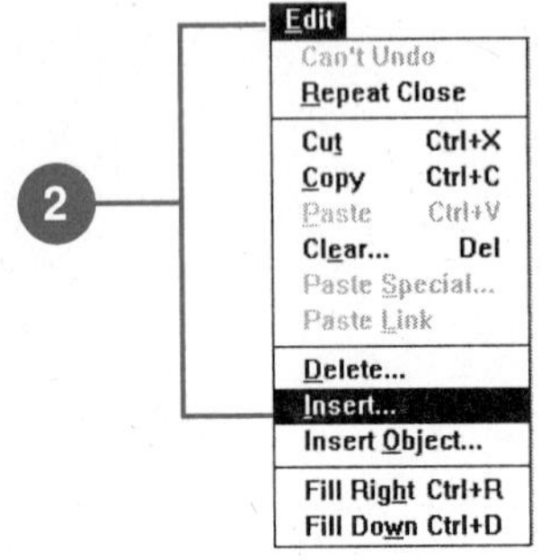

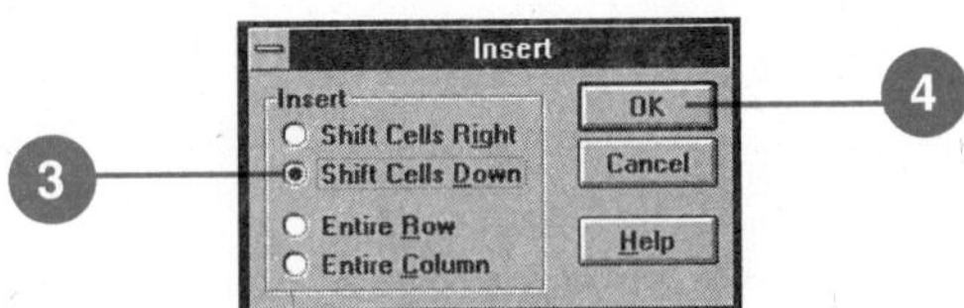

Filling the New Rows with Data

The new rows you added in the previous section are empty. To prepare them for calculation, you need to add the appropriate months and link the Actual column to the INPUT table. This section uses Excel's new AutoFill feature. To use this feature, choose **O**ptions **W**orkspace and then select Cell **D**rag and Drop.

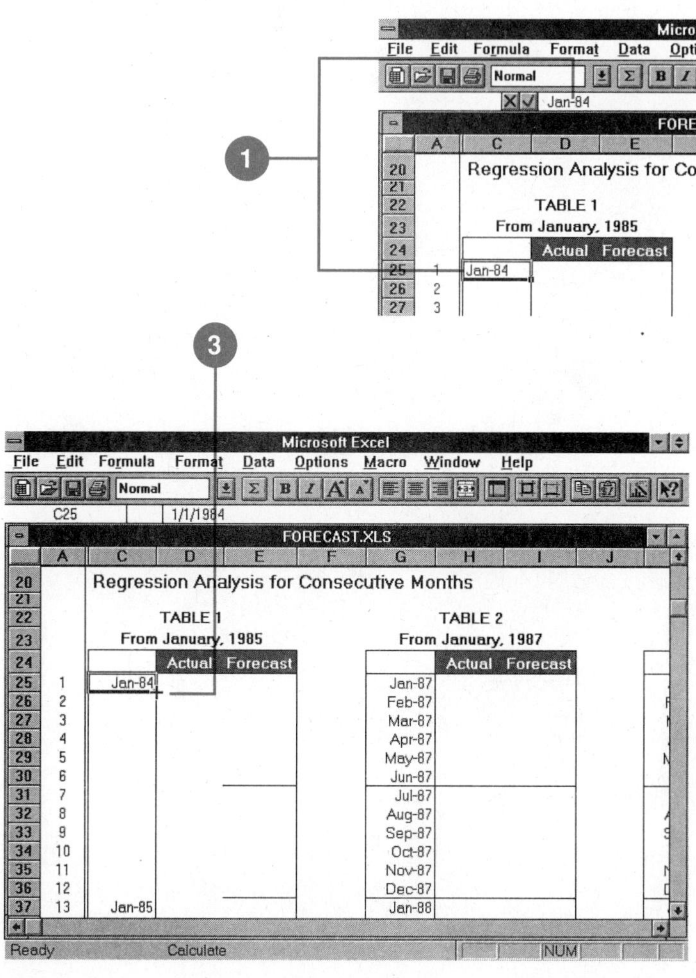

1. Select cell C25 and type **Jan-84**.
2. Press Enter.
3. Select cell C25 and position the mouse on the lower right corner of the cell. The pointer changes to a black cross.
4. Press and hold down the left mouse button.
5. Drag the mouse to cell C36.
6. Release the mouse button. Excel fills the cells with the other months.
7. Select cell D25.
8. Type **=C6** to link the cell with the January 1984 value in the INPUT table.
9. Repeat steps 7–8 to link the other new cells in the Actual column.

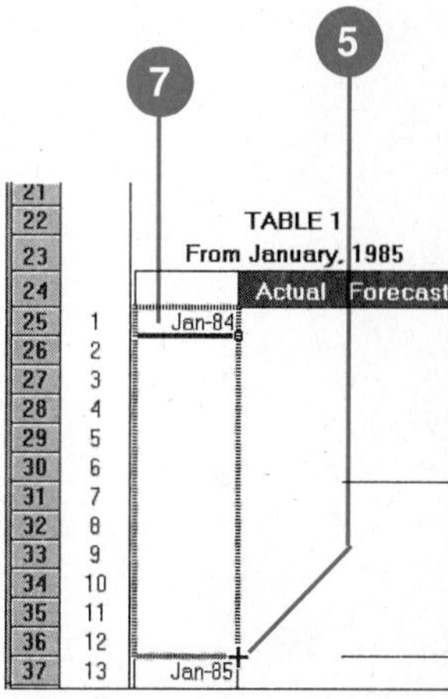

Redefining the TABLE 1 Data Range

After you have added the data for the new years, you need to redefine the TABLE 1 data range.

1. Choose Formula Define Name. Excel displays the Define Name dialog box.
2. In the Names in Sheet list box, select From_Jan_85.
3. In the Name text box, change the name to **From_Jan_84**.
4. In the Refers to text box, change the upper left coordinate of the range to **$D$25**.
5. Select OK or press Enter.

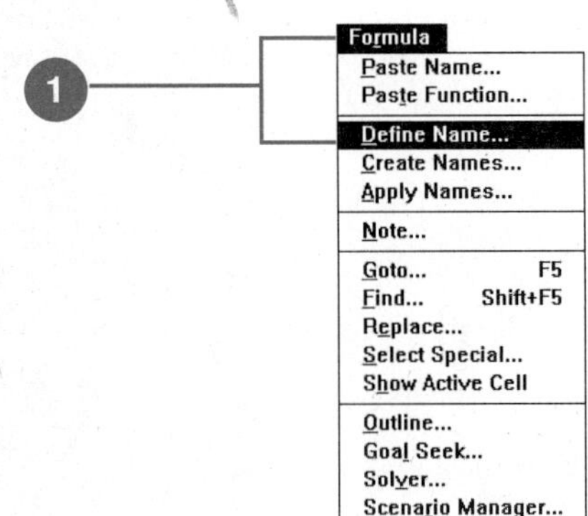

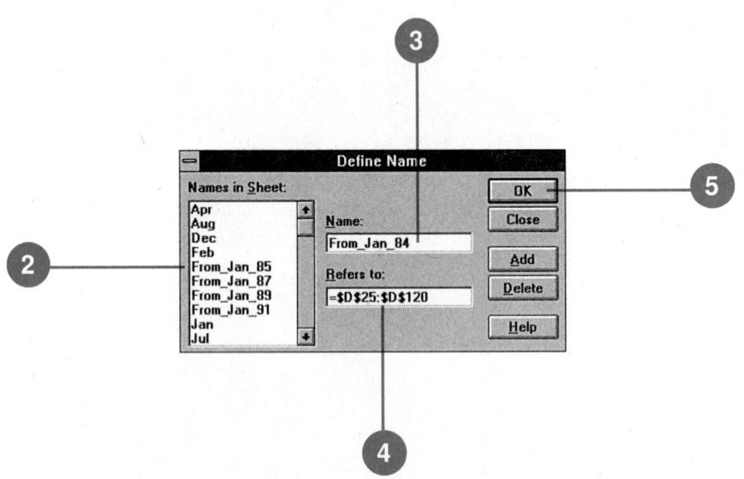

Extending the Time Periods

When you added the new rows to TABLE 1, the old rows were shifted down. You now need to extend the time periods in Column A to the bottom of the table.

1. Highlight the range A156:A168.
2. Choose Data Series.
3. Select Columns.
4. Select Linear.
5. Enter 1 for the **S**tep Value.
6. Select OK or press Enter. Excel fills in the time periods.

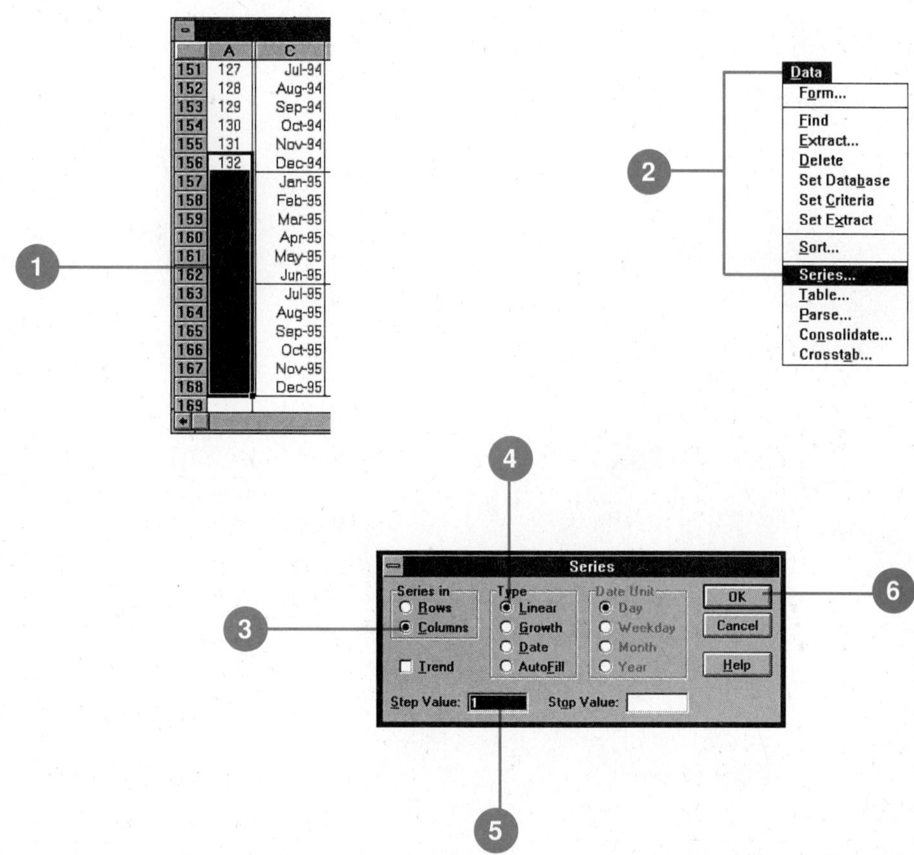

Modifying the Forecast Formulas

To get the proper forecast values, you need to modify the TREND functions used in TABLE 1 so that they refer to the new data range and the new time periods.

1. Select cell E25.
2. Enter `=TREND(From_Jan_84,,A25)`.
3. Select cell E25 and position the mouse on the lower right corner of the cell. The pointer changes to a black cross.
4. Press and hold down the left mouse button.
5. Drag the mouse to cell E168.
6. Release the mouse button. Excel fills the cells with the new formula.
7. Press F9 to recalculate the forecasts.

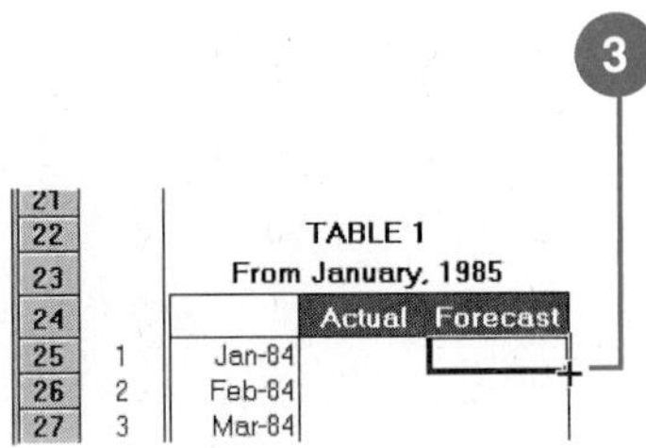

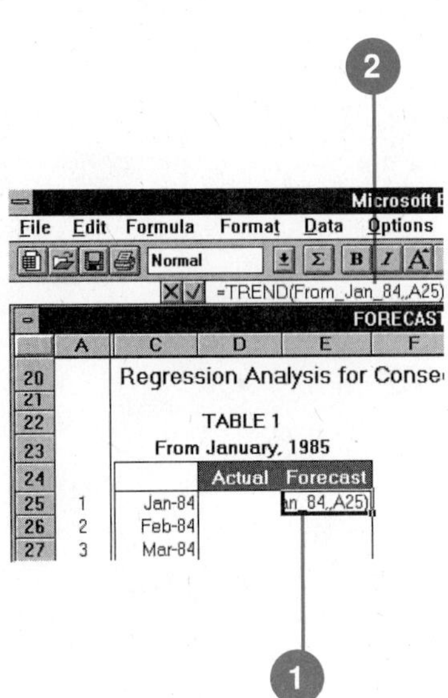

5

	A	C	D	E
159	135	Mar-95		
160	136	Apr-95		
161	137	May-95		
162	138	Jun-95		
163	139	Jul-95		
164	140	Aug-95		
165	141	Sep-95		
166	142	Oct-95		
167	143	Nov-95		
168	144	Dec-95		
169				

Adding New Actual Sales

To keep the worksheet up to date, you need to enter your monthly sales numbers as you get them. The easiest way to do this is to simply replace the forecast value with the actual value in the appropriate cell of the OUTPUT table. Later, at the end of the year, you can move these new actual sales figures from the OUTPUT table to the INPUT table.

After you have replaced a forecast value with an actual value for a given month, you can use the new value to update the remaining forecasts for that month. You also need to adjust the data ranges in each of the Regression Analysis for Consecutive Months tables.

For convenience, the default FORECAST.XLS worksheet assumes you will enter historical data only up to December 1991. By the time you use this worksheet, you may have a number of months of actual 1992 sales. To "catch up," you can use the method described in this section to add any actual sales figures you may have from 1992.

Replacing OUTPUT Table Forecasts with Actual Sales

After entering an actual sales figure in the appropriate OUTPUT table cell, you also need to adjust the data range for the month to include the new value. In this way, you include the new value in the remaining forecasts for that month. As an example, the steps in this section enter an actual sales figure for January 1992. The cell references assume you are using the default FORECAST.XLS worksheet.

1. Select cell C14 (January 1992 in the OUTPUT table).
2. Enter the actual sales figure.
3. Choose Formula Define Name.
4. In the Names in Sheet list box, select Jan.
5. In the **R**efers to text box, change the coordinates of the range to `$C$6:$C$12,$C$14`.
6. Select OK or press Enter.
7. Select cell C15.
8. Modify the formula to read `TREND(Jan,,ROWS(Jan)+1)`.
9. Select cell C16.
10. Modify the formula to read `TREND(Jan,,ROWS(Jan)+2)`.
11. Select cell C17.
12. Modify the formula to read `TREND(Jan,,ROWS(Jan)+3)`.

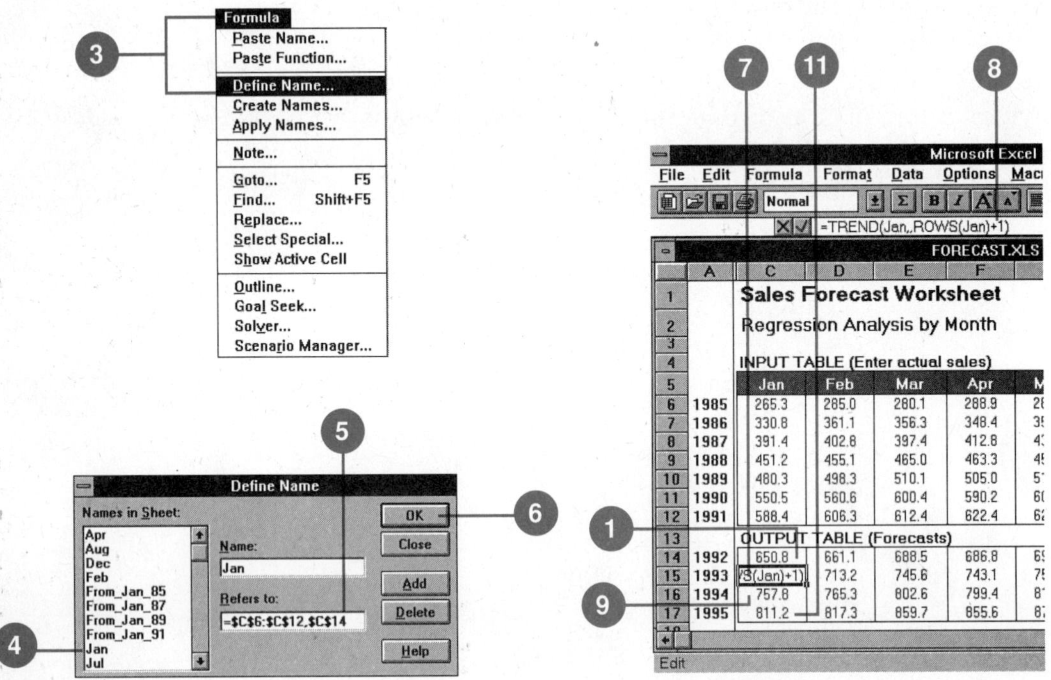

	A	C	D	E	F
5		Jan	Feb	Mar	Apr
6	1985	265.3	285.0	280.1	288.9
7	1986	330.8	361.1	356.3	348.4
8	1987	391.4	402.8	397.4	412.8
9	1988	451.2	455.1	465.0	463.3
10	1989	480.3	498.3	510.1	505.0
11	1990	550.5	560.6	600.4	590.2
12	1991	588.4	606.3	612.4	622.4
14	1992	650.8	661.1	688.5	686.8
15	1993	S(Jan)+1)	713.2	745.6	743.1
16	1994	757.8	765.3	802.6	799.4
17	1995	811.2	817.3	859.7	855.6

Updating the Consecutive Month Tables

To update the Regression Analysis for Consecutive Months tables for the new data, you need to link the appropriate cell to the new sales value and adjust the data range for each table. This section assumes that you have entered a new actual sales figure in the OUTPUT table. The cell references assume that you are using the default FORECAST.XLS worksheet. As an example, the steps update the tables for a new actual sales figure for January 1992.

1. Select the January 1992 cell in TABLE 1 (cell D108).
2. Enter **=C14**. (January 1992 in the OUTPUT table).
3. Repeat steps 1–2 for TABLE 2 (cell H84), TABLE 3 (cell L60), and TABLE 4 (cell P36).
4. Choose Formula Define Name.
5. In the Names in **S**heet list box, select From_Jan_85.
6. In the **R**efers to text box, change the coordinates of the range to **$D$24:$D$108**.
7. Repeat steps 5–6 for TABLE 2 (From_Jan_87, **$H$24:$H$84**), TABLE 3 (From_Jan_89, **$L$24:$L$60**), and TABLE 4 (From_Jan_91, **$P$24:$P$36**).
8. Select OK or press Enter.

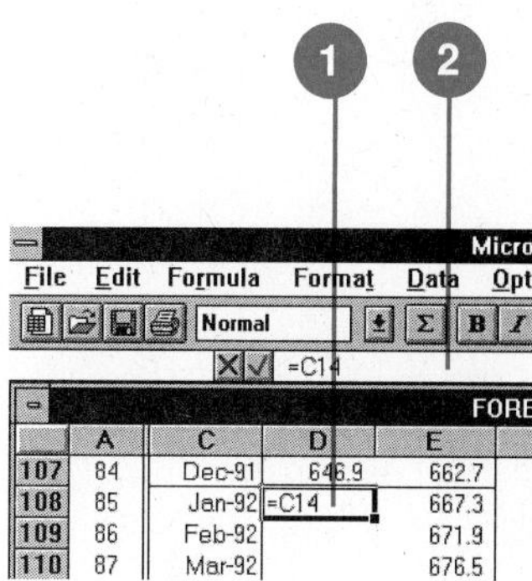

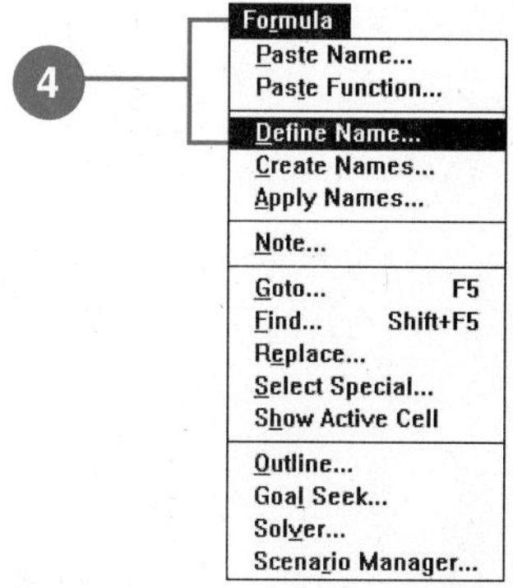

Saving FORECAST.XLS Under a New Name

Besides sales figures, you can use FORECAST.XLS to forecast expenses, profits, returns, and any other item where you have enough monthly historical data. To preserve the default FORECAST.XLS worksheet, you need to save your work under a different name.

1. Choose File Save As.
2. Replace the file name in the File Name text box with the new name you want to use.
3. Select OK or press Enter.

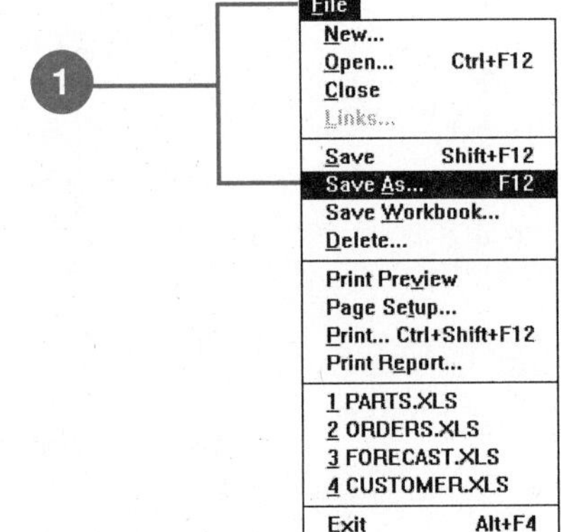

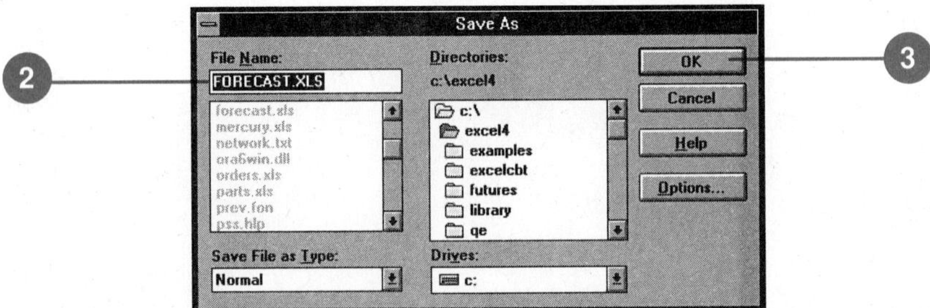

Summary

Business forecasting always gains added importance in uncertain economic times. In today's world, managers need to make intelligent predictions about their company's (or their division's) sales, expenses and profits. If you have some idea of what these numbers will look like a few months—or a few years—down the road, you will be better equipped to plan the future course of your business.

This project provided you with a forecasting model that uses linear regression analysis. You can use this powerful statistical technique to determine the trend over time of your sales and profits, and then use this trend to develop a forecast by month or by year.

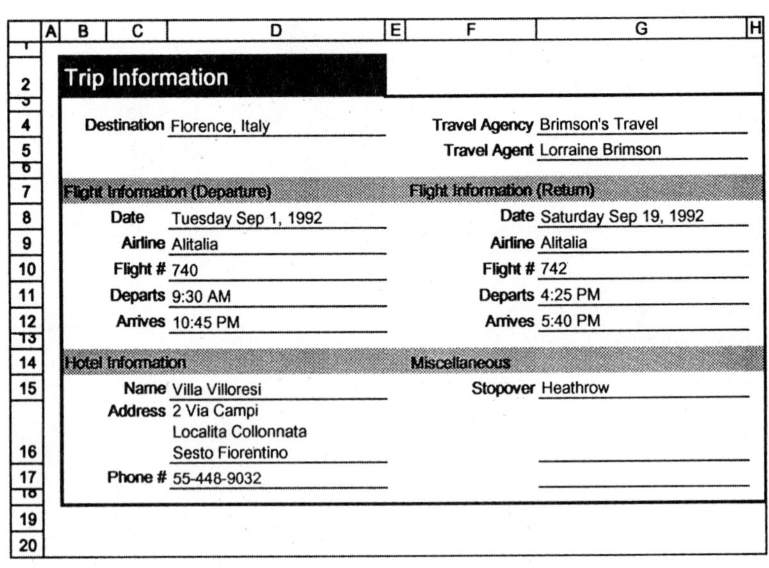

Trip Information

Destination	Florence, Italy	**Travel Agency**	Brimson's Travel
		Travel Agent	Lorraine Brimson
Flight Information (Departure)		**Flight Information (Return)**	
Date	Tuesday Sep 1, 1992	**Date**	Saturday Sep 19, 1992
Airline	Alitalia	**Airline**	Alitalia
Flight #	740	**Flight #**	742
Departs	9:30 AM	**Departs**	4:25 PM
Arrives	10:45 PM	**Arrives**	5:40 PM
Hotel Information		**Miscellaneous**	
Name	Villa Villoresi	**Stopover**	Heathrow
Address	2 Via Campi Localita Collonnata Sesto Fiorentino		
Phone #	55-448-9032		

Project

12

Trip Planner Worksheet

Whether you are traveling for business or pleasure, across the country or across the ocean, for a few days or a few weeks, planning your trip carefully is the best way to avoid headaches and problems. By taking care of the details in a timely manner before you leave, you will be free to get the most out of your trip.

To help you with these details, this project presents a trip planner worksheet. No matter what kind of trip you take, you can use this worksheet to:

- ▲ Record vital trip information.
- ▲ Calculate trip costs.
- ▲ Set up a preparation schedule.
- ▲ Run through a packing checklist.

You will also learn how to customize the worksheet for your own needs, because no two trips or travelers are alike.

Opening the Worksheet

The trip planner worksheet is called TRIPPLAN.XLS. To follow along with the steps in this project, you need to open this file.

1. Choose File Open.

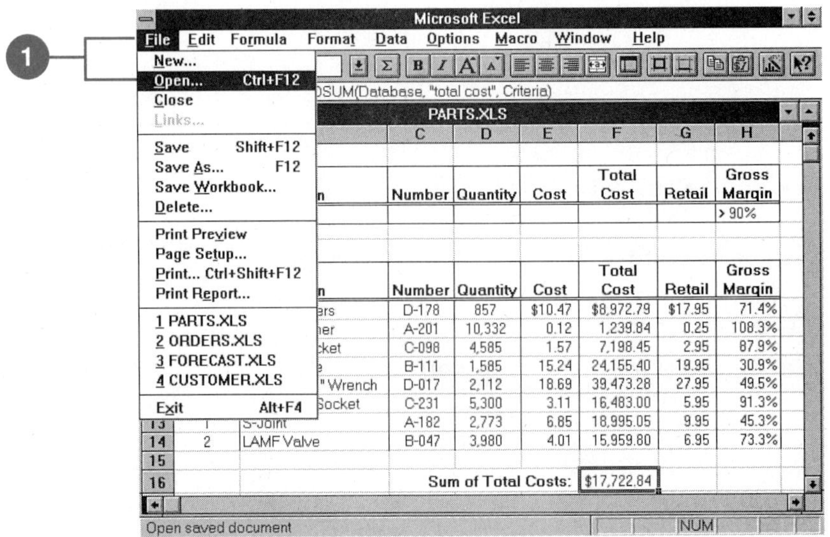

2. Select the drive and directory where you copied the disk files.

3. Highlight the TRIPPLAN.XLS file.

4. Select OK or press Enter. Excel opens TRIPPLAN.XLS.

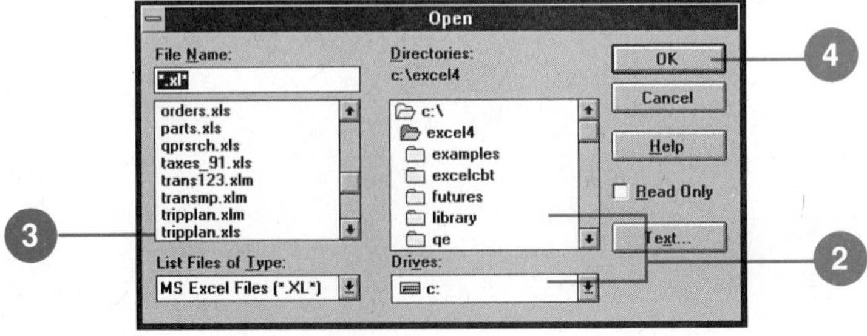

About TRIPPLAN.XLS

TRIPPLAN.XLS is divided into five sections:

Trip Information. Use this section to record basic information about your trip (e.g., destination, departure and return dates, and flight information).

Emergency Information. Use this section to record important data (e.g., passport number, ticket information, and credit card numbers).

Cost Calculation. Use this section to calculate the costs of your trip (e.g., flight, hotel, and car rental).

Preparation Schedule. Use this section to set up a schedule for your trip preparation.

Packing Checklists. Use this section to run through various checklists of items to pack for your trip.

Each of these sections has been set up to be as general as possible. You may find that individual sections contain too much or too little information. In this case, you can easily customize each section to suit your needs.

When you load TRIPPLAN.XLS, the worksheet adds an extra menu option to the normal Excel menu bar. This menu, called **P**lanner, contains five options that enable you to move quickly between the five sections of the worksheet. When you close TRIPPLAN.XLS, the menu bar is returned to its previous state.

The TRIPPLAN.XLM macro sheet controls the **P**lanner menu and its associated macros. This sheet is opened automatically every time you open TRIPPLAN.XLS. To examine this file, use the **W**indow **U**nhide command and select the file from the Unhide dialog box that appears.

Entering Trip Information

You use the Trip Information screen to enter some basic information about your trip. This information includes your destination, travel agent, flight data, and hotel particulars. You can print out the Trip Information for a handy at-a-glance summary of your trip (see the section entitled "Printing the Trip Planner").

Filling in the First Section

In the first section of the Trip Information screen, you enter your destination and travel agent data.

1. If the Trip Information screen is not currently displayed, choose Planner Trip Information.
2. Select cell D4 and enter your destination.
3. Select cell G4 and enter the name of your travel agency.
4. Select cell G5 and enter the name of your travel agent.

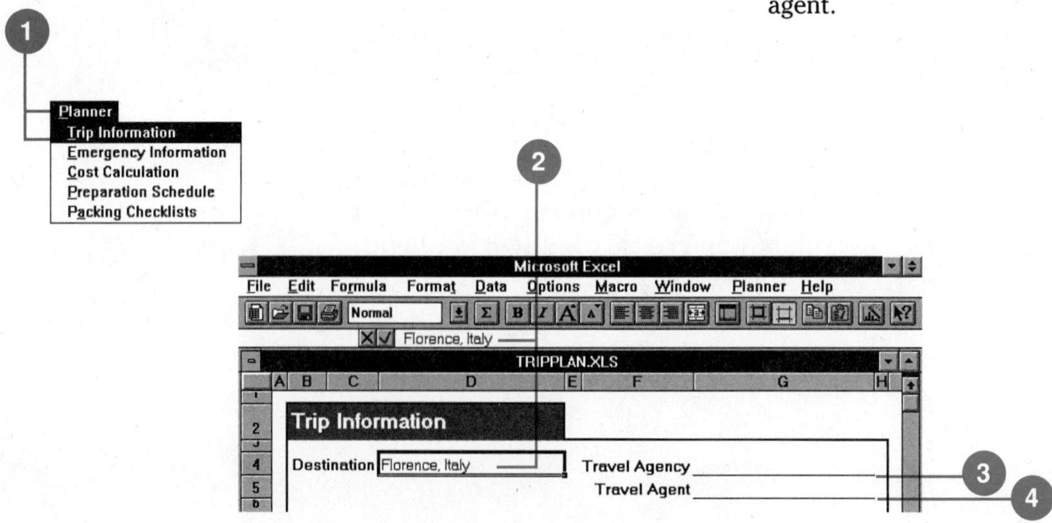

Entering the Flight Information

In the next section of the Trip Information screen, you enter your flight data, including the date, airline, flight number, and times for both your departure and return.

1. Select cell D8 and enter your departure date. This field is preformatted to accept data entered in any Excel date format.
2. Select cell D9 and enter the name of your departure airline.
3. Select cell D10 and enter your departure flight number.
4. Select cell D11 and enter your departure time. This field is preformatted to accept data entered in any Excel time format.
5. Select cell D12 and enter the local time of your arrival. This field has a time format.
6. Select cell G8 and enter your return date. This field has a date format.
7. If your return airline is not the same as your departure airline, select cell G9 and enter the name of your return airline.
8. Select cell G10 and enter your return flight number.
9. Select cell G11 and enter the departure time for your return flight. This field has a time format.
10. Select cell G12 and enter the time of your arrival. This field has a time format.

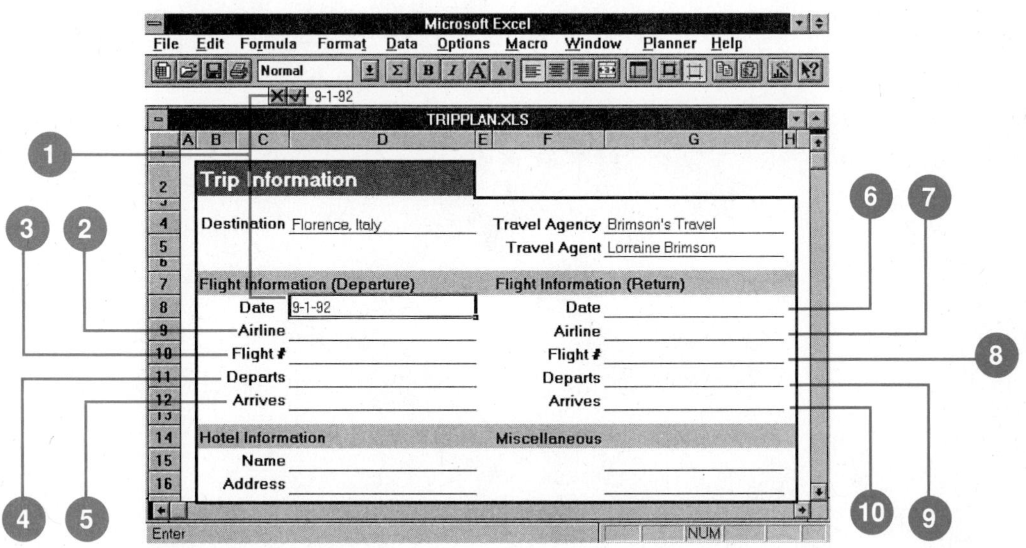

Entering the Hotel Information

In the next section of the Trip Information screen, you enter your hotel data, including the hotel's name, address, and phone number. (To enter hotel costs, use the Cost Calculation screen.)

1. Select cell D15 and enter the name of your hotel.
2. Select cell D16 and enter the address of your hotel. The word wrap feature is turned on for this field so you can enter as much information as you need.
3. Select cell D17 and enter the hotel phone number.

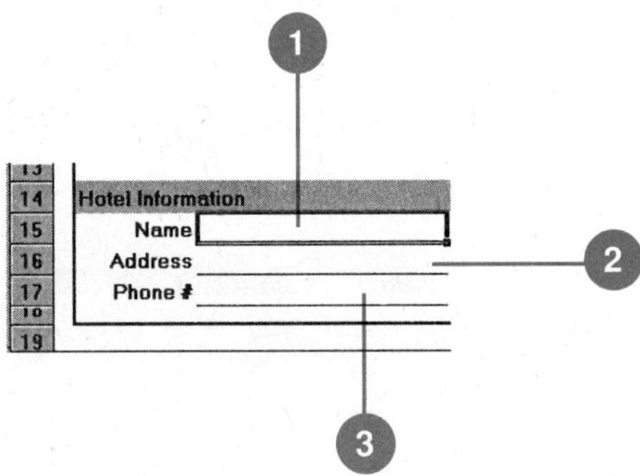

Customizing the Trip Information Screen

The Trip Information screen contains only the very basic information about your trip. If there is other information you want to include (such as flight stop-overs or extra hotel information), you can use the Miscellaneous section to enter the data.

1. Select cell F15 and enter a label for the first field.
2. Select cell G15 and enter the information.
3. Select cell F16 and enter a label for the second field.
4. Select cell G16 and enter the information.
5. Select cell F17 and enter a label for the third field.
6. Select cell G17 and enter the information.

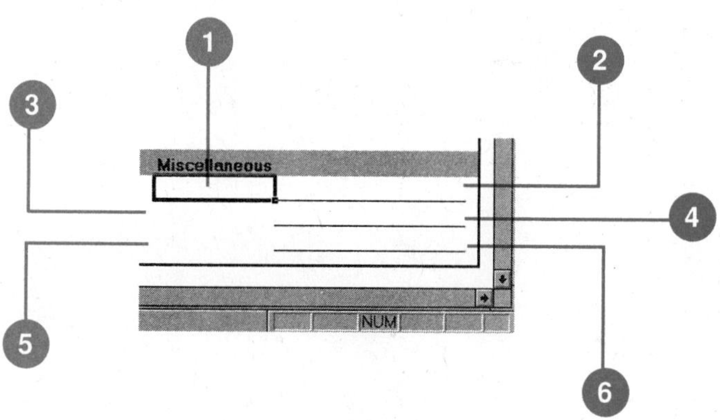

Entering the Emergency Information

You use the Emergency Information screen to record vital data about your airline tickets, passport, home bank, traveler's checks, and credit cards. Print out this information and take it with you when you travel (see the section entitled "Printing the Trip Planner"). When you arrive at your destination, store the printout in a safety deposit box or other secure area. If any of these items are lost or stolen, having a record of the appropriate information will make it easier to obtain replacements.

Displaying the Emergency Information Screen

Use the Planner menu to move to the Emergency Information screen.

1. Choose Planner Emergency Information. Excel displays the Emergency Information screen.

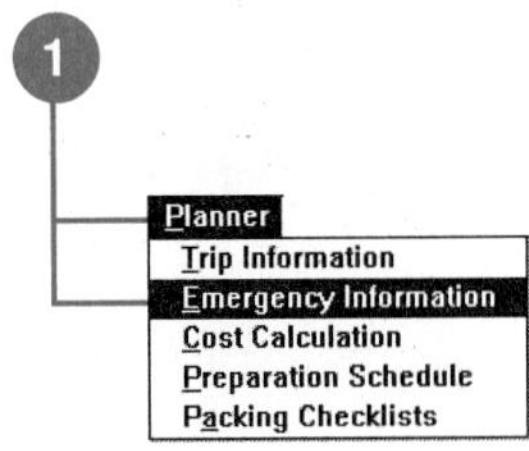

Completing the Airline Ticket Information

If you entered your Trip Information, most of the Airline Tickets section will be filled in automatically. All you need to do to complete this section is enter the ticket numbers.

1. Select cell O32 and enter your departure ticket numbers.
2. Select cell S32 and enter your return ticket numbers.

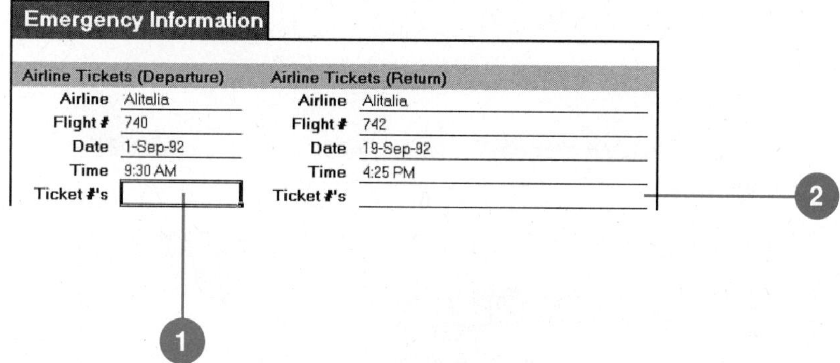

Entering Your Passport and Bank Information

This section holds your passport information (number, the place where it was issued, and the date of issue) and your home bank information (name, address, account number, and phone number).

1. Select cell O35 and enter your passport number.
2. Select cell O36 and enter where your passport was issued.
3. Select cell O37 and enter the date your passport was issued.
4. Select cell S35 and enter the name of your bank.
5. Select cell S36 and enter the address of your bank.
6. Select cell S37 and enter your bank account number.
7. Select cell S38 and enter the phone number of your bank.

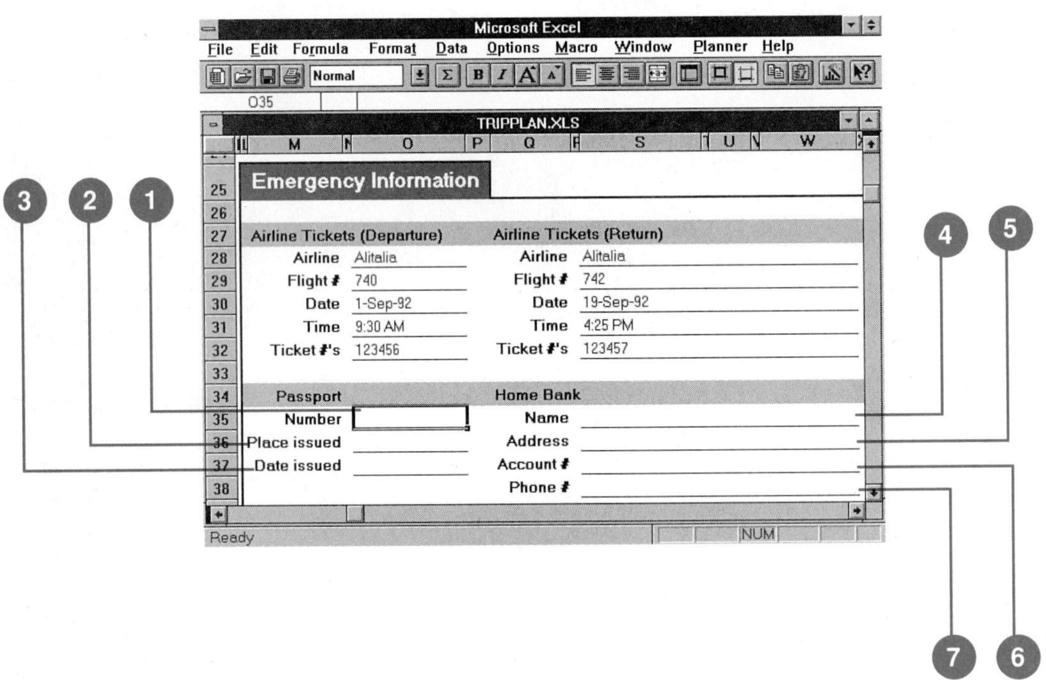

Entering Your Traveler's Check Information

Don't leave home without recording your traveler's checks information. Record the name of the company, its emergency phone number, and the denominations and numbers of your checks.

1. Select cell O41 and enter the name of the traveler's checks company.
2. Select cell O42 and enter the company's emergency phone number.
3. Select cell M44 and enter one of the denominations of your traveler's checks.
4. Select cell O44 and enter the range of check numbers for that denomination.
5. As needed, repeat steps 3–4 in the other traveler's checks fields.

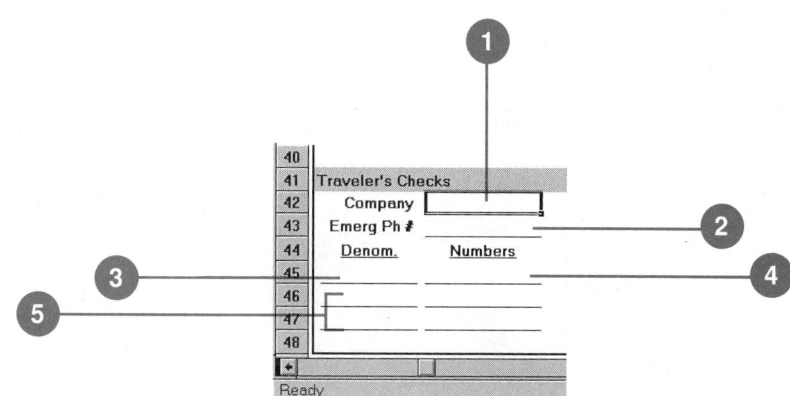

Entering Credit Card Information

For each credit card you take with you, enter the company, the card number, the expiration date, and the company's emergency telephone number.

1. Select cell Q42 and enter the name of the credit card company.
2. Select cell S42 and enter the card number.
3. Select cell U42 and enter the card expiration date.
4. Select cell W42 and enter the credit card company's emergency phone number.
5. As needed, repeat steps 1–4 in the other credit card fields.

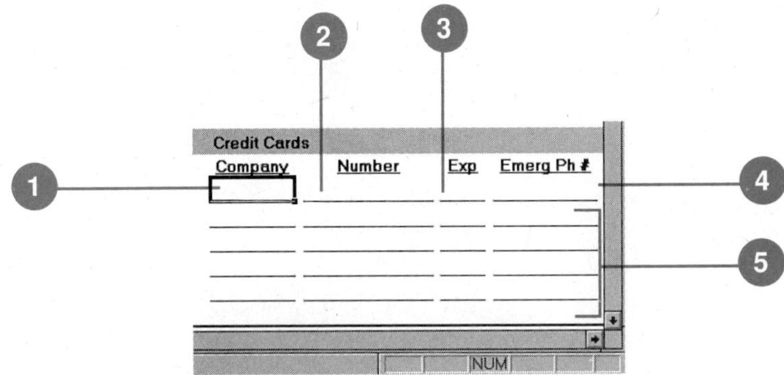

Calculating Trip Costs

The total cost of a trip is more than your airfare and a few nights at a hotel. You also need to factor in meals, entertainment, car rentals, and fees such as trip insurance. The Cost Calculation screen enables you to itemize these expenses and, where appropriate, to break them down by day to get the most accurate estimate of your total costs.

Displaying the Cost Calculation Screen

Use the Planner menu to move to the Cost Calculation screen.

1. Choose Planner Cost Calculation. Excel displays the Cost Calculation screen.

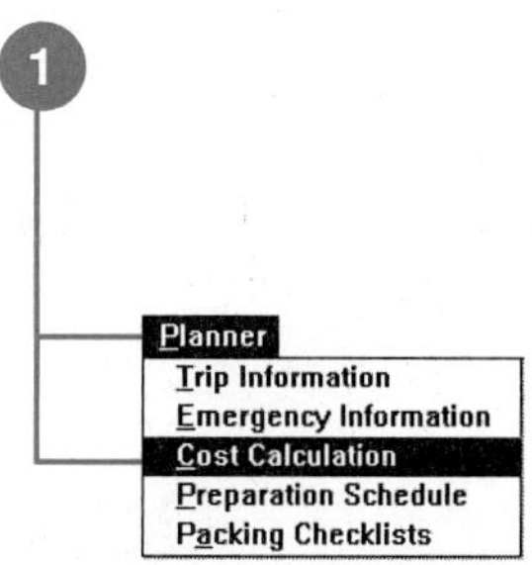

Entering Daily Costs

Use the Daily Costs section to calculate the total cost for your hotel, meals, entertainment, and souvenirs. You will be able to enter an exact daily rate for your hotel, but the other items will require an estimate.

1. Select cell AD57 and enter your daily hotel rate (include taxes, if applicable).
2. Select cell AE57 and enter the number of nights you will be staying at the hotel. The Total is calculated automatically.
3. Select cell AD58 and enter an estimate of your daily spending on meals.
4. Select cell AE58 and enter the number of days on your trip. The Total is calculated automatically.
5. Select cell AD59 and enter an estimate of your daily spending on entertainment.
6. Select cell AE59 and enter the number of days on your trip. The Total is calculated automatically.
7. Select cell AD60 and enter an estimate of your daily spending on souvenirs.
8. Select cell AE60 and enter the number of days on your trip. The Total is calculated automatically.

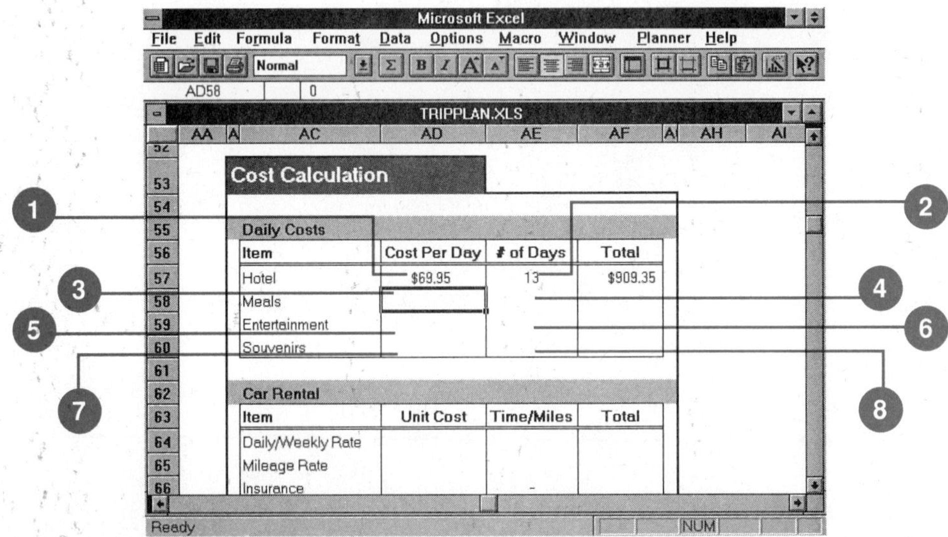

Entering Car Rental Costs

Use the Car Rental section to calculate the costs involved in renting a car. Enter the daily or weekly rate, the mileage rate, the insurance fee (if any), and any other costs such as a drop-off fee.

1. Select cell AD64 and enter the daily or weekly rental rate.
2. Select cell AE64 and enter the number of days or weeks you will be using the car. The Total is calculated automatically.
3. Select cell AD65 and enter the mileage rate.
4. Select cell AE65 and enter an estimate for the number of miles you will drive. The Total is calculated automatically.
5. Select cell AD66 and enter your insurance costs for the rental.
6. Select cell AD67 and enter any other costs for the rental.

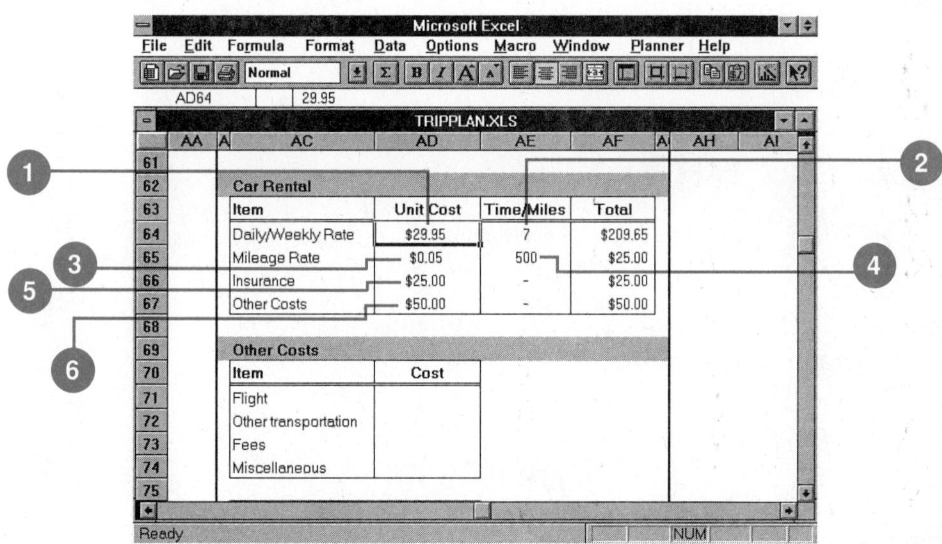

Entering Other Trip Costs

Use the Other Costs section to enter expenses such as your flight, other transportation costs (parking, buses, taxis), fees (passport, visa, trip insurance), and any miscellaneous expenses you can think of. After you have entered all your trip costs, the grand total appears in cell AD76.

1. Select cell AD71 and enter the cost of your flight.
2. Select cell AD72 and enter a total for other transportation costs.
3. Select cell AD73 and enter a total for fees.
4. Select cell AD74 and enter a total for miscellaneous expenses.
5. Select cell AD76, which calculates the grand total of the trip costs you entered.

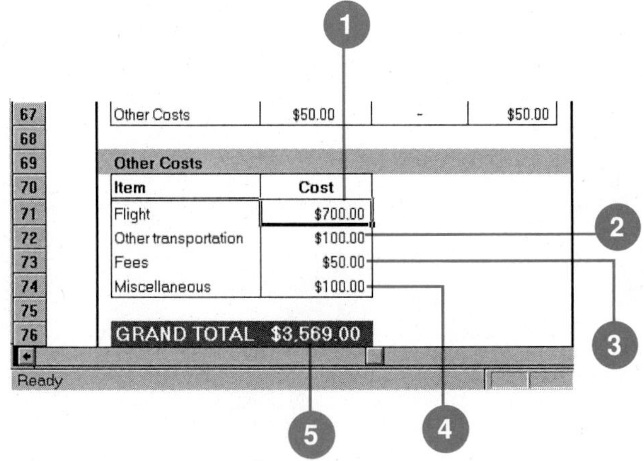

Tracking Trip Preparation

Successful trip planning involves more than simply attending to details. You have to attend to the details at the proper time. For example, if the country to which you are traveling requires a visa, it won't do you much good to apply the day before you leave. Instead, you need to get your application in at least 3 months before departing.

To help you avoid any last-minute rushing around, the trip planner includes a Preparation Schedule. This section of the worksheet is set up much like a time line. A number of trip preparation tasks are listed, and each task is assigned one of the times listed across the top of the schedule (the assignment is indicated by a shaded cell). These values represent the number of months, weeks, or days before your departure that you should consider performing the task. The idea is that when you complete each task, you indicate the completion by changing the cell shading.

Displaying the Preparation Schedule Screen

Use the Planner menu to move to the Preparation Schedule screen.

1. Choose Planner Preparation Schedule. Excel displays the Preparation Schedule screen.

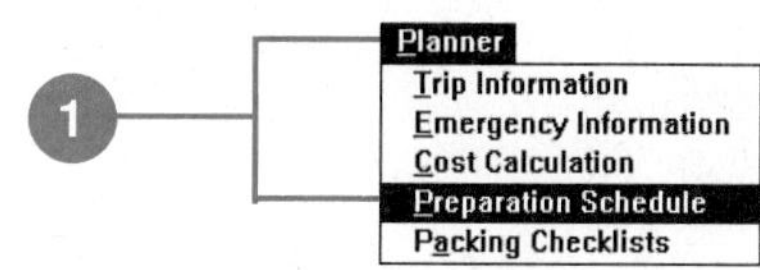

Marking a Completed Task

After you have completed a task, you should indicate the completion by changing the cell shading. Changing the cell to a solid black gives the best contrast.

1. Select the shaded cell for the task you have completed.
2. Choose Format Patterns.
3. In the **P**atterns list box, select the solid black pattern below None.
4. Select OK or press Enter. Excel shades the cell solid black.

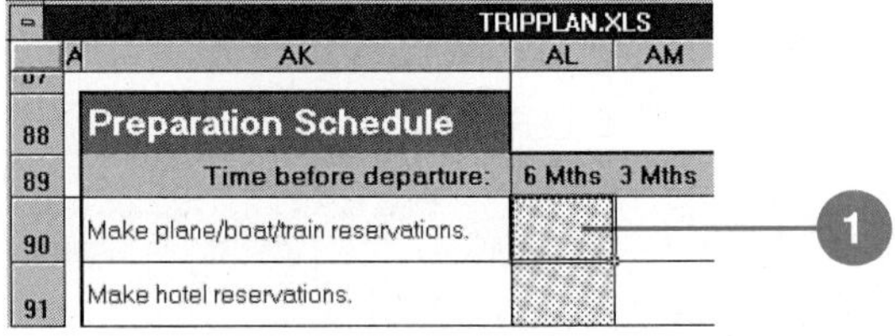

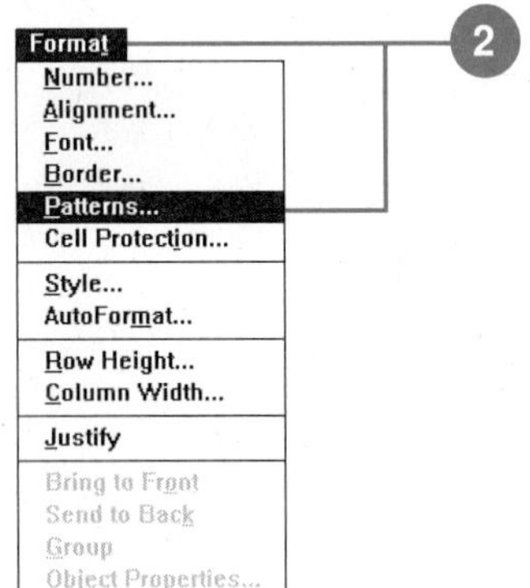

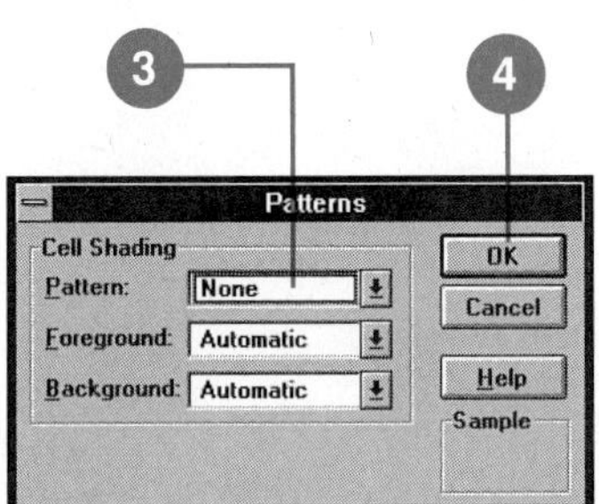

Adding a Task to the Schedule

The Preparation Schedule tasks are not meant to be an exhaustive list of items you need to take care of before a trip. Depending on the type of trip you are taking, you may have a number of tasks you need to add. For example, if you are traveling on business, you might want to include the preparation of reports and presentations.

1. Decide which time frame you want to use for your task.
2. Select a cell in one of the rows from that time frame. Use any row except the first one in the time frame.
3. Choose Edit Insert.
4. Select Entire Row.
5. Select OK or press Enter. Excel inserts the row.
6. In the inserted row, select the cell in column AK.
7. Enter a description of the task.

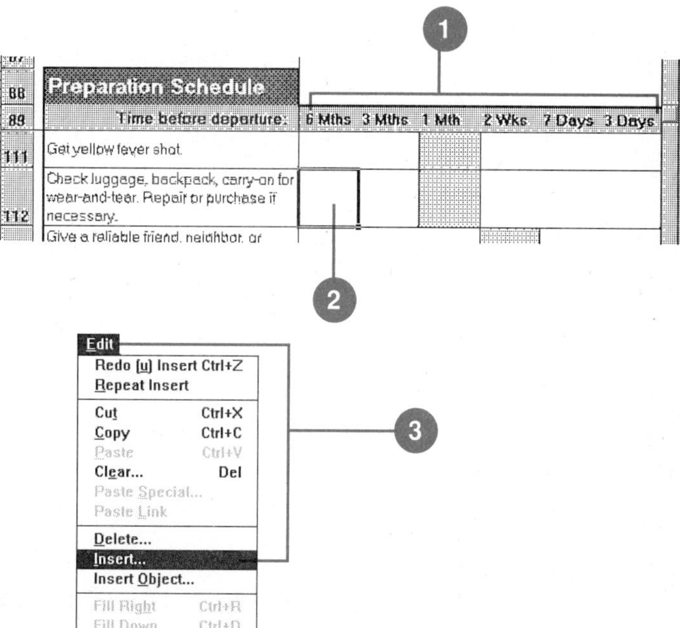

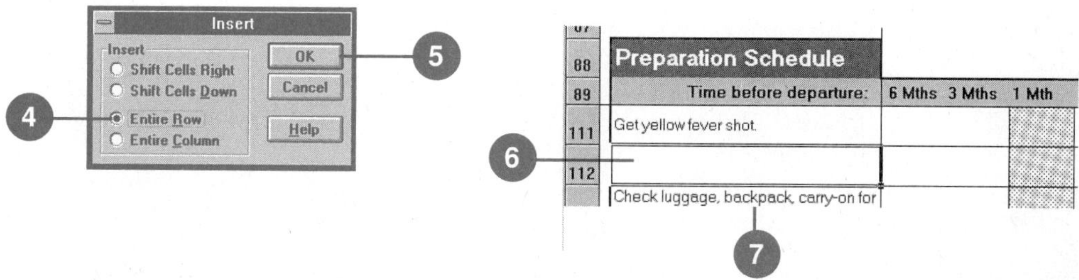

Deleting a Task from the Schedule

Not all of the Preparation Schedule tasks may apply to your situation. For example, if most of your traveling is domestic, it is unlikely you will ever need to start antimalarial medication. To make the schedule more manageable, you can delete these tasks.

1. Select a cell in the row you want to delete.
2. Choose Edit Delete.
3. Select Entire Row.
4. Select OK or press Enter.

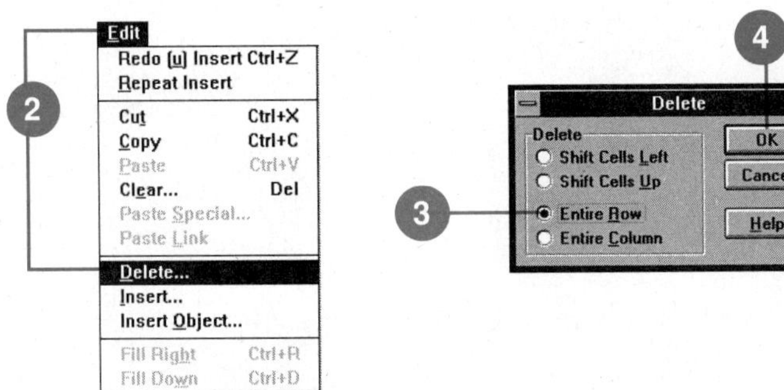

Using the Packing Checklists

Forgetting to pack something seems to be one of those inevitable travel problems. It's not surprising, however, when you consider that even a short trip may require us to pack a few dozen items. The trip planner includes several packing checklists that will help you make sure you have everything you need. There are five checklists: Clothes, Toiletries, First Aid, Laundry, and Miscellaneous.

Displaying the Packing Checklists Screen

Use the Planner menu to move to the Packing Checklists screen.

1. Choose Planner Packing Checklists. Excel displays the Packing Checklists screen.

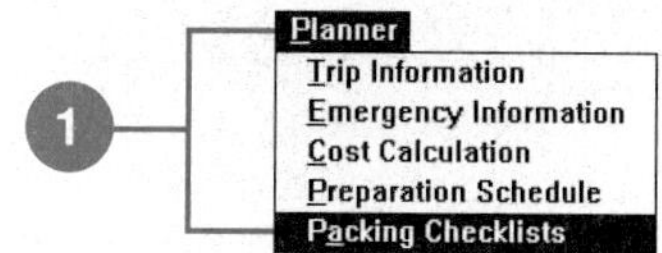

Checking Packed Items

The checklists are probably best used by printing them out and checking off the items by hand (see the section entitled "Printing the Trip Planner"). However, if you prefer to check them on-screen, the check field (column AY) has been formatted to show large, bold marks (an X is probably best).

1. For the item you want to check, select the cell in column AY.
2. Enter **X** into the cell.

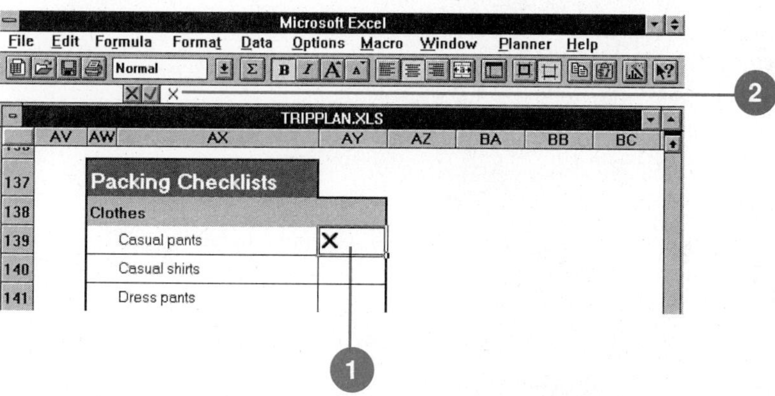

Adding an Item to a Checklist

The items you normally take on a trip will likely differ significantly from those shown in the Packing Checklists. Because the checklists are not meant to be exhaustive, you may want to add a number of items to the lists. One way to do this is to use the extra half a dozen lines provided at the bottom of the Miscellaneous checklist. You can also insert rows in the other checklists.

1. Decide in which checklist you want your item to be included.
2. Select a cell in one of the rows from that checklist. Use any row except the first one in the checklist.
3. Choose Edit Insert. Excel displays the Insert dialog box.
4. Select Entire Row.
5. Select OK or press Enter. Excel inserts the row.
6. In the inserted row, select the cell in column AX.
7. Enter a description of the item.

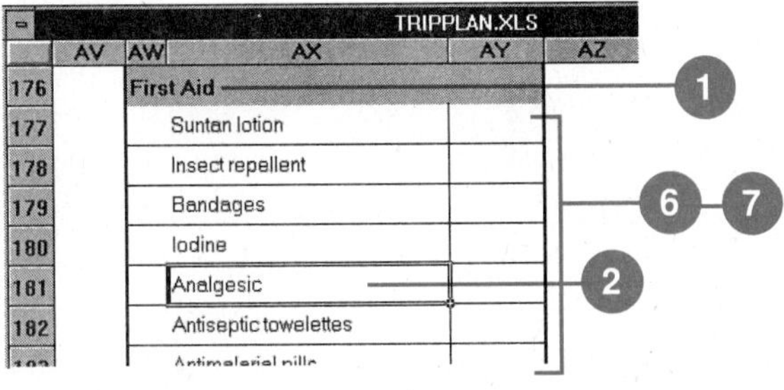

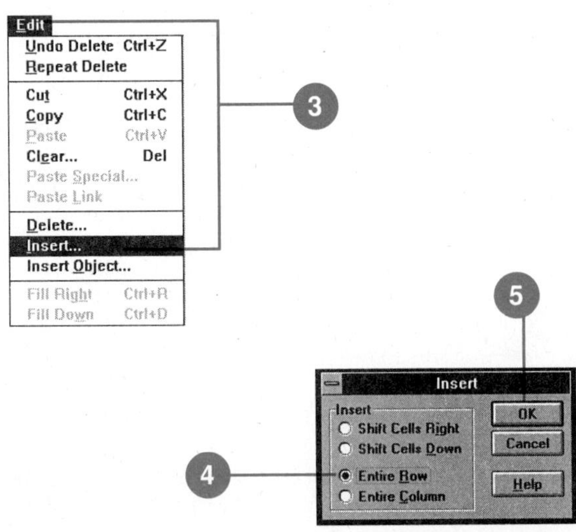

Deleting an Item from the Checklist

Not all of the Packing Checklists items may apply to your situation. For example, if your destination is tropical, you won't need to pack boots, gloves, or long underwear. To make the schedule more manageable, you can delete these tasks.

1. Select a cell in the row you want to delete.
2. Choose Edit Delete. Excel displays the Delete dialog box.
3. Select Entire Row.
4. Select OK or press Enter.

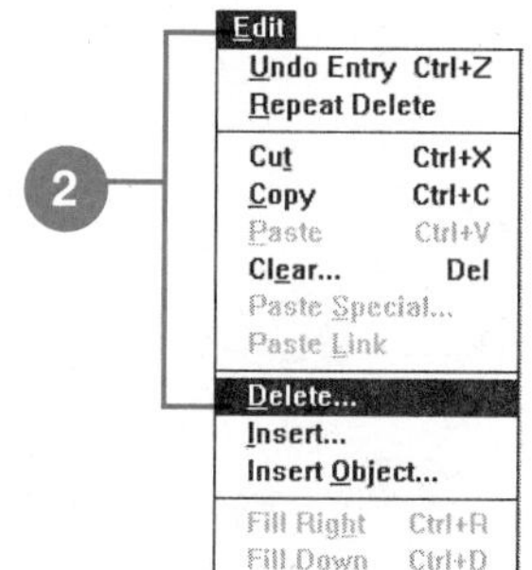

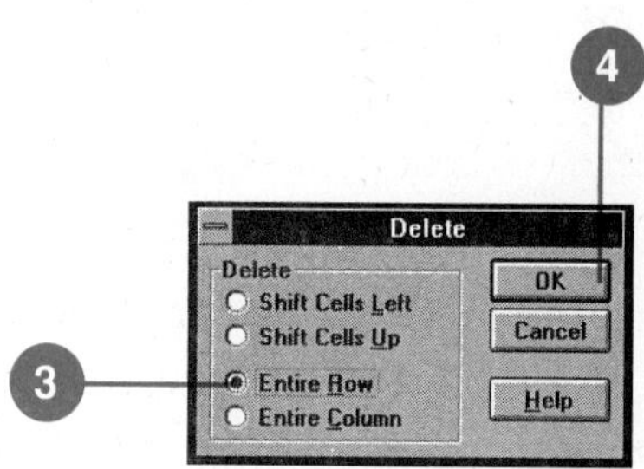

Printing the Trip Planner

You can print any section of the trip planner worksheet. You will need to do this, for example, if you want to take a copy of the Emergency Information with you, or if you want to refer to a hard copy of the Packing Checklists while you pack. To make is easier to print individual sections of the worksheet, each section has been defined as a range with a range name. Here are the names associated with each part of the worksheet:

Worksheet Area	*Range Name*
Trip Information	Trip_Info
Emergency Information	Emerg_Info
Cost Calculation	Cost_Calc
Preparation Schedule	Prep_Sched
Packing Checklists	Checklists
All five areas	Trip_Planner

You print an area by selecting the range and defining it as your print area.

1. Choose Formula Goto.
2. Select the range name you want from the Goto list.
3. Select OK or press Enter. Excel moves to and highlights the range.
4. Choose Options Set Print Area.
5. Choose File Print or press Ctrl+Shift+F12.
6. Set your page setup or print options, as needed.
7. Select OK or press Enter. Excel prints the section.

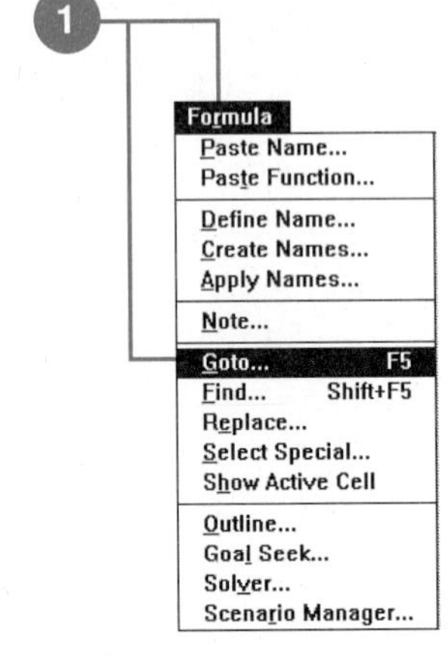

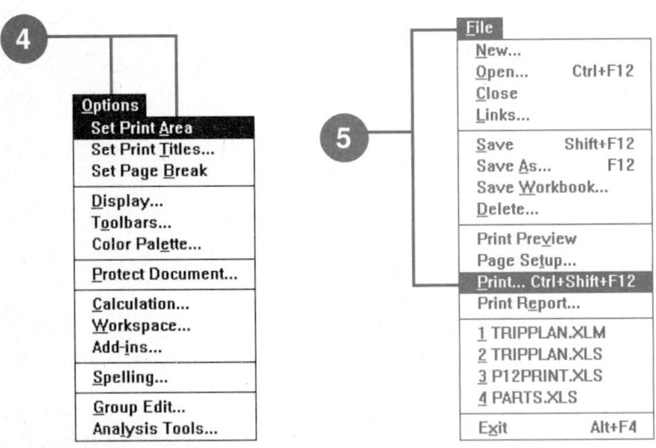

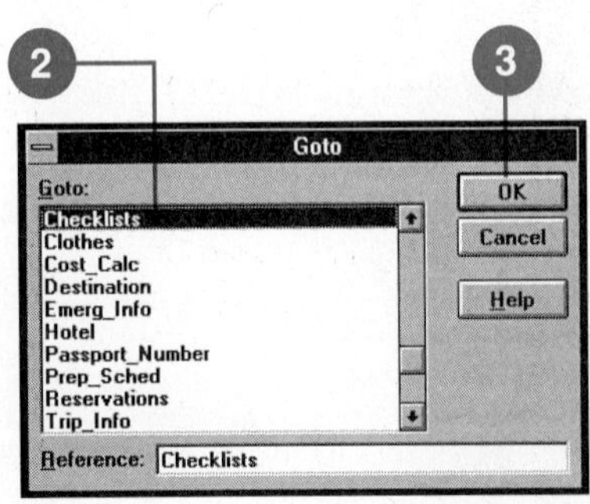

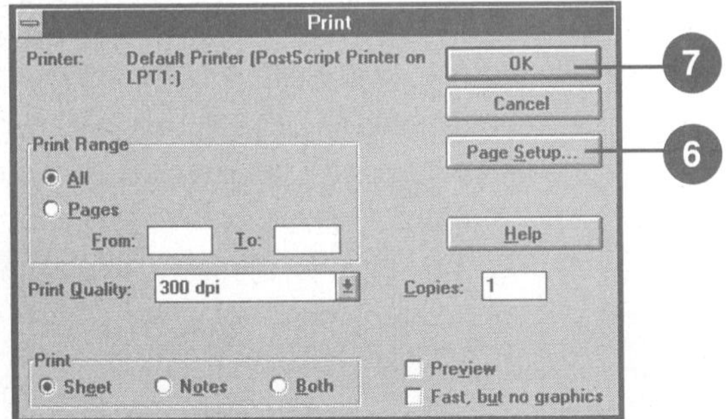

Saving TRIPPLAN.XLS Under a New Name

By customizing TRIPPLAN.XLS, you can use it for any kind of trip. To preserve the default TRIPPLAN.XLS worksheet, you need to save your work under a different name.

1. Choose File Save As. Excel displays the Save As dialog box.
2. Replace the file name in the File Name text box with the new name you want to use.
3. Select OK or press Enter.

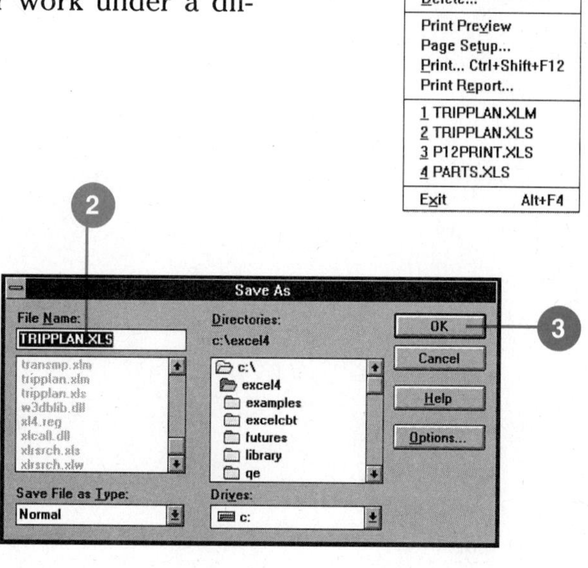

Summary

No matter what kind of trip you take, a few minutes of preparation before you go can save you hours of frustration when you arrive. To help you organize your trip preparation, this project presented you with a trip planner. You can use the trip planner to record your most vital trip and emergency information, calculate the cost of your trip, set up a preparation schedule, and run through a packing checklist. This won't make every trip perfect, but it will help you avoid most of the problems that plague the average traveler.

Command Reference

The first part of this reference, the Command Reference, lists all menu commands in alphabetical order and provides instruction for the use of each. In addition, this reference includes an explanation of each of Excel's macro commands (in alphabetical order, of course), so you can make full use of Excel's powerful macro language.

Command Reference

The Command Reference lists all menu commands in alphabetical order. Each command includes the following information:

- A description of the command.
- Instructions for selecting the command.
- Brief steps showing how to use the command.
- Pointers to other parts of the book that discuss the command in more detail.

Chart Menu Commands

Chart Add Arrow

Adds an arrow to the active chart.

Usage

1. Display a chart in the active window.
2. Select Chart Add Arrow. Excel adds an arrow to the chart.

Move the arrow by clicking and dragging it to a new location. Change the direction of the arrow by dragging a black selection handle.

Select this tool on the Chart toolbox to add an arrow to the active worksheet.

NOTE: When you select an arrow, the command name changes to Chart Delete Arrow.

See also Skill Session 27, "Adding Objects to a Chart."

Chart Add Legend

Adds a legend to the active worksheet, placing it in a text box that can be repositioned.

Usage

1. Display a chart in the active window.
2. Select Chart Add Legend. Excel adds a legend to the chart.

Click and drag any of the selection handles to reposition the legend on the chart.

Select this tool on the Chart toolbar to automatically add a legend to the active chart.

NOTE: The command name changes to Chart Delete Legend when a legend has been added to the active chart.

See also Skill Session 26, "Enhancing Charts."

Chart Add Overlay

Creates a chart that overlays the active chart. You can't add an overlay chart to a 3-D chart. The command name changes to Chart Delete Overlay when you add an overlay to the active chart.

Usage

1. In the active window, display the chart for which you want to create an overlay chart.
2. Select Chart Add Overlay. Excel adds a line chart overlaying the existing chart. You can change the initial overlay line chart to a different type of chart by selecting the Format Overlay command.

See also Skill Session 30, "Working With Chart Overlays."

Chart Attach Text

Allows you to attach text to a chart title, axis, or data point.

Usage

1. Display a chart in the active window.
2. Select Chart Attach Text or select Attach Text from the shortcut menu. Excel displays the Attach Text dialog box.
3. Select an option in the Attach Text To box. If you select the Series and Data Point option, specify a series number and a point number in the appropriate boxes.
4. Select OK.

Select this tool on the Chart toolbar to add a text box to the active chart.

See also Skill Session 27, "Adding Objects to a Chart."

Chart Axes

Allows you to display or hide X- and Y-axis labels and markers.

Usage

1. Display a chart in the active window.
2. Select Chart Axes or select Axes from the shortcut menu.
3. Select the check box for the X-axis, Y-axis, or both. Excel displays the axis label. Clear the check boxes to hide axis labels.
4. Select OK.

See also Skill Session 26, "Enhancing Charts."

Chart Calculate Now

Calculates any worksheet files that are open and updates all dependent charts.

Usage

1. In the active window, display the chart you want to update.
2. Select Chart Calculate Now. Excel automatically recalculates all open worksheets and updates all dependent charts.

> **TIP:** Press F9 to recalculate quickly without selecting the **C**hart Calculate **N**ow command.

> **NOTE:** Excel calculates based on the settings in the Calculation Options dialog box. To change these settings, select Options Calculation.

Select this tool on the Utility toolbar to recalculate all open worksheets now.

See also **O**ptions **C**alculation.

Chart Color Palette

Allows you to customize colors in the active chart or copy colors from another chart or worksheet.

Usage

To customize colors:

1. In the active window, display the chart for which you want to create custom colors.
2. Select Chart Color Palette. Excel displays the Color Palette dialog box.
3. Double-click on the color to change, or select a color, then select the Edit button. Excel displays the Color Picker dialog box.

4. Adjust the color by clicking in the color box (the large colored box) and then adjusting the brightness using the slide arrow at the far right of the dialog box.

   OR

   Adjust the **H**ue, **S**at (saturation), and **L**um (lumination) settings or the **R**ed, **G**reen, or **B**lue settings.

5. The Color|Solid box displays the color you create on the left and the nearest solid color on the right. To use the solid color, double-click on it.

6. Select OK. Excel returns to the Color Palette dialog box.

7. To customize other colors, repeat steps 3–6, then select OK.

To copy colors from another chart or worksheet:

1. In the active window, display the chart for which you want to copy colors.
2. Select Chart Color Palette. Excel displays the Color Palette dialog box.
3. Select a file from the **C**opy Colors From box, then select OK.

> **NOTE:** The **C**hart Color Pal**e**tte command is not available for charts that are embedded in worksheets. Use the Options Color Palette command to set colors for worksheets with embedded charts.

See also Skill Session 27, "Adding Objects to a Chart," and Skill Session 28, "Data Series Editing."

Chart Edit Series

Allows you to edit a data series in the active chart or create a new series.

Usage

1. In the active window, display the chart for which you want to add or edit a data series.
2. Select Chart Edit Series or select Edit Series from the shortcut menu. Excel displays the Edit Series dialog box.
3. In the **S**eries box, select a series to edit or select New Series to add a series.
4. Edit the **N**ame box to add a cell reference or to change the cell reference that defines the series name.

5. Edit the **X** Labels box to add a cell reference or to change the cell reference that defines the X-axis labels.

6. Edit the **Y** Values box to add a cell reference or to change the cell reference that defines the data for the series.

7. Edit the **P**lot Order box to define the order in which a new data series is plotted or to change the order in which data is plotted.

8. Select OK.

See also Skill Session 28, "Data Series Editing."

Chart Gridlines

Allows you to control the display of major and minor gridlines (both horizontal and vertical) in the active chart. Major gridlines define the tick marks on the graph. Minor gridlines are positioned between tick marks.

Usage

1. In the active window, display the chart for which you want to add gridlines.

2. Select **C**hart **G**ridlines or select Gridlines from the shortcut menu. Excel displays the Gridlines dialog box.

3. In the Category (X) Axis box, select check boxes **M**ajor Gridlines, M**i**nor Gridlines, or both.

4. In the Value (Y) Axis box, select check boxes Maj**o**r Gridlines, Mi**n**or Gridlines, or both.

5. Select OK.

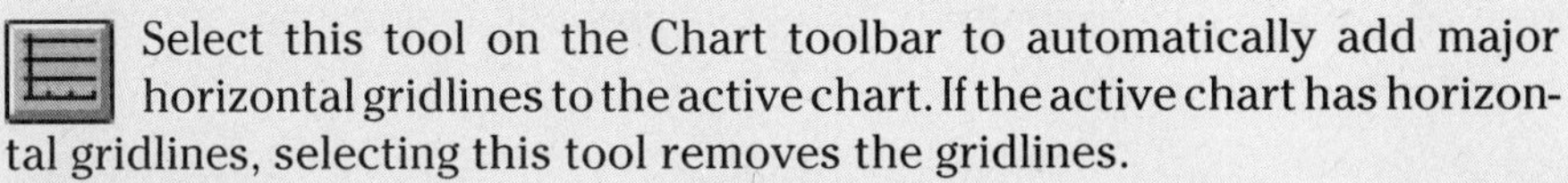

Select this tool on the Chart toolbar to automatically add major horizontal gridlines to the active chart. If the active chart has horizontal gridlines, selecting this tool removes the gridlines.

This tool adds major vertical gridlines to the active chart. If the active chart already has vertical gridlines, selecting this tool removes the gridlines. (This custom tool is available only if you have added it to a toolbar. See Skill Session 48.)

See also Skill Session 26, "Enhancing Charts."

Chart Protect Document

Allows you to protect a chart from changes to the data and formatting.

Usage

1. In the active window, display the chart you want to protect.
2. Select Chart Protect Document. Excel displays the Protect Document dialog box.
3. Select the Chart check box.
4. To prevent other users from turning off document protection, enter a password in the **P**assword box. Note that Excel asks you to enter the password twice.
5. To prevent the chart window from being moved, resized, or hidden, select the Window check box.
6. Select OK.

Chart Select Chart

Selects the entire active chart, including legends, labels, and attached text.

Usage

1. Display a chart in the active window.
2. Select Chart Select Chart. Excel selects the chart by surrounding it with selection squares.

 **TIP:** Click just outside the plot area of the chart to select the entire chart.

Chart Select Plot Area

Selects the plot area of the active chart, excluding legends, labels, and attached text.

Usage

1. Display a chart in the active window.
2. Select Chart Select Plot Area. Excel selects the plot area of the chart by surrounding it with selection squares.

TIP: Click anywhere within the plot area to select the plot area.

Chart Spelling

Checks the active chart for misspelled or unrecognized words that are not part of the chart's worksheet (e.g., titles and attached text).

Usage

1. In the active window, display the chart for which you want to check the spelling.
2. Select Chart Spelling. If Excel finds misspelled or unrecognized words in the chart, it displays the Spelling dialog box. Otherwise, Excel displays a message saying the spell checker is finished.
3. The first word Excel questions is displayed in the Not in Dictionary box. The Change To box displays the suggested replacement word. Other replacement words appear in the Suggestions box. To correct the error, you may:
   - Use the word in the Change To box
   - Select a word from the Suggestions box
   - Edit the Change To box and enter a new word

   If the word is correct as is, you may select Ignore and move on.
4. Select the appropriate command button, as described in the following list. Repeat steps 3 and 4 for subsequent words found. Excel displays a message when the spell checker is finished checking the chart.

Spell Checker Command Button	*Choose This Button to . . .*
Ignore	Ignore the current word.
Ignore All	Ignore every occurrence of the current word. To have Excel ignore uppercase words, check the Ignore Words in UPPERCASE box.
Change	Replace the current word with the word in the Change To box.
Change All	Replace every occurrence of the current word with the word in the Change To box.

Spell Checker Command Button	*Choose This Button to . . .*
Add	Add the current word to an Excel dictionary so it will not be questioned in the future. Select a dictionary file name from the Add **W**ords To box.
Cancel	Close the Spelling dialog box.
Suggest	Display a list of suggested replacement words if the Always Suggest check box is not checked.

 Select this tool on the Utility toolbar to check the spelling of the current chart.

Data Menu Commands

Data Consolidate

Allows you to summarize data from multiple ranges across multiple worksheets. For example, you could consolidate January sales figures for five different divisions into one set of sales figures for January.

Usage

To consolidate data, specify the ranges or *source areas* of the data you want to consolidate, and the range that will hold the results, the *destination area*. You can consolidate data by its *position* in the worksheet when the source areas are in the same location on multiple worksheets. For example, when the January sales figures for five different divisions are located in column B on five separate worksheets, you can consolidate by position. When the source areas are in different locations in the worksheets, you must consolidate by category, using labels.

1. Select the destination area in which you want the consolidation results displayed.

2. Select Data Consolidate to display the Consolidate dialog box.
3. In the Function box, select the function Excel will use to consolidate the data, or use the default function, SUM.
4. In the Reference box, enter the cell reference for the first source area, or select the area in the worksheet using the mouse. If you are consolidating by category using labels, be sure to include the labels in the source area.

   If the source area is on a separate worksheet, use the Window menu to activate an open worksheet. If the worksheet file is not open, use the Browse button in the Consolidate dialog box to locate the file.
5. Select the Add button. Excel adds the reference to the All References box.
6. Repeat steps 3 and 4 for each source area you want to consolidate.
7. To consolidate by category using labels, check either Top Row or Left Column in the Use Labels In box. To consolidate by position using references, clear both of these boxes.
8. Select OK. Excel consolidates the data from the source areas into the destination area.
9. Select Delete to delete the source area reference selected in the All References box.
10. To link the destination and source areas, check the Create Links to Source Data check box. When these are linked, the destination area is updated automatically when the source data changes.

See also Skill Session 42, "Advanced File Operations."

Data Crosstab

Displays the Crosstab ReportWizard used for creating, recalculating, and modifying a cross tabulation table. A *cross tabulation table* is a report that categorizes and tallies data from a database file.

Usage

1. Create and define a database range, using the Data Set Database command. Excel names the range Database.
2. Select Data Crosstab to start the Crosstab ReportWizard.

3. Select the Create A New Crosstab button, then follow the instructions on the screen. If you have already created a crosstab table, choose Recalculate Current Crosstab or Modify Current Crosstab to recalculate or modify the existing table.

See also Data Set Database, and Skill Session 39, "Using Crosstab Tables."

Data Delete

Allows you to delete all records from a database file that meet the criteria you specify using the **D**ata Set **C**riteria command.

Usage

1. Make the database worksheet the active worksheet.
2. Define the criteria and a criteria range, using the **D**ata Set **C**riteria command. Excel names the range Criteria.

> **CAUTION:** Including blank rows in the criteria range will cause Excel to select and delete all records.

3. Select Data Delete. Excel displays a warning message that all matching records will be permanently deleted.
4. Select OK. Excel deletes all records with matching criteria.

> **TIP:** Be sure to save your worksheet before using the **D**ata **D**elete command, as the **E**dit **U**ndo command will not restore the deleted records.

See also **D**ata Set **C**riteria, and Skill Session 36, "Working with Records."

Data Extract

Finds the database records that meet the criteria you specify, and copies them to an extract range in the worksheet.

Usage

1. Make the database worksheet the active worksheet.
2. Define your criteria and the criteria range, using the **D**ata Set **C**riteria command. Excel names the range Criteria.

3. Copy the field names for the fields that will be extracted to the first row of the extract range. Be sure the area below this row is blank.
4. Select the cell range (large enough to hold all extracted records) that will contain the field names and extracted records.
5. Select Data Set Extract. Excel names the range Extract.
6. Select Data Extract. The Extract dialog box appears.
7. To eliminate multiple copies of duplicate records, check the Unique Records Only check box.
8. Select OK.

See also **D**ata Set **C**riteria, **D**ata Set E**x**tract, and Skill Session 36, "Working with Records."

Data Find

Finds records in a database worksheet that meet the criteria you specify.

Usage

1. Make the database worksheet the active worksheet.
2. Define your criteria and the criteria range, using the **D**ata Set **C**riteria command.
3. Select Data Find. Excel finds the first record that matches the criteria in the criteria range.

When you use the **D**ata **F**ind command to find database records, Excel enters Find mode. While you are in Find mode, use the scroll bar to locate next (or previous) matching record(s) within the specified range. Use the **D**ata **E**xit **F**ind command to exit Find mode and restore the scroll bars to normal operation.

> **TIP:** Before selecting the **D**ata **F**ind command, make the first cell in the database the active cell; this ensures that all records are found.

See also Data Set Criteria, and Skill Session 36, "Working with Records."

Data Form

Allows you to display database field names and records, one record at a time. Excel displays the record in a separate dialog box; this can be used to view, change, add, or delete records in the database, and to set criteria for finding records.

Usage

1. Create and define a database range, using the **D**ata Set Data**b**ase command.
2. Select Data Form. Excel displays a dialog box showing the first record in the database.
3. The buttons in the Data Form dialog box have the following uses when viewing, adding, changing, or deleting records:

Close	Closes the Data Form dialog box.
Criteria	Displays a dialog box in which you can specify criteria to find matching records.
Delete	Deletes the current record.
Find Next	Finds the next matching record.
Find Previous	Finds the previous matching record.
Form	Returns you to the regular data form from the Criteria form.
New	Moves to the first blank record at the end of the database.
Restore	Restores data in a record's fields to the previous entry before editing. You must use the Restore button before pressing Enter or scrolling to another record.
Clear	In the Criteria form, this button clears the current entry.

See also Data Set Data**b**ase, and Skill Session 37, "Data Forms."

Data Parse

The **D**ata **P**arse command is often used after you have copied data from another application into Excel. The data from the other application is sometimes condensed from several columns into one column when it is copied into Excel. The Parse command separates the data into multiple columns.

Usage

1. Select the range of cells that contain the data you want to separate. The range must be only one column wide.

2. Select **Data Parse**. Excel displays the Parse dialog box. The first record is displayed in the Parse Line box and includes brackets where Excel thinks the fields should be broken.

3. Change, add, or delete brackets in the Parse Line box.

4. Enter a destination cell in the **D**estination box, or use the suggested reference. Note that cells which already contain entries will be overwritten.

5. Click OK.

Data Series

Using the **D**ata Se**r**ies command, you can fill a range of cells with numbers or dates automatically, in rows or columns. The *step value* determines the amount of increase or decrease from cell to cell. When filling a series with dates, you can choose to increment by day, weekday, month, or year.

Usage

1. Enter a number in the cell where you want the series to begin.

2. Select all cells in the range to be filled with a series, including the cell that contains the starting number.

3. Select **Data Series** to display the Series dialog box.

4. In the Series in box, select either **Rows** or **Columns**.

5. Enter a number in the **S**tep Value box, or use the default (1). Enter a negative number to *decrease* the values in the series.

6. Select an option in the Type box; descriptions of the options follow:

   Linear — Adds the step value to each successive number in the series.

   Growth — Multiplies the number in each cell by the number in the Step Value box.

   Date — Fills the range with a series of dates according to the Date Unit chosen (see step 7).

   AutoFill — Fills blank cells in the selected range automatically, on the basis of the type and step value of the cells in the selected range.

7. If you chose the **D**ate option in the Type box, select an option in the Date Unit box (**Day**, **Weekday**, **Month**, or **Year**).

8. (Optional) In the Stop Value box, enter a number at which you want the series to end. If the range is filled before reaching this number (the *stop value*), the number is ignored.

9. Select OK.

Data Set Criteria

Specify records to find, extract, or delete by defining a criteria range. The *criteria range* consists of a row containing criteria names, and one or more rows specifying the criteria. Choose a blank area of the worksheet in which to create a criteria range.

Usage

1. Copy or enter the criteria names into the first row of the criteria range.
2. In the next row, enter the criteria for each name.
3. Select the cells that make up the criteria range, including the criteria names.
4. Select Data Set Criteria. Excel names the range Criteria.

See also Skill Session 36, "Working with Records."

Data Set Database

Defines the ranges of cells that contain database field names and records. A *database* consists of a row of field names and all the records in the set of data. Enter the field names and data before defining a database.

Usage

1. Select the range of cells that make up the database, including the field names.
2. Select Data Set Database. Excel names the range Database.

See also Skill Session 35, "Creating and Sorting a Database."

Data Set Extract

Defines the range of cells in which extracted database records are copied.

Usage

You must define a database using the Data Set Database command before using the Data Set Extract command. You must also define a criteria range using Data Set Criteria.

1. Copy or enter the field names of the extracted records to a blank area of the worksheet. Make sure the area is large enough to accommodate the number of extracted.
2. Select the range of cells, including the field names, into which the extracted data will be copied.
3. Select Data Set Extract. Excel names the range Extract.

See also Skill Session 36, "Working with Records."

Data Sort

Reorganizes the selected cells in rows or columns, on the basis of the criteria you specify. When you select multiple rows or columns, you can sort on several *keys* (up to three), which are the specification criteria (such as LastName in an employee database).

Usage

1. Select the range of cells in a row or column (or multiple rows or columns) to sort.
2. Select Data Sort. Excel displays the Sort dialog box.
3. In the Sort By box, select to sort by either Rows or Columns.
4. In the **1**st key box, enter the cell address for the sort criteria.
5. In the **1**st key box, select either Ascending or Descending.
6. To sort up to three keys, repeat steps 4 and 5 for the **2**nd and **3**rd key boxes.
7. Select OK.

Click this tool on the Utility toolbar to sort the selected range of cells tomatically, in descending order.

Click this tool on the Utility toolbar to sort the selected range of cells in descending order.

See also Skill Session 35, "Creating and Sorting a Database."

Data Table

Creates a *data table*—a range of cells that display a formula's results after substituting different input values for one of the formula's variables. The variable for which these values are substituted is the *input cell*.

Usage

You must first set up a data table before using the **D**ata **T**able command to fill in the formula's results. To set up a data table, follow these steps:

1. In a column or row, enter the input values to be substituted in the input cell.
2. Enter the formula that refers to the input cell:

   If you entered the input values in a *column*, enter the formula in the row above the first of these numbers, and one cell to the right of the column of numbers.

   If you entered the input values in a *row*, enter the formula in the column to the left of the first of these numbers, and one cell below the row of numbers.

To fill in the data table with the results for each input value, follow these steps:

1. Select the entire range of cells containing the formula and the input values.
2. Select Data Table. Excel displays the Table dialog box.
3. Enter the cell reference for the input cell:

   If you entered the input values in a *row*, enter the cell reference for the input cell in the **R**ow Input cell box, and then select OK.

   If you entered the input values in a *column*, enter the cell reference for the input cell in the **C**olumn Input cell box, and then select OK.

See also Skill Session 36, "Working with Records."

Edit Menu Commands

Edit Clear

Allows you to remove the values, format, formulas, notes, or all content—from the selected cells in the worksheet.

Usage

1. Select the cells you want to clear.
2. Select Edit Clear to display the Clear dialog box.
3. In the Clear box, select All, Formats, Formulas, or Notes, then select OK.

> **TIP:** Press the Delete key to display the Edit Clear dialog box.

> **TIP:** Press Ctrl+Del to clear formulas from selected cells.

> **TIP:** To clear a single cell, select the cell, then press the spacebar.

> **NOTE:** The Clear Formulas and Clear Formats tools are custom tools, available only if you have added them to a toolbar. See Skill Session 48.

See also Edit Delete.

Edit Copy

Copies the selection onto the Windows Clipboard. The selection may be a cell, range of cells, contents of the formula bar, a chart or graphic object, or an entire document.

Usage

1. Select the text to be copied.

2. Select Edit Copy. Excel copies the selection to the Clipboard.
3. Choose a new location for the selection, then select Edit Paste or press Enter.

 **TIP:** Press Ctrl+C to select the **C**opy command.

 Click this tool on the standard toolbar to select the **E**dit **C**opy command.

See also Skill Session 8, "Copying, Moving, and Clearing Cells."

Edit Copy Picture

Copies a picture of the selected cell, cell range, graphic object, or chart onto the Clipboard. Note that this command appears on the Edit menu in place of the **C**opy command only when you hold down Shift while selecting the Edit menu.

Usage

1. Select the cell, cell range, graphic object, or chart to be copied.
2. Hold down the Shift key, and then select Edit Copy Picture. Excel displays the Copy Picture dialog box.
3. Select an option in the Appearance box. The As Shown on **S**creen option copies the selection the same size as it appears on the screen. The As Shown When **P**rinted option copies the selection the same size it would appear when printed.
4. Select an option in the Format box. The Pic**t**ure copies option will copy the picture in Windows metafile format, so it can be displayed on screens with different resolutions. The **B**itmap option copies the picture in bitmap format, which can be displayed correctly only on a screen of the same type and resolution.
5. Select OK or press Enter.

See also **E**dit **P**aste Picture.

Edit Copy Tool Face

Copies the picture on the selected tool onto the Clipboard. Note that this command appears on the Edit menu in place of the Copy command only when the Toolbars dialog box or the Customize dialog box is displayed.

Usage

1. Display either the Customize dialog box or the Toolbars dialog box.
2. Select the tool whose picture you want to copy.
3. Select Edit Copy Tool Face.

Edit Cut

Removes the selection from the document, and places it on the Windows Clipboard. The selection may be a cell, range of cells, contents of the formula bar, a chart or graphic object, or an entire document.

Usage

1. Select the text or object to be cut.
2. Select Edit Cut. Excel places the selection onto the Clipboard.
3. As the status line indicates, choose a new location for the selection, then select Edit Paste or press Enter.

TIP: Press Ctrl+X or Shift+Delete to cut the selected text or object.

Click this tool to cut the selected text or object. (Note that this is a custom tool, available only if you have added it to a toolbar.)

See also Skill Session 8, "Copying, Moving, and Clearing Cells."

Edit Delete

Allows you to remove selected cells, rows, or columns from a worksheet, including cell contents and formatting. Surrounding cells are moved to fill the empty space.

Usage

1. Select the cells to delete. To delete an entire row or column, select the row or column heading. If you don't select an entire row, the Delete dialog box is displayed.
2. Select Edit Delete. The Delete dialog box appears.
3. Select an option from the Delete box, then select OK.

 **TIP:** Press Ctrl+minus sign (–) to delete the selected cells.

NOTE: To delete an entire row or column, select the row or column heading, then select Edit Delete. The Delete dialog box is not displayed, but the selected row or column is deleted.

 Click this tool to delete the selected cells.

 Click this tool to delete the selected row.

 Click this tool to delete the selected column.

NOTE: All delete tools are custom tools that are only available if you have added them to a toolbar.

See also Skill Session 9, "Inserting and Deleting Cells, Rows, and Columns."

Edit Fill Down

Allows you to vertically fill a selections of cells with the value or format contained in the first cell.

Usage

1. Select a range of cells to fill down, including the first cell containing a value or format. You can select cells across multiple columns.
2. Select Edit Fill Down. Excel fills each selected cell below the first cell with the value or format in the first cell.

 **TIP:** Press Ctrl+D to select the **E**dit Fill Do**w**n command.

NOTE: The Fill Down and Fill Right tools are custom tools, available only if you have added them to a toolbar.

See also Skill Session 8, "Copying, Moving, and Clearing Cells," **E**dit Fill Left (**h**), **E**dit Fill Rig**h**t, and **E**dit Fill Up (**w**).

Edit Fill Group

Fills the same range of cells in a group of worksheets with the selection from the active worksheet. This command is only available when a group of worksheets is active.

Usage

1. Start a Group editing session (see **O**ptions **G**roup Edit).
2. Select the range of cells in the active document that you want to copy to other documents in the group.
3. Select Edit Fill **G**roup. Excel displays the Fill Workgroup dialog box.
4. Select an option from the dialog box, and then select OK or press Enter.

Edit Fill Left (h)

Horizontally fills a selection of cells with the contents and format in the cell on the right. Note that this command appears on the Edit menu in place of the Fill Rig**h**t command only when you hold down the Shift key, and then select the **E**dit menu.

Usage

1. Select a range of cells to fill to the left, including the cell from which the contents and format will be copied. You can select cells in multiple rows.
2. Hold down the Shift key, and then select Edit Fill Left (**h**).

See also Edit Fill Rig**h**t.

Edit Fill Right

Allows you to fill a selection of cells horizontally with the number or format contained in the first cell.

Usage

1. Select a range of cells to fill to the right, including the first cell containing a number or format. You can select cells in multiple rows.
2. Select Edit Fill Rig**h**t.

 **TIP:** Press Ctrl+R to select the **E**dit Fill Rig**h**t command.

See also Skill Session 8, "Copying, Moving, and Clearing Cells," **E**dit Fill Do**w**n, **E**dit Fill Left (**h**), and **E**dit Fill Up (**w**).

Edit Fill Up (w)

Vertically fills a selection of cells with the contents and format in the cell at the bottom of the selection. Note that this command appears on the Edit menu in place of the Fill Do**w**n command only when you hold down the Shift key, and then select the **E**dit menu.

Usage

1. Select a range of cells to fill, including the cell at the bottom of the range from which the contents and format will be copied. You can select cells in multiple columns.
2. Hold down the Shift key, and then select Edit Fill Up (**w**).

See also Edit Fill Down.

Edit Insert

Allows you to insert a blank row, column, or range of blank cells that are the same size and shape as the selected cells.

Usage

To insert a row or column:

1. Select the entire row below the point where you want to insert a row, or the entire column to the right of the point where you want to insert a column.
2. Select Edit Insert.

To insert a range of cells:

1. Select the range of cells where you want to insert new cells.
2. Select Edit Insert. Excel displays the Insert dialog box.
3. Select an option in the Insert dialog box, then select OK. Excel inserts the blank cells as specified.

NOTE: When you copy or cut selected text using the Edit Copy or Edit Cut commands, the Insert command changes to Insert Paste. This allows you to insert the Clipboard's contents between existing cells.

Click this tool to insert a blank cell.

Click this tool to insert a blank row.

Click this tool to insert a blank column. To use the equivalent keyboard shortcut instead, press Ctrl+plus sign (+).

> **NOTE:** All of the insert tools are custom tools, available only if you have added them to a toolbar. See Skill Session 48 for instructions on customizing toolbars.

See also Skill Session 9, "Inserting and Deleting Cells, Rows, and Columns."

Edit Insert Object

Allows you to insert an embedded object into a worksheet. The choice of objects is determined by the applications you installed.

Usage

1. Select Edit Insert Object. Excel displays the Insert Object dialog box.
2. From the **O**bject Type box, select an object to insert.
3. Select OK. Depending on the object you choose, Excel displays a separate dialog box in which you can specify the object to insert.

Edit Paste

Allows you to place a selection from the Clipboard into the worksheet, macro sheet, chart, or project window.

Usage

1. Use the Cu**t** or **C**opy command to place selected text into the Clipboard.
2. Select Edit Paste.

Click the Paste tool to use the **P**aste command. (Note that this is a custom tool and is only available if you have added it to a toolbar.)

TIP: Press Enter, Ctrl+V, or Shift+Ins to use the **P**aste command.

See also Skill Session 8, "Copying, Moving, and Clearing Cells."

Edit Paste Link

Allows you to paste copied data into selected worksheet cells, while creating a link to the source of the data.

Usage

1. Copy the cells to be pasted to the Clipboard.
2. Select the cell or range where the Clipboard contents will be pasted.
3. Select Edit Paste Link. Excel pastes the Clipboard contents into the destination range, and links it to the source data.

Edit Paste Picture

Pastes a picture of the Clipboard contents into an Excel document. Note that this command appears on the Edit menu in place of the Paste command only when you hold down the Shift key while selecting the Edit menu.

Usage

1. Select the cell or cells where you want to paste the picture from the Clipboard.
2. Hold down the Shift key, and then select Edit Paste Picture. Excel pastes a copy of the picture from the Clipboard to the selected cells.

See also Edit Copy Picture.

Edit Paste Picture Link

Pastes a picture of the Clipboard contents into an Excel document, and creates a link between the picture and the document from which the Clipboard's contents were copied. Note that this command appears on the Edit menu in place of the Paste command only when you hold down the Shift key while selecting the Edit menu.

Usage

1. Select the cell or cells where you want to paste the picture from the Clipboard.
2. Hold down the Shift key, and then select Edit Paste Picture Link. Excel pastes a copy of the picture from the Clipboard to the selected cells. When the source document changes, the pasted picture is updated.

See also Edit Paste Picture.

Edit Paste Special

Allows you to copy any of the following special elements of a cell's contents: formula, value, format, or note.

Usage

1. Select the range of cells to copy.
2. Select Edit Copy.
3. Select the cell in the upper left corner of the destination range.
4. Select Edit Paste Special to display the Paste Special dialog box.
5. Select an option from the Paste box, then select OK.

Click this tool on the Standard toolbar to automatically paste the format of the selected cell or cells.

Click this tool to paste only the values from the selected cells.

NOTE: This custom tool is available only if you have added it to a toolbar. See Skill Session 48.

See also Skill Session 8, "Copying, Moving, and Clearing Cells."

Edit Paste Tool Face

Pastes the picture on the Clipboard onto the selected tool. Note that this command replaces the **Paste** command only when the Toolbars dialog box or the Customize dialog box is displayed.

Usage

1. Use the Edit Copy Tool Face command to copy the picture you want to the Clipboard.
2. Display the Toolbars dialog box or the Customize dialog box.
3. Select the tool that you want to change.

4. Select Edit Paste Tool Face. Excel pastes the picture from the Clipboard to the selected tool.

See also Edit Copy Face Tool.

Edit Repeat

Allows you to repeat the last command, if possible. (Some commands cannot be repeated.) When the command can be repeated, the command name is appended to the Repeat command name on the Edit menu (such as Repeat Clear, or Repeat Font). When a command can't be repeated, the command changes to Edit Can't Repeat, and is grayed (dimmed) on the menu.

Usage

1. Select the cell or cells in which you want the last command repeated.
2. Select Edit Repeat.

 **TIP:** Press Alt+Enter to use the Repeat command.

 Click this tool on the Utility toolbar to use the Repeat command.

Edit Undo

Allows you to reverse the last command used, if possible. (Some commands cannot be reversed.) When a command can be reversed, the command name is added to the Undo command name (as in Undo Cut, or Undo Clear). Some actions can't be reversed. In this case, the menu command changes to Edit Can't Undo, and is dimmed on the menu.

Usage

Immediately after using the command you want to undo, select Edit Undo. Excel reverses the action taken.

 **TIP:** Press Ctrl+Z or Alt+Backspace to use the Edit Undo command.

 Click this tool on the Utility toolbar to undo the most recent action.

 **NOTE:** You can Undo the Undo command by selecting it twice in a row.

See also Skill Session 5, "Entering and Editing Data."

File Menu Commands

File Close

Closes the document in the active window.

Usage

1. Make the window you want to close the active window.
2. Select File Close. If you have not saved recent changes to the document, Excel asks if you want to save the changes.
3. Select Yes to save the changes and close the document, select No to close the document without saving changes, or select Cancel to return to the document without saving changes.

 **TIP:** Press Ctrl+F4 to close the active document.

See also Skill Session 6, "Working with Worksheets and Workbooks."

File Close All

Closes all windows of all open documents. This command is available only when you hold down the Shift key and select the File menu.

Usage

1. Select File Close All. If you have made changes to any of the open documents, Excel displays a dialog box asking if you want to save the changes.
2. Select Yes to save your changes, No to abandon the changes, or Cancel to return to Excel without saving the changes.

See also File Close.

File Delete

Allows you to delete any file (not just an Excel for Windows file) from the disk.

Usage

1. Select File Delete. Excel for Windows displays the Delete Document dialog box.
2. If necessary, select a drive from the Drives box. Select a directory from the Directories box.
3. Select the file to delete from the File Name box.

> **TIP:** You can display files of a specific file type by selecting a type from the List Files of Type box.

4. Select OK. Excel displays a warning. Select Yes to delete the file, No to cancel.

File Exit

Closes the Excel program, and returns to the Program Manager.

Usage

1. Select File Exit. If you have made changes to any of the open documents, Excel displays a dialog box which asks if you want to save the changes.
2. Select Yes to save the changes, No to abandon the changes, or Cancel to return to Excel without saving the changes.

> **TIP:** Press Alt+F4 to exit Excel.

See also File Close.

File Links

Displays a list of source documents for the active dependent worksheet. Also allows you to change links on the basis of the type of link used.

Usage

1. Open a dependent worksheet.
2. Select File Links. Excel displays the Links dialog box.
3. Select the type of link you want to display in the Link **T**ype box.
4. Select a source document from the **L**inks box.
5. Select Open to open the source document; to open the document as Read Only, select the Read Only button.

Following are descriptions of the command buttons in the Links dialog box.

Change	Allows you to redirect links to the dependent worksheet.
Update	Updates the active dependent document with the latest changes from the selected source document.
Options	Displays the Dynamic Data Exchange (DDE) Options dialog box.

See also Skill Session 42, "Advanced File Operations."

File New

Allows you to create a new worksheet, chart, macro sheet, workbook document, or slides—or a new document—using a template you have already created.

Usage

1. Select File New to display the New dialog box.
2. Select the type of document to create in the **N**ew box.
3. Select OK.

 To create a new worksheet, click this tool on the Standard toolbar.

 **TIP:** Press Shift+F11 or Alt+Shift+F1 to create a new worksheet.

 To create a new chart, click on this tool on the Standard toolbar.

 To create a new macro sheet, click on this tool on the Macro toolbar.

 Click on this tool to create a new workbook file. (Note that this is a custom tool, available only if you have added it to a toolbar. See Skill Session 48.)

See also Skill Session 6, "Working with Worksheets and Workbooks."

File Open

Allows you to open an existing Excel file in its own window. You can also open files from other programs such as Lotus 1-2-3. You can open more than one document at a time in Excel.

Usage

1. Select File Open to display the File Open dialog box.
2. To list files of a type other than the one shown in the File **N**ame box, select a type from the List Files of **T**ype box.
3. If necessary, select a drive from the Dri**v**es box. Select a directory from the **D**irectories box, then select a file from the list shown.
4. To open the file in a Read Only format, select the Read Only option.
5. Select OK.

 Click on the Open file tool on the Standard toolbar to display the File Open dialog box.

TIP: To open one of the four most recently opened documents, select the File menu, then select a file from the list at the bottom of the File menu.

> TIP: Press Ctrl+F12 or Alt+Ctrl+F2 to display the Open dialog box.

See also Skill Session 5, "Working with Worksheets and Workbooks."

File Page Setup

Use to specify special page and paper settings (such as margin widths, page orientation, headers and footers, and so on). The settings you choose are saved with the document.

Usage

1. Select File Page Setup to display the Page Setup dialog box.
2. Select the settings you want, then select OK.

Following is a description of the settings in the Page Setup dialog box:

Portrait	Prints from top to bottom on standard-sized paper.
Landscape	Prints sideways on standard-sized paper.
Center Horizontally	Centers the document between specified top and bottom margins.
Center Vertically	Centers the document between specified left and right margins.
Cell Gridlines	Prints gridlines.
Black & White Cells	Prints color-formatted cells in patterns. Leave blank to print cells in black and white.
Down, then Over	Prints pages from top to bottom, then right.
Over, then Down	Prints pages from left to right, then down.
Fit To	Fits the selected print area to the specified page layout.
Paper Size	Selects a paper size from the drop-down box.
Reduce/Enlarge to	Specifies the percentage of enlargement or reduction.
Start Page No.'s At	Enter the number to be used as the first page number.

Row & **C**olumn Headings	Select this option to print row and column headings on the printed worksheet.

Following is a description of the settings you can choose when you select the command buttons in the Page Setup dialog box.

Options	Allows you to set and remove page breaks.
He**a**der	Allows you to specify header information, which prints at the top of each page.
Footer	Allows you to specify footer information, which prints at the bottom of each page.
Print	Allows you to print the document directly from this dialog box.
Pri**n**ter Setup	Displays the list of printers installed for your system, and allows you to change the printer setup.

See also Skill Session 12, "Basic Printing," and Skill Session 22, "Advanced Print Operations."

File Print

Allows you to print a document or preview a document before printing.

Usage

1. Display the document you want to print in the active window.
2. Select File **P**rint. Excel displays the Print dialog box.
3. Select the print options, then select OK.

Following is a description of each dialog box setting:

Pages	Prints ALL of the document, or a range of pages. To print a range of pages, enter page numbers in the **F**rom and **T**o boxes.
Print **Q**uality	Selects a resolution level offered by the printer currently selected.
Copies	Enters the number of copies to print.
Sh**e**et	Prints only the worksheet.
N**o**tes	Prints worksheet notes only.

Both	Prints both the worksheet and notes on separate pages.
Preview	Peviews the document before printing.
Fast, but no graphics	Prints quickly without graphics.

TIP: Press Ctrl+Shift+F12 to display the Print dialog box. Another shortcut is to press Alt+Ctrl+Shift+F2.

 Select this tool on the Standard toolbar to print the active document without displaying the Print dialog box.

When you select the Setup button, Excel displays the Page Setup dialog box. See **File Page Setup.**

See also File Print Preview, Skill Session 12, "Basic Printing," and Skill Session 22, "Advanced Print Operations."

File Print Preview

Allows you to see, on the screen, how a document will look when it is printed using the current layout and print settings. Header and footer text is displayed as well.

Usage

1. Display the document you want to preview in the active window.
2. Select File Preview.

 **NOTE:** You can't edit a document on the Preview screen.

 **NOTE:** The Print Preview tool is a custom tool, available only if you have added it to a toolbar. See Skill Session 48.

The command buttons on the Preview screen have the following functions:

Next	Displays the next page.
Previous	Displays the previous page.
Zoom	Toggles between full-page view and actual-size view.
Prin**t**	Displays the Print dialog box.
Setup	Displays the Page Setup dialog box.
Margins	Displays the current margin and column settings. Drag the margin or column markers to adjust the settings.
Close	Closes the Preview screen, and returns to the document window.

See also Skill Session 12, "Basic Printing," and Skill Session 22, "Advanced Printing Operations."

File Print Report

Prints a preset sequence of views and scenarios.

Usage

1. Select File Print Report to display the Print Report dialog box.
2. Select the report you want to print from the Reports box.
3. Select the Print button.
4. In the Print box, select the print options you want.
5. Select OK.

You can also add, delete, or edit the reports listed in the Reports box. Simply select a report name, then select Add, Delete, or Edit.

See also Skill Session 23, "Working with Reports."

File Record Macro

Opens a macro sheet, and then records your keystrokes, commands, and other actions as a macro function. This command appears on the **F**ile menu only when all windows are closed or hidden. You can also access this command (Record) on the **M**acro menu.

Usage

1. Select File Record Macro. Excel displays the Record Macro dialog box.
2. Enter a name in the Name box, or use the suggested name.
3. Enter a letter for the shortcut key in the Key box, or use the suggested letter.
4. Select an option in the Store Macro In box.
5. Select OK. The status line indicates that you are now recording. Enter the actions and keystrokes you want to include in the macro. Select Macro Stop Recorder to end the macro.

 Select this tool on the Macro toolbar to begin recording a macro.

See also Macro Record and Macro Stop Recorder.

File Save

Allows you to save the most recent changes or additions to an existing document.

Usage

1. Display the document you want to save in the active window.
2. Select File Save. The status bar indicates that the file is being saved. If the file has not been previously saved, Excel displays the File Save As dialog box.

 **TIP:** To save a file instantly, click on the Save File tool or press Shift+F12.

See also File Save As, and Skill Session 6, "Working with Worksheets and Workbooks."

File Save As

Allows you to save a new or existing document.

Usage

1. Make the document you want to save the active window.
2. Select File Save As. Excel displays the File Save As dialog box.

3. Enter a name in the File **N**ame box.
4. (Optional) From the **D**irectories list, select a different directory in which to save the file.
5. (Optional) From the Dri**v**es box, select a different drive on which to save the file.
6. (Optional) In the Save File as **T**ype, select a different file type.
7. Select OK.

 **TIP:** Press F12 or Alt+Shift+F2 to display the Save As dialog box.

See also Skill Session 6, "Working with Worksheets and Workbooks," and Skill Session 44, "More About Workbooks."

File Save Workbook

Saves changes made to all documents in a workbook.

Usage

1. Select **F**ile Save **W**orkbook. Excel displays the Save As dialog box.
2. In the File Name box, enter a file name or use the suggested name.
3. Select OK.

See also Skill Session 6, "Working with Worksheets and Workbooks," and **F**ile Save **A**s.

File Unhide

Redisplays a window that was previously hidden. This command appears on the **F**ile menu only when all open windows are hidden. When one or more windows are open, the **U**nhide command appears on the **W**indow menu.

Usage

1. Select **F**ile **U**nhide.
2. Select a window from the **U**nhide box, and then select OK.

See also Window **U**nhide and **W**indow **H**ide.

File Update

Updates information in a document that contains an Excel object. This command replaces the **S**ave command on the **F**ile menu when you are editing an Excel object embedded in a separate document.

Usage

1. Made the worksheet that contains the object the active document.
2. Select File Update.

See also Skill Session 27, "Adding Objects to a Chart."

Format Menu Commands

Format Alignment

Allows you to choose an alignment style for data within selected cells.

Usage

1. Select the cells you want to align.
2. Select Forma**t** Alignment to display the Alignment dialog box.
3. Select alignment options as described in Table Format.1.
4. Select OK.

Table Format.1 Alignment Options

Setting	*Description*
Horizontal	Aligns cells horizontally.
General	Left-aligns text, right-aligns numbers.
Left	Left-aligns data.
Center	Centers data.
Right	Right-aligns data.

continues

Table Format.1 continued

Setting	*Description*
Fill	Repeats characters in the cell across the entire cell.
Justify	Aligns data at right and left borders of cell (must use Wrap Text option with this option).
Center Across selection	Centers text across a range of cells.
Vertical	Aligns cells vertically.
Top	Aligns data at top border of cell.
Center	Aligns data at vertical center of cell.
Bottom	Aligns data at bottom cell border.
Orientation	Selects a text orientation style.
Wrap Text	Displays a long entry on multiple lines within the cell.

Format AutoFormat

Automatically formats the selected range of cells using one of Excel's built-in formats for tables.

Usage

1. Select the cells you want to format.
2. Select Format, AutoFormat. Excel displays the AutoFormat dialog box.
3. From the Table Format box, select a format type. A sample of the format type you choose is displayed in the sample box.
4. Select OK.

To apply selected elements of the format style (such as numbers or fonts only), select the Options button in the AutoFormat dialog box.

> To automatically apply the last format style chosen to the selected range of cells, select the AutoFormat tool on the Standard or Formatting toolbar.

Format Border

Allows you to create a border around a selected cell or group of cells.

Usage

1. Select the cell or cells you want to border.
2. Select Format Border to display the Border dialog box.
3. Select a Border and a Style option.
4. (Optional) Select a Color from the **C**olor palette.
5. (Optional) Select the Shade check box to shade the cell.

> **TIP:** You can make borders stand out by hiding the worksheet gridlines. Select the Options Display then deselect the Gridlines check box.

Select this tool on the Standard toolbar to add a bottom border without selecting style, color, or shade options.

Select this tool on the Standard toolbar to add an outline border without selecting style, color, or shade options. Keyboard shortcut: Press Ctrl+Shift+& to outline the selected cells. Press Ctrl+Shift+minus sign (–) to remove all borders.

Select this tool to add a top border without selecting style, color, or shade options.

Select this tool to add a left border without selecting style, color, or shade options.

Select this tool to add a right border without selecting style, color or shade options. Note that the top border, left border, and right border tools are custom tools and are only available if you have added them to a toolbar. See Skill Session 48.

See also Format Patterns.

Format Bring to Front

Places the selected object on top of all other objects. This command takes no action if the selected object is already on top.

Usage

1. Select the object you want to place on top of all other objects.
2. Select Format Bring to Front.

Click this tool on the Drawing toolbar to place the selected object on top of all other objects.

See also Format Send to Back.

Format Cell Protection

Selecting the Format Cell Protection command gives you the option of locking cells or hiding cells when a range of cells is selected. If the worksheet is not already protected, select the Options Protect Document command to activate the locked or hidden feature. Hidden cells do not display the formula in the formula bar when the file is protected using the **O**ptions **P**rotect Document command.

Usage

1. Select a range of cells to protect.
2. Select Format Cell Protection to display the Cell Protection dialog box.
3. Select the Locked, the Hidden, or both check boxes.
4. Select OK.

TIP: When an object is selected rather than a cell range, the Format Cell Protection command changes to Format Object Protection.

Click this tool on the Utility toolbar to automatically lock the selected range of cells.

See also Options Protect Document.

Format Column Width

Set the column width for selected columns in a worksheet.

Usage

1. Select a cell in the column whose width you want to change. (You can select a range of cells across multiple columns.)
2. Select Format Column Width to display the Format dialog box.
3. Enter a number (an integer or decimal fraction) in the Column Width box, or select the Best Fit button to have Excel adjust the width automatically based on cell contents in the column. (The entered number represents the number of characters, based on the current font setting.)
4. To reset the selected column to standard width, check the Use Standard Width check box. To alter the standard width used by Excel, enter a new number in the Standard Width box.
5. Select OK.

To hide a column, select the Hide button in the Column Width dialog box.

To redisplay a hidden column:

1. Select any range of cells that spans the column to the left and to the right of the hidden column.
2. Select Format Column Width to display the Column Width dialog box.
3. Select the Unhide button in the Column Width dialog box.

TIP: To select Best Fit quickly, double-click on the right border of the column heading.

TIP: To resize a column quickly, set a new width by clicking and dragging the right border of the column heading to the right or left.

See also Format Row Height.

Format Font

Allows you to change the font, font style, font size, effects, and color for the selected text. Use this command to add strikeout or underlining to the font.

TIP: Press Ctrl+B to bold the selected cells. Press Ctrl+I to italicize the selected cells.

Usage

1. Select the text for which you want to change the font.
2. Select Format Font to display the Font dialog box.
3. Select the settings you choose from the Font, Font Style, Size, and Color boxes. To return selected text to its normal font, select the Normal Font check box.
4. (Optional) Select Strikeout or Underline from the Effects box.
5. Select OK.

Click this tool on the Standard toolbar to decrease the font size of the selected text to the next smallest size.

Click this tool on the Standard toolbar to increase the font size of the selected text to the next largest size.

Format Group

Makes a connection between selected graphic objects (charts, drawn objects, buttons, text boxes) that allows you to treat them as a single graphic object. When the selected objects are already grouped, the **G**roup command on the Forma**t** menu changes to the **U**ngroup command.

Usage

1. Select the first object to group.
2. Press and hold the Shift key, then select the second object to group.
3. Select Forma**t** **G**roup or select the **G**roup Objects tool on the Drawing toolbar. The two objects now behave as a single object.

You can also choose the Select Objects tool on the Drawing toolbar to select objects to group. Then, click and drag the crosshair to enclose all objects to be grouped within the dotted line.

To ungroup two or more grouped objects, select the group, then select Forma**t** **U**ngroup or select the Ungroup Objects tool on the Drawing toolbar.

Click this tool on the Drawing toolbar to link the selected objects into one object.

Format Justify

Distributes the characters in a cell, text box, or button evenly across the object. The Word Wrap check box in the Alignment dialog box must be selected in order for this command to work.

Usage

1. Select the cell, object, or button to justify.
2. Select the **J**ustify command from the Forma**t** menu, or select the Justify Align tool from the Formatting toolbar.

Click this tool on the Formatting toolbar to distribute the contents of the selected cell, text box, or button evenly across the object.

See also Forma**t** **A**lignment.

Format Number

Determines the format of numbers in the selected cells.

Usage

1. Select the range of cells to which you want to apply a number format.
2. Select Format Number to display the Number Format dialog box.
3. Select a category from the **C**ategory list.
4. Select a format from the **F**ormat Codes list. The format you selected is displayed in the C**o**de box.
5. Select OK to apply the format to the selected cells.

Click this tool on the Formatting toolbar to apply the format to the selected cells.

Click this tool on the Formatting toolbar to apply the format to the selected cells.

Click this tool on the Formatting toolbar to apply the format to the selected cells.

You can apply formats quickly by pressing the keyboard combination Ctrl+Shift+ with any of various other keys. Table Format.2 shows these combinations, and the formats they apply.

Table Format.2 Formatting Shortcuts Using the Keyboard

Press Ctrl+Shift+	*To apply this format:*
!	0.00
@	h:mm
#	d-mmm-yy
$	$#,##0.00 or $#,###.00
%	percent
^	0.00E+00

See also Skill Session 13, "Formatting Numbers, Dates, and Times."

Format Object Properties

Determines how graphical objects are attached to cells as well as their position, size, and movement.

Usage

1. Select the graphical object to reposition.
2. Select Format Object Properties to display the Object Properties dialog box.
3. Choose one of these options from the Object Placement box:
   - Move and **S**ize with Cells
   - **M**ove but Don't Size with Cells
   - **D**on't Move or Size with Cells
4. To print the object when the worksheet is printed, check the **P**rint Object check box.
5. Select OK.

Format Patterns

Allows you to add shading to selected cells and graphics objects.

Usage

1. Select the cells or objects you want to shade.
2. Select Format **P**atterns to displays the Patterns dialog box. The available options depend on the object selected in step 1.
3. Select options as described in Table Format.2, then select OK.

Table Format.3 Patterns Options

Setting	*Description*
Pattern	Displays multiple fill patterns for selected cells or objects.
Foreground	The foreground color of the fill pattern.
Background	The background color of the fill pattern.
Shadow	Shading on the right and lower sides of text box, rectangle, oval, or chart.

continues

Table Format.3 continued

Setting	*Description*
Round Corners	Rounds the corners of a text box, rectangle, or chart.
Arrow Head	Displays style, length, and width options for arrowheads applied to a line. Select an arrowhead style before using length and width options.

Click this tool on the Formatting toolbar to apply the Drop-Shadow format to the selected cells.

Format Row Height

Allows you to change the height of selected rows.

Usage

1. Select a cell in the row or rows you want to change.
2. Select Format Row Height to display the Row Height dialog box.
3. In the Row Height box, type the number of points for the row height. The number can be an integer or decimal fraction.
4. To change selected rows back to standard height, select the Use Standard Height check box.
5. Select the Hide button to hide selected rows; select Unhide to display a hidden row.

To change the height of a row you only need to select one cell in the row. To change the height of all rows in a worksheet, select the entire worksheet or select any column.

TIP: To hide the selected row, press Ctrl+9. To redisplay a hidden row, press Ctrl+Shift+(.

Format Send to Back

Places the selected object beneath all other objects. This command takes no action if the selected object is already on the bottom.

Usage

1. Select the object you want to place beneath all other objects.
2. Select Format Send to Back.

Click this tool on the Drawing toolbar to place the selected object beneath all other objects.

TIP: When you select the Send to Back tool in conjunction with the Shift key, it places the object on top of all other objects.

See also Format Bring To Front.

Format Style

Applies a cell style to the selected cells. (A *cell style* is a named collection of cell formats.) Also allows you to modify an existing style or create a new one.

Usage

1. Select the range of cells you want to format.
2. Select Format Style to display the Style dialog box.
3. From the Style Name drop-down box, select a style.
4. Select OK.

To change or define a new style, select the Define button in the Style dialog box.

Click the drop-down arrow for this tool on the Standard toolbar to select a stored cell style.

Formula Menu Commands

Formula Apply Names

Searches formulas in the selected cells and replaces cell references with range names, if they exist.

Usage

1. Select the range of cells to search.
2. Select Formula Apply Names to display the Apply Names dialog box. The Options button in the Apply Names dialog box contains settings for omitting column name, omitting row name, and specifying the naming order.
3. From the Apply Names list, select the name to apply. To select more than one name, hold down the Control key, while pressing the up or down arrow keys to make your selection. Press the space bar to add a name to the selection.
4. Select OK. Excel changes all cell references to range names in the formulas found in the selected range.

   Check the Ignore Relative/Absolute box to replace all references, whether relative or absolute.

   When you check the Use Row And Column Names box, Excel replaces cell references with the name of the row or the column if the exact name for the referenced cell can't be found.

See also Formula Create Names and Formula Define Name.

Formula Create Names

Creates a range name for a selected range of cells using the label for the selected range.

Usage

Excel names ranges using the name that appears:

- at the top row
- at the bottom row
- in the left column
- in the right column

These choices appear in the Create Names dialog box. Excel suggests a range name based on the cells you select.

1. Select the range of cells to create a name for.
2. Select Formula Create Names. Excel displays the Create Names dialog box.
3. Select an option from the dialog box, then select OK.

> **TIP:** Press Ctrl+Shift+F3 to display the Formula Create Names dialog box for the selected range of cells.

See also Formula Apply Names and Formula Define Name.

Formula Define Name

Allows you to define a name for the selected range of cells. The range may be adjacent or non-adjacent.

Usage

1. Select an adjacent or a non-adjacent range of cells to name.
2. Select Formula Define Name to display the Define Name dialog box.
3. Check to make sure the range shown in the Refers To box is correct. If not, enter the correct range.
4. In the Name box, enter a range name for the selected range.
5. To define this and other range names, select Add, otherwise select OK. When you select Add, the dialog box remains on the screen until you select Close or OK.

> **TIP:** Press Ctrl+F3 to display the Define Name dialog box for the selected range of cells.

See also Formula Apply Names and Formula Create Name.

Formula Find

Finds any character, including letters, numbers, punctuation marks, and wildcard characters. (Type the wildcard character * to represent any number of unknown characters, or ? to represent a single unknown character.) Table Formula.1 summarizes ways you can narrow the scope of the search by using the Find dialog box.

Table Formula.1 Using the Find dialog box to search for specified characters

In This Box:	*Select:*	*Excel will search:*
Look In	**F**ormulas	For formulas.
	Values	For values.
	Notes	For notes.
Look By	**R**ows	Row by row.
	Co**l**umns	Column by column.
Look At	Wh**o**le	For exact matches only.
	Part	For any occurrence that matches in whole or in part.
Match Case	(checked)	For the case identical to that shown in the Find What box.

Usage

1. Select the range to search. (Otherwise Excel searches the whole worksheet.)
2. Select Formula **F**ind to display the Find dialog box.
3. Enter the character or characters to search for in the Find **W**hat box.
4. Choose the desired settings in the dialog box, then select OK.

> **TIP:** Press Shift+F5 to display the Find dialog box, press F7 to find the next occurrence, press Shift+F7 to return to the previous occurrence.

Formula Goal Seek

Adjusts the number in a cell referenced by a formula until the formula returns the number you specify. Use this command to find a specific solution to a formula.

Usage

1. Select the cell that contains the formula.
2. Select Formula Goal Seek to display the Goal Seek dialog box.
3. Check to see that the reference in the **S**et cell box is the cell in which the formula is located. If not, enter the correct cell address.
4. In the To **v**alue box, enter the number that represents the result you want the formula to produce.
5. In the By **c**hanging cell box, enter the cell address for the number you want Excel to adjust.
6. Select OK. Excel displays the Goal Seeking Status box as it adjusts the specified cell. Select OK to accept the change, or Cancel to restore the original operand.

See also Skill Session 49, "Using Goal Seeker."

Formula Goto

Moves directly to and selects the cell, cell range, or named cells you specify.

Usage

1. Select Formula Goto to display the Goto dialog box.
2. In the **R**eference box, enter the cell, cell range, or named cells to go to.
3. Select OK. Excel moves to and selects the cells you specify.

   The **G**oto box lists the last four cell references from which you selected the Goto command. Click on any item in the list to insert the reference in the **R**eference box, then select OK to go to that location.

 **TIP:** Press F5 to display the Goto dialog box instantly.

Formula Note

Attaches a note to the active cell, and places a note indicator in the upper right corner of the cell. The Formula Note command displays the Cell Note dialog box. The Notes in **S**heet box displays cell references in the current worksheet, along with the beginning text of each note. (Notes are not visible in the worksheet itself.) Use this dialog box to add, view, delete, or edit a note.

Usage

1. Select the cell to which you want to attach a note.
2. Select Formula Note to display the Cell Note dialog box.
3. Check to see that the cell referenced in the **C**ell box is the correct cell. If not, enter the correct cell address.
4. In the **T**ext Note box, enter the text for the note.
5. Select OK.

To add more than one note at once while the Cell Note dialog box is open, select the Add button to add the note. Enter the next cell reference in the **C**ell box, and then enter the next note in the Text Note box.

To display or edit a note in the Cell Note dialog box, double-click on the cell (or select the cell), then select Formula Note. Select the note from the Notes in **S**heet list, and then click in the Text Note box to edit the note. To delete a note, select a note from the Notes in Sheet box, and then select the Delete button.

> **TIP:** Press Shift+F2 to display the Cell Note dialog box, or double-click on a cell that has a note attached.

See also Skill Session 5, "Entering and Editing Data," and Skill Session 21, "Using Text Notes and Arrows."

Formula Outline

Allows you to outline the data in a worksheet with up to eight levels of detail or supporting data. In order for Excel to create an outline from a worksheet, the summation formulas in the worksheet must be constructed consistently. For example, if a formula that sums a rows is located below the detail, *all* summary formulas for rows must also be located below the detail. If a formula that sums a column is located to the right of the detail, all formulas that sum columns must be constructed the same way. (It is also possible to locate a *row's* summary formula *above* the detail, or a *column's* summary formula to the *left* of the detail. Although this is not common, it is acceptable as long as all rows and columns in the worksheet are summed the same way.)

Usage

1. Select the range of cells to outline. (Select a single cell to outline the entire worksheet.)

2. Select Formula Outline to display the Outline dialog box.
3. In the Direction box, the summary options for summing rows below the detail and summing columns to the right of the detail are both checked. If your worksheet is not constructed this way, clear these boxes.
4. If you want Excel to apply built-in styles to the summary rows and columns in the outline, check the Automatic Styles box. To apply styles to row and column levels, select the Apply Styles button.
5. To create the outline, select Create, then select OK.

Once an outline is created, you can move up, or *promote*, an item one level at a time in the outline structure. You can also move down, or *demote*, an item one level at a time in the outline structure.

Click this tool on the Utility toolbar, or press Alt+Shift+left arrow to move an item up one level in the outline structure.

Click this tool on the Utility toolbar, or press Alt+Shift+right arrow to move an item down one level in the outline structure.

Click this tool on the Utility toolbar to display or hide outline symbols in a worksheet.

Click this tool on the Utility toolbar to select the visible cells within the current selection.

Formula Paste Function

Allows you to paste a function into the formula bar for the active cell.

Usage

1. Select the cell in which you want to insert a formula.
2. Select Formula Paste Function to display the Paste Function dialog box.

3. Select a category from the Function Category box.
4. Select a function from the Paste Function box.
5. To have Excel paste *argument place holders* along with the function, check the Paste Arguments check box. If the function has more than one form, select a set of arguments from the Select Arguments box that Excel displays.
6. Select OK. Excel pastes the function into the formula bar for the active cell. The formula bar is still active. Once a function is pasted into the formula bar, you can edit the formula, and replace argument place holders with actual numbers or references.
7. Press Enter.

> Click this tool to display the Paste Function dialog box, or press Shift+F3. (Note that this is a custom tool, available only if you have added it to a toolbar. See Skill Session 48.)

See also Skill Session 11, "Using Built-In Functions," and Skill Session 46, "Advanced Formulas and Functions."

Formula Paste Name

Pastes a defined name you have selected into the formula bar for the active cell. Also allows you to paste a list of all defined names into a blank area of the worksheet.

Usage

1. Select the cell in which you want to paste a name.
2. Select Formula, Paste Name to display the Paste Name dialog box.
3. Select a name from the Paste Name box.
4. Select OK.

You can also use this dialog box to paste a list of all defined names into the worksheet. Worksheet names are pasted into an area two columns wide. Macro names are pasted into an area five columns wide. Be sure to allow enough blank space in your worksheet to avoid overwriting existing cells.

To paste a list of defined names into the worksheet:

1. Move to the cell in the upper left corner of the area where the list will be pasted.
2. Select Formula Paste Name to display the Paste Name dialog box.
3. Select the Paste List button.

> Click this tool or press F3 to display the Paste Name dialog box. (Note that this is a custom tool, available only if you have added it to a toolbar. See Skill Session 48.)

See also Formula Define Name.

Formula Reference

Allows you to change the type of cell reference (relative or absolute) in the selected cell without retyping the entry. Note that this command is only available on the Formula menu when the formula bar is active.

Usage

1. Select the cell containing the cell reference type you want to change.
2. Press F2 to activate the formula bar.
3. In the formula bar, select the cell reference for which you want to change the reference type.
4. Select Formula Reference, or press F4. Excel changes the reference type in the following ways:

Reference type:	*Changes to:*
relative (A1)	absolute ($A$1)
absolute ($A$1)	mixed (A$1)
mixed (A$1)	mixed ($A1)
mixed ($A1)	relative (A1)

   Continue to select Formula Reference (or to press F4) until the reference type you want is displayed.

5. Press Enter (or select the Enter box) to confirm the entry. Press Esc (or select the Cancel box) to cancel the change.

Formula Replace

Searches for and replaces characters you specify, in an entire worksheet or within a selected range of cells. The search and replacement characters can include letters, numbers, formulas, parts of formulas, and wildcards. (Type the wildcard character * to search for an unknown number of characters, and ? to search for a single unknown character.)

The Replace dialog box contains the following settings:

Look By	Select Rows to have Excel search row by row, select Columns to have Excel search column by column.
Look At	Select Whole to have Excel replace exact matches only. Select Part to have Excel replace any occurrence that matches in whole or in part.
Match Case	Check this box to search for the case identical to that shown in the Find What box.

The Match Case dialog box contains the following buttons:

Replace All Button	Select this button to replace all occurrences in the entire worksheet or the selected range without displaying each occurrence.
Find Next Button	Select this button to have Excel find the next occurrence.
Replace Button	Select this button to have Excel replace the current selection.

Usage

1. Select the range of cells you want searched. (Otherwise Excel searches the whole worksheet.)
2. Select Formula Replace to display the Replace dialog box.
3. In the Find What box, enter the characters to search for.
4. In the Replace With box, enter the replacement characters.
5. Choose the desired dialog box settings.
6. Select the Find Next button.
7. Select Replace, Replace All, or Find Next Button.

8. If you chose the Replace or Find Next Button, you can repeat step 7 until all desired occurrences are replaced.
9. Select Close to return to the worksheet window.

See also Formula Find.

Formula Scenario Manager

Allows you to create and save different input values for a worksheet model. Each of these sets of numbers represents a separate *scenario*. Use scenarios to view different results in a worksheet, based on each scenario's input values. Using this command, you can also create a summary report that shows the changing input values, and the changing results of each scenario.

Usage

To create one or more scenarios for the active worksheet:

1. Select Formula Scenario Manager to display the Scenario Manager dialog box.
2. In the Changing Cells box, type the range address for the changing cells, or select the correct range in the worksheet window.
3. Select the Add button. Excel displays the Add Scenario dialog box.
4. Enter a name for the scenario in the Name box.
5. Enter the numbers that change for each cell referenced.
6. You have two options for adding this scenario:

   To add the scenario to the list and create another one, select the Add button, then repeat steps 4 and 5 for each scenario you want to add.

   To add the scenario and return to the Scenario Manager dialog box, select OK. The scenario you added appears in the Scenarios box.
7. Select the Close button to return to the worksheet.

To display the input values and results of an existing scenario in the worksheet window:

1. Select Formula Scenario Manager to display the Scenario Manager dialog box.
2. Select a scenario to display from the Scenarios list.
3. Select the Show button. Excel changes the numbers in the worksheet and displays the new results.

4. Repeat steps 2 and 3 to display other scenario results.
5. Select Close to return to the worksheet.

> **NOTE:** The numbers in the last scenario you show remain in the worksheet when you select the Close button. To ensure that the previous numbers will be restored, select the scenario they belong to, *before* you select the Close button.

To create a summary report of all scenarios for a worksheet:

1. Select Formula Scenario Manager to display the Scenario Manager dialog box.
2. Select the Summary button. Excel displays the Scenario Summary dialog box.
3. Check to make sure the Changing Cells reference is correct.
4. (Optional) If you want the summary report to include scenario results, enter the cell reference for the result cell (or cells) in the **R**esult Cells box.
5. Select OK. Excel creates a summary report, and displays it in a separate worksheet. To save this report, rename and save the worksheet in which it appears.

To use the Scenario Manager dialog box to *edit* a scenario:

1. Select a scenario from the Scenarios list.
2. Select the Edit button. Excel displays a dialog box in which you can edit the name of the scenario, and the numbers to change for the changing cells.

To use the Scenario Manager dialog box to *delete* a scenario:

1. Select a scenario from the Scenarios list.
2. Select the Delete button.

Formula Select Special

The Formula Select Special command displays the Select Special dialog box from which you can choose characteristics for the cells you want Excel to select. For example, you can select all blank cells, or you can select all cells with notes attached. For a description of each option in the Select Special dialog box, see Help.

Usage

1. To select cells in a range, select the range. To search the entire worksheet, select only one cell.
2. Select Formula Select Special to display the Select Special dialog box.
3. Select one of the option buttons. If you select either Constants or Formulas, you can select zero, or else more check boxes.
4. Select OK. Excel selects all cells that match the characteristics you chose.

Formula Show Active Cell

Displays the active cell in the worksheet.

Usage

When the active cell is not visible in the worksheet window, select Formula Show Active Cell. Excel repositions the worksheet window to display the active cell.

Formula Solver

Displays Solver Parameters dialog box, in which you can define the problem you want to solve.

Usage

Working with the Solver requires more detailed instruction than is available in this command reference. After selecting Formula Solver, which displays the Solver Parameters dialog box, follow the general guidelines below for using the Solver. For detailed instructions on using this tool, refer to Skill Session 51, "Using Solver."

1. Specify the cell for which you want to maximize the value, minimize the value, or hit a target value.
2. Specify the cells for which values may be adjusted to find a solution.
3. Specify the cells for which values must fall within certain limits, or meet certain target values.
4. Select the Solve button.

See also Skill Session 51, "Using Solver."

Gallery Menu Commands

Gallery 3-D Area

Changes the active chart to a 3-D area chart type.

Usage

1. With a chart displayed in the active window, select Gallery 3-D Area. Excel displays the Chart Gallery dialog box showing different styles of the 3-D area chart.
2. Select a chart style, then select OK.

Select this tool on the Chart toolbar to change the chart in the active window to a 3-D area chart type.

See also **G**allery **A**rea.

Gallery 3-D Bar

Changes the active chart to a 3-D bar chart type.

Usage

1. With a chart displayed in the active window, select Gallery 3-D Bar. Excel displays the Chart Gallery dialog box showing different styles of the 3-D bar chart.
2. Select a chart style, then select OK.

Select this tool on the Chart toolbar to change the chart in the active window to a 3-D bar chart type.

See also Skill Session 29, "Working with 3-D Charts," and **G**allery **B**ar.

Gallery 3-D Column

Changes the active chart to a 3-D column chart type.

Usage

1. With a chart displayed in the active window, select Gallery 3-D Column. Excel displays the Chart Gallery dialog box showing different styles of the 3-D column chart.
2. Select a chart style, then select OK.

Select this tool on the Chart toolbar to change the chart in the active window to a 3-D column chart type.

See also Skill Session 29, "Working with 3-D Charts," and **G**allery **C**olumn.

Gallery 3-D Line

Changes the active chart to a 3-D line chart type.

Usage

1. With a chart displayed in the active window, select Gallery Line. Excel displays the Chart Gallery dialog box, showing different styles of the 3-D line chart.
2. Select a chart style, then select OK.

Select this tool on the Chart toolbar to change the chart in the active window to a 3-D line chart type.

See also Skill Session 29, "Working with 3-D Charts," and **G**allery Li**n**e.

Gallery 3-D Pie

Changes the active chart to a 3-D pie chart type.

Usage

1. With a chart displayed in the active window, select Gallery 3-D Pie. Excel displays the Chart Gallery dialog box, showing different styles of the 3-D pie chart.
2. Select a chart style, and then select OK.

Select this tool on the Chart toolbar to change the chart in the active window to a 3-D pie chart type.

See also Skill Session 29, "Working with 3-D Charts," and **G**allery **P**ie.

Gallery 3-D Surface

Changes the active chart to a 3-D surface chart type.

Usage

1. With a chart displayed in the active window, select **G**allery 3-D S**u**rface. Excel displays the Chart Gallery dialog box, showing different styles of the 3-D surface chart.
2. Select a chart style, and then select OK.

Select this tool on the Chart toolbar to change the chart in the active window to a 3-D surface chart type.

See also Skill Session 29, "Working with 3-D Charts."

Gallery Area

Changes the active chart to an area chart type.

Usage

1. With a chart displayed in the active window, select **G**allery **A**rea. Excel displays the Chart Gallery dialog box, showing different styles of the area chart.
2. Select a chart style, and then select OK.

Select this tool on the Chart toolbar to change the chart in the active window to an area chart type.

See also Skill Session 24, "Creating Charts," and **G**allery 3-D **A**rea.

Gallery Bar

Changes the active chart to a bar chart type.

Usage

1. With a chart displayed in the active window, select Gallery Bar. Excel displays the Chart Gallery dialog box, showing different styles of the bar chart.
2. Select a chart style, and then select OK.

Select this tool on the Chart toolbar to change the chart in the active window to a bar chart type.

See also Skill Session 24, "Creating Charts," and **G**allery **3**-D Bar.

Gallery Column

Changes the active chart to a column chart type.

Usage

1. With a chart displayed in the active window, select Gallery Column. Excel displays the Chart Gallery dialog box, showing different styles of the column chart.
2. Select a chart style, and then select OK.

Select this tool on the Chart toolbar to change the chart in the active window to a column chart type.

See also Skill Session 24, "Creating Charts," and **G**allery 3-D C**o**lumn.

Gallery Combination

Changes the active chart to a combination chart type.

Usage

1. With a chart displayed in the active window, select Gallery Combination. Excel displays the Chart Gallery dialog box, showing different styles of the combination chart.
2. Select a chart style, and then select OK.

Select this tool on the Chart toolbar to change the chart in the active window to a line and column chart type.

Select this tool on the Chart toolbar to change the chart in the active window to a combination volume/hi-low-close chart type.

See also Skill Session 24, "Creating Charts."

Gallery Line

Changes the active chart to a line chart type.

Usage

1. With a chart displayed in the active window, select Gallery Line. Excel displays the Chart Gallery dialog box, showing different styles of the line chart.
2. Select a chart style, and then select OK.

Select this tool on the Chart toolbar to change the chart in the active window to a line chart type.

See also Skill Session 24, "Creating Charts," and **G**allery 3-D Li**n**e.

Gallery Pie

Changes the active chart to a pie chart type.

Usage

1. With a chart displayed in the active window, select Gallery Pie. Excel displays the Chart Gallery dialog box, showing different styles of the pie chart.
2. Select a chart style, and then select OK.

Select this tool on the Chart toolbar to change the chart in the active window to a pie chart type.

See also Skill Session 24, "Creating Charts," and **G**allery 3-D P**i**e.

Gallery Preferred

Changes the chart in the active window to the style you have previously defined as the preferred type.

Usage

1. Display the chart you want to change in the active window.
2. Select Gallery Preferred. Excel changes the chart to the style previously set as "preferred."

Select this tool on the Chart toolbar to change the chart in the active window to the chart type previously set as "preferred."

See also **G**allery Se**t** Preferred.

Gallery Radar

Changes the active chart to a radar chart type.

Usage

1. With a chart displayed in the active window, select Gallery Radar. Excel displays the Chart Gallery dialog box showing different styles of the radar chart.
2. Select a chart style, then select OK.

Select this tool on the Chart toolbar to change the chart in the active window to a radar chart type.

See also Skill Session 24, "Creating Charts."

Gallery Set Preferred

Makes the chart type currently displayed in the active window the "preferred" chart type.

Usage

1. In the active window, display a chart in the type you want to set as the preferred type.
2. Select Gallery Set Preferred. Excel makes the current chart type the preferred type.

See also Gallery Preferred.

Gallery XY (Scatter)

Changes the active chart to an XY (scatter) chart type.

Usage

1. With a chart displayed in the active window, select Gallery XY (Scatter). Excel displays the Chart Gallery dialog box, showing different styles of the XY chart.
2. Select a chart style, and then select OK.

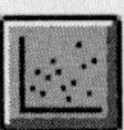

Select this tool on the Chart toolbar to change the chart in the active window to an XY chart type.

See also Skill Session 24, "Creating Charts."

Help Menu Commands

Most commands on the Help menu display an Excel Help window similar to the one shown in the figure below.

Help About Microsoft Excel

Displays the current version number of Excel and the copyright date. Also displays the name of the licensee and the serial number.

Usage

1. Select Help About Microsoft Excel to display the Excel information window.
2. Select OK to close the window.

Help Contents

Displays the table of contents for Excel Help.

Usage

1. Select Help Contents. Excel displays the Help Contents screen in a separate Help window.
2. Select a topic from the list. In most cases, Excel displays a list of subtopics.
3. Repeat step 2 until the description for the topic you selected is displayed. Use the scroll bars or the Page Up and Page Down arrows to view the entire topic.

> **TIP:** Press F1 from any cell in a worksheet to display the Help Contents window.

Help Introducing Microsoft Excel

Starts a Help tutorial in a separate window. Introductory topics include a look at the basics of Excel, new features of Excel 4.0, and information for Lotus 1-2-3 users.

Usage

1. Select Help Introducing Microsoft Excel. Excel starts an introductory tutorial in a separate window.
2. Follow the instructions given on the screen.
3. Select Exit to Microsoft Excel to end the tutorial.

Help Learning Microsoft Excel

Starts a Help tutorial in a separate window. Describes the fundamental skills for using Excel, including topics about worksheets, charts, databases, macros, and toolbars.

Usage

1. Select Help Learning Microsoft Excel. Excel starts a tutorial in a separate window.
2. Follow the instructions given on the screen.
3. Select Exit.

Help Lotus 1-2-3 Help

Provides help to Lotus 1-2-3 users who are learning to use Excel. Describes equivalent commands and procedures. You can choose to display instructions for equivalent commands or a demonstration of Excel's procedures.

Usage

1. Select Help Lotus 1-2-3 Help. Excel displays the Help for Lotus 1-2-3 Users dialog box.
2. Follow the instructions given in the dialog box.
3. Select Close.

Help Multiplan

Provides help to Multiplan users on equivalent Excel commands.

Usage

1. Select Help Multiplan Help. Excel displays the Multiplan Help dialog box.
2. Enter a Multiplan command in the Command box, then select OK or select Cancel to close the dialog box and return to Excel. When you enter a Multiplan command, Excel displays the equivalent Excel command.

Help Product Support

Provides information on all product support services for Excel, including how to contact Microsoft Product Support.

Usage

1. Select Help Product Support. Help displays a list of product support topics.
2. Select a topic from the list.
3. If necessary, select a subtopic until a description of the topic is displayed.

Help Search

Displays a Search dialog box from which you can specify a Help topic to search for.

Usage

1. Select Help Search. Excel displays the Search dialog box.
2. In the upper portion of the window, type an entry to search for, and then select

Show Topics. A list of all topics matching your entry is displayed in the lower portion of the Search box.

3. Select a topic from the list, then select Go To. Excel displays the Help topic you choose in a separate window.

Macro Menu Commands

Macro Absolute Record

Sets Excel to record cell references as absolute rather than relative when recording a macro. When the macro is run, it operates on absolute cells rather than on cells a fixed distance from the active cell.

Usage

Select Macro Absolute Record. Excel is now set to record absolute cell references when the next macro is recorded. This command toggles between Absolute Record and Relative Record.

See also Macro Relative Record.

Macro Assign to Object

Assigns a macro to an existing button or an object on a worksheet or a macro sheet. The mouse pointer changes to a hand when it is pointing to an object with a macro assigned to it. The macro runs when you click on the object.

Usage

1. Open the macro sheet that contains the macro you want to assign to an object. If you are assigning a macro from the global macro sheet, go to step 2.
2. Select the graphic object to which you want to assign the macro.
3. Select Macro Assign to Object or select Assign to Object from the shortcut menu. Excel displays a dialog box.
4. In the Assign to Object box, select a macro to assign or type the macro name in the Reference box.
5. Select OK.

See also Skill Session 54, "Running a Macro."

Macro Record

Records subsequent actions as a macro so that the actions can be repeated later using the Run Macro command.

Usage

To record a macro on the global macro sheet or a new macro sheet, use these steps.

1. Select Macro Record. Excel displays the Record Macro dialog box.
2. Enter a name for the macro in the **N**ame box or use the suggested name.
3. Enter a letter for the shortcut key in the **K**ey box or use the suggested letter.
4. Select an option in the Store Macro In box.
5. Select OK. The status line indicates that you are now recording.
6. Enter the actions to be included in the macro. To stop recording, select Macro Stop Recorder.

To record a macro on an existing macro sheet, use these steps:

1. Display a new or an existing macro sheet in the active window.
2. Select the cell or cell range on the macro sheet where you want to begin recording.
3. Select Macro Set Recorder.
4. Make the document from which you will record actions the active document.
5. Select Macro Record. Excel displays the Record Macro dialog box.
6. Enter a name for the macro in the **N**ame box or use the suggested name.
7. Enter a letter for the shortcut key in the **K**ey box or use the suggested letter.
8. Select an option in the Store Macro In box.
9. Select OK. The status line indicates that you are now recording.
10. Enter the actions to be included in the macro. To stop recording, select Macro Stop Recorder.

Click on this tool on the Macro toolbar to begin recording a macro.

Click on this tool on the Macro toolbar to stop recording a macro.

See also Skill Session 52, "Recording a Macro," **M**acro Stop Rec**o**rder, and **M**acro Se**t** Recorder.

Macro Relative Record

Sets Excel to record cell references as relative rather than absolute when recording a macro. When the macro is run, it operates on cells a fixed distance from the active cell rather than on absolute references.

Usage

Select Macro Relative Record. Excel is now set to record relative cell references when the next macro is recorded. This command toggles between Rel**a**tive Record and **A**bsolute Record.

See also **M**acro **A**bsolute Record.

Macro Resume

Resumes the operation of a macro after choosing the Pause button or after running a Pause macro function.

Usage

Select Macro Resume to resume a paused macro.

Click on this tool on the Macro toolbar to automatically resume the running of a paused macro.

Macro Run

Runs a macro from the global macro sheet or an open macro sheet.

Usage

1. Select Macro Run. Excel displays the Run Macro dialog box.
2. From the **R**un box, select the macro you want to run.
3. Select OK.

Select this tool on the Macro toolbar to run the selected macro at the active cell.

Macro Set Recorder

Defines a selection on the active macro sheet as the recorder range.

Usage

For information on using the **M**acro Se**t** Recorder command, refer to the instructions for recording a macro on a new or existing macro sheet under **M**acro **R**e**c**ord.

See also Macro Re**c**ord.

Macro Start Recorder

Begins recording subsequent actions again after you have paused your recording.

Usage

Select Macro Start Recorder when you are ready to resume recording actions after the recorder has been paused.

See also Macro Stop Re**c**order and **M**acro Re**c**ord.

Macro Stop Recorder

Temporarily stops recording subsequent actions so you can exclude keystrokes and mouse operations from the macro currently being recorded. This command appears on the Macro menu in place of the Record command, only when you are recording a macro.

Usage

Select Macro Stop Recorder when you have been recording actions and want to pause to ignore subsequent actions. Select Macro **Start Recorder** when you are ready to begin recording actions again.

Select this tool on the Macro toolbar to stop recording a macro.

See also Macro **S**tart Recorder and **M**acro Re**c**ord.

Options Menu Commands

Options Add-Ins

Allows you to select a set of add-in macros that are automatically available each time you run Excel. The Options Add-Ins command displays the Add-In Manager dialog box, from which you can edit, remove, or install add-in files.

Usage

1. Select Options Add-Ins. Excel displays the Add-In Manager dialog box. The Add-Ins Installed box lists all add-ins that are currently installed.
2. To edit or remove an add-in, select an item from the Add-Ins Installed box and then select the Edit or the Remove button.
3. To install an add-in file, select the Add button. Excel displays the File Open dialog box from which you can choose the add-in file to open. (Add-in files have a .XLA file extension.) Select a file from the list, then select OK. Excel returns to the Add-In Manager dialog box.
4. Repeat steps 2 and 3 as desired.
5. Select Close to close the Add-In Manager dialog box and return to the worksheet window.

Options Analysis Tools

Displays a list of special statistical and engineering analysis tools.

Usage

1. Select Options Analysis Tools. Excel displays a list of statistical and engineering analysis tools in the Analysis Tools dialog box.
2. Select the tool you want to use and then select OK.
3. Excel displays a special dialog box for the particular tool you chose. At a minimum, the dialog box asks for an input and an output range. Supply the requested information in the dialog box, then select OK.

Options Calculation

Allows you to specify how and when you want Excel to perform calculations on formulas in open documents.

Usage

1. Select Options Calculation. Excel displays the Calculation Options dialog box.
2. In the Calculation box, select one of the following options:

   Automatic. Excel recalculates automatically whenever you make a change to a document.

   Automatic Except Tables. Excel automatically recalculates everything except tables whenever you make a change to a document.

   Manual. Allows you want to control recalculations manually.

   Recalculate Before Save. Excel recalculates each time you save a document.
3. To change the iteration for goal seeking and for resolving circular references, enter new values in the Maximum Iterations and Maximum Change boxes.
4. Select the desired settings in the Sheet Options box.
5. Select the Calc Now button to recalculate all open documents now.
6. Select the Calc Document button to recalculate the active document now.
7. Select OK.

> **TIP:** If you have selected manual calculation, press F9 from anywhere within an Excel document to recalculate all open documents. Press Shift+F9 to recalculate only the active document.

Options Color Palette

Allows you to customize colors in the active document or copy colors from another document.

Usage

1. Select Options Color Palette. Excel displays the Color Palette dialog box.
2. Double-click on the color to change, or select a color, then select the Edit button. Excel displays the Color Picker dialog box.

3. Adjust the color by clicking in the color box (the large colored box) and then adjusting the brightness using the slide arrow at the far right of the dialog box.

   OR

   Adjust the **H**ue, **S**at (saturation), and **L**um (lumination) settings or the **R**ed, **G**reen, or **B**lue settings.

4. The Color | Solid box displays the color you create on the left and the nearest solid color on the right. To use the solid color, double-click on it.

5. Select OK. Excel returns to the Color Palette dialog box.

6. To customize other colors, repeat steps 2–5 and then select OK.

To copy colors from another document:

1. Select **O**ptions Color Pal**e**tte. Excel displays the Color Palette dialog box.

2. Select a file from the **C**opy Colors From box and then select OK.

> Select this tool to change the color of text in the selected cell. (Note that this custom text-formatting tool is available only if you have added it to a toolbar. See Skill Session 48 for information about customizing toolbars.)

See also Skill Session 17, "Using Color in Worksheets."

Options Display

Allows you to select display settings for cells (formulas, row and column headings, gridlines, zero values, and so on) and for objects.

Usage

1. Select **O**ptions **D**isplay. Excel displays the Display Options dialog box.

2. In the Cells box, select the options that you want Excel to display.

3. In the Objects box, select one of the options for displaying objects.

4. To customize gridline and heading colors, select an option from the Gridline & Heading **C**olor box.

5. Select OK.

TIP: To format cells to display formulas rather than their calculated results, press Ctrl+‘ from any cell.

Options Group Edit

Allows you to specify multiple worksheets as a group so that the commands you select apply to all worksheets in the group.

Usage

1. Open all documents to include in a group.
2. Select Options Group Edit. Excel displays the Group Edit dialog box. The Select Group box lists all worksheets that are currently open.
3. Select all worksheets to include in a group by holding down the Ctrl key and clicking on the sheet name.
4. Select OK.

See also Skill Session 42, “Advanced File Operations.”

Options Protect Document

Allows you to prevent a document’s data, format, and window from being changed.

Usage

1. Select Options Protect Document. Excel displays the Protect Document dialog box.
2. To protect cells, select the Cells check box.
3. To protect objects, select the Objects check box.
4. To protect the window from being resized, moved, or hidden, select the Windows check box.
5. To prevent other users from removing the document protection, enter a password in the **Password** box.
6. Select OK.

See also Skill Session 41, “Protecting Data.”

Options Set Page Break

Inserts a manual page break. Manual page breaks override the page breaks that Excel inserts automatically.

Usage

1. Select a cell one row below and one column to the right of the gridline where you want to insert a page break.
2. Select **O**ptions Set Page **B**reak. Excel inserts a dotted line in the worksheet indicating the location of the page break.

To insert only a horizontal page break, select the entire row below the gridline where you want to insert the page break. To insert only a vertical page break, select the entire column to the right of the gridline where you want to insert the page break.

To remove a manual page break, select any cell directly below or to the right of the page break. Select **O**ptions Remove Page **B**reak. (The **O**ptions Set Page **B**reak command changes to **O**ptions Remove Page **B**reak when the active cell is positioned correctly.)

See also Skill Session 22, "Advanced Print Operations."

Options Set Print Area

Defines the range of cells in a worksheet that will be printed.

Usage

1. In the worksheet, select the range of cells you want to print.
2. Select **O**ptions Set Print **A**rea. Excel outlines the print area with a dotted line and names the cell range Print_Area.

Select this tool on the Utility toolbar to set the print area.

See also Skill Session 12, "Basic Printing."

Options Set Print Titles

Lets you specify selected rows and columns of your worksheet as titles. When the worksheet is printed, titles appear on each page.

Usage

1. Select Options Set Print Titles. Excel displays the Set Print Titles dialog box.
2. To set column titles, select the Titles For Columns box and then select the cells in the row you want to use for column titles.
3. To set row titles, select the Titles For Rows box and then select the cells in the column you want to use for row titles.
4. Select OK.

Options Spelling

Checks the active worksheet for misspelled or unrecognized words.

Usage

1. Select Options Spelling. If Excel finds misspelled or unrecognized words in the active document, it displays the Spelling dialog box. Otherwise, Excel displays a message saying the spell checker is finished checking the current document.
2. The first word Excel questions is displayed in the Not in Dictionary box. The Change To box displays the suggested replacement word. Other replacement words appear in the Suggestions box. To correct the error, you may:

   - Use the word in the Change To box.
   - Select a word from the Suggestions box.
   - Edit the Change To box and enter a new word.

   If the word is correct, you may select Ignore and move on.
3. Select the appropriate command button, as described in the following list. Respond to each unrecognized word by selecting the appropriate command button. Excel displays a message when the spell checker is finished checking the document.

Spell Checker Command Button	*Choose This Button to ...*
Ignore	Ignore the current word.
Ignore All	Ignore every occurrence of the current word.
Change	Replace the current word with the word in the Change To box.

Spell Checker Command Button	*Choose This Button to ...*
Change All	Replace every occurrence of the current word with the word in the Change To box.
Add	Add the current word to an Excel dictionary. When selecting this button, select a dictionary file name from the Add Words To box.
Cancel	Close the Spelling dialog box.
Suggest	Display a list of suggested replacement words if the Always Suggest check box is not checked.

Select this tool on the Utility toolbar to check spelling in the active document.

Options Toolbars

Allows you to select which toolbars to display and to create custom toolbars.

Usage

1. Select Options Toolbars. The Toolbars dialog box appears.
2. From the Show Toolbars box, select a toolbar.
3. Select a command button. If you select Show or Hide, Excel closes the dialog box and reflects the change in the worksheet window. If you select Reset, Excel restores the selected toolbar to its default settings and keeps the Toolbars dialog box open. If you select Customize, Excel displays the Customize dialog box. Follow the instructions in the dialog box, then select Close. Excel then returns to the Toolbars dialog box.
4. Select Close.

TIP: Point to a blank area on any toolbar and click the right mouse button to display the Toolbars shortcut menu.

See also Skill Session 4, "Using Excel's Toolbars," and Skill Session 48, "Managing Toolbars."

Options Workspace

Controls Excel settings used for the current session. Options include settings for the default number of decimal places, cell addressing style, status bar, formula bar, scroll bars, and alternate menus or Help keys.

Usage

1. Select Options Workspace. Excel displays the Workspace Options dialog box.
2. To set a fixed number of decimal places, select the Fixed Decimal check box and then enter the number of decimal places to use in the Places box.
3. Select the display options you want to use from the Display box.
4. To define a different key for accessing Excel Help menus or Lotus 1-2-3 Help, enter a character in the Alternate Menu or Help Key box.
5. To use alternate navigation keys, select the Alternate Navigation Keys check box.
6. To ignore remote requests made to Excel by other applications, check the Ignore Remote Requests box.
7. To automatically move the active cell down one row after pressing Enter, select the Move Selection After Enter check box.
8. To enable the drag and drop method of moving and copying cells, select the Cell Drag and Drop check box.
9. Select OK.

Window Menu Commands

Window Arrange

Arranges all open Excel windows so they are all visible at once. Also allows you to synchronize scrolling between windows of the active document.

Usage

1. With two or more documents open, select Window Arrange. Excel displays the Arrange Windows dialog box.
2. In the Arrange box, select an arrangement option.
3. To arrange only those windows of the active document, select the Windows of Active Document check box.
4. To synchronize scrolling in the windows of the active document, select either the Sync Horizontal or the Sync Vertical check box.
5. Select OK.

Window Freeze Panes

In a window that is not split, creates panes and then freezes the top pane, the left pane, or both in the active worksheet.

Usage

1. In the active window, display the document for which you want to freeze the panes.
2. If the window is not split, select a cell below and to the right of the point where you want to split the window. (To create a horizontal split only, select the entire row below the point where you want to split the window. To create a vertical split only, select the entire column to the right of the point where you want to split the window.)
3. Select Window Freeze Panes.

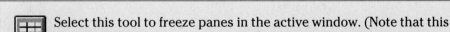

Select this tool to freeze panes in the active window. (Note that this custom utility tool is available only if you have added it to a toolbar. See Skill Session 48 for information about customizing toolbars.)

See also Window Unfreeze Panes.

Window Hide

Hides the active window from view without closing it.

Usage

1. Click in the window you want to hide.
2. Select Window Hide.

See also Window Unhide.

Window New Window

Opens an additional window for the active document so you can view different parts of the worksheet at once.

Usage

1. Display the document for which you want to create a new window.
2. Select Window New Window. Excel opens another copy of the active document in a new window and adds the notation ":2" to the name in the title bar.

> **NOTE:** The new window scrolls separately, but all other editing changes you make occur in both windows.

Window Split

Splits a window into two or four panes so that different areas of the worksheet can be viewed at once.

Usage

1. In the active window, display the worksheet you want to split.
2. To split the window into four panes, place the active cell below and to the right of the point where you want the split to occur. To split the window into two horizontal panes, select the entire row below the point where you want the split to occur. To split the window into two vertical panes, select the entire column to the right of the point where you want the split to occur.
3. Select Window Split.

> **TIP:** You can split a window without using the **W**indow **S**plit command by dragging the horizontal and vertical split boxes to the point where you want the split to occur.

See also **W**indow **F**reeze Panes and **W**indow **N**ew Window.

Window Unhide

Allows you to redisplay windows that have been hidden with the **W**indow **H**ide command.

Usage

1. Select Window Unhide.
2. Select the file you want to redisplay from the Unhide dialog box.
3. Select OK.

> **TIP:** The **W**indow **U**nhide command is not available unless at least one window is hidden.

See also **W**indow **H**ide.

Window View

Allows you to create different views of a worksheet with different print settings, panes, hidden rows and columns, window size and position, and so on.

Usage

1. Display the worksheet for which you want to create a separate view.
2. Select Window View. Excel displays the Views dialog box.
3. Select the Add button. Excel displays the Add View dialog box.
4. In the Name box, enter a name for the view.
5. In the View Includes box, select the options to include in the view.
6. Select OK. All views are saved when the file is saved.

Window Zoom

Allows you to magnify or reduce the worksheet shown in the active window.

Usage

1. Display the worksheet you want to magnify or reduce.
2. Select Window Zoom. Excel displays the Zoom dialog box.

3. In the magnification box, select the percent magnification to use. To fit selected cells to the size of the active window, select Fit Selection. If you select Custom, enter a number in the % box.

4. Select OK.

Select this tool on the Utility toolbar to magnify (to the next higher magnification level) the cells shown in the worksheet window.

Select this tool on the Utility toolbar to reduce (to the next lower magnification level) the view of the cells in the active worksheet.

Excel 4 Macro Functions

Introduction

Microsoft Excel contains over 400 *macro functions*. These are formulas that can automate any task you can perform manually with Excel. As explained in Skill Session 52, you can choose **M**acro Re**c**ord to create macros as you perform the tasks. The Excel Macro Recorder builds macro functions as you perform tasks, and enters these functions into a *macro sheet*.

You can also paste macro functions into a macro sheet (when a macro sheet is active) by choosing Formula Paste Function, and you can enter macro functions by following the syntax rules contained in this macro command reference. In the cases where a macro function is a command-equivalent function, there is no advantage to entering or pasting the argument into the macro sheet. Because of the lengthy and complex nature of many of the command-equivalent macro functions, it is much more efficient to use the Macro Recorder to enter the macro functions into a macro sheet.

Note: When you use these macros, remember that in every case, the last line in the function must be

```
=RETURN( )
```

or

```
=HALT( )
```

A macro without one of these last lines will not run.

Unlike worksheet functions, there is little on-line Help for macro functions. Therefore, you may find this alphabetical command reference that lists most of the macro commands of great help. In addition to being listed in alphabetical order, each macro function has a brief description along with its syntax and arguments. A macro function's syntax shows the name of the function including required and optional arguments. Arguments are values, references, and information you supply to macro functions so they can perform a task. In most cases, a brief example is provided for each function. A few macro functions in this section are not accompanied by examples because providing an example would require complex or lengthy macros that are beyond the reference nature of this section. For other examples of macro functions or additional macro functions, consult the Microsoft Excel Function Reference that is part of the documentation provided with the software.

A1.R1C1

Displays row and column headings and cell references in either R1C1 or A1 reference style.

Syntax

A1.R1C1(*logical*)

logical A logical value. If *logical* is TRUE, Excel uses A1 references; if it is FALSE, Excel uses the R1C1 style.

Example

```
=A1.R1C1(FALSE)
=RETURN( )
```

The cell reference is displayed in RC format as a result of the above macro (for example, B2 is displayed as R2C2).

ABSREF

Returns the absolute reference of the cells specified by the argument *reference* that are offset by the value specified by the argument *ref_text*.

Syntax

ABSREF(*ref_text,reference*)

ref_text Specifies a position relative to *reference*.

reference A cell or range of cells specifying a starting point that *ref_text* uses to locate another range of cells.

Example

The following formula returns the reference PLAN.XLS!A$B$2:

```
=ABSREF("R[1]C[1]",PLAN.XLS!A1)
```

ACTIVATE

Switches to a window if more than one window is open. Switches to a pane of a window if the window is split.

Syntax

ACTIVATE(*window_text,pane_num*)

window_text The text that specifies the window to switch to.

pane_num A number from 1 to 4 that specifies which pane to switch to.

Pane_num (number)	*Location*
1	Upper left pane
2	Upper right pane
3	Lower left pane
4	Lower right pane

Example

The following macro switches to the upper left pane of the window of an open worksheet named RENTBUY.XLS.

```
=ACTIVATE("RENTBUY.XLS",1)
=RETURN()
```

ACTIVE.CELL

Returns the reference of the active cell.

Syntax
ACTIVE.CELL()

Example
If the document in the active window is FINANCE.XLS and B7 is the active cell, then ACTIVE.CELL() equals FINANCE.XLS!$B$7.

ADD.ARROW

Adds an arrow to the active chart. The arrow remains selected after it is added so that it can be moved or sized within the chart.

Syntax
ADD.ARROW()

Example
The following macro activates a chart named AREA.XLC and adds an arrow to the chart.

```
=ACTIVATE("AREA.XLC")
=ADD.ARROW( )
=RETURN( )
```

ADD.BAR

Creates a new but empty menu bar and returns the bar's ID number.

Syntax
ADD.BAR(*bar_num*)

bar_num The number of a built-in menu bar that you want to restore.

Example
The following macro creates a new menu bar and assigns the next available bar ID number but does not display the menu bar. Note: The *bar_num* argument is necessary only if you want to restore a built-in menu bar.

```
=ADD.BAR( )
```

ADD.COMMAND

Adds a command to a menu.

Syntax

ADD.COMMAND(*bar_num,menu,command_ref,position*)

bar_num A number that corresponds to a menu bar or a type of shortcut menu.

menu The menu to which the new command is to be added; can be either the name of a menu as text, or the number of a menu.

command_ref An array or a reference to an area on the macro sheet that describes the new command.

position Specifies the placement of the new command; *position* can be a number indicating the position of the command on the menu, beginning with the number 1 at the top of the menu. If *position* is omitted, the command is added to the bottom of the menu.

Example

The following macro command adds a command before the Edit Paste command on the worksheet menu bar:

```
=ADD.COMMAND(1,"Edit",A1:B10,"Paste")
```

For ID numbers of the built-in menu bars and shortcut menus, consult the *Microsoft Excel Function Reference*, which is part of the documentation provided with the software.

ADD.MENU

Adds a menu to a menu bar.

Syntax

ADD.MENU(*bar_num,menu_ref,position*)

bar_num The number of the menu bar you want to add a menu to.

menu_ref A reference to an area on the macro sheet that describes the new menu or name of a deleted built-in menu you want to restore.

position A number that indicates the placement of the new menu. Menus are numbered from left to right, starting with 1. If *position* is omitted, the menu is added to the end of the menu bar.

Example

The following macro adds a new menu, described in the range B15:C20, to the second position in the Worksheet menu bar:

```
=ADD.MENU(1,B15:C20,2)
```

ADD.OVERLAY

Adds an overlay to a 2-D chart.

Syntax

ADD.OVERLAY()

Example

The following macro activates a chart, maximizes the chart window, and then adds the overlay to the chart:

```
=ACTIVATE("Sheet1 Chart 1")
=WINDOW.RESTORE()
=WINDOW.MAXIMIZE()
=ADD.OVERLAY()
=RETURN()
```

ADD.TOOL

Adds one or more tools to a toolbar.

Syntax

ADD.TOOL(*bar_id,position,tool_ref*)

bar_id Either a number from 1 to 9, indicating one of the built-in toolbars, or the name of a custom toolbar.

Bar_id number	*Built-in toolbar*
1	Standard
2	Formatting
3	Utility
4	Chart
5	Drawing
6	Excel 3.0
7	Macro
8	Macro recording
9	Macro paused

position Specifies the position of the tool within the toolbar; starts with 1 at the left side (if horizontal) or at the top (if vertical).

tool_ref Either a number indicating a built-in tool, or a reference to an area on the macro sheet that defines a custom tool or set of tools.

Example

The following macro adds the percentage tool (54) to the 13th position of the Standard toolbar:

```
=ADD.TOOL(1,13,54)
```

ADD.TOOLBAR

Creates a new toolbar.

Syntax

ADD.TOOLBAR(*bar_name*,*tool_ref*)

bar_name A text string that identifies the toolbar you want to create.

tool_ref Either a number specifying a built-in tool, or a reference to an area on the macro sheet that defines a custom tool.

Example

The following macro creates Toolbar10:

```
ADD.TOOLBAR("Toolbar10",A1:B10)
```

ALERT

Displays a dialog box and message and waits for you to choose a button.

Syntax

ALERT(*message_text*,*type_num*,*help_ref*)

message_text The message displayed in the message box.

type_num A number from 1 to 3 that indicates which type of dialog box to display. A *type_num* 1 displays a dialog box containing the OK and Cancel buttons. ALERT returns TRUE if you choose OK, and FALSE if you choose Cancel. If *type_num* is a 2 or 3, ALERT displays a dialog box containing an OK button. You choose the OK button to continue, and ALERT returns TRUE. The only difference between a *type_num* of 2 or 3 is the type of icon ALERT displays on the left side of the dialog box.

help_ref An optional reference to a custom on-line Help topic. If the *help_ref* is included, a Help button appears in the lower right corner of the ALERT dialog box. The *help_ref* must be in the form *filename! topic_number*.

Example

The following formula returns a dialog box that displays `Delete all files in directory?` and containing OK and Cancel buttons:

```
=ALERT("Delete all files in directory?",1)
```

ALIGNMENT

Aligns the contents of the selected cells.

Syntax

ALIGNMENT(*horiz_align,wrap,vert_align,orientation*)

horiz_align A number from 1 to 7, indicating the type of horizontal alignment.

Horiz_align	*Horizontal alignment*
1	General
2	Left
3	Center
4	Right
5	Fill
6	Justify
7	Center across selection

wrap A logical value that determines the status of the Wrap Text check box in the Alignment dialog box. If *wrap* is TRUE, then Excel selects the check box. If *wrap* is FALSE, Excel clears the check box.

vert_align A number from 1 to 3, indicating the vertical alignment of the text.

Vert_align	*Vertical alignment*
1	Top
2	Center
3	Bottom

orientation A number from 0 to 3, specifying the orientation of the text.

Orientation number	*Text orientation*
0	Horizontal
1	Vertical
2	Upward
3	Downward

Example

The following formula left-aligns the text in the selected cell, turns on the word wrap feature, with a top alignment, and a horizontal orientation:

```
=ALIGNMENT(2,TRUE,1,0)
```

APP.ACTIVATE

Switches to an application.

Syntax

APP.ACTIVATE(*title_text,wait_logical*)

title_text The name of an application as displayed in its title bar.

wait_logical A logical value that determines when to switch to the application. If *wait_logical* is TRUE, Excel waits to be switched to, before switching to the application specified by *title_text*. If *wait_logical* is FALSE or omitted, Excel switches to the application specified by *title_text*.

Example

The following formula switches to Ami Pro, which is currently displaying a document named PLAN.SAM:

```
=APP.ACTIVATE("Ami Pro - PLAN.SAM")
```

APP.MAXIMIZE, APP.MINIMIZE

Maximizes or Minimizes the Excel window.

Syntax

APP.MAXIMIZE()

Example

The following macro minimizes the Excel window, activates the Windows Cardfile, copies the contents of the Clipboard to the Cardfile, and then maximizes the Excel window:

```
=APP.MINIMIZE()
=EXEC("cardfile.EXE",1)
=SEND.KEYS("%ep",TRUE)
=APP.MAXIMIZE()
=RETURN()
```

APP.MOVE

Moves the Excel window.

Syntax

APP.MOVE(*x_num*,*y_num*)

x_num Specifies the horizontal position of the Excel window, measured in points from the left edge of the screen to the top of the Excel window.

y_num Specifies the vertical position of the Excel window, measured in points from the top edge of your screen to the top of the Excel window.

Note: APP.MOVE? is the equivalent of pressing Alt+space bar+M. If you specify coordinates (*x_num*,*y_num*), the window is moved there (though you can still use the keyboard or mouse to move it).

Example

The following macro formula moves the Excel window 70 points from the left edge of the screen and 25.75 points from the top edge of the screen:

```
=APP.MOVE(70,25.75)
```

APP.RESTORE

Restores the Excel window to its previous size and location.

Syntax

APP.RESTORE()

APP.SIZE

Changes the size of the Excel window.

Syntax

APP.SIZE(*x_num,y_num*)

x_num Indicates the width of the Excel window in points.

y_num Indicates the height of the Excel window in points.

Note: APP.SIZE?(*x_num,y_num*) resizes the window according to coordinates; it is the equivalent of pressing Alt+spacebar+S or dragging a window border with the mouse. You are also able to use the keyboard and mouse to resize further.

Example

The following macro formula resizes the Excel window so that it has a width of 477 points and a height of 276 points.

```
=APP.SIZE(477,276)
```

APP.TITLE

Changes the title of the Excel application workspace to the title that you specify.

Syntax

APP.TITLE(*text*)

text The title you want to give to the Excel application workspace. If *text* is omitted, the title is restored to `Microsoft Excel`.

Example

The following formula changes the title of the Excel workspace to Balance Sheet:

```
APP.TITLE("Balance Sheet")
```

APPLY.STYLE

Applies a previously defined style to the current selection.

Syntax

APPLY.STYLE(*style_text*)

style_text The name, in text, of a previously defined style.

Example

The following applies a style called SUBTOTAL to the current selection:

```
=APPLY.STYLE("Subtotal")
```

ARGUMENT (Syntax 1 and Syntax 2)

Describes the arguments used in a custom function.

Syntax 1

ARGUMENT(*name_text,data_type_num*)

Syntax 2

ARGUMENT(*name_text,data_type_num,reference*)

name_text is the name of the argument or of the cells containing the argument.

data_type_num A number that determines what type of values Excel accepts for the argument.

Data_type_num (number)	*Type of value*
1	Number
2	Text
4	Logical
8	Reference
16	Error
64	Array

reference The cell or cells in which you want to store the argument's value.

Example

The following macro uses ARGUMENT to define the arguments in a custom function that computes a sinking fund amount:

```
=RESULT(1)
=ARGUMENT("FUTURE_VALUE",1)
=ARGUMENT("INTEREST_Rate",1)
=ARGUMENT("PERIODS",1)
=FUTURE_VALUE/((((1+INTEREST_Rate)^PERIODS)-1)/INTEREST_Rate)
=RETURN(A6)
```

ARRANGE.ALL

Rearranges open windows and icons and resizes open windows.

Syntax

ARRANGE.ALL(*arrange_num*,*active_doc*,*sync_horiz*,*sync_vert*)

arrange_num A number from 1 to 6 indicating how to arrange the windows.

Arrange_num	*Arrangement*
1 or omitted	Tiled
2	Horizontal
3	Vertical
4	None
5	Horizontal arrangement and size based on position of active cell.
6	Vertical arrangement and size based on position of active cell.

active_doc A logical value indicating which windows to arrange. If *active_doc* is TRUE, Excel arranges only windows of the active document. If *active_doc* is FALSE or omitted, all open windows are arranged.

sync_horiz A logical value corresponding to the Sync Horizontal check box of the Arrange Windows dialog box. If *sync_horiz* is TRUE, Excel selects the check box. If *sync_horiz* is FALSE or omitted, the check box is cleared.

sync_vert A logical value corresponding to the Sync Vertical check box. If *sync_vert* is TRUE, Excel selects the check box. If *sync_vert* is FALSE or omitted, the check box is cleared.

Example

The following formula specifies a horizontal arrangement of windows in the active document with synchronized horizontal scrolling:

```
=ARRANGE.ALL(2,TRUE,TRUE,FALSE)
```

ASSIGN.TO.OBJECT

Assigns a macro to an object so that when that object is clicked with the mouse, the macro will run.

Syntax

ASSIGN.TO.OBJECT(*macro_ref*)

> *macro_ref* The name of, or reference to, the macro you want to assign to an object.

Example

The following macro selects an object named Button 1 and assigns the macro named Macro1!Record3 to the button:

```
=SELECT("Button 1")
=ASSIGN.TO.OBJECT("Macro1!Record3")
=RETURN()
```

ASSIGN.TO.TOOL

Assigns a macro to be run when a tool is clicked with the mouse.

Syntax

ASSIGN.TO.TOOL(*bar_id,position,macro_ref*)

> *bar_id* Specifies the number or name of a toolbar to which you assign a macro.
>
> *position* Indicates the position of the tool within the toolbar, starting with 1 at the left side (if horizontal) or at the top (if vertical).
>
> *macro_ref* The name of, or reference to, the macro you want to assign to a tool.

Example

The following macro formula assigns the macro named Macro1 to the tool in position 2 on Toolbar4:

```
=ASSIGN.TO.TOOL("Toolbar4",2,Macro1)
```

ATTACH.TEXT

Attaches text to selected chart.

Syntax

ATTACH.TEXT(*attach_to_num,series_num,point_num*)

> *attach_to_num* A value that indicates which item on a chart to attach text to (lists follow for 2-D and 3-D charts).

For 2-D charts:

Attach_to_num	*Attaches text to . . .*
1	Chart title
2	Value (Y) axis
3	Category (X) axis
4	Series and data points
5	Overlay value (Y) axis
6	Overlay category (X) axis

For 3-D charts:

Attach_to_num (number)	*Attaches text to . . .*
1	Chart title
2	Value (Y) axis
3	Series (Y) axis
4	Category (X) axis
5	Series and data point

series_num Indicates the series number if *attach_to_num* specifies a series or data point. If *attach_to_num* indicates a series or data point, and *series_num* is omitted, the macro is interrupted.

point_num Indicates the number of the data point, but only if you specify a series number; *point_num* is necessary if *series_num* is specified, unless the chart is an area chart.

Example

The following macro attaches the text CPI to the value (Y) axis:

```
=ATTACH.TEXT(2)
=FORMAT.FONT(0,1,FALSE,"Helv",10,TRUE,FALSE,FALSE,FALSE)
=FORMULA("=""CPI""")
=RETURN( )
```

AXES (Syntax 1 and Syntax 2)

Controls the visibility of the axes on a chart.

Syntax 1 (for 2-D Charts)
AXES(*x_main,y_main,x_over,y_over*)

Syntax 2 (for 3-D Charts)
AXES(*x_main,y_main,z_main*)

All the arguments are logical values, corresponding to the check boxes in the Chart Axes dialog box. If an argument is TRUE, Excel selects the check box and displays the axis. If an argument is FALSE, the check box is cleared and the axis is hidden.

x_main Corresponds to the category (X) axis on the main chart.

y_main Corresponds to the value (Y) axis on the main chart.

x_over Corresponds to the value (X) axis on the overlay chart.

y_over Corresponds to the value (Y) axis on the overlay chart.

z_main Corresponds to the value (Z) axis on the 3-D main chart.

Example
The following macro formula hides the category (X) axis on the selected 3-D chart:

```
=AXES(FALSE,TRUE,TRUE)
```

BEEP

Sounds a tone.

Syntax
BEEP(*tone_num*)

tone_num A number from 1 to 4, specifying the tone to be played. If *tone_num* is omitted, 1 is the default.

Example
The following macro formulas sound a beep and display a dialog box that displays `Delete all files in directory?` and contains OK and Cancel buttons:

```
=ALERT("Delete all files in directory?",1)
=BEEP(1)
```

BORDER

Adds a border to the selected cell, range of cells, or object.

Syntax

BORDER(*outline,left,right,top,bottom,shade,outline_color,left_color,right_color, top_color,bottom_color*)

outline, *left*, *right*, *top*, and *bottom* are numbers from 0 to 7 that correspond to the line styles in the Border dialog box.

Number	*Line Type*
0	No border
1	Thin line
2	Medium line
3	Dashed line
4	Dotted line
5	Thick line
6	Double line
7	Hairline

shade Corresponds to the Shade check box in the Border dialog box. If *shade* is TRUE, then the check box is selected; if *shade* is FALSE, the check box is cleared.

outline_color, *left_color*, *right_color*, *top_color*, and *bottom_color* are numbers from 1 to 16 corresponding to the Color box in the Border dialog box.

Example

The following macro formula adds a double line outline border to a selected cell or range of cells:

```
=BORDER(6,0,0,0,0,,0)
```

BREAK

Interrupts a FOR-NEXT, a FOR.CELL-NEXT, or a WHILE_NEXT loop.

Syntax

BREAK()

Example

The following macro formula interrupts a macro if cell A5 equals zero:

```
=IF(A5=0,BREAK( ))
```

BRING.TO.FRONT

Puts the selected object or objects on top of all other objects.

Syntax

BRING.TO.FRONT()

Example

The following macro selects a chart named Chart 1 and then puts the chart on top of all other documents:

```
=SELECT("Chart 1")
=BRING.TO.FRONT()
=RETURN()
```

CALCULATE.DOCUMENT

Calculates only the active document.

Syntax

CALCULATE.DOCUMENT()

Example

The following macro opens a document named INC_TAX.XLS that is saved in the C:\FINANCE directory, and then calculates that document.

```
=OPEN("C:\FINANCE\INC_TAX.XLS")
=CALCULATE.DOCUMENT()
=RETURN()
```

CALCULATE.NOW

Calculates all open documents.

Syntax

CALCULATE.NOW()

Example

The following macro opens a workbook named FINANCE.XLW and a worksheet named DEBT_PAY.XLS, and calculates both documents:

```
=OPEN("C:\EXCEL4\finance.xlw")
=OPEN("debt_pay.xls")
```

```
=CALCULATE.NOW( )
=RETURN( )
```

CALCULATION

Controls how and when formulas in open documents are calculated.

Syntax

CALCULATION(*type_num,iter,max_num,max_change,update,precision, date_1904,calc_save,save_values,alt_exp,alt_form*)

All arguments correspond to check boxes and options in the Calculation dialog box.

type_num A number from 1 to 3 specifying the type of calculation.

Type_num	*Type of calculation*
1	Automatic
2	Automatic except tables
3	Manual

iter Corresponds to the Iteration check box. If *iter* is TRUE, the check box is selected; if it is FALSE, the check box is cleared.

max_num The maximum number of iterations with the default set at 100.

max_change The maximum change of each iteration with the default set at 0.001.

update Corresponds to the Update Remote References check box. If *update* is TRUE, the check box is selected; if it is FALSE, the check box is cleared.

precision Corresponds to the Precision As Displayed check box. If *precision* is TRUE, the check box is selected; if it is FALSE, the check box is cleared.

date_1904 Corresponds to the 1904 Date System check box with the default set at FALSE. If *date_1904* is TRUE, the check box is selected; if it is FALSE, the check box is cleared.

calc_save Corresponds to the Recalculate Before Save check box. If *calc_save* is TRUE, the document is recalculated before saving; if it is FALSE, the document is not recalculated before saving.

save_values Corresponds to the Save Eternal Link Values check box. If *save_values* is TRUE, the check box is selected; if it is FALSE, the check box is cleared.

alt_exp Corresponds to the Alternate Expression Evaluation check box. If *Alt_exp* is TRUE, the check box is selected and uses a set of rules compatible with Lotus 1-2-3 when calculating formulas. If it is FALSE or omitted, the check box is cleared and Excel calculates normally.

alt_form Corresponds to the Alternate Formula Entry check box. If *alt_form* is TRUE, the check box is selected and Excel accepts formulas entered in the Lotus 1-2-3 format. If it is FALSE or omitted, the check box is cleared and Excel accepts only formulas entered in Excel format.

Example

The following macro formula sets the calculation at manual with recalculation before saving, the iterations at 100, and the maximum change at 0.001. It also turns on the update remote reference, the 1904 Date System, the save external link values, and the capability to accept formulas entered in Lotus 1-2-3 format.

```
=CALCULATION(3,FALSE,100,0.001,TRUE,FALSE,TRUE,TRUE,TRUE,FALSE,TRUE)
```

CALLER

Returns information about the cell, range of cells, command on a menu, tool on a toolbar, or object that called the macro that is currently running.

Syntax

CALLER()

Example

The following macro formula returns the value 2 for an entry in cell B3 of a worksheet.

```
=COLUMN(CALLER( ))
```

CANCEL.COPY

Equivalent to pressing Esc to cancel the marquee after you copy or cut a selection.

Syntax

CANCEL.COPY()

CANCEL.KEY

Controls what happens when a macro is interrupted. Disables macro interruption or specifies a macro to run when a macro is interrupted.

Syntax

CANCEL.KEY(*enable*,*macro_ref*)

enable Specifies whether the macro can be interrupted by pressing Esc, on the basis of the following if-then table:

If enable is . . .	*Then . . .*
FALSE	Esc does not interrupt the macro
TRUE and *macro_ref* is omitted	Esc interrupts the macro
TRUE and *macro_ref* is specified	*Macro_ref* runs when Esc is pressed

macro_ref A cell reference or name of a macro that runs when *enable* is TRUE and Esc is pressed.

Example

The following macro formula runs the macro named MACRO1 when Esc is pressed (when a particular macro is running):

```
=CANCEL.KEY(TRUE,MACRO1)
```

CELL.PROTECTION

Controls cell protection and display.

Syntax

CELL.PROTECTION(*locked*,*hidden*)

locked Corresponds to the Lock check box of the Cell Protection dialog box. If *locked* is TRUE, then the check box is selected; if it is FALSE, the check box is cleared.

hidden Corresponds to the Hidden check box of the Cell Protection dialog box.

Example

The following macro formula unlocks and hides the selected cells when the Protect Document command is chosen:

```
=CELL.PROTECTION(FALSE,TRUE)
```

CHANGE.LINK

Changes a link from one supporting document to another.

Syntax

CHANGE.LINK(*old_text*,*new_text*,*type_of_link*)

old_text The path of the link from the active dependent document you want to change.

new_text The path of the link you want to change to.

type_of_link The number 1 or 2 specifying what type of link you want to change. A *type_of_link* of 1 or if *type_of_link* is omitted, the link is a Microsoft Excel Link. A *type_of_link* of 2 is a DDE link.

Example

The following formula changes the link on the active document from INCOMEA.XLS in the current directory to INCOMEB.XLS in the FINANCE directory:

```
=CHANGE.LINK("INCOMEA.XLS","C:\FINANCE\INCOMEB.XLS")
```

CHART.WIZARD

Formats a chart.

Syntax

CHART.WIZARD(*long*,*ref*,*gallery_num*,*type_num*,*plot_by*,*categories*,*ser_titles*,*legend*,*title*,*x_title*,*y_title*,*z_title*)

long A logical value that determines which type of ChartWizard tool CHART.WIZARD is equivalent to. If *long* is TRUE or omitted, CHART.WIZARD is equivalent to using the five-step ChartWizard tool. If *long* is FALSE, then CHART.WIZARD is equivalent to using the two-step ChartWizard tool; in that case, the arguments *gallery_num*, *type_num*, *legend*, *title*, *x_title*, *y_title*, and *z_title* are ignored.

ref A reference to the range of cells on the active worksheet that contains the source data for the chart or the object identifier of the chart if it had previously been created.

gallery_num A number from 1 to 14, indicating the type of chart you want to create.

Gallery_num (number)	*Type of chart*
1	Area
2	Bar
3	Column
4	Line
5	Pie
6	Radar
7	XY (Scatter)
8	Combination
9	3-D Area
10	3-D Bar
11	3-D Column
12	3-D Line
13	3-D Pie
14	3-D Surface

type_num A number identifying a formatting option that corresponds to the type of chart specified with *gallery_num*. For a complete list of galleries, refer to the section entitled "Changing the Chart Type or Format," in Chapter 12 in Book 1 of the *Microsoft Excel User's Guide*, which is part of the documentation provided with the program.

plot_by The number 1 or 2, indicating whether the data for each data series is in rows or columns. The number 1 specifies rows, while 2 indicates columns.

categories The number 1 or 2, specifying whether the first row or column contains a list of X-axis labels or data for the first data series. The number 1 specifies X-axis labels, while 2 indicates the first data series.

ser_titles The number 1 or 2, specifying whether the first column or row contains series titles or data for the first data point in each series. The number 1 specifies series titles while 2 indicates the first data point.

legend The number 1 or 2, indicating whether to include a legend. The number 1 indicates a legend, while 2 specifies no legend.

title The text for the chart title.

x_title The text for the X-axis title.

y_title The text for the Y-axis title.

z_title The text for the Z-axis title.

Example

The following macro selects a bar chart named "Chart 1," and formats the chart:

```
=SELECT("Chart 1")
=CHART.WIZARD(TRUE,"Sheet1!R15C1:R18C2",2,2,2,2,2,2,"","","","")
=RETURN()
```

CHECK.COMMAND

Adds a Check Mark tool or removes a check mark from a command name on a menu.

Syntax

CHECK.COMMAND(*bar_num,menu,command,check*)

bar_num A number corresponding to the menu bar containing the command to which you want to add a check mark or from which you want to remove a check mark.

menu The menu containing the command and can be either the name of the menu as text or the number of the menu.

command The command you want to check; can be the name of the command as text or the number of the command.

check A logical value corresponding to the check. If *check* is TRUE, then Excel adds a check mark to the command; if it is FALSE, Excel removes the check mark.

Example

The following formula adds a check mark to the Options Profit command:

```
=CHECK.COMMAND(1,"Options","Set Print Area",TRUE)
```

CLEAR

Clears formulas, formats, notes, or all of these from the active macro sheet or worksheet.

Syntax

CLEAR(*type_num*)

type_num A number from 1 to 4, indicating what to clear on a worksheet or macro sheet.

Type_num	*Clears*
1	All
2	Formats
3	Formulas
4	Notes

Example

The following formula clears the formats from a cell or range of cells:

```
=CLEAR(2)
```

CLOSE

Closes the active window and the active file.

Syntax

CLOSE(*save_logical*)

save_logical A logical value that specifies whether to save the file before closing the window. If *save_logical* is TRUE, the file will be saved before it is closed; if it is FALSE, the file is not saved; and if it is omitted and if you have made changes to the file, a dialog box is displayed that asks if you want to save the file.

Example

The following formula will save the file and then close the active window:

```
=CLOSE(TRUE)
```

CLOSE.ALL

Closes all protected and unprotected windows, all hidden windows, and worksheet files.

Syntax

CLOSE.ALL()

COLOR.PALETTE

Copies a color palette from an open document to the active document.

Syntax

COLOR.PALETTE(*file_text*)

file_text The name of a document, as a text string that you want to copy a color palette from.

Example

The following formula copies the color palette from a worksheet named BALANCE.XLS:

```
=COLOR.PALETTE(BALANCE.XLS)
```

COLUMN.WIDTH

Changes the width of columns.

Syntax

COLUMN.WIDTH(*width_num,reference,standard,type_num,standard_num*)

width_num Specifies how wide you want the columns to be as measured in units of one character.

reference Specifies the columns for which you want to change width (if *reference* is omitted, this command changes the width of selected columns).

standard A logical value corresponding to the Use Standard Width check box in the Column Width dialog box. If *standard* is TRUE, Excel sets the column width to the currently defined standard (default) width, and ignores *width_num*. If *standard* is FALSE or omitted, Excel sets the width according to *width_num* or *type_num*.

type_num A number from 1 to 3 which corresponds to the Hide, Unhide, or Best Fit buttons (respectively) in the Column Width dialog box .

Type_num	*Action*
1	Hides column; sets width to zero
2	Unhides column; sets width to width prior to hiding it
3	Sets width to a best-fit width

standard_num Measured in points, and specifies how wide the standard width is. If *standard_num* is omitted, the standard width setting remains unchanged.

Example

The following formula sets the width of selected columns to 16:

```
=COLUMN.WIDTH(16)
```

COMBINATION

Changes format of a chart to a combination format.

Syntax

COMBINATION(*type_num*)

type_num A number corresponding to the chart number in the Combination dialog box. For corresponding numbers, choose the Gallery Combination command that is available when a chart is active.

Example

The following formula formats a chart using the first combination format shown in the Combination dialog box:

```
=COMBINATION(1)
```

CONSOLIDATE

Consolidates data from multiple ranges on multiple worksheets into a single range on a worksheet.

Syntax

CONSOLIDATE(*source_refs,function_num,top_row,left_col,create_links*) *source_refs* An external reference, in text form, to ranges on other worksheets that contain data to be consolidated on a worksheet.

function_num A number from 1 to 11 that indicates one of 11 functions you can use to consolidate data.

Function_num (number)	*Function*
1	AVERAGE
2	COUNT
3	COUNTA
4	MAX
5	MIN
6	PRODUCT
7	STDEV
8	STDDEVP
9	SUM
10	VAR
11	VARP

Each of the following arguments correspond to text and check boxes in the Consolidate dialog box. Arguments that correspond to check boxes are logical values; TRUE indicates the box will be checked, and FALSE indicates the box will be cleared.

top_row Corresponds to the Top Row check box with the default set at FALSE.

left_col Corresponds to the Left Column check box with the default set at FALSE.

create_links Corresponds to the Create Links To Source Data check box.

Example

The following formula consolidates data from A1:B3 of the worksheets GP1.XLS and GP2.XLS:

```
=CONSOLIDATE({"'C:\EXCEL4\GP1.XLS'!R1C1:R3C2","'
C:\EXCEL4\GP2.XLS'!R1C1:R3C2"},9,FALSE,FALSE,TRUE)
```

CONSTRAIN.NUMERIC

Constrains handwriting recognition to numbers and punctuation only when using Microsoft Windows for Pen Computing.

Syntax

CONSTRAIN.NUMERIC(*numeric_only*)

numeric_only A logical value that turns the numeric constraint on or off. If *numeric_only* is TRUE, only numbers and digits are recognized; if it is FALSE, all characters are recognized.

COPY

Copies selected data or objects and pastes them to a cell or range of cells.

Syntax

COPY(*from_reference,to_reference*)

from_reference A reference to the cell or range of cells to be copied. If you omit *from_reference*, the current selection is copied.

to_reference A reference to the cell or range of cells where you want to paste.

Example

The following formula copies the data in the range A5:D10 to S5:

```
=COPY(!A5:D10,!S5)
```

CREATE.NAMES

Creates names from text labels on a worksheet.

Syntax

CREATE.NAMES(*top,left,bottom,right*)

All the arguments are logical values corresponding to check boxes in the Create Names dialog box. If the argument is TRUE, the check box is selected; if it is FALSE, the check box is cleared.

top Corresponds to the Top Row check box.

left Corresponds to the Left Column check box.

bottom Corresponds to the Bottom Row check box.

right Corresponds to the Right Column check box.

Example

The following formula creates names using the text labels in the left column:

```
=CREATE.NAMES(FALSE,TRUE,FALSE,FALSE)
```

CROSSTAB.CREATE

Creates a cross tabulation table.

Syntax

CROSSTAB.CREATE(*rows_array,columns_array,values_array,create_outline,create_names, mult_values,auto_drilldown,new_sh*)

rows_array A two-dimensional array specifying a set of fields that appears in each row of the cross tabulation table.

columns_array A two-dimensional array specifying a set of fields that appears in each column of the cross tabulation table.

values_array A two-dimensional array specifying each field that appears as a value field.

create_outline A logical value that, if TRUE, creates names for the values in the table and, if FALSE, does not create an outline for the table.

create_names A logical value that, if TRUE, creates names for the values from the table and, if FALSE, does not create names for the values.

mult_values A numerical value from 1 to 4, specifying how to handle multiple summaries.

Mult_values	*Description*
1	Inner columns
2	Outer columns
3	Inner rows
4	Outer rows

auto_drilldown A logical value that, if TRUE, places drilldown formulas in the result cells and, if FALSE, does not place drilldown formulas in the result cells.

new_sh A logical value that, if TRUE, creates the cross tabulation table on a new sheet and, if FALSE, creates the cross tabulation table on the existing sheet.

CROSSTAB.CREATE?

Activates the Crosstab ChartWizard.

Syntax

CROSSTAB.CREATE?(*rows_array*,*columns_array*,*values_array*,*create_outline*,*create_names*, *mult_values*,*auto_drilldown*,*new_sh*)

For definitions of arguments, see CROSSTAB.CREATE.

CROSSTAB.DRILLDOWN

Performs a database query to retrieve the records that are summarized in the cell. This is the equivalent to double-clicking a cell that contains a summary value in a cross tabulation table.

Syntax

CROSSTAB.DRILLDOWN()

CROSSTAB.RECALC

Recalculates a cross tabulation table.

Syntax

CROSSTAB.RECALC(*rebuild*)

rebuild A logical value that specifies the type of recalculation you want to execute. If *rebuild* is TRUE, the cross tabulation table is recreated from row, column, and value definitions; if it is FALSE or omitted, Excel recalculates the cross tabulation table with its current layout and elements.

Example

The following formula recalculates the cross tabulation table with its current layout and elements:

```
CROSSTAB.RECALC(FALSE)
```

CUSTOM.REPEAT

Allows custom commands to be repeated using the Repeat tool or the **E**dit **R**epeat command.

Syntax

CUSTOM.REPEAT(*macro_text,repeat_text,record_text*)

macro_text The name of or a reference to the macro you want to run when the **E**dit **R**epeat command is chosen.

repeat_text The text you want to use as the **E**dit **R**epeat command.

record_text The formula you want to record.

Example

The following formula specifies that the macro REPEAT WORK on the MACRO1.XLM macro sheet be run when the REPEAT WORK command is chosen from the Edit menu:

```
=CUSTOM.REPEAT("MACRO1.XLM!REPEAT WORK", "REPEAT WORK")
```

CUSTOM.UNDO

Creates a customized Undo tool and Edit Undo command for custom commands.

Syntax

CUSTOM.UNDO(*macro_text,undo_text*)

macro_text The name of or an R1C1 style reference to the macro you want to run when the Edit Undo command is chosen.

undo_text The text you want to use as the Edit Undo command.

Example

The following formula runs a macro named Undoalign when **E**dit **U**ndo Align is chosen:

```
=CUSTOM.UNDO("Undoalign","Undo Align")
```

CUSTOMIZE.TOOLBAR

Displays the Customize toolbar dialog box.

Syntax

CUSTOMIZE.TOOLBAR(*category*)

category A number from 1 to 10 that indicates which category of tools to display in the dialog box.

Category	*Category of Tools*
1	File
2	Edit
3	Formula
4	Formatting (nontext)
5	Text Formatting
6	Drawing
7	Macro
8	Charting
9	Utility
10	Custom

Example

The following formula displays the Formula tools in the Customize toolbar dialog box:

```
=CUSTOMIZE.TOOLBAR?(3)
```

CUT

Cuts or moves data or objects.

Syntax

CUT(*from_reference,to_reference*)

from_reference A reference to the cell or range of cells to be cut.

to_reference A reference to the cell or range of cells where the cut data or object is to be pasted.

Example

The following formula cuts the cell range B7:D10 and pastes it at cell S100:

```
=CUT(!$B$7:$D$10,!$S$100)
```

DATA.DELETE

Deletes data that matches the current criteria in the current data base.

Syntax

DATA.DELETE()

DATA.FIND

Selects records in the database range that match criteria in the criteria range.

Syntax

DATA.FIND(*logical*)

> *logical* A logical value that indicates whether to exit the Data Find mode. If *logical* is TRUE, Excel executes the Find command; if it is FALSE, Excel executes the Exit Find command.

Example

The following formula executes the Exit Find command:

```
=DATA.FIND(FALSE)
```

DATA.FIND.NEXT

Finds the next matching record in the data base.

Syntax

DATA.FIND.NEXT()

Example

The following formulas find the first two records in the data base that match the criteria and then find the previously matching record:

```
=DATA.FIND.NEXT( )
=DATA.FIND.NEXT( )
=DATA.FIND.PREV( )
```

DATA.FIND.PREV

Finds the previous matching record in the data base.

Syntax

DATA.FIND.PREV()

Example

The following formulas find the first two records in the data base that match the criteria and then find the previously matching record:

```
=DATA.FIND.NEXT( )
=DATA.FIND.NEXT( )
=DATA.FIND.PREV( )
```

DATA.FORM()

Displays the data form.

Syntax

DATA.FORM()

Example

The following macro defines the data base and then displays the data form so that you can review, edit, or enter new records:

```
=SET.DATABASE( )
=DATA.FORM( )
```

DATA.SERIES

Enters an interpolated or incrementally increasing or decreasing series of numbers or dates on a worksheet or macro sheet.

Syntax

DATA.SERIES(*rowcol,type_num,date_num,step_value,stop_value,trend*)

rowcol The number 1 or 2 that specifies where the series should be entered. If *rowcol* is 1, the series must be entered in rows; if *rowcol* is 2, the series must be entered in columns.

type_num A number from 1 to 4 that specifies the type of series.

Type_num	*Series type*
1 or omitted	Linear
2	Growth
3	Date
4	AutoFill

date_num A number from 1 to 4 that indicates the date unit of the series. To use *date_num*, the *type_num* argument must be 3.

Date_num	*Date unit*
1 or omitted	Day
2	Weekday
3	Month
4	Year

step_value A number that specifies the step value for the series.

stop_value A number that specifies the stop value for the series. If *stop_value* is omitted, DATA.SERIES continues filling the series until the end of the selected range.

trend A logical value corresponding to the Trend check box. If *trend* is TRUE, Excel generates a linear or exponential trend; if it is FALSE or omitted, Excel creates a standard data series.

Example

The following macro enters a series of dates, beginning with 2/10/92 that increase in weekly increments and fill D1:D6:

```
=SELECT("R1C4")
=FORMULA("2/10/92")
=SELECT("R1C4:R6C4")
=DATA.SERIES(2,3,1,7,,FALSE)
=RETURN()
```

DEFINE.NAME

Defines a name on an active macro sheet or worksheet.

Syntax

DEFINE.NAME(*name_text,refers_to,macro_type,shortcut_text,hidden,category*)

name_text The text that you want to use for the name.

refers_to The value that is named with *name_text*. The value can be a number, text, a logical value, an external reference, or a formula. The following two arguments are necessary only if the document is a macro sheet.

macro_type A number from 1 to 3 that specifies the type of macro.

Macro_type	*Type of macro*
1	Custom function
2	Command macro
3 or omitted	None (*name_text* does not refer to a macro)

shortcut_text A single text letter that specifies the shortcut key.

hidden A logical value that specifies whether to define the name as a hidden name. If *hidden* is TRUE, Excel defines the name as a hidden name; if it is FALSE or omitted, the name is a normal name.

category A number or text identifying the category of a custom function and corresponds to categories in the Function Category list box.

Example

The following formula assigns the name profit to the cell A2:

```
=DEFINE.NAME("profit","=R2C1")
```

DEFINE.STYLE (Syntax 1 through Syntax 7)

Creates and changes cell styles.

Syntax 1

DEFINE.STYLE(*style_text,number,font,alignment,border,pattern,protection*)

number A logical value. If number is TRUE, the Number check box of the Style dialog box is selected; if FALSE, the check box is cleared.

font A logical value. If font is TRUE, the Number check box of the Style dialog box is selected; if FALSE, the check box is cleared.

alignment A logical value. If alignment is TRUE, the Number check box of the Style dialog box is selected; if FALSE, the check box is cleared.

border A logical value. If border is TRUE, the Number check box of the Style dialog box is selected; if FALSE, the check box is cleared.

pattern A logical value. If pattern is TRUE, the Number check box of the Style dialog box is selected; if FALSE, the check box is cleared.

protection A logical value. If protection is TRUE, the Number check box of the Style dialog box is selected; if FALSE, the check box is cleared.

Syntax 2

DEFINE.STYLE(*style_text,attribute_num,format_text*)

Syntax 3

DEFINE.STYLE(*style_text,attribute_num,name_text,size_num,bold,underline, strike,color,outline,shadow*)

Syntax 4

DEFINE.STYLE(*style_text,attribute_num,horiz_align,wrap,vert_align,orientation*)

Syntax 5

DEFINE.STYLE(*style_text,attribute_num,left,right,bottom,left_color,right_color, top_color,bottom_color*)

Syntax 6

DEFINE.STYLE(*style_text,attribute_num,apattern,afore,aback*)

Syntax 7

DEFINE.STYLE(*style_text,attribute_num,locked,hidden*)

style_text The name, in text form (quotation marks), that you want to assign to the style.

attribute_num A number from 2 to 7 that indicates which attribute of the style you want to specify.

Attribute_num	*Specifies*
2	Number Format
3	Font Format
4	Alignment
5	Border
6	Pattern
7	Cell protection

For the definition of the *format_text* argument, see FORMAT.NUMBER.

For argument definitions for *name_text*, *size_num*, *bold*, *underline*, *strike*, *color*, *outline*, and *shadow*, see FORMAT.FONT.

For argument definitions for *horiz_align*, *wrap*, *vert_align*, and *orientation*, see ALIGNMENT.

For argument definitions for *left*, *right*, *bottom*, *left_color*, *right_color*, *top_color*, and *bottom_color*, see BORDER.

For argument definitions for *apattern*, *afore*, and *aback*, see PATTERNS. For argument definitions for *locked* and *hidden*, see CELL.PROTECTION.

Example

The following formula creates a style including a number ("Currency",3) and font style ("TimesNewRomanPS",10):

```
=DEFINE.STYLE("Currency",3,"TimesNewRomanPS",10,
FALSE,FALSE,FALSE,FALSE,0)
```

DELETE.ARROW

Deletes the selected arrow.

Syntax

DELETE.ARROW()

Example

The following formulas select an arrow and then delete it:

```
=SELECT("Arrow 1")
=DELETE.ARROW( )
```

DELETE.BAR

Deletes a custom menu bar.

Syntax

DELETE.BAR(*bar_num*)

bar_num The ID number of the custom menu bar that you want to delete.

Example

The following formula deletes the menu bar created by ADD.BAR in a cell named REPORT:

```
=DELETE.BAR(REPORT)
```

DELETE.COMMAND

Removes a command from a custom or built-in menu.

Syntax

DELETE.COMMAND(*bar_num*,*menu*,*command*)

bar_num The ID number of a built-in or custom menu bar from which you want to delete the command.

menu The menu from which you want to delete the command; can be the name of text or the number of the menu. Menus are numbered from left to right on the screen, beginning with 1.

command The command you want to delete; can be the name of the command, expressed as text or by number (the first command on a menu is number 1, the second command is the number 2, and so on).

Example

The following formula deletes the BALANCE command from the Financial menu on a custom menu bar created by the ADD.BAR function in a cell named BAR:

```
DELETE.COMMAND(Bar,"Financial","Balance")
```

DELETE.FORMAT

Deletes a specified custom number format.

Syntax

DELETE.FORMAT(*format_text*)

format_text The custom format as a text string.

Example

The following formula deletes a custom percentage format:

```
=DELETE.FORMAT("0.000%")
```

DELETE.MENU

Deletes a menu from a menu bar.

Syntax
DELETE.MENU(*bar_num*,*menu*)

bar_num The ID number of the menu bar from which you want to delete.

menu The menu you want to delete; can be the name of the menu, expressed as text or as a number. (Menus are numbered from left to right on the screen, beginning with 1).

Example
The following formula deletes the Income menu from the custom menu bar created by ADD.BAR in a cell named State:

```
=DELETE.MENU(State,"Income")
```

DELETE.NAME
Deletes a name on the active document.

Syntax
DELETE.NAME(*name_text*)

name_text A text value indicating the name to delete.

Example
The following formula deletes the name profit from a worksheet:

```
=DELETE.NAME("profit")
```

DELETE.OVERLAY
Deletes an overlay from a chart.

Syntax
DELETE.OVERLAY()

Example
The following formula reformats an existing chart, adds an arrow, and then deletes the overlay:

```
=COMBINATION(4)
=ADD.ARROW( )
=DELETE.OVERLAY( )
```

DELETE.STYLE

Deletes a style from a document.

Syntax

DELETE.STYLE(*style_text*)

style_text The name of a style to be deleted.

Example

The following formula deletes a particular currency style from a worksheet:

```
=DELETE.STYLE("Currency [0]")
```

DELETE.TOOL

Deletes a tool from a toolbar.

Syntax

DELETE.TOOL(*bar_id,position*)

bar_id The name or number of a toolbar from which you want to delete a tool.

position The position of the tool within the toolbar starting with the number 1 at the left side (if horizontal) or at the top (if vertical).

Example

The following formula deletes the second tool from the left in Toolbar1:

```
=DELETE.TOOL("Toolbar1",2)
```

DELETE.TOOLBAR

Deletes a custom toolbar.

Syntax

DELETE.TOOLBAR(*bar_name*)

bar_name A text string that identifies the toolbar you want to delete.

Example

The following formula deletes Toolbar1:

```
=DELETE.TOOLBAR("Toolbar1")
```

DEMOTE

Demotes the selected rows or columns in an outline.

Syntax

DEMOTE(*row_col*)

> *row_col* Indicates whether to demote rows or columns. A *row_col* of 1 (or omitted) denotes rows, and a 2 denotes columns.

Example

The following formula demotes rows in an outline:

```
=DEMOTE(1)
```

DEREF

Returns the value of the cells in a reference.

Syntax

DEREF(*reference*)

> *reference* The cell or cells you want to obtain a value for.

Example

The following formula returns the value in cell A1:

```
=DEREF(R1C1)
```

DIALOG.BOX

Displays the dialog box defined in a dialog definition table on a worksheet or macro sheet.

Syntax

DIALOG.BOX(*dialog_ref*)

> *dialog_ref* A reference to a dialog box definition table. The dialog box definition table must be at least seven columns wide by two rows high.

Example

The following formula displays a dialog box that is defined in the range named Dtable in a worksheet:

```
=DIALOG.BOX(Dtable)
```

DIRECTORY

Sets the current drive and directory to the specified path and returns the name of the new directory as text.

Syntax

DIRECTORY(*path_text*)

path_text The drive and directory you want to change to.

Example

The following formula sets the directory to \EXCEL\FINANCE on the current drive:

```
=DIRECTORY(" \EXCEL\FINANCE")
```

DISPLAY (Syntax 1 and Syntax 2)

Controls which commands on the Info window are in effect.

Syntax 1

DISPLAY(*cell,formula,value,format,protection,names,precedents,dependents, note*)

All arguments correspond to commands in the Info menu. With the exception of *precedents* and *dependents*, the arguments are logical values; TRUE indicates that the corresponding Info item will be displayed, and FALSE indicates that the corresponding Info item will not be displayed.

cell A logical value. If cell is TRUE, Info Window displays the cell's reference; if FALSE, Info Window does not display the cell's reference.

formula A logical value. If formula is TRUE, Info Window displays the contents of the cell; if FALSE, Info Window does not display the contents of the cell.

value A logical value. If value is TRUE, Info Window displays the value in the cell in General format; if FALSE, Info Window does not display the value in the cell in General format.

format A logical value. If format is TRUE, Info Window displays the number format, alignment, font, borders, and shading of the cell; if FALSE, Info Window does not display the number format, alignment, font, borders, and shading of the cell.

protection A logical value. If protection is TRUE, Info Window displays the protection status of the cell; if FALSE, Info Window does not display the protection status of the cell.

names A logical value. If names is TRUE, Info Window displays the names that include references to the cell; if FALSE, Info Window does not display the protection status of the cell.

precedents A number from 1 to 3 that indicates which precedent to list.

dependents A number from 1 to 3 that indicates which dependents to list.

Precedents or dependents	*List*
0	None
1	Direct
2	All levels

note A logical value that corresponds to the note command on the Info menu. If TRUE, Excel displays the cell note; if FALSE, the cell note will not be displayed.

Example

The following formula displays cell, formula, and value in the Info window:

```
=DISPLAY(TRUE,TRUE,TRUE,FALSE,FALSE,FALSE,0,0,FALSE)
```

Syntax 2

DISPLAY(*formulas,gridlines,headings,zeros,color_num,reserved,outline, page_breaks,object_num*)

Syntax 2 controls the options in the Options Display dialog box; arguments correspond to options and check boxes. Arguments that correspond to check boxes are logical values. If an argument is TRUE, the check box is selected; if it is FALSE, the check box is cleared.

formulas Corresponds to the Formulas check box.

gridlines Corresponds to the Gridlines check box.

headings Corresponds to the Row & Column Headings check box.

zeros Corresponds to the Zero Values check box.

color_num A number from 0 to 16, corresponding to the gridline and heading colors in the Display dialog box; 0 indicates automatic color.

reserved Reserved for international versions of Excel.

outline Corresponds to the outline Symbols check box.

page_breaks Corresponds to the Automatic Page Breaks check box.

object_num A number from 1 to 3, corresponding to the display options in the Object box.

Object_num	*Corresponds to . . .*
1 or omitted	Show all
2	Show placeholders
3	Hide

Example

The following formula displays formulas, gridlines, and headings along with showing all objects in a worksheet:

```
=DISPLAY(TRUE,TRUE,TRUE,FALSE,0,,FALSE,FALSE,1)
```

DOCUMENTS

Returns a horizontal array of specified open documents in alphabetical order.

Syntax

DOCUMENTS(*type_num*,*match_text*)

type_num A number indicating whether to include add-in documents in the array of documents.

Type_num	*Returns*
1 or omitted	Names of all open documents except add-in documents
2	Names of add-in documents only
3	Names of all open documents

match_text Specifies all the documents whose names you want returned. If *match_text* is omitted, Excel returns the names of all open documents.

Example

The following formula equals a three-cell array containing "BALANCE.XLS", "INCOME.XLS", and "FINANCE.XLW" when the workspace contains three documents with those names:

```
=DOCUMENTS(1)
```

DUPLICATE

Duplicates the selected object.

Syntax

DUPLICATE()

EDIT.COLOR

Defines color for one of the 16 color palette boxes.

Syntax

EDIT.COLOR(*color_num,red_value,green_value,blue_value*)

color_num A number from 1 to 16 specifying one of the 16 color palette boxes for which you want to set color.

red_value, green_value, blue_value Numbers that specify how much red, green, and blue are in each color; each can be a value from 0 to 255.

Example

The following formula changes the *blue_value* to 150, which changes the blue in the palette to a different shade of blue:

```
=EDIT.COLOR(5,0,0,150)
```

EDIT.DELETE

Deletes selected cells from the worksheet and shifts other cells to close up the space.

Syntax

EDIT.DELETE(*shift_num*)

shift_num A number from 1 to 4, indicating how to shift the cells after deleting.

Shift_num	*Result*
1	Shifts cells left
2	Shifts cells up

3	Deletes entire row
4	Deletes entire column

Example

The following formula deletes a cell and shifts cells up one row:

```
=EDIT.DELETE(2)
```

EDIT.OBJECT

Starts the application associated with a selected object or makes the object available for editing or other actions.

Syntax

EDIT.OBJECT(*verb_num*)

verb_num The number 1 or 2 indicating what you want to do with the object. The number 1 specifies that you want to edit the object while 2 specifies starting the application associated with the object (i.e., sound or animation).

EDIT.REPEAT

Repeats actions and commands.

Syntax

EDIT.REPEAT()

Example

The following formulas run a macro that is attached to a button and then repeats the macro:

```
=SELECT("Button 3")
=EDIT.REPEAT()
```

EDIT.SERIES

Creates or changes chart series by adding a new SERIES formula or by modifying an existing SERIES formula in a chart.

Syntax

EDIT.SERIES(*series_num,name_ref,x_ref,y_ref,z_ref,plot_order*)

series_num The number of the series you want to modify.

name_ref The name of the data series, as an external reference, defined name, or text string.

x_ref An external reference to the name of the worksheet and the cells that contain category labels for all charts (except XY scatter charts) or X-coordinate data for XY scatter charts.

y_ref An external reference to the name of the worksheet and the cells that contain values (or Y-coordinate data in XY scatter charts) for all 2-D charts.

z_ref An external reference to the name of the worksheet and the cells that contain values for all 3-D charts.

plot_order A number specifying whether the data series is plotted first, second, and so on, in the chart. The maximum value for *plot_order* is 255.

Example

The following formula modifies the X label so that it is Months:

```
=EDIT.SERIES(1,"","={""Months""}","=Sheet1!R1C1:R1C2",,1)
```

ELSE

Used with IF, ELSE.IF, and END.IF to determine which functions are carried out in a macro. If the results of all preceding groups of IF and ELSE.IF statements are FALSE, then the formulas between the ELSE function and the END.IF function are executed.

Syntax

ELSE()

ELSE.IF

Used with IF, ELSE, and END.IF to determine which functions are carried out in a macro. If the results of all preceding groups of IF and ELSE.IF are FALSE, then the ELSE.IF is executed.

Syntax

ELSE.IF(*logical_test*)

logical_test A logical value that determines where to branch. If logical_test is TRUE, Excel carries out the functions between ELSE.IF and the next ELSE.IF, ELSE, and END.IF function.

ENABLE.COMMAND

Enables or disables a custom command or menu.

Syntax

ENABLE.COMMAND(*bar_num,menu,command,enable*)

bar_num The menu bar that contains the command; can be the number of a built-in menu bar, or the number returned by a previously-run ADD.BAR function. NOTE: For ID numbers of the built-in menu bars and shortcut menus, consult the Microsoft Excel Function Reference.

menu The menu which contains the command; can be either the name of the menu as text, or the number of the menu. Menu numbering starts at the left of the screen and begins with 1.

command The command you want to enable or disable; can be either the name of the command as text, or the number of the command. Command numbering starts at the top of a menu, and begins with 1.

enable A logical value indicating whether the command should be enabled or disabled. If enable is TRUE, Excel enables the command; if FALSE, it disables the command.

Example

The following formula disables a custom command named Report that had been added previously to the Formula menu on the worksheet menu bar.

```
=ENABLE.COMMAND(1,"FORMULA","Report", FALSE)
```

ENABLE.TOOL

Enables or disables a tool on the toolbar.

Syntax

ENABLE.TOOL(*bar_id,position,enable*)

bar_id Either a number from 1 to 9 (indicating one of the built-in toolbars) or the name of a custom toolbar.

Bar_id	*Built-in toolbar*
1	Standard
2	Formatting
3	Utility

4	Chart
5	Drawing
6	Excel 3.0
7	Macro
8	Macro recording
9	Macro paused

position Specifies the position of the tool within the toolbar, and starts with 1 at the left side (if horizontal) or at the top (if vertical).

enable A logical value indicating whether the tool can be accessed. If *enable* is TRUE or omitted, you can access the tool; if FALSE, you cannot access it.

Example

The following formula enables the third tool in Toolbar 2:

```
=ENABLE.TOOL("Toolbar 2",3,TRUE)
```

END.IF

Ends a block of functions associated with the preceding IF function.

Syntax

END.IF()

ENTER.DATA

Turns on Data Entry mode; allows you to select only unlocked cells, and to enter data into those cells.

Syntax

ENTER.DATA(*logical*)

logical A logical value. If *logical* is TRUE, the Data Entry mode is turned on; if FALSE, the Data Entry mode is turned off.

Example

The following formula turns on Data Entry mode.

```
=ENTER.DATA(TRUE)
```

ERROR

Indicates what action to take if an error occurs when a macro is running.

Syntax

ERROR(*enable_logical,macro_ref*)

enable_logical A logical value or number that selects or clears error-checking. If *enable_logical* is TRUE or 1, you can select normal error checking or specify a macro to run when an error occurs; if FALSE or 0, all erroneous checking is cleared. If *enable_logical* is 2 and *macro_ref* is omitted, error checking is normal. If *enable_logical* is 2 and *macro_ref* is given, the macro branches to the *macro_ref.*

macro_ref Specifies a macro to run if *enable_logical* is TRUE, 1, or 2 and an error occurs; can be the name of the macro or a cell reference.

Example

The following formula selects error-checking and runs the macro named Clear.

```
=ERROR(TRUE,Clear)
```

EVALUATE

Evaluates a formula or expression that is in the form of text and returns the result.

Syntax

EVALUATE(*formula_text*)

formula_text The expression (in the form of text) you want to evaluate; is similar to selecting an expression within a formula in the formula bar and pressing the Recalculate (F9) key.

Example

The following formula calculates the value of a cell named Return.

```
=EVALUATE("Return")
```

EXEC

Starts another program.

Syntax

EXEC(*program_text,window_num*)

program_text A text string which indicates the name of an executable file.

window_num A number from 1 to 3 that specifies the appearance of the window containing the program.

Window_num	*Window Appearance*
1	Normal size
2 or omitted	Minimized size
3	Maximized size

Example

The following macro opens the Windows Cardfile and then pastes the contents of the Clipboard to the card file before reactivating Excel.

```
=EXEC("cardfile.EXE",1)
=SEND.KEYS("%ep",TRUE)
=APP.ACTIVATE(FALSE)
=RETURN()
```

EXECUTE

Executes commands in another program.

Syntax

EXECUTE(*channel_num,execute_text*)

channel_num A number returned by a previously-run INITIATE function.

execute_text A text string representing commands you want to carry out in the program specified by *channel_num*.

Example

The following formula sends the number 20 and a carriage return to the application identified by *channel_num* 13.

```
=EXECUTE(13,"20~")
```

EXPON

Predicts a value based on the forecast for the prior period.

Syntax

EXPON(*inprng,outrng,damp,stderrs,chart*)

inprng The input range.

outrng Specifies the starting location of the output range.

damp The damping factor.

stderrs A logical value. If TRUE,standard values are included in the output table; if FALSE, standard errors are not included.

chart A logical value; if TRUE, EXPON creates a chart for the actual and forecast values; if FALSE, the chart is not generated.

EXTEND.POLYGON

Adds vertices to a polygon. NOTE: This function must immediately follow a CREATE.OBJECT function.

Syntax

EXTEND.POLYGON(*array*)

array An array of values or a reference to a range containing values that indicate the position of the vertices in the polygon. Position is measured in points relative to the upper left corner of the polygon's bounding rectangle.

Example

The following formula adds vertices to a polygon based on values contained in cells A1:B10.

```
=EXTEND.POLYGON(A1:B10)
```

EXTRACT

Finds database records that match the criteria defined in the criteria range, and copies them into a separate extract range.

Syntax

EXTRACT(*unique*)

unique A logical value corresponding to the Unique Records Only check box in the Extract dialog box.

Example

The following formula extracts records that match criteria defined in the criteria range, and copies them to an extract range defined on the worksheet.

```
=EXTRACT(TRUE)
```

FILE.CLOSE

Closes the active document.

Syntax

FILE.CLOSE(*save_logical*)

save_logical A logical value indicating whether to save the document before closing it.

▲ For documents other than workbooks:

Save_logical	*Result*
TRUE	Saves the file.
FALSE	Does not save the file.
Omitted	If you've made changes to the file, displays a dialog box asking if you want to save the file.

▲ For workbooks:

Save_logical	*Result*
TRUE	Saves changes to all of the documents in the workbook.
FALSE	Does not save any changes to documents in the workbook.
Omitted	For the workbook and for each unbound document in the workbook that you have made changes to, display a dialog box asking if you want to save the changes made to the document.

Example

The following formula closes the active workbook documents and saves changes.

```
=FILE.CLOSE(TRUE)
```

FILE.DELETE

Deletes a file from disk.

Syntax

FILE.DELETE(*file_text*)

file_text The name of the file to delete.

Example

The following formula deletes a chart named CPI.XLC from the current directory.

```
=FILE.DELETE("CPI.XLC")
```

FILES

Returns a horizontal text array of the names of all files in the specified directory.

Syntax

FILES(*directory_text*)

directory_text Specifies which directories to return filenames from.

Example

The following formula returns the names of all files starting with the letter S in the current directory.

```
=FILES("S*.*")
```

FILL.AUTO

Copies cells or automatically fills a selection.

Syntax

FILL.AUTO(*destination_ref,copy_only*)

destination_ref The range of cells into which you want to fill data.

copy_only A logical value indicating whether to copy cells or perform an AutoFill operation. If *copy_only* is TRUE, Excel copies the current selection into *destination_ref*; if FALSE or omitted, Excel automatically fills cells in *destination_ref* based on the size and contents of the current selection.

Example

The following formula performs an AutoFill operation on the selected cell and the 6 rows below the selected cell.

```
=FILL.AUTO("RC:R[6]C",FALSE)
```

FILL.DOWN

Copies the contents and formats of the cells in the top row of a selection into the rest of the rows in the selection.

Syntax

FILL.DOWN()

Example

The following formula selects the range A32:A39 and copies the contents of A32 down through A39.

```
=SELECT("R32C1:R39C1")
=FILL.DOWN()
=RETURN()
```

FILL.GROUP

Copies the contents of the active worksheet's selection to the same area on all other worksheets in the group.

Syntax

FILL.GROUP(*type_num*)

type_num A number from 1 to 3 that corresponds to one of the choices in the Fill Group dialog box.

Type_num	*Type of information filled*
1	All
2	Formulas
3	Formats

Example

The following formula copies the formulas of the active worksheet's selection (R32C1:R39C1) to the same area on all other worksheets in the group.

```
=SELECT("R32C1:R39C1")
=FILL.GROUP(2)
```

FILL.LEFT, FILL.RIGHT, FILL.UP

Copies the contents and cell formats of the cells in the right column of a selection into the rest of the columns in the selection.

Syntax

FILL.LEFT()

Example

The following formula copies the contents and cell formats of the cells in the right column (R32C13:R39C13) of a selection into the rest of the columns in the selection (R32C10:R39C12).

```
=SELECT("R32C10:R39C13")
=FILL.LEFT()
```

FOPEN

Establishes a channel with a file (so you can exchange data with it), but does not display the file.

Syntax

FOPEN(*file_text,access_num*)

file_text The name of the file you want to open.

access_num A number from 1 to 3, indicating what type of permission.

Access_num	*Permission type*
1 or omitted	Can read and write to the file
2	Can read the file but cannot write to it
3	Creates a new file with read/write permission

Example

The following formula opens a file you can read but not write to.

```
=FOPEN(BALANCE,2)
```

FOR

Starts a FOR-NEXT loop.

Syntax

FOR(*counter_text,start_num,end_num,step_num*)

counter_text The name of the loop counter in the form of text.

start_num The value initially assigned to *counter_text.*

end_num The last value assigned to *counter_text.*

step_num A value added to the loop counter after each iteration.

FOR.CELL

Starts a FOR.CELL-NEXT loop.

Syntax

FOR.CELL(*ref_name,area_ref,skip_blanks*)

ref_name The name Excel gives, as text, to the cell in the range currently being operated on.

area_ref The range of cells on which you want the FOR.CELL-NEXT loop to operate; this argument can have a multiple selection.

skip_blanks A logical balance indicating whether Excel skips blank cells as it operates on the cells in area_ref.

Skip_blanks	*Result*
TRUE	Skips blank cells in the *area_ref* argument.
FALSE or omitted	Operates on all cells in the *area_ref* argument.

FORMAT.AUTO

Formats the selected range of cells from a built-in gallery of formats.

Syntax

FORMAT.AUTO(*format_num,number,font,alignment,border,pattern,width*)

format_num A number corresponding to the formats in the Table Format list box in the AutoFormat dialog box.

The following arguments are logical values corresponding to the Formats To Apply check boxes in the AutoFormat dialog box. If an argument is TRUE or omitted the check box is selected; if FALSE, the check box is cleared.

number Corresponds to the Number check box.

font Corresponds to the Font check box.

alignment Corresponds to the Alignment check box.

border Corresponds to the Border check box.

pattern Corresponds to the Pattern check box.

width Corresponds to the Width check box.

Example

The following formula selects the Table Format called Classic 3.

```
=FORMAT.AUTO(3,TRUE,TRUE,TRUE,TRUE,TRUE,TRUE)
```

FORMAT.FONT (Syntax 1 through Syntax 3)

Applies a font to a selection.

Syntax 1 (for Cells)

FORMAT.FONT(*name_text,size_num,bold,italic,underline,strike,color,outline, shadow*)

Syntax 2 (for Text Boxes and Buttons on Worksheets and Macro Sheets)

FORMAT.FONT(*name_text,size_num,bold,italic,underline,strike,color,outline, shadow,object_id_text,start_num,char_num*)

Syntax 3 (for Chart Items)

FORMAT.FONT(*color,backgd,apply,name_text,size_num,bold,italic,underline, strike,outline,shadow*)

Some of the following arguments correspond to check boxes or options in the Font dialog box. Arguments that correspond to check boxes are logical values. If an argument is TRUE, Excel selects the check box; if FALSE, the check box is cleared.

name_text   The name of the font as it appears in the Font dialog box.

size_num   The font size in points.

bold   Corresponds to the Bold check box in previous versions of Excel; makes the selection bold.

italic   Corresponds to the Italic check box in previous versions of Excel; makes the selection italic.

underline   Corresponds to the Underline check box.

strike   Corresponds to the to the Strikeout check box.

color   A number from 0 to 16 corresponding to the colors in the Font dialog box.

outline   This argument is ignored for Microsoft Excel for the IBM.

shadow   This argument is ignored for Microsoft Excel for the IBM.

object_id_text Specifies the text box to be formatted. If *object_id_text* is ignored, Excel formats the currently selected text box.

start_num Specifies the first character to be formatted.

char_num Specifies how many characters to format.

backgd A number from 1 to 3 indicating which type of background to apply to text in a chart.

Backgd	*Type of background applied*
1	Automatic
2	Transparent
3	Opaque

apply Corresponds to the Apply To All check box, and applies to data labels only.

Example

The following formula applies a format for worksheet cells.

```
=FORMAT.FONT("NewsGothic",10,FALSE,FALSE,FALSE,FALSE,0)
```

FORMAT.LEGEND

Determines the position and orientation of the legend on a chart.

Syntax

FORMAT.LEGEND(*position_num*)

position_num A number from 1 to 5 indicating the position of the legend.

Position_num	*Position of legend*
1	Bottom
2	Corner
3	Top
4	Right
5	Left

Example

The following formula positions the legend at the bottom of the chart.

```
=FORMAT.LEGEND(1)
```

FORMAT.MAIN

Formats a chart according to the arguments you specify.

Syntax

FORMAT.MAIN(*type_num,view,overlap,gap_width,vary,drop,hilo,angle, gap_depth,chart_depth,up_down,series_line,labels*)

type_num A number from 1 to 13 indicating the type of chart.

Type_num	*Chart*
1	Area
2	Bar
3	Column
4	Line
5	Pie
6	XY (Scatter)
7	3-D Area
8	3-D Column
9	3-D Line
10	3-D Pie
11	Radar
12	3-D Bar
13	3-D Surface

view A number indicating one of the views in the Data View box in the Main Chart dialog box.

overlap A number from –100 to +100 indicating how to position bars or columns.

gap_width A number from 0 to 500 specifying the space between bar or column clusters as a percentage of the width of a bar or column.

Several of the following arguments correspond to check boxes; they are logical values that if TRUE select the check box, and if FALSE, clear the check box.

vary Corresponds to the Vary By Categories check box, and applies only to charts with one data series.

drop Corresponds to the Drop Lines check box, and is available only for area and line charts.

hilo Corresponds to the Hi-Lo Lines check box, and is available only for line charts.

angle A number from 0 to 360 indicating the angle of the first pie slice (in degrees) if the chart is a pie chart.

gap_depth A number from 0 to 500 indicating the depth of the gap in front of and behind a bar, column, area, or line as a percentage of the depth of the bar, column, area, or line (for 3-D charts only).

chart_depth A number from 20 to 2000 indicating the visual depth of the chart as a percentage of the width of the chart.

up_down Corresponds to the Up/Down Bars check box, and is available only for line charts.

series_line Corresponds to the Series Lines check box, and is available only for stacked bar and column charts.

labels Corresponds to the Radar Axis Labels check box, and is available only for radar charts.

Example

The following formula formats a 3-D column chart.

```
=FORMAT.MAIN(8,1,,50,FALSE,FALSE,FALSE,,0,100,FALSE,FALSE,TRUE)
```

FORMAT.MOVE (Syntax 1)

Moves the selected object to the specified position.

Syntax 1

FORMAT.MOVE(*x_offset,y_offset,reference*)

x_offset Indicates the horizontal position to which to move the object; measured in points from the upper left corner of the object to the upper left corner of the cell specified by reference.

y_offset Specifies the vertical position to which to move the object; measured in points from the upper left corner of the object to the upper left corner of the cell specified by reference.

reference Indicates the cell or range of cells in which to place the object.

Example

The following formula moves an object to a new location in a worksheet.

```
=FORMAT.MOVE(3,4.5,"R41C3")
```

FORMAT.MOVE (Syntax 2)

Moves the base of the selected object to the specified position.

Syntax 2

FORMAT.MOVE(*x_pos,y_pos*)

x_pos Indicates the horizontal position to which to move the object; measured in points from the base of the object to the lower left corner of the window.

y_pos Indicates the vertical position to which to move the object; measured in points from the base of the object to the lower left corner of the window.

Example

The following formulas move an arrow within a chart.

```
=SELECT("Arrow 1")
=FORMAT.MOVE(40,126.25)
=RETURN()
```

FORMAT.NUMBER

Formats numbers, dates, and times in selected cells.

Syntax

FORMAT.NUMBER(*format_text*)

format_text A format string indicating which format to apply to the selection.

Example

The following formula applies a currency format to a number.

```
=FORMAT.NUMBER("$#,##0_);($#,##0)")
```

FORMAT.OVERLAY

Formats the overlay chart.

Syntax

FORMAT.OVERLAY(*type_num,view,overlap,gap_width,vary,drop,hilo,angle, series_dist,series_num,up_down,series_line,labels*)

type_num A number from 1 to 6 indicating the type of chart.

Type_num	*Chart*
1	Area
2	Bar
3	Column
4	Line
5	Pie
6	XY (Scatter)

view A number indicating one of the views in the Data View box in the Overlay dialog box.

overlap A number from –100 to +100 indicating how to position bars or columns.

gap_width A number from 0 to 500 specifying the space between bar or column clusters as a percentage of the width of a bar or column.

Several of the following arguments correspond to check boxes; they are logical values that if TRUE select the check box, and if FALSE, clear the check box.

vary Corresponds to the Vary By Categories check box .

drop Corresponds to the Drop Lines check box.

hilo Corresponds to the Hi-Lo Lines check box.

angle A number from 0 to 360 indicating the angle of the first pie slice (in degrees) if the chart is a pie chart.

series_dist The number 1 or 2 and indicates automatic or manual series distribution.

series_num The number of the first series in the overlay chart and corresponds to the First Overlay Series box in the Overlay dialog box.

up_down Corresponds to the Up/Down Bars check box, and is available for line charts only.

series_line Corresponds to the Series Lines check box, and is available only for stacked bar and column charts.

labels Corresponds to the Radar Axis Labels check box, and is available only for radar charts.

Example

The following formula formats an overlay chart.

```
=FORMAT.OVERLAY(4,2,,,FALSE,FALSE,FALSE,,1,,FALSE,FALSE,TRUE)
```

FORMAT.SHAPE

Inserts, moves, or deletes vertices of the selected polygon.

Syntax

FORMAT.SHAPE(*vertex_num,insert,reference,x_offset,y_offset*)

vertex_num A number corresponding to the vertex you want to insert, move, or delete.

insert A logical value specifying whether to insert, move, or delete a vertex. If *insert* is TRUE, Excel inserts a vertex between the vertices designated vertex_num and vertex_num–1; if FALSE, Excel deletes the vertex, or moves it to the position specified by the remaining arguments.

reference The reference (cell or range) from which the vertex being inserted or moved is measured.

x_offset The horizontal distance from the upper left corner of *reference* to the vertex; measured in points.

y_offset The vertical distance from the upper left corner of *reference* to the vertex; measured in points.

Example

The following formulas select a polygon and then reshape it.

```
=SELECT("Drawing 9")
=FORMAT.SHAPE(3,FALSE,,33,-2.25)
=FORMAT.SHAPE(1,FALSE,,-9,-0.75)
=FORMAT.SHAPE(21,FALSE,,-4.5,10.5)
```

FORMAT.SIZE

Sizes the selected object.

Syntax

FORMAT.SIZE(*width,height*)

width Indicates the width of the selected object in points.

height Indicates the height of the selected object in points.

Example

The following formula resizes an arrow on a chart.

```
=FORMAT.SIZE(88.5,-21)
```

FORMAT.SIZE

Sizes the selected worksheet object relative to a cell or range of cells.

Syntax

FORMAT.SIZE(*x_off,y_off,reference*)

x_off Specifies the width of the selected object; measured in points from the lower right corner of the object to the upper left corner of *reference*.

y_off Specifies the height of the selected object; measured in points from the lower right corner of the object to the upper left corner of *reference*.

reference Indicates the cell or range of cells to use as the basis for the offset and for sizing.

Example

The following formula resizes an oval object on a worksheet.

```
=FORMAT.SIZE(5.25,0,"R40C8")
```

FORMAT.TEXT

Formats the selected worksheet text box, button, or any text item on a chart.

Syntax

FORMAT.TEXT(*x_align,y_align,orient_num,auto_text,auto_size,show_key, show_value*)

Arguments correspond to check boxes or options in the Text dialog box. Arguments that correspond to check boxes are logical values. If an argument is TRUE, Excel selects the check box; if FALSE, the check box is cleared.

x_align A number from 1 to 4 indicating the horizontal alignment of the text.

X_align	*Horizontal alignment*
1	Left
2	Center
3	Right
4	Justify

y_align A number from 1 to 4 indicating the vertical alignment of the text.

Y_align	*Vertical alignment*
1	Top
2	Center
3	Bottom
4	Justify

orient_num A number from 0 to 3 indicating the orientation of the text.

Orient_num	*Text orientation*
0	Horizontal
1	Vertical
2	Upward
3	Downward

auto_text Corresponds to the Automatic Text check box.

auto_size Corresponds to the Automatic Size check box.

show_key Corresponds to the Show Key check box.

show_value Corresponds to the Show Value check box.

Example

The following formulas format the text in a worksheet button, and then resize the button.

```
=FORMAT.TEXT(2,2,1,,FALSE)
```

```
=FORMAT.SIZE(7.5,4.5,"R47C15")
=RETURN()
```

FORMULA

Enters a formula in the active cell or in a reference. Use the following syntax to enter numbers, text, references, and formulas in a worksheet.

Syntax

FORMULA(*formula_text,reference*)

formula_text Can be text, a number, a reference, or a formula; the formula can be in the form of text, or a reference to a cell (which in turn can contain text, a number, a reference, or a formula in the form of text).

reference Indicates where *formula_text* is to be entered; can be a reference to a cell in the active worksheet, or an external reference to a worksheet.

Example

The following formula enters a sum function in a cell.

```
=FORMULA("=SUM(R[-3]C:R[-1]C)")
```

FORMULA.ARRAY

Enters an array formula in the range specified or in the current selection.

Syntax

FORMULA.ARRAY(*formula_text,reference*)

formula_text Text you want to enter in the array; can be text, a number, a reference, or a formula. The formula can be in the form of text, or a reference to a cell (which in turn can contain text, a number, a reference, or a formula in the form of text).

reference Specifies where *formula_text* is entered; can be a reference to a cell in the active worksheet, or an external reference to a worksheet.

Example

The following formula enters the array formula {=A5:a10+A5:A10} into a selected cell.

```
=FORMULA.ARRAY("=R[-35]C[-8]:R[-30]C[-8]+R[-35]C[-8]:R[-30]C[-8]")
```

The result of this formula depends on current cursor position. For example, if the selected cell is 140, the macro returns the above formula.

FORMULA.FILL

Enters a formula in the range specified or in the current selection.

Syntax

FORMULA.FILL(*formula_text,reference*)

formula_text The text with which you want to fill the range. Can be text, a number, a reference, or a formula; the formula can be in the form of text, or a reference to a cell (which in turn can contain text, a number, a reference, or a formula in the form of text).

reference Specifies where *formula_text* is entered; can be a reference to a cell in the active worksheet, or an external reference to a worksheet.

Example

The following formula selects a range of cells then enters a formula in each of the cells in the range.

```
=SELECT("R38C10:R41C10")
=FORMULA.FILL("=SUM(R[-3]C:R[-1]C)")
```

FORMULA.FIND

Selects the next or previous cell containing the specified text.

Syntax

FORMULA.FIND(*text,in_num,at_num,by_num,dir_num,match_case*)

text The text to find.

in_num A number from 1 to 3 specifying where to search.

In_num	*Searches*
1	Formulas
2	Values
3	Notes

at_num The number 1 or 2, specifying whether to find cells containing only *text* or cells containing *text* within a longer string of characters.

At_num	*Searches for text as*
1	A whole string
2	Either a whole string or part of a longer string

by_num The number 1 or 2, determining whether to search by rows or columns.

By_num	*Searches by*
1	Rows
2	Columns

dir_num The number 1 or 2, determining whether to search for the next or previous occurrence of text.

Dir_num	*Searches*
1	Next
2	Previous

match_case A logical value corresponding to the Match Case check box in the Find dialog box. If *match_case* is TRUE, Excel matches characters exactly; if FALSE or omitted, the search is not case-sensitive.

Example

The following formula searches a range for a formula.

```
=FORMULA.FIND("=sum(a10:a15)",1,2,1,1,FALSE)
```

FORMULA.FIND.NEXT, FORMULA.FIND.PREV

Finds the next or previous cells on the worksheet as specified in the Find dialog box.

Syntax

FORMULA.FIND.NEXT()

Example

The following formulas find a match of a formula in a range, and then find the next match.

```
=SELECT("R26C10:R33C14")
=FORMULA.FIND("=sum(125:126)",1,2,1,1,FALSE)
=FORMULA.FIND.NEXT()
```

FORMULA.GOTO

Scrolls through the worksheet and selects a named area or reference.

Syntax

FORMULA.GOTO(reference,corner)

reference Specifies where to scroll and what to select; can be an external reference to a document, an R1C1-style reference in text form, or a name.

corner A logical value that indicates whether to scroll through the window so that the upper left cell in *reference* is in the upper left corner of the window; if FALSE or omitted, Excel scrolls through normally.

Example

The following formula jumps the cell pointer to cell A10.

```
=FORMULA.GOTO("R10C1")
```

FORMULA.REPLACE

Finds and replaces characters in cells on your worksheet.

Syntax

FORMULA.REPLACE(*find_text,replace_text,look_at,look_by,active_cell, match_case*)

find_text The text to find; can include wildcard characters, question mark, and asterisk.

replace_text The text to replace *find_text*.

look_at A number indicating whether you want *find_text* to match the entire contents of a cell or any string of matching characters.

Look_at	*Looks for find_text*
1	As the entire contents of a cell
2 or omitted	As part of the contents of a cell

look_by A number specifying whether to search horizontally (through rows) or vertically (through columns).

Look_by	*Looks for find_text*
1	By rows
2 or omitted	By columns

active_cell A logical value specifying the cells in which *find_text* is to be replaced. If *active_cell* is TRUE, *find_text* is replaced in the active cell; if FALSE, *find_text* is replaced in the entire selection (or if the selection is a single cell, in the entire document).

match_case A logical value corresponding to the Match Case check box in the Replace dialog box. If *match_case* is TRUE, Excel selects the check box; if FALSE, Excel clears the check box.

Example

The following formula replaces the number 1 with 10 in a selected range.

```
=FORMULA.REPLACE("1","10",2,1,FALSE,FALSE)
```

FREEZE.PANES

Splits the active window into panes, creates frozen panes, or freezes or unfreezes existing panes.

Syntax

FREEZE.PANES(*logical,col_split,row_split*)

logical A logical value that specifies whether to freeze or unfreeze panes. If *logical* is TRUE, the function freezes panes if they exist (if panes do not exist, the function creates them, splits them at a specified position, and freezes them); if FALSE, the function unfreezes the panes.

col_split Specifies where to split the window vertically; measured in columns from the left.

row_split Specifies where to split the window horizontally; measured in rows from the top.

Example

The following formula splits the window vertically at the 5th column from the left and the 6th row from the top.

```
=FREEZE.PANES(TRUE,5,6)
```

GALLERY.3D.AREA,GALLERY.3D.BAR,GALLERY.3D.COLUMN, GALLERY.3D.LINE,GALLERY.3D.PIE,GALLERY.3D.SURFACE

Changes the format of the active chart to the specified 3-D chart.

Syntax

GALLERY.3D.AREA(*type_num*)

type_num A number of a format (in the 3-D Area dialog box) to apply to the 3-D area chart.

Example

The following formula applies the first format in the 3-D Area dialog box to the main chart.

```
=GALLERY.3D.AREA(1)
```

GALLERY.AREA,GALLERY.BAR,GALLERY.COLUMN, GALLERY.LINE,GALLERY.PIE,GALLERY.RADAR, GALLERY.SCATTER

Changes the format of the active chart to the specified chart.

Syntax

GALLERY.AREA(*type_num,delete_overlay*)

type_num The number of a format (in the 3-D Area dialog box) you want to apply to the 3-D area chart.

delete_overlay A logical value specifying whether to delete an overlay chart. If *delete_overlay* is TRUE, Excel deletes the overlay chart; if FALSE or omitted, Excel applies the new format to either the main chart or the overlay chart, depending on the location of the selected series.

Example

The following formula deletes the overlay chart (if present), and applies the first format in the gallery to the main chart.

```
=GALLERY.AREA(1,TRUE)
```

GET.BAR (Syntax 1 and Syntax 2)

Returns information to be used with functions that manipulate menu bars.

Syntax 1

GET.BAR()

Syntax 2

GET.BAR(*bar_num,menu,command*)

Syntax 2 returns the name or position number of a specified command on a menu, or of a specified menu on a menu bar.

bar_num The menu bar that contains the command; can be the number of a built-in menu bar, or the number returned by a previously-run ADD.BAR function. NOTE: For ID numbers of the built-in menu bars and shortcut menus, consult the Microsoft Excel Function Reference.

menu The menu which contains the command; can be either the name of the menu as text, or the number of the menu. Menu numbering starts at the left of the screen, and begins with 1.

command The command whose name or number you want returned; can be the command as text (in which case the number of the command is returned), or the number of the command (in which case the name of the command is returned). Numbering starts at the top of a menu, beginning with 1.

GET.CELL

Syntax

GET.CELL(*type_num,reference*)

type_num A number from 1 to 53 that specifies what type of cell information you want. Refer to the Microsoft Excel Function Reference for descriptions of each of the 53 *type_num* numbers.

reference A cell or range of cells from which you want information.

Example

The following formula returns TRUE if cell A5 on worksheet Sheet2 is italic.

```
=GET.CELL(21,Sheet2!$A$5)
```

GET.DEF

Returns, as text, a name that is defined for a particular area, value, or formula.

Syntax

GET.DEF(*def_text,document_text,type_num*)

def_text Can be a reference, value, or formula with references given in the R1C1 style.

document_text Specifies the worksheet or macro sheet that contains *def_text*.

type_num A number from 1 to 3 specifying which types of names are returned.

Type_num	*Returns*
1 or omitted	Normal names only
2	Hidden names only
3	All names

Example

The following formula returns "FIRST" if cell A1 of a worksheet named Sheet1 is named FIRST.

```
=GET.DEF("R1C1","SHEET1")
```

GET.DOCUMENT

Returns information about a document.

Syntax

GET.DOCUMENT(*type_num,name_text*)

type_num A number that specifies the type of document information. There are 65 possibilities for *type_num*; they are listed in the Microsoft Function Reference (see GET.DOCUMENT).

name_text The name of an open document; if *name_text* is omitted, the macro returns information about the active document.

Example

The following formula returns TRUE if the document is read-only recommended.

```
=GET.DOCUMENT(34)
```

GET.FORMULA

Returns the contents of a cell as they appear in the formula bar.

Syntax

GET.FORMULA(reference)

reference A cell or range of cells on a worksheet or macro sheet.

Example

The following formula returns the contents of the active cell on the active document.

```
=GET.FORMULA(ACTIVE.CELL())
```

GET.LINK.INFO

Returns information about the specified link.

Syntax

GET.LINK.INFO(*link_text,type_num,type_of_link,reference*)

link_text The path of the link as displayed in the Links dialog box.

type_num The number 1, which returns the value 1 if the link is set to automatic update; otherwise it returns 2.

type_of_link A number from 1 to 6 that specifies what type of link you want to obtain information about.

Type_of_link	*Link type*
1	Not applicable
2	DDE
3	Not applicable
4	Not applicable
5	Publisher
6	Subscriber

reference Specifies the cell range (in the R1C1 format) of the publisher or subscriber that you want information about.

GET.NAME

Returns the definition of a name as it appears in the Refers To box of the Define Name dialog box.

Syntax

GET.NAME(*name_text*)

name_text Can be a name defined on the macro sheet, an external reference to a name on the active document, or an open worksheet.

Example

The following formula equals "=$A$1" where A1 has been named Profit.

```
=GET.NAME("Profit")
```

GET.NOTE

Returns characters from a note.

Syntax

GET.NOTE(*cell_ref,start_char,num_chars*)

cell_ref The cell to which the note is attached.

start_char The number of the first character in the note to return.

num_chars The number of characters to return (must be less than or equal to 255).

Example

The following formula returns the first 50 characters in the note attached to cell A10.

```
=GET.NOTE(!$A$10,1,50)
```

GET.OBJECT

Returns information about an object.

Syntax

GET.OBJECT(*type_num,object_id_text,start_num,count_num*)

type_num A number indicating the type of information to be returned about an object. There are 47 different *type_num* numbers. To review the information that a *type_num* can return, consult the Microsoft Excel Function Reference, which is part of the documentation provided with the program.

object_id_text The name and number (or only the number) of the object you want information about; the text displayed in the reference area when an object is selected.

start_num The number of the first character in a text box or button, or the first vertex in a polygon you want information about.

count_num The number of characters in a text box or button, or the number of vertices in a polygon (starting at *start_num*) that you want information about. *Count_num* is ignored unless a text box, button, or polygon is specified.

Example

The following formula returns the cell reference E2 when the upper left corner of the object Rectangle 2 is in cell E2.

```
=GET.OBJECT(4,"Rectangle 2")
```

GET.TOOL

Returns information about a tool or tools on a toolbar.

Syntax

GET.TOOL(*type_num,bar_id,position*)

type_num A number from 1 to 7 that specifies what type of information you want.

Type_num	*Returns*
1	The tool's ID number
2	The reference of the macro assigned to the tool

3	If the tool button is down (was selected), returns TRUE; if the button is up (not selected), returns FALSE
4	If the tool is enabled, returns TRUE; if disabled, returns FALSE
5	A logical value identifying the type of face on the tool: TRUE for bitmap, FALSE for default toolface
6	The *help_text* reference associated with the custom tool
7	The *balloon_text* reference associated with the custom tool

bar_id A number from 1 to 9 (indicating a built-in toolbar or the name of a custom toolbar), or the actual name of a toolbar for which you want information.

Bar_id	*Built-in toolbar*
1	Standard
2	Formatting
3	Utility
4	Chart
5	Drawing
6	Excel 3.0
7	Macro
8	Macro recording
9	Macro paused

position Indicates the position of the tool on the toolbar, starting with 1 at the left side (if the bar is horizontal) or 1 starting at the top (if the bar is vertical).

Example

The following formula requests the Help text associated with the second tool in Toolbar3.

```
=GET.TOOL(6,"Toolbar3",2)
```

GET.TOOLBAR

Returns information about one toolbar or all toolbars.

Syntax

GET.TOOLBAR(*type_num,bar_id*)

type_num A number from 1 to 9 that specifies what type of information to return.

Type_num	*Returns*
1	A horizontal array of all tool IDs on the toolbar
2	A number indicating the horizontal position (x-coordinate) of the toolbar in the docked or floating region
3	A number indicating the vertical position (y-coordinate) of the toolbar in the docked or floating region
4	Number indicating the width of the toolbar in points
5	A number indicating the height of the toolbar in points
6	A number indicating the toolbar location in the workspace: 1 for the top dock, 2 for the left dock, 3 for the right dock, 4 for the bottom dock, 5 for floating
7	TRUE if the toolbar is visible; FALSE if it is hidden
8	An array of toolbar IDs for both visible and hidden toolbars
9	An array of toolbar IDs for all visible toolbars

bar_id A number from 1 to 9 (indicating a built-in toolbar or the name of a custom toolbar), or the actual name of a toolbar for which you want information.

Bar_id	*Built-in toolbar*
1	Standard
2	Formatting
3	Utility
4	Chart
5	Drawing
6	Excel 3.0
7	Macro
8	Macro recording
9	Macro paused

Example

The following formula returns TRUE if Toolbar2 is visible.

```
=GET.TOOLBAR(7,"Toolbar2")
```

GET.WINDOW

Returns information about a window.

Syntax

GET.WINDOW(*type_num,window_text*)

type_num A number from 1 to 25 that specifies what type of window information you want. To review the information that a *type_num* can return, consult the Microsoft Excel Function Reference.

window_text The name that appears in the title bar of the window that you want information about; if omitted, the active window will be used.

Example

The following formula returns TRUE if gridlines are displayed in the active window.

```
=GET.WINDOW(9)
```

GET.WORKBOOK

Returns information about a workbook document.

Syntax

GET.WORKBOOK(*type_num,name_text*)

type_num A number from 1 to 4 that indicates the type of workbook information you want.

Type_num	*Returns*
1	The names of all documents in the workbook as a horizontal array of text values
2	The name of the active document in the workbook
3	The names of the currently selected documents in the workbook as a horizontal array of text vales
4	The number of documents in the workbook

name_text The name of an open workbook; if omitted, information about the active window will be returned.

Example

The following formula returns the number of documents in the workbook named PROFITS.

```
=GET.WORKBOOK(4,"PROFITS.XLW")
```

GOAL.SEEK

Calculates the values necessary to achieve a goal.

Syntax

GOAL.SEEK(*target_cell,target_value,variable_cell*)

target_cell Corresponds to the Set Cell box in the Goal Seek dialog box, and is a reference to the cell containing the formula.

target_value Corresponds to the To Value box in the Goal Seek dialog box, and is the value you want the formula in *target_cell* to return.

variable_cell Corresponds to the By Changing Cell box in the Goal Seek dialog box, and is the single cell you want Excel to change so that the formula in the *target_cell* returns *target_value*.

Example

The following formula forces a monthly loan payment (cell B4) to equal $700 by adjusting the loan amount (cell B1).

```
=GOAL.SEEK("R4C2",700,"R1C2")
```

GOTO

Directs the macro to continue executing at a specified cell.

Syntax

GOTO(*reference*)

reference A cell reference or a name that is defined as a reference.

Example

The following formula branches to a macro named FORMAT.

```
=GOTO(Format)
```

GRIDLINES

Allows you to turn chart gridlines on and off.

Syntax

GRIDLINES(*x_major,x_minor,y_major,y_minor,z_major,z_minor*)

All arguments are logical values that correspond to the check boxes in the Gridlines dialog box. If an argument is TRUE, Excel selects the check box; if FALSE, excel clears the check box.

x_major Corresponds to the Category (X) Axis: Major Gridlines check box.

x_minor Corresponds to the Category (X) Axis: Minor Gridlines check box.

y_major Corresponds to the Value (Y) Axis: Major Gridlines check box. On 3-D charts, *y_major* corresponds to the Series (Y) Axis: Major Gridlines check box.

y_minor Corresponds to the Value (Y) Axis: Minor Gridlines check box. On 3-D charts, *y_minor* corresponds to the Series (Y) Axis: Minor Gridlines check box.

z_major Corresponds to the Value (Z) Axis: Major Gridlines check box (3-D only).

z_minor Corresponds to the Value (Z) Axis: Minor Gridlines check box (3-D only).

Example

The following formula turns on the X_major and X_minor gridlines.

```
=GRIDLINES(TRUE,TRUE,FALSE,FALSE,FALSE,FALSE)
```

GROUP

Creates a single object from several selected objects, and returns the object identifier from the group.

Syntax

GROUP()

Example

The following formula selects three objects on a worksheet, and then groups then as one object identified as Group 1.

```
=SELECT("Rectangle 2,Oval 3,Drawing 4")
=GROUP( )
=RETURN( )
```

HALT

Stops all macros from running.

Syntax

HALT(*cancel_close*)

cancel_close A logical value that determines whether a macro sheet (in an Auto_Close macro) should be closed. If *cancel_close* is TRUE, Excel stops the macro and prevents the document from being closed; if FALSE or omitted, Excel stops the macro and allows the document to be closed.

Example

The following formula at the end of an Auto_Close macro ends the macro and prevents the document from being closed.

```
=HALT(TRUE)
```

HELP

Starts or switches to Help and displays the specified custom Help topic.

Syntax

HELP(*help_ref*)

help_ref A reference to a topic in a Help file, in the form "filename!topic_number" (must be given as text).

Example

The following formula displays the Help topic numbered 91 in the file NEWHELP.DOC.

```
=HELP("NEWHELP.DOC!91")
```

HIDE

Hides a window.

Syntax

HIDE()

Example

The following formula makes the Macro1 document active, and then hides its window.

```
=ACTIVATE("Macro1")
=HIDE()
```

HIDE.OBJECT

Hides or displays the specified object.

Syntax

HIDE.OBJECT(*object_id_text,hide*)

object_id_text The name and number (or only the number) of the object, as text, as it appears in the reference area when the object is selected.

hide A logical value that specifies whether to hide or display the object. If *hide* is TRUE or omitted, Excel hides the object; if FALSE, it displays the object.

Example

The following formula hides the object.

```
=HIDE.OBJECT("Rectangle 2",TRUE)
```

HISTOGRAM

Calculates individual and cumulative percentages for a range of data and a corresponding range of data bins.

Syntax

HISTOGRAM(*inprng,outrng,binrng,pareto,chartc,chart*)

inprng The input range.

outrng The first cell (the upper left cell) in the output table.

binrng An optional set of numbers that define the bin ranges (must be in ascending order).

pareto A logical value. If *pareto* is TRUE, data in the output table is presented in both ascending bin order and descending frequency order. If *pareto* is FALSE or omitted, data in the output table is presented in ascending bin order only.

chartc A logical value; if TRUE, HISTOGRAM creates a cumulative percentages column in the output table. If both *chartc* and *chart* are TRUE, then HISTOGRAM includes a cumulative percentage line in the histogram chart.

chart A logical value; if TRUE, HISTOGRAM creates a histogram chart in addition to the output table.

Example

The following formula creates a histogram chart and a table of percentages, in the range beginning at C1 on a worksheet named Sheet1.

```
=HISTOGRAM(Sheet1!$A$1:$A$8,Sheet1!$C$1:$E$7,,TRUE,TRUE,TRUE)
```

HLINE

Scrolls through the active window by a specific number of columns.

Syntax

HLINE(*num_columns*)

num_columns The number of columns in the active worksheet or macro sheet that you want to scroll through horizontally. A negative *num_columns* scrolls to the left; a positive *num_columns* scrolls to the right.

Example

The following formula scrolls the screen 10 columns to the right.

```
=HLINE(10)
```

HPAGE

Horizontally scrolls through the active window one window or screen at a time.

Syntax

HPAGE(*num_windows*)

num_windows Specifies the number of windows to scroll through. If *num_windows* is positive, the screen scrolls to the right; if negative, the screen scrolls to the left.

Example

The following formula scrolls the screen 10 windows or screens to the right.

```
=HPAGE(10)
```

HSCROLL

Horizontally scrolls through the active document by percentage or column number.

Syntax

HSCROLL(*position,col_logical*)

position Specifies the column you want to scroll to; can be an integer representing the column number, or a fraction (or percentage) representing the horizontal position of the column in the document.

col_logical A logical value indicating how the scroll will work. If *col_logical* is TRUE, the function will scroll through the document to column position. If *col_logical* is FALSE or omitted, then the function scrolls through the document to the horizontal position represented by the fraction *position*.

Example

The following formula scrolls to column K.

```
=HSCROLL(11,TRUE)
```

IF

Used with ELSE, ELSE.IF, and END.IF to control which formulas in a macro are executed.

Syntax

IF(*logical_test*)

*logical_*test A logical value that is used to determine which functions to carry out next (where to branch). If *logical_test* is TRUE, Excel carries out the functions between the IF function and the next ELSE, ELSE.IF, and END.IF function. If *logical_test* is FALSE, Excel branches to the next ELSE.IF, ELSE, or END.IF function.

INITIATE

Opens a dynamic data exchange (DDE) channel to an application and returns the number of the open channel.

Syntax

INITIATE(*app_text,topic_text*)

app_text The DDE name of the application.

topic_text The description of something you are accessing.

Example

The following formula opens a channel to a document named REPORT in an application named DATA.

```
=INITIATE("DATA","REPORT")
```

INPUT

Displays a dialog box for user input, and returns the information entered in the dialog box.

Syntax

INPUT(*message_text,type_num,title_text,default,x_pos,y_pos,help_ref*)

message_text The text to be displayed in the dialog box (must be enclosed in quotation marks).

type_num A number indicating the type of data to be entered.

Type_num	*Data type*
0	Formula
1	Number
2	Text
4	Logical
8	Reference
16	Error
64	Array

title_text Text specifying a title to be displayed in the title bar of the dialog box.

default Indicates a value to be shown in the Edit box when the dialog box is initially displayed.

x_pos, y_pos These specify, in points, the horizontal and vertical position of the dialog box and if omitted, the dialog box is centered on the screen.

help_ref A reference to a custom online Help topic in a text file. The form "filename!topic_number" is used for *help_ref*.

Example

The following formula displays a dialog box which requests that you enter the address of the customer.

```
=INPUT("Enter the address of the customer:",2,
"Address",,,,"ADDRHELP.DOC!101")
```

INSERT

Insert a blank cell or range of cells or pastes cells from the Clipboard into a worksheet.

Syntax

INSERT(*shift_num*)

shift_num A number from 1 to 4, specifying which way to shift the cells.

Shift_num	*Direction*
1	Shifts cells right

Shift_num	*Direction*
2	Shifts cells down
3	Shifts entire row
4	Shifts entire column

Example

The following formula inserts the contents of the Clipboard by shifting the entire row.

```
=INSERT(3)
```

INSERT.OBJECT

Creates an embedded object whose source data is supplied by another application.

Syntax

INSERT.OBJECT(*object_class*)

object_class A text string containing the classname for the object you want to create.

Example

The following formula embeds a new Microsoft Word object.

```
=INSERT.OBJECT("WordDocument")
```

JUSTIFY

Rearranges the text in a range so that it fits the range.

Syntax

JUSTIFY()

Example

The following formula selects a range, and makes the text from the first cell of that range fit into the range.

```
=SELECT("R1C3:R1C6")
=JUSTIFY()
```

LAST.ERROR

Returns the reference of the cell where the last macro sheet error occurred. If no error has occurred, the function returns the #NA error value.

Syntax

LAST.ERROR()

LEGEND

Adds a legend to (or removes a legend from) a chart.

Syntax

LEGEND(*logical*)

logical A logical value that if TRUE or omitted adds a legend to the chart; if FALSE, it deletes the legend from the chart.

Example

The following formula adds a legend to a chart.

```
=LEGEND(TRUE)
```

LINKS

Returns a horizontal array (as text values) of the names of all worksheets referred to by external references.

Syntax

LINKS(*document_text,type_num*)

document_text The name of a document, including its path.

type_num A number from 1 to 6, specifying the type of linked document to return.

Type_num	*Returns*
1 or omitted	Excel Link
2	DDE link
3	Reserved
4	Not applicable

Type_num	*Returns*
5	Publisher
6	Subscriber

Example

The following formula returns an array of the names of the files referred to by external Excel links in a worksheet named PROJECT.XLS and found in the current default directory.

```
=LINKS("PROJECT.XLS",1)
```

LIST.NAMES

Lists all names defined on a worksheet.

Syntax

LIST.NAMES()

Example

The following formulas create a list of the names defined on the worksheet COST.XLS.

```
=ACTIVATE("COST.XLS")
=LIST.NAMES()
```

MCORREL

Returns a matrix that measures the correlation between two or more data sets which are scaled to be independent of the unit of measurement.

Syntax

MCORREL(*inprng,outrng,grouped,labels*)

inprng The input range.

outrng The first cell (the upper left cell) in the output table.

grouped A text character that determines whether the data in the input range is organized by row or column. If *grouped* is "C" or omitted, then the data is organized by columns. If *grouped* is "R," then the data is organized by row.

labels A logical value that describes where the labels are located in the input range. If *labels* is TRUE and grouped is "C," then labels are in the first row of the input range. If *labels* is TRUE and grouped is "R," then labels are in the first column of the input range. If *labels* is FALSE or omitted, then there are no labels; all cells in the input range are data.

Example

The following formula returns a correlation matrix.

```
=MCORREL(A10:D20,E21,"C",TRUE)
```

MERGE.STYLES

Merges all the styles from another document into the active document.

Syntax

MERGE.STYLES(*document_text*)

document_text The name of a document from which you want to merge styles into the active document.

Example

The following formula merges the styles from the document BALANCE.XLS.

```
=MERGE.STYLES("BALANCE.XLS")
```

MESSAGE

Displays and removes messages in the message area of the status bar.

Syntax

MESSAGE(*logical,text*)

logical A logical value indicating whether to display or remove a message. If *logical* is TRUE, Excel displays the text specified by the argument text (see below) in the message area of the status bar; if FALSE, Excel removes any messages and the status bar is returned to normal.

text The text you want to display as a message in the status bar.

Example

The following formula displays the message "Processing" in the status bar.

```
=MESSAGE(TRUE,"Processing")
```

MOVE.TOOL

Moves or copies a tool from one toolbar to another.

Syntax

MOVE.TOOL(*from_bar_id,from_bar_position,to_bar_id,to_bar_position, copy,width*)

from_bar_id Specifies the number or name of a toolbar from which to copy or move a tool.

from_bar_position Indicates the current position of the tool.

to_bar_id The number of a built-in toolbar, or the name of a toolbar to which you want to move or paste the tool.

To_bar_id	*Built-in toolbar*
2	Formatting
3	Utility
4	Chart
5	Drawing
6	Excel 3.0
7	Macro
8	Macro recording
9	Macro paused

to_bar_position Specifies the position within the toolbar to which you want to move or paste the tool.

copy A logical value indicating whether to copy the tool. If *copy* is TRUE, the tool is copied; if FALSE or omitted, the tool is moved.

width The width (in points) of a drop-down list.

Example

The following formula moves the first tool on the Chart toolbar to the third position on the Standard toolbar.

```
=MOVE.TOOL(4,1,1,4)
```

MOVEAVG

Forecasts values based on a moving average.

Syntax

MOVEAVG(*inprng,outrng,interval,stderrs,chart*)

inprng The input range.

outrng The first cell (the upper left cell) in the output table.

interval The number of values to include in the moving average.

stderrs A logical value. If *stderrs* is TRUE, standard error values are included in the output table; if FALSE or omitted, standard errors are not included in the output table.

chart A logical value. If *chart* is TRUE, the function creates a chart for actual and forecast values; if FALSE or omitted, the chart is not created.

Example

The following formula calculates a 3-month sales moving average (based on 12 months of sales contained in the range A1:A12), and creates a chart of the actual and forecasted data.

```
=MOVEAVG(A1:A12,B1,3,TRUE,TRUE)
```

NAMES

Returns a horizontal array of names defined in a document.

Syntax

NAMES(*document_text,type_num,match_text*)

document_text Text that indicates the document whose names you want to return.

type_num A number from 1 to 3 that specifies whether to include hidden names in the array of defined names.

Type_num	*Names returned*
1 or omitted	Normal names only
2	Hidden names only
3	All names

match_text Text that specifies the names you want returned; can include wildcard characters. If *match_text* is omitted, all names are returned.

Example

The following formula returns all names defined in the worksheet COST.XLS that begin with the letter M.

```
=NAMES("COST.XLS",3,"M*")
```

NEW

Creates a new document or opens a template.

Syntax

NEW(*type_num,xy_series,add_logical*)

type_num Specifies the type of file to create.

Type_num	*Document*
1	Worksheet
2	Chart
3	Macro sheet
4	International macro sheet
5	Workbook
Quoted text	Template

xy_series A number from 0 to 3 that specifies how data is arranged in a chart.

add_logical Indicates whether or not to add the active document to the open workbook. If *add_logical* is TRUE, the document is added; if FALSE or omitted, it is not added.

Example

The following formula creates a new workbook.

```
=NEW(5)
```

NEW.WINDOW

Creates a new window for the active document.

Syntax
NEW.WINDOW()

Example
```
=NEW.WINDOW( )
```

NEXT
Ends a FOR-NEXT, FOR.CELL-NEXT, or WHILE_NEXT loop, and continues carrying out the current macro with the macro formula that follows the next function.

Syntax
NEXT()

NOTE
Creates a note or replaces characters in a note.

Syntax
NOTE(*add_text,cell_ref,start_char,num_chars*)

add_text Text you want to add to a note. *Add_text* can be up to 255 characters.

cell_ref The cell to which to add the note text.

start_char The number of the character at which you want *add_text* to be added.

num_chars The number of characters you want to replace in the note.

Example
The following formula attaches a new note to cell A10.

```
=NOTE("This is the equity in the investment",!$A$10)
```

OBJECT.PROPERTIES
Determines how the selected object or objects are attached to cells and whether they are printed.

Syntax
OBJECT.PROPERTIES(*placement_type, print_object*)

placement_type A number from 1 to 3 indicating how to attach the selected object or objects.

Placement_type	*What happens to the object*
1	Moved and sized with the cells
2	Moved but not sized with the cells
3	Not affected by moving and sizing cells

print_object A logical value specifying whether to print the selected object or objects. If *print_object* is TRUE or omitted, the objects are printed; if FALSE, they are not printed.

Example

The following formula specifies that the selected object is to be moved and sized with the slected objects, and printed when included in a print range.

```
=OBJECT.PROPERTIES(1,TRUE)
```

OBJECT.PROTECTION

Changes the protection status of a selected object.

Syntax

OBJECT.PROTECTION(*locked,lock_text*)

locked A logical value that determines whether the selected object is locked or unlocked. If *locked* is TRUE, the object is locked; if FALSE, the object is unlocked.

lock_text A logical value that determines whether text in a text box or button can be changed. If *lock_text* is TRUE or omitted, text cannot be changed; if FALSE, text can be changed.

Example

The following formula unlocks the selected object and allows the text of the object to be changed.

```
=OBJECT.PROTECTION(FALSE,FALSE)
```

ON.DATA

Runs a specified macro when another application sends data to a document through the dynamic data exchange.

Syntax

ON.DATA(*document_text,macro_text*)

document_text The name of the document to which the data will be sent, or the name of the source of the remote data.

macro_text The name of (or an R1C1-style reference to) a macro to run when data comes into the document. (Both the name and the reference are in text form).

Example

The following formula runs the macro VARIANCE when data is sent to the worksheet COST.XLS.

```
=ON.DATA("COST.XLS","VARIANCE")
```

ON.DOUBLECLICK

Runs a macro when you double-click any cell, object, or any item on a chart.

Syntax

ON.DOUBLECLICK(*sheet_text,macro_text*)

sheet_text A text indicating the name of a document.

macro_text The name of (or an R1C1-style reference to) a macro to run when when you double-click the document specified by *sheet_text*. (Both the name and the reference are in text form).

Example

The following formula runs the macro VARIANCE when you double-click any cell or object in the worksheet COST.XLS.

```
=ON.DOUBLECLICK("COST.XLS","VARIANCE")
```

ON.ENTRY

Runs a macro when you enter data into any cell of a document.

Syntax

ON.ENTRY(*sheet_text,macro_text*)

sheet_text A text value indicating the name of a document.

macro_text The name of (or an R1C1-style reference to) a macro to run when you enter data into the document specified by *sheet_text*. (Both the name and the reference are in text form.)

Example

The following formula runs the macro Variance when data is entered into the worksheet COST.XLS.

```
=ON.ENTRY("COST.XLS","VARIANCE")
```

ON.KEY

Runs a macro when a particular key or key combination is pressed.

Syntax

ON.KEY(*key_text,macro_text*)

key_text Can specify any key, a combination of a key with Alt, Ctrl, or Shift, or any combination of those keys.

macro_text The name of (or an R1C1-style reference to) a macro to run when the key or keys defined by *key_text* are pressed. (Both the name and the reference are in text form.)

Example

The following formula specifies that the key combination Shift+Ctrl+RIGHT will run the macro named Print.

```
=ON.KEY("+^{RIGHT}","Print")
```

ON.RECALC

Runs a macro when a document is recalculated.

Syntax

ON.RECALC(*sheet_text,macro_text*)

sheet_text A text indicating the name of a document.

macro_text The name of (or an R1C1-style reference to) a macro to run when the document specified by *sheet_text* is recalculated. (Both the name and the reference are in text form.)

Example

The following formula specifies that the macro named Invoice on the macro sheet BILLS.XLM be run when the worksheet named ACCOUNTS.XLS is recalculated.

```
=ON.RECALC("ACCOUNTS.XLS","BILLS.XLM!Invoice")
```

ON.TIME

Runs a macro at a specified time.

Syntax

ON.TIME(*time,macro_text,tolerance,insert_logical*)

time The time and date (as a serial number) when the macro is to be run. (Note: if *time* does not include a date, the macro runs the next time the time occurs.)

macro_text The name of (or an R1C1-style reference to) a macro to run at the time specified in the *time* argument. (Both the name and the reference are in text form.)

tolerance The time and date (as a serial number) that you are willing to wait and still have the macro run. It specifies a period beyond which you do not want to wait.

insert_logical A logical value specifying whether you want the macro to run at the time specified by *time*. If *insert_logical* is TRUE or omitted, the macro is executed at *time*. If *insert_logical* is FALSE, the macro will not run at *time*.

Example

The following formula runs a macro named Update at 6:00 pm when Excel is in the ready mode.

```
=ON.TIME("6:00:00 PM","Update")
```

ON.WINDOW

Runs a macro when you switch to a particular window.

Syntax

ON.WINDOW(*window_text,macro_text*)

window_text The name of a window (in text form).

macro_text The name of (or an R1C1-style reference to) a macro to run when you switch to the window specified by *window_text*. (Both the name and the reference are in text form.)

Example

The following formula runs the macro named Update when you switch to the window containing SALES.XLS.

```
=ON.WINDOW("SALES.XLS","Update")
```

OPEN

Opens an existing document.

Syntax

OPEN(*file_text,update_links,read_only,format,prot_pwd,write_res_pwd, ignore_rorec,file_origin,custom_delimit,add_logical*)

file_text The name (as text) of the document to open.

update_links Determines whether and how to update external and remote references. If *update_links* is omitted, Excel displays a message asking if you want to update links.

Update_links	*What Excel updates*
0	Neither external nor remote references
1	External references only
2	Remote references only
3	External and remote references

read_only Corresponds to the Read Only check box in the Open dialog box. If *read_only* is TRUE, the document can be modified but changes cannot be saved; if FALSE or omitted, changes to the document can be saved.

format Specifies what to use as a delimiter when opening text files.

Format	*Text files separated by*
1	Tabs
2	Commas
3	Spaces
4	Semicolons

continues

Format	*Text files separated by*
5	Nothing
6	Custom characters

prot_pwd The password (as text) required to unprotect a file.

write_res_pwd The password (as text) required to open a Read-Only file with write privileges.

ignore_rorec A logical value that determines whether the Read-Only Recommended message is displayed. If *ignore_rorec* is TRUE, the message is not displayed; if FALSE or omitted, the alert message is displayed after opening a Read-Only Recommended document.

file_origin A number indicating the original operating environment in which the file was created.

File_origin	*Original operating environment*
1	Macintosh
2	Windows
3	MS-DOS
Omitted	Current operating environment

custom_delimit The character (as text) you want to use as a custom delimiter when opening text files.

add_logical A logical value that determines whether or not to add the text in the argument file_text to the open workbook. If *add_logical* is TRUE, the document is added; if FALSE or omitted, it is not added.

Example

The following formula opens the file INC_TAX.XLS as a read-only file, updates both external and remote references, and supplies the password Smith.

```
=OPEN("INC_TAX.XLS",3,TRUE,,"Smith")
```

OPEN.LINKS

Equivalent to choosing the Links command from the file menu.

Syntax

OPEN.LINKS(*document_text1,document_text2,...,read_only,type_of_link*) *document_text1,document_text2,...* From 1 to 12 arguments that are the names of supporting documents in the form of text, or the names of arrays or references that contain text.

read_only To the Read Only check box in the Open dialog box. If *read_only* is TRUE, the document can be modified, but changes cannot be saved; if FALSE or omitted, changes to the document can be saved.

type_of_link A number from 1 to 3 that indicates what type of link you want to get information about.

Type_of_link	*Link type*
1	Excel Link
2	DDE Link
3	Reserved

Example

The following formula opens documents that are linked to the active document, and opens them as Read-Only files.

```
=OPEN.LINKS("C:\EXCEL4\LINK1.XLS",C:\EXCEL4\COST.XLS",TRUE,1)
```

OUTLINE

Creates an outline.

Syntax

OUTLINE(*auto_styles,row_dir,col_dir,create_apply*)

The arguments *auto_styles*, *row_dir*, and *col_dir* correspond to check boxes in the Outline dialog box. If an argument is TRUE, the check box is selected; if FALSE the check box is cleared.

auto_styles Corresponds to the Automatic Styles check box.

row_dir Corresponds to the Summary Rows Below Detail check box.

col_dir Corresponds to the Summary Columns To Right Of Detail check box.

create_apply The number 1 or 2, corresponding to the Create button and the Apply styles button.

Create_apply	*Result*
1	Creates an outline with the current settings

continues

Create_apply	*Result*
2	Applies outlining styles to the selection based on outline levels
Omitted	Corresponds to choosing the OK button to set the other outline settings

Example

The following formula creates an outline, turns on automatic styles, and specifies that the summary columns and rows are to the right and below the detail.

```
=OUTLINE(TRUE,TRUE,TRUE,1)
```

PAGE.SETUP (Syntax 1 and Syntax 2)

Controls the printed appearance of your documents.

Syntax 1 (for Worksheets and Macro Sheets)

PAGE.SETUP(*head,foot,left,right,top,bot,hdng,grid,h_cntr,v_cntr,orient, paper_size,scale,pg_num,pg_order,bw_cells*)

Arguments that correspond to check boxes are logical values. If an argument is TRUE, the check box is selected; if FALSE, the check box is cleared.

head Specifies the text and formatting codes for the header.

foot Specifies the text and formatting codes for the footer.

left Corresponds to the Left box, and is a number specifying the left margin.

right Corresponds to the Right box, and is a number specifying the right margin.

top Corresponds to the Top box, and is a number specifying the top margin.

bot Corresponds to the Bottom box, and is a number specifying the Bottom margin.

hdng Corresponds to the Row & Column Headings check box.

grid Corresponds to the Cell Gridlines check box.

h_cntr Corresponds to the Center Horizontally check box in the Page Setup dialog box.

v_cntr Corresponds to the to the Center Vertically check box in the Page Setup dialog box.

orient The number 1 or 2, determining the orientation of the document when printed. If *orient* is 1, the orientation is Portrait; if 2, it is Landscape.

paper_size A number from 1 to 26 that specifies the size of the paper.

Paper_size	*Paper size*
1	Letter
2	Letter (small)
3	Tabloid
4	Ledger
5	Legal
6	Statement
7	Executive
8	A3
9	A4
10	A4 (small)
11	A5
12	B4
13	B5
14	Folio
15	Quarto
16	10x14
17	11x17
18	Note
19	ENV9
20	ENV10
21	ENV11
22	ENV12
23	ENV14
24	C Sheet
25	D Sheet
26	E Sheet

scale A number that is the percentage to increase or decrease the size of the document. *Scale* can also be the logical value TRUE, which means that the scale will be set to fit the print area on a single page.

pg_num Specifies the number of the first page.

pg_order The number 1 or 2 which determines whether pagination is left-to-right and then down, or top-to-bottom and then right.

Pg_order	*Pagination*
1	Top-to-bottom, then right
2	Left-to-right, then down

bw_cells A logical value that specifies whether to print cells and text boxes in color. If *bw_cells* is TRUE, then cell text and borders will be printed in black, and cell backgrounds will be printed in white; if FALSE, then cell text, borders, and background will be printed in color.

Example

The following formula sets up a worksheet page for printing and excludes headers and footers.

```
=PAGE.SETUP("","",0.5,0.5,0.5,0.5,FALSE,FALSE,FALSE,FALSE,
1,1,TRUE,1,1,FALSE)
```

Syntax 2 (for Charts)

PAGE.SETUP(*head,foot,left,right,top,bot,size,h_cntr,v_cntr,orient,paper_size, scale,pg_num*)

head Specifies the text and formatting codes for the header.

foot Specifies the text and formatting codes for the footer.

left Corresponds to the Left box, and is a number specifying the left margin.

right Corresponds to the Right box, and is a number specifying the right margin.

top Corresponds to the Top box, and is a number specifying the top margin.

bot Corresponds to the Bottom box, and is a number specifying the Bottom margin.

size A number corresponding to the options in the Chart Size box. *Size* determines how the chart is printed within the margins.

Size	*Chart print size*
1	Screen size
2	Fit to page
3	Full page

h_cntr Corresponds to the Center Horizontally check box in the Page Setup dialog box.

v_cntr Corresponds to the to the Center Vertically check box in the Page Setup dialog box.

orient The number 1 or 2, determining orientation of the document when printed. If *orient* is 1, the orientation is Portrait; if 2, it is Landscape.

paper_size A number from 1 to 26 that specifies the size of the paper.

Paper_size	*Paper size*
1	Letter
2	Letter (small)
3	Tabloid
4	Ledger
5	Legal
6	Statement
7	Executive
8	A3
9	A4
10	A4 (small)
11	A5
12	B4
13	B5
14	Folio
15	Quarto
16	10x14

continues

Paper_size	*Paper size*
17	11x17
18	Note
19	ENV9
20	ENV10
21	ENV11
22	ENV12
23	ENV14
24	C Sheet
25	D Sheet
26	E Sheet

scale A number that is the percentage to increase or decrease the size of the document. *Scale* can also be the logical value TRUE, which means the scale will be set to fit the print area on a single page.

pg_num Specifies the number of the first page.

Example

The following formula sets up the page to print a chart, and sizes it to fit on the page.

```
=PAGE.SETUP("&F","Page &P",0.75,0.75,1,1,2,FALSE,FALSE,
1,1,100,1)
```

PARSE

Distributes the contents of a single column to fill several adjacent columns.

Syntax

PARSE(*parse_text,destination_ref*)

parse_text The parse line (in the form of text); a copy of the first nonblank cell in the selected column. If *parse_text* is omitted, the macro parses the current selection.

destination_ref A reference to the upper left corner of the range of cells where the parsed data is to be placed.

Example
The following formula parses the current selection and places the parsed data starting in cell C1 of the active worksheet.

```
=PARSE(,!$C$1)
```

PASTE
Pastes a selection or object that you copied or cut.

Syntax
PASTE(*to_reference*)

to_reference A reference to the cell or range where you want to paste.

Example
The following formulas select a range, copy it to the Clipboard, and paste it to a cell.

```
=SELECT("R64C8:R67C8")
=COPY()
=VLINE(2)
=SELECT("R69C8")
=PASTE()
=RETURN()
```

PASTE.LINK
Pastes the copied data or objects and establishes a link to the source of the data or object.

Syntax
PASTE.LINK()

Example
The following formulas select a cell in the active worksheet, copy the contents of that cell to the Clipboard, select another worksheet, and paste the contents of the Clipboard to the worksheet while linking it to the previously-active worksheet (source worksheet).

```
=SELECT("R20C2")
=COPY()
=ACTIVATE("COST7.XLS")
```

```
=PASTE.LINK( )
=RETURN( )
```

PASTE.PICTURE

Pastes a picture of the Clipboard contents onto a worksheet.

Syntax

PASTE.PICTURE()

Example

The following formulas select a range of cells, copy the cells to the Clipboard, select another worksheet, paste a picture of the Clipboard contents, and then select the object (the pasted picture).

```
=SELECT("R24C1:R24C2")
=COPY( )
=ACTIVATE("COST7-1.XLS")
=SELECT("R11C1")
=PASTE.PICTURE( )
=SELECT("Picture 1")
=RETURN( )
```

PASTE.PICTURE.LINK

Pastes a linked picture of the Clipboard contents.

Syntax

PASTE.PICTURE.LINK()

Example

The following formulas copy the selection, select another worksheet, and paste a picture of the Clipboard contents—which is linked to the source document, so that as the data in the source document changes, the picture will change.

```
=COPY( )
=ACTIVATE("COST7-1.XLS")
=SELECT("R13C1")
=PASTE.PICTURE.LINK( )
=RETURN( )
```

PASTE.SPECIAL (Syntax 1 through Syntax 4)

Pastes the specified components of a copy area into the current selection.

Syntax 1 (for Pasting from Another Application)

PASTE.SPECIAL(*format_text,pastelink_logical*)

format_text Text that specifies the type of data you want to paste from the Clipboard and depends upon the application from which the data was copied. For example, if the data was copied from Microsoft Word, "Microsoft Document Object," "Picture," and "Text" are possible *format_text* arguments.

pastelink_logical A logical value indicating whether to link the pasted data to the source application. If *pastelink_logical* is TRUE, a link is created; if FALSE or omitted, no link is established.

Example

The following formula pastes a linked picture from Word for Windows to an Excel worksheet.

```
=PASTE.SPECIAL("Picture",TRUE)
```

Syntax 2 (Pastes from a Copy Area to a Chart)

PASTE.SPECIAL(*paste_num*)

paste_num A number from 1 to 3 specifying what to paste.

Paste_num	*What Excel pastes*
1	All (formats and data series)
2	Formats only
3	Formulas (data series) only

Example

The following formula pastes formats and data series from the copy area into a chart.

```
=PASTE.SPECIAL(1)
```

Syntax 3 (Pastes from a Worksheet to Another Worksheet)

PASTE.SPECIAL(*paste_num,operation_num,skip_blanks,transpose*)

Syntax 3 pastes the specified components from the copy area into the current selection.

paste_num A number from 1 to 5 specifying what to paste.

Paste_num	*What Excel Pastes*
1	All
2	Formulas
3	Values
4	Formats
5	Notes

operation_num A number from 1 to 5 specifying which operation to perform when pasting.

Operation_num	*What it does*
1	Nothing
2	Adds
3	Subtracts
4	Multiplies
5	Divides

skip_blanks A logical value corresponding to the Skip Blanks check box in the Paste Special dialog box. If *skip_blanks* is TRUE, Excel skips blanks in the copy area when pasting; if FALSE, Excel pastes normally.

transpose A logical value corresponding to the Transpose check box in the Paste Special dialog box. If *transpose* is TRUE, Excel transposes rows and columns when pasting; if FALSE, Excel pastes normally.

Example

The following formula pastes all formulas, values, formats, and notes, subtracts the numeric contents of the Clipboard from the numbers in the current selection, and skips blank cells.

```
=PASTE.SPECIAL(1,3,TRUE,FALSE)
```

Syntax 4 (Pastes from a Worksheet to a Chart)

PASTE.SPECIAL(*rowcol,series,categories,replace*)

Syntax 4 pastes the specified components from the copy area into a chart.

rowcol The number 1 or 2; determines whether the values corresponding to a data series are in rows or columns. The number 1 is for rows, while 2 is for columns.

series A logical value corresponding to the Series Names In First Column (or First Row, depending on the value for rowcol. If *series* is TRUE, Excel selects the check box, and uses the contents of the cell in the first column of each row (or the first row of each column) as the name of the data series in that row (or column). If *series* is FALSE, Excel clears the check box, and uses the contents of the cell in the first column of each row (or first row of each column) as the first data point of the data series.

categories A logical value corresponding to the Categories (X Labels) in First Row (or First Column) check box in the Paste Special dialog box. If *categories* is TRUE, Excel selects the check box, and uses the contents of the first row (or column) of the selection as the categories for the chart; if FALSE, the check box is cleared, and Excel uses the contents of the first row (or column) as the first data series in the chart.

replace A logical value corresponding to the Replace Existing Categories check box in the Paste Special dialog box. If *replace* is TRUE, Excel selects the check box and applies categories, while replacing existing categories with information from the copied cell range; if FALSE, the check box is cleared, and Excel applies new categories without replacing any old ones.

Example

The following formula pastes to a chart while specifying that values are in columns with the series name in the first row.

```
=PASTE.SPECIAL(2,TRUE,FALSE,FALSE)
```

PASTE.TOOL

Pastes a toolface from the Clipboard to a specified position on a toolbar.

Syntax

PASTE.TOOL(*bar_id,position*)

bar_id Specifies the number or name of the toolbar into which to paste the toolface. The built-in toolbars are specified by numbers from 1 to 9.

Bar_id	*Built-in toolbar*
1	Standard
2	Formatting
3	Utility
4	Chart
5	Drawing
6	Excel 3.0
7	Macro
8	Macro recording
9	Macro paused

position Specifies the position (within the toolbar) of the tool you want to paste to; starts with 1 at the left side (if horizontal) or at the top (if vertical).

Example

The following formula pastes a toolface onto the tool found in position 5 of the Macro toolbar.

```
=PASTE.TOOL(7,5)
```

PAUSE

Pauses a macro.

Syntax

PAUSE(*no_tool*)

no_tool A logical value determining whether to display the Resume toolbar when the macro is paused. If *no_tool* is TRUE, the toolbar is not displayed; if FALSE, the toolbar is displayed.

Example

The following formula pauses a macro and displays the Resume toolbar.

```
=PAUSE(FALSE)
```

PRECISION

Controls the precision with which values are stored in cells.

Syntax

PRECISION(*logical*)

logical A logical value, corresponding to the Precision As Displayed check box in the Calculation dialog box. If *logical* is TRUE, future cell entries will be stored at full precision (15 digits); if FALSE or omitted, Excel stores values exactly as they are displayed.

Example

If a macro encounters the following formula, future entires will be stored with up to 15 digits.

```
=PRECISION(TRUE)
```

PREFERRED

Changes the format of the active chart to the format defined by the Set Preferred command or the SET.PREFERRED macro function.

Syntax

PREFERRED()

Example

The following formulas change the format of Chart 2 to the format currently defined by the Set Preferred command.

```
=ACTIVATE("Sheet1 Chart 2")
=PREFERRED( )
```

PRESS.TOOL

Depresses a tool.

Syntax

PRESS.TOOL(*bar_id,position,down*)

bar_id Specifies the number or name of the toolbar in which to depress the toolface. The built-in toolbars are specified by numbers from 1 to 9.

Bar_id	*Built-in toolbar*
1	Standard
2	Formatting

continues

Bar_id	*Built-in toolbar*
3	Utility
4	Chart
5	Drawing
6	Excel 3.0
7	Macro
8	Macro recording
9	Macro paused

position Specifies the position (within the toolbar) of the tool to which you want to paste; starts with 1 at the left side (if horizontal) or at the top (if vertical).

down A logical value, specifying the appearance of the tool. If *down* is TRUE, the tool appears depressed; if FALSE or omitted, the tool appears normal.

Example

The following formula depresses the fourth tool on the Utility toolbar.

```
=PRESS.TOOL(3,4,TRUE)
```

PRINT

Prints the active document.

Syntax

PRINT(*range_num,from,to,copies,draft,preview,print_what,color,feed,quality, y_resolution*)

range_num A number specifying the pages to print.

Range_num	*Pages to be printed*
1	All the pages
2	Prints a specified range

from Specifies the first page to print.

to Specifies the last page to print.

copies Specifies the number of copies to print.

draft Corresponds to the Fast, but no graphics check box. If *draft* is TRUE, the check box is selected; if FALSE, it is cleared.

preview Corresponds to the Preview check box. If preview TRUE, the check box is selected; if FALSE, it is cleared.

print_what A number from 1 to 3 that specifies the parts of the worksheet or macro sheet to print.

For more about *y_resolution*, see the Excel Function Reference.

Print_what	*Prints*
1	Sheet only
2	Notes only
3	Sheet and then notes

color Corresponds to the Print Using Color check box, and is only available in Excel for the Macintosh.

feed A number specifying the type of paper feed (only available in Excel for the Macintosh).

quality Corresponds to the Print Quality box and specifies the DPI output quality desired.

Example

The following formula prints three copies of pages 2 through 5 including notes and previews the pages on screen before printing.

```
=PRINT(2,2,5,3,FALSE,TRUE,3,FALSE,1)
```

PRINT.PREVIEW

Previews the pages and page breaks of the active document on screen before printing.

Syntax

PRINT.PREVIEW()

PRINTER.SETUP

Specifies the printer you want to use.

Syntax

PRINTER.SETUP(*printer_text*)

printer_text The name of the printer as it would be entered in the Setup dialog box.

Example

The following formula identifies the LaserJet Plus as connected to LPT1

```
=PRINTER.SETUP("PCL / HP LaserJet on LPT1:")
```

PROMOTE

Promotes the currently selected rows or columns in an outline.

Syntax

PROMOTE(*rowcol*)

rowcol The number 1 or 2, determining whether to promote rows or columns.

Rowcol	*Promotes*
1 or omitted	Rows
2	Columns

Example

The following formula promotes columns.

```
=PROMOTE(2)
```

PROTECT.DOCUMENT

Adds protection to or removes protection from the active worksheet, macro sheet, workbook, or chart.

Syntax

PROTECT.DOCUMENT(*contents,windows,password,objects*)

contents A logical value, corresponding to a check box in the Protect Document dialog box. For worksheets or macro sheets, *contents* corresponds to the Cells check box. For charts, *contents* corresponds to the Chart check box. For workbooks, *contents* corresponds to the Contents check box. If *contents* is TRUE or omitted, the check box is selected and cells of sheets or contents of workbooks are protected; if FALSE, Excel clears the check box, and removes protection if the correct password is supplied.

windows A logical value, corresponding to the Windows check box in the Protect Document dialog box for all document types.

password A password (in the form of text) that you must specify in order to protect or unprotect the file.

objects A logical value that corresponds to the Objects check box in the Protect Document dialog box; applies only to worksheets and macro sheets. If *objects* is TRUE or omitted, Excel selects the check box, and protects all locked objects on the worksheet or macro sheet; if FALSE, Excel clears the check box.

Example

The following formula protects a worksheet, but does not utilize a password.

```
=PROTECT.DOCUMENT(TRUE,FALSE,,TRUE)
```

QUIT

Quits Excel and closes open documents.

Syntax

QUIT()

Example

The following formulas save the active document and then quit from Excel.

```
=SAVE( )
=QUIT( )
```

RANDOM (Syntax 1 through Syntax 7)

Fills a range with randomly generated numbers.

Syntax 1 (Uniform Distribution)

RANDOM(*outrng,variables,points,distribution,seed,from,to*)

Syntax 2 (Normal Distribution)

RANDOM(*outrng,variables,points,distribution,seed,mean,standard_dev*)

Syntax 3 (Bernoulli Distribution)

RANDOM(*outrng,variables,points,distribution,seed,probability*)

Syntax 4 (Binomial Distribution)

RANDOM(*outrng,variables,points,distribution,seed,probability,trials*)

Syntax 5 (Poisson Distribution)

RANDOM(*outrng,variables,points,distribution,seed,lambda*)

Syntax 6 (Patterned Distribution)

RANDOM(*outrng,variables,points,distribution,seed,from,to,step,repeat_num, repeat_seq*)

Syntax 7 (Discrete Distribution)

RANDOM(*outrng,variables,points,distribution,seed,inprng*)

outrng The cell (the upper left cell) in the output table.

variables Number of random number sets to generate.

points The number of data points per random number set.

distribution Specifies the type of number distribution.

Distribution	*Distribution type*	*Description*
1	Uniform	Characterized by lower and upper bounds with variables drawn with equal probability.
2	Normal	Characterized by a mean and a standard deviation.
3	Bernouli	Characterized by a probabilty of success on a given trial.
4	Binominal	Characterized by a probability of success for a number of trials.
5	Poisson	Characterized by a value lambda, equal to 1/mean and is used to predict the number of events that occur per unit of time.
6	Patterned	Uses a lower and upper bound, a step, a repetition rate for values, and a repetition rate for the sequence.

Distribution	Distribution type	Description
7	Discrete	Characterized by a value and the associated probability range and must include two columns, with the left column containing values and the right column containing probabilities for those values.

seed An optional value with which to begin generating random numbers.

from The lower bound.

to The upper bound.

mean The mean value of the randomly generated numbers.

standard_dev The standard deviation of the randomly generated numbers.

probability The probability of success on each trial.

trials The number of trials.

lambda The Poisson distribution parameter.

step The increment between from and to.

repeat_num The number of times to repeat each value.

repeat_seq The number of times to repeat each sequence of values.

inprng A two-column range of values and their probabilities.

Example

The following formula creates a column of 10 randomly generated numbers that fall between the values 1 and 10, using a Uniform distribution.

```
=RANDOM(Sheet1!$A$1,1,10,1,,1,10)
```

REFTEXT

Converts a reference to an absolute reference in the form of text.

Syntax

REFTEXT(*reference,A1*)

reference The reference that you want to convert.

A1 A logical value, specifying the A1 or R1C1-style references. If *A1* is TRUE the function returns an A1-style reference; if FALSE or omitted, the function returns an R1C1-style reference.

Example

The following formula returns $B$2

```
=REFTEXT(B2,TRUE)
```

RELREF

Returns the reference of a cell or cells relative to the upper left cell of *rel_to_ref*.

Syntax

RELREF(*reference,rel_to_ref*)

reference The cell or cells to which you want to create a relative reference.

rel_to_ref The cell from which you want to create the relative reference.

Example

The following formula returns the "R[-2]C[-2]" relative reference.

```
=RELREF($A$1,$C$3)
```

REMOVE.PAGE.BREAK

Removes manual page breaks.

Syntax

REMOVE.PAGE.BREAK()

Example

The following formula selects a worksheet, removes the page break, then prints the worksheet.

```
=ACTIVATE("Sheet1")
=REMOVE.PAGE.BREAK()
=PRINT(1,,,1,FALSE,FALSE,1,FALSE,1,-4)
=RETURN()
```

RENAME.COMMAND

Changes the name of a built-in or custom menu command of the name of a menu.

Syntax

RENAME.COMMAND(*bar_num,menu,command,name_text*)

bar_num The number of a built-in menu bar, or the number returned by a previously-run ADD.BAR function.

menu Can be either the name of a menu (as text) or the number of the menu. Menus are numbered starting with 1 (from the left of the screen).

command Can be either the name of the command (as text) or the number of the command to be renamed.

name_text The new name for the command.

For ID numbers of the built-in menu bars and shortcut menus, consult the Microsoft Excel Function Reference.

Example

The following formula renames the Show Graph command to Hide Graph.

```
=RENAME.COMMAND(1,"FILE","Show Graph","Hide Graph")
```

REPORT.DEFINE

Creates or replaces a report definition.

Syntax

REPORT.DEFINE(*report_name,views_scenarios_array,pages_logical*)

report_name The name of the report.

views_scenarios_array An array that contains one or more rows of view and scenario pairs.

pages_logical A logical value. If pages_logical is TRUE or omitted, continuous page numbers for multiple sections is specified; if FALSE, resets page numbers to 1 for each new section.

Example

The following formula creates a report with continuous page numbers for multiple sections called Income_Statement.

```
=REPORT.DEFINE("Income_Statement",TRUE)
```

REPORT.DELETE

Removes a report definition from the active document.

Syntax
REPORT.DELETE(*report_name*)

report_name The name of the report that you want to remove from the active document.

Example
The following formula removes the report called Income_Statement from the active document.

```
=REPORT.DELETE("Income_Statement")
```

REPORT.GET

Returns information about reports defined for the active document.

Syntax
REPORT.GET(*type_num,report_name*)

type_num A number from 1 to 3 indicating the type of information to return.

Type_num	*Returns*
1	An array of reports from the active document.
2	An array of view and scenario pairs from the report specified by *report_name*.
3	If continuous page numbers are used, returns TRUE. If page numbers start at 1 for each section, returns FALSE.

report_name The name of the report from the active document.

Example
The following formula returns an array of reports from the active document.

```
=REPORT.GET(1)
```

REPORT.PRINT

Prints a report.

Syntax
REPORT.PRINT(*report_name,copies_num,show_print_dlg_logical*)

report_name The name of the report from the active document that you want to print.

copies_num The number of a report in the active document. If *copies_num* is omitted, the default is 1.

show_print_dlg_logical A logical value. If *show_print_dlg_logical* is TRUE, Excel displays a dialog box asking how many copies to print; if FALSE or omitted, prints the report immediately using existing settings.

Example

The following formula prints a report named Income_Statement.

```
=REPORT.PRINT("Income_Statement")
```

RESET.TOOL

Resets a tool to its original toolface.

Syntax

RESET.TOOL(*bar_id,position*)

bar_id Either a number from 1 to 9 (indicating one of the built-in toolbars), or the name of a custom toolbar.

Bar_id	*Built-in toolbar*
1	Standard
2	Formatting
3	Utility
4	Chart
5	Drawing
6	Excel 3.0
7	Macro
8	Macro recording
9	Macro paused

position Specifies the position of the tool within the toolbar, and starts with 1 at the left side (if horizontal) or at the top (if vertical).

Example

The following formula resets the second tool on the Utility toolbar to its original toolface.

```
=RESET.TOOL(3,2)
```

RESET.TOOLBAR

Resets built-in toolbars to the default set.

Syntax

RESET.TOOLBAR(*bar_id*)

bar_id Either a number from 1 to 9 indicating one of the built-in toolbars or the name of a custom toolbar.

Bar_id	*Built-in toolbar*
1	Standard
2	Formatting
3	Utility
4	Chart
5	Drawing
6	Excel 3.0
7	Macro
8	Macro recording
9	Macro paused

Example

The following formula rests the Utility toolbar to its default.

```
=RESET(3)
```

RESTART

Restarts a macro by removing RETURN statements from the stack.

Syntax

RESTART(*level_num*)

level_num A number specifying the number of previous RETURN statements you want ignored.

Example

The following formula removes one level of RETURN statements from memory.

```
=RESTART(1)
```

RESULT

Specifies the type of data a macro or custom function returns.

Syntax

RESULT(*type_num*)

type_num A number specifying the data type.

Type_num	*Type of data returned*
1	Number
2	Text
4	Logical
8	Reference
16	Error
64	Array

Example

The following formula specifies that the data type to be returned is text.

```
=RESULT(2)
```

RESUME

Resumes a paused macro.

Syntax

RESUME(*type_num*)

type_num A number from 1 to 4, specifying how to resume.

Type_num	*How resumed*
1 or omitted	If paused by a PAUSE function, the macro continues running. If paused from the Single Step dialog box, returns to that dialog box.
2	Halts the paused macro.
3	Continues running the macro.
4	Opens the Single Step dialog box.

Example

The following formula resumes the running of the macro.

```
=RESUME(3)
```

RETURN

Ends the currently running macro.

Syntax

RETURN(*value*)

value Specifies what value to use if the macro is a function or subroutine. If the macro is a command macro, *value* should be omitted.

Example

The following macro switches to the upper left pane of the window of an open worksheet named RENTBUY.XLS.

```
=ACTIVATE("RENTBUY.XLS",1)
=RETURN()
```

ROW.HEIGHT

Changes the height of the rows in a reference.

Syntax

ROW.HEIGHT(*height_num,reference,standard_height,type_num*)

height_num Specifies how height of the rows (in points).

reference Specifies the rows for which you want to change their heights.

standard_height A logical value that sets the row height dependent upon the size of the fonts in the row. If *standard_height* is TRUE, Excel sets the row height to a standard height that varies according to the size of the fonts in each row; if FALSE or omitted, Excel sets the row height according to *height_num*.

type_num A number from 1 to 3, corresponding to selecting the Hide or Unhide button in the Row Height dialog box or setting the selected rows to a best-fit height.

Type_num	*Action*
1	Hides the row(s) by setting the row height to 0.
2	Unhides the row(s) by setting the row height to the value set before the selection was hidden.
3	Sets the row(s) to a best-fit height.

Example

The following formula restores row 2 to a best-fit height.

```
=ROW.HEIGHT(,"R2",,3)
```

RUN

Runs a macro.

Syntax

RUN(*reference,step*)

reference A reference to the macro to run or is a number from 1 to 4, specifying an Auto macro to run.

Reference	*Specifies to run*
1	All Auto_Open macros.
2	All Auto_Close macros.
3	All Auto_Activate macros.
4	All Auto_Deactivate macros.

step A logical value, specifying that the macro is to be run in a single-step mode. If *step* is TRUE, Excel runs the macro in the single-step mode; if FALSE or omitted, Excel runs the macro normally.

Example

The following formula runs the macro found at a range named DOLLARS in a macro sheet named FORMATS.XLM.

```
=RUN(FORMATS.XLM!DOLLARS).
```

SAMPLE

Creates a sample from a population of data.

Syntax

SAMPLE(*inprng,outrng,method,rate*)

inprng The input range that contains the population of values from which you want to create a sample.

outrng The first cell (the upper left cell) in the output column that will contain the sample.

method A text character that specifies the type of sampling. If *method* is "P", then periodic sampling is used, with the input range sampled every *n*th (*n* is equal to the value of the *rate* argument). If *method* is "R", then random sampling is used.

rate The sampling rate if *method* is "P". If *method* is "R", then *rate* is the number of samples to take.

Example

The following formula creates a random sample from the range A1:A100.

```
=SAMPLE(Sheet1!$A$1:$A$100,Sheet1!$B$1,"R",1)
```

SAVE

Saves the active document.

Syntax

SAVE()

Example

The following formula prints the active document, then saves it.

```
=PRINT(1,,,1,FALSE,FALSE,1,FALSE,1,-4)
=SAVE()
```

SAVE.AS

Saves a file and gives you the opportunity to specify a new filename, file type, protection password, write-reservation password, or backup file.

Syntax

SAVE.AS(*document_text,type_num,prot_pwd,backup,write_res_pwd,read_only_rec*)

document_text Specifies the name of a document to save.

type_num A number from 1 to 29 that specifies the file format in which to save the document.

Type_num	*File format*
1 or omitted	Normal
2	SYLK
3	Text
4	WKS
5	WK1
6	CSV
7	DBF2
8	DBF3
9	DIF
10	Reserved
11	DBF4
12	Reserved
13	Reserved
14	Reserved
15	WK3
16	Microsoft Excel 2.x
17	Template

continues

Type_num	*File format*
18	Add-in macro
19	Text (Macintosh)
20	Text (Windows)
21	Text (MS-DOS)
22	CSV (Macintosh)
23	CSV (Windows)
24	CSV (MS-DOS)
25	International macro
26	International add-in macro
27	Reserved
28	Reserved
29	Microsoft Excel 3.0

prot_pwd A password of 15 characters of text (or less), or a reference to a cell containing this type of value.

backup A logical value. If *backup* is TRUE, a backup file is created; if FALSE, no backup file is created.

write_res_pwd A password that allows the user to write to a file.

read_only_rec A logical value. If *read_only_rec* is TRUE, Excel saves the document as read only recommended; if FALSE, saving is done as normal.

Example

The following formula saves a file with "smith" as the password.

```
=SAVE.AS("C:\EXCEL4\FINANCE.XLS",1,"smith",FALSE,"",FALSE)
```

SAVE.TOOLBAR

Saves one or more toolbar definitions to a specified file.

Syntax

SAVE.TOOLBAR(*bar_id,filename*)

bar_id Specifies the number or name of the toolbar whose definition you want to save. The built-in toolbars are specified by numbers from 1 to 9.

Bar_id	*Built-in toolbar*
1	Standard
2	Formatting
3	Utility
4	Chart
5	Drawing
6	Excel 3.0
7	Macro
8	Macro recording
9	Macro paused

filename Text specifying the name of the destination file.

Example

The following formula saves Toolbar 1 as TOOLBAR1.XLB.

```
=SAVE.TOOLBAR("Toolbar 1","C:\EXCEL4\TOOLBAR1.XLB")
```

SAVE.WORKBOOK

Saves the workbook to which the active document belongs.

Syntax

SAVE.WORKBOOK(*document_text,type_num,prot_pwd,backup,write_res_pwd, read_only_rec*)

document_text Specifies the name of a document to save.

type_num A number from 1 to 29 that specifies the file format in which to save the document.

Type_num	*File format*
1 or omitted	Normal
2	SYLK
3	Text

Type_num	*File format*
4	WKS
5	WK1
6	CSV
7	DBF2
8	DBF3
9	DIF
10	Reserved
11	DBF4
12	Reserved
13	Reserved
14	Reserved
15	WK3
16	Microsoft Excel 2.x
17	Template
18	Add-in macro
19	Text (Macintosh)
20	Text (Windows)
21	Text (MS-DOS)
22	CSV (Macintosh)
23	CSV (Windows)
24	CSV (MS-DOS)
25	International macro
26	International add-in macro
27	Reserved
28	Reserved
29	Microsoft Excel 3.0

prot_pwd A password of 15 characters of text (or less), or a reference to a cell containing this type of value.

backup A logical value. If *backup* is TRUE, a backup file is created; if FALSE, no backup file is created.

write_res_pwd A password that allows the user to write to a file.

read_only_rec A logical value. If *read_only_rec* is TRUE, Excel saves the document as read only recommended; if FALSE, saving is done as normal.

Example

The following formula saves the file FINANCE.XLS, using "smith" as the password.

```
=SAVE.AS("C:\EXCEL4\FINANCE.XLS",1,"smith",FALSE,"",FALSE)
```

SCENARIO.ADD

Defines specified values as scenarios.

Syntax

SCENARIO.ADD(*scen_name,value_array*)

scen_name The name of the scenario to be defined.

value_array A horizontal array of values to be used as input for the model on the worksheet.

Example

The following formula defines an array of cells {1;100;2;250;3;320;4;820} as the Best_Case scenario.

```
=SCENARIO.ADD("Best_Case",{1;100;2;250;3;320;4;820})
```

SCENARIO.CELLS

Defines the changing cells for a model on your worksheet.

Syntax

SCENARIO.CELLS(*changing_ref*)

changing_ref A reference to the cells you want to define as input cells for a worksheet model.

Example

The following formula defines the changing cells in a scenario as A1:B4.

```
=SCENARIO.CELLS(!$A$1:$B$4)
```

SCENARIO.DELETE

Deletes the specified scenario.

Syntax

SCENARIO.DELETE(*scen_name*)

scen_name The name of the scenario you want to delete.

Example

The following formula deletes the Best_Case scenario.

```
=SCENARIO.DELETE("Best_Case")
```

SCENARIO.GET

Returns specified information about the scenarios defined on your worksheet.

Syntax

SCENARIO.GET(*type_num*)

type_num A number from 1 to 4, specifying the type of information you want.

Type_num	*Information returned*
1	A horizontal array of all scenario names in the form of text
2	A reference to the changing cells
3	A reference to the result cells
4	An array of scenario values

Example

The following formula returns an array of scenario values.

```
=SCENARIO.GET(4)
```

SCENARIO.SHOW

Recalculates a model using the specified scenario and displays the result.

Syntax

SCENARIO.SHOW(*scen_name*)

scen_name The name of the scenario whose result you want to display.

Example

The following formula recalculates a worksheet model and displays the results of the scenario named Worst_Case.

```
=SCENARIO.SHOW("Worst_Case")
```

SCENARIO.SHOW.NEXT

Recalculates a worksheet and displays the results of the next scenario in the Scenarios list.

Syntax

SCENARIO.SHOW.NEXT()

SCENARIO.SUMMARY

Creates a table summarizing the results of all the scenarios for a worksheet model.

Syntax

SCENARIO.SUMMARY(*result_ref*)

result_ref A reference to the result cells you want to include in the summary report.

Example

The following formula creates a table summarizing the results of scenarios that are using cell B5 of the active worksheet as a results cell.

```
=SCENARIO.SUMMARY(!$B$5)
```

SELECT (Syntax 1 through Syntax 3)

Selects cells on a worksheet or macro sheet or objects in a worksheet or chart.

Syntax 1 (for Chart Items)

SELECT(*item_text,single_point*)

item_text A selection code that specifies which item of a chart to select.

To select	*Item_text*
Entire chart	"Chart"
Plot area	"Plot"
Legend	"Legend"
Main chart value axis	"Axis 1"
Main chart category axis	"Axis 2"
Overlay chart value axis or 3-D series axis	"Axis 3"
Overlay chart category axis	"Axis 4"
Chart title	"Title"
Label for the main chart value axis	"Text Axis 1"
Label for the main chart category axis	"Text Axis 2"
Label for the main chart series axis	"Text Axis 3"
*n*th floating text item	"Text *n*"
*n*th arrow	*"Arrow n"*
Major gridlines of value axis	"Gridline 1"
Minor gridlines of value axis	"Gridline 2"
Major gridlines of category axis	"Gridline 3"
Minor gridlines of category axis	"Gridline 4"
Major gridlines of series axis	"Gridline 5"
Minor gridlines of series axis	"Gridline 6"
Main chart droplines	"Dropline 1"
Overlay chart droplines	"Dropline 2"
Main chart hi-lo lines	"Hiloline 1"
Overlay chart hi-lo lines	"Hiloline 2"
Main chart up bar	"Up Bar 1"
Overlay chart up bar	"Up Bar 2"
Main chart down bar	"Down Bar 1"
Overlay chart down bar	"Down Bar 2"

To select	*Item_text*
Main chart series line	"Series line 1"
Overlay chart series line	"Series line 2"
Entire series	"S*n*"
Data associated with points *m* in series *n* if *single_point* is TRUE	"S*n*P*m*"
Text attached to point *m* of series *n*	"Text S*n*P*m*"
Series title text of series *n* of an area chart	"Text S*n*"
Base of a 3-D chart	"Floor"
Back of a 3-D chart	"Walls"
Corners of a 3-D chart	"Corners"

single_point A logical value that determines whether to select a single point. If *single_point* is TRUE, Excel selects a single point; if FALSE or omitted, Excel selects a single point (if there is only one series in the chart), or selects the entire series (if there is more than one series in the chart).

Syntax 2 (for Worksheets and Macro Sheets)

SELECT(*object_id_text,replace*)

object_id_text Text that identifies the object to select. *Object_id_text* can be either the text form of the number, or the name and number of the object as it would appear in the reference area when the object is normally selected.

replace A logical value that specifies whether previously selected objects are included in the selection. If replace is TRUE or omitted, Excel selects only the objects indicated by *object_id_text*; if FALSE, it includes any objects that were previously selected.

Syntax 3 (for Cells on a Worksheet or Macro Sheet)

SELECT(*selection,active_cell*)

selection The cell or range of cells you want to select.

active_cell The cell in the selection argument you want to make the active cell.

Example

The following formulas selects a chart named Chart 1, and then puts the chart on top of all other documents.

```
=SELECT("Chart 1")
=BRING.TO.FRONT()
```

SELECT.END

Selects the cell at the edge of the range in the direction specified.

Syntax

SELECT.END(*direction_num*)

direction_num A number from 1 to 4, specifying the direction in which to move.

Direction_num	*Direction*
1	Left
2	Right
3	Up
4	Down

Example

The following formula selects the cell that is one row below the current selection if that cell contains data. Otherwise, it will select the last cell in the column.

```
=SELECT.END(4)
```

SELECT.LAST.CELL

Selects the cell at the intersection of the last row and column that contains a formula, value, or format, or that is referred to in a formula or name.

Syntax

SELECT.LAST.CELL()

SELECT.PLOT.AREA

Selects the plot area of the active chart.

Syntax

SELECT.PLOT.AREA()

SELECT.SPECIAL

Select groups of similar cells in one of a several categories.

Syntax

SELECT.SPECIAL(*type_num,value_type,levels*)

type_num A number from 1 to 13 that corresponds to options in the Select Special dialog box and describes what to select.

Type_num	*Description*
1	Notes
2	Constants
3	Formulas
4	Blanks
5	Current region
6	Current array
7	Row differences
8	Column differences
9	Precedents
10	Dependents
11	Last cell
12	Visible cells only
13	All objects

value_type A number specifying which types of constants or formulas to select.

Value_type	*Selects*
1	Numbers
2	Text
4	Logical values
16	Error values

levels A number specifying how precedents and dependents are selected. If *levels* is 1, then Excel selects only direct precedents and dependents; if 2, all levels are selected.

Example

The following formula selects only visible cells in a worksheet.

```
=SELECT.SPECIAL(12)
```

SEND.TO.BACK

Sends the selected object or objects to the back, behind other objects.

Syntax

SEND.TO.BACK()

Example

The following formula selects a chart named Chart 1 and then puts the chart on behind all other objects.

```
=SELECT("Chart 1")
=SEND.TO.BACK()
=RETURN()
```

SET.CRITERIA

Defines the name criteria for the selected range on a worksheet or macro sheet.

Syntax

SET.CRITERIA()

Example

The following formulas select a range, and then define it as a criteria range.

```
=SELECT("R13C1:R14C2")
=SET.CRITERIA()
=RETURN()
```

SET.DATABASE

Gives the name Database to the selected range on a worksheet or macro sheet.

Syntax

SET.DATABASE()

Example

The following formulas select the range and define it as the database range.

```
=SELECT("R13C1:R137C6")
=SET.DATABASE()
=RETURN()
```

SET.EXTRACT

Gives the name Extract to the selected range on a worksheet or macro sheet.

Syntax

SET.EXTRACT()

Example

The following formulas select the range and define it as the extract range.

```
=SELECT("R13C1:R137C6")
=SET.EXTRACT()
=RETURN()
```

SET.NAME

Defines a name on a macro sheet to refer to a value.

Syntax

SET.NAME(*name_text,value*)

name_text The name (in text form) that refers to value.

value The value you want to store in *name_text*.

Example

The following formula assigns the value 10 to the name DECADE.

```
=SET.NAME("DECADE",10)
```

SET.PAGE.BREAK

Sets manual page breaks for a printed worksheet.

Syntax
SET.PAGE.BREAK()

SET.PREFERRED

Changes the default format used when creating a new chart or when you format a chart with the Preferred command from the Gallery menu.

Syntax
SET.PREFERRED()

SET.PRINT.AREA

Defines the print are that is printed when you choose the File Print command.

Syntax
SET.PRINT.AREA()

Example
The following formula selects a worksheet range, sets it as the print area, then prints the range.

```
=SELECT("R1C1:R9C8")
=SET.PRINT.AREA()
=PRINT(1,,,1,FALSE,FALSE,1,FALSE,1,-4)
=RETURN()
```

SET.PRINT.TITLES

Sets up or defines the current selection as the titles in the document that will be printed.

Syntax
SET.PRINT.TITLES(*titles_for_columns_ref,titles_for_rows_ref*)

titles_for_columns_ref A reference to the row to be used as a title for columns.

titles_for_rows_ref A reference to the column to be used as a title for rows.

Example

The following formula specifies column A as the source for row titles and omits column titles.

```
=SET.PRINT.TITLES("",$A:$A)
```

SET.VALUE

Changes the value of a cell or cells on the macro sheet—not the worksheet—without changing any formulas entered in those cells.

Syntax

SET.VALUE(*reference,values*)

reference Specifies the cell or cells on the macro sheet to which you want to assign a new value or values.

values The value or set of values to which you want to assign the cell or cells in reference.

Example

The following formula changes the value of cell B10 to the value 150.

```
=SET.VALUE($B$10,150)
```

SHOW.ACTIVE.CELL

Scrolls the active window so that the active cell becomes visible.

Syntax

SHOW.ACTIVE.CELL()

SHOW.BAR

Displays the specified menu bar.

Syntax

SHOW.BAR(*bar_num*)

bar_num The number of the menu bar you want to display; can be the number of one of the Excel built-in menu bars, the number returned by a previously-executed ADD.BAR function, or a reference to a cell containing a previously-executed ADD.BAR function.

SHOW.CLIPBOARD

Displays the contents of the Clipboard in the Clipboard window if the Clipboard is active; otherwise shows the Clipboard icon (which you double-click to open).

Syntax

SHOW.CLIPBOARD()

SHOW.DETAIL

Expands or collapses the detail under the specified expand or collapse button in an outline.

Syntax

SHOW.DETAIL(*rowcol, rowcol_num, expand*)

rowcol A number that specifies whether to operate on rows or columns of data.

Rowcol	*Operates on*
1	Rows
2	Columns

rowcol_num A number that specifies the row or column to expand or collapse.

expand A logical value. If *expand* is TRUE, Excel expands the detail under the row or column; if FALSE, Excel collapses the detail.

Example

The following formula collapses the detail under row 5.

```
=SHOW.DETAIL(1,5)
```

SHOW.INFO

Controls the display of the Info Window.

Syntax

SHOW.INFO(*logical*)

logical Controls the display of the Info window. If *logical* is TRUE, Excel switches to the Info Window; if FALSE, Excel switches to the document linked to the Info Window.

Example

The following formula switches to the Info Window.

```
=SHOW.INFO(TRUE)
```

SHOW.LEVELS

Displays the specified number of row and column levels of an outline.

Syntax

SHOW.LEVELS(*row_level,col_level*)

row_level Specifies the number of row levels of an outline to display.

col_level Specifies the number of column levels of an outline to display.

Example

The following formula displays row levels 1 through 10.

```
=SHOW(10,1)
```

SHOW.TOOLBAR

Hides or displays a toolbar.

Syntax

SHOW.TOOLBAR(*bar_id,visible,dock,x_pos,y_pos,width*)

bar_id Either a number from 1 to 9 indicating one of the built-in toolbars, or the name of a custom toolbar.

Bar_id	*Built-in toolbar*
1	Standard
2	Formatting
3	Utility
4	Chart
5	Drawing
6	Excel 3.0
7	Macro

continues

Bar_id	*Built-in toolbar*
8	Macro recording
9	Macro paused

visible A logical value that, if TRUE, specifies that the toolbar is visible—or, if FALSE, specifies that the toolbar is hidden.

dock Specifies the docking location of the toolbar.

Dock	*Position of toolbar*
1	Top of workspace
2	Left edge of workspace
3	Right edge of workspace
4	Bottom of workspace
5	Floating

x_pos Specifies the horizontal position of the toolbar; measured in points from the left edge of the toolbar to the left edge of the toolbar's docking area.

y_pos Specifies the vertical position of the toolbar; measured in points from the top edge of the toolbar to the top edge of the toolbar's docking area.

width Specifies the width of the toolbar and is measured in points.

Example

The following formula displays the formatting toolbar as a floating toolbar.

```
=SHOW.TOOLBAR(2,TRUE,5)
```

SOLVER.ADD

Adds a constraint to the current problem.

Syntax

SOLVER.ADD(*cell_ref,relation,formula*)

cell_ref A reference to a cell or range of cells on the active worksheet; forms the left side of the constraint.

relation Specifies the relationship between the left and right sides, or whether *cell_ref* must be an integer.

Relation	*Relationship*
1	<=
2	=
3	>=
4	Int (*cell_ref* is an integer)

formula The right side of the constraint; can be a single number, formula (as text), or a reference.

Example

The following formula adds the following constraint to a Solver problem: B5 must be less than or equal to 3000.

```
=SOLVER.ADD(!$B$5,1,"<=3000")
```

SOLVER.CHANGE

Changes the right side of an existing constraint.

Syntax

SOLVER.CHANGE(*cell_ref,relation,formula*)

cell_ref A reference to a cell or range of cells on the active worksheet; forms the left side of the constraint.

relation Specifies the relationship between the left and right sides, or whether *cell_ref* must be an integer.

Relation	*Relationship*
1	<=
2	=
3	>=
4	Int (*cell_ref* is an integer)

formula The right side of the constraint; can be a single number, formula (as text) or a reference.

SOLVER.DELETE

Deletes an existing constraint.

Syntax

SOLVER.DELETE(*cell_ref,relation,formula*)

cell_ref A reference to a cell or range of cells on the active worksheet and forms the left side of the constraint.

relation Specifies the relationship between the left and right sides, or whether *cell_ref* must be an integer.

Relation	*Relationship*
1	<=
2	=
3	>=
4	Int (cell_ref is an integer)

formula The right side of the constraint; can be a single number, formula (as text), or a reference.

Example

The following formula deletes a previously-defined constraint.

```
=SOLVER.DELETE(!$B$5,1,"4000")
```

SOLVER.FINISH

Finishes the solver solution.

Syntax

SOLVER.FINISH(*keep_final,report_array*)

keep_final The number 1 or 2; determines whether to keep the final solution. If *keep_final* is 1 or omitted, the final solution values are kept in the changing cells. If *keep_final* is 2, the final solution values are discarded; the former values of the changing cells are restored.

report_array An array, that can be any combination of the numbers 1,2,3, indicating what reports to create when Solver is finished.

Report_array	*Excel creates*
{1}	An answer report
{2}	A sensitivity report
{3}	A limit report

Example

The following formula produces an answer report and a sensitivity report.

```
=SOLVER.FINISH(1,{1,2})
```

SOLVER.GET

Returns information about current settings for Solver.

Syntax

SOLVER.GET(*type_num,sheet_name*)

type_num A number specifying the type of information you want.

Type_num	*Returns*
1	The reference in the Set Cell box
2	A number, corresponding to the Equal To option: 1 = Max 2 = Min 3 = Value of
3	The value in the Value Of box
4	The reference (as a multiple reference if necesssary) in the By Changing Cells box
5	The number of constraints
6	An array of the left sides of the constraints in the form of text
7	An array of numbers, corresponding to the relationships between the left and right sides of the constraints: 1 equals <= 2 equals = 3 equals >= 4 equals int
8	An array of the right sides of the constraints, in the form of text

The following settings are specified in the Solver Options dialog box:

Type_num	*Returns*
9	The maximum calculation time
10	The maximum number of iterations
11	The precision
12	The integer tolerance value
13	TRUE if the Assume Linear Model check box is selected; FALSE if otherwise
14	TRUE if the Show Iteration Results check box is selected; FALSE if otherwise
15	TRUE if the Use Automatic Scaling check box is selected; FALSE if otherwise
16	A number, corresponding to the type of estimates: 1 equals Tangent 2 equals Quadratic
17	A number, corresponding to the type of derivatives: 1 equals Forward 2 equals Central
18	A number, corresponding to the type of search: 1 equals Quasi-Newton 2 equals Conjugate Gradient

sheet_name The name of the document that contains the scenario for which you want information. If *sheet_name* is omitted, it is assumed to be the active document.

Example

The following formula returns the number of constraints.

```
=SOLVER.GET(5)
```

SOLVER.LOAD

Loads Solver problem specifications that have been previously saved in the worksheet.

Syntax

SOLVER.LOAD(*load_area*)

load_area A reference on the active worksheet to a range of cells from which you want to load a complete specification. The first cell in *load_area* contains a formula for the Set Cell box, the second cell contains a formula for the changing cells, and subsequent cells contain constraints in the form of logical formulas.

Example

The following formula uses the data in the range A1:A5 to provide a formulas for the Set Cell box, a formula for the changing cells, and logical formulas for the constraints.

```
=SOLVER.LOAD($A$1:$A$5)
```

SOLVER.OK

Specifies basic Solver options.

Syntax

SOLVER.OK(*set_cell,max_min_val,value_of,by_changing*)

set_cell Corresponds to the Set Cell box in the Solver Parameters dialog box, and is a reference to a cell on the active worksheet.

max_min_val Corresponds to the options Max, Min, and Value Of in the Solver Paramenters dialog box and is a number from 1 to 3.

Max_min_val	*Option specified*
1	Maximize
2	Minimize
3	Match specific value

value_of A number that becomes the target for the cell in the Set Cell box if the *max_min_val* is 3.

by_changing Indicates the changing cells, as entered in the By Changing Cells box; must be a cell reference on the active worksheet.

Example

The following formula specifies that the set cell is A1, and the solution is to be maximized by changing cell A2.

```
=SOLVER.OK(!$A$1,1,0,(!$A$2))
```

SOLVER.OPTIONS

Specifies the available options. Controls the solution process, such as solution time, iterations, precision, and integer tolerance.

Syntax

SOLVER.OPTIONS(*max_time,iterations,precision,assume_linear,step_thru,estimates, derivatives,search,int_tolerance,scaling*)

max_time An integer greater than zero; corresponds to the Max Time box. *Max_time* limits the time taken by the solution process.

iterations An integer greater than zero; corresponds to the Iterations box. Controls the number of iterations made by the solution process.

precision A number between zero and one, but not equal to zero or one; corresponds to the Precision box. *Precision* controls the precision of the answers that Solver finds.

assume_linear A logical value, corresponding to the, assume Linear Model check box; allows Solver to arrive at a solution more quickly. If *assume_linear* is TRUE, Solver assumes the underlying model is linear; if FALSE, it does not assume a linear model.

step_thru A logical value, corresponding to the Show Iteration Results check box. If *step_thru* is TRUE, Solver pauses at each trial solution; if FALSE, it does not pause at each trial solution.

estimates The number 1 or 2; corresponds to the Estimates options. If *estimates* is 1, the option is Tangent; if 2, the option is Quadratic.

derivatives The number 1 or 2; corresponds to the Derivatives options. If *derivatives* is 1, the option is Forward; if 2, the option is Central.

search The number 1 or 2; corresponds to the Search options. If *search* is 1, the option is Quasi-Newton; if 2, the option is the Conjugate Gradient.

int_tolerance A decimal number, corresponding to the Tolerance box in the Solver Options dialog box; controls the amount of time the Solver spends searching for better integer solutions.

scaling A logical value, corresponding to the Use Automatic Scaling check box. If *scaling* is TRUE, then if two or more constraints differ by several orders of magnitude, Solver scales the constraints to similar orders of magnitude during computation. If scaling is FALSE, Solver calculates normally.

Example

The following formula sets the Solver options to 60 seconds for maximum time, 100 iterations, a precision of .000001, linear solution, and integer tolerance of .05.

```
=SOLVER.OPTIONS(60,100,0.000001,TRUE,FALSE,1,1,1,0.05,FALSE)
```

SOLVER.RESET

Erases all cell selections and constraints from the Solver Parameters dialog box, and restores all the settings in the Solver Options dialog box to their defaults.

Syntax

SOLVER.RESET()

SOLVER.SAVE

Saves the Solver problem specifications on the worksheet.

Syntax

SOLVER.SAVE(*save_area*)

save_area A reference on the active worksheet to a range of cells (or to the upper left corner of a range of cells) into which you want to paste the current problem specification.

Example

The following formula saves the Solver problem specifications in the worksheet range A1:A3.

```
=SOLVER.SAVE(!$A$1:$A$3)
```

SOLVER.SOLVE

Equivalent to choosing the Solver command from the Formula menu, and choosing the Solve button in the Solver Parameters dialog box.

Syntax

SOLVER.SOLVE(*user_finish,show_ref*)

user_finish A logical value specifying whether to display the standard Finish dialog box. If *user_finish* is TRUE, the function returns its integer value without displaying anything; if FALSE or omitted, Solver displays the standard Finish dialog box, which allows you to keep or discard the final solution and run reports.

show_ref A macro to be called in place of the Show Trial Solution box.

SORT

Sorts the rows or columns of the selection according to the contents of a key row or column within the selection.

Syntax

SORT(*sort_by,key1,order1,key2,order2,key3,order3*)

sort_by The number 1 or 2; specifies whether to sort by rows or columns. If *sort_by* is 1 the function sorts by rows; if 2, then it sorts by columns.

key1 A reference to the cell or cells you want to use as the first sort key. The sort key identifies which column to sort by when sorting rows, or which row to sort by when sorting columns.

order1 Determines whether to sort the row or column containing *key1* in ascending or descending order. If *order1* is 1, then the function sorts in ascending order; if 2, then it sorts by descending order.

key2, *order2*, *key3*, and *order3* Similar to *key1* and *order1*, except that *key2* specifies the second sort key, *order2* determines ascending or descending order, and so on.

Example

The following formula sorts by rows with the first key as C1 and the order as descending.

```
=SORT(1,"R1C3",2)
```

SPLIT

Splits the active window into panes.

Syntax

SPLIT(*col_split,row_split*)

col_split Specifies where to split the window vertically; measured in columns from the left of the window.

row_split Specifies where to split the window horizontally; measured in rows from the top of the window.

Example

The following formula splits the window horizontally after the third row and removes a vertical split if there is one.

```
=SPLIT(0,3)
```

STANDARD.FONT

Sets the attributes of the standard font for the active worksheet or macro sheet, and is included for compatibility with earlier versions of Excel.

Syntax

STANDARD.FONT(*name_text,size_num,bold,italic,underline,strike,color,outline, shadow*)

Some of the following arguments correspond to check boxes or options in the Font dialog box. Arguments that correspond to check boxes are logical values. If an argument is TRUE, Excel selects the check box; if FALSE, the check box is cleared.

name_text The name of the font as it appears in the Font dialog box.

size_num The font size in points.

bold Corresponds to the Bold check box in previous versions of Excel; makes the selection bold.

italic Corresponds to the Italic check box in previous versions of Excel; makes the selection italic.

underline Corresponds to the Underline check box.

strike Corresponds to the to the Strikeout check box.

color A number from 0 to 16, corresponding to the colors in the Font dialog box.

outline This argument is ignored for Microsoft Excel for the IBM.

shadow This argument is ignored for Microsoft Excel for the IBM.

Example

The following formula sets the standard font for the active worksheet at News Gothic 10-point.

```
=STANDARD.FONT("NewsGothic",10,FALSE,FALSE,FALSE,FALSE,0)
```

STEP

Stops the normal flow of a macro, and calculates it one cell at a time.

Syntax

STEP()

TABLE

Creates a table based on the input values and formulas you define on a worksheet.

Syntax

TABLE(*row_ref,column_ref*)

> *row_ref* Specifies the one cell to use as the row input for your table.
>
> *column_ref* Specifies the one cell to use as the column input for your table.

Example

The following formula creates a two-input table in the selection on the active sheet, using B1 and B2 as input cells.

```
=TABLE(!$B$1,!$B$2)
```

TEXT.BOX

Replaces characters in a text box or button with new characters.

Syntax

TEXT.BOX(*add_text,object_id_text,start_num,num_chars*)

> *add_text* The text you want to add to the text box or button.
>
> *object_id_text* The name of the text box or button to which you want to add text.
>
> *start_num* A number that indicates the position of the first character you want to replace.
>
> *num_chars* The number of characters you want to replace. If *num_chars* is 0, then no characters are replaced.

Example

The following formula inserts the words "Net Income for" at the beginning of a text box named Text 1.

```
=TEXT.BOX("Net Income for","Text 1",1,0)
```

UNDO

Reverses certain actions and commands.

Syntax

UNDO()

UNGROUP

Separates a grouped object into individual objects.

Syntax

UNGROUP()

UNHIDE

Displays hidden windows.

Syntax

UNHIDE(*window_text*)

window_text The name of the window to unhide.

Example

The following formula unhides the global macro sheet.

```
=UNHIDE("GLOBAL.XLM")
```

UPDATE.LINK

Updates a link to another document.

Syntax

UPDATE.LINK(*link_text,type_of_link*)

link_text Text describing the full path of the link as displayed in the Links dialog box.

type_of_link A number from 1 to 4 that specifies the type of link to update.

Type_of_link	*Link document type*
1 or omitted	Microsoft Excel Link
2	DDE link
3	Not available
4	Not available

Example

The following formula updates a link to a worksheet named COST.XLS.

```
=UPDATE.LINK("C:\EXCEL4\COST.XLS",1)
```

VPAGE

Vertically scrolls window by window or screen by screen.

Syntax

VPAGE(*num_windows*)

num_windows The number of windows (20 rows) to scroll through. If *num_windows* is positive, the function scrolls down; if negative, it scrolls up.

Example

The following formula scrolls down 15 windows or screen by screen.

```
=VPAGE(15)
```

VSCROLL

Vertically scrolls through the active document by percentage or by row number.

Syntax

VSCROLL(*position,row_logical*)

position The row you want to scroll to.

row_logical A logical value specifying how the function scrolls. If *row_logical* is TRUE, the function scrolls through the document to row position defined by the argument position; if FALSE or omitted, it scrolls through the document to the vertical position represented by the fraction defined by the argument position.

Example

The following formula scrolls to row 150.

```
=VSCROLL(150,TRUE)
```

WAIT

Pauses the macro until the time specified by the serial_number argument.

Syntax

WAIT(*serial_number*)

> *serial_number* The date-time number used by Excel for date and time calculations.

Example

The following formulas pause a macro for 10 seconds.

```
=WAIT(NOW()+"00:00:10")
```

WHILE

Executes the statements between the WHILE function and the next NEXT function, until *logical_test* is FALSE.

Syntax

WHILE(*logical_test*)

> *logical_test* A value or formula that evaluates to TRUE or FALSE. If *logical_test* is FALSE the first time the WHILE function is encountered, the macro skips the loop, and resumes executing at the statement after the next NEXT function.

WINDOW.MAXIMIZE

Changes a window from its normal size to full size.

Syntax

WINDOW.MAXIMIZE(*window_text*)

> *window_text* Specifies which window to make active and then maximize; can be text (enclosed in quotation marks) or a reference to a cell containing text. If this argument is omitted, the macro maximizes the active window.

Example

The following formula maximizes the window for the file CONS1.XLS.

```
=WINDOW.MAXIMIZE("CONS1.XLS")
=RETURN()
```

WINDOW.MINIMIZE

Shrinks a window to an icon.

Syntax

WINDOW.MINIMIZE(*window_text*)

> *window_text* Specifies which window to make active and then minimize; can be text (enclosed in quotation marks) or a reference to a cell containing text. If this argument is omitted, the macro minimizes the active window.

Example

The following formula shrinks the window for the file CONS1.XLS to an icon.

```
=WINDOW.MAXIMIZE("CONS1.XLS")
=RETURN()
```

WINDOW.MOVE

Moves a window so that its upper left corner is at the specified horizontal and vertical positions.

Syntax

WINDOW.MOVE(*x_pos,y_pos,window_text*)

> *x_pos* The horizontal position to which you want to move the window; measured in points from the left edge of your workspace to the left edge of the window.
>
> *y_pos* The vertical position to which you want to move the window; measured in points and is measured from the top edge of the workspace to the top edge of the window.
>
> *window_text* Specifies the window to move; can be text (enclosed in quotation marks) or a reference to a cell containing text. If this argument is omitted, the macro moves the active window.

Example

The following formula places the active window against the upper left edge of the workspace.

```
=WINDOW.MOVE(1,1)
=RETURN()
```

WINDOW.RESTORE

Changes a window to its previous size.

Syntax

WINDOW.RESTORE(*window_text*)

window_text Specifies the window to restore; can be text (enclosed in quotation marks) or a reference to a cell containing text. If this argument is omitted, the macro restores the active window.

Example

The following formula restores the window of the worksheet CONS1.XLS.

```
=WINDOW.RESTORE("CONS1.XLS")
=RETURN()
```

WINDOW.SIZE

Changes the size of a window by moving its lower right corner, so that the window has the width and height you specify.

Syntax

WINDOW.SIZE(*width,height,window_text*)

width The width of the window measured in points.

height The height of the window measured in points.

window_text The window to size; is text (enclosed in quotation marks) or a reference to a cell containing text. If this argument is omitted, the macro sizes the active window.

Example

The following formula changes the size of the window which contains the file CONS1.XLS to 250 by 125 points.

```
=WINDOW.SIZE(250,125,"CONS1.XLS")
=RETURN( )
```

WINDOW.TITLE

Changes the title of the active window.

Syntax

WINDOW.TITLE(*text*)

text The title (enclosed in quotation marks) to assign to the window.

Example

The following formula assigns the title First to the active window.

```
=WINDOW.TITLE("FIRST")
=RETURN( )
```

WINDOWS

Returns the names of open Excel windows.

Syntax

WINDOWS(*type_num,match_text*)

type_num A number from 1 to 3 that specifies which types of document names are returned by the function.

Type_num	*Returns window names from these types*
1 or omitted	All windows except those belonging to add-in documents.
2	Add-in documents only.
3	All types of documents.

match_text Text (enclosed in quotation marks) that specifies the windows whose names you want to return; can include wildcard characters. If *match_text* is omitted, the function returns the names of all open windows.

Example

The following formula returns the names of all open windows that begin with the letter S.

```
=WINDOWS(3,"S*")
```

WORKBOOK.ACTIVATE

Activates a document in a workbook.

Syntax

WORKBOOK.ACTIVATE(*sheet_name,new_window_logical*)

sheet_name The name of the document you want to activate.

new_window_logical A logical value. If *new_window_logical* is TRUE, Excel displays the document in a new window; if FALSE or omitted, Excel displays the document at the same size (and in the same location) as the workbook contents window.

Example

The following formula activates the document INCOME.XLS, and displays it at the same size (and in the same location) as the workbook contents window.

```
=WORKBOOK.ACTIVATE("[BOOK1.XLW]INCOME.XLS",FALSE)
=RETURN()
```

WORKBOOK.ADD

Adds one or more documents to a workbook.

Syntax

WORKBOOK.ADD(*name_array,dest_book,position_num*)

name_array The name of a document or an array of names of documents that are to be added to a workbook.

dest_book The name of the workbook to which you want to add the document(s) specified by *name_array*.

position_num A number that specifies the position of the document within the workbook.

Example

The following formula adds the document CONS1.XLS to the workbook BOOK1.XLW and places it fourth in the workbook contents.

```
=WORKBOOK.ADD("CONS1.XLS","BOOK1.XLW",4)
=RETURN()
```

WORKBOOK.COPY

Copies one or more documents from their current workbook into another workbook at the specified position.

Syntax

WORKBOOK.COPY(name_array,dest_book,position_num)

name_array The name of a document or an array of names of documents to be copied from one workbook to another.

dest_book The name of the workbook to which you want to copy the document(s) specified by name_array.

position_num A number that specifies the position of the document(s) within the workbook.

Example

The following formula copies the document CONS1.XLS from its current workbook to the fourth position in the workbook named BOOK.XLW.

```
=WORKBOOK.COPY("CONS1.XLS","BOOK.XLW",4)
=RETURN()
```

WORKBOOK.SELECT

Selects individual documents in the active workbook window.

Syntax

WORKBOOK.SELECT(*name_array,active_name*)

name_array A horizontal array of text names of documents to select.

active_name The name of a single sheet in the workbook that should become the active sheet when the selection is made.

Example

The following formula selects two worksheets in the active workbook.

```
=WORKBOOK.SELECT({"INCOME.XLS","SALES.XLS"},"SALES.XLS")
=RETURN()
```

WORKGROUP

Creates a group of worksheets and macro sheets.

Syntax

WORKGROUP(*name_array*)

name_array The list of open worksheets and macro sheets (as text) to be included in a group.

Example

The following formula creates a group of four worksheets.

```
=WORKGROUP({"CONS1.XLS","INCOME.XLS","INFLATE.XLS","LOAN.XLS"})
=RETURN( )
```

ZOOM

Syntax

ZOOM(*magnification*)

magnification A logical value or a number (from 10 to 400) specifying the size of the document. If *magnification* is TRUE or omitted, the current selection is enlarged or reduced to completely fill the active window; if FALSE, the document is restored to normal 100% magnification.

Example

The following formula enlarges the worksheet in the active window to twice its normal size.

```
=ZOOM(200)
```

ZTESTM

Performs a two-sample z test for means, assuming the two samples have known variances.

Syntax

ZTESTM(*inprng1,inprng2,outrng,labels,alpha,difference,var1,var2*)

inprng1 The input range for the first data set.

inprng2 The input range for the second data set.

outrng The first cell (the upper left cell) in the output table.

labels A logical value. If *labels* is TRUE, then labels are in the first row or column of the input ranges (*inprng1* and *inprng2*); if FALSE or omitted, all cells in the input ranges are data (*inprng1* and *inprng2*).

alpha The confidence level for the test. If you omit the *alpha* argument, Excel uses a confidence level of .05.

difference The hypothesized mean difference. If you omit the *difference* argument, Excel uses a hypothesized mean difference of 0.

var1 The variance of the first data set.

var2 The variance of the second data set.

Appendix

A

Installing Excel 4 for Windows

To install Excel 4 for Windows on your system:

1. Before you install this or any program, make copies of your original installation disks. This protects them against accidental damage.
2. Start Windows by typing `WIN` at the DOS prompt. The Program Manager appears on-screen.
3. Insert Excel disk labeled "Setup" in drive A or B.
4. Open the Program Manager **F**ile menu by pressing Alt-F or clicking on File. Select Run by clicking on it or pressing R.
5. Beside Command Line, type `A:SETUP`. (If you are using drive B for installation, type `B:SETUP`.)
6. Press Enter.
7. Follow the on-screen instructions. The easiest type of installation is Complete Installation.

Windows then installs the Excel 4 program on your system, creating a separate program group called Microsoft Excel 4.0. When the installation program is over, click on OK; Windows returns you to the Windows Program Manager.

Appendix

B

Microsoft Windows Primer

Microsoft Windows is a *graphical user interface* (GUI) that runs on top of DOS (your computer's disk operating system). Although many users consider the Windows screen (interface) easier to use, you need to know how to use it before it will seem easy.

In addition to a graphical interface, Windows offers a *multitasking* environment. What this means is that you can run two or more programs at the same time (each in a separate window) and smoothly switch from one program to the other.

Starting Windows

To start Windows, follow these steps:

1. Change to the drive that contains your Windows files. For example, type `C:` at the DOS prompt and press Enter.

2. Change to the directory that contains your Windows files. For example, if the name of the directory is WINDOWS, type **`CD\WINDOWS`** at the prompt and press Enter.

3. Type **`WIN`** and press Enter. DOS starts Windows. The Windows title screen appears for a few moments, and then you see a screen like the one in Figure B.1.

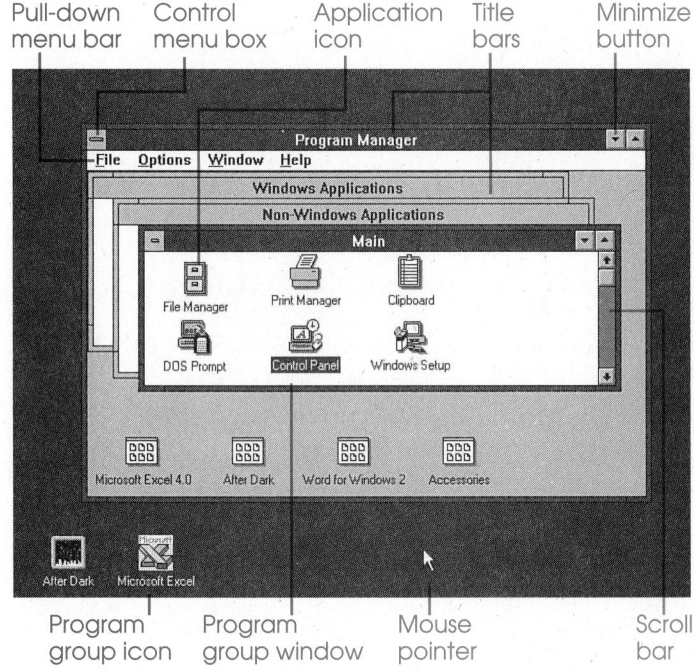

Figure B.1 The Program Manager allows you to run other programs from Windows.

The Windows Interface

As shown in Figure B.1, the Windows interface contains several unique elements. The following list briefly describes each element:

Title bar—The title bar contains the name of the window or program.

Program group windows and icons—Each program group window contains application icons. You can shrink any window down to the size of an icon to clear screen space.

Application icons—To run an application, you select one of these icons from a program group window.

Minimize and Maximize buttons—The Minimize button shrinks the window to the size of an icon. The Maximize button expands the window to take up most of the screen. The button then changes to a double-headed *Restore* button, which allows you to return the window to its original size.

Control menu box—At the upper left corner of the active window is a Control menu box. Selecting this box pulls down a menu that allows you to control the size and location of the window.

Pull-down menu bar—This bar contains a list of the pull-down menus available in the program.

Mouse Pointer—Somewhere on the screen, a mouse pointer should appear (if you are using a mouse). If you don't see it, move the mouse to bring the pointer into view.

Scroll bars—If a window contains more information than can be displayed, a scroll bar appears. Use the scroll arrows on each end of the bar to scroll incrementally. Drag the scroll box along the bar to scroll more quickly.

Using a Mouse

To work most efficiently in Windows, you should use a mouse. You can press mouse buttons and move the mouse in various ways to change the way it acts:

Point means to move the mouse pointer onto the specified item. Part of the mouse pointer must be touching the item.

Click on an item means to move the pointer onto the specified item and press the mouse button once. Unless specified otherwise, use the left mouse button.

Double-click on an item means to move the pointer onto the specified item and press and release the mouse button twice quickly.

Drag means to move the mouse pointer onto the specified item, hold down the mouse button, and move the mouse while holding down the button.

Figure B.2 shows how to use the mouse to perform common Windows activities, including running programs and moving and resizing windows.

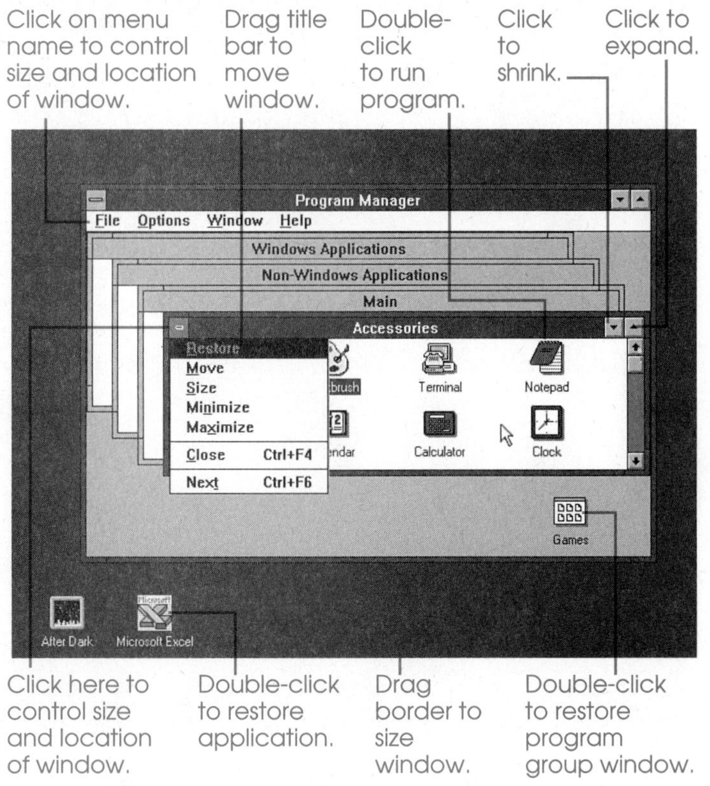
Click on menu name to control size and location of window.
Drag title bar to move window.
Double-click to run program.
Click to shrink.
Click to expand.
Program Manager
File Options Window Help
Windows Applications
Non-Windows Applications
Main
Accessories
Restore
Move
Size
Minimize
Maximize
Close Ctrl+F4
Next Ctrl+F6
Terminal
Notepad
Calculator
Clock
Games
After Dark
Microsoft Excel
Click here to control size and location of window.
Double-click to restore application.
Drag border to size window.
Double-click to restore program group window.

Figure B.2 Use your mouse to control Windows.

Using the Keyboard

Although Windows works best with a mouse, you can also use your keyboard. The following keyboard shortcuts explain how.

Press	*To*
Alt+Esc	Cycle through the application windows and icons
Ctrl+F6 (or Ctrl+Tab)	Cycle through program group icons and windows
Alt+spacebar	Open the Control menu for an application window or icon
Alt+ – (hyphen)	Open the Control menu for a program group window or icon
Arrow keys	Move from one icon to another in the active window
Alt (or F10)	Activate the pull-down menu bar
Alt+*menu letter*	Pull down a menu from the menu bar
Enter	Run the application whose icon is highlighted, or restore a window that's been reduced to an icon
Esc	Close a menu or dialog box
Ctrl+Esc	View the task list, which allows you to switch to a different program
F1	Get help
Ctrl+F4	Minimize the selected program group window
Alt+F4	Exit the active application or exit Windows

Managing Directories and Files with the Windows File Manager

Windows includes a special program called the File Manager, which simplifies many of the DOS file-related tasks, including listing, copying, and deleting files. To open the File Manager, double-click on the File Manager icon in the Main Program Group window. If the Main window is not shown, pull down the **Window** menu and select Main. The following list tells you how to move around in the File Manager:

- To change drives, click on the drive letter at the top of the Directory Tree window. Or, press the Tab key to move up to the drive list, highlight a drive letter with the arrow keys, and press Enter.
- To display the subdirectories of a directory, click on the plus sign to the left of the directory's name, or highlight the directory and press the + (plus) key. To reverse the process, press the – (hyphen) key or click on the minus sign.
- To open a directory, double-click on it, or highlight it and press Enter. You can open more than one directory window at a time.
- To activate a directory window, click anywhere on the window or use the Control menu to switch windows.
- To close the File Manager, select File Exit or double-click on the Control menu box in the upper left corner of the screen.

Making Directories with the File Manager

To use the File Manager to create a directory, follow these steps.

1. Highlight the directory under which you want the new directory.
2. Select File Create Directory.
3. Type the name of the new directory in the dialog box.
4. Click on OK or press Enter.

Selecting Files to Copy, Move, or Delete

Before you can copy, move, or delete files, you must select the files using one of the following methods.

With a Mouse

You can use the mouse to select the files.

- To select a group of consecutive files, hold down the Shift key and click on the first and last files in the group.
- To select a group of nonconsecutive files, hold down the Ctrl key and click on each file. To deselect a file, click on it again.

With the Keyboard

You can also use the keyboard to select the files.

- To select a group of consecutive files, highlight the first file, hold down the Shift key, and use the arrow keys to stretch the highlight over the desired group.
- To select a group of nonconsecutive files, press Shift+F8, and then select each file by highlighting it and pressing the spacebar. To deselect a file, highlight it and press the spacebar.

Copying Files

Follow these steps to copy files from one drive or directory to another.

1. Select the files you want to copy.
2. Select File Copy or press F8. The Copy dialog box appears.
3. Type the destination drive, directory, and file name in the To text box.
4. Press the Copy button. Windows copies the file to the specified location.

Moving Files

Follow these steps to move files from one drive or directory to another.

1. Activate the directory window for the directory that contains the files you want to move.

2. Select the files you want to move.

3. Select File Move or press F7. The Move dialog box appears, prompting you to specify a destination directory for the selected files.

4. Type a complete path to the destination directory and then press the Move button. The selected files are moved to the destination directory you specified.

Deleting Files

Follow these steps to delete files.

1. Select the files you want to delete.

2. Select File Delete. The Delete dialog box appears, prompting you to confirm the operation.

3. Press the Delete button to delete the selected files or Cancel to cancel the operation.

For More Information . . .

For more information about using Windows, try these other books from SAMS:

10 Minute Guide to Windows 3.1

The First Book of Windows 3.1

Index

Symbols

A

DIRECTORY
Basic Skills Workshop 1-144
Publishing and Printing Workshop 145-308
Graphics Workshop 309-470
Database Workshop 471-574
File Management Workshop 575-670
Advanced Topics Workshop 671-750
Macros Workshop 751-800
Projects Workshop 801-1078
Command Reference 1079-1336
Appendices 1337-1348

B

DIRECTORY
Basic Skills Workshop 1-144
Publishing and Printing Workshop 145-308
Graphics Workshop 309-470
Database Workshop 471-574
File Management Workshop 575-670
Advanced Topics Workshop 671-750
Macros Workshop 751-800
Projects Workshop 801-1078
Command Reference 1079-1336
Appendices 1337-1348

C

DIRECTORY
Basic Skills Workshop 1-144
Publishing and Printing Workshop 145-308
Graphics Workshop 309-470
Database Workshop 471-574
File Management Workshop 575-670
Advanced Topics Workshop 671-750
Macros Workshop 751-800
Projects Workshop 801-1078
Command Reference 1079-1336
Appendices 1337-1348

DIRECTORY
Basic Skills Workshop 1-144
Publishing and Printing Workshop 145-308
Graphics Workshop 309-470
Database Workshop 471-574
File Management Workshop 575-670
Advanced Topics Workshop 671-750
Macros Workshop 751-800
Projects Workshop 801-1078
Command Reference 1079-1336
Appendices 1337-1348

DIRECTORY
Basic Skills Workshop 1-144
Publishing and Printing Workshop 145-308
Graphics Workshop 309-470
Database Workshop 471-574
File Management Workshop 575-670
Advanced Topics Workshop 671-750
Macros Workshop 751-800
Projects Workshop 801-1078
Command Reference 1079-1336
Appendices 1337-1348

DIRECTORY
Basic Skills Workshop 1-144
Publishing and Printing Workshop 145-308
Graphics Workshop 309-470
Database Workshop 471-574
File Management Workshop 575-670
Advanced Topics Workshop 671-750
Macros Workshop 751-800
Projects Workshop 801-1078
Command Reference 1079-1336
Appendices 1337-1348

DIRECTORY
Basic Skills Workshop 1-144
Publishing and Printing Workshop 145-308
Graphics Workshop 309-470
Database Workshop 471-574
File Management Workshop 575-670
Advanced Topics Workshop 671-750
Macros Workshop 751-800
Projects Workshop 801-1078
Command Reference 1079-1336
Appendices 1337-1348

D

DIRECTORY
Basic Skills Workshop 1-144
Publishing and Printing Workshop 145-308
Graphics Workshop 309-470
Database Workshop 471-574
File Management Workshop 575-670
Advanced Topics Workshop 671-750
Macros Workshop 751-800
Projects Workshop 801-1078
Command Reference 1079-1336
Appendices 1337-1348

DIRECTORY
Basic Skills Workshop 1-144
Publishing and Printing Workshop 145-308
Graphics Workshop 309-470
Database Workshop 471-574
File Management Workshop 575-670
Advanced Topics Workshop 671-750
Macros Workshop 751-800
Projects Workshop 801-1078
Command Reference 1079-1336
Appendices 1337-1348

E

F

DIRECTORY
Basic Skills Workshop 1-144
Publishing and Printing Workshop 145-308
Graphics Workshop 309-470
Database Workshop 471-574
File Management Workshop 575-670
Advanced Topics Workshop 671-750
Macros Workshop 751-800
Projects Workshop 801-1078
Command Reference 1079-1336
Appendices 1337-1348

DIRECTORY
Basic Skills Workshop 1-144
Publishing and Printing Workshop 145-308
Graphics Workshop 309-470
Database Workshop 471-574
File Management Workshop 575-670
Advanced Topics Workshop 671-750
Macros Workshop 751-800
Projects Workshop 801-1078
Command Reference 1079-1336
Appendices 1337-1348

G

DIRECTORY

H

I

DIRECTORY
Basic Skills Workshop 1-144
Publishing and Printing Workshop 145-308
Graphics Workshop 309-470
Database Workshop 471-574
File Management Workshop 575-670
Advanced Topics Workshop 671-750
Macros Workshop 751-800
Projects Workshop 801-1078
Command Reference 1079-1336
Appendices 1337-1348

J

K

L

M

N

O

P

DIRECTORY
Basic Skills Workshop 1-144
Publishing and Printing Workshop 145-308
Graphics Workshop 309-470
Database Workshop 471-574
File Management Workshop 575-670
Advanced Topics Workshop 671-750
Macros Workshop 751-800
Projects Workshop 801-1078
Command Reference 1079-1336
Appendices 1337-1348

Q

R

DIRECTORY
Basic Skills Workshop 1-144
Publishing and Printing Workshop 145-308
Graphics Workshop 309-470
Database Workshop 471-574
File Management Workshop 575-670
Advanced Topics Workshop 671-750
Macros Workshop 751-800
Projects Workshop 801-1078
Command Reference 1079-1336
Appendices 1337-1348

S

DIRECTORY

Basic Skills Workshop 1-144

Publishing and Printing Workshop 145-308

Graphics Workshop 309-470

Database Workshop 471-574

File Management Workshop 575-670

Advanced Topics Workshop 671-750

Macros Workshop 751-800

Projects Workshop 801-1078

Command Reference 1079-1336

Appendices 1337-1348

T

DIRECTORY
Basic Skills Workshop 1-144
Publishing and Printing Workshop 145-308
Graphics Workshop 309-470
Database Workshop 471-574
File Management Workshop 575-670
Advanced Topics Workshop 671-750
Macros Workshop 751-800
Projects Workshop 801-1078
Command Reference 1079-1336
Appendices 1337-1348

W

DIRECTORY
Basic Skills Workshop **1-144**
Publishing and Printing Workshop **145-308**
Graphics Workshop **309-470**
Database Workshop **471-574**
File Management Workshop **575-670**
Advanced Topics Workshop **671-750**
Macros Workshop **751-800**
Projects Workshop **801-1078**
Command Reference **1079-1336**
Appendices **1337-1348**

DIRECTORY
Basic Skills Workshop 1-144
Publishing and Printing Workshop 145-308
Graphics Workshop 309-470
Database Workshop 471-574
File Management Workshop 575-670
Advanced Topics Workshop 671-750
Macros Workshop 751-800
Projects Workshop 801-1078
Command Reference 1079-1336
Appendices 1337-1348

X

Y-Z

IF YOUR COMPUTER USES 3.5" DISKS

While most personal computers use 5.25" disks to store information, some newer computers use 3.5" disks. If your computer uses 3.5" disks, you can return this form to Sams to obtain a 3.5" disk to use with this book.

Print the required information on this reply form and mail the form to:

Excel 4 Superbook

SAMS

A Division of Prentice Hall Computer Publishing

11711 North College, Carmel, Indiana 46032 USA

Name: ____________________________________

Address: ____________________________________

City: ____________________ State: ____ Zip: ____

Phone: ____________________________________

Sams—Covering The Latest In Computer And Technical Topics!

Audio

Advanced Digital Audio $39.95
Audio Systems Design and Installation $59.95
Compact Disc Troubleshooting and Repair . . $24.95
Handbook for Sound Engineers: The New Audio Cyclopedia, 2nd Ed. . . $99.95
How to Design & Build Loudspeaker & Listening Enclosures $39.95
Introduction to Professional Recording Techniques $29.95
The MIDI Manual $24.95
Modern Recording Techniques, 3rd Ed. $29.95
OP-AMP Circuits and Principles $19.95
Principles of Digital Audio, 2nd Ed. $29.95
Sound Recording Handbook $49.95
Sound System Engineering, 2nd Ed. $49.95

Electricity/Electronics

Active-Filter Cookbook $24.95
Basic Electricity and DC Circuits $29.95
CMOS Cookbook, 2nd Ed. $24.95
Electrical Wiring $19.95
Electricity 1-7, Revised 2nd Ed. $49.95
Electronics 1-7, Revised 2nd Ed. $49.95
How to Read Schematics, 4th Ed. $19.95
IC Op-Amp Cookbook, 3rd Ed. $24.95
IC Timer Cookbook, 2nd Ed. $24.95
RF Circuit Design $24.95
Transformers and Motors $29.95
TTL Cookbook $24.95
Understanding Digital Troubleshooting, 3rd Ed. $24.95
Understanding Solid State Electronics, 5th Ed. $24.95

Games

Master SimCity/SimEarth $19.95
Master Ultima $16.95

Hardware/Technical

First Book of Modem Communications $16.95
First Book of PS/1 . . . . $16.95
Hard Disk Power with the Jamsa Disk Utilities $39.95
IBM PC Advanced Troubleshooting & Repair $24.95
IBM Personal Computer Troubleshooting & Repair $24.95
Microcomputer Troubleshooting & Repair . . $24.95
Understanding Fiber Optics $24.95

IBM: Business

10 Minute Guide to PC Tools 7 . . . . $ 9.95
10 Minute Guide to Q&A 4 . . . . $ 9.95
First Book of Microsoft Works for the PC . . $16.95
First Book of Norton Utilities 6 . . . . $16.95
First Book of PC Tools 7 . . . . $16.95
First Book of Personal Computing, 2nd Ed. . . $16.95

IBM: Database

10 Minute Guide to Harvard Graphics 2.3 . . . $9.95
Best Book of AutoCAD $34.95
dBASE III Plus Programmer's Reference Guide $24.95
dBASE IV Version 1.1 for the First-Time User $24.95
Everyman's Database Primer Featuring dBASE IV Version 1.1 . . . . $24.95
First Book of Paradox 3.5 . . . . $16.95
First Book of PowerPoint for Windows $16.95
Harvard Graphics 2.3 In Business $29.95

IBM: Graphics/Desktop Publishing

10 Minute Guide to Lotus 1-2-3 . . . . $ 9.95
Best Book of Harvard Graphics $24.95
First Book of Harvard Graphics 2.3 . . . . $16.95
First Book of PC Paintbrush $16.95
First Book of PFS: First Publisher $16.95

IBM: Spreadsheets/Financial

Best Book of Lotus 1-2-3 Release 3.1 . . . . $27.95
First Book of Excel 3 for Windows $16.95
First Book of Lotus 1-2-3 Release 2.3 . . . . $16.95
First Book of Quattro Pro 3 . . . . $16.95
First Book of Quicken In Business $16.95
Lotus 1-2-3 Release 2.3 In Business $29.95
Lotus 1-2-3: Step-by-Step $24.95
Quattro Pro In Business $29.95

IBM: Word Processing

Best Book of Microsoft Word 5 . . . . $24.95
Best Book of Microsoft Word for Windows . $24.95
Best Book of WordPerfect 5.1 . . . . $26.95
First Book of Microsoft Word 5.5 . . . . $16.95
First Book of WordPerfect 5.1 . . . . $16.95
WordPerfect 5.1: Step-by-Step $24.95

Macintosh/Apple

First Book of Excel 3 for the Mac $16.95
First Book of the Mac $16.95

Operating Systems/Networking

10 Minute Guide to Windows 3 . . . . $ 9.95
Best Book of DESQview $24.95
Best Book of Microsoft Windows 3 . . . . $24.95
Best Book of MS-DOS 5 . . . . $24.95
Business Guide to Local Area Networks . . . $24.95
DOS Batch File Power with the Jamsa Disk Utilities $39.95
Exploring the UNIX System, 2nd Ed. $29.95
First Book of DeskMate $16.95
First Book of Microsoft Windows 3 . . . . $16.95
First Book of MS-DOS 5 . . . . $16.95
First Book of UNIX $16.95
Interfacing to the IBM Personal Computer, 2nd Ed. $24.95
The Waite Group's Discovering MS-DOS, 2nd Edition $19.95
The Waite Group's MS-DOS Bible, 4th Ed. . $29.95
The Waite Group's MS-DOS Developer's Guide, 2nd Ed. $29.95
The Waite Group's Tricks of the UNIX Masters $29.95
The Waite Group's Understanding MS-DOS, 2nd Ed. $19.95
The Waite Group's UNIX Primer Plus, 2nd Ed. $29.95
The Waite Group's UNIX System V Bible . . $29.95
Understanding Local Area Networks, 2nd Ed. $24.95
UNIX Applications Programming: Mastering the Shell $29.95
UNIX Networking $29.95
UNIX Shell Programming, Revised Ed. . . . $29.95
UNIX: Step-by-Step $29.95
UNIX System Administration $29.95
UNIX System Security $34.95
UNIX Text Processing $29.95

Professional/Reference

Data Communications, Networks, and Systems $39.95
Handbook of Electronics Tables and Formulas, 6th Ed. $24.95
ISDN, DECnet, and SNA Communications . $49.95
Modern Dictionary of Electronics, 6th Ed. . . $39.95
Reference Data for Engineers: Radio, Electronics, Computer, and Communications, 7th Ed. $99.95

Programming

Advanced C: Tips and Techniques $29.95
C Programmer's Guide to NetBIOS $29.95
C Programmer's Guide to Serial Communications $29.95
Commodore 64 Programmer's Reference Guide $24.95
Developing Windows Applications with Microsoft SDK $29.95
DOS Batch File Power $39.95
Graphical User Interfaces with Turbo C++ . $29.95
Learning C++ $39.95
Mastering Turbo Assembler $29.95
Mastering Turbo Pascal, 4th Ed. $29.95
Microsoft Macro Assembly Language Programming $29.95
Microsoft QuickBASIC Programmer's Reference $29.95
Programming in ANSI C $29.95
Programming in C, Revised Ed. $29.95
The Waite Group's BASIC Programming Primer, 2nd Ed. $24.95
The Waite Group's C Programming Using Turbo C++ $29.95
The Waite Group's C: Step-by-Step $29.95
The Waite Group's GW-BASIC Primer Plus . $24.95
The Waite Group's Microsoft C Bible, 2nd Ed. $29.95
The Waite Group's Microsoft C Programming for the PC, 2nd Ed. $29.95
The Waite Group's New C Primer Plus . . . $29.95
The Waite Group's Turbo Assembler Bible . . $29.95
The Waite Group's Turbo C Bible $29.95
The Waite Group's Turbo C Programming for the PC, Revised Ed. $29.95
The Waite Group's Turbo C++Bible $29.95
X Window System Programming $29.95

Radio/Video

Camcorder Survival Guide . . . . $ 14.95
Radio Handbook, 23rd Ed. $39.95
Radio Operator's License Q&A Manual, 11th Ed. $24.95
Understanding Fiber Optics $24.95
Understanding Telephone Electronics, 3rd Ed. $24.95
VCR Troubleshooting & Repair Guide . . . $19.95
Video Scrambling & Descrambling for Satellite & Cable TV $24.95

For More Information, See Your Local Retailer Or Call Toll Free

1-800-428-5331

All prices are subject to change without notice. Non-U.S. prices may be higher. Printed in the U.S.A.